FIFTH EDITION

Child Development

A THEMATIC APPROACH

Danuta Bukatko
College of the Holy Cross

Marvin W. Daehler
University of Massachusetts, Amherst

Houghton Mifflin Company   Boston   New York

To Don and Nicholas
D. B.

To June, and to Curtis and Angela, Joshua, and Renée
M. W. D.

155.4

Learning
Resource Center
Stockton
Riverside C...

Editor-in-Chief: Charles Hartford
Senior Sponsoring Editor: Kerry Baruth
Development Editor: Rita Lombard
Editorial Assistant: Caryn Yilmaz
Senior Project Editor: Aileen Mason
Editorial Assistant: Liliana Ritter
Production/Design Coordinator: Jodi O'Rourke
Senior Manufacturing Manager: Jane Spelman
Senior Marketing Manager: Katherine Greig
Marketing Assistant: Anne Tousey

Copyright © 2004 by Houghton Mifflin Company. All rights reserved.

No part of this work may be reproduced or transmitted in any form or by any means, electronic or mechanical, including photocopying and recording, or by any information storage or retrieval system without the prior written permission of the copyright owner unless such copying is expressly permitted by federal copyright law. With the exception of nonprofit transcription in Braille, Houghton Mifflin is not authorized to grant permission for further uses of copyrighted selections reprinted in this text without the permission of their owners. Permission must be obtained from the individual copyright owners as identified herein. Address requests for permission to make copies of Houghton Mifflin material to College Permissions, Houghton Mifflin Company, 222 Berkeley Street, Boston, MA 02116-3764.

Printed in the U.S.A.

Library of Congress Control Number: 2002116641

ISBN: 0-618-33338-X

2 3 4 5 6 7 8 9-VHP-07 06 05 04 03

Brief Contents

Contents

FEATURES

RESEARCH APPLIED TO PARENTING/EDUCATION

ATYPICAL DEVELOPMENT

CONTROVERSY: THINKING IT OVER

EXAMINING RESEARCH METHODS

CHRONOLOGY CHARTS

When we first wrote this text more than a decade ago, we had some very explicit goals in mind. Given the vast amount of information about child development gathered by researchers, how do we as teachers help students understand the most important aspects of that process? And given the tendency for researchers to hone in on very specific aspects of child development, how do we give students a meaningful sense of the child as a whole being? Those goals have become even more important to us as we approached this fifth edition, largely because technology has created even more of an information explosion than ever before. Certainly, the Internet has become a vast storehouse of material about child development. In addition, it has become more common for other media—television, magazines, and newspapers—to cover various aspects of the psychological growth of children.

The availability of so many sources for information has made it evident that we should emphasize still another important teaching goal—helping students to refine their critical thinking skills so they can become educated consumers in our "information age." We also remain as committed as we have been since the first edition to the goal of presenting the story of child development from the perspective of scientific theory and research. We believe that it is important for students to be well grounded in the scientific approach to the study of the child and to carry this viewpoint with them as they continue to learn about children after leaving our classes.

One other important line of thinking went into the changes for the fifth edition. We tried to pay more deliberate attention to pedagogy, to help students learn the information presented in the text and to encourage them to be actively engaged with it. Several of the new features described later were created with these objectives in mind. The more widespread availability of technology shaped the way we thought about some of these pedagogical enhancements. In particular, we sought to provide more direct links between the text and information (including multimedia materials) now available on the Internet. We hope that students and instructors will find value in these new additions.

A Thematic Approach

To meet our goals, we hold to our commitment of providing a comprehensive, topically organized, up-to-date picture of development from conception to adolescence. Most important, we draw students' attention to the themes that replay themselves throughout the course of development, fundamental issues that resurface continually and that provide coherence to sometimes seemingly disparate research. The themes, we believe, can serve as frameworks to help students further understand and remember the multitude of facts about child development. They can also serve as organizing ideas for lectures or for the questions instructors pose on examinations or other assignments. We highlight the following six themes throughout our discussion of child development:

- What roles do nature and nurture play in development?
- How does the sociocultural context influence development?
- How does the child play an active role in development?
- Is development continuous or discontinuous?
- How prominent are individual differences in development?
- How do the various domains of development interact?

Additionally, by drawing out these themes, we hope to stimulate readers to think about the process of development, or why development proceeds as it does. We believe that when students engage in this sort of reflection, they will become more adept critical thinkers. We also believe that they are more likely to appreciate the ramifications of theory and research for applied issues such as parenting practices, education, and social policy for children, which are ultimately concerns for us all.

Organizational Changes and Updated Coverage

Preparing the fifth edition provided us with new ways to do justice to our goals. We sought to respond to the needs of various instructors who wanted us to reduce and expand coverage of various topics and refine and revisit some of the features we've introduced over time. Several organizational changes have taken place as a result. Chapter 1 has been reworked to streamline the amount of theoretical detail by moving some of the more extensive points to more appropriate later chapters. Other changes include moving the brief summary of the history of child development from Chapter 2 into Chapter 1. Chapter 16 has been retitled "Beyond Family and Peers" and now adds discussion of broader issues of neighborhood and community. In this reorganized chapter, we begin with a discussion of the influence on development of television, followed by a consideration of computers, the school, and neighborhoods, including new sections on school violence, as well as war and its effects on children. A new vignette opens the chapter, and a new Controversy on children's access to the Internet has also been added to this chapter.

We have tried to pay attention to important emerging themes and concepts in the research literature and have added new research, studies, and citations as appropriate. As a result of our efforts to provide an up-to-date portrait of contemporary research, this edition of the text includes approximately six hundred new references. New and updated information has been added on a number of key topics throughout the book, among them the following:

- Research regarding thumb sucking to illustrate principles of learning theory (Chapter 1)
- A recent study (Ginsburg, Pappas, & Seo, 2001) to illustrate naturalistic observation (Chapter 2)
- A new study (Ram & Ross, 2001) and figure to illustrate structured observation (Chapter 2)
- A recent study and new figure illustrating sequential study design by Cole et al. (2001) (Chapter 2)
- Information on ethnography in the section on Cross-Cultural Studies of Development (Chapter 2)
- Information on proteomics, a new field of study that attempts to understand how genes influence one's phenotype (Chapter 3)
- Detailed information on Williams syndrome (Chapter 3)
- More updated research on phenylketonuria (PKU), fragile X syndrome, and Down syndrome (Chapter 3)
- Reorganized presentation of prenatal screening tests (Chapter 3)
- Updated research on behavioral genetics (Chapter 3)
- Updated references on spina bifida, and a new figure demonstrating the decline in neural tube defects associated with increased folic acid supplements (Chapter 4)
- Reorganization and updating of material on children born to parents by means of in vitro fertilization and other forms of assisted reproduction (Chapter 4)
- Presentation of new, revised views of the effects of fetal exposure to cocaine (Chapter 4)

- New data showing the decline in HIV/AIDS transmitted to offspring, and updated text on HIV/AIDS (Chapter 4)
- Further consideration of the long-term effects of cesarean deliveries for mothers and infants (Chapter 4)
- An introduction to "kangaroo care" and its effects on development in premature infants (Chapter 4)
- Reorganization of material to emphasize increasing information on brain development (Chapter 5)
- New growth charts and updated references on body growth and development (Chapter 5)
- Greater emphasis and a new figure on trends in overweight boys and girls in the United States (Chapter 5)
- A new section on implicit learning in the discussion of Basic Learning Processes in Infancy and Childhood (Chapter 6)
- A recently published study (Johnson & Mason, 2002) and new figure to demonstrate the habituation procedure under the Examining Research Methods section (Chapter 6)
- A separate section on Atypical Development focusing on visual problems in infancy including a discussion of cataracts, amblyopia (lazy eye), and strabismus (crossed eyes) (Chapter 6)
- More recent information in the discussion of depth perception along with two new figures ("Avoiding a Risky Fall" and "Surface Contour as a Cue Implying Depth") (Chapter 6)
- New discussion concerning the possible primacy of intermodal perception in infancy (Chapter 6)
- New research in the section on Early Responses to Human Speech (Chapter 7)
- A new section on Later Phonological Development (Chapter 7)
- New information on critical periods and language learning (Chapter 7)
- New research on statistical learning in infancy and language learning (Chapter 7)
- New information and figure on private speech in preschoolers (Chapter 7)
- Extended discussion of the core knowledge hypothesis, and a new figure on the concept of solidity (Chapter 8)
- A separate section and more studies on the "A-not-B Error" (Chapter 8)
- Additional studies in the section retitled Early Number Concepts and Counting, and a new figure on how infants represent number (Chapter 8)
- New research on infants' shifts of attention (Chapter 9)
- New information on ADHD, including the role of executive control processes (Chapter 9)
- Updated studies on infants' recognition memory (Chapter 9)

- A new section and information on elicited imitation (Chapter 9)

- A new figure on generating retrieval cues for memory (Chapter 9)

- A new section on Executive Function including a discussion of metacognition (Chapter 9)

- New information on intelligence and working memory (Chapter 10)

- New information on stereotype threat in the section on Group Differences in IQ Scores, along with a new figure on the impact of stereotype threat on test performance (Chapter 10)

- A new figure on the long-term impact of early intervention on IQ (Chapter 10)

- More information on parent-child interactions that involve mutual reciprocal influences (Chapter 11)

- New research on the cultural differences in emotion (Chapter 11)

- New information on the role of internal working models of relationships in later friendships and romantic relationships (Chapter 11)

- New research in the sections on Cross-Cultural Variations in Patterns of Attachment and Child Care and Attachment (Chapter 11)

- The section on adoption now includes foster care (Chapter 11)

- Updated research and references on the self as object and developmental changes in views of self (Chapter 12)

- A new figure on gender differences in self-concept (Chapter 12)

- More research on cultural differences in the section on self-definition (Chapter 12)

- New research on the impact of maternal feedback to two-year-olds following problem-solving tasks (Chapter 12)

- Updated research on ethnic identity (Chapter 12)

- Additional information on developmental changes in compliant behavior and self-regulation (Chapter 12)

- New information on the regulation of behavior in the section on The Influence of Language and Attention (Chapter 12)

- Additional discussion of the antecedents of guilt and the emergence of a conscience (Chapter 12)

- A new section on prosocial behavior and academic achievement (Chapter 12)

- Updated research and references on children's knowledge of gender stereotypes (Chapter 13)

- New information on girls' increased rates of depression (Chapter 13)

- New research on children's sex-segregated groups (Chapter 13)

- Current research on girls' shifting attitudes about their mathematical abilities (Chapter 13)

- Cross-cultural research on sex differences in academic self-evaluation (Chapter 13)

- A new section on Effective Parenting, with sections on the roles of parental warmth and parental control (Chapter 14)

- A new figure on levels of parental expressions of warmth (Chapter 14)

- A new section titled The Child's Characteristics and Behavior (Chapter 14)

- Updated statistics and research on child abuse (Chapter 14)

- A new table on the characteristics of victims of child maltreatment (Chapter 14)

- Updated research on maternal employment (Chapter 14)

- Updated research on child care (Chapter 14)

- Updated research on adjusting to divorce (Chapter 14)

- New research on how adolescents spend their time, along with a corresponding table depicting the data (Chapter 15)

- Updated research on peer group formation (Chapter 15)

- Updated research on the role emotion regulation plays in peer relationships (Chapter 15)

- New research, with an accompanying figure, on the impact of peer rejection (Chapter 15)

- New research added on the long-term consequences of television viewing (Chapter 16)

- Updated evaluations of the benefits of computers on academic performance, including the decreasing gap in boys' and girls' use of the computer (Chapter 16)

- Further consideration of cross-cultural differences in school achievement, including a new figure showing average math and science scores of students by nation (Chapter 16)

- New information on the benefits of mentoring for academic success (Chapter 16)

- Further consideration of the effects of classroom climate, the teacher's influence, and teacher expectancy effects on children's academic achievement (Chapter 16)

- A new section on School Violence (Chapter 16)

- A new section on Neighborhoods (Chapter 16)

- A new section on War and Children (Chapter 16)

New Features

Thanks in large part to the suggestions of many reviewers, we have refined and added to our many well-established features.

NEW! Our **Controversy** boxes continue to serve as the foundation for debate and extended discussion in the classroom. However, they have now been organized into a new three-question framework to better promote critical thinking and a deeper appreciation of all sides of a theoretical debate:

1. What Is the Controversy?
2. What Are the Opposing Arguments?
3. What Answers Exist/What Questions Remain?

As well as reorganizing and updating existing Controversies, we have added a number of new ones:

- What Should Sex Education Programs Emphasize? (Chapter 5)
- Should the Fetus Undergo a Sensory Curriculum? (Chapter 6)
- Is Praise Always a Good Thing? (Chapter 12)
- Is Gender Identity Disorder Really a Disorder? (Chapter 13)
- Should Parents Spank Their Children? (Chapter 14)
- What Regulations Should Exist for Children's Access to the Internet? (Chapter 16)

NEW! **What Do You Think?** As an extension of the Controversy feature, critical thinking questions have been added in each chapter to promote active learning and reinforce important concepts in the text. These questions, linked to recommended resources on the text web site, encourage students to review other materials related to contemporary controversies and to apply their acquired knowledge.

NEW! **See For Yourself** This icon—located in the text margins—integrates resources available on the text web site. These resources encourage students to actively explore material related to the text and again apply information or "see for themselves."

NEW! **For Your Review** bulleted recaps at the end of major sections of the text provide an active way for students to recap and verify their understanding of the material just covered. In addition, reworked **Chapter Recaps** are now bulleted into more manageable and readily digestible chunks of material to increase their efficiency as a review tool.

Successful Features Retained in This Edition

EXAMINING RESEARCH METHODS

The **Examining Research Methods** boxes continue to provide a close-up examination of a particular research strategy, using a contemporary study as a case example. Our two-fold purpose continues in this edition. First, we wish to highlight the diverse and creative research methodologies that have been particularly useful in illuminating the process of development, strategies such as habituation, the microgenetic approach, and cross-cultural studies, for example. We want, in particular, to remind students that, as they read about the hundreds of studies that are described in this book, there are fundamentally sound and interesting methods that underlie the summaries of results. Second, we believe that an analysis of methodologies can be a useful way to help students develop their critical thinking skills. Hence, each example of this feature includes questions for students' thought and possibly for class discussion.

KEY THEMES IN DEVELOPMENT

Within each chapter, some or all of the six developmental themes previously identified serve to organize and provide coherence for the material. We see these **Key Themes** as pedagogical tools designed to help students discern the importance and interrelatedness of various facts, and as vehicles for instructors to encourage critical analysis among students. The themes are highlighted for students in several ways.

1. The themes most immediately relevant to a chapter are listed at its start.
2. Indicators in the margins of the chapter point to discussions of each key theme.
3. Each chapter closes with a brief synopsis of how the key themes are illustrated in the domain explored by the chapter.

Students and instructors may, of course, find additional instances of the six themes we have identified. They may also locate new and additional themes. We encourage this process in keeping with our desire to set in motion a search on the part of readers for integration and coherence in the vast material that constitutes the scientific study of child development.

CHRONOLOGY CHARTS

From our own experience as teachers who have adopted a topical approach to child development, we know that students often get so immersed in the information on a given topic that they lose sense of the child's achievements over time. Consequently, in most chapters, we include one or two **Chronology Charts** that summarize the child's specific developmental attainments at various ages. We caution students that these figures are meant only to give a picture of the overall trajectory of development, a loose outline of the sequence of events we expect to see in many children. Nonetheless, we believe that these guidelines will give students a sense of the patterns and typical timing of important events in the child's life, and that they will serve as another organizing device for the material presented in each chapter. For comparative and review purposes, students can locate all the Chronology Charts by consulting the list on the inside front cover and in the features page at the end of the table of contents.

RESEARCH APPLIED TO PARENTING/EDUCATION

Designed to identify some of the implications of research that extend beyond the laboratory, our goal is to help students think about questions and concerns that typically affect parents and teachers in their interactions with children. The **Research Applied to Parenting/Education** feature addresses such topics as the steps parents might take to reduce the risk of sudden infant death syndrome and the strategies teachers might follow to promote gender equity in the classroom. Each topic covered in this feature is introduced with a continuation of the chapter-opening vignette and is followed by a set of points that, based on our current knowledge, leads to positive consequences for children and their development. These points, of course, should not be considered the final word on the subject, but they will help readers to understand how research has led to practical benefits for children, parents, and teachers. For a complete list of topics covered in this and other features, see the inside front cover and the list of features at the end of the table of contents.

ATYPICAL DEVELOPMENT

Rather than include a separate chapter focused on developmental problems, we continue to include within most chapters an **Atypical Development** feature. In doing so, we hope to emphasize that the same processes that help to explain normal development can also help us understand development that is different from the norm. We believe that the reverse applies as well: that understanding atypical development can illuminate the factors that guide more typical child development. Thus, we consider such topics as attention deficit hyperactivity disorder, conduct disorders, and language impairment. A complete list of topics appears on the inside front cover and in the features list at the end of the table of contents.

STUDY AIDS

The chapter outlines, For Your Review lists, marginal and end-of-text glossaries, and restructured bulleted chapter summaries all serve to underscore important themes, terms, and concepts. We hope that students will actively utilize these aids to reinforce what they have learned in the chapter body. In addition, we employ several strategies to make the material in this text more accessible to students: vignettes to open the chapter, the Research Applied to Parenting/Education feature, the liberal use of examples throughout the text, and an extensive program of illustrations accompanied by instructive captions.

Organization and Coverage

We begin the text with two chapters that set the stage for the balance of the book. Chapter 1 introduces the six developmental themes, followed by a brief history of views of childhood and the major theories of development. Chapter 2 considers the research methodologies the field typically employs today.

The next three chapters deal primarily with the biological underpinnings and physical changes that characterize child development. Chapter 3 explains the mechanisms of heredity and evaluates the role of genetics in the expression of many human traits and behaviors. Chapter 4 sketches the major features of prenatal development and focuses on how environmental factors such as teratogens can modify the genetic blueprint for physical and behavioral development. Chapter 5 begins our consideration of the influence of brain differentiation and continues with the major features of motor skill and physical development.

The next group of chapters focuses on the development of the child's various mental capacities. Chapter 6 reviews the literature on both children's learning and the development of perception. Chapter 7 describes language development, highlighting the contemporary research on infant language and the social context of language acquisition. Chapter 8 features Piaget's and Vygotsky's theories of cognitive development, as well as recent research spurred by their ideas. Chapter 9 continues the discussion of cognitive development from the information-processing perspective. Chapter 10 provides students with a picture of traditional and more recent views of intelligence.

The child's growing social and emotional achievements constitute the focus of the next group of chapters. We devote Chapter 11 to a treatment of emotional development. Chapter 12 covers social cognition and, under the broader framework of the concept of self, values, and moral development. Chapter 13 discusses the most recent ideas on gender development, including substantial treatment of gender schema theory.

In the final portion of the text, we consider the most important external forces that shape the path of child development—the family, peers, and "beyond," such as media, schools, and neighborhoods. Chapter 14 adopts a family systems approach to emphasize how various family members continually influence one another. A separate chapter entirely dedicated to the influence of peers, Chapter 15, covers the expanding research on this topic. Chapter 16 considers the special influence of television and computers, schools, and neighborhoods on child development.

Teaching and Learning Support Package

Many useful materials have been developed to support the study of *Child Development*. Designed to enhance the teaching and learning experience, they are well integrated with the text and include some of the latest technologies. Several components are new to this edition.

PRINT ANCILLARIES

Accompanying this book are, among other ancillaries, a *Test Bank,* an *Instructor's Resource Manual*, and a *Study Guide.* All three are unified by a shared set of learning objectives, and all three have been revised and enhanced for the fifth edition.

Test Bank

The *Test Bank*, revised by Ashley E. Murphy, University of Minnesota, and Marvin W. Daehler, University of Massachusetts, Amherst, includes nearly two thousand multiple-choice items. Each is accompanied by a key that provides the learning objective, the text page number on which the answer can be found, type of question (Fact, Concept, or Application), and correct answer. We continue our commitment to the idea that students should be encouraged to engage in critical thinking about child development and have retained a set of essay questions for each chapter.

Instructor's Resource Manual

The *Instructor's Resource Manual*, revised by Michelle K. Demaray, Northern Illinois University, and Danuta Bukatko, College of the Holy Cross, contains a complete set of chapter outlines and learning objectives, as well as lecture topics, classroom exercises, demonstrations, and handouts. It also features recommended readings, videos, and Internet sites.

Study Guide

The *Study Guide*, revised by Karen L. Yanowitz, Arkansas State University, and Marvin W. Daehler, University of Massachusetts, Amherst, contains the same set of learning objectives that appear in the *Instructor's Resource Manual* and the *Test Bank*. Each chapter also contains a detailed study outline, a key terms section, and a self-quiz consisting of thirty multiple-choice questions. An answer key tells students not only which response is correct but also why each of the other choices is incorrect.

ELECTRONIC AND VIDEO ANCILLARIES

In keeping with the technological needs of today's campus, we provide the following electronic and video supplements to *Child Development.*

For the Student

Student CD-ROM   This brand new *Student CD-ROM*, which comes packaged with the textbook, contains videos illustrating key concepts and classic and contemporary studies in child development (such as Eating Disorders and the Bobo Doll Study). It also offers supportive peda-

gogy that helps students test their comprehension of these key concepts.

Student Web Site   The student web site contains additional study aids, such as self-tests (ace quizzes) and flashcards, as well as follow up activities accompanying the textbook features See For Yourself and What Do You Think? It also contains chapter outlines, learning objectives, and essay and concept questions to better focus students' study. Testing material on the free Student CD-ROM is also available on the web site for ease of use. All web resources are keyed to the textbook and can be found by following the links at **psychology.college.hmco.com**.

For the Instructor

HMClassPrep CD-ROM with HM Testing 6.1   This instructor CD-ROM collects in one place materials that instructors might want to have available electronically. It contains PowerPoint lecture outlines and art from the textbook. In addition, it includes the *Computerized Test Bank* (as well as word files of the *Test Bank*) in an easy-to-use new interface with complete cross-platform flexibility. It also offers electronic versions of much of the *Instructor's Resource Manual* to make it easy to incorporate into a web site or lecture/activity and a transition guide to direct instructors through this new edition. Lastly, for reference, it offers the extensive testing material available on the *Student CD-ROM* that tests students on topics such as attachment, eating disorders, and the Bobo Doll Study.

Child Development in Context: Voices and Perspectives   This innovative reader by David N. Sattler, Geoffrey P. Kramer, Virginia Shabatay, and Douglas A. Bernstein features personal narratives taken from popular and literary authors covering concepts, issues, and topics related to child development. Concept guides, critical-thinking questions, and research questions promote analysis of the articles. Featured authors include, among others, Brian Hall, Anne Lamott, Frank McCourt, Annie Dillard, Russell Baker, Richard Rodriguez, and Nora Ephron.

Instructor's Web Site   Much of the material from the *HMClassPrep CD-ROM* is also available on the web, as well as information on how to integrate the students' technology package into the course. All web resources keyed to the text can be found by following the links at **psychology.college.hmco.com**.

Course Cartridges for WebCT and Blackboard   Ask your Houghton Mifflin representative for details about these course management cartridges. You can utilize many of the instructor resources available with this edition including chapter outlines, learning objectives, and PowerPoint slides. Additionally, you can access a wealth of testing material specifically developed for this edition including multiple-choice quizzes, NetLabs, Critical Thinking exercises, and Evaluating Research web exercises.

Lecture Starter Video and Guide   The Lecture Starter Video contains a series of high-interest, concise segments that instructors can use to begin a class meeting or change to a new topic. The accompanying guide briefly describes each segment, indicates concepts that can be addressed using each segment, and offers suggestions on how to use each segment.

Lecture Starter CD-ROM   An additional set of video clips is available on CD-ROM.

Online Teaching Tools   Links to useful and practical information on online teaching tools can be found on the *Child Development* web site, including a link to useful print resources such as *Teaching Online: A Practical Guide* (0-618-00042-9).

Other Multimedia Offerings   A range of videos, CD-ROMs, and other multimedia materials relevant to child development are available free to qualified adopters. Houghton Mifflin sales representatives have further details.

Acknowledgments

Our students at Holy Cross and the University of Massachusetts continue to serve as the primary inspiration for our work on this text. Each time we teach the child development course, we see their enthusiasm and appreciation for what we teach, but we also find that we learn from them how to communicate our messages about developmental processes more effectively.

We also appreciate the insightful comments and criticisms provided by the reviewers of this text. Their classroom experiences have provided a broader perspective than our own, and we believe our book becomes stronger because of their valued input. We would like to express our thanks to the following reviewers of the fourth edition, whose influence continues to be felt:

Lakshmi Bandlamudi, *LaGuardia Community College, City University of New York*

Debora Bell-Dolan, *University of Missouri*

Jeffrey T. Coldren, *Youngstown State University*

Michelle K. Demaray, *Northern Illinois University*

Daniel Fasko, Jr., *Morehead State University*

S. A. Fenwick, *Augustana College*

Janice H. Kennedy, *Georgia Southern University*

Beverly R. King, *South Dakota State University*

Cynthia Legin-Bucell, *Edinboro University of Pennsylvania*

Doug Needham, *Redeemer College*

Susan Sonnenschein, *University of Maryland, Baltimore College*

Nanci S. Woods, *Austin Peay State University*

We would also like to thank the reviewers who helped fashion this fifth edition:

Victor K. Broderick, *Ferris State University*

Jeffrey T. Coldren, *Youngstown State University*

Margaret Dempsey, *Tulane University*

Michelle K. Demaray, *Northern Illinois University*

K. Laurie Dickson, *Northern Arizona University*

Rebecca Eaton, *The University of Alabama in Huntsville*

Lynn Haller, *Morehead State University*

Robert F. Rycek, *University of Nebraska at Kearney*

In addition, we would like to express our gratitude to colleagues at our respective institutions for reading and commenting on various chapters or just plain sharing ideas that were helpful in our revision. Special thanks go to Patricia Porcaro and Sr. Irene Mazula at Holy Cross, who so graciously and promptly helped with reference questions and interlibrary loan requests. At the University of Massachusetts, colleagues in the Developmental Psychology Program, Daniel Anderson, Carole Beal, Neal Berthier, Elliott Blass, Richard Bogartz, Rachel Clifton, and Nancy Myers have provided a wealth of information and stimulating ideas in formal seminars and informal hallway conversations. Just as these faculty colleagues have offered insightful perspectives, so too have a spirited company of former and present graduate students at the University of Massachusetts who have carried out research on a number of aspects of development. Their number is too great to identify individually, so they must be thanked collectively. They will, however, surely be aware of our admiration for their efforts to enhance our knowledge of development. Among them, Zhe Chen, Monica Sylvia, Laura L. Mitchell, Dawn Melzer, and Laura Claxton deserve special mention because, in addition to their individual contributions, they have often had to accommodate their schedules and endeavors to the demands imposed by this work. Several former undergraduates, among them Kristen E. Miller, Monica V. Mitchell, Mona Mody, and Ashley E. Murphy, have provided inspiring contributions, each in remarkably unique ways, to confirm why teaching and writing about child development is an especially important enterprise. Additionally, to our wonderful ancillary author team Michelle K. Demaray, Northern Illinois University (*Instructor's Resource Manual*), Ashley E. Murphy, University of Minnesota (*Test Bank*), Christine Vanchella, South Georgia College (*Student CD-ROM*), and Karen L. Yanowitz, Arkansas State University (*Study Guide*), we say a sincere thank you for the exceptional quality of their work, always completed with a great degree of good humor!

As with previous editions, several individuals at Houghton Mifflin have demonstrated their talent, dedication, and professionalism. Kerry Baruth, senior sponsoring editor, has always shown exceptional enthusiasm and support for this project; Rita Lombard, development editor, has managed to maintain a continuing calming presence throughout her expert and insightful guidance of the development of the fifth edition; and Aileen Mason, senior project editrix, has worked what can only be described as miracles in carrying out the necessary steps involved in production of this text. Ann Schroeder and Jessyca Broekman did an outstanding job of capturing visually the concepts we were trying to convey with words under the guidance of production design coordinator, Jodi O'Rourke. Our thanks to Henry Rachlin, designer, who gave this edition a wonderful fresh new look; and to Elaine Lauble Kehoe and Charleen Akullian for their comprehensive copyediting and proofreading. Giuseppina Davanzo and Daniel Stone helped produce our new *Student CD-ROM* and instructor *ClassPrep CD-ROM*, respectively, and Katherine Greig, senior marketing manager, and Anne Tousey, marketing assistant, have provided unfailing support in their efforts to promote our text. We thank them all for their outstanding contributions.

Lastly, we would like to thank our families for their support during still another revision of this text. Nick's willingness to help out in day-to-day tasks and to defer on some family activities is much appreciated. Don also accepted with good will and supportiveness the adjustments that the book schedule required. Special thanks to June, who continued to accept the demands that such a project entails, and also thanks to Curtis, Joshua, and Renée, who have now joined the ranks of young adulthood. The progress and success they continue to demonstrate in their chosen professions bear witness to the value and rewards of understanding the extraordinary spectacle that is the focus of this book: children and their development.

Danuta Bukatko
Marvin W. Daehler

CHAPTER 1

Themes and Theories

Andrew had spent an enormous amount of time carefully aligning the beams, braces, and other equipment at just the right locations on his building project. He was fascinated by how he could make the crane swing up and down and how it would lift and drop the small metal pieces with the magnet. But six-year-old Andrew was so absorbed in his play that he failed to notice his one-year-old sister, Heather, rapidly crawling toward these shiny new objects. Fourteen-year-old Benjamin, the oldest member of the family, placed in charge of watching both Andrew and Heather as their parents prepared dinner in the kitchen, had also become distracted by the challenging new computer game he had just borrowed from his friend.

As she crawled within reach of Andrew's construction set, Heather grabbed the truck on which the crane was mounted and pulled it sharply, pitching beams, equipment, and everything else into a chaotic heap. For one brief instant, Andrew froze in horror as he observed the devastation his little sister had just wrought. Then came the almost reflexive, inevitable shriek at the top of his lungs: "HEATHER! GET OUTTA HERE!" as he simultaneously swung his arm in Heather's direction in an uncontrollable burst of emotion. Andrew's shout was more than enough to produce a wail from Heather, but the sting across her back from Andrew's hand didn't help, either. Benjamin, startled by the uproar, anticipated the melee about to begin and raced to the kitchen, knowing full well that his mother and father were the only ones who would be able to reinstate tranquility after this unfortunate exchange between his little brother and sister.

Although the specifics may be very different, this type of exchange between siblings is probably not uncommon in families and households around the world. The sequence of events serves to introduce a few of the many issues central to this book. For example, consider some of the developmental differences displayed by Heather, Andrew, and Benjamin during this interaction. Heather, only one year of age, does not move about or handle objects in the same way as her older siblings. Perhaps more important for our purposes, Heather seems to have very little appreciation for the consequences her impulsive reach might have on both Andrew and the construction set. Her six-year-old brother displays far greater physical dexterity and more sophisticated planning and thinking about the toys that are part of his play. Andrew also has excellent verbal skills with which to express his thoughts and emotions, although he still has some difficulty regulating the latter. Yet Andrew's reasoning about his world pales in comparison with that of his older brother, Benjamin, who is captivated by a complex computer game. Moreover, at the age of fourteen, Benjamin has been given increased responsibility, such as that of looking after both younger siblings. Although he is not always as careful and conscientious in this task as his mother and father might like, his parents feel reasonably assured that if things are not going well, Benjamin knows where to seek assistance.

How did these enormous developmental differences come about? That is a primary question that we address in this book. But there are other questions of interest to us in the sequence of events described here. How should their parents now deal with the conflict in order to bring about peace between Heather and Andrew? How would you? How should his parents respond to the angry outburst from Andrew? How might they have encouraged Benjamin to take his baby-sitting responsibilities more seriously?

When we think about trying to understand how children develop and become competent individuals in interactions with one another and their physical environment, common sense seems like the place to start. For generations common sense provided the parenting wisdom by which caregivers understood and reared children. For example, when Heather, Andrew, and Benjamin could not get along with each other, their parents often spanked the child whom they thought might be at fault. They followed a commonly accepted approach to dealing with conflict, a method that seems to be shared in many cultures. As an illustration, among the proverbs expressed by the

Ovambo of southwest Africa is the saying, "A cranky child has not been spanked," and Korean parents may say, "Treat the child you love with the rod; treat the child you hate with another cake." Proverbs like these promoting physical discipline for children can be found in many cultures around the world (e.g., Palacios, 1996).

Although common sense is extremely important in child rearing, in some circumstances it may yield unexpected and perhaps even undesirable consequences. For example, is physical punishment the best way to prevent unacceptable behaviors in children? Caregivers in many societies believe spanking is an effective method of dealing with angry outbursts such as that displayed by Andrew. However, researchers have found that the children of parents who routinely resort to physical punishment often initiate more aggressive acts than do the children of parents who rely on alternative methods of disciplining undesirable conduct (Bandura & Walters, 1959; Dodge, Pettit, & Bates, 1994). This relationship has been observed in Native American (McCord, 1977) and British working-class homes (Farrington, 1991), as well as in families in the United States, Australia, Finland, Poland, and Israel (Eron, Huesmann, & Zelli, 1991). In other words, under some circumstances, physical punishment appears to encourage rather than discourage aggressive actions and may escalate into increasingly coercive interactions between parent and child. Thus the common-sense practice of disciplining by physical punishment, a practice supported by various cultural proverbs and recommendations, may need to be examined more closely. This is precisely the point at which the need for the scientific study of children and their development enters.

What Is Development?

Development, as we use the term, means all the physical and psychological changes a human being undergoes in a lifetime, from the moment of conception until death. The study of human development is, above all, the study of change (Overton, 1998). From the very moment of birth, changes are swift and impressive. Within a few short months, the newborn who looked so helpless (we will see that the true state of affairs is otherwise) comes to control his or her own body, to locomote, and to master simple tasks such as self-feeding. In the years that follow, the child begins to understand and speak a language, engages in more and more complex thinking, displays a distinct personality, and develops the skills necessary to interact with other people as part of a social network. The range and complexity of every young person's achievements in the first two decades of life can only be called extraordinary.

One of the goals of this book is to give you an overview of the most significant changes in behavior and thinking processes that occur in this time span. In the pages that follow we describe the growing child's accomplishments in many domains of development. For example, we detail the basic physical and mental capabilities in infants and children and examine the social and emotional skills children acquire as they reach out to form relationships with their family members, peers, and others. In addition, we discuss more thoroughly, for example, the issue of aggressive behavior and what research suggests about how parents, teachers, and society might address this problem. A second important goal is to help you appreciate just why children develop in the specific ways they do. That is, we also try to explain developmental outcomes in children. How do the genetic blueprints inherited from parents shape the growing child? What is the role of the environment? How does the society or culture in which the child lives influence development? Does the child play a passive or an active role in his or her own development? We are repeatedly concerned with some other questions about development. Do the changes that take place occur gradually or suddenly? Do all children follow a common developmental pathway, and if not, what factors explain these individual differences? And how do the many facets of development influence one another? As you may imagine, although we often seek simple answers to these questions, they are neither simple nor always obvious (Horowitz, 2000).

development Physical and psychological changes in the individual over a lifetime.

As suggested here, the activity of reading together provides a context for learning that extends to sharing thoughts about mutual interests and ideas between friends. Among the many topics of interest to developmental psychologists are understanding how children establish close relationships with one another. In *theorizing* about this developmental accomplishment, researchers may explore what the members of a group gain from their peers, the cognitive skills that are required to form friendships, and how various kinds of experiences help children to become sensitive and responsive to others.

Developmental psychology is the discipline concerned with the scientific study of changes in human behaviors and mental activities as they occur over a lifetime. *Developmental psychologists* rely on research to learn about growth and change in children. This approach has its limitations: researchers have not studied every important aspect of child development, and sometimes studies do not point to clear, unambiguous answers about the nature of development. Indeed, psychologists often *disagree* on the conclusions they draw from a given set of data. Nonetheless, scientific fact-finding has the advantage of being verifiable and is also more objective and systematic than personal interpretations of children's behavior. As you read about development in the chapters that follow, the controversies as well as the unequivocal conclusions, we hope you will use them to sharpen your own skills of critical analysis.

An essential ingredient of the scientific process is the construction of a **theory,** a set of ideas or propositions that helps to organize or explain observable phenomena. For many students, theories seem far less interesting than the vast assortment of intellectual, linguistic, social, physical, and other behaviors and capabilities that undergo change with time. However, by describing children's accomplishments in a systematic, integrated way, theories *organize* or make sense of the enormous amount of information researchers have gleaned. Theories of development also help to *explain* our observations. Is your neighbor's little boy shy because he inherited this trait, or did his social experiences encourage him to become this way? Did your niece's precocious mathematical skills develop from her experience with her home computer, or does she just have a natural flair for numbers? Was Andrew's angry reaction to his baby sister a biological response or something he had learned? Psychologists are interested in understanding the factors that contribute to the emergence of behavioral skills and capacities, and their theories are ways of articulating ideas about what causes various behaviors to develop in individual children.

A good theory goes beyond description and explanation, however. It leads to *predictions* about behavior, predictions that are clear and easily tested. If shyness results from social experiences, for example, the withdrawn four-year-old should profit from a training program that teaches social skills. If, on the other hand, shyness is a stable, unchangeable personality trait, even extensive training in sociability may have very little impact. Explaining and predicting behavior is not only gratifying but also essential for translating ideas into applications—creating meaningful programs and ways to assist parents, teachers, and others who work to enhance and promote the development of children. For example, when a theory proposes that adults are an im-

developmental psychology
Systematic and scientific study of changes in human behaviors and mental activities over time.

theory   Set of ideas or propositions that helps to organize or explain observable phenomena.

portant source of imitative learning and that parents who display aggressive behavior provide a model for responding to a frustrating situation, we can begin to understand why common proverbs such as "spare the rod and spoil the child" sometimes need to be reevaluated.

The knowledge that developmental psychologists acquire through their research can also address many concerns about **social policy.** *Social policies* are plans and efforts established by local, regional, or national organizations and agencies. These are often government programs, but businesses, private foundations, and other groups attempt to implement social policies that are designed to achieve a particular purpose with respect to the members of a society as well. The goals of many of these policies are geared to alleviating social problems. Social policies may, for example, be concerned with increasing the effectiveness of education for children, improving their health, reducing teenage pregnancy, eliminating child abuse, reducing low birth weight and infant deaths, preventing young people from smoking cigarettes, encouraging parents to enforce the use of seat belts, promoting self-esteem, and a host of other goals. Research can help identify social problems that limit or interfere with children's development and can assist policymakers in establishing programs to reduce or eliminate the factors that hinder psychological health and competence in children. At the same time, research may shed further light on the mechanisms and processes that underlie behavior. We have the opportunity to consider many social policies that bear on children in the chapters that follow.

In this chapter, our discussion focuses on several broad theories, and some of their historical antecedents, that have influenced explanations of children's behavior. No one theory is sufficient to provide a full explanation of all behavior. Some theories strive to make sense of intellectual and cognitive development; others focus on social, emotional, personality, or some other aspect of development. Theories also vary in the extent to which they present formalized, testable ideas. Thus some are more useful than others in providing explanations for behavior that can be rigorously evaluated. And they often disagree in their answers to the fundamental questions of development. In fact, before we examine specific theories, let us consider a cluster of basic questions that all theories of development must address.

SEE FOR YOURSELF
psychology.college.hmco.com
Developmental Research and Social Policies

Six Major Themes in Developmental Psychology

As you read about different aspects of child development—language acquisition, peer relationships, motor skills, emergence of self-worth, and many others—you will find that certain questions about development surface again and again. We call these questions the *themes in development*. Various theories provide different answers to these questions. Good theories, grounded in careful research, help us to think about and understand these major themes. What are these key questions?

What Roles Do Nature and Nurture Play in Development?

We have all heard expressions such as "He inherited a good set of genes" or "She had a great upbringing" to explain some trait or behavior. These explanations offer two very different answers to a basic question that has fueled controversy among theorists since the beginnings of psychology and that continues to rage even today. Dubbed the **nature-nurture debate,** the dispute centers on whether the child's development is the result of genetic endowment or environmental influences.

Do children typically crawl at nine months and walk at twelve months of age as part of some inborn unfolding program or because they have learned these motor responses? Do they readily acquire language because their environment demands it or because they are genetically predisposed to do so? Are boys more aggressive than girls because of cultural conditioning or biological factors? In some areas, such as the

social policy Programs and plans established by local, regional, or national public and private organizations and agencies designed to achieve a particular social purpose or goal.

nature-nurture debate Ongoing theoretical controversy over whether development is the result of the child's genetic endowment or the kinds of experiences the child has had.

development of intelligence and the emergence of gender roles, the debate over nature versus nurture has been particularly heated.

Why all the uproar about such a question? One reason is that the answer has major implications for children's developmental outcomes, for parenting practices, for the organization of schooling, and for other practical applications concerning research. If, for example, experiments support the view that intelligence is guided largely by heredity, providing children with rich learning experiences may have minimal impact on their eventual levels of intellectual skill. If, on the other hand, research and theory more convincingly show that intellectual development is shaped primarily by environmental events, it becomes vital to provide children with experiences designed to optimize their intellectual growth. Answers to this type of question are likely to have an impact on social policy by affecting how funds are allocated to health, educational, and many other programs.

Psychologists now recognize that both nature and nurture are essential to all aspects of behavior and that these two forces combine to mold what the child becomes. Thus the controversy has shifted away from a concern with identifying *which* of these two factors is critical in any given situation. Instead, the question is *how,* specifically, each contributes to development. The problem for researchers is to determine the manner in which heredity and environment *interact* to fashion the behaviors we see in children and eventually in adults. As will soon be apparent, developmental theories have taken very different positions on this question.

How Does the Sociocultural Context Influence Development?

Development is influenced by more than just the immediate environment of the family. Children grow up within a larger social community, the *sociocultural context.* The sociocultural context includes unique customs, values, and beliefs about the proper way to rear children and the ultimate goals for their development. Think back to your family and the cultural standards and values that determined how you were reared. Were you allowed to be assertive and to speak your mind, or were you expected to be compliant toward adults and never challenge them? Were you encouraged to fend for yourself, or were caregivers, relatives, and even cultural institutions such as the school, church, or some other agency expected to assist with your needs throughout childhood, adolescence, and perhaps even into your early adult years?

Children grow up in many different cultures and social settings. This Malaysian American family, celebrating the Chinese New Year at their home in San Francisco, has adopted some customs and values from American culture, yet maintains many traditions and practices brought with them from their native country. Various sociocultural contexts provide the backdrop in which specific parenting practices are carried out. Researchers must consider these different kinds of experiences to fully understand development.

How was your development affected by your family's economic status and educational attainments? By your gender and ethnic identity?

Sociocultural factors affect everything from the kinds of child-rearing practices parents engage in to the level of health care and education children receive; they affect, for example, children's physical well-being, social standing, sense of self-esteem, "personality," and emotional expressiveness. As you explore the various domains of development, you will come to appreciate that many developmental outcomes are heavily influenced by the sociocultural context. And, as with the nature-nurture debate, the precise relationship of sociocultural context to various areas of development has generated much heated discussion among theorists.

How Does the Child Play an Active Role in Development?

Do children learn to speak by passively listening to their language and reproducing it as if they were playing back a tape recording? Or are they actively operating on the sounds, grammar, and meanings of words to express themselves in new ways? Do children exhibit masculine and feminine gender stereotypes simply by mirroring the behaviors of males and females around them? Or do they construct mental interpretations of "male" and "female" activities that in turn drive their own behavior? Do parents establish the emotional tone for interactions with their young infants? Or do infants take some initiative in determining whether playing or bathing will be stressful or happy events? In other words, do infants and children somehow regulate and determine their own development?

Most researchers today believe that children take an active role in their own growth and development. That active role may be evident at two different levels. The first begins with certain attributes and qualities that children possess and exhibit, such as curiosity about and eagerness to engage in the physical and social world surrounding them. By virtue of being a male or a female, being placid or active, being helpful or refusing to cooperate, and by eventually taking an interest in such things as dinosaurs, music, or sports, children elicit reactions from others. Thus children are not simply passive recipients of the environment or blank slates on which it writes; their own capacities and efforts to become immersed in, to get "mixed up" with, their physical and social world often modify what happens to them and can affect their development in profound ways.

A second, perhaps more fundamental, way in which children contribute to their own development is through actively constructing and organizing ways of thinking, feeling, communicating, and so forth to assist them in making sense of their world. Children may formulate these conceptualizations to help them respond to and understand the rich array of physical and social events they experience. As you will soon see, questions about how children directly influence their own development are theoretically controversial as well.

Is Development Continuous or Discontinuous?

Everyone agrees that children's behaviors and abilities change, sometimes in dramatic ways. However, there is much less consensus on how best to explain these changes. On the one hand, development can be viewed as a *continuous* process in which new attainments in thinking, language, and social behavior are characterized by gradual, steady, small *quantitative* advances. For example, substantial progress in reasoning or problem solving may stem from the ability to remember more and more pieces of information. Or, as neural coordination and muscle strength gradually increase, the infant may advance from crawling to walking—a progression that, by anyone's account, has substantial consequences for both child and caregiver. Thus, even though at two given points in time the child's ability to think or locomote may look very different, the transformation may arise from gradual, quantitative improvements in the speed, efficiency, or strength with which mental or physical processes are carried out rather than from a dramatic reorganization of some underlying capacity.

FIGURE 1.1
Development as a
Continuous Versus a
Discontinuous Process

**Children display many changes
in their abilities and behaviors
throughout development. According to some, the best way
to explain these changes is in
terms of the gradual acquisition
of the structures and processes
that underlie growth (A).
Others believe development
undergoes a series of stagelike
transformations during which
underlying structures and
processes exhibit rapid
reorganization followed by a
period of relative stability (B).
However, other approaches
suggest that at any given time
children may exhibit multiple
ways of demonstrating some
ability or capacity, as is evident
in the "overlapping waves"
(Siegler, 1998) depiction of development (C). According to
this view, the ability or capacity
displayed by children will depend on a variety of situational
and developmental factors.**

stage Developmental period
during which the organization of
thought and behavior is qualitatively different from that of an
earlier or later period.

Alternatively, some theories explain development in terms of the child's progress through a series of **stages,** or periods during which innovative developmental accomplishments abruptly surface, presumably because some fundamental reorganizations in thinking or other capacities underlying behavior have taken place. In this view, development undergoes rapid transitions as one stage ends and a new one begins, followed by relatively stable periods during which the child's behaviors and abilities change very little (see Figure 1.1). Abrupt or rapid changes resulting in a dramatic reorganization in how children perceive, think, feel, or behave are interpreted as *qualitative advances* in development. From this perspective, children establish new ways of thinking—for instance, during the early school years—that change problem solving, moral judgment, interactions with peers, and other activities. In adolescence they move to yet another level of thinking that influences these various domains of behavior in still different ways.

Evidence to support continuity or discontinuity in human development is difficult to obtain. Perhaps one reason is that these perspectives have underestimated the variability that exists in individual children's skills. Many ways of behaving and thinking are available to children at any given time. Which one will be expressed depends on a variety of circumstances. Robert Siegler (1996, 1998) has suggested that different strategies or ways of responding can best be described as "overlapping waves" because they often coexist in the child's repertoire. Some methods of responding may be exhibited more frequently at younger ages and others at older ages. Although some strategies may be lost as the child gains more experience and as others are freshly formulated, at any particular time children are likely to be able to use several competing approaches for responding to a situation. For example, when young children demonstrate the ability to add two numbers, say 4 plus 3, they may do so using several different strategies such as counting from one, counting beginning with the larger of the pair of numbers, comparing the problem to another whose answer is already known, or directly retrieving the information from memory. Which specific strategy is employed will depend on how much experience the child has had with the problem, how familiar he or she is with each of the numbers, how quickly the answer must be determined, and how much effort is required to carry out the strategy, among other things. Thus to conclude that a child has moved into a stage or phase in which he or she is able to carry out addition profoundly underestimates the variety of competencies he or she can draw on to demonstrate that capacity.

Few, if any, aspects of human growth appear to mimic the dramatic transformations found in the life cycle of an insect as it changes from egg to larva to pupa and finally to adult periods in which a stable physical organization is followed by rapid reorganization and emergence of a new period in the life cycle. Yet over the months and years, children do become quite different. Whether these changes are best understood as quantitative or qualitative advances are points of frequent disagreement among theories of development.

How Prominent Are Individual Differences in Development?

Parents of two or more children frequently comment on how unique each child is. One child may have learned to speak before reaching one year of age, another not until eighteen months. One may have shown an interest in music, another in athletics. Perhaps one child repeatedly challenged the parent's authority, whereas another cheerfully complied with parental demands and requests. No "average" or "typical" child exists.

Biological and experiential differences certainly contribute to wide variations in behavior and competency displayed by children, even those born to and reared by the same set of parents. Although human growth must go forward within certain constraints, development may proceed along many paths and at quite different rates from one individual to another. One especially important reason that differences emerge is that individual children are exposed to various kinds and levels of benefits and risks during their development. For example, risk may be a consequence of genetic or biological complications, as well as rearing or cultural events, that promote development in less than optimal ways. An accidental head injury, exposure to a disease such as AIDS, being reared by an abusive parent, experiencing parents' divorce, attending an unstimulating daycare center, and the absence of close friends are just a few of the many factors that can affect the course of development and may limit healthy progress. Individual children, because of their genetic or biological makeup or because of other resources available in their environment, respond to these risks in different ways. *Resilient* children, those who seem able to most effectively resist the negative consequences of risk, tend to have a constellation of individual qualities that include a relatively relaxed, self-confident character that permits them to adapt and to respond intelligently in difficult situations and circumstances. In addition, they are likely to have the benefits of a close, encouraging relationship with at least one member of their family and with others beyond the family, such as a teacher or close friend, through their membership in some supportive agency or organization such as a club or church (Luthar, Ciccheti, & Becker, 2000; Masten & Coatsworth, 1998; Runyan et al., 1998; Rutter, 1990; Werner, 1995). Theories differ as to how and to what extent this diversity is emphasized and can be explained.

Individual differences in development arise from many influences. Genetic, biological, parenting, and social factors can play a role. For example, not all children have a grandparent available to directly influence their lives. For this preschooler, her grandmother is an important person who encourages and inspires an interest in reading. As a result of her grandmother's influence, she gains some of the skills necessary to succeed when she enters school.

How Do the Various Domains of Development Interact?

Many times the child's development in one domain will have a direct bearing on her attainments in other domains. Consider just one example: how a child's physical growth might influence her social and emotional development. A child who has become taller than her peers may experience very different interactions with adults and peers than a child who is small for his age. The taller child might be given more responsibilities by a teacher or be asked by peers to lead the group more frequently. These opportunities may instill a sense of worth and offer occasions to practice social skills less frequently available to the smaller child. As these social skills are exercised and become more refined and advanced, the taller child may receive still more opportunities that promote social and even cognitive development. Our ultimate aim is to understand the child as a whole individual, not just as someone who undergoes, for example, physical, perceptual, emotional, cognitive, or social development. To do so, we must keep in mind that no single component of development unfolds in isolation from the rest.

In the discussions that follow concerning various historical contributions to developmental psychology and the major theoretical approaches still important to the field today, it will be apparent that answers pertaining to the themes often differ. Moreover, the themes, summarized in Figure 1.2, will continue to have an important influence on our discussion of developmental psychology throughout this book. Perhaps one of the best ways to review them is to take a few minutes to consider your stand on each of these themes.

FIGURE 1.2
Six Major Themes in Developmental Psychology

The study of children and their development must address a number of questions, or what are identified here as themes in development. Answers to these issues are often influenced by the theoretical orientations that guide research. Throughout this chapter and the chapters that follow, we repeatedly consider these themes and the ways developmental psychologists attempt to answer these questions. Charts like the one here will appear in every chapter dealing with particular areas of development.

Key Themes in Child Development

- **Nature/Nurture**
  What roles do nature and nurture play in development?
- **Sociocultural Influence**
  How does the sociocultural context influence development?
- **Child's Active Role**
  How does the child play an active role in the process of development?

- **Continuity/Discontinuity**
  Is development continuous or discontinuous?
- **Individual Differences**
  How prominent are individual differences in development?
- **Interaction Among Domains**
  How do the various domains of development interact?

FOR YOUR REVIEW

- What do we mean by the debate between nature and nurture? Do you think development is more greatly influenced by one or the other?

- How and to what extent do you feel that society's concerns, values, and resources affect an individual's development?

- To what extent do you think that children actively influence their own development?

- Do you find it easier to understand development in terms of continuous or discontinuous stagelike change?

- In your view, how pervasive and important are individual differences in children's development?

- To what extent do you think advances or difficulties in one domain affect the child's development in other domains?

The Study of the Child: Historical Perspectives

Human development became a focus of serious study comparatively late in the history of science, having its origins only a little over one hundred years ago. Despite its relatively short history, however, developmental psychology has grown at an astonishing rate in the last several decades and is a thriving modern-day field of study. Each year hundreds of books and thousands of articles about children's growth are published for professionals interested in specific theoretical issues and for parents or teachers. Scientists and laypersons, however, have not always had such a focused and conscious desire to understand the process of child development. In fact, societal attitudes toward childhood *as a concept* have shifted considerably over the last several centuries.

The Concept of Childhood

Contemporary society views childhood as a separate, distinct, and unique period, a special time when individuals are to be protected, nurtured, loved, and kept free of most adult responsibilities and obligations. Child labor laws try to ensure that children are not abused in the work world, and the institution of public education signals a willingness to devote significant resources to their academic training. But childhood was not always viewed in this way (Borstelmann, 1983).

In many regions of the world, children spend much of their time engaged in physical labor. This girl, helping to harvest rice in Cambodia, very likely had little opportunity to learn to read or write. Historically, and in some cultures yet today, attitudes about childhood differ greatly from those held in recent times in most Western societies.

● **Children in Medieval and Renaissance Times**   From the Middle Ages through premodern times, European society's attitudes toward children differed strikingly from those of our contemporary society. Though their basic needs to be fed and clothed were tended to, children were not coddled or protected in the same way infants in our society are. As soon as they were physically able, usually at age seven or so, children were incorporated into the adult world of work; they harvested grain, learned craft skills, and otherwise contributed to the local economy. In medieval times, Western European children did not have special clothes, toys, or games. Once they were old enough to shed swaddling clothes, they wore adult fashions and pursued adult pastimes such as archery, chess, and even gambling (Ariès, 1962).

In certain respects, however, premodern European society regarded children as vulnerable, fragile, and unable to assume the full responsibilities of adulthood. Medical writings alluded to the special illnesses of young children, and laws prohibited marriages of children under age twelve (Kroll, 1977). Religious movements of this era proclaimed the innocence of children and urged that they be educated. Children's souls, as well as adults', must be saved, said clerics, and they held that parents were morally responsible for their children's spiritual well-being. Parents recognized that children were also a financial responsibility and helped them to set up their own households as they approached adulthood and marriage (Pollock, 1983; Shahar, 1990). Thus, even though medieval children were incorporated quickly into the adult world, they were recognized both as different from adults and as possessing special needs.

A noticeable shift in attitudes toward children occurred in Europe during the sixteenth century. In 1545, English physician and lawyer Thomas Phayre published the first book on pediatrics. In addition, the advent of the printing press during that century made possible the wide distribution of other manuals on the care of infants and

In premodern Europe, children often dressed like adults and participated in many adult activities. At the same time, though, children were seen as fragile and in need of protection.

children. The first grammar schools were established to educate upper-class boys in economics and politics. Upper-class girls attended convent schools or received private instruction intended to cultivate modesty and obedience as well as other skills thought to be useful in their future roles as wives and mothers (Shahar, 1990).

Probably one of the most significant social changes occurred as a result of the transition from agrarian to trade-based economies in the sixteenth and seventeenth centuries and the subsequent growth of industrialization in the eighteenth century. As people relocated from farms to towns and as the production of goods shifted outside the home, the primary role of the family in Western society changed from ensuring economic survival to the nurturing of children (Hareven, 1985). Closeness and emotional attachment increasingly became the hallmarks of parent-child relations.

● **The Age of Enlightenment**   The impact of these sweeping social changes was consolidated by the writings of several key thinkers who shaped the popular understanding of childhood. In the seventeenth and eighteenth centuries, two philosophers proposed important but distinctly different ideas about the nature and education of children. In his famous treatise *An Essay Concerning Human Understanding* (1961), originally published in 1690, the British philosopher John Locke (1632–1704) described his views on the acquisition of human knowledge. Virtually no information is inborn, according to Locke. The newborn's mind is a *tabula rasa*, literally a "blank slate," on which perceptual experiences are imprinted. Locke's philosophy of **empiricism,** the idea that environmental experiences shape the individual, foreshadowed the modern-day psychological school of behaviorism. Locke believed that rewards and punishments from others, imitation, and the associations the child forms between stimuli are key elements in the formation of the mind.

In a second work, *Some Thoughts Concerning Education* (1693/1964), Locke expounded further on his philosophy of training children:

> *The great mistake I have observed in people's breeding their children . . . is that the mind has not been made obedient to discipline and pliant to reason when it was most*

empiricism   Theory that environmental experiences shape the individual; more specifically, that all knowledge is derived from sensory experiences.

tender, most easy to be bowed. . . . He that is not used to submit his will to the reason of others when he is young, will scarce hearken to submit to his own reason when he is of an age to make use of it.

Locke further argued in support of the importance of early experiences and proper training but also that child rearing and education should proceed through the use of reason rather than harsh discipline. In his view, parents must find a balance between being overly indulgent and overly restrictive as they manage their child's behavior. As we will see, many of these same themes resound in contemporary research on good parenting and represent a contrast to the strict discipline characteristic of Western society before the eighteenth century.

The second influential philosopher of the Enlightenment was Jean Jacques Rousseau (1712–1778), a French thinker who embraced the ideal of the child as a "noble savage." According to Rousseau, children are born with a propensity to act on impulses, but not necessarily with the aim of wrongdoing. They require the gentle guidance of adult authority to bring their natural instincts and tendencies in line with the social order. In *Émile* (1762/1895), Rousseau set forth these beliefs about child rearing:

Never command him to do anything whatever, not the least thing in the world. Never allow him even to imagine that you assume to have any authority over him. Let him know merely that he is weak and that you are strong; that by virtue of his condition and your own he is necessarily at your mercy.
. . . Do not give your scholar any sort of verbal lesson, for he is to be taught only by experience. Inflict on him no species of punishment, for he does not know what it is to be in fault.

Rousseau emphasized the dynamic relationship between the curious and energetic child and the demands of his or her social environment as represented by adults. Adults should not stifle the child's natural development and spirit through domination. Contemporary theories that acknowledge the active role of the child in the process of development have distinct roots in Rousseau's writings.

Rousseau also advanced some radical ideas about education. Children, he held, should not be forced to learn by rote the vast amounts of information that adults perceive as important. Instead, teachers should capitalize on the natural curiosity of children and allow them to discover on their own the myriad facts and phenomena that make up the world. Rousseau's ideas on the nature of education would be incorporated in the twentieth-century writings of Jean Piaget.

Both Locke and Rousseau emphasized the notion of the child as a developing, as opposed to a static, being. Both challenged the supposition that children are merely passive subjects of adult authority, and both advanced the idea that children should be treated with reason and respect. Having been elevated by the efforts of these worthy thinkers to an object of intellectual interest, the child was now ready to become the subject of scientific study.

The Origins of Developmental Psychology

By the mid to late 1800s, scholars in the natural sciences, especially biology, saw in the study of children an opportunity to support their emerging theories about the origins of human beings and their behaviors. Charles Darwin, for example, hypothesized that the similarities between the behaviors of humans and those of other species were the result of common evolutionary ancestors. Similarly, Wilhelm Preyer, another biologist, was initially interested in the physiology of embryological development but soon extended his investigations to behavioral development after birth. In the United States and Europe, key researchers who participated in the birth of psychology as an academic discipline also began to show an interest in studying children. By the beginning of the twentieth century, developmental psychology was established as a legitimate area of psychological inquiry.

G. Stanley Hall is considered to be the founder of modern child psychology.

● **The Baby Biographers: Charles Darwin and Wilhelm Preyer**   One of the first records of the close scrutiny of a child for the purpose of scientific understanding comes from the writings of Charles Darwin. Eager to uncover important clues about the origins of the human species, Darwin undertook to record in great detail his infant son's behaviors during the first three years of life. Darwin documented the presence of early reflexes, such as sucking, as well as the emergence of voluntary motor movements, language, and emotions such as fear, anger, and affection. When he saw similarities, he linked the behaviors of the young child to other species, such as when, for example, he concluded that the infant's comprehension of simple words was not unlike the ability of "lower animals" to understand words spoken by humans (Darwin, 1877).

In 1882, the German biologist Wilhelm Preyer published *The Mind of the Child* (1882/1888–1889), a work that described in great detail the development of his son Axel during his first three years of life. Preyer wrote meticulously of his son's sensory development, motor accomplishments, language production, and memory, even noting indications of an emerging concept of self. Although Preyer followed in the footsteps of several previous "baby biographers," including Darwin, he was the first to insist that observations of children be conducted systematically, recorded immediately and unobtrusively, and repeated several times each day. By advocating the application of scientific techniques to the study of children, the baby biographers, and Preyer in particular, set in motion the beginnings of the child development movement in the United States.

● **G. Stanley Hall: The Founder of Modern Child Psychology**   The psychologist perhaps most responsible for launching the new discipline of child study in the United States was G. Stanley Hall, who, in 1878, became the first American to obtain a Ph.D. in psychology. Hall is also known for founding the first psychological journal in the United States in 1887 and, in 1891, the first journal of developmental psychology, *Pedagogical Seminary* (now called the *Journal of Genetic Psychology*). In addition, he founded and served as the first president of the American Psychological Association.

As the first American to study in Europe with the pioneer psychologist Wilhelm Wundt, G. Stanley Hall returned to the United States in 1880 with an interest in studying the "content of children's minds." Adopting the questionnaire method he had learned about in Germany, he had teachers ask about two hundred kindergarten-age children questions such as "Have you ever seen a cow?" or "What are bricks made of?" The percentage of children who gave particular answers was tabulated, and comparisons were made between the responses of boys and girls, city children and country children, and children of different ethnic backgrounds (Hall, 1891). For the first time, researchers were collecting data to compare groups of children, in contrast to previous approaches that had emphasized the detailed examination of individual children.

● **Alfred Binet: The Study of Individual Differences**   The French psychologist Alfred Binet is known primarily as the developer of the first formal assessment scale of intelligence. Binet was a pioneer in the study of **individual differences,** those unique characteristics that distinguish one person from others in the larger group.

Binet's original interest lay in the general features of children's thinking, including memory and reasoning about numbers. To that end, he closely scrutinized the behaviors of his two daughters as they progressed from toddlerhood to the teenage years. He noted, in particular, how one daughter, Madeleine, was serious and reflective as she tried to solve problems, whereas the other daughter, Alice, was more impulsive and temperamental (Fancher, 1998). His studies of children's thinking had two significant outcomes: first, they demonstrated that a description of individual differences contributed to the understanding of human development, and second, they provided the basis for more formal tests of children's mental abilities (Cairns, 1998). In response to a request from the Ministry of Public Instruction in Paris for a tool to screen for students with learning problems, Binet and another colleague, Théodore Simon, developed a series of tasks to systematically measure motor skills,

individual differences   Unique characteristics that distinguish a person from other members of a larger group.

vocabulary, problem solving, and a wide range of other higher-order thought processes (Binet & Simon, 1905). This instrument could identify patterns in mental capabilities that were unique to each child.

The idea of mental testing caught on very quickly in the United States, especially among clinicians, school psychologists, and other professionals concerned with the practical side of dealing with children. For the first time, it was legitimate, even important, to consider variation in mental abilities from person to person.

● **James Mark Baldwin: Developmental Theorist** Considered the founder of academic psychology in Canada (Hoff, 1992), James Mark Baldwin established a laboratory devoted to the systematic study of movement patterns, handedness, and color vision in infants at the University of Toronto (Cairns, 1992). Soon, however, his interests shifted away from gathering empirical data. He became one of the most important developmental theorists of the early twentieth century.

One of Baldwin's most important propositions was that development is a dynamic and hierarchical process such that "every genetic change ushers in a real advance, a progression on the part of nature to a higher mode of reality" (Baldwin, 1930, p. 86). Baldwin applied these ideas to the domain of cognitive development by suggesting that mental advances occur in a stagelike sequence in which the earliest thought is prelogical but gives way to logical and eventually hyperlogical or formal reasoning—ideas that today are often linked to Piaget.

Baldwin is also recognized for his unique perspective on social development and the formation of personality. Instead of characterizing the child as a passive recipient of the behaviors and beliefs endorsed by the larger society, he described the child's emerging self as a product of continual reciprocal interactions between the child and others. The proposition that development results from a mutual dynamic between the child and others took a long time to catch on among psychologists, but this idea, so popular today—and one of the themes of development we emphasize throughout this text—is actually almost a century old (Cairns & Ornstein, 1979).

By the start of the 1900s, the foundations of developmental psychology as a scientifically based discipline were firmly established. Psychologists were well poised to begin the study of differences among groups of children, individual differences among children, and the hypotheses generated by emerging theories of development.

● **Sigmund Freud: The Importance of Early Experience** During the early decades of the twentieth century, Sigmund Freud's theory also became extremely influential, particularly with respect to explaining emotional and personality development. Freud proposed in his psychosexual theory of development that many aspects of the individual's personality originate in an early and broad form of childhood sexuality. The fuel that powers human behavior, according to Freud, is a set of biological instincts. The psychological tension induced by these instincts, called *libido* or *libidinal energy,* gradually builds and requires eventual discharge. Under many circumstances, this energy is reduced as rapidly as possible. Sometimes, however, tensions such as those associated with hunger or pain in infants cannot be eliminated immediately. Because of these delays, mental structures and behavioral responses eventually organize into more satisfactory ways of decreasing tension. For example, behavioral acts might include calling out to the caregiver as a signal to be fed or eventually learning to feed oneself, responses that normally lead to a reduction in libidinal urges by effective, rational, and socially acceptable means.

The locus of tension and the optimal ways to reduce needs undergo change with age. Freud identified five stages of psychosexual development, periods during which libidinal energy is usually associated with a specific area of the body. During the *oral stage*, lasting until about one year of age, libidinal energy is focused around the mouth and is reduced through sucking, chewing, eating, and biting. Throughout the subsequent *anal stage*, from about one to three years of age, this energy is centered on the anal region and is lessened via satisfactory expelling of body wastes. The *phallic stage*, typically bridging the period between three and five years of age, is characterized as a time of desire for the opposite-sex parent and other forms of immature gratification surrounding the genitals. A relatively long *latency* period lasts from about five years of age to adolescence, and is a time in which libidinal energy is submerged or expressed, for example, via a more culturally acceptable focus on the acquisition of social or intellectual skills. During the final stage, the *genital stage,* which occurs in adolescence and continues throughout adulthood, mature forms of genital satisfaction are theorized to be an important source of tension reduction.

Freud believed that the individual's progression through these stages is greatly influenced by maturation. However, the environment also plays a critical role. Lack of opportunity to meet needs adequately or to express them during a stage could lead to negative consequences in the way the child relates to others and to feelings of low self-worth. For example, the infant whose sucking efforts are not gratified may become *fixated,* that is, preoccupied with actions associated with the mouth for the rest of his or her life. A child whose toilet training is too lax may become messy, disorderly, or wasteful, whereas one whose toilet training is too strict may display a possessive, retentive (frugal and stingy) personality or show an excessive concern with cleanliness and orderliness in later adulthood.

Freud's view of development has been criticized extensively for its emphasis on libidinal gratification, as well as for its cultural and gender limitations. So also has his method for arriving at his theory, that of asking adults to reflect on their earliest experiences. As a consequence, his contributions have often been discounted. Nevertheless, for Freud, as is true for many developmental psychologists today, events that occur during the earliest years of development and that involve interactions with the family were of paramount importance in understanding and explaining behavior throughout the later years of an individual's life.

The Continued Growth of Developmental Psychology in the Twentieth Century

From the beginning of this century to the mid-1940s, psychologists interested in development increasingly concentrated their efforts on gathering descriptive information about children. At what ages do most children achieve the milestones of motor development such as sitting, crawling, and walking? When do children develop emotions such as fear and anger? What are children's beliefs about punishment, friendship, and morality? It was during this era of intensive fact gathering that many *norms* of development—that is, the ages at which most children are able to accomplish a given developmental task—were established. For example, Arnold Gesell established the norms of motor development for the first five years of life, guidelines that are still useful to psychologists, pediatricians, and other professionals who work with children in diagnosing developmental problems or delays (Gesell & Thompson, 1934, 1938).

Over the years, questions about norms gave way to research on the variables that might be related to specific aspects of development or cause it to occur in the way it does. For example, is maturation or experience responsible for the sequence of motor behaviors most children seem to display? Even almost seventy years ago, researchers found that the answer was not simple. Myrtle McGraw (1935, 1939), in her classic studies of twins Johnny and Jimmy, reported that training Johnny (and not Jimmy) to reach for objects, crawl, and swim during infancy accelerated motor development, but only when he was already showing signs of physiological maturity. Similarly, does the predictable sequence of language development occur because of biological influences or learning? What factors lead to the emergence of emotional ties children form with caregivers? Researchers today continue to ask questions of these sorts, recognizing more and more the complexities of the influences on child development.

The first half of the twentieth century also saw the founding of a number of major institutes or research centers that attracted bright young scholars who dedicated their lives to the scientific study of children. A further sign of the professionalization

In her classic studies of a pair of twins, Myrtle McGraw found that both maturation and experience contributed to motor skill development.

of the discipline was the formation of the Society for Research in Child Development (SRCD) in 1933 for scientists who wished to share their growing knowledge of child behavior and development. Today the membership of this society numbers about five thousand (SRCD, 2002) and includes developmental researchers, practitioners, and professionals working in settings such as colleges, universities, research institutes, and hospitals.

Scholars now approach child development from an assortment of disciplines, including anthropology, sociology, education, medicine, biology, and several subareas of psychology (e.g., neuropsychology, comparative psychology, and clinical psychology), as well as the specialized area of developmental psychology. Each discipline has its own biases, as defined by the questions each asks about development and the methodological approaches it employs to answer those questions. Nonetheless, our pooled knowledge gives us a better understanding of development than we might expect from a field that officially began only a century ago.

A number of major theories also influence our understanding of development today. We introduce them and briefly highlight some of the major concepts and principles associated with each in the sections that follow. However, their contributions will be a major part of our discussion in later chapters as well. In considering these theories in this first chapter, we focus in particular on where each stands with respect to the major themes in developmental psychology.

FOR YOUR REVIEW

- How have views of childhood changed from medieval and Renaissance times to today?

- What were John Locke's and Jean Jacques Rousseau's views of childhood?

- How did Charles Darwin, Wilhelm Preyer, G. Stanley Hall, Alfred Binet, and James Mark Baldwin contribute to developmental psychology?

- What was Sigmund Freud's pyschosexual theory of development?

- What new emphases emerged in research on children during the first half of the twentieth century?

Learning Theory Approaches

Learning theorists study how principles of learning cause the individual to change and develop. **Learning,** the relatively permanent change in behavior that results from experience, undoubtedly contributes to why the infant smiles as her mother approaches, the three-year-old says a polite "thank you" on receiving his grandmother's present, the five-year-old displays newfound skill in tying her shoes, and the adolescent expresses a clear preference about the most fashionable item of clothing to wear.

In the extreme view, some learning theorists believe, as John B. Watson did, that learning mechanisms can be exploited to create virtually any type of person:

> *Give me a dozen healthy infants, well-formed, and my own specified world to bring them up in and I'll guarantee to take any one at random and train him to become any type of specialist I might select—doctor, lawyer, artist, merchant-chief, and yes, even beggar-man and thief, regardless of his talents, penchants, tendencies, abilities, vocations, and race of his ancestors.* (Watson, 1930, p. 104)

Although present-day supporters of learning seldom take such a radical position, they are in agreement that basic principles of learning can have a powerful influence on child development (Bijou, 1989; Gewirtz & Peláez-Nogueras, 1992; Schlinger, 1992).

learning Relatively permanent change in behavior as a result of such experiences as exploration, observation, and practice.

Behavior Analysis

Behavior analysis is a theoretical account of development that relies on several basic principles of learning to explain developmental changes in behavior. Behavior analysis sprang from the radical learning position introduced by John B. Watson and was extended in more recent years by B. F. Skinner (1953, 1974) and others. Nearly a century ago, the Russian physiologist Ivan Pavlov observed that dogs would often begin to salivate at the sound of a bell or some other arbitrary stimulus when the stimulus was accompanied by food. In this type of learning, called *classical conditioning*, a neutral stimulus begins to elicit a response after being repeatedly paired with another stimulus that already elicits that response. We learn certain behaviors and emotions as a result of classical conditioning. For example, children and adults may become anxious on entering a dental office because of its association with previous painful treatments performed by the dentist.

To understand a second basic principle of learning, consider two babies who smile as their caregivers approach. With one baby, the caregiver stops, says "Hi, baby!" and briefly rocks the cradle. With the other baby, the caregiver walks on past, preoccupied. Which baby is more likely to repeat his smiling response when the caregiver nears again? If you reasoned that the first is more likely than the second because the behavior was followed by a positive event (attention or approval) that often increases the frequency of a behavior, you know something about the principle of operant conditioning. *Operant conditioning* (also called *instrumental conditioning*) refers to the process by which the frequency of a behavior changes depending on response consequences in the form of a desirable or undesirable outcome. Behavior analysts have used this principle to account for the emergence of such straightforward behaviors as the one-year-old's waving good-bye to far more sophisticated skills involving memory, language, social interaction, and complex problem solving.

Operant and classical conditioning have been shown to have enormous potential to change behavior. *Behavior modification*, sometimes called *applied behavior analysis*, involves the systematic application of operant conditioning to modify human activity. To illustrate, Jason Stricker and his colleagues (Stricker et al., 2001) investigated whether thumb sucking could be reduced in children who engaged in such activity at an age when it is no longer considered appropriate. They identified a seven-year-old child with an attention deficit hyperactivity disorder who often sucked his thumb while watching television and in other situations. Would consistent feedback to the child help him to become aware of this activity and reduce this behavior? To test this possibility, the researchers attached two small transmitters to the child, one to his wrist and a second to his shirt, just below his mouth. When the child raised his hand to his mouth to engage in thumb sucking, bringing the wrist and shirt transmitter close to each other, the transmitters triggered a nearby device that began to produce a beeping tone. The researchers recorded the percentage of time the child engaged in thumb sucking during ten-minute sessions of television viewing over a number of weeks. During a baseline period the child did not wear the transmitters. In other sessions, he wore transmitters that were either activated or not activated to provide feedback. The findings of this experiment are shown in Figure 1.3. The results clearly demonstrate the elimination of the thumb sucking when the transmitters produced feedback about the activity. The feedback may have helped the child to become aware of his thumb sucking; in addition, the sound also may have been annoying enough to yield the change in his behavior.

Applied behavior analysis has become a powerful approach used by teachers, therapists, and caregivers to bring about changes in behavior ranging from the elimination of temper tantrums and other disruptive responses to encouraging healthy diets and safe driving habits. Even some of its detractors have suggested that behavior analysis may have done more to benefit human welfare than any other psychological theory (Hebb, 1980). For this reason alone, learning theory has appealed to many in their efforts to understand development. Yet behavior analysis has drawn extensive criticism. Its critics, including some learning theorists, remain unconvinced that a

behavior analysis   Learning theory perspective that explains the development of behavior according to the principles of classical and operant conditioning.

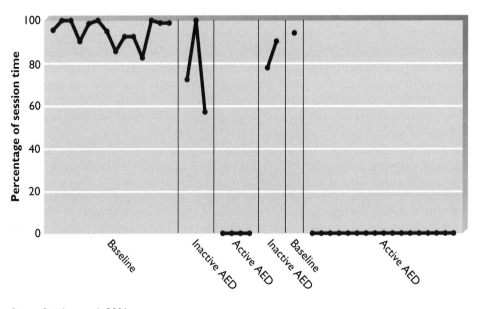

FIGURE 1.3
A Behavioral Approach to Reducing Thumb Sucking in Children

Source: Stricker et al., 2001.

The seven-year-old child observed in this study often sucked his thumb. During the baseline period sessions in which he was simply observed watching television, he engaged in this activity a high percentage of time. Next, a set of transmitters, called an awareness enhancement device (AED), was attached to the child. When the device did not activate a beeping tone (Inactive AED), he continued to display such behavior frequently. However, when the tone was activated whenever the child sucked his thumb (Active AED), the practice ceased. As predicted by behavorial theories, response consequences can have a powerful effect on behavior.

behavior can be understood without taking into account the child's feelings and reasons for engaging in that behavior. In other words, mental, emotional, and motivational factors also play a prominent role in how a child interprets and responds to stimulation. Among various learning perspectives, social learning theory attempts to incorporate these factors into its explanation of behavior and development.

Social Learning Theory

Social learning theory emphasizes the importance of learning through observation and imitation of the behaviors displayed by others. Social learning theorists start with the assumption that whether an individual will be friendly, outgoing, confident, and honest rather than shy and perhaps hostile and untrustworthy largely depends on the socialization practices of parents and caregivers throughout that person's childhood. Although operant and classical conditioning play a substantial role, social learning theorists underscore **observational learning,** the acquisition of behaviors from listening to and watching other people, as a particularly important means of acquiring new behaviors. The two-year-old who stands before a mirror pretending to shave in imitation of his father is displaying observational learning. Similarly, you may have witnessed the embarrassment of a parent whose three-year-old has uttered a profanity, a behavior probably acquired by the same process.

According to Albert Bandura, psychology's best-known spokesperson for social learning, a society could never effectively convey complex language, social and moral customs, or other achievements to its younger members without extensively relying on observational learning. Bandura (1965) notes that significant learning occurs, often completely without error, through the act of watching and imitating another person, a *model.* For example, girls in one region of Guatemala learn to weave simply by watching an expert, an approach to learning new skills common to the fields, homes, and shops of communities all over the world. Social learning theorists propose that many kinds of complex social activities, including the acquisition of gender roles, aggression, prosocial responses (such as willingness to assist others), resistance to temptation, and other facets of moral development, are learned primarily through observing others (Bandura & Walters, 1963).

In accounting for the acquisition of complex behaviors, Bandura has often referred to cognitive processes within his theory, now known as *social cognitive theory.* Bandura (1989) believes that four sets of cognitive processes are especially important

social learning theory
Theoretical approach emphasizing the importance of learning through observation and imitation of behaviors modeled by others.

observational learning
Learning that takes place by simply observing another person's behavior.

Social learning theory emphasizes the important role that observation of another person's behavior plays in learning. By brushing her doll's hair, this preschooler is imitating the same activity that she herself is experiencing—having her own hair brushed by her mother. Social learning provides an important mechanism by which she and others acquire many desirable customs and behaviors in their society.

in observational learning. Attentional processes determine what information will be acquired from models, and memory processes convert these observations into stored mental representations. Production processes then transform these mental representations into matching behaviors, and motivational processes define which behaviors are likely to be performed. As each of these processes becomes more sophisticated, observational and other forms of learning become increasingly refined and proficient, and the child becomes more effective in regulating his or her own behavior (Grusec, 1992).

Learning Theory and Themes in Development

As our discussions of behavior analysis and social cognitive theory suggest, not all learning theorists share the same views about the prime determinants of development. What stance do behavior analysts and social cognitive theorists take on the six major developmental themes we introduced at the beginning of this chapter?

■ *Nature/Nurture*   Behavior analysts believe that although biological and genetic factors may limit the kinds of responses that can be performed and help to define which events are reinforcing or punishing, it is the environment that controls behavior. For behaviorists, a child's functioning is the outcome of a history of associated behaviors and consequences. In social cognitive theory, biological and other internal factors along with the environment are believed to play a mutual, interactive role in contributing to development (Bandura, 1989).

■ *Sociocultural Influence*   Behaviorists believe that although societies differ in the responses viewed as desirable or unacceptable, the mechanisms of learning are universal for individuals in all cultures. Rewards and punishments delivered in the immediate environment are a key to understanding development. Social learning theorists give sociocultural context more emphasis than behaviorists do by pointing out, for example, that advances in communication technology such as television expand the opportunity for children and adults to acquire many novel skills and patterns of behavior through observational learning.

■ *Child's Active Role*   In keeping with their strong experiential emphasis, behaviorists believe the child's role in development is passive. Skinner claimed that "a person does not act upon the world, the world acts upon him" (1971, p. 211). According to Skinner, psychologists should abolish references to unobservable mental or cognitive constructs such as motives, goals, needs, or thoughts in their explanations of behavior. Bandura's social cognitive theory differs from behavior analysis by embracing mental and motivational constructs and processes for interpreting and understanding others as well as the self. Social cognitive theory therefore confers a much more active status on the child than does behavior analysis.

■ *Continuity/Discontinuity*   Both behavior analysts and social learning theorists consider development to be continuous rather than stagelike. Any departure from this pattern would stem from abrupt shifts in environmental circumstances, such as when the child enters school or the adolescent enters the work environment.

■ *Individual Differences*   The general principles of learning apply to all individuals. Individual differences arise primarily from the unique kinds of experiences each person receives, for example, the specific models she or he is exposed to or the particular behaviors rewarded by others in the environment.

■ *Interaction Among Domains*   Whereas behavior analysts explain development in all domains in terms of the basic principles of learning, social cognitive theorists stress that learning is linked to the child's physical, cognitive, and social development. Thus this latter perspective acknowledges the interaction among different domains of development by recognizing that the child's learning is a consequence of what he or she feels, believes, and thinks.

Cognitive-Developmental Approaches

According to **cognitive-developmental theory,** behavior reflects the emergence of various cognitive *structures,* organized units or patterns of thinking, that influence how the child interprets experience. Cognitive-developmental theories tend to share the fundamental assumption that normal children display common intellectual, emotional, and social capacities despite widely varying experiences. Most three- and four-year-olds around the world, for example, believe that a gallon of water, when poured from one container to another of a different shape, changes in amount or quantity, an error children rarely make once they reach seven or eight years of age. Cognitive-developmental theorists explain this profound change in reasoning in terms of children acquiring new ways of understanding their world.

The most extensive and best-known cognitive-developmental theory was put forward by Jean Piaget. His vigorous defense of physical and mental *action* as the basis for cognitive development (Beilin & Fireman, 1999) and his belief that intellectual capacities undergo *qualitative* reorganization at different stages of development have had a monumental impact, not only on developmental psychologists but also on educators and other professionals working with children.

Piaget's Theory

Piaget's vision of human development was based on two overriding assumptions about intelligence: (1) it is a form of biological adaptation, and (2) it becomes organized as the individual interacts with the external world (Piaget, 1971). Thus, for Piaget, thinking exhibits two inborn qualities. The first is **adaptation,** a tendency to adjust or become more attuned to the conditions imposed by the environment. The second is **organization,** a tendency for intellectual structures and processes to become more systematic and coherent. Just as arms, eyes, lungs, heart, and other physical structures assemble and take shape to carry out biological functions, so do mental structures array themselves in ever more powerful patterns to support more complex thought. These changes, however, depend on the opportunity to look and touch, handle and play with, and construct and order the rich assortment of experiences stemming from action on the environment. From the abundant encounters provided in commonplace physical and social experiences, the child confronts unexpected and puzzling outcomes that ultimately lead to reorganizations in thought.

● **Schemes** The basic mental structure in Piaget's theory is a **scheme,** a coordinated and systematic pattern of action or way of reasoning. A scheme is a kind of template for acting or thinking applied to similar classes of objects or situations. The infant who sucks at her mother's breast, at her favorite pacifier, and at her thumb is exercising a scheme of sucking. The toddler who stacks blocks, pots and pans, and then shoe boxes is exercising a scheme of stacking. The six-year-old who realizes that his eight Matchbox cars can be stored in an equal number of boxes regardless of how they are scattered about the floor is also exercising a scheme, this time one concerned with number.

The infant's schemes are limited to patterns of action applied to objects: sucking, grasping, shaking, and so forth. The older child's schemes will often involve mental processes and be far more complex as he or she reasons about such things as classes of objects, number, or spatial relations, and, by adolescence, the meaning of life and the origins of the universe. For Piaget, earlier schemes set the stage for constructing new and more sophisticated schemes. From simple reflexes such as grasping and sucking emerge schemes for holding or hugging or hitting. And from these actions children construct new schemes—for categorizing objects, for relating to family and friends, and so forth.

● **Assimilation and Accommodation** Piaget believed that schemes change through two complementary processes. The first, **assimilation,** refers to the process

Jean Piaget's keen observations and insights concerning the behavior of children laid the groundwork for his theory of cognitive development. Piaget's ideas about how thinking develops have influenced psychologists, educators, and many others in their attempts to understand children.

cognitive-developmental theory Theoretical orientation, most frequently associated with Piaget, emphasizing the active construction of psychological structures to interpret experience.

adaptation In Piagetian theory, the inborn tendency to adjust or become more attuned to conditions imposed by the environment; takes place through assimilation and accommodation.

organization In Piagetian theory, the inborn tendency for structures and processes to become more systematic and coherent.

scheme In Piagetian theory, the mental structure underlying a coordinated and systematic pattern of behaviors or thinking applied across similar objects or situations.

assimilation In Piagetian theory, a component of adaptation; process of interpreting an experience in terms of current ways (schemes) of understanding things.

of interpreting an experience in terms of current ways of understanding things. The second, **accommodation,** refers to the modifications in behavior and thinking that take place when the old ways of understanding, the old schemes, no longer fit. To illustrate these two processes, consider the toddler who has begun to walk. He freely moves about the floor of his home, but when approaching the steps leading to either the bedroom upstairs or the basement below, he pauses, says "Stairs," and turns away. He does the same thing when coming across sets of stairs while visiting his grandmother's or neighbor's house. He recognizes, in other words, perhaps after repeatedly hearing his parents say, "Stop! You'll fall down!" and maybe even experiencing a fall on some steps, that stairs are forbidden and *assimilates* other instances of staircases within this scheme or knowledge of "things that can cause me to fall."

One early winter day, when the temperature has dropped below freezing, this same toddler and his father go for a walk outdoors. Following some distance behind, the father suddenly shouts, "Stop! You'll fall down!" The toddler appears puzzled, looks around as if searching for something, and utters, "Stairs." His father, sensing his son's confusion, points to the ice on the sidewalk and adds, "There aren't any stairs here, but you can fall down on ice, too." Through this new encounter, the child comes to *accommodate* his understanding of "things that cause me to fall" to include not just stairs but also ice and, eventually, perhaps a slippery rug or toys left lying about on the floor. So, too, when the baby first begins to drink from a cup instead of feeding from her mother's breast, she must accommodate to this new experience: shape her lips and mouth in new ways to take in the milk. In a similar manner throughout development, the child's intellectual capacities become reshaped and reorganized as the child attempts to adjust—that is, accommodate—to new experiences.

For Piaget, assimilation and accommodation are complementary aspects of all psychological activity, processes engaged in a constant tug of war in the never-ending goal of acquiring understanding (Valsiner, 1998). Fortunately, adaptation in the form of newer and more complex schemes is the result of this continuous dynamic. The outcome of adaptation is a more effective fitting together of the many pieces of knowledge that make up the child's understanding. The process by which assimilation and accommodation bring about more organized and powerful schemes for thinking is called **equilibration.** Each new experience can cause imbalance, which can be corrected only by modification of the child's schemes. In trying to make sense of his or her world, the child develops more adaptive ways of thinking.

● **The Piagetian Stages**   During some periods of development, schemes may undergo rapid and substantial modification and reorganization. The more effective levels of knowledge that emerge from these restructurings are the basis for different stages in Piaget's theory of development. Piaget proposed that development proceeds through four stages: *sensorimotor, preoperational, concrete,* and *formal.* Much more will be said about each of these stages in the chapter titled "Cognition: Piaget and Vygotsky"; however, Table 1.1 briefly identifies them. Each higher stage is defined by the appearance of a qualitatively different level of thinking, an increasingly sophisticated form of knowledge through which the child displays greater intellectual balance for responding to the environment. However, each new stage does not suddenly appear full-blown; it arises from the integration and incorporation of earlier ways of thinking.

Piaget's wide range of observations, his frequently surprising findings about what infants and children can and cannot do, and his challenging theoretical explanations and assumptions have sparked a wealth of research on cognitive, social, and moral development. Many researchers applaud his innovative conceptualizations concerning development but disagree with Piaget's specific interpretations for them. For example, Piaget vigorously embraced the notion of children as active participants in their own development, a viewpoint that others have widely adopted (Siegler & Ellis, 1996). However, the central concept of qualitative differences in thinking between children and adults, and particularly of stagelike transformations, has been far less favorably received (Fischer & Bidell, 1998; Thelen & Smith, 1994). We will consider

accommodation   In Piagetian theory, a component of adaptation; process of modification in thinking (schemes) that takes place when old ways of understanding something no longer fit.

equilibration   In Piagetian theory, an innate self-regulatory process that, through accommodation and assimilation, results in more organized and powerful schemes for adapting to the environment.

TABLE 1.1	Piaget's Stages of Cognitive Development	
Stage	**Emerging Cognitive Structure (schemes)**	**Typical Achievements and Behaviors**
Sensorimotor (birth until 1½–2 years)	Sensory and motor actions, initially reflexes, quickly differentiate by means of accommodation and co-ordinate to form adaptive ways of acting on the environment.	Infants suck, grasp, look, reach, and so forth, responses that become organized into complex activities such as hand-eye coordination, knowledge of space and objects, and eventually rudimentary symbols designed to solve problems and understand the physical world.
Preoperational (1½–7 years)	Symbols stand for or represent objects and events, but communication and thought remain relatively inflexible.	Children begin to acquire language and mental representations, but thought remains unidimensional and oriented around the self.
Concrete Operational (7–11 years)	Cognitive operations permit logical reasoning about concrete objects, events, and relationships.	Children are no longer fooled by appearance, and they can reason more systematically with respect to classes, number, and other characteristics of their physical and social world.
Formal Operational (11 years and above)	Operations can be performed on operations. Thought becomes abstract, and all possible outcomes can be considered.	Adolescents and adults are able to reason about hypothetical outcomes. Abstract issues (e.g., religion, morality, alternative lifestyles) are systematically evaluated.

Piaget's theory and the many pieces of evidence that support or challenge his views more fully in the chapter titled "Cognition: Piaget and Vygotsky."

Piaget's Theory and Themes in Development

How does Piaget's theory address the six major themes of development?

■ *Nature/Nurture*   Piaget theorized that a number of biologically based factors contribute to cognitive development. Among them is maturation, the gradual unfolding over time of genetic programs for development. Another factor is the child's inherent tendency to act, physically or mentally, on the environment. Nevertheless, for Piaget development is clearly the product of the interaction of these factors with experience.

■ *Sociocultural Influence*   For Piaget, children develop in much the same way in all cultures around the world because of their similar biological makeups and the common physical and social world to which all humans must adapt. Different cultural or educational opportunities, however, can affect the speed and ultimate level of achievement in cognitive development.

■ *Child's Active Role*   In Piaget's theory, knowledge is *constructed,* that is, created and formed by the continuous revision and reorganization of intellectual structures in conjunction with experience. Piaget's constructivist model depicts a mind actively engaged in knowing and understanding its environment. Thinking is active. That activity leads to increasingly effective ways of thinking. Children, then, are highly active participants in determining what they learn and how they understand reality.

■ *Continuity/Discontinuity*   Although recognizing continuous changes, Piaget's theory focuses on the ways schemes undergo reorganization and change to form distinctive stages in development. In his later writings and conversations, Piaget began to downplay the importance of stages (Piaget, 1971; Vuyk, 1981). He believed that an overemphasis on stages had led to too much concern with describing periods of intellectual stability or equilibrium when, in fact, cognition is always undergoing development. Cognitive development, he eventually concluded, is more like a spiral in which change constantly occurs, although sometimes at faster rates than at other times (Beilin, 1989).

■ *Individual Differences*   Piaget placed very little emphasis on individual differences in development. His goal was to identify the principles that applied to cognitive and other aspects of development in all children.

■ *Interaction Among Domains*   Piaget's theory has implications for many domains of development. For example, his ideas about cognitive development have been used to explain changes in communication, moral thinking, and aspects of *social cognition* such as how children understand the thoughts, intentions, feelings, and views of others. Nevertheless, Piaget has been criticized for paying relatively little attention to how social and emotional domains influence cognitive development.

Information-Processing Approaches

Computer information processing as a metaphor for human thinking has generated so many models and theories that it is difficult to single out any one approach as a prototype (Klahr & MacWhinney, 1998). However, one common thread evident in any **information-processing** point of view is the notion that humans, like computers, have a *limited capacity* for taking in and operating on the vast amount of information available to them. Thus changes in cognitive structures (for example, short- and long-term memory) and processes (e.g., strategies, rules, and plans associated with attending, remembering, and decision making) are an essential component to explaining how older children might process information more fully and effectively than younger children.

What sets an information-processing theory apart from many other theories is its detailed effort to explain exactly how the child comes to identify the letters of the alphabet, remember the multiplication tables, recall the main ideas of a story, give a classmate directions to his or her home, or decide whether it is safe to cross the street. For example, how does a six-year-old solve addition problems? She may have practiced this activity over and over and learned the answer to each particular problem by rote over many months of exposure to them. Or she may rely on some kind of strategy that permits her to consistently arrive at the correct answer. For example, she could start with the first number of the addition problem and then add one unit the number of times indicated by the second number. Thus, for the problem 3 + 5, she may begin at 3 and add 1 to it the necessary five times to arrive at the correct answer.

How could we tell whether one child was engaging in the first procedure, retrieving information from long-term rote memory, and another child the second procedure of utilizing a rule to determine the answer? One clue could come from the length of time it takes to solve various addition problems. If a child is using the first technique, she can be expected to solve each problem in about the same length of time. If she uses the second technique, however, she will likely take somewhat longer to answer a problem in which the second number is very large than when it is very small. We may also see the child producing other observable behaviors, such as holding up three fingers to begin with and counting off additional fingers to arrive at the correct answer.

As this example illustrates, information-processing theorists frequently attempt to describe the rules, strategies, and procedures that children employ to complete a task and that help them to remember, make inferences, and solve problems. Why has this approach become popular in developmental psychology? One reason is disenchantment with learning, Piagetian, and other perspectives for explaining behavior. For instance, although learning theories attempt to identify which abilities are learned, they have offered few insights into how the child's mind changes with age in learning these abilities. Piaget's cognitive-developmental theory is concerned with this issue,

information processing
Theoretical approach that views humans as having a limited ability to process information, much like computers.

but his explanations have been difficult to translate into ideas about how the mind actually functions. Moreover, the information-processing approach can be extended to account for development in many other domains, including language acquisition, peer relationships, and even social and personality development. Not surprisingly, given its breadth of application, information-processing approaches are discussed further in a number of the chapters that follow.

Information-Processing Approaches and Themes in Development

Because of the wide variety of information-processing models theorized to account for changes in cognitive development, we can draw only broad conclusions concerning their positions on the various themes in development.

■ *Nature/Nurture*   Information-processing models have said little about the nature versus nurture debate. Some basic capacities to perceive and process information are assumed at or before birth, and the system may be attuned to respond in certain ways, for example, to language and other kinds of information. The environment has an obvious impact on development because it provides input for processing by the mind. The implicit assumption in most models is that basic cognitive structures and processes interact with experience to produce changes in the system.

■ *Sociocultural Influence*   As in the case of learning theory, the sociocultural context of development has largely been ignored by information-processing theorists. This is probably because researchers have typically focused on identifying how the mind operates on specific problems rather than on how the mind is affected by the kinds of problems a culture presents to it.

■ *Child's Active Role*   The computer is often viewed as a metaphor for human information processing and is generally perceived as a passive machine that must be programmed. However, few information-processing theorists extend this notion to the human mind. Although we do, of course, react to the environment, we also initiate and construct strategies and procedures that assist in processing information more effectively. From this perspective, children take an increasingly active role in controlling their own learning and development.

■ *Continuity/Discontinuity*   In most information-processing models, cognitive development is theorized to undergo quantitative rather than qualitative changes. For example, children retain increasing numbers of items in both short-term and long-term memory and interpret information and apply various strategies more efficiently and effectively with development. Similarly, the acquisition of new strategies for storing and retrieving information, new rules for problem solving, and new ways of thinking about and processing information are interpreted as shifts in ability that come about because of relatively small, continuous improvements in the capacity to process information.

■ *Individual Differences*   Many information-processing theories pay little heed to individual differences in development. However, their potential to explain such differences in terms of variations in rules, strategies, and other procedures for processing information is considerable.

■ *Interaction Among Domains*   A notable limitation of many information-processing models is their failure to consider emotional, motivational, and other domains of behavior. How social factors such as instructions, modeling, and the cultural context of learning lead to developmental changes in processing information is also rarely spelled out (Klahr, 1989). However, as already noted, information-processing approaches have been extended to other domains of development including language and social and personality development.

TABLE 1.2	Erikson's Stages of Psychosocial Development	
Stage	**Adaptive Mode**	**Significant Events and Outcomes**
Basic Trust Versus Mistrust (birth to 1 year)	Incorporation—to take in (and give in return)	Babies must find consistency, predictability, and reliability in their caregivers' behaviors to gain a sense of trust and hope.
Autonomy Versus Shame and Doubt (1–3 years)	Control—to hold on and to let go	The child begins to explore and make choices in order to understand what is manageable and socially acceptable.
Initiative Versus Guilt (3–6 years)	Intrusion—to go after	The child begins to make plans, set goals, and persist in both physical and social exchanges to gain a sense of purpose and remain enthusiastic even in the face of inevitable frustration.
Industry Versus Inferiority (6 years to puberty)	Construction—to build things and relationships	The child acquires skills and performs "work" in the form of becoming educated and supporting the family in order to feel competent and attain a sense of achievement.
Identity Versus Identity Confusion (puberty to adulthood)	Integration—to be oneself (or not be oneself)	The adolescent attempts to discover his or her identity and place in society by trying out of many roles in order to answer the question, "Who am I?"
Intimacy Versus Isolation (young adulthood)	Solidarity—to lose and find oneself in another	Having achieved a sense of identity, the young adult can now share himself or herself with another to avoid a sense of isolation, self-absorption, and the absence of love.
Generativity Versus Stagnation (middle adulthood)	Productivity—to make and to take care of	The adult produces things and ideas through work and creates and cares for the next generation to gain a sense of fulfillment and caring.
Integrity Versus Despair (old age)	Acceptance—to be (by having been) and to face not being	The older adult reviews and evaluates his or her life and accepts its worth, even if he or she has not reached all goals, to achieve a sense of wisdom.

Erikson's Psychosocial Approach

For the most part, the theoretical models we have examined so far have been concerned with learning and cognitive development. With *psychosocial* models, we shift to a substantially greater focus on emotions and personality. At one time, Freud's theory of personality was extremely influential in explaining emotional and personality development. However, Erikson's theory has gained far greater attention in recent years. Like Freud, Erikson theorized that personality development progresses through stages. During each stage, the child must resolve conflicts between needs or feelings and external obstacles. The satisfactory resolution of these conflicts leads to a healthy personality and a productive lifestyle. But in contrast to Freud, Erikson included several additional stages during adulthood, and he gave socialization and society far greater importance in his theory.

Psychosocial Theory

In his classic work *Childhood and Society* (1950), Erikson outlined eight stages of development, as summarized in Table 1.2. During the first stage, for example, Erikson theorized that *incorporation* or taking in is the primary mode for acting adaptively toward the world. In Erikson's view, this mode of activity extends beyond the mouth and includes other senses, such as looking and hearing, and motor systems, such as reaching and grasping, systems designed to expand the infant's resources for absorbing and responding to reality. Each subsequent stage identified another important mode for adapting to the environment.

Society, according to Erikson, plays a critical role in shaping and forming reality for the child. Communities create their own demands and set their own criteria for socializing the child. In one society an infant may be permitted to breast-feed whenever hungry over a period of several years, whereas infants in another society may be nursed or bottle-fed on a rigid schedule and weaned within the first year of life. In another example, the timing and severity of toilet training, as well as the means by which caregivers initiate it, may differ vastly from one society to another. Cultures differ in the requirements imposed on the child, yet each child must adapt to his own culture's regulations. Thus Erikson's **psychosocial theory of development** highlights the child's composite need to initiate adaptive modes of functioning while meeting the variety of demands framed by the society in which she lives.

Erikson theorized that the individual confronts a specific crisis as society imposes new demands in each stage. The resolution of each crisis may or may not be successful, but triumphs at earlier stages lay the groundwork for the negotiation of later stages. Moreover, each society has evolved ways to help individuals meet their needs. Caregiving practices, educational programs, social organizations, occupational training, and moral and ethical support are examples of cultural systems established to foster healthy, productive psychosocial development.

A common theme underlying the various features of Erikson's theory is the search for **identity,** or the acceptance of both self and one's society. At each stage, this search is manifested in a specific way. The needs to develop a feeling of trust for a caregiver, acquire a sense of autonomy, initiate exchanges with the world, and learn and become competent in school and other settings are examples of how the infant and child discovers who and what she or he is and will become. During adolescence, the individual confronts the issue of identity directly. But the answer to "Who am I?" is elaborated and made clearer as the individual progresses through each psychosocial stage.

In summary, Erikson's views of personality development highlighted the practices society uses to encourage and promote healthy social and personality development. However, he painted development with a broad brush, and consequently his theory is frequently criticized for its vagueness. Still, just as Piaget identified meaningful issues in cognitive development, Erikson—regardless of the precision of his specific formulations—had a flair for targeting crucial issues in social and personality development.

Erik Erikson outlined eight stages of personality development. His psychosocial theory emphasized that at each stage, individuals must successfully adapt to new forms of demands placed on them by society. He also stressed that cultures frequently differ in how they help individuals to negotiate these demands.

Psychosocial Theory and Themes in Development

Our discussion of Erikson's theory has already focused on a number of themes in development, but let's consider them once more.

■ *Nature/Nurture* A biological contribution to behavior, extended from Freud's theory, is evident in Erikson's positions as well. Yet psychosocial theory must be considered interactionist, given the momentous role the presence and absence of appropriate socializing experiences play in resolving conflicts that arise at every stage.

■ *Sociocultural Influence* The broader sociocultural context in which caregivers encourage children to master, explore, and engage in their physical and social environment, especially during the early years of life, plays a critical role in Erikson's theory of development. For Erikson, the sociocultural context is a key factor in understanding an individual's personality and social relationships.

■ *Child's Active Role* In Erikson's theory, the emphasis on establishing an identity for self within society suggests an active role for the child in development. Each stage, in fact, identifies a particular task or way to effectively adapt to sustain a healthy personality.

■ *Continuity/Discontinuity* Erikson identified eight stages in personality development. The successful negotiation of earlier stages lays the groundwork for continued psychological growth. The individual unable to work through a crisis at one time, however, may still effectively resolve it at a later stage.

psychosocial theory of development Erikson's theory that personality develops through eight stages of adaptive functioning to meet the demands framed by society.

identity In Eriksonian psychosocial theory, the acceptance of both self and society, a concept that must be achieved at every stage but is especially important during adolescence.

■ *Individual Differences*   The psychosocial stages are common to every individual in every culture. However, the success with which each stage is negotiated can vary dramatically from one individual to another and from one society to another. Although not specifically focused on individual differences in development, Erikson's theory offers many insights into how and why these differences might come about.

■ *Interaction Among Domains*   Erikson links social, emotional, and cognitive development together in the individual's efforts to achieve identity. For example, a sense of trust emerges from taking in through the senses as well as the motor system; a sense of industry reflects intellectual competence as well as the ability to interact effectively with others; and discovering one's identity requires the integration of all of one's psychological skills and competencies.

Contextual Approaches

Psychologists have long recognized that children live in vastly different circumstances and that these differences can have a dramatic influence on development. Some children grow up in households with a single parent, others with two parents, and still others with grandparents and perhaps aunts and uncles; children in foster care, on the other hand, may be shuffled frequently from one family to another. In addition, siblings within the same family may receive quite different experiences as a function of being the eldest or youngest or being singled out for certain kinds of treatment and expectations by family members. Number of siblings, economic resources, space and privacy, independence, and emotional atmosphere are among the vast assortment of factors that vary in the immediate surroundings of children.

Differences in the contexts of development extend far beyond a child's immediate family, however. Physical surroundings, access to schools, job opportunities, technological innovations, natural disasters, political systems, and war, as well as the cultural dictates of the community, influence the way children are reared. Some of these circumstances will be more supportive of development than others. Apart from the physical and sociocultural contexts in which each child lives is still another factor: the innate and species-specific predispositions, the biological context that equips the child to learn and develop.

Developmental theories usually focus on immediate experience, defined narrowly in terms of contemporary circumstances and recent events, and how it affects devel-

Contextual approaches to development give recognition to the dramatic impact that broad sociocultural factors can have on children's lives. These children in Ethiopia attend an overcrowded school with few educational resources, a setting far different from classrooms in most Western countries. Schooling and work, family structure, economic resources, and many other social contexts vary tremendously for children living in different cultures. Researchers need to consider these types of broad factors affecting children's lives in order to fully understand development.

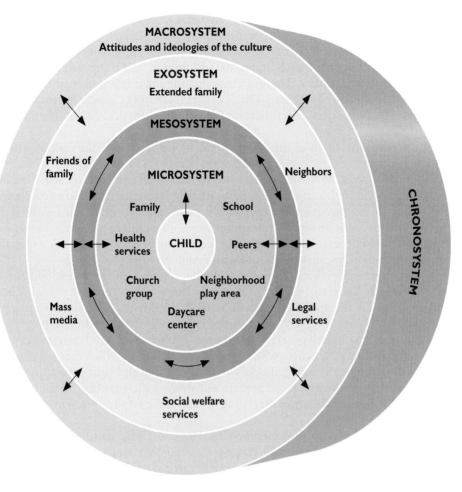

FIGURE 1.4
Bronfenbrenner's
Ecological Model

At the core of Bronfenbrenner's ecological model is the child's biological and psychological makeup, based on individual genetic and developmental history. This makeup continues to be affected and modified by the child's immediate physical and social environment (*microsystem*), as well as interactions among the systems within this environment (*mesosystem*). Other broader social, political, and economic conditions (*exosystem*) influence the structure and availability of microsystems and the manner in which they affect the child. Social, political, and economic conditions are themselves influenced by the general beliefs and attitudes (*macrosystem*) shared by members of the society, and all of these systems are affected by changes that occur over time (*chronosystem*).

Source: Adapted from Garabino, 1982.

opment. Yet culture, the historical legacy of earlier generations of a given social group, as well as the evolutionary pressures that have shaped humans to exist in their natural environment, are also major factors affecting growth. Put another way, the transformation from infant to child to adult takes place via a complex, multidirectional system of influences (Gottlieb, Wahlsten, & Lickliter, 1998). Contextual models, sometimes called *systems views,* are concerned with understanding this broad range of biological, physical, and sociocultural settings and how they affect development.

Ecological Systems Theory

The most extensive description of the context in which development proceeds has been put forth in the **ecological systems theory** proposed by Urie Bronfenbrenner (1989, 1995). Ecological theories in general stress the need to understand development in terms of the everyday environment in which children are reared, a concern that is seldom the focus of many other theories. For example, Bronfenbrenner claims that "much of contemporary developmental psychology is the science of the strange behavior of children in strange situations with strange adults for the briefest possible periods of time" (Bronfenbrenner, 1977, p. 513). Development, Bronfenbrenner believes, must be studied not only in the laboratory but also in the homes, schools, neighborhoods, and communities in which it takes place.

One of Bronfenbrenner's major theoretical contributions has been his comprehensive portrait of the environment—the ecological forces and systems that exist at several different but interrelated levels—and the bidirectional and reciprocal relationships that exist among them. These levels are shown in Figure 1.4. At the center

ecological systems theory
Bronfenbrenner's theory that development is influenced by experiences arising from broader social and cultural systems as well as a child's immediate surroundings.

is the child's biological and psychological makeup, including her cognitive capacities and socioemotional and motivational propensities (e.g., temperament and personality) for responding to and acting on the environment. Settings with the most immediate and direct impact on an individual's biological and psychological qualities make up the **microsystem.** These settings include the home and members of the household, social and educational circumstances (including classmates, teachers, and classroom resources), and neighborhoods (including physical layout, friends, and acquaintances).

The **mesosystem** includes the many interrelationships among the various settings within the microsystem. For example, opportunities and expectations within the family, such as access to books and learning to read or an emphasis on acquiring basic academic and socialization skills, may critically influence the child's experiences and success in another microsystem, the school. As another example, a child of divorced parents living in separate neighborhoods may undergo frequent moves between the two homes. Such a living arrangement may have repercussions for the range and kinds of friendships the child can establish with peers.

Social, economic, political, religious, and other settings can affect development either directly or indirectly via their impact on those who care for the child. These wider contexts make up the **exosystem.** In many countries today, for example, the child seldom is part of either parent's work environment. Nevertheless, the parent who encounters a difficult problem at work may bring frustrations home and express them through angry exchanges with members of the family. Urban renewal planned at city hall may have dramatic consequences for children and their interactions with peers, hopefully for the better, but perhaps not always with that effect. Skirmishes between rival villages or countries may bring poverty if the family breadwinner is killed in fighting.

The broadest context is the **macrosystem.** The macrosystem includes the spiritual and religious values, legal and political practices, and ceremonies and customs shared by a cultural group. Cultural beliefs about child rearing, the role of schools and family in education, the importance of maintaining kinship affiliations, tolerance for different lifestyles, and the ethical and moral conventions of a society affect the child both directly (through the socialization practices of the caregivers) and indirectly (through the cultural norms and strictures defining acceptable and desirable behavior).

These four systems do not remain constant over time. Historical events such as famines, wars, or other natural disasters can disrupt and devastate conventional microsystems such as schools and neighborhoods, as well as the social, economic, political, and religious framework of a community provided by the exosystem. The arrival of a new family member, the separation of parents, the move to a new home, and the loss of a peer are examples of other changes a child may experience at different times. The **chronosystem** is Bronfenbrenner's (1995) term for this temporal dimension of influence. Change is always taking place, and these time-linked shifts and transitions may have greater or lesser impact depending on when they occur during the child's development. Thus temporal events, too, have far-reaching consequences for each individual's psychological development.

Vygotsky's Sociohistorical Theory

Bronfenbrenner's ecological systems theory highlights the many different contexts in which development proceeds. Lev Vygotsky's sociohistorical theory blends these different levels into one overarching concept: culture. What is culture? It is, of course, the many facets of the environment that humans have created and continue to produce, including physical artifacts such as tools and furnishings. But even more important, culture includes language and the practices, values, and beliefs accumulated and communicated from one generation to the next via that language system. Culture, in other words, is the human-generated, historical accumulation of one's surroundings, and it has an enormous influence on the way children are reared. Vygotsky's **sociohistorical theory** emphasizes the unique collective wisdom com-

microsystem In Bronfenbrenner's ecological systems theory, the immediate environment provided in such settings as the home, school, workplace, and neighborhood.

mesosystem In Bronfenbrenner's ecological systems theory, the environment provided by the interrelationships among the various settings of the microsystem.

exosystem In Bronfenbrenner's ecological systems theory, environmental settings that indirectly affect the child by influencing the various microsystems forming the child's immediate environment.

macrosystem In Bronfenbrenner's ecological systems theory, major historical events and the broad values, practices, and customs promoted by a culture.

chronosystem In Bronfenbrenner's ecological systems theory, the constantly changing temporal component of the environment that can influence development.

sociohistorical theory Vygotsky's developmental theory emphasizing the importance of cultural tools, symbols, and ways of thinking that the child acquires from more knowledgeable members of the community.

Lev Vygotsky's sociohistorical theory emphasizes that the cultural experiences to which children are exposed become an indispensable part of their development. This Maya Indian father in Guatemala is teaching his young child how to make bricks. In doing so, the parent is transmitting important information to his offspring. By becoming aware of how communities transmit knowledge to their younger members, we can begin to appreciate how culture influences attitudes, beliefs, and values, as well as cognitive development.

piled by a culture and transmitted to the child through ongoing, daily interactions with the more knowledgeable members of that society.

A central tenet of Vygotsky's sociohistorical theory is that as children become exposed to and participate in their communities, they begin to internalize and adopt, often with the guidance of a skilled partner such as a parent or teacher, the culturally based, more mature and effective methods of thinking about and solving problems (Wertsch, 1985; Wertsch & Tulviste, 1992). For example, in sitting down with and reading to the child, the caregiver demonstrates how important this activity is so that eventually the child comes to value it in her own behavior. Vygotsky believed that language is an especially important tool in this dialogue because it too is internalized by the child to affect thinking and problem solving.

One quality that permeates both ecological systems theory and sociohistorical views of development is the seamless alloy that embodies development as the child is affected by and, in turn, actively influences his or her surroundings (Sameroff, 1994). Development is dynamic, a never-ending *transaction* involving continuing, reciprocal exchanges: people and settings transform the child, who in turn affects the people and settings surrounding him, which further reshape the child in an endless progression.

Consider the baby born with low birth weight. Such an infant often displays a sharp, shrill cry and has difficulty nursing. Because of these factors and the baby's fragile appearance, a mother who might otherwise feel confident may become anxious and uncertain about her caregiving abilities. Her apprehensions may translate into inconsistent behaviors to which the baby, in turn, responds with irregular patterns of feeding and sleeping. These difficulties further reduce the mother's confidence in her abilities and enjoyment of her baby, leading to fewer social interactions and less positive stimulation for the infant. As a consequence, achievements in other areas of development, such as language acquisition, may be delayed. But what factor, precisely, caused these delays? To answer this question, we might point to the child's low birth weight or the mother's avoidance of her infant. However, these explanations fall far short of capturing the many complex elements that contributed to the mother's behaviors and the child's development.

Consider, also, the teenager unable to resist her boyfriend's urgings to engage in sexual activity. The consequences may set in motion a course of events that dramatically alters her role from that of a student with many friends and freedoms to that of mother with many responsibilities and little time to herself. We can single out her pregnancy and the birth of a baby as critical factors in this turn of events. However, many other factors undoubtedly contributed, and to isolate any single cause does injustice to the complexity of human development.

The importance of these complex transactions becomes especially apparent when psychologists and others attempt to modify the course of development. The mother who has avoided her low-birth-weight infant because of a widening gulf of anxious reactions brought about by disappointments and unhappy exchanges will need more than simply to be told to start talking to her child to encourage his language development. She may need to gain a greater understanding of the typical problems such babies face, receive support and reinforcement for her efforts to initiate confident caregiving skills, and acquire richer insights into how development is affected by experiences, only some of which she can control. Will, for example, telling an adolescent to "Just Say NO" be effective, or must other programs be included in efforts to reduce teenage pregnancy?

Dynamic Systems Theory

It should be evident by now that contextual theories champion the importance of many interacting events to account for development. **Dynamic systems theory** captures this idea and at the same time stresses the emergence over time of more advanced, complex behaviors from these many interactions (Lewis, 2000). Of particular interest in this theoretical orientation is the notion that development reflects more than an accumulation of past events; it is, instead, the product of reorganizations that arise from the interactions of various levels of the system that could not be observed or expected from each component level by itself. One outcome of this reorganization is a stable, more adaptive way of responding (Novak, 1996; Thelen & Smith, 1994, 1998). When the right combinations of elements are present, new, sometimes unexpected, capacities emerge.

One of the more important implications of dynamic systems theory is that development is not controlled or regulated by any one particular factor, for example, by the brain, the genes, child-rearing practices, or any other specific influence. Instead, these various components are parts of a process that induces more organized and advanced behaviors or ways of thinking. Perhaps one of the best examples illustrating a dynamic systems view is learning to walk. As Thelen and Smith indicate, "Learning to walk is less a prescribed, logically inevitable process than a confluence of available states within particular contextual opportunities" (1994, p. 72). In more concrete terms, learning to walk results from a necessary combination of inherited human anatomical and neural systems, opportunities to exercise muscles, the desire to move around more effectively, the availability of acceptable surfaces and other supportive physical environments, and parenting that fosters exploration and sensorimotor development. Walking begins when the right blend of these come together. So, too, do new accomplishments in perception, language, cognition, and social behavior.

Ethological Theory

dynamic systems theory
Theoretical orientation that explains development as the emerging organization arising from the interaction of many different processes.

ethology   Theoretical orientation and discipline concerned with the evolutionary origins of behavior and its adaptive and survival value in animals, including humans.

Development is influenced by yet one more broad context: the biological history and constraints that have been a part of human evolution. In the nineteenth century, Darwin and other biologists concluded that adaptive traits—those that improved the likelihood of survival and thus ensured a greater number of offspring for further reproduction—were more likely to be found in succeeding generations of a species. Darwin hypothesized that through *evolution,* the descent of living species from earlier species of animals, humans inherited biological traits and capacities that improved their rate of survival. **Ethology** is the discipline specifically concerned with understanding how adaptive behaviors evolved and what functions they still serve for the continuation of the species.

Ethological theory surfaced in the 1930s when European zoologists such as Konrad Lorenz (1963/1966) and Niko Tinbergen (1951) investigated aggressive actions and the courtship and mating rituals of species such as the mallard duck and stickleback fish. Their observations led to explanations that took into account the *mutual* interchange between the inherited, biological bases of behavior and the environment in which that behavior was exhibited (Hinde, 1989). Ethological studies propose answers to questions such as the following: Why do babies cry or smile? Why might the ten-year-old fight or be friendly? Ethologists point out the adaptive value of such activities for the individual in the specific environment in which he or she is growing up.

Ethological theory proposes that human infants, as well as the offspring of other species of animals, begin life with a set of innate, *species-specific* behaviors common to all members. In human babies, these include reflexes such as sucking and grasping and may also include more complex activities such as babbling, smiling, and orienting to interesting sensory events—behaviors exhibited by normal infants around the world. These species-specific behaviors help infants meet their needs either directly, as in the case of sucking as a means of ingesting food, or indirectly, as in the case of smiling, a behavior that attracts caregivers and encourages them to provide support.

Besides innate behaviors, the young of many species are predisposed to certain kinds of learning that are not easily reversed, learning that may occur only during limited sensitive or *critical* periods in development. A **sensitive period** occurs when an organism is highly responsive or vulnerable to specific kinds of environmental stimulation. One of the best-known examples is found in various species of birds, including geese. Usually, shortly after hatching, the gosling begins to follow and prefers being near a particular object. Normally, that stimulus will be another goose, its mother. In displaying this tendency, the gosling not only learns about its species more generally but also increases the likelihood of being fed and protected. This form of learning that takes place during a brief interval early in life and is difficult to modify once established is known as **imprinting.**

Do other animals show imprinting? Mammals such as horses and sheep do. What about human infants? John Bowlby's (1969) theory of attachment suggests that they do, at least to some degree. Bowlby noted that the crying, babbling, and smiling behaviors of young infants signal needs and elicit supportive and protective responses from adults. These behaviors, along with following and talking in older infants, become organized and integrated with social and emotional reactions of caregivers to form the basis for attachment, a mutual system of physical, social, and emotional stimulation and support between caregiver and young. Many experts believe that the failure to form this strong emotional bond with a caregiver in infancy is linked to serious emotional and other problems that occur later in childhood, an issue that will be discussed more fully in the chapter titled "Emotion."

Konrad Lorenz, an ethologist, is being followed by young geese who have imprinted to him. Imprinting in young animals typically occurs to other members of the same species who, under normal circumstances, are present shortly after hatching or the birth of an animal. One question posed by ethologists is whether human infants also show some form of imprinting.

Contextual Approaches and Themes in Development

Contextual models generally agree on many of the themes in development, and where differences exist, they are most often found in ethological theories.

■ *Nature/Nurture* Contextual theories differ widely in their emphasis on nature and nurture, but all recognize the importance of both to development. For ethologists, however, behaviors are closely linked to nature because they have helped, or continue to help, humans survive.

■ *Sociocultural Influence* Perhaps more than any other theoretical orientation, contextual theories are concerned with the ways broad sociocultural patterns affect development. Contextual approaches often search for evidence of how the larger social systems and settings in which children are reared affect their behavior and shape their minds.

■ *Child's Active Role* Contextual models, even those having an ethological focus, tend to view the child as actively engaged with the environment. In calling for

sensitive period Brief period during which specific kinds of experiences have significant positive or negative consequences for development and behavior. Also called *critical period*.

imprinting Form of learning, difficult to reverse, during a sensitive period in development in which an organism tends to stay near a particular stimulus.

their caregivers, exploring and playing, and seeking out playmates, infants and children elicit reactions from the adults and peers around them. Both individual and environment change in highly interdependent ways, and the relationship between the two is *bidirectional,* each influencing the other (Bell, 1968).

■ *Continuity/Discontinuity*　Most contextual models place little emphasis on qualitative changes in development. Instead, such models describe the continuous ebb and flow of interactions that transpire throughout development to produce incremental change. However, ethologists often emphasize that particular periods in development are critical for establishing certain competencies. For example, infancy is considered a crucial time for forming emotional ties with caregivers.

■ *Individual Differences*　Aside from ethological theories, contextual perspectives focus less on highlighting universal experiences that promote development and more on the unique configuration of circumstances that foster cognitive, linguistic, social, and personality development. Given the immense number of factors potentially affecting the child, individual differences are often an important aspect to be explained by such theories.

■ *Interaction Among Domains*　Not surprisingly, most contextual models are typically concerned with the entire fabric of human growth and claim substantial interactions among cognitive, linguistic, social, and other domains. Ethological theorists especially focus on the interrelationship between biological and other aspects of development.

FOR YOUR REVIEW

- What is learning? What are some of its basic mechanisms? How do behavior analysis and social learning theory differ in explaining what takes place during learning?

- What are the primary factors underlying change in Piaget's theory of cognitive development? How do schemes, assimilation, accommodation, and equilibration help to explain the increasingly adaptive and organized nature of cognition?

- What characteristics distinguish information-processing approaches from other theories of development?

- What is the focus and a common underlying theme in Erikson's theory of psychosocial development?

- What common assumptions underlie various contextual approaches to development, for example, Bronfenbrenner's ecological systems theory, Vygotsky's sociohistorical theory, dynamic systems theory, and ethological theory? How do they differ?

What Develops?

All theories of development, of course, are ultimately concerned with the simple question, "What develops?" As you have seen in this chapter, the answers differ. For learning theorists, what develops is a set of responses. For Piaget, it is a set of cognitive structures. For information-processing enthusiasts, it is mental structures and strategies for responding. For psychosocial theorists, it is identity. For most contextual theorists, it is a pattern of mutually supportive individual and cultural relationships. For ethologists, it is adaptive behaviors.

Theories, by giving us models for observing and interpreting behavior, have had an enormous influence on the way we view children and their development. Why so many different theories? The reason is that each brings an important perspective to our understanding of development. Some remind us of the importance of emotions, others of cognitive structures. Some keep us honest about the role of our biological nature; others perform the same service for the culture in which we are born and reared. Various theories enrich and broaden our understanding of development. We will frequently draw on their contributions for interpreting the many behaviors of children. We hope you will, too.

As we have introduced developmental theories, we have also discussed their positions on six major themes of development. Table 1.3 summarizes these positions for the major theories introduced in this chapter. As you read further, you may find yourself revising your own stand on the six themes. We trace their presence throughout the remainder of this book with marginal cues placed beside important research and discussion that bear on each theme. Beginning with the chapter titled "Genetics and Heredity," we also open each chapter with a list of the most relevant themes discussed in it and conclude by summarizing how the themes have applied to the developmental domain under discussion.

WHAT DO YOU THINK?

Should Child Rearing Be Regulated?
psychology.college.hmco.com

TABLE 1.3	The Main Developmental Theories and Where They Stand on the Six Themes of Development				
Theme	**Learning Theories**	**Piagetian Theory**	**Information-Processing Approaches**	**Erikson's Psychosocial Approach**	**Contextual Theories**
What roles do nature and nurture play in development?	Environment is more important than heredity.	Maturation sets limits on how rapidly development proceeds, but experience is necessary for the formation of cognitive structures. Interaction between nature and nurture.	Structures and processes presumably have an inherent basis, but experience is likely to be important for their effective operation.	Erikson stressed an interactional position that emphasizes the socialization demands of the society in which a child is reared, along with a biological contribution.	A major emphasis is the environmental factors that interact with biological structures. For ethologists, the environment elicits and influences biologically based patterns of behavior.
How does the sociocultural context influence development?	Sociocultural factors determine which behaviors are reinforced, punished, or available from models, but the principles of learning are considered to be universal.	The cognitive structures underlying thought are universal. Sociocultural context might affect the rapidity or final level of thinking, but sociocultural differences are not stressed.	The rules, strategies, and procedures acquired to perform tasks may differ from one culture to another but cultural differences have received little attention.	Sociocultural context is a major component of Erikson's theory.	Culture is a critical determinant of behavior although ethological principles of development are presumed to apply in all cultures.
How does the child play an active role in development?	In behavior analysis the child is not considered to be an active agent, but in social cognitive theory the child more actively engages the environment to determine what is learned.	Knowledge is based on underlying cognitive structures constructed by the child.	The child determines what information is processed and the rules, strategies, and procedures initiated to perform tasks.	The child is actively in search of an identity.	Biologically equipped to interact with the environment, the child plays a central role in determining what kind of environment is established, how it changes, and how it further affects behavior.
Is development continuous or discontinuous?	Continuous. Development is cumulative, consisting of the acquisition of greater numbers of learned responses.	Stagelike. Four qualitatively different stages emerge, each involving a reorganization of cognitive structures that permits more effective adaptation to the world.	Usually continuous. Development consists of the acquisition of more effective structures and processes for performing tasks.	Stagelike, although the individual may return to earlier stages to work through unresolved conflicts.	Continuous. Development involves transactions between the individual and the environment. Abrupt reorganization may take place, according to dynamic systems approaches.
How prominent are individual differences in development?	Individual differences are not emphasized; the laws of learning are universal. However, variations in experience can be a major source of individual differences.	Individual differences are not a primary focus of Piaget's theory.	Little emphasis is placed on individual differences. Variations in structures, strategies, and other processes help to explain individual differences in behavior.	Psychosocial stages are universal; however, individuals may proceed through and resolve each need in quite different ways.	Stresses the unique configuration of events that contribute to individual differences in explaining behavior.
How do the various domains of development interact?	Learning proceeds on many different fronts and is highly situational.	Stagelike advances in cognition have implications not only for thinking and problem solving but also for moral and social development.	Development is usually considered to be domain specific. However, recent efforts have been made to understand social and emotional relationships in terms of information-processing models.	Failure to progress through psychosocial stages may disrupt progress in many different domains besides personality development.	Because of the strong mutual interdependence between individual and environment, all aspects of development are closely interrelated.

CHAPTER RECAP

SUMMARY OF TOPICS

What Is Development?

- Development refers to all the physical and psychological changes that occur throughout a human's lifetime.

- *Developmental psychology*, the discipline concerned with these changes, has several goals. One goal is to describe changes in behavior and mental processes that occur over time. A second goal is to understand the reasons development occurs in the way that it does. Another is to assist in the creation of *social policies* that will achieve particular objectives with respect to children and their development.

- Different theories have been proposed to assist in describing, explaining, and predicting behavior and its development. These theories differ in their answers to several important questions concerning the themes of development.

Six Major Themes in Developmental Psychology

- Six recurring issues must be addressed by every developmental theory.

What Roles Do Nature and Nurture Play in Development?

- Often described as the *nature-nurture debate,* this issue is concerned with how genetic and experiential variables interact to influence behavior.

How Does the Sociocultural Context Influence Development?

- Children grow up in a social environment and cultural community that can have a tremendous impact on the behaviors that are displayed.

How Does the Child Play an Active Role in Development?

- The interests, skills, and qualities displayed by children influence those who interact with them, but in addition, children may actively construct ways of interpreting their world.

Is Development Continuous or Discontinuous?

- Changes in behavior may stem from quantitative, incremental developmental advances or qualitative reorganization. Children's behavior also may be influenced by multiple strategies or ways of responding.

How Prominent Are Individual Differences in Development?

- No "average" child exists; this issue is concerned with the extent to which children display individual differences in various domains and how those differences come about.

How Do the Various Domains of Development Interact?

- Developmental psychologists are concerned with the "whole" child; thus they are interested in how skills and capacities acquired in some area affect other aspects of behavior.

The Study of the Child: Historical Perspectives

- Attitudes toward children have changed over the centuries.

The Concept of Childhood

- In medieval times, although recognized as vulnerable, children quickly became a part of adult society.
- Philosophers such as John Locke emphasized *empiricism,* the view that experience shapes the development of the individual, whereas others such as Jean Jacques Rousseau wrote about the curious and active nature of the child.

The Origins of Developmental Psychology

- The formal establishment of developmental psychology began with the careful study of children by several influential contributors during the nineteenth and early twentieth centuries.
- Baby biographers such as Charles Darwin and Wilhelm Preyer carried out the first systematic observations of individual children.
- G. Stanley Hall introduced the questionnaire method for studying large groups of children.
- Alfred Binet initiated the movement to study *individual differences* in children's behavior and abilities.
- Theorist James Mark Baldwin viewed the child as an active participant in his or her own cognitive and social development.
- Freud emphasized the importance of early experience on development and posited a series of *psychosexual stages* that children must successfully negotiate in order to demonstrate normal personality development.

The Continued Growth of Developmental Psychology in the Twentieth Century

- For much of the first half of the twentieth century, work was carried out on gathering descriptive information about children. Arnold Gesell and others focused on establishing norms of behavior. Other research began to be initiated to investigate the variables that might cause development.

Learning Theory Approaches

- *Behavior analysis* relies on two basic forms of learning, classical and operant conditioning to bring about behavioral change. *Social cognitive theory*, as outlined by Albert Bandura, adds *observational learning* as an important mechanism by which behavior is continuously modified and changed.

Cognitive-Developmental Approaches

- Jean Piaget's *cognitive-developmental theory* highlights the child's construction of *schemes* or patterns of acting on and thinking about the world. Through *assimilation* and *accommodation,* a child's schemes actively adapt to the demands of the environment by becoming more organized, conceptual, and logical. Cognitive development progresses through a series of qualitatively different stages according to Piaget's theory.

Information-Processing Approaches

- *Information-processing models* use the computer as a metaphor in accounting for cognitive development. Developmental differences in cognitive structures and processes such as rules, strategies, and procedures account for changes in attention, memory, thinking, and problem solving.

Erikson's Psychosocial Approach

- Erikson's *psychosocial theory of development* focuses on the sociocultural context in which behavioral needs are met. Personality development proceeds through a series of stages in which self and societal demands are resolved to construct one's *identity*. Individuals who successfully negotiate these demands become contributing members of society.

Contextual Approaches

- *Contextual models* view human development from a broader framework involving multiple, bidirectionally interacting levels of influence.

Ecological Systems Theory

- *Ecological systems theory* looks beyond the immediate experiences of family, peers, and friends and considers the broader sociocultural contexts in which development proceeds.

Vygotsky's Sociohistorical Theory

- Vygotsky's *sociohistorical theory* views culture as the historical legacy of a community and emphasizes the social interactions by which this heritage is transferred from others and adopted by the child to become part of his or her way of thinking.

Dynamic Systems Theory

- *Dynamic systems theory* proposes that new, complex, and sometimes qualitatively different behaviors arise from the interaction of events at many different levels in the system.

Ethological Theory

- *Ethological theory* pays special attention to the biological, evolutionary heritage each individual brings to the world as the basis for species-specific behaviors found to be adaptive in interacting with the environment.

What Develops?

- Theories differ greatly in their answers to what develops. However, each can bring an important perspective to an understanding of development and help to interpret the many behaviors displayed by children.

CHAPTER 2

Studying Child Development

To me, research is discovery: *an odyssey of surprises, confirmations, and unexpected twists and turns that contribute to the excitement of a research career. . . . The excitement of a research career is that the story told by the data is always more interesting than the one you expect to confirm. In this sense, human behavior is far more interesting and provocative than even the most thoughtful theories allow, and this means that the scientist must be instructed by the lessons revealed by unexpected research findings— while maintaining humility about her or his capacity to predict the next turn in the road.* (Thompson, 1996, p. 69)

These words, written by developmental researcher Ross Thompson, reveal the genuine enthusiasm of the scientist for the task of systematically observing and making sense of human behavior. Like investigators in many disciplines, developmental psychologists are firmly committed to the idea that theories and hypotheses, such as those described in the chapter titled "Themes and Theories," should be thoroughly and systematically tested using sound principles of science. But as Thompson suggests, researchers must be prepared to modify or even cast off theories if their observations suggest other truths. At first glance, this outcome may seem discouraging. But as many researchers can attest, great rewards lie in the simple notion of discovering something new.

Part of the reason that researchers get drawn into the enterprise of developmental psychology is that they are captivated by and want to understand the fascinating, complex, and oftentimes surprising array of behaviors children display. Moreover, there is the sheer fun of being a "child watcher." As even the most casual of observers can confirm, children are simply delightful subjects of study. Research can also make a real difference in the lives of children. For example, newborn nurseries for premature infants now contain rocking chairs so that parents and nurses can rock and stimulate babies previously confined to isolettes. Bilingual education programs capitalize on the ease with which young children master the complexities of language. The benefit of each of these approaches has been revealed through the systematic study of the child.

Collecting data about children, then, is an essential and rewarding aspect of scientific developmental psychology, and being well grounded in research techniques is important for students of the discipline. With this principle in mind, we devote this chapter to methodological issues in developmental psychology. In addition, from time to time throughout the book, we highlight the research methodology used in particular studies. We hope that by alerting you to important issues in the research process, we will better equip you to think critically about the findings of the numerous studies you will encounter in subsequent chapters.

Research Methods in Developmental Psychology

Like their colleagues in all the sciences, researchers in child development seek to gather data that are objective, measurable, and capable of being replicated in controlled studies by other researchers. Their studies, in other words, are based on the **scientific method.** Frequently they initiate research to evaluate the predictions of a specific theory (e.g., is cognitive development stagelike, as Piaget suggests?). The scientific method dictates that theories must be revised or elaborated as new observations confirm or refute them. The process of scientific fact-finding involves a constant cycle of theorizing, empirical testing of the resulting hypotheses, and revision (or even outright rejection) of theories as the new data come in. Alternatively, the investigators may formulate a research question to determine an application of theory to a real-world situation (e.g., can early intervention programs for preschoolers

scientific method Use of objective, measurable, and repeatable techniques to gather information.

boost IQ scores?). Regardless of the motivation, the general principles of good science are as important to research in child development as they are to any other research arena. Although many of the methods child development researchers use are the very same techniques psychologists routinely employ in other specialized areas, some methodological approaches are particularly useful in studying changes in behavior or mental processes that occur over time.

Measuring Attributes and Behaviors

All researchers are interested in identifying relationships among **variables,** those factors in a given situation that have no fixed or constant value. In child development studies, the variables are individual attributes, experiences, or behaviors that differ from one time to the next or from one person to another. Ultimately, researchers are interested in determining the causal relationships among variables; that is, they wish to identify those variables directly responsible for the occurrence of other variables. Does watching television cause children to behave aggressively? Do withdrawn children have academic problems once they enroll in school? Does the way a parent interacts with a toddler raise or lower the child's later intelligence? In posing each of these questions, researchers are hypothesizing that some attribute or experience of the child is causally related to another attribute or behavior.

The first problem the researcher faces is that of **operationally defining,** or specifying in measurable terms, the variables under study. Take the case of aggression. This term can be defined as parental ratings of a child's physical hostility, the child's own reports of his or her level of violent behavior, or the number of hits and kicks recorded by an observer of the child's behavior. The key point is that variables must be defined in terms of precise measurement procedures that other researchers can use if they wish to repeat the study.

The measurement of variables must also be valid and reliable. **Validity** refers to how well an assessment procedure actually measures the variable under study. Parental reports of physical violence, for example, or even the child's own self-reports may not be the best indicators of aggression. Parents may not want a researcher to know about their child's misbehavior, or they may lack complete knowledge of how their child behaves outside the home. Children's own reports may not be very accurate because the children may wish to present themselves to adults in a certain way. If a trained observer records the number of hits or kicks the child displays during a school day, the resulting measurement of aggression is likely to be valid.

Reliability is the degree to which the same results will be obtained consistently if the measure is administered repeatedly or if several observers are viewing the same behavior episodes. In the first case, suppose a child takes an intelligence test one time, then two weeks later takes the test again. If the test has high *test-retest reliability,* she should obtain similar scores on the two testing occasions. In the second case, two or more observers viewing a child's behavior should agree about what they are seeing (e.g., did the child smile in the presence of a stranger?); if they do agree, the test has high *inter-rater reliability*. Both types of reliability are calculated mathematically and are usually reported by researchers in their published reports of experiments; both are very important factors in good scientific research. Measurements of behavior that fluctuate dramatically from one observation time to another or from one observer to another are virtually useless as data.

Methods of Collecting Data

What is the best way for researchers in developmental psychology to gather information about children? Should they simply watch children as they go about their routines in natural settings? Should children be brought into the researcher's laboratory to be observed? Should the researcher ask the child questions about the topic under study? Each approach offers advantages and disadvantages, and the choice of re-

variable Factor having no fixed or constant value in a given situation.

operational definition Specification of variables in terms of measurable properties.

validity Degree to which an assessment procedure actually measures the variable under consideration.

reliability Degree to which a measure will yield the same results if administered repeatedly.

search tactic will often depend on the nature of the investigator's questions. If we are interested in exploring children's spontaneous tendencies to behave aggressively as they play (e.g., do boys play more aggressively than girls?), we will probably find a *naturalistic approach* most appropriate. If we want to see whether children's behavior is influenced by the presence of an aggressive model, we might use a *structured observation* to systematically expose some children to this manipulation in a laboratory setting. If we want to examine how children understand aggression, its antecedents, and its consequences, we might adopt another strategy, such as a *structured interview* or a *questionnaire*. Sometimes researchers combine two or more of these data collection methods within a study or series of studies.

● **Naturalistic Observation**   Researchers have no better way to see how children really behave than to observe them in natural settings: in their homes, playgrounds, schools, and other places that are part of their everyday lives. After all, the ultimate goal of developmental psychology is to describe and explain changes in behavior that actually occur. **Naturalistic observations** do not involve the manipulation of variables; researchers simply observe and record behaviors of interest from the natural series of events that unfold in a real-world setting.

A study by Herbert Ginsburg and his colleagues (Ginsburg, Pappas, & Seo, 2001), for example, used naturalistic observations to assess the degree to which preschool-age children used mathematical concepts in their spontaneous free-play activities. The study was conducted in four daycare centers that enrolled children from different ethnic and social class backgrounds. Each of the eighty children in the study was videotaped for fifteen minutes during free-play time. Then raters coded the videotapes for the presence of six types of mathematical activities: classification, dynamics (or transformation of objects), enumeration, magnitude comparison, spatial relations, and pattern and shape exploration. The results showed that children spent almost half of the observation period engaged in some form of mathematical activity. Furthermore, there were no gender or social class differences in the tendency to use mathematical concepts in free play.

Several methodological issues are especially relevant to naturalistic observations. First, as researchers code the stream of activities they observe, they need to use clear operational definitions of the behaviors of interest. Ginsburg and his colleagues did

In naturalistic observations, researchers observe and record children's behaviors in real-life settings such as playgrounds, schools, or homes.

naturalistic observation
Study in which observations of naturally occurring behavior are made in real-life settings.

so by specifying the elements that constituted each particular form of mathematical activity. For example, enumeration was defined as counting, use of one-to-one correspondence, estimation of quantity, or any statement of number words. Second, researchers must be aware that children (and others) might react to the presence of an observer by behaving in untypical or "unnatural" ways. To reduce such **participant reactivity,** children in this study were acclimated to the video camera and cordless microphone they wore before the recordings began. Finally, to minimize the effects of **observer bias,** the possibility that the researcher would interpret ongoing events to be consistent with his or her prior hypotheses, pairs of independent observers coded thirty of the eighty children to ensure the reliability of the findings. Researchers usually require that at least one of the observers is unfamiliar with the purposes of the study.

An important advantage of naturalistic observations is that researchers can see the events and behaviors that precede the target behaviors they are recording; they can also note the consequences of those same target behaviors. In this way, they may be able to discern important relationships in sequences of events. Moreover, naturalistic observations give researchers powerful insights into which variables are important to study in the first place, insights they may not derive solely by observing children in the laboratory. For example, a laboratory study might not reveal the high level of unguided engagement preschoolers have with mathematical concepts. Often the trends or phenomena identified in such preliminary studies become the focus of more intensive, controlled laboratory experiments. Naturalistic observations also have the distinct advantage of examining real-life behaviors as opposed to behaviors that may emerge only in response to some contrived laboratory manipulation.

Some cautions regarding this method are in order, however. A wide range of variables may influence the behaviors under observation, and it is not always possible to control them. Cause-and-effect relationships, therefore, cannot be deduced. Do preschoolers evidence mathematical thinking because they are in a "school" environment or because certain kinds of toys or materials are available to them? Or do none of these environmental circumstances matter? Answering questions such as these requires the systematic manipulation of variables, a tactic that is part of other research approaches.

● **Structured Observation**   Researchers cannot always depend on a child to display behaviors of scientific interest to them during observation. Researchers who observe a child in the home, school, or other natural setting may simply not be present when vocalization, sharing, aggression, or other behaviors they wish to study occur. Therefore, developmental psychologists may choose to observe behaviors in a more structured setting, usually the laboratory, in which they devise situations to elicit those behaviors of interest to them. **Structured observations** are the record of specific behaviors the child displays in a situation the experimenter constructs. Structured observations, like naturalistic observations, are a way to collect data by looking at and recording the child's behaviors, but this form of looking takes place under highly controlled conditions.

A recent study of the ways in which siblings resolve potential conflicts illustrates how structured observations are typically conducted (Ram & Ross, 2001). Pairs of siblings ages four and six years and six and eight years, respectively, were brought to a laboratory. First, each child was escorted to a private room and was asked to rate the quality of his or her relationship with the sibling. Each child was also asked to indicate how much he or she liked six toys that the siblings could later take home. Next, the siblings were reunited and instructed to divide up the toys between themselves. The researchers were interested in the types of negotiation strategies these children used. A portion of the results is shown in Figure 2.1. As the graph shows, the most prevalent strategy was "problem solving," attempting to achieve a solution that satisfied both children. Least frequent was a class of behaviors the researchers called "struggle," the display of some form of overt conflict.

participant reactivity   Tendency of individuals who know they are under observation to alter natural behavior.

observer bias   Tendency of researchers to interpret ongoing events as being consistent with their research hypotheses.

structured observation   Study in which behaviors are recorded as they occur within a situation constructed by the experimenter, usually in the laboratory.

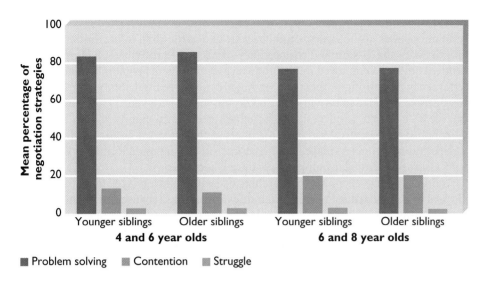

Source: Adapted from Ram & Ross, 2001.

FIGURE 2.1
A Structured Observation

What happens when siblings are instructed to divide up desirable toys? Ram and Ross (2001) structured a laboratory task in which children had to decide which of six toys each sibling would get. Their negotiation strategies were coded as *problem solving* **(attempts to satisfy each child in the pair),** *contention* **(attempts to satisfy one's own desire), and** *struggle* **(withdrawing from the negotiation or using an aggressive strategy). The results show that the predominant strategy used by both older and younger children was problem solving.**

Although these researchers could have attempted to conduct their study of sibling interactions through naturalistic observations in children's homes, they might have had to wait a long time for the targeted interactions to take place spontaneously. Furthermore, by doing this study in a laboratory, the researchers were able to keep tight control over the instructions the children received and the specific toys they had to divide between themselves.

At the same time, structured observations may have limitations, especially if they are conducted in a laboratory setting. Children may not react in the same ways in the research room as they do in "real life." They may be reticent to display negative behaviors, such as lack of cooperation with a brother or sister, in front of the researcher, or they may show heightened distress or shyness because of the unfamiliar setting. One solution to this problem is to confirm the results of laboratory studies by conducting similar studies in children's natural environments.

Structured observations can focus on a variety of types of behaviors. Like many structured observations, the study by Ram and Ross focused on children's overt actions, in this case their physical and verbal behaviors. Researchers often record other behaviors, such as the number of errors children make in a problem-solving task, the kinds of memory strategies they display, or the amount of time they take to learn a specified task. When structured observations are conducted in the laboratory, it is also possible for researchers to obtain *physiological measures,* the shifts in heart rate, brain wave activity, or respiration rate that can indicate the child's reaction to changes in stimuli. Physiological measures are especially useful in examining the behavior of infants, because the range of overt responses very young children usually display is more limited than that of older children.

● **The Interview and the Questionnaire**   Sometimes the best way to glean information about what children know or how they behave is not simply to observe them but to ask them directly. Researchers have found that talking with children about their conceptions of friendships, gender roles, problem-solving skills—in fact, almost anything in the child's world—has yielded a wealth of material for analysis.

Many investigators use the technique of **structured interviews,** studies in which each participant is asked the same sequence of questions. For example, the goal of a study conducted by Mary Levitt and her colleagues (Levitt, Guacci-Franco, & Levitt, 1993) was to explore the sources of social support for seven-, ten-, and fourteen-year-old children from different ethnic backgrounds. More than three hundred African American, Anglo American, and Hispanic American children were interviewed

structured interview   Standardized set of questions administered orally to participants.

individually about the people most important in their lives. Each child was questioned by an interviewer of the same cultural background as the child to maximize the child's comfort with the session and the accuracy of his or her responses. Examples of the standard questions employed in this study include "Are there people who make you feel better when something bothers you or you are not sure about something?" and "Are there people who like to be with you and do fun things with you?" The results showed that for all children, regardless of ethnic background, the family was an important source of social support. Moreover, members of the extended family (such as grandparents, aunts, or uncles) played an increasing role during middle childhood, whereas peers assumed a significant support role during adolescence.

Another "asking" technique researchers use with children is to obtain written responses to a standard set of items in a **questionnaire.** Because questionnaires can be administered to large numbers of children at the same time, researchers can use this method to obtain a large set of data very quickly. Questionnaires can also be scored quickly, particularly if the items ask participants to pick from a set of multiple-choice items or to rate items on a numerical scale. Children, however, may have difficulty understanding the items and may not be able to answer accurately without guidance from an adult. Under those conditions, oral interviews with individual children may provide more reliable and valid information about how children think and feel.

Researchers who use interviews and questionnaires to collect data from children must be careful, though. Sometimes young respondents, like their adult counterparts, will try to present themselves in the most favorable light or answer questions as they think the researcher expects them to. In the study of children's sources of social support, for example, participants may have said they talked with their parents when they had problems because they knew this was the expected response. To prompt participants to answer as honestly as possible, researchers try not to react positively or negatively as the participant responds and also try to explain the importance of answering truthfully before the start of the interview or questionnaire.

Another way to collect data by interview is the **clinical method,** a flexible, openended technique in which the investigator may modify the questions in reaction to the child's response. A notable example was Jean Piaget's use of the clinical method to explore age-related changes in children's thinking capabilities. Consider the following segment, in which Piaget (1929) questions a six-year-old boy about the sun:

> *Piaget:* How did the sun begin?
> *Child:* It was when life began.
> *Piaget:* Has there always been a sun?
> *Child:* No.
> *Piaget:* How did it begin?
> *Child:* Because it knew that life had begun.
> *Piaget:* What is it made of?
> *Child:* Of fire . . .
> *Piaget:* Where did the fire come from?
> *Child:* From the sky.
> *Piaget:* How was the fire made in the sky?
> *Child:* It was lighted with a match. (p. 258)

Note how Piaget follows the child's line of thinking with each question he asks. The format of the interview changes with an older boy, age nine years:

> *Piaget:* How did the sun start?
> *Child:* With heat.
> *Piaget:* What heat?
> *Child:* From the fire.
> *Piaget:* Where is the fire?
> *Child:* In heaven.
> *Piaget:* How did it start?

questionnaire Set of standardized questions administered to participants in written form.

clinical method Flexible, open-ended interview method in which questions are modified in reaction to the child's responses.

Child: God lit it with wood and coal.
Piaget: Where did he get the wood and coal?
Child: He made it. (p. 265)

Piaget gained some enormous insights into the thinking processes of children by using the probing, interactive questions typical of the clinical method. Having the flexibility to follow the child's train of thought rather than sticking to a rigid protocol of predetermined questions allows the researcher to gather fresh insights. The weakness of this approach, however, lies precisely in this flexibility. Because the questions asked of different participants are likely to vary, systematic comparisons of their answers are difficult to make. Moreover, the researcher may be tied to a theoretical orientation that biases the formulation of questions and the interpretation of answers. Nonetheless, the clinical method can be a valuable research tool, particularly in exploring the way children think and reason.

● **The Meta-analytic Study**   Sometimes researchers do not actually collect empirical data themselves but instead make a statistical analysis of a body of previously published research on a specific topic that allows them to draw some general conclusions. Instead of looking or asking, they "crunch" data; that is, they combine the results of numerous studies to assess whether the central variable common to all has an important effect. This technique, called **meta-analysis,** is particularly useful when the results of studies in the same area are inconsistent or in conflict with one another.

A good example of meta-analysis is a study conducted by Janet Hyde and her colleagues to assess the existence of sex differences in children's mathematical skills (Hyde, Fennema, & Lamon, 1990). Many researchers have concluded that boys perform better than girls on tests of mathematical skill, particularly after age twelve or thirteen (Halpern, 1986; Maccoby & Jacklin, 1974). Such observations have spawned numerous debates about the origins of this sex difference. Is mathematical skill biologically given, or is it learned through experiences in the environment? The answer to this question has important educational implications for male and female students. Hyde and her colleagues collected one hundred studies conducted from 1967 through 1987 that examined the question of sex differences in mathematics performance. (This body of studies represented the participation of more than 3 million participants!) For each study, a statistical measure representing *effect size* was computed, a mathematical way of expressing the size of the difference in male and female scores. Hyde and her colleagues (1990) found that the average difference between males and females across all studies was small, leading the researchers to conclude that sex differences in mathematical ability are not large enough to be of great scientific significance.

Conducting a meta-analysis requires the careful transcription of hundreds of statistical figures, a powerful computer, and a good deal of computational skill. Because the researcher taking this approach did not design the original studies, she or he cannot always be sure the central variables have been defined in identical ways across studies. Moreover, studies that do not present their data in the form necessary for analysis may have to be eliminated from the pool; potentially valuable information may thus be lost. Despite these difficulties, the meta-analytic approach allows researchers to draw conclusions based on a large corpus of research, not just individual studies, and thereby to profit from an accumulated body of knowledge. This technique has recently become increasingly popular in developmental research and has provoked the reevaluation of more than one traditional notion about children.

From our discussion it should be clear that there is no one right way to study children. Researchers must consider their overall goals and their available resources as they make decisions about how to construct a research study. Table 2.1 summarizes the advantages and disadvantages of the four general types of data collection just described.

meta-analysis   Statistical examination of a body of research studies to assess the effect of the common central variable.

TABLE 2.1	Advantages and Disadvantages of Information-Gathering Approaches		
Approach	**Description**	**Advantages**	**Disadvantages**
Naturalistic Observations	Observations of behaviors as they occur in children's real-life environments.	Can note antecedents and consequences of behaviors; see real-life behaviors.	Possibility of participant reactivity and observer bias; less control over variables; cause-and-effect relationships difficult to establish.
Structured Observations	Observations of behaviors in situations constructed by the experimenter.	More control over conditions that elicit behaviors.	Children may not react as they would in real life.
Interviews and Questionnaires	Asking children (or parents) about what they know or how they behave.	Quick way to assess children's knowledge or reports of their behaviors.	Children may not always respond truthfully or accurately; systematic comparisons of responses may be difficult; theoretical orientation of researcher may bias questions and interpretations of answers.
Meta-analytic Studies	Statistical analysis of other researchers' findings to look for the size of a variable's effects.	Pools a large body of research findings to sort out conflicting findings; no participants are observed.	Requires careful mathematical computation; variables may not have been defined identically across all studies.

Research Designs

Besides formulating their hypotheses, identifying the variables, and choosing a method of gathering information about children, investigators must select the research design they will use as part of their study. The *research design* is the overall conceptual approach that defines whether the variables will be manipulated, how many children will be studied, and the precise sequence of events as the study proceeds. Research designs may be fairly complex, and an investigator might choose more than one design for each part of a large study. Generally, however, researchers select from one of three study types: the correlational, the experimental, and the single-case design.

● **The Correlational Design**   Studies in which the researcher looks for systematic relationships among variables use the correlational design and are called **correlational studies.** Instead of manipulating the variables, in this design the investigator obtains measures of two or more characteristics of the participants and sees whether changes in one variable are accompanied by changes in the other. Some variables show a **positive correlation;** that is, as the values of one variable change, scores on the other variable change in the same direction. For example, if a positive correlation exists between children's television viewing and their aggression, as the number of hours of TV viewing increases, the number of aggressive acts committed increases as well. A **negative correlation** indicates that as scores on one variable change, scores on the other variable change in the opposite direction. Thus, using our example, a negative relationship exists if aggression decreases as TV viewing increases.

The statistic used to describe the strength of a relationship between two variables is called the **correlation coefficient,** or *r.* Correlation coefficients may range from +1.00 (perfectly positively correlated) to −1.00 (perfectly negatively correlated). As the correlation coefficient approaches 0.00 (which signifies no relationship), the relationship between the two variables becomes weaker. A rule of thumb is that correlations of .70 or higher usually signify strong relationships, whereas those below .20

correlational study   Study that assesses whether changes in one variable are accompanied by systematic changes in another variable.

positive correlation   Relationship in which changes in one variable are accompanied by systematic changes in another variable in the same direction.

negative correlation   Relationship in which changes in one variable are accompanied by systematic changes in another variable in the opposite direction.

correlation coefficient (*r*)   Statistical measure, ranging from +1.00 to −1.00, that summarizes the strength and direction of the relationship between two variables; does not provide information about causation.

represent weak relationships. In most cases, values falling in between indicate a moderate relationship between two variables.

We can use a portion of a study conducted by Carol MacKinnon-Lewis and her colleagues (MacKinnon-Lewis et al., 1994) to illustrate the key features of correlational research. One objective of these investigators was to see if relationships existed between boys' aggressive behaviors and several family variables, such as the number of negative life events the child experienced. The latter included experiences such as a parent leaving home or a divorce between parents. The investigators found a statistically significant correlation of $r = .40$ between the number of negative life events reported by boys and the number of fights they started with peers. Thus, the more stress the boys experienced within the family, the more fights they initiated in school. In contrast, the number of negative life events experienced by boys correlated $r = .04$ with the mothers' tendency to judge their sons as having hostile intentions in interactions with others, suggesting no relationship between these two variables.

Because researchers do not actively manipulate the variables in correlational studies, they must be cautious about making statements about cause and effect when strong relationships are found. In the previous study, for example, do negative life events cause boys to be aggressive? Or does their aggression contribute to stress and negative events within the family? Still another possibility is that some third factor not measured by the researchers influences both variables. Perhaps, for example, the child's father is aggressive and that factor influences both the son's aggression and the number of negative life events in the family.

Despite these limitations on interpretation, correlational studies are often a useful first step in exploring which variables might be causally related to one another. In addition, in many instances experimenters are unable to manipulate the variables that are the suspected causes of certain behavior. In the preceding study, for example, it would be impossible to systematically vary the number of negative life events experienced by boys. In such cases, correlational studies represent the only approach available to understanding the influences on child development.

● **The Experimental Design**   The **experimental design** involves the manipulation of one or more **independent variables**—the variables that are manipulated or controlled by the investigator, often because they are the suspected cause of a behavior—to observe the effects on the **dependent variable,** the suspected outcome. One major goal of this type of study is to control for as many as possible of the factors that can influence the outcome, aside from the independent variables. Experimental studies are frequently conducted in laboratory situations, in which it is possible to ensure that all participants are exposed to the same environmental conditions and the same task instructions. In addition, **random assignment** of participants to different treatment groups (in which one group is usually a *control group* that receives no treatment) helps to avoid any systematic variation aside from that precipitated by the independent variables. As a consequence, one distinct advantage of the experimental study design is that cause-and-effect relationships among variables can be identified.

To illustrate the experimental design, consider the following questions: Can young infants recognize their own faces as compared with the faces of other infants? Do they distinguish social stimuli—that is, the faces of babies—from the face of a nonsocial stimulus, a puppet? In one portion of a study reported by Maria Legerstee and her colleagues (Legerstee, Anderson, & Schaffer, 1998), five-month-old children were shown video images (without sounds) of their own faces, the face of a peer, and the face of a puppet with scrambled features. The amount of time infants spent looking and smiling at, as well as vocalizing to, each of the stimuli was recorded. In this experiment, the independent variable was the type of stimulus presented in the video, and the dependent variables were the three infant behaviors: looking, smiling, and vocalizing.

On the surface, it may seem that the design of this study was relatively straightforward. However, infants may prefer to look and smile at or vocalize to stimuli for any

experimental design   Research method in which one or more independent variables are manipulated to determine the effect on other, dependent variables.

independent variable   Variable manipulated by the experimenter; the suspected cause.

dependent variable   Behavior that is measured; suspected effect of an experimental manipulation.

random assignment   Use of principles of chance to assign participants to treatment and control groups; avoids systematic bias.

FIGURE 2.2
Stimuli for the Study of Infants' Responses to Faces

Shown in these photographs are examples of the stimuli used by Legerstee et al. (1998) to examine an infant's reactions to his or her own face (left), to the face of a peer (middle), and to the scrambled face of a puppet (right).

number of reasons, such as a preference for the color of one stimulus item over another or the unique movement patterns of a given stimulus figure. Therefore, it was important for the researchers to control for as many variables as possible—in this case by holding them constant—such that only the independent variable changed across conditions. Under these circumstances, the experimenter can be more confident that the independent variable is causing changes in the dependent variable. The experimenters took great care in this regard. Each stimulus figure was clothed in a yellow robe. Each infant's own hair and skin color were matched to those of the peer and the puppet. Even the movements of each stimulus figure on the video were constructed to be as similar as possible. Figure 2.2 shows the stimulus items that were used for one of the participants.

The results of this experiment, shown in Figure 2.3, indicated that infants looked longer at the peer than at the self. As we discuss in the chapter titled "Basic Learning and Perception," infants show a fairly distinct preference for novelty. Thus the findings for looking behavior are as expected if we assume that infants recognize their own faces as familiar. They also looked at the puppet longer than at any of the other stimuli. Moreover, babies directed fewest of their social signals, smiles and vocalizations, to the nonsocial object, the puppet. The experimental approach suggests that it was the degree of humanlike qualities of the stimulus items that was responsible for these variations in infant responses rather than some other aspect of the stimuli. Thus, early in development, infants are well equipped to respond to the social features of their environment. (By the way, do you think the researchers should have used a puppet with a normal face configuration instead of an abstract one? Why or why not?)

The experimental approach has been the traditional design choice for many developmental psychologists because of the "clean" answers it provides about the causes of developmental phenomena. Yet it has also been criticized for providing a narrow portrait of child development. Development in the real world is likely to be caused by many variables; few changes are likely to be the result of a single or even a few independent variables. In that sense, experimental studies typically fail to capture the complexities of age-related changes. Moreover, we have already mentioned that children may not react normally when they are brought into the laboratory setting, where most experiments are conducted. Children may "clam up" because they are shy about being in unfamiliar surroundings with strangers and mechanical equipment. Or they may rush through the experimental task just to get it over with.

In recognition of these problems, many researchers have tried to achieve a more homelike feeling in their laboratories, with comfortable couches, chairs, tables, and rugs instead of sterile, bare-walled rooms filled with equipment. Another tactic has been to conduct **field experiments,** in which the experimental manipulations are actually carried out in a natural setting, such as the child's home or school. In one such field experiment, Grover Whitehurst and his colleagues (Whitehurst et al., 1994) randomly assigned children attending their preschools to one of three experimental conditions to see if the type of reading experiences they had influenced their language skills. For six weeks, a ten-minute period was allocated each day to one of the following conditions: (1) school reading, in which the teacher read a book and concurrently asked children numerous questions about the story and promoted discussion; (2) school plus home reading, in which teachers read to children in the same special

field experiment   Experiment conducted in a "natural," real-world setting such as the child's home or school.

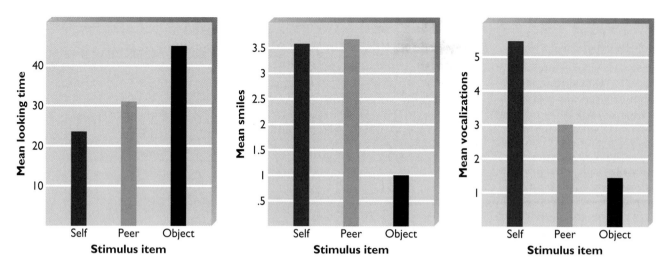

Source: Data from Legerstee et al., 1998.

manner but parents were also trained to read to children at home using an active discussion approach; and (3) control, in which children engaged in ten minutes of teacher-supervised play. The groups were formed such that no more than five children participated in each at any single time. The results, displayed in Figure 2.4, showed that at the end of six weeks, children in both reading groups scored significantly higher on a test of vocabulary compared with the control group and that the school plus home reading group scored higher than the school reading group. In the follow-up phase six months later, both reading groups continued to show advantages over the control group in language skills. Because the only known variation in children's experiences was systematically introduced by the researchers in their manipulation of the independent variable (the type of reading group children were exposed to), changes in behavior could be attributed to type of reading program. In addition, the natural setting of this field experiment minimized the problems associated with bringing children into the artificial surroundings of a laboratory.

In some instances, it is not possible for the researcher to randomly assign participants to treatment groups because of logistical or ethical difficulties. In these cases, the researcher may take advantage of the natural separation of participants into different groups. **Quasi-experiments** are studies in which researchers investigate the effects of independent variables that they do not manipulate themselves but that occur as a result of children's natural experiences. Suppose a researcher wanted to investigate the effects of a longer school year on children's academic skills. One way to make sure that it is the length of the school year that influences performance rather than the initial characteristics of the children is to randomly assign children to the two groups, one with a longer school year and one with a regular school year. That way, children with higher and lesser abilities, for example, would be equally likely to appear in both groups. However, it would be unethical, and also logistically very difficult, to assign children to different schools in this way. Julie Frazier and Frederick Morrison (1998) learned of one elementary school that was extending its school year from 180 to 210 days and took the opportunity to assess the impact on the achievement of kindergartners in mathematics, reading, general knowledge, and vocabulary. The researchers found that children with additional time in school during the year showed greater gains in achievement, especially in mathematics, compared with students who attended a school with a regular 180-day calendar.

The results of quasi-experimental designs must be interpreted with caution. The children who experienced an extended school year may have differed in systematic ways from children who had a regular academic year, ways that could have accounted for their better performance. For example, the former group may have had parents who were very concerned with academic achievement and spent more time teaching

FIGURE 2.3
An Experimental Study

These three graphs show the mean duration of looking and the number of smiles and vocalizations that five-month-old infants made when viewing the self, a peer, and a puppet. The type of stimulus item was the independent variable. Looking time, smiling, and vocalizations were the three dependent variables, each one shown separately on its own graph. Because the researchers controlled for extraneous variables that could have affected looking, smiling, and vocalizing, it is plausible to conclude that there was something about the familiarity of the self and the "humanness" of the self and peer that was responsible for differential responding.

quasi-experiment Study in which the assignment of participants to experimental groups is determined by their natural experiences.

FIGURE 2.4
A Field Experiment

The data from Whitehurst et al.'s (1994) field study show that children who had special reading experiences at school and at school plus home received higher scores on a test of vocabulary on a posttest (six weeks after the program began) and a follow-up (six months later) compared with the control group. A field experiment employs many of the features of an experiment but is conducted in a natural setting.

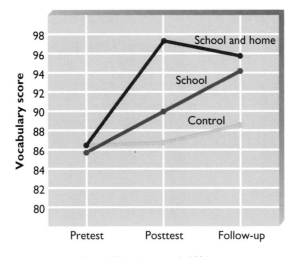

Source: Adapted from Whitehurst et al., 1994.

them at home. The investigators took great care to try to make the two groups equivalent at the outset of the study by matching them on intelligence test scores, medical history, parents' occupations, parents' expectations about school, and several other dimensions. Could other competing explanations for the outcomes be ruled out? Because they were in the same district, the curricula in the two schools were equivalent. Most revealing, though, was the pattern of exactly at what time gains in achievement were made. Through the winter, when the two school programs still had an equivalent number of days, the students in both groups showed similar patterns of growth in achievement. However, it was during the summer, after the extended days occurred, that student achievement patterns diverged. Thus researchers who conduct quasi-experimental studies must be very concerned with ruling out alternative explanations for their findings. Despite these methodological difficulties, quasi-experimental studies offer a way to address important questions about the complex influences on child development, questions that often have powerful real-world implications.

● **Case Studies and the Single-Case Design** Some notable discoveries about developmental processes have come from the in-depth examination of a single child or just a few children. At times, psychologists make an intensive description of an individual child, much as the baby biographers did. Freud and Piaget both relied heavily on such **case studies** of individuals to formulate their broad theories of personality and cognitive development, respectively. Case studies can be particularly revealing when researchers discover a child with an unusual ability or disability or an uncommon past history. The details of a child's background, cognitive skills, or behaviors can, in some cases, provide important insights about the process of development or even a critical test of a theory. For example, researchers (Fletcher-Flinn & Thompson, 2000) recently reported the case of a three-and-a-half-year-old child who was able to read at the level of an eight-and-a-half-year-old. Did this precocious reader focus on the sounds made by each letter in a word, a process that many reading specialists say is essential to skilled reading? Extensive tests and observations indicated that this child had little awareness of the correspondence between individual letters and their sounds, a finding that suggests that successful reading may not depend on phonics skills for all children. Although case studies can provide a rich picture of a given aspect of development, they must also be interpreted with caution. The observations reported in case studies can be subjective in nature and thus vulnerable to the phenomenon of observer bias that was discussed earlier in this chapter.

In other instances, researchers introduce experimental treatments to one or a few children and note any changes in their behavior over time. The emphasis is on the systematic collection of data, rather than on providing a detailed narrative, as is often done in case studies. Frequently the purpose of these **single-case designs** is to

case study In-depth description of psychological characteristics and behaviors of an individual, often in the form of a narrative.

single-case design Study that follows only one or a few participants over a period of time, with an emphasis on systematic collection of data.

evaluate a clinical treatment for a problem behavior or an educational program designed to increase or decrease specific activities in the child.

Suppose we wish to evaluate the effectiveness of a treatment for stuttering in children. One team of researchers selected four boys, ages ten to eleven years, who had difficulties with stuttering (Gagnon & Ladouceur, 1992). Their first step was to record the percentage of stuttered syllables each boy spoke during the baseline period, prior to the start of the treatment. Next, the treatment began. During two one-hour sessions per week, each boy received instruction on how to recognize stuttering and how to regulate breathing during stuttering. Special speaking exercises and parent information sessions were also introduced. Finally, the participants' speech was assessed at one month and six months following the end of treatment. Figure 2.5 shows the decline in percentage of stuttered syllables among the children from baseline through follow-up periods. Was the treatment effective? The facts that all four participants showed similar declines in

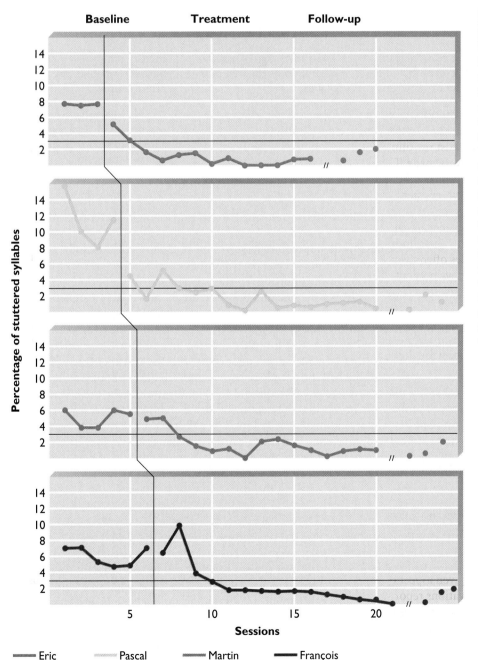

FIGURE 2.5
A Single-Case Design

In this example of a single-case design, four boys with stuttering problems were observed during a baseline period. Next, a program to treat their speech problems was begun. The graph shows that the percentage of stuttered syllables declined dramatically following the onset of treatment and remained low during the follow-up period. Because the four children showed similar patterns of behavior change, and because the behavior change was maintained long after the treatment ended, the researchers concluded that their treatment was effective.

Source: Gagnon & Ladouceur, 1992.

TABLE 2.2	Strengths and Weaknesses of Research Designs		
Design	**Description**	**Strengths**	**Weaknesses**
Correlational Design	Researcher sees if changes in one variable are accompanied by systematic changes in another variable.	Useful when conditions do not permit the manipulation of variables.	Cannot determine cause-and-effect relationships.
Experimental Design	Researcher manipulates one or more independent variables to observe the effects on the dependent variable(s).	Can isolate cause-and-effect relationships.	May not yield information about real-life behaviors.
Field Experiment	Experiment conducted in real-life, naturalistic settings.	Can isolate cause-and-effect relationships; behaviors are observed in natural settings.	Less control over treatment conditions.
Quasi-experiment	Assignment of participants to groups is determined by their natural experiences.	Takes advantage of natural separation of children into groups.	Factors other than independent variables may be causing results.
Case Study/ Single-Case Design	In-depth observation of one or a few children over a period of time.	Does not require large pool of participants.	Can be vulnerable to observer bias; ability to generalize to the larger population may be limited.

stuttering and that the stuttering remained low during follow-up several months later suggest that it was.

Single-case designs do not require large groups of children or the random assignment of participants to groups. Each participant essentially serves as his or her own control by experiencing all conditions in the experiment over a period of time. As with any study involving only one or a few individuals, however, researchers' ability to generalize to a larger group of children may be limited. Perhaps the child or children they selected for the study were particularly responsive to the treatment, a treatment that might not work as well for other children. In addition, the researcher must be aware of any other circumstances concurrent with the treatment that may have actually produced the behavior changes. For example, did the children in the stuttering study mature neurologically, and did that maturation cause the reduction in speech problems? The fact that the treatment started at different times for each of the four children and was immediately followed by a decrease in stuttering suggests that the treatment and not some other factor caused the changes.

Table 2.2 presents an overview of the strengths and weaknesses of case studies and single-case designs, as well as other research designs we have briefly examined here.

Strategies for Assessing Developmental Change

The developmental researcher faces a problem unique to this field: how to record the changes in behavior that occur over time. The investigator has two choices: to observe individual children repeatedly over time or to select children of different ages to participate in one study at a given time. Each approach has its strengths and limitations, and each has contributed substantially to our understanding of child development.

● **The Longitudinal Study**   **Longitudinal studies** assess the same sample of participants repeatedly at various points in time, usually over a span of years. This approach has the longest historical tradition in developmental psychology. The early baby biographies were in essence longitudinal observations, and several major longi-

longitudinal study   Research in which the same participants are repeatedly tested over a period of time, usually years.

Longitudinal studies assess the same individuals over a span of years, sometimes ranging from infancy through adolescence. This strategy for assessing developmental change allows researchers to identify the stability of many human characteristics.

tudinal projects that were initiated in the early 1900s continued for decades. One of the most famous is Lewis Terman's study of intellectually gifted children, begun in 1921 (Terman, 1925; Terman & Oden, 1959).

Terman identified 952 children aged two to fourteen years who had scored 140 or above on a standardized test of intelligence. He was interested in answering several questions about these exceptionally bright children. Would they become extraordinarily successful later in life? Did they possess any specific cluster of common personality traits? Did they adapt well socially? The sample was followed until most participants reached sixty years of age, and a wealth of information was collected over this long span of time. One finding was that many individuals in this sample had highly successful careers in science, academics, business, and other professions. In addition, contrary to many popular stereotypes, high intelligence was associated with greater physical and mental health and adaptive social functioning later in life.

Longitudinal research is costly and requires a substantial research effort. Participants followed over a period of years often move or become unavailable for other reasons; just keeping track of them requires constant and careful recordkeeping. In addition, one might raise questions about the characteristics of the people who remain in the study: perhaps they are less mobile, or perhaps those who agree to participate in a thirty-year study have unique qualities that can affect the interpretation of the project's results (e.g., they may be less energetic or be more curious about themselves and more introspective). Another difficulty lies in the fact that participants who are tested repeatedly often get better at the tests, not because of any changes in their abilities but because the tests become more familiar over time. Participants who take a test of spatial skill again and again may improve due to practice with the test and not as a result of any developmental change in their abilities. If the researcher attempts to avert this outcome by designing a different version of the same test, the problem then becomes whether the two tests are similar enough!

One of the biggest methodological drawbacks of longitudinal research is the possibility of an **age-history confound.** Suppose a researcher began a twenty-year

age-history confound In longitudinal studies, the co-occurrence of historical factors with changes in age; affects the ability to interpret results.

FIGURE 2.6
A Cross-Sectional Study

In this example of a cross-sectional study, children of different ages were asked two progressively misleading questions about each of several portions of a video clip they watched. Kindergarten children made significantly more incorrect responses to the second set of misleading questions. Cross-sectional studies allow researchers to examine age differences in performance quickly and efficiently.

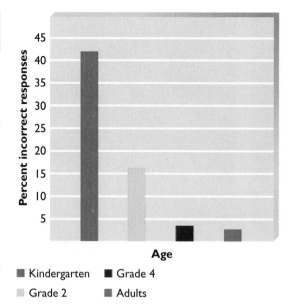

■ Kindergarten   ■ Grade 4
■ Grade 2   ■ Adults

Source: Data from Cassel, Roebers, & Bjorklund, 1996.

longitudinal study in 1970 and found that individuals' gender-role beliefs became less stereotyped as the years progressed; that is, participants were less likely to believe that females are dependent, passive, and emotional and males are independent, aggressive, and logical. Are these shifts in attitude associated with development? Or did some historical factor, such as the women's movement, bring about the changes in beliefs? Because participants age as cultural and historical events occur, it is often difficult to decide which factor affects the results of a longitudinal study. Moreover, consider a twenty-year longitudinal study begun in the 1940s versus a similar study begun in the 1990s. Many of the factors that are likely to influence children's development today—television, daycare, and computers, to name a few—probably would not have been included in studies begun five decades ago.

Despite all these difficulties, the longitudinal approach has distinct advantages no other research tactic offers; in fact, certain research questions in child development can *only* be answered longitudinally. If a researcher is interested in identifying the *stability* of human characteristics—that is, how likely it is that early attributes will be maintained later in development—the longitudinal approach is the method of choice. Only by observing the same person over time can we answer such questions as "Do passive infants become shy adults?" or "Do early experiences with peers affect the child's ability to form friendships in adolescence?" For researchers interested in understanding the process of development and the factors that precede and follow specific developmental phenomena, particularly with respect to individual differences, the longitudinal strategy remains a powerful one.

● **The Cross-Sectional Study**   Possibly the most widely used strategy for studying developmental differences is the **cross-sectional study,** in which children of varying ages are examined at the same point in time. Cross-sectional studies take less time to complete and are usually more economical than longitudinal studies.

A good example of cross-sectional research is the investigation of children's responses to repeated questions about a past event conducted by William Cassel and his colleagues (Cassel, Roebers, & Bjorklund, 1996). Children from kindergarten, second, and fourth grades, as well as adults, watched a video of two children fighting over a bicycle. One week later, participants were asked to recall what they saw. In one portion of the experiment, they were also asked two increasingly misleading questions about each of several segments in the videotaped episode. Figure 2.6 shows the results: kindergartners gave significantly more incorrect responses to the second set of misleading questions compared with the other age groups.

cross-sectional study   Study in which individuals of different ages are examined at the same point in time.

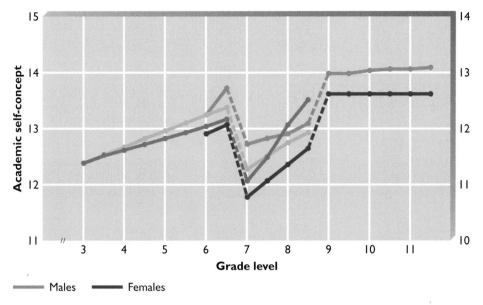

Source: Adapted from Cole et al., 2001.

FIGURE 2.7
A Sequential Study

Age differences in behavior patterns over time can be assessed with sequential studies. In a study of children's self-concepts from elementary school through high school, Cole and his colleagues (Cole et al., 2001) assessed two groups of children over a period of six years. The first was a group of third-graders. The data in the graph show changes in their academic self-concept from third through eighth grade (based on a test with the scale shown on the left y-axis). The second group was in the sixth grade at the start of the study. The data in the graph show changes in their self-concepts from sixth through eleventh grade (based on a test for older children with the scale shown on the right y-axis). Thus information about a nine-year age span was obtained in six years.

The cross-sectional approach allowed the researchers to make a rapid assessment of the children's performance without waiting for them to grow several years older. They were, however, unable to draw conclusions about individual children and about how characteristics observable at one age might be related to characteristics at another age. Would the children who were most resistant to misleading suggestions also resist those suggestions years later? The cross-sectional approach does not provide answers to these kinds of questions. Most cross-sectional studies involve pooling the scores of individual participants such that the average performance of an entire group of children of a specified age is reported; the average scores of two or more groups of children are then compared. The result is that information about individuals is not the focus of data analysis in this type of study.

Another difficulty with cross-sectional designs is that cohort effects may interfere with our ability to draw clear conclusions. **Cohort effects** are all the characteristics shared by children growing up in a specific social and historical context. For example, many of today's five-year-olds have had extensive peer experience through their enrollment in daycare and other preschool programs, whereas many fifteen-year-olds probably have not. A researcher comparing the two groups might mistakenly conclude that younger children are more sociable than older children, but the differential exposure to agemates early in life—that is, the cohort effect—may be responsible for the findings rather than changes in sociability with age. Cross-sectional studies are a quick means of providing descriptions of age changes in all sorts of behaviors. Where they sometimes fall short is in helping us to understand the processes underlying those age-related changes.

● **The Sequential Study** One way to combine the advantages of both the longitudinal and cross-sectional approaches is the **sequential study,** in which groups of children of different ages are followed repeatedly but for only a few years. For example, David Cole and his colleagues (Cole et al., 2001) examined changes in children's self-concepts from the elementary to high school years. Two groups of children—a group of third-graders and a group of sixth-graders—were followed for a period of six years. Every six months, children took a battery of tests assessing several aspects of self-confidence, such as academic competence, social acceptance, and physical appearance. Thus, by the end of the study, data were available for children in the third through eleventh grades.

Figure 2.7 shows the results for academic competence. Both boys and girls showed gains in this domain from third through sixth grade but evidenced a decline in

SEE FOR YOURSELF
psychology.college.hmco.com
Childhood Today

cohort effects Characteristics shared by individuals growing up in a given sociohistorical context that can influence developmental outcomes.

sequential study Study that examines groups of children of different ages over a period of time; usually shorter than a longitudinal study.

T034600

TABLE 2.3	Strategies for Assessing Developmental Change		
Approach	**Description**	**Advantages**	**Disadvantages**
Longitudinal Study	Repeated testing of the same group of children over an extended period of time.	Can examine the stability of characteristics.	Requires a significant investment of time and resources; problems with participant attrition; can have age-history confound.
Cross-Sectional Study	Comparison of children of different ages at the same point in time.	Requires less time; less costly than longitudinal study.	Cannot study individual patterns of development or the stability of traits; subject to cohort effects.
Sequential Study	Observation of children of two or more different ages over a shorter period of time than in longitudinal studies.	Combines the advantages of both longitudinal and cross-sectional approaches; can obtain information about stability of traits in a short period of time.	Has same problems as longitudinal studies, but to a lesser degree.

seventh grade, followed by increases in successive years. (Note that both groups of children were measured in sixth, seventh, and eighth grades.) Because subsets of the children were assessed repeatedly, information about the stability of self-concept for individual children was available just as it would have been in a longitudinal study. The benefit of the sequential design was that it allowed information about a nine-year span to be obtained in six years.

Although most developmental researchers still prefer to conduct cross-sectional studies because of their expediency, the sequential study provides a convenient way to reap the advantages of both cross-sectional and longitudinal approaches to studying developmental change.

Table 2.3 summarizes the relative benefits of each of the research strategies for assessing developmental change.

Cross-Cultural Studies of Development

Some of the most fundamental questions about the nature of development concern the universality of the various features of psychological growth. Do all children learn language in the same way, regardless of the specific language they acquire? Does children's thinking develop in a universal sequence? Are certain emotions common to all children regardless of attitudes about the appropriateness of crying, smiling, or feeling angry in the larger social group in which they live?

If psychological development does display universal features, this circumstance has far-reaching implications. It could imply, for a start, that a child's behavior is largely shaped by biological factors and, more specifically, by the genes that govern the unfolding of some human behaviors. Variations in aspects of psychological development across cultures, on the other hand, imply that the differences in the child's experiences weigh heavily in bringing about those behaviors. **Cross-cultural studies,** which compare children from different cultural groups on one or more behaviors or patterns of abilities, can be extremely useful in answering questions such as these.

Take, for example, the development of play. One hypothesis put forward by Piaget is that there is a general progression in early childhood from *exploratory play,* in which the toddler throws, manipulates, and otherwise learns about the functions of objects, to *symbolic play,* in which he or she pretends with objects, for example, sipping from an empty cup or using a block as a telephone. Marc Bornstein and his colleagues

cross-cultural study   Study that compares individuals in different cultural contexts.

Cross-cultural studies allow researchers to explore the extent to which children's behaviors are universal or specific to a given culture. For example, are the emotions expressed by these Dominican children as they make music also seen among children from other cultures?

(1999) recorded and coded the naturally occurring play behaviors of twenty-month-old children and their mothers in two countries, the United States and Argentina. Mother-child pairs were provided with the same set of eight toys and were told to play as they normally would for ten minutes. These researchers found that despite being the same age, children in the United States engaged in more exploratory play with their mothers, whereas Argentine children engaged in more symbolic play. Moreover, mothers' play behaviors were strongly related to children's patterns of play. Thus there were clear cultural differences, perhaps linked to the different social goals in the two groups. Exploratory play patterns, which involve manipulating and combining objects, are consistent with the emphasis on individual achievement, independence, and self-reliance in the United States. On the other hand, symbolic play patterns among Argentine mothers and their children often included social behaviors, such as feeding or putting a doll to sleep. These social behaviors are compatible with the orientation of Argentine society toward the larger, collective group. Thus the transition from one form of play to another may be less influenced by universal processes, as suggested by Piaget, than by culture-specific experiences.

Cross-cultural studies can present unique challenges to the researcher. If children from two cultural backgrounds are being compared, the researcher must make sure the tasks are well understood and have equivalent forms despite differences in language or the kinds of activities the children are used to doing. For example, children in some cultures may never have seen a photograph or a two-dimensional drawing. Asking these children to categorize objects in pictorial form may place them at an unfair disadvantage if they are to be compared with children who have extensive experience with two-dimensional representations. Moreover, if the researcher is an outsider to the cultural group being observed, he or she may provoke atypical reactions from the individuals under study. Parent-child interactions, peer play, and many other behaviors may not occur as they would in the natural course of events because of the presence of an outside observer. Cross-cultural researchers must thus pay special attention to the possibility of participant reactivity.

For some researchers, cross-cultural studies play a different sort of role in that they provide a way of understanding human development as it is shaped and formed by the unique contexts in which it occurs. From this perspective, a researcher may try to avoid imposing the values and concepts of his or her own culture on another, trying instead to discover the particular beliefs, values, and modes of thinking in the group under study. The goal is not to compare cultures in order to document similarities and differences; rather, it is to study cultures in an in-depth fashion in order to describe behaviors and underlying meaning systems *within* that culture (Miller, 1999; Saarni, 1998; Shweder et al., 1998; Super & Harkness, 1997). A research approach that is often used to achieve these goals is **ethnography,** a set of methods that includes observations of behaviors within the natural environment and interviews with individuals about values and practices within the culture. Ethnographers often live within a particular culture as *participant-observers,* immersing themselves over an extended period of time in the daily routines and practices of a culture (Weisner, 1996). Using these methods, researchers have obtained rich descriptions of what it means to be a child in cultures as diverse as the Gusii tribe of western Kenya (LeVine et al., 1994), Samoa (Ochs, 1988), and the poor neighborhoods of modern-day Brazil (Scheper-Hughes, 1992).

The cross-cultural approach has benefits in terms of understanding human development as it occurs not only in other countries but also in our own society, in which cultural diversity is increasingly becoming a characteristic of the population. Consider some statistics. In Canada, almost 15 percent of children age fourteen years and under come from non-Caucasian background cultures (Statistics Canada, 1999). In the United States, 32 percent of children under age eighteen are African American, Hispanic, Native American, or Asian (U.S. Bureau of the Census, 2001). By the year 2010, the majority of children under eighteen will be of these ethnic heritages in several states, including Hawaii, California, Texas, New York, and New Mexico (McLoyd, 1998). Thus, in order to capture the elements of human development in the broadest and most meaningful sense, researchers will have to study concepts that are relevant and indigenous to these cultures. Individual autonomy and competition may be valued goals of socialization in middle-class Caucasian culture, for example, but they have less relevance for African American or Native American cultures (McLoyd, 1998). Cross-cultural studies can provide important insights into almost all aspects of child development. For this reason, we draw on available cross-cultural work as we discuss each aspect of the growth of children.

FOR YOUR REVIEW

- What issues must researchers pay attention to when they measure attributes and behaviors?

- What four information-gathering techniques do developmental researchers generally have available to them? What are the advantages and disadvantages of each approach?

- What are the different research designs that researchers might employ to study child development? What are the strengths and weaknesses of each design?

- What three research tactics allow researchers to address questions about developmental change? What are the strengths and weaknesses of each approach?

- What functions do different types of cross-cultural studies serve in developmental research?

Ethical Issues in Developmental Research

All psychologists are bound by professional ethics to treat the participants under study humanely and fairly. In general, researchers try to minimize the risk of any physical or emotional harm that might come to participants from taking part in research and to maximize the benefits that will accrue from the findings of their work. The American Psychological Association has drawn up the following specific guide-

ethnography Set of methods, including observations and interviews, used by researchers to describe the behaviors and underlying meaning systems within a given culture.

lines for the use of human participants. First, participants must give **informed consent** before participating in a research project; that is, they must be told the purposes of the study and informed of any potential risks to their well-being, and then they must formally agree to participate. Second, participants have the right to decline to participate or to stop participation, even in the middle of the experiment. Third, if participants cannot be told the true purpose of the experiment (sometimes knowing the experimenter's objective will influence how participants behave), they must be *debriefed* at the conclusion of the study. When participants are **debriefed,** they are told the true objective of the study and the reasons for any deception on the part of the experimenter. Finally, data collected from participants must be kept confidential. Names of participants must not be revealed, and care must be taken to protect their anonymity. To ensure that experimenters comply with these guidelines, virtually all research institutions in the United States are required to have review boards that evaluate any potential risks to participants and the researchers' compliance with ethical practice.

The same ethical guidelines apply to using children as participants in research, but frequently the implementation of these guidelines becomes a difficult matter. Who provides informed consent in the case of an infant or a young toddler, for example? (The parents do.) Is it proper to deceive children about the purposes of a study if they cannot understand the debriefing? (In general, it is a good idea to avoid any kind of deception with children, such as telling them you are interested in how quickly they learn a game when you are really interested in whether they will be altruistic with their play partner.) Are some subjects of study taboo, such as asking children about their concepts of death, suicide, or other frightening topics that might affect them emotionally? (Such studies, if conducted, must be planned very carefully and conducted only by trained professionals.) What about cases in which treatments are suspected to have beneficial outcomes for children? Can the control group properly have the treatment withheld? For example, if we suspect that children's participation in an early intervention preschool program will have real benefits for them, should children in the control group be kept out of it? (One solution to this thorny problem is to offer the control group the beneficial treatment as soon as possible after the conclusion of the study, although this is not always a satisfactory compromise. The control group still has to wait for a beneficial treatment or intervention.)

Many researchers assume that children's vulnerability to risk as they participate in psychological experiments decreases as they grow older. Because infants and young children have more limited cognitive skills and emotional coping strategies, they are viewed as less able to protect themselves and to understand their rights during participation in research. This assumption certainly has some logical basis and, in fact, is confirmed by research showing that second-graders have difficulty understanding the concept of confidentiality, as well as the contents of a debriefing statement (Hurley & Underwood, 2002). Some types of research, however, may actually pose a greater threat to older children. As Ross Thompson (1990) has pointed out, older children are developing a self-concept and a more elaborate understanding of the ways others evaluate them. Older children may thus be more susceptible to psychological harm than younger children when the researcher compares their performance with that of others or when they think teachers or parents may learn about their performance. In addition, older children may be more sensitive to research results that reflect negatively on their families or sociocultural groups. These situations require awareness on the part of the researcher of the subtle ways children can be adversely affected by the research enterprise.

Table 2.4 sets forth the ethical guidelines on using children as participants in research established by the Society for Research in Child Development (1996). Probably the overriding guiding principle is that children should not be subjected to any physical or mental harm and should be treated with all possible respect. In fact, because children are frequently unable to voice their concerns and have less power than adults do, developmental researchers must be especially sensitive to their comfort and well-being.

WHAT DO YOU THINK?

Which Ethical Principles Apply?
psychology.college.hmco.com

informed consent Participant's formal acknowledgment that he or she understands the purposes, procedures, and risks of a study and agrees to participate in it.

debriefing Providing research participants with a statement of the true goals of a study after initially deceiving them or omitting information about its purposes.

TABLE 2.4	Ethical Guidelines in Conducting Research with Children

- *Nonharmful procedures:* The investigator may not use any procedures that could impose physical or psychological harm on the child. In addition, the investigator should use the least stressful research operation whenever possible. If the investigator is in doubt about the possible harmful effects of the research, he or she should consult with others. If the child will be unavoidably exposed to stress in research that might provide some diagnostic or therapeutic benefits to the child, the study should be reviewed by an institutional review board.

- *Informed consent:* The investigator should inform the child of all features of the research that might affect his or her willingness to participate and should answer all questions in a way the child can comprehend. The child has the right to discontinue participation at any time.

- *Parental consent:* Informed consent should be obtained in writing from the child's parents or from other adults who have responsibility for the child. The adult has the right to know all features of the research that might affect the child's willingness to participate and can refuse consent.

- *Deception:* If the research necessitates concealment or deception about the nature of the study, the investigator should make sure the child understands the reasons for the deception after the study is concluded.

- *Confidentiality:* All information about participants in research must be kept confidential.

- *Jeopardy:* If, during research, the investigator learns of information concerning a jeopardy to the child's well-being, the investigator must discuss the information with the parents or guardians and experts to arrange for assistance to the child.

- *Informing participants:* The investigator should clarify any misconceptions that may have arisen on the part of the child during the study. The investigator should also report general findings to participants in terms they can understand.

Source: Adapted from the ethical standards set by the Society for Research in Child Development, 1996.

CONTROVERSY: THINKING IT OVER

Should Researchers Reveal Information They Learn About Participants in Their Studies?

Researchers often study issues that are sensitive but that can have important consequences for the well-being of children. For example, a researcher might be interested in finding out the factors that predict the emergence of eating disorders in adolescents or the consequences of parental drug abuse for the child. However, research that can be very illuminating about the nature of childhood problems often raises difficult ethical dilemmas (Fischer, 1994).

What Is the Controversy?
Suppose the researcher discovers that a particular child has a serious eating disorder or that a young child has ingested harmful illegal drugs kept by the parents in the home. What are the ethical obligations of the researcher in such situations? Should the concerns about the welfare of individual children override any potential benefits of the research for children in general? Furthermore, should the identities of children with serious problems be revealed to parents, school personnel, or others responsible for their well-being at the risk of violating children's trust that data will be kept confidential?

What Are the Opposing Arguments?
Ethical guidelines state that researchers who discover that a child is at risk must take steps to make sure that the child obtains appropriate assistance. Such action is based on the concept of "jeopardy" outlined by the Society for Research in Child Development and referred to in Table 2.4. The idea is that ethical concerns about the welfare of children should be a primary concern and override any potential benefits of the research for children in general. Also implicit in the concept of jeopardy is the notion that in some circumstances, confidentiality must be broken to protect the best interests of the child.

However, as a consequence of such actions, the child may drop out of the study in order to receive some form of treatment or intervention. If several children in the study thus drop out, the opportunity to complete the research project could be lost, along with the potential benefits of the results of the study for a larger group of children (Beauchamp et al., 1982). Some researchers believe that the benefits of a well-conducted study can override the obligation to help a particular child for whom a problem has been revealed.

What Answers Exist? What Questions Remain?

In some cases, researchers may have a legal obligation to enforce the principle of jeopardy. A federal law, the Child Abuse Prevention and Treatment Act enacted in 1974, resulted in the creation of mandatory reporting procedures for suspected cases of child abuse and neglect in every state. In many states, researchers are included among individuals who are required to report. Thus a researcher who discovers that a child has been abused or neglected, as in the preceding example of a child who has ingested parents' illegal drugs, may be required by law to report the case to the proper authorities. The fact that the child might drop out of the study or that confidentiality is broken is simply a necessary consequence.

In other cases, the issue may be more difficult to resolve. Research can be of help, though, by supplying information on how children themselves feel when such ethical dilemmas arise. Celia Fisher and her colleagues (Fisher et al., 1996) asked adolescents to judge what researchers should do if they discover that a child has a substance abuse problem, has been physically or sexually abused, displays a life-threatening behavior, or engages in delinquent behaviors. Most adolescents favored reporting instances of child abuse or threats of suicide to a responsible adult. For less severe problems, such as cigarette smoking and nonviolent delinquent acts, adolescents were more inclined to say that the researcher should do nothing. In cases such as the latter, rather than reporting children to parents or authorities, researchers might decide to urge children to seek assistance on their own.

Other questions remain. Does the age of the child matter in such ethical decisions? Should these decisions be handled differently with adolescents than with younger children? How can research help us to address questions such as these?

CHAPTER RECAP

SUMMARY OF TOPICS

Research Methods in Developmental Psychology

- Like other scientists, developmental psychologists are concerned with using sound methodologies to glean information about children. The *scientific method* is used not only to test theories but also to gather information that can have applications in the lives of children.

Measuring Attributes and Behaviors

- Researchers need to be concerned with *operationally defining* the *variables* in the study. That is, the variables must be specified in measurable terms.

- Variables must be *valid*, that is, actually measure the concept under consideration.

- Variables must also be *reliable*, that is, obtained consistently from one time to another or from one observer to another.

Methods of Collecting Data

- *Naturalistic observations* involve the systematic recording of behaviors as they occur in children's everyday environments. Two special concerns in this approach are *participant reactivity*, the chance that children will react to the presence of an observer by behaving in untypical ways, and *observer bias*, the possibility that the researcher will interpret observations to be consistent with his or her hypotheses.

- *Structured observations*, usually conducted in the laboratory, allow the experimenter more control over situations that accompany children's behaviors. Researchers can measure children's overt behaviors or obtain physiological measures such as heart rate or brain wave activity. One limitation of this approach is that children may not act as they would in a natural context.

- Researchers can employ *structured interviews* or *questionnaires* if they are interested in children's own reports of what they know or how they behave. Alternatively, they can use a more open-ended technique, the *clinical method*. Researchers need to be aware that children may not always answer questions truthfully and that systematic comparisons and unbiased interpretations by the researcher may be difficult to obtain, especially with the clinical method.

- *Meta-analysis* permits investigators to analyze the results of a large body of published research to draw general conclusions about behavior.

Research Designs

- In the *correlational design*, the investigator attempts to see whether changes in one variable are accompanied by changes in another variable. Researchers may observe a *positive correlation*, in which increases in one variable are accompanied by increases in another, or a *negative correlation*, in which increases in one variable are accompanied by decreases in the other. The statistic used to assess the degree of relationship is the *correlation coefficient*. One caution about this design is that cause-and-effect conclusions cannot be drawn.

- In the *experimental design*, the researcher manipulates one or more *independent variables* to see if they have an effect on the *dependent variable*. *Random assignment* of participants to different treatment groups helps to ensure that only the independent variable varies from one group to the other. Therefore, cause-and-effect relationships among variables can be identified. Variations on this technique are *field experiments*, in which the experimental manipulations are carried out in a natural setting, and *quasi-experiments*, in which the assignment of participants to experimental groups is determined by the participants' natural experiences. Because of this circumstance, researchers conducting quasi-experiments must be concerned with ruling out alternative explanations for their findings.

- In *case studies* or the *single-case design*, the researcher intensively studies one or a few individuals over a period of time. The former usually involves a detailed narrative description, whereas the latter involves the systematic collection of data. The ability to generalize to a larger population may be limited with these approaches.

Strategies for Assessing Developmental Change

- *Longitudinal studies* test the same participants repeatedly over an extended period of time. This approach requires a significant investment of time, may involve attrition of participants, and could be vulnerable to the *age-history confound*. It is the only method that allows researchers to examine the stability of traits.

- *Cross-sectional studies* examine participants of different ages at the same time. Although this approach requires less time and fewer resources than the longitudinal approach, it is vulnerable to *cohort effects*.

- *Sequential studies* examine children of two or more ages over a period of time, usually shorter than that used in longitudinal studies. This approach combines the advantages of the cross-sectional and longitudinal approaches but is also vulnerable to the problems associated with each.

Cross-Cultural Studies of Development

- *Cross-cultural studies*, which compare individuals from different cultural groups, can be especially helpful in answering questions about universals in development. Researchers must make sure that tasks are comparable across cultural groups, however.

- An important methodological tool, especially for those who wish to learn about the meaning systems within a culture, is *ethnography*, the use of observations and interviews by a researcher who acts as a participant-observer.

Ethical Issues in Developmental Research

- Researchers must be concerned with obtaining *informed consent*, allowing participants to decline participation, *debriefing* participants, and protecting participants' confidentiality.

- The overriding principle is that children should not be subjected to physical or mental harm and should be treated with all possible respect.

CHAPTER 3
Genetics and Heredity

Key Themes in Genetics and Heredity

- **Nature/Nurture** What roles do nature and nurture play in development?

- **Child's Active Role** How does the child play an active role in the effects of heredity on development?

- **Individual Differences** How prominent are individual differences in development?

"**M**ake a wish before you blow out the candles!" But before Sheila could finish speaking, all twelve candles had been extinguished. It had been a great birthday party for the two five-year-olds and their guests. Fortunately, enough candles had been found to signal each year of growth and to continue the custom of adding "one to grow on."

When Sheila first learned that she would become a mother, she had not realized just how much work it would be to rear a child, even though her husband had been an enormous help. Then again, she had not planned on having identical twins! Thus, for this party (as for just about everything else) there were two cakes to be decorated, two presents to be wrapped, two sets of friends to invite for the festivities. Jasmine and Alyssa seemed to bask in the attention they were receiving on their special day. Their excited voices sounded so much alike, indistinguishable by others, including their parents, unless the listener could see which of the twins was speaking (and could remember what each was wearing for the day). The twins enjoyed many of the same games and activities; they displayed the same impatience when others couldn't tell whether they were speaking with Jasmine or Alyssa. But there were differences, too. Jasmine was more impulsive, willing to try new things, likely to jump into the fray of things without a second thought, and less sensitive to the concerns of others. Alyssa was more cautious and careful and seemed to become upset easily, but she was also more willing to help her friends. And although they shared many friends, each twin had preferences for certain playmates. For their mother it was a puzzle: Why were they similar in so many ways but at the same time clearly different?

Parents of more than one child are aware of similarities among them. However, they often take particular notice of the differences; for example, by pointing out how one child "takes after," perhaps, his mother and another after her father. In the case of identical twins, of course, the similarities are far more striking, although parents of twins, like Jasmine's and Alyssa's mother, are able to quickly identify differences in the two children. What are the mechanisms by which such resemblances and differences come about? Though we may grant the contribution of nature to eye color, gender, height, and many other physical traits, heredity's role in other characteristics, such as whether we are contented or quick-tempered, prone to alcoholism, likely to suffer depression, bright and quick-witted, active or more sedentary, is far less certain. Is Jasmine more impulsive and Alyssa more cautious because these qualities developed untouched by the common genetic pattern the twins share or because their parents and others encouraged them to develop individual interests and styles? Or did their individuality come about, perhaps, because the twins actively pursued different paths of responding to their daily experiences despite their common genetic circumstance?

In this chapter, we examine hereditary contributions to development. Major advances in our understanding of the basic biological units of inheritance and their effects on behavior help us to better appreciate the mutual, interactive relationship between nature and nurture. Experiences mold, modify, and enhance biological predispositions, and in a similar manner, genetic endowment influences, perhaps even

64

actively promotes, selection and preference for certain kinds of environments. Our goal is to understand just how such complex interactions evolve.

We begin with a brief overview of the principles of heredity. The blueprint for development is replicated in nearly every cell of our body. This blueprint includes genetic instructions that distinguish us from other species of plants and animals. Regardless of the language we speak, the work we do, the color of our skin, or how friendly we are, we share a genetic underpinning that makes each of us a human being. This biological inheritance also contributes to our individuality. With the exception of identical twins such as Jasmine and Alyssa, each of us begins with a different set of genetic instructions. But even for identical twins, in whom genetic makeup is the same, the influence of distinctive experiences ensures that each of us is a unique individual, different from everyone else.

In this chapter, we also examine several examples of hereditary variations that pose problems for development. As researchers learn more about the ways in which genetic influences occur, we can design environments to help minimize the restrictions imposed by certain hereditary conditions. We consider too how genetic counseling assists parents in deciding whether to have children or how to prepare for a child who is likely to experience developmental problems.

Most psychological development, of course, cannot be linked to simple genetic instructions. Intelligence, temperament, and personality, along with susceptibility to various diseases and conditions, are the outcome of complex interactions between genetic and environmental events. In the final section of this chapter, we consider research involving identical and fraternal twins, siblings, adopted children, and other family relationships to help us understand the complex tapestry genetic and environmental factors weave for cognitive, social-emotional, and personality development (Gottlieb, Wahlsten, & Lickliter, 1998; Rutter, 2002).

Principles of Hereditary Transmission

KEY THEME
Nature/Nurture

Whether we have freckles, blonde hair, or a certain type of personality can be influenced by genetic factors, but none of these characteristics is bestowed on us at conception any more directly than is our ultimate height. We must make a distinction, then, between what our genetic makeup consists of and the kind of individual we eventually become. Thus, we must distinguish between the **genotype**, a person's constant, inherited genetic endowment, and the **phenotype**, his or her observable, measurable features, characteristics, and behaviors. A given phenotype is the product of complex interactions involving the genotype and the many events that are part of an individual's *experience.*

Modern theories of the genotype can be traced to a series of experiments reported in 1866 by Gregor Mendel, an Austrian monk. From his observations of the characteristics of successive generations of peas, Mendel theorized that hereditary characteristics are determined by pairs of particles called *factors* (later termed **genes,** the specialized sequences of molecules that form the genotype). He also proposed that the information provided by the two members of a pair of genes is not always identical. These different forms of a gene are today known as **alleles.** The terms *gene* and *allele* are often used interchangeably, but an allele refers to the specific variation, and sometimes many possible alternative versions exist for a particular gene.

Mendel also outlined the basic principle by which genes are transferred from one generation to another. He concluded that offspring randomly receive one member of every pair of genes from the mother and one from the father. This is possible because the parents' **gametes,** or sex cells (egg and sperm), carry only one member of each pair of genes. Thus, when egg and sperm combine during fertilization, a new pair of genes, one member of the pair inherited from each parent, is reestablished in the offspring. That individual, in turn, may transmit either member of this new pair to subsequent children. Thus, genetic information is passed on from one generation to the next.

genotype Total genetic endowment inherited by an individual.

phenotype Observable and measurable characteristics and traits of an individual; a product of the interaction of the genotype with the environment.

gene Large segment of nucleotides within a chromosome that codes for the production of proteins and enzymes. These proteins and enzymes underlie traits and characteristics inherited from one generation to the next.

allele Alternate form of a specific gene; provides a genetic basis for many individual differences.

gametes Sperm cells in males, egg cells in females, normally containing only twenty-three chromosomes.

At about the same time Mendel's research was published, biologists discovered **chromosomes,** long, threadlike structures in the nucleus of nearly every cell in the body. In the early 1900s, several researchers independently hypothesized that genes are located on chromosomes. Yet another major breakthrough occurred in 1953 when James Watson and Francis Crick deciphered the structure of chromosomes and, in so doing, proposed a powerfully elegant way by which genes are duplicated during cell division. By 1956, researchers had documented the existence of forty-six chromosomes in normal human body cells. Today, the monumental effort to map the entire sequence of the **human genome,** that is, the nearly 3 billion chemical base pairs that make up every human's biological inheritance, is essentially complete (Celera Genomics Sequencing Team, 2001; International Human Genome Mapping Consortium, 2001).

The Building Blocks of Heredity

How could hereditary factors play a part in the similarities displayed by Jasmine and Alyssa or in a child's remarkable mathematical ability or in yet another's mental retardation? To understand the genotype and its effects on appearance, behavior, personality, or intellectual ability, we must consider genetic mechanisms at many different levels.

To begin with, every living organism is composed of cells—in the case of mature humans, trillions of cells. As Figure 3.1 indicates, within the nucleus of nearly all cells are the chromosomes that carry genetic information critical to the cells' functioning. Genes, regions within the strands of chromosomes, determine the production of specific proteins in the cell. The genes, in turn, are made up of various arrangements of four different chemical building blocks called **nucleotides** that contain one of four nitrogen-based molecules (*adenine, thymine, cytosine,* or *guanine*). The nucleotides pair together in one of only two ways to form the rungs of a remarkably long, spiral staircaselike structure called **DNA** or **deoxyribonucleic acid** (see Figure 3.1). An average of about one thousand nucleotide pairs make up each gene, although some genes have substantially more pairings (National Research Council, 1988). Genes differ from one another in number and sequence of nucleotide pairings and in their location on the chemical spiral staircases, or chains of DNA that we call the chromosomes.

Just as Mendel had theorized, hereditary attributes are, in most cases, influenced by pairs of genes or, more specifically, the two allelic forms of the pair. One member of the pair is located on a chromosome inherited from the mother, the other on a similar, or *homologous,* chromosome acquired from the father. Figure 3.2 shows a **karyotype** or photomicrograph of the forty-six chromosomes that males normally possess.

As can be seen in Figure 3.2, the homologous sets of chromosomes that are not genetically involved in the determination of sex, called **autosomes,** can be arranged in pairs and numbered from 1 to 22 on the basis of their size. However, the remaining two chromosomes specify the genetic sex of an individual and differ for males and females. In females this pair consists of **X chromosomes;** both are relatively large and similar in size. The normal male, however, has one X chromosome and a much smaller **Y chromosome.** The Y chromosome is believed to carry only a few dozen genes, in sharp contrast to the two to three thousand genes estimated to be on the X chromosome (Jegalian & Lahn, 2001). Thus, although most genes are present in pairs, males typically have only one instance of each gene found on the sex chromosomes. Nevertheless, the Y chromosome carries a specific gene that promotes the development of the male *gonads* (testes) and, as a consequence, provides an important first step in determining whether an individual is likely to be identified as male or female.

Cell Division and Chromosome Duplication

Each of us began life as a single cell created when a sperm cell, normally containing twenty-three chromosomes, from the father united with an ovum (egg), normally containing an additional twenty-three chromosomes, from the mother. The develop-

chromosomes   Threadlike structures of DNA, located in the nucleus of cells, that form a collection of genes. A human body cell normally contains forty-six chromosomes.

human genome   Entire inventory of nucleotide base pairs that compose the genes and chromosomes of humans.

nucleotide   Repeating basic building block of DNA consisting of nitrogen-based molecules of adenine, thymine, cytosine, and guanine.

deoxyribonucleic acid (DNA) Long, spiral staircaselike sequence of molecules created by nucleotides identified with the blueprint for genetic inheritance.

karyotype   Pictorial representation of an individual's chromosomes.

autosomes   Twenty-two pairs of homologous chromosomes. The two members of each pair are similar in size, shape, and genetic function. The two sex chromosomes are excluded from this class.

X chromosome   Larger of the two sex chromosomes associated with genetic determination of sex. Normally females have two X chromosomes and males only one.

Y chromosome   Smaller of the two sex chromosomes associated with genetic determination of sex. Normally males have one Y chromosome and females none.

| FIGURE 3.1 | The Building Blocks of Heredity |

Hereditary contributions to development can be observed at many levels. This figure depicts five major levels. Nearly every cell in the human body carries the genetic blueprint for development in the chromosomes. Specific regions on each chromosome, the genes, regulate protein production. Looked at in even more detail, the human genome consists of chemical molecules that are the building blocks for the genes. Each of these different levels of the individual's biological makeup can offer insights into the mechanisms by which the genotype affects the phenotype, the observable expression of traits and behaviors.

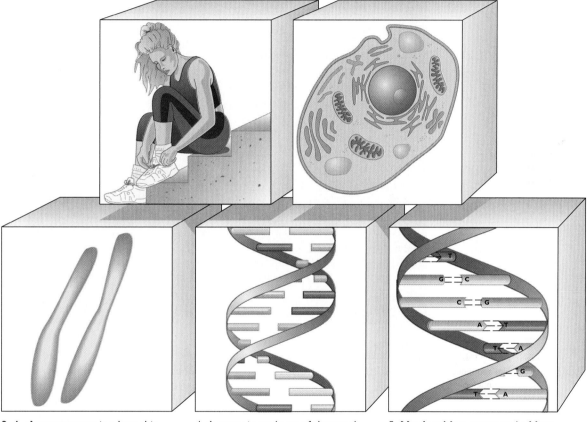

1. The **human body** has about 10 trillion cells. Proteins determine the structure and function of each cell.

2. Most **cells** contain a nucleus. Located within the nucleus are forty-six chromosomes that carry the instructions that signal the cell to manufacture various proteins.

3. A **chromosome** is a long thin strand of DNA organized as a coiled double helix. A full set of forty-six chromosomes in humans is believed to contain somewhere between 26,000 and 38,000 genes, far fewer than had been believed before the human genome was mapped.

4. A **gene** is made up of thousands of nucleotide pairs. Each gene typically has information designed to specify the production of one or more particular proteins.

5. **Nucleotides,** composed of four different kinds of chemical building blocks—adenine (A), thymine (T), cytosine (C), and guanine (G)—are the smallest genetic unit and are paired in specific combinations. Nearly 3 billion pairs of nucleotides make up the total complement of DNA in humans.

Source: Adapted from Isensee, 1986.

mental processes started by this fertilized egg cell, called a **zygote,** are more fully described in the chapter titled "The Prenatal Period and Birth." Remarkably, however, nearly every one of the millions of different cells in the newborn, whether specialized for bone or skin, heart or brain, or in some other way, contains the same genetic blueprint established in the initial zygote.

How does this extraordinary duplication of DNA from one cell to another and from one generation to the next take place? Most cells divide through the process

zygote   Fertilized egg cell.

FIGURE 3.2
Chromosomes in the
Normal Human Male

**This karotype depicts the
twenty-two homologous pairs
of autosomes and the two sex
chromosomes in the normal
human male. In females, the
twenty-third pair of chromosomes consists of an XX pair
instead of an XY pair.**

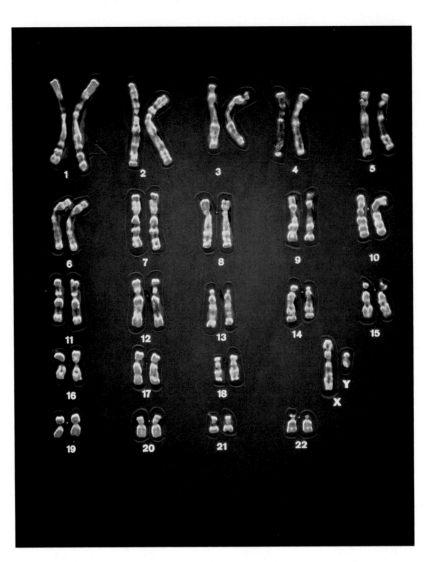

called **mitosis.** During mitosis, genetic material in the nucleus of the cell is reproduced such that a full complement of DNA becomes available to each new cell. Even
before cell division occurs, the chemical bonds linking the nucleotides that form the
rungs of the DNA ladder weaken. The pairs of nucleotides separate as though they
were being unzipped from each other. At the same time, additional nucleotides are
manufactured in the cell and attach to the separated nucleotides. Because each nucleotide can combine with only one other type, the two newly formed strands of
DNA are rebuilt exactly as in their original sequence. The two newly formed copies
of DNA eventually separate completely so that one becomes a member of each of
the two new daughter cells, as depicted in Figure 3.3.

The process of cell division associated with the gametes (the sex cells) is called
meiosis. Meiosis, which results in twenty-three chromosomes in the egg and sperm
cells, actually involves *two* successive generations of cell divisions. In the first stage,
each of the forty-six chromosomes begins to replicate in much the same way as mitosis begins. However, before the identical replicas split apart, the cell divides, so that
each daughter cell receives only one chromosome from each of the twenty-three
pairs, as pictured in Figure 3.4. In the second stage, the replicas of the twenty-three
chromosomes completely separate, and the cell divides once more, each cell again receiving one of the replicas. Thus, from these two successive divisions, four cells are
produced, each with twenty-three chromosomes.

Random segregation of the twenty-three homologous chromosome pairs in the
first stage of meiosis yields more than 8 million possible combinations of gametes
with one or more different sets of chromosomes. Along with an equivalent number

mitosis   Process of cell division
that takes place in most cells of
the human body and results in a
full complement of identical material in the forty-six chromosomes
in each cell.

meiosis   Process of cell division
that forms the gametes; normally
results in twenty-three chromosomes in each human egg and
sperm cell rather than the
full complement of forty-six
chromosomes.

| FIGURE 3.3 | The Process of Mitosis |

The process of mitotic cell division generates nearly all the cells of the body except the gametes. During mitosis, each chromosome replicates to form two chromosomes with identical genetic blueprints. As the cell divides, one member of each identical pair becomes a member of each daughter cell. In this manner, complete genetic endowment is replicated in nearly every cell of the body.

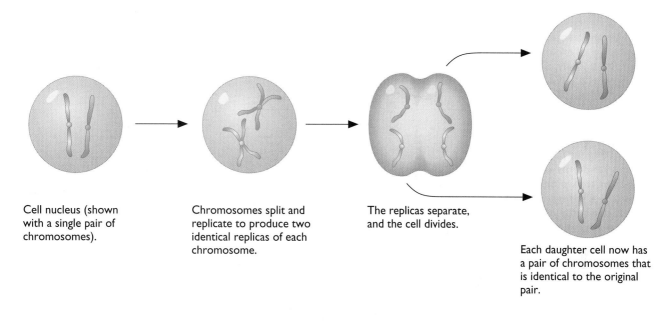

Cell nucleus (shown with a single pair of chromosomes).

Chromosomes split and replicate to produce two identical replicas of each chromosome.

The replicas separate, and the cell divides.

Each daughter cell now has a pair of chromosomes that is identical to the original pair.

| FIGURE 3.4 | The Process of Meiosis for Sperm Cells |

As meiosis begins (A), DNA replicates as in mitotic cell division. However, before the replicated arms split apart, one member of each pair of homologous chromosomes moves to become part of each first-generation daughter cell (B). Once the first generation of daughter cells is established, DNA replicas split as part of the second meiotic division (C). Thus one replica of one member of the pair of homologous chromosomes is contributed to each second-generation daughter cell (D). From these two successive divisions, four cells, each with twenty-three chromosomes, are produced.

Cell with forty-six chromosomes (only one pair of homologous chromosomes is shown here). Each member of the pair has begun to replicate similar to mitotic cell division.

First meiotic cell division begins but does not proceed as in mitosis. Instead of the replicated chromosome splitting apart, one member of each homologous pair becomes a part of the first-generation daughter cell.

The second meiotic division proceeds after the first is completed; now the replicated chromosome acquired in the first-generation daughter cell splits apart.

Each of the four gametes produced by the two-step process now has acquired one member of the pair of homologous chromosomes.

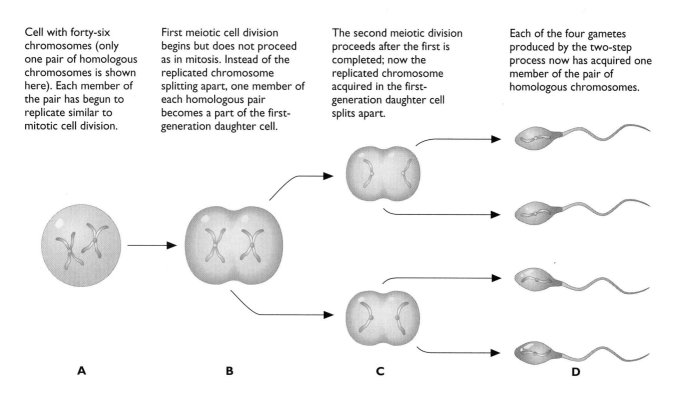

A   B   C   D

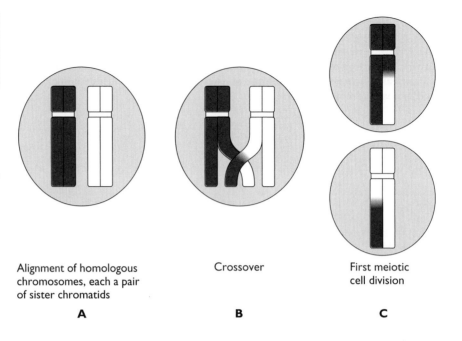

FIGURE 3.5

Crossing Over: The Exchange of Genetic Material Between Chromosomes

In the process known as crossing over, genetic material is exchanged between homologous pairs of chromosomes during the first stage of meiotic cell division. (A) Initially, autosomes that have begun DNA replication align with each other. (B) Genetic material between homologous chromosomes is exchanged. (C) One member of each homologous pair of chromosomes randomly segregates or relocates to two different regions of the parent cell, and the first generation of cell division in meiosis takes place.

Alignment of homologous chromosomes, each a pair of sister chromatids

A

Crossover

B

First meiotic cell division

C

WHAT DO YOU THINK?

Should Research on Cloning Humans Be Permitted?

psychology.college.hmco.com

crossing over   Process during the first stage of meiosis when genetic material is exchanged between autosomes.

homozygous   Genotype in which two alleles of a gene are identical, thus having the same effects on a trait.

heterozygous   Genotype in which two alleles of a gene are different. The effects on a trait will depend on how the two alleles interact.

dominant allele   Allele whose characteristics are reflected in the phenotype even when part of a heterozygous genotype. Its genetic characteristics tend to mask the characteristics of other alleles.

recessive allele   Allele whose characteristics do not tend to be expressed when part of a heterozygous genotype. Its genetic characteristics tend to be masked by other alleles.

of possible unique arrangements from a mate, mother and father together have a gene pool of about 64 trillion different combinations from which their offspring may derive. But the potential for genetic variability is actually far greater because of the phenomenon known as **crossing over,** a key part of the first stage of meiosis. Before homologous chromosome pairs separate in the first cell division, they mysteriously align, and segments of DNA transfer, or cross over, from one member to the other member of the pair, as shown in Figure 3.5. The genetic variability ensured by crossing over makes it virtually impossible for two individuals to have the same genetic makeup, even siblings, unless the two are identical twins.

Gene Expression

We have briefly described key structures of inheritance—nucleotides, genes, and chromosomes—and the way these are replicated in cells of the body, including gametes. But how does the genotype affect the phenotype? That is, how does the underlying genetic blueprint promote the appearance of blue eyes, baldness, and dark skin or such complex traits as shyness, schizophrenia, and intelligent problem solving? The answer begins with the alleles, the specific form a particular gene may take.

We have already learned that each of us typically inherits two genes that code for a particular protein in the cell, one from our mother and the other from our father. These may be identical—that is, have the same allelic form—or they may differ. When both have the same allelic form, a person's genotype is said to be **homozygous** for whatever characteristic that gene affects. For example, three different alleles exist for the gene that governs blood type: A, B, and O. When both inherited alleles are A, both B, or both O, a person has a homozygous genotype for blood type. But if an individual inherits two different alleles of the gene for blood type, let's say A and B, that person's genotype is **heterozygous;** he or she has Type AB blood.

The consequences of a homozygous genotype are usually straightforward: the child's phenotype will be influenced by whatever characteristics are specified by that particular allelic form. But the effects of a heterozygous genotype depend on how the alleles influence each other. When a child's phenotype shows the effects of only one of the two allelic forms, the one whose characteristics are observed is **dominant;** the allelic form whose influence is not evident in the phenotype is **recessive.** For example, a person who inherits both an A and an O allele for blood type will still be classified as having Type A; the allele for Type A is dominant and the allele for Type O recessive.

Father's genotype (Ff)

Meiosis

	F sperm	f sperm
F ovum	FF zygote (homozygous) phenotype–normal	Ff zygote (heterozygous) phenotype–normal
f ovum	fF zygote (heterozygous) phenotype–normal	ff zygote (homozygous) phenotype–cystic fibrosis

Mother's genotype (Ff) — Meiosis

FIGURE 3.6

The Pattern of Inheritance for Cystic Fibrosis

The inheritance of cystic fibrosis is one of many traits and diseases that are influenced by a single pair of genes. In this figure, F symbolizes a normal allele and f represents the allele for cystic fibrosis. When parents with a heterozygous genotype for this disease have children, their offspring may inherit a homozygous genotype with normal alleles (FF), a heterozygous genotype with one normal and one abnormal allele (Ff or fF), or a homozygous genotype with two abnormal alleles (ff). Because the normal allele dominates, children with a heterozygous genotype will not exhibit cystic fibrosis. When both alleles carry genetic information for the disease, however, cystic fibrosis will occur.

KEY THEME

Individual Differences

Cystic fibrosis, the most common autosomal recessive disorder in Western Europe (Mueller & Cook, 1997) and a leading cause of childhood death among Caucasian children, provides another example of a dominant-recessive relationship between alleles. The shortened lifespan typically stems from a thickening of the mucus lining the respiratory tract that interferes with breathing. Most Caucasian children inherit a gene pair that does not include the allelic form that codes for cystic fibrosis; they have a homozygous genotype that contributes to normal development. About one in twenty-five people of Caucasian ancestry, however, has a heterozygous genotype in which one gene is normal and the other carries the genetic information that results in cystic fibrosis. The normal allele is *dominant.* Thus someone who is heterozygous for this condition can lead an ordinary, productive life. But a child of a mother and father, each of whom has a heterozygous genotype, may inherit either two normal alleles, both a normal and an abnormal allele, or two alleles coding for cystic fibrosis (see Figure 3.6). In the latter homozygous condition, the two recessive alleles are no longer masked by a normal gene; this child (about 1 in every 2,500 Caucasian children) will suffer from cystic fibrosis. Medical researchers today are actively investigating the potential for *gene therapy,* the replacement of the gene that codes for a disorder, to reduce and even eliminate the devastating consequences of cystic fibrosis and other inherited diseases (Friedmann, 1997).

For other genes, the child's phenotype will reflect the influence of both allelic forms if they differ. When the characteristics of both alleles are observed, they exhibit **codominance.** For example, a child with Type AB blood has inherited a gene for Type A blood from one parent and another gene for Type B blood from the other parent.

Table 3.1 summarizes a number of traits and characteristics of individuals who are affected by genes exhibiting dominant-recessive patterns. But we must be cautious when drawing inferences about these relationships. Many traits are **polygenic,** that is, determined by several genes, each located, perhaps, on different sets of chromosomes. For example, even eye color, although largely governed by the dominant-recessive relationship between allelic forms of a single gene, as suggested in Table 3.1, is affected by other genes as well.

Gene Functioning and Regulation of Development

How do genes influence the development of a phenotype? A major new field of study called *proteomics* has emerged precisely to attempt to answer that question (Ezzell, 2000). We can only give a brief glimpse into this rapidly evolving area. Although exceptions exist, genetic information is typically conveyed from the DNA in the cell's nucleus to the organic and inorganic substances in other parts of the cell. This

codominance Condition in which individual, unblended characteristics of two alleles are reflected in the phenotype.

polygenic Phenotypic characteristic influenced by two or more genes.

TABLE 3.1	Alleles of Genes That Display a Dominant and Recessive Pattern of Phenotypic Expression	
Dominant Traits		**Recessive Traits**
Brown eyes		Gray, green, blue, hazel eyes
Curly hair		Straight hair
Normal hair growth		Baldness
Dark hair		Light or blond hair
Nonred hair (blond, brunette)		Red hair
Normal skin coloring		Albinism (lack of pigment)
Immunity to poison ivy		Susceptibility to poison ivy
Normal skin		Xeroderma pigmentosum (heavy freckling and skin cancers)
Thick lips		Thin lips
Roman nose		Straight nose
Earlobe free		Earlobe attached
Cheek dimples		No dimples
Extra, fused, or short digits		Normal digits
Second toe longer than big toe		Big toe longer than second toe
Double-jointedness		Normal joints
Normal color vision		Red-green colorblindness
Farsightedness		Normal vision
Normal vision		Congenital eye cataracts
Retinoblastoma (cancer of the eye)		Normal eye development
Normal hearing		Congenital deafness
Type A blood		Type O blood
Type B Blood		Type O blood
Rh-positive blood		Rh-negative blood
Normal blood clotting		Hemophilia
Normal metabolism		Phenylketonuria
Normal blood cells		Sickle cell anemia
Familial hypercholesterolemia (error of fat metabolism)		Normal cholesterol level at birth
Wilms tumor (cancer of the kidney)		Normal kidney
Huntington's disease		Normal brain and body maturation
Normal respiratory and gastrointestinal functioning		Cystic fibrosis
Normal neural and physical development		Tay-Sachs disease

process is performed by *messenger ribonucleic acid,* or *mRNA,* a molecule somewhat similar to DNA. mRNA replicates some segment of the DNA. This copy is transported outside the nucleus of the cell, where it can then initiate a series of events that produce proteins to give the cell its unique ability to function. Important to remember here is that the genes do not directly cause appearance, behavior, or any other phenotypic expression. Instead, our appearance and behavior are, in part, the end result of an extensive chain of biochemical processes started by the instructions provided by the DNA.

The instructions conveyed by different alleles of a gene may cause one or more biochemical events in the chain to be modified or disrupted. Such a disruption occurs, for example, in **phenylketonuria (PKU),** a genetic condition in which *phenylalanine,* an amino acid in milk and high-protein foods such as meat, cannot be metabolized normally by the liver. As a result, phenylalanine and other metabolic products accumulate in the blood, and the nervous system becomes deprived of needed nutrients. The eventual consequences are often convulsions, severe mental retardation, hyperactivity, and other behavioral problems. Remember, however, that a phenotype is the product of the interaction between genotype and environment. In the case of PKU, intervention in the form of reducing phenylalanine in the diet can help prevent severe mental retardation. Here, then, is an excellent example illustrating that genes do not have all the information built into them to cause particular developmental outcomes; environmental factors interact with the genotype to yield a specific phenotype.

KEY THEME
Nature/Nurture

Many mysteries remain concerning how genes influence development. For example, humans are believed to have between twenty-six and thirty-eight thousand *structural genes* that code for the production of proteins that govern the physiological functions of a cell (Pääbo, 2001). Yet structural genes account for only 1 to 2 percent of the nearly 3 billion base pairs estimated to make up the human genome (Pennisi, 2001). Some of the remaining DNA, for example, consists of other types of genes that start and stop or modify the functioning of structural genes. But large stretches of DNA are made up of repeat sequences of base pairs or of other patterns that seem to have simply replicated themselves and the functions of which, if any, remain unknown.

Other new discoveries are continuing to be made about genes and how they influence development. For example, sometimes it matters whether a particular gene has been inherited from the mother or the father. This phenomena, called **genomic imprinting,** is best illustrated by the *Prader-Willi* and *Angelman* syndromes, estimated to affect about one in ten thousand persons. Individuals with Prader-Willi syndrome display, among other physical and behavioral characteristics, short stature, obesity, and mild to moderate mental retardation. In contrast, individuals with Angelman syndrome display disturbances in gait suggestive of marionettelike movements, epilepsy, and more severe learning difficulties, including minimal or no speech. Prader-Willi syndrome stems from the absence of a particular gene or set of genes on chromosome 15 inherited from the father and the inability of the mother's genetic material on the homologous chromosome to compensate for this loss. In contrast, Angelman syndrome arises from the absence of that same gene or set of genes inherited from the mother and the inability of the father's genetic material to compensate for the loss (Everman & Cassidy, 2000; Lombroso, 2000). Susceptibility to certain cancers, growth disorders, and some types of diabetes are also known to occur as a result of genomic imprinting.

KEY THEME
Individual Differences

Substantial progress in understanding genetic influences has been made in recent years. However, important questions still exist concerning the effects of the human genome on a wide range of complex human behaviors of interest to psychologists. In the section that follows, we highlight additional examples of several specific gene mutations as well as chromosomal disturbances that can have profound repercussions for development. Keep in mind, however, that serious consequences associated with gene and chromosomal deviations affect a relatively small number of individuals. Nevertheless, the consequences often reverberate and extend well beyond those individuals and to their family and others within the community.

FOR YOUR REVIEW

- What roles do genotype and the environment play in determining a phenotype?

- What is the human genome? How do the nucleus of the cell, chromosomes and DNA, genes, and nucleotides play a role in genetic influences on development?

- How many autosomes exist in the human karyotype? Of what importance are the X and Y chromosomes?

phenylketonuria (PKU) Recessive genetic disorder in which phenylalanine, an amino acid, fails to be metabolized. Unless dietary changes are made to reduce intake of phenylalanine, severe mental retardation occurs.

genomic imprinting Instances of genetic transmission in which the expression of a gene is determined by whether the particular allelic form has been inherited from the mother or the father.

- What is the difference between mitosis and meiosis, and what is the impact of the phenomenon of crossing over?

- How do homozygous and heterozygous genes and the presence of dominant, recessive, and codominant allelic forms account for the inheritance patterns associated with various phenotypes? What are polygenic traits?

- How do genes regulate the development of the genotype? What is genomic imprinting?

KEY THEME
Individual Differences

Gene and Chromosomal Abnormalities

Changes in the structure of genes, or **mutations,** introduce genetic diversity among individuals. Mutations occur surprisingly often; perhaps as many as half of all human conceptions occur with some kind of genetic or chromosomal change (Plomin, DeFries, & McClearn, 1990). Most mutations are lethal, resulting in loss of the zygote through spontaneous abortion very soon after conception, often before a woman even knows she is pregnant. A small number of other mutations will have little impact on development. However, some can have enduring, often negative, consequences for an individual and his or her quality of life, consequences that may be passed on from one generation to the next. In fact, more than 5 percent of all diseases observed in individuals before the age of twenty-five are at least in part the result of some type of genetic or chromosomal anomaly (Rimoin, Connor, & Pyeritz, 1997). Moreover, birth defects and genetically based diseases contribute to a disproportionately high number of hospitalizations and medical expenses in the United States (Yoon et al., 1997). We consider here the consequences of just a few of the more than fourteen hundred gene and chromosome anomalies that have been identified as influencing physical and behavorial development (Peltonen & McKusick, 2001).

Gene Variations

An estimated 100,000 infants are born each year in the United States alone with some kind of problem caused by a single dominant or recessive gene. For about twenty thousand of these babies, the problem is serious (Knowles, 1985). Table 3.2 lists a few of the more serious of these. In many cases, the effects are evident at birth (*congenital*), but the consequences of some are not observed until childhood or even late adulthood. We will discuss several dominant and recessive disorders to illustrate their effects on development, the interventions and treatments available for them, and the insights they provide concerning the genotype's contribution to intellectual and behavorial capacities.

● SEE FOR YOURSELF
psychology.college.hmco.com
**Gene Locations for
Various Disorders**

● **Williams Syndrome: Discordances in Language, Cognition, and Social Behavior**   About one in 10,000 children are born with **Williams syndrome,** caused by the deletion of a small number of genes on chromosome 7. The syndrome is autosomal dominant, although most occurrences are the result of a mutation. Children with Williams syndrome possess a distinctive set of facial features including a short, upturned nose and full lips. They also display knee and hip inflexions that produce an unusual postural appearance and gait, and they often have heart and kidney abnormalities.

Individuals with Williams syndrome are typically mildly to moderately retarded. Perhaps most puzzling, however, is their strikingly uneven profile of cognitive and social strengths and weaknesses. For example, as young children they seem especially preoccupied with the faces of adults and show relatively few social inhibitions, even among strangers, despite evidence of underlying anxiety in some contexts (Mervis, 2001). When young, they are also extremely sensitive to certain sounds, such as those made by a drill or vacuum cleaner, or the loud noises produced by fireworks or the bursting of a balloon. Their ability to acquire language is initially slow and may never reach a high

mutation Sudden change in molecular structure of a gene; may occur spontaneously or be caused by an environmental event such as radiation.

Williams syndrome Dominant genetic disorder involving the deletion of a set of genes that results in affected individuals typically having a strong social orientation, good musical ability, and some unusual linguistic capabilities; accompanied by mental retardation and severe deficits in numerical and spatial ability.

The smiling face of this girl with Williams syndrome epitomizes one of the behavorial characteristics common to such children, a strong orientation to initiating and maintaining social relationships. Their unusual pattern of strengths and weaknesses in various areas of cognition and language as well as their inquisitiveness about other people are of considerable interest to those who study child development. Such observations support the view that some aspects of development may be domain specific rather than more broadly determined by intelligence or personality.

TABLE 3.2	Some Inherited Gene Syndromes		
Syndrome	**Estimated Frequency (live births in U.S.)**	**Gene Located on Chromosome**	**Phenotype, Treatment, and Prognosis**
Autosomal Dominant Syndromes			
Huntington's Disease	1 in 10,000–20,000	4	Personality changes, depression, gradual loss of motor control and memory caused by massive neuronal cell death that often begins in mid-adulthood. Thus affected individuals may transmit the disease to another generation of offspring before becoming aware of the disease. In some individuals, symptoms may begin earlier and be more severe if the dominant gene is transmitted by the father, another example of genomic imprinting.
Marfan Syndrome	1 in 10,000–20,000	15	Tall, lean, long limbed, with gaunt face (some believe Abraham Lincoln had syndrome). Frequent eye and heart defects. Cardiac failure in young adulthood common. Suicide second most common cause of death. Associated with increased paternal age.
Neurofibromatosis Type I	1 in 3,500	17	Symptoms range from a few pale brown spots on skin to severe tumors affecting peripheral nervous system and distorting appearance. Minimal intellectual deficits in about 40% of cases. Other forms of neurofibromatosis are associated with genes located on other chromosomes.
Williams Syndrome	1 in 10,000	7	See text.

(continued)

TABLE 3.2	Some Inherited Gene Syndromes *(continued)*		
Syndrome	**Estimated Frequency (live births in U.S.)**	**Gene Located on Chromosome**	**Phenotype, Treatment, and Prognosis**
Autosomal Recessive Syndromes			
Albinism	1 in 10,000–20,000. Several forms. Most common occurs in about 1 in 15,000 African Americans, 1 in 40,000 Caucasians, but much more frequently among some Native American tribes (1 in 200 among Hopi and Navajo, 1 in 132 among San Blas Indians of Panama).	11 (also 15)	Affected individuals lack pigment *melanin*. Extreme sensitivity to sunlight and visual problems.
Cystic Fibrosis	Most common genetic disease in Caucasian populations in U.S., especially those of Northern European descent, affecting about 1 in 2,500. Less common among African American and Asian American populations.	7	Respiratory tract becomes clogged with mucus; lungs likely to become infected. Death often in young adulthood, but individuals may have children. Prognosis for females poorer than for males. Pulmonary therapy to remove mucus accumulation in lungs helps delay effects.
Galactosemia	1 in 60,000	9	Mental retardation, cataracts, cirrhosis of the liver caused by accumulation of galactose in body tissues because of absence of enzyme to convert this sugar to glucose. Heterozygous individuals have half the normal enzyme activity, enough for normal development. Galactose-free diet is only treatment, although many still display learning and behavioral problems.
Gaucher Disease	1 in 600 Ashkenazic Jews. Other, rarer forms found in all populations.	1	Enlarged spleen contributing to pain, cardiac failure, and failure to thrive. Frequent bone fractures, bruising, and bleeding. Limited treatment available.
Phenylketonuria	1 in 15,000. Somewhat higher rate of incidence in Caucasian than in Asian or African American populations.	12	See text.
Sickle Cell Disease	1 in 400 African Americans. Also frequently found in malaria-prone regions of world.	11	See text.
Tay-Sachs Disease	1 in 3,600 Ashkenazic Jews. Very rare in other populations.	15	Signs of mental retardation, blindness, deafness, and paralysis begin 1 to 6 months after birth. No treatment available. Death normally occurs by 3 or 4 years of age.
ß–Thalassemia (Cooley's anemia)	1 in 800–3,600 in populations of Greek and Italian descent. Much less frequent in other populations.	11	Severe anemia beginning within 2 to 3 months of birth, stunted growth, increased susceptibility to infections. Death usually occurs in 20s or 30s.

TABLE 3.2	Some Inherited Gene Syndromes *(continued)*		
Syndrome	**Estimated Frequency (live births in U.S.)**	**Gene Located on Chromosome**	**Phenotype, Treatment, and Prognosis**
Sex-Linked Syndromes			
Colorblindness (red-green)	About 1 in 100 males of Caucasian descent see no red or green. About 1 in 15 Caucasian males experience some decrease in sensitivity to red or green colors.	X	If completely red-green colorblind, lack either green-sensitive or red-sensitive pigment for distinguishing these colors and see them as yellow. If decreased sensitivity to red or green, reds are perceived as reddish browns, bright greens as tan, and olive greens as brown.
Duchenne Muscular Dystrophy	1 in 3,500 males. Most common of many different forms of muscular dystrophy. Several forms, including Duchenne, are X linked.	X	Progressive muscle weakness and muscle fiber loss. Mental retardation in about ⅓ of cases. No cure, and few live long enough to reproduce. Responsible gene located on short arm of X chromosome; appears to be massive in number of nucleotide pairs.
Fragile X Syndrome	1 in 4000 males; 1 in 8,000 females.	X	See text.
Hemophilia A	1 in 10,000 Caucasian male births for the most common form.	X	Failure of blood to clot. Several different forms; not all are sex linked. Queen Victoria of England was carrier for the most common form. Potential for bleeding to death, but administration of clot-inducing drugs and blood transfusions reduces hazard.

Sources: Adapted from Beaudet et al., 1995; Committee on Genetics, 1996; Laskari, Smith, & Graham, 1999; McKusick & Amberger, 1997; Scriver et al., 1995.

level of grammatical complexity. However, children with Williams syndrome accumulate a surprisingly large vocabulary that permits them to engage in relatively sophisticated, although somewhat stereotyped, verbal interactions (Moldavsky, Lev, & Lerman-Sagie, 2001). Complementing these verbal abilities tend to be some rather uncommon abilities with respect to creating and imitating music (Levitin & Bellugi, 1998). For example, some, after hearing a selection only once and regardless of the language in which it may have been sung, are able to reproduce the piece with extraordinary skill. Despite these strengths, children with Williams syndrome show poor visual and spatial abilities, planning and problem solving, and little competence in acquiring numerical skills, although some can achieve relatively high levels of reading ability.

Individuals with Williams syndrome have become of special interest to developmental, cognitive, and social psychologists because of their unusual, and quite uneven, profile of intellectual and behavioral strengths and weaknesses. As is shown in the chapter titled "Cognition: Piaget and Vygotsky," many cognitive abilities may be modular; that is, they may undergo relatively specific patterns of development. Extensive debate occurs as well about whether to best view the nature of intelligence as a general capacity or as a set of more specific abilities (see the chapter titled "Intelligence"). The observations being carried out on children with Williams syndrome are helping to provide valuable new insights about the ways in which genes may have highly targeted consequences for intellectual, social, and other developmental capacities and about how best to conceptualize the concepts of cognition and intelligence.

Individuals who suffer from sickle cell anemia, a genetically inherited disorder, have a large proportion of crescent-shaped red blood cells like the one shown at the bottom left. A normal red blood cell (upper right) is round and doughnut-shaped. Sickle-shaped cells are ineffective in transporting oxygen and may cause damage to various organs and pain by blocking small blood vessels.

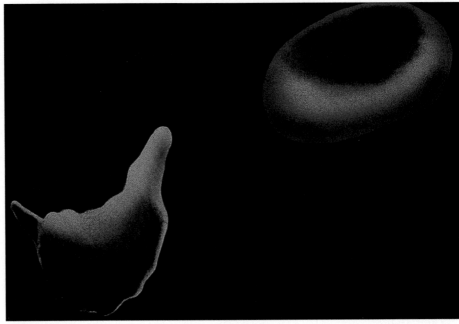

● Sickle Cell Disease: A Problem Arising Out of Adaptive Circumstance

Sickle cell disease is a genetic disorder whose incidence is extremely high in many regions of West Africa and around the Mediterranean basin. Sickle cell disease is also found in about 1 out of every 400 African Americans (Ashley-Koch, Yang, & Olney, 2000) and in high numbers of Greek Americans and others whose ancestors came from regions in which malaria commonly occurs. The defect introduces a change in a single amino acid in hemoglobin, the molecule that permits the red blood cells to carry oxygen. As a result, red blood cells become crescent shaped rather than round.

Sickle-shaped cells are ineffective in transporting oxygen; they also survive for a much shorter duration than normal red blood cells, and the bone marrow has difficulty replacing them. The consequences are often anemia, jaundice, low resistance to infection, and susceptibility to stroke, severe pain, and damage to various organs when the distorted cells block small blood vessels. Blood transfusions can help to alleviate the more serious problems, and recent research in both Europe and the United States raises the possibility that bone marrow transplants can provide a cure (Davis & Roberts, 1996). Despite the physical limitations, elementary school children with sickle cell disease appear quite similar to unaffected peers in terms of emotional well-being and view themselves no differently in terms of social satisfaction, competencies, and feelings of depression. Still, children with sickle cell disease, especially girls, tend to be somewhat less popular in the classroom and boys somewhat less aggressive, perhaps because of their more limited energy and slower physical development (Noll et al., 1996).

About one in every twelve African Americans are carriers of the sickle cell gene. These individuals, who possess a heterozygous genotype, have the **sickle cell trait.** They manufacture a relatively small proportion of cells with abnormal hemoglobin. Few of these individuals show symptoms of sickle cell disease; most live normal lives. But insufficient oxygen, which may occur in high-altitude regions, when flying in unpressurized airplane cabins, or after strenuous exercise, can trigger sickling of red blood cells in those who have the trait. Nevertheless, carriers of the sickle cell gene are more resistant to malaria than are individuals who have normal hemoglobin—an adaptive feature that accounts for the high incidence and persistence of the trait in populations in which malaria is present.

● Phenylketonuria: A Genetic Problem Modifiable by Diet

Phenylketonuria (PKU), a recessive metabolic disorder, provides a good illustration of how changing

sickle cell disease   Genetic blood disorder common in regions of Africa and other areas where malaria is found and among descendents of the people of these regions. Abnormal blood cells carry insufficient oxygen.

sickle cell trait   Symptoms shown by those possessing a heterozygous genotype for sickle cell anemia.

the child's environment, in this case diet, can reduce its more harmful consequences. An infant with PKU appears normal at birth. However, retardation sets in soon thereafter and becomes severe by four years of age if the condition is untreated. Fortunately, screening using blood samples collected a day or two after birth can detect elevated levels of phenylalanine. An infant identified as having PKU can then be placed on a diet low in phenylalanine to prevent its more serious effects. Experts agree the diet must be started relatively early, within the first few weeks after birth, and continued at least through adolescence to ensure nearly normal mental development (Phenylketonuria, 2000).

KEY THEME
Nature/Nurture

Even though the more serious consequences of phenylketonuria can be prevented, a completely normal prognosis for these children remains problematic. The diet is difficult to maintain; it requires a careful balance between excessive phenylalanine to prevent neural damage and sufficient nutrients. Weekly blood tests may be necessary to keep metabolite concentrations within an acceptable range, a regimen for which child, parents, and testing centers may be ill prepared. The bland and unappetizing diet can be a source of conflict between child and caregiver as well, creating management problems within households attempting to lead relatively normal lives (Phenylketonuria, 2000).

KEY THEME
Child's Active Role

Even under optimal conditions, children with PKU may show some growth and intellectual deficiencies. For example, these children seem to have difficulty in planning and problem-solving tasks in which working memory or sustained attention is required to inhibit well-learned, simpler reactions in order to master new, more complex responses (Diamond et al., 1997; Ris et al., 1994). Moreover, individuals with PKU who successfully reach adulthood still need to be concerned about their diets. For example, children born to mothers who continue to display elevated levels of phenylalanine during pregnancy show increased risk for heart defects and mental retardation (Platt et al., 2000; Rouse et al., 2000). If a mother returns to a low-phenylalanine diet before or early in her pregnancy, the risks can be reduced substantially. Although dietary modifications are helpful, it remains unclear whether this intervention completely eliminates some negative consequences of PKU.

● **Sex-Linked Syndromes** As already indicated, only a few dozen genes may be located on the Y chromosome, whereas the X chromosome carries many. This imbalance has substantial implications for a number of phenotypes said to be sex linked because the gene associated with them is carried only on the X chromosome. Hemophilia, red-green colorblindness, and Duchenne muscular dystrophy (see Table 3.2) have nothing to do with differentiation of sex but are sex linked because they are inherited via specific genes on the X chromosome. Thus, they occur much more frequently in males than in females.

As with genes for autosomes, those that are sex linked often have a dominant-recessive relationship. Females, who inherit two genes for sex-linked traits, one on each X chromosome, are much less likely to display the deleterious effects associated with an abnormal recessive gene than are males, who, if they inherit the damaging allele, have no second, normal allele to mask its effects. Hemophilia, a condition in which blood does not clot normally, is a good example because it is nearly always associated with a defective gene on the X chromosome. Because the allele for hemophilia is recessive, daughters who inherit it typically do not exhibit hemophilia; the condition is averted by an ordinary gene on the second X chromosome that promotes normal blood clotting. A female can, however, be a carrier. If she possesses a heterozygous genotype for hemophilia, the X chromosome with the abnormal allele has a fifty-fifty chance of being transmitted to either her son or her daughter. When a son inherits the abnormal allele, he will exhibit hemophilia because the Y chromosome does not contain genetic information to counter the allele's effects. If a daughter inherits the abnormal allele, she will be a carrier who may then transmit it to her sons and daughters, as has occurred in several interrelated royal families of Europe.

● Fragile X Syndrome: A Sex-Linked Contributor to Mental Retardation

Geneticists have identified a structural anomaly that consists of a pinched or constricted site near the end of the long arm of the X chromosome in some individuals (see Figure 3.7). This anomaly, termed **fragile X syndrome,** may be the most frequently inherited source of mental retardation associated with a specific gene (Moldavsky et al., 2001). Males with fragile X syndrome commonly have a long, narrow face, large or prominent ears, and large testes. Cardiac defects and relaxed ligaments (permitting, e.g., hyperextension of finger joints) are also frequent components of the disorder. Behavioral attributes include poor eye contact and limited responsiveness to external stimulation, as well as hand flapping, hand biting, and other unusual mannerisms such as mimicry. Females who possess a heterozygous genotype often show, to a much lesser extent, some of the physical characteristics of the disorder. Many of these women display a normal or nearly normal level of intelligence, although, as with other sex-linked gene disorders, they are carriers for the syndrome.

An unusual feature of fragile X syndrome is that its severity seems to increase as the abnormal gene is passed on from one generation to the next, a phenomenon termed *anticipation.* This progression begins when one set of three nucleotides, which repeats between five and fifty times in the normal gene, for some reason expands to fifty to two hundred repetitions. Once this expansion begins, the gene seems to become unstable for subsequent offspring so that more copies of the three nucleotides are spewed out, as though the replication process has difficulty turning off (Eliez & Reiss, 2000). The inheritance of this unchecked expansion is accompanied by a spectrum of learning difficulties ranging from mild to severe mental retardation. Thus the size of the abnormal segment of the gene, along with the severity of the disorder, appears to increase as it is passed from a grandfather, in whom the initial amplification may occur (even if he shows no evidence of the disorder), to a daughter (who may be minimally affected because she has an additional X chromosome to compensate for the disorder), to a grandson (who now displays full-blown fragile X syndrome).

Chromosome Variations

Mutations in specific genes are only one of several sources of variation in the human genome. Occasionally whole sections of a chromosome are deleted, duplicated, or relocated to another chromosome, or an extra chromosome is transmitted to daughter cells during cell division. When this happens, normal development is often dis-

FIGURE 3.7
Chromosome Illustrating Fragile X Syndrome

Fragile X syndrome is one of the most frequently occurring genetic causes of mental retardation. This photomicrograph illustrates the pinched or constricted portion of one of the pair of X chromosomes in a heterozygous female and the X chromosome in an affected male.

fragile X syndrome Disorder associated with a pinched region of the X chromosome; a leading genetic cause of mental retardation in males.

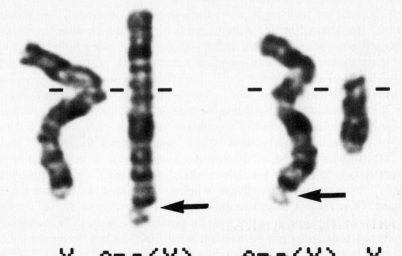

X   fra(X)   fra(X)   Y

rupted. Perhaps as many as half of all conceptions that result in spontaneous abortion include such chromosomal abnormalities (Garber, Schreck, & Carlson, 1997; Jacobs & Hassold, 1995). But this is not always the case. For example, the deletion of a small segment of the fifth chromosome is responsible for *cri du chat* or *cat-cry syndrome,* in which infants exhibit a cry similar to a cat's (hence its name), severe mental retardation, microcephaly (very small head size), short stature, and other congenital anomalies. Mental retardation and severe physical deformations often accompany structural aberrations observed in other chromosomes as well.

Human embryonic growth virtually never proceeds when a complete pair or even a member of one pair of autosomes is missing or when an extra pair of autosomes is inherited. **Trisomy,** the inheritance of an extra chromosome, also very often results in the loss of the zygote or miscarriage in early pregnancy (Jacobs & Hassold, 1995). However, three copies of chromosomes 13, 18, and 21 may be observed in surviving human newborns. Of these, trisomy 21, or Down syndrome, occurs most frequently. Even with this syndrome, however, fewer than 25 percent of conceptions survive to birth (Tolmie, 1997).

- **Trisomy 21 (Down Syndrome)**   Trisomy 21, one of the most common genetic causes of mental retardation, arises in about one out of every eight hundred live births (Tolmie, 1997). Physically observable features include an epicanthal fold that gives an almond shape to the eye, flattened facial features, poor muscle tone, short stature, and short, broad hands, including an unusual crease of the palm. About 40 percent of infants with Down syndrome have congenital heart defects. Cataracts or other visual impairments, as well as deficiencies in the immune system, are also common. Physical development is slowed compared with normal children, as is intellectual development.

Approximately 95 percent of babies born with Down syndrome have an extra twenty-first chromosome. Nearly 90 percent of these errors originate in egg cells, and the remainder arise from errors during the production of sperm cells (Jacobs & Hassold, 1995). A small percentage of infants with Down syndrome have a segment of chromosome 21, perhaps as little as its bottom third, shifted to another chromosome (Moldavsky et al., 2001). Another small percentage display a mosaic genotype, that is, have chromosomal deviations in only a portion of their body cells. The severity of Down syndrome in these latter individuals seems to be related to the proportion of cells exhibiting trisomy.

This 13-year-old boy with trisomy 21, or Down syndrome, has learned to read. He has made considerable progress in academic subjects as is evident from his contribution to this geography project. By being provided with an enriching environment, many with Down syndrome are able to accomplish levels of skill that permit them to engage in meaningful work and be active members of their community.

trisomy   Condition in which an extra chromosome is present.

FIGURE 3.8
Relationship Between
Maternal Age and the
Incidence of Down Syndrome

The incidence of Down syndrome increases dramatically as a function of the mother's age. One in every 1,500 babies born to a mother age twenty-one has Down syndrome. For forty-nine-year-old mothers, the incidence is much higher: one in every ten babies has Down syndrome. Several different explanations have been offered to account for these findings.

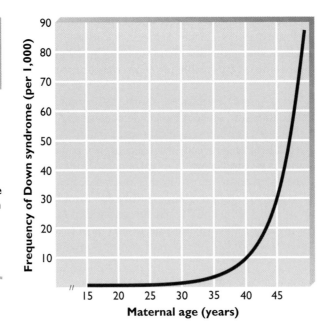

Source: Data from Epstein, 1989.

The probability of giving birth to an infant with trisomy 21 increases with the age of the mother, as is true for most other forms of trisomy (see Figure 3.8). Although mothers over thirty-five years of age give birth to only about 16 percent of all babies, they bear more than half of the infants with Down syndrome. The father's age shows virtually no relationship to the incidence of Down syndrome (Epstein, 1995). To explain these findings, experts have often proposed an "older egg" hypothesis. According to this view, the ova, which begin the first phases in meiosis even before the mother's own birth, change with age, either from the passage of time or perhaps because of increased exposure to potentially hazardous biological and environmental conditions. These older egg cells, released during ovulation in the later childbearing years, are then more susceptible to chromosomal errors while undergoing the final steps of meiosis. Other researchers have proposed a "relaxed selection" hypothesis to account for the increased frequency of Down syndrome in older mothers. According to this view, older mothers are less likely than younger mothers to spontaneously abort a zygote with trisomy 21. Still another view is that egg cells containing the extra chromosome are unlikely to be selected during ovulation. However, as they become a proportionally larger pool of the available ova over time, the possibility that one is released during ovulation increases (Tolmie, 1997).

Thanks to better medical and physical care, the majority of individuals born with Down syndrome may be expected to live more than fifty years (Tolmie, 1997). Many show considerable proficiency in reading and writing. But we still have much to discover about Down syndrome. For example, individuals with trisomy 21 who survive beyond age forty frequently develop the abnormal brain cells and show some of the same behavioral symptoms found in adults who acquire Alzheimer's disease (Janicki & Dalton, 2000). Alzheimer's disease is characterized by memory and speech disturbances, personality changes, and increasing loss of intellectual functioning, typically in individuals between fifty and seventy-five years of age, although the symptoms may begin much earlier. At least one form of Alzheimer's disease is thought to be inherited, and, not surprisingly, the responsible gene appears to be located on chromosome 21.

KEY THEME
Individual Differences

● **Sex Chromosome Syndromes**   As we have already noted, males normally have an X and a Y sex chromosome and females have two X chromosomes. However, variations in the number of sex chromosomes as a result of errors during meiosis can occur in humans. For example, an individual may inherit only a single X, an extra chromosome (XXX, XXY, XYY), and, on rare occasions, even pairs of extra chromosomes (for example, XXXX, XXYY, XXXY). Table 3.3 describes several of these variations in more detail.

When it was first discovered that some humans possess an extra sex chromosome, these individuals were typically thought to display intellectual deficits, along with an assortment of abnormal and socially unacceptable behaviors. For example, in the 1960s some researchers claimed that an extra Y chromosome contributed to more aggressive and antisocial behavior. Males with an XYY chromosomal makeup tend to be taller than other males and display some learning difficulties but show a nearly normal range of intelligence. Furthermore, the majority of individuals who have this chromosomal pattern, along with those who possess other combinations of sex chromosome patterns, lead normal lives. In fact, variation in phenotypes associated with sex chromosome anomalies may be due as much, perhaps more, to experiential factors than to inheritance.

Bruce Bender and his colleagues at the University of Colorado School of Medicine studied forty-six children with variations in number of sex chromosomes such as those described in Table 3.3 (Bender, Linden, & Robinson, 1987). These children, born between 1964 and 1974, were identified by screening forty thousand consecutive births in the Denver area. Those with sex chromosome modifications were more likely to have

KEY THEME
Nature/Nurture

TABLE 3.3	Examples of Observed Sex Chromosome Syndromes		
Disorder	**Estimated Frequency (live births in U.S.)**	**Phenotype**	**Prognosis**
45, XO (Turner syndrome)	I in 2,500 females (more than 90% are spontaneously aborted); 80% of cases involve the absence of the paternal X chromosome.	Short stature, usually normal psychomotor development but limited development of secondary sexual characteristics. Failure to menstruate and sterility due to underdeveloped ovaries. About 50% have webbed, short neck. Near-average range of intelligence but serious deficiencies in spatial ability and directional sense.	Increased stature and sexual development, including menstruation, but not fertility, can be induced through administration of estrogen and other hormones. In vitro fertilization permits carrying of child when adult.
47, XXX (Triple-X syndrome)	I in 1,200 females; 90% have received two copies of maternal X chromosome.	Not generally distinguishable. Some evidence of delay in speech and language development, lack of coordination, poor academic performance, and immature behavior. Sexual development usually normal. Tendency for tall stature.	Many are essentially normal, but substantial proportion have language, cognitive, and social-emotional problems.
47, XXY (Klinefelter syndrome)	I in 600 males (increased risk among older mothers); 56% received two maternal chromosomes, 44% two paternal sex chromosomes.	Tend to be tall, beardless, with feminine body contour, high-pitched voice. Some evidence for poor auditory short-term memory and difficulty with reading. Testes underdeveloped, individuals usually sterile.	Many with normal IQ, but about 20% may have occasional mild to moderate retardation.
47, XYY (XXY syndrome)	I in 1,000 males	Above-average height, some have learning disabilities, but near-average range of intelligence.	Most lead normal lives and have offspring with a normal number of chromosomes. Higher proportion than normal incarcerated, but crimes no more violent than those of XY men.

Sources: Adapted from Beaudet et al., 1995; Jacobs & Hassold, 1995; McGinniss & Kaback, 1997; McKusick & Amberger, 1997; Robinson & de la Chappelle, 1997.

neuromotor, psychosocial, language, and school problems than siblings who had a normal XX or XY complement. But this was true for school and psychosocial problems only if children were growing up in a family in which they experienced severe stress, such as exposure to drug abuse or considerable illness, lack of effective parenting by caregivers, or poverty. In the absence of such tensions, children with sex chromosome variations showed no greater evidence of school or psychosocial problems than their siblings, although they did continue to show more neuromotor and language impairment.

Bender and his colleagues followed the progress of thirty-nine of these children as they moved through adolescence (Bender et al., 1995). As Figure 3.9 shows, more of these students, compared with their siblings with a normal complement of sex chromosomes, needed special education assistance in high school and were less likely to graduate. This was especially true for girls with an extra X chromosome. These groups also exhibited somewhat more depression in psychiatric interviews and lower overall functioning and adaptation to adolescence. Even so, children with a mosaic pattern of abnormal sex chromosomes showed just as much progress in school as their siblings did. And, as in their earlier studies, the researchers note that the presence of a stable and supportive family environment seemed to promote more positive development in adolescents with sex chromosome variations, particularly those with XXY and X complements. These findings, then, further suggest that children and adolescents with different sex chromosome complements may be more vulnerable to disruptions in the caregiving environment than children with a normal complement of sex chromosomes.

FOR YOUR REVIEW

- What is the basis for each of the following genetically influenced disorders?

  Williams syndrome   Sickle cell disease and sickle cell trait
  Phenylketonuria   Fragile X syndrome

  What phenotypes are associated with each? Why is each of interest to developmental psychologists?

- What variations in the chromosomal makeup of an individual are possible? What is the most common example of chromosomal trisomy? What are examples of chromosomal variation associated with the sex chromosomes?

- What is the role of the environment in influencing behavioral outcomes for children with chromosomal variations?

KEY THEME
Individual Differences

FIGURE 3.9

Need for Educational Intervention Among Adolescents with Various Sex Chromosome Complements and Their Siblings

Adolescents who inherit an extra sex chromosome (**X** or **Y**) or only one X chromosome (Turner syndrome) often need more assistance in high school and may be somewhat less likely to graduate than their siblings who have a normal complement of sex chromosomes (**XY** or **XX**). Academic progress among high schoolers with a mosaic pattern of normal and abnormal sex chromosomes appears similar to that of their siblings. Closer inspection of the circumstances in which adolescents are reared also reveals that those with sex chromosome variations who are more successful academically live in families that provide more stable and supportive environments. Thus individuals with sex chromosome deviations may be more susceptible to disruptions or stress than their siblings.

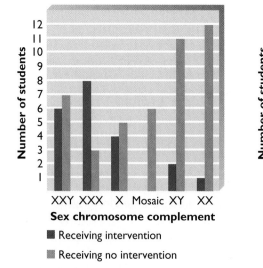

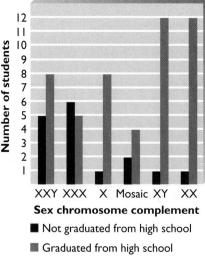

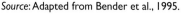

Source: Adapted from Bender et al., 1995.

Genetic Counseling

Advances in detecting gene and chromosomal defects, as well as in understanding the biochemical and metabolic consequences of various inherited disorders, have led to a rapidly expanding medical and guidance specialty called **genetic counseling.** Obtaining a family history to summarize the occurrence of various diseases among ancestors and other relatives is usually the first step. If warranted, *parental* **genetic screening** may be carried out. For example, chromosomal abnormalities, as well as dominant and recessive genes associated with all of the disorders listed in Tables 3.2 and 3.3 (and many more not listed in these tables), can be detected through parental screening. Thus genetic counselors can provide prospective parents with estimates of the likelihood of bearing a child with a specific problem, although parental screening, of course, does not identify new mutations that may arise in offspring. Prospective parents can then use this information to decide whether, for example, adoption or other new reproductive technologies, such as those discussed in the chapter titled "The Prenatal Period and Birth," may be a better choice than bearing their own children.

Many reasons exist to carry out such tests. For example, prenatal testing is often recommended for women who are older than thirty-five because of the increased risk for Down syndrome; when a genetic disorder has been reported in the family history; if a previous child was born with a chromosomal variation or genetic disorder; if there has been difficulty in completing prior pregnancies; or if delayed or unusual development of the fetus occurs during pregnancy (Committee on Genetics, 1994). The finding of a serious inherited disorder may lead to a decision to terminate the pregnancy if religious and ethical values allow such a choice. However, prenatal screening tests, along with neonatal screening carried out shortly after birth, can serve another important purpose, that of suggesting therapy and treatment designed to prevent or minimize the more devastating consequences of some metabolic disorders (Erbe & Levy, 1997).

Prenatal Diagnosis

Procedures now exist that can be performed prenatally to detect hundreds of genetically and environmentally induced defects in fetal development. Some of these procedures provide unequivocal answers about the presence or absence of a problem. Other, often less invasive, procedures provide estimates of increased likelihood of the presence of some defect. If they are suggestive of a developmental disability, they are followed by more conclusive diagnostic tests. One of the best known definitive tests is **amniocentesis,** in which a small amount of amniotic fluid is withdrawn via a syringe inserted (under the guidance of an ultrasound image) in the woman's abdominal wall. Cells in the amniotic fluid are extracted and submitted to biochemical and chromosomal examination (see Figure 3.10). Amniocentesis is an especially effective procedure for detecting chromosomal variations, and it provides information about some metabolic problems as well. The test is usually performed between the thirteenth and eighteenth weeks of pregnancy. However, researchers are studying whether it can be safely carried out a few weeks sooner. Even when amniocentesis is performed later in pregnancy, the possibility of some increased risk exists from infections and spontaneous abortion (Elias & Simpson, 1997; Tongsong et al., 1998).

Another test that provides much the same information as amniocentesis but that can be carried out somewhat earlier in pregnancy (between ten and twelve weeks) is **chorionic villus sampling.** In this diagnostic procedure, a small sample of hairlike projections (*villi*) from the chorion, the outer wall of the membrane in which the fetus develops and that attaches to the woman's uterus, is removed by suction through a thin tube inserted through the vagina and cervix or, in some cases, through the abdominal wall. Information gained at this earlier time can reduce uncertainty and anxiety about the possibility of a developmental disability (Caccia et

◉ **SEE FOR YOURSELF**
psychology.college.hmco.com
Genetic Counseling

genetic counseling Medical and counseling specialty concerned with determining and communicating the likelihood that prospective parents will give birth to a baby with a genetic disorder.

genetic screening Systematic search using a variety of tests to detect developmental risk due to genetic anomalies.

amniocentesis Method of sampling the fluid surrounding the developing fetus by insertion of a needle. Used to diagnose fetal genetic and developmental disorders.

chorionic villus sampling Method of sampling fetal chorionic cells. Used to diagnose embryonic genetic and developmental disorders.

FIGURE 3.10
The Process of
Amniocentesis

In this prenatal screening procedure, a needle is inserted into the amniotic fluid surrounding the fetus. A small amount of fluid is withdrawn, and cells shed by the fetus are separated from the fluid by centrifuge. The cells are cultured and submitted to various biochemical and other tests to determine whether chromosomal, genetic, or other developmental defects exist.

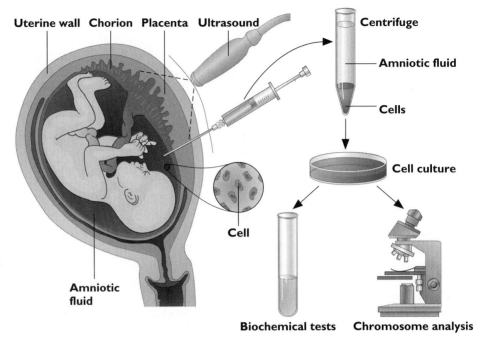

Source: Adapted from Knowles, 1985.

al., 1991). However, chorionic villus sampling, in contrast to amniocentesis, does not provide information about possible neural tube defects, the procedure is somewhat more difficult to carry out unless performed by skilled technicians, and some researchers report a slightly increased risk of miscarriage and limb malformations (Elias & Simpson, 1997; Hsieh et al., 1995).

In **fetal blood sampling,** blood is directly withdrawn from the umbilical cord of the fetus for biochemical and chromosomal examination. This particular procedure, normally carried out from about the eighteenth week of pregnancy onward, permits the detection of various chromosomal and genetic errors and is especially useful in evaluating disorders associated with the blood. Although relatively safe, the procedure does appear to be slightly more risky than other invasive tests, although adequate evaluation of the risks remains to be carried out (Elias & Simpson, 1997).

Because of the possible increase in risk and their relatively high cost, amniocentesis, chorionic villus sampling, and fetal blood sampling are normally performed only when there is some reason to believe fetal abnormalities may occur. Testing can also be carried out to analyze fetal cells circulating in the pregnant woman's blood, but this and other new procedures remain experimental and of limited availability (Steele et al., 1996). Other, less invasive procedures are often performed to determine whether a fetal anomaly may exist. For example, several types of **maternal blood screening** tests such as the *alpha fetoprotein test* and the more extensive and accurate *triple screen test* can be carried out at around fifteen to twenty weeks of gestational age to provide evidence of increased risk for Down syndrome, neural tube defects, and certain kidney and other problems. Certainly the most widespread of the noninvasive diagnostic procedures, however, is **ultrasonography,** often called *ultrasound.* Ultrasound is now used routinely in many countries to help determine whether fetal growth is proceeding normally. Sound waves, reflecting at different rates from tissues of varying density, are represented on video monitors and even printed to form a picture of the fetus. The picture can reveal such problems as microcephaly (small head size), cardiac malformations, cleft lip and palate, and other physical disabilities. However, it is not possible to detect many other developmental disorders with great accuracy using this technique (Dooley, 1999; Grandjean et al., 1999).

fetal blood sampling   Method of withdrawing blood from the umbilical cord of the fetus. Used to diagnose genetic disorders, especially those that affect the blood.

maternal blood screening Tests preformed on a woman's blood to determine if the fetus she is carrying has an increased risk for some types of chromosomal and metabolic disorders.

ultrasonography   Method of using sound wave reflections to obtain a representation of the developing fetus. Used to estimate gestational age and detect fetal physical abnormalities.

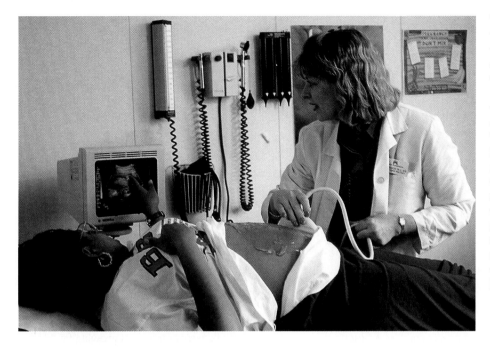

The use of ultrasound to provide a visual image of the developing fetus has become a common practice in medical facilities around the world. Prospective parents are often thrilled by this opportunity to obtain a glimpse of the fetus. The use of ultrasound also can be important for obtaining a more accurate assessment of the age of the fetus. It provides assistance in carrying out other tests to determine if development is proceeding normally and, in some cases, permits surgical procedures designed to improve the likelihood of a healthy newborn.

Ultrasonography is widely used to assist in carrying out other prenatal diagnostic tests, to verify the age of the fetus (interpretation of maternal and fetal blood tests are often highly dependent on an accurate assessment of age), and to monitor life-saving operations that may on rare occasions be performed on the fetus within the womb (Harrison, 1996). Although not universally recommended in the United States because of its limits as a diagnostic tool, ultrasound has become a popular tool for informing specialists and parents about the course of prenatal development.

Ethical and Social Issues

The major prenatal diagnostic tests are summarized in Table 3.4. Note that many of these tests are carried out relatively late in pregnancy, and prospective parents may have to wait several weeks longer before they learn of the results. This waiting period, and even the somewhat shorter time frame required to obtain information from other procedures, can create enormous apprehension, especially among those who, on the basis of genetic counseling or less definitive tests such as maternal blood screening, have reason to believe that a problem may exist. Moreover, some expectant women almost feel coerced into using these technological advances to learn more about their pregnancies (Henifin, 1993; Wertz & Fletcher, 1993). Yet a physician who fails to at least offer prenatal diagnosis in circumstances in which it can be informative runs legal risks for incompetent obstetric practice (Wertz & Fletcher, 1998).

Prospective parents have choices regarding whether or not to have such tests performed. In many cases those about to become parents would like to know about possible problems, if for no other reason than to effectively prepare for and address them even before birth. In fact, a substantial number of expectant women who learn that the fetus carries some abnormality still elect to continue the pregnancy, especially if the problem is less severe and possibilities exist for prenatal or postnatal therapy (Pride et al., 1993). On the other hand, in some countries such tests may not be available. But even when they are, not everyone takes advantage of them. For example, women of African American and Hispanic ethnic identity, at least in some areas of the United States, are far less likely to undergo prenatal testing than Caucasian or Asian women (Kuppermann, Gates, & Washington, 1996).

TABLE 3.4	Prenatal Screening Tests		
Prenatal Test	**When Usually Administered (gestational age)**	**Typical Waiting Period for Results**	**Other Comments**
Amniocentesis	13–18 weeks	About 2 weeks	Can be administered in weeks 11–14 but normally is not because the available supply of amniotic fluid is more limited.
Chorionic villus sampling	10–12 weeks	24–48 hours	Possibly a slightly greater risk than associated with amniocentesis, including limb deformities.
Fetal blood sampling	18 weeks or later	24–48 hours	Possibly somewhat greater risk than associated with amniocentesis.
Maternal blood screening	15–20 weeks	One week	Not definitive but provides information about increased risk for Down syndrome, and neural tube and some metabolic defects.
Ultrasonography	About 6 weeks and later	None	Provides picture of growing fetus. Not definitive for identifying many disorders. Little evidence of any risk. Often used to accompany other test procedures.

Another issue concerns access to the results of these tests. For example, might insurance companies or other health organizations drop coverage if they become aware of results that indicate expensive medical treatment in the future? What about employers who might choose to hire on the basis of fewer health risks, as, for example, when genetic information provides a hint of susceptibility to major diseases, such as cancer, diabetes, or heart disease, that could affect an individual's subsequent employment capability? There is also the issue of sex preselection.

CONTROVERSY: THINKING IT OVER

Should Sex Preselection Be Permitted?

At one time in medieval Germany couples placed a hammer under their bed if they wished to conceive a boy; in Denmark they chose a pair of scissors if they desired a girl (Golden, 1998). In China and India, where abortion is more widely practiced, evidence already exists that sex selection has been exercised; a disproportionate number of males have been born in these countries in recent years. As a consequence, China and India, as well as some other countries, have passed laws forbidding the use of prenatal tests solely to determine the sex of the fetus and to influence the course of pregnancy when the fetus is male or female (Wertz & Fletcher, 1998).

What Is the Controversy?

Although many adamantly oppose the use of a procedure that leads to the selective abortion of a healthy fetus on the basis of sex, *preselection*, the effort to tilt the probability toward having either a male or female conception, may be far less objectionable. In fact in 1996, 40 percent of individuals in the United States already supported the unrestricted availability of sex preselection if an effective procedure became available (Wertz & Fletcher, 1998).

We are, in fact, at the point at which this possibility exists. Previous efforts have focused on the timing or technique involved in procreation to increase conception of a male or female. These attempts have generally failed to provide a reliable method of conceiving a boy or a girl. However, in 1998, a new, far more effective procedure was reported, at least for promoting the conception of females (Fackelmann, 1998). This new procedure is based on the difference in the amount of DNA found in the X and Y chromosomes. With the help of a dye that attaches to the DNA and glows when exposed to the light of a laser, sperm cells carrying a second X chromosome and containing about 2.8 percent more DNA than sperm cells carrying a Y chromosome shine more brightly. By introducing lopsided distributions of cells carrying the second X chromosome into the uterus during periods when a woman might become pregnant, these specialists claim to have attained markedly higher numbers of successful pregnancies resulting in girls, a procedure that could also be expected to be successful in skewing the odds toward boys. Other techniques associated with assisted reproduction (see the chapter titled "The Prenatal Period and Birth") can also be used to increase the likelihood of, or even virtually guarantee, a boy or a girl.

What Are the Opposing Arguments?

Proponents of sex preselection claim that parents in most Western countries do not show a strong preference for having a boy or a girl first; but family balancing, having one boy and one girl, is frequently seen as the ideal family complement (Silver, 1998). Having the opportunity to rear children of both sexes also is often viewed as a desirable experience for parents. For other couples, sex preselection may serve to prevent a sex-linked genetic disease from being passed on to their offspring.

Opponents of sex preselection are concerned that even among countries in which no strong preference exists for rearing either boys or girls, the practice supports the potential for sexual bias or increased sexism, a potential that may become more visible once a choice is available to prospective parents (Fackelmann, 1998). A second argument is that determining a conception on the basis of sex is but the first step in the emergence of a preference mentality that can ultimately lead to preselection on the basis of other desired traits and attributes intended to create "perfect" children. Thus the potential for discrimination against those who do not meet the ethnic, cultural, or community ideal may increase substantially.

What Answers Exist? What Questions Remain?

The American College of Obstetricians and Gynecologists (2002) currently supports the notion that sex preselection is ethical and justified in cases in which it will prevent sex-linked genetic disorders in offspring. In the United States, the public also seems to be in support of this position. Opinion is much more divided, however, with respect to sex preselection for other purposes. Recent advertisements have appeared in the United States that target some ethnic groups and emphasize, "Choose the sex of your next baby" and "Desire a son?" Perhaps to help address the controversy, psychologists need to conduct research on the extent to which such preferences exist and on what social and cultural factors promote them in order for the public to gauge whether regulations should be considered. Declarations in favor of sex preselection for the purpose of family balancing and even for selecting the sex of a child in a first pregnancy also have been made by individuals associated with committees and organizations—for example, the American Society for Reproductive Medicine—established to deal with these kinds of issues (Kolata, 2001; Sachs, 2001). Perhaps research on whether raising offspring of both sexes leads to different outcomes for children or results in more successful and effective parenting would provide informative data. Given advances in sex preselection, are we nearing a time when professionals will be recruited to help create "designer" children with respect to other traits? Could such efforts actually contribute to harmful effects because of the potential for lessening genetic diversity in humans? What other kinds of psychological research might be conducted to help answer whether a need exists for regulation of sex and other kinds of trait preselection?

FOR YOUR REVIEW

- What are the major diagnostic tests for prenatal development? What are their limitations and their advantages?

- What ethical and social issues emerge from the use of prenatal diagnostic tests?

- What is sex preselection, and what are arguments for and against the practice of it?

Developmental and Behavioral Genetics

KEY THEME
Nature/Nurture

As our previous discussion indicates, chromosomal errors and particular genes can have drastic, often devastating, effects on physical, intellectual, and social development. Yet similarities observed among relatives—the quick tempers of two brothers; the wry sense of humor in a mother and daughter; the musical talent of a grandfather and his grandchildren; and, as we saw at the beginning of the chapter, Jasmine's and Alyssa's impatience when others could not tell them apart—are not likely to be linked to a single, isolated gene. Might these attributes and behaviors reflect a contribution from many genes? Or are these phenotypic resemblances primarily the result of experiences shared by kin? Researchers engaged in **behavior genetics** attempt to learn to what extent the diversity of human traits, abilities, and behaviors stem from combinations of genes versus experience. Behavioral geneticists are helping to show that the entire realm of human behavior is influenced by nature and nurture in a variety of complex, sometimes surprising, ways (Plomin et al., 2001; Rutter et al., 1999a, 1999b).

The Methods of Behavioral Geneticists

When studying the fruit fly or mouse, behavior geneticists can use *selective breeding* experiments to learn whether certain phenotypic expressions can be increased or decreased in offspring. Members of a species that display a specific attribute are bred to each other, usually over many generations. If the attribute is inherited, subsequent generations of offspring can be expected to display it more and more frequently or strongly. For example, after thirty generations of selective breeding in which either highly active mice were bred only to each other or mice showing only a low level of activity were bred to each other, researchers observed no overlap in terms of the amount of activity displayed by members of the two groups (DeFries, Gervais, & Thomas, 1978). Those bred for high activity were thirty times more active; they would run the equivalent of a football field during two three-minute test periods compared to the other mice, which would not even run the equivalent of a first down (Plomin et al., 2001).

Selective breeding in various species of animals has revealed genetic contributions to many different attributes, including aggressiveness, emotionality, maze learning, and sex drive (Plomin et al., 2001). But selective breeding, of course, cannot be used to examine human behavior. Instead, behavior geneticists gain information about hereditary and environmental influences on human behavior by examining resemblances among family members. These studies investigate similarities among *identical* and *fraternal twins,* siblings, and other members of families who are genetically different from one another to varying degrees.

Identical, or *monozygotic,* twins come from the same zygote: a single egg fertilized by a single sperm. A cell division early in development creates two separate embryos from this zygote, and the twins are genetically identical. **Fraternal,** or *dizygotic,* twins come from two different zygotes, each created from a separate egg and separate sperm. Fraternal twins are no more genetically similar than siblings born at different times, each averaging about half of their genes in common. However, they do share some aspects of their prenatal environment and, by virtue of their being the same age, may share other experiences to a greater extent than siblings born at different times.

behavior genetics   Study of how characteristics and behaviors of individuals, such as intelligence and personality, are influenced by the interaction between genotype and experience.

identical twins   Two individuals who originate from a single zygote (one egg fertilized by one sperm), which early in cell division separates to form two separate cell masses. Also called *monozygotic twins.*

fraternal twins   Siblings who share the same womb at the same time but originate from two different eggs fertilized by two different sperm cells. Also called *dizygotic twins.*

If identical twins resemble each other more than fraternal twins in intelligence or shyness, one *potential* explanation for this similarity is their common genotype. The degree of resemblance is usually estimated from one of two statistical measures: concordance rate or correlation coefficient. The **concordance rate** is the percentage of pairs of twins in which both members display a specific attribute when one twin is identified as having it. Concordance rate is used when measuring characteristics that are either present or absent, such as schizophrenia or depression. If both members of every twin pair have a particular trait, the concordance rate will be 100 percent. If only one member of every pair of twins has some particular trait and the other does not, the concordance rate will be 0 percent.

When attributes vary on a continuous scale such that they can be measured in terms of amount or degree, resemblances are estimated from a *correlation coefficient.* This statistic helps to determine whether variables such as intelligence or shyness, which have some quantitative value, are more similar for identical than for fraternal twins or more similar among siblings than among unrelated children.

Identical twins may resemble one another more than fraternal twins do because identical twins share the same genotype. However, another explanation for any greater resemblance may be that identical twins share more similar experiences. One way to potentially reduce the effects of similarity in experience is to study biologically related family members who have been adopted or reared apart from one another. If an attribute is influenced by genetic factors, children should still resemble their biological siblings, parents, or other family members more than their adoptive relatives. On the other hand, if the environment is the primary determinant of an attribute, separated children can be expected to resemble their adoptive parents or other adopted siblings more closely than their biological parents or siblings.

Adoption studies, just as in the case of twin studies, pose many challenges for evaluating hereditary and environmental influences (Rutter et al., 1999a). For example, in the past adopted children were often placed in homes similar to those of their biological parents. Under these circumstances, the relative contributions of family environment and heredity to an attribute are extremely difficult to distinguish. In addition, information on the biological family has not always been readily available in the case of adoption. Nevertheless, a number of large-scale investigations of genotype-environment effects involving twins, adopted children, siblings, half-siblings, and unrelated children in blended families are currently under way. For more than twenty-five years, the Colorado Adoption Project, for example, has been conducting longitudinal research on resemblances between (1) parents and their natural children, (2) adoptive parents and their adopted children, and (3) parents and their biological children who have been adopted into other homes (Plomin, DeFries, & Fulker, 1988). Another project, the Minnesota Study of Twins Reared Apart, has assessed a variety of psychological and physiological characteristics in identical and fraternal twins reared together or reared apart and having virtually no contact with each other prior to adulthood (Bouchard, 1997; Bouchard et al., 1990). The MacArthur Longitudinal Twin Study (MALTS), started in 1986, has been following 300 identical and fraternal twins, beginning at about one year of age, to investigate cognitive, social, emotional, and temperamental aspects of development (Emde & Hewitt, 2001). Yet another project, the Nonshared Environment in Adolescent Development (NEAD) study, has been observing 720 families, which include identical and fraternal twins, nontwin siblings in traditional families, and full, half, and unrelated siblings in stepfamilies, to explore the relationship between genetic and environmental influences in adolescence (Reiss et al., 2000). These and other studies are just beginning to illuminate the complex interactions and correlations that exist between heredity and experience, intricate relationships that we must consider more fully as well.

A major goal of many of these studies is to provide an estimate of the **heritability** of complex traits and various behaviors. Heritability refers to the extent to which the variability in a sample of individuals on some characteristic such as shyness or assertiveness is a result of genetic differences among those individuals. Of course, the variability that is not accounted for by the genotype must then be a result of the

If you were given their names, would you be able to tell these twins apart once they moved and were no longer seated side by side? Virtually everyone would have a great deal of difficulty with such an assignment unless they could constantly keep an eye on at least one of them as he moved about. Because their genetic makeup is the same, identical or monozygotic twins typically look very much alike and display very similar traits and behaviors as can be seen here. Twin studies provide important information about the contributions of heredity and enviroment to development.

concordance rate Percentage of pairs of twins in which both members have a specific trait identified in one twin.

heritability Proportion of variability in the phenotype that is estimated to be accounted for by genetic influences within a known environmental range.

FIGURE 3.11
The Concept of Range of
Reaction for Intellectual
Performance

As the product of the interaction between genotype and the environment, the phenotype for any attribute shows a broad range of reaction. For example, the intelligence score of any child, even one who is born with the potential for high intellectual ability, is likely to be limited when the environment is severely restricted. An enriched environment will benefit all children, although perhaps those with greater intellectual potential (Child A or B) more than a child with less intellectual potential (Child C).

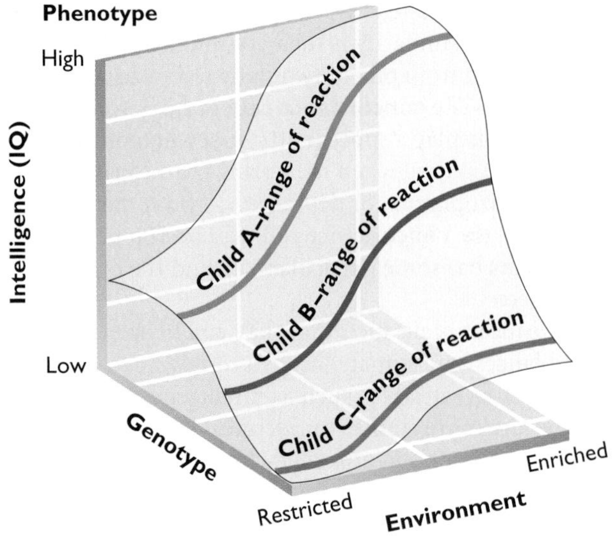

Source: Adapted from Turkheimer, Goldsmith & Gottesman, 1995.

environmental circumstances those individuals have had the opportunity to experience. Thus, although research on heritability was initially designed to provide answers about the contribution of the genotype, it also helps to shed light on the role of experience in development (Plomin et al., 2001). Unfortunately, estimates of heritability are not always easy to obtain because, as we discuss next, complex interactions and correlations exist between the genotype and experience.

Conceptualizing the Interaction Between Genotype and Environment

Neither genotype nor experience in isolation of one another explain development. Instead, how a genotype influences development depends to a great extent on the environment. Similarly, how an environment affects behavior often depends on the genotype. These conditional relationships are the basis for complex *interactions* between heredity and experience; the influence of one on the other is not constant across individuals or environmental circumstances or even during different periods of development (Collins et al., 2000; Rutter & Silberg, 2002).

● **Range of Reaction**   The interactive relationship between genotype and environment can be conceptualized in terms of the concept of **range of reaction,** the notion that, depending on environmental conditions, a broad range of phenotypes may be expressed as a function of the genotype (Turkheimer, Goldsmith, & Gottesman, 1995). Figure 3.11 illustrates this concept for intellectual performance. Consider a child with Down syndrome (represented, e.g., by Child C in Figure 3.11). Transferring this child from an unstimulating institutional setting (a restricted environment) and engaging him in supportive learning activities (more enriched environments) very likely will help him to achieve a much higher level of cognitive functioning (Feuerstein, Rand, & Rynders, 1988). The performances of children with other genotypes (as represented by Child A and Child B in Figure 3.11) can be enormously affected, too, perhaps even more greatly, depending on whether they are reared in deprived or stimulating conditions.

We need to be cautious, however, in thinking about the concept of range of reaction. It reflects only what we presently know about the way genotypes are expressed in environments familiar to us (Gottlieb, 1995; Rutter et al., 1999a). For example, some day, when the ways in which trisomy 21 affects proteins essential to neural

KEY THEME
Nature/Nurture

range of reaction   Range of phenotypic differences possible as a result of different environments interacting with a specific genotype.

events are more fully understood, an environment may be fashioned to promote far higher levels of intelligent behavior in children with Down syndrome. New advances in knowledge of biological processes and the other, much broader complex of multi-directional influences that we call environment may help to drastically modify the way a genotype is expressed in specific behavior (Bronfenbrenner & Ceci, 1994).

● **Canalization**   The principle of **canalization,** a kind of "channeling" of development, suggests yet another way to think about genotype-environment relationships. This principle helps to shed light on the emergence of behaviors common to all members of a species, as well as individual differences. As originally proposed, a highly canalized attribute is one influenced primarily by the genotype; experiential factors can have an impact on the course of development, but only under extreme conditions (Waddington, 1971). Imagine an emerging capacity as something like water flowing through terrain in which channels of varying depth have been cut. The channels help to steer the flow in one of several possible directions. However, the channels are so deeply cut by the genotype that only extreme environmental pressures can change the course of some phenotypes.

KEY THEME
Individual Differences

Various aspects of early motor development tend to emerge on a fairly regular basis during infancy. Presumably the genotype has carved a relatively deep course for their appearance. However, as you will learn in the chapter titled "Physical Growth and Motor Skills," the emergence of early motor skills is not completely protected from disturbances in experience. Other aspects of early development, including the onset of babbling and smiling at interesting events, which are important components of social responsivity, may also be highly canalized, as may some aspects of language acquisition.

Gilbert Gottlieb (1991) has extended these ideas, proposing that the channeling process may come about not only through the genotype but also from early experiential influences. Thus exposure to certain types of stimulation during a critical period may steer development just as hereditary information can. As an example, Gottlieb cites research on mallard ducklings. If prevented from hearing their own vocalizations and instead exposed to a chicken's call early in development, the ducklings later show a preference for the chicken's call rather than for sounds produced by members of their own species.

Gottlieb (2000) has also argued that the genome itself is not "encapsulated" or isolated from the influences of the environment. A classic example is evident in some reptiles—the temperature during incubation determines the sex of the offspring. As we learn more about how genetic information is transcribed into proteins, we may discover other ways in which events both within and outside the organism change how the genetic transcription process takes place. In other words, we may begin to more fully appreciate that development is the outcome of bidirectional influences between the genotype and levels of experience that range from neural activity to behavior to social and cultural events.

Conceptualizing the Correlation Between Genotype and Environment

KEY THEME
Nature/Nurture

The task of determining what proportion of various traits such as activity level, sociability, or intelligence derives from the genes and what proportion comes from the environment is laden with further difficulties. Not only do genotype and environment interact, but they are also linked or *correlated* with each other in several complex ways (Plomin & Rutter, 1998; Rutter et al., 1999a; Scarr, 1992; Scarr & McCartney, 1983).

● **Passive Links**   One correlation between genotype and experience arises from the tendency for parents to establish a child-rearing environment in harmony with their own interests and preferences. Assume, for example, that sociability has some genetic basis. Sociable parents may transmit this orientation to their children either through

canalization   Concept that the development of some attributes is governed primarily by the genotype and only extreme environmental conditions will alter the phenotypic pattern for these attributes.

their genes, through the social environment created in their home, or through both mechanisms. This kind of correlation between genotype and environment is labeled as *passive,* because it has been created for the child by the parents.

In most families, the correlation between the genetic and environmental components of child rearing is likely to be positive; that is, the environment will contain features that support and complement the child's genetic potential. But a negative correlation is also possible, as in cases in which a highly active child is adopted into a sedentary family or in which parents elect to rear their children in ways that depart from their own backgrounds and genetic propensities. A parent who feels he or she was too shy during childhood and, as a consequence, missed out on many social opportunities may actively initiate play groups and other projects designed to promote sociability in a child.

● **Evocative Links**   Another type of correlation between genotype and environment, termed *evocative* or *reactive,* occurs when aspects of the environment, particularly other people, support or encourage behaviors that may have a genetic component; that is, other people's behavior occurs in response to or is evoked by the child's genotype. For example, an active preschooler is likely to prompt teachers to provide large-muscle toys to dissipate some of her energy. A ten-year-old's eagerness to read may encourage a teacher to offer additional opportunities for learning. A sociable child is more likely to attract the attention of peers than a shy or passive child. Thus attributes that have a biological basis are likely to evoke patterns of behavior from others that complement the child's genetic tendencies.

Adoption studies are especially valuable for examining evocative genotype-environment correlations because the genetic makeup of the adopted child is independent of the genetic makeup of the adoptive parents. For example, Thomas O'Connor and his colleagues (O'Connor et al., 1998) wondered whether parental behaviors might be influenced by genetic factors that children bring to the caregiving situation. More specifically, could a child adopted shortly after birth whose biological parent had reported a history of antisocial behavior influence the way the adoptive parents treated him or her? In particular, would the adoptive parents of such children engage in more negative interactions than the adoptive parents of children whose biological parents did not report a history of antisocial behavior? Indeed, this was the finding, suggesting that something about the genotype inherited by the child was evoking more negative reactions from the adoptive parents. These children were, in fact, reported to engage in more antisocial behavior, thus perhaps drawing out the more negative reactions of their adoptive parents. However, the researchers also emphasize that other unknown environmental factors also seemed to play a role in increased negative parental reactions in some of these families.

KEY THEME
Child's Active Role

● **Active, Niche-Picking Links**   In yet another type of correlation between genotype and environment, termed *active,* the child may be attracted by and eagerly seek out experiences more compatible with his or her genotype. Bright children could prefer to exercise their intellect and to play with peers who are also bright. The athletic child may find little pleasure in practicing the piano but spend countless hours skateboarding and playing basketball. Thus any genetic basis for various traits and activities influences the kind of environment a child attempts to create and experience. Sandra Scarr and Kathleen McCartney (1983) described this kind of linkage as **niche picking** to emphasize that children and adults selectively construct and engage environments responsive to their genetic orientations.

Scarr and McCartney (1983; Scarr, 1992) believe that the strength of passive, evocative, and active correlations between genotype and environment changes with development. The experiences infants receive are often determined for them by their caregivers. Thus initial correlations between genotype and environment are more likely to be influenced by passive factors. As children gain greater independence and control of their environment, however, others around them are likely to notice and support their individual differences, and niche picking becomes an increasingly im-

niche picking   Tendency to actively select an environment compatible with a genotype.

Niche picking, the tendency for an individual to seek out and become attracted to activities that are compatible with his or her genotype, is an important aspect of the interaction between nature and nurture. Because of her talent at playing the piano, this young person may be drawn to a future career or avocation involving music. She is also likely to pursue additional training and opportunities to become even more skilled as a musican.

portant factor as children have the opportunity to choose their own interests and activities.

An important implication of these changing relationships is that children within the same family may become less similar to one another as they grow older and become freer of the common environment their parents provide. Older siblings can select niches befitting their individual genotypes more easily than can younger children. When Sandra Scarr and Richard Weinberg (1977) studied adopted children, they obtained support for this prediction. During early and middle childhood, adopted but biologically unrelated children in the same families showed similarities in intelligence, personality, and other traits. Perhaps these resemblances came about both as a result of adoption procedures that encouraged the placement of children in homes somewhat like their biological homes and from the common family environment the adopted children now shared. As adopted siblings neared the end of adolescence, however, they no longer exhibited similarities in intelligence, personality, or other traits; the passive influence of the common environment established by the adoptive parents had become supplanted by active niche picking.

The notion of niche picking provides us with an even more startling prediction. When identical twins are reared apart, they may, with increasing age, actually come to resemble each other more, and perhaps as much as, identical twins reared together! This greater correspondence would emerge as others react to their similar behaviors and as opportunities arise for the twins to make more choices. In the Minnesota Study of Twins Reared Apart, pairs of identical twins, separated as infants and having no interactions with each other until well into adulthood, revealed remarkable similarities not only in gait, posture, gestures, and habits such as straightening eyeglasses but also in storytelling skill, spontaneous giggling, phobic tendencies, hobbies, and interests, resemblances rarely observed between fraternal twins reared apart and usually not considered to have a strong genetic basis (Bouchard, 1984; Bouchard et al., 1990; Lykken et al., 1992). Furthermore, identical twins reared apart showed as high a correlation on many intellectual tasks and personality variables as those reared together. These results suggest that niche picking can be a powerful means of maintaining behaviors supported by the genotype.

Hereditary and Environmental Influences on Behavior

KEY THEME
Nature/Nurture

Research findings involving studies of family resemblances, adopted children, and identical and fraternal twins can be, and often are, interpreted in many different ways precisely because of the complex interactions and relationships that genotype and environment share in shaping behavior. These interpretations sometimes have powerful implications for intervention and social policy (Baumrind, 1993; Jackson, 1993; Scarr, 1992, 1993). Should families or communities, for example, expend resources for educational and mental health efforts if a substantial biological basis for behavior exists? Or does this kind of question, concerned with *how much* heredity contributes to variations in the human phenotype, fail to recognize that educational and social opportunities are essential to maximize competencies, even where genetic contributions are considerable?

Consider the following: about 90 percent of the variability in height among individuals reared in a typical community is believed to be a consequence of genetic factors. However, even though height is strongly influenced by the genotype, its average increase among young adult males in Japan since the end of World War II has been about three-and-a-half inches (Angoff, 1988). Clearly changes in the environment have had a profound impact on a characteristic that receives a significant contribution from the genes. Environmental factors can surely be expected to have an impact on other inherited characteristics as well (Collins et al., 2000; Rutter, 2002).

Robert Plomin (1996) emphasizes one other interesting point about the work that often has revealed a substantial genetic contribution to various kinds of behaviors. Environmental influences frequently account for *more* of the variability in human behavior than does the genotype. Moreover, research in behavioral genetics has begun to provide intriguing insights into *how* environmental factors affect development. Let's examine some of the findings more closely.

● **Intelligence**   Despite its many limitations (see the chapter titled "Intelligence"), most studies have relied on IQ to measure the contributions of genotype and environment to intelligence. Table 3.5 summarizes correlations on IQ test scores among individuals who share different genetic relationships with one another. Environmental contributions are revealed by findings that individuals reared together show somewhat higher correlations for intelligence scores than those with the same genetic relationship reared apart. Nevertheless, the impact of the genotype on intelligence is also evident. The correlations for IQ increase as the similarity in genotypes rises.

We can make sense of several additional findings by considering correlations between genotype and environment. For example, IQ scores for younger adopted children reared together are positively correlated (about .20), as indicated in Table 3.5. However, they are much closer to .00 for adolescents. Moreover, intelligence has been found to be highly correlated in infancy and early childhood for *both* identical and fraternal twins and, with increasing age, to become *even greater* for identical twins but decline to the level reported in Table 3.5 for fraternal twins (Fischbein, 1981; Wilson, 1986). These findings probably reflect the impact of passive links (the similar rearing environment created by the parents) on intelligence early in childhood and more opportunity for niche picking later in development.

Identical twins, however, do not always become more similar as they grow older. As twins who have been reared together become older, fraternal, and to some extent identical, twins become more dissimilar on many aspects of intelligence tests (McCartney, Harris, & Bernieri, 1990). Perhaps they actively attempt to establish a *unique* niche in the family and community, efforts that may also be encouraged by parents of the twins (Schachter, 1982).

Despite the evidence that the heritability of intelligence is high, a classic investigation by Marie Skodak and Harold Skeels (1949) illustrates the substantial impact experience still has. One hundred children born to mentally retarded mothers, most of whom were from low socioeconomic backgrounds, were adopted before six months of age into homes that were economically and educationally well above average. These children displayed above-average intelligence throughout childhood and adolescence and substantially higher IQs than their biological parents, an outcome reflecting the contribution of environmental factors. Nevertheless, the children's IQs

KEY THEME
Child's Active Role

TABLE 3.5	Correlation in IQ as a Function of Genetically Related and Unrelated Individuals Living Together and Apart	
Relationship	**Raised**	**Observed**
Monozygotic twins	Together	0.85
Monozygotic twins	Apart	0.74
Dizygotic twins	Together	0.59
Siblings	Together	0.46
Siblings	Apart	0.24
Midparent/child	Together	0.50
Single parent/child	Together	0.41
Single parent/child	Apart	0.24
Adopting parent/child	Together	0.20

Note: The data are based on a meta-analysis of 212 IQ correlations reported in various studies. In the case of twins and siblings, the heritability estimates are increased by an unspecified amount because of the common environmental contribution from the prenatal environment shared simultaneously by twins and sequentially by siblings. "Midparent" refers to the mean of the IQ scores of both parents.

Source: From B. Devlin, S. E. Feinberg, D. P. Resnick, & K. Roeder (Eds.), *Intelligence, genes, and success: Scientists respond to* The Bell Curve, pp. 45–70. Copyright © 1997. Used by permission of Springer-Verlag and the author.

were still correlated with those of their biological mothers, indicating a hereditary contribution to these scores as well.

● **Temperament and Personality** Genetic influences typically account for 20 to 50 percent of the variability in personality differences within a population (Plomin et al., 2001; Saudino, 1997). The higher heritability estimates tend to be found when parental reports rather than direct observation of social behavior are recorded (Collins et al., 2000). **Temperament,** an early-appearing constellation of personality traits, has been of particular interest in terms of possible genetic influences. A number of broad qualities characterize temperament. One of these is *sociability,* the tendency to be shy or inhibited and somewhat fearful of new experiences versus outgoing and uninhibited, characteristics that are likely precursors to introversion and extroversion, respectively, in older children and adults. Another trait is *emotionality,* the ease with which an individual becomes distressed, upset, or angry and the intensity with which these emotions are expressed. A third trait is *activity,* as evidenced by the tempo and vigor with which behaviors are performed. Identical twins consistently show higher correlations on these characteristics (typically between .40 and .60) than fraternal twins (typically between .10 and .30), suggesting an inherited component (Emde et al., 1992; Goldsmith, Buss, & Lemery, 1997; Robinson et al., 1992). Perhaps inherited differences in physiological reactivity underlie these differences. For example, with respect to sociability, young children who remain aloof and are reluctant to play with novel toys display increased heart rate and muscle tension in unfamiliar situations compared with children who are more outgoing and spontaneous (Kagan, 1994).

KEY THEME
Individual Differences

Consistent racial and ethnic differences have been reported and attributed to genetic differences in temperament as well. When Daniel Freedman (1979) compared Caucasian and Chinese American newborns, he found that Caucasian babies were more irritable and harder to comfort than Chinese American infants. Similarly, research with four-month-olds from Boston, Dublin, and Beijing indicated that American infants were more active and fretful than those in Dublin, who in turn were more reactive than those in China (Kagan et al., 1994).

Does the environment also play some important role in temperament and other personality differences? Studies comparing the personalities of unrelated children in

temperament Stable, early-appearing constellation of individual personality attributes believed to have a hereditary basis; includes sociability, emotionality, and activity level.

the same household report that the correlations are fairly low and often approach zero, especially in later childhood and adolescence (Plomin et al., 2001). Behavioral geneticists have uncovered some other surprising findings. *Shared environment,* the kinds of experiences children in a home or community bear in common and that are assumed to foster similarity in children within the same family, simply does not have much effect for many aspects of personality (Goldsmith, Buss, & Lemery, 1997; Plomin et al., 2001). In contrast, *nonshared environment,* the experiences unique to individual children as they interact with parents, peers, and others, can play a powerful role in development, one that tends to make children in the family *different* rather than similar (Harris, 1998; Plomin et al., 2001).

How can this be? One possibility is that peers, as well as genes, play a pivotal role in determining the differences in personality and social adjustment displayed by children reared in the same family. This view has sometimes escalated to suggest that parenting matters relatively little with respect to offspring's personality and social adjustment. Needless to say, such a conclusion has been heatedly debated (Collins et al., 2000; Harris, 2000; Vandell, 2000).

Perhaps, too, parents actually do treat their children differently, even though they claim not to. Although mothers and fathers typically do not report much differential treatment, siblings frequently express another take on the matter. Observations of how parents interact with their sons and daughters seem to provide some ammunition in support of the children's perceptions. For example, the toys boys and girls are encouraged to play with may differ considerably in some families (Lytton & Romney, 1991). And when siblings perceive that they are being treated unfairly by their parents, the quality of their relationships with one another deteriorates (Kowal & Kramer, 1997).

RESEARCH APPLIED TO PARENTING

Treating Siblings Fairly

As the party was nearing its end, the twins began opening their presents. Jasmine, just as she approached many of her other ventures, impulsively grabbed one of the brightly wrapped packages and without hesitation tore it open; Alyssa was more refined and systematic in her procedure, opening each box carefully, as carefully as any excited five-year-old might be expected to in such a situation. Their mother looked on with pride but with some apprehension as well. Should she encourage Jasmine to be less impetuous and Alyssa to be more spontaneous? Or should she promote their differences, respecting the individual styles each child showed even if it meant that each twin was treated very differently? She knew that Jasmine's impish streak would require more disciplining and that Alyssa's more cautious character would lead to fewer tests of limits. But she did not want her children to think that she favored one of the twins more than the other.

KEY THEME
Individual Differences

Should parents treat their children differently or in the same way? The answer is far from clear. For example, historically, identical twins were often dressed alike and treated almost as if they were one and the same individual. Today parents are advised to recognize their twins' individuality by encouraging them to gain unique experiences and to "pick out" their own niche in the family and community. As a consequence, they may be treated differently by parents and others. Other siblings, of course, share only about half of their genes and are quite distinct in physical appearance, personality, intellectual ability, and other characteristics. When is differential treatment a good thing? When is it a source of conflict? Research indicates parents might consider some of these points when confronting this matter.

1. *Expect siblings to kindle different reactions from others.*   Because all children, with the exception of identical twins, are born with different genotypes, they are likely to evoke distinctive kinds of responses from family members, teachers, peers, and others. These responses can, in turn, serve to magnify existing differences in the behaviors of siblings.

2. *Assume siblings will actively search out ways to be different from one another.* Children very likely will engage in niche picking to set themselves apart from others within the family—a process called *sibling deidentification* (Feinberg & Hetherington, 2000). Such efforts may be observed even in identical twins such as Jasmine and Alyssa, as one twin takes on a more active role in leadership, becomes more studious, or engages in more social interactions than the other. Whether it stems from biology or experience, the opportunity to find one's niche within the family, as well as the larger community, is an important aspect of development for all children.

KEY THEME
Child's Active Role

3. *Anticipate that siblings will experience family events in different ways and will need to be treated differently in some circumstances.* Siblings within the family—by virtue of their birth order, spacing, and unique events such as an illness, the death of a grandparent, or a move to a new neighborhood—will necessarily receive unique experiences because of their specific developmental status. In fact, distinct socialization practices for children of different ages is the norm because treatment by caregivers could otherwise be developmentally inappropriate. Younger children typically need more nurturance and care, older children increased independence and greater responsibility. Caregivers recognize that differential treatment is sometimes necessary (Dunn & McGuire, 1994). Children as young as five years of age notice these differences. Moreover, younger children would prefer being the oldest in the family; that is, in their eyes older siblings seem to have higher status (McHale et al., 1995). Furthermore, children and adolescents perceive greater differential treatment of same-sex siblings than brother-sister dyads by parents (McHale et al., 2000). Stress within the family may magnify these differences (Crouter, McHale, & Tucker, 1999). Children do not always find differential treatment to be unfair. In fact, when children experience differential treatment on the part of their parents but feel it is justified, that is, equitable even though not equal, sibling relationships are generally positive (Kowal & Kramer, 1997)

KEY THEME
Individual Differences

4. *Treat siblings impartially when possible and appropriate.* Impartial treatment of siblings by parents, to the extent that it is appropriate, is associated with less conflict between siblings and between children and their parents (Brody & Stoneman, 1994; McHale et al., 1995). In other words, parents who maintain a balance between socialization practices that are equitable within the limits of age-appropriate differences have children who interact effectively and in constructive ways with others, including their siblings. Differences in parenting arising from the individual needs of children can have positive consequences, but only as long as these differences do not reflect a form of parental "favoritism."

Parents with more than one child often want to treat each of them equally but need to fine-tune their parenting efforts to the needs and age-appropriate activities of individual children. Fine motor skills demonstrated by the older sibling may permit her to color or carry out other activities that are beyond the capacity of the younger sibling, who, as shown here, has found her own way to keep busy. By providing individual support and avoiding "favoritism," parents seem to help siblings learn to appreciate each other's abilities.

● **Behavioral and Personality Disorders**   Table 3.6 summarizes the concordance rate for identical and fraternal twins for a variety of behavioral and personality disorders. None of these findings indicates 100 percent concordance even in identical twins, despite the identity of their genetic makeup. Thus environmental factors play an important role in the manifestation of each of these problems. In fact, concordance measures for *conduct disorders* (fighting and aggressive behavior, failure to accept parental discipline) in both identical and fraternal twins are relatively high, suggesting that environmental factors contribute substantially to their appearance in both groups.

The genetic contribution to *bipolar disorder,* a disorder characterized by rapid and wide mood swings between feverish activity and withdrawn, depressed behaviors, appears to be substantial. Family studies reveal that children of a parent with bipolar disorder are at far greater risk for displaying the illness than children without such a parent. Research on adoptees provides further evidence that genotype plays a role; the risk for adopted children whose biological parents have the illness is about three times greater than for adopted children whose biological parents do not have it (Rutter et al., 1999b). Recent work on *autism* (more fully described in the chapter titled "Cognition: Piaget and Vygotsky"), a disorder that historically was assumed to be largely the consequence of improper caregiving, also reveals an ample hereditary contribution (Rutter et al., 1999b).

Alcoholism, although not linked to a single gene, shows a modest genetic component. In fact, more recent studies now put the concordance rate at over .50 for identical twins and over .30 for fraternal twins who are male, somewhat higher than shown in Table 3.6 for the general population (Kendler et al., 1997; McGue, 1999). *Schizophrenia,* a form of psychopathology that includes disturbances in thoughts and emotions, such as delusions and hallucinations, also exhibits some genetic contribution. As the biological relationship to someone diagnosed as having schizophrenia increases, an individual's risk for the same diagnosis rises. When one twin has schizophrenia, the other twin is about three times more likely to display schizophrenia if identical than if fraternal. Adoption studies further confirm a role for the genotype; schizophrenia is far more prevalent among adopted children who are the biological offspring of a schizophrenic parent than among those of a nonschizophrenic parent (Gottesman & Shields, 1982). At the present time, no single gene seems to be responsible for the findings; instead, polygenic contributions are more likely.

Recent behavioral genetic research raises the possibility that the same genes could have some role in different manifestations of psychopathology, including anxiety and depression or aggressive behavior and antisocial behavior (Eley, 1997). These "general" genes, in other words, may contribute to wide variations in characteristics and behaviors that are often problematic for the individual. Although psychologists have long assumed that environmental conditions play a part in different expressions of

Evidence for the genetic basis of behavioral and personality disorders is often supported by studies of twins. For these disorders, the likelihood that both members of a pair will display the disorder, if exhibited by one, is greater when the pair are identical twins rather than fraternal twins. However, environmental factors may contribute to high concordance rates for both identical and fraternal twins, as is likely for conduct disorders.

TABLE 3.6	The Genetic Basis of Selected Behavioral and Personality Disorders: Twin Data	
Twin Concordances	**Identical Twins**	**Fraternal Twins**
Conduct disorder	.85	.70
Bipolar disorder	.65	.20
Autism	.65	.10
Unipolar depression	.45	.20
Alcoholism—males	.40	.20
Schizophrenia	.40	.10
Alcoholism—females	.30	.25

Source: Data from Plomin, 1994.

psychopathologies, the finding that a subset of genes may contribute to this phenomenon raises interesting questions about how biochemical processes affect behavioral and personality disorders and their development.

● **Other Characteristics** A host of other characteristics, including empathy, reading disabilities, sexual orientation, obesity, susceptibility to various illnesses such as heart disease and cancer, and even a propensity to watch television, have a genetic linkage (Castles et al., 1999; LeVay & Hamer, 1994; Pérusse & Chagnon, 1997; Plomin, Corley, et al., 1990; Plomin, Owen, & McGuffin, 1994). In addition, how individuals perceive their family environments also appears to be influenced by the genotype (Hur & Bouchard, 1995; Plomin et al., 1994), as does the way caregivers parent and how children adjust to that parenting (Neiderhiser et al., 1999). The influence of the genotype affects the entire breadth of human behavior, although exactly how it does so remains uncertain.

FOR YOUR REVIEW

- What methods do behavior geneticists use to investigate the extent to which behavior is influenced by combinations of genes versus experience? Why are identical and fraternal twins—as well as adopted children—important in work designed to evaluate the heritability of behavior?

- How do concordance rate and correlation differ as measures in investigating genetic and environmental contributions to development?

- How are conceptualizations of the interaction between genotype and environment advanced by notions of a range of reaction and canalization?

- How do passive, evocative, and active niche-picking correlations between the genotype and experience differ from one another?

- To what extent are behavioral phenotypes such as intelligence, personality and temperament, personality disorders, and other characteristics influenced by heredity?

- To what extent are shared and nonshared environments important in accounting for similarities and differences in children's behavior?

- Why might parents treat siblings differently, and how do children interpret these differential treatments?

CHAPTER RECAP

SUMMARY OF DEVELOPMENTAL THEMES

■ **Nature/Nurture** *What roles do nature and nurture play in development?*

The phenotype, the observable behaviors and characteristics of an individual, is the product of a complex interaction between genotype and environment. Environment includes biological contexts, such as the foods we eat, but more frequently we consider it to be the experiences provided by caregivers and others. The relationship between genotype and environment is complicated by their interaction with each other and by passive, reactive, and niche-picking correlations. As a consequence, experiential factors are tightly interwoven with genotype to produce the range and variety of behaviors and characteristics an individual displays. Both genotype and environment are indispensable to development.

■ **Child's Active Role** *How does the child play an active role in the effects of heredity on development?*

Researchers recognize the child's active efforts to seek out environments that support and maintain behavioral orientations and preferences influenced by hereditary factors. As the child achieves greater control over the environment, he or she has increasing opportunities to find a niche. In other words, behaviors, activities, and skills the child displays not only are a consequence of imposed social and physical experiences but also reflect the selective efforts of the child to discover interesting, challenging, and supportive environments. Inherited and environmentally imposed influences may be met with eager support or active resistance to determine each child's unique life history.

■ **Individual Differences**   *How prominent are individual differences in development?*

Individual differences are pervasive in intellectual, temperamental, and a host of other cognitive, social, and emotional aspects of development. Hereditary and environmental factors determine these differences. Alleles of genes contribute to the wide range of physical, cognitive, emotional, and social adaptations displayed by individuals. These individual differences are not solely produced by genes; they are also the product of a rich medley of physical, social, and cultural contexts in which each individual matures. A distinctive combination of genes and experiences promotes the abundant diversity we observe in human abilities and behavior.

▌ SUMMARY OF TOPICS

Principles of Hereditary Transmission

■ The observable and measurable characteristics of an individual are the result of his or her *genotype,* or inherited endowment, and experience. A *phenotype* refers to the traits and behaviors displayed by an individual.

The Building Blocks of Heredity

■ The structures associated with the principles of heredity must be examined at several different levels.

■ An individual's body is composed of trillions of cells. Twenty-three pairs of *chromosomes* (a total of forty-six), consisting of *deoxyribonucleic acid* or *DNA,* are located in the nucleus of most cells in the human body.

■ The central unit of hereditary information is the *gene,* a segment of a chromosome. *Nucleotides* are two different sets of pairs of repeating molecules that form the biochemical building blocks for the genes and the basic structure of the chromosomes.

■ Males and females differ in the composition of the twenty-third pair of chromsomes. In females, both members of the pair normally are *X chromosomes.* In males, one is normally an X chromosome and the other is a *Y chromosome.*

■ The entire inventory of nucleotide base pairs in humans, which has recently been mapped, is called the *human genome.*

Gene Expression

■ Variants of genes on the twenty-three pairs of chromosomes, or *alleles,* often interact with one another in a *dominant-recessive* pattern or in other ways to establish different probabilities of inheritance for particular traits or characteristics.

■ Cell division in the human body takes place in two different ways. *Mitosis* is the process of cell division by which the forty-six chromosomes are duplicated in the body cells. The *gametes,* or sperm and egg cells, are formed by *meiosis,* a process of a cell division that results in twenty-three chromosomes in each of these cells.

■ The random process by which a member of each of the twenty-three pairs of chromosomes is selected for the gametes, combined with *crossing over* during meiosis, ensures that every individual, with the exception of identical twins, has a unique hereditary blueprint.

Gene and Chromosomal Abnormalities

■ A number of inherited diseases and abnormalities associated with chromosomes and alleles can lead to severe disruptions in physical and behavior development.

Gene Variations

■ The likelihood of inheriting a genetic disease or disorder such as Williams syndrome, sickle cell disease, or phenylketonuria depends on whether it is caused by a dominant or a recessive allele. Gene disorders such as fragile X syndrome that are associated with the XX or XY chromosomes are said to be *sex-linked.*

Chromosome Variations

■ The most common disorder contributing to mental retardation, trisomy 21 (Down syndrome), is associated with inheritance of an extra chromosome.

■ Variations in number of sex chromosomes also occur but do not always contribute to behavioral or other developmental problems, especially if a supportive environment is available.

Genetic Counseling

■ *Genetic counseling* provides prospective parents with information on the probability of having children affected by birth defects.

Prenatal Diagnosis

■ Various tests, including *amniocentesis, chorionic villus sampling, fetal blood sampling, maternal blood screening,* and *ultrasonography,* can be carried out to assess the likelihood of the developing fetus having a genetic defect or one of many other abnormalities.

■ Controversial ethical and social issues, including the opportunity to carry out sex preselection, confront parents and professionals as a result of advances in prenatal tests.

Developmental and Behavioral Genetics

■ *Behavior genetics* is a method of attempting to determine the relative contribution of heredity and environment to traits and behaviors that are often the result of combinations of genes.

The Methods of Behavorial Geneticists

■ To determine contributions from combinations of genes, behavioral geneticists frequently engage in selective breeding with lower organisms or compare findings between various family members, such as *identical twins, fraternal twins,* siblings, and adopted children, because these groups differ in the extent to which they share a common genotype. The *concordance rate* refers to the extent that both members of pairs of twins display the same characteristics.

■ *Heritability* refers to the extent to which the variability on some characteristic in a sample of individuals is accounted for by genetic differences among those individuals.

Conceptualizing the Interaction Between Genotype and Environment

■ The concept of *range of reaction* highlights the fact that a trait or behavior influenced by a person's genotype may be unique to a particular kind of environment.

■ The principle of *canalization* emphasizes that some traits and characteristics are highly determined by the genotype or, conversely, that some environments may have a powerful influence in how these are displayed.

Conceptualizing the Correlation Between Genotype and Environment

■ Determining the relative contribution of genotype and environment to variations in behavior is made complicated by interactions and correlations between these two factors, as well as by other limitations in our understanding of their relationship to one another.

■ Correlations between genotype and environment may be *passive* in that caregivers with specific genotypes are likely to provide environments supportive of their children's genotypes; *evocative* in that parents, peers, and others are likely to react in ways that accommodate genetic inclinations; and *active* in that children may attempt to find or create environments that support their individual genetic propensities, that is, engage in *niche picking*.

Hereditary and Environmental Influences on Behavior

■ Intelligence, temperament and other personality variables, social adjustment and behavioral disorders, and other traits and characteristics often display considerable heritability, suggesting that the genotype contributes substantially to variability among children for many aspects of development.

■ The shared environment provided by the family increases similarity among siblings, often to a limited extent. However, the nonshared environment that children within the same family experience contributes substantially to individual differences among children.

■ Siblings perceive differential treatment from their parents, but when the differential treatment is interpreted as equitable, even if not equal, positive relationships between siblings are fostered.

CHAPTER 4

The Prenatal Period and Birth

Key Themes in the Prenatal Period and Birth

- **Nature/Nurture**   What roles do nature and nurture play in prenatal development and birth?

- **Sociocultural Influence**   How does the sociocultural context influence prenatal development and birth?

- **Continuity/Discontinuity**   Is development before and after birth continuous or discontinuous?

- **Individual Differences**   How prominent are individual differences in prenatal development and the newborn?

She was expecting. It was great news. But this time her concerns outweighed the joy. Carole was already caring for two little ones, both under the age of five, and also working full-time to provide income to help ends meet. Her job paid only a little above the minimum wage. Never enough, even when added to her husband's paycheck. However, neither she nor her husband had gone to college. Nor did either have the kinds of skills to permit them to obtain a really high-paying job. It would be a struggle to provide for another child.

Although only four weeks into her pregnancy, Carole knew the embryo was undergoing rapid developmental changes and would continue to do so for many more weeks. She avoided alcohol as soon as she learned of her pregnancy. She had stopped smoking even before her first child was born. But was there enough money for prenatal care? Did she need to make modifications in her diet or adjustments in her work to ensure that her unborn would have a healthy start? Would her persistent anxieties take a toll as well? She wanted the best for this new addition coming into the family. But she wasn't sure she would always be able to give it.

Most women experience both pride and apprehension when they learn they are pregnant. Those feelings are often influenced by a multitude of social and cultural views and ideas about pregnancy. Although societies differ enormously in their specific beliefs, anthropologists report that expectant women around the world are often urged to avoid certain activities and to carry out various rituals for the sake of their unborn. In Western civilizations, admonitions about pregnancy exist as well; obstetricians may advise a pregnant woman to stop smoking, avoid alcohol, and let someone else clean the cat's litterbox, and they may recommend taking supplements containing folic acid and other nutrients.

Fortunately, the mysteries surrounding this remarkable time are beginning to become clearer. Our discussion of prenatal development will open with a brief description of the amazing sequence of events taking place between conception and birth. At no other time does growth take place so rapidly or do so many physical changes occur in a matter of weeks, days, and even hours. Some cultures, such as the Chinese, tacitly acknowledge these dramatic events by granting the baby a year of life when born. In the typical nine months of confinement to the womb, the fetus has indeed undergone an epic journey.

Although fetal growth proceeds in a highly protected environment, we are also discovering the ways in which drugs, diseases, and other factors affect prenatal development. We summarize our current understanding of these influences as well. We then consider the birth process and take a first brief look at the newborn's states and characteristics.

The Stages of Prenatal Development

KEY THEME
Continuity/Discontinuity

👁 SEE FOR YOURSELF
psychology.college.hmco.com
Prenatal Development

prenatal development   Period in development from conception to the onset of labor.

perinatal period   Period beginning about the seventh month of pregnancy and continuing until about four weeks after birth.

postnatal development   Period in development following birth.

germinal period   Period lasting about ten to fourteen days following conception before the fertilized egg becomes implanted in the uterine wall. Also called *period of the zygote.*

embryonic period   Period of prenatal development during which major biological organs and systems form. Begins about the tenth to fourteenth day after conception and ends about the eighth week after conception.

fetal period   Period of prenatal development, from about the eighth week after conception to birth, marked by rapid growth and preparation of body systems for functioning in the postnatal environment.

Three major overlapping periods define the life of a human organism. **Prenatal development** is launched from the moment of conception and continues to the beginning of labor. All but the first few days of this period are spent within the confines of the womb. The **perinatal period** dawns about the seventh month of pregnancy and extends until twenty-eight days after birth. This phase is associated with the impending birth, the social and physical setting for delivery, and the baby's first adjustments to his or her new world. Among the events included in the perinatal period are the medical and obstetrical practices associated with delivery and the preparations and care provided by parents and others to assist in the transition from the womb to life outside. **Postnatal development** begins after birth. The child's environment now includes the broader physical and social world afforded by caregivers and others responsible for the infant's continued growth.

Prenatal development is further divided into three stages. The **germinal period,** also known as the *period of the zygote,* encompasses the first ten to fourteen days following conception. Cell division and migration of the newly fertilized egg, culminating with its implantation in the uterine wall, characterize the germinal period. The second stage, the **embryonic period,** continues from about two to eight weeks after conception. The formation of structures and organs associated with the nervous, circulatory, respiratory, and most other systems mark the embryonic period. The final stage, the **fetal period,** lasts from about eight weeks after conception to birth. This period is distinguished by substantial physical growth, and organs and systems are refined in preparation for functioning outside the womb. This entire process begins the moment sperm and egg fuse.

Fertilization

Even before her own birth, Carole, like most other human females, had formed approximately 5 million primitive egg cells in her ovaries. Their numbers, however, declined with development; by puberty perhaps only thirty thousand remained. Of this abundant supply, about four hundred will mature and be released for potential fertilization during the childbearing years (Samuels & Samuels, 1986). In contrast, male sperm production begins only at puberty, when an incredible 100 to 300 million sperm may be formed daily.

The opportunity for human conception begins about the fourteenth day after the start of the menstrual period. At this time, a capsulelike *follicle* housing a primitive egg cell in one of the ovaries begins to mature. As it matures and changes position, the follicle eventually ruptures and discharges its valuable contents from the ovary. After being expelled, the egg cell, or *ovum,* is normally carried into the Fallopian tube. This organ serves as a conduit for the egg, which moves toward the uterus at the leisurely rate of about one-sixteenth inch per hour. The Fallopian tube provides a receptive environment for fertilization if sperm are present. If unfertilized, the ovum survives only about twenty-four hours.

Sperm reach the Fallopian tube by maneuvering from the vagina through the cervix and the uterus. Sperm can migrate several inches an hour with the assistance of their tail-like appendages. From 300 to 500 typically negotiate the six- or more hour trip into the Fallopian tube; these usually survive about forty-eight hours and sometimes substantially longer.

If an ovum is present, sperm seem attracted to it (Roberts, 1991). The egg also prepares for fertilization in the presence of sperm. Cells initially surrounding the ovum loosen their protective grip, permitting the egg to be penetrated (Nilsson, 1990). As soon as one sperm cell breaks through the egg's protective linings, enzymes rapidly transform its outer membrane to prevent others from invading. Genetic material from egg and sperm quickly mix to establish a normal complement of forty-six chromosomes. The egg, the body's largest cell, barely visible to the naked eye, weighs about 100,000 times more than the sperm, the body's smallest cell. Despite the enor-

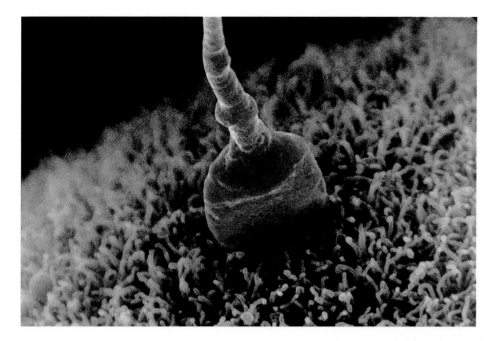

Human development begins with the penetration of the egg by a single sperm as shown here (egg and sperm are magnified greatly). Although the egg is the body's largest cell and the sperm its smallest, each contributes twenty-three chromosomes to form the hereditary basis for the development of a new living entity.

mous difference in size, both contribute equivalent amounts of genetic material to the zygote.

The Germinal Period

After fertilization, the zygote continues to migrate down the Fallopian tube (see Figure 4.1). Within twenty-four to thirty hours after conception, the single cell divides into two cells, the first of a series of mitotic divisions called *cleavages*. At roughly twenty-hour intervals these cells divide again to form four, then eight, then sixteen cells. During the cleavages, the zygote remains about the same size; thus individual cells become smaller and smaller.

After three days, about the time the zygote is ready to enter the uterus, it has become a solid sphere of sixteen cells called a *morula*. Each cell is alike in its capacity to generate a separate identical organism. About the fourth day after conception, however, the cells begin to segregate and carry out specific functions. One group forms a spherical outer cellular layer that eventually becomes various membranes providing nutritive support for the embryo. A second, inner group of cells organizes into a mass that will develop into the embryo (Cross, Werb, & Fisher, 1994). This differentiated group of cells is now called a *blastocyst*.

About the sixth day after conception, the blastocyst begins the process of attaching to the uterine wall to tap a critical new supply of nutriments. By about the tenth to fourteenth day after conception, the implantation process is completed. In preparing for this event, the blastocyst began secreting hormones and other substances to inhibit menstruation, or the shedding of the uterine lining, and to keep the woman's immune system from rejecting the foreign object. One of these hormones eventually becomes detectable in the woman's urine as a marker in pregnancy tests.

If the zygote fails to attach to the uterine wall, it is expelled; the frequency of such events is unknown because a woman seldom realizes that a potential pregnancy has terminated. However, the possibility exists for the zygote to also implant and begin development at some location other than in the uterus. Such an event is called an **ectopic pregnancy.** The most likely site is somewhere in the Fallopian tube, although it may implant on occasion within the abdominal cavity, ovary, or cervix. Ectopic pregnancies occur relatively infrequently, but they are the leading cause of maternal death during the first trimester of pregnancy (Grimes, 1995). Thus they pose a serious health risk for a woman. For example, if the embryo continues to grow, it may rupture the narrow Fallopian tube and cause life-threatening hemorrhaging. The rate of

ectopic pregnancy Implantation of the fertilized ovum in a location outside of the uterus.

FIGURE 4.1 | Fertilization and the Germinal Period

During the early development of the human embryo, an egg cell is released from a maturing follicle within the ovary, and fertilization takes place in the Fallopian tube, transforming the egg cell or ovum into a zygote. Cleavage and multiplication of cells proceed as the zygote migrates toward the uterus. Differentiation of the zygote begins within the uterus, becoming a solid sixteen-cell sphere known as the *morula,* then a differentiated set of cells known as the *blastocyst,* which prepares for implantation in the uterine wall. Once implanted, it taps a vital source of nutriments to sustain further development. (The numbers indicate days following fertilization.)

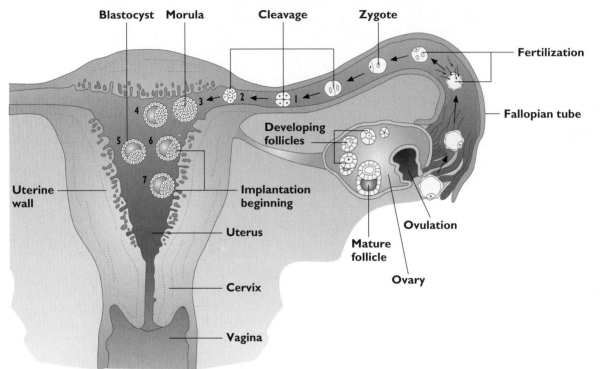

ectopic pregnancies has shown a worrisome increase in recent years. For example, in the United States its occurrence increased from 4.5 to 19.7 per 1,000 pregnancies between 1970 and 1992, and in Norway, from 12.5 to 18.0 per 1,000 pregnancies between 1979 and 1993 (Pisarska & Carson, 1999).

Numerous factors may account for the increase in ectopic pregnancies. For example, pelvic infections, many caused by sexually transmitted diseases, and surgery, especially involving the Fallopian tubes, elevate the risk substantially. So, too, although to a lesser extent, do new methods of assisted reproduction (see later in this section) and certain aspects of lifestyle, including multiple sexual partners or early sexual activity and cigarette smoking (Frishmuth, 1998; Pisarska & Carson, 1999). Regardless of its cause, however, ectopic pregnancy is serious for the mother and does not allow for the continued development of the embryo or fetus.

The Embryonic Period

The embryonic period, which begins with the implantation of the blastocyst in the uterine wall and continues until about the eighth week after conception, is marked by the rapid differentiation of cells to form most of the organs and systems within the body. This differentiation, known as *organogenesis,* is achieved by the production and migration of specialized cells having distinctive functions.

● **Formation of Body Organs and Systems**   The first step in the formation of various body organs and systems involves the migration of unspecialized embryonic cells to establish a three-layered embryo. The three layers serve as the foundation for all tissues and organs in the body. The *endoderm,* or inner layer, will give rise to many of the linings of internal organs such as lungs, the gastrointestinal tract, the liver, the pancreas, the bladder, and some glands. The *mesoderm,* or middle layer, eventually develops into skeleton and muscles, the urogenital system, the lymph and cardiovascular systems, and other connective tissues. The *ectoderm,* or outer layer, will form skin, hair, and nails, but its earliest derivatives will be the central nervous system and nerves.

How, by simply migrating to a layered configuration, do undifferentiated cells come to establish a highly distinctive set of organs and systems? Understanding this process remains one of the most important unresolved issues in prenatal development (Barinaga, 1994). However, the immediate environment surrounding a cell appears to play a major role. Although at first unspecialized, a cell's potential becomes constrained by its association with neighboring tissues. In other words, cells are induced by their surroundings to take on certain forms and functions. For example, if cells from the ectodermal layer are removed and placed in a culture so that they grow in isolation from other cell layers, they form epidermal, or skinlike, tissues. If placed with a layer of mesodermal cells, however, a nervous system will emerge (Abel, 1989).

Because the embryonic period is the major time for development of organs and systems, many possibilities for disruption exist. However, under normal conditions the sequence of primary changes in prenatal development proceeds in a fairly regular pattern, as summarized in the Prenatal Development chronology.

● **Early Brain and Nervous System Development**   About the fifteenth day after conception, a small group of cells at one end of the ectoderm starts to grow rapidly. The growth creates a reference point for the cephalo (head) and the caudal (tail) regions of the embryo and helps to distinguish left from right side. The cells induce the development of the *neural* tube, which in turn initiates the formation of the spinal cord, nerves, and eventually the brain.

Rapid changes in the neural tube begin about the third week. At first, the neural tube is open at both ends. The tube begins closing in the brain region and, a few days later, in the caudal region. Its failure to knit shut at either end can have drastic consequences for development. In *anencephaly,* a condition in which the cephalic region of the neural tube does not close, the cerebral hemispheres fail to develop, and most of the cortex is missing at birth. Newborns with such a condition survive only a short time.

Spina bifida is a condition that arises when the caudal region of the neural tube fails to close. The resulting cleft in the vertebral column permits spinal nerves to grow outside the protective vertebrae. In more serious cases, the infant may be paralyzed and lack sensation in the legs. Surgery often must be performed. Sometimes it can be done even before birth to keep the condition from getting worse. But lost capacities cannot be restored, and malformations in brain development and impaired intellectual development may accompany spina bifida (Northrup & Volcik, 2000).

The frequency of both neural tube defects, now about one in every one thousand births in the United States, has declined sharply over the last thirty years. This decline, as illustrated in Figure 4.2 for the state of South Carolina, appears to be the consequence of two factors. A better understanding of the benefits of nutritional supplements taken early in pregnancy, particularly of folic acid and other components of the vitamin B complex, have helped to prevent neural tube defects in the first place (Stevenson et al., 2000). In addition, in the case of more serious neural tube defects such as anencephaly, the pregnancy is often not carried to term (Limb & Holmes, 1994).

The second month after conception is marked by continued rapid development of the head and brain. Nerve cells show an explosive increase in number, with as many as 100,000 neurons generated every minute (Nilsson, 1990). Neurons also undergo extensive migration once the neural tube closes and soon make contact with one another. The region of the head greatly enlarges relative to the rest of the embryo to account for about half of total body length. Nevertheless, the embryo is still tiny; it is less than one-and-a-half inches long and weighs only about half an ounce. However, nearly all organs are established by this time, and the embryo is recognizably human.

KEY THEME
Nature/Nurture

KEY THEME
Nature/Nurture

CHRONOLOGY: *Prenatal Development*

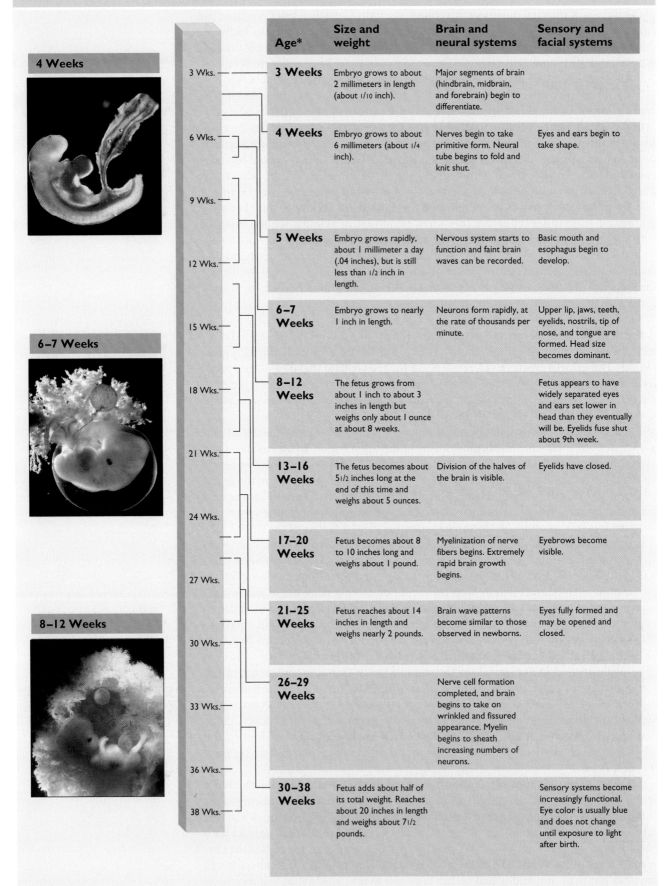

4 Weeks

6–7 Weeks

8–12 Weeks

Age*	Size and weight	Brain and neural systems	Sensory and facial systems
3 Weeks	Embryo grows to about 2 millimeters in length (about 1/10 inch).	Major segments of brain (hindbrain, midbrain, and forebrain) begin to differentiate.	
4 Weeks	Embryo grows to about 6 millimeters (about 1/4 inch).	Nerves begin to take primitive form. Neural tube begins to fold and knit shut.	Eyes and ears begin to take shape.
5 Weeks	Embryo grows rapidly, about 1 millimeter a day (.04 inches), but is still less than 1/2 inch in length.	Nervous system starts to function and faint brain waves can be recorded.	Basic mouth and esophagus begin to develop.
6–7 Weeks	Embryo grows to nearly 1 inch in length.	Neurons form rapidly, at the rate of thousands per minute.	Upper lip, jaws, teeth, eyelids, nostrils, tip of nose, and tongue are formed. Head size becomes dominant.
8–12 Weeks	The fetus grows from about 1 inch to about 3 inches in length but weighs only about 1 ounce at about 8 weeks.		Fetus appears to have widely separated eyes and ears set lower in head than they eventually will be. Eyelids fuse shut about 9th week.
13–16 Weeks	The fetus becomes about 5 1/2 inches long at the end of this time and weighs about 5 ounces.	Division of the halves of the brain is visible.	Eyelids have closed.
17–20 Weeks	Fetus becomes about 8 to 10 inches long and weighs about 1 pound.	Myelinization of nerve fibers begins. Extremely rapid brain growth begins.	Eyebrows become visible.
21–25 Weeks	Fetus reaches about 14 inches in length and weighs nearly 2 pounds.	Brain wave patterns become similar to those observed in newborns.	Eyes fully formed and may be opened and closed.
26–29 Weeks		Nerve cell formation completed, and brain begins to take on wrinkled and fissured appearance. Myelin begins to sheath increasing numbers of neurons.	
30–38 Weeks	Fetus adds about half of its total weight. Reaches about 20 inches in length and weighs about 7 1/2 pounds.		Sensory systems become increasingly functional. Eye color is usually blue and does not change until exposure to light after birth.

3 Wks. —
6 Wks. —
9 Wks. —
12 Wks. —
15 Wks. —
18 Wks. —
21 Wks. —
24 Wks. —
27 Wks. —
30 Wks. —
33 Wks. —
36 Wks. —
38 Wks. —

* From conception.

Muscle, skin, and skeletal systems	Other systems	Reflexive and behavioral responses
Precursors to vertebrae begin to organize.	Blood vessels form and connect to precursor of umbilical cord. Primitive one-chambered heart starts to beat by 21st day.	
Stripe of tissue forms on either side of trunk to begin chest and stomach muscle production. Arm buds appear by about 26 days. Similar swelling begins about 2 days later to form early buds for lower limbs. Tail-like cartilage appears to curve under rump.	Rudimentary liver, gall bladder, stomach, intestines, pancreas, thyroid, and lungs created. Red blood cells are formed by yolk sac.	
Elbow, wrist regions, and paddle-shaped plate with ridges for future fingers take shape.	Heart differentiates into upper and lower regions.	
Embryo possesses short webbed fingers, and foot plate has also begun to differentiate. Many muscles differentiate and take final shape. Tail-like cartilage regresses.	Heart divides into four chambers.	Embryo begins to show reflexive responses to touch, first around the facial region. Spontaneous movements of head, trunk, and limbs becomes possible.
Bones start to grow. Fingernails, toenails, and hair follicles form.	Fetus begins to show differentiation of external reproductive organs (if male about 9th week, if female, several weeks later).	Startle and sucking responses first appear. Fetus displays hiccups, flexes arms and legs, and also displays some facial expressions.
Spinal cord begins to form. Fingerprints and footprints established. Fetus sprouts soft, downlike hair at the end of this period.	If female, large numbers of primitive egg cells are created.	Other reflexes, including swallowing, emerge. Begins to display long periods of active movement.
Fetus becomes covered by cheeselike, fatty material secreted by oil glands that probably protects the skin constantly bathed in amniotic fluid. Hair becomes visible.		Fetus often assumes a favorite position and displays sleep/wake cycles.
Skin appears wrinkled and has a pink to reddish cast caused by blood in capillaries, which are highly visible through translucent skin.	Lung functioning becomes possible but uncertain.	Fetus can see and hear and produces crying if born prematurely. Some indicators of stable states of sleep and wakefulness are exhibited.
Fat deposits accumulate beneath surface of skin to give fetus a much less wrinkled appearance. Hair may begin to grow on head, lungs are sufficiently developed to permit breathing of air should birth occur.	Red blood cells now produced by bone marrow.	
Fat continues to accumulate, giving full-term newborn chubby appearance and helping to insulate baby from varying temperatures once born. Skin color turns from red to pink to white to bluish pink for all babies regardless of racial makeup.		Seeing, hearing, and learning are now possible.

13–16 Weeks

17–20 Weeks

26–29 weeks

FIGURE 4.2
Decline in Neural Tube Defects Associated with the Increased Use of Folic Acid Supplements

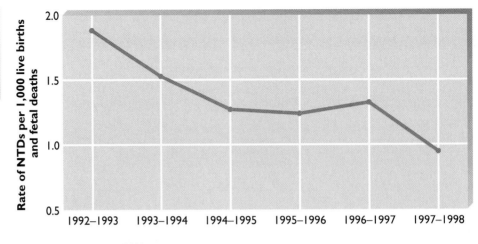

Source: Stevenson et al., 2000.

Some regions of the United States, including South Carolina, historically have shown relatively high rates of neural tube defects (NTDs) such as spina bifida and anencephaly. However, as shown here, those rates have dropped substantially in South Carolina since 1992. In fact, the rate is now close to that found throughout the United States. During this same period, the use of folic acid supplements by women in their childbearing years in South Carolina increased more than fourfold, a factor that very likely contributed to the substantial decline in neural tube defects.

One of the most striking milestones is reached about the sixth week after conception, when the nervous system begins to function. Now irregular and faint brain wave activity can be recorded. Soon, if the head or upper body is touched, the embryo exhibits reflex movements. In a few more weeks muscles may flex, but it will still be some time before the woman is able to feel any movement.

The Fetal Period

The change from embryo to fetus is signaled by the emergence of bone tissue at about the eighth week after conception. Organ differentiation continues, particularly in the reproductive system and the brain. However, the fetal period is best known for growth in size and the genesis of processes that assist organs and systems to function. One positive consequence is that the fetus becomes much less susceptible to many potentially damaging environmental factors.

During the third month after conception, the fetus increases to about three-and-a-half inches in length and about one-and-a-half ounces in weight. Its movements become more pronounced. At nine weeks, the fetus opens and closes its lips, wrinkles its forehead, raises and lowers its eyebrows, and turns its head. By the end of twelve weeks, the behaviors have become more coordinated. The fetus can, for example, display sucking and the basic motions of breathing and swallowing. Fingers will bend if the arm is touched, and the thumb can be opposed to fingers, an indication that peripheral muscles and nerves are functioning in increasingly sophisticated ways (Samuels & Samuels, 1986).

● **The Second Trimester**   In the second of the three trimesters into which prenatal development is sometimes divided, the fetus's body grows more rapidly than at any other time. By the end of the fourth month, the fetus is about eight to ten inches long, although it still weighs only about six ounces. During the sixth month, the fetus rapidly starts to gain weight, expanding to about one-and-a-half pounds and reaching a length of about fourteen inches.

By the middle of the second trimester, fetal movements known as *quickening* are unmistakable to the woman. The fetus stretches and squirms as well. Near the end of this trimester, brain wave patterns begin to look like those observed in the newborn. Should birth occur at this time, there is some chance of survival if specialized medical facilities are available.

● **The Third Trimester**   The final months add finishing touches to the astonishing progression in prenatal development. The cerebral hemispheres, the regions of the brain most heavily involved in complex mental processing, grow rapidly, folding and developing fissures to give them a wrinkled appearance. *Myelin,* which helps to insulate and speed the transmission of neuronal impulses, begins to form and surround some nerve fibers. Brain wave patterns indicating different stages of sleep and wakefulness can also be observed. The sense organs are developed sufficiently to enable the fetus to smell and taste, as well as to hear, see, feel, and even learn, as we show in the chapter titled "Basic Learning and Perception." The fetus continues to gain weight rapidly (nearly half a pound per week), although growth slows in the weeks just preceding birth. Control of body temperature and rhythmic respiratory activity remain problematic if birth occurs at the beginning of the third trimester. Nevertheless, **viability,** or the ability of the fetus to survive outside the womb, dramatically improves over the course of these three months.

The onset of birth can be expected when the fetus reaches a gestational age of about 277 days. **Gestational age,** commonly employed in the medical profession to gauge prenatal growth, is derived from the date of onset of the woman's last menstrual period before conception. This method of calculation makes the embryo or fetus about fifteen days older than determining age from the date of conception (Reece et al., 1995). However, as any parent knows, variability in the timing of birth is the norm. The average gestational period appears to be a few days shorter for Japanese and African American babies compared to Caucasian babies, for infants born to mothers younger than nineteen or older than thirty-four years, and for second and later children compared with firstborns (Mittendorf et al., 1990, 1993).

KEY THEME
Individual Differences

Assisted Reproduction

For many prospective parents, conceiving and having a baby proceeds as a normal part of the process of establishing a family. However, for many men and women the opportunities to become a parent are limited or require special consideration. For example, an estimated 5 to 6 million couples in the United States alone (Collins, 1995; Wright, 1998) have difficulty conceiving. Other couples who may be carriers of genetic diseases (see the chapter titled "Genetics and Heredity") wish to avoid the risk of passing these disorders to their offspring. For these couples, recent advances in the field of reproductive technology have opened up many alternatives in addition to adoption in their efforts to become parents; these advances also are dramatically affecting traditional notions about what it means to be a mother or father.

If a male is infertile or carries a genetic disorder, for example, couples may elect *artificial insemination by donor* (see Table 4.1). In this procedure, a donor, who is usually anonymous and is often selected because of similarity in physical and other characteristics to a prospective father, contributes sperm that are then artificially provided to the mother when ovulation occurs. If a female is infertile, a carrier of a genetic disease, or unable to complete a pregnancy for various reasons, options may include one or a combination of new reproductive technologies involving *fertility drugs, egg donation, in vitro fertilization (IVF), gamete intrafallopian transfer (GIFT), surrogacy,* or other, more experimental techniques currently under investigation. Surrogate motherhood has sometimes been termed the "renting" of another woman's womb, but this concept can be misleading because, in many cases, the surrogate mother may donate an egg for prenatal development, as well as her womb. The surrogate is thus the biological mother, as well as the bearer of the child who has been conceived by artificial insemination using the prospective father's sperm. Alternatively, with in vitro fertilization, eggs can be removed from a woman's ovaries, fertilized in a laboratory dish with the prospective father's sperm, and transferred to another woman's uterus. In this situation, the biological and social mothers may be one and the same except during the gestational period, when the surrogate mother's womb is used. Furthermore, a woman who cannot or chooses not to conceive in the traditional way might undergo in vitro fertilization and carry her own or another woman's fertilized egg during her pregnancy.

Legal, medical, and social controversies swirl around the technologies associated with assisted reproduction (Collins, 1995; Wright, 1998). For one thing, those who

viability Ability of the baby to survive outside the mother's womb.

gestational age Age of fetus derived from onset of mother's last menstrual period.

TABLE 4.1	Examples of New Technologies Associated with Assisted Reproduction
Artificial Insemination by Donor	Sperm from a donor (often anonymous) are artificially provided to a woman during ovulation.
Egg Donation	An egg is harvested from a donor, fertilized, and inserted in another woman's uterus.
Fertility Drugs	Drugs given to stimulate the development and release of egg cells from the ovary to increase the likelihood of conception by traditional means or to increase the harvest of eggs for other assisted reproduction technologies.
Gamete Intrafallopian Transfer (GIFT)	Surgical insertion of both sperm and eggs in the Fallopian tube, where fertilization normally occurs. Zygote intrafallopian transfer (ZIFT) is similar except that fertilization occurs in vitro and the zygote is inserted in the Fallopian tube.
In Vitro Fertilization (IVF)	Eggs harvested from the ovaries and fertilized in a petri dish for subsequent implantation into a woman's uterus.
Surrogacy	A contractual arrangement in which a woman carries a pregnancy to term and in which the pregnancy involves either the surrogate's egg and sperm donated by the father or a couple's zygote established through in vitro fertilization.

In vitro fertilization is one of several reproductive technologies that can assist men and women with fertility problems in their attempts to have healthy offspring. In this procedure, an egg cell is surgically removed from the woman's ovary to permit it to be fertilized by a sperm cell. After cell division begins, the zygote is inserted in the woman's uterus where it can implant and continue to grow. Prior to its insertion in the uterus, individual cells also can be tested to determine whether the zygote carries a hereditary defect.

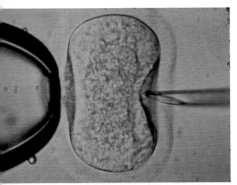

offer artificial insemination, apart from fertility clinics, are not always licensed, nor are they required to receive special training. Thus the competence of the practitioners, the safety of their various activities, and the frequency of this practice are unknown (Guinan, 1995). In addition, whereas adopted children are often informed of their status, children born as a result of new reproductive technologies may not know about their biological history. And even if told, for example, that their legal and biological fathers may be two different individuals, these offspring typically would be unable to obtain further information, because doctors who draw on sperm banks are not required to keep records linking donors and recipients (Guinan, 1995). In some other countries, however, such as England and Sweden, legislation has been enacted to permit individuals to obtain such information (Daniels & Taylor, 1993). Legal debates can also erupt over who is the rightful father or mother when, for example, a surrogate mother resolves to keep the child she has carried to term.

Medical concerns are linked to the use of fertility drugs because they increase the rate of multiple pregnancies perhaps to as much as 25 percent, compared with 1 or 2 percent in the general population without the use of such drugs (Wright, 1998). Multiple pregnancies, especially when they involve more than two fetuses, increase risks both to the woman and to her offspring. Evidence exists, too, that single children born to mothers who receive assisted reproduction, even with various factors such as maternal age controlled, tend to be of lower birth weight (Dhont et al., 1999; Tough et al., 2000). Controversies further extend to the costly medical procedures associated with assisted reproduction. Should insurance companies be mandated to pay expenses accompanying the repeated efforts often required to conceive (Collins, 1995)?

The desire to have their own children is a powerful motive for many couples. This is evident from the large number of fertility clinics—perhaps as many as three hundred operating in the United States alone and probably twenty or so more in Canada (Nemeth, 1997; Wright, 1998). In Western societies about one in every one hundred conceptions involving first-born children may be completed by means of in vitro fertilization (Van Balen, 1998). Studies conducted in Europe, the United States, and Taiwan reveal that children conceived by means of assisted reproduction show few emotional, behavioral, or other problems during their development (Hahn & DiPietro, 2001; Van Balen, 1998). For example, Susan Golombok and her colleagues (Golombok et al., 1995; Golombok, MacCallum, & Goodman, 2001; Golombok et al., 2002) have followed samples of children from the United Kingdom who were conceived by in vitro fertilization or donor insemination and who are now entering into adolescence. They found no differences between these children and children who were conceived without assistance on scales evaluating ability to function in school, peer relationships, or self-esteem. Parents, especially mothers, of these children are sometimes reported to display greater warmth and more concern than other parents, perhaps an indicator of their commitment to and the value they place on their children (Hahn & DiPietro, 2001). The general conclusion from research is that the risks to children born to parents who have been assisted in their reproductive efforts is low and that their development is similar to that found in the larger population of children.

FOR YOUR REVIEW

- What constitutes the prenatal, perinatal, and postnatal periods of development?

- What are the major changes that take place following conception during the germinal, embryonic, and fetal periods of prenatal development?

- What is an ectopic pregnancy? What factors may account for its increasing frequency in recent decades?

- When are the major organs and systems of the body established? What is the course of brain and nervous system development in the embryo and fetus?

- How can various kinds of assisted reproduction help those couples who have difficulty conceiving or are concerned about the inheritance of genetic disorders in their offspring? What are some of the medical and legal issues associated with various forms of assisted reproduction?

Environmental Factors Influencing Prenatal Development

We can readily imagine that a host of events must occur, and at the right times, for prenatal development to proceed normally. What kinds of environmental support do embryo and fetus receive in their liquid, somewhat buoyant, surroundings, and how well protected are they from intrusions that can disrupt their development?

Support Within the Womb

The embryo and fetus are sustained by a number of major structures, including the placenta, the umbilical cord, and the amniotic sac. The **placenta,** formed by cells from both the blastocyst and the uterine lining, produces essential hormones for the fetus. Just as important, it serves as the exchange site at which oxygen and nutrients are absorbed from the woman's circulatory system and carbon dioxide and waste products are excreted from the embryo's circulatory system (Cross, Werb, & Fisher, 1994). The transfer takes place via a network of intermingling blood-rich capillaries originating in the woman's and the fetus's circulatory systems. Thus blood is not normally exchanged between a woman and the fetus. Although blood cells are too large to cross the membranes separating the two systems, smaller molecules of oxygen, carbon dioxide, nutrients, and hormones can traverse the barrier. So can some chemicals, drugs, and diseases that interfere with fetal development, as we will see shortly.

The **umbilical cord** is the conduit to and from the placenta for the blood of the fetus. The fetus lives in the womb surrounded by the fluid-filled **amniotic sac.** Amniotic fluid helps to stabilize temperature, insulates the fetus from bumps and shocks, and contains substances necessary for the development of the lungs. The fluid is constantly recirculated and renewed as the fetus ingests nutrients and urinates.

placenta Support organ formed by cells from both blastocyst and uterine lining; serves as exchange site for oxygen, nutrients, and waste products.

umbilical cord Conduit of blood vessels through which oxygen, nutrients, and waste products are transported between placenta and embryo.

amniotic sac Fluid-filled, transparent protective membrane surrounding the fetus.

Principles of Teratology

Most fetuses negotiate the average thirty-eight-week period from conception to birth as healthy, vigorous newborns. Yet, as we discuss in the chapter titled "Genetics and Heredity," genetic factors can modify normal progress. So too can environmental factors. The study of disabilities and problems that arise from environmental influences during the prenatal period is called *teratology*. Environmental agents that cause disruptions in normal development are known as **teratogens.**

The fact that external agents can upset the course of prenatal development in humans was first appreciated in 1941 when McAllister Gregg, an ophthalmologist, confirmed that rubella, commonly called German measles, caused visual anomalies in the fetus. During this same decade, many infants born to women exposed to the atomic bomb were reported to have birth defects. This finding, along with studies involving animals, implicated radiation as a teratogen (Warkany & Schraffenberger, 1947). The import of these early observations became more fully appreciated when researchers documented that women who had taken a presumably harmless antinausea drug called *thalidomide* frequently bore infants with severe arm and leg malformations (McBride, 1961).

The widely publicized thalidomide tragedy made it abundantly clear that human embryos could be harmed seriously by environmental agents without adversely affecting the woman or others during postnatal development (Wilson, 1977). In fact, the embryo may be susceptible to virtually any substance if exposure to it is sufficiently concentrated (Samuels & Samuels, 1986). A number of broad generalizations have emerged from research on teratogens since the 1960s (Abel, 1989; Hanson, 1997; Vorhees, 1986). These principles help to explain the sometimes bewildering array of adverse consequences that specific drugs, diseases, and other agents can have on development.

■ *The Principle of Susceptibility: Individuals within species, as well as species themselves, show major differences in susceptibility to different teratogens.* Thalidomide provides a good example of this principle. Scientists knew that extremely large amounts of the drug caused abnormal fetal development in rats (Cohen, 1966). However, the doses given to pregnant women in Europe and Canada, where thalidomide was available as an over-the-counter preparation to reduce morning sickness and anxiety, were considerably smaller. For reasons unknown, the embryos of humans between twenty and thirty-five days after conception are extremely sensitive to small amounts of thalidomide. More than ten thousand babies were born without limbs or with limb defects and intellectual retardation. The genotype of an individual woman and her fetus may also affect susceptibility. Some fetuses were exposed to thalidomide during this sensitive period, yet at birth these babies showed no ill effects from the drug (Kajii, Kida, & Takahashi, 1973).

■ *The Principle of Critical or Sensitive Periods: The extent to which a teratogen affects the fetus depends on the stage of development during which exposure occurs.* Figure 4.3 shows that many human organs and systems are most sensitive to toxic agents during the third to eighth week after conception, when they are still being formed. However, vulnerability to teratogens exists throughout much of prenatal development. In fact, the brain continues to undergo substantial neural differentiation, migration, and growth during the second and third trimesters of pregnancy, as well as after birth. As a consequence, exposure to teratogens throughout prenatal development may have especially important behavioral consequences.

■ *The Principle of Access: The accessibility of a given teratogen to a fetus or an embryo influences the extent of its damage.* Many factors determine when and to what extent an embryo or a fetus is exposed to a teratogen. At one level, cultural and social practices may prevent or encourage a pregnant woman to use drugs, be inoculated for certain diseases, or become exposed to chemicals and other toxins. For example, use of cocaine may be socially approved in one segment of a culture and avoided in another. However, even when a teratogen is present, it must still gain ac-

KEY THEME
Nature/Nurture

KEY THEME
Individual Differences

KEY THEME
Continuity/Discontinuity

teratogen Any environmental agent that can cause deviations in prenatal development. Consequences may range from behavioral problems to death.

FIGURE 4.3 | Sensitive Periods in Prenatal Development

During prenatal development, organs and systems undergo periods in which they are more or less sensitive to teratogenic influences, environmental agents that can cause deviations in development. The potential for major structural defects (blue-colored sections) is usually greatest during the embryonic period, when many organs are forming. However, many regions of the body, including the central nervous system, continue to have some susceptibility to teratogens (yellow-colored sections) during the fetal period.

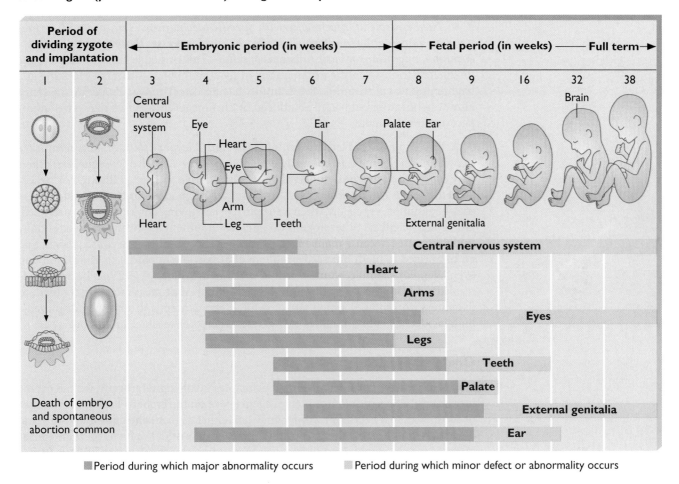

■ Period during which major abnormality occurs   ■ Period during which minor defect or abnormality occurs

Source: Moore & Persaud, 1998.

cess to the uterine environment, for example, by a woman inhaling, ingesting, or injecting a drug intravenously. How a woman has been exposed to the agent, the way she metabolizes it, and how it is transported to the womb influence whether a teratogen reaches a sufficient threshold to have some effect.

■ *The Principle of Dose-Response Relationships: The amount of exposure or dosage level of a given teratogen influences the extent of its damage.* The severity of a teratogen often is related to level of dosage. The more a woman smokes, for example, the greater the likelihood that her baby will be of low birth weight. The concentration of a toxic agent reaching the fetus, however, cannot always be determined from the woman's exposure to it. The severity of an illness a woman experiences, for example, from rubella, does not always predict the effect of the disease on the fetus.

■ *The Principle of Teratogenic Response: Teratogens do not show uniform effects on prenatal development.* Teratogens may cause death or disrupt development of specific organs and systems. They may also have behavioral consequences, impairing sensorimotor, cognitive, social, and emotional development. The principles of species and individual differences, as well as timing, duration, and intensity of exposure

KEY THEME
Sociocultural Influence

to the teratogen, govern the effect a specific teratogen will have on prenatal development. Alcohol, for example, can cause congenital defects during the embryonic period, but may interfere with prenatal weight gain and contribute to postnatal behavioral problems during the second and third trimesters of pregnancy (Abel, 1989). One other important implication of this principle is that very different teratogenic agents can produce a similar pattern of disabilities. Thus efforts to pinpoint why a baby was born with a given anomaly are not always successful.

■ *The Principle of Interference with Specific Mechanisms: Teratogens affect prenatal development by interfering with biochemical processes that regulate the differentiation, migration, or basic functions of cells.*   This principle helps to differentiate folk beliefs from scientific explanations of fetal anomalies. A woman's looking at a frightening visual stimulus, for example, has no direct consequence for the fetus. However, hormonal imbalances induced by chronic levels of stress may have an impact on development.

■ *The Principle of Developmental Delay and "Sleeper Effects": Some teratogens may delay development temporarily with no long-term negative consequences; others may cause developmental problems only late in development.*   Although some teratogenic effects can be observed at birth and are permanent and irreversible, others may be nullified, especially when a supportive caregiving environment is provided. However, the effects of teratogens on later development are probably substantially underestimated because many produce "sleeper effects." These are consequences that go unnoticed at birth but seed problems that become apparent in childhood and even later. For example, women treated with *diethylstilbestrol (DES)*, a hormone administered from the 1940s through the 1960s to prevent miscarriages, gave birth to daughters who showed a high rate of genital tract cancers and sons who displayed a high incidence of abnormalities of the testes when they reached adulthood.

Drugs as Teratogens

Now that we have considered general principles involving teratogens, we can examine the effects specific environmental agents have on the embryo or fetus. A number of substances that expectant women may use, either as medicine or as mood-altering devices, frequently become part of the intrauterine world. We focus on their consequences for embryonic and fetal development because the primary impact during the germinal stage is likely to be a disruption in implantation and thus the loss of the zygote.

KEY THEME
Sociocultural Influence

● **Alcohol**   Because alcohol readily crosses the placenta, its concentration in the fetus is likely to be similar to that in the woman (Abel, 1981). Moreover, because it lacks some enzymes to effectively degrade alcohol, the fetus may be exposed to it for a longer period of time (Reece et al., 1995). Among pregnant women in the Western world, alcohol is more widely used than any other teratogen and, according to some experts, is the single most frequent cause of mental retardation in industrialized countries (Reece et al., 1995). Although the percentage of pregnant women in the United States indicating that they consume alcohol began to decline in the late 1980s, that percentage now appears to be rising again (Ebrahim et al., 1998). Part of this upturn may stem from recent reports that alcohol, when taken in limited amounts, can have health benefits for adults. Moreover, the percentage of pregnant women who drink and who drink frequently is probably substantially greater in some other Western European nations (such as France and Italy) and in many countries around the world in which alcohol consumption is more generally accepted and in which concerns about its teratogenic effects are less extensively publicized.

Widespread recognition of the dangers of alcohol emerged in the early 1970s, when three sets of characteristics were observed in a number of babies of alcoholic women (Jones & Smith, 1973). They included prenatal and postnatal growth retardation, microcephaly, and abnormal facial features, and mental retardation and other behavioral problems, such as hyperactivity and poor motor coordination, suggestive of central nervous system dysfunction. This constellation of deficits, known as **fetal alcohol syndrome (FAS),** appears in as many as 6 percent of infants born to alcoholic mothers (Day & Richardson, 1994). *Alcohol-related neurodevelopmental disabilities* (ARND) have been identified in many other children prenatally exposed to alcohol. These children exhibit retardation or learning difficulties, along with other behavioral problems (Mattson et al., 1997; Stratton, Howe, & Battaglia, 1996). Perhaps as many as one in every one hundred births in the United States displays FAS or ARND (Sampson et al., 1997).

Binge drinking, usually identified as five or more drinks within a short time, even if it takes place infrequently, can be especially hazardous because it exposes the fetus to highly concentrated levels of alcohol (Chasnoff, 1986; Streissguth et al., 1994). However, even limited alcohol consumption, some researchers report, is linked to an increase in spontaneous abortions and to reduced alertness, less vigorous body activity, more tremors, and slower learning in newborns compared with babies of women who do not drink (Jacobson & Jacobson, 1996; Streissguth et al, 1994). Work by Anne Streissguth and her colleagues shows that prenatal exposure to relatively moderate amounts of alcohol contributes to measurable deficits in attention and school performance, small declines in IQ, and more frequent behavioral problems in children and adolescents (Bookstein et al., 1996; Streissguth et al., 1994; Streissguth et al., 1999). For example, these children and adolescents tended to be more impulsive and had difficulty organizing their work, especially under stress. Moreover, the tendency to display neurocognitive deficits was related to the amount of alcohol exposure prenatally, an example of the dose-related principle, and was especially evident when the expectant woman engaged in occasional binge drinking. Nevertheless, there was no clear threshold at which negative consequences began to appear. As a result, Streissguth et al. (1999) concluded that even small amounts of alcohol can be harmful.

How does alcohol produce such effects? One way is by directly modifying cell functioning, including cell differentiation, migration, and growth. Examination of infants with fetal alcohol syndrome who died shortly after birth reveals structural changes in the brain caused by delays and errors in the way neurons migrate to form the cortex, or outer layer, of the brain (Clarren et al., 1978). Greater alcohol consumption has also been linked to delayed growth of the frontal cotex (Wass, Persutte, & Hobbins, 2001). The metabolism of alcohol also requires substantial amounts of oxygen so less oxygen may be available for normal cell functions. These findings provide further justification for the recommendation of the American Academy of Pediatrics for complete abstinence during pregnancy because no "safe dose for alcohol has been established" (American Academy of Pediatrics, 1993).

● **Cigarette Smoking** About 13 percent of women in the United States smoke during pregnancy, a percentage that has been declining in recent years (Hoyert et al., 2001). The percentage is higher among Caucasian (15 percent) and African American women (10 percent) than among Hispanic women (5 percent). It may also be far higher in other countries in which less effort has been directed at publicizing the negative health consequences of smoking.

No evidence exists to indicate that smoking during pregnancy causes major congenital defects. However, nicotine and some other of the more than twenty-five hundred chemicals found in tobacco smoke (American College of Obstetricians, 1994) do have serious consequences for fetal and infant mortality, birth weight, and possibly postnatal development. Spontaneous abortions, stillbirths, and neonatal deaths increase in pregnant women who smoke (Streissguth et al., 1994). The most consistent finding from studies of babies born to smokers compared with nonsmokers, however, is their smaller size (Ernst, Moolchan, & Robinson, 2001; Secker-Walker et al., 1997). The more and the longer a woman smokes during pregnancy, the lower her baby's average weight at birth, even when equated for length of gestation, because babies of women who smoke are also likely to be born a few days early (Pollard, 2000; Shah & Bracken, 2000). Babies of women who smoke ten to twenty cigarettes a day

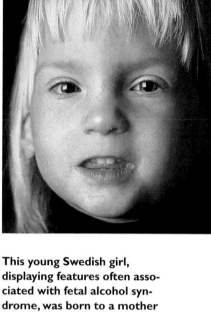

This young Swedish girl, displaying features often associated with fetal alcohol syndrome, was born to a mother who was alcoholic. Physical characteristics, including microcephaly (small head size), eyes widely set apart, and flat thin upper lip are often accompanied by delayed physical growth and mental retardation.

fetal alcohol syndrome (FAS) Cluster of fetal abnormalities stemming from mother's consumption of alcohol; includes growth retardation, defects in facial features, and intellectual retardation.

weigh an average of nearly three hundred grams (about ten ounces) less than other babies.

As with alcohol consumption, a reduction in oxygen may account for the effects. Smoking increases carbon monoxide, which displaces oxygen, in the red blood cells of both woman and fetus. Nicotine also reduces blood flow to the placenta. Moreover, a fetus's heart rate goes up when a woman smokes, a reaction that may be designed to maintain adequate oxygen (Samuels & Samuels, 1986). Babies of women who use tobacco have larger placentas and more frequent placental abnormalities than babies of the same weight born to nonsmoking women (Meyer & Tonascia, 1977; Weinberger & Weiss, 1988). Nicotine may also interfere with metabolic activity important to cell regulation and differentiation.

KEY THEME
Individual Differences

The long-term behavioral consequences of prenatal exposure to smoke are less well understood (Ernst et al., 2001). Some researchers have failed to find evidence of poorer performance on cognitive, academic, or other tasks for children exposed to smoke prenatally. However, other researchers have reported that infants born to smokers display poorer learning (Martin et al., 1977), a higher-pitched cry (Nugent et al., 1996), and reduced visual and auditory alertness (Franco et al., 1999; Landesman-Dwyer, Keller, & Streissguth, 1978). Moreover, studies carried out in the United States, the Netherlands, and New Zealand reveal a small but significant increase in behavioral problems in children and adolescents whose mothers smoked during pregnancy (Fergusson, Woodward, & Horwood, 1998; Orlebeke, Knol, & Verhulst, 1999; Weitzman, Gortmaker, & Sobel, 1992). Although efforts to control other factors potentially contributing to these observations have often been undertaken, genetic, family differences, continued passive exposure to smoke from a caregiver or others in the family, and transmission of smoking-related substances during breastfeeding cannot be eliminated as possible causal contributors to these outcomes (Becker et al., 1999; American Academy of Pediatrics Committee on Drugs, 2001; Orlebeke et al., 1999). For example, passive exposure to environmental tobacco smoke created by others in the child's household is associated with significantly increased health risks such as sudden infant death (see the chapter titled "Brain, Motor Skill, and Physical Development") and other respiratory problems (American Academy of Pediatrics Committee on Environmental Health, 1997; Brown, 2001).

● **Prescription and Over-the-Counter Drugs**   Legal drugs in addition to alcohol and tobacco can be hazardous for fetal development. Some are known teratogens (see Table 4.2), but knowledge of the effects of many remains perilously limited. Aspirin, for example, has been demonstrated to impair behavioral competence in the offspring of lower animals. One well-controlled study found that aspirin may also be associated with lower IQ in early childhood (Streissguth et al., 1984). Certainly large doses of aspirin, but also alternative pain relievers such as acetaminophen, may increase risk to the fetus (Reece et al., 1995).

Caffeine too has been implicated in birth defects in animals, although studies have failed to reveal any consistent link in humans. However, babies born to mothers who consume higher amounts of caffeine tend to have lower birth weight than babies of mothers who drink less coffee (Eskenazi et al, 1999). Caffeine also has a behavioral impact on the fetus. Lawrence Devoe and his colleagues (1993) used ultrasound to record biweekly two-hour observations of fetal activity during the final ten weeks of pregnancy in ten heavy caffeine consumers (>500 milligrams, or five cups of coffee, daily) and ten low caffeine consumers (<200 milligrams, or two cups of coffee, daily). Fetuses exhibited considerably more arousal (defined by irregular heart rate and breathing activity, frequent body movements, and rapid eye movements) when exposed to the higher amounts of caffeine. The more highly aroused infants may have consumed more energy, a factor that could contribute to their lower birth weight. However, the long-term implications of this difference in activity remain unknown.

KEY THEME
Individual Differences

Perhaps an even greater concern is the number of prescription and over-the-counter drugs consumed during pregnancy. Most expectant women use at least one medication, and the average is more than three (Buitendijk & Bracken, 1991). Little is

TABLE 4.2	Prescription and Other Frequently Used Drugs and Their Effects on Prenatal Development
Drug	**Description and Known or Suspected Effects**
Alcohol	See text.
Amniopterin	Anticancer agent. Facial defects and a number of other congenital malformations as well as mental retardation (Hanson, 1997).
Amphetamines	Stimulants for the central nervous system, some types frequently used for weight control. Readily cross placental barrier. Fetal intrauterine growth retardation often reported but may be a result of accompanying malnutrition or multiple-drug use. Increased amounts and duration of exposure prenatally found to be correlated with aggressive behavior in 8-year-olds (Billing et al., 1994).
Antibiotics (streptomycin, tetracycline)	Streptomycin associated with hearing loss. Tetracycline associated with staining of baby's teeth if exposure occurs during second or third trimester (Friedman & Polifka, 1996).
Aspirin	Possibility of increased bleeding in both mother and infant (Hanson, 1997). See text for other complications that can arise.
Barbiturates (pentobarbital, pheno-barbital, secobarbital)	Sedatives and anxiety reducers. Considerable evidence of neurobiological and behavioral complications in rats. Readily cross human placenta; concentrations in fetus may be greater than in woman. Newborns may show withdrawal symptoms (Friedman & Polifka, 1996). No consistent evidence of long-term effects in humans.
Benzodiazepines (chlor-diazepoxide, diazepam)	Tranquilizers. Not shown to have teratogenic effects although newborns may display withdrawal symptoms with diazepam (Friedman & Polifka, 1996).
Caffeine	See text.
Hydantoins (Anticonvulsants)	Treatment for epilepsy. Produce *fetal hydantoin syndrome*, including heart defects, cleft lip or palate, decreased head size, and mental retardation. Controversy continues over whether effects are entirely caused by drug or by conditions associated with the mother, including her epilepsy (Hanson, 1986).
Lithium	Treatment for bipolar disorder. Crosses placenta freely. Known to be teratogenic in premammalian animals. Strong suggestive evidence of increased cardiovascular defects in human infants. Behavioral effects unknown. Administration at time of delivery markedly reduces infant responsivity (Friedman & Polifka, 1996).
Retinoids	Antiacne medicine. Effects similar to large amounts of vitamin A.
Sex Hormones (androgens, estrogens, progestins)	Contained in birth control pills, fertility drugs, and other drugs to prevent miscarriages. Continued use of birth control pills during pregnancy associated with heart and circulatory disorders. Behavioral and personality implications suspected. Masculinization of female embryo from exposure to high doses of androgens or progestins.
Thalidomide	Reduces morning sickness and anxiety. Deformities of the limbs, depending on time of exposure, often accompanied by mental retardation (Friedman & Polifka, 1996).
Tobacco	See text.
Tricyclics (imipramine, desimipramine)	Antidepressants. Some tricyclics cross the placenta. Studies with rats reveal developmental and behavioral disturbances. Studies with humans reveal no consistent findings (Friedman & Polifka, 1996).
Vitamins	Large amounts of vitamin A known to cause major birth defects. Excessive amounts of other vitamins may also cause prenatal malformations (Reece et al., 1995).

Note: This listing is not meant to be exhaustive, and other drugs may have teratogenic effects. No drug should be taken during pregnancy without consultation with a qualified physician.

known about the effects of many of these products, and even less is known about the interactive consequences when multiple drugs are used. For these reasons expectant women are often advised to take *no* drugs during pregnancy, including over-the-counter remedies, or to take them only under the close supervision of their physicians.

● **Illegal Drugs**   The effects of illegal drugs such as marijuana, heroin, and cocaine on prenatal development are even more difficult to untangle than the effects of prescription and over-the-counter medications. Drug users are rarely certain of the contents or concentrations of the drugs they consume. Wide variation in frequency of use, the possibility of interactions from exposure to multiple drugs, poor nutritional status, inadequate or no prenatal care, and potential psychological and physiological differences both before and after taking such drugs compound the problem of isolating their teratogenic effects. The lifestyles of many illegal-drug users can be described as essentially chaotic (Chasnoff, 1992), so that conclusions about the impact of the drug itself are often difficult to make.

Research with animals has shown that the psychoactive ingredients associated with marijuana cross the placenta and are stored in the amniotic fluid (Harbison & Mantilla-Plata, 1972). They may also be transferred postnatally through the mother's milk (Dalterio & Bartke, 1979). Still, efforts to determine the effects of marijuana on the human fetus and postnatal development reveal few consistent findings (Zuckerman & Bresnahan, 1991). As with tobacco, fetal weight and size appear to be reduced. Length of gestation may also be shorter for heavy marijuana users, a finding consistent with giving marijuana to speed labor, a practice carried out at one time in Europe.

A higher pitched cry, visual problems, lower scores on memory and verbal tasks, and more restless sleep patterns in early childhood are reported with prenatal exposure to marijuana (Dahl et al., 1995; Fried, Watkinson, & Gray, 1998; Lester & Dreher, 1989). However, social and economic differences in the backgrounds of the children could account for these findings. In fact, in some cultures, such as Jamaica, marijuana use correlates positively with neonatal test performance (Dreher, Nugent, & Hudgins, 1994).

The effects of heroin and morphine became a public concern as early as the late 1800s when doctors reported withdrawal symptoms in newborns whose mothers used these substances (Zagon & McLaughlin, 1984). By the early 1900s, heroin and morphine were known to be transmitted through the placenta, as well as through the mother's milk. Today an estimated nine thousand infants born in the United States each year are exposed to heroin or *methadone,* a pharmacologically similar product (Sprauve, 1996). Often given under regulated conditions as a heroin substitute, methadone's effects on fetal development are just as powerful as heroin's. So, too, may be the effects of a newer synthetic form of heroin, OxyContin, a prescribed pain killer that has recently achieved the status of a widely sought after street drug.

Although congenital defects have not been positively linked to heroin and methadone, stillbirths and infant deaths are more frequent and lower birth weight is common (American College of Obstetricians and Gynecologists, 1994). About 60 to 70 percent of infants born to heroin- and methadone-addicted women also undergo withdrawal symptoms such as diarrhea, sweating, a distinctive high-pitched cry, tremors, and irritability (Sprauve, 1996). Developmental difficulties continue to be observed in infants and children exposed to heroin and methadone. However, high quality caregiving can play a powerful role in lessening the negative impact of prenatal exposure to heroin in children, at least for those who do not experience neurological damage (Orney et al., 1996).

Each year in the United States alone, more than 200,000 infants are estimated to be born to mothers who use illegal drugs (National Institute on Drug Abuse, 1995). However, probably none of these drugs has received more widespread attention than cocaine. Cocaine in its many forms—including *crack,* an especially potent and addictive variation—readily crosses the placenta. Once it reaches the fetus, it stays longer than in adults because the immature organs of the fetus have difficulty breaking it down. Cocaine also can continue to influence the baby after birth through the mother's milk.

KEY THEME
Individual Differences

KEY THEME
Sociocultural Influence

Dire effects for the fetus and subsequently for postnatal development as a result of exposure to cocaine have been widely publicized (Chavkin, 2001; Frank et al., 2001). Indeed, evidence exists that cocaine may be associated with premature and low birth weight (Bendersky & Lewis, 1999), as well as attentional, motor, and some early neurobehavioral difficulties (Eyler et al., 1998; Fried et al., 1998; Singer, Arendt, et al., 1999; Stanwood & Levitt, 2001). However, these observed relationships often can be explained by other factors known to interfere with development. In fact, a recent detailed review of the results of a number of well-controlled studies by Deborah Frank and her colleagues concluded that exposure to cocaine for those undergoing a normal gestational period is *not* a factor that leads to poor physical growth or delayed acquisition of motor skills, lowered cognitive abilities, or behavioral, attentional, or affective disturbances in young children (Frank et al., 2001).

The primary position of Deborah Frank and her colleagues, and a common thread of agreement emerging among researchers, is that other risk factors regularly associated with the use of cocaine—such as increased exposure to tobacco and alcohol, poor nutrition, diminished parental responsiveness, abuse and neglect, social isolation of the family, and the increased stress typically accompanying poverty—play a *far more important* role in negative outcomes for development during early childhood than does cocaine itself (Bendersky & Lewis, 1999; Frank et al., 2001; Miller & Boudreaux, 1999). Thus the prognosis for children subjected to cocaine and other illegal drugs in utero should and does improve substantially when interventions are undertaken to reduce or eliminate these other risk factors (Butz et al., 2001; Field et al., 1998; Kilbride et al., 2000). In other words, although the potential for negative consequences of prenatal exposure to cocaine cannot be ruled out, intervention at other levels appears to be the key to improving the developmental outlook for children exposed to this and other drugs. So, too, may be the need to educate the public, as well as professionals, about the known consequences of exposure to cocaine for development.

Nancy Stewart Woods and her colleagues (Stewart Woods et al., 1998) asked college students to rate a videotape of infants who were described as having been exposed to cocaine. Their assessments of the infants were significantly more negative than assessments of these same infants not described as cocaine-exposed. Perhaps the heavily promoted image of alarming consequences for development as a result of exposure to cocaine needs to be brought into greater accord with recent research findings in order to prevent the potential self-fulfilling prophecy of continued difficulties for such children.

Because prenatal development is so closely tied to the intrauterine environment, little research has been conducted on the father's abuse of drugs or other teratogens and their effects on the fetus. Studies with lower animals, and some with humans, suggest that the sperm of men who consume alcohol or use cocaine or other drugs may carry toxic substances that can disrupt normal prenatal development (Yazigi, Odem, & Polakoski, 1991). However, the woman is regularly assigned far greater responsibility for prenatal events, as the following controversy reveals.

CONTROVERSY: THINKING IT OVER

Should a Drug-Abusing Expectant Woman Be Charged with Child Abuse?

Consider the circumstances surrounding the prosecution of Cornelia Whitner of South Carolina. Her son was born with cocaine in his system. In 1992 Cornelia pled guilty to a charge of child neglect after admitting to the use of cocaine in her third trimester of pregnancy. She was sentenced to eight years in prison.

What Is the Controversy?

Although the conviction of Cornelia Whitner has since been overturned, the issues surrounding this and similar cases deeply divide law enforcement, medical, and social service agencies in the United States, Canada, and many Western European countries (Capron, 1998; Peak & Del Papa, 1993). Since the mid-1980s, more than two hundred American women in thirty states have been prosecuted on charges of child abuse and neglect, delivery of drugs to a minor, or assault with a deadly weapon for allegedly harming their offspring through prenatal exposure to cocaine or other illegal drugs (Paltrow et al., 2000). Court cases with policy implications for whether a woman can or should be arrested if she exposes a fetus to illegal drugs are continuing to be debated at the highest judicial levels including the Supreme Court in the United States (Greenhouse, 2000; Paltrow et al., 2000). Is this an effective way to reduce the likelihood of drug use and any of its accompanying risks for the fetus?

What Are the Opposing Arguments?

Some say a concerned society should impose criminal or other charges on a pregnant woman who uses a drug that may be dangerous to the fetus. A number of jurisdictions in the United States and provinces in Canada have implemented laws permitting a newborn to be removed from a parent on the grounds of child abuse or neglect because of drug exposure during pregnancy. In some cases, the woman has been ordered to be confined to a drug-treatment facility during pregnancy. After all, anyone found to provide such illegal substances to a child would certainly expect to face criminal or other charges. Are the circumstances that much different in the case of a pregnant woman and her fetus?

Others believe the situation is vastly different and further claim that criminal charges, imprisonment, or mandatory treatment are counterproductive (Beckett, 1995; Farr, 1995). Legislation specifically targeted to pregnant drug users might actually drive prospective mothers, out of fear of being prosecuted, away from the care and treatment needed for both themselves and their fetuses. Moreover, the tendency to rely on criminal procedures could limit the resources available for the implementation of innovative, well-funded public health efforts for treating addiction and its consequences for the fetus (Chavkin, 2001).

What Answers Exist? What Questions Remain?

At the present time no research has been carried out on whether threats of criminal procedures or other forms of punishment dissuade a woman from using drugs during her pregnancy. If studies with this or other populations demonstrate that these kinds of actions are effective in reducing drug use, perhaps greater justification would exist for the extension of this approach to expectant women. But given the recent findings that the negative consequences for the fetus often stem less from the illegal drugs themselves than from the myriad of other factors that are associated with drug use, would such actions be helpful? In other words, are poor nutrition and a host of other social and economic factors, as well as the chaotic lifestyle that often accompanies drug use and over which a woman may not always have control, the primary culprits in impaired fetal development? If so, then intervention must take place at the public health level. And do your views about how to address this issue change given that alcohol and tobacco have been shown to have more serious consequences for fetal development than many illegal drugs (Bendersky & Lewis, 1999; Frank et al., 2001; Miller & Boudreaux, 1999; Streissguth et al., 1999)? If laws are introduced to protect the fetus from illegal drugs, should these laws not also be extended and applied to those who use readily available, heavily advertised, and common drugs that are known to have even more serious teratogenic effects? Research has begun to shed light on some of these issues by providing knowledge about the effects of exposure to drugs on fetal development. What other kinds of developmental research would be useful in helping to resolve these competing views? Are there alternatives that might be proposed to help solve a very complex problem, that of ensuring an optimal start for every child at birth?

Diseases as Teratogens

Somewhere between 2 and 8 percent of babies born to American women are exposed to one or more diseases or other forms of illness during pregnancy (Saltzman & Jordan, 1988). Fortunately, most babies are unaffected. Moreover, significant progress has been made in eliminating the potential negative fetal consequences of several diseases, such as mumps and rubella (German measles), at least in some countries. Unfortunately, rubella, for example, a highly preventable illness, continues to be a major cause of fetal malformations and death worldwide because vaccination programs are limited in some regions of the world. Other diseases, some of which are described in Table 4.3, continue to pose risks for the fetus in even the most medically advanced countries. Their impact on the fetus can be serious, sometimes devastating, even when a woman is completely unaware of illness.

● **Toxoplasmosis** Toxoplasmosis is caused by a parasite found in many mammals and birds. Twenty to 40 percent of adults in the United States and Great Britain have been exposed to it (Feldman, 1982; Peckham & Logan, 1993). However, the disease is found with greater frequency in some European countries, including France and Austria, and in tropical regions. An unusual aspect of the parasite is that part of its life cycle can be completed only in cats. Humans occasionally contract the disease by touching cat feces containing the parasite or, even more frequently, by eating raw or partially infected cooked meat, especially pork and lamb. Children and adults are often unaware of their exposure, because the infection may have no symptoms or cause only a minor fever or rash.

Infections early in pregnancy can have devastating consequences; fortunately, risk of transmission to the fetus at this time is lowest (Foulon et al., 1999). Growth retardation, jaundice, accumulation of fluid in the brain, and visual and central nervous system damage are the most frequent teratogenic outcomes. Some infants show no symptoms at birth; only later may mental retardation, neuromuscular abnormalities, impaired vision, and other eye problems become apparent. Research carried out in Europe indicates that early treatment with antibiotics can help to reduce some of its more devastating consequences (Foulon et al., 1999).

● **Cytomegalovirus** Cytomegalovirus (CMV), a member of the herpes family of viruses, causes swelling of the salivary glands and mononucleosis-like symptoms in adults. It is the single most frequent infection found in newborns today, affecting one to two of every one hundred babies. As many as 10 percent of infected infants can be expected to sustain some congenital damage (Demmler, 1991). No effective treatment exists.

CMV is most frequently reported in Asia and Africa and among lower socioeconomic groups, in which up to 85 percent of the population may be infected. Yet 45 to 55 percent of middle- and high-income groups in Europe and the United States are infected as well (Hagay et al., 1996). Transmission occurs through various body fluids. CMV can be passed easily between children playing together, for example, in daycare centers and in family daycare settings (Bale et al., 1999) and from child to adult through physical contact.

Fortunately, the aftermath of contracting the virus in early childhood is generally not serious. Infection can occur within the womb, during birth, and through breastfeeding with more severe consequences (Adler, 1992; Stagno & Cloud, 1994). The negative outcomes are typically greatest for the fetus if a woman contracts the disease for the first time during her pregnancy (Guerra et al., 2000). For example, growth retardation, jaundice, skin disorders, and small head size are common consequences. About one-third of infants showing these characteristics at birth will die in early infancy; a large percentage of those who survive will be mentally retarded. About half of infants sustaining congenital damage from CMV show no symptoms at birth, but many will subsequently display progressive loss of hearing or other,

KEY THEME
Sociocultural Influence

TABLE 4.3	Diseases and Maternal Conditions That May Affect Prenatal Development
Disease	**Physical and Behavioral Consequences for the Fetus**
Sexually Transmitted Diseases	
Acquired Immunodeficiency Syndrome (AIDS)	See text.
Chlamydia	Nearly always transmitted to infant during delivery via infected birth canal. Estimated 100,000 (of 155,000 exposed in the United States) become infected. Often causes eye infection in infant and some increased risk of pneumonia. Other adverse effects suspected (McGregor & French, 1991).
Gonorrhea	If acquired prenatally, may cause premature birth (Reece et al., 1995). Most frequently contracted during delivery through infected birth canal and may then attack eyes. In the United States and many other countries, silver nitrate eye drops are administered to all newborns to prevent blindness.
Hepatitis B	Associated with premature birth, low birth weight, increased neonatal death, and liver disorders (Pass, 1987). Most frequently contracted during delivery through birth canal or postnatally.
Herpes Simplex	Of its two forms, only one is transmitted primarily through sexual activity. Both forms, however, can be transmitted to the fetus, causing severe damage to the central nervous system (Pass, 1987). Most infections occur during delivery through birth canal containing active herpes lesions. The majority of infants will die or suffer central nervous system damage (Nahmias, Keyserling, & Kernick, 1983). If known to carry the virus, women may need to be tested frequently during pregnancy to determine if the disease is in its active, contagious state because symptoms may not be present even when active. If the disease is active, cesarean delivery is used to avoid infecting the baby.
Syphilis	Damage to fetus does not begin until about 18 weeks after conception. May then cause death, mental retardation, and other congenital defects (Reece et al., 1995). Infected newborns may not show signs of disease until early childhood.
Other Diseases	
Cytomegalovirus	See text.
Influenza	Some forms linked to increased heart and central nervous system abnormalities, as well as spontaneous abortions (Reece et al., 1995).
Mumps	Increased risk of spontaneous abortion and stillbirth.
Rubella	Increased risk of spontaneous abortion and stillbirth. Growth retardation, cataracts, hearing impairment, heart defects, mental retardation also common and especially if exposure occurs in the first or second month of pregnancy.
Toxoplasmosis	See text.
Varicella-zoster (chicken pox)	Skin and muscle defects, intrauterine growth retardation, limb reduction.
Other Maternal Conditions	
Diabetes	Risk of congenital malformations and death to fetus two to three times higher than for babies born to nondiabetic women (Coustan & Felig, 1988). Excessive size at birth also common. Effects are likely to be a consequence of metabolic disturbances rather than of insulin. Rapid advances in care have helped reduce risks substantially for diabetic women.
Hypertension (chronic)	Probability of miscarriage or infant death increased.
Obesity	Increased risk of diabetes and large-for-gestational-age babies (Lu et al., 2001).

TABLE 4.3	Diseases and Maternal Conditions That May Affect Prenatal Development *(continued)*
Disease	**Physical and Behavioral Consequences for the Fetus**
Other Maternal Conditions (continued)	
Pregnancy-Induced Hypertension	5%–10% of expectant women experience significant increase in blood pressure, often accompanied by *edema* (swelling of face and extremities as a result of water retention), rapid weight gain, and protein in urine during later months of pregnancy. Condition is also known as *pre-eclampsia* (or *eclampsia,* if severe) and *toxemia.* Under severe conditions, woman may suffer seizures and coma. The fetus is at increased risk for death, brain damage, and lower birth weight. Adequate protein consumption helps minimize problems. Drugs used to treat high blood pressure may be just as hazardous to fetus as the condition itself.
Rh Incompatibility	Blood containing a certain protein is Rh positive, Rh negative if it lacks that protein. Hereditary factors determine which type the individual possesses. If fetus's blood is Rh positive, it can cause formation of antibodies in blood of woman who is Rh negative. These antibodies can cross the placental barrier to destroy red blood cells of fetus. May result in miscarriage or stillbirth, jaundice, anemia, heart defects, and mental retardation. Likelihood of birth defects increases with succeeding pregnancies because antibodies are usually not present until after birth of first Rh-positive child. A vaccine (Rhogam) can be administered to the mother within 3 days after childbirth, miscarriage, or abortion to prevent antibody formation.

subtler defects, including minimal brain dysfunction, visual or dental abnormalities, or motor and neural problems (Pass, 1987; Saltzman & Jordan, 1988).

● **Sexually Transmitted and Other Diseases**   Several diseases identified as teratogenic are transmitted primarily through sexual contact, or the infection and its symptoms are usually concentrated in the genitourinary tract (see Table 4.3). Syphilis and certain strains of herpes simplex, for example, are virtually always contracted from infected sexual partners. On the other hand, some diseases, such as acquired immunodeficiency syndrome (AIDS) and hepatitis B, can be acquired through exposure to infected blood as well.

Sexually transmitted diseases (STDs) can interfere with reproduction in a number of ways. They may compromise the woman's health (AIDS, gonorrhea, hepatitis B, herpes simplex, syphilis), scar or disturb reproductive organs so that conception and normal pregnancy cannot proceed (chlamydia, gonorrhea), directly infect the fetus (AIDS, herpes simplex, syphilis), and interfere with healthy postnatal development (AIDS, hepatitis B, herpes simplex, syphilis) (Lee, 1988). In recent years, their frequency has risen rapidly in populations around the world. None, however, has had as dramatic an impact as AIDS.

Of the estimated 16,000 children having human immunodeficiency virus type 1 (HIV) in the United States and the more than 1.1 million children currently living with the disease worldwide, most were infected prenatally, during birth, or shortly after birth through an infected mother's breast milk (Burgess, 2001; Lindegren, Steinberg, & Byers, 2000). Prior to 1995, about 25 percent of infants born to HIV-positive women could be expected to eventually acquire AIDS. However, as can be seen in Figure 4.4, new medical treatments have reduced the transmission rate by more than one-third, at least in countries in which expensive drugs such as zidovudine are available (Lindegren et al., 2000).

Of those infants who do become infected with HIV, about 20 percent show rapid progression to AIDS and death in early childhood. However, with new advances in treatment, about two-thirds live more than five years; the average length of survival in Western countries is now greater than nine years; and about 25 percent of children do not show severe symptoms of AIDS until after ten years (Barnhart et al., 1996; Brown, Lourie, & Pao, 2000; European Collaborative Study, 2001). Children

FIGURE 4.4
Decline in HIV/AIDS
Transmitted to Offspring
Via HIV-Infected Women

The transmission of HIV/AIDS infection to infants and children via HIV-infected women has declined dramatically in the United States in recent years. The data from thirty-two reporting states reveal that introducing treatment with zidovudine (represented by the shaded bars as the percentage of women receiving treatment with the drug) has been an important factor in reducing the number of cases of infants and children reported with HIV/AIDS. Unfortunately, about 90% of the approximately 1.1 million children around the world with HIV/AIDS are born in sub-Saharan Africa, where this method of treatment is often too expensive or unavailable.

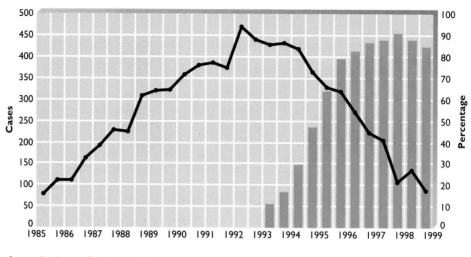

Source: Lindegren, Steinberg, & Byers, 2000.

KEY THEME
Nature/Nurture

receiving medication for HIV also show substantial benefits in terms of maintaining more normal levels of cognitive functioning throughout much of their childhood (Brown et al., 2000). Thus the negative course of the disease can be slowed for cognitive and other aspects of development (Tardieu et al., 1995). Unfortunately, however, for many children around the world, limited medical services, poverty, and the absence of social support will adversely affect their development while living with the disease.

Environmental Hazards as Teratogens

Radiation was one of the earliest confirmed teratogens, and it can cause genetic mutation as well. Radiation's effects include spontaneous abortion, small head size, and other defects associated with the skeleton, genitals, and sensory organs. Even low doses of radiation have been linked to increased risks of cancer and neural damage; pregnant women are urged to avoid unnecessary x-rays and other circumstances in which exposure might occur.

Chemicals and other elements in the environment pose another significant source of potential risks. Known teratogens include lead, mercury, and polychlorinated biphenyls or PCBs (a synthetic hydrocarbon once used in transformers, hydraulic fluids, and other industrial equipment), as well as many elements found in paints, dyes and coloring agents, solvents, oven cleaners, pesticides, herbicides, food additives, artificial sweeteners, and cosmetic products (cf. Needleman & Bellinger, 1994). Careless handling and disposal of such elements and their excessive production and use—they pervade the foods we eat and the air we breathe—are one problem. In addition, many women of childbearing age are exposed to hazardous substances in the workplace (see Table 4.4).

Women's Conditions and Prenatal Development

In addition to teratogens, a number of health conditions are associated with increased risk during pregnancy. Several of these conditions (diabetes, pregnancy-induced and chronic hypertension, Rh incompatibility) and their consequences for the fetus are summarized in Table 4.3. Additional factors influencing the prenatal environment include the age of the woman, her nutritional status, and her emotional state.

TABLE 4.4	Occupational Hazards for Women of Childbearing Age
Occupation	**Hazardous Substances**
Cleaning personnel	Soaps, detergents, solvents
Electronic assemblers	Lead, tin, antimony, trichloroethylene, methyl chloride, resins
Hairdressers and cosmetologists	Hair-spray resins, aerosol propellants, solvents, dyes
Health personnel	Anesthetic gases, x-rays, laboratory chemicals
Painters	Lead, titanium, toluene
Photographic processors	Caustics, bromides, iodides, silver nitrate
Plastic workers	Formaldehyde, vinyl chloride
Printing personnel	Ink mists, methanol, carbon tetrachloride, lead, solvents, trichloroethylene
Textile and garment workers	Formaldehyde, dyes, asbestos, solvents, flame retardants
Transportation personnel	Carbon monoxide, lead

Source: Adapted from Samuels & Bennett, 1983.

● **Age**   The number of older mothers is on the rise in industrialized countries as women postpone pregnancy to establish careers or for other reasons. Is pregnancy riskier as women become older? As we show in the chapter titled "Genetics and Heredity," the likelihood of having a child with Down syndrome increases markedly during the later childbearing years, especially after age thirty-five. Some studies also report increased prematurity, mortality, and greater difficulty during labor for women over thirty-five having their first child (Gilbert, Nesbitt, & Danielsen, 1999; Reece et al., 1995). The findings are likely due, in large part, to greater health-related problems (hypertension, diabetes, and others) that can accompany increased age. Despite these elevated risks, healthy women older than thirty-five routinely deliver healthy infants, just as do women between twenty and thirty-five years of age.

Teenagers, on the other hand, may be at considerably greater risk for delivering less healthy babies (McAnarney, 1987). Lack of adequate prenatal care is one reason; pregnant teenagers in the United States, particularly those who are very young and unmarried, often do not seek medical services. Another reason pregnancy at these early ages poses more problems is the complicated nutritional needs of adolescents; many teenagers are still growing themselves. Although the rate of births to teenagers has declined steadily throughout the 1990s in the United States (Hoyert et al., 2001), it is still substantially higher than in other industrialized nations and double or even triple those of most Western European countries. In any given year, about one in twenty-five teenagers is likely to bear a child; over 90 percent of the nearly 500,000 births to teenagers each year will be to unmarried teens (Children's Defense Fund, 2001).

● **Nutrition**   What foods are needed for the health of the woman and her fetus? The seemingly obvious but important answer is a well-balanced diet. Extreme malnutrition during prenatal development can be especially detrimental. During World War II, famines occurred in parts of Holland and in Leningrad in the former Soviet Union. When the malnutrition occurred during the first few months of pregnancy, death, premature birth, and nervous system defects were especially frequent. When famine occurred later in prenatal development, retardation in fetal growth and low

KEY THEME
Sociocultural Influence

Teenage mothers give birth to nearly 500,000 babies in the United States each year. Many of them will be unmarried teens who have received little or even no prenatal care, factors that increase the risk for delivering less healthy babies.

birth weights were more likely (Antonov, 1947). Although not everyone agrees about the guidelines, women of normal weight for their height are typically advised to gain about twenty-five to thirty-five pounds during pregnancy.

Diets must not only be sufficient in number of calories but also balanced with respect to adequate protein, vitamins, and other nutrients. In fact, intake of many nutrients should be increased during pregnancy, as Table 4.5 indicates. Fortunately, unless deficiencies are so severe that malformations and deficits in neuron formation cannot be overcome, many cognitive problems associated with prenatal undernutrition and the lowered birth weight that often accompanies it may still be reversed when adequate nourishment and stimulation are provided following birth (Pollitt, 1996).

KEY THEME
Sociocultural Influence

● **Stress**   Cultural beliefs about potentially harmful consequences of frightening or stressful events on fetal development are pervasive, and many societies encourage a calm atmosphere for pregnant women (Samuels & Samuels, 1986). In studies in which researchers have carefully measured anxiety, family conflict, positive and negative life events, and the availability of physical and social support for the woman, stress has been linked to greater complications during both pregnancy and birth. Anxiety appears to lengthen labor, increase the need for more anesthesia during delivery, and produce more birthing complications. High stress, particularly early in pregnancy, seems to contribute to a shorter length of gestation and therefore to more frequent preterm births and more infants with lower birth weight (Wadhwa et al., 1993). For example, women who had experienced an earthquake in the first trimester of pregnancy viewed the event as more stressful and also delivered their infants sooner than those who had experienced the earthquake in the second or third trimester (Glynn et al., 2001). In addition, fatigue associated with long hours at work, especially work that involves prolonged standing, increases preterm birth and health problems for a pregnant woman (Gabbe & Turner, 1997; Luke et al., 1999). Stress also may indirectly affect prenatal development by leading a woman to increase smoking, consume more alcohol, or engage in other activities known to have negative effects on the fetus (McAnarney & Stevens-Simon, 1990).

TABLE 4.5	Nutritional Need Differences Between Nonpregnant and Pregnant Women 24 Years of Age			
Nutrient	**Nonpregnant**	**Pregnant**	**Percent Increase**	**Dietary Sources**
Folic acid	180 mcg	400 mcg	+ 122	Leafy vegetables, liver
Vitamin D	5 μg	10 μg	+ 100	Fortified dairy products
Iron	15 mg	30 mg	+ 100	Meats, eggs, grains
Calcium	800 mg	1200 mg	+ 50	Dairy products
Phosphorus	800 mg	1200 mg	+ 50	Meats
Pyridoxine	1.6 mg	2.2 mg	+ 38	Meats, liver, enriched grains
Thiamin	1.1 mg	1.5 mg	+ 36	Enriched grains, pork
Zinc	12 mg	15 mg	+ 25	Meats, seafood, eggs
Riboflavin	1.3 mg	1.6 mg	+ 23	Meats, liver, enriched grains
Protein	50 g	60 g	+ 20	Meats, fish, poultry, dairy
Iodine	150 mcg	175 mcg	+ 17	Iodized salt, seafood
Vitamin C	60 mg	70 mg	+ 17	Citrus fruits, tomatoes
Energy	2200 kcal	2500 kcal	+ 14	Proteins, fats, carbohydrates
Magnesium	280 mg	320 mg	+ 14	Seafood, legumes, grains
Niacin	15 mg	17 mg	+ 13	Meats, nuts, legumes
Vitamin B-12	2.0 mcg	2.2 mcg	+ 10	Animal proteins
Vitamin A	800 μg	800 μg	0	Dark green, yellow, or orange fruits and vegetables, liver

Source: Reece et al., 1995.

The social support a pregnant woman receives from family and friends is an important factor that can lessen the consequences of stress during pregnancy (Feldman et al., 2000). Among women who experience a variety of life changes before and during pregnancy, those with strong social and personal assistance—for example, those who can obtain a ride to work, get help when sick, or borrow needed money—have far fewer complications than women without such resources (Norbeck & Tilden, 1983). In fact, women who receive as little as twenty minutes of psychosocial support addressing their concerns and offering encouragement during regular prenatal visits have babies who weigh more than the babies of women who do not receive this benefit (Rothberg & Lits, 1991). How well a family functions during stressful times may be a more important predictor of complications during and after pregnancy than how many stressful events are actually experienced (Smilkstein et al., 1984).

In the chapter-opening vignette, Carole expressed concern about the considerable pressure of her work and caring for her other children. She, like many other women, is unable to completely eliminate stress from her life. Pregnant women must juggle work, family, and many other obligations. Perhaps additional support from family and friends could help Carole manage her stress and minimize the potentially negative outcomes. Efforts that families initiate to reduce stress or respond to it in adaptive ways can be effective preventive medicine both during pregnancy and after (Samuels & Samuels, 1986).

A Final Note on Environment and Prenatal Development

After learning about the many teratogens and other factors that can affect prenatal development, we may be surprised that babies manage to be born healthy at all. But they do so every day. We should wonder, rather, at the rich complexity of prenatal development and appreciate more deeply that it proceeds normally so much of the time. Ninety to 95 percent of babies born in the United States are healthy and fully prepared to adapt to their new environment. Knowledge of teratogens allows prospective parents as well as others in the community to maximize the chances that all infants will be equipped to enter the world with as many resources as possible.

FOR YOUR REVIEW

- What kinds of supportive functions do the placenta, umbilical cord, and amniotic sac provide for the embryo and the fetus?

- What are teratogens? What principles apply to how teratogens have their effects?

- How do alcohol, cigarette smoke, prescription and over the counter drugs, and illegal drugs affect prenatal development? What are the methodological difficulties associated with determining the consequences of use of such drugs on the embryo, the fetus, and the child?

- How should society treat women charged with using drugs during their pregnancy?

- What kinds of risks exist for the embryo and fetus exposed to rubella, toxoplasmosis, cytomegalovirus, and sexually transmitted diseases?

- What maternal conditions affect the well-being of the fetus and embryo?

Birth and the Perinatal Environment

KEY THEME
Sociocultural Influence

Societies vary enormously in the techniques and rituals that accompany the transition from fetus to newborn. Some interpret pregnancy and birth as natural and healthy, others, as an illness requiring medical care and attention (Newton, 1955). The !Kung, a hunting-and-gathering people living in the Kalahari Desert of Africa, build no huts or facilities for birthing. They view birth as part of the natural order of events, requiring no special intervention (Shostak, 1981). In contrast, pregnancy and childbirth in the United States and many other countries throughout much of the twentieth century has been regarded more as an illness to be managed by professionally trained medical personnel (Dye, 1986). In 1900 fewer than 5 percent of babies were born in hospitals in the United States. Today about 99 percent of all babies in the United States are born in hospitals (Declercq, 1993; Hosmer, 2001).

Preparing for Childbirth

With the shift from childbirth at home to childbirth in the hospital came an increase in the use of medication during delivery. Concerns about the impact of these medications, along with reports of unmedicated but seemingly pain-free delivery by women in other cultures, prodded professionals and expectant parents alike to reconsider how best to prepare for the birth of a baby. After observing one woman who reported a pain-free delivery, Grantley Dick-Read, a medical practitioner in Great Britain, concluded that difficult childbirth was fostered largely by the tension and anxiety in which Western civilization cloaked the event. Dick-Read (1959) proposed that women be taught methods of physical relaxation, given information about the process of childbirth, and encouraged to cultivate a cooperative relationship with their doctors to foster a more natural childbirth experience. Others, including Fernand Lamaze (1970), adopted similar ideas, adding procedures to divert thoughts from pain and encouraging breathing activities to support the labor process.

In recent years, **prepared** (or **natural**) **childbirth,** which involves practicing procedures designed to minimize pain and reduce the need for medication during delivery, has become a popular alternative for prospective mothers. Women who attend classes and adhere to the recommendations of Lamaze and other childbirth education programs (including the National Childbirth Trust in the United Kingdom) generally require fewer and lower amounts of drugs during delivery than women who have not participated in prepared childbirth. Women who attend childbirth classes may experience no less pain, but relaxation techniques and an additional element frequently promoted in these programs—the assistance of a coach or trainer, sometimes the father—seem to help counter the discomfort and lead to a more positive evaluation of childbirth (Waldenström, 1999).

prepared childbirth   Type of childbirth that involves practicing procedures during pregnancy and childbirth that are designed to minimize pain and reduce the need for medication during delivery. Also called *natural childbirth.*

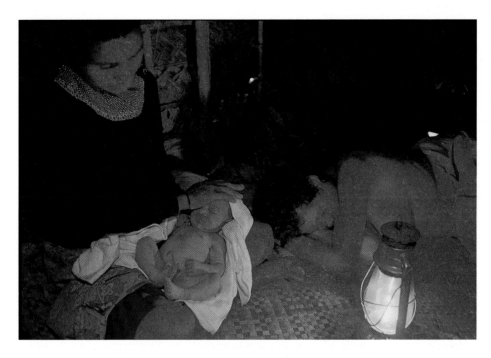

Societies differ enormously in their approach to the birth of a baby. In the United States, most births occur in hospitals. In contrast, more than four of every five births in the Trobriand Islands (part of Papua New Guinea) take place in villages where a midwife is in charge.

RESEARCH APPLIED TO PARENTING

Nurturing and Caring During Labor

Carole knew the signs for the onset of labor; after all, she had already gone through two deliveries. Birthing had proceeded smoothly for her other two children despite her anxieties about the whole process, especially the first time. Maybe it helped to have her husband participate with her in childbirth classes. During those pregnancies she had learned about the various options, ranging from massage to hypnosis to traditional medication, even delivering the baby in water, an alternative the birthing center offered for those who wished to do so. One other thing had been extremely helpful: the presence of a doula, *another woman to accompany her throughout the entire period of labor. Carole was not certain about some of the other alternatives for making the delivery easier and more comfortable. But of one thing she was very sure: she would have a doula with her throughout the birthing process this time as well.*

In addition to exhilaration, most women delivering a baby go through a lot of hard work and some, perhaps considerable, discomfort. It can be a very anxious time. Human birth differs from that of other species of mammals in that it typically requires some form of assistance (Rosenberg & Trevathen, 2001). In many cultures, the help comes from friends and relatives or from midwives, just as it did in the United States many decades ago. With the relocation of childbirth to hospitals, however, women became isolated from family and friends, and a more private and impersonal procedure emerged. Perhaps with that change something very important was lost. Research has helped to identify this loss and has led to alternatives in birthing practices that may benefit both men and women as they become new parents.

1. *Include a partner or some other trusted companion in preparing for and assisting during childbirth.* Studies carried out in Botswana, Guatemala, several European countries, and the United States demonstrate that having a continuously supportive companion during delivery is helpful to women and their newborns (Kayne, Greulich, & Albers, 2001; Madi et al., 1999; Scott, Berkowitz, & Klaus, 1999). For example, in the Guatamalan studies, first-time mothers were assigned a *doula*, a

KEY THEME

Sociocultural Influence

Today, fathers, and sometimes other friends and family members, are encouraged to furnish social and emotional support to women who are about to deliver a baby. When such support is provided by a trusted companion, labor is shorter, fewer drugs are required, and babies are born exhibiting less distress. Nurse midwives, such as the one here discussing the progress of labor with this expectant woman, also have demonstrated an excellent record in helping with the delivery of newborns.

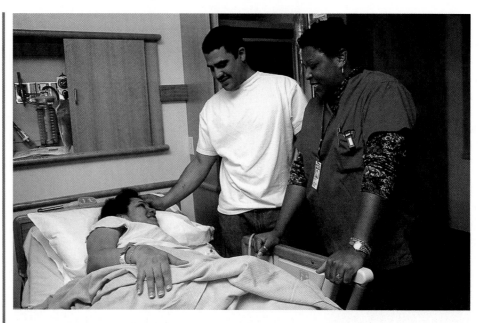

woman experienced with delivery who stayed with the mother to provide emotional support, increase her physical comfort, inform her about what was happening during labor, and advocate for her needs (Klaus & Kennell, 1982). Women given these personal attendants spent far shorter times in labor, required drugs or forceps less frequently, and delivered babies who showed less fetal distress and difficulty breathing than women who received only routine nursing care. Sometimes fathers or other partners are actively encouraged to take on some of these functions as well and can be very effective (Cunningham, 1993), although a doula may be able to provide a more balanced and informative perspective on the sequence of unfolding events.

2. *Consider what type of practitioner might be most beneficial during childbirth.* Of course, fathers or other partners who assist in labor are not likely to be experts in the process. Midwives, nurses, or others far more experienced in childbirth, whose additional primary function is to provide personal assistance while managing labor, have received positive evaluations as well. Compared with physicians, midwives who oversee birthing produce, for example, lower rates of deliveries undergoing cesarean births or other surgical procedures, less use of medication by the mother, and greater satisfaction with care (Butler et al., 1993; Oakley et al., 1996; Sakala, 1993). Whereas about 5 percent of births in the United States are now accompanied by midwives, this figure is nearly 75 percent in many European countries (Alan Guttmacher Institute, 1993).

3. *Explore the different alternatives available to assist in delivering a baby.* The positive outcomes achieved by midwives appear to stem from an attitude that inspires women to not just deliver babies but also draw on their own inner resources, as well as their support networks, for giving birth. For example, midwives are likely to suggest greater flexibility in positioning and moving about during labor, perhaps even soaking in a tub. Standing, squatting, or sitting in special chairs, or even hanging from a bar, are increasingly being offered as alternatives to the traditional recumbent position for delivery. These choices can increase a woman's comfort through the natural benefits of gravity and thus reduce stress for both mother and baby. In fact, in nonwestern cultures, these alternative positions for childbirth are the norm (Rosenberg & Trevathen, 2001).

Labor and Delivery

When labor begins, the wet, warm, and supportive world within the uterus undergoes a rapid transformation, and the fetus must adjust to an earthshaking series of changes. During normal birth, the fetus begins to be subjected to increasingly stronger pressure. Because the birth canal is typically smaller than the size of the head, pressure—as great as thirty pounds of force—will probably cause the head to become somewhat elongated and misshapen (Trevathen, 1987). This is possible because the cerebral plates are not yet knitted together, allowing them to slide up and over one another. At times the fetus may experience brief disruptions in oxygen as the flow of blood in the umbilical cord is temporarily obstructed. And then the infant emerges head first into a strange, new world, one drier, possibly colder, and often much brighter and noisier. Within minutes the new arrival must begin to take in oxygen. The baby must also soon learn to coordinate sucking, swallowing, and breathing to obtain sufficient nutrients.

Labor is a complicated, interactive process involving the fetus, the placenta, and the woman. What brings about its onset? The answer begins with the hypothalamus, pituitary, and adrenal glands of the fetus. When these become mature enough, they help to produce a cascading sequence of hormones and other events, including some in the placenta, that are especially important in initiating labor (Nathanielsz, 1996). In fact, measurement of one hormone in the placenta as early as the sixteenth to twentieth week of pregnancy can predict whether a delivery will occur somewhat before, somewhat after, or about the time of the anticipated due date (Smith, 1999).

The first of the three traditional stages of labor (see Figure 4.5) begins with brief, mild contractions perhaps ten to fifteen minutes apart. These contractions become increasingly frequent and serve to alter the shape of the cervix, preparing it for the fetus's descent and entry into the narrow birth canal. Near the end of the first stage, which on average lasts about eleven hours for firstborns and about seven hours for later-borns, dilation of the cervix proceeds rapidly to allow passage through the birth canal. The second stage consists of the continued descent and the birth of the baby. This stage usually requires a little less than an hour for firstborns and about twenty minutes for later-borns. It also normally includes several reorientations of both the head and shoulders to permit delivery through the tight-fitting passageway (Rosenberg & Trevathen, 2001). In the third stage, which lasts about fifteen minutes, the placenta is expelled. These durations are, however, averages; enormous variation exists from one woman to another.

WHAT DO YOU THINK?

Are Home Deliveries a Safe Alternative? psychology.college.hmco.com

This woman, who has just given birth, now has the opportunity to see and hold her infant for the first time. In contrast to earlier practices, parents in most hospital settings today are allowed ample time to become acquainted with their newborns immediately after birth.

| FIGURE 4.5 | The Three Stages of Childbirth |

In the first stage of labor the cervix, the neck of the uterus, dilates and thins to open a passage through the birth canal. The amniotic fluid, if not already lost, helps by exerting firm, even pressure on the cervix. When the pressure becomes too great, the sac containing the amniotic fluid will rupture, a process known as "breaking the water." The head of the fetus will soon enter the birth canal, and the second stage of labor begins. During the second stage of labor, each contraction continues to push the fetus farther along the approximately four inches of the birth canal. During a normal delivery, the head emerges first (known as *crowning*), much as though pushing through the neck of a tight turtleneck sweater. The orientation of the head toward the mother's back is one of the reasons birthing for humans often needs the assistance of others (Rosenberg & Trevathen, 2001). Once the head has emerged, shoulders twist around in the birth canal, and the head turns sideways to permit delivery of the rest of the body. In the final stage of labor, the placenta is delivered.

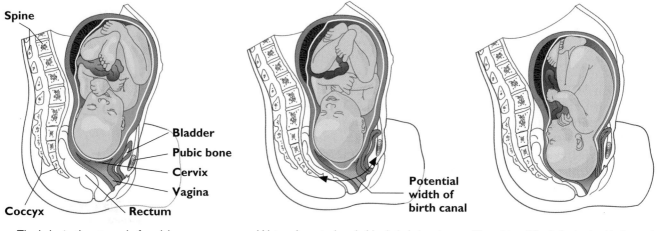

The baby in the uterus before labor

Water about to break (the baby's head now rests inside the cervix)

Transition: The baby in the birth canal

STAGE 1

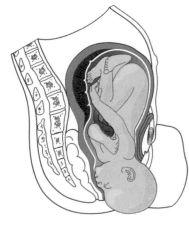

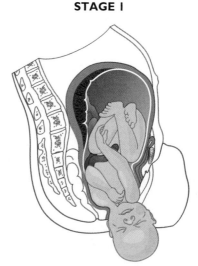

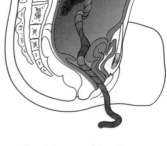

The baby about to be born

The head rotates sideways after it emerges

The delivery of the placenta

STAGE 2

STAGE 3

● **Medication During Childbirth**   In Western societies, births are often accompanied by some form of medication. Anesthesia blocks the transmission of pain, analgesics lessen feelings of discomfort, and sedatives help the woman to relax. All of these drugs readily pass through the placenta and enter the fetus's circulatory system. Critics of the routine use of drugs point out that babies whose mothers receive high doses during labor are less attentive and responsive to caregivers, are more irritable, and gain weight more slowly than babies exposed to small amounts or no drugs at all (Brazelton, Nugent, & Lester, 1987; Emory, Schlackman, & Fiano, 1996). Moreover, some behavioral differences may persist well beyond infancy. Heavy use of drugs during labor has been associated, for example, with an increased incidence of learning disorders among school-age children (Brackbill, McManus, & Woodward, 1985).

Developmental differences between babies born to medicated and nonmedicated women, however, are not consistent. Some experts believe the negative effects of exposure to drugs at birth have been markedly overstated and occur only when medications are used excessively (Kraemer et al., 1985). Thus women need not experience unreasonable pain or feel guilty if drugs are administered. Efforts to make the birth process gentler, such as by reducing illumination and noise or delivering the baby under water, have also been proposed (Daniels, 1989; LeBoyer, 1975), although the advantages of these practices for either women or infants have not been documented. Furthermore, the use of other complementary and alternative medical procedures, such as acupuncture and various relaxation techniques, remain unproven with respect to benefits to mother or newborn as well (Allaire, 2001). However, as we have already discussed, providing a network of social support does help.

● **Cesarean Birth** A *cesarean birth* is the delivery of a baby through a surgical incision in the woman's abdomen and uterus. Cesarean births are recommended, for example, when labor fails to progress normally, when the baby's head is very large, or when birth is *breech* (foot or rump first) rather than head first. Concerns about stress on the fetus that might lead to increased risk of brain damage, vaginal infections that might be transmitted to the baby, and expensive malpractice suits (should things go awry during vaginal delivery) have led to more than a fivefold increase in the frequency of cesarean sections in the past thirty years in the United States. Today nearly 23 percent of deliveries in the United States are cesarean rather than vaginal (Hoyert et al., 2001), a rate that is far higher than in all other countries except Brazil and Puerto Rico (Centers for Disease Control, 1993).

KEY THEME
Individual Differences

KEY THEME
Sociocultural Influence

Women who undergo cesarean section face an increased risk of infection and a longer hospital stay than women who give birth vaginally. Moreover, cesarean babies are likely to be exposed to greater maternal medication. Other concerns center on the different experiences both mother and infant receive under such circumstances. For example, when cesarean babies are delivered before labor begins, they do not have a misshapen head and appear perfectly healthy. However, they have substantially lower levels of two stress hormones, adrenaline and noradrenaline, known to facilitate respiration by helping to keep the lungs open and clear. The hormones also enhance cell metabolism, circulation of the blood to the brain, and activity level, factors that help the infant make the transition to his or her new environment and to become responsive to caregivers. Thus cesarean babies generally tend to have more trouble breathing, are less active, sleep more, and cry less than other babies (Trevathen, 1987). Mothers, too, tend to evaluate their experience of a cesarean delivery, especially if unplanned, less positively than those who deliver vaginally. Nevertheless, the quality of mother-infant interactions and the psychosocial functioning of the infants a year after their births appear quite similar regardless of type of delivery, suggesting that there are few long-term negative consequences of cesarean births (DiMatteo et al., 1996; Durik, Hyde, & Clark, 2000).

● **Birth Trauma** The increase in the frequency of cesarean sections in the United States has come about partly because of concerns about birth trauma, or injuries sustained at birth. A potentially serious consequence is *anoxia,* or deprivation of oxygen. Anoxia can result from, for example, damage to or lengthy compression of the umbilical cord or head during birth, problems associated with the placenta, or failure of the baby to begin regular breathing after birth. If oxygen deprivation lasts more than a few minutes, severe damage to the central nervous system, including cerebral palsy, can result.

Fortunately, brief periods of anoxia have few long-lasting effects. Furthermore, an adequate postnatal caregiving environment can help to counter potentially negative outcomes for infants experiencing periods without oxygen (Sameroff & Chandler, 1975). Concerns about anoxia and other birth traumas, however, have led to the widespread use of **fetal monitoring devices** during labor. Most of these devices record fetal heartbeat to determine whether the fetus is undergoing stress during delivery. However, some experts argue that reliance on medically sophisticated equipment promotes a cascading series of interventions that only exacerbate the difficulty of delivery. In fact, by focusing on a supportive context to reduce anxiety, less birth trauma will occur than that which the technology was designed to prevent (Hafner-Eaton & Pearce, 1994; Sakala, 1993).

KEY THEME
Individual Differences

Low Birth Weight

As infant and childhood diseases have come under greater control in recent decades, the treatment and prevention of low-birth-weight infants (those weighing less than twenty-five hundred grams, or five-and-a-half pounds) has gained increased attention. Mortality rate rapidly declines as birth weight increases to near normal levels. The United States has a higher proportion of infants born with low birth weight than many other developed countries, a major reason that its infant mortality rate is also higher than in many other industrialized countries (see Figure 4.6).

Babies with low birth weight fall into two major groups: those born preterm (less than thirty-five weeks conceptual age) whose development has generally proceeded

KEY THEME
Sociocultural Influence

FIGURE 4.6
Infant Mortality in Selected Developed Countries

The infant mortality rate (deaths before one year of age per thousand live births) is a measure that provides an indication of the overall health of a nation. A number of countries have a lower infant mortality rate than the United States.

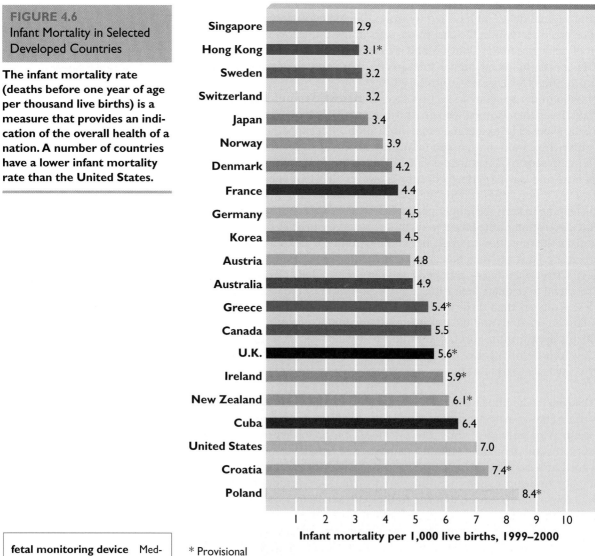

Infant mortality per 1,000 live births, 1999–2000

* Provisional

Source: Data from United Nations, *Population and Vital Statistics Report,* 2001.

fetal monitoring device Medical device used to monitor fetal heartbeat during delivery.

normally but has been cut short by early delivery, and those born near their expected arrival date but are *small for gestational age (SGA)*, that is, who display intrauterine growth retardation. Thus, low-birth-weight infants compose a heterogeneous group, perhaps needing separate types of medical treatment and intervention and facing different developmental outcomes. Congenital anomalies are somewhat more frequent in SGA infants, for example, whereas respiratory distress is more likely among infants who are born preterm.

● **Caring for Infants with Low Birth Weight**   In general, infants born with low birth weight face numerous obstacles, not only in terms of survival but also throughout subsequent development (Agustines et al., 2000; Chan et al., 2000). Cerebral palsy, seizure disorders, neurological difficulties that include hemorrhaging associated with regions of the brain, respiratory difficulties, and eye disorders are some examples of the problems observed. These difficulties are found especially frequently among infants born with very low birth weight (less than fifteen hundred grams) and even more so among those with extremely low birth weight (less than 1,000 grams) or who are born at less than twenty-seven weeks gestational age. In addition to these problems, all low-birth-weight and premature infants face the major task of maintaining physiological stability and achieving regular cycles of activity involving sleep and wakefulness. To deal with these problems, premature infants spend much of their time in an isolette, a small plexiglass chamber that carefully controls temperature and air flow with the aid of a respirator. They may be fed via a stomach tube and are often given painful heel pricks and other interventions to monitor the effects of medication and treatment.

The types of experience that premature infants have typically received has been of considerable concern in terms of their social and psychological consequences for development. At one time parents were either excluded completely from neonatal intensive care units (NICUs), the specialized medical facilities designed to care for low-birth-weight infants (called *special care baby units* in Great Britain), or were given little opportunity to see or care for their newborns. However, that policy has changed substantially as evidence emerged showing the importance of appropriate stimulation for postnatal development (Ramey, Bryant, & Suarez, 1987; Thoman, 1993). NICUs and parents now sometimes provide *compensatory stimulation*. This experience attempts to duplicate what the baby would have gained while still in the womb. For instance, the baby might be exposed to oscillating devices or waterbeds to simulate the movements the fetus experiences prenatally; muffled recordings of a human voice, a

KEY THEME
Nature/Nurture

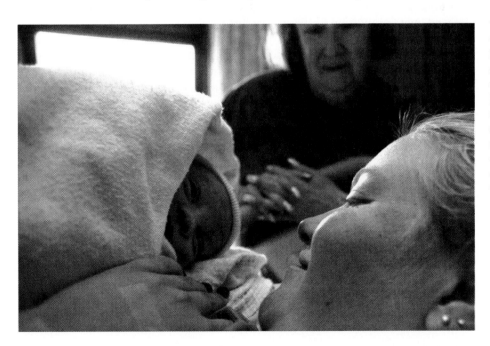

The opportunity to interact with each other shortly after birth typically has positive consequences for both mother and child. For children born with low birth weight these occasions may be more difficult to arrange. Nevertheless, research reveals that encouraging parents to engage in these kinds of experiences are beneficial to all children.

heartbeat, or other sounds to match those usually heard in the womb; reduced light and exposure to noise; and opportunities for nonnutritive sucking, an activity in which the fetus occasionally engages (Thoman, 1993). Caregivers and others may also be encouraged to provide suitable *enriching* visual and auditory experiences, prudent handling, and social and body contact more akin to the environment to which normal newborns are exposed. Researchers have identified benefits from both compensatory and enriching stimulation: more rapid weight gain, shorter hospital stays, fewer medical and eating problems, more regular breathing and heart rate, improvements in sensorimotor development, more stable and longer periods in quiet states, and smoother transitions from one state to another (Gorski, 1991; Thoman, 1993).

More recently, many hospitals have begun to implement *kangaroo care,* another kind of caregiving that combines both compensatory and enriching elements. First used in Bogotá, Colombia, about a decade ago, kangaroo care involves resting the unclothed premature infant on the mother's body between her breasts for an hour or longer each day. This procedure helps the mother's own body temperature regulate the infant's body temperature, permits opportunity for nursing activity, and assists mother and child to establish a social relationship with one another (Charpak et al., 1997; Ludington-Hoe & Swinth, 1996). Research has revealed that this experience, given to premature infants in the NICU for as little as an hour a day for fourteen days, facilitates infants' ability to regulate arousal, maintain a more consistent sleep-wake pattern, and engage in more mature attentional and exploratory behaviors as much as six months later, compared with premature infants not receiving kangaroo care (Feldman et al., 2002). In addition, the experience appears to positively affect how mothers view their infants and their role as a parent (Neu, 1999).

● Promoting Development in Low-Birth-Weight Children   In general, low-birth-weight infants lag behind other children in later development. A higher proportion, especially those with extremely low birth weights, display visuomotor and language deficits, learning disabilities, behavior problems, and fewer social skills, and suffer more peer rejection as children (Bregman, 1998; Taylor, Klein, & Hack, 2000; Vohr et al., 2000). The problems are likely to culminate in poorer school achievement and the need for more special education intervention (Klebanov, Brooks-Gunn, & McCormick, 1994; Saigal et al., 2000). Fortunately, many low-birth-weight children still do surprisingly well, as revealed by an analysis of data from more than eighty studies conducted in North America, Europe, Australia, and New Zealand (Aylward et al., 1989). Indeed, the enormous, although justified, concern about the development of some of these children often overshadows the fact that the ones who display disabilities represent only a proportion of all very low-birth-weight children (McCormick, 1997).

As we have begun to see in other examples of children with special needs, one very important factor contributing to positive developmental outcomes appears to be the support and encouragement of parents. Providing parents with opportunities to engage in suitable caregiving in the hospital setting, instructing them to recognize the specific needs of their infant and what behaviors to expect, and extending the emotional support of professional staff and other parents are types of assistance that have proven beneficial to low-birth-weight children (Achenbach et al., 1993; McCormick et al., 1993; Ramey et al., 1992). For example, Jeanne Brooks-Gunn and her colleagues (1993) found that low-birth-weight children who participated in educational daycare programs and whose families received regular home visits and joined in frequent parent group meetings were able to maintain higher levels of performance on cognitive tests than children in families for whom these resources were unavailable (see Figure 4.7).

Parenting a low-birth-weight infant, especially one who shows medical complications, can be very stressful (Taylor et al., 2001). Despite the continuing demands and increased burdens that are often a part of such child rearing, mothers of very low-birth-weight children report similar levels of satisfaction and positive feelings with respect to their parenting as mothers of normal-birth-weight children by the time their offspring reach three years of age (Singer, Salvator, et al., 1999). Moreover, the caregivers of children born with extremely low birth weight are as enthusiastic and

KEY THEME
Nature/Nurture

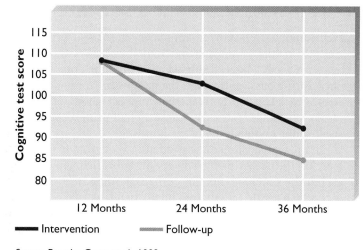

FIGURE 4.7
Low-Birth-Weight Children's Cognitive Development as a Function of Intervention

In a large-scale study investigating the effects of providing home visits and educational child care for low-birth-weight infants and their families, Brooks-Gunn and her colleagues (1993) found that performance on measures of intellectual development was substantially better for those who received the intervention than for those who did not. Although some decline in scores occurred even for the group receiving intervention, it was far less than for those who did not receive the intervention. Both groups performed similarly at the youngest age (twelve months), perhaps because tests measuring cognitive skills often are not very sensitive to differences at that age.

Source: Brooks-Gunn et al., 1993.

supportive of making every effort to provide the best medical care possible for these children as parents of children born with normal birth weights (Streiner et al., 2001). In bringing up a low-birth-weight child, however, providing family- and child-oriented services appears to be especially important in helping to reduce stress, especially for those mothers who are less educated and may have fewer other resources available (Klebanov, Brooks-Gunn, & McCormick, 2001).

Attempts to reduce complications associated with low birth weight have proceeded on two fronts. Improved medical care in NICUs and supportive caregiving have permitted more low-birth-weight, especially extremely low-birth-weight, infants to survive and develop normally. These positive findings reflect more effective treatment (e.g., for respiratory distress) and management of the NICU (e.g., reductions in bright light, loud noise, and sleep interruptions) designed to reduce stress in individuals who are among the least capable of responding to stress (Als et al., 1994; Bregman, 1998). Yet despite this increased number of survivors, the proportion of children showing neurological or cognitive problems has remained stable (Lorenz et al., 1997; O'Shea et al., 1997; Piecuch, Leonard, & Cooper, 1998; Stevenson et al., 1998). Thus, a second major assault on the problem has been in the form of prevention. Researchers have catalogued a long list of demographic, medical, and behavioral factors associated with low birth weight, for example, inadequate prenatal care and nutrition, heavy smoking, and drug use. Because many of these factors are preventable, educational programs targeted to pregnant women at high risk, including teenagers, have become increasingly important. These programs can reduce the incidence of low birth weight, especially when offered consistently and early in the course of pregnancy (Fangman et al., 1994; Seitz & Apfel, 1994). Indeed, future progress in addressing the problems that accompany low birth weight is likely to be closely tied to improved and more widespread programs of prevention as much as to new medical advances.

FOR YOUR REVIEW

- What are the benefits of prepared childbirth and a supportive relationship with another individual for both parent and newborn child?

- What are the stages of delivery? How does medication during delivery affect the newborn?

- What are the benefits and disadvantages of cesarean births for mother and child? Why is this procedure often carried out?

- How do premature and small for gestational age infants differ? What are the factors that increase the likelihood of low birth weight? What practices help children born with low birth weight?

Newborn Assessment and States

Even parents of a healthy infant may be in for a surprise when they see their baby for the first time. Unless delivered by cesarean section, the baby is likely to have a flattened nose and a large, distorted head from the bones of the skull overriding one another during passage through the narrow birth canal. The skin of all babies, regardless of racial background, is a pale pinkish color and often is covered by an oily, cheeselike substance (the vernix caseosa) that protects against infection. Sex organs are swollen due to high levels of sex hormones.

An infant's most immediate need after emerging from the womb is to breathe. Pressure on the chest during delivery probably helps to clear the baby's fluid-filled lungs, but the shock of cool air, perhaps accompanied by jiggling, a slap, or some other less than gentle activity by a birth attendant, makes the first breath more like a gasp, quickly followed by a reflexive cry. The umbilical cord may continue to pulse for several minutes after birth, and in many societies the cord is not cut until after it ceases to do so (Trevathen, 1987).

The second major task the baby must accomplish upon entering the world is to regulate body temperature. Babies lose body heat about four times more rapidly than adults because of their lower fat reserve and relatively large body surface (Bruck, 1962). As a consequence, newborns, although they can effectively maintain their temperature when held close to a caregiver's body, are often quickly placed under heaters.

Assessing Newborns

KEY THEME
Individual Differences

Newborns typically weigh five-and-a-half to ten pounds and measure eighteen to twenty-two inches in length. Many procedures for evaluating their health have become available in recent years, but one routinely administered is the *Apgar Scale* (Apgar, 1953). Typically assessed at both one and five minutes after birth, the Apgar measures five vital signs: heart rate, respiratory effort, muscle tone, reflex responsivity, and color. Each vital sign is scored 0, 1, or 2 based on the criteria described in Table 4.6. In the United States, 90 percent of infants receive a total score of 7 or better; those who score less than 4 are considered to be at risk.

A more extensive measure, developed by T. Berry Brazelton (1973) and given several days after birth, is the *Neonatal Behavioral Assessment Scale (NBAS)*. The NBAS evaluates, for example, the baby's ability to interact with the tester, responsiveness to objects in the environment, reflex motor capacities, and ability to control behavioral state. Newborn performance on the NBAS has been used to assess neurological con-

This two-day-old baby, holding her father's hand, has entered a world in which new forms of physical and social stimulation can be experienced. Although newborns and young infants spend much of their time sleeping, this infant is engaged in alert inactivity, a time in which she may be learning much about her environment.

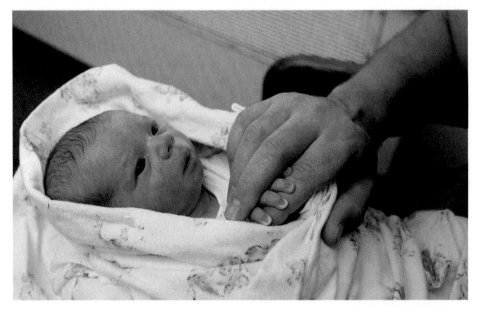

dition and can indicate whether certain prenatal or perinatal conditions, as well as intervention programs, have had an effect (Korner, 1987; Tronick, 1987). An NBAS score can also predict later developmental outcomes. Babies who score poorly on the scale continue to be somewhat less responsive to caregivers in the first few months after birth (Vaughn et al., 1980). In general, however, the predictive validity of the NBAS (along with other infant tests) for long-term development is only modest at best (Brazelton, Nugent, & Lester, 1987). Nevertheless, parents who observe while examiners give the NBAS or who are trained to give it themselves seem to become more responsive to and effective in interactions with their infants (Worobey, 1985).

Newborn States

Babies sleep. They sleep a lot. But newborns and young infants display a wide variety of states: regular and irregular sleep, drowsiness, alert inactivity, alert activity, and crying. Crying or distress usually begins with whimpering but swiftly shifts to full-scale cries, often accompanied by thrashing of arms and legs. During alert activity the infant also exhibits vigorous, diffuse motor activity, but such exertions are not accompanied by signs of distress. During alert inactivity the baby is relatively quiet, at least in terms of motor activity, but actively engages in visual scanning of the environment. In this state, the baby appears to be most responsive to sensory stimulation and may be learning a great deal.

Although individual differences are great, newborns average sixteen to seventeen hours of sleep a day. Sleep and wake cycles are extremely short, and babies are easily disrupted by external stimulation. As the weeks pass, infants gradually sleep less but for longer periods; by about three to five weeks of age, a pattern begins to emerge in which the longest sleep periods take place at night (Thompson, 1982). But naps during the day continue to be a regular occurrence through the preschool years. In fact, in some cultures, such naps are never eliminated.

KEY THEME
Individual Differences

The development of sleep patterns differs substantially across various cultures. In most industrialized countries, parents eagerly look forward to having their infants adopt a routine that matches their own. A significant milestone is reached when the baby of three or four months finally sleeps through the night. In some cultures, such as the Kipsigi of rural Kenya, however, infants are permitted more flexibility and will not sleep through the night until much older (Super & Harkness, 1982).

KEY THEME
Sociocultural Influence

Like adults, infants (even before they are born) display two distinct sleep states (Groome et al., 1997). During active or *REM (rapid-eye-movement)* sleep, eye movements and muscle jerks are frequent and breathing and heart rate are irregular. During quiet sleep *(NREM),* eye and muscle movements are few and physiological activity is more regular. The proportion of time spent in the two states, however,

	Ratings		
Vital Sign	*0*	*1*	*2*
Heart rate	Absent	Slow (below 100)	Over 100
Respiratory effort	Absent	Slow, irregular	Good, crying
Muscle tone	Flaccid	Some flexion of extremities	Active motion
Reflex responsivity	No response	Grimace	Vigorous cry
Color	Blue, pale	Body pink, extremities blue	Completely pink

TABLE 4.6
The Apgar Scoring System

The Apgar Scale is used at and shortly after birth to diagnose the physical condition of a newborn. The ratings for each vital sign are added for a total score ranging from 0 to 10. An infant who scores less than 4 is considered to be at risk.

Source: Adapted from Apgar, 1953. From V. Apgar, "A Proposal for a New Method of Evaluation of the Newborn Infant," *Anesthesia and Analgesia: Current Researches, 32,* 260–267. Copyright © 1953. Used by permission of Lippincott Williams & Wilkins. www.anesthesia-analgesia.org

shifts dramatically with development. About eight in sixteen hours of sleep is spent in REM sleep as a newborn, but only about two in seven hours of sleep as an adult.

Active or REM sleep has been linked to dreaming, but it is not clear whether young infants dream. However, REM sleep is believed to be important for normal brain activity (Roffwarg, Muzio, & Dement, 1966). *Autostimulation theory* proposes that REM sleep provides powerful stimulation to the central nervous system, which in adults is interpreted as sensory and motor activity associated with dreaming. According to this theory, stimulation during REM sleep compensates for the relatively brief number of hours each day the infant is awake. Infants kept awake for relatively lengthy periods of time show reduced amounts of REM sleep, and premature infants, whose wakeful periods are even shorter, show more REM sleep than full-term babies (Halpern, MacLean, & Baumeister, 1995). If autostimulation theory is correct, it is a further demonstration of how important stimulation is for development, even at those times when a large amount of sleep is essential as well.

FOR YOUR REVIEW

• What are the first tasks for the newborn following birth?

• Why are scores on the Apgar and Neonatal Behavioral Assessment Scale important?

• What states do newborns display? What kinds of sleep patterns are found in newborns?

CHAPTER RECAP

SUMMARY OF DEVELOPMENTAL THEMES

■ **Nature/Nurture**   *What roles do nature and nurture play in prenatal development and birth?*

Prenatal development is the product of complex interactions involving genetic instructions inherited from parents (see the chapter titled "Genetics and Heredity") and the expectant woman's physical and emotional conditions, as well as exposure to drugs, diseases, hazardous chemicals, and medications before and during pregnancy and during labor. We have seen, for example, that differentiation of organs and systems in the embryo typically obeys principles established by biochemical and physiological processes. Yet these processes do not operate in a vacuum. Teratogens and various intrauterine conditions can radically alter the normal developmental path. Thus events in the life of the woman may change the immediate environment within her womb, with drastic consequences for the fetus. The reactions, attitudes, and availability of the newborn's caregivers and the stimulation they provide are other major sources of potential influence on the baby's development.

■ **Sociocultural Influence**   *How does the sociocultural context influence prenatal development and birth?*

The immediate internal environment of the fetus and the perinatal environment provided for the newborn can be influenced dramatically by the larger social, economic, and cultural settings in which pregnancy and birth take place. The woman's actions during pregnancy are often modified or regulated by a network of expectations, advice, and resources within the culture in which she lives. An expectant woman in one community, for example, may have access to medical and other kinds of care that provide a more or less healthy environment for the fetus than a woman in another community. Industry or governing units may legislate controls on chemical pollution in one country and ignore them in another. Scientific and technological advances in prenatal testing, birthing practices, and newborn care may be available in one region of the world but not another; even when available, however, not all parents may have the economic resources or desire to use them.

■ **Continuous/Discontinuous**   *Is development before and after birth continuous or discontinuous?*

When the zygote attaches to the uterine wall and taps a new source of nourishment, its course of development changes dramatically. Once the various organs and systems are formed and become less susceptible to environmental disruptions, the fetus achieves a vastly different status. The process of birth itself is a major transition. Such spectacular changes fit with discontinuous or stagelike descriptions of development. So do the marked shifts in vulnerability to teratogens observed during prenatal development. Underlying the progressions, however, are biochemical and physiological processes governing cell proliferation, differentiation, and the emergence and functioning of biological systems that can be seen as continuous. Many dramatic changes are essentially the product of modest accumulative modifications in the multifaceted, complex environment that promotes development.

■ **Individual Differences** *How prominent are individual differences in prenatal development and the newborn?*

Newborns everywhere undergo many common gestational experiences; however, individual differences already have begun to surface. Many differences arise because, contrary to once widely held beliefs, the fetus is not immune to the influences of the larger world. Because of exposure to teratogens and other maternal conditions, babies will differ in their physical and behavioral qualities and their ability to cope with and adapt to their new environment. Greater knowledge of and sensitivity to those differences by caregivers, whether exhibited by a newborn with special needs such as one with low birth weight or by an infant who falls within the typical range for newborns, can help to ensure success for the continued development of every child.

SUMMARY OF TOPICS

The Stages of Prenatal Development

■ *Prenatal development* is the period that extends from conception to birth. During this time, a single-celled *zygote* is transformed into the complex, active organism that is the newborn.

Fertilization

■ Fertilization normally takes place in the Fallopian tube when an ovum, or egg cell, is penetrated by a single sperm cell.

The Germinal Period

■ During the *germinal period*, about the first ten to fourteen days after conception, the zygote migrates from the Fallopian tube to the uterus, becomes multicelled, and implants itself in the uterine wall to gain access to a new source of nutrients obtained from the mother.

■ If implantation of the zygote occurs in a location other than the uterus, an *ectopic pregnancy* has occurred. Such a pregnancy is potentially life threatening to a woman.

The Embryonic Period

■ The *embryonic period* begins after implantation and continues until about the eighth week after conception.

■ The embryonic period is marked by development of the *placenta* and other supportive structures within the uterine environment and by the differentiation of cells into tissues that form the major organs and systems of the embryo.

The Fetal Period

■ The *fetal period*, beginning in about the eighth week after conception and lasting until birth, is marked by substantial growth and by refinement of organs and systems.

■ Neurons continue to form and migrate during the fetal period. Brain activity, sensory reactions, and movement are exhibited by the fetus. *Viability*, that is, the ability to survive outside the womb, improves rapidly over the last three months of pregnancy.

■ *Gestational age* differs from conceptual age by about two weeks, because it is based on the woman's last menstrual period rather than the time at which conception occurs.

Assisted Reproduction

■ Various forms of assisted reproduction offer couples who are unable to conceive naturally the opportunity to have their own biological children. Among the technologies associated with these procedures are artificial insemination by donor, egg donation, fertility drugs, gamete intrafallopian transfer, in vitro fertilization, and maternal surrogacy.

■ Medical concerns, as well as legal and social issues concerning the many different categories of parenting offered by these new technologies, continue to be debated. Nevertheless, children born as a result of assisted reproduction typically appear to show normal psychological and social development.

Environmental Factors Influencing Prenatal Development

■ Many environmental circumstances influence prenatal development.

Support Within the Womb

■ The placenta serves as the major organ for transfer of nutrients from the mother's circulatory system and for the expelling of waste products from the fetus. The *umbilical cord* connects the fetus to the placenta. The *amniotic sac* provides a fluid-filled, protective surrounding in which development of the fetus occurs.

Principles of Teratology

■ During both embryonic and fetal development, *teratogens*, or environmental agents harmful to the organism, can disrupt development and interfere with later behavior.

■ The effects of teratogens differ depending on the genetic susceptibility of the embryo or fetus, how the teratogen reaches the prenatal environment, its level of dosage and manner of exposure, and where it interferes with cellular activity. A teratogen's effects also differ depending on the time at which exposure occurs during prenatal development. Not all the consequences are observed immediately; they may not even be evident until well into the postnatal years.

Drugs as Teratogens

■ Many different drugs are able to cross the placental barrier and can have teratogenic effects. Among those known to have the greatest impact on fetal development are alcohol, which can result in *fetal alcohol syndrome*, and cigarette smoke.

■ The effects of prescription and over-the-counter drugs on prenatal development are not always well known. Of considerable concern is the potential harmful outcome from interactions involving the use of many such drugs.

■ Teratogenic effects are linked to the use of illegal drugs. However, their effects are often confounded with other factors known to have significant negative consequences for the fetus. These factors include lack of proper nutrition, poor health of the mother, absence of medical care, lack of emotional and social support, and high levels of stress. These factors may well be more damaging to the fetus than the drugs themselves.

Diseases as Teratogens

■ Although some diseases known to have teratogenic effects are no longer common, at least in some regions of the world, others, including sexually transmitted diseases such as HIV, can have serious repercussions on both prenatal and postnatal development.

Environmental Hazards as Teratogens

■ Certain chemicals found in the environment, as well as in various workplaces, can have teratogenic effects.

Women's Conditions and Prenatal Development

■ Being either very young or in the late childbearing years, poor nutrition, a high level of stress, and lack of social support, in addition to certain conditions such as diabetes, obesity, and pregnancy-induced hypertension, are associated with less positive outcomes in prenatal development.

A Final Note on Environment and Prenatal Development

■ Despite the possibility of negative consequences from teratogens, most infants in technologically advanced countries are born healthy and normal.

Birth and the Perinatal Environment

■ The practices and procedures surrounding the birth and initial care of a baby are part of the *perinatal period* of development.

Preparing for Childbirth

■ Cultures differ enormously in the support and types of assistance provided for the delivery of a child. These preparations may include the prospective parent engaging in *prepared* or *natural childbirth* designed to make birthing easier. Other social and cultural differences include place of delivery (home, hospital, or some other facility specifically de-

signed for birthing), who is present and assists in the birth, and what function those assistants serve.

■ The presence of a *doula*, someone familiar with the birth process but continuously present to provide emotional support and information to the mother, appears to have benefits for both mother and newborn.

Labor and Delivery

■ Childbirth proceeds through three stages. In the first and longest stage, labor helps to initiate preparation of the birth canal. Passage of the fetus through the birth canal makes up the second stage. During the third stage, the placenta is delivered. Labor appears to be initiated by hormones produced by the fetus and the placenta.

■ Concerns about too much reliance on medication during labor have led to efforts to initiate procedures that permit delivery with the use of fewer pain-relieving drugs.

■ Cesarean deliveries continue to be relatively common in the United States, despite their greater expense and the fact that vaginal births may produce some benefits for the infant. The large number of cesarean births in the United States may stem, in part, from the extensive use of *fetal monitoring devices* that signal distress to the fetus during delivery and concerns about the long-term negative consequences of birth trauma.

Low Birth Weight

■ As infant and childhood diseases have come under increasing control, researchers have directed attention to the prevention and treatment of small-for-gestational-age and low-birth-weight infants. Although many low-birth-weight infants develop into healthy children and adults, a significant number, especially among those with very or extremely low birth weight, experience various developmental disorders.

■ Compensatory and enrichment programs for low-birth-weight infants increase early weight gains and other developmental outcomes. They also help to reduce stress among mothers, especially those for whom other support from family and community may be limited.

Newborn Assessment and States

■ The newborn's initial appearance may be far different from what most parents expect. Respiration and maintenance of body temperature are two immediate critical goals for the newborn.

Assessing Newborns

■ Tests given to the newborn shortly after birth, such as the Apgar Scale and Neonatal Behavioral Assessment Scale, provide some indication of the baby's physiological state and ability to interact with caregivers and respond to stimulation.

Newborn States

■ Newborns display a number of states ranging from deep sleep to intense crying. A relatively large proportion of an infant's time involves REM sleep, a state that may provide them with stimulation even when asleep.

Key Themes in Brain, Motor Skill, and Physical Development

- **Nature/Nurture** What roles do nature and nurture play in brain, motor skill, and physical development?

- **Sociocultural Influence** How does the sociocultural context influence brain, motor skill, and physical development?

- **Child's Active Role** How does the child play an active role in the process of brain, motor skill, and physical development?

- **Continuity/Discontinuity** Are brain, motor skill, and physical development continuous or discontinuous?

- **Individual Differences** How prominent are individual differences in brain, motor skill, and physical development?

- **Interaction Among Domains** How do brain, motor skill, and physical development interact with other domains of development?

She stared intently at the thirteen-year-old who had just finished her routine. Danielle couldn't believe what she had just seen. How could any girl her own age do that? Danielle's words expressed admiration and awe, but her voice was tinged with envy as she confided to her best friend, "We've been in gymnastics ever since we were five. If we tried that, we'd probably break our necks!"

Even as a toddler, Danielle seemed captivated by leaping and tumbling. Her parents took great pride in their daughter's graceful athleticism and precocious motor skills. Danielle enrolled in ballet and gymnastics at an early age. Both activities had been fun. As Danielle became older and more skilled, however, she especially seemed to thrive on the competition that permeated the gymnastics meets. She liked being good at what she did; she preferred being the best. However, she couldn't imagine anyone at her age with the dexterity and endurance to carry out that kind of routine. Through the applause, her friend had no difficulty hearing Danielle mutter, "I'll bet I can do that. I don't care if I do break my neck."

Physical growth and advances in motor skills are among the most readily apparent signs of development as it progresses from infancy through childhood and into adolescence. Few children become Olympic gymnasts, but virtually all acquire a sophisticated set of motor skills and physical abilities. The transformation is accompanied by less obvious, but no less revolutionary, changes in the brain.

Development of the brain, the acquisition of physical skills, and the growth of the body from infancy to adolescence affect virtually every behavior displayed by the child and are, in turn, influenced by the social, emotional, and cognitive demands in which their growth occurs. Consider how newfound motor coordinations may, for example, dramatically awaken cognition. The six-month-old who begins to reach for and grasp objects acquires a fresh and powerful means of gaining information and, at the same time, a new way to control and influence her environment. So, too, the child who just learned to ride his bike opens up broader vistas to explore and, at the same time, must learn to avoid new dangers that may accompany this feat.

The reactions of others to changing stature and accomplishments can arouse a child's pride and promote renewed efforts, or they can lead to discouragement and apprehension. For example, when children begin to crawl, they may confront new barriers and repeated choruses of "no, don't do that." How these freshly imposed limits, inspired by burgeoning physical and mental capacities, are faced and resolved can affect many other aspects of solving problems or building relationships with others. Danielle, who is physically poised and skilled, displays confidence in the demands of learning a new and difficult gymnastic routine. That self-assurance very easily could extend to her social interactions and to her academic challenges. In contrast, the child who fails to display certain competencies or lacks physical attributes valued in a society—for example, is shorter, less coordinated, or otherwise physically distinctive—may receive strikingly different treatment compared with the child who is tall, strong, or athletic. Interpreting and orchestrating all these changes is the increasingly sophisticated and complex brain.

How do brain, motor skills, and body develop? To what extent do parenting, culture, or other environmental events influence their course? How important are appearance, early maturity, and physical prowess to achievements in other domains of development? In this chapter we explore these kinds of questions. First, we turn to the developing brain, the structure that plays a central role in controlling and integrating the many changes in all aspects of behavior, including physical development.

The Brain and Nervous System

In no other decade before the 1990s has the brain and its influence on the development of human behavior received more attention. Major advances in the field of *cognitive neuroscience*, the study of neural and other structures and systems of the brain associated with behavior, have produced insights and generated widespread interest among neuroscientists, child psychologists, parents, and the public about the relationship between the brain and behavior. In large part, much of this enthusiasm has been spurred by the emergence of fascinating new technologies for studying the brain (Thompson & Nelson, 2001). Among these innovative procedures are *positron emission tomography* (PET scans), *functional magnetic resonance imaging* (fMRI), and the recording of *event-related potentials* (ERP). These techniques measure metabolic activity, blood flow, and electrical events and provide clues about which areas of the brain are functioning when an individual is engaged in motor, sensory, linguistic, emotional, and other information processing. At the present time, PET scans have limited utility for studying normal infants and children because they require injection of a radioactive substance. However, fMRI (which measures cerebral blood flow) and ERP (which is a measure of electrical activity generated by the synchronous firing of neurons) are among the more widely available noninvasive procedures that hold considerable promise for investigating normal and abnormal brain development (Casey, Thomas, & McCandless, 2001; Nelson & Monk, 2001).

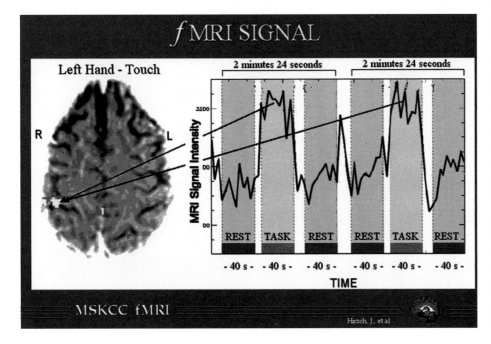

Cognitive neuroscientists employ many newer methods to understand how the brain functions as it processes information. One procedure involves functional magnetic resource imaging (fMRI). In this procedure information about blood flow and the availability of oxygen to various regions of the brain, an indicator of neural activation, is measured. Here, while the left hand is receiving tactile stimulation, one section of the brain (the right post central gyrus) shows activation, as indicated by the bright yellow and red coloration in that region. When the hand was not being touched (rest periods), the intensity of the fMRI signal was much less. This and other emerging technologies hold great promise for learning which specific areas of the brain are involved in various kinds of cognitive processing.

Theoretical and practical questions about the importance of early experience, the possibility of critical periods for receiving certain kinds of stimulation, and whether neural growth continues during later childhood, adolescence, and even well into adulthood have further fueled enthusiasm for studying the brain (Bruer, 1999). Much remains to be learned about these issues, and we continue to address some of them in other chapters. However, we summarize here a few of the major developmental changes that take place in the brain.

The Developing Brain

◉ SEE FOR YOURSELF
psychology.college.hmco.com
Early Brain Development

Even before birth, brain growth is rapid. As Figure 5.1 shows, the size of the brain swiftly increases, from about 4 percent of its adult weight at five months after conception to about 25 percent at birth and about 80 percent by four years of age (Spreen et al., 1994). However, the total volume of the brain does not change very much after about the age of five. Such a statement is a bit misleading, because the volume of the white matter increases throughout childhood and into adulthood largely because of continuing myelination of neurons. In contrast, the volume of gray matter, usually associated with the neurons, decreases largely as a result of pruning and perhaps cell death (Durston et al., 2001).

The *brainstem* and *midbrain* (see Figure 5.2), which are involved in basic reflexes and sensory processing, as well as such essential biological functions as digestion, elimination, and respiration, are fairly well established at birth (Joseph, 2000). In con-

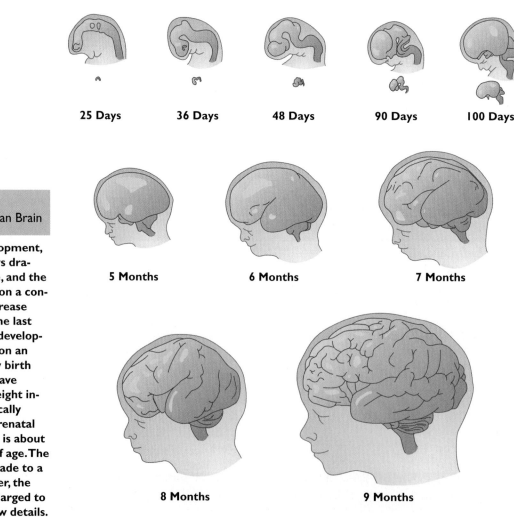

FIGURE 5.1
The Developing Human Brain

During prenatal development, the human brain shows dramatic increases in size, and the cerebral cortex takes on a convoluted pattern to increase surface area. During the last trimester of prenatal development, the brain takes on an adultlike shape, and by birth most of the neurons have formed. The brain's weight increases most dramatically from about the fifth prenatal month until the infant is about two-and-a-half years of age. The drawings have been made to a common scale; however, the first five have been enlarged to a common size to show details.

25 Days   36 Days   48 Days   90 Days   100 Days

5 Months   6 Months   7 Months

8 Months   9 Months

Source: Adapted from Cowan, 1979.

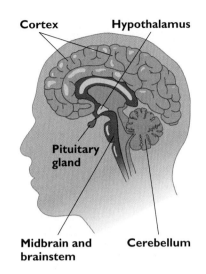

Cortex   **Hypothalamus**

Pituitary gland

Midbrain and brainstem   **Cerebellum**

FIGURE 5.2
Cross-Section of the Human Brain

Certain regions of the brain are closely associated with specific functions. The overarching cortex is essential for most of behavior and includes regions associated with processing sensory and motor information, as well as areas heavily involved in thinking, planning, and problem solving. The early-developing midbrain and brain stem are important to basic biological functioning. The cerebellum is centrally involved in coordination and control of voluntary movements. Both the hypothalamus and pituitary glands are believed to play a major role in the regulation of physical growth.

trast, neural changes in the cortex, the part of the brain most closely linked to sensation, motor responses, thinking, planning, and problem solving, continue to take place well after birth. Within the cortex, regions associated with sensory and motor functions tend to be among the earliest to mature. The frontal cortex, the region of the brain most directly involved in higher levels of cognition, tends to be among the latest.

With development, **neurons,** cells that carry electrochemical messages as neural impulses, *proliferate,* that is, increase in number. Neurons also *migrate*—move to various regions of the brain—and *differentiate*—increase in size, complexity, and functioning. One notable aspect of differentiation is the increased number and kinds of *synapses,* the space-filled junctures associated with the branches or dendrites of the neuron that permit it to communicate with other neurons. Parts of many neurons also become surrounded by **myelin,** a sheath of fatty material that serves to insulate and speed neural impulses by about tenfold. An estimated ten times more **glial cells** (from the Greek word for *glue*) than neurons also form within the brain (Blinkov & Glezer, 1968). Glial cells establish a scaffolding for neuron migration, provide the material from which myelin develops, facilitate the transfer of nutrients to neurons, and instruct the neurons to form synapses with other neurons (Ullian et al., 2001).

● **Neuron Proliferation**   The production of new nerve cells is known as *neuron proliferation.* Neuron production in humans begins near the end of the first month of prenatal development, shortly after the neural tube closes, and much of it, at least in the cerebral cortex, is completed by the sixth month of prenatal development (Nelson, 1999). Thus, at a very early age, a finite but very large number—certainly well over 100 billion—of young neurons have formed (Shatz, 1992).

● **Neuron Migration**   Shortly after their formation, neurons move from the neural tube, where they were produced, to other locations. In some regions of the brain this movement occurs passively, so that as additional neurons are born, older neurons are pushed further to the outside of that portion of the brain. This type of growth takes place, for example, in the hypothalamus, the brain stem, and the cerebellum. However, for many other regions of the brain such as the cerebral cortex, the neurons may migrate a great distance, passing through levels of older neurons that already have reached their final destination. These regions of the brain are formed by an *inside-out pattern* of development in which layers of nerve cells nearer the outer surface are younger than layers deeper in the cortex (Rakic, 1981). Under these circumstances, how do neurons know where to migrate and when to stop migrating? Both neurochemical and mechanical information probably play a role. Young neurons attach to and maneuver along the surfaces of fibers of glial cells radiating to the region of their destination, detaching from their guide, as shown in Figure 5.3, at programmed locations. Both the production and migration of large numbers of neurons

neuron   Nerve cell within the central nervous system that is electrochemically designed to transmit messages between cells.

myelin   Sheath of fatty cells that insulates and speeds neural impulses by about tenfold.

glial cells   Brain cells that provide the material from which myelin is created, nourish neurons, and provide a scaffolding for neuron migration.

This color-enhanced photo, taken with a scanning electron microscope, shows a neuron. Neurons carry the electro-chemical messages that are the basis for behavior. Even before birth, massive numbers of neurons are manufactured and migrate to various regions of the brain, where they begin to establish connections with other neurons.

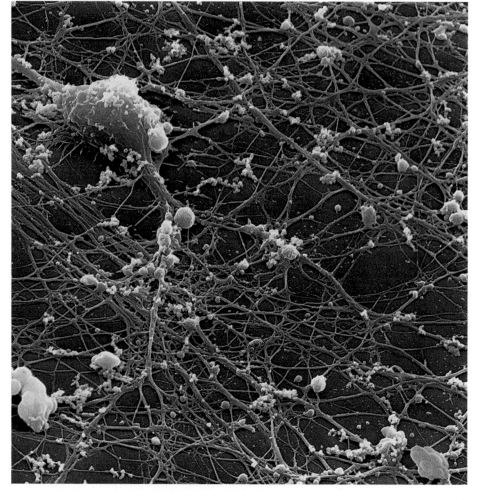

KEY THEME
Nature/Nurture

in the cortex occur in waves, especially during the seventh and eleventh weeks of gestational age (Spreen et al., 1984). However, some teratogens, including mercury and alcohol, are known to interfere with the onset and path of neuron migration. In fact, developmental defects ranging from mental retardation to behavioral disorders have been linked to interference in the migratory patterns of nerve cells (Gressens, 2000).

● **Neuron Differentiation**   Whereas neuron proliferation and migration take place prenatally for the most part, neuron differentiation—the process of enlarging, forming synapses with other neurons, and beginning to function—flourishes postnatally. Neural differentiation, along with the growth of glial cells and other supportive tissues, including myelin, contributes to the substantial postnatal increase in the size of the brain. Moreover, growing evidence exists to indicate that at least in some regions remodeling of the brain, in the form of neuron differentiation and even neuron production, continues well into adulthood (Spear, 2000; Tanapat, Hastings, & Gould, 2001).

Some aspects of neuron differentiation proceed without external stimulation. Experience, however, plays a major role in the selection, maintenance, and strengthening of connections among many neurons (Nelson, 2000). Work investigating the effects of vision on brain development in cats illustrates the complex relationship (Hubel & Wiesel, 1979). By the time a kitten's eyes open, neurons in the visual receptor areas of the cerebral cortex have already established some connections and can respond, for example, to sensory information from either eye or to visual patterns with a broad range of characteristics. But the neurons become far more selective and tuned to particular kinds of sensory information as the kitten experiences specific forms of visual stimulation. Some neurons may, for example, begin to respond to

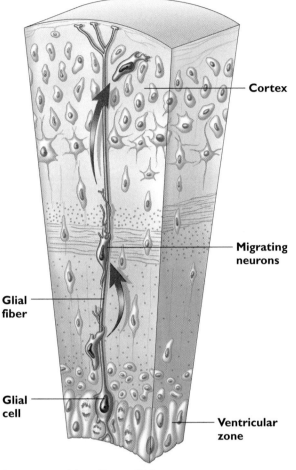

FIGURE 5.3
The Migration of Neurons
via Glial Fiber

Wrapping themselves around glial fibers, neurons climb in spiral fashion to a particular layer in the cortex of the brain. Because the cortex of the brain develops in an inside-out pattern, earlier waves of neurons need to progress across shorter distances, and their migration may be completed within a day. However, later waves of neurons pass through earlier layers of the cortex and migrate across a greater distance, so that their journey may require several weeks. Some teratogens can interfere with this migratory pattern and, if the disruption is severe, result in a variety of developmental defects.

Cortex

Migrating neurons

Glial fiber

Glial cell

Ventricular zone

Source: Adapted from Kunzig, 1998.

input arising from one or the other eye only and to transitions in dark-light patterns in the visual field that are vertical or horizontal or at some other spatial orientation.

Without stimulation and the opportunity to function, neurons are unlikely to establish or maintain many connections with other neurons; their synaptic density becomes substantially reduced. For example, in the visual cortex the total number of synapses rises meteorically in the first few months after birth; but then the connections show a small decline from about eight months of age to the late preschool years followed by a more substantial decline between about four and ten years. These dramatic changes in the visual cortex can be seen in Figure 5.4. Neurons may even die if no synapses are formed with other neurons. In fact, one theory holds that massive cell death, perhaps as great as 50 to 75 percent of neurons, occurs during normal development in the brains of some animals and perhaps in some regions of the human brain, although probably not in the cerebral cortex (Huttenlocher, 1994). Thus, the typical infant is genetically equipped with the capacity for neurons to generate many synaptic connections, perhaps far more than a person will ever need. That surplus provides the opportunity for a rich variety of experiences to affect development; it also means that if damage or destruction occurs to some synapses early in life, others may replace them.

KEY THEME
Nature/Nurture

Plasticity in Brain Development

Because of the unspecialized nature of young neurons, the immature brain displays substantial **plasticity,** or the ability, within limits, of alternate regions of the cerebral cortex to take on specialized sensory, linguistic, and other information-processing requirements (Johnson, 2000). Infants or children who suffer damage to regions of the cerebral cortex that process speech, for example, are often able to recover, because

plasticity Capacity of immature systems, including regions of the brain and the individual neurons within those regions, to take on different functions as a result of experience.

FIGURE 5.4
Estimated Number of
Synapses for Neurons in the
Human Visual Cortex as a
Function of Age

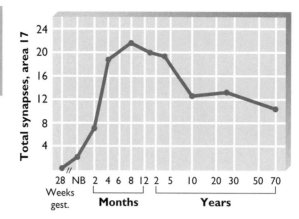

Source: Adapted from Huttenlocher, 1994.

Differentiation of the neurons in the human visual cortex proceeds rapidly shortly after birth and reaches a peak before the end of the first year. The number of synapses ($\times 10^{11}$), connections of dendrites to other neurons, then declines to about half of the original peak number over the lifespan. The rapid increment is associated with visual stimulation after birth and accompanies significant improvements in visual abilities before a year of age, as is discussed in the chapter titled "Basic Learning and Perception." The number of synapses reflects an initial overproduction; those that become functional are then likely to be maintained over the remaining years. Other regions of the cortex may show a similar pattern of rapid increase and then decline in number of synapses, although perhaps at different periods in development.

neurons in other parts of the cortex take on this function. On the other hand, although considerable plasticity is retained by some regions of the mature adult brain (Thompson & Nelson, 2001), the prognosis for recovery of language in adults after an accident or a stroke is usually much poorer, because the remaining neurons in various regions of the brain have become dedicated to processing certain kinds of experiences.

William Greenough and his colleagues contend that neurons in human and other mammalian brains exhibit two different kinds of plasticity (Greenough, Black, & Wallace, 1987). Some neurons are sensitive to *experience-expectant information.* As a result of a long evolutionary process, these neurons begin to grow and differentiate rapidly about the time they can be expected to receive the kinds of stimulation important to their functioning. In many mammals, for example, parts of the visual cortex involved in depth or pattern perception develop quite rapidly shortly before and after the eyes open or, in the case of humans, shortly before and after birth. Research with lower animals indicates that visual deprivation during these periods—being reared in the dark or without patterned light, for example—results in the permanent loss of some kinds of depth and pattern vision, losses that do not occur when equivalent lengths of deprivation occur during other periods.

Other neurons are sensitive to *experience-dependent information.* Many opportunities for learning occur at unpredictable times during development. Each person learns different and unique things, even into old age. The distinctive perceptual features forming the image of a neighbor or the attributes defining the concept of democracy are unique representations registered within an individual's neural system. Here, then, is a form of plasticity that implicates neural differentiation as a critical aspect of brain functioning throughout a person's lifetime.

Brain Lateralization

One of the brain's most obvious physical characteristics is its two mirrorlike structures, a *left* and *right* hemisphere. By and large, sensory information and motor responses on the left side of the body in humans are processed by the right hemisphere and those on the right side of the body are processed by the left hemisphere. In addition, in most adults the left hemisphere is especially involved in language functioning, whereas the right hemisphere is more typically engaged in processing certain types of spatial, emotional, or other nonverbal information (Kosslyn et al., 1999). But these differences are by no means absolute. For example, speech is controlled primarily by the left hemisphere in about 95 percent of right-handed adults but in only about 70 percent of left-handed adults (Kinsbourne & Hiscock, 1983).

Does hemispheric specialization exist already at birth, or does the brain show progressive **lateralization,** the process by which one hemisphere comes to dominate the other in terms of a particular function? Based on research on left-hemisphere damage in children, Eric Lenneberg (1967) proposed that at least until age two, both

lateralization   Process by which one hemisphere of the brain comes to dominate the other, for example, processing of language in the left hemisphere or of spatial information in the right hemisphere.

hemispheres are capable of carrying out language functions equally well and that lateralization increases only gradually until adolescence. Other researchers, however, suggest that lateralization begins much earlier (Kinsbourne & Hiscock, 1983), perhaps as a consequence of exposure to fetal testosterone (Geschwind & Galaburda, 1987; McManus & Bryden, 1991). For example, some physical differences in the two hemispheres exist already at birth (Kosslyn et al., 1999). Perhaps such brain asymmetries contribute to the observation that most infants lie with the head oriented to the right rather than to the left, an orientation that later predicts hand preference (Michel, 1988). Even before three months of age, most babies more actively use and hold objects longer in the right hand than in the left (Hawn & Harris, 1983). They also turn to stimulation coming from the right side more frequently (Siqueland & Lipsitt, 1966). Furthermore, infants are able to better identify changes in speech sounds heard in their right ear and to detect shifts in the timbre of musical notes better in their left ear (Best, Hoffman, & Glanville, 1982).

FOR YOUR REVIEW

- What are the major methodological procedures that have permitted advances in the study of the developing brain?

- Which regions of the brain develop earliest and latest? To what functions do those regions contribute?

- What developmental changes occur in neurons? How do myelin and glial cells contribute to neuronal development?

- When does the plasticity of the brain decline? What is the difference between experience-expectant and experience-dependent information?

- What evidence exists for brain lateralization in infancy and early childhood?

Motor Skill Development

During postnatal development, cartilage continues to be transformed into bone, and bones elongate and increase in number to become scaffolding to support the body in new physical orientations. As the brain and nervous system mature, neural commands begin to coordinate thickened and enlarged muscles, permitting more powerful and refined motor activities. Two complementary patterns are evident in the emergence of motor activity: *differentiation,* the enrichment of global and relatively diffuse actions with more refined and skilled ones, and *integration,* the increasingly coordinated actions of muscles and sensory systems. Throughout infancy and childhood, motor skills become more efficient, coordinated, and deliberate or automatic as the task requires. Toward the end of childhood, many skills become highly specialized talents: youngsters such as Danielle are already accomplished athletes; others her age are concert musicians.

For Piaget, sensorimotor activity served as the prototype and first stage in the construction of knowledge. Thus, the acquisition, coordination, and integration of basic motor skills is not only an interesting topic of study in itself but also can give us important insights into early cognitive and perceptual development.

KEY THEME
Interaction Among Domains

The First Actions: Reflexes

At first glance, newborns seem helpless and incompetent. Babies eat, sleep, and cry; their diapers always seem to need changing. Yet a more careful look reveals that infants enter their new world with surprisingly adept sensory abilities (see the chapter titled "Basic Learning and Perception"), along with **reflexes,** involuntary reactions to touch, light, sound, and other kinds of stimulation, some of which are exhibited even prenatally.

reflex Involuntary movement in response to touch, light, sound, or other form of stimulation; controlled by subcortical neural mechanisms.

Among the reflexes that babies display is the swimming reflex. When young infants are placed in water, breathing is suspended, and they engage in swim-like movements with their arms and legs.

TABLE 5.1	Typical Reflexes Observed in Newborns and Infants

Considerable variability exists among infants in their reflexes and the ages at which they can be elicited (Touwen, 1974). The presence or absence of any single reflex provides only one among many indicators of healthy or atypical development.

Name of Reflex	Testing Procedure	Response	Developmental Course	Significance
Primitive Reflexes				
Palmar or Hand Grasp	Place finger in hand.	Hand grasps object.	Birth to about 4 months.	Absence may signal neurological defects; persistence could interfere with voluntary grasping.
Rooting	Stroke corner of mouth lightly.	Head and tongue move toward stimulus.	Birth to about 5 months.	Mouth is brought to stimulus to permit sucking.
Sucking	Place finger in mouth or on lips.	Sucking begins.	Birth to about 6 months.	Ensures intake of potential nutrients.
Moro	(1) Sit child up, allow head to drop about 20 degrees backward, or (2) make a loud noise, or (3) lower baby rapidly.	Baby extends arms outward, hands open; then brings hands to midline, hands clenched, spine straightened.	Birth to about 5–7 months.	Absence may signal neurological defects; persistence could interfere with acquisition of sitting.
Babinski	Stroke bottom of foot.	Toes fan and then curl.	Birth to about 1 year.	Absence may signal neurological defects.
Asymmetric Tonic Neck Reflex	Place baby on back, arms and legs extended, and rotate head 90 degrees.	Arm on face side extends, arm on back side of head flexes.	About 1 month to 4 months.	Absence may signal neurological defects; persistence could prevent rolling over, coordination.

TABLE 5.1	Typical Reflexes Observed in Newborns and Infants *(continued)*			
Name of Reflex	**Testing Procedure**	**Response**	**Developmental Course**	**Significance**
Postural Reflexes				
Stepping	Hold baby under arms, upright, leaning forward.	Makes walk-like stepping movements.	Birth to about 3 months.	Absence may signal neurological defects.
Labyrinthine	(1) Place baby on back.	Extends arms and legs.	Birth to about 4 months.	Absence may signal neurological defects.
	(2) Place baby on stomach.	Flexes arms and legs.		
Swimming	Place baby in water.	Holds breath involuntarily; arms and legs move as if trying to swim.	Birth to about 4–6 months.	Absence may signal neurological defects.
Placing	Hold baby under arms, upright, top of foot touching bottom edge of table.	Lifts foot and places on top of table.	Birth through 12 months.	Absence may signal neurological defects.
Landau Reaction	Place baby on stomach, hold under chest.	Lifts head, eventually other parts of body, above chest.	Head at 2 months, other parts of body later.	Absence may signal neurological defects; inadequate muscle tone for motor development.
Body Righting	Rotate hips or shoulder.	Rotates remainder of body.	4 months to more than 12 months.	Absence may signal neurological defects; difficulty in gaining postural control and walking.

Reflexes are among the building blocks that soon give rise to voluntary movements and the acquisition of developmental milestones or significant achievements in motor skills. Along with breathing and swallowing, *primitive reflexes* such as rooting and sucking (see Table 5.1) provide nourishment for survival of the infant. Among our evolutionary ancestors, other reflexes, such as the Moro and palmar reflexes, helped to protect newborns from danger. *Postural reflexes,* including stepping, swimming, and body righting (which are surprisingly similar to later voluntary movements), appear to be designed to maintain a specific orientation to the environment. If primitive or postural reflexes are absent, are too strong or too weak, display unequal strength when normally elicited from either side of the body, or continue to be exhibited beyond certain ages, a pediatrician may begin to suspect cerebral palsy or some other neurological impairment and developmental difficulties for the baby (Blasco, 1994).

RESEARCH APPLIED TO PARENTING

Reducing Sudden Infant Death Syndrome

Danielle's parents faithfully attended her gymnastics meets and were ardent supporters of her efforts. Danielle wasn't always pleased by the watchful presence they exhibited toward her, their only daughter. But she was beginning to more fully understand it. When Danielle was four, her parents introduced her to a baby brother. Danielle remembered how proud she had been to hold him and to "help her mother." But all that changed a few months later. On that tragic morning, she had been awakened by the frantic voices of her parents and strangers—emergency medical technicians, she learned later—in her baby brother's room. She suspected something terrible had happened, and it had: her brother had died. She was frightened then and for a long time thereafter. Her fears subsided only gradually as her parents picked up the pieces of their lives.

To survive in the postnatal environment, the infant must synchronize rooting and sucking with swallowing and breathing. In fact, the inability to coordinate these reflexes often makes nursing difficult for premature infants (Rosenblith & Sims-Knight, 1985). But organizing and controlling breathing can be a problem for a small number of older infants as well. The abrupt, unexplained death of an infant less than one year of age who stops breathing during sleep is known as **sudden infant death syndrome (SIDS).** The deaths, most frequently reported in babies about two to four months of age, are particularly tragic because they occur with no identifiable warnings. The highest incidence appears to occur at a time when basic automatic respiratory reflexes governed by the brain stem begin to be supplemented by voluntary, cortex-regulated breathing essential for vocalization and the emergence of speech.

SIDS, once known as *crib death* or *cot death,* claimed the lives of between one and two of every one thousand babies born in the United States in recent decades. Much higher rates had been reported in some other countries such as New Zealand (Mitchell et al., 1997). It continues to be the third leading cause of infant mortality in the United States and in most Western countries. Only congenital malformations and low birth weight or prematurity contribute to more deaths among infants (Hoyert et al., 2001). Although researchers still do not know what causes SIDS, specific steps that parents can take are now known to reduce its risk of occurring:

1. *"Back to Sleep."*   Up until the 1990s, parents were often advised to place their babies in a prone position (on their stomachs) when ready for sleep. However, research conducted around the world (Australia, Britain, New Zealand, the Netherlands, Norway, Sweden, and many other countries, including the United States) reveals that when parents stop this practice, the incidence of SIDS declines (Hauck & Hunt, 2000). Thus in 1994 pediatricians initiated a "Back to Sleep" campaign to encourage parents to place healthy infants on their backs to sleep. This single change has been estimated to reduce the incidence of SIDS as much as 50 percent in some nations, and greater than 40 percent in the United States (American Academy of Pediatrics, 2000).

2. *Eliminate exposure to cigarette smoke and other drugs.*   Numerous studies have confirmed that a mother's smoking or use of other drugs during pregnancy is associated with a greater likelihood of SIDS (Mitchell & Milerad, 1999). However, exposure even to passive smoke after birth (from mother, father, or other live-in adults) increases the risk as well.

3. *Provide firm bedding.*   The incidence of SIDS in Australia and New Zealand had been among the highest in the world. In these countries, less firm bedding (use of wool or of bark from the ti tree) appears to have contributed to the risk of SIDS, especially for infants sleeping prone, perhaps because of a tendency for this softer bedding to trap carbon dioxide.

4. *Avoid overheating.*   High room temperature and high body temperature because of excessive bedding and/or clothing are also known to increase the incidence of SIDS (Guntheroth & Spiers, 2001). Adequate ventilation also helps to prevent overheating of the infant, as well as to disperse carbon dioxide.

SIDS is associated with a number of other factors, including the colder months of the year, economically depressed neighborhoods, having a cold, being male, being either a later-born or one of a multiple birth, and low birth weight. In addition to susceptibility to the buildup of carbon dioxide and increased temperature, other infant characteristics that are hypothesized to play a causative role include a deficit in arousal and anomalies associated with heart rate (Hauck & Hunt, 2000). Parents

KEY THEME
Sociocultural Influence

sudden infant death syndrome (SIDS) Sudden, unexplained death of an infant or a toddler as a result of cessation of breathing during sleep.

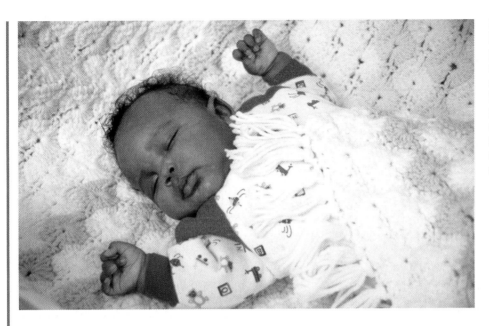

Placing infants on their backs in preparation for sleep appears to have reduced the frequency of sudden infant death syndrome (SIDS). The decline in SIDS associated with this practice is reported in many countries, including the United States, where pediatricians in the 1990s launched a "back to sleep" campaign.

may have little control over some of these factors. Unfortunately, efforts to educate everyone about a better sleeping position or use of firmer bedding have not reached all caregivers (Brenner et al., 1998; Kemp et al., 1998). The rate of placing infants on their stomachs is higher than average among African American families, younger mothers, and low-income families, and in some regions of the United States, in daycare centers where infants are put to sleep during nap periods (Moon & Biliter, 2000; Willinger et al., 2000). As more and more parents turn to daycare centers, family daycare providers, or other family members (e.g., grandparents or siblings) to care for their young infants, it is vital that these alternative caregivers also be informed about the importance of infants being placed on their backs for naps and during other sleep periods (Flick et al., 2001; Moon, Patel, & McDermott Shaefer, 2000). Research indicates that babies accustomed to sleeping on their backs, if placed prone or on their sides (because of the possibility of rolling into a prone position), are particularly susceptible to increased risk of SIDS (Hauck & Hunt, 2000; Mitchell et al., 1999).

Although the benefits far outweigh the drawbacks, one unintended outcome of having infants sleep on their backs has been more frequent reports of misshapen heads, particularly, flattening of the back of the head (Najarian, 1999). The problem, not normally serious, can be substantially reduced by varying head position each time the baby is placed for sleep and giving the infant plenty of experience on his or her stomach during periods when awake and under the watchful eye of a parent. Adequate "tummy time" also helps to strengthen the shoulders and arms and minimizes possible delays in achieving various milestones of motor development associated with the upper body (American Academy of Pediatrics, 2000).

Controversy continues over the question of where an infant should sleep. Historically, and in most cultures today (such as Japan), an infant and mother sleeping together (co-sleeping) is the norm (Latz, Wolf, & Lozoff, 1999). In fact, Mayan mothers view putting very young children in a separate room at night as almost equivalent to child neglect (Morrelli et al., 1992). However, American mothers typically justify such a practice, especially after the baby is a few months old, as a way to encourage self-reliance and independence.

Decisions about sleeping arrangements are deeply ingrained in cultural beliefs concerning the values of closeness and interdependence and of privacy and self-reliance. James McKenna and his colleagues contend that in co-sleeping arrangements, mothers and infants engage in greater synchronized sleep, breathing, and arousal patterns that serve to protect infants from *apnea,* irregular patterns of temporary cessations in breathing (Mosko, Richard, & McKenna, 1997). However, little evidence has been found to demonstrate that this practice has a protective effect

KEY THEME
Sociocultural Influence

against SIDS. Co-sleeping is especially hazardous on a couch or if the parent smokes, consumes alcohol, or uses other drugs (Hauck & Hunt, 2000). A far safer alternative to bed sharing for those who wish to be in close contact appears to be having the baby sleep within arm's length but in an infant crib.

Motor Milestones

Reflexes are often viewed as fixed responses to a stimulus. However, many early motor behaviors that young infants soon produce consist of coordinated actions. For example, babies exhibit **rhythmical stereotypies,** repeated sequences of motions performed with no apparent goal (Thelen, 1996). Rubbing one foot against the other, rocking back and forth, bouncing up and down, swaying side to side, striking or banging objects, mouthing and tonguing activities, and shaking and nodding the head are just a few of the movements that exercise bones, joints, and muscles. Stereotypies, along with early reflexes, appear to be the bits and pieces of the primitive melody of behavior that eventually are recruited and integrated into organized voluntary motor skills and activities (Thelen, 1996).

KEY THEME
Child's Active Role

Many more organized goal-directed voluntary actions emerge during the first year as infants gradually gain neuromotor control of their heads, arms, and legs. Some of these actions—grasping, crawling, and walking, for example—are motor milestones: once mastered, new worlds open up to the infant. Moreover, they lead caregivers to respond in different ways: childproofing the home to prevent accidents, allowing greater independence, expecting more mature behavior. Most gains in infant movement illustrate progress in coordinating (1) *postural control,* the ability to maintain an upright orientation to the environment; (2) *locomotion,* the ability to maneuver through space; and (3) *manual control,* the ability to manipulate objects (Keogh & Sugden, 1985).

● **Postural Control** Keeping the head upright and stable at about two to three months of age represents one of the first milestones in infant motor development. As the Motor Skill Development chronology indicates, this achievement is followed by mastery of other significant postural skills, such as maintaining an upright sitting position, moving to a standing position, and standing without assistance. The milestones, built on various postural reflexes among other things, often reflect a cephalocaudal progression. **Cephalocaudal development** (*cephalocaudal* combines the Greek words for *head* and *tail*) describes the tendency for systems and parts of the body near the head to become organized sooner than those more distant from the head. Head control, for example, precedes control of the trunk, and command of the legs is the last to develop. The integration of postural skills is also important. For example, the ability to keep the head upright while sitting or while standing on a stable surface is one thing; the ability to do this when being carried about or during self-movement requires integration of far more information to retain motor control.

● **Locomotion** Achievements in the ability to move about the environment are also summarized in the chronology. One early milestone in locomotion is the capacity to roll over. Then comes success at initiating forward motion, a skill marked by considerable variation (Adolph, Vereijken, & Denny, 1998; Freedland & Bertenthal, 1994). Some infants use arms to pull and legs to push, others use only arms or legs, and still others scoot forward while sitting. *Crawling,* locomotion with stomach touching the floor, may soon give way to *creeping,* locomotion on hands and knees— and then again it may not. The varieties of forward motion invented by babies often generate lively discussions among caregivers.

Once babies are able to pull themselves upright, they often *cruise,* that is, move by holding onto furniture or other objects to help maintain their balance while stepping sideways (Barela, Jeka, & Clark, 1999). Forward walking while holding onto someone's hand typically follows. By about twelve months of age, about half of American

rhythmical stereotypies
Repeated sequences of movements, such as leg kicking, hand waving, or head banging, that have no apparent goal.

cephalocaudal development
Pattern in which organs, systems, and motor movements near the head tend to develop earlier than those near the feet.

CHRONOLOGY: *Motor Skill Development*

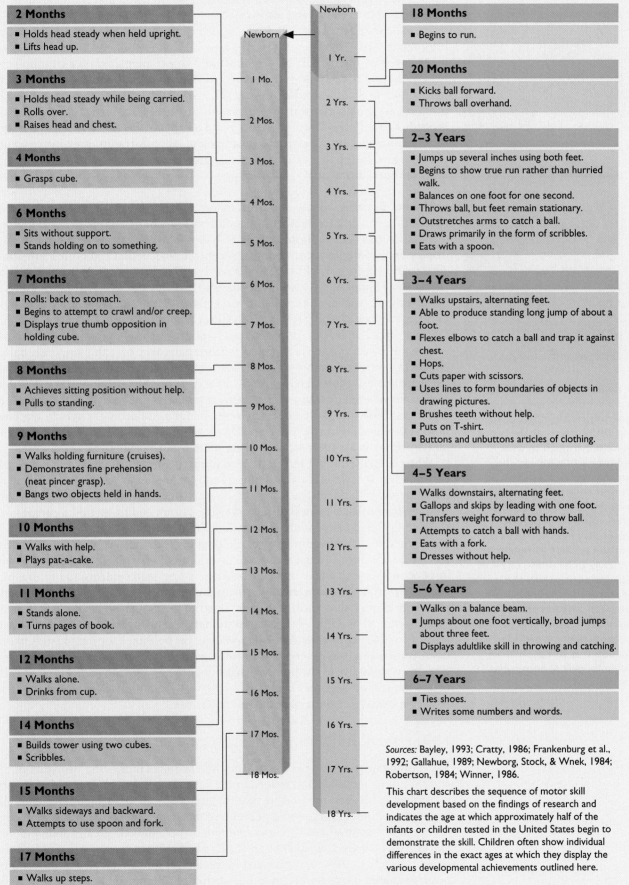

Newborn

2 Months
- Holds head steady when held upright.
- Lifts head up.

3 Months
- Holds head steady while being carried.
- Rolls over.
- Raises head and chest.

4 Months
- Grasps cube.

6 Months
- Sits without support.
- Stands holding on to something.

7 Months
- Rolls: back to stomach.
- Begins to attempt to crawl and/or creep.
- Displays true thumb opposition in holding cube.

8 Months
- Achieves sitting position without help.
- Pulls to standing.

9 Months
- Walks holding furniture (cruises).
- Demonstrates fine prehension (neat pincer grasp).
- Bangs two objects held in hands.

10 Months
- Walks with help.
- Plays pat-a-cake.

11 Months
- Stands alone.
- Turns pages of book.

12 Months
- Walks alone.
- Drinks from cup.

14 Months
- Builds tower using two cubes.
- Scribbles.

15 Months
- Walks sideways and backward.
- Attempts to use spoon and fork.

17 Months
- Walks up steps.

Newborn · 1 Mo. · 2 Mos. · 3 Mos. · 4 Mos. · 5 Mos. · 6 Mos. · 7 Mos. · 8 Mos. · 9 Mos. · 10 Mos. · 11 Mos. · 12 Mos. · 13 Mos. · 14 Mos. · 15 Mos. · 16 Mos. · 17 Mos. · 18 Mos.

Newborn · 1 Yr. · 2 Yrs. · 3 Yrs. · 4 Yrs. · 5 Yrs. · 6 Yrs. · 7 Yrs. · 8 Yrs. · 9 Yrs. · 10 Yrs. · 11 Yrs. · 12 Yrs. · 13 Yrs. · 14 Yrs. · 15 Yrs. · 16 Yrs. · 17 Yrs. · 18 Yrs.

---

18 Months
- Begins to run.

20 Months
- Kicks ball forward.
- Throws ball overhand.

2–3 Years
- Jumps up several inches using both feet.
- Begins to show true run rather than hurried walk.
- Balances on one foot for one second.
- Throws ball, but feet remain stationary.
- Outstretches arms to catch a ball.
- Draws primarily in the form of scribbles.
- Eats with a spoon.

3–4 Years
- Walks upstairs, alternating feet.
- Able to produce standing long jump of about a foot.
- Flexes elbows to catch a ball and trap it against chest.
- Hops.
- Cuts paper with scissors.
- Uses lines to form boundaries of objects in drawing pictures.
- Brushes teeth without help.
- Puts on T-shirt.
- Buttons and unbuttons articles of clothing.

4–5 Years
- Walks downstairs, alternating feet.
- Gallops and skips by leading with one foot.
- Transfers weight forward to throw ball.
- Attempts to catch a ball with hands.
- Eats with a fork.
- Dresses without help.

5–6 Years
- Walks on a balance beam.
- Jumps about one foot vertically, broad jumps about three feet.
- Displays adultlike skill in throwing and catching.

6–7 Years
- Ties shoes.
- Writes some numbers and words.

Sources: Bayley, 1993; Cratty, 1986; Frankenburg et al., 1992; Gallahue, 1989; Newborg, Stock, & Wnek, 1984; Robertson, 1984; Winner, 1986.

This chart describes the sequence of motor skill development based on the findings of research and indicates the age at which approximately half of the infants or children tested in the United States begin to demonstrate the skill. Children often show individual differences in the exact ages at which they display the various developmental achievements outlined here.

A major motor milestone that babies around a year of age typically reach is that of walking. Although this baby is not quite old enough to walk independently, infants show surprisingly coordinated leg movements well before this milestone is reached. Do you think this kind of practice might also help her to begin walking earlier? Although we typically think of the onset of walking as primarily the result of maturation, cross-cultural research suggests that in communities in which a great deal of opportunity is provided to acquire this ability, children begin to walk at somewhat earlier ages.

babies and infants in many other countries walk alone, a skill that continues to be refined throughout infancy and early childhood.

Prewalking and walking skills likely depend on the growth of higher brain centers, but even before independent walking, many of the components of this ability are evident. For example, when babies six months of age are placed on a treadmill and held so they do not have to support their full weight, they display alternating stepping similar to that involved in walking (Thelen & Ulrich, 1991). Even six-week-olds produce surprisingly coordinated leg movements when lying on their backs (Thelen, Skala, & Kelso, 1987). Thus even though the coordinated action pattern underlying these abilities may be available much earlier, the task constraints of maintaining upright posture, lifting the leg against gravity, moving forward, and other factors may delay the onset of walking.

● **Manual Control**   In the weeks that follow birth, infants make enormous progress in reaching. Moving the hand to the mouth appears to be among the earliest goal-directed actions (Lew & Butterworth, 1997; Rochat, 1993). However, newborns also display *prereaching* in their attempts to contact objects that catch their attention. These early efforts are neither accurate nor coordinated with grasping. Still, movements show speeding up, slowing down, and changes in direction, just as in later, more accurate reaches (Rönnqvist & von Hofsten, 1994; von Hofsten & Rönnqvist, 1993). Systematic reaching for objects begins at about three months of age. By about five to six months, infants display mature, *ballistic* reaches to rapidly and accurately retrieve an object in the visual field. In gaining mastery over this response, babies engage in a series of submovements, not always perfectly executed but often quickly corrected to meet the goal of obtaining the target (Berthier, 1996; Berthier & Robin, 1998) and will even intercept a target moving past their line of sight (Robin, Berthier, & Clifton, 1996). The ability to see their own hands is not necessary in early reaching; however, infants eventually make greater use of visual cues to help them retrieve an object (Clifton et al., 1993; McCarty et al., 2001; Robin, Berthier, & Clifton, 1996).

When first attempting to reach, very young infants typically keep their hands closed in fistlike fashion. By about four months of age, infants awkwardly pick up an object by grasping it with the palm of the hand. Over the next few months, they shift from using the inner palm to using opposing thumb and fingertips, a progression that culminates in a *neat pincer grasp* at about nine months of age.

Another important component of motor skill is increased coordination between the two hands. Very young infants often attempt to grasp objects with both hands, but once babies gain an ensemble of skills, including head control and postural balance while sitting by themselves and when leaning forward, one-handed reaches and more consistent, stable reaching become a part of their repertoire (Rochat & Goubet, 1995; Spencer et al., 2000). Increased coordination is further reflected in the appearance of complementary hand orientations, such as holding a toy dump truck in one hand while using the other hand to fill it with sand. This *functional asymmetry* emerges at about five to six months of age but becomes especially refined as the child enters the second year and begins to display self-help and advanced motor tasks requiring sophisticated use of both arms and hands.

Motor Skills in the Preschool and Later-Childhood Years

Many fundamental motor skills that the child acquires in the first two years of life continue to be modified and refined in the preschool and elementary school years. For example, between two and six months after learning to walk, children typically begin to run. In the months and years that follow, they show increasingly effective body and eye-hand or eye-foot *coordination*, evident in their greater ability to hop and skip or, perhaps, kick, dribble, and catch a ball. With increasing age, children also demonstrate better *balance*, reflected in the ability to walk greater distances on a beam or stand on one foot for a longer period of time; increased *speed*, shown by running short distances more rapidly; improved *agility*, revealed, for example, in the

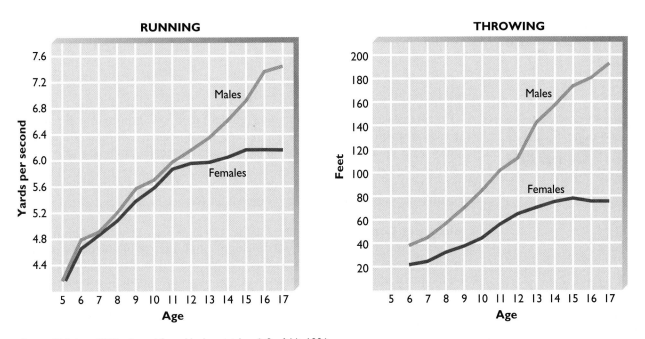

Source: Gallahue, 1989, adapted from Haubenstricker & Seefeldt, 1986.

ability to shift directions quickly while running; and greater *power,* shown by jumping higher or longer distances or throwing a ball farther and faster than at younger ages. The Motor Skill Development chronology summarizes major accomplishments for some of these abilities during early childhood.

In general, activities that exercise large muscles attract the interest of toddlers and preschoolers—pulling and pushing things, stacking and nesting large objects, and, eventually, riding toys such as kiddie cars and tricycles. As preschoolers begin to organize and display more interest in energetic games and athletic activities—jumping, hopping, running, balancing, and catching or throwing a ball—feats that emphasize speed, strength, and efficiency of performance become frequent ingredients of their everyday schedule. When first attempting to execute these skills, young children often fail to prepare or follow through on their actions, and the speed or force needed to complete them in a mature way is absent. Before finally demonstrating mastery of a skill, children may have difficulty synchronizing all of the complex movements.

Older preschoolers supplement their large-muscle and athletic exercises with coloring and drawing, cutting and sculpting, and other activities that demand greater neural control and small-muscle coordination, a longer attention span, and more sophisticated planning and organization. Motor skills during middle childhood become more efficient and better controlled, involve complex and coordinated movements, and are exhibited quickly and in a wider variety of contexts and circumstances (Keogh & Sugden, 1985). With the exception of balance, boys tend to slightly outperform girls on many gross motor tasks by the time they enter elementary school (Gallahue, 1989). However, differences between boys and girls may become especially large for some activities as children enter the adolescent years, as Figure 5.5 indicates for running speed and the distance a youngster can throw a ball.

Fine motor coordination improves dramatically during the school years. For example, writing as a motor production activity independent of drawing emerges around six years of age (Adi-Japha & Freeman, 2001). In addition, model construction or needlework, mastering the complex finger sequencing needed to play musical instruments, and more detailed drawings confirm that motor skills are undergoing significant developmental advances.

As children grow older, differences in individual abilities often increase. The effect may, of course, stem from practice, because some children focus on acquiring particular competence relevant to their social and cultural milieus. The acquisition of expertise or specialized motor skills in sports, dance, crafts, hobbies, playing musical

FIGURE 5.5
Running Speed and Throwing Distance for Boys and Girls at Different Ages

Boys tend to outperform girls on many motor skill tasks during the elementary school years, as indicated by these data on speed of running and distance throwing a ball, summarized from a number of studies carried out since 1960. The differences between girls and boys often increase substantially as children enter adolescence.

KEY THEME
Individual Differences

instruments, and, in some cultures, trade- or work-related endeavors permits older children to become more effective members of their society, and gain greater social status among peers and adults.

Determinants of Motor Development

KEY THEME
Nature/Nurture

Are the emergence, refinement, and integration of motor skills primarily dependent on genetic or maturational factors? Or are they the consequence of practice, cultural, or other experiential factors? Many pioneers in developmental psychology advocated a strong maturational theory to explain the orderly acquisition of motor skills. But changes, just as in other domains of development, are better understood in terms of the confluence of both biological and experiential factors.

● **Biological Contributions**   One of the strongest arguments in support of a genetic or maturational basis for the development of motor skills is their tendency to be displayed at predictable times and in similar ways in normal children. More-over, the onset of such skills as sitting and walking show greater concordance for identical than for fraternal twins. Greater similarity in gross motor activities such as running, jumping, and throwing is found in children who are more closely related biologically (Malina, 1980). Even intellectually and physically disabled babies attain major milestones in an orderly manner, although at a later age than other children. For example, blind children who show substantial delays in acquiring postural, loco-motion, and manual coordination skills eventually acquire them nonetheless (Tröster & Brambring, 1993).

● **Experiential Contributions**   Could experiential variables also play a role in motor development? With respect to the acquisition of expert motor skill, the answer is most certainly yes. However, it may be true for attaining basic developmental mile-stones as well. Lack of opportunity to engage in physical activity seriously interferes with reaching developmental milestones. For example, babies who spent most of their first year in an orphanage lying in cribs and receiving few other forms of stimu-lation typically did not walk before age three or four (Dennis, 1960). When special programs encourage blind infants to acquire self-initiated movement, they do so at ages more comparable to their sighted peers' (Fraiberg, 1977).

In the Navajo culture babies are often swaddled for most of the day. Wayne Dennis's re-search with Hopi infants who were also cared for in this way suggests that this baby, despite the lack of opportunity to prac-tice sitting up, crawling, and standing alone, will begin to walk about the same time as an infant who has not been swaddled.

Several investigators in the 1930s conducted studies with sets of twins to test the role of experience in motor skill development. Typically, one twin received extensive training in, say, handling blocks, climbing stairs, or roller skating; the other twin did not (Gesell & Thompson, 1934; Hilgard, 1932; McGraw, 1935). When given a chance to acquire the skills, the untrained twin often rapidly achieved the same level of accomplishment displayed by the trained twin. In another early study, Wayne and Marsena Dennis investigated child-rearing practices among the Hopi Indians (Dennis & Dennis, 1940). Some Hopi Indian mothers followed the tribal tradition of tightly swaddling their babies in a cradleboard; the mother would strap the board to her back for all but about an hour a day during her waking hours for the first six to twelve months of her child's life. These Hopi babies had little opportunity to practice sitting up, crawling, and walking. Other Hopi mothers reared infants without swaddling. The researchers found that swaddling had little bearing on when infants initiated walking, an observation reconfirmed in a later study of the effects of Hopi rearing customs (Harriman & Lukosius, 1982).

What can we conclude from these investigations? Perhaps that the typical range of daily activities and experiences in which infants and children are engaged is sufficient to promote normal locomotor development. But consider other findings. Infants from one to seven weeks of age, given a few minutes of daily practice with the placing and stepping reflexes, retain them and begin walking earlier than infants who receive no special training or whose legs are passively moved back and forth (Zelazo, 1983). Moreover, practice in sitting helps infants acquire these skills (Zelazo et al., 1993).

Esther Thelen and her colleagues (Thelen & Smith, 1994, 1998) have applied a far broader perspective to the role of experience in motor development. Thelen has argued that all complex motor skills require the assembling and reassembling of multiple processes involving, among other things, motivation, elements of the nervous system that regulate posture and balance, increased bone and muscle strength, and changes in body proportions. The assemblages are further constrained by the biodynamics of the human body, as well as the situational context. However, when the right improvisation of components exists, infants display mastery of motor skills or advance to new levels of competence. Neither biological nor experiential factors alone are responsible. Instead, motor development is a dynamic system; its multiple components become "tuned" into sequences of more effective, self-organized actions over time (Lockman & Thelen, 1993).

> **KEY THEME**
> **Individual Differences**

Cross-Cultural Differences

> **KEY THEME**
> **Sociocultural Influence**

Given the multiple processes involved, it should not be surprising to learn that ethnic and cultural differences in motor development exist as well. At birth and throughout their first year, African American babies, as well as infants among the Wolof of Senegal, Gusii of Kenya, Yoruba of Nigeria, Bantu of South Africa, and Ganda of Uganda, typically outperform Caucasian infants on a variety of motor skills (Lester & Brazelton, 1982; Werner, 1972). Parents in a fairly prosperous rural community in Kenya made extensive efforts to teach their infants to sit or walk (Super, 1976). In fact, their language, as in some other regions of East Africa, contained distinctive words to denote the specialized training. The more caregivers promoted specific motor skills, the earlier their children tended to display them. For example, 93 percent of one group of caregivers said they taught their babies to crawl, and babies in this group began crawling at about five-and-a-half months of age. In contrast, only 13 percent of the caregivers in a nearby group expressed support for teaching their infants to crawl, and these babies did not crawl until about eight months of age.

Many factors could contribute to the cultural differences, but one finding strongly implicates child-rearing efforts. Advanced motor development in this part of Kenya was limited to sitting, standing, and walking, skills considered culturally important. Other milestones not taught or valued, such as head control or the ability to roll over, were acquired later than they are by American infants. A similar observation comes from Jamaica. Some mothers in that country perform special stretching and massaging exercises to encourage their infants to sit and walk alone (Hopkins & Westra, 1990). Children of these mothers sit by themselves and walk earlier than other children.

We cannot be certain whether training focused on particular skills or more general experiences are responsible for cultural differences. Children in East Africa, for example, spend more time in an upright position, seated on a caregiver's lap or riding on her back, than children in the United States (Super, 1976). The activities may strengthen trunk and leg muscles to aid the earlier appearance of sitting, standing, and walking. However, gains achieved from training in one of two particular skills, such as stepping or sitting, do not appear to generalize to the other (Zelazo, 1998; Zelazo et al., 1993). Infants who become increasingly proficient in crawling up and down a slope have to relearn how to go up and down the same slope when they start to walk (Adolph, 1997).

Children of the Ache of Eastern Paraguay are significantly delayed in acquiring a host of motor skills. For example, walking is not exhibited until twenty-one to twenty-three months of age (Kaplan & Dove, 1987). This small band, which engages in hunting and gathering, does not encourage the acquisition of motor skills in infants. When families migrate to the forests, the women closely supervise their children younger than three years, preventing them from venturing more than a yard or so into the uncleared vegetation (Kaplan & Dove, 1987). For the Ache, keeping infants close by may be crucial for their continued survival, but it gives little opportunity for infants to practice motor skills. Because the Ache have been relatively isolated and the total population at times quite small, genetic factors cannot be ruled out as contributing to the delay, but cultural concerns and efforts to either promote or discourage the acquisition of motor skills appear to have a significant effect on their development.

FOR YOUR REVIEW

- How do primitive and postural reflexes differ? What purpose do they serve for the infant?

- What are the factors associated with SIDS? What steps can caregivers take to reduce the likelihood of its occurring?

- Why does controversy exist concerning the sleeping arrangements for young infants?

- When are rhythmical stereotypies exhibited?

- What are the major milestones associated with the development of postural control, locomotion, and manual control? How does the principle of cephalocaudal development apply to the emergence of the major motor milestones?

- What kinds of improvements in motor skills are observed in the preschool and later childhood years?

- What are factors that contribute to motor development? How do cultural practices influence their acquisition?

Body Growth and Development

Just as the emergence of increasingly sophisticated motor skills provides a highly visible indicator of development, so too does the change in physical size. For parent and child alike, the ever-higher marks penciled on the bathroom wall give eloquent testimony to increasing maturity. A long-absent aunt who cries, "My, how you've grown!" may summon a grin from the wary seven-year-old or a blush from the self-conscious thirteen-year-old. She is, however, confirming for both children the social importance of this sign of change.

We tend to use the words *grow* and *develop* interchangeably in describing the physical transformations of childhood, but they do not refer to the same processes.

Strictly speaking, *growth* is the increase in size of the body or its organs, whereas *development* refers not only to changes in size but also to the orderly patterns, such as growth spurts, and the more complicated levels of functioning that often accompany increases in height and weight.

Norms of Growth

By recording information about the height and weight of large numbers of children from diverse populations, we can determine whether a particular child's individual growth falls within the range expected for his or her chronological age and ethnic background. These **norms,** quantitative measures that provide typical values and variations in height and weight for children, have become an essential reference for attempting to answer questions about how biological and experiential factors influence growth.

● **Length and Height**   The most rapid increase in body length occurs during the fourth month of prenatal development, when the fetus grows about 1.5 millimeters a day. The fetus continues to grow rapidly, albeit at a somewhat slower rate, during the remaining prenatal weeks. The newborn maintains a high rate of growth for several months following birth. In fact, if growth rate during the first six months after birth were sustained, the average ten-year-old would be about one hundred feet tall (McCall, 1979). Girls can be expected to reach approximately half their adult height a little before two years of age and boys a little after two years of age (Fredriks et al., 2000).

Throughout infancy and childhood boys and girls grow at similar rates, although individual children, of course, may differ enormously. For example, sudden growth spurts of one-quarter to one-half inch can occasionally occur literally overnight in infants and toddlers (Lampl, Veldhuis, & Johnson, 1992). Over a longer span of time, growth rate generally follows a slow and steady pace throughout much of childhood. At about ten or eleven years of age, however, many girls begin an adolescent growth spurt, a period in which height increments occur at nearly double the rate in childhood. Because the growth spurt usually does not start in boys until about two years later, girls may tower over their male peers for a brief period in early adolescence. During the approximately three years over which the growth spurt occurs, girls add about twenty-eight centimeters (eleven inches) and boys about thirty centimeters

KEY THEME
| **Individual Differences**

Variation in height and weight are just two of the many ways that children of similar ages differ in their physical development. These children in junior high school joining together to socialize after school illustrate a wide variation in height. Some may not have begun their adolescent growth spurt, others may be in the middle of this developmental phase, and still others may have already completed it.

norms   Measures of average values and variations in some aspect of development, such as physical size and motor skill development, in relation to age.

| FIGURE 5.6 | Growth in Height and Weight over the First Twenty Years |

Height and, to a lesser extent, weight rapidly increase in the first two years following birth. Changes in height and weight continue at a fairly modest rate throughout childhood, followed by a brief, more rapid upturn sometime during the preadolescent or adolescent years. However, there is a wide range in height and weight among children, especially during the adolescent years. For example, this figure (based on children in the United States) shows height and weight growth charts for boys and girls between the 3rd and 97th percentiles.

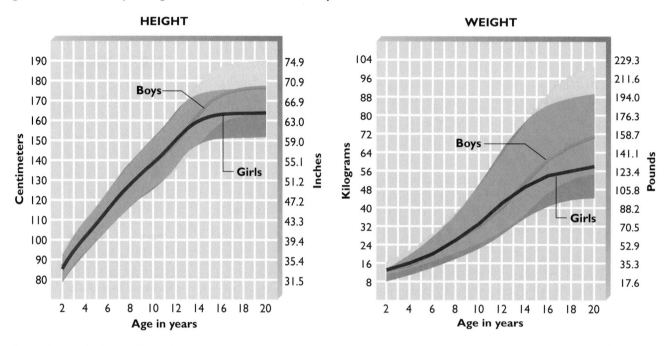

Source: Centers for Disease Control and Prevention, National Center for Health Statistics, 2000.

(twelve inches), or about 17 percent of their total height (Abbassi, 1998). Figure 5.6 illustrates the growth typically observed in many populations of children during their first eighteen years.

● **Weight**   In contrast to that of height, the maximum rate of increase in weight takes place shortly after birth. In their first few days, newborns typically lose excess body fluids and shed 5 to 10 percent of their birth weight. They then usually make rapid weight gains, normally doubling their birth weight in about five months and nearly tripling it by the end of the first year (Pinyerd, 1992). If the gains for the first six months were sustained, the average ten-year-old would weigh in at about 240,000 tons (McCall, 1979). Weight gains are smallest during childhood between ages two and three and gradually increase until just before adolescence (see Figure 5.6).

Patterns in Body Growth

Specific organs and systems of the body often develop at rates different from that for the body as a whole. The most dramatic example probably is head size. Two months after conception, the head constitutes nearly 50 percent of total body length. By birth, however, head size represents only about 25 percent, and by adulthood only about 12 to 13 percent of total body length, as Figure 5.7 shows. The central nervous system, along with the head, undergoes an early and extremely rapid increase in weight. By five or six years of age, the child has reached 90 percent of the adult level for brain and head size.

Other organs, for example, the muscles and the respiratory and digestive systems, follow the pattern of overall weight change: substantial gains during the first two years; a slower, more stable increase throughout childhood; and a rapid increase during

FIGURE 5.7 Changes in Body Proportions During Prenatal and Postnatal Growth

The size of the human head in proportion to the rest of the body shows striking changes over the course of prenatal to adult development. Two months after conception, the head takes up about half of the entire length of the body. By adulthood, the head makes up only about 12 to 13 percent of total body length. The head's tendency to grow more rapidly than regions of the body near the "tail" demonstrates the pattern of cephalocaudal development.

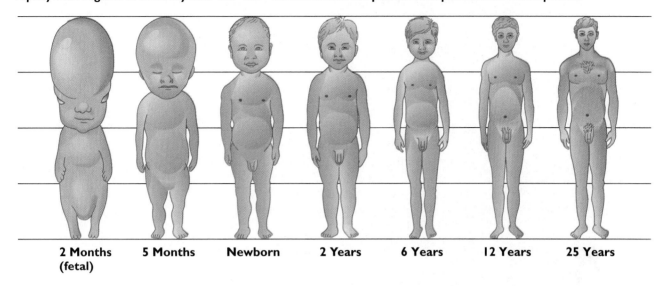

| 2 Months (fetal) | 5 Months | Newborn | 2 Years | 6 Years | 12 Years | 25 Years |

Source: Adapted from Robbins et al., 1928.

adolescence. However, the reproductive system follows a strikingly different pattern: only during adolescence do organs associated with reproduction begin to mature and rapidly approach their adult size. These different patterns mirror the functional importance of various systems of the body at specific points in development.

● **Directionality of Growth**   In addition to growth that generally follows the *cephalocaudal principle* (the region nearer the head matures more quickly than other areas), body growth also tends to reflect a pattern of **proximodistal development.** This principle points up the fact that regions nearer the trunk of the body tend to grow and become more differentiated earlier than those more peripheral to the body. A good example is the ability of infants to gain control of their arms and legs much sooner than of areas more distant, such as their fingers and toes. However, not all physical growth conforms to either the cephalocaudal or proximodistal principles of development. During the adolescent growth spurt, for example, some parts of the body undergo rapid growth in a pattern almost the reverse of the proximodistal principle. We are all familiar with the teenager who seems to be all hands and feet. Hands and feet are in fact among the first body parts to show a dramatic change during this period; they are followed by arms and legs and, last of all, the trunk (Tanner, 1978). An adolescent, in other words, is likely to outgrow his shoes first, then his trousers, and finally his jacket.

● **Individual and Group Differences**   Children show substantial deviations from the norm in their rates of physical growth and development. Individual variations in size are already noticeable at birth; for example, boys tend to be slightly longer and heavier than girls at this time (Copper et al., 1993). Individual differences in growth become especially evident during the adolescent years, when children are likely to show enormous variation in the timing, speed, and duration of the adolescent growth spurt. In the United States, the onset of rapid adolescent growth typically occurs between ages ten and fourteen for girls and between ages twelve and sixteen for boys (Sinclair, 1985). A girl who once towered over her childhood girlfriends may suddenly find at age thirteen that she is looking up to them, temporarily at least. A

KEY THEME
Individual Differences

proximodistal development
Pattern in which organs and systems of the body near the middle tend to develop earlier than those near the periphery.

boy whose athletic skills were unremarkable may find himself the starting center for the junior high basketball team if he undergoes an early adolescent growth spurt.

Variability in growth occurs among ethnic and cultural groups as well. For example, although individual differences account for much of the variability in size, American infants of African heritage tend to weigh slightly less than American infants of European heritage at birth, even when social class, gestational age, and other factors known to affect birth weight are equated (Goldenberg et al., 1991). Variability in height among ethnically and culturally diverse populations is also exhibited throughout childhood.

Determinants of Body Growth and Development

KEY THEME
Nature/Nurture

What are the roles of nature and nurture in human physical growth? On the one hand, the contributions of nature, or heredity, are suggested by research indicating significant biological influences on physical development, as well as correlations among related family and cultural members in mature size and in the onset and pattern of physical changes. On the other hand, nurture, or environment—including diet, disease, and social and emotional circumstances—has a bearing on physical growth as well.

● **Genetic Factors**   A person's height is likely to be closely related to that of his or her mother and father. A late-maturing adolescent often shares late maturity with other family members (Rallison, 1986). What is true for the family in miniature is also true for larger human populations that are genetically related. The Lese of Zaire, for example, are much taller as a group than their nearby neighbors the Efe, the pygmies of the Ituri rain forest. Even body proportions differ among groups. For example, although many individual differences and much overlap occur among people of different ethnic backgrounds, leg and arm lengths tend to be relatively greater in individuals of African descent, and even more so in Australian aborigines, than in other ethnic groups when length of the torso is equated (Eveleth & Tanner, 1990). Such similarities and differences implicate genetic factors in physical development. But genes do not control growth *directly*. Genes regulate physical development by means of neural and hormonal activity in different organs and body systems.

● **Neural Control**   Many researchers believe the brain includes a growth center, a genetically established program or template that monitors and compares expected and actual rates and levels of growth for the individual. The claim has been supported by observations of **catch-up growth,** an increase in growth rate that often occurs if some environmental factor interferes with normal increases in height during infancy or childhood. Illness or malnutrition, for example, may disrupt physical growth. However, if the duration and severity are limited and do not occur at some critical time, the child's rate of growth often accelerates once she or he recovers. The acceleration continues until height "catches up" to the level expected had no disruption occurred.

The presence of a growth center is also suggested by the converse finding: **lagging-down growth** (Prader, 1978). Some rare congenital and hormonal disorders produce unusually rapid growth. If the disorder is corrected, growth halts or slows until actual and projected height match the trajectory established before the disruption. Where might this neural control center be located? Researchers theorize that the *hypothalamus,* a small region near the base of the brain (see Figure 5.2), orchestrates the genetic instructions for growth.

catch-up growth   Increase in growth rate after some factor, such as illness or poor nutrition, has disrupted the expected, normal growth rate.

lagging-down growth Decrease in growth rate after some factor, such as a congenital or hormonal disorder, has accelerated the expected, normal growth rate.

hormones   Chemicals produced by various glands that are secreted directly into the bloodstream and can therefore circulate to influence cells in other locations of the body.

● **Hormonal Influences**   Hormones, chemicals produced by various glands that are secreted directly into the bloodstream and can therefore circulate to influence cells in other locations of the body, furnish another key mechanism for converting genetic instructions into physical development. For example, hormones produced by cells in the hypothalamus, the suspected site of the growth center, trigger or inhibit production of still other hormones in the nearby *pituitary gland* (see Figure 5.2), including one known as *human growth hormone (HGH)*. Infants with insufficient HGH may be nearly normal in size at birth, but their growth slows dramatically over the ensuing months and years; they typically reach an adult height of only about four to four-and-a-half feet. HGH, however, only indirectly promotes growth. It spurs the production of *somatomedins,* specialized hormones manufactured by many other cells in the body that directly regulate cell division for growth (Underwood, 1991).

The hypothalamus and pituitary gland produce still other hormones important for physical changes, including those that occur during puberty. However, variations in amounts of many hormones, as long as they fall within a reasonable range, do not account for individual differences in height. Individual differences seem to depend on the sensitivity of cells to the hormones (Tanner, 1978). For example, the pygmy Efe produce normal quantities of HGH but seem unable to use it to produce one kind of somatomedin important for growth to heights typical of other groups (Merimee, Zapf, & Froesch, 1981).

● **Nutrition and Health**   For a large proportion of the world's children, adequate nutrition and exposure to diseases may be the primary determinants of whether physical growth proceeds normally or even at all. We pointed out some consequences of malnutrition for fetal development in the chapter titled "The Prenatal Period and Birth." Illness and nutritional deprivation can affect postnatal growth as well. During much of the first half of the twentieth century in Western Europe, for example, the average height gain of children at various ages increased gradually over the years except during World Wars I and II and periods of agricultural and economic crises, when food was far more limited. In 1984, a severe, three-month-long drought struck Kenya while researchers were engaged in a study of malnutrition in that region (McDonald et al., 1994). Food intake was cut sharply. The normal rate of weight gain among elementary school children was halved.

Severe protein-energy malnutrition can have a particularly devastating effect on growth. Infants with *marasmus* fail to grow because they lack sufficient calories. Consequences include eventual loss in weight; wrinkly, aged-looking skin; an abdomen that is often shrunken; and a hollow appearance to the body, suggesting emaciation. Another prevalent form of protein-energy malnutrition is *kwashiorkor,* or failure to develop because the diet either contains an inadequate balance of protein or includes potentially harmful toxins. Kwashiorkor typically appears in one- to-three-year old children who have been weaned, usually because of the arrival of a newborn sibling, and whose subsequent sources of protein are inadequate or contaminated.

● **SEE FOR YOURSELF**
psychology.college.hmco.com
Hunger and Nutrition in Children

In many countries, large numbers of young children suffer from *kwashiorkor.* This young child, living in a refugee camp at Bakauu, Rwanda, displays the distended, bloated stomach so typical of this nutritional disorder because his diet either does not include sufficient protein or contains toxins.

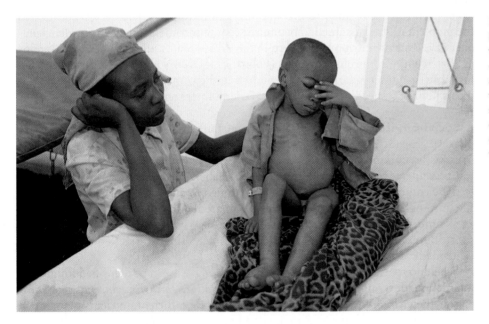

The symptoms of kwashiorkor include lethargic behavior and an apathetic look, wrinkled skin, and a thin, wispy, reddish-orange cast to the hair, but most defining is edema or swelling, especially of the stomach, to give the child a bloated appearance (Balint, 1998). Kwashiorkor leads not only to disruption in growth of the body but also to deterioration of the brain. Although some of the damage can be quickly reversed when adequate nutrition is reinstated early (Gunston et al., 1992), long-term cognitive deficits and poorer school-related performance may persist due to impaired attention and memory (Galler et al., 1990). Studies of the effects of supplementary feeding during the first few years of life provided for nutritionally deprived families in Colombia, Guatemala, Jamaica, Taiwan, and Indonesia indicate that both motor and mental development are enhanced (Pollitt, 1994). Benefits to intellectual development extend into adolescence even when the supplementary diet is discontinued in the preschool years (Pollitt et al., 1993).

KEY THEME
Interaction Among Domains

As Figure 5.8 suggests, malnutrition operates at many levels to produce negative consequences for development. For example, cognitive deficits may stem from lessened motivation or curiosity and an inability to respond to or engage the environment (Brown & Pollitt, 1996). To illustrate, during the relatively brief drought in Kenya, schoolchildren became less attentive in class and less active on the playground (McDonald et al., 1994). To counter the disruption in motivation, attention, and activity level that can accompany malnutrition, some projects have been designed to encourage mothers to become more competent and effective teachers and caregivers for their young children. When nutritionally deprived children in Jamaica have been given extra play opportunities and mothers have been taught how to positively influences their children's development, children have shown substantially higher performance on developmental and intelligence tests over a fourteen-year time period compared to children not receiving the intervention (Grantham-McGregor et al., 1994). However, the scores of malnourished children, even those given this kind of intervention, continue to fall below those of children who have been adequately nourished, a finding consistently reported in studies on the long-term consequences of malnutrition (Drewett et al., 2001). Even in the United States, lower academic performance and less positive interpersonal relationships are reported among large numbers of children living in families in which inadequate amounts of nutritional food are available (Alaimo, Olson, & Frongillo, 2001).

Deficiencies in specific nutritional elements—for example, vitamins A, B complexes, D, and K, as well as iron and calcium—are also linked to growth disorders affecting hundreds of thousands of children throughout the world (Balint, 1998; Hansen, 1990). Some of these disorders, especially iron-deficiency anemia, spawn lower performance on intelligence and other kinds of psychological tests. Although the problem is often assumed to be limited to low-income countries, iron-deficiency anemia is a major nutritional concern in the United States, affecting perhaps as many as 20 percent of some ethnic groups (Pollitt, 1994). More alarming is the claim that, for more than three-quarters of the children in the United States, the quality of their diet is poor or in need of improvement (Federal Interagency Forum, 1999).

● **Social-Emotional Factors**   How important are social-emotional factors in physical growth? Early studies of institutionalized children painted vivid images of massive disruption in physical growth, or even death, if a warm, consistent caregiver was unavailable to the infant (Spitz, 1946b). A label of **failure to thrive** was attached to these children. Today this label is often applied to any boy or girl who falls below the third percentile in weight or height compared with other children of the same age. Some children fall into this classification simply because they have inherited short stature or are normally slow in growth; others qualify due to disease or some other medical cause.

When no specific genetic, biological, or medical basis can be identified for growth retardation, the condition is labeled *nonorganic failure-to-thrive syndrome.* For some reason, these children are not taking in or processing sufficient nutrients to maintain normal growth despite the availability of adequate nutritional resources. Why might

failure to thrive   Label applied to any child whose growth in height or weight is below the third percentile for children of the same age.

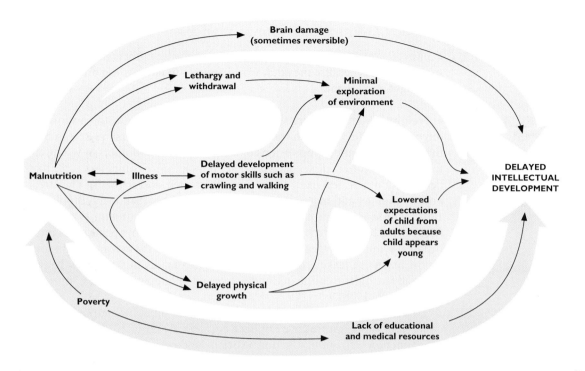

Brain damage
(sometimes reversible)

Lethargy and
withdrawal

Minimal
exploration
of environment

Malnutrition → Illness

Delayed development
of motor skills such as
crawling and walking

DELAYED
INTELLECTUAL
DEVELOPMENT

Lowered
expectations
of child from
adults because
child appears
young

Delayed physical
growth

Poverty

Lack of educational
and medical resources

Source: From *Malnutrition, Poverty and Intellectual Development* by J. Larry Brown and Ernesto Pollitt. Copyright © 1996 by Scientific American, Inc. All rights reserved.

FIGURE 5.8
The Many Routes by Which Malnutrition Affects Development

Nutritional deprivation can influence development at many different levels. More frequent and severe illness, delayed growth, and slower motor skill development are among the more visible consequences. Lower intellectual development is often an outcome as well. Malnutrition can damage the brain directly. However, limited capacity to engage the environment and other repercussions from the kinds of experiences a malnourished child receives may take a further toll on intellectual development. The context in which it often persists, such as poverty and the lack of essential resources, must also be factored into a consideration of how nutritional deprivation affects development.

this be the case? Research has not yet uncovered the answer. However, characteristics associated with both parent and child may be involved. These infants and young children with the syndrome tend to be more passive and apathetic and display less facial expressivity than other infants and children (Maggioni & Lifshitz, 1995). They may also be fussier about what they eat, despite the best efforts of parents to encourage food intake. These responses, in turn, can contribute to feelings of incompetence in the parents (Bithoney et al., 1995).

Parental behavior can further complicate the situation. For example, mothers of failure-to-thrive infants are often reported to display less pleasure, positive affect, and support in their communications and tend to be more abusive or neglectful (Drotar, 1991; Liggon et al., 1992). Concerned about their children becoming overweight or about allergic reactions, still other parents restrict the amounts of food (often healthy) or overemphasize some foods (often unhealthy) at the expense of others (Roesler, Barry, & Brock, 1994; Dennison, Rockwell, & Baker, 1997). One consistent long-term consequence of failure to thrive is decreased height, although evidence for continuing cognitive or social deficits remains mixed (Boddy, Skuse, & Andrews, 2000; Drewett, Corbett, & Wright, 1999).

● **Secular Trends**   Increased knowledge of nutrition and the ability to treat disease have yielded dramatic changes in patterns of growth in many societies in recent generations. These generational changes are termed **secular trends.** Children today grow faster and become taller as adults than did previous generations in most regions of the world. Between 1880 and 1950, the average height of Western European and American children increased by nearly four inches. A slower increase or even stability in size has been found since the 1960s. Similar findings have been reported for other cultures, although at different times. For example, in Japan the most substantial changes in height took place between 1950 and 1970 (Tanner, 1978). Improved nutrition, better medical care, and the abolition of child labor account not only for secular trends in greater height across generations but also for the larger size of children from professional, highly educated, and urban families compared with children of poorer families and those in rural populations (Tanner, 1978).

secular trend   Consistent pattern of change over generations.

KEY THEME
Interaction Among Domains

KEY THEME
Individual Differences

KEY THEME
Sociocultural Influence

The Social-Emotional Consequences of Body Growth

Is physical size important to development and the way others interact with a child? If so, perhaps it is because the adult world appears to have strong preferences concerning height and weight.

● **Height**   Many societies share a mystique about tallness, the notion that height directly correlates with such traits as competence and leadership. Research has shown that height does affect impressions of a child's abilities. Mothers of young children of the same age, for example, perceive taller boys as more competent (able to get along better with others, less likely to cry when frustrated, and so forth). They treat smaller boys as younger and in a more overprotective manner (Sandberg, Brook, & Campos, 1994). The same is true of children judged on the basis of maturity of facial features (Zebrowitz, Kendall-Tackett, & Fafel, 1991). Moreover, boys believe it is important to be tall and muscular; those substantially shorter than the average height for their age report extensive teasing from their peers; greater dissatisfaction with their skills, especially in athletic endeavors; and increasing unhappiness as they approach adolescence (Finch, 1978).

Despite these observations, lower self-esteem or other behavorial problems among children of short stature have not been consistently reported. And short adults typically function well within the norm socially and intellectually (Kranzler et al., 2000; Sandberg et al., 1994; Zimet et al., 1997). Until 1985, little could be done to alter the course of growth or eventual height for most children. Today, however, human growth hormone can be produced synthetically. For children whose lack of growth stems from insufficient HGH or because of other genetic or physiological conditions, the breakthrough represented an enormously positive step toward more typical growth. However, increasing numbers of children who are genetically short or whose delay in growth is a normal part of their pattern of maturation are also being given HGH to speed up growth or increase their height, even though this practice is not officially recommended in many countries, including the United States (Cuttler et al., 1996).

Should such treatments, which tend to be motivated by perceptions and expectations about the benefits of being tall rather than by a medical condition, be encouraged? It is an expensive course of treatment and many children who are not HGH deficient gain few long-term benefits from its administration (Brook, 2000). Nor is the potential for negative side effects fully understood (Betts, 2000; Drug and Therapeutics Committee, 1995), although some pediatric endocrinologists believe it is very safe. In some countries HGH is officially approved for use with individuals born with Turner syndrome (e.g., France, Japan, and Sweden) and with children of short stature or who are simply failing to grow at normal rates (Bercu, 1996). However, attempting to alter normal physical development to conform to a cultural stereotype is a drastic action that raises many ethical issues.

**WHAT DO
YOU THINK?**

When Should HGH Be
Prescribed for Children?
psychology.college.hmco.com

● **Obesity**   Most estimates of obesity today make use of a measure called the *body mass index (BMI)*. The BMI is determined by dividing the weight of a child or adult (in kilograms) by the square of his or her height (in meters). Children and adults above the 95th percentile for their age on this measure compared with a reference population (which for the United States usually has been a large sample of children and adults who were tested in this country in the 1970s) or whose BMI is above 30 are considered obese. Children between the 85th and 95th percentile or who show rapid changes in weight relative to other children their age also are considered at risk for becoming obese (Strauss, 1999; Styne, 2001).

KEY THEME
Sociocultural Influence

Being overweight has strong social-emotional consequences in most cultures. At earlier times it carried positive connotations of substance and prosperity in industrialized societies and still does in many developing countries today (Sobal & Stunkard, 1989). For example, adolescent females in some regions of the world are encouraged to increase their body fat in preparation for marriage (Brown & Konner, 1987). However, in contemporary Western cultures obesity is often viewed negatively. For example, children as young as six, when describing drawings or photographs of people who are chubby or thin, are likely to label obese figures as "lazy," "cheater," or "liar," although they seldom apply such terms to their overweight friends (Kirkpatrick & Sanders, 1978; Lawson, 1980). In addition, overweight ten- and eleven-year-olds experience more negative interactions involving peers than do other children (Baum & Foreham, 1984). Although research has revealed a mixed pattern of findings, self-esteem may suffer as well (Klesges et al., 1992; Pierce & Wardle, 1997), especially for children who feel (or are made to feel) that they are responsible for being overweight (e.g., because of over-eating or insufficient exercise) even as early as five years of age in girls (Davidson & Birch, 1999).

Genetic factors predispose some children to obesity. At least five single gene disorders are known to be related to its early onset (Farooqi & O'Rahilly, 2000). Behavioral genetics studies further suggest a relationship as a function of multiple genes, perhaps because of inherited differences in metabolic processes (Strauss, 1999). Not surprisingly, either because of a genetic component or because parents serve as models for their children's eating and exercise habits, overweight parents are more likely to have obese children (Birch & Davison, 2001). Early obesity as well as the longer a child continues to be overweight increase the likelihood he or she will be obese as an adult (Strauss, 1999; Whitaker et al., 1997).

KEY THEME
Nature/Nurture

Controlling weight is complicated by the tendency of heavy children to be more sensitive to external food-related cues and less responsive to internal hunger cues compared with their normal-weight peers (Ballard et al., 1980; Costanzo & Woody, 1979). Infants and children are responsive to the amount of energy provided by the foods they consume (Birch & Davison, 2001; Fomon, 1993). However, eleven-year-old obese children tend to eat faster than other children. They also fail to slow down their rate of food intake as they near the end of their meal, a pattern of responding that is at odds with what is typically observed in children of normal weight (Barkeling, Ekman, & Rössner, 1992). Obese children also are somewhat less accurate in reporting how much they eat (Maffeis et al., 1994).

Leann Birch and her colleagues (cf. Birch & Davison, 2001) believe that children can learn to become unresponsive to internal satiation cues through child-feeding practices imposed by parents. For example, some parents, perhaps many, express concerns about their infants gaining sufficient weight. As a consequence, they may initiate meal-related practices designed to encourage food consumption (e.g., to "clean their plates") and use certain foods such as sweets to reward good behavior and to calm and quiet the child. These efforts, however, could have the unintended effect of shifting the child's reliance on internal signals for hunger to external signals based on how much has been eaten and of increasing preferences for some foods that may not be so healthy for the child. In addition, if concerns begin to emerge about becoming overweight, parents may attempt to restrict ingestion of high caloric foods, an action that seems to have the unintended consequence of making the forbidden foods even more attractive to children.

KEY THEME
Individual Differences

Recent health surveys reveal a worrisome increase in obesity among children and adolescents in the United States (see Figure 5.9). Increases have been greatest among African American, Hispanic American, and Native American children (Crawford et al., 2001). Although less information is available from other countries, increases in obesity in children also have been reported in England (Reilly & Dorosty, 1999) and are taking place in many other regions of the world if the reports of the rise of obesity for adults are any indication (Taubes, 1998).

What are the reasons for this secular trend? Researchers have advanced various hypotheses. For example, compared with a generation ago, children spend more time in sedentary activities such as watching television. In general, children who watch more television per day have a higher BMI (Andersen et al., 1998; Robinson, 2001); the likelihood of becoming overweight is correlated with the number of hours

KEY THEME
Sociocultural Influence

FIGURE 5.9 | Trends in Overweight (BMI ≥ 95th Percentile): United States

These data, collected from a series of studies carried out in the United States between 1963 and 1999, reveal the marked increase that has taken place in the number of children and adolescents who are considered obese. Some believe obesity has become a health epidemic in this and in other countries because of the dramatic change and accompanying health risks that are associated with being overweight.

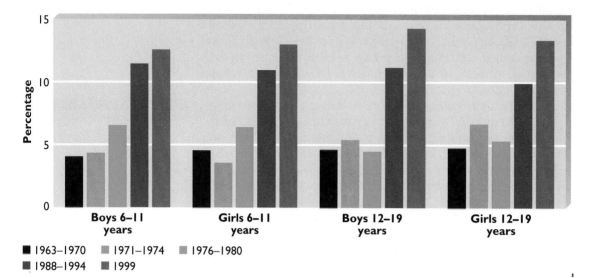

■ 1963–1970   ■ 1971–1974   ■ 1976–1980
■ 1988–1994   ■ 1999

Source: Centers for Disease Control and Prevention, 2002.

FIGURE 5.10

The Relationship Between Becoming Overweight and Hours of Television Viewing per Day

The more time children spend watching television each day, the more likely they are to be overweight. Ten- to fifteen-year-olds who were reported to watch more than five hours of television each day in 1990 were greater than eight times (8× in the figure) more likely to have become overweight (BMI greater than 85th percentile) between 1986 and 1990 than children who watched less than two hours each day. These findings provide powerful arguments for the view that obesity is increasing among children because they do not spend enough time engaging in physical activity or because the advertising messages on television encourage excessive food consumption.

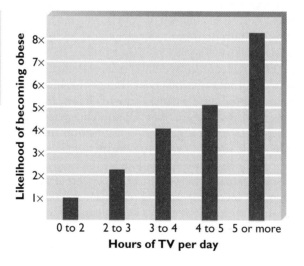

Source: Adapted from Strauss, 1999. Data from Gortmaker et al., 1996.

children watch television, as can be seen in Figure 5.10. Perhaps an even greater influence stems from television advertising, which rarely promotes consumption of fresh fruits and vegetables over calorie-laden snack and convenience foods; consumption of these latter foods has gone up substantially over the last twenty-five years (Jahns, Siega-Riz, & Popkin, 2001). Although culture may attach a negative label to being overweight on the one hand, television may actively serve to promote it on the other.

In many cultures, the concern with being overweight seems to have contributed to another problem: efforts to initiate dieting, even by children who are within a normal weight range.

ATYPICAL DEVELOPMENT

Dieting and Eating Disorders

In the United States, many young people, especially women, are dissatisfied with their weight. Concerns about becoming obese are expressed as early as age five (Feldman, Feldman, & Goodman, 1988). These concerns continue to be expressed among eight-year-olds from nearly all ethnic groups (Robinson et al., 2001), and various studies report that up to half of third-grade girls have attempted to diet (Strauss, 1999). In fact, more than 40 percent of high school women report that they are dieting (Centers for Disease Control, 1991), and as many as 75 percent indicate that they have attempted to lose five or more pounds at some time (Emmons, 1996). Similar percentages of girls have been found to be dieting in Australia, and the levels may be the same in many other countries (Paxton et al., 1991).

Repeated messages from fashion magazines, and perhaps from family and peers (that occasionally escalate to the level of teasing), stress the importance of slenderness for beauty and success and undoubtedly place enormous pressure even on preteenagers to control weight. During the adolescent years, girls believe it is increasingly important to have a boyfriend and to be physically attractive. Having dates, at least among Caucasian girls and African American girls whose mothers are more highly educated, is correlated with lower body fat, an indication that concern about weight has some basis in real experience (Halpern et al., 1999).

The large number of girls who attempt to diet has become an almost normative, although troubling, aspect of growing up in many cultures. Sometimes, however, young people initiate more drastic steps to encourage weight loss. For example, in one recent study nearly 10 percent of girls and 4 percent of boys in the sixth through eighth grades indicated they have resorted to vomiting or use of laxatives in their efforts to remain thin (Krowchuck et al., 1998). A substantial number of teenagers, especially girls, including many who are not obese, go to great and even life-threatening lengths to reduce their weight. Anorexia nervosa and bulimia nervosa are two self-initiated forms of extreme weight control efforts, disorders that affect perhaps as many as 3 percent of women in industrialized countries at some time during their lifetime (Walsh & Devlin, 1998). *Anorexia nervosa* is a kind of self-imposed starvation. Individuals with anorexia appear to be obsessed with the fear of appearing too heavy and as a consequence become dangerously thin. As weight loss becomes severe, muscle tissue degenerates, bone marrow changes, menstrual periods are disrupted in girls, and cardiac stress and arrhythmias can occur. *Bulimia nervosa* is an eating disorder in which the individual often engages in recurrent bouts of binge eating, sometimes consuming enormous quantities of high-calorie, easily digested food. For many, binge eating alternates with self-induced vomiting, actions sometimes accompanied by use of laxatives or diuretics. Although they share with anorexics an intense concern about their bodies, individuals suffering from bulimia often fall within a normal weight range for their age and height.

A substantial increase in these disorders, particularly the more frequent of the two, bulimia, has been reported since the 1970s (Bryant-Waugh & Lask, 1995). Its incidence is greatest among Caucasian, middle- to upper-income young women (Harris, 1991), but both disorders appear to be increasing in males and in some cultural groups that have begun to adopt Western values. Their frequency may also be greater in certain groups, such as athletes and dancers, who are especially concerned about weight gain. Eating disorders may begin as part of the larger spectrum of anxieties children, adolescents, and young adults experience about physical changes, especially as they approach and continue through puberty (Keel, Fulkerson, & Leon,

KEY THEME
Child's Active Role

KEY THEME
Sociocultural Influence

1997). For some individuals, an inherited, biological susceptibility, particularly in cases of anorexia nervosa, may exist (Katzman et al., 2000). Because sociocultural, psychological, and biological factors appear to interact, it should not be surprising that the treatments most effective for dealing with such disorders have been difficult to identify. However, about two-thirds of individuals who display anorexia nervosa show good recovery if treatment is begun early (Herpetz-Dahlmann et al., 2001). Because eating disorders can have serious long-term consequences, individuals experiencing one of them should be strongly encouraged to seek professional help.

FOR YOUR REVIEW

- What are norms for growth? How do they provide information about whether physical growth is proceeding appropriately?

- What are the patterns of growth observed from infancy through adolescence? How do they differ for various parts of the body? How do they differ between individuals and ethnic groups? What evidence is there for secular trends in growth?

- Does growth always conform to the cephalocaudal and proximodistal principles of development?

- How do genetic factors, neural control, and hormonal variations affect growth? What are catch-up and lagging-down growth?

- What are the consequences of poor nutrition and social-emotional factors for growth? What are marasmus, kwashiorkor, and failure to thrive?

- What are the concerns about short stature and obesity in many cultures? What factors may be contributing to the increase in obesity observed in many Western nations?

- Why are dieting and eating disorders of concern, and what factors lead to such efforts to control weight?

Concerns about attractiveness, physical size, and especially weight become especially common among girls during adolescence. Repeated messages in fashion magazines and on television often portray unrealistic body shape and weight-control efforts.

Physical Maturity

Having learned about major advances in the brain, motor skills, and physical size, we can now turn to the many changes that signal the transition from childhood to adulthood. The growth spurt of early adolescence is only one of numerous indicators of approaching physical maturity. Accompanying the growth spurt are important progressions indicating sexual maturity. We briefly consider these and the psychological issues a young person may confront during the passage from late childhood to early adulthood.

Defining Maturity

Because rate and final level of growth vary so greatly among individuals and for different parts of the body, researchers have turned to other criteria to define physical maturity. One reliable indicator is **skeletal maturity,** the extent to which *ossification,* the chemical transformation of cartilage into bony tissue, has been completed. The change begins prenatally about the eighth week after conception, when cartilage in the ribs and in the center of the long bones of the arms and legs is transformed. The process continues into late adolescence or early adulthood, when bones in the wrist and ankle are finally completely formed. Although skeletal maturity has become the standard for defining the end of physical growth, other, visible markers of approaching maturity appear just before and during the adolescent years. These important markers comprise a series of events associated with **puberty,** the developmental milestone reached when a young person gains the ability to reproduce.

During puberty, the *primary sexual organs*—testes and penis in males; vagina, uterus, and ovaries in females—enlarge and become capable of functioning. *Secondary sexual characteristics* that distinguish men from women, such as facial hair or breasts, also mature. Boys take on a more muscular and angular look as shoulders widen and the fat tissue of childhood is replaced with muscle. Girls' hips broaden, a change especially adaptive to bearing children. Girls also tend to retain a higher proportion of fat to muscle tissue and assume a more rounded appearance overall than boys.

Like the growth spurt, the timing of each of the many events associated with puberty differs enormously from one young person to another. As a rule, however, this cluster of characteristics tends to appear somewhat earlier in girls than in boys. The Adolescent Sexual Development chronology summarizes the approximate ages at which many of the developmental changes typically associated with the adolescent years take place for girls and boys growing up in North America and Europe.

Although there are numerous indicators of increasing sexual maturity, perhaps none are more significant than **menarche,** the first menstrual period in females, and **spermarche,** the occurrence of the first ejaculation of sperm in males. Menarche typically takes place between about twelve and thirteen years of age for females and spermarche between thirteen and fourteen years of age in males. However, as with other indicators of puberty, their initial appearance varies considerably from one individual to the next. For example, in the United States, the events accompanying sexual maturity begin somewhat earlier in African American girls than in Caucasian American girls (Biro et al., 2001).

What triggers these remarkable changes? The brain, including the hypothalamus and pituitary gland, and various hormones are centrally involved. *Adrenarche* initiates many of the changes taking place during early adolescence (McClintock & Herdt, 1996). Adrenarche refers to the maturation of the adrenal glands, small glands located above the kidneys. These glands release hormones important for the growth spurt and the emergence of underarm and pubic hair in girls. In addition, adrenarche may play an important role in the emergence of sexual attraction, which Martha McClintock and Gilbert Herdt (1996) argue typically occurs as early as ten years of age. In girls the hypothalamus may monitor metabolic cues associated with body size or the ratio of fat to muscle, because body mass index appears to be a good, although not the only, predictor of onset of menarche (Kaplowitz et al., 2001).

KEY THEME
Continuity/Discontinuity

KEY THEME
Individual Differences

skeletal maturity Extent to which cartilage has ossified to form bone; provides the most accurate estimate of how much additional growth will take place in the individual.

puberty Developmental period during which a sequence of physical changes takes place that transforms the person from an immature individual to one capable of reproduction.

menarche First occurrence of menstruation.

spermarche The first ejaculation of sperm by males entering puberty.

CHRONOLOGY: *Adolescent Sexual Development*

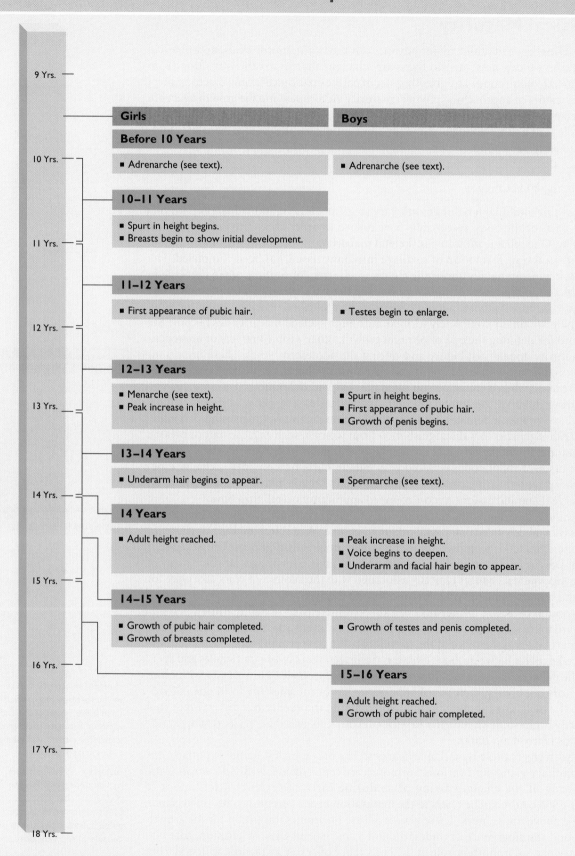

Girls	Boys
Before 10 Years	
■ Adrenarche (see text).	■ Adrenarche (see text).
10–11 Years	
■ Spurt in height begins. ■ Breasts begin to show initial development.	
11–12 Years	
■ First appearance of pubic hair.	■ Testes begin to enlarge.
12–13 Years	
■ Menarche (see text). ■ Peak increase in height.	■ Spurt in height begins. ■ First appearance of pubic hair. ■ Growth of penis begins.
13–14 Years	
■ Underarm hair begins to appear.	■ Spermarche (see text).
14 Years	
■ Adult height reached.	■ Peak increase in height. ■ Voice begins to deepen. ■ Underarm and facial hair begin to appear.
14–15 Years	
■ Growth of pubic hair completed. ■ Growth of breasts completed.	■ Growth of testes and penis completed.
15–16 Years	
	■ Adult height reached. ■ Growth of pubic hair completed.

9 Yrs. — 10 Yrs. — 11 Yrs. — 12 Yrs. — 13 Yrs. — 14 Yrs. — 15 Yrs. — 16 Yrs. — 17 Yrs. — 18 Yrs.

Sources: Malina & Bouchard, 1991; McClintock & Herdt, 1996; Tanner, 1990.

These ages are typical for individuals reared in the United States and many other Western nations.
However, considerable individual differences exist in the ages at which these various developmental changes occur.

Still other *gonadotropic* (gonad-seeking) hormones released by the pituitary gland stimulate, in the case of females, the production of estrogen and progesterone by the ovaries and regulate the menstrual cycle. Estrogen promotes the development of the breasts, uterus, and vagina, as well as the broadening of the pelvis. Even family relationships, such as greater stress in the family, which can affect hormonal balances, may accelerate female development (Ellis & Garber, 2000). In the case of males, gonadotropic hormones contribute to the production of sperm and elevate the production of testosterone by the testes. Testosterone, in turn, promotes further growth in height, an increase in size of the penis and testes, and the appearance of secondary sexual characteristics such as pubic and facial hair.

Early Versus Late Maturity

KEY THEME
Individual Differences

Today adult height in most industrialized societies is typically reached by about age seventeen; a century ago, it often was not achieved until about age twenty-three (Rallison, 1986). Changes in the age of menarche reveal a similar trend toward increasingly early occurrences over recent generations (see Figure 5.11). The secular changes stem from improved socioeconomic conditions, including more adequate nutrition. Do the individual differences that are a part of this transition affect socioemotional development? The answer appears to be yes. For example, girls who are unprepared for menarche, either due to lack of information or because of its early onset, perceive the event more negatively than other girls, whose reactions are often a mixture of positive and negative feelings (Koff & Rierdan, 1995; Ruble & Brooks-Gunn, 1982). Thanks to greater communication within the family, including emotional support and assurance that menstruation is normal and healthy, girls' reactions to menarche today seem more positive (Brooks-Gunn & Ruble, 1980; Koff & Rierdan, 1995).

KEY THEME
Interaction Among Domains

The limited research conducted with boys suggests that they are often uninformed, surprised, and confused about spermarche (Stein & Reiser, 1994). For many boys, sex education classes may either fail to explain what they need to know or are provided too late to prepare them. Their feelings about the event are mixed, and they seldom talk about it with others (Gaddis & Brooks-Gunn, 1985; Stein & Reiser, 1994). Nevertheless, early maturity seems to have positive aspects for boys (Alsaker, 1992; Petersen, 1988). Compared with early maturers, late-maturing boys report

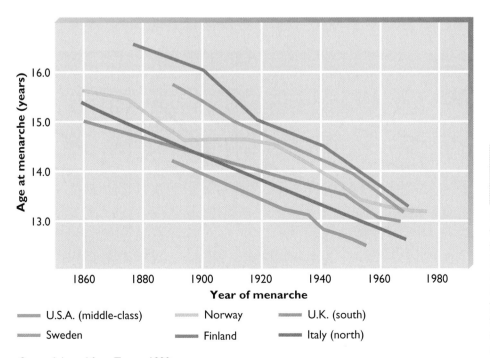

FIGURE 5.11
Secular Trends in the Age of Menarche

Evidence exists for a secular trend in the decrease in age of the onset of menarche from 1845 through 1960. Although most of the data were obtained by questioning adolescents and young adults, some, especially those from earlier generations, depended on the memories of older individuals.

Source: Adapted from Tanner, 1990.

more negative feelings about themselves, feel more rejected, express stronger dependency and affiliative needs, and are more rebellious toward their parents (Mussen & Jones, 1957). Although late maturers want to be well liked and accepted, their efforts to obtain social approval often translate into attention-getting, compensatory, and childish behaviors disruptive to success with peers and adults (Mussen & Jones, 1958). The differences continue to be observed even into adulthood (Jones, 1965).

What are girls' reactions to early and late maturity? Here the picture differs (Alsaker, 1992; Greif & Ulman, 1982; Simmons, Blyth, & McKinney, 1983). Early maturity may enhance status and prestige for girls just as for boys, but it can also be embarrassing; decrease their popularity, at least among agemates; and lead to greater social pressure and expectations from older friends, parents, and other adults to conform to more mature behavior patterns (Brooks-Gunn, 1989). In research carried out in Sweden, girls who reached menarche early were more likely than late-maturing girls to engage in a variety of norm-breaking activities, such as staying out late, cheating on exams, pilfering, or using alcohol (Magnusson, Stattin, & Allen, 1986). Early maturing girls preferred older and more mature friends who may have inspired their greater independence from socially approved conventions of behavior. Indeed, among those maturing early but reporting no older friends, the frequency of norm-breaking activities was about the same as for girls who matured later.

As they grew older, early maturers with and without older friends began to look more alike in their frequency of many norm-breaking activities, and late maturers began to engage in such activities as use of alcohol as often as early maturers. Still, a few unacceptable behaviors, such as the use of drugs, remained higher throughout adolescence among early-maturing than among late-maturing girls. As illustrated in Figure 5.12, another important component of girls' responses to early maturity appears to be whether their group of friends includes only other girls or also boys (Ge, Conger, & Elder, 1996). Early-maturing girls growing up in a rural area of the United States reported that they felt somewhat more stress than their on-time or late-maturing counterparts. They continued to report this greater stress over several years but particularly if their friends included boys. Although peer influences may be a factor in norm-breaking, other changes taking place within the family, including less careful monitoring by parents, may contribute as well (Dick et al., 2000).

Some of the negative consequences of early maturity for females may also spring from the cultural ideals of beauty and maturity that exist in most Western societies. Slenderness and long legs are considered desirable traits in women. Although initially

KEY THEME
Sociocultural Influence

FIGURE 5.12

Psychological Distress Reported by Early-, On-Time, and Late-Maturing Girls as a Function of Sex Composition of Their Friends

In general, early-maturing girls report somewhat greater stress than girls who mature late or on time. However, this increased stress in early maturers is especially evident when their group of friends includes boys, as well as girls. Early-maturing girls undergoing greater stress may initiate friendships that include boys, which continue to heighten their concerns throughout the adolescent years.

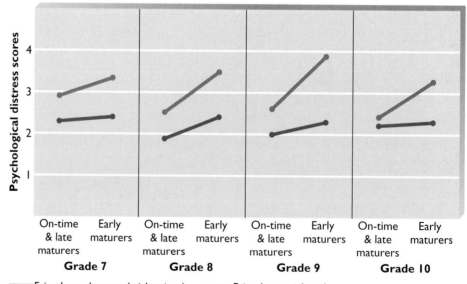

Source: Ge, Conger, & Elder, 1996.

taller than their peers during the growth spurt, early-maturing girls have less opportunity to grow tall and often end up somewhat shorter, heavier, and more robust than their later-maturing peers (Biro et al., 2001). Not surprisingly, early-maturing girls are therefore initially less satisfied with their weight and appearance than late-maturing girls (Williams & Currie, 2000). Personality disturbances such as depression are also slightly more frequent among girls who mature early (Stice, Presnell, & Bearman, 2001). In contrast, early-maturing boys more quickly assume the rugged, muscular physique stereotypically portrayed in American society as ideal for men and are more pleased by their weight and appearance than late-maturing boys (Petersen, 1988).

Girls who mature early and boys who mature late are also out of step with most of their classmates. Young people usually prefer friends who share interests, and interests change with increasing maturity. Late-maturing boys may find that their peers move on to other pursuits, making it more difficult to maintain positive relationships with their friends. Early-maturing girls may redirect friendships to older peers and boys. But this desire can be a problem, because it can contribute to increased behavior and school problems and greater personal unhappiness caused by pressures to conform to the interests of these older peers or boys. In other words, biological, immediate social, and broader cultural factors combine to help define the consequences of early and late maturity.

Sexual Behavior

Few changes accompanying puberty are as contentious in many families as the increased sexuality that attends physical maturity. Anthropological research indicates that the majority of cultures are likely to permit or at least tolerate some sexual activity during the teen years. But Western societies have generally been more restrictive in its expression (Schlegel & Barry, 1991). Many mothers in the United States tend to underestimate the extent of sexual activity among their offspring; their children, in turn, tend to underestimate the degree to which their mothers disapprove of this activity (Jaccard, Dittus, & Gordon, 1998). Nevertheless, large numbers of teenagers are sexually active, and at young ages. To further illustrate this point, 30 percent of students entering sixth grade (averaging 11.7 years of age) in impoverished areas of one major city in the United States report that they have engaged in sexual intercourse (Kinsman et al., 1998). Levels of sexual activity similar to those found in the United States are often reported in other Western nations (Newcomer & Baldwin, 1992).

What factors play a role in whether a teenager will engage in sexual activity? Several different family variables seem to be instrumental, according to a recent review by Brent Miller, Brad Benson, and Kevin Galbraith (2001). One especially important parameter is how the members of the family "connect" with each other. More specifically, when parents are warm and supportive of their children, that is, seem to be close and responsive to them, teenagers are more likely to remain sexually abstinent until somewhat older. Additionally, a similar outcome occurs when parents maintain relatively closer supervision and monitoring of their children's behavior, although evidence exists that there is a limit to this factor; when parents become intrusive and overcontrolling, sexual activity may be started somewhat earlier by their offspring. Not surprisingly, another important factor is the values the parents hold concerning the appropriateness of sexual activity among teenagers. On the other hand, research on the extent to which parents communicate with their sons and daughters about sexual issues does not appear to be related to the timing in which sexual activity is initiated. However, few studies have examined when such communications begin; information about this subject may often be initiated by parents only after they become aware that their children are sexually active.

Other contextual variables associated with the family also are related to sexual activity. In general, children in families living in neighborhoods in which there is greater poverty, higher crime rates, and less stability—factors that are generally correlated with lower education and income—tend to engage in earlier onset of sexual activity. Children of single parents are more likely to initiate sexual behavior earlier,

KEY THEME
Child's Active Role

KEY THEME
Individual Differences

and so are children who are growing up in abusive family environments or who have older teenage siblings who are already parents (East & Jacobson, 2001).

Aside from the moral and ethical issues that adolescent sexual behavior raises, there are important health and social consequences. Among the most frequent concerns are sexually transmitted diseases (STDs), teenage pregnancy, and the tendency of teenage parents to drop out of school. Adolescents appear to be more susceptible than adults to STDs, and an estimated 3 million are infected each year by one of these diseases—a number that has spread considerable alarm among members of the medical profession (Eng & Butler, 1997; McIlhaney, 2000). In the 1980s approximately 20 percent of unmarried American women of European heritage eighteen years or younger and 40 percent of African heritage became pregnant during their adolescent years (Furstenberg, Brooks-Gunn, & Chase-Lansdale, 1989). The rate of teen pregnancy has shown some decline throughout the 1990s but still remains far higher in the United States than in other technologically advanced countries. Moreover, approximately 300,000 of the nearly half million teenage women delivering their first child and 75 percent of all adolescents giving birth to a child each year will remain unmarried, a substantial increase from 40 years ago when only 15 percent who gave birth were unmarried (Allen et al., 1997; Coley & Chase-Lansdale, 1998). Only about half of these women will finish high school (Hotz, McElroy, & Sanders, 1997). Moreover, their children will often have difficulty when they begin school (Brooks-Gunn & Chase-Lansdale, 1995).

CONTROVERSY: THINKING IT OVER

What Should Sex Education Programs Emphasize?

Because of the risks associated with sexual activity, such as pregnancy and contracting AIDS or other STDs, many individuals working with elementary, junior high, and high school students in the United States and other countries around the world have argued that young people need to be better educated about their sexuality.

What Is the Controversy?

Nearly everyone agrees that sex education should begin in the home at a young age, taught by parents. Moreover, parents generally wish to see instruction about sexuality provided in the schools (Henry J. Kaiser Family Foundation, 2000). For example, it is not unusual to find that about 80 percent of adults in the United States believe that sex education is appropriate, and, when given the opportunity, only a small proportion of parents ask to have their children excused from sex education classes (Fine, 1988). In fact, sex education is either required or recommended in all states today and in most other countries in which formal education is offered. But beyond that, much less accord exists about sex education and, in particular, on what the focus of the instructional content should be, especially in the United States. Should the emphasis be on encouraging young people to abstain from sexual relationships until they are married? Or should sex education in the schools attempt to promote the acquisition of skills to handle maturely the complexities and consequences of interpersonal relationships and provide clear information and access to resources that will help young people to think clearly about and be comfortable with their emerging sexuality?

What Are the Opposing Arguments?

From the perspective of some, the only effective way for teenagers to avoid the potentially negative outcomes associated with sexual relationships is to abstain from them. Harmful consequences, both psychological and physical, are the inevitable result of such premature activity. Moreover, to promote anything other than abstinence in sex education classes sends a mixed message that communicates a double standard: "Avoid sexual relationships, but in case you can't, here is what you should know."

To others, however, a message that focuses only on abstinence ignores the fact that many teenagers are already engaging in sexual relationships. In fact, somewhere between 800,000 and 900,000 adolescent girls less than nineteen years of age will become pregnant each year in the United States alone, and about half of them can be expected to deliver babies (Centers for Disease Control, 2000). The number who are sexually active is substantially higher. Youths need information on the best ways to avoid pressure to initiate sexual activity and to prevent becoming infected with sexually transmitted diseases and becoming pregnant. Thus a more balanced perspective is to encourage postponing sexual involvement but, for those already involved or likely to initiate it, to emphasize engaging in it responsibly and safely.

What Answers Exist? What Questions Remain?

Tests of the effectiveness of various sex education curricula have yielded mixed results, although some success has been reported. Knowledge of sexuality typically increases, but young people do not consistently report that they are involved in fewer sexual relationships or practice sex more responsibly or safely after exposure to many of these programs. Moreover, little evidence exists to indicate that abstinence-only programs are any more effective than other programs in reducing initiation into sexual activity or risky behaviors associated with it. Rarely have sex education programs been found to lead to an increase in sexual activity, another fear that is occasionally expressed (Grunseit et al., 1997). Nevertheless, some types of programs seem to hold considerable promise for delaying the onset of sexual activity or in reducing the number of partners, unplanned pregnancies, or rate of sexually transmitted diseases (Franklin et al., 1997; Grunseit et al., 1997; Kirby, 1997). One example is Teen Outreach. This program is designed to involve high schoolers in voluntary community service and encourages them to reflect on the normative tasks of adolescence, such as career goals and appropriate social relationships; only a small component of the curriculum is geared to sex education. Students participating in it, however, displayed a significant decline in pregnancy and other school-related problems compared with other students who did not participate (Allen et al., 1997). What makes this or other sex education programs more effective? At the present time, the essential ingredients are unknown. In that many young people are already sexually active before they participate in sex education classes, do programs need to be offered at earlier ages? Should the curricula include emphasis on more than the biology of reproduction? For example, could young people benefit from learning the social skills needed to respond to the many pressures they face to engage in sexual relationships? Have programs stressing abstinence, which for the most part have only recently gained widespread adoption, not been in schools long enough to prove themselves? Or are these programs too biased and narrow in their focus, often emphasizing fear instead of knowledge, extolling a simplistic solution to a complex problem that can have life-and-death consequences? What do you think is required for a successful program?

FOR YOUR REVIEW

- How is maturity defined?

- What are the developmental changes that accompany puberty?

- What are the social and behavior consequences of early and late maturity for males and females?

- What factors are related to sexual behavior in adolescents? What are the health implications of such behavior?

- What are the controversies associated with sex education programs in the public schools?

CHAPTER RECAP

SUMMARY OF DEVELOPMENTAL THEMES

■ Nature/Nurture   *What roles do nature and nurture play in brain, motor skill, and physical development?*

Brain development, the acquisition of motor skills, and physical growth are the product of complex systems influenced by both biology and experience. Biological processes, both genetic and hormonal, augment the proliferation and migration of neurons, events associated with the development of motor skills and growth. At the same time, the transformation from relatively immature infant to increasingly competent child and adolescent is affected by experience and the many different forms of influence caregivers provide. Important stimulation ranges from providing adequate emotional, social, and nutritional support for physical growth to practice and training in encouraging the acquisition of motor skills and talents.

■ Sociocultural Influence   *How does the sociocultural context influence brain, motor skill, and physical development?*

Motor skill and physical growth are embedded within settings, resources, and beliefs promoted by the society in which the child lives. For example, the extent to which a culture encourages specific skills, from the acquisition of motor milestones to skilled athletic ability, or values a particular physical attribute, such as being slender, affects the efforts of children to display these qualities. Knowledge of nutrition, views about physical appearance, and the availability of leisure time, as well as educational practices, have produced changing secular trends for many aspects of development, including growth in height, prevalence of obesity, and onset of menarche.

■ Child's Active Role   *How does the child play an active role in the process of brain, motor skill, and physical development?*

Babies seem to be intrinsically motivated to exercise rudimentary motor skills. Once a child attains locomotion or other skills, she or he provokes new reactions from caregivers that may include being denied access to cupboards and light sockets or being prevented from pouncing on the usually patient family dog. New physical competencies may also be exercised to improve their speed, accuracy, and efficiency. From these efforts can emerge expertise that fuels further progress in athletic, artistic, and other endeavors. Rapid growth or early maturity may affect not only the child's interests but also the expectations and reactions of others. Excessive concerns about weight, for example, and the emergence of sexual maturity may influence the kinds of interactions in which the child or adolescent engages both within and outside the home, interactions that can have dramatic consequences for future development.

■ Continuity/Discontinuity   *Are brain, motor skill, and physical development continuous or discontinuous?*

Brain development, the acquisition of motor skills, and physical development show spurts at certain times in development. The patterns often give rise to conceptions of stagelike development. But even dramatic changes such as those exhibited in attaining motor milestones in infancy or during the pubertal changes of adolescence are grounded in processes undergoing continuous transformations. Small, incremental changes in the relative strength of muscles or production of hormones, for example, may initiate substantive dynamic reorganizations in complex systems of behavior. Physical and skill changes observed in children may bring about dramatic reactions from others that are interpreted as stagelike.

■ Individual Differences   *How prominent are individual differences in brain, motor skill, and physical development?*

Individual differences are a hallmark of motor skill development and physical growth. Variations may arise from biological or experiential factors that can limit or augment development and physical growth. The differences can significantly influence the child and the reactions of others, as early or late maturity or precocious or delayed skill acquisition demonstrates. Individual differences are pervasive and readily apparent, and an important aspect of behavior to be appreciated as well as explained.

■ Interaction Among Domains   *How do brain, motor skill, and physical development interact with other domains of development?*

A child's physical size and weight, as well as improvements in the execution and coordination of motor skills, have dramatic influences on the responses and expectations of caregivers, peers, and others and, in turn, on how the child feels about his or her body and abilities. For example, once capable of walking, the child has a greater ability to initiate independence, which may lead parents to grant more freedoms and at the same time demand more responsibilities. Similarly, the young adolescent's status with peers is often influenced by signs of his or her physically maturing body and other aspects of physical stature, coordination, and skill. These qualities are evaluated by others and influence the child's evaluation of self.

SUMMARY OF TOPICS

The Brain and Nervous System

- New methodologies to investigate the brain, including positron emission tomography (PET), functional magnetic resonance imaging (fMRI), and recording of event-related potentials, have recently promoted widespread attention to the brain and its development.

The Developing Brain

- Brain growth proceeds rapidly during the fetal and early postnatal period. Much of *neuron* proliferation and migration to various regions of the brain occurs before birth; however, extensive neuron differentiation continues throughout the first few years after birth. New neuron formation, as well as their continued differentiation, may take place into adulthood.

- *Glial cell* formation, *myelination,* and the operation and organization of nervous system networks also begin prenatally and continue after birth.

Plasticity in Brain Development

- The unspecialized nature of early neurons permits the brain to exhibit considerable *plasticity*; various regions of the brain take on different functions should injury occur to regions that normally process that information.

- Neuron differentiation may proceed at critical or sensitive times for experience-expectant information but occurs throughout development for experience-dependent information.

Brain Lateralization

- Infants display behaviors suggestive of hemispheric specialization, or *lateralization,* at birth. However, both hemispheres may have equal potential for higher order processing of information.

Motor Skill Development

- Two complementary patterns, differentiation—the substitution of global, diffuse actions with more refined skills—and integration—the emergence of increasingly coordinated actions—characterize the major dimensions of change in the development of motor skills.

The First Actions: Reflexes

- *Reflexes,* involuntary responses to stimulation controlled by subcortical processes, are among the earliest motor actions displayed in newborns. Primitive reflexes help to increase the likelihood of survival, whereas postural reflexes help the infant to maintain a specific orientation in his or her environment.

- Failure to integrate higher order voluntary and lower order brain reflex mechanisms that control breathing may be one factor contributing to *sudden infant death syndrome (SIDS).* Parents can take a number of steps to reduce SIDS, including placing the infant on his or her back for sleeping, avoiding smoking in the infant's presence, providing firm bedding, ensuring adequate ventilation, and preventing the infant from becoming overheated.

Motor Milestones

- *Rhythmical stereotypies,* repeated motor actions with no apparent goal, are among the earliest organized motor behaviors displayed by infants.

- Postural, locomotor, and manual control undergo regular patterns of development. The *cephalocaudal principle* highlights the fact that regions nearer the head tend to undergo more rapid development than regions farther away from the head.

Motor Skills in the Preschool and Later-Childhood Years

- Throughout infancy and childhood, motor skills become more efficient, more coordinated, and more powerful and reveal an increase in balance, speed, and agility when being performed.

Determinants of Motor Development

- Genetic preadaptation may contribute to the emergence of motor skills, but research indicates that experience can be important as well.

Cross-Cultural Differences

- Some societies promote the acquisition of basic motor skills, and, as a consequence, such skills often appear somewhat earlier among infants and very young children in those societies.

Body Growth and Development

- The term *grow* essentially applies to the increase in size of the body or its organs. *Grow* and *develop* are often used interchangeably; however, the latter refers not only to changes in size but also to any orderly pattern of change.

Norms of Growth

- *Norms* derived from measurements carried out on a large sample of individuals within a population provide an estimate of the range of what is considered typical in development. Growth norms reveal rapid height and weight just before and after birth, much slower but regular increases in size beginning at about two years of age, and a final growth spurt before or during early adolescence in most humans.

Patterns in Body Growth

- Some regions of the body, for example, the head, do not show the typical pattern of continued growth during childhood and into adolescence. Regions nearer the center of the body also tend to develop somewhat sooner than regions more peripheral, a reflection of the principle of *proximodistal development*.

Determinants of Body Growth and Development

- Biological factors help to regulate physical development. Cells in the hypothalamus may determine whether growth is proceeding according to genetic instructions. *Catch-up growth*, the tendency for the rate of growth to increase for a period of time after disease or illness, and *lagging-down growth*, the tendency for it to decrease for a period of time after rapid gains, suggest a template in the brain for growth.

- Human growth hormone interacts in complex ways with other hormones to influence growth. Nutrition and disease are key factors affecting growth as well.

- Some children display *failure to thrive* because of inability to process or take in sufficient nutrients to grow normally as a result of social and emotional factors.

- Improved nutrition and prevention of disease have yielded a *secular trend* of increased height in humans in many regions of the world over the past several centuries.

The Social-Emotional Consequences of Body Growth

- Although children, especially boys, prefer being tall, little evidence exists to indicate that those who develop normally but who are constitutionally small are seriously disadvantaged. Nevertheless, parents of children with short stature often request synthetic growth hormone for their children despite lack of evidence that it provides long-term benefits in terms of height.

- Being overweight in today's society typically has negative connotations for children. The numbers of children and adolescents who are obese has shown a dramatic increase over the past several decades. The reasons may include a more sedentary lifestyle, as well as the increasing availability of calorie-laden convenience foods and drinks.

- Control of weight by efforts to diet are frequently reported among children. Of additional concern is the increased number of individuals, especially girls, who display eating disorders such as anorexia nervosa and bulimia.

Physical Maturity

- The growth spurt associated with early adolescence is only one of many indicators of the transition from childhood to adulthood.

Defining Maturity

- Maturity is defined not by size but by ossification of bone material, or *skeletal maturity*. *Puberty* is defined as the period during which the individual gains the ability to reproduce. *Menarche*, or the first occurrence of menstruation, and *spermarche*, the initial occurrence of ejaculation of sperm, signal the ability to reproduce in females and males, respectively.

- Many signs of approaching sexual maturity, including the adolescent growth spurt, begin earlier in girls than in boys.

Early Versus Late Maturity

- Boys seem to benefit from early maturity, but the consequences for girls are less positive. The different consequences may stem from the reactions and pressures of peers and perceived cultural values regarding body size and shape.

Sexual Behavior

- Among the factors that seem to be related to whether youth engage in sexual behavior appear to be the "connectedness" they feel with their families, the extent to which they are supervised, and the attitudes their parents hold with respect to such activity. Fewer resources in the family, as well as the presence of an older teenage sibling who is already a parent, also are associated with increased sexual activity in young people.

- Health concerns associated with sexual activity among young people include substantial increases in the incidence of sexually transmitted diseases and pregnancy. Although the number of teenagers giving birth to children in the United States has shown some decline over the past decade, it still remains higher than in virtually all other Western societies.

- The effectiveness of various kinds of education programs designed to reduce the risk associated with sexual activity among young people remains uncertain.

CHAPTER 6

Basic Learning and Perception

Key Themes in Basic Learning and Perception

- **Nature/Nurture**   What roles do nature and nurture play in learning and perceptual development?

- **Sociocultural Influence**   How does the sociocultural context influence learning and perceptual development?

- **Child's Active Role**   How does the child play an active role in learning and perceptual development?

- **Individual Differences**   How prominent are individual differences in learning and perceptual development?

- **Interaction Among Domains**   How do learning and perceptual development interact with development in other domains?

The apartment had suddenly grown terribly quiet. The three other babies and their mothers who had been helping to celebrate Chad's first birthday had departed. Only Tanya, Chad's mother, remained with him as the light faded at the end of the day. Picking up the torn gift wrappings, Tanya reflected on the events of the past year. She thought back to her first glimpse of Chad. She had counted his toes and fingers to make sure all were there. She had wondered aloud, as she first held him, "What do you see? Can you hear me? What are you thinking?" Tanya had vowed to be a good mother, to help Chad learn. As she began to vacuum the cake crumbs from the floor, she wasn't sure she was keeping her promise. She couldn't afford the colorful playland that had beckoned to him at the toy store. She never seemed to have enough money now that Chad's father had moved out. Was it fair for Chad not to have things that delighted him and from which he could learn so much? Chad also sometimes challenged her, and she became angry with him. What was he learning from these kinds of exchanges?

What can a newborn learn or hear, or see or feel? Only thirty or forty years ago obstetricians and pediatricians, and even some psychologists, might have answered, "Very little and perhaps nothing at all" (Haith, 1990). But a far different answer has emerged in recent years. Newborns are already engaging in the lifelong process of learning. Their vision provides enormous amounts of information from which to learn. If newborns can see, can they also hear—for example, a mother's lullaby? Can they identify the subtle smells of their mothers' bodies, feel the prick of a nurse's pin or the pain of circumcision? If the answer to these questions is yes, they also have the potential to learn a great deal about their world right from birth, maybe even before. What had Chad been learning? Being reared in the angular world of city skyscrapers, might he, for example, see and learn in a far different way than a child growing up in a tropical rain forest? How important are these early experiences for his development?

These are precisely the kinds of questions psychologists have often asked. Why? Because learning and perception are fundamental processes by which children come to understand their world. Perception, the interpretation of sensory information from visual, auditory, and other receptors, is the vehicle by which we glean information about the world. Learning, a means of acquiring new skills and behaviors from experience, is an extremely important form of adaptation. Through learning children avoid dangers, achieve satisfactions, and become contributing members of the families, communities, and cultures in which they live. We begin this chapter by discussing basic processes in learning; then we consider sensory and perceptual development in infants and children. These processes serve as the foundation for the more complex aspects of cognitive, intellectual, emotional, and social development examined in the chapters that follow.

Basic Learning Processes in Infancy and Childhood

Learning permits adaptation to the environment. It helps infants and children to respond to the demands of their physical and social world and to achieve goals and solve problems. Children learn, for example, that a stove can be hot, that hitting a sibling will make their parents angry, and that a symbol of a male on a rest room door signals the right (or wrong) one to enter. What are the basic forms of learning? How early do these important capacities appear? Consider first one of the simplest forms of learning: *habituation*.

Habituation

The gradual decline in intensity, frequency, or duration of a response to the repeated occurrence of a stimulus is known as **habituation.** Even newborns display habituation. For example, they may show less arousal—that is, reductions in heart rate or fewer searching eye movements—as they are shown a colorful toy or hear the same bell ringing over and over. Habituation is thus a simple, adaptive form of learning to ignore things that offer little new information and that, in a sense, have become boring.

The finding that, once babies have habituated to an event, they often display a renewed response to a change in the stimulus indicates that habituation is a form of learning rather than merely fatigue or an inability to continue responding. For example, if touched on the leg instead of the arm or exposed to a sound other than the ringing of a bell, they may become aroused once again. The return of a response is an example of **recovery from habituation** (sometimes called **dishabituation**) and suggests that the baby perceives the new stimulus as different from the old one.

Low-birth-weight, brain-damaged, and younger babies tend to habituate less rapidly than older, more mature infants (Krafchuk, Tronick, & Clifton, 1983; Rovee-Collier, 1987). In fact, as we will see in the chapter titled "Intelligence," an infant's rapid habituation and recovery from habituation to new stimuli is associated with greater intelligence and cognitive capacities in later childhood. Thus, although it is a simple form of learning, habituation may nonetheless be an important process in intellectual development.

Classical Conditioning

As we learned in the chapter titled "Themes and Theories," in *classical conditioning* a neutral event paired with a stimulus that triggers an inborn reaction can begin to elicit a response similar to the one initiated by the original stimulus. Consider a nipple placed in a newborn's mouth; it tends to elicit sucking. The nipple is an **unconditioned stimulus (UCS);** the sucking response is an **unconditioned response (UCR).** After a series of trials in which a neutral stimulus—say, a distinctive odor—is paired with the nipple (the UCS), the odor may also begin to elicit sucking even when the nipple is not present. The odor has become a **conditioned stimulus (CS),** and the sucking response it initiates a **conditioned response (CR).** Table 6.1 summarizes the sequence of steps in classical conditioning for this and other typical examples.

Infants display classical conditioning within hours of birth. Elliot Blass and his colleagues (Blass, Ganchrow, & Steiner, 1984) paired a tactile stimulus, stroking of the newborn's forehead (CS), with the delivery of a sugar solution to the mouth (UCS) that elicited sucking (UCR). Newborns learned to orient and initiate sucking (CR) with stroking of the forehead (CS) alone. Thus, important associations, particularly those surrounding feeding activity, can be acquired through classical conditioning shortly after birth. But some types of classical conditioning are difficult for infants to learn. For example, researchers have not been able to successfully condition infants

habituation Gradual decline in intensity, frequency, or duration of a response over repeated or lengthy occurrences of the same stimulus.

recovery from habituation Reinstatement of the intensity, frequency, or duration of a response to a stimulus that has changed. Also called *dishabituation*.

dishabituation See *recovery from habituation*.

unconditioned stimulus (UCS) Stimulus that, without prior training, elicits a reflexlike response (unconditioned response).

unconditioned response (UCR) Response that is automatically elicited by the unconditioned stimulus (UCS).

conditioned stimulus (CS) Neutral stimulus that begins to elicit a response similar to the unconditioned stimulus (UCS) with which it has been paired.

conditioned response (CR) Learned response that is exhibited to a previously neutral stimulus (CS) as a result of pairing the CS with an unconditioned stimulus (UCS).

| TABLE 6.1 | Examples of Classical Conditioning |

Classical conditioning is learning in which a neutral event (conditioned stimulus), through its association with a cue (unconditioned stimulus) that naturally elicits a reflexlike response (unconditioned response), comes to elicit the same response (conditioned response).

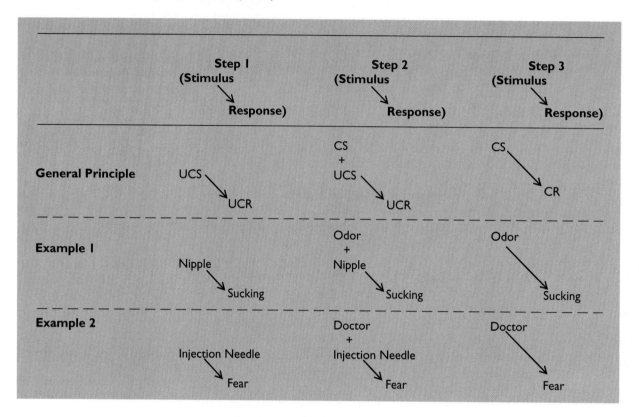

younger than three or four weeks to respond to aversive stimuli, such as foot withdrawal at loud noises or a painful prick. Perhaps the youngest infants lack the motor and neural abilities needed to escape noxious events; they must depend on caregivers for protection until they acquire simple locomotor skills for avoiding aversive stimuli (Rovee-Collier, 1987). As infants become older, classical conditioning occurs more rapidly and involves a broader range of stimuli.

Operant Conditioning

In *operant* (or *instrumental*) *conditioning*, the frequency of spontaneous, sometimes novel behaviors changes as a result of positive and negative consequences. Put another way, behaviors tend to increase when followed by rewards (**positive reinforcement**) or the removal of aversive events (**negative reinforcement**) and to decrease when followed by the loss of rewards (**negative punishment**) or an aversive outcome (**positive punishment**). The term *positive* in this context indicates that when a behavior occurs, it causes a stimulus event that either increases the rate of the response (reinforcement) or decreases it (punishment). The term *negative* in this context indicates that when a behavior occurs, it leads to the removal of a stimulus that either increases the rate of the response (reinforcement) or decreases it (punishment). Figure 6.1 summarizes these relationships and provides examples of positive and negative reinforcement and punishment.

Operant conditioning can also be observed in infants within the first few hours of birth. For example, newborns will either increase or decrease pressure during sucking when the availability of milk, a positive reinforcer, is contingent on an increase or

positive reinforcement
Occurrence of a stimulus that strengthens a preceding response. Also known as a *reward*.

negative reinforcement
Removal of an aversive stimulus that strengthens a preceding response.

negative punishment
Removal or loss of a desired stimulus or reward that weakens or decreases the frequency of a preceding response.

positive punishment
Occurrence of an aversive stimulus that serves to weaken or decrease the frequency of a preceding response.

Rate of response

	Increases	Decreases
Response leads stimulus to be Delivered	**Positive reinforcement** (Increases behavior by delivering a desired stimulus) Example: Infant says, "cookie" → Mother gives praise	**Positive punishment** (Decreases behavior by delivering an aversive stimulus) Example: Toddler throws toys → Father yells, "Stop it"
Response leads stimulus to be Removed	**Negative reinforcement** (Increases behavior by removing an aversive stimulus) Example: Child cleans messy room → Parent stops "nagging"	**Negative punishment** (Decreases behavior by removing a desired stimulus) Example: Teenager out past curfew → Parent grounds teenager

FIGURE 6.1
Positive and Negative Reinforcement and Punishment

Reinforcement leads to an increase in the rate of responding; punishment leads to a decrease in the rate of responding. *Positive* refers to the presentation of a stimulus following a response; *negative* refers to the removal of a stimulus following a response.

a decrease in pressure (Sameroff, 1972). And as with classical conditioning, operant conditioning seems to work best with behaviors important to infants, such as searching for (head turning, mouthing) and obtaining (sucking) food or other stimuli that are comforting. In other words, babies seem to be biologically prepared to learn about some things that are especially important for them.

Visual and auditory events can be especially powerful reinforcers for infants. Babies will work hard, modifying the frequency or rate of sucking, vocalizing, smiling, and other behaviors under their control, to see and hear things. These kinds of stimulation, of course, typically occur in the presence of parents, grandparents, neighbors, and siblings who, as major sources of reinforcers, encourage the baby to become responsive to them.

RESEARCH APPLIED TO PARENTING

Reducing Sleep Disturbances Through Changes in Learned Behavior

As the last rays of sun disappeared, Tanya shifted her focus to preparing Chad for bed. After putting on his pajamas and playing with him a few more minutes, she rocked him and sang a lullaby before giving him a final hug and kiss. But just as she was about to lay him in his crib, Chad started to cry. Tanya tried to ignore his sobs, but as they intensified to screams, she knew Chad, still wound up from the party, would not go to sleep right away this night. Indeed, he had been doing the same thing for the last several weeks. Why would this evening be any different? Tanya picked him up, played with him a bit longer, and then lay down with him in her own bed until he finally fell asleep. She moved Chad to his own crib later that evening.

Even more distressing for Tanya, however, were Chad's frequent awakenings. Usually, two or three times each night, he would cry so hard that she would have to go through the same bedtime routine until he fell asleep again. Tanya was having difficulty getting the sleep that she desperately needed, and it was beginning to take a toll on her relationship with Chad.

Surveys of parents reveal that somewhere between 10 and 40 percent of infants and young children have difficulty going to sleep or returning to sleep after awakening in the middle of the night (Blampied & France, 1993; Johnson, 1991). Most of

Establishing bedtime routines can help young children prepare for sleep. Quiet activities such as looking at and reading a book together with a parent, as well as the availability of a comforting toy such as a teddy bear, should help these toddlers make the transition from wakefulness to sleep.

these difficulties do not stem from serious developmental problems, but they can become a major challenge for parents as they try to obtain sufficient rest for themselves.

Principles of classical and operant learning can account for most sleep difficulties; they can also provide answers to eliminating the problem. For example, for a variety of reasons, such as illness, teething, or some other discomfort, an older infant or a young child may have considerable difficulty falling asleep. Under such circumstances, parents often—and in such cases, quite appropriately—pick up, rock, or otherwise soothe the child. However, such activities are usually powerful reinforcers that can strengthen fussing, crying, or other attention-getting behaviors. Thus, long after the initial distress has been resolved, a child may still display sleep difficulties at bedtime or after awakening in the middle of the night. The principles of learning suggest a number of steps to take to address this issue (Adair et al., 1992; Blampied & France, 1993; Ferber, 1985):

1. *Provide positive routines in preparation for bedtime.*   Older infants and young children need to learn to associate certain cues with preparing themselves for sleep. These should include regular, quiet activities such as reading or gentle rocking about the same time each evening to reduce arousal level and increase expectations—that is, set the stage—for sleep onset.

2. *Arrange for falling asleep in the child's own crib or bed.*   Children need to associate certain rooms and other spatial cues with falling asleep. Otherwise, particularly if they awaken in the middle of the night, those cues are not available to help them return to sleep.

3. *Offer comforting resources to substitute for parental attention.*   A favorite toy, blanket, or other item may help young children soothe themselves in preparing for sleep. Once such items become associated with falling asleep, they can also be important cues for subsequently promoting sleep if the child awakens later in the night.

4. *Reduce and eventually eliminate parental cues for falling asleep.*   Parental attention can be a highly positive reinforcer. Sleep difficulties often arise when parents rock, hold, or otherwise engage their children in trying to get them back to sleep; the parents' presence and falling asleep become a learned association (Ferber, 1985).

Infants less than four to six months of age should not be expected to adopt a sleep schedule. Parents need to follow their young infant's lead, feeding and providing other care and assistance even when tired themselves. However, older infants and young children may need to learn to fall asleep. If soothing and rocking seem to be effective, parents can feel more confident that hunger, pain, or some other problem is not the reason for difficulty in sleeping. In considering learning principles to help reduce sleep problems, Richard Ferber and others suggest that when an older infant or a young child has difficulty, parents implement a progressive *delayed-responding* or "controlled-crying" *technique* to change the association between caregiver presence and falling asleep. If a young child starts to cry after being put to bed, wait a few minutes. Then check to see that she or he is all right and does not need to be fed, changed, or provided with other care; but limit the visit to two or three minutes and to reassuring behaviors other than picking up, feeding, and so forth. Leave while the child is still awake to promote cues for falling asleep without the parent's presence. If crying continues, wait for gradually increasing periods of time before returning and follow the same procedure. On subsequent days, start with gradually longer intervals before confirming that the child is all right.

By sticking to such a schedule, parents promote fewer and less severe sleeping problems (Hiscock & Wake, 2002). Of course, an illness or a significant change in the child's life can upset a child so that sleep disturbances return. But once the immediate problem is addressed, parents may need to reimplement the steps that encourage sleep both for their child and themselves.

Classical and operant conditioning can explain the acquisition of many other behaviors throughout infancy and childhood. Through repeated associations of events and from positive outcomes, including the reinforcing actions of caregivers or "instructors," children become more skilled and proficient in a rich variety of endeavors. Consider the six-year-old learning to write the letters of the alphabet. At first, of course, neither the sizes nor the shapes of the letters are skillfully reproduced, but the teacher may express enormous satisfaction with these early efforts. With practice and as the child's fine motor skills improve, the teacher begins to expect far more legible symbols before granting praise to the student. Precisely these kinds of contingencies are central to *applied behavior analysis,* described in the chapter titled "Themes and Theories."

It is difficult to imagine, however, that habituation, classical conditioning, and the systematic implementation of reinforcers and punishment are the basis for mastering all the vital tasks of childhood. One element that seems to be missing from this discussion so far is children's active roles in observing and interpreting events that occur in their surroundings. As we see in the chapter titled "Themes and Theories," social learning theorists have also considered observational learning an important means by which children acquire many complex social and cognitive skills (Bandura, 1977b). Individuals often learn behaviors important to the community by observing the activities of others, who in turn provide further guidance. Imitation has become an increasingly important element in explaining learning throughout development.

KEY THEME
Child's Active Role

Imitation

When does imitation become possible? How important is this ability in the learning of infants and children? Andrew Meltzoff and M. Keith Moore (1999) argue that even newborns and very young infants imitate a variety of responses, including tongue protrusion, mouth opening, and possibly even facial expressions portraying such emotions as happiness, sadness, and surprise (Field et al., 1982). Although some investigators have been unable to replicate these results, many others, including the authors of one study involving infants from Nepal (see Figure 6.2), report amazing imitative competence in neonates (Reissland, 1988).

More controversial, though, is what the imitative behaviors mean. Piaget (1962), for example, claimed that infants younger than eight to twelve months could imitate someone else's behavior, but only when able to see themselves making these responses. Because babies cannot view their own faces, imitative facial gestures would be impossible, according to Piaget, until after about a year of age, when symbolic capacities emerge. From this perspective, then, facial gestures are stereotyped, rigid responses triggered by or tethered, so to speak, to limited forms of stimulation. For example, perhaps tongue

FIGURE 6.2
Facial Imitation in Newborns

Within an hour after birth, babies in Nepal showed different responses when an experimenter used pursed versus widened lip movements. On the left, the baby broadens his lips in response to widened lips by the model. On the right, the baby exposes his tongue in response to pursed lips by the model. The findings support the highly controversial position that even newborns are capable of imitating facial gestures.

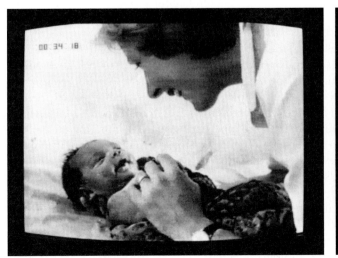

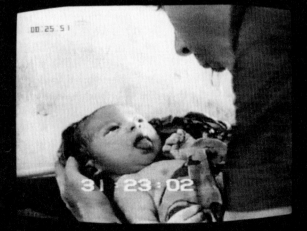

protrusion by a model arouses the infant, which in turn promotes a sucking response that naturally invokes tongue protrusion from the infant (Karmiloff-Smith, 1995). Alternatively, perhaps this behavior reflects an active effort to explore an interesting object available in the infant's visual field (Jones, 1996). In either case, infants could be responding to just one or two types of stimuli and producing a kind of reflexive motor activity that is not really a form of imitation (Anisfeld, 1996).

Meltzoff and Moore (1999) counter that very young infants imitate a variety of responses, modify their imitations to increasingly match the modeled behavior over time, and exhibit their imitations primarily to other people and not to inanimate objects. These arguments contradict the view that such behaviors are simply a fixed pattern of reflexive actions. They propose instead that infants imitate in order to continue interacting with others. In fact, babies as young as six weeks will imitate behaviors of a model up to twenty-four hours later. The infant produces these imitative actions, according to Meltzoff and Moore, to help determine whether the model is the same person seen earlier, that is, as a way to help to identify and communicate with the model. If this interpretation is correct, imitation has an important social-communicative function and signals one of the earliest games babies play to learn about others in their surroundings.

KEY THEME
Interaction Among Domains

Between six and twelve months of age, infants clearly display far more frequent and precise imitations, matching a wide range of modeled behaviors (Kaye & Marcus, 1981; Meltzoff & Moore, 1999). Piaget and others (McCall, Parke, & Kavanaugh, 1977) believed that **deferred imitation,** the ability to imitate well after some activity has been demonstrated, was not possible until about eighteen to twenty-four months of age. Piaget held that deferred imitation, along with pretend play and the emergence of language, provides one of the first major pieces of evidence for symbolic capacities (see the chapter titled "Cognition: Piaget and Vygotsky"). However, as we have already seen, Meltzoff and Moore observed infants as young as six weeks reproducing a model's behavior a day after seeing it.

Other research confirms that deferred imitation can be observed far earlier than Piaget claimed. For example, six-month-olds will remove a mitten from a puppet's hand, shake it, and try to put it back on the puppet after observing this sequence of actions performed by a model twenty-four hours earlier (Barr, Dowden, & Hayne, 1996). Moreover, toddlers as young as fourteen months who see a peer pulling, pushing, poking, and inserting toys in the laboratory or at a day care center will reproduce the behaviors in their own homes as much as two days later when given the same toys and will imitate other novel behaviors as much as a week later (Meltzoff & Moore, 1999). The capacity for deferred imitation, then, appears to emerge much sooner than previously assumed. In fact, the results accord well with research on memory (discussed in the chapter titled "Cognition: Information Processing") showing that infants younger than one year can recognize stimuli hours and even days later.

The findings of imitation at very young ages provide clear and compelling evidence that infants, as well as older children, learn many new behaviors by observing others. In fact, fourteen- to eighteen-month-olds are more likely to imitate an adult's action that is accompanied by the verbal expression "There!"—indicating it was performed intentionally—than an action accompanied by the verbal expression "Whoops!"—implying a mistake (Carpenter, Akhtar, & Tomasello, 1998). This finding suggests that very young children are capable of selectively imitating the deliberate actions of others, an important achievement for learning the more important social and cultural skills valued by other members of the community. Mothers also report that two-year-olds increasingly imitate responsible behaviors such as chores and self-care (pretending to cook, brushing teeth) rather than affective or attention-getting actions such as laughing, sighing, shouting, or pounding (Kuczynski, Zahn-Waxler, & Radke-Yarrow, 1987). Thus observational learning, along with the parent's direct application of reinforcers and punishments, undoubtedly plays a powerful role in the socialization of young children.

deferred imitation   Ability to imitate a model's behavior hours, days, and even weeks after observation.

Implicit Learning

Humans, including infants and young children, probably learn in many other ways. **Implicit learning** has become of increasing interest to researchers because it may help to explain the acquisition of some fundamental aspects of knowledge, including language, categories, and procedural routines that accompany many motor behaviors in infants and children. Implicit learning refers to abstract knowledge that is not available to conscious reflection. It is knowledge incidentally acquired from processing structured information; the learning is unintentional. Because much of the stimulation to which we are exposed—for example, the visual-spatial environment and language—is organized by patterns and rules, learning these systematic relationships is important for adaptation to both the physical and social worlds. Essentially, as a result of the frequent covariation of specific features and attributes in experience, we implicitly become sensitive to these patterns or rules. We present a claim for such learning in the chapter titled "Language," in the discussion of how infants might acquire some aspects of linguistic abilities, such as detecting the boundaries of words within the continuous stream of speech sound. Implicit learning may also be a significant aspect of perceptual learning, a topic discussed more fully later in this chapter.

Research by Annie Vinter and Pierre Perruchet (2000) illustrates the concept of implicit learning applied to a motor skills task. When we draw a figure such as a circle, we tend to do so either clockwise or counterclockwise, depending on the position of the starting point. For example, if the starting point is above an imaginary line drawn to connect the positions of approximately eleven o'clock and five o'clock on the circle, we tend to draw it counterclockwise; if below the line, clockwise. Of course, the task requirement of drawing the entire circle is the same no matter which direction is employed. In Vinter and Perruchet's study, children practiced drawing the circle but were instructed at what point to start and in which direction to draw it. Some children received far more experience drawing the circle in the direction opposite to the one they would spontaneously employ. When no longer instructed to draw the circle in a particular direction, they were much more likely to draw it in the direction with which they had more experience. The children (as is true of adults as well) did not realize that they had drawn the circle in one direction more frequently than the other during the practice session. Nevertheless, they continued to display this behavior, a kind of procedural learning, as much as an hour after the practice session. These findings suggest that learning takes place in many contexts and situations of which we are totally unaware and by different mechanisms than those involved in, for example, classical and operant conditioning. In other words, even infants' and young children's behavior could be dramatically influenced and driven by the various kinds of regularities that they experience in their world.

Knowing how to address a revered elder, care for a flock of sheep, read and solve complex mathematics problems, and navigate from one location to another within the city, over mountainous terrain, or between widely dispersed islands are just a few of the many complex skills children acquire that involve various facets of learning. Because learning is exhibited within the confines of a rich context of additional social and cognitive processes, its importance will continue to be evident in our discussion of many other aspects of development.

FOR YOUR REVIEW

- What are the basic principles of habituation, classical conditioning, and operant conditioning? What does recovery from habituation tell us about the habituation process? What are an unconditioned stimulus, an unconditioned response, a conditioned stimulus, and a conditioned response? How do positive reinforcement, negative reinforcement, negative punishment, and positive punishment affect behavior?

implicit learning Abstract knowledge not available to conscious reflection acquired incidentally from processing structured information.

- How can learning principles affect the sleep patterns of toddlers and young children? How might they play a role in the emergence of other acceptable and unacceptable behaviors in children?

- Why is imitation an important component of learning theory? What evidence exists for imitation in early infancy? What is the significance of deferred imitation?

- What is implicit learning?

Sensory and Perceptual Capacities

Although various kinds of learning contribute to mastering new behaviors and enriching each individual's skills and competencies, these depend on other basic processes, including sensation and perception. Tanya's queries about whether Chad could see or hear as she first held her son are the kinds of questions many parents pose to their newborns even as they seem to provide their own answers by vocalizing, making funny facial expressions, touching, caressing, and rocking the baby. Still, the uncertainty remains: what do infants sense and perceive?

Sensation refers to the basic units of information recorded by a sensory receptor and the brain. **Perception** refers to the process of organizing and interpreting sensations. Sensations consist of, for example, registering different regions of brightness or of *contours,* the transitions in dark-light shading that signal borders and edges of elements in a visual array. With respect to auditory input, sensation refers to, for example, being able to discriminate a difference in the intensity or frequency of a sound. Perception, on the other hand, takes place when the infant recognizes his mother's face by sight or interprets a sequence of sounds as a familiar lullaby. Thus, sensations are typically thought to be the building blocks; perception, the order and meaning imposed on those basic elements.

Is the sensory world of the newborn a "big blooming buzzing confusion" caused by a barrage of unorganized sensations, a view proposed by William James (1890) more than a century ago? If so, the young infant would not apprehend objects or meaningful events at first but would acquire the ability to do so only from learning, over a lengthy period of time, which pattern of basic sensory features is associated with a particular perceptual array (Gordon & Slater, 1998). Perhaps, then, as a result of repeated experience with distinctive sensory input, the infant comes to recognize the human face or to perceive how far away an object is located or to hear a sequence of sounds as a lullaby. According to this viewpoint, perceptual development is a *constructive* process, that is, one of imposing sense and order on the multisensory external world.

James and Eleanor Gibson and many of their students offer a strikingly different opinion of the early sensory capacities of infants (Pick, 1992). For them, babies come into the world well equipped to respond to the structure and organization of many stimuli and readily perceive the patterns afforded by objects and other sensory events. Some go even further. According to the *nativist* position, the newborn from very early on has, for example, a set of core principles and mechanisms to process complex visual cues signifying objects and three-dimensional space and to interpret other sensory input (Spelke & Newport, 1998). Of course, even within this framework, experience provides ever greater opportunity to refine knowledge about which properties processed by the senses are stable and important and which can be ignored as relatively uninformative.

Before considering some of the findings bearing on these issues, we can make two broad observations about work on perceptual development. First, vision has been studied far more than any other sensory domain. To some extent, this bias reflects the widespread view that sight provides the major source of information for humans. Vision, however, has also been easier to study than hearing, smell, and other senses. Second, knowledge of sensory and perceptual development in newborns and young infants has expanded far more rapidly than knowledge of their development in older infants and children (Aslin & Smith, 1988). The disparity reflects the efforts of researchers to un-

KEY THEME
Nature/Nurture

sensation Basic information in the external world that is processed by the sensory receptors.

perception Process of organizing and interpreting sensory information.

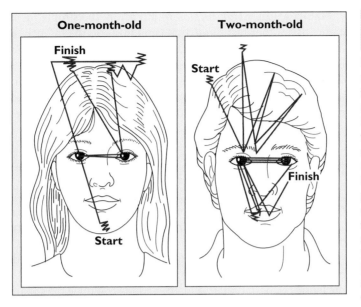

One-month-old   **Two-month-old**

Finish

Start

Start

Finish

Start

Source: Adapted from Salapatek, 1975.

FIGURE 6.3
Visual Scanning

Using specialized techniques, researchers can often pinpoint the specific features in a visual stimulus at which infants are looking. Here the typical patterns of scanning these facelike stimuli by a one- and a two-month-old have been recorded. Note how the younger infant's gaze tends to be directed to the outer or external regions of the facial stimulus, that is, hair and chin. The older infant's gaze is more frequently directed to inner features such as the eyes and mouth.

cover the earliest appearance of sensory and perceptual capacities, the finding that many important changes in these domains occur in the first few months after birth, and interest in trying to determine whether perceptual abilities are innate or acquired.

Measuring Infant Sensory and Perceptual Capacities

How can we possibly know what babies see, hear, or smell when they are unable to tell us about it in words? Researchers have devised ingenious techniques, some quite simple, to help answer this question. Most of these procedures are based on measures of **attention,** that is, alertness or arousal focused on a specific aspect of the environment. For example, when infants display attentional preferences, that is, look longer at one thing than at another, they are communicating that they perceive differences between visual arrays.

● **Preferential Behaviors**   In 1958 Robert Fantz placed babies on their backs in an enclosed, criblike chamber. Through a peephole, he and his colleagues observed how long the babies gazed at different visual stimuli inserted in the top of the brightly illuminated chamber. Observers were able to determine where the infants were looking because the reflection of the stimulus could be seen on the *cornea,* the outer surface of the babies' eyes, as they looked at the objects. Using this method, Fantz (1961) found that one- to six-month-olds attended to disks decorated with bull's eyes, stripes, newsprint, or facelike figures far longer than to solid-colored circles.

The simple methodology encouraged many researchers to study the visual capacities of infants by observing their preferential looking. The procedure has some limitations, however. What can we conclude, for example, when the infant attends to both members of a pair of stimuli for the same length of time? Is the baby unable to discriminate the two, or does she prefer to look at one just as much as the other? Nor can we be certain about what features the infant is processing when gazing at a stimulus.

Despite the limitations, babies often show preferences in what they attend to, and this simple procedure has proven enormously useful in assessing whether they prefer a human face over equally complex patterns; features such as edges, corners, or movement within a visual array; and other patterns or characteristics of visual information. By using special photographic techniques involving infrared lights and appropriate film, researchers can pinpoint specific regions and aspects of a figure at which the baby looks and how she or he inspects a stimulus. Such procedures have revealed, for example, which features of a human face infants are most likely to scan, as Figure 6.3 shows.

attention   State of alertness or arousal that allows the individual to focus on a selected aspect of the environment.

● **Habituation**   *Habituation* of attention, the simple form of learning described earlier, is another technique that capitalizes on the infant's tendency to prefer looking at some things more than others. Babies shown the same stimulus for relatively lengthy periods or over a series of trials pay less and less attention to it. A change in the stimulus, however, may elicit *recovery from habituation,* or, if the habituated stimulus is paired with one that is dissimilar, the infant may show a preference for the new one, both indicators that the child has perceived a difference.

EXAMINING RESEARCH METHODS

Habituation Procedures

To illustrate the use of a habituation procedure, consider a recent study carried out by Scott P. Johnson and Uschi Mason (2002). They were interested in whether two-month-old infants could detect the illusory shape of a black square or a cross with points of light on the surface when the figure was embedded in an equally black background containing similar points of light (see Figure 6.4). Not surprisingly, when the figures were stationary, not even adults could see the square or the cross; the figure literally fused with the background. However, when the illusory figure moved, the accretion and deletion of the points of light on the background, as well as the relative motion of the points within the shape, "revealed" the appearance of the figure, at least to adults. Would two-month-olds be able to process these same **kinetic cues**—cues provided by changes in the flow of visual elements within the perceptual array—and perceive the illusory shape as well?

To answer this question, Johnson and Mason (2002) presented a series of trials during which either the square or the cross moved along a square path in the center of the background. Not surprisingly, the infants' attention declined over these trials; they habituated to the display. How were the researchers able to measure the babies' attention? The answer, of course, was by having observers watching through peepholes positioned at the side of the monitor on which the displays were presented and recording the amount of time the infants looked at the array before turning away for two seconds. When looking times on trials decreased to less than 50 percent of the time the infant had attended on the beginning trials—a conventional way of assessing habituation—test trials were presented. These test trials consisted of alternate presentations of a gray square and a gray cross of the same size and moving in the same pattern as the shape on the habituation trials.

Would infants show greater looking time at the test pattern that differed from the textured pattern to which they habituated? The answer was yes. If they had been presented the square during the habituation trials, most infants preferred looking at the cross; if they were shown the cross during the habituation trials, most infants preferred looking at the square. In other words, their findings indicated that the infants must have perceived the figure that appeared during the familiarization period, as their attention to the novel shape was greater on the test trials. Could the researchers have reached the same conclusion had the infants shown a preference for the figure that had appeared on habituation trials? Probably yes, although the general finding in research of this type is that infants prefer to attend to novel arrays. What could they conclude if the infants showed no preference for either figure on test trials?

Johnson and Mason (2002) went on to show in additional experiments that infants this young can detect the shape on the basis of either the accretion and deletion of the background points or from the relative motion of the light points. These findings suggest a rather remarkable ability to perceive shape as a result of motion via simple textural cues very early in development; the infants did not need to have boundary information to convey the shape in order to perceive it. The ingenuity of these researchers, along with that of many others relying on a simple habituation procedure, has yielded extraordinary insights into the sensory and perceptual capacities of even very young infants.

kinetic cue   Perceptual information provided by movement of objects in the environment or of eyes, head, or body. Important source of information for depth perception.

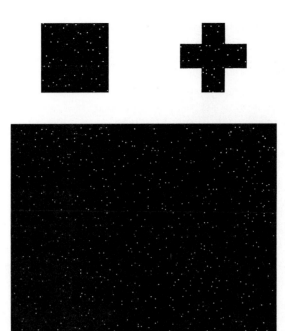

Source: Johnson & Mason, 2002, p. 24.

FIGURE 6.4
Using Kinetic Cues to See
an Illusory Figure

The habituation and recovery from habituation procedures can be used to demonstrate that even very young infants perceive illusory shapes. Johnson and Mason (2002) showed two-month-olds a black background with points of light randomly distributed on it. A square or a cross with the same background and containing similar points of light was imposed on the background to test whether accretion and deletion of the light points in the background, as well as the relative movement of the points of light, were cues that the infants could use to "see" the square or the cross. When not moving, the shapes were undetectable (the square is in the left portion of the background, the cross in the right portion). When only one of the shapes was presented moving within the background, even two-month-olds recognized the figure, as evidenced by their showing greater attention during test trials to the other (novel) figure than to the one shown during habituation trials. Infants could form a coherent percept of the moving figure, even though its appearance was undefined by contour boundaries.

● **Operant Conditioning**   More complex forms of learning, such as operant conditioning, can be used to further test an infant's ability to process sensory cues. To receive milk and other tangible rewards, such as interesting visual and auditory patterns, babies will learn to suck faster or slower, turn their heads, look, and perform other behaviors that indicate that they discriminate the arrays.

Operant conditioning procedures figure prominently in research on auditory perception. One procedure, established by Peter Eimas and his colleagues (1971), has proven especially informative. Babies are given a special nipple designed to record their rate of sucking. A baby who sucks energetically or at a rapid rate may be rewarded by hearing some pleasant sound, for example, the consonant-vowel pairing *pa*. After hearing *pa* repeatedly, the rate of sucking typically declines as the infant habituates to the stimulus. What will the baby do when a different sound, such as *ba*, is introduced? Infants as young as one month begin to suck at a high rate again in order to keep hearing *ba*. They can discriminate the new consonant-vowel pair from *pa*; they are already able to distinguish some important sounds that occur in language.

In addition to behavioral methods—preferential looking, habituation, and operant conditioning—physiological measures such as heart rate or the neurological activity of the brain and even the firing of individual neurons can be recorded to clarify the sensory and perceptual abilities of infants (de Haan & Nelson, 1997; Teller, 1998). Fortunately, the results of the various methods often complement one another in providing information about what infants are processing.

Vision

Because newborns have limited motor skills, we are often tempted to assume that their sensory systems—their eyes, ears, noses, mouths, and skin—must be passive receptors awaiting stimulation. But Eleanor J. Gibson and James J. Gibson convincingly argue that perceiving is an active process (Gibson, 1966). "We don't simply see, we look" (Gibson, 1988, p. 5). Even neonates mobilize sensory receptors to respond to stimulation flowing from their bustling environment.

KEY THEME
Child's Active Role

This young infant appears to be attentively examining his mother's smiling face. Such an interesting stimulus undoubtedly helps the baby to make sense of the various features that differentiate the face of the mother from the face of others. Visuomotor and other visual abilities rapidly improve during the first few months of life, and the ability to recognize a caregiver's face is acquired very early in development.

● **Visuomotor Skills**   The eye includes a lens designed to refract, or bend, light. The lens focuses visual images onto the *retina,* the back of the eye that houses the *rods,* which are responsive to the intensity of light, and the *cones,* which are sensitive to different wavelengths of light. The lens of the human eye is variable; small, involuntary muscles change its shape so that images of objects viewed at different distances are brought into focus on the retina, a process called **visual accommodation.** When the lens works effectively, we can see things clearly.

Newborns display limited visual accommodation. However, the process improves rapidly to nearly adultlike levels by about three months of age (Aslin, 1987a). Improvements in the physical characteristics of the eye and in paying attention to visual information may contribute to the developmental change (Hainline, 1998). In addition, the *pupillary reflex,* which controls the amount of light entering the eye, is sluggish during the first few months after birth, further reducing the ability to focus (Aslin, 1987a). As a result, infants are unable to see details of stimuli. However, they discriminate best those patterns and objects about eight to twenty inches away, the typical distance of a caregiver's face when holding or feeding the baby.

Eye movements are another essential part of looking. **Saccades,** rapid movements of the eye to inspect an object or to look at something in the periphery of the visual field, are produced within hours of birth (Lewis, Maurer, & Kay, 1978). At first, the saccades are initiated slowly and cover only small distances; neonates must launch a sequence of them to "catch up" to a peripheral target (Aslin, 1993). Saccades typically become more accurate, however, during the first three to four months and continue to improve in accuracy throughout childhood (Fioravanti et al., 1995).

Humans exhibit another pattern of eye movements, **smooth visual pursuit,** which consists of maintaining fixation on a slowly moving target almost as though

visual accommodation
Visuomotor process by which small involuntary muscles change the shape of the lens of the eye so that images of objects seen at different distances are brought into focus on the retina.

saccade   Rapid eye movement to inspect an object or view a stimulus in the periphery of the visual field.

smooth visual pursuit   Consistent, unbroken tracking by the eyes that serves to maintain focus on a moving visual target.

FIGURE 6.5
What the Two-Month-Old Sees

Although adults with normal vision would see a clear image of this individual (**A**), the two-month-old would perceive the same individual in far less detail as suggested by the photo on the right (**B**). Acuity in young infants, however, rapidly improves and typically approaches a normal level sometime between about six and twelve months of age.

the eyes were locked onto it. Newborns display only brief periods of smooth pursuit, but its execution continues to improve through six to eight months of age (von Hofsten & Rosander, 1997), when it begins to appear adultlike. The development of both saccadic and smooth visual pursuit eye movements is closely linked to the improving capacity of infants to sustain attention to visual arrays (Richards & Holley, 1999).

In looking for an object, both eyes normally move together in the same direction. Sometimes, however, the eyes must rotate in opposite directions, turning toward each other as, for example, when a person tries to see a fly that has landed on his or her nose. This response, called **vergence,** occurs when fixations shift between far and near objects; otherwise, we would see double images. Vergence occurs irregularly in infants younger than two months, especially when objects are not static and move to different depths (Hainline & Riddell, 1995; Thorn et al., 1994). For example, young babies' eyes may fail to rotate far enough toward each other to converge on a visual target.

● **Acuity** How well are young infants able to see despite their immature visuomotor skills? The question concerns **visual acuity.** One common test of visual acuity, the *Snellen test,* is based on identifying letters or other symbols on a chart twenty feet away. Babies, of course, cannot name letters, so other procedures are used to test their visual acuity. Several methods have been devised, but one that has proven reasonably good relies on preferential looking. As an array of, say, black and white stripes appears more frequently (the stripes become narrower), the pattern becomes more difficult to see, and the stimulus eventually appears gray. Infants unable to detect the stripes quickly lose interest, preferring to attend instead to a pattern they can still detect. By pairing stimuli with different frequencies of stripes and observing preferential looking, researchers can gauge the visual acuity of infants.

Two key findings emerge from the many investigations of visual acuity and *contrast sensitivity,* another more complex measure of visual capacity that takes into consideration ability to discriminate when illumination, orientation, and other aspects of contour also vary. First, even newborns detect contours, although their acuity and sensitivity to contrast is estimated to be about forty times poorer than in children or adults as suggested in Figure 6.5 (Maurer et al. 1999). Second, acuity and contrast sensitivity improve rapidly during the first six months after birth and continue to improve at a slower rate for several years thereafter (Adoh & Woodhouse, 1994; Tschopp et al., 1999). The gain, especially during early infancy, is owed to enhanced visuomotor skills and neural pathways for vision, changes in the shape and physical characteristics of the eye, and greater efficiency in the functioning of visual receptors in the retina.

● **SEE FOR YOURSELF**
psychology.college.hmco.com
Perceptual Abilities in Infants

vergence Ability of the eyes to rotate in opposite directions to fixate on objects at different distances; improves rapidly during first few months after birth.

visual acuity Ability to make fine discriminations among elements in a visual array by detecting contours, transitions in light patterns that signal borders and edges.

ATYPICAL DEVELOPMENT

Visual Problems in Infancy

How important is visual sensory stimulation during infancy and early childhood for the development of the normal capacity to see? In the chapter titled "Brain, Motor Skill, and Physical Development," we describe research carried out on young kittens suggesting that early perceptual stimulation was essential for the growth of neurons in the visual receptor areas of the cortex. Although experimental procedures cannot be carried out on human infants, several naturally occurring problems in infancy suggest similar consequences for the development of human visual abilities.

Approximately 1 in every 10,000 babies is born with cataracts, a clouding of part or all of the lens of the eye that impairs the capacity to see patterned stimulation (Sireteanu, 1999). If uncorrected, the baby's visual acuity, as well as other visual abilities, can be seriously impaired. Moreover, if the cataract is located in only one eye, the normal eye will actively suppress whatever responsiveness exists in the affected eye. The result is a lack of improvement in acuity in the affected eye, as well as impairment in depth perception because of the loss of binocular vision. Fortunately, cataracts are often relatively easy to detect. They can be surgically removed if medical resources are available, and substitute contact lenses can be implanted so that visual input will be focused on the retina. When such procedures are followed early in infancy, acuity in the affected eye or eyes improves rapidly, even after only an hour of patterned visual experience, and continues to improve rapidly with an outcome of normal visual development (Maurer et al., 1999).

Perhaps an even more frequent visual problem affecting as many as 5 percent of infants and young children is *amblyopia*, a condition sometimes called "lazy eye." Amblyopia refers to the failure of vision to develop in one eye, again because of suppression of visual input by the other eye. A common cause of amblyopia is *strabismus,* or the inability of the two eyes to display vergence. In many circumstances, strabismus is also relatively easy to detect; the eyes appear misaligned, or the child appears "cross-eyed" because muscles controlling the directionality of one of the eyes may be too strong or too weak. When strabismus is corrected early, normal depth perception and vision again become possible, as the two eyes begin to work together. However, for some infants and young children, the complementary functioning of the two eyes may go awry even without visible evidence of strabismus if, for example, the ability of one eye to focus is better than the other. A child with amblyopia displays the progressive loss of depth perception that vergence provides (Banks, Aslin, & Letson, 1975), and the weaker eye may become functionally blind. Fortunately, many procedures are available to correct such conditions, including patching the stronger eye for a period of time to strengthen the weaker one. If not performed early, preferably in toddlers and especially before the end of the preschool years, the loss of visual capacities can be permanent. However, parents, and sometimes even pediatricians, may not always be aware of these visual problems. Thus caregivers need to take the initiative in ensuring that their infants' and toddlers' vision is evaluated by experts who can conduct relatively simple tests for amblyopia; adequate perceptual stimulation early in development is an essential ingredient to the emergence of normal visual capacities.

● **Color Perception**   Can babies also see colors? Once again the answer is yes, at least after a few months of age. Although very young infants may not see a full range of colors, perception of several hues is possible. For example, shortly after birth babies can detect red hues, especially if they are highly saturated, that is, contain relatively few wavelengths of other light (Adams & Courage, 1998). Detection of some hues may even become adultlike by three months of age (Kellman & Banks, 1998; Teller, 1998).

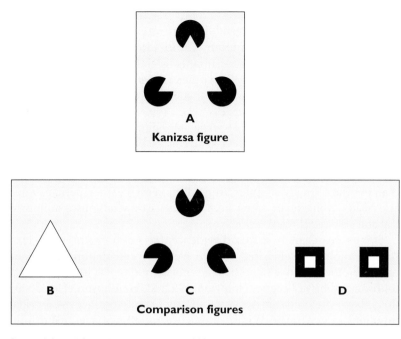

A
Kanizsa figure

B   C   D
Comparison figures

Source: Adapted from Treiber & Wilcox, 1980.

FIGURE 6.6
Infants' Subjective
Perception of Form

Infants, as well as adults, perceive the subjective triangular figure (A) even though no contour is present to define it. After becoming habituated to the Kanizsa figure, babies are shown other figures, including a standard triangle formed by visible contours (B), the indented circular figures rotated to eliminate the subjective triangle (C), or a completely different array of stimuli (D). Infants show the least recovery from habituation to the traditional triangle (B), suggesting that they perceived the triangular shape produced by the Kanizsa figure.

● **Perception of Pattern and Form**   Few questions fascinate psychologists more than when and how infants recognize patterns and other configurations of visual arrays. Are babies born with the ability to perceive wholes and units? Some researchers think so. Others have argued the more traditional view, that this capacity is acquired only through extensive visual experience; infants become aware of or construct perceptions of integrated, holistic, and meaningful visual figures through repeated opportunities to process contours, angles, shading, and other primary sensory features.

As we have already learned, very young infants detect contours of visual stimuli, as well as movement associated with contours. Does that necessarily mean that they see a unitary object or pattern? Perhaps not, but evidence suggests that by two or three months of age, babies are likely to see the whole. Furthermore, infants now inspect and analyze the components of complex stimuli, scanning a variety of their visual properties and carrying out a much more deliberate, organized search (Bronson, 1994). A good example of this developmental change is demonstrated by the **externality effect:** infants younger than about two months of age typically focus on the outer contours of a complex stimulus as if caught by this sensory feature, so that little systematic exploration of its internal characteristics takes place. However, older infants tend to scan its internal features as well (Maurer, 1983; Salapatek, 1975). We saw an illustration of the externality effect in the discussion of preferential looking. Babies younger than two months tend to fixate on the outer contours of the face, such as hair or the chin line; older infants much more frequently inspect internal features, such as the eyes or mouth (see Figure 6.3).

Other experiments provide further evidence that babies perceive entire forms and patterns at least within a few months after birth but continue to show improvement in form perception throughout infancy (Kellman & Arterberry, 1998). One especially convincing illustration involves subjective, or gradient-free, contours. Look at the Kanizsa figure shown in Figure 6.6. You should see a highly visible white triangle appearing to stand "above" three black, disklike figures at each of its corners. But closer inspection will reveal that the brain subjectively assumes the triangular form; no contour is present to mark its edges. Infants, perhaps when as young

KEY THEME
Nature/Nurture

KEY THEME
Child's Active Role

externality effect   Tendency for infants younger than two months to focus on the external features of a complex stimulus and explore the internal features less systematically.

as one or two months and certainly by three to four months, perceive the subjective figures too, another powerful demonstration that perception of form is not always based on a detectable contour (Ghim, 1990; Treiber & Wilcox, 1980). In addition to seeing the illusory figure, infants by eight months of age treat it as residing above the circular elements. When other elements are moving in the array, they are perceived as disappearing "behind" the illusory figure and coming out its other side (Csibra, 2001).

Some perceptual patterns are especially significant to the infant. One is the human face. Do even newborns recognize faces, perhaps the faces of their caregivers? Based on the discussion so far, it should not be surprising to learn that by about two months of age infants do assign great importance to the face, attending to it more than to other, equally complex arrays. But an even earlier, perhaps innate preference also makes evolutionary sense, because faces are a vital source of information for social and emotional relationships.

KEY THEME
Interaction Among Domains

KEY THEME
Nature/Nurture

Some researchers have found evidence that newborns prefer, at least for moving configurations, a facelike image—two eyelike representations above a mouthlike feature—to other arrangements of the same components (Johnson et al., 1991). Mark Johnson and his colleagues (Johnson, 1992; M. H. Johnson et al., 2000) suggest that this inborn preference arises from a fairly primitive subcortical visual system that functions in newborns. Within about two months of age, this primitive system is supplanted by a more sophisticated cortical visual system that explores and discriminates faces from other, equally complex stimuli (Mondloch et al., 1999). The primitive system helps to ensure, however, that the infant gets off to the right start by preferring this extremely important perceptual array. Moreover, newborns display preferences for certain kinds of faces. Alan Slater and his colleagues (Slater et al., 1998) showed babies between one and six days of age pairs of female faces that had been judged by adults as attractive and unattractive. These infants gazed at the attractive faces longer than the unattractive faces. By five months of age, they also prefer looking at pictures of faces with larger eyes, just as do adults (Geldart, Maurer, & Carney, 1999).

When does a baby discriminate his or her mother's face from that of another person? Perhaps within days after birth (Bushnell, Sai, & Mullin, 1989). However, as you might guess, this recognition is based on outer elements, such as hairline or head contours, rather than on a full appreciation of a mother's facial features (Pascalis et al., 1995). By six months of age, differences in brain wave patterns are evident when a baby looks at her mother's face compared with a stranger's face (de Haan & Nelson, 1997). The conclusion is that infants are attracted to and identify significant aspects of the human face early in their development and make rapid strides in perceiving and recognizing this important social stimulus.

KEY THEME
Child's Active Role

● **Perception of Objects**   Much of the visual environment is made up of objects and their surfaces. How does a baby perceive a rattle apart from the table on which it lies or the family dog as distinct from the floor on which it sits? James J. Gibson (1979) argued that the dynamic flow of visual information provided by kinetic cues is essential to this capacity.

Research carried out by Philip Kellman, Elizabeth Spelke, and others supports Gibson's position regarding the importance of kinetic information for perceiving objects, even in infants as young as three months of age (Kellman, 1996; Kellman & Spelke, 1983). Kellman, Spelke, and their colleagues initiated similar studies investigating how a variety of movements associated with an occluded rod influences the infant's inferences about object unity. Figure 6.7 illustrates some of the variations that infants were shown. Babies interpreted the rod as complete, not broken, as long as its two protruding ends appeared to move together in the same direction and independently of the block during habituation trials, even if the two visible ends were of quite different shapes (Kellman & Banks, 1998). If neither the

FIGURE 6.7 Inference of Unity and Coherence

Under some conditions, four-month-olds respond as if they perceived an occluded rod as a single complete figure. Infants are habituated to one of the seven familiarization displays shown here and are then presented with the test displays. After viewing conditions A, B, and C, infants respond to the complete rod in the test display as novel, indicating they perceived the rod in A, B, and C as being broken. When shown conditions D, E, F, or G, however, infants appear to perceive the rod as a connected whole, showing less attention to the complete rod than to the broken rod in the test display. The results indicate that young infants are able to infer unity and coherence for objects. Research suggests newborns do not make these perceptual inferences.

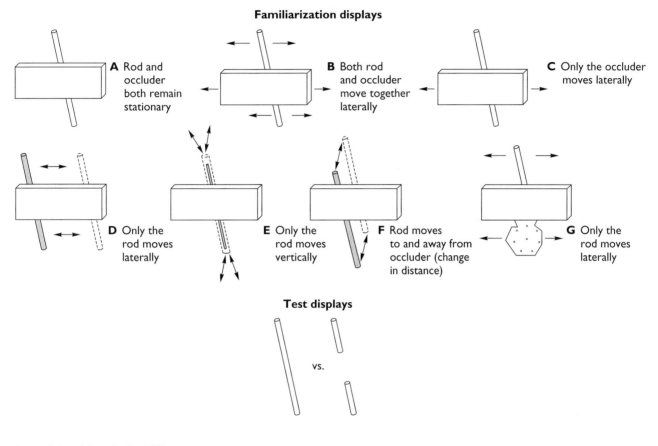

Familiarization displays

A Rod and occluder both remain stationary

B Both rod and occluder move together laterally

C Only the occluder moves laterally

D Only the rod moves laterally

E Only the rod moves vertically

F Rod moves to and away from occluder (change in distance)

G Only the rod moves laterally

Test displays

vs.

Source: Adapted from Spelke, 1985.

rod nor the block moved, or if the rod and block shifted together in the same direction, or if only the occluding block moved during habituation trials, the infants did not "fill in" the unseen portion of the rod; they treated the stimulus as two short pieces separated by an intervening space. By about six months of age or older infants are more likely to infer a unitary rod when its ends move together in a different direction—for example, when it rotates behind an occluder (Eizenman & Bertenthal, 1998).

Kinetic cues associated with viewing three-dimensional arrays are not the only way for infants to infer object unity (Mareschal & Johnson, 2002). A recent set of studies involved two-dimensional computer-generated figures in which a rectangular surface was displayed on a textured background (much like that shown in Figure 6.4) and appeared to bisect the end projections of a rodlike element. The cues provided by the appearance and disappearance of the dots on the textured background were necessary for infants to infer the unity of the end projections of the rod, as it and the rectangular shape were shown moving independently in the two-dimensional array. However, when the end projections were misaligned so that they did not appear to project toward one another, the infants did not infer their unity as part of a single occluded rod (S. P. Johnson et al., 2000). Thus characteristics of the occluded form, as well as its movement in the textured background, contribute to its perception of connectedness.

Is the perception of a coherent object possibly innate? Might newborns interpret the rod as being complete as well? Alan Slater and his colleagues think the answer is no (Slater et al., 1996). Under movement conditions in which older infants treat the separated segments as novel, newborns see the complete rod as novel; they do not fill in or make the perceptual inferences about the occluded segment of the stimulus.

Amy Needham (2001) and her colleagues (Needham & Baillargeon, 1998; Needham & Modi, 2000) have argued for yet one other important factor in object perception for infants, especially when perception takes place in a relatively cluttered environment in which many contours and surfaces are intermingled. Such a condition might exist, for example, when the infant is able to see a pacifier stuck among numerous toys in a box or among kitchen utensils in a drawer. Needham suggests that in these circumstances having viewed or manipulated the object as a separate entity at an earlier time is critical. Because the infant has memory for the segmented visual display on the basis of experience with it, he or she is able to perceive it in other contexts. Needham's work, then, points out the role that the infant's emerging cognitive capacities (see the chapters titled "Cognition: Piaget and Vygotsky" and "Cognition: Information Processing") might play in the very young infant's perception. In other words, perceiving an object may stem not only from processing features and characteristics of the external sensory environment but also from what the infant brings to the perceptual task in the form of memory for having interacted with it before.

● **Biological Motion**   The role of kinetic cues, and motion in general, for early infant perceptual development is demonstrated in yet another phenomenon known as *biological motion.* Bennett Bertenthal (1993) and his colleagues (Proffitt & Bertenthal, 1990) carried out a series of studies in which infants were shown points of light moving as though attached to the head and major joints of a person walking. Adults who observe the pattern readily interpret the light movement as though it were someone walking. In other conditions, the pattern of lights was inverted or an equivalent amount of motion was shown but with the lights scrambled so that the motion did not simulate the appearance of a person walking. Using attentional and habituation measures, these experiments demonstrated that by the time infants have reached three to five months of age, the "walker" has taken on special meaning to them compared with other patterns of light motion.

● **Depth Perception**   From our earlier discussion of visual problems in infancy, it should be apparent that, in addition to seeing to the left and right and above and below, babies see depth or distance. Yet visual images are recorded on the retina in two dimensions. When and how do we acquire the ability of depth perception? One source of information is *binocular vision.* Sensory information differs slightly for each eye. The ability to fuse the two distinct images to perceive a single object is called **stereopsis,** a capacity that improves markedly during the first four months after birth. Stereopsis provides clues to depth as effectively for six-month-olds as for adults (Fox et al., 1980; Held, Birch, & Gwiazda, 1980).

Still other sources of information about depth and distance are available to infants. A classic series of studies involving the **visual cliff** suggests that kinetic cues are among them. The visual cliff consists of a large sheet of glass bisected by a relatively

KEY THEME
Nature/Nurture

stereopsis   Ability to perceive a single image of an object even though perceptual input is binocular and differs slightly for each eye; significant source of cues for depth perception.

visual cliff   Experimental apparatus used to test depth perception in which the surface on one side of a glass-covered table is made to appear far below the surface on the other side.

narrow plank. A patterned surface is placed immediately under the glass on one side, but much farther below it on the other side. Richard Walk (1968) found that an infant old enough to crawl can usually be coaxed to cross the shallow side but was much less likely to crawl over the deep side. The kinetic cues provided by their own head and body movements signaled depth; the babies showed the same response regardless of whether they could use one or both eyes.

Even babies too young to crawl react to the shallow and deep sides of the visual cliff differently. When placed face down on the glass surface, two- to three-month-olds become quieter, are less fussy, and show a greater decrease in heart rate on the deep side than on the shallow side (Campos, Langer, & Krowitz, 1970). Such reactions suggest that infants have not yet associated anxiety or fear with depth and find the visual information provided by the deep side more interesting than that on the shallow side. In fact, depth cues may already influence attention at birth, because newborns prefer looking at three-dimensional objects to looking at two-dimensional figures (Slater, Rose, & Morison, 1984).

Surprisingly, however, learning to avoid a drop-off occurs relatively independently when babies are acquiring the ability to sit, crawl, and walk. Karen Adolph has observed infants as they attempt to either reach across or crawl over a gap and as they attempt to negotiate crawling or walking down a steeply inclined surface (Adolph, 1997, 2000). Whereas infants may avoid reaching across a gap that would cause them to lose their balance and fall from their seated position, they may readily attempt to crawl across a gap that is far too wide for them to avoid falling (see Figure 6.8). Similarly, even though they may have learned to safely crawl down an inclined plane, they seem to have to relearn the dangers of that same slope when beginning to walk. Although infants may perceive depth, awareness of the risks accompanying it does not transfer to the acquisition of later postural and motor milestones. Instead, infants need to learn to coordinate their perception of depth with safe actions for negotiating their surroundings as each new kind of postural and motor ability is acquired.

Finally, other cues, collectively described as *pictorial,* signal depth in photos or two-dimensional arrays. Pictorial cues include relative size (near objects appear larger), shadows, interposition of surfaces (one surface hides another), and linear perspective (lines converging toward a horizon), as well as the surface contour cues depicted in Figure 6.9. Infants begin to use many of the cues to identify nearer configurations by about five to seven months of age (Kellman & Arterberry, 1998; Sen, Yonas, & Knill, 2001; Yonas & Owsley, 1987). Thus infants respond very early on to an abundant array of cues signaling depth and the three-dimensionality of objects. Many aspects of visual development during infancy are summarized in the Visual Development chronology.

FIGURE 6.8
Avoiding a Risky Fall

Although infants at a very young age can perceive depth, their understanding of its consequences has to be relearned to fit the postural limitations associated with different motor skills. An infant may resist leaning too far to reach an attractive object located across a gap when sitting (A). However, that infant may readily try to crawl across a gap of a similar width and would fall if not caught by the experimenter (B). Similarly, in learning to locomote down an inclined plane, the child seems to have to relearn that he or she will fall down a steep slope that he or she can successfully negotiate when crawling. Coordinating perceptual information with permissible actions has to be relearned with each motor milestone in development.

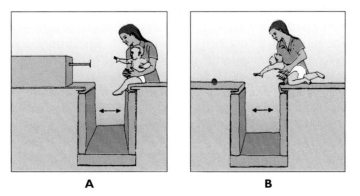

A   **B**

Source: Adolph, 2000, p. 292.

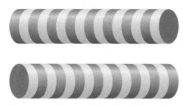

Source: Sen, Yonas, & Knill, 2001, p. 168.

FIGURE 6.9

Surface Contour as a
Cue Implying Depth

**Objects with certain kinds
of markings can produce the
illusion of depth in a two-
dimensional array. One end
of one of the cylinders in each
pair shown here appears to
be closer than the other, depending on the pattern of
surface contours. When shown
these two-dimensional arrays,
infants seven months of age
also process this kind of pictorial depth cue; they are more
likely to reach toward the end
of the cylinder that looks
closer. Five-month-olds do
not consistently reach to the
apparently closer end; these
surface cues do not yet provide a source of information
about depth for them. These
and other findings indicate
that infants begin to use a
variety of pictorial cues to
interpret depth in the layout
of two-dimensional visual
arrays at around five to seven
months of age.**

KEY THEME
Nature/Nurture

FOR YOUR REVIEW

- What is the difference between sensation and perception?

- How are attention and other behavioral and physiological responses used to investigate infant sensory and perceptual capacities?

- What limitations exist in infant visual accommodation, saccadic eye movements, smooth visual pursuit, vergence, and other visuomotor capacities? How quickly do these achieve adultlike ability?

- What kinds of visual problems are found among infants? Why is the correction of these problems important in infancy or early childhood?

- What is the ability of infants to perceive color?

- How early do infants see patterns and forms in the visual world? What is the externality effect? What is the developmental course of infant perception of faces? When can an infant distinguish the faces of caregivers from the faces of others?

- How early and what kinds of cues can be used by infants to perceive objects in their world? What is meant by the perception of biological motion?

- How early and what kinds of cues can be used by infants to perceive depth? What evidence exists to indicate that its perception does not always produce appropriate responses to the dangers associated with depth?

- Why do developmental psychologists no longer believe the infant's visual world is simply a "blooming buzzing confusion?"

Audition

Just as opinion once held that newborns are blind, so did it assert that newborns are deaf (Spears & Hohle, 1967). However, the fetus is listening well before birth. Brain wave patterns, heart rate changes, and activity level observed on ultrasound scans reveal responses to vibroacoustic stimulation (Kisilevsky, Hains, & Low, 1999; Kisilevsky & Muir, 1991). Low-frequency sounds, the kind that are produced in human speech, are detected by the fetus sometimes as early as twenty-three weeks of age (Kisilevsky & Low, 1998; Lecanuet, 1998). Sensitivity to a wide range of sounds at lower and lower intensities increases dramatically during the remainder of the prenatal period (Hepper & Shahidullah, 1994).

Persuasive evidence that fetuses hear also comes from several studies indicating that newborns prefer to listen to the sounds they heard before birth. Anthony DeCasper and Melanie Spence (1986) asked expectant women to read aloud a passage from Dr. Seuss's *The Cat in the Hat.* Women read the passage twice a day during the last six weeks of pregnancy; their fetuses were exposed to the story for a total of about three-and-a-half hours before birth. Two or three days after birth, the babies listened to either the same passage or a new story while outfitted with a special pacifier that recorded rate of sucking. Depending on rate of sucking, the recording of the story would turn on or off. When newborns heard *The Cat in the Hat,* they changed

Newborn

- Shows minimal accommodation; limited, sluggish saccades; incomplete vergence.
- Detects contours, but acuity and contrast sensitivity remain relatively poor.
- Prefers attending to highly visible contours, angles, features in motion, and three-dimensional over two-dimensional stimuli.
- Exhibits externality effect.

1–3 Months

- Shows accommodation; near normal adultlike vergence.
- Smooth visual pursuit emerges.
- Discriminates cues to depth.
- Responds to rapidly expanding visual images.
- Explores internal as well as external features of stimuli.
- Recognizes shape of simple figures and more detailed patterns and objects.
- Prefers attending to increasingly complex patterns, including those with facelike organization.
- Detects basic colors.
- Infers "subjective" contour if defined by movement cues.

4–8 Months

- Exhibits stereopsis.
- Saccadic eye movements become larger, more rapid, and accurate.
- Shows adultlike smooth visual pursuit.
- Acuity and contrast sensitivity approach normal.
- Displays fear of depth on visual cliff.
- Discriminates many pictorial (two-dimensional) cues to depth.
- Distinguishes symmetrical from asymmetrical patterns.
- Processes "subjective" contours even if arrays are static.
- Perceives occluded objects as wholes.
- Becomes responsive to "biological motion."

Newborn

Newborn
1 Mo.
2 Mos.
3 Mos.
4 Mos.
5 Mos.
6 Mos.
7 Mos.
8 Mos.
9 Mos.
10 Mos.
11 Mos.
12 Mos.
13 Mos.
14 Mos.
15 Mos.
16 Mos.
17 Mos.
18 Mos.

Newborn

Newborn
1 Yr.
2 Yrs.
3 Yrs.
4 Yrs.
5 Yrs.
6 Yrs.
7 Yrs.
8 Yrs.
9 Yrs.
10 Yrs.
11 Yrs.
12 Yrs.
13 Yrs.
14 Yrs.
15 Yrs.
16 Yrs.
17 Yrs.
18 Yrs.

This chart describes the sequence of visual development in infancy based on the findings of research. Children often show individual differences in the exact ages at which they display the various developmental achievements outlined here.

their rate of sucking to listen to it but did not do so for the new story. Some kind of learning about the Dr. Seuss story apparently took place prenatally.

What precisely does the fetus hear, and what is it learning from these exposures? We are not really sure. As newborns, infants prefer to listen to their mothers' voice rather than the voice of a stranger (DeCasper & Fifer, 1980), especially the lower frequency sounds associated with their mother's voice (Spence & Freeman, 1996). Because the mother's body tissue and bones are very good conductors of sound, the newborn already has had considerable exposure to characteristics of the mother's speech (Lecanuet, 1998). However, the fetus can also learn something about the cadence of sound as well. After expectant women in France repeatedly recited a rhyme from the thirty-third to thirty-seventh week of their gestation period, changes in fetal heart rate in response to the rhyme revealed that the fetus differentiated it from another novel rhyme even when recited by someone else (DeCasper et al., 1994).

CONTROVERSY: THINKING IT OVER

Should the Fetus Undergo a Sensory Curriculum?

Many prospective parents are eager to assist their child's development in any way they can. That desire extends to the fetus as well. An expectant mother, as we saw in the chapter titled "Prenatal Period and Birth," can initiate many practices that will foster healthy development during pregnancy. But with the advent of public awareness about the auditory and learning abilities of the fetus has come a new type of training that some parents have adopted to promote development, this time in terms of giving their infants a psychological head start.

What Is the Controversy?

With the finding that the fetus has sensory capacities, a new kind of "curriculum" has entered the caregiving market. This one involves the planned and regular exposure of the fetus to patterned sounds—simple ones, such as a heartbeat or drumbeat, or complex auditory and vibroacoustic events, such as classical or other kinds of music; sometimes even words, numbers, and letters are steadily relayed to the fetus via a belt worn by the expectant woman. Such technological gadgetry is really only one example of such efforts; others may expose the fetus to "daily lessons" in music or other forms of sensory stimulation via other means. Does this practice give the newborn a head start in life by stimulating intellectual processes or by arranging a relaxing and comforting continuity to its world after birth? Could it have some negative consequences?

What Are the Opposing Arguments?

Some claim that this kind of early stimulation can have lasting beneficial effects on cognitive development, literally helping children to become smarter. Others suggest that these early memories promote emotional stability as well, a kind of "security blanket" in the form of a soothing environmental context for the infant, who is experiencing many additional stresses in negotiating the new world after birth. Countering these views is the concern about whether such extra stimulation, especially if too intense, might actually damage delicate sensory organs that are just beginning to function. For example, low-frequency sounds emanating from outside the womb are somewhat amplified for the fetus (Richards et al., 1992), and expectant women exposed to noisy workplaces or rock concerts sometimes report considerable activity in their fetuses. No one really knows what level of sound intensity the fetus might be exposed to by an enthusiastic prospective parent. Could such experiences, then, disrupt sleep patterns that occur prenatally, overstimulating and discomforting the fetus with the potential outcome of disrupting normal brain development?

What Answers Exist? What Questions Remain?

At this time, despite some claims to the contrary, no scientific studies have demonstrated that a prenatal sensory curriculum promotes cognitive, creative, or any other form of intellectual development. Nor is there any evidence supporting its potential benefits for emotional or social development. It would be extremely difficult to conduct experimental research that could show that development is enhanced by a sensory curriculum rather than by some other characteristic of parenting activity practiced either before or after the birth of the baby. Perhaps, if there are benefits, they may be as much for the prospective parents as for the baby. Gently talking to the fetus and reserving and organizing time for it may provide a kind of prelude to the type of attention and schedule that the infant will very likely demand after birth. And listening to music may be good for adults as well. But one thing all agree on, even those who champion a sensory curriculum, is that moderation is essential (Van De Carr & Lehrer, 1996).

● **Hearing**   Little research exists on exactly how well babies hear immediately after birth. Physiological measures taken from the auditory brain stem suggest that responsivity is nearly adultlike for some frequencies, especially those in the middle range, of sounds that humans can detect (Sininger, Doyle, & Moore, 1999). However, work using attentional and behavioral measures with older infants reveals marked improvement in most auditory skills throughout the first few months. Certainly by about six months of age, babies are able to detect and discriminate numerous features of sound, such as its frequency and intensity, almost as well as do adults (Aslin, Jusczyk, & Pisoni, 1998).

Not all babies, however, are able to hear at birth. Deafness and other hearing disabilities strike an estimated one to three out of every thousand infants born in the United States (Stein, 1999). That translates into perhaps as many as 20,000 infants each year who are hearing impaired. Lower rates are found in some Western European nations such as France (Baille et al., 1996), but higher rates are found in many other regions of the world. New screening techniques—for example, physiological measurements of neural activity in the auditory brain stem—can be used with infants to detect the possibility of hearing loss. Auditory screening is often administered to those infants born at risk in families with a history of hearing impairment or to those exposed to cytomegalovirus and other diseases or drugs known to affect hearing. However, auditory screening of infants is not universal in many countries, including the United States and the United Kingdom, despite the known benefits of early intervention (Joint Committee on Infant Hearing, 2000; Kennedy, 2000). In fact, congenital hearing impairment is detected in only about half of the infants who have the impairment in the United States during the first year of life (Eilers & Berlin, 1995).

KEY THEME
Individual Differences

● **Sound Localization and Patterns of Sound**   Shortly after birth babies display **sound localization,** the ability to locate a sound in space, by turning their heads or eyes in the direction of the sound. This early ability, which may be reflexive, declines during the first two months and then reemerges at about four months of age in the form of a more deliberate search for sound (Field et al., 1980). Ability to locate the precise position from which a sound originates markedly improves throughout infancy and into early childhood (Ashmead, Clifton, & Perris, 1987; Morrongiello, Fenwick, & Chance, 1990). By six to eight months of age, infants also begin to appreciate the distance from which a sound emanates. At this age, babies hearing a sound in the dark produced by an object beyond their reach are less likely to attempt to retrieve it than an object producing a sound that is within their reach (Clifton, Perris, & Bullinger, 1991).

In every culture that has been observed, caregivers sing to their infants (Trehub, Unyk, & Trainor, 1993). Can babies distinguish music from noise? Might they even have a preference for some kinds of music? Two- and three-month-olds do recognize changes in tempo (the rate at which sounds occur; Baruch & Drake, 1997) and in

sound localization   Ability to determine a sound's point of origin.

intervals between brief bursts of sound that denote simple rhythmic change (De-many, McKenzie, & Vurpillot, 1977). Between six months and one year of age, they also begin to distinguish between more complex rhythms and patterns of sounds (Clarkson, 1996; Morrongiello, 1984). For example, at eight months of age babies recognize changes in short (six-note) melodies, including a transposition in key and the shift to either a higher or a lower frequency of a single note in a sequence (Tre-hub, Bull, & Thorpe, 1984; Trehub, Thorpe, & Morrongiello, 1985). Surprisingly, un-der some circumstances eight-month-olds are able to keep track of absolute pitch better than adults (Saffran & Griepentrog, 2001).

In addition to detecting differences between sound patterns, infants show clear pref-erences for certain auditory events. Perhaps because of its voice quality or tempo, they prefer to listen to a song or lullaby directed by an adult to another infant over the same song or lullaby of the adult singing alone (Trainor, 1996). In fact, four-and-a-half- to six-month-olds can boast of some budding capacities as music critics! Carol Krum-hansl and Peter Jusczyk (1990) chose short passages of Mozart minuets and introduced brief pauses at locations judged by adults to be either natural or awkward places for a musical phrase to end. Babies preferred looking at a loudspeaker that played only natural versions of the music to those passages that played unnatural versions of the Mozart selections. Other research has shown that infants prefer the original passages of Mozart minuets over versions in which the intervals between sequences of notes have been altered to create a more dissonant, less pleasing sound, as heard by adults (Trainor & Heinmiller, 1998). In addition, after hearing two Mozart sonatas daily over several weeks' time, seven-month-olds can distinguish these from other Mozart sonatas, even when tested two weeks later (Saffran, Loman, & Robertson, 2000).

Babies are indeed sensitive to rhythmic and melodic contour. Hemispheric asym-metries in responsiveness to melodic changes (a left-ear/right-hemisphere advan-tage), as well as to speech sounds (right-ear/left-hemisphere advantage), are found in many young infants just as they are observed in adults (Balaban, Anderson, & Wis-niewski, 1998). Moreover, the ability to detect satisfying musical phrasings may be important not only for appreciating music but also for the phrasing and sound rhythms that commonly underlie speech. The Auditory Development chronology summarizes some of the early abilities displayed in this domain.

● **Speech**   Research on infants' hearing abilities has often been conducted to an-swer another question: how soon do babies perceive human speech? The ability to interpret speech sounds as meaningful elements of language probably begins in the second six months of life. That developmental story is discussed in the chapter titled "Language." However, can even younger infants discriminate speech sounds?

The smallest unit of sound that affects the meaning of a word is called a **phoneme.** Phonemes are surprisingly complicated bursts of acoustic energy. For example, a dif-ference of less than one-fiftieth of a second in the onset or transition of a frequency of sound is enough for adults to discriminate the distinctive phonemes /p/, /b/, and /t/ in the sounds *pa, ba,* and *ta.* (Linguists use slashes to identify the phonemes of a language.) Are infants able to hear the differences? Indeed they are. In fact, before six months of age babies distinguish all the important sounds in any of the hundreds of languages spoken around the world (Werker & Desjardins, 1995).

From these findings, some who study language acquisition argue that babies are born with a "speech module," an innate capacity to detect and process the subtle and complicated sounds that make up human language (Fodor, 1983). The complexity of language acquisition, according to this view, requires a specialized ability because the cognitive skills of infants and young children are so limited. Another view is that phoneme discrimination hinges on general auditory capacities, capacities not limited to processing speech sounds or even necessarily unique to humans but that infants are able to exploit quite early in development.

What evidence exists for either of these positions? Two research findings lend support to the view that speech perception involves special language-oriented

?

**WHAT DO
YOU THINK?**

Is There a "Mozart Effect"?
psychology.college.hmco.com

KEY THEME
Nature/Nurture

phoneme   Smallest unit of sound that changes the meanings of words.

Newborn

- Recognizes auditory events that were repeatedly produced by the woman when fetus was still in utero.
- Discriminates mother's and stranger's voices.
- Localizes sound reflexively.

1–3 Months

- Recognizes simple auditory patterns.
- Discriminates many, if not all, basic sounds used in language.
- Makes deliberate efforts to locate sound, an ability that continues to improve throughout early childhood.

4–8 Months

- Detects and discriminates high-frequency tones nearly as well as, sometimes better than, children or adults; ability to detect low-frequency tones continues to improve throughout childhood.
- Recognizes melodic rhythms, transposition in key, note changes, phrasing in music.

9–12 Months

- Begins to lose some phoneme discriminations if not heard in native language.

Newborn

1 Mo.

2 Mos.

3 Mos.

4 Mos.

5 Mos.

6 Mos.

7 Mos.

8 Mos.

9 Mos.

10 Mos.

11 Mos.

12 Mos.

13 Mos.

14 Mos.

15 Mos.

16 Mos.

17 Mos.

18 Mos.

Newborn

1 Yr.

2 Yrs.

3 Yrs.

4 Yrs.

5 Yrs.

6 Yrs.

7 Yrs.

8 Yrs.

9 Yrs.

10 Yrs.

11 Yrs.

12 Yrs.

13 Yrs.

14 Yrs.

15 Yrs.

16 Yrs.

17 Yrs.

18 Yrs.

This chart describes the sequence of auditory development in infancy based on the findings of research. Children often show individual differences in the exact ages at which they display the various developmental achievements outlined here.

mechanisms. The first comes from the extremely complex relationship between the acoustic properties of phonemes and their perception. For example, the /b/ phoneme in the words *beak* and *book* are quite different acoustically, although people treat the sounds as equivalent. Researchers argue that the absence of a simple set of rules for signaling the phoneme /b/ in the two words makes the presence of a special mechanism for speech perception highly likely (Kuhl, 1987).

A second finding is based on **categorical perception,** the classification of sounds as the same even when they differ on some continuous physical dimension, except when on opposite sides of a critical juncture. For example, the English consonants /b/ and /p/ in the sounds *ba* and *pa* differ only in voice onset time (VOT), the period during which the vocal chords begin to vibrate relative to the release of air by the vocal apparatus. Small changes in VOT are typically not heard as more or less like *ba* or *pa.* Instead, English speakers hear only *ba* as long as VOT continues to fall on one side of the categorical boundary and only *pa* when it falls on the other side. But if the difference in VOT crosses a critical point, the phoneme boundary, the two sounds are readily distinguishable. Infants as young as one month already demonstrate categorical perception for many different speech sounds (Aslin, 1987b; Kuhl, 1987).

Researchers remain uncertain about whether babies are born with a special sensory mode for speech (Aslin, Jusczyk, & Pisoni, 1998). Categorical perception can be observed with some sounds other than those found in speech. Monkeys, even chinchillas, also distinguish speech sounds categorically (Kuhl & Miller, 1978; Kuhl & Padden, 1983), a finding that further argues against a specialized innate ability to process phonemes in humans.

KEY THEME
Sociocultural Influence

Regardless of what accounts for phoneme perception, younger infants appear to be more sensitive than older infants to phonemes found in languages other than their own (Best et al., 1995; Werker & Desjardins, 1995). In one study, six- to eight-month-olds reared in an English-speaking environment could readily discriminate among phonemes used only in Hindi, whereas eleven- to thirteen-month-olds had more difficulty with this task (Werker & Lalonde, 1988). Adults can regain the lost discriminations only with considerable practice or under highly restricted listening conditions (Werker, 1989). Thus it does not appear that we completely lose the capacity to make these discriminations. Instead, toward the end of the first year of exposure to speech, our auditory and, perhaps, our attentional and cognitive functioning undergo a reorganization that limits our sensitivity to the sounds not utilized in the language we hear (Lalonde & Werker, 1995). As with vision, psychologists have often been surprised at the many competencies infants display with respect to their auditory abilities.

Smell, Taste, Touch, and Sensitivity to Pain

Developmental researchers have given far less attention to smell, taste, and the *cutaneous senses*—the receptor systems of the skin responsible for perceiving touch, pressure, pain, and temperature—than to vision or hearing. Each of these senses also functions shortly after birth and furnishes crucial adaptive and survival cues for the baby. Smell, for example, may be critical for determining what is edible and may also be involved in early attachment to the caregiver.

KEY THEME
Nature/Nurture

categorical perception
Inability to distinguish among sounds that vary on some basic physical dimension except when those sounds lie at opposite sides of a critical juncture point on that dimension.

● **Smell** Facial expressions, changes in rate of respiration and blood flow in the brain, and approach-avoidance activities involving head turning are just a few of the responses indicating that newborns detect odors. Do babies turn up their noses at the unpleasant smell of rotten eggs? Can they detect the food-related smells of fish, butter, banana, or vanilla? They most certainly can (Steiner, 1979). Moreover, newborns become increasingly sensitive to these and other smells during the first few days of life (Marlier, Schaal, & Soussignan, 1998).

Parent-infant recognition occurs by odor among many species of animals. Can human infants identify their caregivers this way as well? Again, the answer is yes. By five days of age infants turned their heads longer in the direction of a breast pad that had been worn by the mother than to an unused one. By six days of age, infants also preferred a pad obtained from their own mothers to one from an unfamiliar mother (MacFarlane, 1975).

Can other family members also identify their infants on the basis of odor? Indeed, within the first few days of birth and after brief contact, not only mothers but also fathers, grandmothers, and aunts can recognize newborn kin by their smell alone. In other words, humans may inherit some family olfactory signature about which they are sensitive or learn very quickly (Porter, Balogh, & Makin, 1988).

● **Taste**   Receptors for the basic tastes of sweet, sour, salty, and bitter, located mostly on the tongue, develop well before birth; the fetus may already taste as it swallows amniotic fluid. Facial expressions and rate of sucking reveal that newborns can also discriminate tastes (see Figure 6.10). Sweet stimuli, for example, elicit a relaxed facial expression resembling a smile; sour stimuli produce lip pursing or a puckered expression; and bitter stimuli elicit mouth opening as though expressing disgust (Steiner, 1979).

Innate preferences for some tastes may help infants to meet nutritional needs and protect them from harmful or dangerous substances. Preferences can, however, be modified by experience. For example, babies fed sweeter fluids in the first few months after birth ingest more sweet water at six months of age than babies not given this experience (Beauchamp & Moran, 1982). The desire for salt in a specific food may

KEY THEME
Nature/Nurture

| FIGURE 6.10 | Discriminating Tastes |

Babies produce different facial expressions depending on what they taste. The first column shows the resting faces of three newborns. Column 2 shows the same babies after they received distilled water—their expressions show very little change. After sweet stimulation, the babies' facial expressions are more positive and relaxed, resembling a smile or licking of the upper lip, as shown in column 3. However, their mouths become more pursed after sour stimulation (column 4) and more arch-shaped after bitter stimulation (column 5).

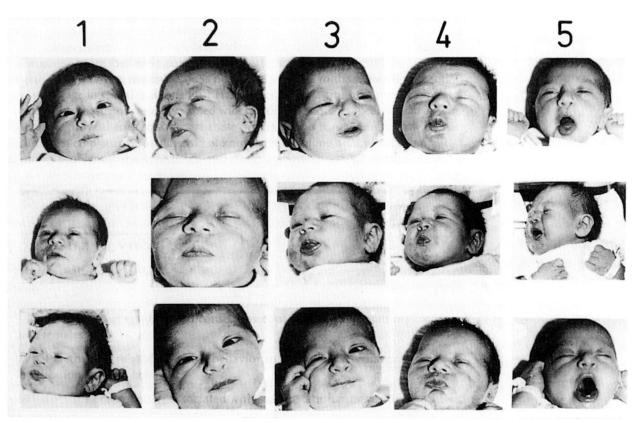

also be established early in infancy (Beauchamp & Cowart, 1990; Sullivan & Birch, 1990). Infants can detect flavors from their mothers' milk as well—for example, garlic, alcohol, and vanilla—an ability that might familiarize them to the foods common to their families and cultures (Mennella & Beauchamp, 1996). Although learning appears to be important in the emergence of odor and taste preferences, we should emphasize that until about two years of age, children will put just about anything into their mouths. Thus among the most important things they must learn is what *not* to taste (Rozin, 1990).

● **Touch and Temperature**   Skin contains more than one hundred types of receptors sensitive to touch, pressure, temperature, and pain (Reisman, 1987). As we see in the chapter titled "The Prenatal Period and Birth," even the fetus responds to touch. In the newborn, stimulation can also elicit a variety of reflexes (see the chapter titled "Brain, Motor Skill, and Physical Development"). And just as caregivers recognize their babies by odor shortly after birth, so can they recognize them by touch. After only sixty minutes of contact, mothers and fathers can identify their infants on the basis of stroking the backs of the babies' hands (Bader & Phillips, 1999; Kaitz et al., 1992; Kaitz et al., 1994). This ability, which may be adaptive in encouraging caregivers to be responsive to their offspring, is another illustration of the sensory communication that can facilitate social interactions between infant and caregiver.

KEY THEME
Interaction Among Domains

A difficult problem for newborns, particularly premature infants, is regulation of body temperature (Moffat & Hackel, 1985). Cooling awakens babies, makes them more restless, and increases their oxygen consumption, responses that facilitate heat production. Because many newborns are unable to sweat or pant, exposure to high temperatures produces reddening skin, less activity, and more sleep, events that decrease heat production and assist heat loss (Harpin, Chellappah, & Rutter, 1983). When warm, babies also assume a sunbathing position, extending their extremities, perhaps a good clue for a caregiver who is trying to decide whether a baby is too warm (Reisman, 1987).

● **Sensitivity to Pain**   Heel pricks, circumcision, and other medical procedures involving newborns and young infants have come under increasing scrutiny in recent years because of concerns about the pain they may cause. Historically, newborns experiencing such invasive procedures were rarely given pain reduction medication (Ramenghi et al., 1996), and even major operations on very young infants were carried out with little or no effort to diminish pain. Why was this the case? The answer is that newborns were believed to have neither the neurological capacity to experience pain nor the ability to remember it. An additional concern was the potential negative side effects of pain medication on an immature organism.

Today we know that brain centers involved in the detection of pain are well developed prenatally and that behavioral responses (crying, facial expressions, etc.) consistent with the discomfort associated with pain are readily displayed by preterm and other newborns (Anand et al., 2001). Moreover, evidence has been gathered to suggest that exposure to painful circumstances early in infancy can lead to lasting changes in the endocrine and immune systems and to continued behavioral sensitivity to pain later in development (Porter, Grunau, & Anand, 1999; Taddio et al., 1995). And although medications may be an important part of efforts to manage pain, offering sucrose or the opportunity to engage in nonnutritive sucking and even exposure to music during minor operations have comforting effects for infants in painful situations (Anand et al., 2001; Joyce, Keck, & Gerkensmeyer, 2001).

Intermodal Perception

We have considered the development of seeing, hearing, and other senses in isolation from one another, but, of course, most objects and events bombard us with multiple sensory inputs. The sight of a cup provides information about how to shape the mouth to drink from it. The toddler who hears his mother's voice from another room expects to see her when he walks into that room. We often perceive these experiences as integrated and coordinated, and draw perceptual inferences because of the typical relationships observed from multimodal stimulation. Sometimes, of course, we can be fooled by all these correlated experiences: a good ventriloquist really does make the dummy appear to be talking!

How does the capacity to integrate several sensory inputs, referred to as **intermodal perception,** begin, and how important is it for development? One traditional view is that input received via the various senses is initially unimodal, that is, the senses function separately and independently. Only after repeated multimodal experiences, this argument runs, do babies come to recognize the correlations among various sensory inputs. Thus intermodal perception involves, for example, learning that when objects are shaken, some rattle and make a noise but others do not; that material that feels soft can also look soft; and that a square-looking peg will not fit into a round-looking hole. According to this viewpoint, intermodal perception stems from *integration* or *enrichment* by the repeated association of sensations from two or more modalities. Alternatively, from a more Piagetian perspective, it is the outcome of constructing multisensory schemes from correlated sensory experiences (Lickliter & Bahrick, 2000).

But others have suggested that some intermodal perception is already possible at birth (Gibson, 1982; Gibson, 1979). According to this perspective, a primitive unity

KEY THEME
Nature/Nurture

This toddler appears to be enjoying both the visual and tactual effects of playing with the water leaking from the flower pot. In fact, it would not be too surprising if she even began to taste it as well, although a caregiver might quickly discourage this behavior. Infants and young children experience events through multiple sensory modalities. At a very early age, they expect things to look, feel, taste, or sound in a particular way based on the information received from just one of these modalities.

intermodal perception Coordination of sensory information to perceive or make inferences about the characteristics of an object.

exists among the senses in early infancy, and with development and experience, **perceptual differentiation,** the ability to distinguish information coming through each particular sensory modality, occurs. A related aspect of this point of view is that important sensory information is often *amodal,* that is, not tied to a particular sensory modality but shared across two or more of them. Examples of amodal characteristics of sensory input are temporal synchrony, that is, the correlated onset and offset of stimulation that can occur between two or more sensory modalities (e.g., hearing someone begin and stop speaking while simultaneously seeing their lips start and stop), and tempo and rhythm, common components of both auditory and visual experience.

Some researchers believe that the ability to process amodal properties is especially important for early perceptual development (Bahrick & Lickliter, 2000; Lewkowicz, 2000). For example, Lorraine Bahrick and Robert Lickliter (2000) suggest that the intermodal redundancy that characterizes temporal synchrony attracts the infants' attention to patterns of stimulation that belong together and that it, along with other amodal properties, is among the earliest perceptual cues they process. As a consequence of the attentional bias, infants also begin to learn about other arbitrarily correlated properties and qualities of objects and events, such as the voice that belongs to a particular parent, the bark that signifies the family's pet dog, or the verbal label for a particular color. Some go so far as to claim that this kind of learning begins very shortly after birth (Slater et al., 1999). But regardless of how early it begins, this perspective emphasizes that both differentiation and integration of intermodal properties cannot be ignored as important components in perceptual development very early in infancy.

● **Sight and Sound**   To determine whether infants link visual and auditory events, Elizabeth Spelke (1976) developed a simple procedure in which four-month-olds could look at either of two films shown side by side. At the same time, the infants could hear a soundtrack coming from a speaker located between the two viewing screens. The soundtrack matched events in one of the two films, for example, an unfamiliar woman engaged in a game of peek-a-boo or someone playing a percussion instrument. Would infants pay more attention to the film synchronized with the soundtrack? Spelke found this to be the case, at least when the percussion sounds could be heard.

Four-month-olds can match other auditory-visual cues as well. In one study babies were shown two films, one depicting wet sponges being squeezed, the other two blocks being clapped together (Bahrick, 1983). When the babies heard a squishing sound, they attended more to the film showing the sponges; when they heard a banging sound, they attended more to the film of the rigid blocks. Before four months of age, they also infer that a sound made by one object or multiple objects hitting a surface extends to other, somewhat similar visual arrays containing one object or multiple objects (Bahrick, 2002). Five-month-olds even link sounds such as an auto or a train coming or going with concordant visual progressions of approaching and retreating movement (Pickens, 1994; Walker-Andrews & Lennon, 1985).

Experience may have permitted the three- to five-month-olds to learn about these relationships. However, other research suggests that newborns quickly master the association between a sound and a visible toy. After seeing a toy presented in several different locations and making a particular sound for brief periods of time, neonates displayed increased attention if the sound originated apart from the toy or if it accompanied a different toy (Morrongiello, Fenwick, & Chance, 1998). Thus even newborns possess some kind of amodal process that guides and unifies sensory information from separate senses such as hearing and vision (Kellman & Arterberry, 1998).

perceptual differentiation
Process postulated by Eleanor and James Gibson in which experience contributes to the ability to make increasingly finer perceptual discriminations and to distinguish stimulation arising from each sensory modality.

Intermodal perception in infants extends to social information and relationships as well. For example, three-and-a-half-month-olds are likely to look at that parent, seated to one side, whose voice is coming from a speaker centered in front of the baby (Spelke & Owsley, 1979). By six months of age, babies hearing a strange male or female voice recite a nursery rhyme look longer at a face of the same sex than at a face of the opposite sex (Walker-Andrews et al., 1991). In addition, babies are able to match the maturity of a face with its voice; they look more at the face of an adult or a child, depending on who is heard talking from a central speaker (Bahrick, Netto, & Hernandez-Reif, 1998).

Intermodal cues can influence perception in some perhaps unexpected ways. Speech perception, for example, may be greatly affected by what a person sees. Harry McGurk and John MacDonald (1976) played videotapes of an adult uttering simple syllables such as *ba ba*. Sometimes, however, the video picture was synchronized with another sound, such as *ga ga*. Three-year-olds through adults often reported hearing something quite different, for example, *da da* or another utterance. By five months of age, babies also recognize auditory-visual correspondence, attending more to facial expressions articulating sounds that match than facial expressions that do not match what they hear (Meltzoff & Kuhl, 1994; Rosenblum, Schmuckler, & Johnson, 1997).

● **Sight and Touch** By six months of age, infants who explore an object with their hands alone can recognize it by sight alone (Pineau & Streri, 1990; Rose, Gottfried, & Bridger, 1981; Ruff & Kohler, 1978). But coordination of some visual and tactile information exists much earlier when the mouth is used to explore objects. In one experiment, one-month-olds showed greater visual attention to a hard rigid object or a soft, deformable object, depending on which they had been given time to suck (Gibson & Walker, 1984). Other research reveals that infants five months of age exhibit intermodal perception between proprioceptive and visual cues deriving from self-movement. Infants showed differential attention to point light displays (similar to those used in studying sensitivity to biological motion) depending on whether the display mirrored the motion produced by the movement of their own hidden legs or the noncontingent movement of the legs of another infant (Schmuckler & Fairhall, 2001).

Babies can even be surprised by a discrepancy between vision and touch. Emily Bushnell (1981) showed infants a solid object within a box. Its location was distorted by mirrors. When babies reached for it, they touched another object that differed in size, shape, and texture. Infants younger than nine months failed to investigate the novel object actively or search for the one they could see, but older infants did both. Thus there is substantial evidence that infants before a year of age make inferences about their world based on intermodal perception.

FOR YOUR REVIEW

- What evidence exists to show that the fetus can detect vibroacoustic stimulation? Are there advantages or disadvantages to exposing the fetus to auditory stimulation?

- What are the basic auditory capacities of the infant, and what sound patterns do they prefer to listen to? How does sound localization develop?

- What arguments exist for or against the view that infants possess an innate capacity to detect phonemes?

- Can newborns and very young infants discriminate smells, tastes, touch, and temperature differences? Can they feel pain?

- How does intermodal perception develop? What evidence exists to show that infants recognize the correlation between visual and auditory information as well as visual and tactual cues?

Perceptual Development Throughout Childhood

Richard Aslin and Linda Smith (1988) have noted a predicament facing anyone interested in learning about perceptual development after infancy. As research has increasingly documented sophisticated abilities in newborns and infants, the importance of studying perceptual development at older ages appears to have faded. Nonetheless, researchers do find evidence of improved sensory processing during childhood (Ellemberg et al., 1999; Tschopp et al., 1999).

Perception also becomes more difficult to investigate without considering at the same time the child's developing attentional, linguistic, and cognitive skills. These factors may contribute to the observation that perceptual skills become more focused, organized, and confined to the meaningful and important features of the environment; in other words, perception becomes increasingly efficient with development. Eleanor Gibson (1969, 1982, 1988) has outlined a view of perceptual learning to account for these kinds of findings.

Perceptual Learning

Eleanor Gibson's theory of perceptual learning emphasizes three changes with age: increasing specificity in perception, improved attention, and more economical and efficient acquisition of perceptual information. Much of the infant's first year is spent learning the sensory properties of objects, the spatial layout of the infant's world, and the perceptual repercussions of his or her actions. But perceptual learning continues. For example, children acquire new kinds of visual discriminations when they learn to read. They must begin to pay attention to consistencies and variations in letters and text.

Eleanor Gibson and her colleagues (Gibson et al., 1962) created different sets of letterlike figures such as those shown in Figure 6.11. One member of each set was designated a standard, but each set included variations of that standard. A straight line, for example, might be redrawn as a curved line, the standard rotated or reversed, a break introduced in a continuous line, or the line's perspective changed by tipping or elongating some aspect of the figure. Children four through eight years of age

KEY THEME
Interaction Among Domains

FIGURE 6.11
Sensitivity to Perceptual Differences

Column 1 gives different letterlike forms used as standards in a sorting task. Columns 2 through 6 display various transformations of each standard. Four- to eight-year-olds, when shown a stack of the figures and asked to select only those identical to the standard, commit relatively few errors on variations that involve a break in the figure, presumably because the distinction is important for identifying many objects, as well as alphabetic symbols. With increasing age, errors involving rotation, reversal, and line/curve variations decrease substantially because, according to Eleanor Gibson, children who are beginning to learn to read must pay attention to these features of the stimuli. Errors involving perspective remain high at all ages, perhaps because the transformation is not important for identifying either objects or letters of the alphabet.

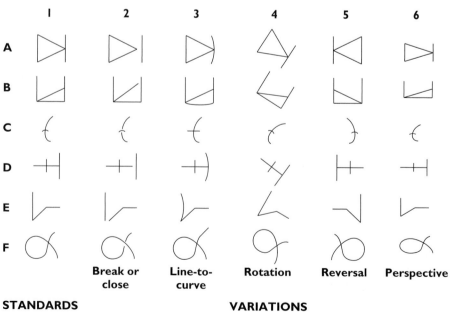

STANDARDS　　　　　VARIATIONS

Source: Adapted from Pick, 1965.

were shown a stack of each set of figures and asked to pick out only those identical to the standard.

Children made many more errors for some kinds of variations than others. Children of all ages seldom confused the standard with versions that contained breaks, perhaps because these features are important for identifying objects in the environment, as well as letters of the alphabet. On the other hand, older children did substantially better than younger children in discriminating rotations and reversals and line/curve transformations, presumably because children who are learning to read must begin to distinguish such variations. Finally, children of all ages found it difficult to discriminate changes in perspective from the standard, a variation that can and normally should be ignored for identifying both physical objects and letters of the alphabet.

Eleanor Gibson believes the age-related improvements in performance on this activity do not come about by reinforcing children to make the discriminations. In fact, when asked to classify the letterlike forms over a series of trials, children showed steady improvement in sorting without any feedback about their accuracy. Gibson argues that through repeated exposure to and inspection of letters of the alphabet, children are afforded the opportunity to recognize certain critical features distinguishing such figures, an example of the powerful influence of implicit learning discussed earlier.

Still other changes are evident in perceptual development. Young children, for example, have difficulty making precise and systematic judgments about the similarity of objects based on a single dimension or attribute (Smith, 1989). Preschoolers might put a red rubber ball with a slightly smaller ball of pink yarn because the overall appearance of the two is similar, whereas older children are likely to lump the red rubber ball with a white foam ball on the basis of their being the exact same size. Preschoolers also do not perceive the two distinctive interpretations that typically can be given to ambiguous figures (see Figure 6.12). Even after looking at an ambiguous figure for a long period of time, children less than about five years of age fail to see the figures reverse as do older children and adults (Gopnik & Rosati, 2001). Perhaps cognitive limitations in organizing perceptual information and in understanding that arrays can have multiple meanings is a factor in the difficulty young children have with these kinds of perceptual tasks.

Experience and Perceptual Development

How do experience and inborn sensory capacities interact to determine perception? Throughout the history of psychology this has been an important question, and it continues to be so as medical and technical advances provide opportunities to compensate for some kinds of sensory disabilities. For example, blind children can perceive the existence of distant objects, presumably from changes in auditory cues they receive while moving about (Ashmead, Hill, & Talor, 1989). As a consequence, blind infants are now being fitted with sonic devices to help them hear echoes to signal the direction, distance, and other qualities of objects.

Source: Gopnik & Rosati, 2001, p. 176.

FIGURE 6.12
Perceiving Ambiguous Figures

What do you see in these ambiguous figures? If you look at each figure long enough, you will most likely see (in one or the other order) a vase and two people looking at each other, a duck and a rabbit, and a rat and an old man with glasses. In fact, your perception of the figures may often shift back and forth between the two interpretations. If you did not see both initially, you will readily detect them when told about the two possible representations. However, children less than five years of age seem unable to see more than one representation even when told about the alternative interpretation. Cognitive limitations associated with attributing multiple representations to a stimulus may be a factor in seeing both aspects of the ambiguous figures.

The effects of these efforts with blind children are still to be demonstrated, but we can be sure of one thing from research we discussed earlier that showed evidence for sensitive periods in the development of vision: experience is extremely important for maintaining many perceptual capacities. Experience also helps to explain cross-cultural differences in perception. Environments around the world differ in their degree of "carpenteredness" (Segall, Campbell, & Herskovits, 1966). In most urban, technically advanced societies, houses are constructed on rectilinear principles, which involve perpendicular and right-angle dimensions. Even the layouts of roads and other artifacts of the environment often follow these principles. In other environments, such as in Oceanic and many African cultures, walls and roofs may be curved, and straight lines and angular intersections may be few.

In one study, field workers administered several optical illusions, such as the Müller-Lyer and horizontal-vertical illusions whose effects depend on straight lines that intersect, to samples of children and adults in Africa, the Philippines, and the United States (Segall et al., 1966). The researchers theorized that individuals living in a carpentered environment, who often see rectangular intersecting contours, would be more susceptible to these illusions than people living in noncarpentered environments. In fact, their results conformed to their prediction. In a related set of findings children and adults in cultures with minimal formal education, little experience with pictures, or artworks that incorporate few depth cues are unlikely to perceive pictures or photos in three dimensions (Pick, 1987). Thus the ways in which children and adults interpret their sensory environment can be greatly affected by cultural opportunities, a finding that fits well with the conclusion that perception is influenced by experience.

FOR YOUR REVIEW

• What kinds of developmental changes are accounted for by Gibson's perceptual learning theory?

• What aspects of objects do children have difficulty perceiving?

• How might cross-cultural factors influence perceptual development?

These children in the Sudan receive their education in front of a round schoolhouse. Does a child who grows up in a culture in which linear perspective is uncommon, as in many parts of Africa and island regions in the Pacific Ocean, perceive things differently than a child who grows up in an environment filled with straight lines, right angles, and many opportunities to see distances based on orderly linear cues?

CHAPTER RECAP

SUMMARY OF DEVELOPMENTAL THEMES

■ **Nature/Nurture** *What roles do nature and nurture play in learning and perceptual development?*

We cannot help but be impressed by the remarkably adaptive resources immediately available to infants for gaining knowledge of their environment. The basic mechanisms of learning—habituation, classical and operant conditioning, and perhaps even imitation—are ready to influence behavior at or shortly after birth. A newborn's sense organs are sufficiently developed to provide rudimentary capacities to see, hear, feel, taste, and smell, and often function even before birth. We have also seen, however, that sensory and perceptual capacities improve substantially as a result of experiential fine-tuning. Thus the environment plays an early and powerful role in determining which capacities are acquired and maintained.

■ **Sociocultural Influence** *How does the sociocultural context influence learning and perceptual development?*

Experiences the culture provides—the behaviors that are reinforced and punished and opportunities to observe others engaged in work, play, and social interactions—have substantial effects on what a child learns. Although formal instruction and education assist learning in some societies, in all cultures the actions of caregivers and other models provide plentiful opportunities for children to gain knowledge of what is socially accepted and expected. Specific cultural demands, such as discriminating the printed word, and culturally related physical layouts, such as carpentered environments, may have considerable bearing on perceptual development.

■ **Child's Active Role** *How does the child play an active role in learning and perceptual development?*

Mechanisms of learning typically do not emphasize an active role for the child. Yet what the child learns certainly affects the kinds of interactions she or he will experience and opportunities for further learning. In this sense, the knowledge and skills a child possesses actively contribute to further social interactions, learning, and development. With respect to perceptual development, Eleanor Gibson's theory highlights the important role the activity of the child, including visuomotor and other sensorimotor mechanisms, plays in perceptual development. Children construct perceptions of whole, multisensory arrays at an early age, and their perceptual learning increasingly reflects deliberate and organized exploration of the environment.

■ **Individual Differences** *How prominent are individual differences in learning and perceptual development?*

All normal children are equipped with the basic capacities to learn and perceive. But individual differences are built on those capacities as each child experiences various role models, educational practices, cultural conventions, and other phenomena unique to his or her circumstances. What the child learns establishes the knowledge base on which he or she displays a rich variety of accomplishments and skills. Accompanying these achievements may also be different ways of using the senses and perceiving the environment that contribute to the individual's unique view of the world.

■ **Interaction Among Domains** *How do learning and perceptual development interact with development in other domains?*

Learning plays a substantial role in almost every aspect of development. The child learns social skills, acceptable ways to express thoughts and feelings, techniques to achieve academic and occupational success, and numerous other behaviors. The child who learns about the alphabet, about having to sit quietly in the classroom, about when and when not to speak to an adult, or about behaviors effective in hunting, shepherding, domestic, or other activities of the culture can be expected to achieve social status, prestige, and other resources that will benefit development in many other domains. Furthermore, gains in perception are substantially influenced by physiological and neural advances. Rapidly improving intellectual and motor skills introduce demands for making new perceptual discriminations (such as reading) that, once mastered, lead to further progress in cognitive, social, and other domains.

SUMMARY OF TOPICS

Basic Learning Processes in Infancy and Childhood

■ Learning includes mechanisms that permit adaptation to the environment. Many forms of learning are already evident in infancy.

Habituation

■ *Habituation* refers to the gradual decline in responding as a result of repeated exposure to an event, a basic form of learning that helps in orienting to new information in the environment. Increased attention to new information following habituation indicates *recovery of habituation*.

Classical Conditioning

- Classical conditioning involves the pairing of a neutral stimulus with one that naturally elicits a response. The neutral stimulus then begins to elicit the response as well.

Operant Conditioning

- Operant conditioning involves the delivery or removal of a reinforcing or punishing stimulus so that behaviors preceding the stimulus increase or decrease.

Imitation

- Imitation plays a major role in socialization, as well as in the acquisition of knowledge. Caregivers and tutors often rely on observational learning to assist children in the acquisition of a wide range of behaviors.

Implicit Learning

- Implicit learning takes place as a result of unintentionally abstracting patterns and rules that often organize the structure of physical, linguistic, and social information.

Sensory and Perceptual Capacities

- *Sensations* refer to the basic units of information recorded by the various receptor systems and the brain; *perception* refers to the organization and interpretation of these sensations.

- Although all of the senses operate at birth and, in some cases, well before, debates exist concerning the roles that nature and nurture play in their continued development.

Measuring Infant Sensory and Perceptual Capacities

- Researchers rely on infants' *attentional* preferences, habituation and recovery of habituation to familiar stimuli, learning, and other physiological indicators to provide evidence that they are able to discriminate objects and events.

Vision

- Vision involves actively looking and seeing. Although infants possess some capacities at birth, they typically show rapid advances within the first six months in *accommodation,* the ability of the lens of the eye to focus visual input on the retina; *saccadic* eye movements, shifts of the eye to attend to visual targets at different locations; *smooth visual pursuit,* the tracking of a slowly moving object; and *vergence,* the capacity to orient both eyes toward an object at different distances.

- *Visual acuity,* the ability to discriminate contour and fine details, is limited in newborns but improves rapidly. However, cataracts, or clouding of the lens, or the failure of both eyes to focus together, if left uncorrected, can result in the failure of visual acuity to improve and loss of stereoptic depth perception.

- Color vision and *stereopsis,* the ability to see depth as a function of the slight discrepancy in the images available to the two eyes, normally are evident shortly after birth.

- Newborns do not examine visual patterns systematically and are often attracted to the more salient external features that show high contrast (the *externality effect*) or movement. Within a few months, they engage in more systematic exploration of visual arrays. They prefer attending to the human face and show signs of this preference for certain features shortly after birth. Their perception of the unity and coherence of objects is enhanced by kinetic cues and prior experience with the stimuli.

- Depth information is provided to infants by *kinetic cues,* the differential flow of optic information that derives from self-induced movement or as a result of movement among arrays in the visual field and stereopsis. Infants process depth provided by pictorial cues beginning about five to seven months of age.

Audition

- The ability to hear exists prenatally, undergoes substantial improvement during the first few months after birth, and continues to improve throughout childhood. Some kinds of auditory information experienced prenatally are remembered after birth. These observations have led some parents to provide regular vibroacoustic experiences in the form of music or other sounds to the fetus. At the present time, no research has shown long-term benefits to the child, and some believe that potentially negative consequences can occur under some conditions of exposure.

- Newborns demonstrate *sound localization,* the ability to determine the location from which a sound emanates, and this capacity undergoes improvement over the following months. Auditory perception of patterns of sound is displayed early, and infants show a preference for listening to musical patterns that conform to acceptable phrasing.

- Infants can detect *phonemes,* the basic unit of sound used to differentiate the meaning of words in languages. However, by the end of the first year, as a result of exposure to only a subset of these sounds, they often discriminate only those phonemes heard in their own language. This observation, along with evidence of *categorical perception* for phonemes, has given rise to theoretical debates about whether speech sounds are processed by special acoustic mechanisms available only to humans or by more general auditory processes.

Smell, Taste, Touch, and Sensitivity to Pain

- Newborns discriminate basic tastes and pleasant and unpleasant smells. Behavioral and other responses indicate that the newborn can feel pain.

Intermodal Perception

■ Babies also display *intermodal perception,* the ability to integrate information arising from more than one sensory modality. However, the role that learning plays in this capacity is uncertain. Some amodal properties of stimulation, information common to more than one sensory modality such as temporal synchrony, may be highly salient to young infants and assist in their acquiring an understanding of the correlations that exist among the various sensory properties of objects and events.

Perceptual Development Throughout Childhood

■ Compared with the extensive research carried out on infants, relatively few investigations of perceptual development have been carried out on children.

Perceptual Learning

■ Research based on Eleanor Gibson's theory of perceptual learning has revealed that perception becomes more focused, organized, and confined to the meaningful and important features of the environment with development.

Experience and Perceptual Development

■ Perceptual learning may have an important bearing on observations of some cultural differences in perception of the environment.

CHAPTER 7
Language

Key Themes in Language

- **Nature/Nurture**   What roles do nature and nurture play in language development?

- **Sociocultural Influence**   How does the sociocultural context influence language development?

- **Child's Active Role**   How does the child play an active role in the process of language development?

- **Continuity/Discontinuity**   Is language development continuous or discontinuous?

- **Individual Differences**   How prominent are individual differences in language development?

- **Interaction Among Domains**   How does language development interact with development in other domains?

The family reunion had been scheduled for months, and Jennifer and Bill were looking forward to showing off their one-year-old son, Devon, to aunts, uncles, and cousins who had not yet met him. They were especially eager to compare notes with Jennifer's cousin Gayle, who had a little girl born two days after Devon. Although they had seen pictures of little Meagen on e-mail, they hadn't yet officially met her. As they pulled into the driveway of the family cottage, they could see a distant figure holding a child in her arms. Sure enough, it was Gayle walking carefully down the driveway with Meagen. As they got closer, Jennifer rolled down her window and was met with Meagen's eager squeals, "Baby! Mama! Baby!" as she pointed to Devon in the back seat. Jennifer was surprised, to say the least. Their own son Devon, while a real pro at walking, was not saying much more than a few "Dadas." Could two children the same age really be so different in their ability to speak?

Parents often compare their children's latest feats with other parents, and, aside from walking, there are few accomplishments they focus on more than their baby's first use of language. At about one year of age, most children make their formal entrance into the world of human communication by saying their first words, and parents respond with equal delight and amazement. As in many domains of development, there can be noticeable differences in the accomplishments of two children who are the same age. Nonetheless, by age five, most children have moved from Meagen's effective but rudimentary mix of verbal and nonverbal messages to more complex achievements. They have mastered the bewildering variety of sounds in their native language to produce thousands of recognizable words, and they understand the meanings of words reasonably well. They also become aware of the interactive and sociocultural rules of communication.

By age five, in fact, most children have become highly proficient listeners and speakers, a marvel indeed given the overwhelming abundance of sounds, vocabulary words, grammatical rules, and social conventions that go into producing mature, adult-sounding speech. You probably do not have a vivid memory of how you learned to speak; most of us have little specific recall of this extremely complex, yet entirely natural process. But if you have ever tried to learn a foreign language, you probably have some sense of how remarkable children's mastery of communication is. How do infants and children manage such a seemingly overwhelming task?

In this chapter, we will first examine the major milestones in the acquisition of communication and language skills from infancy through childhood, the sequence of events that unfolds as the child comes to comprehend and produce language. Next, we will look at the most important theories of language development and how they account for our observations of children's language attainments. Of all the themes of development, none has been more central to theories of language development than the nature-versus-nurture debate, the extent to which either biological predispositions or environmental influences dictate the child's developing linguistic competence. Finally, we will briefly examine the functions of language, particularly as they interact with children's growing cognitive skills and ability to regulate their own behavior.

The Course of Language Acquisition

A baby's contact with language is—initially, at least—noticeably one-sided. Although she may gurgle or coo, most of her experience is as a listener. Among her first tasks is to learn to identify the myriad sounds that make up her native language. That is, she must distinguish specific sounds in the stream of spoken language, note the regularities in how they are combined, recognize which combinations constitute words, and eventually, when she makes the transition from listener to speaker, form the consonant-vowel combinations that are the building blocks of words and sentences. The fundamental sound units and the rules for combining them in a given language make up that language's **phonology.** If you have studied a foreign language, you will recognize that some sounds appear only in certain languages, such as the prolonged nasal *n* sound in Spanish and the French vowel that is spoken as though *e* and *u* are combined. Furthermore, each language has its own rules for combining sounds. In English, for example, the *sr* combination does not occur, whereas *sl* and *st* appear frequently. An important task for the child is to absorb the sounds and combinations of sounds that are acceptable in her native language and, eventually, to detect which of these sounds form words.

Another basic language skill the child must master is linking the combinations of sounds he hears to the objects, people, events, or relationships they label. **Semantics** refers to the meanings of words (sometimes called the *lexicon*) or combinations of words. For example, *cookie* is an arbitrary grouping of sounds, but speakers of English use it to refer to a specific class of objects. The child thus attaches words to conceptual groups, learning when it is appropriate to use them and when it is not (for example, *cookie* does not refer to all objects or edible goods found in the bakery). The child also learns that some words describe actions (*eat*), whereas others describe relationships (*under or over*) or modify objects (*chocolate cookie*). Mapping combinations of sounds to their referents (that is, the things to which words refer) is a central element of language acquisition.

As the child begins to combine words, she learns the principles of **grammar,** the rules pertaining to the structure of language. Grammar includes two components, *syntax* and *morphology*. **Syntax** refers to the rules that dictate how words can be combined. The order in which words are spoken conveys meaning; for example, "Eat kitty" and "Kitty eat" do not mean the same thing, even in the simplified language of the young child. A word's position in a sentence can signify whether the word is an agent or the object of an action, for example. The rules of syntax vary widely from one language to another, but within a given language they operate with consistency and regularity. **Morphology** refers to the rules for combining the smallest meaningful units of language to form words. For example, the word *girl* has one morpheme. Adding *-s* to form *girls* makes the number of morphemes two and changes the meaning from singular to plural. Similarly, morphemes such as *-ed* and *-ing* create a change in the tense of words. One of the most remarkable features of language acquisition is the child's ability to detect the rules of syntax and morphology and use them to create meaningful utterances of his own with little direct instruction.

The process of acquiring language also includes learning **pragmatics,** the rules for using language effectively and appropriately according to the social context. The effective use of language includes a host of nonverbal behaviors, rules of etiquette, and even changing the content of speech according to the identity of the listener and the situation surrounding the communication. How do you ask someone for a favor? Not, the child soon learns, by saying, "Hey, you, get me that ball!" The child also learns that if someone did not hear what she said, she can sometimes add a gesture to complete the communication. And the proper way to speak to an adult who has

phonology Fundamental sound units and combinations of units in a given language.

semantics Meanings of words or combinations of words.

grammar Rules pertaining to the structure of language.

syntax Grammatical rules that dictate how words can be combined.

morphology Rules for how to combine the smallest meaningful units of language to form words.

pragmatics Rules for using language effectively within a social context.

some authority will probably include more polite forms and fewer terms of familiarity than when speaking to a peer. As they acquire language, then, children also absorb the equally important sociocultural dimension of pragmatics.

Clearly, language is a multifaceted skill with many overlapping dimensions, from understanding and uttering sounds to appreciating the sometimes subtle rules of social communication. Despite the complexities, by the time they are four or five years old, most children speak much as adults do. Their progress in mastering vocabulary, syntax, and pragmatics continues during the school years and thereafter, but they acquire the essential elements of the language system in an impressively brief period.

Phonology

What does it take to learn a language? The infant's first steps consist of attending to the sounds of speech as a special type of auditory stimulation, deciphering the units of sound that occur in her language, and discerning which clusters of sounds constitute words, clauses, and phrases. Thus, during much of the infant's first year, the emphasis is on phonological development, both in receiving messages from others and in being able to produce them on his own.

● **Early Responses to Human Speech**   Right from birth, the human infant has a special sensitivity to the sounds other human beings make. Newborns show a distinct preference for human voices over other sounds and like to hear their own mothers' voices more than a stranger's (DeCasper & Fifer, 1980; Gibson & Spelke, 1983). Most important, however, infants respond in specific ways to small acoustic variations in human speech that distinguish one word or part of a word from another.

As we discuss in the chapter titled "Basic Learning and Perception," the basic building blocks of spoken language are called *phonemes,* the smallest units of sound that change the meanings of words. In the words *pat* and *bat,* for example, the phonemes /p/ and /b/ make a big difference in the meaning of the word. Recall also that infants as young as one month can discriminate different phonemes and do so categorically, ignoring small acoustic variations in a sound unless the sound pattern crosses a phonemic boundary (Aslin, Pisoni, & Jusczyk, 1983; Kuhl, 1987). At two months of age, infants add to their repertoires the ability to discriminate vowels (Marean, Werner, & Kuhl, 1992). Remarkably, young infants show an ability to detect phonemes and vowel sounds from a variety of languages. However, by six to ten months of age, infants show a decline in the ability to distinguish those basic sounds that do not appear in their native language (Kuhl et al., 1992; Polka & Werker, 1994; Werker & Tees, 1984). That is, their experiences with the language spoken around them quickly begin to constrain the small units of sound to which they are sensitive.

Infants also show an early sensitivity to **prosody,** the patterns of intonation, stress, and rhythm that communicate meaning. One example of a prosodic feature is the pattern of intonation that distinguishes questions from declarative statements. When you raise your voice at the end of a question, you are signaling a different communicative intent than when you let your voice fall at the end of a declarative sentence. Researchers have found that infants prefer the prosodic features associated with the high-pitched, exaggerated, musical speech, often called "baby talk," that mothers typically direct to their young children. Figure 7.1 illustrates some of the acoustical properties of mothers' speech to infants. In one study, Anne Fernald (1985) trained four-month-olds to turn their heads to activate a loudspeaker positioned on either side of them. The infants were more likely to make this response if their "reward" was a female stranger's voice speaking as the woman would speak to a baby than if she used normal adult speech. Other research has shown that it is the positive affective tone of "baby talk" that infants are particularly attracted to (Singh, Morgan, & Best, 2002). In light of these preferences, it seems fitting that mothers from cultures as diverse as France, Italy, Germany, Britain, Japan, China, and the Xhosa tribe of southern Africa have been found to raise their pitch when they speak to their young infants (Fernald, 1991; Papoušek, 1992).

KEY THEME
Nature/Nurture

prosody   Patterns of intonation, stress, and rhythm that communicate meaning in speech.

FIGURE 7.1
The Acoustical Properties of
Maternal Speech to Infants

These two samples of maternal
speech show the special
acoustical qualities that make
speech to infants (bottom)
distinct from speech to adults
(top). The vertical axis represents fundamental frequency,
a measure of auditory pitch.
Note the frequent use of modulation of pitch and the pre-
dominance of high pitch in
maternal speech to infants.
Babies seem to be especially
responsive to the qualities of
this type of speech.

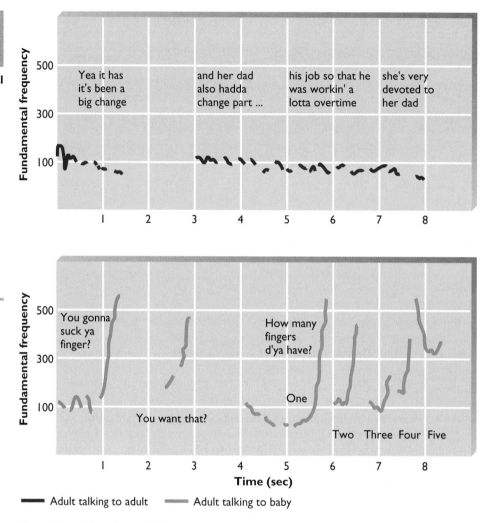

Source: Adapted from Fernald, 1985.

Infants' sensitivity to the prosodic features of speech prepares them for the more
complex aspects of language learning that lie before them. As early as two days of age
they show a clear preference for hearing a stream of speech from their native language as opposed to a foreign language (Moon, Cooper, & Fifer, 1993). Sometime between six and nine months of age, infants begin to show a preference to listen to
unfamiliar isolated words from their native language. For example, American infants
prefer unfamiliar English words over Dutch words. At ten months of age, they also
prefer words with a strong-weak stress pattern (e.g., *crossing* versus *across*) that are
more common in English (Jusczyk, Cutler, & Redanz, 1993; Jusczyk, Friederici, et al.,
1993). Young infants thus seem to be especially tuned in to the rhythmic properties
that distinguish one language from another (Nazzi, Bertonciui, & Mehler, 1998).

Perhaps most impressive is the finding that by about eight months of age, infants
show that they can detect the beginnings and endings of specific words in a stream
of their native speech (Jusczyk & Aslin, 1995), a skill that should strike you as remarkable if you have ever tried to detect the presence of particular words when listening to someone speak a foreign language. To explore this ability, Sven Mattys and
Peter Jusczyk (Mattys & Jusczyk, 2001) first familiarized infants with a single word
such as *dice*. Next, infants heard the target word within a passage, such as "Two dice
can be rolled without difficulty," or they heard the same sound pattern but across two
different words, as in "Wired ice no longer surprises anyone." Infants showed a clear
preference for the first type of correctly segmented passage, probably using rhythmic
cues, as well as noting the different acoustic properties that phonemes have at the be-

ginnings versus the ends of words (e.g., /d/ sounds slightly different at the beginning than at the end of a word). Words starting with vowels, though, are much harder for infants to locate in speech segments than words starting with consonants. Only sixteen-month-olds could locate words such as *ice* or *eel.*

Once infants can locate words, the pathway is prepared for the next critical aspect of learning a language, namely, learning the meanings of words. Word recognition skills improve dramatically in the second year, especially as infants begin to use their knowledge of word meanings to decipher the sounds they hear. At eighteen months of age, for example, toddlers need to hear only the very first portion of a word, such as *daw* in *doggie,* in order to look at the picture the word represents (Fernald, Swingley, & Pinto, 2001). This relationship between meaning and sound is only one example of how the various facets of language are, in fact, very much interrelated.

● **Cooing and Babbling: Prelinguistic Speech**   Well before the child utters her first word, she produces sounds that increasingly resemble the language spoken in her environment. At birth, the infant's vocal capabilities are limited to crying and a few other brief sounds such as grunts, sighs, or clicks. Between six and eight weeks, a new type of vocalization, **cooing,** emerges. These brief, vowel-like utterances are sometimes accompanied by consonants, usually those produced in the back of the mouth, such as /g/ or /k/. Infants coo when they are in a comfortable state or when a parent has made some attempt to communicate, either with speech or coos of his or her own. In the weeks that follow, the infant's vocalizations become longer and begin to include consonants formed at the front of the mouth, as in /m/ or /b/.

The next significant accomplishment is the emergence of **babbling,** the production of consonant-vowel combinations such as *da* or *ba.* Most children begin to babble at about three to six months and refine their skills in the succeeding months. To many listeners, the infant's babbling sounds like active experimentation with the production of different sounds. These vocalizations are especially likely to occur in the context of mutually coordinated caregiver-child interactions (Hsu & Fogel, 2001), and they are often accompanied by facial expressions such as smiles or frowns (Yale et al., 1999), perhaps to emphasize the child's communicative intent. At about seven months, the infant will repeat well-formed syllables, such as *baba* or *dada,* a phenomenon called **canonical babbling.** It is almost as if the infant is trying to say words. At nine or ten months, the child's babbling includes more numerous and complex consonant-vowel combinations, as well as variations in intonation (Davis et al., 2000).

The changes in children's productive capabilities are linked to physiological changes in their vocal apparatus and central nervous systems that occur during the first year. In the months after birth, the infant's larynx descends farther into the neck, the oral cavity grows, and the baby can place her tongue in different positions in her mouth (not just forward and backward as at birth). At the same time, the cortex of the brain replaces the brain stem in controlling many of the child's behaviors. In general, early reflexlike vocalizations, such as cries, fade as more controlled voluntary utterances, such as coos and babbles, enter the child's repertoire (Stark, 1986).

The fact that most infants, regardless of their culture, begin to coo and babble at similar ages suggests that biological factors direct the onset of these behaviors. Even deaf children vocalize with coos and babbles in the first few months of life (Stoel-Gammon & Otomo, 1986), and both deaf and hearing children exposed to sign language make repetitive, rhythmic hand gestures akin to babbling prior to full-fledged signing (Petitto et al., 2001; Petitto & Marentette, 1991; Takei, 2001). Nature thus plays a distinct role in the emergence of the child's utterances. But even at this early stage of language development, the form the child's vocalizations take is influenced by the language spoken around her. Studies have shown identifiable differences in babbling among infants from varying cultures. One group of researchers conducted a spectral analysis of the vowel sounds made by ten-month-olds in Paris, London, Algiers, and Hong Kong. The procedure involved translating the acoustic properties of speech into a visual representation of the intensity, onset, and pattern of vocalization. Infants from different countries varied in the average frequencies of the sounds

SEE FOR YOURSELF
psychology.college.hmco.com
Children's Speech

KEY THEME
Interaction Among Domains

KEY THEME
Nature/Nurture

cooing   Vowel-like utterances that characterize the infant's first attempts to vocalize.

babbling   Consonant-vowel utterances that characterize the infant's first attempts to vocalize.

canonical babbling   Repetition of simple consonant-vowel combinations in well-formed syllables.

they produced; the differences paralleled those of adult speakers from the same countries (Boysson-Bardies et al., 1989). Thus the child's linguistic environment has a distinct effect on his own speech before he can speak true words.

● **Later Phonological Development**   At around one year of age, some of the child's babbles begin to sound like words, a major achievement that is discussed in greater detail later. From the perspective of phonology, though, the infant's ability to make different sounds is still somewhat restricted. Infants say a limited number of consonants and vowels, usually the same ones that appear in their babbles (Ingram, 1999). Some sounds, such as /m/ and /b/, are more common than others, such as /l/ and /r/ (Leonard, Newhoff, & Meselam, 1980). As the child's ability to speak improves, she adds consonants to the ends of words (e.g., *bite* instead of *bi*), although not consistently (Sternberger, 1992). Perhaps the best characterization of this phase is that infants say words, and sometimes change them, in accordance with the sounds they are capable of articulating.

Once children enter a period of rapid vocabulary acquisition, between eighteen months and two years of age, the range of sounds they produce expands. Certain kinds of errors are common, though, and may persist until children are in preschool or even elementary school. They might replace a *k* sound with a *t* to say *tootie* instead of *cookie* or substitute *w* for *r* in the word *rabbit*. Or children might delete a syllable that is unstressed, for example, saying *nana* for *banana*, or use reduplication, calling a bottle *baba* (Vihman, 1998).

By about age five, the speech of most children sounds like that of adults. In addition, they are beginning to understand the components of sound in the language they speak, especially as they learn to read. Phonology is something children can both use and think about in a conscious and reflective manner.

ATYPICAL DEVELOPMENT

Language-Impaired Children

About 7 percent of children fail to develop normal speech and language despite having normal hearing and general intellectual skills (Leonard, 1998). They may have trouble pronouncing words, have a limited spoken vocabulary, and show poor language comprehension. For many of these children, delayed language skills can mean severe reading difficulties, called *dyslexia,* once they enter school. Many researchers now believe that this wide array of problems is due to phonological processing deficits (Olson, 1994; Siegel, 1993; Stanovich, 1993; Whitehurst & Fischel, 2000). These children have particular difficulty in discriminating phonemes, precisely the type of skill at which many infants are so adept. Compared with normal children, these children are slower and less accurate when asked to read nonsense words such as *calch* and *tegwop*; they also have difficulty when asked to make words into a familiar children's language called Pig Latin (e.g., making the word *pig* into *ig-pay*) (Connors & Olson, 1990). These processing deficits can persist well into adulthood (Bruck, 1993). They also occur among poor readers from a wide variety of language backgrounds, including Arabic, Chinese, Punjabi, and Norwegian (Chiappe & Siegel, 1999; Høien et al., 1995; Siegel, 1998).

Paula Tallal and her colleagues (1996) have found that many of these children can be helped by being trained with taped exercises in which speech has been modified to help them identify auditory sounds that change quickly. In these exercises, the speech signal was slowed down by 50 percent, but its natural quality was preserved. In addition, the elements of speech that typically change rapidly were amplified in volume. The children had to act out commands they heard in the exercises or repeat syllables, words, and phrases. The program was intensive; children worked on the exercises three hours each weekday and were also given homework every night. At the end of only one month, the children's scores on several measures of language development improved by two years on average.

Just why language-impaired children lag behind in phonological processing skills is still not completely understood. Tallal and her colleagues believe that the problem lies in a general deficit in processing auditory stimuli of any sort, be they speech sounds or not (Tallal et al., 1997). Another ingredient may be poor executive processing skills, such as the ability to maintain two pieces of information in memory at once or to select the best strategy from a number of competing options in a task (Swanson, Mink, & Bocian, 1999). Other experts argue that the problem is not cognitive but rather is specific to processing linguistic stimuli, because children from a wide range of intellectual levels—even those with high IQs—can show dyslexia (Siegel, 1998). Whatever the explanation, this body of research makes very clear the importance of mastering phonology in the acquisition of language and reading for all children, not just those who have dyslexia. The ability to decipher the basic sound units of language is now a widely recognized predictor of children's eventual skill in reading (Comeau et al., 1999; Ehri, 1998; Ho & Bryant, 1997).

Semantics

Few moments in life rival the excitement parents feel when they hear their children say their first words, typically at about one year of age. "Cookie," "Mama," and "Dada" are joyfully entered into the baby book alongside other momentous events, such as the infant's first steps. Certainly the uttering of first words is a major accomplishment, marking the visible entry of the child into the world of spoken, shared communication. The child's comprehension and production of words also signal a new focus in the mastery of language: semantic development.

● **Gesture as a Communication Tool** Late in the first year, before or as they speak their first words, many children begin to use such gestures as pointing, showing, or giving as a means to communicate with other people (Bates, Camaioni, & Volterra, 1975). Carlotta, a ten-month-old infant observed by Elizabeth Bates and her colleagues, provides some good examples of several kinds of nonverbal communication that seem to express meaning. In one observation, Carlotta held up her toy and extended her arm in a showing motion to an adult. Here she was using a **protodeclarative communication** that, much as a declarative sentence does, called the adult's attention to the object. Another time, Carlotta pointed to the kitchen sink and said, "Ha!," a **protoimperative communication** intended to get the adult to do something (Bates, 1979). Often children's gestures are accompanied by direct eye contact with the communication's recipient. As children get older, they may add a vocalization to the gesture for added emphasis (Messinger & Fogel, 1998), much as Carlotta did when asking for water. Children may also repeat their communications if the messages are not understood. This constellation of behaviors and the context in which they occur suggest that children use gestures as a purposeful means to an end (Scoville, 1983).

Linda Acredolo and Susan Goodwyn (1988) found that a child between eleven and twenty-four months of age uses gestures not just to show or request but also to symbolize objects or events. The child may signify a flower, for example, by making a sniffing gesture or the desire to go outside with a knob-turning motion. A significant number of children's gestures recreate the functions of objects rather than their forms or shapes. For example, participants in the study would put their fist to one ear to signify a telephone or wave their hands to represent a butterfly.

Acredolo and Goodwyn believe a strong relationship exists between the development of symbolic gestures and verbal abilities because both appear at approximately the same point in development, with gestures usually preceding words by a few weeks (Acredolo & Goodwyn, 1988; Goodwyn & Acredolo, 1993). Recognizing that one thing

⊙ SEE FOR YOURSELF
psychology.college.hmco.com
Baby Signs

protodeclarative communication Use of a gesture to call attention to an object or event.

protoimperative communication Use of a gesture to issue a command or request.

Late in the first year, many young children use gestures to communicate, either to call an adult's attention to an object or to get an adult to do something. Gestures typically drop out of the child's repertoire, though, as spoken language develops.

can symbolize another represents a major cognitive advance, one that is essential for the use of both gestures and spoken language. By the middle of the second year, however, children are less likely to use gestures as their sole means of communication. Gestures unaccompanied by verbalization are less useful when the "listener" is out of view and they are usually correctly understood by only a limited number of adults. Parents also probably tend to encourage the child's verbalizations more than they do the use of gestures (Acredolo & Goodwyn, 1990a). So oriented do hearing children become to words as a means of expression that by two years of age, they are much more likely to learn new names for objects as opposed to new gestures to represent them (Namy & Waxman, 1998).

All of this is not meant to say that children stop using gestures entirely. In fact, quite the contrary is true. Both adults and children tend to use gestures as an accompaniment to their speech, giving emphasis to what they are saying or elaborating on a concept visually. Children begin to use gesture in these ways as their speech gets more complex, at ages two and three (Mayberry & Nicoladis, 2000). Even blind children gesture while they speak to others, suggesting that this behavior is not merely an imitation of the communication styles of adults (Iverson & Goldin-Meadow, 2001). Rather, gesture seems to be very much intertwined with the communicative process.

● **The One-Word Stage**   From about twelve to twenty months of age, most children speak only one word at a time. Children's first words are most frequently **nominals,** labels for objects, people, or events, although action words (*give*), modifiers (*dirty*), and personal-social words (*please*) also occur (Bates et al., 1994; Nelson, 1973). Children's early words usually refer to people or objects important in their lives, such as parents and other relatives, pets, or familiar objects. Children are also

nominals   Words that label objects, people, or events; the first type of words most children produce.

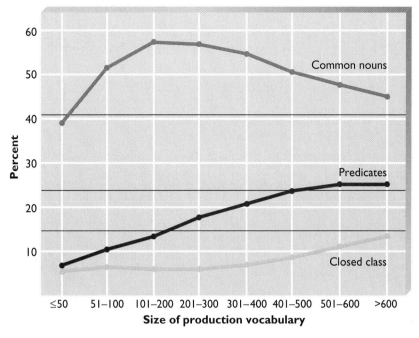

FIGURE 7.2
Changes in the Proportion of Word Types in Children's Vocabularies

As children's vocabularies grow from only a few words to several hundred (the horizontal axis on the graph), the proportion of nouns rises and remains high. The proportion of other types of words children learn, such as predicates (verbs and adjectives) and closed-class words (prepositions, conjunctions, and other relational words), remains lower. The children in this study ranged in age from sixteen to thirty months.

Source: Bates et al., 1994.

more likely to acquire labels for dynamic objects (*clock, car, ball*) or those they can use (*cup, cookie*) than for items that are stationary (*wall, window*). Figure 7.2 shows how the proportion of word types changes in the vocabularies of children between one and two-and-a-half years of age.

Children acquire their first ten words slowly; the typical child adds about one to three words to his or her repertoire each month (Barrett, 1989). From about age eighteen months onward, however, many children show a virtual explosion in the acquisition of new words. This remarkable period in language development is called the **vocabulary spurt** (Barrett, 1985; Bloom, 1973). In one longitudinal study of vocabulary growth in one- to two-year-olds, some learned to say as many as twenty new words, mostly nouns, during each week of the vocabulary spurt (Goldfield & Reznick, 1990). Figure 7.3 shows the rapid rate of vocabulary growth for three children in the middle of their spurt. Within the same period, children also typically show a spurt in the number of words they understand (Reznick & Goldfield, 1992). When rapid vocabulary growth first begins, children also show a temporary increase in the number of errors they make in naming objects, forgetting words they recently learned. The influx of new words may temporarily interfere with knowledge that has been recently stored, a finding that is perhaps to be expected at this transitional time in language development (Dapretto & Bjork, 2000; Gershkoff-Stowe, 2001; Gershkoff-Stowe & Smith, 1997).

Some of the child's first words are bound to a specific context: that is, the child uses the word to label objects in limited situations. Lois Bloom (1973) observed that one nine-month-old used the word *car* only when she was looking out the living room window at cars moving on the street. She did not say "car" to refer to parked cars, pictures of cars, or cars she was sitting in. This type of utterance, used when the child applies a label to a narrower class of objects than the term signifies, is called an **underextension.** Over time, the child begins to use single words more flexibly in a wider variety of contexts (Barrett, 1986).

Children may also show **overextension,** applying a label to a broader category than the term signifies. For example, a toddler may call a horse or a cow "doggie." The child often applies the same word to objects that look alike perceptually (Clark, 1973). At other times, the child may misuse a word when objects share functions, such as calling a rolling quarter a "ball" (Bowerman, 1978). As with underextensions, the child's use of overextensions declines after the second year.

vocabulary spurt Period of rapid word acquisition that typically occurs early in language development.

underextension Application of a label to a narrower class of objects than the term signifies.

overextension Tendency to apply a label to a broader category than the term actually signifies.

FIGURE 7.3
The Vocabulary Spurt in
Three Young Children

Many children show a vocabulary spurt, a sharp rise in the
number of new words they
learn, as they approach two
years of age. However, children
may begin their spurts at different ages, as the graph clearly
shows. Child A showed an
early spurt, beginning at fifteen
months. Child B's spurt began
at the more typical age of eighteen months. Child C showed
a late spurt at twenty-one
months.

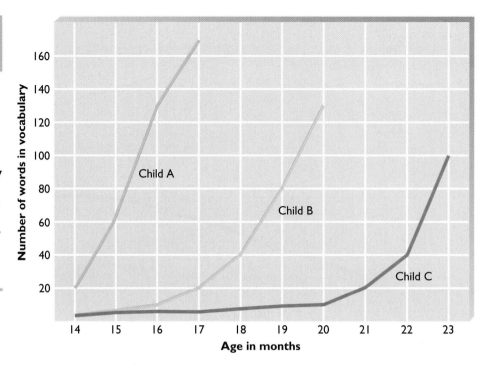

Source: Adapted from Goldfield & Reznick, 1990.

Most noticeable at this phase of language learning is the child's intense desire to
communicate her thoughts, feelings, and desires. Even though her language skills are
limited to one or at most two words at a time, the young child is enormously eager to
find ways of talking about favorite people, toys, and objects (Bloom, 1998; Dromi,
1999).

● **Comprehension Versus Production**   If you have ever tried to learn a new language, you undoubtedly found it easier to understand what another speaker was saying than to produce a sentence in the new language yourself. An important point to
remember about children's early language is that their **receptive language,** what they
comprehend, far exceeds their **productive language,** their ability to say and use the
words. In one study, parents reported an average of 5.7 words produced by their ten-
month-olds but a comprehension average about three times greater, 17.9 words
(Bates, Bretherton, & Snyder, 1988).

Infants show distinct signs of comprehending words as early as six months of age,
well before they utter their first words. In one study, infants heard the word
"mommy" or "daddy" produced by a synthetic voice in a gender-neutral frequency.
As each word was repeated, they also saw side-by-side videos of their parents. Infants
showed a clear preference for looking at the video of the parent who matched the
spoken word. This preference was not evident in another group of infants who
viewed strange men and women on videotape while listening to the words (Tincoff
& Jusczyk, 1999). Thus six-month-old infants show that they know the specific
meanings of words, at least for people who are important in their lives.

In general, infants comprehend the labels for nouns before they understand the
labels for verbs (Tomasello & Farrar, 1986). For example, although eighteen-month-
olds show that they can learn what it means for a Lego car to *neem* (push), fourteen-
month-olds have difficulty (Casasola & Cohen, 2000). One hypothesis for this delay
in understanding verbs has to do with the notion that many verbs denote the actions
or motions of objects. Thus, in order to understand a verb, the child has to first understand something about the object involved and the actions and motions it is
capable of (Kersten, 1998). In fact, when young children are learning new verbs

receptive language   Ability to
comprehend spoken speech.

productive language   Meaningful language spoken or otherwise produced by an individual.

(e.g.,. "This one is *spogging*"), they often attend to how objects look as much as what they do (Kersten & Smith, 2002).

That young children understand so much of what is said to them means they have acquired some important information about language before they actually speak. They know that people, objects, and events have names. They know that specific patterns of sounds represent objects and events in their environment. Most important, they begin to appreciate the usefulness of language as a means of expressing ideas, needs, and feelings.

● **Individual and Cultural Differences in Language Development**   Although children show many common trends in the way they acquire language, they also show significant individual differences in rates and types of language production. You may have heard a family member or friend report that her child said virtually nothing for two or three years and then began speaking in complete sentences. Although such dramatic variations in language milestones are not frequent, children sometimes show unique patterns in their linguistic accomplishments, patterns that still lead to the attainment of normal language by later childhood.

One example of wide individual variation is the age at which children say their first word. Some children produce their first distinguishable word as early as nine months, whereas others may not do so until sixteen months (Barrett, 1989). Similarly, some children show good pronunciation, whereas others have difficulty making certain sounds, consistently substituting *t* for *k* or *b* for *v*, for example (Smith, 1988). In addition, not all children display the vocabulary spurt (Acredolo & Goodwyn, 1990b), or they may start their spurts at different ages, as Figure 7.3 indicates. The results of a study of more than eighteen hundred children underscore just how variable the size of children's vocabularies can be: at sixteen months of age, some children spoke 10 or fewer words, whereas others spoke as many as 180 words (Fenson et al., 1994).

Children may also differ in the content of their one-word speech. Most one-year-olds tend to use nominals predominantly, displaying what Katherine Nelson (1973) termed a **referential style.** Other children show a different pattern: rather than naming objects, they frequently use words that have social functions, such as *hello* or *please,* thus displaying an **expressive style.** Expressive children use words to direct or comment on the behavior of other people. According to some research, referential children tend to have larger vocabularies and show more rapid advances in language development, at least in the early stages (Bates et al., 1988; Nelson, 1973).

How do we explain these individual differences in the rates and styles with which children acquire language? There are several hypotheses. Perhaps individual differences result from differences in the neurological structures that control language or from inborn differences in temperament. For example, referential children tend to have long attention spans, smile and laugh a lot, and be easily soothed (Dixon & Shore, 1997). Children who are more advanced in language comprehension and production show a similar profile (Dixon & Smith, 2000). This style might allow them to profit from incoming information about the names of objects. Another possibility is that parents influence the rate and form of children's vocabulary development. Some parents, for example, may spend a great deal of time encouraging their infants to speak, focusing especially on labeling objects. Others may be more relaxed about letting the infant proceed at his or her own pace. Researchers have confirmed that the overall amount and variety of speech parents produce to their infants is related to the acceleration of vocabulary growth (Hoff & Naigles, 2002; Huttenlocher et al., 1991).

Cultural differences in how children speak in the one-word stage bolster the idea that what children hear others say influences what they themselves say. Unlike American children, Korean toddlers show a "verb spurt" before a "noun spurt" (Choi, 1998; Choi & Gopnik, 1995); similarly, Mandarin-speaking toddlers utter more verbs than nouns as they and their mothers play with toys (Tardif, 1996; Tardif, Gelman, & Xu, 1999). Mothers from both Asian groups pepper their speech with many more verbs

KEY THEME
Individual Differences

KEY THEME
Nature/Nurture

referential style   Type of early language production in which the child uses mostly nominals.

expressive style   Type of early language production in which the child uses many social words.

Chinese mothers use more verbs and action sequences in their speech to children than American mothers. It is interesting to note that Chinese-speaking toddlers use more verbs than nouns in their early speech. Thus, the form of early speech is influenced by the sociocultural context in which the child lives.

KEY THEME
Sociocultural Influence

and action sequences, saying things such as "What are you doing?" and "You put the car in the garage"; American mothers, in contrast, use far more nouns (e.g., "That's a ball") and ask questions that require a nominal as an answer (e.g., "What is it?").

● **Deriving the Meanings of Words**   The number of new words the child learns grows rapidly from age eighteen months through the preschool years. By the time they enter school, children know more than fourteen thousand words (Carey, 1978); by age ten, they comprehend almost forty thousand words. These numbers translate into an astonishing rate of learning of between six and twelve new words per day among school-age children (Anglin, 1993)!

Many researchers believe that certain biases operate in the child's literal "search for meaning." Consider the toddler who hears a new word such as *eggbeater*. What does that word mean? Logically, it could refer to a host of objects or perhaps an action instead of an object. Testing the numerous hypotheses could take an inordinate amount of time. Several researchers argue that children are biased to form more restricted hypotheses about the meanings of words; if they were not, they would not learn language so rapidly and with so few errors. *Constraints* on word learning give young children an edge in figuring out the meanings of words from the vast array of possibilities.

KEY THEME
Child's Active Role

One way that the child acquires word meanings is by a process called **fast-mapping,** in which the context in which the child hears words spoken provides the key to their meanings. Often the child's initial comprehension of a word is an incomplete guess, but a fuller understanding of its meaning follows from successive encounters with it in other contexts (Carey, 1978). Upon hearing the word *eggbeater* while watching someone unload various implements from the dishwasher, the child may think it is some kind of cooking tool; hearing the word again as someone uses a specific object to stir a bowl of eggs refines the meaning of the word in the child's mind. Children are often able to derive the meanings of words quickly, even when the exposure is brief, if the context in which they hear those words is meaningful (Rice & Woodsmall, 1988).

fast-mapping   Deriving meanings of words from the contexts in which they are spoken.

Young children also tend to assume that new words label unfamiliar objects, a phenomenon called the **mutual exclusivity bias** (Littschwager & Markman, 1994; Markman, 1987, 1990). Researchers have been able to demonstrate that children tend to treat new words as labels for new objects rather than as synonyms for words they already know. For example, Ellen Markman and Gwyn Wachtel (1988) showed three-year-olds pairs of objects; in each set, one object was familiar and the other was unfamiliar (for example, a banana and a pair of tongs). When children were told, "Show me the *x*" where *x* was a nonsense syllable, they tended to select the unfamiliar objects. The mutual exclusivity bias emerges at about age three and is evident even in deaf children who use American Sign Language (Lederberg, Prezbindowski, & Spencer, 2000).

Other biases in word learning include the child's assumption that a new word labels an entire object, specifically its shape. Young children learning that a new object is called a *zup*, for example, apply that word to other objects similar in shape, but not in color, rigidity, or other characteristics (Graham & Poulin-Dubois, 1999; Samuelson & Smith, 2000). Children extend new words to objects that come from a similar conceptual category, too. Consider a study conducted by Ellen Markman and Jean Hutchinson (1984). Four- and five-year-olds looked at a picture as the experimenter labeled it with a nonsense syllable. For example, a cow was called a *dax*. Then two other pictures were presented, in this case a pig and milk. When asked, "Can you find another *dax*?" most children pointed to the pig, not the milk. In contrast, when children heard no label for the cow and were simply instructed to "find another one," they tended to associate the cow with milk.

Where do constraints on word learning come from? Some researchers believe they are innate and unique to word learning (e.g., Waxman & Booth, 2000). Others suggest they arise from growth in general knowledge about objects and their relationships to one another (Smith, 1995; Smith, 1999). It may also be that some word learning biases, such as the "whole object bias," are more important in the early stages of semantic development, whereas others, such as the "category bias," play a larger role in later stages (Golinkoff, Mervis, & Hirsh-Pasek, 1994). Another set of hypotheses, called the *social-pragmatic approach*, focuses on children's ability to interpret the rich cues about word meaning provided in early parent-child interactions. For example, parents of infants tend to label many objects, often in the context of joint book reading or the child's manifest interest in a particular object or person in her surroundings (Ninio & Bruner, 1978). A typical scenario goes like this: The infant turns his head, points, and maybe even coos as the family dog enters the room. The mother also turns and looks, and says "Doggie." Such interactions, in which the parent follows the child's attention and labels the target of her interest, are common between nine and eighteen months of age. Researchers have noted that these are precisely the conditions under which infants seem to remember the words that name objects. Children's vocabulary development is strongly related to the tendency of parents to label objects at which the child points (Masur, 1982).

Young language learners are also able to use more subtle social cues to figure out which objects labels map onto. Suppose an adult says, "Let's find the *gazzer*" and looks at an object, rejects it, and excitedly picks up another object without naming it. The infant assumes the second object is the *gazzer* (Tomasello, Strosberg, & Akhtar, 1996). Or suppose an adult and an infant are playing with several unfamiliar, unnamed objects; then the adult introduces a new object, saying, "Look, I see a *modi*!" without pointing to any object. Again, the infant assumes the newest object is the *modi* (Akhtar, Carpenter, & Tomasello, 1996). These studies demonstrate that infants have an impressive ability to interpret social cues in deciding how labels and objects match up. They also show that episodes of **joint attention,** those times in which child and caregiver share the same "psychological space," are important contexts for language acquisition. In fact, researchers have found that the amount of time infants spend in joint attention with their caregivers predicts their early language skills (Carpenter, Nagell, & Tomasello, 1998). According to Paul Bloom (2000), studies such as these indicate that the child is actively seeking to find out what is on the minds of the

KEY THEME
Nature/Nurture

KEY THEME
Child's Active Role

mutual exclusivity bias
Tendency for children to assume that unfamiliar words label new objects.

joint attention   Episodes in which the child shares the same "psychological space" with another individual.

Episodes of joint attention between child and caregiver are
important contexts for the acquisition of language and particularly for learning the meaning of words. Research shows
that the amount of time infants spend in joint attention
with their caregivers predicts
their early language skills.

adults with whom she is interacting—what their words refer to and what they are intending to communicate.

Even though researchers continue to debate vigorously the specifics of how word
meanings are acquired, the general consensus today is that children arrive at semantic understanding as a result of a multitude of factors (Hollich, Hirsh-Pasek, &
Golinkoff, 2000; Woodward, 2000). Constraints and social-pragmatic cues, along
with developments in memory and attention (Samuelson & Smith, 1998) and the
child's own internal motivations and efforts (Bloom & Tinker, 2001), all play important roles, with any one of these rising in importance depending on the developmental phase or the particular context.

Grammar

Around the child's second birthday, another significant achievement in language
production appears: the child becomes able to produce more than one word at a time
to express ideas, needs, and desires. At first, two-word utterances such as "Doggie go"
and "More juice" prevail, but the child soon combines greater numbers of words in
forms that loosely resemble the grammatical structure of his or her native language.
When children combine words, they are stating more than just labels for familiar
items; they are expressing relationships among objects and events in the world. Most
impressive is that most of this process is conducted with relatively little deliberate
instruction about grammar from adults. All of this represents no small feat for a
two-year-old.

● **Early Grammars: The Two-Word Stage**   At first, children's two-word utterances consist of combinations of nouns, verbs, and adjectives and omit the conjunctions, prepositions, and other modifiers that give speech its familiar flow. In addition,
young talkers use very few morphemes to mark tense or plurals. Because speech at

no bed	boot off	more car	airplane all gone
no down	light off	more cereal	Calico all gone
no fix	pants off	more cookie	Calico all done
no home	shirt off	more fish	all done milk
no mama	shoe off	more high	all done now
no more	water off	more hot	all gone juice
no pee	off bib	more juice	all gone outside
no plug		more read	all gone pacifier
no water		more sing	salt all shut
no wet		more toast	
		more walk	
		outside more	

TABLE 7.1
One Child's Early Grammar

This table shows several examples of one two-year-old's two-word speech. Frequently, one word—the pivot word— is repeated while several other words fill the other slot. The pivot word can occupy either the first or second position in the child's utterances.

Source: Adapted from Braine, 1976.

this stage usually contains only the elements essential to getting the message across, it has sometimes been described as **telegraphic speech.**

In his systematic observations of the language of three children, Martin Braine (1976) noted that speech at this stage contained a unique structure that he dubbed *pivot grammar.* The speech of the children he observed contained noticeable regularities: one word often functioned in a fixed position, and other words filled in the empty slot. For example, one child said, "More car, more cookie, more juice, more read." Table 7.1 contains several other examples of a two-year-old's early word combinations.

More recent research has confirmed that children use nouns, in particular, in these pivot-type constructions, even when the noun is a nonsense word such as *wug.* Thus, if a caregiver says, "Look! A wug!" children would say "More wug" or "Wug gone" (Tomasello et al., 1997). Children do not yet produce utterances according to a well-developed grammar, though; their constructions are probably based on the phrasings they hear as the adults around them speak (Tomasello & Brooks, 1999).

Roger Brown (1973) also studied the regularities of child speech in the two-word stage in ten different cultures. Table 7.2 summarizes some of the results. In children's verbalizations, agents consistently precede actions, as in "Mommy come" or "Daddy sit." At the same time, inanimate objects are usually not named as agents. The child rarely says, "Wall go." To avoid making this utterance, the child must know the meaning of *wall* and that walls do not move. Thus the child's semantic knowledge is related to the production of highly ordered two-word utterances.

Many experts believe that no one syntactic system defines the structure of early language for all children (Maratsos, 1983; Tager-Flusberg, 1985). Some children speak with nouns, verbs, adjectives, and sometimes adverbs, whereas others pepper their speech with pronouns and other words such as *I, it,* and *here* (Bloom, Lightbown, & Hood, 1975). Most researchers agree, however, that individual children frequently use consistent word orders and that their understanding of at least a small set of semantic relationships is related to that word order. Moreover, numerous detailed observations of children's language indicate that they never construct "wild grammars"; some utterances, such as "Big he" or "Hot it," are simply never heard (Bloom, 1990). Such observations have distinct implications for explanations of syntactic development.

As we saw with semantics, children just starting to use more complex speech are able to comprehend more information conveyed by different grammatical structures than they are able to produce. Two-year-olds, for example, demonstrate an understanding of the difference between past, present, and future tenses, even though these

KEY THEME
Individual Differences

telegraphic speech Early two-word speech that contains few modifiers, prepositions, or other connective words.

TABLE 7.2
Examples of Semantic Relations in Child Syntax

Children's word orders often reflect knowledge of semantic relationships, such as the idea that agents precede actions or that actions are followed by locations. Roger Brown believes the semantic relations shown in this table are incorporated into the syntactic constructions of children in many different cultures.

Semantic Relation	Examples
agent + action	Mommy come; Adam write
action + object	eat cookie; wash hand
agent + object	Mommy sock; Eve lunch
action + location	sit chair; go park
entity + location	lady home; baby highchair
possessor + possession	my teddy; Daddy chair
entity + attribute	block yellow; box shiny
demonstrative + entity	dat book; dis doggie

Source: Adapted from Brown, 1973.

distinctions do not typically appear in their own speech (Wagner, 2001). They also show that they understand the different meanings conveyed by transitive versus intransitive verbs (those with and without objects, respectively). In one study, twenty-five-month-old children saw a video of a duck bending a bunny over as both animals made arm circles. The experimenter said either, "The duck is blicking the bunny" or "The duck and the bunny are blicking," constructions that are more complex syntactically than the child's own spontaneous utterances. Then children saw two screens, one that portrayed bending and one that portrayed arm-circling. When asked to "Find blicking!" children who had heard the term as a transitive verb looked at bending, and those who had heard the term as an intransitive verb looked at arm-circling (Naigles, 1990). What cues are children using to make this correct distinction? Two-year-olds can detect the difference between transitive and intransitive verbs when subject and object are represented by nouns and also when they are made more ambiguous in the form of pronouns, as in "She pilks her back and forth" versus "She pilks back and forth." These results suggest that information denoted by the number of arguments or relationships expressed in the sentence helps children decipher its meaning (Fisher, 2002).

● **Later Syntactic Development**   At age two-and-a-half, children's speech often exceeds two words in length and includes many more of the modifiers and connective words that enrich the quality of speech. Adjectives, pronouns, and prepositions are added to the child's repertoire (Valian, 1986). Between ages two and five, the child's speech also includes increasingly sophisticated grammatical structures. *Morphemes,* such as -s, -ed, and -ing, are added to words to signal plurals or verb tense, and more articles and conjunctions are incorporated into routine utterances. Also, the child comes to use negatives, questions, and passives correctly.

Several other sophisticated forms of speaking emerge after age two, one of which is the use of negatives. In her examination of language acquisition in four children, Lois Bloom (1991) found a predictable sequence in the use of negatives. Initially, children use the negative to express the *nonexistence* of objects, as in "no pocket," said as the child searches for a pocket in her mother's skirt. In the second stage, children use the negative as they *reject* objects or events. For example, one of Bloom's participants said "no sock" as she pulled her sock off her foot. Finally, negatives are used to express *denial,* such as when the child states "No dirty" in response to his mother's comment about his dirty sock. This sequence has also been observed cross-culturally, among Chinese children learning to speak Cantonese (Tam & Stokes, 2001). Young children form negatives not just by putting the negative marker at the beginning of an utterance but also by embedding it deep within a statement, as in "My sweetie's no gone" (de Villiers & de Villiers, 1979).

Questions too are formed in a fairly consistent developmental sequence, although not all children display the pattern we are about to describe (Maratsos, 1983). Children's earliest questions do not contain inverted word order but consist instead of an affirmative sentence or a declarative preceded by a *wh-* word (*who, what, why, when, where*), with a rising intonation at the end of the statement ("Mommy is tired?"). Subsequently, children form questions by inverting word order for affirmative questions ("Where will you go?") but not negative ones ("Why you can't do it?"). Finally, by age four, children form questions for both positive and negative instances as adults do (Klima & Bellugi, 1966).

One of the more difficult linguistic constructions for children to understand is the passive voice, as in "The car was hit by the truck." Children typically begin to comprehend the meaning of a passive construction by the later preschool years, but they may not use this grammatical form spontaneously and correctly until several years later. Prior to age four, children are also limited in their ability to generate sentences using subject-verb-object (the transitive) with novel verbs they have just learned, as in "He's meeking the ball" (Tomasello & Brooks, 1998). Michael Tomasello maintains that when two- and three-year-olds do use more complex syntactic constructions such as the passive and transitive voices, they are initially imitating what adults say. Only later in the preschool and early school years do they have a deeper appreciation for the forms that grammatical constructions can take (Brooks & Tomasello, 1999; Tomasello, 2000).

One particularly interesting phenomenon of the preschool and early school years is the child's tendency to use **overregularizations,** the application of grammatical rules to words that require exceptions to those rules. From time to time, for example, young children use words such as *goed* or *runned* to express past tense even if they previously used the correct forms, *went* and *ran*. Perhaps children make these mistakes because they forget the exception to the general rule for forming a tense (Marcus, 1996). Whatever the reason, these constructions suggest that the child is learning the general rules for forming past tense, plurals, and other grammatical forms (Marcus et al., 1992).

How exactly do children master the rules of syntax? Some clues may come from the phonology or sounds of language. Is the word *record* a noun or a verb, for example? The answer depends on which syllable is stressed; if the first, the word is a noun; if the second, it is a verb. Children may pick up cues from stress, the number of syllables in a word, or other tips from the sounds of language to help them classify words as nouns, verbs, or other grammatical categories (Kelly, 1992). Other cues about syntax may come from the meanings of words. According to the **semantic bootstrapping hypothesis,** for example, when children learn that a certain animal is called a *dog,* they also notice that it is a thing (noun) and, later in development, that it is an agent (subject) or a recipient (object) of action (Pinker, 1984, 1987). Noticing that adults use certain patterns of speech and understanding their contents may help, too. For example, when young children hear adults say, "Look! The dog's hurling the chair. See? He's hurling it," the pronouns in the pattern "He's [verb] -ing it!" may help children understand the unfamiliar verb *hurling* and its use with a subject and object in a transitive sentence. In other words, children's knowledge of semantics influences their mastery of grammar (Childers & Tomasello, 2001).

Pragmatics

Just as important as semantic and syntactic rules are cultural requirements or customs pertaining to the proper use of speech in a social context. Is the child speaking with an elder or a peer? Is the context formal or informal? How does the speaker express politeness? Each situation suggests some unique characteristics of speech, a tone of voice, a formal or more casual syntactic structure, and the choice of specific words. In the context of playing with a best friend, saying "Gimme that" might be perfectly appropriate; when speaking with the first-grade teacher, saying "Could I please have that toy?" will probably produce a more favorable reaction. These examples demonstrate the child's grasp of pragmatics.

overregularization Inappropriate application of syntactic rules to words and grammatical forms that show exceptions.

semantic bootstrapping hypothesis Idea that children derive information about syntax from the meanings of words.

● Acquiring Social Conventions in Speech   When do children first understand that different situations call for different forms of speech? When Jean Gleason and Rivka Perlmann (1985) asked two- to five-year-olds and their parents to play "store," they observed that at age three some children modified their speech depending on the role they were playing. For example, one three-and-a-half-year-old boy who was the "customer" pointed to a fake milk bottle and said, "I want . . . I would like milk." His revision showed an understanding that an element of politeness is required of a customer. Preschoolers also have some limited understanding that different listeners are typically spoken to in different ways. In a study in which four- and five-year-olds were asked to speak to dolls portraying adults, peers, or younger children, the participants used more imperatives with dolls representing children and fewer with dolls representing adults and peers (James, 1978).

The child's facility with social forms of politeness increases with age. Researchers in one study instructed two- to six-year-olds to *ask* or *tell* another person to give them a puzzle piece. Older children were rated by adults as being more polite than the younger children, particularly when they were asking for the puzzle piece. Usually, older children included such words as *please* in their requests of another person (Bock & Hornsby, 1981).

Parents undoubtedly play a significant role in at least some aspects of the acquisition of pragmatics, especially because they deliberately train their children to speak politely. Esther Greif and Jean Gleason (1980) observed the reactions of parents and children after children had received a gift from a laboratory assistant. If the child did not say "thank you" spontaneously (and most of the preschoolers in the sample did not), the parent typically prompted the child with "What do you say?" or "Say thank you." Parents also serve as models for politeness routines; most parents in the study greeted the laboratory assistant upon entry and said goodbye when the assistant departed. In cultures such as Japan, in which politeness is a highly valued social behavior, children begin to show elements of polite language as early as age one year (Nakumura, 2001), probably because parents model and reinforce these verbal forms.

Incorporating social conventions into language often involves learning subtle nuances in behaviors, the correct words, vocal intonations, gestures, or facial expressions that accompany speech in different contexts. Children may get direct instruction on the use of verbal forms of politeness, but it is not yet clear exactly how they acquire the other behaviors that accompany socially skilled communication.

KEY THEME
Nature/Nurture

KEY THEME
Sociocultural Influence

When speaking to children younger than themselves, four- and five-year-olds often repeat their utterances and use attention-getting devices. These behaviors indicate that young children are sensitive to the requirements of the listener, an important aspect of *referential communication.* Thus, during the preschool years, children show progress in understanding the pragmatic aspects of language.

Source: Adapted from Krauss & Glucksberg, 1969.

FIGURE 7.4
An Experiment in Referential Communication

In Krauss and Gluckberg's (1969) study of referential communication, four- and five-year-olds had to describe a series of unfamiliar geometric forms (pasted on blocks) to other children who could not see them. In this illustration, for example, the speaker on the left must explain to the listener on the right which forms to place on the stacking peg. The results showed that children this age are generally ineffective in transmitting this type of information. Research in more naturalistic settings, however, demonstrates that preschoolers can engage in effective referential communication.

● **Referential Communication**   A group of experiments that has been especially useful in providing information on children's awareness of themselves and others as effective communicators centers on **referential communication,** situations that require the child to either talk about a topic specified by the experimenter or evaluate the effectiveness of a message describing some sequence of events. Researchers note whether the child's message is sufficient to communicate his or her intent or, alternatively, whether the child is able to detect ambiguous or uninformative components in the messages heard.

In a classic study of referential communication, Robert Krauss and Sam Glucksberg (1969) asked four- and five-year-olds to describe a series of unfamiliar geometric forms to another child who could not see them (see Figure 7.4). The speaker had to provide the listener with enough information to duplicate an array the speaker was constructing. The results showed that children this age often rely on personal descriptions of the stimuli (e.g., "It looks like Daddy's shirt"), messages that are not at all helpful to the listener. Thus young children's ability to understand the requirements of the listener and to adjust their speech accordingly is limited when they are describing unfamiliar items and when the interaction is not face to face.

On the other hand, observations of children in more natural interactions with one another suggest that well before they enter school, children appreciate at least some of the requirements of the listener and can modify their speech to make their communication effective. In a study of the communication skills of preschool-age children, Marilyn Shatz and Rochel Gelman (1973) asked four-year-olds to describe a toy to either an adult or a two-year-old listener. When the children spoke to the younger child, they shortened their utterances, used simple constructions, repeated utterances, and employed more attention-getting devices than when they spoke to the adult. Other researchers have also observed that even two-year-olds use techniques to make sure their messages get across during the normal interactions that occur in a nursery school. Children point, seek eye contact with listeners, and use verbal attention-getters such as "hey" to ensure that listeners hear what they have to say (Wellman & Lempers, 1977). In addition, when a listener somehow indicates that he has misunderstood or says "What?" two- and three-year-olds attempt to make their communication more effective. They may repeat their statement or restate the utterance with a better choice of words, a change in a verb form, or some other linguistic correction (Ferrier, Dunham, & Dunham, 2000; Levy, 1999; Shwe & Markman, 1997).

referential communication
Communication in situations that require the speaker to describe an object to a listener or to evaluate the effectiveness of a message.

Children ages seven to thirteen show wide individual differences in the ability to interact effectively with others (Anderson, Clark, & Mullen, 1994). The mature use of language involves the ability to understand the demands of the situation, be sensitive to the needs of the listener, and employ subtle nuances in speech that are compatible with the situation. The child's failure to acquire the social skills that are a part of effective communication can have broad consequences for the qualities of relationships she or he establishes with parents, teachers, and peers, among others.

KEY THEME
Interaction Among Domains

Metalinguistic Awareness

During the period of most rapid language learning, from about eighteen months through age five, children may lack a full understanding of what it means for a sentence to be grammatical or how to gauge their linguistic competencies, even when their speech is syntactically correct and effective in delivering a communication. The ability to reflect abstractly on the properties of language and to conceptualize the self as a more or less proficient user of this communication tool is called **metalinguistic awareness.** By most accounts, the child does not begin to think about language in this way until at least the early school years. However, there are some indicators that a rudimentary ability begins sometime before that.

● **Reflecting on Properties of Language**   One of the first studies to explore children's ideas about the function of grammar was conducted by Lila Gleitman and her colleagues (Gleitman, Gleitman, & Shipley, 1972). The investigators had mothers read grammatically correct and incorrect passages to their two-, five-, and eight-year-old children. After each sentence, an experimenter said "Good" at the end of an acceptable passage, such as "Bring me the ball," or "Silly" at the end of an unacceptable one, such as "Box the open." When the children were given the opportunity to judge sentences themselves, even the youngest children were generally able to discriminate between correct and incorrect versions. They were not able, however, to correct improper constructions or to explain the nature of the syntactic problem until age five.

Not until age six or seven do most children appreciate that words are different from the concepts to which they are linked. For example, four-year-olds frequently believe *train* is a long word because its referent is long (Berthoud-Papandropoulou, 1978). Some changes in metalinguistic understanding are undoubtedly linked to advances in cognition, particularly the development of more flexible and abstract thought.

● **Humor and Metaphor**   One visible way in which children demonstrate their metalinguistic awareness is through language play: intentionally mislabeling objects, creating funny words, telling jokes or riddles, or using words in a figurative sense. The earliest signs of humor have been documented shortly after the child begins speaking. Researcher Carolyn Mervis noted that her son Ari, at age 15 months, called a hummingbird a "duck" (a word he had previously used correctly) and then looked at his mother and laughed (Johnson & Mervis, 1997). However, the ways in which children comprehend and produce humorous verbalizations undergo clear developmental changes from the preschool to later school years. Three- to five-year-olds frequently experiment with the sounds of words, altering phonemes to create humorous facsimiles (for example, *watermelon* becomes *fatermelon*) (McGhee, 1979). By the early school years, the basis of children's humor expands to include riddles or jokes based on semantic ambiguities, as in the following:

> *Question*: How can hunters in the woods find their lost dogs?
> *Answer*: By putting their ears to a tree and listening to the bark.

metalinguistic awareness
Ability to reflect on language as a communication tool and on the self as a user of language.

Still later—as every parent who has ever had to listen to a seemingly endless string of riddles and jokes from a school-age child can testify—children begin to understand and be fascinated by jokes and riddles that require them to discern syntactic ambiguities (Hirsch-Pasek, Gleitman, & Gleitman, 1978), as in the following:

Question: Where would you go to see a man-eating shark?
Answer: A seafood restaurant.

Thus children's appreciation of humor mirrors their increasingly sophisticated knowledge of the various features of language, beginning with its fundamental sounds and culminating with the complexities of syntactic and semantic rules.

Similarly, children's understanding of **metaphor,** figurative language in which a term that typically describes one object or event is applied to another context (for example, calling a shadow a "piece of the night" or skywriting a "scar in the sky"), undergoes developmental change. Even preschoolers show a rudimentary ability to understand and produce figurative language, especially when it refers to perceptual similarities between two objects (Gottfried, 1997). A four-year-old understands expressions such as "A string is like a snake," for example (Winner, 1979). In later childhood and adolescence, children understand and even prefer metaphors grounded in conceptual relationships, such as "The volcano is a very angry man" (Silberstein et al., 1982).

The development of metalinguistic skills necessarily follows the acquisition of phonological, semantic, and syntactic knowledge (the sequence of which is described in the Language Development chronology). After all, the ability to reflect on and even play with the properties of language demands that a person first possess a basic understanding of those properties. In addition, metalinguistic skill is probably tied to advances in thinking skills in general. Just how children move from concrete to abstract thinking and come to reflect on their thought processes are topics to which we will return in the next chapter, when we discuss the development of cognition.

> **KEY THEME**
> **Interaction Among Domains**

FOR YOUR REVIEW

- What are four different kinds of skills that children master in the course of language development?

- What kinds of phonological skills and preferences have researchers observed among infants? Among toddlers and preschoolers?

- What kinds of processing deficits do language-impaired children display?

- What are some of the features of infants' early vocalizations? What do they suggest about the roles of nature and nurture in language development?

- How do young children use gestures as tools for communication?

- What are the important features of children's language during the one-word stage?

- What are some of the individual and cultural variations in language acquisition that have been observed by researchers?

- What are the two main sets of hypotheses concerning how children derive the meanings of words? Identify research findings that provide support for each position.

- What are the major grammatical accomplishments of children in the two-word stage of language acquisition? What syntactic accomplishments follow the two-word stage?

- What aspects of pragmatics do children acquire in the preschool years?

- What are some examples of children's metalinguistic awareness?

> **metaphor** Figurative language in which a term is transferred from the object it customarily designates to describe an object or event in another context.

CHRONOLOGY: *Language Development*

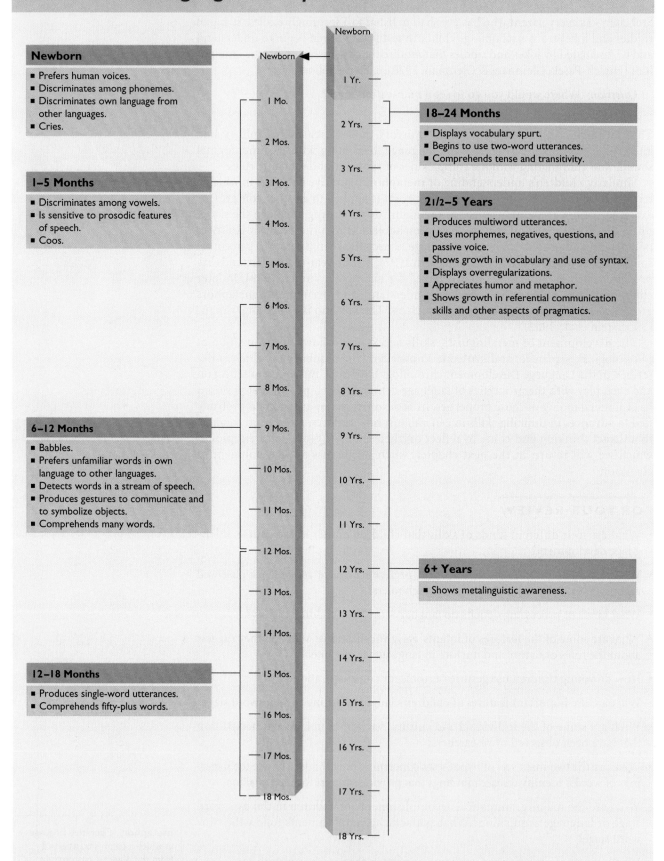

Newborn

- Prefers human voices.
- Discriminates among phonemes.
- Discriminates own language from other languages.
- Cries.

1–5 Months

- Discriminates among vowels.
- Is sensitive to prosodic features of speech.
- Coos.

6–12 Months

- Babbles.
- Prefers unfamiliar words in own language to other languages.
- Detects words in a stream of speech.
- Produces gestures to communicate and to symbolize objects.
- Comprehends many words.

12–18 Months

- Produces single-word utterances.
- Comprehends fifty-plus words.

18–24 Months

- Displays vocabulary spurt.
- Begins to use two-word utterances.
- Comprehends tense and transitivity.

2 1/2–5 Years

- Produces multiword utterances.
- Uses morphemes, negatives, questions, and passive voice.
- Shows growth in vocabulary and use of syntax.
- Displays overregularizations.
- Appreciates humor and metaphor.
- Shows growth in referential communication skills and other aspects of pragmatics.

6+ Years

- Shows metalinguistic awareness.

Newborn · 1 Mo. · 2 Mos. · 3 Mos. · 4 Mos. · 5 Mos. · 6 Mos. · 7 Mos. · 8 Mos. · 9 Mos. · 10 Mos. · 11 Mos. · 12 Mos. · 13 Mos. · 14 Mos. · 15 Mos. · 16 Mos. · 17 Mos. · 18 Mos.

Newborn · 1 Yr. · 2 Yrs. · 3 Yrs. · 4 Yrs. · 5 Yrs. · 6 Yrs. · 7 Yrs. · 8 Yrs. · 9 Yrs. · 10 Yrs. · 11 Yrs. · 12 Yrs. · 13 Yrs. · 14 Yrs. · 15 Yrs. · 16 Yrs. · 17 Yrs. · 18 Yrs.

This chart describes the sequence of language development based on the findings of research. Children often show individual differences in the exact ages at which they display the various developmental achievements outlined here.

Explaining Language Acquisition

W hen you consider the sequence of language acquisition we have just described, three points are especially noteworthy. First, language development proceeds in an orderly fashion. Although individuals may vary in the ages at which they attain language milestones or in the precise form of those achievements, children do not acquire language in a haphazard fashion. Second, children learn language rapidly and with seemingly little effort. With the exception of those with some serious physical or psychological problem, all children learn to speak within only a few years, despite the diverse range of skills required. Third, children produce *generative* language; that is, they do not merely duplicate what others say but create novel and unique expressions of their own. Any theoretical explanation of language must account for these remarkable achievements. Although we have already alluded to some possibilities in describing language development, it is time to more closely examine several major theoretical positions.

There are two fundamental questions that divide the various camps. First, to what extent are the child's language skills based on innate capabilities? Although most developmental researchers staunchly insist that nature and nurture interact, some posit a fairly substantial role for innate factors, whereas others emphasize the role of experience. Second, are the processes that children use to learn language unique to human speech, or are they the result of more general capabilities for processing information? Some experts believe that language skills are modular packages of skills dedicated to language processing. Others maintain that the attention, memory, and problem-solving skills that children apply to a wide array of thinking problems are used in the service of language acquisition as well. We should not be surprised if each of the following theories makes some contribution to our full understanding of language development. On some issues, though, there are still debates remaining to be settled.

The Role of Biology

The human brain contains several areas associated with the understanding and production of language. As we saw in the chapter titled "Brain, Motor Skill, and Physical Development," the right and left hemispheres of the brain have specialized functions, a phenomenon called *lateralization*. The primary regions that control language processing in most people are found in the left hemisphere. A major question arising from knowledge of the brain's involvement in language is the extent to which the milestones of language acquisition are controlled by physiological maturation of brain structures and, more specifically, by lateralization.

● **The Brain and Language** *Neuropsychological studies* reveal that several portions of the temporal, prefrontal, and visual areas of the brain are involved in language processing (Neville et al., 2001). However, studies of individuals who have suffered brain damage due to stroke, traumatic injury, or illness have pinpointed two specific regions in the left hemisphere that play a special role in the ability to use language. The first is **Broca's area,** located in the left frontal region near the motor cortex (see Figure 7.5). Patients who have damage in this region evidence **expressive aphasia,** or the inability to speak fluently, although their comprehension abilities remain intact. The second region, **Wernicke's area,** is in the temporal region of the left hemisphere, close to the areas of the brain responsible for auditory processing. Damage to Wernicke's area results in **receptive aphasia,** in which speech seems fluent—at least on the surface—but contains nonsense or incomprehensible words; the ability to understand the speech of others is also impaired. An important finding is that children are more likely than adults to recover language functions following injury to the left hemisphere (Annett, 1973; Basser, 1962), an illustration of the brain's greater *plasticity* during childhood.

KEY THEME
Nature/Nurture

Broca's area Portion of the cerebral cortex that controls expressive language.

expressive aphasia Loss of the ability to speak fluently.

Wernicke's area Portion of the cerebral cortex that controls language comprehension.

receptive aphasia Loss of the ability to comprehend speech.

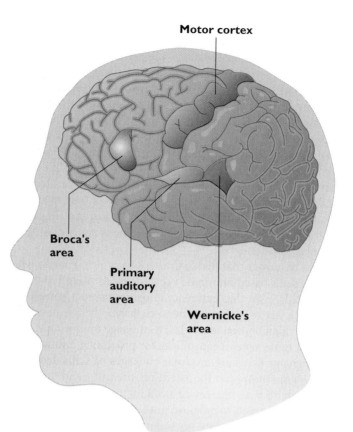

FIGURE 7.5
The Two Portions of the Left Cortex of the Brain Responsible for Language Processing

Broca's area governs the production of speech, and Wernicke's area is responsible for the comprehension of speech. Damage to the former produces expressive aphasia, whereas damage to the latter leads to receptive aphasia.

Recent advances in the ability to record electrical activity and blood flow in the brain have yielded further information on the brain's involvement in language. Before young children begin speaking, brain wave activity as they listen to words they comprehend is distributed across many regions of the brain. Once they start speaking, brain waves become more focused in the left hemisphere (Mills, Coffey-Corina, & Neville, 1993, 1994, 1997). In addition, children for whom fMRI data (see the chapter titled "Brain, Motor Skill, and Physical Development) indicate left hemisphere damage at sixteen to twenty-four months of age show delayed language acquisition at age four years (Chilosi et al., 2001). Studies such as these suggest that some (but not all) language processing is localized in the left hemisphere shortly after the first year. By the time children reach age seven years, patterns of brain activation indicate adultlike lateralization of language in the left hemisphere (Lee et al., 1999). Even deaf individuals learning sign language show brain activity in the left hemisphere similar to that of hearing individuals (Corina et al., 1999; McGuire et al., 1997).

Several other features of language acquisition suggest a strong biological component. Like motor milestones, language milestones are attained in a predictable sequence, regardless of the environment in which the child grows up (except for a few rare cases of extreme environmental deprivation). In addition, all languages share such features as phonology, semantics, and grammar, elements that Erik Lenneberg (1967) and others believed derive from the biologically determined capabilities of human beings. Indeed, children do seem to be driven to learn language, even in the absence of linguistic stimulation. One group of researchers studied a group of congenitally deaf preschool-age children who had not been taught sign language because parents were led to believe it would impede their ability to learn oral communication. None of them had learned to speak yet. Even so, the children had developed a unique gestural system of communication that followed the same sequence used by hearing children, that is, a one-symbol stage, followed by a two-symbol stage, and so forth (Feldman, Goldin-Meadow, & Gleitman, 1978). For these children, language literally "dripped" out of their fingers.

● **Critical Periods and Language Learning**   Lenneberg (1967) claimed that to speak and comprehend normally, children must acquire all language basics by adolescence, when physiological changes in the brain make language learning more difficult. He thus proposed a *critical period* for the acquisition of language. A few rare case studies of children who have been isolated from social contact or linguistic experience for protracted periods support his position. One girl, Genie, had minimal human contact from age twenty months until thirteen years due to isolation imposed by her parents. She did not speak at all. After she was found and received extensive therapy, Genie made some progress in learning words but never learned to speak normally, showing special difficulty in completely mastering the rules of syntax (Curtiss, 1977). Another nineteen-year-old boy from rural Mexico, deaf since birth but given hearing aids at age fifteen years, spoke only in one- or two-word utterances and had difficulties with verb tenses, negation, and other elements of syntax despite three years of exposure to language (Grimshaw et al., 1998). Studies of deaf people who learned American Sign Language (ASL) at different times in life provide additional support for the critical-period hypothesis. Elissa Newport (1990) found that individuals who learned ASL after age twelve showed consistent errors in the use of grammar, whereas those who were exposed to ASL from birth displayed a normal course in the development of the language.

Lenneberg's hypothesis also implies that children will find it difficult to learn a second language if they begin during or after adolescence. Here too there is evidence to support his ideas. Jacqueline Johnson and Elissa Newport (1989) assessed the ability of Chinese and Korean immigrants who learned English as a second language to judge the grammatical correctness of more than two hundred English sentences. Some participants started to learn English as early as age three, others not until age seventeen or later. The older they were before learning English, the poorer were their scores on the grammar test. Moreover, factors such as length of experience with English, amount of formal instruction in English, or identification with American culture could not account for the findings. Early exposure to a second language can also affect one's ability to pronounce it. One recent study found that when individuals merely overheard Spanish before age six, they sounded more like native speakers when they went on to study Spanish as adults, as compared with individuals without that early experience (Au et al., 2002). Newport (1990) aptly summarizes findings like these by stating that "in language . . . the child, and not the adult, appears to be especially privileged as a learner" (p. 12).

Neuropsychological findings with bilingual speakers complement the preceding findings. Participants in one recent study were Chinese adults who had acquired English as a second language at different points in their lifetimes. While participants read sentences that were either correct or violated semantic or syntactic rules, the researchers monitored their brain wave activity. Brain wave patterns suggested that the age of second-language acquisition made a special difference for syntactic tasks; if English had been acquired after age four, electrical activity in the left hemisphere showed a different pattern than if English had been acquired earlier in childhood (Weber-Fox & Neville, 1996). In another study, magnetic resonance imaging was used to study patterns of brain activation as bilingual individuals performed linguistic tasks in their native and second languages. When the second language was learned in adulthood, images of brain functioning showed that two adjoining but separate regions in Broca's area were activated (see the left panel of Figure 7.6). In contrast, when the second language was learned during infancy, overlapping regions in Broca's area showed activity (see the right panel of Figure 7.6) (Kim et al., 1997). Thus the brain seems to respond, and perhaps become organized, differently depending on when the second language was learned.

Critics point to problems in interpreting some of the research cited in support of the critical-period hypothesis. Genie, for example, may have suffered serious cognitive, physiological, and emotional deficits because of her prolonged isolation from other humans, deficits that could well account for her lack of mature language. Furthermore, most studies of second-language learning, although controlling for many

KEY THEME
█ Continuity/Discontinuity

?

**WHAT DO
YOU THINK?**

?

**Should Deaf Children
Receive Cochlear
Implants?**
psychology.college.hmco.com

FIGURE 7.6 | Brain Functioning in Bilingual Individuals

These two panels show activity patterns in the brains of two bilingual individuals as they engage in linguistic tasks in their native and second languages. The panel on the left shows brain activity for a native speaker of English who learned French in adulthood. Notice that two adjacent areas show activation. The panel on the right shows brain activity for a native speaker of Turkish who learned English in infancy. Here the areas activated for each language overlap. Neuropsychological findings such as these provide support for the critical-period hypothesis of language acquisition.

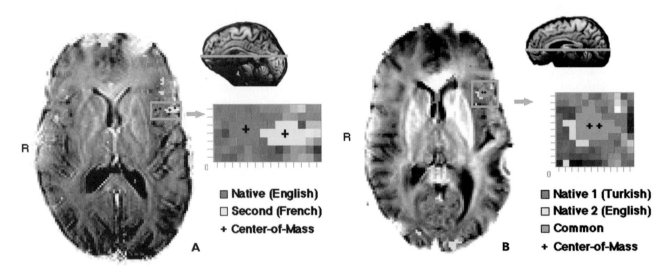

Source: Kim et al., 1997.

KEY THEME
Sociocultural Influence

relevant variables, have not taken into account how much the later-learned second language is actually used (Bruer, 2001). One recent study showed that even though they were learning English at age seventeen or later, the amount of English spoken by native Spanish speakers used in speaking to others predicted their facility with English (Birdsong & Molis, 2001). Finally, some individuals who learn a second language in adulthood acquire the phonology, vocabulary, and syntax of that language with nativelike proficiency (Birdsong & Molis, 2001; Bongaerts, 1999; Snow, 1987). Thus the window of opportunity for learning language may not be as restricted by biology as initially thought. Nonetheless, most experts would probably agree that children have a distinct advantage over adults in language learning, which makes early childhood an ideal time to acquire a second language.

Ample and convincing evidence exists for the role of biology in language acquisition—few would debate that claim. Yet a biological account, although necessary for a comprehensive understanding of language development, is not sufficient. The world's languages often differ, for example, in how they express ideas, some using patterns of intonation instead of words for a given concept (Maratsos, 1989). How would brain structures account for such cultural variations? In addition, knowing that biology is involved still does not reveal the details of many aspects of language development that we reviewed earlier in this chapter—children's early facility with nouns in one culture versus verbs in others, for example. In other words, we need to be able to explain how the language environment to which the child is exposed feeds into whatever biological language structures exist.

The Linguistic Perspective

Noam Chomsky (1980, 1986) and other linguists emphasize the structures that all languages share, those syntactic regularities that the young language learner quickly identifies in the course of everyday exposure to speech, such as when the child learning English notices that nouns representing agents precede verbs and nouns representing the objects of actions follow verbs. According to Chomsky, children possess an innate system of language categories and principles, called *universal grammar,* that predisposes them to notice the general linguistic properties of any language. As children are exposed to a specific language, a process called *parameter setting* takes place; that is, "switches" for the grammatical rules that distinguish English from Japanese or Arabic from French are set. After abstracting the general rules of language, children apply them to form their own novel and creative utterances. Language learning, say most linguists, is different from other forms of learning; there are constraints on what the child will be predisposed to learn, and language learning is governed by its own set of principles. In other words, language learning is *modular,* separate and distinct from other kinds of processing. Furthermore, many linguists believe language is a uniquely human enterprise, one that is not part of the behavioral repertoire of other species.

KEY THEME
Nature/Nurture

KEY THEME
Child's Active Role

Research evidence generally supports the idea that learning and applying rules is part of the process of learning language. Children learn syntactic rules for forming plurals, past tense, and other grammatical forms rapidly in their first five years and can even apply them to words they have never heard before. In a famous experiment, Jean Berko (1958) demonstrated this phenomenon by presenting children with several nonsense words such as *wug.* Children were able to state correctly that the plural form of *wug* is *wugs,* although they had never heard made-up words such as these. Even seven-month-old infants show evidence of being able to learn rules that can help them to learn language. In one study, infants heard several three-word sentences from an artificial language until they showed a decline in interest in them. For example, they heard constructions that had an ABA form such as "ga ti ga" and "li na li." During the test phase, though, they showed a distinct preference for sentences with an ABB construction, such as "wo fe fe." Likewise, infants who were habituated to the ABB structure preferred sentences with the ABA structure during the test phase. (Marcus et al., 1998). Moreover, linguistic theories provide a plausible explanation of the occurrence of overregularizations; these can be seen as the product of a language learner who has done too good a job, implementing rules even in cases in which exceptions exist. The drive to find structure in language is evident in another interesting way—in the development of *creole* languages, in which children in a particular cohort permanently embellish or expand the organization of the language they hear. Researchers have discovered a deaf community in Nicaragua in which individuals created their own version of sign language. With each new generation of children, the complexity of that language's structure has increased (Senghas & Coppola, 2001). The implication is that children do not simply pattern their speech after what they hear; rather, they use language in creative and highly organized ways.

Linguistic approaches help to explain just how children can master the complex, abstract rules that characterize all languages, given what some have called the "impoverished input"—the incomplete or ungrammatical utterances—that they typically hear (Lightfoot, 1982). They also help us understand how children learn language without explicit teaching of the rules of grammar or lists of vocabulary words. However, critics point out that linguistic approaches may reflect more closely the biases of adult theoreticians who attempt to describe the logical necessities of language achievements than the actual processes children use. Michael Tomasello (2000), for example, maintains that young children's use of language does not always reflect an appreciation of abstract principles of syntax. When children first learn how to use verbs, they use some in very restricted ways (e.g., "cut paper," "cut it") and others in varied types of constructions (e.g., "I draw on man," "Draw it by Santa Claus"). This lack of consistency suggests that children are not using general rules about how verbs work to produce their utterances.

What about the linguists' claim that language is uniquely human? In the past several decades, numerous attempts have been made to train members of the ape family to use language, all with some apparent success (Gardner & Gardner, 1971; Premack, 1971; Rumbaugh, Gill, & von Glasersfeld, 1973), although many early studies were criticized on methodological grounds (Terrace et al., 1979). Nevertheless, in one

SEE FOR YOURSELF
psychology.college.hmco.com
Ape Language

well-controlled study, an ape named Kanzi was raised from infancy with exposure to human speech similar to that provided to a young girl named Alia. When Kanzi was eight years old and Alia was two, they were tested on their ability to comprehend an assortment of novel sentences, such as "Take the potato outdoors." On many of the sentences, ape and child performed equally well (Savage-Rumbaugh et al., 1993). Scientists have also identified areas in the left hemisphere of the chimpanzee brain that seem to correspond to Broca's area and Wernicke's area in humans (Cantalupo & Hopkins, 2001; Gannon et al., 1998). However, compare the ages of Kanzi and Alia; it took many more years to bring the ape to the two-year-old child's level of mastery. Furthermore, although apes may be able to use visual props or sign language to form two-word communications, they rarely generate more complex grammatical structures. Perhaps most important, when observed in their natural habitats, apes do not point to or show objects to other apes. That is, although they do use highly patterned signals to communicate with one another, they do not use signs or gestures in referential or symbolic ways (Tomasello, 1998). Perhaps their limitation is a cognitive rather than a linguistic one, so questions about the modularity of language skills in humans cannot be answered from these observations. Even so, apes are evidently limited in their ability to use language despite intensive efforts to teach them.

Learning and Cognition

B. F. Skinner (1957) and other behaviorists regarded language as a behavior like any other, whose appearance and development could be accounted for by the basic principles of learning. Learning theorists believe productive language is initially shaped through the selective reinforcement of the child's earliest vocalizations. At first, utterances that even remotely resemble the child's native language are rewarded by caregivers with smiles, hugs, or an enthusiastic "Good!", whereas other, random sounds are ignored or discouraged. Gradually, parents and others expect the child's verbalizations to conform more closely to the phonological and syntactic structure of their language before they will reward her. Imitation also plays a significant role, according to learning theorists. As parents and other more experienced users of language label objects for children and speak in syntactically correct sentences, they provide models of competent and mature language use for young language learners. Children do, after all, learn the phonology, syntax, and conversational rules of the culture into which they are born.

Traditional learning theory plays a lesser role in current explanations of language development than it did a few decades ago. As an alternative way to capture how general knowledge acquisition might account for language, some theorists emphasize changes in the child's cognitive, or thinking, processes. Elizabeth Bates found that abilities such as imitation, tool use, and the complex manipulation of objects predict language attainments (Bates, 1979). Alison Gopnik and Andrew Meltzoff (1986) have identified still other skills that seem to emerge just before certain language accomplishments. For example, children who can find a hidden object after it has been moved from one location to another begin within a few weeks to use words such as *gone* to signify disappearance. Similarly, they begin to use words representing success and failure (for example, *there* and *uh-oh*) after learning to solve a complex means-ends task, such as using a stick to obtain an object. Gopnik and Meltzoff (1987, 1992) also noted that children who are able to sort groups of toys into two distinct categories, such as dolls and cars or boxes and balls, have more words in their vocabulary. According to these researchers, children develop linguistic labels consistent with cognitive problems that interest them at a given stage of development. In addition, it may be no accident that children's first words tend to be nouns such as *dog* and not *animal* or *collie*. Learning to organize objects at this intermediate level seems to be easier for young children than using either broader or more specific categories (Mervis, 1984; Mervis & Crisafi, 1982; Rosch et al., 1976), and the child's language reflects this cognitive preference.

KEY THEME
Nature/Nurture

KEY THEME
Interaction Among Domains

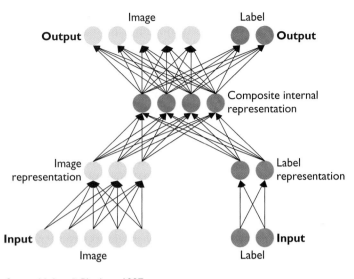

Source: Nobre & Plunkett, 1997.

FIGURE 7.7

A Connectionist Model of Vocabulary Acquisition

Connectionist models emphasize the formation of elaborate networks of associations between incoming stimuli (images and labels, in this case) and internal representations, as well as associations of internal representations with outputs (e.g., saying a word). Connectionist models have been successful in simulating many aspects of language acquisition, including vocabulary development and syntax acquisition, suggesting that general cognitive processes may underlie the child's language achievements.

Recent studies are also beginning to specify how memory capabilities are involved in language acquisition. For example, at eight months of age, infants show a remarkable ability to remember particular words from stories they had heard two weeks earlier (Jusczyk & Hohne, 1997). This is precisely the age at which infants begin to show an increase in their comprehension of words spoken by others. Among older children, short-term memory skills, such as the ability to repeat a string of digits, are related to the ease with which children learn the sound patterns of new words (Gathercole et al., 1997).

Finally, infants have been shown to be capable of extracting information about the probability that one sound will follow another in a stream of speech, a phenomenon called *statistical learning*. In one experiment, researchers exposed eight-month-olds to an unbroken stream of speech, such as *tibudopabikudaropigolatupabikuti*, for two minutes. In this example, every instance of *pa* was followed by *bi*. On the other hand, *pi* was followed by *go* only one-third of the time. When later presented with *pabiku* versus *pigola*, infants showed a clear attentional preference for *pigola*, suggesting that they were sensitive to the likelihood that one sound follows another (Saffran, Aslin, & Newport, 1996). This process may be an important part of infants' ability to detect words as they listen to ongoing streams of natural speech (Saffran, 2001).

Some researchers now argue that language acquisition is less modular and rule-based than originally thought. These theorists maintain that many apparently uniquely linguistic phenomena actually have their roots in broader cognitive processing abilities such as the ones we have just described. One contemporary approach that emphasizes the role of general learning processes includes *connectionist models* of language acquisition. Connectionist models describe language development in terms of networks of associations that are organized in interconnected layers, much like the associations that form among neurons (see Figure 7.7 for one example). Repeated experiences with the linguistic environment are responsible for forming and strengthening associations between stimuli and the network of associations, among items within the network, and between the network and the individual's output or response (Klahr & MacWhinney, 1998; Plunkett, 1995). So far, connectionist models have done a good job of simulating some aspects of children's language acquisition, such as vocabulary and syntactic development (MacWhinney, 1998; Nobre & Plunkett, 1997; Plunkett & Marchman, 1996).

KEY THEME
Nature/Nurture

The Social Interaction Perspective

Many researchers of child language hold as a central tenet that language is a social activity, one that arises from the desire to communicate with others and that is nurtured

KEY THEME
Interaction Among Domains

KEY THEME
Nature/Nurture

in social interactive contexts. Though these researchers acknowledge the biological and innate predispositions of the young human organism to learn language, they emphasize the role that experiences with more mature, expert speakers play in fostering linguistic skill. Children, they say, need models whose speech does not exceed their processing abilities. Many qualities of parental speech directed at children are well suited to the child's emerging receptive and productive skills, providing a *scaffolding* or framework from which the child can learn.

As we saw earlier in this chapter, parents have a unique way of talking to their young children. Most parents present a scaled-down version of spoken language as they interact with their young offspring, a version that contains simple, well-formed sentences and is punctuated by exaggerated intonation, high pitch, and clear pauses between segments of speech (Newport, 1977). Caregivers describe concrete events taking place in the present and often refer to objects with diminutives such as *kitty* or *doggie*. **Motherese,** or **parentese,** as this form of communication is called, also includes repetitions of what the child has said, as well as many questions. Questions in particular serve to facilitate the occurrence of **turn taking,** the alternating vocalization by parent and child. Some questions are also used as **turnabouts,** elements of conversation that explicitly request a response from the child, as in "You like that, don't you?" or "What did you say?" Also, parents often follow the child's verbalization with a **recast,** repeating what the child has said but correcting any errors. **Expansions**—more elaborate verbal forms—may be added, too. Thus, when a child says, "Ball fall," his mother might reply, "Yes, the red ball [expansion] fell [recast]." Recasts and expansions provide children with cues that their verbalization needs improvement and a model for how to improve. Children, in fact, often imitate and retain their parent's recasts (Farrar, 1992; Saxton, 1997).

When caregivers talk to infants and young children, they employ simple sentences, exaggerate their intonation, and speak with a high pitch. Infants are especially responsive to these qualities of "motherese," which seem to provide a helpful framework for learning language.

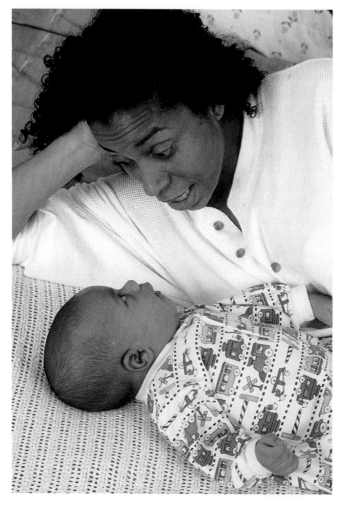

motherese/parentese Simple, repetitive, high-pitched speech of caregivers to young children; includes many questions.

turn taking Alternating vocalization by parent and child.

turnabout Element of conversation that requests a response from the child.

recast Repetition of a child's utterance along with grammatical corrections.

expansion Repetition of a child's utterance along with more complex forms.

The following exchange between one seven-month-old, Ann, and her mother illustrates several of these concepts (Snow, 1977):

MOTHER	ANN
Ghhhhh ghhhhh ghhhhh ghhhhh	
Grrrrr grrrrr grrrrr grrrrr	
	(protest cry)
Oh, you don't feel like it, do you?	
	aaaaa aaaaa aaaaa
No, I wasn't making that noise.	
I wasn't going *aaaaa aaaaa*.	
	aaaaa aaaaa
Yes, that's right.	

Notable in the exchange is the mother's pattern of waiting for her child's vocalization to end before she begins her response, an example of turn taking. If the child had spoken actual words, a real conversation would have taken place. The mother also repeated the child's vowel-like sound but embedded it in more elaborate speech. By the time the infant reaches eighteen months, the mother's tendency to expand or explain her utterances becomes even more pronounced, as in the following brief episode (Snow, 1977):

MOTHER	ANN
	(blowing noises)
That's a bit rude.	
	Mouth.
Mouth, that's right.	
	Face.
Face, yes, mouth is in your face.	
What else have you got in your face?	
	Face. (closing eyes)
You're making a face, aren't you?	

According to Snow (1984), two general principles operate during caregiver-child interactions. First, parents generally interpret their infants' behaviors as attempts to communicate, even when that interpretation may not seem warranted to an objective observer. Second, children actively seek relationships among objects, events, and people in their world and the vocal behaviors of their caregivers. The result of these two tendencies is that parents are motivated to converse with their children and children have a mechanism for learning language.

Parentese may serve a number of functions in the child's growing competence with language. First, this form of speech may assist the child's acquisition of word meaning. Mothers tend to say the names for objects more loudly than other words in their speech to infants, and often they place the object label in the last position in their sentence, as in "Do you see the *rattle*?" (Messer, 1981). Mothers also tend to highlight new words by raising their pitch as they say them (Fernald & Mazzie, 1991) or moving an object as they label it (Gogate, Bahrick, & Watson, 2000). Second, the intonations of motherese may facilitate the child's acquisition of syntax. One study demonstrated that seven- to ten-month-olds oriented more frequently to motherese that contained pauses at clausal boundaries (e.g., "Cinderella lived in a great big house/but it was sort of dark . . .") than to motherese that was interrupted within clauses (e.g., "Cinderella lived in a great big house but it was/sort of dark . . ."). Infants did not show these differential preferences in response to regular adult speech (Kemler Nelson et al., 1989). Infants show a similar sensitivity to even smaller grammatical units, the phrases and even the words within a sentence, but only when sentences are spoken in motherese (Jusczyk et al., 1992; Myers et al., 1996; Nazzi et al., 2000). The prosodic features of motherese may thus assist the infant in identifying syntactically relevant elements of language. Finally, exposure to motherese may provide lessons in conversational turn taking, one aspect of pragmatics that governs speech in interactions with others.

Are there any other effects of interactions with caregivers on child language development? Researchers have observed that the more mothers talk with their children, the more words their children acquire (Huttenlocher et al., 1991; Olson, Bayles, & Bates, 1986). It is not just how much mothers talk to their children that makes a difference, however; *how* they talk also matters. When mothers use many directives to control their children's behaviors and are generally intrusive, language development is slowed. When mothers (or teachers) use questions, expansions, and conversational turn taking to elicit language from children or follow the children's vocalizations with a response, language development proceeds more rapidly (Hoff-Ginsberg, 1986; Nelson, 1973; Tamis-LeMonda, Bornstein, & Baumwell, 2001; Valdez-Menchaca & Whitehurst, 1992). Among older children, about age five, exposure to sophisticated words (e.g., *cholesterol, gulping,*) at mealtimes and play times predicts vocabulary development in the early school years (Weizman & Snow, 2001).

As important as motherese may seem, it is not a universal phenomenon. Although features of motherese have been observed in many languages and even among deaf mothers signing to their deaf infants (Gleason & Weintraub, 1978; Masataka, 1996), mothers in some cultures adopt a distinctly different style in talking with their infants. Consider the following two examples of maternal speech, one American and the other Japanese, as observed by Anne Fernald and Hiromi Morikawa (1993):

> *American mother*: That's a car. See the car? You like it? It's got nice wheels.
> *Japanese mother*: Here! It's a vroom vroom. I give it to you. Now you give it to me. Give me. Yes! Thank you.

KEY THEME
Sociocultural Influence

Whereas American mothers tend to name objects and focus on the exchange of information, Japanese mothers rarely name objects, using them instead to engage their infants in social routines. Perhaps it is not surprising, then, that American infants use substantially more nouns in their speech at nineteen months of age. Similarly, other researchers have noted that Japanese mothers ask fewer questions but use more nonsense sounds and songs than American mothers (Bornstein et al., 1992; Toda, Fogel, & Kawai, 1990). Thus mothers may have different agendas as they speak with their children, and their style of speech may subtly shape the children's utterances.

Another example of variation in the use of motherese can be found in the Kaluli society of Papua New Guinea. In this culture, talking with others is a highly valued social skill, yet few adult verbalizations are directed to infants. Infants may be called by their names, but until they pass their first year, little else is said to them. When mothers do begin to talk to their babies, their speech contains few of the elements of motherese. Turn taking, repetitions, and elaborations are absent; usually mothers simply make directive statements that require no response from the child. Nevertheless, Kaluli children become proficient users of their language within developmental norms (Schieffelin & Ochs, 1983). Joint linguistic interactions between caregiver and child thus may not be essential to the emergence of language.

Linguistic exchanges with other interaction partners—fathers, siblings, peers, and others—may uniquely influence the child's eventual level of linguistic skill. For example, when fifteen-month-olds "converse" with their fathers, they experience more communication breakdowns than when they talk with their mothers. Fathers more often request clarification, change the topic, or do not acknowledge the child's utterance after they fail to understand what she or he said (Tomasello, Conti-Ramsden, & Ewert, 1990). Thus, in communicating with fathers, children are challenged to make adjustments to maintain the interaction. Children also learn language by overhearing it on educational television (Wright et al., 2001), in conversations between mothers and older siblings (Ashima-Takane, Goodz, & Derevensky, 1996), or even between two strangers (Akhtar, Jipson, & Callanan, 2001). Children are normally exposed to a rich and varied range of linguistic stimuli from different sources in the environment; many theorists believe this fact ensures that children will learn the details of linguistic structures that may not be present in the verbalizations of a single conversation partner, such as the mother (Gleitman, Newport, & Gleitman, 1984; Wexler, 1982).

RESEARCH APPLIED TO PARENTING

Reading to Children

*I*t was several months later before Devon began to say a few different words. But after that his vocabulary expanded rapidly, and he started stringing words together. Jennifer marveled at the progress Devon was making as she prepared her son's bed and eavesdropped on Devon and his father in their evening ritual. This was Bill's favorite time of day. Every night, just before Devon was put to bed, Bill would pull him up in his lap and take a picture book from the shelf. At first, he just pointed to and named things in the book, often encouraging Devon to participate by asking, "What's that?" As Devon's vocabulary increased, Bill elaborated on his answers and asked other questions: "What does the doggie say?" "Woof-woof!" squealed Devon, enjoying the ritual perhaps every bit as much, maybe even more, than his father.

The research findings discussed earlier show that how and how often parents speak to children can influence language development. One context in which mothers' speech tends to be particularly lavish is during book reading. Erika Hoff-Ginsberg (1991) found that when mothers and two-year-olds were reading books, mothers showed the greatest diversity in the vocabulary they used, the greatest complexity of syntax, and the highest rate of replies to their children compared with other contexts, such as mealtime or toy play. Other research has shown that the amount of time parents spent reading stories to their twenty-four-month-olds predicted children's language ability up to two years later (Crain-Thoreson & Dale, 1992). As a result of such findings, many child development experts encourage parents to read to their young children.

Grover Whitehurst and his colleagues have developed a program called *dialogic reading* to stimulate language development in preschool children at risk for academic failure, but the general principles can be applied by any parent interested in promoting his or her child's language development. Here is some advice the researchers have developed for parents of two- and three-year-olds:

1. *Ask* what *questions (such as "What is this?") to stimulate the child to speak.* Avoid yes/no questions that require only brief answers.
2. *Follow the child's answer with a question.* Ask, for example, what shape or color an object has or what it is used for.
3. *Repeat the child's utterance in the form of a recast.* For example, follow "Cow" with "Yes, that's right, it's a cow." This gives the child feedback that she is correct.

Researchers have identified several techniques that parents can use to promote language development in the context of reading to their children. Among them are asking "what" questions, following the child's answer with another question, and using recasts. Making the experience positive and fun for the child is also important.

4. *If the child doesn't have an answer, provide a model and ask him to repeat.*   For example, say "That's a bottle. Can you say *bottle*?"

5. *Be generous with praise and encouragement.*   Make comments such as "Good talking" or "Nice job."

6. *Be responsive to the child's interests.*   When the child expresses an interest in a picture or part of the story, follow her interest with encouragement to talk.

7. *Have fun.*   Do not pressure the child; take turns with the child, and even make the activity a game.

Dialogic reading has been shown to increase language skills in children from different social classes when used by daycare teachers as well as parents (Arnold & Whitehurst, 1994). Of course, children learn language skills in many other contexts, such as mealtime conversations (Snow, 1993). Thus children whose parents do not read to them often are not necessarily fated to have poor language skills (Scarborough & Dobrich, 1993). Nonetheless, reading to children, perhaps especially when they are infants, leads to desirable outcomes in language development (DeBaryshe, 1993).

FOR YOUR REVIEW

- What have neuropsychological studies revealed about the involvement of the brain in language acquisition?

- What evidence supports a critical period hypothesis of language acquisition? What evidence is inconsistent with a critical period hypothesis?

- How does a linguistic perspective account for language acquisition? What research findings are consistent with a linguistic perspective?

- How does learning theory account for the development of language?

- Which cognitive skills have been suggested as correlates of language acquisition?

- What are the unique features of a social interaction perspective on language acquisition? What research findings are consistent with a social interaction explanation? What parental activities can promote children's language skills?

The Functions of Language

Aside from its obvious usefulness as a social communication tool, what functions does language serve? Does the human propensity to learn and employ language affect other aspects of functioning, specifically, mental processes, the regulation of behavior, and socialization? At the very least, language enriches the human experience by providing a useful vehicle for enhancing cognition and behavior; it also exerts powerful influences on other areas of human activity. In this section, we will examine briefly some broad effects of language on the domains of cognition, behavior, and socialization.

Language and Cognition

KEY THEME
Interaction Among Domains

The relationship between language and cognition has been a controversial subject for many years, especially with respect to which activity precedes the other. Some psychologists and anthropologists have argued that language shapes thinking, whereas others contend that cognition paves the way for language. Most now acknowledge that the link between language and cognition is bidirectional and that each domain

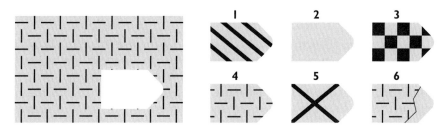

Source: Raven, 1962.

FIGURE 7.8
Cognitive Achievements of Bilingual and Monolingual Children

Bilingual children outperform monolingual children on nonverbal tests such as the Raven Progressive Matrices, which requires participants to select the segment that correctly fits into the larger pattern. Bilingual children generally seem to be more analytical than monolingual children in their approach to various problem-solving tasks.

influences the other. We have already pointed out some ways cognition might influence language. How might language have a powerful influence on the child's cognitive attainments?

● **Language, Memory, and Classification** If you ask a child to perform a cognitive task, such as remembering a list of words or grouping a set of similar objects, you will notice that he will often spontaneously use language to aid his performance. The best examples of this behavior come from research findings on developmental changes in children's memory. There are distinct differences in the way preschool and school-age children approach the task of remembering. Older children are far more likely than younger children to employ deliberate strategies for remembering, strategies that typically involve the use of verbal skills. In one study, John Flavell and his colleagues (Flavell, Beach, & Chinsky, 1966) asked kindergarteners and second- and fifth-graders to watch as the experimenter pointed to three pictures in an array of seven. The children's job was to point to the same three pictures either immediately or after a delay of fifteen seconds. During the delay, the experimenters noticed that most children in the oldest group made spontaneous lip movements, suggesting that they were verbally repeating the items to be recalled. Moreover, the superior performance of the oldest group on the memory test was attributed to their spontaneous repetition of the names of the items. The use of verbal labels seemed to bridge the gap between the time the items were first seen and the time they were to be recalled.

Language can also influence how children categorize related groups of objects. Stan Kuczaj and his colleagues showed children twelve unfamiliar objects that could be grouped into three sets (Kuczaj, Borys, & Jones, 1989). Children who were taught the names of one category member from each group were more successful in sorting the objects than children who were not given labels. Language provides children with cues that classes of stimuli differ from one another, and these cues can influence how children form conceptual groups. If some four-legged animals are called *dogs* and others are called *cats,* the different linguistic labels will highlight for the child that the features of these two groups differ.

● **Bilingualism and Cognition** One of the more interesting ways in which the influence of language on thought has been studied has been to compare, on a variety of tasks, the performances of bilingual children equally fluent in two languages with monolinguals fluent in only one. Bilingual children have been characterized as more analytic and flexible in their approach to different types of thought problems. For example, bilingual children perform better than monolinguals on certain nonverbal problems, such as the Raven Progressive Matrices (see Figure 7.8) (Hakuta & Diaz, 1985). Bilingual children have also been found to display greater metalinguistic awareness than monolingual children, even those who are chronologically older. When given sentences such as "Why is the cat barking so loudly?" bilingual children were more likely than monolingual children to ignore conflicting semantic information and state that the sentences were grammatically correct (Bialystok, 1986). Finally, bilingual children perform better than monolingual children on tasks that require selective attention. If instructed to sort a deck of cards based on one dimension, say color, and then re-sort the deck on the basis of a different dimension, say shape, bilingual children are better able to inhibit responses from the first task (Bialystok, 2001).

One hypothesis to explain their superior performance is that bilingual children are forced to think more abstractly and analytically because they have had experience with analyzing the structure and detail of not just one language but two. A second possibility is that they are generally more verbally oriented in their thinking and have a greater tendency to produce verbalizations that enhance their performance even in nonverbal tasks. Finally, they may have more control over cognitive processing because they are constantly having to inhibit one language when they speak (Bialystok, 1999, 2001; Diaz & Klingler, 1991). Whatever the mechanism, these studies demonstrate that speaking a second language affects cognitive processes, often in a favorable way.

CONTROVERSY: THINKING IT OVER

How Should Bilingual Education Programs Be Structured?

Estimates are that almost 10 percent of school-age children in the United States have limited English proficiency (National Clearinghouse for English Language Acquisition, 2002), a characteristic that could understandably hinder success in school. Given the ease with which young children learn language and the apparent connection between bilingualism and certain cognitive processes, are there any implications for how children learning English as a second language should be taught?

What Is the Controversy?

Philosophies of teaching language-minority children have varied. Some believe that children should receive most of their education in their primary language, whether it is Spanish, Cambodian, or French, and make the transition to English only when they are ready. At the other extreme are the advocates of immersion, the idea that children should be totally surrounded by the second language, learning it in the same way the young child learns the first language. Immersion has been in the public spotlight as states such as California and Massachusetts have mandated this approach to teaching children with limited English proficiency. Many bilingual programs, in reality, fall in between these two extremes, such that English is taught as an extra subject by a bilingual teacher while children take their core academic subjects in their native languages.

What Are the Opposing Arguments?

Proponents of easing children into English by starting them in classes in their native languages say that this approach promotes basic language development, which in turn creates the foundation for acquiring the second language. In addition, children will develop a sense of belonging in the school, and their self-esteem will be high (Fillmore & Meyer, 1992). Advocates of immersion generally say that children will have to learn English eventually and that it is better not to delay. This view is also consistent with a belief that language learning is generally easier for younger than for older children.

What Answers Exist? What Questions Remain?

Some research findings suggest that allowing students to build their competence in their own native language assists in learning both core academic subjects and English (Bialystok, 2001; Meyer & Fienberg, 1992). On the other hand, immersion programs have been successful in Canada, Spain, and other countries (Artigal, 1991; Tucker & d'Anglejan, 1972). Unfortunately, evaluations of the effectiveness of bilingual education programs have been fraught with methodological difficulties (Willig & Ramirez, 1993). One issue is that many language-minority children come from backgrounds of poverty, the effects of which may contribute to difficulties with school (Hakuta, 1999). Another problem is that the goal of most bilingual education programs for language-minority children is not, in reality, to make them bilingual but to emphasize speaking English (Hakuta & Mostafapour, 1996). In contrast, many successful immersion programs in Europe involve teaching *both* the native language and another highly valued language (Brisk, 1998).

What does the research on the process of language development suggest about the best way to structure bilingual education programs? Aside from economic status, what other variables should future research evaluating bilingual education take into account?

Language and Self-regulation

Language takes on an increasingly important role in regulating behavior as the child develops, according to prominent Russian psychologist Lev Vygotsky. Vygotsky (1962) believed the child's initial utterances serve an interpersonal function, signaling others about the child's affective state. In the preschool years, however, speech takes on a different function. Specifically, the child's **private speech,** or overt, audible "speech-for-self," comes to guide his or her observable activities. If you have ever observed a toddler coloring and simultaneously saying something like "Now, I'll use the blue crayon. I'll make the sky blue," you have seen an example of private speech. Eventually, speech-for-self becomes interiorized; **inner speech** dictates the direction of the child's thoughts.

KEY THEME
Interaction Among Domains

How important is private speech in directing behavior? You may have noticed that you tend to talk to yourself when you are under stress or when you have a lot to do. Research has confirmed that children, like adults, use private speech when they find tasks difficult or when they make errors. In one recent study, researchers found that about 13 percent of three- and four-year-olds used private speech in some way during their spontaneous activities in preschool, but as Figure 7.9 shows, the older children were more likely to use private speech in the context of focused, goal-directed activities, such as doing a puzzle, rather than non-goal-directed activities, such as wandering around the classroom (Winsler, Carlton, & Barry, 2000).

Young children often use private speech when they are engaged in new or challenging tasks. This overt "speech-for-self" guides children's actions and eventually becomes interiorized into a form called *inner speech*. Language thus helps children to regulate their own behavior.

private speech   Children's vocalized speech to themselves that directs behavior.

inner speech   Interiorized form of private speech.

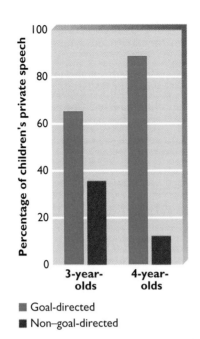

FIGURE 7.9
Private Speech in
Preschoolers

Both three- and four-year-olds use private speech in the natural context of preschool, but four-year-olds are more likely to use private speech when they are engaged in focused, goal-directed activities. Private speech is one way in which language can regulate children's behaviors.

Source: Winsler, Carleton, & Barry, 2000.

Similarly, Laura Berk (1986) noted that when first-graders were solving math problems in school, they engaged in high levels of externalized private speech to guide their problem solving. Third-graders also showed evidence of private speech, but a more internalized form—through mutterings and lip movements—as they attempted to solve math problems. When children use task-relevant private speech, their performance on a variety of tasks improves (Berk, 1992). One longitudinal study demonstrated that as children progress from overt to more internal private speech, they also show fewer distracting body movements and greater sustained attention in school (Bivens & Berk, 1990). Such studies suggest that language becomes an increasingly powerful regulator of children's behavior as they develop.

Language and Cultural Socialization

KEY THEME
Sociocultural Influence

KEY THEME
Interaction Among Domains

Still another way in which language can have a broad influence on development is by helping children discern the social roles, relationships, and values of their culture. Many languages have specific grammatical forms that are used to convey gender, age, or social power. In acquiring language, children are sensitized to the specific ways their own culture creates social order. For example, in Japanese, the word particle *zo* signifies affective intensity and a male speaker, and the particle *wa* conveys hesitancy and a female speaker. Children learning Japanese are therefore likely to associate hesitancy with females and forcefulness with males (Ochs, 1990). In many other languages, specific words have formal and informal versions, with the formal used when speaking with individuals who have more authority or power and the informal with individuals who share equal status or are related. Again, such linguistic distinctions highlight important social relationships within the cultural group.

A good example of how language can influence socialization comes from traditional Samoan culture, which emphasizes community and group accomplishments over the attainments of individuals. In Samoan speech, few verbalizations include praise or blame for individuals. Most statements concern the success or failure of the group and emphasize the life of the community. When Samoan children are exposed to verbalizations of this type, they are being socialized into the collective orientation of their culture (Ochs, 1990).

Researchers are just beginning to explore the ways in which the words and social conventions within a specific language are related to cultural values and beliefs. However, it is apparent that through language, children learn far more than simply how to communicate; they also learn about the broader belief systems of their society.

FOR YOUR REVIEW

- In what ways does language influence cognitive processing? What are the particular effects of bilingualism on cognition?

- What are the functions of private speech for the developing child?

- In what ways does language provide cues about cultural values and socialization goals?

CHAPTER RECAP

SUMMARY OF DEVELOPMENT THEMES

■ Nature/Nurture *What roles do nature and nurture play in language development?*

There are several indicators that for humans, nature sets early predispositions to develop language: the infant's sensitivity to phonemes and prosody, the child's tendency to progress through language milestones in a predictable sequence, and the devotion to language functions of certain portions of the brain are just some examples. Nurture, in the form of the child's experiences with more mature language users, interacts with these biological tendencies to lead the child to acquire the phonology, semantics, and grammar of a particular language and to learn the social conventions that accompany spoken language in his or her culture.

■ Sociocultural Influence *How does the sociocultural context influence language development?*

Cultures vary in the extent to which caregivers use motherese with their growing children, a factor that may influence the rate of language acquisition. The specific elements of phonology, semantics, grammar, and pragmatics also vary across languages. Often the content and structure of a specific language provide cues to the culture's social order and values.

■ Child's Active Role *How does the child play an active role in the process of language development?*

Even in the earliest stages of language acquisition, children often influence which objects or people caregivers will label when they look at or point to specific items. Although children do benefit by merely listening to language use in the environment, they also actively use context to derive the meanings of words. In addition, their rapid acquisition of the rules of grammar suggest that children abstract the regularities in language to generate their own verbalizations.

■ Continuous/Discontinuous *Is language development continuous or discontinuous?*

Descriptions of early language production often seem stagelike because children appear to spend distinct periods of time in a babbling stage, a one-word stage, and so on. However, there are continuities among different events in language acquisition. For example, the sounds in infant babbling are related to the language the child will eventually speak.

■ Individual Differences *How prominent are individual differences in language development?*

Children frequently show striking differences in the rate at which they achieve language milestones. They may differ, for example, in the age at which they say their first words or when (even if) they show a vocabulary spurt. Some may develop a referential style of speech, whereas others may speak expressively. Nonetheless, there is a pronounced regularity in the sequence of language attainments among children, regardless of the culture in which they grow up.

■ Interaction Among Domains *How does language development interact with development in other domains?*

In early childhood, the ability to produce spoken language parallels the physiological maturation of the vocal apparatus and the central nervous system. The emergence of language also coincides with the onset of certain cognitive skills, such as conceptual understanding. Language is nurtured largely within the context of social interactions with caregivers. Thus physical, cognitive, and social factors affect the process of language acquisition. By the same token, language has a clear effect on other domains. Children's use of language enhances their ability to remember, form concepts, and, as studies of bilingual individuals suggest, may even promote analytic thinking and mental flexibility. In addition, children's ability to be successful communicators can have important repercussions for social relationships with parents, peers, and others.

▇ Summary of Topics

The Course of Language Acquisition

■ Language is a multifaceted skill with many overlapping dimensions. To learn language, children must master *phonology*, the basic sound units of a language; *semantics*, or the meanings of words; *grammar*, the rules pertaining to the structure of language (including *syntax* and *morphology*); and *pragmatics*, the rules for using language within a social context.

Phonology

■ Newborns show a tendency to respond to language as a unique auditory stimulus.

■ Young infants detect phonemes and vowel sounds from a variety of languages but show a decline in this ability by the second half of the first year.

■ Infants show an early sensitivity to *prosody*, patterns of intonation, stress, and rhythm that mothers around the world include in their speech to young children. Children's sensitivity to rhythmic properties of language helps them to differentiate their native language from others and possibly to detect the presence of specific words in a stream of speech.

■ Infants typically *coo* at six to eight weeks, *babble* at three to six months, and produce syllable-like *canonical babbling* at seven months. Biology seems to guide the emergence of these different types of vocalizations in universal sequence, although the environment also plays a role in shaping the acoustic properties of children's early speech.

■ As children mature, the range of sounds they make expands, although certain pronunciation errors may persist until the elementary school years.

Semantics

■ Many children start producing communicative behaviors by gesturing. They might use a *protodeclarative communication* to call attention to an object or a *protoimperative communication* to make a request. Sometimes children's gestures symbolize objects; later in development, gestures may accompany verbalization in order to elaborate a point.

■ By one year of age, most children are speaking one-word utterances, usually *nominals*, or nouns. At about eighteen months or so, children may show a particularly rapid phase of growth in word acquisition called the *vocabulary spurt*. At the earlier stages of word learning, children may restrict their use of some words to particular contexts (*underextension*) or apply them to too broad a category (*overextension*).

■ Children comprehend word meanings much earlier than they are able to produce words. Their *receptive language* exceeds their *productive language*. Labels for verbs are harder for children to understand than labels for nouns.

■ Some children's early speech is *referential*; it includes mostly nominals. Other children are *expressive*; they use words with social functions. Fairly substantial individual differences also occur for the rate of language acquisition. Culture, too, can have an influence on the types of words children produce in the early stages of acquisition.

■ Some researchers believe that children learn the meanings of words by relying on constraints such as *fast-mapping*, the *mutual exclusivity bias*, the whole object bias, and the category bias. In contrast, the social-pragmatic view emphasizes children's ability to interpret the rich social cues about word meaning provided in early parent-child interactions, such as episodes of *joint attention*.

Grammar

■ Two-year-olds begin to use two-word utterances, sometimes called *telegraphic speech* because it contains few modifiers, prepositions, and connective words. They also use few morphemes to mark tense or plurals. Although no single syntactic system defines the structure of language at this stage, acquisition for individual children is orderly and may rely on semantic knowledge.

■ Children show that they understand more complex syntactic structures, such as transitive versus intransitive constructions, than they can produce.

■ As children progress through the preschool years, they add morphemes, modifiers, prepositions, pronouns, and connective words. They begin to use negatives, questions, and eventually, the passive voice. One interesting type of error they sometimes make is called *overregularization*, the application of grammatical rules to words that are exceptions.

■ Children seem to derive some information about syntax through phonology and *semantic bootstrapping*.

Pragmatics

■ Children begin to show that different situations call for different forms of speech around age three. They adjust their speech, depending on the listener, and begin to use polite forms, probably because parents instruct them to.

■ Although preschool children's *referential communication* skills are limited in some tasks, two-and three-year-olds show sensitivity to the needs of listeners by making adjustments to their speech to ensure successful communication.

Metalinguistic Awareness

■ Children begin to show *metalinguistic awareness* in the preschool and early school years. They begin to use word play to create humor and show an understanding of *metaphor*.

Explaining Language Acquisition

■ Two important questions are raised by theories of language development: the extent to which biology and experience are responsible for the sequence of acquisition and the degree to which language skills are either modular or based on broader cognitive skills.

The Role of Biology

- Specific brain structures are associated with *expressive aphasia* (*Broca's area*) and *receptive aphasia* (*Wernicke's area*). Children sustaining damage to these areas show a greater ability to recover language functions than adults do.

- Neuropsychological studies suggest that language functions begin to become lateralized shortly after the first year and look adultlike by age seven. The predictability of language milestones and the universality of certain language structures also support the role of biology.

- Research on later language learners and neuropsychological evidence support a critical period for language learning, although perhaps not a strong version of it.

The Linguistic Perspective

- Linguistic theorists emphasize the child's abstraction of general grammatical principles from the stream of speech. They tend to take a nativist stance and believe that language skills are modular.

- Data showing that children are able to learn rules, that they creolize language, and that animals are limited in their ability to learn language are consistent with linguistic theory, but some aspects of children's verb learning are not.

Learning and Cognition

- Learning theorists have emphasized the roles of shaping, reinforcement, and imitation in language acquisition.

- The cognitive perspective adds that certain advances in thinking, such as classification skills, memory, and statistical learning, are involved in language attainment.

- Connectionism is a recent approach that emphasizes networks of associations.

The Social Interaction Perspective

- Social-interaction theorists highlight the characteristics of caregiver-child speech, called *motherese* or *parentese*, that facilitate development. Specific techniques include *turn taking*, *turnabouts*, *recasts*, and *expansions*.

- The amount and content of maternal speech to children predicts the rate and form of children's language acquisition.

The Functions of Language

Language and Cognition

- Language has been shown to influence specific cognitive processes such as memory and classification.

- Bilingual children are more flexible and analytic in certain cognitive tasks. They also perform better than monolingual children on tasks that require response inhibition.

Language and Self-regulation

- Children often use *private speech*, and later, *inner speech*, to direct their behavior. They tend to use private speech when tasks are difficult or goal directed.

Language and Cultural Socialization

- Language can be a vehicle to transmit to children the specific values and expectations of their native culture.

Cognition: Piaget and Vygotsky

Key Themes in Cognition

- **Nature/Nurture** What roles do nature and nurture play in cognitive development?

- **Sociocultural Influence** How does the sociocultural context influence cognitive development?

- **Child's Active Role** How does the child play an active role in the process of cognitive development?

- **Continuity/Discontinuity** Is cognitive development continuous or discontinuous?

- **Individual Differences** How prominent are individual differences in cognitive development?

- **Interaction Among Domains** How does cognitive development interact with development in other domains?

"Jeremy! Let's play hide-and-seek!" shouted Tommy to his three-year-old brother. "See. You hide. I'll count to ten. Then I'll find you. It's fun, Jeremy. Let's try it." Tommy took special pride in being a big brother; with seven years between them, he often baby-sat while his parents did chores around the house, and he especially enjoyed teaching Jeremy new things like this favorite childhood game of his.

"Okay," smiled Jeremy. "I hide." The toddler stepped carefully over the family's Labrador retriever and plunked himself squarely behind the couch, or so he thought since he could not see his older brother. In the distance, he heard Tommy say, "Ten! Ready or not, here I come!" and held his breath. In barely a few seconds, though, Tommy was right in front of him, grinning widely. "Silly Jeremy," chuckled Tommy, "You can't let your legs stick out like that from behind the couch. I can see you!"

One of the most active research areas of child development focuses on **cognition**—those thought processes and mental activities, including attention, memory, concept formation, and problem solving, that are evident from early infancy onward. As the scene above suggests, younger children seem to think differently than older children. They do not understand, for example, that other individuals may have different information about the world than they themselves do. In what other ways do children of different ages think differently? Do young children remember as well as older children do? Do older children solve problems the same way younger children do? These are the types of questions that psychologists interested in cognitive development ask.

Virtually every aspect of a child's development has some connection to emerging cognitive capabilities. We saw in the chapter titled "Language" that a child's use of language is linked to his or her growing conceptual development. Similarly, as we will discuss in later chapters, the child's increasing knowledge of effective social interaction can influence the quality of relations with peers. You should find numerous examples throughout this text of how changes in thinking influence and interact with other areas of the child's development.

In this chapter, we focus our discussion of cognitive development on two of the most important theoretical positions framing research on children's thought: those of Jean Piaget and Lev Vygotsky. Jean Piaget (1896–1980) was a Swiss psychologist whose childhood interest in biology evolved into a general curiosity about how individuals acquire knowledge. Piaget saw himself as a *genetic epistomologist,* a scholar who was interested in the origins of knowledge from a developmental perspective. His desire to understand children's intellectual growth was probably sparked by his experiences working in the laboratories of Alfred Binet, in which the first intelligence test was developed. From the early 1920s, when his first books were published, to 1980, when he died, Piaget authored more than seventy books and scores of articles describing various aspects of children's thinking. Lev Vygotsky (1896–1934), too,

cognition Processes involved in thinking and mental activity, such as attention, memory, and problem solving.

271

began his work in the early part of the twentieth century. Growing up in Russia at a time of great social and political upheaval—the Marxist revolution—and no doubt influenced by the vigorous intellectual debates of the times, Vygotsky authored several landmark essays outlining his ideas on language, thought, and the sociocultural environment. His untimely death at the age of 38 cut short a rich and promising academic career.

We begin by summarizing Piaget's major ideas and evaluating his contributions to our understanding of cognitive development. We also discuss several topics explored by contemporary researchers influenced or provoked by Piaget's writings, including the development of children's understanding of physical objects, their ability to classify objects, and their understanding of concepts such as number, space, and psychological states. Finally, we review the major features of Vygotsky's sociocultural theory of development, along with research that his work has stimulated.

Piaget's Theory of Cognitive Development

As we saw in the chapter titled "Themes and Theories," one of the most important beliefs espoused by Piaget is that children actively construct their knowledge of the world, incorporating new information into existing knowledge structures, or *schemes,* through *assimilation.* As a result, schemes are modified or expanded through the process of *accommodation.* For example, the young infant may attempt to grasp a new, round squeeze toy, relying on a pre-existing scheme for grasping objects. As a consequence, that scheme becomes altered to include information about grasping round objects. The outcome is greater *equilibrium* or balance among the pieces of knowledge that make up the child's understanding. Thus what a child can understand or mentally grasp at any given point in time is heavily influenced by what the child already knows or understands. At the same time, the child's schemes are constantly transformed, as equilibrium is continually disrupted by the never-ending flow of information from the surrounding world.

Piaget maintained that thought processes become reorganized into distinct stages at several points in development. Though the schemes in early stages lay the foundation for later knowledge structures, their reorganization is so thorough that schemes in one stage bear little resemblance to those in other stages. According to Piaget, the child progresses through the *sensorimotor, preoperational, concrete operational,* and *formal operational* stages, reflecting major transitions in thought in which early, action-based schemes evolve into symbolic, then logical, and finally abstract mental structures.

Stages of Development

Piaget maintained that all children progress through the stages of cognitive development in an invariable sequence in which no stage is skipped. In addition, each stage contains a period of formation and a period of attainment. When the child begins a new stage, his schemes are somewhat unstable and loosely organized. By the end of the stage, his schemes are well formed and well organized. Even though Piaget provided age norms for the acquisition of each stage, he believed that because cognitive development is the result of maturational factors working in concert with environmental experiences, some children may reach a stage more quickly or more slowly, depending on the opportunities for learning their environment provided. Ultimately, though, the evolution of thought shows a universal regularity, according to Piaget.

● **The Sensorimotor Stage (Birth to Two Years)**   The most striking characteristic of human thinking during the **sensorimotor stage** is its solid basis in action. Each time the child reaches for an object, sucks on a nipple, or crawls along the floor, she is obtaining varied feedback about her body and its relationship to the environment that becomes part of her internal schemes. At first, the infant's movements are reflexive, not deliberate or planned. As the child passes through each of the six sub-

KEY THEME
Child's Active Role

KEY THEME
Continuity/Discontinuity

KEY THEME
Nature/Nurture

sensorimotor stage   In Piagetian theory, the first stage of cognitive development, from birth to approximately two years of age, in which thought is based primarily on action.

TABLE 8.1	The Six Substages of Piaget's Sensorimotor Stage	
Substage	**Major Features**	**Object Concept**
Reflexive Activity (Birth–1 month)	Formation and modification of early schemes based on reflexes such as sucking, looking, and grasping	No attempt to locate objects that have disappeared
Primary Circular Reactions (1–4 months)	Repetition of behaviors that produce interesting results centered on own body (e.g., Lucienne accidentally, then repeatedly, touches her quilt)	No attempt to locate objects that have disappeared
Secondary Circular Reactions (4–8 months)	Repetition of behaviors that produce interesting results in the external world (e.g., Lucienne accidentally, then repeatedly, kicks the dolls in her bassinet)	Search for objects that have dropped from view or are partially hidden
Coordination of Secondary Schemes (8–12 months)	Combination of actions to achieve a goal (e.g., Lucienne pulls a doll to make her bassinet hood sway)	Search for completely hidden objects
Tertiary Circular Reactions (12–18 months)	Experimentation with different actions to achieve the same goal or observe the outcomes (e.g., Laurent drops a case of soap, then a piece of bread)	Ability to follow visible displacements of an object
Invention of New Means Through Mental Combinations (18–24 months)	Thinking through of potential solutions to problems and imitation of absent models (e.g., Jacqueline imitates her playmate's tantrum)	Ability to follow invisible displacements of an object

stages of the sensorimotor period, outlined in Table 8.1, her actions become increasingly goal directed and aimed at solving problems. Moreover, she is able to distinguish self from environment and learns about the properties of objects and how they are related to one another.

A significant accomplishment of the sensorimotor stage is the infant's progression toward **means-ends behavior,** the deliberate use of an action to accomplish some goal. During the early substages of sensorimotor development, the infant often initiates actions accidentally rather than purposefully. When Piaget's daughter Lucienne was almost four months old, she was observed to shake her bassinet

> *by moving her legs violently (bending and unbending them, etc.), which makes the cloth dolls swing from the hood. Lucienne looks at them, smiling, and recommences at once.* (Piaget, 1952b, pp. 157–158)

Lucienne repeated her kicking to make the dolls shake in what Piaget calls a *circular reaction,* the repetition of a motor act to experience the pleasure it brings. Her first kick, however, was totally accidental. Several months afterward, when Lucienne was eight months old, Piaget placed a new doll over the hood of her bassinet. This time her behavior revealed a greater degree of intentionality:

> *She looks at it for a long time, touches it, then feels it by touching its feet, clothes, head, etc. She then ventures to grasp it, which makes the hood sway. She then pulls the doll while watching the effects of this movement.* (Piaget, 1952b, p. 256)

Throughout the first two years, the child increasingly uses actions as a means to obtain some end or goal. He also experiments with new means to reach the same goal,

means-ends behavior Deliberate behavior employed to attain a goal.

A significant attainment in infancy is the child's understanding of object permanence. Children under three to four months of age act as if a hidden or obstructed object no longer exists. By age eight months, though, children will remove a barrier to look for a hidden object.

as Piaget's son Laurent did when he successively dropped a soap case and then a piece of bread to investigate how objects fall.

A second aspect of sensorimotor development is the child's gradual separation of self from the external environment. Initially, the child derives pleasure from actions that center on her own body. At three months of age, Lucienne "strikes her quilt with her right hand; she scratches it while carefully watching what she is doing, then lets it go, grasps it again, etc." (Piaget, 1952b, p. 92). The circular reaction, in this case, was repeated because of the satisfying sensations it brought to Lucienne's hand. Weeks later, in the episode of the swinging dolls, Lucienne's kicking in the bassinet produced a gratifying result in the external environment. In general, the child becomes less centered on the self and more oriented to the external world.

A third important accomplishment of this stage is the attainment of the **object concept,** or *object permanence*. Infants who possess the object concept realize that objects continue to exist even though they are not within immediate sight or within reach to be acted on. Up to three months of age, the saying "out of sight, out of mind" characterizes the child's understanding of objects. At about four months of age, he will lift a cloth from a partially covered object or show some reaction, such as surprise or puzzlement, when an object disappears. At about eight months of age, he will search for an object that has completely disappeared, for example, when it has been covered entirely by a cloth. In the last two phases of the attainment of the object concept, he will be able to follow visible and then invisible displacements of the object. In the first instance, the twelve-month-old will follow and find a toy that has been moved from under one cloth to another, as long as the movement is performed while he is watching. In the second instance, the eighteen-month-old can find an object moved from location A to location B, even if the displacement from A to B is done while he is not looking.

The completion of the sensorimotor stage and the beginning of the next stage is signaled by the child's display of *deferred imitation,* the ability to imitate a model who is no longer present. At age sixteen months, Piaget's daughter Jacqueline was playing with a boy who suddenly had a dramatic temper tantrum. The next day, the normally well-behaved Jacqueline mimicked the little boy's behaviors with remarkable accuracy. To do so, she must have had the ability to *represent* the boy's overt behaviors in internal form and to draw on that representation hours later. This ability to represent events and objects internally marks the beginning of a major transition in thought.

object concept   Realization that objects exist even when they are not within view. Also called *object permanence.*

● **The Preoperational Stage (About Two to Seven Years)**   The key feature of the young child's thought in the **preoperational stage** is the *semiotic function,* the child's ability to use a symbol, an object, or a word to stand for something. The child can play with a cardboard tube as though it were a car or draw a picture to represent the balloons from her third birthday party. The semiotic function is a powerful cognitive ability because it permits the child to think about past and future events and to employ language. In fact, Piaget asserted that language would not be possible without this significant characteristic of thought; the child must possess the general cognitive ability to let one thing stand for another before she can use words to represent objects, events, and relationships. The semiotic function is also a prerequisite for imitation, imagery, fantasy play, and drawing, all of which the preschool child begins to manifest.

Despite this tremendous advance in thinking, preoperational thought has distinct limitations. One is that children in this stage are said to be **egocentric,** a term that describes the child's inability to separate his own perspective from those of others. Put into words, his guiding principle might be "You see what I see, you think what I think," much like Jeremy in this chapter's opening scene, who thinks he is hiding from his older brother by crouching behind a couch. Even though his legs and feet might be sticking out for all present to see, the youngster believes he is well concealed because he himself is unable to see anyone. According to Piaget, the preschooler's egocentrism has ramifications for both his social communicative behavior and his perceptual skills. Piagetian theory predicts poor referential communication skills in children under age seven years and, as we will see later in this chapter, the inability to appreciate the perspectives of others in perceptual tasks.

The second limitation of preoperational thought lies in the child's inability to solve problems flexibly and logically. The major tasks Piaget used to assess the status of the child's cognitive development are called the **conservation tasks.** These "thinking problems" generally require the child to observe some transformation in physical quantities that are initially equivalent and to reason about the impact of the transformation. Figure 8.1 shows several conservation tasks.

We can use the conservation of liquid quantity task to illustrate how the preoperational child thinks. The four- or five-year-old will usually quickly agree that two equal-size glasses of water contain the same amount of liquid. If the liquid from one glass is poured into a tall cylinder, however, the child will state that the cylinder now contains more than the glass does. According to Piaget, this error is the result of several limitations in preoperational thinking. One is **centration,** that is, focusing on one aspect of the problem—in this case, the height of the cylinder—to the exclusion of all other information, such as its narrower width, that could help to produce a correct solution. A second cognitive trait at work here is lack of **reversibility.** The preoperational child cannot mentally reverse the action of pouring from the tall cylinder to the shorter glass; if she could, she would realize that the two containers still hold the same amount of liquid that they did at the start of the problem. Third, the preoperational child tends to **focus on states** rather than on the events that occur between states. It is as though he has stored two static photographs of the two equal-size glasses, followed by static photographs of the shorter glass and the tall cylinder, rather than a video of the sequence of events. He fails to realize the connection between the two components of the conservation problem and, as a result, fails the conservation task.

● **The Concrete Operational Stage (About Seven to Eleven Years)**   Children enter the **concrete operational stage** when they begin to be able to solve the conservation tasks correctly. At first, the six- or seven-year-old may solve only a few of the simpler problems, such as conservation of length, number, or liquid quantity. Later, she will succeed on tasks that involve area or volume. Piaget called this extension of the same cognitive structures to solve increasingly difficult problems within a given stage *horizontal décalage.*

KEY THEME
Interaction Among Domains

preoperational stage   In Piagetian theory, the second stage of development, from approximately two to seven years of age, in which thought becomes symbolic in form.

egocentrism   Preoperational child's inability to separate his or her own perspective from those of others.

conservation tasks   Problems that require the child to make judgments about the equivalence of two displays; used to assess stage of cognitive development.

centration   In Piagetian theory, tendency of the child to focus on only one aspect of a problem.

reversibility   In Piagetian theory, the ability to mentally reverse or negate an action or a transformation.

focus on states   Preoperational child's tendency to treat two or more connected events as unrelated.

concrete operational stage   In Piagetian theory, the third stage of development, from approximately seven to eleven years of age, in which thought is logical when stimuli are physically present.

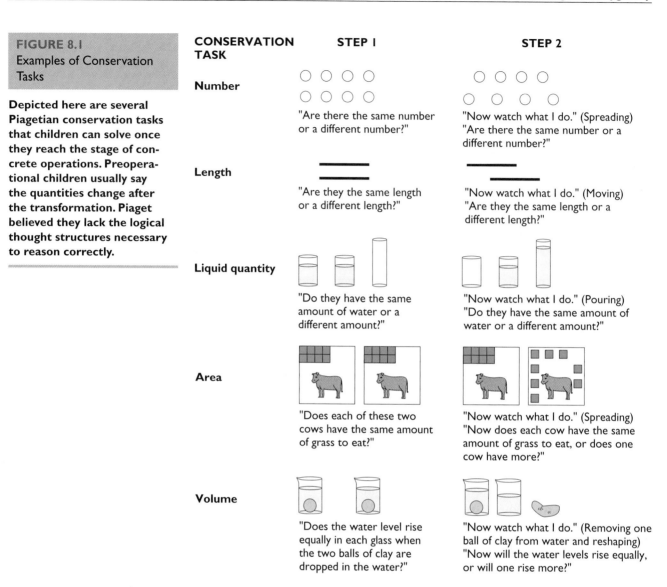

FIGURE 8.1
Examples of Conservation
Tasks

Depicted here are several
Piagetian conservation tasks
that children can solve once
they reach the stage of concrete operations. Preoperational children usually say
the quantities change after
the transformation. Piaget
believed they lack the logical
thought structures necessary
to reason correctly.

The reason for this shift is that the child is now capable of performing **operations,** mental actions such as *reversibility,* that allow him to reason about the events that have transpired. He can pour the liquid back from the cylinder to the glass "in his head" or think about the narrow width of the tall cylinder as compensating for its height. In other words, the child now thinks logically, although the physical components of the problem must still be present (if not externally in the world, then as images in the mind). The child's growing logical capabilities are also manifested in his ability to *seriate* objects, putting sticks of varied lengths into a systematic series arranged from shortest to longest, for example. Unlike the preoperational child who performs this task in a haphazard way, the concrete operational child starts with the shortest (or tallest) and compares each successive stick with those that are shorter and longer so that an orderly array results. The child's thought in this stage is also less egocentric, allowing him to understand that other individuals' perceptions, beliefs, and feelings may differ from his own. The concrete operational child is becoming a true "thinker," as long as there are specific objects or events to which he can apply his logic.

● **The Formal Operational Stage (About Eleven Years and Beyond)**   By the time the child reaches adolescence, she will most likely have moved to the final stage in Piaget's theory, the **formal operational stage.** Thinking in this stage is both logical and abstract. Problems such as "Bill is shorter than Sam but taller than Jim. Who is

operation   In Piagetian theory, a mental action such as reversibility.

formal operational stage   In Piagetian theory, the last stage of development, from approximately eleven to fifteen years of age, in which thought is abstract and hypothetical.

tallest?" can now be solved without seeing the individuals or conjuring up concrete images of them. The adolescent can also reason **hypothetically;** that is, she can generate potential solutions to problems in a thoroughly systematic fashion, much as a scientist approaches an experiment.

Piaget's pendulum problem allows us to examine the thinking of the formal operational adolescent. In this task, the person is shown an object hanging from a string and asked to determine the factor that influences the frequency of oscillation, or the rate at which the pendulum swings. The length of the string, the weight of the object, the force of the push on the object, and the height from which the object is released can all be varied. How do children in earlier Piagetian stages approach this problem? Children in the preoperational and concrete operational stages typically try various manipulations in a haphazard fashion. They might compare the effect of a long string attached to a heavy weight and a short string tied to a light weight. Or they might vary the weight of the object and force of the push but leave out the length of the string. In contrast, formal operational children are both systematic and complete in testing the potential influences on oscillation. For example, while keeping weight constant, they observe the effects of varying length, push, and height; while keeping length the same, they investigate the effects of varying weight, push, and height; and so forth. Most adolescents, Piaget observed, could correctly determine that the length of the string was the critical factor in how fast the pendulum swings (Inhelder & Piaget, 1958).

In the social realm, achieving abstract thought means the adolescent can think about the nature of society and his own future role in it. Idealism is common at this developmental stage because he understands more fully concepts such as justice, love, and liberty and thinks about possibilities rather than just realities. In some ways, the adolescent may be more of a "dreamer" or utopian than the adult because he has not yet had to confront the practical facts of living and working in the world (Inhelder & Piaget, 1958).

The contemplative nature of adolescent thought may manifest itself in two other ways, according to David Elkind (1976, 1981). First, adolescents may believe others scrutinize and evaluate them as much as they think about themselves. This belief, called the **imaginary audience,** may cause a young girl to avoid going out because she just got braces on her teeth ("Everybody will see me!") or make a teenage boy avoid answering a question in class because he is certain all his classmates will think he is "dumb." Second, adolescents may show signs of holding a **personal fable,** the belief that they are unique, that no one can fully understand them, and even that they are invulnerable. A teenage boy prohibited from going to a late-night rock concert by his parents might say, "You just don't understand how important this is to me!"

The development of formal operational thought represents the culmination of the reorganizations in thought that have taken place throughout each stage in childhood. By adolescence thought has become logical, flexible, and abstract, and its internal guiding structures are now highly organized.

Implications for Education

Piaget's theory carries some clear implications for teaching children. The first is that the individual child's current stage of development must be carefully taken into account as teachers plan lessons. For example, a seven-year-old who is in the stage of concrete operations should be given problems involving actual physical objects to observe or manipulate rather than abstract word problems or diagrams (Flavell, 1963). Similarly, a four-year-old preoperational child may have difficulty with tasks requiring the use of logic; a more fruitful strategy might be to foster the imagination and creativity that result from the recently acquired semiotic function. By encouraging drawing, pretend play, and vocal expression, teachers can capitalize on the preschooler's cognitive strengths.

A second, related implication is that what the child knows already will determine what new information she is able to absorb. Because her current cognitive structures

hypothetical reasoning Ability to systematically generate and evaluate potential solutions to a problem.

imaginary audience Individual's belief that others are examining and evaluating him or her.

personal fable Belief that one is unique and perhaps even invulnerable.

Piaget believed that active learning promotes deeper and more enduring understanding than rote memorization. One implication of this hypothesis is that educators should try to provide children with hands-on activities to promote their understanding of subjects such as mathematics and science.

KEY THEME
Child's Active Role

limit what she will be able to assimilate, it is important that the teacher be aware of the child's current state of knowledge. In addition, cognitive advances are most optimally made when new material is only slightly different from what the child already knows (Ginsburg & Opper, 1988). Thus the teacher's task is to plan lessons that are tailored to the needs of the individual child rather than to the class as a whole and to be flexible in devising instructional materials that stretch the child one step beyond what she already knows.

One of Piaget's most important statements about cognitive development is that it is the result of the *active engagement of the child*. Early sensorimotor schemes and later mental operations are all founded first on the child's physical activity and later on mental actions. Thus education too must be structured in such a way that it will promote the child's active participation. Instead of emphasizing rote learning, teachers following a Piagetian model provide children with experiments that allow them to discover scientific principles on their own. Children do not memorize numerical relationships, such as the multiplication tables, but discover them by manipulating sets of objects under the close guidance of the teacher. According to Piagetian thinking, active learning of this sort promotes deeper and more enduring understanding.

Evaluating Piaget's Theory

Piaget is widely acknowledged as being one of the most influential of all thinkers in the history of psychology and a founder of the study of cognitive development as we know it (Brainerd, 1996; Flavell, 1996). By introducing questions about *what* develops as well as *how* development occurs, Piaget went well beyond the descriptions of norms of behavior that had been the staple of the early years of research in developmental psychology. Moreover, once American psychologists learned of his ideas in the 1960s and early 1970s, they could no longer conceptualize development solely in terms of learning theory, which was a dominant psychological view at that time. Finally,

Piaget's method of closely watching the nuances of children's behaviors and listening as they explained their reasoning provided an important and inspiring lesson for developmental psychologists: that "grand questions can actually be answered by paying attention to the small details of the daily lives of our children" (Gopnik, 1996, p. 225).

The fact that Piaget's theory has stimulated so much research in developmental psychology is not surprising, given its wide-ranging scope. In sheer numbers of empirical studies generated by the writings of one person, Jean Piaget has no rival in developmental psychology. Like all good theories, Piaget's has spawned a host of debates about the fundamental nature of cognitive change. These debates are a tribute to the power of his ideas and his contribution to the scientific process.

● **How Competent Are Young Children?**   One criticism of Piaget's theory is that Piaget underestimated the abilities of infants and young children. Many researchers have found that when cognitive tasks are simplified or restructured, children display cognitive skills at much earlier ages than Piaget believed possible.

Take the object concept, for example. Piaget maintained that the first real notions about the permanence of objects do not emerge until about eight or nine months of age, when infants will search for objects that are completely covered. In an experiment more fully described in the next Examining Research Methods feature, however, Renée Baillargeon (1987a) believes she has obtained evidence that infants as young as four months of age have a rudimentary understanding of the continuing existence of objects. Even though this study has been criticized on methodological grounds, other research suggests that young infants possess a surprising degree of knowledge about objects and their properties (Bremner, 1998). For example, six-and-a-half-month-old infants will reach in the dark for an object they had earlier seen in the light. Simply reaching is a much easier sequence of motor actions than reaching for and uncovering a hidden object (Goubet & Clifton, 1998). Thus these infants apparently had some form of the object concept.

Many other studies described later in this chapter and in the chapter titled "Cognition: Information Processing" indicate that young children are not as egocentric and illogical as Piaget thought. Piaget himself was less concerned with the specific ages at which children acquire cognitive skills than with the sequence of development. However, the fact that many cognitive attainments occur earlier than he suggested challenges the notion that young children must gradually build up their knowledge of the world over time.

EXAMINING RESEARCH METHODS

Ensuring Experimental Control in Studying the Object Concept

Is it possible to demonstrate knowledge about the continuing existence of objects in very young infants? Renée Baillargeon (1987a) conducted a unique experiment in which four-month-olds behaved as if they understood that an object continued to exist even when it was concealed by a screen. Figure 8.2 shows the phases of this experiment. At first, infants observed a screen that rotated back and forth 180 degrees over repeated trials. As you might expect, they eventually showed habituation of visual fixation to this display. Next, a box was placed behind the screen. Initially, when the screen was still flat against the table, the box was visible, but as the screen rotated away from the child, it hid the box from view. In the possible-event condition, the screen stopped moving at the point where it hit the box. In the impossible-event condition, the box was surreptitiously removed and the screen passed through the space the box would have occupied. As you learned in the chapter titled "Basic Learning and Perception," infants in a habituation experiment should look longer at the novel event, in this case, the screen that rotated only 112 degrees. However, infants looked significantly longer at the impossible event, apparently drawn in by the fact that the screen was moving through the space where the object should have

● SEE FOR YOURSELF
psychology.college.hmco.com
Testing Object Concept

FIGURE 8.2

Do Infants Have an Object Concept?

In Baillargeon's experiment, infants were habituated to a screen rotating 180 degrees (A). Next, infants in the *impossible-event* condition saw the screen appearing to pass through the location of a box (B, on left), whereas infants in the possible-event condition saw the screen stop at the location of the box (C, on left). Infants in the *impossible-event* condition looked significantly longer at this event, suggesting that they were puzzled by what they saw and therefore had an object concept. The control conditions (shown at right) were included to make sure the infants were not responding to the arc of the screen's movement.

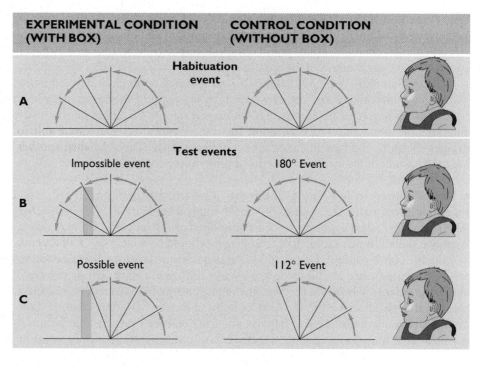

EXPERIMENTAL CONDITION (WITH BOX)   **CONTROL CONDITION (WITHOUT BOX)**

Habituation event

A

Test events

Impossible event   180° Event

B

Possible event   112° Event

C

Source: Adapted from Baillargeon, 1987a.

been. Because infants are presumed to look longer at the stimulus display that goes against their internal knowledge, this procedure is often called the *violation-of-expectation* method.

Before the researcher could conclude that infants had the object concept, however, she had to rule out alternative explanations for the results. This tactic is the hallmark of the experimental method, by which researchers try to make sure that only one variable (and not other simultaneously occurring factors) explains the results. For example, what if infants simply prefer an arc of 180 degrees compared with an arc of 112 degrees, whether there is a box or not? Baillargeon included a control group of infants who saw the original habituation event followed by each of the test events (180 and 112 degrees) but without a box. In this condition, infants did not show preferences for the 180-degree rotation, indicating that the arc of the movement did not influence infants' responses.

Are there any other explanations for the results Baillargeon obtained? As noted, the possible test event was conceptualized by the experimenter as a novel occurrence. Some researchers point out, though, that the impossible test event (the screen rotating 180 degrees apparently through the box) also contains novel elements; the presence of the box makes the event different from the original habituation event. Thus novelty, and not knowledge about objects, could account for looking at the impossible event. In addition, there are some circumstances, particularly in the early stages of processing, in which infants may show a preference for familiar, rather than novel, stimuli. Preference for the impossible event could actually be based on a preference for *familiarity*, the 180-degree rotation, as opposed to knowledge about objects (Bogartz & Shinskey, 1998; Bogartz, Shinskey, & Speaker, 1997).

As you can see from this experiment, establishing experimental control is not always easy or simple. On the surface, the original Baillargeon experiment seemed to be well designed, with the appropriate experimental controls. Researchers should always be asking themselves, though, whether any other competing variables could explain the observed data—that is, have they controlled for all the variables that could possibly be present?

● **Is Cognitive Development Stagelike?** If cognitive development proceeds in stages, children should show common features in how they think within a stage and distinctive differences in how they think across stages. One problem with Piagetian theory is that it posits more consistency in performance within a given stage than is actually found in the behavior of children. In one study, Ina Uzgiris (1968) tested children who should have been in the stage of concrete operations on conservation of quantity, weight, and volume. The same tasks were tested with different materials, such as plasticine balls, metal cubes, and plastic wires. Many children were able to conserve when one material (say, plasticine balls) was used but not when another (say, metal cubes) was employed. If conservation is indeed tied to the presence of logical thought structures, it should not matter which materials are used to conduct the conservation tests.

KEY THEME
Continuity/Discontinuity

Other researchers have noted that the correlations among various abilities predicted to co-occur within the stage of concrete operations are much lower than would be expected if development were truly stagelike (Gelman & Baillargeon, 1983). Piaget maintained, for example, that before children can conserve number they must understand the principle of class inclusion, the idea that some groups of objects are subsets within a larger set. "Dogs" are a subset of "animals," just as "five" is a set contained within "six." Yet children can conserve number by age six or seven and still not fully understand the concept of class inclusion (Brainerd, 1978a).

Many contemporary researchers now believe development shows more continuity than Piaget suggested. What seems to vary among children of different ages, say the critics, is not their cognitive skills but the degree to which the same basic skills are displayed in a wide variety of increasingly complex situations (Brainerd, 1978b).

● **Is Cognitive Development a General Process?** Piaget maintained that, for the most part, changes in mental structures are broad, sweeping reorganizations that influence thinking in multiple domains. Development, in this view, is said to be *domain-general*. However, some theorists maintain that advances in thinking occur more rapidly in some domains than others; that is, development is seen as *domain-specific* (Hirschfeld & Gelman, 1994).

One example of domain-specific processes is children's rapid acquisition of certain concepts, such as the properties of biological entities. Children seem to acquire a vast amount of information about animals, plants, and other living things at very young ages and at a particularly rapid pace (Gelman & Williams, 1998). In addition, this knowledge does not seem to "spill over" into other kinds of conceptual understanding. Children's acquisition of basic numerical concepts and their understanding of physical causality are other candidates for domain-specific knowledge. We will have more to say about each of these concepts in the next section of this chapter, "Concept Development."

● **Are There Alternative Explanations for Development?** Many studies have confirmed Piaget's general claims about the patterns of behavior children display at different ages. Without special training, for example, most children under age six or seven years fail conservation tasks, whereas older children perform them successfully. Adolescents are indeed capable of solving problems more systematically and abstractly than their younger counterparts. Yet many psychologists disagree with Piaget about the precise mechanisms that account for such patterns in the development of thinking processes.

The basic challenge to Piaget's theory centers on whether cognitive development is best understood in terms of emerging symbolic, logical, and hypothetical thought structures or whether some other explanation is more tenable. A case in point is the successful training of conservation by Rochel Gelman (1969). Gelman suggests that young children normally fail conservation tasks because they fail to attend to the correct portions of the problem, not because they lack mental operations such as reversibility. If children's attention is directed to the salient cues, such as length or number, Gelman and others argue, they will be successful in conserving. Younger children may also be less skilled at remembering than older children, forgetting elements of problems that are essential to reaching the correct solutions. Thus cognitive development may result from a change in how information is gathered, manipulated, and stored rather than from the alteration of cognitive structures themselves.

Another central Piagetian tenet is that maturation, in conjunction with experience, is responsible for the unfolding of more sophisticated thought structures. The emphasis Piaget places on maturation implies that the sequence of development is universal. Yet not all children reach the stage of formal operations, and some do not even attain the highest levels of concrete operations. Many American adults, in fact, fail to display formal operational thought (Neimark, 1979). Members of many non-Western cultures do not display formal operational thinking, especially when they have little experience with formal schooling (Dasen, 1972; Rogoff, 1981). At the same time, specific kinds of cultural experiences may accelerate the emergence of conservation and formal operational thought. Douglass Price-Williams and his colleagues examined two groups of rural Mexican children six to nine years old on standard conservation problems (Price-Williams, Gordon, & Ramirez, 1969). Half of the children came from pottery-making families, the other half from families that practiced other trades. Children who had experience in manipulating clay for pottery making were far more likely to conserve than the other children. Other research shows that adolescents today receive higher scores on tests of formal operations than adolescents did twenty and thirty years ago (Flieller, 1999). Studies such as these imply that the child's experiences in the sociocultural context may shape the nature of thought to a greater degree than Piaget acknowledged.

Neo-Piagetian Approaches

Several developmental psychologists have modified and expanded Piaget's theory to address some of the criticisms discussed here. Because their ideas build on those Piaget initially proposed, these theorists are often called *neo-Piagetians*. Like Piaget, neo-Piagetians believe children show distinct, even stagelike advances in general thinking skills, probably because of maturation. They also agree that what children know at a given time heavily influences what they will be able to learn and think about. Neo-Piagetians, though, are much more willing than Piaget was to acknowledge the role specific experiences play in shaping the child's knowledge in a given area (Flavell, 1992).

● **Fischer's Skill Theory**   Kurt Fischer, like Piaget, believes the emergence of general, broad thinking skills contributes to cognitive development (Fischer, 1980; Fischer & Farrar, 1988; Fischer & Pipp, 1984). These skills, he proposes, are organized into four stages or "tiers": reflex, sensorimotor, representational, and abstract. Unlike Piaget, though, Fischer adds that within the same individual, skills may develop more rapidly in some domains—say, numerical understanding or classifying familiar objects—than others, depending on the child's experiences. The child who is given ample access to art materials but not to math problems, for example, may show greater skill in the first area than the second.

In Fischer's theory, skills are similar to Piaget's schemes: mental structures that stem from action. In contrast to schemes, however, which are highly generalized structures, skills are more specific to particular objects and tasks. If the environment supports a variety of skills, development in all skills will proceed relatively evenly. Fischer suggests, however, that uniform access to skill development is unlikely. At any one time in development, most children show different levels of skill depending on the domain, be it numerical reasoning, spatial understanding, classification of objects, or some other. Specific skills used in limited contexts eventually become more powerful and are used in more generalized contexts (Fischer & Bidell, 1991). By emphasizing the emergence of separate skills that are heavily dependent on the specific experiences available to the child, Fischer offers a picture of development that is more continuous and gradual than that proposed by Piaget.

KEY THEME
Nature/Nurture

KEY THEME
Individual Differences

KEY THEME
Sociocultural Influence

KEY THEME
Continuity/Discontinuity

KEY THEME
Nature/Nurture

KEY THEME
Individual Differences

● **Case's Theory**   Robbie Case (1985, 1992) proposed four stages of development similar to those outlined by Piaget. He theorized that infants begin life with certain innate but limited capacities and attentional resources. Through both maturation and sensorimotor practice, the infant's actions gradually become more efficient and automatic, eventually permitting the child to think about as well as act on these objects and entities and, still later, integrate information about their dimensions, features, and qualities to solve problems.

Beyond infancy, the increasing efficiency of cognitive *operations,* processes such as identifying stimuli and recognizing relationships among them, paves the way for greater memory capacity. If children expend a substantial amount of mental effort on identifying or recognizing stimuli, fewer resources will be available for storage and retention of information. Conversely, as children become more proficient at identifying letters, colors, and other features of stimuli, they will have more resources available for remembering. A simple experiment illustrates how these principles work. Three- and six-year-olds were asked to repeat a list of words one at a time as rapidly as possible and then recall that same list of words. Children who were quick to repeat the words had better memory scores than children who were slower at repetition (Case, Kurland, & Goldberg, 1982). As operational efficiency increased with development, more cognitive resources were available for remembering.

According to Case, increases in children's ability to process information quickly are tied to maturational changes in the nervous system as well as to practice with various cognitive activities. One important physiological change that occurs through adolescence is the *myelinization* of areas of the cortex that control alertness and higher-order thinking processes; portions of some neurons develop a fatty coating that speeds neural transmission (Yakovlev & Lecours, 1967). It is plausible that this process is related to the increasing speed of cognitive processing. Practice also helps. In contrast to Piaget, Case allowed a greater role for experience in pushing the child's abilities forward. The more times the child identifies numbers, words, or other stimuli, the more facile she or he will become in this activity. As a result of practice and experience, children develop *central conceptual structures* that guide their performance in specific domains, such as numerical or spatial reasoning. As you will see in the chapter titled "Cognition: Information Processing," many of the ideas Case proposed draw from another theoretical school of cognitive development: the information-processing perspective.

> **KEY THEME**
> **Nature/Nurture**

> **KEY THEME**
> **Interaction Among Domains**

FOR YOUR REVIEW

- What are the infant's chief accomplishments during the sensorimotor stage? What is the primary basis of thought in this stage?

- What are the major characteristics of thinking in the preoperational stage?

- What are the major features of thinking in the concrete operational stage?

- What are the major characteristics of thinking in the formal operational stage?

- What are the implications of Piaget's theory for education?

- What are the most important criticisms of Piaget's theory? What research evidence supports these criticisms?

- What are the basic elements of neo-Piagetian approaches to cognitive development?

Concept Development

When and how does the child begin to understand that horses, dogs, and cats all belong to a common category called "animals"? When does she realize that numbers such as "2" or "4" represent specific quantities, no matter what objects are being counted? And how does she mentally organize her spatial environment, such as the layout of her house or the path from home to school? In each case, we are concerned with the ways the child organizes a set of information about the world, using some general or abstract principle as the basis for that organization. In other words, we are describing the child's use of **concepts.**

As one psychologist put it, "Concepts and categories serve as the building blocks for human thought and behavior" (Medin, 1989). Concepts allow us to group isolated pieces of information on the basis of common themes or properties. The result is greater efficiency in cognitive processing. Suppose someone tells you, "A quarf is an animal." Without even seeing one, you already know many of the quarf's properties: it breathes, eats, locomotes, and so on. Because concepts are linked to one of the most powerful human capabilities—language—as well as other aspects of cognition, understanding how concepts develop is an important concern of developmental psychologists. Many modern-day accounts of concept development arose out of attempts to test or expand the groundbreaking ideas Piaget set forth concerning children's understanding of objects, classes of objects, number, and space.

Properties of Objects

The most fundamental early concepts, of course, have to do with the objects infants and young children encounter. What exactly do they understand about the properties of objects, for example, the fact of their continual existence or how one object might cause another to launch forward or zigzag across the room?

● **The Object Concept** We already discussed how Piaget believed that significant accomplishments such as the object concept emerge late in the first year of life and do not become fully elaborated until the second year. We have also seen that experiments such as those of Renée Baillargeon suggest that by three to four months of age, infants may understand far more about the properties of physical objects, such as the object concept, than Piaget surmised (Baillargeon, 1987a; Baillargeon & DeVos, 1991).

According to Baillargeon, such young infants not only understand that objects exist when out of sight but also understand that the objects' size continues to be preserved as well (Baillargeon, 1987b). In a series of experiments involving the rotation of a screen similar to that shown in Figure 8.2, the rectangular box was either upright (as shown in the figure) or lying flat. Three- and four-month-olds seemed to understand that the screen could not rotate as far when the box was in the upright position as it could when lying down. Moreover, if the object was something that could be squeezed, such as a ball of gauze the infants had previously played with, they were not surprised by the continued rotation of the screen in front of it. They did show surprise when the screen seemed to rotate past the position of a hard and rigid box. Apparently, young infants quickly move beyond simply understanding that an object exists under a cover or behind a barrier; they also develop ideas about physical properties of objects such as their height and rigidity (Baillargeon, 1995).

Similarly, experiments by Elizabeth Spelke and her colleagues show that infants seem to appreciate the concept of *solidity,* the fact that one object cannot pass through the space occupied by another object. In one study, represented in Figure 8.3, two-and-a-half-month-old infants saw a ball roll across a ramp and behind a screen for several trials. Next they saw the ball roll as a partially visible box blocked its path. When the screen was removed, infants viewed the ball either resting in front of the box or at the end of the ramp. Infants looked significantly longer at the impossible result, the ball at the end of the ramp, suggesting to Spelke that infants recognize the concept of solidity. Some of Spelke's other experiments imply that young infants also understand the principle of *continuity,* the idea that objects move continuously in time and space (Spelke et al., 1992).

The results of the violation-of-expectation experiments have led some researchers to formulate the **core knowledge hypothesis,** the idea that young infants possess innate knowledge concerning important fundamental properties of objects (Baillargeon,

concept Definition of a set of information on the basis of some general or abstract principle.

core knowledge hypothesis The idea that infants possess innate knowledge of certain properties of objects.

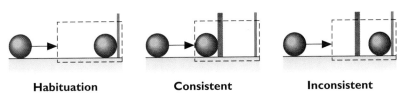

Habituation	Consistent	Inconsistent

Source: Spelke et al., 1992.

FIGURE 8.3
Infants' Concepts of Solidity

In an experiment conducted by Elizabeth Spelke and her colleagues, two-and-a-half-month-old infants were habituated to the scene on the left, a ball rolling across a ramp. In the test phase, infants saw events that were either consistent or inconsistent with the principle that one object cannot pass through the space occupied by another. The infants looked longer at the inconsistent event, leading Spelke and her colleagues to postulate that this early knowledge about objects is innate.

2001; Spelke & Hespos, 2001). The implication is that even young infants possess a startling degree of competence as they encounter items and events in the world. Core knowledge becomes elaborated with experience, according to these theorists, but the infant starts out with much more capability than Piaget presumed. There are some problematic findings for those in this camp, however. For example, Neil Berthier and his colleagues (Berthier et al., 2000) had two- and three-year-olds participate in a task similar to the one shown in Figure 8.3. In this case, however, the researchers asked the children to retrieve the ball from behind one of several doors positioned in front or in back of the wall. Children under age three performed poorly; they did not open the door right in front of the wall. If infants have early knowledge of the concept of solidity and can represent hidden objects, why would children several years older fail to locate the object? At the very least, the findings suggest that a great deal of knowledge about the locations of objects develops in the first three years (Butler, Berthier, & Clifton, 2002).

The contrasting point of view is that infants' performance in the violation-of-expectation tasks is not due to innate core knowledge but rather to perceptual and memory processes that detect that "something is different" or "something is familiar" (Bogartz, Shinskey, & Schilling, 2000). It is wrong, say the critics, to imbue young infants with more advanced or specialized cognitive and representational skills than is warranted (Haith, 1998; Smith, 1999). Rather, it is better to assume that basic, general cognitive processes are responsible for the behaviors we observe. Knowledge about objects is built, say many of these theorists, through rapid advances in attention and memory abilities, as well as the child's experiences in the world. Experts hope that well-designed experiments that rule out competing explanations will help to resolve this controversy (Aslin, 2000).

Given the behaviors of young infants in the violation-of-expectation tasks, why do they fail to retrieve a covered object prior to eight months of age? One possibility is that infants do not yet have the skill to solve means-ends tasks, that is, to develop and execute a plan to reach for and uncover the hidden object. However, seven-month-old infants will pull down a transparent screen to reach for an object behind it; they do not make this response when the screen is opaque (Shinskey & Munakata, 2001). Seven-month-olds can also push a button to make a shelf drop and deliver a visible toy; they do not push the button if the toy is invisible or if button-pushing simply lights a set of lights on the shelf (Munakata et al., 2002; Munakata et al., 1997). A means-ends deficit cannot account for such results, as, under some circumstances, we see that infants can put into action a sequence of steps in order to obtain an object. Yuko Munakata and her colleagues hypothesize that infants' representations of hidden objects are weaker than for visible objects and thus make search tasks more demanding (Munakata et al., 1997). As infants have more experiences in the world, however, and the neural networks that underlie representations of objects become strengthened, children become more successful in retrieving hidden objects (Munakata, 2001).

KEY THEME
Nature/Nurture

● **The A-Not-B Error**   A common error that occurs when the child is about seven to nine months of age is the A$\overline{\text{B}}$ (or "A-not-B") error. In this task, an object is hidden in location A, found by the infant, and then, in full view of the infant, moved to location B. Piaget observed that the child would mistakenly but persistently search for the object in location A. He hypothesized that the infant's incomplete knowledge

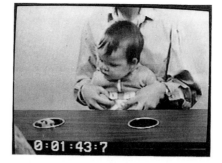

FIGURE 8.4
Alternative Explanations for
the AB̄ Error

**A toy has been hidden first in
the right well (location A), then
is placed in the well on the left
(location B) as shown in the
first photograph. The next
three photographs show that
after the object is hidden, the
infant reaches for location A
even though he looks persistently at location B. The looking behavior suggests that he
has the object concept when
there are visible displacements
of the object. Diamond (1991)
believes that one reason infants
reach for the incorrect location
is because they fail to inhibit
motor responses.**

of the object concept leads to this error, in large part because the sensorimotor
scheme for searching in location A still controls the child's thought. Researchers,
however, have generated several alternative hypotheses about the reasons for the A-
not-B error.

For one thing, memory difficulties may play a role. Eight- to twelve-month-old
infants are less likely to make the AB̄ error when they can search for the object at B
immediately as opposed to after a delay. In addition, when watching infants make
the AB̄ error, Adele Diamond noticed that even though some infants mistakenly
reached for A, they actually *looked* at B, the correct location of the hidden toy (see
Figure 8.4) (Diamond, 1985). They behaved as though they knew the correct location of the toy but could not stop themselves from reaching to A. In other studies,
adult monkeys, which normally perform successfully on the AB̄ task, make mistakes
identical to those of seven-to-nine-month-old human infants when lesions are
made in very specific areas of their frontal cortex; these are the brain areas that control the inhibition of responses (Diamond & Goldman-Rakic, 1989). Diamond
(1991) proposes that infants have the object concept well before age seven months
but, due to the physical immaturity of this special cortical area, they cannot suppress their tendency to reach for location A. Lending support to this hypothesis are
data showing that infants who are successful in the AB̄ task display more powerful
brain electrical activity from the same frontal region of the cortex (Bell & Fox,
1992). Moreover, when infants' responses to the AB̄ situation are assessed using the
habituation procedure rather than by the child's motor response, they look longer
at an impossible event (a toy moves from A to B and is then found at A) than at a
possible event (a toy moves from A to B and is found at B) (Ahmed & Ruffman,
1998). Thus infants seem to know the correct location of the transposed object but
do not show this knowledge when tasks require reaching.

Another account of the AB̄ error states that infants may not be able to efficiently
update their representation of the object's location after it is moved to B; in fact, they
perform better when the A and B locations are covered with distinctive shapes and
colors (Bremner & Bryant, 2001). Perhaps the most comprehensive description
comes from a dynamic systems perspective. In this view, the infant's errors arise from
competing tendencies of different strengths: the strong memory of the object at A
and a deteriorating plan to look at location B in the face of few perceptual cues

Direct launching

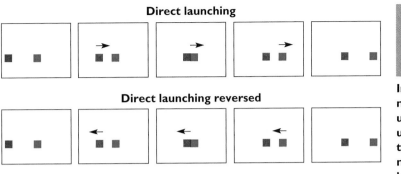

Direct launching reversed

Source: Leslie & Keeble, 1987.

FIGURE 8.5

A Demonstration of Infant Discrimination of Physical Causality

In Leslie's experiment, six-month-old infants viewed stimulus sequences that occurred under different conditions. The top row shows a red brick moving and touching a green brick, after which the green brick moves. Infants habituated to this sequence showed dishabituation when the reverse sequence, the green brick moving and striking the red brick, was shown (view the direct launching condition in the figure from right to left); that is, they noticed when the object causing the physical movement switched. In another condition, the red brick moved and touched the green brick, but the green brick moved only after a delay; that is, the cues did not suggest the red brick was causing the green brick to move. Infants habituated to this latter sequence showed less dishabituation to the reversal.

(Smith et al., 1999; Spencer, Smith, & Thelen, 2001). Any of several factors can improve performance: better memory for spatial locations, stronger perceptual cues about the object's location, or heightened attention to the events in the task. As you can see, we now have several alternatives to Piaget's notion that the object concept relies on an internal sensorimotor-based scheme, all of them emphasizing changes in the ability of infants to process information.

● **Physical Causality**   Imagine the following scene: a red brick moves halfway across a screen, hits a green brick, and the green brick moves across the rest of the screen. Most adults would conclude that the red brick caused the green brick to glide across the screen. They would not reach that conclusion, however, if they saw that the bricks did not touch each other or if there was a pause between the time the two bricks made contact and the time the green brick started to move (Michotte, 1963).

In a series of experiments, Alan Leslie showed that infants as young as six months exhibit similar reactions (Leslie, 1982, 1984; Leslie & Keeble, 1987). In one condition, infants observed one object collide with another object and propel it forward for a series of trials. After they showed habituation to this scene, they viewed the reverse situation, in which the second object hit and launched the first. Infants showed dishabituation; that is, they treated the two event sequences (depicted in Figure 8.5) as though they were different. In a control condition, infants were habituated to the same events, but the second object moved only after a delay. Now, though, when the event was reversed, little dishabituation was observed. These experiments showed that infants notice something unique about causal events, a result, says Leslie, of an innate propensity to perceive causality. Other research has demonstrated that for infants to react to physical causality, the same objects must be used repeatedly during habituation trials. Reactions to physical causality diminish when the objects themselves change from trial to trial or when the objects are more complex (Cohen & Oakes, 1993; Oakes, 1994; Oakes & Cohen, 1990). In this view, the infant's conceptual understanding of physical causality develops as a result of repeated experiences with specific, simple objects rather because of an innate "causality" module.

Of course, the infant studies just described do not suggest a full-blown appreciation of the concept of causality; they simply imply that before age one year, infants notice something unique about contiguous event sequences in which one object seems to "cause" another to do something. How do slightly older children—preschoolers—understand concepts of causality?

Piaget (1930, 1974) believed that up until the early school years, ages seven or eight years, children lack an awareness of physical causality. Once they are verbal and can discuss causality, they make some interesting errors. One type of error is **animism,** attributing lifelike properties to inanimate objects. In one of Piaget's examples of animism, a six-year-old boy named Vern was asked why a boat floats on water but a little stone sinks. Vern answered, "The boat is more intelligent than the stone" (Piaget, 1929, p. 223). Another child, age seven, is asked if the sun can do whatever it likes. The child responds affirmatively; asked why the sun doesn't stop

animism   Attribution of lifelike qualities to inanimate objects.

giving light, the child says, "It wants it to be fine weather" (Piaget, 1929, p. 227). Animism is often accompanied by **artificialism,** the belief that people cause naturally occurring events. Piaget provides the example of a six-year-old named Hub:

Piaget: Has the sun always been there?
Hub: No, it began.
Piaget: How?
Hub: With fire . . . .
Piaget: How did that start?
Hub: With a match . . . .
Piaget: Who struck it?
Hub: A man. (Piaget, 1929, p. 266)

In Piaget's view, children are slow to shed their animistic and artificial beliefs; the latter may persist until age ten years or so (Piaget, 1929).

Susan Gelman and Kathleen Kremer (1991) attempted to replicate some of Piaget's studies by asking preschoolers, "Do you think people made (or make)——?" in which the blank was filled in by an object such as the sun, the moon, dogs, flowers, dolls, and shoes. Few of the children showed evidence of artificialism; most recognized that objects such as dolls are made by humans, but the sun and moon are not. Moreover, these young children often cited natural causes for the behaviors of living things (e.g., birds fly because they have wings) and human causes for the things artificial objects do (e.g., cars go uphill because people make them do so). Why the discrepancy from Piaget's observations? Gelman and Kremer (1991) postulate that direct questions, such as the ones they used, were more likely to tap children's underlying knowledge of causality than the free-ranging interview questions Piaget employed.

Classification

Aside from learning about the properties of single objects, as in the object concept, children also quickly learn about relationships that can exist among sets of objects. Sometimes objects resemble one another perceptually and seem to "go together" because they are the same color or shape. At other times, the relationships among objects can be more complex; the perceptual similarities may be less obvious and, moreover, some sets can be embedded within others. Cocker spaniels and Great Danes, two different-looking dogs, can be classified together in the group "dogs," and both breeds fit into a larger category of "animals." As with many other cognitive skills, Piaget believed that before age seven years, children's ability to classify objects, particularly in the hierarchical manner of the latter example, is limited. Ask a young child who sees six brown beads and three white beads, all of which are wooden, "Do I have more brown beads or wooden beads?" Chances are the four- or five-year-old will respond, "More brown beads." According to Piaget, preoperational children lack the logical thought structures to permit understanding that some classes can be subsets of others (Piaget, 1952a). Piaget was right in claiming that classification skills undergo changes with development, but the research that followed his work has revealed a far more complex portrait of this cognitive skill.

● **Early Classification**   One of the earliest signs of classification skills in young children occurs toward the end of the first year, when children begin to group *perceptually similar* objects together. Susan Sugarman (1982, 1983) carefully watched the behaviors of one- to three-year-olds as they played with successive sets of stimuli that could be grouped into two classes, such as plates and square blocks or dolls and boats. Even the youngest children displayed a spontaneous tendency to group similar-looking objects together by pointing consecutively to items that were alike. With the habituation paradigm, it has also been possible to show that three- and four-month-old infants respond to different items, such as dogs, cats, and horses, on the basis of

---

artificialism   Belief that naturally occurring events are caused by people.

perceptual similarity (Oakes, Coppage, & Dingel, 1997; Quinn, Eimas, & Rosenkranz, 1993). Thus the tendency to group objects together on the basis of shared perceptual characteristics emerges early in development.

Between ages one and three years, children experience a rapid growth in classification skills. Infants as young as fourteen months successively touch objects that appear in common contexts, such as "kitchen things" and "bathroom things" (Mandler, Fivush, & Reznick, 1987). Two-year-olds will match items on the basis of *thematic relations*, clustering items that function together or complement one another, such as a baby bottle and a baby (Markman & Hutchinson, 1984). They will also occasionally classify items *taxonomically*, grouping objects that may not look alike on the basis of some abstract principle, such as a banana with an apple (Ross, 1980). Taxonomic classification is easier for young children when they hear that objects from the same category share the same label even though they may not look very much alike (e.g., a panther and a tabby house cat are both called "cats") or when their similarities are pointed out in some other way (Deák & Bauer, 1996; Nazzi & Gopnik, 2001).

In fact, mothers often provide varied information of this sort to their young children about objects and their membership in categories, saying such things as, "That's a desk. That's a desk, too," or pointing sequentially to objects that come from the same conceptual group (Gelman et al., 1998). As children encounter new instances of a category, they incorporate information about those examples into their prior knowledge about the category (Carmichael & Hayes, 2001). As children grow older, they become capable of using a wider range of relations to classify objects, their exclusive reliance on shared perceptual features lessens, and they display spontaneous hierarchical knowledge of categories.

● **Basic-Level Categories**   Some groupings of objects can be described as *basic level;* that is, objects go together when they look alike and can be used in similar ways, and when we can think of "average" members of the class. "Chair" is an example of a basic-level concept because virtually all chairs have seats, legs, and backs; all are used for sitting; and we can think of such a thing as a "typical" chair. In contrast, other concepts are *superordinate level*. Members of superordinate-level groups, such as "furniture," do not necessarily share many perceptual attributes, and they are broader and more general than basic-level concepts. Figure 8.6 illustrates this example of a basic-level and a superordinate-level grouping.

Eleanor Rosch and her colleagues believe that because basic-level groups carry more information, especially perceptual information, than superordinate-level groups, they are easier for children to process. Children under age five years readily put together four pictures of different shoes or four pictures of different cars; that is, they could sort according to basic-level groupings (Rosch et al., 1976). Children in Rosch's study could not, however, proficiently sort on the basis of superordinate category by putting a shoe, shirt, sock, and pants together until they reached age eight or nine years. In fact, other research shows that the ability to sort basic-level stimuli is evident as early as eighteen months of age (Gopnik & Meltzoff, 1992). We also saw in the chapter titled "Language" how many of the child's first words are basic-level terms.

Even though Rosch's theory of basic-level categories has had widespread appeal, there are two important points of contention. First, do children really evidence knowledge and use of superordinate categories later (as opposed to early) in development? Not according to findings by Behl-Chadha (1996), which indicate that three- to four-month-olds can categorize superordinate items when the habituation procedure is used. Second, do children's early categories really rely primarily on perceptual information, as the notion of basic-level concepts suggests? Jean Mandler thinks the answer is no (Mandler, 1997). Consider the items shown in Figure 8.7, which are perceptually similar but belong to two different conceptual categories. A group of seven- to eleven-month-olds was allowed to examine several items from one category, say birds, until they were familiar with them. Then two more objects, a

FIGURE 8.6
Basic- and Superordinate-
Level Categories

The left panel gives an example of objects that are considered a basic-level grouping.
These stimuli share perceptual
features, and an "average"
member of the class can be
conceptualized. The right
panel gives an example of
superordinate-level grouping.
Members of such classes do
not necessarily share many
perceptual features, and it is
more difficult to think of an
"average" class member.
Basic-level categories are
easier for young children to
employ than superordinate-
level groupings.

new bird and a new plane, were presented. Infants spent more time looking at and
manipulating the item from the new category—in this particular instance, planes—
than the item from the familiar category despite the striking perceptual similarities
between the two groups (Mandler & McDonough, 1993). Mandler argues that infants form categories based on *meanings* rather than perceptual similarities during
the latter portion of the first year. Moreover, rather than starting with basic-level categories and progressing to superordinate categories as Rosch has postulated, Mandler and her colleagues maintain that infants begin with broad, general categories.
They understand, for example, that different animals (both a dog and a bird) can
drink water from a cup but that an airplane cannot. These broad categories of "ani-
malness" become increasingly more fine-tuned and refined with experience (Mandler & McDonough, 1998, 2000).

● **Natural Domains**   Recently several developmental psychologists have asserted
that some concepts or categories of objects are easier to acquire than others. Just as
children seem to be biologically "programmed" to learn language rapidly and easily
(see the chapter titled "Language"), so do they seem to learn about certain conceptual domains quickly and effortlessly. In other words, some objects and events in the
environment offer "privileged relationships" for the child to learn about (Gallistel et
al., 1991). Among these so-called **natural domains** is knowledge about biological
entities.

   Children show a dramatically early ability to classify animate versus inanimate objects. For example, a twenty-four-month-old will show obvious surprise when a chair
seems to move forward on its own (Golinkoff et al., 1984), and a twelve-month-old
will fuss and cry more when a robot starts to move as opposed to a human stranger
(Poulin-Dubois, Lepage, & Ferland, 1996). Three-year-olds know that living things
can feel emotions but inanimate objects cannot; they say a person can feel sad, but a
doll or a rock cannot (Gelman, Spelke, & Meck, 1983). Preschoolers also begin to recognize that other processes, such as growth, illness, healing, and death, are unique to
biological organisms (Backscheider, Shatz, & Gelman, 1993; Rosengren et al., 1991;
Siegal, 1988).

natural domains   Concepts or
categories that children acquire
especially rapidly and effortlessly.

Source: Mandler, 1997.

Part of the usefulness of concepts, of course, is that they permit us to make assumptions about other category members, as in our earlier example of the "quarf." That is, we go beyond the information given, perhaps even beyond the similarities of perceptual features of objects, to make conceptually based judgments or inductions about them. According to Susan Carey (1985b) and Frank Keil (1989), children's inductions are largely guided by "theories" they construct about the nature of specific concepts. For the domain of biological entities, Carey found that children's theories undergo revision with development to allow more and more accurate judgments. For example, a four-year-old who is told that humans have "omenta" will say that only other animals that are very similar to humans also have "omenta." The child's theory about biology centers around what he knows about humans. In contrast, an older child would state that even animals physically dissimilar from humans have "omenta." Her theory of biology extends beyond resemblances to human beings to the broader properties that characterize living things. Theories do seem to play a role in children's categorization. When provided with theories about fictitious animals and their features, for example (e.g., "Wugs are animals that like to fight" and "Gillies are animals that like to hide in trees"), children were more successful in categorizing pictures of "wugs" and "gillies" than when they were trained to focus solely on their features (e.g., "Wugs are animals that have claws") (Krascum & Andrews, 1998).

FIGURE 8.7
How Do Infants Group Birds and Airplanes?

According to research by Mandler and McDonough (1993), seven- to eleven-month-old infants treated these stimuli as belonging to two separate categories, birds and planes, despite the strong perceptual similarities between them. Thus, Mandler argues, infants' categories are based on meanings rather than shared perceptual features.

● **Individual and Cultural Variations in Classification**   Implicit in Piagetian ideas about classification is the notion that there should be many similarities in concept development among children, even those from different cultures. However, research suggests that this is not the case. For example, some three-year-olds show a clear propensity to use thematic classification, whereas others prefer taxonomic classification. Interestingly, these individual differences in classification preferences are linked to earlier unique profiles in play and language use. As one-year-olds, "thematic" children have been noted to play with objects in spatial, functional ways and, at age two, use words such as *in* and *down* more than "taxonomic" children do; that is, they have seemingly stable preferences to focus on how objects work in relation to one another (Dunham & Dunham, 1995).

KEY THEME
Individual Differences

Cultural variations in classification occur, too. One group of researchers found that residents of rural Mexico with little formal schooling tended to group objects on the basis of their functional relations. "Chicken" and "egg" were frequently classified together because "the chicken lays eggs." On the other hand, individuals with more education relied on taxonomic classification, grouping "chicken" with "horse" because "they are animals" (Sharp, Cole, & Lave, 1979). It may be that taxonomic classification strategies are taught explicitly in schools or that education fosters the development of more abstract thought, a basic requirement for taxonomic grouping.

KEY THEME
Sociocultural Influence

Any full explanation of the development of classification skills will have to take into account the experiences of children within their specific sociocultural contexts.

Numerical Concepts

Children as young as two years of age frequently use number terms, either to count toys, snacks, or other items or in playful ways, such as shouting, "One, two, three, jump!" as they bounce off their beds (Saxe, Guberman, & Gearhart, 1987). But do young children really understand the full significance of numbers as a tool for establishing quantitative relationships? Or are they merely repeating a series of words they have heard someone else say without fully appreciating the conceptual underpinnings of those words?

Piaget's (1952a) position was that children under age seven years or so, before they enter the concrete operational stage, lack a full grasp of the meaning of numbers. One indication is the failure of preoperational children to succeed in the conservation of number task. In this problem, you will recall, children see two equal rows of objects—say, red and white poker chips—as was shown in Figure 8.1. Initially the rows are aligned identically, and most children will agree that they have equal numbers of chips. But when the chips in one row are spread out, the majority of children state that this row now has more chips even though no chips have been added or subtracted.

Preoperational children, Piaget maintained, fail to comprehend the **one-to-one correspondence** that still exists among items in the two rows; that is, each element in a row can be mapped onto an element in the second row, with none left over. Moreover, he believed young children have not yet attained an understanding of two important aspects of number. The first is **cardinality,** or the total number of elements in a class, as in *six* red poker chips. The second is **ordinality,** the order in which an item appears in the set, as in the *second* poker chip. According to Piaget, the child must grasp both these concepts to judge two sets of items as being equivalent.

Like this four-year-old, many preschoolers are able to count and understand at least some principles of numerical relationships, such as *cardinality.* **By claiming that preoperational children do not have a conceptual understanding of number, Piaget probably underestimated children's numerical competence.**

one-to-one correspondence Understanding that two sets are equivalent in number if each element in one set can be mapped onto a unique element in the second set with none left over.

cardinality Principle that the last number in a set of counted numbers refers to the number of items in that set.

ordinality Principle that a number refers to an item's order within a set.

● **Early Number Concepts and Counting**   Many contemporary researchers believe Piaget underestimated preschool children's understanding of number concepts. For example, two-year-olds will correctly point to a picture with three items, and not a picture with one item, when asked, "Can you show me the three fish?" (Wynn, 1992b). By age four years, many children count—they say number words in sequence and, in so doing, appreciate at least some basic principles of numerical relationships. Rochel Gelman and her associates have argued that young children have knowledge of certain important fundamental principles of counting (Gelman & Gallistel, 1978; Gelman & Meck, 1983). Among these principles are (1) using the same sequence of counting words when counting different sets, (2) employing only one counting word per object, (3) using the last counting word in the set to represent the total number, (4) understanding that any set of objects can be counted, and (5) appreciating that objects can be counted in any order.

When young children count, their words are not devoid of numerical meaning. In one experiment, three- and four-year-olds saw six dolls and five rings and were asked, "There are six dolls. Is there a ring for every doll?" Most of the four-year-olds used number words to answer questions about one-to-one correspondence. For example, many said, "No, because there are six dolls and five rings" (Becker, 1989). In addition, four-year-olds are able to compare quantities, answering correctly such questions as "Which is bigger, five or two?" (Siegler & Robinson, 1982). Thus their understanding of number terms includes relations such as "larger" and "smaller." One interesting pattern, though, is that young children have more difficulty in making such comparisons when the numbers themselves are large (ten versus fourteen) or when the difference between two numbers is small (eight versus nine). The same is true when children have to add, subtract, and perform other calculations with numbers (Levine, Jordan, & Huttenlocher, 1992).

● **Infants' Responses to Number**   Thanks to a growing body of research, we now know that even infants demonstrate sensitivity to basic aspects of numerical relationships. Habituation studies show that newborns can detect differences in small numeric sets, such as two versus three (Antell & Keating, 1983) and six-month-olds differentiate between eight and sixteen dots (Xu & Spelke, 2000). Infants even seem to understand something about additive properties of numbers. In one experiment, five-month-old infants watched as a toy was placed in a case and then was hidden by a screen. The infants watched as a second, identical toy was placed behind the screen (see Figure 8.8). When the screen was removed and only one toy remained—an impossible outcome if the infants appreciated that there should still be two toys—they showed surprise and looked longer than they did when two toys were visible (Wynn, 1992a). Other researchers have confirmed that before age six months, babies show numerical competencies that likely serve as the foundation for more complex reasoning about quantities (Canfield & Smith, 1996; Simon, Hespos, & Rochat, 1995).

But what exactly is the nature of those competencies? The preceding findings raise several interesting questions about the processes that underlie infants' behaviors. First, is sensitivity to number another example of innate core knowledge? To some researchers, the answer is yes, especially because infants only five months old appear to be sensitive to addition and subtraction events (Wynn, 1998). Others disagree and point out that the infants in these experiments might be responding on the basis of changes in the visual display other than number. For example, when stimulus items change in number, they also change in the amount of contour, or exterior boundary length, they contain; two mouse dolls have more total "outline" than one mouse doll. In a study in which the stimuli varied *either* in contour length or number, infants responded on the basis of contour length rather than number (Clearfield & Mix, 1999). Similarly, infants respond to changes in surface area of stimuli as opposed to their number (Clearfield & Mix, 2001). Thus it may be more accurate to say that infants respond on the basis of the *amount* of things rather than the *number* of things (Mix, Huttenlocher, & Levine, 2002).

KEY THEME
Nature/Nurture

FIGURE 8.8

Can Infants Add?

This figure shows the sequence of events used in Wynn's (1992a) experiments with five-month-olds. Infants first saw a hand place a mouse doll in the display. Next, a screen rotated up to hide the doll. A hand appeared with a second doll, placing it behind the screen and leaving the display empty-handed. During the test, the screen dropped down and revealed either two dolls (possible event) or one doll (impossible event). Infants looked longer at the impossible event, suggesting they knew something about the additive properties of numbers.

Sequence of events 1 + 1 = 1 or 2

1. Object placed in case   2. Screen comes up   3. Second object added   4. Hand leaves empty

Then either: possible outcome   **or: impossible outcome**

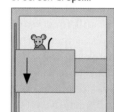   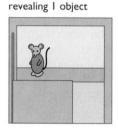

5. Screen drops....   revealing 2 objects   5. Screen drops....   revealing 1 object

Source: Adapted from Wynn, 1992a.

Second, what is the nature of the representations that subserve infants' responses to number? Figure 8.9 presents two possibilities. One is the *analog magnitude* model, in which the representation consists of a general amount in proportion to the actual number of items (Gelman & Cordes, 2001; Whalen, Gallistel, & Gelman, 1999; Wynn, 1998). One item is represented by a small magnitude, two items by a larger magnitude, and so on. These representations are not numerically precise, but they are sufficient to make judgments about how two stimuli compare with one another in quantity. The other is an *object-file* model, in which each item in a set is represented with a file or marker that denotes quantity but not necessarily the properties of the object. Infants are presumed to be limited in the number of object files they can use (Carey, 2001; Feigenson, Carey, & Hauser, 2002). So far, different investigators have claimed to find evidence consistent with each model (Feigenson et al., 2002; Huntley-Fenner & Cannon, 2000). Researchers are eager to find if either of these two accounts, or perhaps some other mechanism, underlies infants' responses to numbers.

FIGURE 8.9

How Do Infants Represent Number?

Researchers currently hypothesize that infants may represent number in one of two ways. In the analog magnitude model, the representation is a general amount in proportion to the actual number. In the object-file model, each item is represented by a marker that denotes quantity.

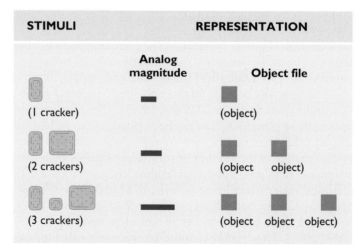

Source: Feigenson, Carey, & Hauser, 2002.

● **Learning Mathematics**   Once children enter school, of course, they are expected to master the formal properties of numbers through mathematics. Lauren Resnick (1986) believes that before children learn the systematic rules for addition, subtraction, algebra, and other mathematical systems, they develop intuitive concepts about how numbers can be manipulated. How would Pitt, one of her seven-year-old participants, add 152 and 149?

> *I would have the two 100's, which equals 200. Then I would have 50 and the 40, which equals 90. So I have 290. Then plus the 9 from 49, and the 2 from the 52 equals 11. And then I add the 90 plus the 11 . . . equals 102. 102? 101. So I put the 200 and the 101, which equals 301. (p. 164)*

All of this came from a young boy who had mastered only first-grade arithmetic!

In fact, children seem to have a good basic grasp of even more complex numerical concepts, such as fractions, by age four. Suppose a preschooler sees three-fourths of a circle hidden by a screen and then one-half of a circle come out from the screen. How much is left behind the screen? A surprising number of four-year-olds can select a picture of one-fourth of a circle from a set of alternatives (Mix, Levine, & Huttenlocher, 1999). In addition, even a brief training session can help young children understand the basic concepts of fractions. When five-year-olds in one study had the opportunity to observe a whole pizza divided among different numbers of recipients, they began to understand that the size of each share of pizza depended on the number of individuals who were going to eat it (Sophian, Garyantes, & Chang, 1997). Given such findings, it is puzzling that many children experience difficulties with mathematics in school. Perhaps, as Resnick suggests, teachers should frame more complex mathematical operations, such as ratios and algebraic expressions, in terms of simple additive properties or other intuitions children have about numbers, at least when they are first being learned (Resnick, 1995; Resnick & Singer, 1993).

Because Asian students score significantly higher than students from the United States on tests of mathematics (Fuligni & Stevenson, 1995; Geary et al., 1993; Stevenson, Chen, & Lee, 1993), examining the source of their mathematical proficiency can be especially instructive. Asian children use different strategies to solve mathematics problems than American children usually do. Korean and Japanese children, for example, add the numbers 8 + 6 by first trying to reach 10; that is, they add 8 + 2 to make 10 and then add the difference between 6 and 2 to reach the answer, 14. It is interesting to note that in these Asian languages, names for numbers in the teens are "ten one" (eleven), "ten two" (twelve), and so on. Thus children may be used to thinking in terms of tens. Addition and subtraction strategies based on a system of tens are also taught explicitly in Korea and Japan (Fuson & Kwon, 1992; Naito & Miura, 2001); as amount of schooling increases, so does children's use of the base ten approach (Naito & Miura, 2001). Findings such as these offer interesting potential ways of enhancing children's already sound mathematical understanding.

KEY THEME
Sociocultural Influence

◉ **SEE FOR YOURSELF**
psychology.college.hmco.com
Tests of Math Skills

Spatial Relationships

From early infancy onward, children organize the objects in their world in still another way: according to relationships in space. Where does the toddler find his shoes or an enticing snack? Usually the infant and the young child have developed a mental picture of their homes and other familiar physical spaces to guide their search for missing objects or to reach a desired location. For the older child, spatial understanding extends to finding her way to school, grandparents' homes, or other, more remote locations. As he did for many other areas of cognitive development, Piaget set forth some of the first hypotheses about the child's concepts of space, ideas that later researchers have modified or enriched.

During infancy, Piaget (1954) stated, the child's knowledge of space is based on her sensorimotor activities within that space. For example, the child searches for objects by using *egocentric* frames of reference. That is, if a ball disappears under a couch or chair, the infant represents its location in relation to her own body ("to the left of my arm") rather than in relation to some other external object ("to the left of the door"). Only with the advent of symbolic ability at the end of the sensorimotor stage are children able to use frames of reference external to the self.

● **Early Spatial Concepts**   Many researchers have confirmed that children, in the absence of environmental cues, indeed rely on the positions of their own bodies in space to locate objects. For example, in one study, nine-month-olds readily learned to locate an item hidden under one of two covers situated to either their left or their right. Shifted to the opposite side of the table, however, they looked in the wrong location because of their egocentric responding (Bremner & Bryant, 1977). When the investigator made the covers of the two hiding locations of distinctively different colors, infants were able to locate the hidden toy even when they were moved to a different position around the table (Bremner, 1978). Thus infants are not egocentric when other information is available to assist them in finding objects.

Toward the end of the year, children quite literally reach out into the world for cues denoting spatial relationships. Infants slightly under nine months of age use **landmarks** denoting the physical locations of objects to find them in larger spatial environments. When playing peekaboo, infants in one study were assisted in locating a face by different colored lanterns positioned by the correct window, even if their own positions were shifted (Lew, Bremner, & Lefkovitch, 2000). Linda Acredolo and her colleagues demonstrated this skill among older children. Three- through eight-year-olds were taken on a walk through an unfamiliar building in one of two conditions (Acredolo, Pick, & Olsen, 1975). In the first condition, the hallway through which the experimenter led each child contained two chairs; in the second, there were no chairs. The children saw the experimenter drop a set of keys during the walk, and in the "landmark" condition this event occurred near one of the chairs. Later, when children were asked to retrieve the keys, performance was best in the "landmark" condition for the preschoolers; older children did well regardless of the experimental condition.

Young children are also able to use distance cues without the benefit of landmarks to search for objects. Janellen Huttenlocher and her colleagues asked children ages sixteen to twenty-four months to find a toy buried in a five-foot-long sandbox that had no distinguishing landmarks. The success rate for these young children was impressively high (Huttenlocher, Newcombe, & Sandberg, 1994). Using the habituation method, this same research team was able to show that five-month-olds reacted when hidden objects unexpectedly reappeared as little as eight inches from their original hiding location in a thirty-inch sandbox (Newcombe, Huttenlocher, & Learmonth, 2000).

Taken together, these findings show that infants have several ways to locate objects in space—referencing their own bodies, using landmarks, and employing distance cues. As with other forms of conceptual knowledge, researchers debate the degree to which this knowledge is innate and specialized versus acquired and due to more general processes. Most agree, though, that infants and young children are far more competent in this domain than Piaget imagined and that they improve these basic skills as they begin to move about in their environments (Newcombe & Huttenlocher, 2000).

● **Map Reading**   One of the practical ways in which spatial skills are exercised is in reading maps. From participating in a "treasure hunt" at a birthday party to traveling or learning geography in school, reading maps, at least occasionally, is part of many children's experiences. Making use of a map involves several types of skills, including understanding that the symbols on the page refer to real objects or places, appreciating the scale and alignment of the map in relation to the actual physical space, and, if one is actually navigating, planning an efficient route in order to get from one place to another.

Four-year-olds begin to show an ability to use simple maps to navigate a U-shaped route through a series of rooms (Uttal & Wellman, 1989). However, their skills are limited to maps for which there is a clear one-to-one correspondence between representations on the map (in this case, photographs of stuffed animals) and real objects in each of the rooms (actual stuffed animals). Also, the map must be aligned to match the actual physical space; rotating it to a different orientation presents problems. Map-reading skills improve in the next two years, though, so that by the time they

landmark   Distinctive location or cue that the child uses to negotiate or represent a spatial environment.

are six, many children can use a map to plan an efficient route through a large-scale space (Sandberg & Huttenlocher, 2001). However, understanding maps that are not oriented in the same direction as the physical space remains challenging for children through the early school years (Liben & Downs, 1993).

Why do children improve in map reading? One way to answer this question is to see which kinds of experiences improve children's ability to use maps. When experimenters highlight the connection between objects on the map and objects in the physical space by making explicit comparisons, young children's performances improve (Loewenstein & Gentner, 2001). Organizing the spatial relations among objects in the map—by making them into a drawing, for example—helps, too (Uttal et al., 2001). Thus improvements in children's ability to reason about relations among objects are one likely source of better performance. Creating an efficient map route to follow also depends on the emergence of good planning skills. In fact, many of the problem-solving skills we will discuss in the chapter titled "Cognition: Information Processing" are relevant to children's facility with maps.

FOR YOUR REVIEW

- What kind of knowledge do infants display about the properties of objects?

- What is the core knowledge hypothesis? What research findings support this position on infants' conceptual knowledge? What are the criticisms of this point of view?

- What developmental changes have researchers observed in children's classification skills?

- What developmental changes have researchers observed in children's numerical skills? What basic forms of mathematical reasoning do young children display?

- What developmental changes have researchers observed in children's spatial concepts, including map reading?

Understanding Psychological States

Our knowledge extends beyond understanding of physical objects, classes, number, and space. It also includes an awareness of our minds and how they and the minds of others work. How do children understand and judge the motives, feelings, needs, interests, capacities, and thoughts of playmates, siblings, parents, and others? And how and when do children come to understand and reflect on the psychological states of the self? This type of cognition, thinking about the self and its relationship to the social world, is called *social cognition* and is a vital aspect of successful communication and social interaction. In comparison to the world of physical objects and events, thinking about the social world presents unique challenges to the developing child. People may act unpredictably; their feelings and moods, and even their appearances, may shift unexpectedly. Just how children piece together their understanding of social experiences has been the focus of several lines of research. Here too contemporary researchers owe Piaget recognition for his initial efforts to study how children think about thinking.

KEY THEME
Interaction Among Domains

Perspective Taking: Taking the Views of Others

Perspective taking is the ability to put oneself in another person's place, to consider that person's thoughts, feelings, or knowledge. One basic element of perspective taking is understanding what others see. For example, does the child realize that his sister, who is standing across the room, cannot see the brightly colored pictures in the book he is eagerly examining? In 1956, Jean Piaget and Barbel Inhelder published a classic experiment illustrating children's limited knowledge of the visual perspectives of others. Children seated in front of three different papier-mâché mountains (see

perspective taking Ability to take the role of another person and understand what that person is thinking, is feeling, or knows.

FIGURE 8.10
Visual Perspective Taking

How well can children adopt another person's perspective? Piaget asked this question by seating a child at a table (location 1) containing three "mountains" of different size and color, then asking the child how the scene would look to a doll (or another person) seated at other locations (locations 2 and 3) around the table. Piaget found that preschoolers often chose a view similar to their own. More recent research indicates that preschoolers can more successfully accomplish this task when familiar and easily distinguishable scenes are used.

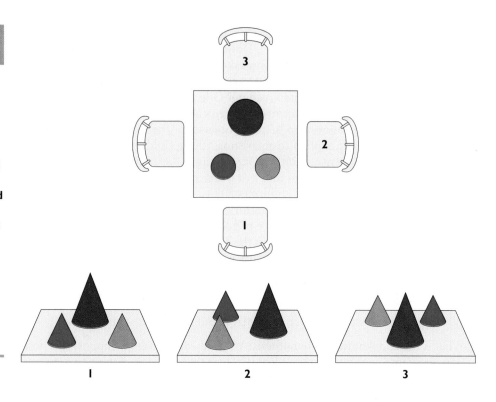

Figure 8.10) were asked to indicate what a doll would see in viewing the array from various locations. Four- to six-year-olds showed considerable *egocentrism* in their responses; they typically indicated that the doll's view would be identical to their own. By six to nine years of age, children began to realize the doll's perspective would differ, although they still had difficulty figuring out what the doll would actually see. Nine- and ten-year-olds were able to determine the doll's perspective accurately. More recent research has shown that the difficulty of the doll and mountain task may have led Piaget and Inhelder to underestimate children's role-taking competence. When simpler visual arrays or familiar everyday scenes are used, or when the method of interviewing children is simplified, three- and four-year-olds can answer some of these kinds of questions reasonably well (Borke, 1975; Newcombe & Huttenlocher, 1992).

Visual perspective taking develops in two phases. At first, from late infancy until about age three years, children come to realize that their own and another's view are not identical. This is called *Level 1 perspective taking.* More advanced *Level 2 perspective taking* appears in three- and four-year-olds and continues to be refined for several years thereafter. Now children can determine the specific limitations of another's view, for example, whether an object or picture another person sees will look right side up or not (Flavell, 1978). These advances reflect cognitive gains in differentiating oneself from another and in knowledge of spatial relationships (Shantz, 1983).

The Child's Theory of Mind

Children's understanding of their social world extends beyond visual perspective-taking skills. Emerging among their competencies is an expanding and increasingly coherent appreciation of the kinds of mental qualities that contribute to the behavior of self and others. Did the playmate who broke a favorite toy *intend* to do the damage? Would a close friend *believe* that Mom will not let them go to the park alone? Many of our social behaviors are guided by the judgments and inferences we make about the desires, feeling states, beliefs, and thoughts of other people (Astington, Harris, & Olson, 1988; Slomkowski & Dunn, 1996; Wellman, 1990). In fact, it would be rare *not* to be concerned with the mental states of others in the normal course of interactions with them.

When and how do children become aware of the concept of mental states, their own and those of others? That is, when and how do children develop a **theory of mind**? Once

KEY THEME
Interaction Among Domains

theory of mind Awareness of the concept of mental states, both one's own and those of others.

again, Piaget has provided much of the impetus for research on this topic. His position was quite clear. As Piaget put it, "The child knows nothing about the nature of thought . . ." (Piaget, 1929, p. 37). Dubbing this characteristic of children **realism,** Piaget maintained that children are not capable of distinguishing between mental and physical entities until the school years. To the child under age eight, dreams and mental images are as real as any event in waking, conscious life. To the same child, thinking is a behavior produced by the body, usually the mouth or the head; physical and mental acts are one and the same.

● **Understanding Mental States**   Despite Piaget's strong claims, developmental researchers have uncovered considerable evidence to the contrary. By age three, children readily distinguish between mental and physical entities and, after that age, show further developments in their understanding of their own mental states and those of others (Flavell, 1993).

In one classic experiment, three-year-olds were told stories such as the following: "Judy doesn't have a kitty, but right now she is thinking about a kitty." Could they see or touch the kitty? Could the kitty be seen by someone else or touched at some time in the future? Children had no problem identifying this as a mental event, one in which the kitty could not be seen or touched. In contrast, when they heard other stories, as in "Judy had a kitty," they correctly stated that these real events could be seen and touched (Wellman & Estes, 1986).

Some of the earliest signs of awareness of mental states are evident at eighteen months, when infants follow the gaze of an adult in episodes of joint attention (see the chapter titled "Language"). Infants react to these actions as if the adult "intends" to communicate something (Butler, Caron, & Brooks, 2000). From there, children display an increasing repertoire of knowledge of mental states. Eighteen-month-olds show a beginning appreciation for what it means to "desire" (Repacholi & Gopnik, 1997). Three-year-olds understand the concept of "pretend" or "make-believe" (Harris et al., 1991; Harris & Kavanaugh, 1993), but they still have difficulty with the concept of "belief" (Lillard & Flavell, 1992). Between ages six and ten, children begin to understand "the mind" as an active entity discrete from the self as they interpret metaphors such as "My mind was racing" or "My mind was hungry" (Wellman & Hickling, 1994). At age ten, children also understand that some mental states, such as "wanting" and "fearing," are more difficult to control than others, such as "paying attention" (Flavell & Green, 1999).

● **False Beliefs**   A particularly useful scenario to assess aspects of children's theory of mind has been the "false belief" task. Children are shown a doll named Maxi who puts some chocolate in a cupboard and leaves the scene. Maxi's mother moves the chocolate to a new location. When Maxi returns, children are asked, "Where will he look for the chocolate?" Most three-year-olds say in the new location. Four-year-olds, though, recognize that Maxi holds a "false belief" and will look for the chocolate in the cupboard (Wimmer & Perner, 1983).

What factors account for the child's growing success on the false belief task and presumably their theory of mind? Currently there is an ongoing debate. On the one hand, some researchers argue that the theory of mind is an innate, prepackaged, modular form of knowledge that becomes more elaborate as the child's cognitive skills develop (Baron-Cohen, 1995; Fodor, 1992; Leslie, 1994). In support of this view, it is interesting to note that children from several cultures, including China, Japan, and the preliterate Baka society of Cameroon, show similar developmental improvements in their understanding of mental state terms such as "desire" and "belief" (Avis & Harris, 1991; Flavell et al., 1983; Gardner et al., 1988; Tardif & Wellman, 2000). Likewise, performance on the false belief task shows consistent developmental trends across many studies (Wellman, Cross, & Watson, 2001). In contrast, other researchers believe that a theory of mind arises from the child's socialization experiences, especially those that encourage an appreciation of others' mental states. Mothers who use more language to describe mental states to their preschoolers, for example, have children who are more successful on the false belief task several months later (Ruffman, Slade, & Crowe, 2002). Theory of mind may also depend on the extent to which a culture emphasizes this type of

KEY THEME
Nature/Nurture

realism Inability to distinguish between mental and physical entities.

KEY THEME
| Sociocultural Influence

understanding. For example, among the Illongot people of the Philippines, there is not a great deal of concern with the concept of mind, so we might not expect to see the emergence of a strong theory of mind (Lillard, 1997, 1998). As you review the child's accomplishments in the Cognitive Development I chronology, you should note that the child's theory of mind, in particular, is a key cognitive attainment bridging the self and social world. Researchers have noted, for example, that performance on the false belief task is related to the child's social skills with peers (Watson et al., 1999). You will encounter several other examples of the link between theory of mind and the child's social and emotional functioning in other chapters.

ATYPICAL DEVELOPMENT

Childhood Autism

Childhood autism is a puzzling disorder affecting about one or two of every one thousand children born. The disorder, more common among boys than girls, is characterized by the child's preference to be alone, poor eye contact and general lack of social skills, often the absence of meaningful language, and a preference for sameness and elaborate routines. Some autistic children show unusual skills, such as being able to recite lengthy passages from memory, put together complex jigsaw puzzles, or create intricate drawings. Often these children show a fascination with spinning objects or repeating the speech patterns of someone else. The hallmark trait, though, is the lack of contact these children have with the social world, starting at an early age. Kanner's (1943) description of one autistic boy captures the syndrome well: "He seems almost to draw into his shell and live within himself" (p. 218).

👁 SEE FOR YOURSELF
psychology.college.hmco.com
Autism

Since Leo Kanner first identified this psychopathology, numerous causes of autism have been proposed, ranging from deprived early emotional relationships with parents to defective neurological wiring in the brain (Waterhouse, Fein, & Modahl, 1996). An intriguing more recent suggestion is that autistic children, for biological reasons, lack the ability to think about mental states; that is, they lack a "theory of mind" that most children begin to develop during the preschool years. Consider how autistic children behave in the "false belief" task described earlier. Whereas most normal four-year-olds are successful, most nine-year-old autistic children fail this problem (Baron-Cohen, Tager-Flusberg, & Cohen, 1993; Frith, 1993). These results suggest that autistic children cannot conceptualize the mental state of another individual. Autistic children, the argument proceeds, have severe deficits in communication and social interaction precisely because they cannot appreciate what the contents of another person's mind might be (Frith & Happé, 1999).

Not all researchers believe the absence of a "theory of mind" explains childhood autism. Some maintain that autistic children cannot disengage their attention from a stimulus on which they are focusing, such as the hiding location in the "false belief" task (Hughes & Russell, 1993). Others suggest that problems with memory or executive control processes are responsible (Bennetto, Pennington, & Rogers, 1996; Carlson, Moses, & Hix, 1998). Moreover, even if autistic children lack a theory of mind, it may not be because of a neurological deficit. Deaf children who are not exposed to sign language for several years, for example, perform similarly to autistic children on the false belief task. Thus, as discussed earlier, the opportunity to engage in conversations from which one might glean information about the mental states of others may be a crucial factor in the development of a theory of mind (Peterson & Siegal, 1999; Woolfe, Want, & Siegal, 2002). Whatever the ultimate basis for autism, however, it seems likely that understanding basic cognitive processes will be helpful in deciphering the mechanisms underlying this perplexing childhood disorder. One outcome of this active area of research, for example, is awareness that autistic children show deficits in joint attention in the preschool years and as early as age one (Dawson et al., 2002; Leekam, Lopez, & Moore, 2000; Osterling & Dawson, 1994), a finding that can be useful in early diagnosis and treatment of this disorder.

FOR YOUR REVIEW

- What developmental changes in visual perspective taking have been identified by researchers?

- What is meant by the child's "theory of mind"? What contrasting positions have been suggested as explanations for the development of theory of mind?

- What is childhood autism? What are some hypotheses about its causes?

Vygotsky's Sociocultural Theory of Cognitive Development

Piaget assumed that cognitive processes function in similar ways across cultures, that the nature and development of thinking have universal qualities. Standing in sharp contrast to these claims are the theoretical ideas of the prominent Russian psychologist Lev Vygotsky (1978). As we saw in the chapter titled "Themes and Theories," Vygotsky wrote that the child's cognitive growth must be understood in the context of the culture in which he or she lives. Vygotsky believed that in formal and informal exchanges with children, caregivers, peers, and tutors cultivate in them the particular skills and abilities their cultural group values. Gradually, regulation and guidance of the child's behavior by others is replaced by internalized self-regulation. Lev Vygotsky made such *social activity* the cornerstone of his theory, which, like Piaget's, has had enormous impact on the field of developmental psychology.

KEY THEME
Sociocultural Influence

Scaffolding

The concept of **scaffolding** is a way of thinking about the social relationship involved in learning from another person (Wood, Bruner, & Ross, 1976). A scaffold is a temporary structure that gives the support necessary to accomplish a task. An effective caregiver or teacher provides such a structure in problem-solving situations, perhaps by defining the activity to be accomplished, demonstrating supporting skills and techniques in which the learner is still deficient, and motivating the beginner to complete the task. The collaboration advances the knowledge and abilities of the apprentice, as illustrated by the following study of a toddler learning to label objects. Anat Ninio and Jerome Bruner (1978) visited the child in his home every two weeks from age eight months to two years. One commonly shared activity they observed was reading from a picture book, with the boy's mother providing the scaffold for the child to learn more about his language.

> *The mother's (often quite unconscious) approach is exquisitely tuned. When the child responds to her "Look!" by looking, she follows immediately with a query. When the child responds to the query with a gesture or a smile, she supplies a label. But as soon as the child shows the ability to vocalize in a way that might indicate a label, she raises the ante. She withholds the label and repeats the query until the child vocalizes, and then she gives the label if the child does not have it fully or correctly.*
>
> *Later, when the child has learned to respond with shorter vocalizations that correspond to words, she no longer accepts an indifferent vocalization. When the child begins producing a recognizable, constant label for an object, she holds out for it. Finally, the child produces appropriate words at the appropriate place in the dialogue. Even then the mother remains tuned to the developing pattern, helping her child recognize labels and make them increasingly accurate.* (Bruner, 1981, pp. 49–50)

Scaffolding involves a teaching/learning relationship that uses the expert or tutor who intervenes as required and gradually withdraws as assistance becomes unnecessary. Patricia Greenfield (1984) observed this phenomenon among girls learning to weave in Zinacantan, Mexico. Beginners, in the presence of at least one expert weaver

scaffolding Temporary aid provided by one person to encourage, support, and assist a lesser-skilled person in carrying out a task or completing a problem. The model provides knowledge and skills that are learned and gradually transferred to the learner.

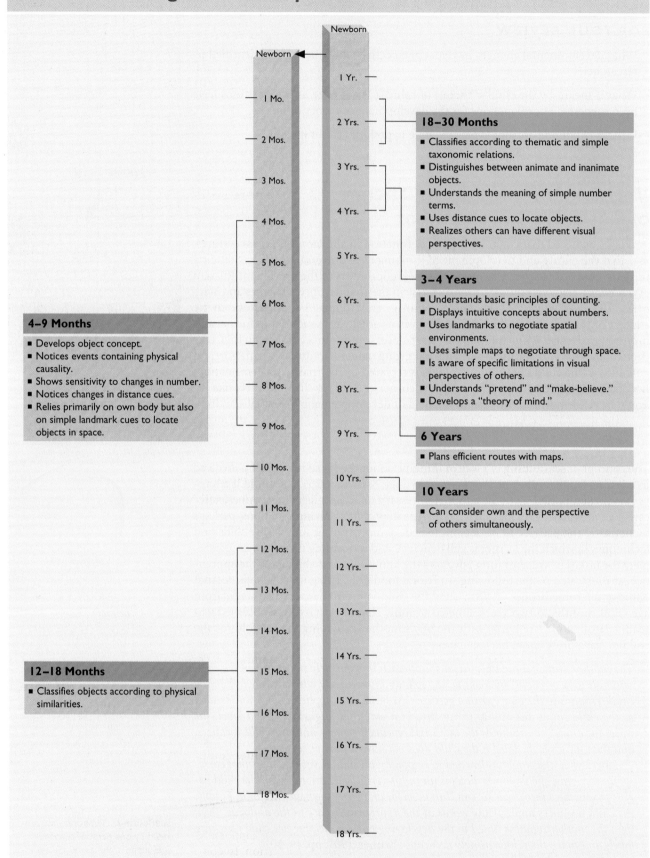

Newborn

Newborn

— 1 Mo.

— 2 Mos.

— 3 Mos.

— 4 Mos.

— 5 Mos.

— 6 Mos.

— 7 Mos.

— 8 Mos.

— 9 Mos.

— 10 Mos.

— 11 Mos.

— 12 Mos.

— 13 Mos.

— 14 Mos.

— 15 Mos.

— 16 Mos.

— 17 Mos.

— 18 Mos.

Newborn

— 1 Yr.

— 2 Yrs.

— 3 Yrs.

— 4 Yrs.

— 5 Yrs.

— 6 Yrs.

— 7 Yrs.

— 8 Yrs.

— 9 Yrs.

— 10 Yrs.

— 11 Yrs.

— 12 Yrs.

— 13 Yrs.

— 14 Yrs.

— 15 Yrs.

— 16 Yrs.

— 17 Yrs.

— 18 Yrs.

4–9 Months

- Develops object concept.
- Notices events containing physical causality.
- Shows sensitivity to changes in number.
- Notices changes in distance cues.
- Relies primarily on own body but also on simple landmark cues to locate objects in space.

12–18 Months

- Classifies objects according to physical similarities.

18–30 Months

- Classifies according to thematic and simple taxonomic relations.
- Distinguishes between animate and inanimate objects.
- Understands the meaning of simple number terms.
- Uses distance cues to locate objects.
- Realizes others can have different visual perspectives.

3–4 Years

- Understands basic principles of counting.
- Displays intuitive concepts about numbers.
- Uses landmarks to negotiate spatial environments.
- Uses simple maps to negotiate through space.
- Is aware of specific limitations in visual perspectives of others.
- Understands "pretend" and "make-believe."
- Develops a "theory of mind."

6 Years

- Plans efficient routes with maps.

10 Years

- Can consider own and the perspective of others simultaneously.

This chart describes the sequence of cognitive development based on the findings of research. Children often show individual differences in the exact ages at which they display the various developmental achievements outlined here.

(usually the mother), started by weaving small items and performed only the simpler parts of the task. The more experienced the learner, the less likely the teacher was to intervene to complete the more technically difficult steps. Novices were more likely to receive direct commands from the teachers, whereas experienced weavers were more likely to receive statements or comments. Both verbal and nonverbal assistance declined as the girls became increasingly proficient weavers, although the expert continued to be a role model for both specific techniques and more general principles of weaving. Remarkably, the scaffolding the tutor provided yielded a woven product from beginners indistinguishable from those completed by expert weavers. These examples illustrate what Vygotsky (1978) called the **zone of proximal development,** the span or disparity between what children are able to do without the assistance of others and what they are often able to accomplish by having someone more expert assist them at key points. Vygotsky claimed the most effective assistance from the expert is that just slightly beyond or ahead of the child's current capacities.

The Role of Skilled Collaborators

As the phenomena of scaffolding and the zone of proximal development suggest, a role model who is sensitive to the learner's level of knowledge contributes greatly to the effective transmission of skills. The effect can be demonstrated in tasks as diverse as the three-year-old's learning to distinguish the colors and shapes of pictures (Diaz, Neal, & Vachio, 1991) to fifth-graders learning how to carry out long division in mathematics assignments (Pratt et al., 1992). Of course, some tutors may be better at these activities than others. Barbara Radziszewska and Barbara Rogoff (1988) examined how nine- and ten-year-olds learned to plan errands. One group of children worked with their parents to organize a shopping trip through an imaginary town, while a second group of children worked with a peer to plan the expedition. Children who worked with adults were exposed to more sophisticated planning strategies; they explored a map of the town more frequently, planned longer sequences of activities, and verbalized more of their plans. Instead of using a step-by-step strategy ("Let's go from this store to the next closest store") as the peer pairs did, children working with adults formulated an integrated sequence of actions ("Let's mark all the stores we have to go to in blue and see what is the best way between them"). In the second part of the experiment, all of the children were observed as they planned a new errand in the same town, this time by themselves. Children who had initially worked with their parents employed more efficient planning strategies than children who had worked with peers.

Why does collaboration with adults work so well? In a follow-up study, Radziszewska and Rogoff (1991) observed that when children worked with adults, they participated in more discussion of the best planning strategy—more "thinking out loud"—than when they worked with peers who had expertise in planning. When working with adults, children were generally more actively involved in the cognitive task, whereas they tended to be more passive observers when their tutor was another child.

Barbara Rogoff and her colleagues (1993) have suggested that the extent to which children and adults take an active role in learning the skills, values, and knowledge of their community differs across cultures. In general, in all communities adults provide a scaffolding for children to begin engaging in mature activities, a process the researchers label *guided participation*. However, children take on a greater burden of responsibility for managing their attention, desire, and interest in mature activities in communities in which they are routinely in the company of adults. The guidance caregivers provide in this context is likely to be in the form of supporting children's observations and efforts rather than in the form of instruction. In contrast, when much of a child's day is spent separate from adults, the child will need more directed lessons and training to acquire mature skills. In this context, the caregivers assume comparatively greater responsibility in helping children to observe and understand the world.

Lev Vygotsky (1896–1934), with his sociocultural theory, made substantial contributions to our understanding of cognitive development.

WHAT DO YOU THINK?

Is Home Schooling a Good Idea?
psychology.college.hmco.com

KEY THEME
Sociocultural Influence

zone of proximal development Range of various kinds of support and assistance provided by an expert (usually an adult) who helps children to carry out activities they currently cannot complete but will later be able to accomplish independently.

By watching skilled collaborators and participating in guided learning, this Afghan boy is learning how to make a basket, an ability that is highly valued in his culture. Vygotsky emphasized the importance of sociocultural context in influencing which skills and abilities will be nurtured among children. Caregivers transmit knowledge by providing children with the *scaffolding* necessary to complete a task, gradually withdrawing as the child gains competence.

Rogoff and her colleagues (1993) found that in communities in India and Guatemala, where young children could watch and enter into adult social and work activities, caregivers were likely to assist and support children in carrying out the more mature responsibilities, such as learning to dress themselves or play with a new toy. On the other hand, in middle-income communities in Turkey and the United States, where children were more likely to be segregated (and parents could not be as consistently attentive and supportive), caregivers were likely to promote play and conversation or provide lessons or learning opportunities in interacting with children to teach them new skills. These interactions, in other words, looked more like the kind typically found with older children in formal school settings. Thus, although all caregivers provided guidance for more mature behavior in each community, its specific form differed, a confirmation of the diverse ways learning may be encouraged in various cultural contexts.

Cognitive development, as you can see, takes place in a distinctly social context, resulting from the child's collaboration with and internalization of social exchanges with parents, peers, and teachers (Rogoff, 1998). An important ingredient in the process of guided participation is the establishment of **intersubjectivity,** the mutual attention and shared communication that take place between expert and learner. We have already seen evidence of intersubjectivity in the chapter titled "Language," in which we discussed how episodes of joint attention contribute to language acquisition. Intersubjectivity is also undoubtedly related to many of the aspects of emotional development discussed in the chapter titled "Emotion" and to the emergence of the child's theory of mind. Infants show the early beginnings of participating in shared attention and communication in the first few months of life in such simple routines as the game of peekaboo (Rochat & Striano, 1999). Researchers are now actively exploring the development of intersubjectivity and how it relates to the various domains of child development.

Developmental psychologists have shown widespread interest in Vygotsky's theory. Many have accepted his claims for the social basis of cognitive development and the importance of understanding the sociocultural context in which the child grows up. Despite the fundamental differences between the ideas of Piaget and Vygotsky, both "theoretical giants" have attempted to capture the dynamism and complexity of how children *develop* in their thinking.

intersubjectivity Mutual attention and shared communication that take place between child and caregiver or learner and expert.

RESEARCH APPLIED TO EDUCATION

Reciprocal Teaching

*A*lthough Craig had always been impressed with Tommy's social skills, he and Marta, his wife, were more concerned with how Tommy was doing in reading in school. Although he could read aloud fairly well, he seemed to have consistent problems in understanding what he read. This was beginning to affect his performance in social studies, science, and other subjects in which students were expected to do quite a bit of independent fact-finding. Tommy seemed to stumble through these assignments and was beginning to feel embarrassed by the grades he was getting. At the last parent-teacher conference, though, Craig and Marta were reassured. The third-grade teacher was trying a new approach to reading called "reciprocal teaching," and she was very encouraged by the visible changes she saw in students' performance and attitudes toward their schoolwork.

Several facets of Vygotsky's theory can be seen in action in a special program developed to foster the emergence of reading comprehension strategies in junior high school students (Brown et al., 1991; Palincsar & Brown, 1984, 1986). The students received instruction in several important reading skills with an instructional method called *reciprocal teaching*. According to this method, teachers should do the following:

1. *Introduce students to four key reading comprehension strategies.* These strategies are summarizing, clarifying word meanings and confusing passages, generating questions about the passage, and predicting what might happen next.

2. *Provide the scaffolding for how to use comprehension strategies.* For one paragraph, the teacher models how to summarize the theme, isolate material that needs to be clarified, anticipate questions, and predict what will happen next.

3. *Ask students to engage in the same four activities for the next paragraph.* The teacher adjusts instructions according to the needs of the individual students, working within what Vygotsky would call each student's *zone of proximal development*. The teacher also provides feedback, praise, hints, and explanations. The teacher invites other students to react to a student's statements, adding other questions, making predictions, or requesting clarification. Teacher and students alternate paragraphs in the early stages of this process.

4. *Become less directive as the students become more skilled in each component of reading.* The students gradually take charge of the process, and the teacher becomes more of an observer, adding suggestions and support when necessary.

Table 8.2 gives an example of the teacher-student exchanges that typically occur with this method.

The results of training were impressive. Whereas during the pretests students averaged 20 percent correct in answering ten questions from reading a paragraph of material, after twenty sessions of reciprocal teaching they averaged 80 percent correct on similar tests. Six months later, students trained in this method moved up from the twentieth percentile in reading ability in their school to the fifty-sixth percentile. Several other studies have documented similar success of reciprocal teaching from as early as first grade (Rosenshine & Meister, 1994).

The key to the success of reciprocal teaching, many experts believe, is the carefully modulated interaction between teacher and students, a point Vygotsky consistently emphasized.

TABLE 8.2
An Example of Reciprocal Teaching

This conversation illustrates the types of exchanges that typify reciprocal teaching. The teacher and, eventually, the students model question asking, summarizing, clarifying, and predicting. In this particular excerpt, students have begun to assume control over their own learning. Students who participated in this program showed significant gains in reading comprehension.

	Reciprocal Teaching
Student 1:	(Question) My question is, what does the aquanaut need when he goes under water?
Student 2:	A watch.
Student 3:	Flippers.
Student 4:	A belt.
Student 1:	Those are all good answers.
Teacher:	(Question) Nice job! I have a question too. Why does the aquanaut wear a belt? What is so special about it?
Student 3:	It's a heavy belt and keeps him from floating up to the top again.
Teacher:	Good for you.
Student 1:	(Summary) For my summary now: This paragraph was about what aquanauts need to take when they go under the water.
Student 5:	(Summary) And also about why they need those things.
Student 3:	(Clarify) I think we need to clarify gear.
Student 6:	That's the special things they need.
Teacher:	Another word for gear in this story might be equipment, the equipment that makes it easier for the aquanauts to do their job.
Student 1:	I don't think I have a prediction to make.
Teacher:	(Prediction) Well, in the story they tell us that there are "many strange and wonderful creatures" that the aquanauts see as they do their work. My prediction is that they'll describe some of these creatures. What are some of the strange creatures you already know about that live in the ocean?
Student 6:	Octopuses.
Student 3:	Whales?
Student 5:	Sharks!

Source: From Palincsar, A. S., & Brown, A. L. (1986, April). Interactive teaching to promote independent learning from text. *The Reading Teacher, 39*(8), 771–777. Reprinted with permission of Annemarie S. Palincsar and the Internation Reading Association. All rights reserved.

FOR YOUR REVIEW

- What are the essential elements of Vygotsky's sociocultural theory of development?

- How do the processes of scaffolding, guided participation with skilled collaborators, and intersubjectivity contribute to development?

CHAPTER RECAP

SUMMARY OF DEVELOPMENTAL THEMES

- **Nature/Nurture** *What roles do nature and nurture play in cognitive development?*

A central tenet of Piaget's theory is that maturation, in conjunction with experience, is responsible for the child's cognitive growth. Neo-Piagetian theorists echo the same theme. When we examine the child's concept development, we may find that certain natural domains offer the child "privileged relationships" to learn about. The role of nature is implicated here. At the same time, studies of concept formation in different cultures suggest that experiences, like formal schooling, also play a role in determining whether children will display specific kinds of classification skills. The role of experts in guiding the child's development—that is, nurture—is emphasized in Vygotsky's theory.

- **Sociocultural Influence** *How does the sociocultural context influence cognitive development?*

Piaget's theory emphasizes the universal cognitive attainments of all children, regardless of their cultural background. However, research has shown that the sociocultural context, the cornerstone of Vygotsky's theory, cannot be ignored. For example, not all children in all cultures attain formal operational thought. We have also seen that children with formal schooling employ taxonomic classification more frequently than unschooled children. Cultural beliefs are often transmitted to children through the scaffolding provided by experts.

- **Child's Active Role** *How does the child play an active role in the process of cognitive development?*

A central assumption in Piaget's theory of cognitive development is that the child actively organizes cognitive schemes and knowledge to more effectively adapt to the demands of the environment. In fact, this idea, a hallmark of Piaget's work, is widely accepted by developmental psychologists of different theoretical persuasions. Vygotsky, too, emphasized the active role of the child, in the sense that what the child has learned contributes to the kinds of interactions to which she or he will be exposed.

- **Continuity/Discontinuity** *Is cognitive development continuous or discontinuous?*

Piaget stressed stagelike attainments in thinking. Others who have empirically reevaluated his work make claims for more continuous changes in cognition in their focus on the underlying basic processes that contribute to development. Unlike Piaget, Vygotsky did not emphasize discontinuities in development.

- **Individual Differences** *How prominent are individual differences in cognitive development?*

Piaget emphasized the common features of thought displayed by all children. His explicit goal was to explain the general characteristics of cognition as children move from the sensorimotor through the formal operational stage of development. Although Piaget acknowledged that some children may reach a given stage earlier or later than others, his main concern was not with individual differences among children. Others, including the neo-Piagetians, argue that children may show greater or lesser abilities within particular domains, depending on the specific experiences to which they are exposed. Thus substantial individual differences in cognitive development may occur among children of similar ages. Finally, Vygotsky argued that children will show differences in development depending on the values of the larger culture and the sensitivity of skilled collaborators to the child's needs in the learning situation.

- **Interaction Among Domains** *How does cognitive development interact with development in other domains?*

The child's emergent cognitive skills interact with almost every other aspect of development. For example, children's decreasing cognitive egocentrism will affect their ability to make judgments in perspective-taking tasks, which have important social ramifications. By the same token, development in other domains can influence cognitive growth. For example, cognition may be affected by maturation of the central nervous system, which is hypothesized to contribute to progress in the speed and efficiency of cognitive processing. The child's thinking is thus both the product of and a contributor to development in many other domains.

SUMMARY OF TOPICS

Piaget's Theory of Cognitive Development

- One of the most comprehensive theories of cognitive development was proposed by Jean Piaget. Piaget championed the active role of the child in the construction of knowledge and the transformation of cognitive schemes as a result of maturation combined with experience.

- Piaget believed that children progressed through four stages of development, each with its own unique characteristics.

Stages of Development

- The chief feature of the *sensorimotor stage* is that thought is based on action. Children develop *means-ends behavior,* separate the self from the external environment, and attain the *object concept.* The end of this stage is signaled by the child's ability to engage in deferred imitation, a form of representation.

- Children in the *preoperational stage* can think using symbols, but their thought is limited in that it is *egocentric*. Children fail *conservation tasks* because they do not yet have the logical thought structures that allow them to think about *reversibility*. They also focus on only one aspect of the problem (*centration*), and they tend to *focus on states*.

- The *concrete operational stage* is characterized by logical thought, but only in the presence of real objects or images. Because children are capable of performing *operations*, they are successful on increasingly difficult conservation tasks, as well as seriation tasks.

- By the time children reach the *formal operational stage,* they can think abstractly and *hypothetically,* generating multiple solutions to a problem. Thought is also systematic. Adolescents in this stage may display beliefs in the *imaginary audience* and the *personal fable.*

Implications for Education

- Piaget's theory implies that teachers must take into account the child's current stage of development and supply activities consistent with his or her capabilities.

- Teachers should also be aware of the individual child's current state of knowledge so that new material can be readily assimilated.

- Piagetian theory supports the active role of the child in the educational process.

Evaluating Piaget's Theory

- One criticism of Piaget's theory is that he underestimated the competence of young children. Evidence for the attainment of the object concept by about six months of age, for example, shows that children may not need to gradually build up certain knowledge over time.

- Another criticism is that children's performance may not be as stagelike as Piaget maintained. There is less consistency in the child's behaviors within a stage than the theory claims.

- Some critics maintain that cognitive development is not a general process, but rather shows more rapid advances in some domains than in others. One example is children's early sensitivity to biological entities.

- Researchers have proposed alternative explanations for the behaviors Piaget observed. Some data suggest that changes in information processing lie behind advances in cognition, and other data imply a larger role for the sociocultural environment than Piaget acknowledged.

Neo-Piagetian Approaches

- Theories such as those of Fischer and Case postulate stages of development but allow a greater role for experience and domain-specific accomplishments than did Piaget.

Concept Development

- A *concept* is a set of information defined on the basis of some general or abstract principle. Concepts result in greater efficiency in information processing.

Properties of Objects

- Young infants seem to be sensitive to the height and rigidity of objects, as well as the concept of solidity, leading some researchers to formulate the *core knowledge hypothesis,* the idea that infants possess innate knowledge of certain properties of objects. Others believe that infants' responses to objects are due to information-processing components such as attention and memory.

- Infants display the A-not-B error at about eight to twelve months of age. Explanations of this error include problems in memory, the failure to suppress an already made motor response, and an inability to update information about an object's changed location.

- Infants show an apparent awareness of the concept of physical causality. Older children fail to show the *animism* and *artificialism* described by Piaget when they are asked direct questions about the causes of things.

Classification

- One-year-olds group items together on the basis of perceptual similarities. Slightly older children rely on thematic and taxonomic relations.

- Some researchers believe that children begin to classify with basic-level (perceptually similar) categories and progress to superordinate relations. Others maintain that children's early concepts are global and based on meanings and that they become more refined with development.

- The learning of concepts in *natural domains* occurs at an accelerated pace. Children also seem to form theories about the meanings of concepts, ideas that become more elaborated with development.

Numerical Concepts

- Piaget maintained that preoperational children fail to comprehend *one-to-one correspondence, cardinality,* and *ordinality*. However, by age four, children are able to count, and they display some knowledge of certain numerical principles. Preschoolers understand relations such as "bigger" and "smaller," but have more difficulty with large number sets and numbers that are close together.

- Newborns detect differences in small number sets, and five-month-olds respond to addition and subtraction of objects in a display. Some researchers believe that sensitivity to number is innate, but others say that infants may be responding on the basis of other attributes of the displays. A fundamental question concerns the nature of infants' underlying representations of number.

- Preschoolers display good intuitions about how to add and form fractions. These understandings can form the basis for mathematical instruction.

Spatial Relationships

- Infants first rely on the locations of objects relative to their own bodies, but they can soon use cues such as color as *landmarks* to locate objects in physical space. Infants and young children are also sensitive to distance cues in locating objects.

- Four-year-olds can use simple maps to navigate a route, but map-reading skills improve over the next few years. Children learn to understand that symbols in the map refer to corresponding real-world objects, understand the scale and alignment of the map, and become able to plan an efficient route using the map.

Understanding Psychological States

- A vital aspect of communication and social interaction is the ability to understand the thoughts, feelings, and motives of others.

Perspective Taking: Taking the Views of Others

- Although Piaget believed that preoperational children were limited in the ability to take the visual perspective of others, children show competence when these tasks are simplified or made more familiar. Children first recognize that their view is not identical to that of another person, and then they can determine the specifics of the other's view.

The Child's Theory of Mind

- According to Piaget, preschoolers display *realism,* the failure to distinguish between physical and mental states. More recent research has shown that mental-state knowledge is acquired much earlier than he suspected.

- Children begin to show knowledge of mental states at about eighteen months, when they follow the gaze of another person and show an understanding of the concept of "desire." In the years that follow, children understand concepts such as "pretend," "belief," and other aspects of the mind as an entity.

- Children under age four and autistic children typically fail the false belief task, a test of acquisition of *theory of mind.* Researchers disagree about the source of the child's theory of mind. Some feel that it is an innate, modular form of knowledge, whereas others claim it arises from the child's experiences with language.

Vygotsky's Sociocultural Theory of Cognitive Development

- A principle feature of Vygotsky's theory is that the child's cognitive growth must be understood in terms of the sociocultural context in which he or she lives.

Scaffolding

- Scaffolding is the temporary support provided by an expert to a learner who is trying to accomplish a task. Novice learners often get more support, but as their skills improve, that support is gradually withdrawn.

- Tutors often work within the child's *zone of proximal development,* the distance between what the child can do alone and what she can do with guidance.

The Role of Skilled Collaborators

- Research shows that adults play a critical role in the transmission of skills, probably because they encourage children to be active and to think out loud.

- Some communities may afford children more opportunities for guided participation than others, especially when the children are routinely in the company of adults.

- An important ingredient in the process of guided participation is the establishment of *intersubjectivity,* a state of mutual attention and shared communication.

Cognition: Information Processing

Key Themes in Cognition

- **Nature/Nurture**   What roles do nature and nurture play in cognitive development?

- **Sociocultural Influence**   How does the sociocultural context influence cognitive development?

- **Child's Active Role**   How does the child play an active role in the process of cognitive development?

- **Continuity/Discontinuity**   Is cognitive development continuous or discontinuous?

- **Individual Differences**   How prominent are individual differences in cognitive development?

- **Interaction Among Domains**   How does cognitive development interact with development in other domains?

"Tomorrow's geography test is going to be really tough," Nate lamented to his friend on the way home from school. "I should have paid more attention in class and kept up with my assignments. Now I have to study so much!" Normally a good student, Nate had been preoccupied with the success of his baseball team. Now there was a price to be paid as he prepared for the next day's test, and he was decidedly anxious about it. Nate had made up one "trick" for remembering the states in the Southeast: he strung their first letters to make the phrase "True aces forget no states" for Tennessee, Alabama, Florida, Georgia, North Carolina, and South Carolina, respectively. And it helped him to identify some of the states by tying their shapes to things he knew; for example, Florida really did look as though it had a "panhandle." But there was so much more to remember! Maybe he could just repeat the capitals of the states over and over to himself. One thing he knew for sure: next time he would not save all of his studying for the night before the test.

Nate, as it turns out, had a pretty good understanding of his mental capabilities. He knew that paying attention in class was helpful and that certain techniques, such as rehearsal, mental imagery, and other "tricks," could help him remember information. He also knew there were limits to what he could accomplish in the few hours he had to prepare for his exam. In fact, many aspects of Nate's own thinking—attention, memory, and even the fact that he could evaluate his thought capabilities—have been topics of great interest to developmental psychologists. In this chapter, we continue our examination of cognitive development, this time from an important alternative viewpoint to the perspectives described in the chapter titled "Cognition: Piaget and Vygotsky": the information-processing perspective. First, we will summarize the major features of this theoretical model. Then we will survey several topics that have been studied extensively from the stance of information-processing theory, including attention, memory, and problem solving.

The Information-Processing Approach

As we saw in the chapter titled "Themes and Theories," information-processing theorists believe that human cognition is best understood as the management of information through a system with limited space or resources. In the information-processing approach, mental processing is usually broken down into several components or levels of activity. For example, memory processes are often partitioned into *encoding, storage,* and *retrieval* phases. Information is assumed to move forward through the system, and each stage of processing takes some time (Massaro & Cowan, 1993; Palmer & Kimchi, 1986).

Many traditional information-processing models are called **multistore models** because they posit several mental structures through which information flows

multistore model Information-processing model that describes a sequence of mental structures through which information flows.

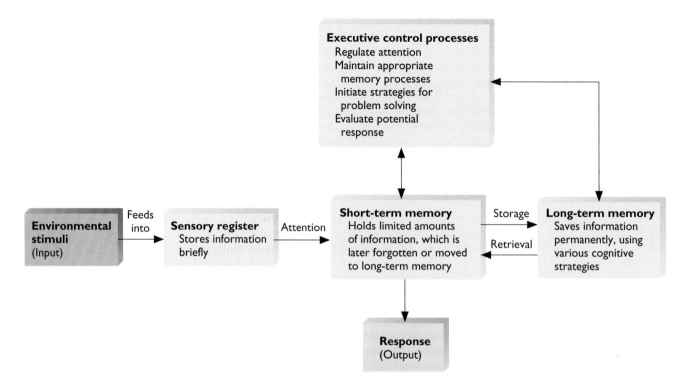

Source: Adapted from Atkinson & Shiffrin, 1968.

FIGURE 9.1
A Schematic Model of Human Information Processing

This highly simplified model includes several cognitive structures and processes that many information-processing theorists believe to be important in cognitive development. As the arrows indicate, information often flows in several directions between various structures. The goal of information-processing models is to identify those structures and processes that are at work when a child responds to his or her environment.

sequentially, much as data pass through a computer. One example of this type of model is shown in Figure 9.1. Most multistore models distinguish between psychological structures and control processes. *Psychological structures* are analogous to the hardware of a computer. The *control processes* are mental activities that move information from one structure to another, much as software functions for the computer.

Suppose someone asks you to repeat a list of words, such as *shoe, car, truck, hat, coat, bus.* If you have paid attention to all of the words and, like an efficient computer, "input" them into your cognitive system, processing will begin in the **sensory register.** Information is held here for a fraction of a second in a form very close to the original stimuli, in this case the audible sounds you experienced. Next, the words may move to the *memory stores.* **Working memory** (sometimes called *short-term memory*) holds information for no more than a couple of minutes. Many researchers consider working memory to be a kind of work space in which various kinds of cognitive tasks can be conducted. If you were to repeat the words over and over to yourself—that is, rehearse them—you would be employing a *control process* to retain information in working memory. You might also use the second memory store, **long-term memory,** the repository of more enduring information, and notice that the items belong to two categories, clothing and vehicles. The *executive control* oversees this communication among the structures of the information-processing system. Finally, when you are asked to say the words aloud, your *response system* functions to help you reproduce the sounds you heard moments earlier.

Other theorists in this field have advanced a **limited-resource model** of the cognitive system that emphasizes a finite amount of available cognitive energy that can be deployed in numerous ways, but only with certain tradeoffs. Limited-resource models emphasize the allocation of energy for various cognitive activities rather than the mental structures themselves. The basic assumption is that the pool of resources available for processing, retaining, and reporting information is finite (Bjorklund & Harnishfeger, 1990). In one such model, introduced in the chapter titled "Cognition: Piaget and Vygotsky," Robbie Case proposes an inverse relationship between the amount of space available for operating on information and that available for storage (Case, 1985; Case, Kurland, & Goldberg, 1982). *Operations,* as we have seen,

sensory register   Memory store that holds information for very brief periods of time in a form that closely resembles the initial input.

working memory   Short-term memory store in which mental operations such as rehearsal and categorization take place.

include processes such as identifying the stimuli and recognizing relationships among them; *storage* refers to the retention of information for use at a later time. If a substantial amount of mental effort is expended on operations, less space is available for storage or retention.

In the simple memory experiment we just examined, the effort used to identify the words and notice the categorical relationships among them will determine the space left over for storing those words. If we are proficient at recognizing words and their relationships, storage space will be available. If these tasks cost us substantial effort, however, our resources will be taxed and little will be left for the task of remembering. Robert Kail's research (1986, 1991a, 1991b) supports the idea that a central component of cognitive development is an increase in processing speed with age. As children grow older, they can mentally rotate images, name objects, or add numbers more rapidly. More resources then become available for other cognitive tasks.

How do these two general information-processing frameworks, the multistore model and the limited-resource model, account for cognitive development? Multistore models allow for two possibilities. Changes in cognition can stem from either an increase in the size of the structures—the "hardware"—or increasing proficiency in employing the "software," or control processes. For example, the capacity of the mental structure working memory may increase with age, or, as children grow older, they may increase their tendency to rehearse items to keep information in working memory or even push it into long-term memory. Limited-resource models suggest that what changes during development is processing efficiency. As children become more proficient in manipulating information, more internal space is freed up for storage.

The Development of Attention

Have you ever noticed that sometimes a teenager can spend hours absorbed in a single activity, such as doing a jigsaw puzzle or playing a video game, whereas a toddler seems to bound from activity to activity? Most of us have a sense that older children are better able than younger ones to "pay attention" to a given task. Researchers have documented how children's attentional processes undergo recognizable changes with development.

Attention has been conceptualized as a process that allows the individual to focus on a selected aspect of the environment, often in preparation for learning or problem solving (Kahneman, 1973). Attention represents the first step in cognitive processing and, as such, is a critical phase. Unless information enters the system in the first place, there will be few opportunities to develop memory, concepts, or other cognitive skills. Children with a poor capacity to attend will have difficulties in learning, the ramifications of which can be enormous, especially as they enter school. Research evidence corroborates that children who have greater attention spans and persistence in tasks at ages four to five years have higher intelligence scores and school achievement by the time they get to second grade (Palisin, 1986). Even at three months of age, infants who pay greater attention to stimuli have better recognition memory for them (Adler, Gerhardstein, & Rovee-Collier, 1998).

Sustaining Attention

One of the most obvious developmental trends is the dramatic increase in the child's ability to *sustain* attention on some activity or set of stimuli. Holly Ruff and Katharine Lawson (1990) observed one-, two-, and three-and-a-half-year-olds while the children played with an array of six toys. They observed a steady increase with age in the amount of attention directed to individual toys. On average, one-year-olds showed focused attention for 3.33 seconds, two-year-olds for 5.36 seconds, and three-and-a-half-year-olds for 8.17 seconds. Generally, at ages two and three, children

long-term memory Memory that holds information for extended periods of time.

limited-resource model Information-processing model that emphasizes the allocation of finite energy within the cognitive system.

show longer periods of attention to television and to toys they are playing with than to highly structured tasks. Between ages three and five years, though, children show growth in the ability to attend to tasks arranged by an adult (Ruff, Capozzoli, & Weissberg, 1998). The attention span continues to increase throughout the early school years and adolescence and shows a particularly marked improvement around age ten years (Milich, 1984; Yendovitskaya, 1971).

Why does sustained attention increase with age? Maturation of the central nervous system is partly responsible. The reticular activating system, the portion of the lower brainstem that regulates levels of arousal, is not fully mature until adolescence. Another factor may be the increasing complexity of the child's interests. Young children seem to be intrigued by the physical properties of objects, but because these are often not too complex, simply looking at or touching objects quickly leads to habituation. On the other hand, older children are more concerned with creative and varied ways of playing with objects (Ruff & Lawson, 1990). As children actively generate more possible uses for stimuli, their active engagement with stimuli captivates and feeds back to influence attention.

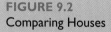

KEY THEME
Interaction Among Domains

KEY THEME
Child's Active Role

Deploying Attention

A second developmental change in attentional processes involves the ability of children to control their attention in a systematic manner; that is, they increasingly *deploy* their attention effectively, such as when they are comparing two stimuli. At three-and-a-half months of age, shifts of attention from one stimulus to another appear to be reflexive in nature, but by five to six months of age, they are more deliberate and planned. Changes in the electrical activity of the cortex accompany this changeover to more controlled attention (Richards, 2000). During the period from about five to seven months, infants also exhibit a marked increase in the rate with which they shift attention from one stimulus to another. More rapid shifts probably reflect the infant's greater efficiency in processing information from the environment. Researchers hypothesize that the infant's ability to *inhibit* processing of one stimulus so that the next one can be attended to underlies more rapid shifts (Rose, Feldman, & Jankowski, 2001a).

The classic studies of Eliane Vurpillot (Vurpillot, 1968; Vurpillot & Ball, 1979) illustrate developmental changes in how older children control their attention. Children were shown a picture of two houses, each having six windows, and were asked to judge whether the houses were identical (see Figure 9.2). As they inspected the houses, their eye movements were filmed. Preschoolers scanned the windows less thoroughly and systematically than older children. For example, when the houses were identical, four- and five-year-olds looked at only about half of the windows

FIGURE 9.2
Comparing Houses

Children were asked to explore houses to make judgments about whether they were the same or different while a camera photographed their eye movements. Preschoolers explored the windows less thoroughly, efficiently, and systematically than older children.

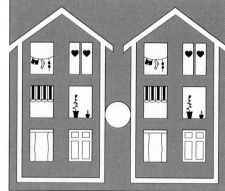

Source: Adapted from Vurpillot, 1968

before making a decision, but older children looked at nearly all of them. When the windows differed, older children were more likely than younger children to stop scanning as soon as they detected a discrepancy. Finally, older children were more likely to look back and forth at windows in the same locations of the two houses; younger children displayed more haphazard fixations, looking at a window in one house, then a different window in the other house.

In another experiment, Patricia Miller and Yvette Harris (1988) found that children not only become more systematic but also use more *efficient* attentional strategies as they grow older. Preschoolers were asked to determine whether one row of six drawings of toys contained the same elements in sequence as a second row of six drawings. To accomplish this task, they had to open doors that covered the pictures. Three-year-olds tended to be systematic but not very efficient: they opened one entire row first, then opened the next row. In contrast, four-year-olds adopted a systematic and more efficient strategy for comparing: they opened each vertically aligned pair from one end of the array to the next. Perhaps as a consequence, the older participants were more accurate in their judgments about whether or not the rows were identical.

Selective Attention

Still another aspect of attention that changes with development is the ability to be *selective*. Older children are much more likely than younger children to ignore information that is irrelevant or distracts from some central activity or problem. For example, in one study children ages six, nine, and twelve years participated in a *speeded classification task*. They were given decks of cards that varied on one or more stimulus dimensions: form (circle or square), orientation of a line (horizontal or vertical), and location of a star (above or below the center). The objective was to sort the cards on the basis of one predetermined dimension as quickly as they could. But what happened when an irrelevant dimension was added to the cards in the deck? This manipulation interfered with the ability of six-year-olds to sort the cards but had little effect on the performance of older children (Strutt, Anderson, & Well, 1975). Other research confirms that the ability to filter out distracting information continues to mature at least until early adolescence (Goldberg, Maurer, & Lewis, 2001).

The ability to attend to some parts of an event or activity to the exclusion of others signals the child's increasing skill at controlling his own cognitive processing. This ability likely depends to some extent on the maturation of the prefrontal cortex, which we know is involved in selective attention in adults (Husain & Kennard, 1997). Also contributing to this change is the child's growing understanding that his attentional capacity is limited and that cognitive tasks are best accomplished with focused attention. Growth in this knowledge occurs during the preschool and early school years. When asked if they would rather listen to pairs of stories simultaneously or one at a time, three-year-olds are willing to listen to two tape recordings at once, but four-year-olds prefer to listen to one at a time (Pillow, 1988). Six-year-olds state that a person who is concentrating on one task will not pay much attention to other things, whereas four-year-olds do not exhibit this understanding (Flavell, Green, & Flavell, 1995).

To some degree, the child's knowledge about attention may be gleaned from the kinds of behaviors that are emphasized in his or her culture. In our society, focusing on one thing at a time is probably considered by most parents and teachers to be a desirable goal (Ruff & Rothbart, 1996). However, this pattern is not universal. Among members of a Mayan community in Guatemala, both toddlers and caregivers spend more time attending simultaneously to several competing events—an interesting toy and a playful sibling, for example—than American children and caregivers (Chavajay & Rogoff, 1999). Cultural preferences may thus guide the particular attentional style a child develops.

⊙ SEE FOR YOURSELF
psychology.college.hmco.com
Testing Selective Attention

KEY THEME
Interaction Among Domains

KEY THEME
Sociocultural Influence

Attention Deficit Hyperactivity Disorder

Between 3 and 5 percent of school-age children in the United States, usually boys, show a pattern of impulsivity, high levels of motor activity, and attention problems called *attention deficit hyperactivity disorder* or *ADHD* (American Psychiatric Association, 2002). The disorder is puzzling because its cause is not completely understood, and an unambiguous diagnosis can be difficult to obtain. At the same time, for parents, teachers, and the children themselves, the consequences of the disorder—poor school achievement, behavior management problems, poor peer relationships, negative moods, and low self-esteem among them—can be serious (Erhardt & Hinshaw, 1994; Rapport, 1995; Whalen et al., 2002). Whereas hyperactivity and impulsivity may decline in adolescence, problems with attention often persist for years (Hart et al., 1995).

As the diagnostic label implies, a major assumption about the nature of ADHD is that these children have some type of deficit in attention. But what precisely is the nature of that deficit? A prominent current hypothesis is that children with ADHD have problems with higher-order executive control processes, especially those that help children to inhibit their tendencies to respond (Barkley, 1997; Pennington, 1998). In one type of experiment, children sitting in front of a computer screen are instructed to hit one key if they see the letter "X" appear and to hit another key if the letter "O" pops up. However, if they first hear a tone, they must not hit a key at all. Children with ADHD have difficulty stopping themselves unless the tone is played much earlier than the letter appears (Schachar et al., 2000).

Children with ADHD also have difficulty in being selective when confronted with numerous stimuli that compete for their attention. An experiment comparing six- to twelve-year-old ADHD boys with non-ADHD boys as they watched television demonstrates this effect (Landau, Lorch, & Milich, 1992). Each boy watched four segments of a show for fourteen minutes, half the time with several distracting toys in the room and half the time without toys. All participants were told they would have to answer some questions about the televised segments at the end of the viewing period. When distracting toys were present, ADHD boys paid about half as much attention to the shows as the non-ADHD boys. However, the two groups did not differ in their attention in the absence of distracting toys. These results suggest that ADHD children do not have a pervasive problem in sustaining attention; rather, they have difficulty in the presence of extraneous stimulation.

Some researchers now hypothesize that the specific cognitive problem that children with ADHD have is with working memory, the memory store in which "cognitive work" occurs (Tannock & Martinussen, 2001). In this line of thinking, the process of selective attention takes place in working memory. A recent study showed that normal adults, too, are distracted by stimuli when they are overloaded with another demanding cognitive task, such as remembering a set of digits. When less stress is placed on the cognitive system, problems in attention diminish (de Fockert et al., 2001).

KEY THEME
Nature/Nurture

Why do children with ADHD have these difficulties? Several studies implicate biological factors. Individuals with ADHD show abnormal brain wave activity, slower blood flow, and lower glucose metabolism in the prefrontal regions of the brain that are associated with regulating attention and motor activity (Rapport, 1995). Also, several brain regions, including the prefrontal cortex, are smaller in children with ADHD than in children without the diagnosis (Giedd et al., 2001). Evidence also indicates that ADHD may have an inherited component. In one investigation, 65 percent of the ADHD children in the sample had at least one relative with the disorder (Biederman et al., 1990). Other risk factors for attention problems include prenatal exposure to alcohol (Streissguth et al., 1995) and possibly nicotine, cocaine, or other drugs that may affect the developing brain of the fetus (National Institute of Mental Health, 1996).

ADHD children are frequently treated with medications, such as Ritalin, that are classified as stimulants but that actually serve to "slow them down." This treatment helps many children, as does a combination of medication and behavior therapy, according to a major national study conducted by the National Institute of Mental Health (MTA Cooperative Group, 1999). But some experts worry that too many children are placed on this medication simply because they exhibit behavior problems rather than genuine ADHD. Clearly, a better understanding of ADHD is needed to sharpen its clinical diagnosis and develop effective treatment strategies for these children.

FOR YOUR REVIEW

- What are the major differences between multistore and limited-resource models of information processing? How do they differ in accounting for developmental changes in cognition?

- What are three major ways in which attention changes with development?

- What factors seem to be responsible for developmental changes in attention?

- What is ADHD? What factors may be responsible for its occurrence?

The Development of Memory

Few cognitive skills are as basic as the ability to store information encountered at a given time for potential retrieval seconds, minutes, days, or even years later. It is hard to imagine how any other cognitive activity, such as problem solving or concept formation, could take place without the ability to draw on previously experienced information. How could we classify dogs, horses, and giraffes into the category "animals" without remembering the shared features of each? How could we solve a problem such as Piaget's pendulum task, described in the chapter titled "Cognition: Piaget and Vygotsky," without remembering the results of each of our mini-experiments with the length of the string, weight of the object, and so on? In one way or another, memory is a crucial element in most of our thinking.

However, memory is far from a simple or unitary construct. One distinction is drawn between episodic and semantic memory. **Episodic memory** is memory for events that occurred at a specific time and place in the past ("What did you do on your first day of school?"). **Semantic memory,** on the other hand, consists of general concepts or facts that are stored without reference to a specific previous event ("How many inches are there in a foot?"). We can make another distinction, one between recognition and recall memory. Tasks that measure **recognition memory** require participants to indicate whether they have encountered a picture, word, or other stimulus before ("Have you seen this picture on previous trials of this experiment?"). Participants are required merely to give a *yes* or *no* answer or some other simple response that signals they have previously encountered an item. In **recall memory** tasks, participants must reproduce previously presented stimuli ("Tell me the twelve words you heard me say a few minutes ago."). The fact that memory can be conceptualized in such different ways has complicated the task of describing developmental processes. Nevertheless, three decades of research on this aspect of cognition have begun to suggest some clear and predictable trends in the development of memory.

Recognition Memory

How early can we demonstrate the presence of memory? How long do those memories last? How much information can be retained through recognition memory? Two techniques useful in documenting young infants' perceptual abilities and discussed

episodic memory Memory for events that took place at a specific time and place.

semantic memory Memory for general concepts or facts.

recognition memory Ability to identify whether a stimulus has been previously encountered.

recall memory Ability to reproduce stimuli that one has previously encountered.

FIGURE 9.3
Infant Recognition Memory

Fagan tested infant recognition memory by using visual stimuli in a paired-comparison procedure. For each row, one of the stimuli was presented repeatedly until habituation occurred. Then one of the other stimuli in the row was paired with the familiar stimulus to see if infants preferred the novel item. Infants only a few months old looked longer at novel items up to fourteen days after the initial familiarization.

Source: Adapted from Fagan, 1974.

in the chapter titled "Basic Learning and Perception," *habituation* and *operant conditioning,* have also been fruitful in yielding answers to these questions about infants' and young children's recognition abilities.

Much of the earliest research on infant recognition memory was conducted by Joseph Fagan, who used the habituation procedure. First, a visual stimulus such as a photograph of a human face or a geometric figure (some examples are shown in Figure 9.3) is presented to the infant for a predetermined period of time. On a subsequent trial, the same stimulus is paired with a completely new item, and the time the infant spends looking at each picture is recorded. In this *paired-comparison procedure,* infants typically look longer at the novel stimulus than at the familiar one, suggesting that they remember the familiar item. Using this basic approach, Fagan (1974) demonstrated that five- to six-month-olds familiarized with black-and-white photos of human faces for only a few minutes retain information about them for surprisingly long periods of time. When the recognition test occurred three hours or up to fourteen days after the initial familiarization, infants showed consistently longer visual fixations to the novel stimulus. This is an impressive level of performance for infants only a few months old!

Carolyn Rovee-Collier and her colleagues have used a different technique, relying on operant conditioning to demonstrate infants' early memory capabilities (Rovee-Collier & Hayne, 1987; Rovee-Collier & Shyi, 1992). As shown in Figure 9.4, an infant lies in a crib with a ribbon running from his ankle to an overhead mobile. Within a few minutes, the infant recognizes the contingency between his foot kicks and the movement of the mobile; his rate of kicking increases dramatically. Suppose, however, that the mobile is removed from the crib for two weeks. When the mobile is reintroduced, does the infant remember that this is the object that he can move with a foot kick? The answer is yes: three-month-olds vigorously kicked when the familiar mobile was replaced over the crib but did not kick as much when a brand-new mobile was put in the same position (Enright et al., 1983).

These early memories are easily disrupted, however, by changes in the context of the task. Suppose an infant learns the original contingency between a foot kick and the movement of the mobile when she is in a playpen lined with a yellow cloth with green squares. Twenty-four hours later, the mobile is reintroduced, but this time the cloth liner is blue with red stripes. Now the infant does not show a memory for the previous day's events; she does not kick nearly as much as she did at the end of training the previous day (Rovee-Collier et al., 1992). Thus infants six months of age and under encode very detailed and specific information about an event, even when that information is not the central focus of attention. Put another way, infants will show

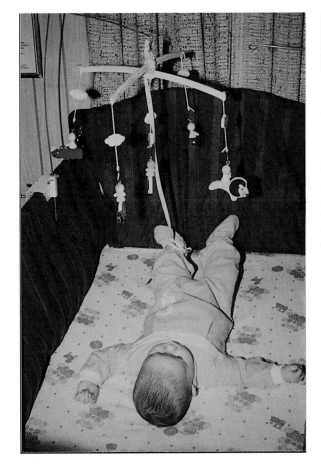

FIGURE 9.4
Using Operant Conditioning
to Study Early Memory

Infants in Rovee-Collier's studies had a ribbon attached between their feet and an interesting mobile overhead. Infants quickly learned that kicking made the mobile move. When the mobile was removed and then reintroduced after a delay interval, infants showed that they "remembered" it by vigorously kicking again.

Source: Stricker et al., 2001.

evidence of memory only when the conditions during training and memory testing are as similar as possible (Hayne & Rovee-Collier, 1995). By the latter portion of the first year, however, infants are more likely to disregard differences in contextual cues when they are tested for memory, perhaps because their memories are more robust (Hartshorn et al., 1998). More broadly speaking, they can remember things that are learned in one place and tested in another (Rovee-Collier, 1999). Thus recognition memory shows distinct developmental changes in the first year.

Reminders of an event can enhance infant recognition, but when they occur is apparently crucial. If infants who had learned to make a foot-kick in the presence of a mobile were given a "memory boost" by seeing the mobile again within three days, they showed memory for the mobile by kicking in its presence eight days later. Reminders given more than three days later did not have this effect; infants seemed to have forgotten the mobile at the eight-day test (Rovee-Collier, Evancio, & Earley, 1995). Figure 9.5 summarizes the results of this experiment. Rovee-Collier (1995) proposes that there are *time windows* within which a reminder can provide an "inoculation" against forgetting. Reminders toward the end of the time window rather than at its beginning seem to be especially effective (Rovee-Collier, Greco-Vigorito, & Hayne, 1993).

At just how young an age do infants display recognition memory? One experiment shows that even newborns can retain information for at least a twenty-four-hour period (Swain, Zelazo, & Clifton, 1993). On the first day of the study, newborns heard a tape of a word, either *beagle* or *tinder,* that was repeated during the experimental session while an observer recorded the number of head turns the infants made toward the sound. As you would expect with the habituation procedure, the number of head turns declined over the session. One day later, one group of infants heard the same word again, whereas a second, experimental group heard a new word.

FIGURE 9.5
Time Windows in
Remembering

In an experiment conducted
by Carolyn Rovee-Collier and
her colleagues, three-month-
old infants were trained to kick
in the presence of a mobile.
The numbers along the horizontal axis give the days on
which the various components
of the study occurred. Day 0
is the day of original training.
Days 1–8 signifies that the
reminder occurred one day
after the initial training and
the long-term memory test
occurred on day 8 and so on.
The graph shows that infants
who had received a "reminder"
of the event up to three days
after the initial training had
improved memories.

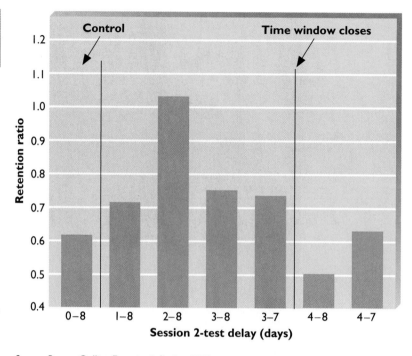

Source: Rovee-Collier, Evancio, & Earley, 1995
Note: The retention ratio on the vertical axis is a mathematical measure of how much
infants remembered. It is the proportion of training kicking rate that infants displayed
during the long-term memory test.

Infants in the first group made fewer head turns toward the stimulus word and more head turns away from it than infants in the second group. Evidently, they remembered some very specific properties of the auditory stimulus for a duration of many hours.

How many items can infants remember? Susan Rose and her colleagues found that at five to seven months of age, infants had trouble recognizing a string of three or four different objects that were presented as part of one memory trial but that, by twelve months of age, almost half of infants were successful (Rose, Feldman, & Jankowski, 2001b). Older infants and preschool-age children are even more impressive. Typically, researchers present children with a large number of pictures, sometimes as many as one hundred. On test trials, the "old" pictures are interspersed with "new" ones, and children state whether they had seen the picture before. Alternatively, researchers note whether children look longer at the novel pictures. In general, children correctly recognize a striking percentage—75 percent or more—of stimulus items even when they are tested several weeks later (Brown & Scott, 1971; Daehler & Bukatko, 1977).

Finally, recent studies that measure brain wave activity as individuals respond to old and new stimuli indicate that the speed of recognition memory, as well as its accuracy, increases from the preschool years to young adulthood (Cycowicz et al., 2001; Marshall et al., 2002). Thus, although recognition memory is present from the child's earliest hours, age-related changes are seen in some of its characteristics.

Recall Memory

Researchers have used different types of tasks to assess the development of recall memory. Some of these tasks have been focused on short-term memory, whereas others have tapped memories over longer durations. Regardless of the delay period involved, the child's use of memory strategies seems to be an important factor in preserving past events. However, alternative conceptualizations of memory development emphasizing different aspects of processing have also offered explanations of memory improvement.

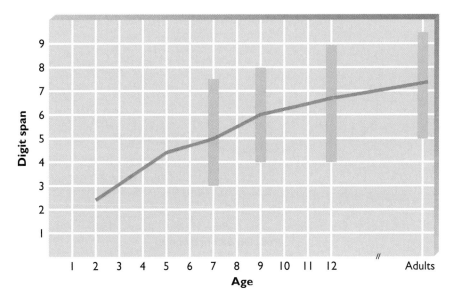

Source: Adapted from Dempster, 1981.

FIGURE 9.6
Developmental Changes in Memory Span

In the memory span task, participants are asked to repeat a string of digits after an interval of a few seconds. The points on the curve represent the average number of digits participants are able to recall. The bars represent the ranges of typical performance at each age. Memory span increases throughout childhood and approaches the adult level between ages ten and twelve years.

● **Memory Span** Suppose someone asks you to repeat a string of digits, such as a phone number. Like most adults, you should be able to repeat between seven and nine digits with relatively little difficulty as long as no more than approximately thirty seconds elapse after you first hear the digits. Tasks such as these measure **memory span,** the number of stimulus items that can be recalled after a brief interval. Children under age ten years remember fewer items than do adults. As Figure 9.6 shows, two-year-olds typically remember only about two items, four-year-olds about three or four, and seven-year-olds about five (Dempster, 1981).

Do these changes in memory span occur because the storage capacity of memory increases? Numerous memory experiments suggest that this is not necessarily the case. Instead, children's ability to employ **memory strategies,** activities to enhance the encoding and retrieval of information, increases with age. Children seven years and older are more likely than younger children to rehearse items or reorganize them into more meaningful, and hence more memorable, units. For instance, noting that the numbers 1, 3, 5, and 7 form the sequence of odd numbers makes the list easier to recall. So does simply repeating them over and over. Alternatively, as we saw at the start of this chapter, Robbie Case and his colleagues have proposed that increases in memory span can be understood as a result of the increasing operational efficiency children display as they mature (Case et al., 1982). As operational efficiency increases, more cognitive resources are available for storage.

Changes in **processing speed,** the rapidity with which cognitive activities are carried out, indeed contribute to developmental gains in memory span. Researchers have suggested that two types of processing speed are important. Among children ages seven to eight, the ability to speak digits or words rapidly—presumably indexing the *rate of verbal rehearsal*—is related to their memory span. Among children ages eleven and twelve, memory span is more closely linked to shorter silent pauses between the items as they are being recalled. This second measure is presumed to index the rate at which items are actually *retrieved* from short-term memory. The data suggest that these different aspects of processing speed mature at different ages (Cowan, 1999; Cowan et al., 1998).

The memory span task is usually believed to tap short-term memory because the interval between presentation of the stimuli and the memory test is relatively brief. Other techniques have been used to study the ability of children to remember lists of words, sentences, or other items for longer than a few seconds.

● **Elicited Imitation** Suppose you want to study recall from long-term memory, but the child you are studying does not yet speak. How can you find out about his or her

KEY THEME
Child's Active Role

memory span Number of stimulus items that can be recalled after a brief interval of time.

memory strategy Mental activity, such as rehearsal, that enhances memory performance.

processing speed The rapidity with which cognitive activities are carried out.

FIGURE 9.7
Developmental Differences in Free Recall

This graph shows the probability that a word will be recalled by third-, sixth-, and eighth-graders in a free-recall task. Few developmental differences appear in memory for the last few items in the list, but older children show elevated levels of recall for the first few items. This pattern suggests that older children are more likely than younger children to employ memory strategies such as rehearsal to remember the early items.

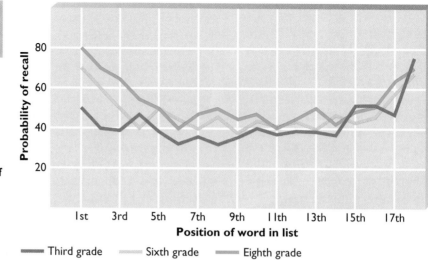

Source: Adapted from Ornstein, Naus, & Liberty, 1975.

memory skills? In the chapter titled "Basic Learning and Perception," you learned about a technique called *deferred imitation,* in which infants are shown a unique sequence of actions and then observed to see whether they imitate those behaviors at a later time. For example, in Andrew Meltzoff's studies, infants typically see the experimenter pull the square ends off a dumbbell or push a button on a box with a stick. When tested as long as four months later, a substantial number of fourteen-month-olds remembered the specific action sequences (Meltzoff, 1995).

Similarly, Patricia Bauer and her colleagues have used a procedure they call **elicited imitation,** in which older infants and preschoolers must repeat a sequence of actions demonstrated by the experimenter. For example, one sequence used in these studies is "making a gong." Children watch as the researcher shows three distinct steps to an event they have never seen before: (1) putting a bar across two posts; (2) hanging a plate from the bar; and (3) hitting the plate with a mallet. Then, weeks or even months later, the children return to the laboratory and are asked to repeat the sequence of actions with the array of parts they see on the table. In other words, they must recall a correctly ordered set of behaviors after a long delay.

Bauer's studies show that by the time most children start their second year, they need to see the sequence only once in order to remember it one month later. By twenty months of age, memories for the sequence last for as long as twelve months (Bauer, 2002; Bauer et al., 2000). These studies provide dramatic evidence for the presence of recall memory well before children have developed their language skills.

● **Free Recall** Many studies of memory with older children have used *free-recall* tasks in which they are given a list of words or objects that they are to repeat, after a specified delay period, in any order they wish. As Figure 9.7 shows, few developmental differences in recall are usually noted for items later in the list (Ornstein & Naus, 1978; Ornstein et al., 1975). Children of all ages recall these items well, at least by the time they are of elementary school age. This elevated recall for later items, called the **recency effect,** is viewed as the extraction of information from more immediate memory, a task that is usually not too demanding for children age four years and older. Older children, however, show a clear advantage for recalling items that appeared in the early or middle positions in the list. The fact that older children show good memory for early items is called the **primacy effect.** Developmental differences in the primacy effect can be explained as the result of the tendency of older children, those age seven years or older, to engage in deliberate strategies to improve recall. They repeat items aloud, make up sentences connecting the items, or think of mental images that connect the items. In fact, much of the research on memory development has centered on detailing the types of strategies children of different ages display.

elicited imitation A way of assessing memory in which children must reconstruct a unique sequence of actions that they have seen in the past; usually used with preverbal children.

recency effect Tendency for individuals to show good recall for the last few items in a list.

primacy effect Tendency for individuals to display good recall for early items in a list.

● **Memory Strategies**   How do you make sure you remember your grocery list or where you hung your coat in a restaurant coatroom? Or, as in the case of Nate, the underprepared student described at the beginning of the chapter, how do you make sure you remember important facts and concepts for a test in school? Ordinarily, you must perform some activity to ensure that the stimuli are correctly and enduringly encoded in the first place. As a mature rememberer, you often capitalize on cues that may later "trigger" retrieval. Thus, you might say the words in your grocery list over and over to yourself ("milk, eggs, bread; milk, eggs, bread") or note the characteristics of the location of an object ("I hung my coat next to the bright red one"). In general, as children grow older, they become more likely to employ self-generated strategies for both encoding and retrieval and to take advantage of external information that can potentially aid recall.

KEY THEME
Child's Active Role

We already identified one useful memory tactic, **rehearsal**—simply repeating, either aloud or silently, items to be remembered. The fact that young children are unlikely to engage spontaneously in rehearsal is well documented. In a study mentioned in the chapter titled "Language," investigators asked kindergartners, second-graders, and fifth-graders to observe as an experimenter pointed to three specific pictures in an array of seven (Flavell, Beach, & Chinsky, 1966). When asked to point to the same sequence after a fifteen-second delay, fifth-graders showed significantly greater accuracy than the other two age groups. More important, during the delay period the researchers recorded any signs that the children may have been rehearsing the items to be remembered, such as moving their lips or vocalizing to themselves. They found that 85 percent of the fifth-graders engaged in spontaneous rehearsal, whereas only 10 percent of the kindergartners did. Moreover, children who rehearsed showed the best recall. In other words, there was a direct link between the children's production of this strategy and memory performance.

Older children also exhibit another important memory strategy called **organization,** the tendency to reorder items to fit some category or higher-order scheme. If the items to be recalled can be grouped conceptually, older children do so, and the amount they recall increases accordingly. For example, if the stimulus list contains words from the categories *animals, furniture, vehicles,* and *clothing* (e.g., *sofa, dog, chair,* etc.), ten- and eleven-year-olds spontaneously cluster conceptually related items together as they recall them, whereas five- and six-year-olds do not (Moely et al., 1969). Furthermore, instructing children to group the words or objects they are to remember into categories significantly enhances recall (Bjorklund, Ornstein, & Haig, 1977; Black & Rollins, 1982).

Still another helpful memory technique is the use of **elaboration,** thinking of a sentence or an image that links together items to be remembered. If you have to remember the list *cat, shoe, piano,* you might construct the sentence "The cat wearing shoes played the piano" or think of a visual image portraying this scene. Elaboration is one of the latest memory strategies to appear; usually children do not spontaneously use images or elaborative verbalizations until adolescence or later (Pressley & Levin, 1977).

The strategies just discussed pertain mostly to *encoding,* or getting information into the memory stores; but older children are also better at *retrieval,* or getting it out. Figure 9.8 shows the sketches made by a first-grader and a seventh-grader who were asked in one recent study to "write or draw anything you want to help you win the game" as they played the memory game "Concentration." Notice how the first-grader's drawing has little to do with the game; it is simply a picture depicting an unrelated event. In contrast, the seventh-grader's notations contain important details about what the items are and their specific locations on the game board. Not surprisingly, the results of the study showed that the better the quality of children's notations, the fewer turns it took for them to win the game (Eskritt & Lee, 2002).

Throughout this discussion, the recurring theme has been the tendency of children over seven years of age to initiate some activity that will improve their recall. Younger children, however, are not completely deficient in the use of strategies. For example, when preschoolers are instructed to "remember" a set of objects, they are

rehearsal Memory strategy that involves repetition of items to be remembered.

organization Memory strategy in which individuals reorder items to be remembered on the basis of category or some other higher-order relationship.

elaboration Memory strategy in which individuals link items to be remembered in the form of an image or a sentence.

FIGURE 9.8
Generating Retrieval Cues
for Memory

Older children are more skilled than younger children at producing notes to help them to remember information. The drawing on the left was made by a first-grader playing a memory game. The items in this child's drawing have little to do with the stimulus items to be remembered. In contrast, the seventh-grader's notations on the right include the stimulus items themselves, as well as their specific locations. Children who produce good external notes are more successful in memory tasks.

Source: Eskritt & Lee, 2002.

more likely to name and look at them than children who are instructed to "play with" the objects (Baker-Ward, Ornstein, & Holden, 1984). However, younger children do not generate memory strategies such as rehearsal or organization on their own, a phenomenon termed **production deficiency** (Flavell, 1970). It is important to note that when younger, nonstrategic children are instructed to employ strategies, their recall markedly improves (Keeney, Cannizzo, & Flavell, 1967; Moely et al., 1969; Ornstein & Naus, 1978). The only exception appears to occur when children are first learning a strategy; there seems to be a transition time during which younger children's recall does not improve substantially when they first employ a memory strategy, a phenomenon called **utilization deficiency** (Miller, Woody-Ramsey, & Aloise, 1991). Recent research has also revealed that children sometimes use multiple strategies—not just one—while engaged in a memory task, employing a mix of rehearsal and organization, for example (Coyle & Bjorklund, 1997). Thus development is not characterized by the replacement of simple strategies such as rehearsal with more sophisticated ones such as organization. Instead, the array of study techniques available to children seems to expand with development.

How can we explain children's tendency to become more strategic and able to plan with age? Parents play at least a partial role. Hilary Ratner (1984) found a positive relationship between three-year-olds' memory performance and the frequency with which their mothers asked them questions about past events, such as "Where did you put your coat?" or "What does an airplane do?" Such memory demands may help children learn about encoding and retrieval processes that aid memory. Children may also learn to use strategies indirectly from environments that provide information in an organized, structured way (Ornstein, Baker-Ward, & Naus, 1988). For example, teachers usually present lessons in a cohesive, integrated manner. Pupils who have this repeated experience may discover on their own memory strategies they can apply to other situations.

production deficiency Failure of children under age seven years to spontaneously generate memory strategies.

utilization deficiency Phenomenon by which a memory strategy, when first applied, may fail to improve memory in a noticeable way.

metamemory Understanding of memory as a cognitive process.

● **Controlling Cognitive Processing** Until recently, most explanations of developmental changes in memory have focused on children's increasing use of deliberate strategies to enhance their recall. However, theorists now recognize that this focus does not capture the full complexities of cognitive processing in children. Developmental changes in memory are now understood in terms of the child's increasing efficiency and control over cognitive processes.

Metamemory, the child's understanding of memory, is one aspect of this process. It includes the ability to assess one's own memory characteristics and limitations, the demands made by different memory tasks, and the strategies likely to benefit memory (Flavell & Wellman, 1977; Guttentag, 1987). It also includes the ability to monitor the contents of one's own memory and to make decisions about how to allocate cognitive resources ("Have I memorized everything thoroughly? Do I still need to study some items?") (Kail, 1990). Advances in each of these aspects of metamemory are, to some degree, related to improvements in memory as children get older. For example, older children have a better understanding than younger children that longer lists are harder to remember than shorter ones and that events from the distant past are more difficult to remember than more recent events (Kreutzer, Leonard, & Flavell, 1975; Lyon & Flavell, 1993; Wellman, 1977). One consequence of this awareness is that children begin to see the need to use strategies (Schneider, 2000).

The child also displays a growing ability to engage in *cognitive inhibition*, to regulate how much irrelevant information gets processed. Older children are better able than younger children to filter out information that is not pertinent to the task at hand so that the space allocated to cognitive processing is greater. For example, older children can selectively forget irrelevant information; they can intentionally keep it "out of mind" (Harnishfeger & Pope, 1996; Pope & Kipp, 1998). Accomplishments like these are good examples of the child's increasing control over the management of his own thinking.

Charles Brainerd and Valerie Reyna's *fuzzy trace theory* (Brainerd & Gordon, 1994; Reyna & Brainerd, 1995) provides still another example of growing cognitive efficiency. According to this theory, a continuum exists for how literally memories are stored. On one end, memories are very true to the original event, containing verbatim information. On the other end, they may be stored as "fuzzy traces" or "gists," containing the essence or core of the event without the literal details. Both types of memory representations coexist, but they are used for different purposes. Gists, according to this theory, are extracted by children of all ages, but younger children are more predisposed toward verbatim memories. Difficulties can arise, though, because verbatim memories are more vulnerable to disruption; they also make more demands on the cognitive system in that they take more time to process. Young children's performance is affected by these demands.

To illustrate this theory, consider a study in which preschoolers and second-graders were given the following problem: "Farmer Brown owns many animals. He owns three dogs, five sheep, seven chickens, nine horses, and eleven cows." Children were then asked verbatim questions such as, "How many chickens does Farmer Brown own, seven or five?" or gist questions such as, "Does Farmer Brown have more cows or horses?" Among preschoolers performance was better on the verbatim questions than the gist questions, whereas the reverse was true for the second-graders. In addition, preschoolers and second-graders performed at equal levels on the verbatim questions, but second-graders had better recall for the gist questions (Brainerd & Gordon, 1994). Children who can focus on the gist of information do not get distracted by irrelevant details and retain the core of essential information for longer periods of time.

● **Memory and the Growth of General Knowledge** Do younger children ever remember more than older children or adults? In a unique experiment, Michelene Chi (1978) found that in certain situations they do. Adults and children averaging ten years of age were asked to remember lists of ten digits presented by the experimenter. Typically, the adults' performance surpassed the children's. However, when the memory task consisted of reproducing chess positions previously seen for only ten seconds on a chessboard, children significantly outperformed adults. How did they accomplish this remarkable feat? Chi explains that the children who participated were experts in the game of chess, whereas the adults (who were college educated) had only casual knowledge of the game. By having greater knowledge, these children probably could encode the familiar patterns of chess pieces more efficiently, whereas adults were probably seeing random arrangements of rooks, knights, and pawns. Thus, *domain-specific knowledge,* information about a specific content area, can influence the individual's ability to remember.

By the time they reach age three or four, many children display organized general knowledge of familiar routines and events, such as birthday parties. Scripts such as these can serve as frameworks within which specific memories are stored.

Knowledge about logical and causal relations among events helps memory, too. When preschoolers witness a logically ordered event such as making "fun dough," they remember more details about the event than when the event consists of arbitrary segments, such as different activities in sand play (Fivush, Kuebli, & Clubb, 1992). Likewise, eleven-month-olds show an excellent ability to imitate the following sequence of causally connected actions: push a button through a slot in a transparent box, then shake it. Imitation will occur even if children are presented with the objects three months after they first saw them; however, arbitrary sequences of actions are not remembered as well (Bauer & Mandler, 1992; Mandler & McDonough, 1995).

The effect of a growing knowledge base on memory has been described in another way: in terms of scripts. **Scripts** are the organized schemes of knowledge individuals possess about commonly encountered events. For example, by the time they are three or four years old, most children have a general schematic representation for the events that occur at dinner time—cooking the food, setting the table, sitting down to eat—as well as for other routine events such as going to school or attending a birthday party (Fivush, 1984; Nelson & Gruendel, 1981). When asked to remember stories based on such familiar scripts, children typically recall script-based activities such as "eating dinner" better than other details less closely related to scripts (McCartney & Nelson, 1981). Thus scripts serve as general frameworks within which specific memories can be stored and may be one of the earliest building blocks for memory.

Conversations with parents and others probably foster the formation of scripts. When parents reminisce about past events with their children with rich and detailed language, children have better recall about the past (Reese & Fivush, 1993; Reese, Haden, & Fivush, 1993). Thus scripts are likely to be influenced by the types of social experiences the child has. Within this framework, memory is better conceptualized as something children *use* rather than something that they *have* (Fivush, 1997).

Autobiographical Memory

Think back to your childhood and try to identify your earliest memory. How old were you? It is unlikely that you will report that you were an infant or perhaps even a toddler. Most people are not able to recount memories for experiences prior to age three years (Pillemer & White, 1989; West & Bauer, 1999), a phenomenon called **infantile**

KEY THEME
Nature/Nurture

script   Organized scheme or framework for commonly experienced events.

infantile amnesia   Failure to remember events from the first two to three years of one's life.

amnesia. The question of why infantile amnesia occurs has intrigued psychologists for decades, especially in light of the ample evidence that infants and young children can display impressive memory capabilities. Many find that understanding the general nature of **autobiographical memories,** that is, memory for events that have occurred in one's own life, can provide some important clues to this mystery. Between ages three and four, children begin to give fairly lengthy and cohesive descriptions of events in their past (Fivush, Haden, & Adam, 1995). What factors are responsible for this developmental turning point?

One explanation goes back to some ideas raised by Piaget, namely that children under age two years represent events in a qualitatively different form than older children. According to this line of thought, the verbal abilities that blossom in the two-year-old allow events to be coded in a form radically different from the action-based codes of the infant. The child's emerging verbal skills are, in fact, related to memory for personal experiences. Preverbal children who see unique events at age two do not describe them in verbal terms six months later when they are able to talk. Thus early memories seem to be encoded in a format that cannot be translated into verbal terms later on (Simcock & Hayne, 2002).

Another suggestion is that before children can talk about past events in their lives, they need to have a reasonable understanding of the self as a psychological entity (Howe & Courage, 1993, 1997). As we will see in the chapter titled "Self and Values," the development of the self becomes evident between the first and second years of life and shows rapid elaboration in subsequent years. The realization that the physical self has continuity in time, according to this hypothesis, lays the foundation for the emergence of autobiographical memory. One recent study has confirmed that the ability to recognize the self at nineteen months of age predicts the frequency with which children talk about past events when they are a few months older (Harley & Reese, 1999).

A third possibility is that children will not be able to tell their own "life story" until they understand something about the general form stories take, that is, the structure of narratives (Nelson, 1993a). Knowledge about narratives arises from social interactions, particularly the storytelling children experience from parents and the attempts parents make to talk with children about past events in their lives (Reese et al., 1993). When parents talk with children about "what we did today" or "last week" or "last year," they guide the children's formation of a framework for talking about the past. They also provide children with reminders about the memory and relay the message that memories are valued as part of the cultural experience (Nelson, 1993b). It is interesting to note that Caucasian children have earlier childhood memories than Korean children (Mullen, 1994). American four-year-olds also provide more extensive, detailed descriptions of events in their past than do Korean and Chinese children (Han, Leichtman, & Wang, 1998). By the same token, Caucasian mother-child pairs talk about past events three times more often than do Korean mother-child pairs (Mullen & Yi, 1995). Moreover, Caucasian mothers who ask their children many questions about past events, elaborating on their children's comments or asking for more details (e.g., "And what'd daddy do on the boat?") tend to have children who talk more about the past (Harley & Reese, 1999). Thus the types of social experiences children have factor into the development of autobiographical memories.

A final suggestion is that children must begin to develop a "theory of mind," as described in the chapter titled "Cognition: Piaget and Vygotsky," before they can talk about their own past memories. Once children begin to accurately answer questions such as "What does it mean to *remember*?" and "What does it mean to *know* something?" improvements in memory seem to occur (Perner & Ruffman, 1995).

It may be that the developments just described are intertwined with and influence one another. Talking with parents about the past may enhance the development of the self-concept, for example, as well as help the child understand what it means to "remember" (Welch-Ross, 1995). No doubt the ability to talk about one's past arises from the interplay of several factors, not just one (Pillemer, 1998).

KEY THEME
Continuity/Discontinuity

KEY THEME
Interaction Among Domains

According to one view, autobiographical memories arise from children's experiences of talking with their caregivers about past events in their lives. These interactions help children learn a narrative structure for how to talk about the past.

autobiographical memory
Memory for specific events in one's own life.

The research on children's memory, particularly recognition memory, suggests that their ability to remember events from the past is very impressive. But as children are increasingly called on to testify in courts after they have witnessed or been victims of abuse, neglect, or other crimes, their capability to render an accurate account of past events has been called into question.

What Is the Controversy?

Just how reliable are children's memories when they are called on to give eyewitness testimony? Children's memories for events, even those that occurred months or years in the past, are remarkably good. On the other hand, children's memories are also susceptible to suggestive or leading questions by attorneys, clinicians, and other interrogators (Bruck & Ceci, 1999; Ceci & Bruck, 1993). The stakes are high regarding these issues. If children have been the victims of crime, the perpetrators should be punished; but if children's memories are inaccurate in these contexts, a criminal suspect might be falsely accused.

What Are the Opposing Arguments?

Some research indicates that children's recall of distinctive events such as a trip to Disney World or a medical emergency is surprisingly complete and accurate even four or five years after the event (Fivush & Schwarzmueller, 1998; Peterson & Whalen, 2001). For example, in one study of two- to thirteen-year-old children who had been treated in a hospital emergency room, even two-year-olds remembered a substantial amount about their injuries when they were interviewed five years later (Peterson & Whalen, 2001). Data such as this suggests that children's memories are reliable.

On the other hand, other studies have shown that children, especially preschoolers, are likely to misreport a past event if they are asked misleading questions. In some of the original studies of "false memories" in children, Stephen Ceci and his colleagues tested children ages three through twelve years on their ability to remember the details of a story (Ceci, Ross, & Toglia, 1987). A day later, children in one of the experimental conditions were asked leading questions that distorted the original information, such as "Do you remember the story about Loren, who had a headache because she ate her cereal too fast?" In the original story, Loren had a stomachache from eating her eggs too fast. Compared with children who did not hear misleading questions, children who heard biased questions made more errors on a subsequent test that required them to select pictures depicting the original story: they chose the pictures showing a girl eating cereal and having a headache. This tendency to err was especially pronounced in children ages four and under.

What Answers Exist? What Questions Remain?

Many factors may influence just how suggestible children are. One is exactly who is doing the questioning. For example, in Ceci's study just described, misinformation provided by an adult tended to distort memory more than misinformation provided by another child; the perceived power of the questioner may make a difference. Second, when children are asked questions repeatedly, particularly *yes-no* questions, they are likely to change their answers or speculate inappropriately (Poole & White, 1991, 1993). Preschoolers especially may perceive the repeated question as a signal that their first answer was incorrect. Repeated questions, even when they are neutral, can lead to false memories because the information contained in them can be incorporated into the "gist" of the real memory (Brainerd & Mojardin, 1998). Third, the use of dolls and props for children to reenact the past event can lead to elevated false reports, especially among younger children (age three) and when this form of interview occurs after a delay of several weeks (Greenhoot et al., 1999). Finally, suggestibility may be reduced when children first are reminded to consider the basis of their information, a phenomenon called *source monitoring* (Poole & Lindsay, 2002; Thierry & Spence, 2002). In one laboratory study, for example, preschoolers were shown a video depicting a story about a boy feeding his dog accompanied by the experimenter's narrative. Some children were first asked to answer "Did you see it on the tape?" or "Did I tell you?" before they were asked leading questions about the story. This group was less likely to be influenced by leading questions compared with a group of children who were asked the leading questions first (Giles, Gopnik, & Heyman, 2002).

An important, and perhaps obvious, consideration in this discussion is that memories—those of both children and adults—generally decline with the passage of time. The results of a recent experiment showed that the amount and accuracy of information children spontaneously recalled about past events went down after two years, especially if they did not have an opportunity to be reminded of the original event. Under the latter conditions, up to 50 percent of the new information children added to their memories after being prompted by an experimenter was found to be inaccurate (Pipe et al., 1999). Because extended periods of time often elapse between a criminal event and the trial, these findings are especially relevant.

Given this information, what is the best way for professionals in the criminal justice system to encourage children to give reliable eyewitness accounts based on what we know from research?

Brain Development and Memory

Ultimately, any account of cognitive development will have to be connected to changes in the structures or processes that occur in the brain. Neuroscientists have been actively exploring brain functioning in both animals and humans to try to establish the underlying substrates of different cognitive processes, including memory. Fruitful approaches have included studying the memory performance of animals that have had different portions of the brain lesioned (or damaged), "scanning" the brain to measure metabolism and blood flow, and recording the electrical activity of the brain while individuals perform memory tasks.

We noted earlier that even very young infants show a robust preference for novel stimuli, indicating their recognition memory for "old" items they have seen before. Infant monkeys show similar patterns of behavior; however, when their hippocampus is removed at fifteen days of age, preferences for novelty disappear (Bachevalier, Brickson, & Hagger, 1993). As Figure 9.9 shows, the hippocampus is a brain structure located below the cerebral cortex that has long been known to be involved in memory functioning. Apparently, the hippocampus, which is a part of the *limbic system,* is an early developing structure that is necessary for the display of fundamental memory processes (Nelson, 1995).

Toward the latter part of the first year, portions of the temporal and prefrontal lobes of the brain (see Figure 9.9) begin to mature, as is revealed by *positron emission tomography,* or PET scans. PET scans allow neuroscientists to measure, among other things, the glucose activity in different portions of the brain. Interestingly, the levels of glucose metabolism in the temporal lobes of monkeys begin to look adultlike at four months of age, the age at which they begin to reach for a novel object after a short delay (Bachevalier, Hagger, & Mishkin, 1991). Similarly, glucose metabolism in the prefrontal lobes begins to appear mature in one-year-old human infants (Chugani, 1994). This is also the age at which infants correctly search for objects in the "A-not-B" task (see the chapter titled "Cognition: Piaget and Vygotsky") and at which they can locate objects after a delay (Nelson, 1995). By the time children reach preadolescence, fMRI data show that their brains respond much as adults' brains do when they engage in a working memory task. Portions of the parietal and prefrontal areas of the cortex, in particular, show unique patterns of activation (Nelson et al., 2000). Thus, as the cortex develops, so does the ability to perform more demanding memory tasks.

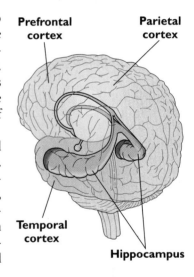

Prefrontal cortex   **Parietal cortex**

Temporal cortex

Hippocampus

FIGURE 9.9
The Brain and Memory Development

Several regions of the brain are implicated in memory development. The hippocampus matures early, and part of its function may be to direct recognition memory. Portions of the temporal and prefrontal cortex mature later in the first year and apparently are involved in more demanding memory tasks.

Researchers have also begun to record the electrical activity of the brain on-line while infants participate in memory tasks. In one recent study, five-month-old infants heard a succession of one hundred identical stimuli, either a click or a tone. The next day, fifty of the "old" stimuli were presented with fifty "new" ones (e.g., a tone if a click had originally been heard). Electrical firing patterns of the brain were more pronounced for familiar than for unfamiliar stimuli. Brain waves also had less variable onset times for familiar stimuli on the second day compared with the first day (Thomas & Lykins, 1995). Put another way, physiological responses were more consistent and prominent for the stimuli that had been put into memory.

Neuropsychological studies hold great promise in unlocking some of the mysteries of brain-behavior relationships. No doubt, they will also provide important information about the factors that influence cognitive development.

FOR YOUR REVIEW

- What are the major features of recognition memory in infancy?

- How does recognition memory change with age?

- What have different types of recall studies (memory span, elicited imitation, and free recall) told us about age changes in memory performance?

- What factors are primarily responsible for developmental improvements in recall memory?

- What explanations have been offered to account for the emergence of autobiographical memory?

- What major changes in the brain accompany developmental improvements in memory?

The Development of Problem-Solving Skills

One of the most powerful and uniquely human cognitive skills is the ability to solve problems. Whether you are completing an analogy, computing an arithmetic solution, or testing a scientific hypothesis, problem solving typically involves several steps or phases. Often you start with planning the steps to the solution of the problem, considering both the information you have at the start and the final goal. Clearly, you must attend to the portions of the problem that are relevant to its solution. You will probably select from a number of strategies to help you achieve your goal (for example, count on your fingers or use a calculator). In many cases, you must rely on your understanding of what different symbols in the problem (e.g., "+" or "=") represent. Frequently you must draw on a body of information from memory and examine relationships among several pieces of that information. Once you have the solution, you will often apply this new knowledge to similar contexts. Given the number of steps involved and the complex, intertwined relationships among them, you can see why problem solving is considered to be an example of what is called "higher-order thinking."

What are the earliest instances of problem-solving activity in humans? Piaget's descriptions of the development of means-ends behavior during the sensorimotor stage of development, discussed in the chapter titled "Cognition: Piaget and Vygotsky," suggest that infants show the beginnings of problem solving. Other researchers have confirmed that infants are capable of solving problems, combining several sub-goals to reach an interesting toy. In an experiment conducted by Peter Willatts (1990), twelve-month-olds saw a barrier in front of a cloth on which was placed a string attached to a toy (Figure 9.10). To get the toy, infants had to remove the barrier, pull the cloth, and then pull the string. In a control condition, the toy was not

attached to the string. Infants in the first group tended to remove the barrier without playing with it, quickly pulled the cloth, and grasped the string to reach the toy. Their behavior suggested that reaching the attractive toy was of utmost interest. In contrast, infants in the control group played with the barrier, were slower to reach for the cloth, and frequently did not grasp the string, probably because they recognized that the barrier, cloth, and string could not help to bring the toy closer. Willatts (1990) concluded that infants are capable of putting together several subgoals with the deliberate intent of reaching a goal.

Problem-solving skills become more elaborate and complex as children pass through the preschool and school years. A major question has been whether the child's increasing proficiency in solving complex and abstract problems results from an abrupt, qualitative shift in the ability to think logically or whether improvements in problem solving result from gradual gains in memory, attention, and other component cognitive skills. As we saw in the chapter titled "Cognition: Piaget and Vygotsky," Piaget believed in abrupt, qualitative shifts; he posited that the cognitive structures that permit completely logical and abstract thought do not evolve until adolescence, when children reach the stage of formal operations. In contrast, many information-processing theorists have emphasized the continuous growth and refinement of component skills involved in problem solving. According to them, children of all ages possess the fundamental ability to manipulate information in a logical fashion but may forget some of those elements during the process of problem solution or fail to attend to them sufficiently in the first place. With age, however, improvements in children's attention, memory, or other cognitive skills result in

FIGURE 9.10
Simple Problem Solving by Infants

This one-year-old knocks down the barrier and pulls the cloth to obtain the string to which an attractive toy is attached. Such behavior suggests that young infants can deliberately put together several subgoals to reach a goal.

KEY THEME
Continuity/Discontinuity

corresponding improvements in problem solving. Let us take a closer look at the components of problem solving that are considered essential in information-processing views of cognitive development.

Components of Problem Solving

Just think about the typical day of the average school-age child and you will undoubtedly discern many problem-solving situations the child encounters: a set of arithmetic problems to complete on a worksheet at school, a computer maze or jigsaw puzzle to solve for fun, or several bus routes to choose from to get to an after-school job. More mature and efficient problem solvers deploy several "executive" cognitive skills, much as the central processor directs the various functions of a computer. For instance, can I add these numbers in my head or should I get a calculator? What is the best strategy to use—should the puzzle be started with the edge pieces or the entire top left corner? Will learning how to do a simple computer maze provide any clues about how to do a more complex one? As researchers have explored children's problem solving, they have discovered a number of developmental changes in important components that characterize higher-order thinking.

● **Representation**   One of the most basic capacities required for problem solving is the ability to use symbols—images, words, numbers, pictures, maps, or other configurations that represent real objects in the world. Piaget argued that children are unable to think with symbols, that is, use representations, until near the end of the sensorimotor stage of development at about eighteen months of age. Others, however, have challenged this position and argue that representational capacities are evident much earlier in infancy. Jean Mandler (1988, 1998) has pointed out a number of early abilities infants display that support this thesis. For example, we noted in the chapter titled "Language" that infants begin to use gestures to stand for objects or events prior to age one year. Similarly, young infants' apparent knowledge about the physical properties of objects, described in the chapter titled "Cognition: Piaget and Vygotsky," suggests that they must hold some internal representation of them.

Although infants may have basic representational capacities, toddlers and older children far more readily recognize that external symbols of real objects in the world can be used to further their problem-solving efforts. For example, Judy DeLoache

An important cognitive skill that emerges at about age three is the understanding that a model may *represent* a real-life event. Representation is a fundamental skill necessary for problem solving.

(1987) asked two- and three-year-olds to search for a small toy hidden in a scale model of a room. Next, the children were brought into a life-size room that corresponded to the scale model they had just seen. Could they find the real-life toy that corresponded to the smaller replica in the previous segment of the experiment? If they saw a small Snoopy toy under a miniature couch, would they look for a large Snoopy under the couch in the life-size room? The three-year-olds could find the hidden object on more than 70 percent of the trials. But the two-year-olds could do so on only 20 percent of the trials. Later, when both age groups were asked to locate the toy back in the scale model, they did so with few errors. Thus the search failures of two-year-olds in the life-size room were not due to memory problems. DeLoache believes that two-year-olds have difficulty with *dual representation*, that is, with understanding that a scale model can be both an object in its own right and a representation of a life-size room. By age three, however, children have the cognitive capacity, flexibility, and conceptual knowledge to appreciate that a symbol such as a model can "stand for" a real-life event. In other words, children gain **representational insight** (DeLoache, 2000; DeLoache & Smith, 1999).

● **Planning**   One of the hallmarks of a mature problem solver is the ability to plan an approach to obtaining a goal. Planning, of course, depends on representational capacities, because symbols may be employed or manipulated as part of the plan. It also depends on having general knowledge about the events being planned for—what is involved in going grocery shopping versus taking a trip to the beach, for example (Hudson, Shapiro, & Sosa, 1995). Moreover, planning has at least two aspects: (1) deciding on the steps one needs to take ahead of time and (2) knowing when to be flexible and perhaps modify or discard advance plans if the situation calls for it (Baker-Sennett, Matusov, & Rogoff, 1993).

Planning can be observed as young children attempt to solve simple novel problems, such as making a gong out of triangular supports, a metal plate, and a mallet. When two-year-olds in one study were shown the fully assembled gong first, they showed a high proportion of actions that would lead to successful problem solution. Showing the children the goal was much more effective than getting them started with the early steps in solving the problem. Thus information about the end state of the problem was critical in prompting these young children to plan (Bauer et al., 1999).

David Klahr's classic research using the Tower of Hanoi problem, illustrated in Figure 9.11, shows that there are also clear developmental improvements in planning (Klahr, 1978; Klahr & Robinson, 1981). In this problem, one of three pegs has three cans of different sizes stacked on it. The goal is to move the cans to the third peg so they end up in the same order they were on the first peg. Two rules apply: only one can may be moved at a time, and a smaller can cannot be placed on a larger one.

Klahr found that six-year-olds were better planners than three-year-olds in two respects: they were more likely to pursue long-term goals, and they could keep more subgoals in mind as they attempted to solve the problem. For example, three-year-olds single-mindedly moved the cans to the third peg without thinking of the intermediate steps that might be necessary; their plan encompassed only the short-term goal to get the cans to the final peg. They could think of only one or two steps to attain the goal and broke the rules of the game. In contrast, six-year-olds used five or six steps to solve the problem, looking ahead a step or more as they planned their moves and anticipating potential traps in or obstacles to their placement of the cans.

With development, children also show changes in the flexibility of their planning. This phenomenon is illustrated by another study in which children were asked to plan a route through a maze (Gardner & Rogoff, 1990). When the task involved no time pressure, seven- to ten-year-olds planned the entire route through the maze before they drew in the path. However, when the experimenter told children to work as fast as they could, these older children used a more efficient approach under the circumstances: they planned less. Younger children, ages four to seven years, were less likely to adapt their planning strategies to the particular demands of the task.

KEY THEME
Child's Active Role

● **SEE FOR YOURSELF**
psychology.college.hmco.com
The Tower of Hanoi

representational insight   The child's ability to understand that a symbol or model can stand for a real-life event.

FIGURE 9.11
The Tower of Hanoi

In the Tower of Hanoi problem, the child must move three cans stacked on the first peg to the third peg so that they end up in the same order. Only one can may be moved at a time, and a smaller can may not be placed on a larger one. This problem gives researchers the opportunity to study developmental changes in children's planning activities as they solve problems.

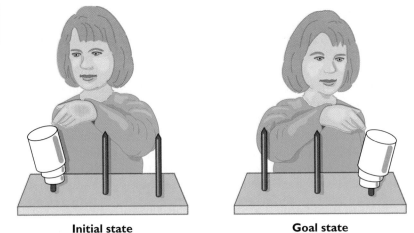

Initial state   **Goal state**

KEY THEME
Nature/Nurture

KEY THEME
Child's Active Role

WHAT DO
YOU THINK?

How Should
Math Be Taught?
psychology.college.hmco.com

Planning is likely to develop as children gain experiences with everyday routines in which specific events occur in a temporal order. Parental verbalizations about plans and the child's own emerging ability to verbalize probably also contribute (Benson, 1997). Another ingredient, according to Marshall Haith, is the child's "future orientation," his or her ability to think about events that are yet to come. Although early signs of future orientation are evident in infants—as they show anticipation about events in familiar routines, for example—a sense about the future probably undergoes more complex elaboration as the child matures (Haith, 1997).

● **Strategy Choice**   When a child encounters a problem—say, an addition problem—he will most likely choose from among several strategies. Robert Siegler has closely examined children's strategies as they solve simple addition problems and has found that children often rely on more than one approach (Siegler & Crowley, 1991; Siegler & Jenkins, 1989; Siegler & Shrager, 1984). Most children, he noted, first turned to one strategy but also usually had a backup strategy or two. Having multiple strategies affords the child useful flexibility as she encounters new situations and gains new knowledge (Siegler, 1989).

Suppose the child's assignment is to add the numbers 3 and 1. Several strategies are possible. The child can represent each number on his fingers and then count to the total. Alternatively, he can represent the larger number on his fingers and then count off the smaller number. Or he can simply retrieve the information from memory. Siegler found that if the problem was simple, children drew on memory for the answer because that approach is the fastest (Siegler & Shrager, 1984). If the problem was more difficult, however, children used other strategies that ensured greater accuracy, such as counting on their fingers.

With development, as children have more successes with solving problems and become more confident about their approach, they are more likely to use memory as opposed to finger counting to solve addition problems. They also learn new strategies, often when they fail to solve a problem and need to search for alternative solutions. But children can learn from their successes, too. Siegler and Jenkins (1989) noticed that children often came up with new strategies for problems they had solved correctly earlier in the experiment. Children may also discover strategies simply by interacting with the materials for a problem (Thornton, 1999) or by hearing an expert explain a successful strategy (Crowley & Siegler, 1998).

Siegler's research shows that children do not merely substitute one strategy for another as they become more mature problem solvers. Rather, they incorporate new blends of strategies as they learn new ones and discard older ones. Children are constantly selecting from a pool of multiple strategies, depending on whether the task demands that they be fast or accurate and on what they remember about the success of the particular strategy in the past (Siegler, 1989). In their use of strategies, children frequently show variability from one problem-solving session to another, from one child to the next, and from one context to another, such as playing a board game versus doing math (Bjorklund & Rosenblum, 2002; Kuhn et al., 1995; Siegler, 1994). Variability, in fact, may enhance learning because it provides experiences with different problem-solving approaches and opportunities to discover those that work (Siegler, 1996).

KEY THEME
Individual Differences

EXAMINING RESEARCH METHODS

Using the Microgenetic Approach to Study Children's Problem-Solving Strategies

According to Robert Siegler (Siegler, 1997; Siegler & Crowley, 1991), cross-sectional and longitudinal studies of cognitive development may not reveal a complete picture of cognitive development. When researchers use these methods, they tend to focus on average differences in performance from one time to the next or from one age group to another. But this approach usually does not tell us much about the precise cognitive processes that change as the child develops. A key feature of the **microgenetic approach** is examining a child's performance *while* she is engaged in a cognitive task, making note of any changes in behaviors that occur from trial to trial. Through this close analysis of the child's progress from one level of understanding to another, we can glean important details about development and have a better appreciation for the mechanisms that are responsible for change.

An experiment conducted by Robert Siegler and Elsbeth Stern (1998) illustrates this method. These researchers were interested in second-graders' tactics as they solved arithmetic problems that involved the principle of inversion—for example, $35 + 8 - 8$. Here, it is possible to use a shortcut to arrive at the answer—the quantity $(8 - 8)$ can be quickly discounted because the result is 0. Only children who did not know the inversion principle were selected to participate. In solving these problems, what kinds of strategies would children use? With repeated practice with these problems, would they eventually learn the inversion principle? Several strategies for solving the inversion problems were defined by the researchers:

- *computation*: adding all of the numbers

- *negation*: adding the first two numbers but then answering without subtracting the third number

- *unconscious shortcut*: a quick answer, with a vague reference to computation or negation in the child's explanation but no evidence of actually computing the second and third numbers (i.e., the child uses the inversion principle but cannot explain it)

- *computation shortcut*: actual computation but then an explanation that the shortcut would work (i.e., the child does not use the inversion principle but can explain it)

- *shortcut*: a quick answer, no evidence of computation, and an explanation of the inversion principle.

The strategies in this list were presumed to increase in sophistication from top to bottom. In the experiment, one group of children received twenty inversion problems, and a second group received ten inversion problems and ten standard problems (e.g., $35 + 8 - 2$) over a total of six practice sessions. After each individual problem was completed, the researcher asked the child how he or she figured out the problem. The researchers noted the child's numerical answer, the time it took to solve the problem, the explanation the child provided, and any other behaviors that occurred during the trial. Figure 9.12 shows a portion of the results for children who received blocks of twenty inversion problems.

microgenetic approach A research approach in which detailed trial-to-trial observations are made of individual children's performances.

FIGURE 9.12
A Microgenetic Analysis of Children's Strategy Use

In Siegler and Stern's (1998) experiment, children were closely observed as they solved a series of problems involving the inversion principle. The best strategy to use was a shortcut (e.g., 8 – 8 = 0). Trial 0 on this graph represents the point at which each child began to use this strategy. Notice that on previous trials (e.g., Trial –3), many children were using an unconscious shortcut, as opposed to computation, to solve the problems. (Note that in this particular portion of the study none of the children used negation.) A microgenetic approach allows researchers to understand more of the details of the *process* of development.

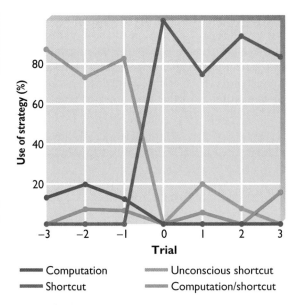

Source: Siegler & Stern, 1998.

In the graph, Trial 0 represents each child's first use of the best strategy, the shortcut (thus 100 percent of the children are represented at this point). Notice that three trials before Trial 0, on Trial –3, 87 percent of the children were using the unconscious shortcut, but very few were using computation or any other strategy. This pattern suggests that right before children discover the actual shortcut, they use it without being fully aware of it or being able to verbalize it. This pattern of results, by the way, did not emerge for children who had mixed sets of inversion and standard problems. Instead, they relied more on computation shortcuts right before they discovered the inversion principle.

As you can see, fine-grained analyses of trial-to-trial changes in children's responses can provide rich information about the way their thought processes change. Can you think of other ways that the microgenetic approach can be used to study various aspects of cognitive development? Are there any disadvantages to using this approach?

• **Transferring Skills** One final essential element in higher-order thinking is the ability to use what you have learned in one situation and apply it to other, similar problems. How well do children extend their existing problem-solving skills to new circumstances? This has been a long-standing question in psychology, particularly among researchers who have studied the role of generalization in learning. It has also been a question of paramount importance to educators, who assume children will find some application in their everyday lives for what they have learned in the classroom.

The ability to transfer knowledge requires that children learn the original problem well, note the resemblance between the old and new problems, and apply the appropriate activities to the new problem. This process is called **analogical transfer** in that the child must notice the one-to-one correspondence that exists between the elements of one problem and those of another and then apply the familiar skills to the novel context.

An experiment by Ann Brown and her coresearchers illustrates how this process can occur (Brown, Kane, & Echols, 1986). Three- to five-year-olds were read a story in which a magical genie had to move his jewels from one bottle across a high wall to another bottle. Several items were available to help the genie: glue, paper clips, sheets of paper, and so on. The experimenter and each child enacted the solution, rolling up the paper into a tube and using it to transport the jewels from one bottle to the other. The children were then presented with a different problem having the same general solution (a rabbit that needs to get its Easter eggs across a river can roll paper

analogical transfer Ability to employ the solution to one problem in other, similar problems.

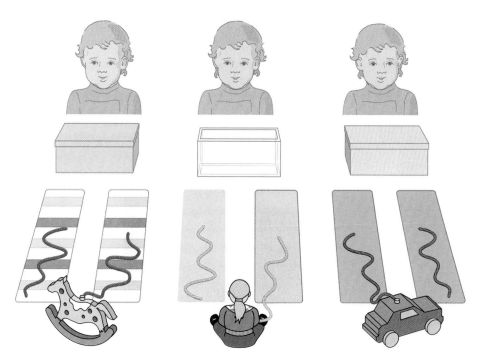

Source: Chen, Sanchez, & Campbell, 1997.

FIGURE 9.13
Transfer of Problem Solutions Among Infants

Even one-year-olds can transfer the solution of one problem to another when the goal sequences are similar. Each of these problems requires the child to bypass a barrier, pull the cloth, and grab the string to obtain the toy. Infants who were successful in solving one of these problems could typically solve the others, even though the problems were not perceptually identical.

into a tube to transport them). Whether the children were able to transfer the solution to a new problem depended on whether they recalled the goal structure of the previous problem. If they remembered the major actor, his goal, and the solution to his problem, even three-year-olds could solve the new problem. In fact, based on children's performance on a variety of problem-solving tasks employed by Ann Brown and other researchers (Baillargeon & DeVos, 1991; Brown, 1990), Usha Goswami (1996) has concluded that certainly toddlers, and possibly even infants, demonstrate analogical transfer.

Brown hypothesized that for transfer of problem solving to take place, the child must represent the problem in general mental terms, that is, abstract out the goal, problem, and solution dissociated from the specific fact that it was a genie who had to transfer jewels. Children can be encouraged to discern such common goal structures in consecutive problems. Zhe Chen and Marvin Daehler (1989) found that when six-year-olds were explicitly prompted to formulate an answer to the question of how problems were alike, they then performed significantly better on a transfer problem than control participants who did not receive this training. Thus parents and teachers may play a crucial role in facilitating the transfer of learning by pointing out commonalities across several problems. In fact, there are some circumstances in which very young children can discern the similarities across problems themselves. For example, when problem-solving situations look perceptually different but share similar goal sequences (e.g., remove a barrier, pull the correct cloth, and pull the correct string to reach a toy, as shown in Figure 9.13), even infants who are one year of age show the ability to transfer the solution to other problems once they have been successful with the first (Chen, Sanchez, & Campbell, 1997).

KEY THEME
Nature/Nurture

RESEARCH APPLIED TO EDUCATION

Facilitating Transfer in the Classroom

As the teacher collected each student's paper, Nate was thinking how glad he was to have the geography test over with. Science was next, and science was without doubt his favorite subject in school. The class was studying electricity and had learned about how to make a circuit, the properties of conductors and insulators, and the role of

One technique that teachers can use to facilitate transfer of knowledge from one situation to another is to present information using an obvious organizational structure. Explaining to students why the material they are learning is important can also be helpful.

a battery. Now the teacher was asking pairs of students to make a series of three light bulbs work by putting together wires and batteries in the correct order. Nate and his partner, Eliza, looked at the equipment before them and were stumped. How would they even begin? As they experimented, though, the principles they discussed in the previous day's lesson began to creep into their thinking. By the end of only a few minutes, their bulbs were assembled and shining as brightly as their proud faces.

If you stop and think about it, probably the greatest overarching goal of education is to ensure that students transfer what they learn in one lesson, problem, or assignment to new situations both in and outside of the classroom. We expect students to go beyond the specific content of one particular mathematics problem, scientific experiment, or writing assignment and apply what they have learned in new situations. Is there anything teachers can do to promote this important process?

Robert Sternberg and Peter Frensch (1993) offer the following suggestions based on their review of numerous studies of both memory and transfer:

1. *"Teach for transfer" by providing multiple settings in which information is encoded.*   This tactic, according to numerous studies of memory, should make retrieval of information more likely because there are more cues associated with it. Teachers should demonstrate to students how information they learn can be applied in different contexts and even ask students to think of applications themselves. That is, knowledge should not be "encapsulated" or taught as a "stand-alone" topic. As an example, principles of algebra could be taught in the context of a science class as well as a math class. The results should be that those principles are remembered well and their usefulness in different subject areas is apparent to students.

2. *Organize information so that transfer is more likely to occur.*   Classroom presentations should have an obvious organizational structure and should be connected to information students already have. Such an approach would provide students with

a framework, much like a *script,* that would enhance understanding and learning. Sternberg and Frensch (1993) add that teachers rarely begin lessons with a discussion of why the information is important in students' lives (i.e., where it fits in their personal scheme of things), but to enhance learning, they should.

3. *Help students see the general features that are common across different content areas to be learned and that are specific to a given lesson.*   Sternberg and Frensch (1993) describe a personal experience in learning Spanish in which the general features of the language were explicitly pointed out. At the same time, pronunciations and vocabulary that were unique to a given region or country were also highlighted for students. Learning should proceed more efficiently under circumstances in which common themes and exceptions to those themes are deliberately highlighted.

4. *Test students on their ability to apply what they have learned to new situations rather than on their ability to recall specific pieces of information.*   This approach would establish in students a "mental set" for the idea that they will have to engage in transfer—that this is an important expectation of them.

All of these pointers have a common aim: to make students aware of transfer as an explicit goal of learning. In a sense, the preceding suggestions ask teachers and students to be more "metacognitive" about the learning process, to overtly and frequently discuss and reflect on how transfer might be promoted. The more teachers incorporate this goal into their daily classroom instruction, according to these researchers, the more likely students will learn in the truest sense of the word.

The Development of Scientific Thinking

Most of us have received at least some formal training in the complex type of reasoning called *scientific thinking*. Scientific reasoning involves formulating a hypothesis, designing experiments in which one factor varies while others are held constant, and deciding on the validity of the hypothesis based on the observable evidence. According to Piaget, you will recall, this form of logical thought is not observed prior to the start of the formal operational stage, usually at preadolescence. Contemporary research confirms that there are indeed observable developmental accomplishments in scientific reasoning; however, children who are just starting school show impressive knowledge about some of the basic tenets of scientific thinking.

One element of scientific thinking is the ability to distinguish between theory and evidence. Preschoolers often behave as if there is no distinction between the two. Shown a series of pictures depicting two runners in a race, younger children typically answer the questions, "Who won?" and "How do you know?" with theory (e.g., "He has fast sneakers") rather than evidence (e.g., "He's holding the trophy"). By age six, though, children are likely to cite objective evidence (Kuhn & Pearsall, 2000).

A related skill is the capacity to see which conclusions are warranted by the evidence. Let us consider one example in which the child is presented with a series of pictures depicting the phases of the moon along with two theories about why they occur: (1) clouds cover different portions of the moon at different times, or (2) the moon has a dark and a light side. Then the child hears the evidence: an astronaut reports that the moon is dry and has no water, that he landed on some white rock, and that he later walked on black gravel. Which theory about the moon could possibly be correct? Most first-, third-, and fifth-graders in this study chose the second theory, the one that was consistent with the evidence (Samarapungavan, 1992). Other researchers have confirmed that first-graders can correctly identify whether a specific piece of empirical evidence provides conclusive or inconclusive support for a hypothesis (Sodian, Zaitchik, & Carey, 1991).

Yet scientific thinking involves greater complexities. For example, hypotheses must be formed in the first place, and usually several hypotheses are concurrently in the mind of the scientist. Often several variables operate at the same time. Experiments

Research shows that when children have the opportunity to engage in repeated scientific problem solving, they become more proficient in designing experiments and drawing valid conclusions from them. For example, several variables can potentially determine the speed of a moving car. With experience, children become better able to propose experiments in which only one variable changes while the others are held constant so that the cause of greater speed can be determined.

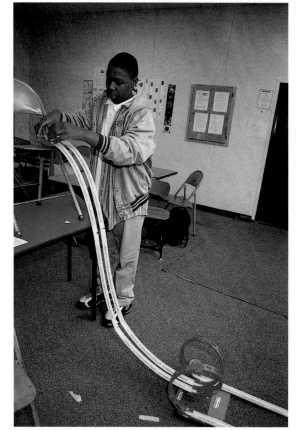

KEY THEME
Nature/Nurture

must be designed and conducted and their outcomes coordinated with the hypotheses to determine which variable causes the observed outcomes (Klahr & Dunbar, 1988). It is here that developmental changes are most apparent. When third-graders are asked to generate and evaluate hypotheses by running a series of experiments, they usually are not systematic in designing experiments that isolate the key variable and do not write down the outcomes of their experiments. Sixth-graders show improvements but still design a limited number of experiments, and their experiments are often difficult to interpret. Adults do the best, but not because their reasoning about the relationship between theory and evidence is stronger. Rather, adults can coordinate the generation of hypotheses with the design of the set of experiments necessary to test them (Klahr, Fay, & Dunbar, 1993).

When children are encouraged to engage repeatedly in scientific problem solving, their skills improve noticeably. Deanna Kuhn and her colleagues (Kuhn, Schauble, & Garcia-Mila, 1992) asked preadolescents to identify which variables affected the speed of a model boat being towed in a tank of water: the water depth, boat size, boat weight, sail color, or sail size. The instructor gave minimal feedback to the students, but they were encouraged to make a plan about what they wished to find out, state what they found out after each experiment, and record their findings in a notebook. The results showed that over only a few weeks of repeated exposure to these problems, students became markedly more proficient at designing valid and focused experiments and at drawing valid inferences from the data they collected. Follow-up studies show that this knowledge is subsequently applied to new problems (Kuhn et al., 1995; Schauble, 1996).

Direct instruction helps children master principles of scientific reasoning, too. In a recent study, seven- to ten-year-olds received explicit training on the concept "controlling variables in an experiment." They were provided with examples of confounded and unconfounded experiments and were then asked to apply their knowledge to a sample experiment. Children who had received this training were

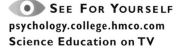
SEE FOR YOURSELF
psychology.college.hmco.com
Science Education on TV

able to apply the principle of "controlling variables" to several different experiments and were more likely to do so than children who had not received instruction. Thus the ability to reason like a scientist is clearly within the grasp of elementary school students (Chen & Klahr, 1999; Klahr, Chen, & Toth, 2001).

A good way to capture the development of scientific thinking is provided by Deanna Kuhn and her colleagues, who say that children acquire increasing control over their own thought processes. By becoming aware of the differences between theory and evidence, fact and opinion, and by coordinating theories with evidence, children begin to be able to "know how they know" (Kuhn & Pearsall, 2000). In that sense, the steps in the development of scientific reasoning may reflect broader accomplishments in the cognitive domain, as we discuss here.

The Executive Function

Numerous times in this chapter, we have mentioned that with development, children are better able to control their cognitive processing—their attention and memory, for example. As children develop, they become better able to analyze the tasks they face, size up their own capabilities, deploy and modify strategies, inhibit certain behaviors if they have to, and monitor the effectiveness of their approaches. The control of cognitive processing is also very important in problem solving, which, as we saw in this chapter, can involve complex tasks such as planning and transfer. Researchers have recently begun to turn their attention to understanding the role and development of this **executive function** that is part of the information-processing model with which we began this chapter. A key aspect of the executive function is *coordination* of components of cognitive processing in order to achieve some goal (Welsh, 2002).

Neuropsychological studies of children who have experienced brain damage indicate that executive function skills seem to stand apart from other cognitive abilities; affected children may show normal language and sensory abilities but have difficulties with planning and inhibition (Espy & Kaufmann, 2002). The prefrontal cortex of the brain has been implicated as one area responsible for the executive function, although there may be others. Thus, as the cortex of the brain matures, we would expect children to show gains in their executive function capabilities.

On the behavioral level, one manifestation of the child's executive function skills is the growth of **metacognition**, the child's awareness and knowledge of cognitive processes. The beginnings of this process are evident in the preschooler's emerging *theory of mind*, discussed in the chapter titled "Cognition: Piaget and Vygotsky." Children become aware of the difference between *thinking* about something and *seeing* it, and they understand the meanings of other psychological states such as *belief* and *desire*. Preschoolers, though, often perform cognitive tasks without being fully reflective about their actions. For example, in one experiment, three-year-olds readily sorted objects on the basis of either color or shape, but they could not switch from one rule to the other. When questioned, they could state the second rule for sorting given to them by the experimenter, but they could not link it to their actions (Zelazo & Frye, 1998).

Metacognitive awareness grows through the school years, as does the ability to act on that awareness, as you saw in our discussions of attention and memory. However, adolescents (or even adults) do not necessarily reach the most mature levels of metacognition (Kuhn, 2000a, 2000b). For example, adolescents and adults engaged in decision making are often influenced by their current belief systems. They are vulnerable to judgment biases, and operate according to their personal beliefs about social groups or how things look. Most adolescents are vulnerable to the gambler's fallacy, for example, saying that if a person has just won 75 percent of the time in video poker, she is destined to lose on the next turn (Klaczynski, 2001). They are also influenced by biases toward their own group, such as the religion to which they belong (Klaczynski, 2000).

KEY THEME
Child's Active Role

KEY THEME
Interaction Among Domains

executive function Portion of the information-processing system that coordinates various component processes in order to achieve some goal.

metacognition Awareness and knowledge of cognitive processes.

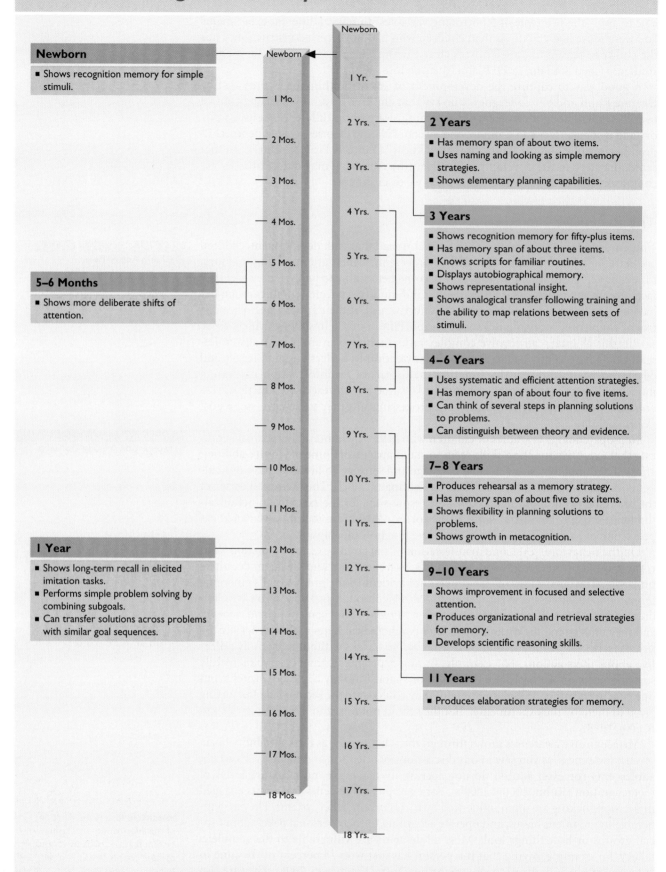

Newborn

- Shows recognition memory for simple stimuli.

5–6 Months

- Shows more deliberate shifts of attention.

1 Year

- Shows long-term recall in elicited imitation tasks.
- Performs simple problem solving by combining subgoals.
- Can transfer solutions across problems with similar goal sequences.

2 Years

- Has memory span of about two items.
- Uses naming and looking as simple memory strategies.
- Shows elementary planning capabilities.

3 Years

- Shows recognition memory for fifty-plus items.
- Has memory span of about three items.
- Knows scripts for familiar routines.
- Displays autobiographical memory.
- Shows representational insight.
- Shows analogical transfer following training and the ability to map relations between sets of stimuli.

4–6 Years

- Uses systematic and efficient attention strategies.
- Has memory span of about four to five items.
- Can think of several steps in planning solutions to problems.
- Can distinguish between theory and evidence.

7–8 Years

- Produces rehearsal as a memory strategy.
- Has memory span of about five to six items.
- Shows flexibility in planning solutions to problems.
- Shows growth in metacognition.

9–10 Years

- Shows improvement in focused and selective attention.
- Produces organizational and retrieval strategies for memory.
- Develops scientific reasoning skills.

11 Years

- Produces elaboration strategies for memory.

This chart describes the sequence of cognitive development based on the findings of research. Children often show individual differences in the exact ages at which they display the various developmental achievements outlined here.

The Cognitive Development II chronology chart summarizes the major developmental changes that occur in the information-processing system. Keeping this concept of executive function in mind, you will find many examples in which children are better able to control and coordinate their thinking as they develop. Because of its influence on learning in school, as well as on the ability to regulate the self (see the chapter titled "Self and Values"), research on executive function is likely to grow in the next several years. In fact, according to some researchers, it may be the most important cognitive skill of all (Kuhn, 2000a).

FOR YOUR REVIEW

- When do children first evidence the ability to engage in problem solving? What types of studies have demonstrated this skill?

- What kinds of changes have researchers observed in young children's ability to demonstrate representational insight?

- What are the major ways in which children show changes in planning skills as they develop?

- How have the results of microgenetic studies of problem solving challenged more traditional beliefs about children's strategy use?

- What factors encourage children to engage in the transfer of skills from one situation to another?

- What basic scientific reasoning skills do children who are just starting school display? What kinds of changes occur in these skills with development?

- What role does the executive function play in cognitive processing? In what ways does the executive function change with development?

CHAPTER RECAP

SUMMARY OF DEVELOPMENTAL THEMES

■ **Nature/Nurture** *What roles do nature and nurture play in cognitive development?*

Some of the changes in cognition documented by information-processing theorists have links to underlying alterations in the structure of the brain. For example, changes in attention and, perhaps, the speed of information processing may be associated with maturation of parts of the central nervous system. Likewise, changes in memory have been observed to accompany the maturation of certain portions of the brain. These connections between cognition and biology point to the role of nature. On the other hand, the child's exposure to specific experiences that nurture the emergence of cognitive skills is also important. As an example, parents and teachers serve as important guides for how to approach cognitive tasks such as planning and transfer of learning.

■ **Sociocultural Influence** *How does the sociocultural context influence cognitive development?*

The culture in which the child grows up plays a vital role in cognitive development. Cognitive skills such as memory strategies or the notion of autobiographical memory may be transmitted directly by parents, teachers, or other experts in the environment. They may also be transmitted more indirectly through the types of problems and tasks children confront.

■ **Child's Active Role** *How does the child play an active role in the process of cognitive development?*

Many of the child's cognitive achievements reflect active rather than passive processing. From the child's increasing control of his or her attention to the deployment of memory strategies, from the use of planning in problem solving to the selection of strategies in problems, the portrait of the child that emerges from studies of cognition is of an engaged, dynamic processor of information.

■ **Continuous/Discontinuity** *Is cognitive development continuous or discontinuous?*

Most information-processing researchers reject the notion that there are qualitative, stagelike changes in cognition with development. Their studies have confirmed that successive increments occur in cognitive skills such as attention and memory.

■ **Individual Differences**　*How prominent are individual differences in cognitive development?*

Information-processing theorists have focused on documenting general changes in cognition with age and, until recently, have been relatively unconcerned with individual differences. Nonetheless, the general features of information-processing skill may vary from child to child. A case in point is ADHD, which appears to involve significant disruptions in attention skills. Individual differences may also be observed in the extent and effectiveness with which strategies are implemented in memory and problem solving.

■ **Interaction Among Domains**　*How does cognitive development interact with development in other domains?*

There are many examples of how cognition is influenced by development in other domains. For example, cognition may be affected by maturation of the central nervous system, which is hypothesized to contribute to the development of sustained attention; the speed of information processing; and memory. Social interactions with parents, teachers, and others form the basis for cognitive development within a given cultural context. At the same time, cognitive development affects how the child functions in other arenas, such as language, emotion, and social interactions.

SUMMARY OF TOPICS

The Information-Processing Approach

■ Information-processing theories emphasize the flow of information through the cognitive system.

■ *Multistore models* include such structures as the *sensory register*, *working memory*, and *long-term memory*, as well as control processes such as rehearsal.

■ *Limited-resource models* describe tradeoffs between energy used to operate on stimuli and the capacity left over for storage.

The Development of Attention

Sustaining Attention

■ An important developmental change occurs in the ability to keep one's attention on some stimulus or activity. This change is due, in part, to maturation of the central nervous system, as well as the growing complexity of the child's interests.

Deploying Attention

■ With development, children gain in the ability to control their attention in a systematic and efficient manner.

Selective Attention

■ As children grow older, they are better able to select certain aspects of the environment to attend to. Physiological maturation and the child's increasing control over cognitive processing are responsible for these changes.

■ ADHD is a developmental disorder linked to problems of attention. Problems with executive control and allocating resources in working memory are thought to underlie this disorder.

The Development of Memory

■ Researchers distinguish between *episodic memory* (memory for events that took place at a specific time and place) and *semantic memory* (memory for general concepts or facts). They also distinguish between *recognition memory* (knowing that a stimulus has already been encountered) and *recall memory* (the ability to reproduce previously encountered stimuli).

Recognition Memory

■ Habituation and operant-conditioning studies show that young infants have very good recognition memory. Stimuli seen for only brief periods can be remembered for days or weeks.

■ Early memories are easily disrupted by changes in context, but they can be enhanced by reminders that occur shortly after the original event.

■ Even newborns display the capacity for recognition memory. Older children show impressive levels of recognition performance.

■ Developmental changes in recognition include an increase in the number of items that can be remembered, as well as an increase in the speed of remembering.

Recall

■ From preschool to preadolescence, children show an increase in *memory span*, the number of items that can be recalled after a brief period of time. Changes in *processing speed*, the rapidity with which cognitive activities can be carried out, contribute to this increase.

■ *Elicited imitation* studies, in which preverbal children must reconstruct a unique past event from an array of stimuli, show that long-term recall is possible in this age group.

■ Children participating in free-recall tasks typically show *primacy* and *recency effects*. The former refers to elevated recall at the beginning of the list and reflects rehearsal. The latter refers to good recall for the last few items in a list.

■ As children progress through the school years, they show an increase in the deliberate production of memory strategies for both encoding and retrieval. Among these are *rehearsal* (repeating items), *organization* (reordering items on the basis of higher-order relationships), and *elaboration* (linking items in an image or sentence). Younger children's failure to generate these strategies is called *production deficiency*.

- At the early stages of strategy use, children may show *utilization deficiencies*, the failure of the strategy to enhance recall.

- Improvements in memory are tied to the child's increasing control over his or her cognitive processing. One aspect of cognitive control is *metamemory*, the child's understanding of memory as a process. Improvements in cognitive inhibition and reliance on the gist of an event are also part of this process.

- Children's memory is particularly impressive in domains in which they have extensive general knowledge. The formation of *scripts*, organized schemes for commonly experienced events, also contributes to improvements in memory.

Autobiographical Memory

- Few people can remember events that occurred prior to age three, a phenomenon called *infantile amnesia*. Improvements in memory for specific events in one's life, or *autobiographical memory*, are tied to the child's emerging verbal skills, growing awareness of the self, and increasing understanding of the form of a narrative.

Brain Development and Memory

- Neuropsychological studies indicate that memory development is tied to maturation of several brain structures, including the hippocampus and temporal, prefrontal, and parietal lobes of the cortex.

- Patterns of electrical activity in the brain change during the process of remembering.

The Development of Problem-Solving Skills

- Infants about one year of age show the ability to solve problems in that they will put together several steps to achieve a goal.

Components of Problem Solving

- By age three, children attain *representational insight*, the ability to use a symbol for a real-world event.

- With development, children are better able to plan the steps in problem solving. They also become more flexible in their strategy use.

- Research using the *microgenetic approach* has found that children usually select from a pool of problem-solving strategies rather than simply switch from one strategy to another.

- With development, children improve in their ability to employ one problem solution to other, similar problems, a process called *analogical transfer*. Several factors can influence the likelihood of transfer, such as making the parallels between problems more obvious to children.

The Development of Scientific Thinking

- One important element of scientific thinking is the ability to distinguish between theory and evidence, a capability that emerges around age six. At this age, children are also able to identify which evidence supports a given hypothesis.

- Developmental changes are most apparent in the ability to design systematic experiments to test hypotheses. This ability can be enhanced, though, with increased experiences in scientific problem solving, as well as direct instruction on how to design an experiment without confounds.

The Executive Function

- Researchers are beginning to recognize that an important element in cognitive development is the ability to control and coordinate one's own cognitive processes, a concept called the *executive function*.

- One element of the executive function is *metacognition*, the child's awareness and knowledge of cognitive processes. Metacognitive awareness grows through the school years and adolescence but may not reach full maturity. Even adults' decisions can be influenced by judgment biases.

CHAPTER 10

Intelligence

Key Themes in Intelligence

- **Nature/Nurture** What roles do nature and nurture play in the development of intelligence?

- **Sociocultural Influence** How does the sociocultural context influence the development of intelligence?

- **Child's Active Role** How does the child play an active role in the development of intelligence?

- **Continuity/Discontinuity** Is the development of intelligence continuous or discontinuous?

- **Individual Differences** How prominent are individual differences in the development of intelligence?

- **Interaction Among Domains** How does the development of intelligence interact with development in other domains?

*S*on Van Nguyen stared intently at the school psychologist's desk. Son was embarrassed to be stuck and especially embarrassed about the nature of the questions he was having trouble with. After three years in America, this ten-year-old was proud of the English he had learned. But he had been having serious problems with his reading and just couldn't stay focused on his work. The teacher had recommended to his parents that he be tested, but he really didn't understand what the test was for. He was relieved when the school psychologist announced that the test was done.

At lunchtime he approached Manuela Gomez, whom he considered to be an "expert" on American life because her family had lived in the States four years longer than his family had. "What does *inscription* mean?" he asked her.

"Oh, that's easy. It's words you write or carve on something, like a tombstone."

Son was impressed but suspicious. "How did you know that?"

"It's the same as in Spanish: *inscripción*."

Manuela was acting so superior that he almost didn't want to confess his ignorance. When he asked her another question from the test, she hooted with laughter. "Are you ever dumb! Don't you know anything? Everybody knows Christopher Columbus discovered America. We all knew that back in Chihuahua before we even moved here."

Son's worst fears about himself had just been confirmed. Although the teacher and the school psychologist had tried to explain to him about the test he was to take, he had not really understood. Now he did. And at that moment the truth seemed all too plain to Son: compared to Manuela, he was not intelligent.

*P*sychologists who have tested large numbers of children and adults on intelligence tests have found noticeable differences in individual performance, such as those that presumably existed between Son and his classmate. What do these differences mean? In contrast to cognitive psychologists, who are interested in identifying *common processes* in children's and adults' thinking, some researchers focus on identifying and explaining *individual differences* in mental capabilities. Researchers look for these differences in participants' responses on tests of word meanings, general knowledge, and visual-spatial performance and describe the results as a measure of intelligence.

But what *is* intelligence? To the layperson, the term usually includes the abilities to reason logically, speak fluently, solve problems, learn efficiently, and display an interest in the world at large (Siegler & Richards, 1982; Sternberg et al., 1981). Most of us probably have a sense that the abilities to profit from experience and adapt to the environment are also part of intelligent human functioning. We might even postulate that intelligent behavior is defined by different kinds of skills at different ages, as did the college-age participants in one study of popular notions of intelligence (see Table 10.1). Yet despite the average person's ability to give what sounds like a reasonable description of intelligent behavior, in the field of psychology the formal definition of

6-Month-Olds	2-Year-Olds	10-Year-Olds	Adults
Recognition of people and objects	Verbal ability	Verbal ability	Reasoning
Motor coordination	Learning ability	Learning ability; problem solving; reasoning (all three tied)	Verbal ability
Alertness	Awareness of people and environment		Problem solving
Awareness of environment	Motor coordination		Learning ability
Verbalization	Curiosity	Creativity	Creativity

Source: Adapted from Siegler & Richards, 1982

TABLE 10.1
Popular Notions of Age-Specific Intelligence

This table shows the five most important traits that characterize intelligence at different ages according to one survey of college students. The students identified perceptual and motor abilities as most important for infants. They saw problem solving and reasoning as abilities that become increasingly important later in development.

intelligence has proven surprisingly elusive. Although the concept has been the subject of research and theorizing for more than a century, no single definition has been commonly agreed on, and no one measurement tool assesses intelligence to everyone's satisfaction.

Despite the lack of consensus on how to define and measure intelligence, we now have many tests designed to measure it in children as well as adults. Most of the commonly used tests assess the kinds of thinking people do in academic settings as opposed to common sense or "practical intelligence" (Sternberg, 1995). These tests are routinely used in schools, as well as in medical, mental health, and employment settings, to make decisions about educational strategies, therapeutic interventions, or job placements. Given this use of intelligence tests in many different contexts, it is vital that we closely examine the concept of intelligence and how it is measured.

Our objective in this chapter is to present both historical and contemporary ideas about intelligence—what it is, how we measure it, and the factors that influence it—while keeping in mind that many of the long-standing controversies surrounding this topic are still unresolved. Particularly contentious is the age-old debate over nature versus nurture, that is, the degree to which intellectual ability is shaped by heredity or by experience. Although virtually all modern-day researchers acknowledge that genes and environment interact to produce intelligence, some experts place greater emphasis on biological concepts of heritability, whereas others focus on how intelligence is shaped by the particular context in which the individual grows up. This controversy highlights the importance of applying sound scientific principles and open-mindedness to a topic that has important implications for the ways individuals think about themselves and for social policy.

What Is Intelligence?

Among the many attempts to define intelligence, one prominent issue has been and continues to be whether intelligence is a unitary phenomenon or whether it consists of various separate skills and abilities. In the first view, an intelligent person has a global ability to reason and acquire knowledge that manifests itself in all sorts of ways, such as memorizing a long poem or solving a maze. Intelligence by this definition is a general characteristic that shows up in the multiple and varied observable behaviors and activities of any one person. In the second view, an intelligent person may possess specific talents in some areas but not in others and so, for instance, may be able to compose a sonata but unable to solve a verbal reasoning problem. The various component skills of intelligence are seen as essentially independent, and each individual may have areas of strength and weakness.

A second major issue has been the best way to conceptualize intelligence. Should it be defined in terms of the *products* individuals generate, such as correct solutions to a series of mathematics problems or giving the precise definitions of words? Or should it be defined in terms of the *processes* people use to solve problems, such as the ability to integrate different pieces of information or to apply knowledge to new situations? The earliest theories about intelligence came from the *psychometric tradition,* which emphasized a product approach, quantifying individual differences in test scores to establish a rank order of capabilities among the participants tested. More recently, psychologists have put forth alternative ideas about the nature of intelligence based on theories about the cognitive processes people employ to acquire knowledge.

Throughout this discussion, you should notice that few theories explicitly describe the *development* of intelligence. Most models of intelligence are derived from data gathered from adults and provide few suggestions about the way intelligence changes from early childhood through adulthood. This state of affairs may surprise you given the rich theories of cognitive development—those of Piaget and Vygotsky—that we discussed in the chapters on cognition. The task of bringing our knowledge of the development of thinking to explaining individual differences in intellectual performance remains to be accomplished.

Psychometric Approaches

The notion that human beings may differ from one another in certain skills originated in the late nineteenth century with the work of Sir Francis Galton. Galton (1883) believed people differ in their ability to discriminate among varying physical stimuli, such as auditory tones of different pitch, and in their speed of reaction to sensory stimuli. Such differences, according to Galton, are largely innate. Expanding on these ideas, James McKeen Cattell (1890) devised a series of psychophysical tests that assessed a person's ability to sense physical stimuli or perform different motor actions. It was Cattell who coined the term *mental test*. Based on subsequent empirical studies, the idea that intelligence is functionally equivalent to psychophysical skill was temporarily shelved, but the notion of testing individuals to compare their levels of performance remained alive.

The first formal intelligence test was created in 1905 by Alfred Binet and Théophilius Simon. Commissioned by the minister of public instruction in Paris to devise an instrument that would identify children who could not profit from the regular curriculum in the public schools due to lower mental abilities, Binet and Simon (1905) designed a test that assessed children's ability to reason verbally, solve simple problems, and think logically. With the Binet-Simon test, the mental testing movement was born, and psychometrics became firmly entrenched as a model for understanding intelligence.

Psychometric models of intelligence are based on the testing of large groups of individuals to quantify differences in abilities. The basic assumption is that some people will perform better than others and that those who perform below some average or normative level are less intelligent, whereas those who perform above that level are more intelligent. Within the general psychometric framework, however, theorists have taken contrasting positions on the exact nature of intelligence.

● **Spearman's Two-Factor Theory** Charles Spearman (1904) believed that intelligence consists of two parts: *g*, a general intelligence factor that he equated with "mental energy," and *s*'s, specific knowledge and abilities such as verbal reasoning or spatial problem solving that are evident only in certain tasks. According to Spearman, *g* is a central aspect of any task requiring cognitive activity and accounts for commonalities in levels of performance that people typically demonstrate in various kinds of intellectual tasks. Thus the influence of *g* might enable a person to obtain a high score on a verbal test, as well as on a test of visual-spatial skill.

Spearman (1923, 1927) claimed to find high correlations among tests of various mental abilities, concluding that they were caused by the presence of the single factor *g*. Not all researchers agree that intelligence is a unitary phenomenon. However, this view

KEY THEME
Individual Differences

psychometric model Theoretical perspective that quantifies individual differences in test scores to establish a rank order of abilities.

continues to be a part of many contemporary ideas about intelligence (Thorndike, 1994).

● **Thurstone's Primary Mental Abilities**   In contrast to Spearman, Louis Thurstone (1938) believed that intelligence is composed of several distinct fundamental capabilities that are completely independent of one another. After analyzing the intelligence test scores of many college students, Thurstone concluded that there was little evidence for *g*. Instead, he proposed that the following seven *primary mental abilities* are components of intelligence: *visual comprehension,* as measured by vocabulary and reading comprehension tests; *word fluency,* the ability to generate a number of words (for example, those beginning with *b*) in a short period of time; *number facility,* the ability to solve arithmetic problems; *spatial visualization,* the mental manipulation of geometric forms or symbols; *memory,* the ability to recall lists of words, sentences, or pictures; *reasoning,* the ability to solve analogies or other problems involving formal relations; and *perceptual speed,* the ability to recognize symbols rapidly.

Subsequent studies found that the correlations among Thurstone's seven skill areas were higher than he initially thought, but Thurstone continued to maintain that any underlying general skill is secondary in importance to the separate skill areas themselves (Thurstone, 1947). In Thurstone's conception of intelligence, individuals possess areas of strength and weakness rather than the global entity of intelligence.

● **Fluid and Crystallized Intelligence**   According to Raymond Cattell and John Horn, a distinction can be made between two types of intelligence, each with a unique developmental course (Cattell, 1971; Horn, 1968; Horn & Cattell, 1967). **Fluid intelligence** consists of biologically based mental abilities that are relatively free of cultural influence, such as the ability to remember a list of words or to group abstract figures together. **Crystallized intelligence** consists of skills one acquires as a result of living in a specific culture, such as knowledge of vocabulary, reading comprehension, or general information about the world. Cattell and Horn believed that fluid intelligence is tied to physiological maturation and that it increases until adolescence, when it levels off, and then declines in later adulthood. On the other hand, they hypothesized that crystallized intelligence increases over much of the life span because individuals continually acquire knowledge from the cultural groups in which they live.

Researchers have found that fluid intelligence does eventually decline with age, especially after ages seventy to eighty. Crystallized intelligence increases through the middle adult years but also declines with aging, although on a somewhat slower trajectory

KEY THEME
| Nature/Nurture

KEY THEME
| Sociocultural Influence

According to Cattell and Horn, *crystallized intelligence* **consists of skills that are acquired as the result of living in a specific culture. These Ugandan schoolgirls, for example, are learning to make baskets, a skill that is not likely to be acquired by children living in highly industrialized countries.**

fluid intelligence   Biologically based mental abilities that are relatively uninfluenced by cultural experiences.

crystallized intelligence   Mental skills derived from cultural experience.

than fluid intelligence (Kaufman, 2001; McArdle et al., 2002). These decreases are probably linked to physiological changes in the ability of the brain and other portions of the nervous system to process information. It is important to note, however, that wide individual differences occur in age-related changes in intelligence (Brody, 1992).

Modern-day versions of the theory of fluid and crystallized intelligence (often called *Gf-Gc*) emphasize a hierarchical structure to intelligence. John Horn (Horn, 1994; Horn & Noll, 1997), for example, believes that just as fluid and crystallized intelligence contribute broadly to the construct of intelligence, visual and auditory skills, short-term memory, processing speed, and quantitative skills make more specific contributions. Similarly, John Carroll (1993) postulates that at one level individuals possess varying degrees of specific abilities, such as speed of processing. Fluid and crystallized intelligence make up a second layer in the model, and *g*, a general intelligence factor, constitutes a third. Models such as these represent interesting ways to conceptualize intelligence as comprising both general *and* specific skills.

Information-Processing Approaches

Newer theoretical ideas about intelligence are directly derived from the information-processing model of cognition discussed in the chapter titled "Cognition: Information Processing." Rather than identifying the structures of mental ability, as the psychometricians did, information-processing theorists have focused on describing the mental processes necessary to accomplish different types of tasks. Thus each step involved in the chain of cognitive processes from encoding to retrieval, such as speed of processing, a growing knowledge base, or metacognitive skill, provides important insights about defining intelligence.

● **Intelligence as Speed of Processing** Individuals vary in the speed with which they conduct certain cognitive activities. For example, consider a typical *choice reaction-time* task. A participant sits in front of an apparatus that contains eight lights, her finger resting on a "home" button. As soon as one of the eight lights comes on, the participant must move her finger to a button below that light to turn it off. People show notable differences in the speed with which they carry out this task. Several researchers have proposed that such individual differences in speed of processing information may be related to intelligence, particularly *g*, the general intelligence originally described by Spearman (Jensen, 1982; Jensen & Munroe, 1979; Vernon, 1983).

Is there evidence that speed of information processing is a component of intelligence? Researchers have observed at least moderate relationships between reaction-time measures and scores on standardized tests of intelligence among adults (Jensen, 1982; Vernon, 1983); these relationships are weaker among young children (Miller & Vernon, 1996). As we will soon see, though, recent research on the speed with which infants engage in visual processing is related to later intelligence test scores.

It is important to keep in mind that individuals may differ in their processing speed because of variations in motivation and attention to the task rather than differences in intellectual ability. Some participants in the choice reaction-time task may be distracted by the equipment in the experimental room or may become anxious, and hence slower, in their attempts to do their best. Because reaction times are measured in fractions of a second, they are particularly vulnerable to these types of disruptions. In addition, different cultures and ethnic groups place varying emphases on the value of speed in mental processes. In our own Western culture, we place high priority on getting things done quickly, but the same may not be true for cultures in which time is not a major factor in daily routines. A person who does not have a heightened consciousness of time and speed may not choose to perform mental tasks rapidly, even when he or she has the capability to do so (Marr & Sternberg, 1987). Finally, not all intelligent problem solving is done in a speedy way. Consider the problem of deciding on a career or whom to marry. Rushing to a solution can hardly be considered "smart" in these situations (Sternberg, 1982). Thus we must be cautious about interpreting the results of tasks that assess speed of processing as an element of intelligence.

KEY THEME
Interaction Among Domains

KEY THEME
Individual Differences

KEY THEME
Individual Differences

KEY THEME
Interaction Among Domains

FIGURE 10.1
The Triarchic Theory
of Intelligence

According to Robert Sternberg, intelligence has three
major facets, or "subtheories,"
all based on the individual's
ability to process information.

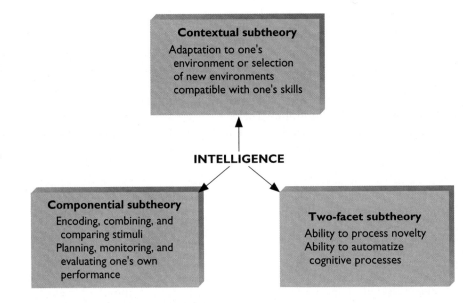

KEY THEME
Sociocultural Influence

triarchic theory Theory developed by Robert Sternberg that
intelligence consists of three major components: (1) the ability to
adapt to the environment, (2) the
ability to employ fundamental information-processing skills, and
(3) the ability to deal with novelty
and automatize processing.

● **Intelligence and Working Memory**   A promising new approach to understanding intelligence involves examining individual differences in working memory.
Recall from the chapter titled "Cognition: Information Processing" that working
memory involves a short-term psychological "work space" in which complex (and
sometimes multiple) tasks are performed on incoming information. Individuals
might be asked to read and confirm the truth value of a sentence and also to remember the last word in the sentence, for example. Researchers have reported that
successful performance on working memory tasks is related to intelligence test
scores and is also linked to specific patterns of brain activity in the parietal and oc-
cipital lobes (Van Rooy et al., 2001). Other research suggests that the capacity of
working memory is an even better predictor of intelligence test scores than processing speed (Conway et al., 2002). Working memory probably involves some form
of attentional control, the ability to regulate the amount of cognitive resources
required to perform the components of a complex task (Engle, 2002; Miyake et al.,
2001). Some researchers postulate that individual differences in this ability represent an element of *g*, the concept of general intelligence identified by Spearman
(Engle, Kane, & Tuholski, 1999). Although this approach has been applied mainly to
studies of adults, it holds promise in illuminating our understanding of developmental aspects of intelligence because of its emphasis on cognitive processes that
have also been studied in children.

● **Sternberg's Triarchic Theory of Intelligence**   Robert Sternberg (1985) has
proposed a broad contemporary theory of intelligence based on the principles of information processing. The **triarchic theory** of intelligence (see Figure 10.1) consists
of three major subtheories that describe mental functioning in terms of what cognitive psychologists have learned in the past three decades about how people think.

The first of these subtheories, called the *contextual subtheory,* asserts that intelligence must be considered as an adaptation to the unique environment in which the
individual lives. This means, for example, that we would not administer an intelligence test designed for children in the United States to children from a completely
different culture, such as that of the Australian aborigines. In Sternberg's words, intelligence consists of "purposive adaptation to, and selection and shaping of, real-
world environments relevant to one's life" (1985, p. 45). Intelligent people are thus
able to meet the specific demands their environment places on them—by learning to
hunt if their culture requires that skill or by perfecting reading or mathematical skills
in societies that stress formal education. By the same token, intelligent people will
change their environment to utilize their unique skills and abilities most effectively.

The contextual subtheory of Sternberg's triarchic theory of intelligence describes an individual's ability to adapt to the demands of the environment. Some cultures, for example, stress verbal abilities and literacy, but these skills may not be equally emphasized in other environments.

For instance, changing jobs or moving to a different locale may demonstrate what Sternberg calls "successful intelligence," which may be equally as important as or more important than "academic intelligence" (Sternberg, 2001).

The *componential subtheory* focuses on the internal mental processes involved in intelligent functioning, including the ability to encode, combine, and compare stimuli—the basic aspects of the information-processing system. Other components of intelligence are higher-order mental processes, such as relating new information to what one already knows. Finally, the ability to plan, monitor, and evaluate one's performance—the metacognitive activities we described in the chapter titled "Cognition: Information Processing"—is also part of intelligent functioning. Thus Sternberg stresses *how* individuals acquire knowledge rather than *what* they know as indicators of intelligence.

The *two-facet subtheory* describes intelligent individuals in terms of (1) their ability to deal with novelty and (2) their tendency to automatize cognitive processes. Devising a creative solution to an unfamiliar problem or figuring out how to get around in a foreign country are examples of coping successfully with novelty. Automatization takes place when the individual has learned initially unfamiliar routines so well that executing them requires little conscious effort. Learning to read is a good example of this process. The beginning reader concentrates on the sounds symbolized by groups of letters and is very aware of the process of decoding a string of letters. The advanced reader scans groups of words effortlessly and may not even be aware of his mental activities while in the act of reading.

By including practical abilities, analytical abilities, and creative abilities, the triarchic theory captures the enormous breadth and complexity of what it means to be intelligent (Sternberg, 1998; Sternberg & Kaufman, 1998). Sternberg believes it is difficult to assess this human quality with one measure or test score because such a number would mask the extremely different patterns of abilities that individuals show. One child may have exceptional componential skills but behave maladaptively in her environment. Another may be highly creative in tackling novel problems but show poor componential skills.

● **Gardner's Theory of Multiple Intelligences**   Howard Gardner defines intelligence as "an ability (or skill) to solve problems or to fashion products which are valued within one or more cultural settings" (1986, p. 74). Like Sternberg, Gardner believes that information-processing abilities are at the core of intelligence. Gardner's (1983, 1998) emphasis, though, is on the idea that people often show marked individual differences in their ability to process specific kinds of information. Accordingly, he identified the following eight distinct intelligences:

Linguistic: A sensitivity to the meanings and order of words, as well as the functions of language

Musical: A sensitivity to pitch, tone, and timbre, as well as musical patterns

Logico-mathematical: The ability to handle chains of reasoning, numerical relations, and hierarchical relations

Spatial: The capacity to perceive the world accurately and to transform and recreate perceptions

Bodily-kinesthetic: The ability to use one's body or to work with objects in highly differentiated and skillful ways

Intrapersonal: The capacity to understand one's own feelings and use them to guide behavior

Interpersonal: The ability to notice and make distinctions among the moods, temperaments, motivations, and intentions of others

Naturalistic: The ability to distinguish among, classify, and see patterns in aspects of the natural environment.

Gardner claims support for the existence of these discrete areas of intelligence on several fronts. For each skill, he says, it is possible to find people who excel or show genius, such as Mozart, T. S. Eliot, and Einstein. It is also possible, in many instances, to show a loss of or a deficit in a specific ability due to damage to particular areas of the brain. Lesions to the parts of the left cortex specifically dedicated to language function, for example, produce a loss of linguistic intelligence. Yet the other intelligences usually remain intact. Finally, it is possible to identify a core of information-processing operations uniquely relevant to each area. For musical intelligence, one core process is sensitivity to pitch. For bodily-kinesthetic intelligence, it is the ability to imitate the movement made by another person.

How do each of the intelligences develop? Gardner believes propensities or talents in certain areas may be inborn, but the child's experiences are also of paramount importance. Some children, for example, may show a unique ability to remember melodies, but all children would profit from exposure to musical sequences. Moreover, Gardner reminds us that it is important to remember the cultural values to which the child is exposed. In our culture, linguistic and logico-mathematical skills are highly valued and are emphasized as measures of school success. Among the Puluwat islanders of the South Pacific, the navigational skills required for successful sailing are critical, and hence spatial intelligence receives great recognition in that culture.

Gardner's theory has refueled the debate over intelligence as a unitary construct versus a set of distinct skills; the theory of multiple intelligences clearly falls into the latter category. However, although the theory has appealed to many educators and parents in its positive emphasis on each child's unique talents, some researchers caution that more independent empirical evidence is necessary to fully evaluate it (Klein, 1997). Tests assessing children's skills in each of the domains of intelligence are now available for preschoolers (Chen & Gardner, 1997; Krechevsky, 1994), and these will no doubt lead to a more thorough assessment of the theory.

According to Gardner's theory of multiple intelligences, children may show exceptional abilities in some domains but not others. Among the eight types of intelligence he hypothesizes is musical intelligence, a sensitivity to pitch, tone, timbre, and musical patterns.

FOR YOUR REVIEW

- What two major questions have surrounded attempts to define intelligence?

- What are the main features of psychometric approaches to intelligence?

- What are the principal ideas underlying the theories of Spearman and Thurstone, and *Gf-Gc* theory?

- What are the main features of information-processing approaches to intelligence?

- What are the principal ideas in Sternberg's and Gardner's theories of intelligence?

- How are speed of processing and working memory related to intelligence?

Measuring Intelligence

Over the years, we have come to use the term *IQ* as a synonym for *intelligence*. In fact, the abbreviation IQ means "intelligence quotient" and refers only to the score a person obtains on the standardized intelligence tests now widely used in Western societies. The results of these tests have become so closely associated with intelligence as an attribute of human functioning that we have virtually ceased to make a distinction between them. Yet, as we saw in the opening scene about Son, the IQ score may or may not be a good indicator of intelligent functioning.

Standardized tests of intelligence are based on many shared assumptions about how this characteristic is distributed among individuals. As Figure 10.2 shows, IQ scores are assumed to be normally distributed in the population, with the majority falling in the middle of the distribution and fewer at the upper and lower extremes. The average or *mean* IQ score on most tests is 100. Usually a statistical measure of the average variability of scores around the mean, or *standard deviation,* is also calculated. The standard deviation gives a picture of how clustered or spread out the scores are around the mean. On many tests, the standard deviation has a value of 15.

The normal distribution of scores can also be partitioned into "standard deviation units." As Figure 10.2 shows, the majority of IQ scores (about 68 percent) fall within one standard deviation on either side of the mean, and almost all scores in the population (about 99 percent) fall within three standard deviations above or below the mean. In reality, the percentage of scores below the mean is slightly greater than the theoretical normal distribution would predict. This fact is probably the result of genetic, prenatal, or early postnatal factors that can put young infants at risk for lower intellectual development (Vandenberg & Vogler, 1985; Zigler, 1967).

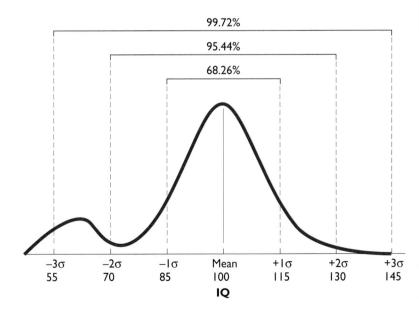

FIGURE 10.2
How Intelligence Is Distributed in the General Population of Intelligence

Intelligence scores are assumed to be normally distributed in the population, with a mean score of 100. Most people's scores fall within 15 points (or one standard deviation) above or below the mean, and almost the entire population falls within three standard deviation units of the mean. In reality, a slightly greater number of individuals than we would theoretically expect fall at the lower end of the distribution, probably due to genetic, prenatal, or early postnatal risks that can affect intelligence.

Exceptional Intelligence

L ess than 3 percent of the population falls outside the typical range of intelligence, that is, beyond two standard deviation units of the mean for IQ scores. A child who obtains an IQ score greater than 130 is generally regarded as gifted, whereas a child who obtains a score below 70 is often classified as mentally retarded.

Giftedness

According to the U. S. Department of Education (1993), gifted children show "high performance capability in intellectual, creative, and/or artistic areas, possess an unusual leadership capacity, or excel in specific academic fields." Gifted children may already display remarkably high levels of performance compared with other children of similar age or background experiences, or they may show the potential to perform at those high levels. Although unusual talent has been measured traditionally by IQ scores, more contemporary views provide alternative ways of understanding giftedness.

For example, drawing on his triarchic theory of intelligence, Robert Sternberg (1981, 1986) has demonstrated that gifted children show several unique information-processing skills. First, when solving problems, they tend to spend much of their time in planning—selecting and organizing strategies and information, for example—and less time in encoding the details stated in the problem. That is, their approach tends to be more "global" than "local," reflecting greater metacognitive skills, an idea that has received support in several studies of gifted children (Alexander, Carr, & Schwanenflugel, 1995). Second, Sternberg hypothesizes that gifted children are better able to deal with novelty and to automatize their information processing. Given novel, unusual insight problems, for example, gifted children are better able than children of average ability to recognize useful strategies for solutions (Sternberg, 1986).

Gifted children are also apparently more efficient and speedier in processing stimuli that match their particular talents. Veronica Dark and Camilla Benbow (1993) asked extremely gifted seventh- and eighth-graders to judge, as quickly as they could, whether two stimuli were the same or different. When the stimuli were digits, the response patterns of students most gifted in mathematics showed faster access to numerical representations than those of other children. The response patterns of students most gifted in verbal skills showed faster access to verbal representations when the stimuli were words. Based on their analyses of many studies of giftedness, Dark and Benbow concluded that the difference between gifted and other children is not qualitative; rather, it is simply a matter of degree, in this case, the degree to which basic cognitive skills are used quickly and efficiently.

What else do we know about the characteristics of gifted children? One of the most extensive studies was conducted by Lewis Terman beginning in 1921 (Terman, 1954; Terman & Oden, 1959). More than one thousand children with IQ scores of 140 or greater were studied longitudinally from early adolescence into their adult years. Contrary to popular stereotypes, they were not frail, sickly, antisocial, "bookish" types. They tended to be taller than average, were physically healthy, and often assumed positions of leadership among their peers. By the time they were young adults, about 70 percent of those in the sample had completed college (a very high proportion for that generation), and many had obtained advanced degrees. The majority entered professional occupations in which they became very productive as adults—authoring books, plays, and scientific articles, for example. Unfortunately, however, because the children in Terman's sample were nominated by their teachers, gifted children who were quieter or did not fit a teacher's conception of a "good student" were probably overlooked. Thus, Terman's results must be viewed with caution. Other more recent research has found that gifted children take advantage of accelerated educational opportunities and are far more likely to pursue postgraduate degrees than is the norm (Lubinski et al., 2001). They generally show healthy peer relationships, good self-concepts, and are well adjusted. Those at the extreme end of the continuum, though, are more likely to be socially isolated and feel unhappy, probably because they are so different from their peers and have trouble "fitting in" (Robinson & Clinkenbeard, 1998; Winner, 1996, 1997).

Does giftedness simply reveal itself naturally during the childhood years? Not according to other researchers examining the underpinnings of exceptional talent. In one study, two children who were expert chess players and one who was an accomplished musician were found to spend many hours practicing their skills under the tutelage of special teachers (Feldman, 1979). In another study, world-class musicians, mathematicians, and athletes reported that their childhood years were marked by strong encouragement of their early natural abilities. Parents, coaches, and teachers were important sources of motivation, and typically these talented individuals spent years in intensive training of their skills (Bloom, 1982). Because of the exceptional drive and hard work that are involved in achieving high levels of success, most gifted children do not become unusually accomplished or eminent adults (Winner, 1997). A special concern for many researchers and educators is that the talents of gifted children be nurtured so that their potential can be realized (Winner, 2000).

Mental Retardation

The American Association on Mental Retardation (2002) defines mental retardation as consisting of limitations in intellectual and adaptive functioning originating before the age of eighteen. *Adaptive functioning* refers to a range of skills typically required to function in the everyday world, such as self-care skills, the ability to get to school or home on one's own, or, eventually, the capacity to find a job and handle personal finances. Within this broad definition, four levels of retardation have been identified: mild, moderate, severe, and profound. Whereas a child with mild retardation can usually be expected to profit from school instruction and eventually hold a job and live independently as an adult, a child with profound retardation will require special assistance throughout life with almost every aspect of daily functioning.

As we saw in the chapters titled "Genetics and Heredity" and "The Prenatal Period and Birth," some instances of mental impairment are linked to genetic factors, as in the case of Down syndrome or PKU, or to experiences in the prenatal or perinatal environment that interfere with brain and central nervous system development and functioning, such as exposure to rubella or oxygen deprivation during birth. When a clear biological cause exists, the retardation is called *organic*. Generally, the most severe forms of retardation fall into this category. In other cases, the retardation has no obvious organic roots but is suspected to have resulted from an impoverished, unstimulating environment, the inheritance of the potential for a low range of intelligence, or a combination of both factors. About 70 to 75 percent of cases of mental retardation fall into this category, called *nonorganic* or *familial retardation* (Zigler & Hodapp, 1986). Usually the level of retardation among children in this second class is mild or moderate.

Do children with mental retardation differ qualitatively from children with at least average intelligence, or do their mental capacities differ only in degree? Psychologists who have studied the cognitive processing of children with familial retardation have noted that they show deficits on a number of fronts. First, they have difficulty focusing attention on the task at hand and become distracted easily. Second, they show notable deficits in working memory and an impoverished general knowledge base. One reason may be that they rarely produce the strategies for remembering typically displayed by children of average or above-average intelligence, strategies such as rehearsal and organization described in the chapter titled "Cognition: Information Processing." Thus their ability to retain information in both short- and long-term memory is hampered. Finally, children who have nonorganic retardation often fail to transfer knowledge from one learning situation to another. If the child was trained, for example, to repeat a string of digits to improve recall, he would fail to employ that strategy when given a new but similar task such as recalling a set of letters (Campione, Brown, & Ferrara, 1982). All of these findings suggest that children with mental

KEY THEME
Nature/Nurture

◉ **SEE FOR YOURSELF**
psychology.college.hmco.com
Savant Syndrome

retardation develop just as children of average intelligence do, only slower. On the other hand, say some experts, we do not know whether children with organic retardation have the same structure of intelligence that others possess. Their developmental progression in attaining cognitive skills may be unique (Zigler & Hodapp, 1986).

With regard to the effective care and education of children with mental retardation, the trend in recent years has been to "deinstitutionalize" all but those with the most profound retardation. Likewise, the placement of children with mental retardation in special education schools and classrooms has given way to the practice of *mainstreaming* these children within normal classrooms, where they are encouraged to participate in and benefit from as many regular classroom activities as their abilities permit.

WHAT DO YOU THINK?

Does Mainstreaming Work?
psychology.college.hmco.com

Standardized Tests of Intelligence

Educators, clinicians, and others who must assess and diagnose children have a number of standardized tests to choose from. Usually intelligence tests are administered in special situations, such as when parents or teachers suspect that a child is unusually gifted. Alternatively, there may be a need to assess a child whose schoolwork falls below the level of other children in the class, as in the case of Son described at the beginning of this chapter. Does the child have a learning disability (which is usually accompanied by normal intellectual functioning), or is the child's general ability to learn impaired? Are there other reasons (for example, emotional factors) the child is not performing well? A special educational plan designed to meet the needs of the student is then implemented. Intelligence tests may also be employed to assess the developmental progress of children who are at risk for any one of a number of reasons; perhaps they were premature at birth or suffered some trauma that could affect the ability to learn. Although many children will not have the experience of taking an IQ test, a variety of special circumstances may dictate administering such a test.

How are IQ tests designed? *Psychometricians,* psychologists who specialize in the construction and interpretation of tests, typically administer a new test to a large sample of individuals during the test construction phase, both to assess the test's *reliability* and *validity* (see the chapter titled "Studying Child Development") and to establish the norms of performance against which to compare other individuals. A central concern is to ensure that each item included in the test is related to the overall concept being measured, in this case, intelligence. Moreover, if the test is valid, the scores obtained should be related to scores on other, similar tests. Needless to say, the business of designing intelligence tests requires careful thought and skill. Some intelligence tests are designed to be administered to individual children; others can be given to large groups. Ethical standards dictate that psychologists be carefully trained in both the administration and scoring of IQ tests before being permitted to administer them.

◉ SEE FOR YOURSELF
psychology.college.hmco.com
Ethics and Testing

● **Infant Intelligence Tests**   Most tests of infant intelligence are based on norms for behaviors that are expected to occur in the first year or two of life. Because most of the infant's accomplishments are in the domains of motor, language, and socioemotional development, these areas appear most frequently on the various tests. Almost without exception, the tests are administered individually to infants.

Perhaps the most widely used infant test is the *Bayley Scales of Infant Development,* designed by Nancy Bayley (1993) to predict later childhood competence. The test consists of two scales. The Mental Scale assesses the young child's sensory and perceptual skills, memory, learning, acquisition of the object concept, and linguistic skill. The Motor Scale measures the child's ability to control and coordinate the body, from large motor skills to finer manipulation of the hands and fingers. Table 10.2 shows some sample items from each scale. Designed for infants from one through forty-two months of age, the test yields a *developmental index* for both the mental

TABLE 10.2	Sample Items from the Bayley Scales of Infant Development	
Age	**Mental Scale**	**Motor Scale**
2 months	Turns head to sound Plays with rattle Reacts to disappearance of face	Holds head erect and steady for 15 seconds Turns from side to back Sits with support
6 months	Lifts cup by handle Looks for fallen spoon Looks at pictures in book	Sits alone for 30 seconds Turns from back to stomach Grasps foot with hands
12 months	Builds tower of 2 cubes Turns pages of book	Walks with help Throws ball Grasps pencil in middle
17–19 months	Imitates crayon stroke Identifies objects in photograph	Stands alone on right foot Walks up stairs with help
23–25 months	Matches pictures Uses pronoun(s) Imitates a 2-word sentence	Laces 3 beads Jumps distance of 4 inches Walks on tiptoe for 4 steps
38–42 months	Names 4 colors Uses past tense Identifies gender	Copies circle Hops twice on 1 foot Walks down stairs, alternating feet

Source: Bayley Scales of Infant Development. Copyright © 1969 by The Psychological Corporation, a Harcourt Assessment Company. Reproduced by permission. All rights reserved. "Bayley Scales of Infant Development" is a registered trademark of The Psychological Corporation.

and the motor scale. That is, the infant's scores are compared with the scores for the standardization sample (the large sample of normal infants whose performance was assessed at the time the test was developed) and are expressed in terms of how much they deviate from the average scores of that sample. The Bayley scales also contain a Behavior Rating Scale to assess the infant's interests, emotions, and general level of activity compared with the standardization sample.

One of the most recently developed measures of infant intelligence is the *Fagan Test of Infant Intelligence,* designed for infants between six and twelve months old and based on infants' recognition memory capabilities. During the test, the child sits on the parent's lap and views a picture for a predetermined period of time. The familiar picture is then presented alongside a novel one, and the infant's looking time to the novel stimulus is recorded. As you saw in the chapter titled "Cognition: Information Processing," infants show their "memory" for the familiar stimulus by looking longer at the new item. Several of these "novelty problems" are presented in succession. The test is designed to screen for children at risk for intellectual deficits based on the premise that their response to novelty is depressed. In one study, scores infants obtained on the Fagan Test of Infant Intelligence correlated in the range of +.44 to +.47 with their scores on several standard tests of intelligence at age eight years (Smith, Fagen, & Ulvund, 2002). Furthermore, a series of studies found that if infants directed fewer than 53 percent of their visual fixations to the novel stimuli, they were especially likely to fall into the category of "intellectually delayed" (Fagan & Montie, 1988).

● **Individual IQ Tests for Older Children**   The two most widely used individually administered intelligence tests for school-age children are the Stanford-Binet Intelligence Scales and the Wechsler Intelligence Scales for Children–III (or WISC-III). Both are based on the psychometric model and measure similar mental skills.

The *Stanford-Binet Intelligence Scales,* adapted from the original Binet scales by Lewis Terman of Stanford University, were most recently revised in 2003 (Terman, 1916; Roid, 2003). When Binet originally designed the test, he chose mental tasks that the average child at each age could perform. He also assumed that children of a specific age—say, eight years—who performed as their older counterparts—say, ten years—did had a higher *mental age.* By the same token, an eight-year-old who passed only the items the average six-year-old could answer had a lower mental age. Thus intelligence was thought to be the extent to which children resemble their agemates in performance.

Terman translated, modified, and standardized the Binet scales for use in the United States. He also borrowed from William Stern, a German psychologist, an equation for expressing the results of the test. The child's **intelligence quotient,** or **IQ,** was computed as follows:

$$IQ = \text{mental age/chronological age} \times 100$$

Thus a ten-year-old who obtained a mental age score of 12 would have an IQ of 120. The Stanford-Binet Intelligence Scale rapidly came into use among educators and clinicians eager to find a useful diagnostic tool for children.

The Stanford-Binet test assesses five broad areas of mental functioning: verbal reasoning, knowledge, visual reasoning, quantitative reasoning, and working memory. The test is scaled for use with individuals from two years of age through adulthood. In the Stanford-Binet, the concept of mental age has been replaced by a **deviation IQ.** The child's score in each of the test areas is compared with those of similar-age children in the standardization sample, and Verbal and Nonverbal IQ scores are obtained. An overall IQ score can also be computed. Thus this test permits psychologists not only to assess the child's overall abilities but also to isolate specific areas of strength and weakness.

The *Wechsler Intelligence Scale for Children,* the major alternative to the Stanford-Binet, is scaled for use with children ages six through sixteen years. The original version was constructed in 1949 by David Wechsler and most recently revised in 1991 (Wechsler, 1991). The revised version, called the WISC-III, contains three scales: (1) the Verbal Scale, which includes items assessing vocabulary, arithmetic skills, digit span performance, and knowledge of general information; (2) the Performance Scale, which includes tests of visual spatial skill, puzzle assembly, and arranging pictures to form a story; and (3) a Full Scale IQ, which represents a composite of the two scales. Thus, like the Stanford-Binet, this test allows the examiner to assess patterns of strength and weakness in the child's mental abilities. In addition, like the Stanford-Binet, the child's score on the WISC-III is computed on the basis of the deviation IQ. Figure 10.3 shows some items resembling those from the Verbal and Performance scales of the WISC-III.

A relatively newer intelligence test for two- through twelve-year-olds is the *Kaufman Assessment Battery for Children* or *K-ABC* (Kaufman & Kaufman, 1983). This test is based on the assumption that intelligence is related to the quality of mental processing; the focus is on how children produce correct solutions to problems rather than on the content of their knowledge. The test includes three scales: (1) the Sequential Processing Scale, which assesses the ability to solve problems in a step-by-step fashion; (2) the Simultaneous Processing Scale, which tests the ability to solve problems through integration and organization of many pieces of information; and (3) the Mental Processing Composite, a combination of the first two scales. The K-ABC also includes an Achievement Scale to assess knowledge the child has acquired in the home and school. Figure 10.4 illustrates some of the items found on the K-ABC.

Most of the items on the K-ABC were specifically designed to be neutral in content so that processing differences among children could be validly assessed; that is, the intent was to minimize the influence of the child's previous learning history on performance. In addition, the emphasis in test administration is on obtaining the child's best performance. Whereas administration of the Stanford-Binet and the WISC-III requires strict adherence to test protocol, examiners giving the K-ABC are encouraged to use alternative wording, gestures, or even languages other than English to make sure the child understands what is expected. Thus, in terms of content and mode of administration, the K-ABC represents a departure from many traditional tests of intelligence.

intelligence quotient (IQ) Numerical score received on an intelligence test.

deviation IQ   IQ score computed by comparing the child's performance with that of a standardization sample.

VERBAL SCALE

General Information
  1. How many nickels make a dime?
  2. Who wrote *Tom Sawyer*?

General Comprehension
  1. What is the advantage of keeping money in a bank?
  2. Why is copper often used in electrical wires?

Arithmetic
  1. Sam had three pieces of candy and Joe gave him four more. How many pieces
     of candy did Sam have all together?
  2. If two buttons cost fifteen cents, what will be the cost of a dozen buttons?

Similarities
  1. In what way are a saw and a hammer alike?
  2. In what way are an hour and a week alike?

Vocabulary
  This test consists simply of asking, "What is a _____?" or "What does _____ mean?"
  The words cover a wide range of difficulty.

PERFORMANCE SCALE

Picture Arrangement

I want you to arrange these pictures in the right order so they tell a story that makes sense.
Work as quickly as you can. Tell me when you have finished.

Object Assembly

Put this one together as quickly as you can.

Source: Simulated items similar to those in the Wechsler Intelligence Scale for Children: Third Edition.
Copyright © 1991 by the Psychological Corporation, a Harcourt Assessment Company. Reproduced
by permission. All rights reserved. "Wechsler Intelligence Scale for Children" and "WISC-III" are registered trademarks of The Psychological Corporation.

FIGURE 10.3
Sample Items from the
Wechsler Intelligence Scale
for Children–III

**The WISC-III contains two
scales, the Verbal Scale and
the Performance Scale. Shown
here are examples that resemble items from the several
subtests that contribute to
each scale.**

Stability and Prediction

Intelligence tests were first developed with the goal of predicting children's future
functioning. Binet, you recall, was asked to design a tool that would anticipate children's achievement in school. Those who followed with other theories and assessment tools for measuring intelligence likewise assumed, either explicitly or implicitly,
that scores on the tests would forecast the individual's successes or failures in some
areas of life. Moreover, many (although not all) psychologists assumed "intelligence"
is a quality people carry with them over the whole life span. They believed, in other
words, that IQ scores would show continuity and stability.

FIGURE 10.4
Sample Items from the
Kaufman Assessment Battery
for Children

The K-ABC contains a Sequential and a Simultaneous Processing Scale. One goal of this test is to assess intelligence apart from the specific content children already have learned.

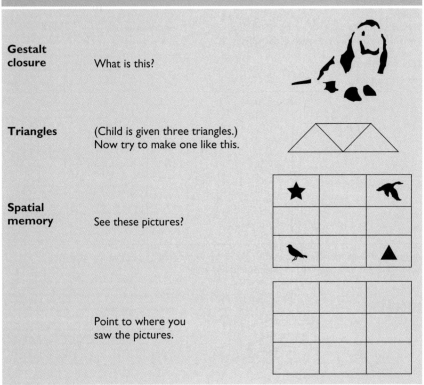

SEQUENTIAL PROCESSING

Hand movements	Watch my hand. Now you try it.	
Number recall	Say these numbers just as I do.	5 – 4 – 8 – 1 – 10
Word order	Cat–hand–shoe–ball. Now touch the pictures that I named.	

SIMULTANEOUS PROCESSING

Gestalt closure	What is this?	
Triangles	(Child is given three triangles.) Now try to make one like this.	
Spatial memory	See these pictures?	
	Point to where you saw the pictures.	

Source: Kaufman & Kaufman, 1983.

● **The Stability of IQ**   If intelligence is a reasonably invariant characteristic, a child tested repeatedly at various ages should obtain approximately the same IQ scores. In one major longitudinal research project, the Berkeley Growth Study, a group of children was given intelligence tests every year from infancy through adulthood. The correlations between the scores obtained during the early school years and scores at ages seventeen and eighteen years were generally high; the correlation between IQ scores at ages seven and eighteen years, for example, was .80 (Jones & Bayley, 1941; Pinneau, 1961). Even though the results point to a moderate degree of stability, however, about half of the sample showed differences of 10 points or more when IQ in the early school years was compared with IQ in adolescence.

In another extensive project, the Fels Longitudinal Study, the stability of intelligence was assessed from the preschool years to early adulthood. Although correlations for scores were high when the ages were adjacent, they were much lower as the years between testing increased; the correlation between IQ score at ages three and four years, for example, was .83, but dropped to .46 between ages three and twelve years. Furthermore, as in the Berkeley data, individual children frequently showed dramatic changes in scores—sometimes as much as 40 points—between ages two and seventeen years (McCall, Appelbaum, & Hogarty, 1973; Sontag, Baker, & Nelson, 1958). Taken together, the results of these two major longitudinal studies suggest that for many children, IQ scores can be stable, especially if the two test times are close together, but large fluctuations in individual scores are also possible.

Why do the scores of some children shift so dramatically? The presence or absence of family stress can be a factor. Children in the Berkeley study who showed significant declines in IQ often experienced a dramatic alteration in life experience, such as loss of a parent or a serious illness (Honzik, Macfarlane, & Allen, 1948). Similarly, a more recent longitudinal study found a relationship between IQ scores and the number of environmental risk factors to which a child is exposed (Sameroff et al., 1993). As children matured from ages four to thirteen years, those with lower IQ scores also experienced a greater number of risks, factors such as unemployment of a parent, physical illness of a family member, or absence of the father from the household. The child's personality attributes or parental interaction styles can also play a role. In the Fels study, children who showed gains in IQ were described as independent, competitive in academics, and self-initiating. In addition, the parents of these children encouraged intellectual achievement and used a discipline style that emphasized moderation and explanation. In contrast, children whose IQ scores decreased with age had parents who were overly restrictive or permissive in discipline style (McCall et al., 1973). Qualities of a parent's personality, a parent's style of interaction with the child, and the type of home environment provided can contribute to instability in IQ scores (Pianta & Egeland, 1994). This body of studies suggests that IQ scores can be vulnerable to environmental influences that can affect the child's performance on a test at a given point in time or, more broadly, his or her motivation to achieve in the intellectual domain.

KEY THEME
Nature/Nurture

● **The Stability of Infant Intelligence**   In general, studies conducted prior to the 1990s have found that correlations between scores on infant intelligence tests and IQ scores in later childhood were low (Kopp & McCall, 1980; McCall, Hogarty, & Hurlburt, 1972). One review of studies measuring IQ at age one year and again at ages three through six years found that the average correlation was only .14 (Fagan & Singer, 1983). In another review, Nancy Bayley (1949) reported essentially no relationships between scores obtained in the first four years of life and those obtained in young adulthood. Only when children reached age five years were correlations of .60 seen with adult scores (see Figure 10.5).

How can we explain these results? One possibility, of course, is that there is no such thing as a general intelligence factor (or *g*) or that, if it exists, it is not a stable trait. Another possibility is that intelligence in infancy differs qualitatively from intelligence in later years, implying that intellectual development is discontinuous. One problem in drawing any conclusions is that the types of skills measured by infant intelligence tests are very different from those measured by tests such as the Stanford-Binet and WISC-III. Recall, for example, some of the items from the Bayley Scales of Infant Development, many of which center on the child's sensory and motor accomplishments: the ability to roll over, reach, or jump on one foot. We have little reason to believe the infant's skill in these areas should be related to the verbal, memory, and problem-solving skills measured by traditional IQ tests for older children.

KEY THEME
Continuity/Discontinuity

As we saw with the Fagen Test of Infant Intelligence, however, some components of infants' information-processing capabilities remain constant over a span of years and are related to IQ scores in later childhood. Several researchers have reported strong relationships among recognition memory, speed of habituation, and visual reaction time measured during infancy and IQ up to age eleven years (Bornstein & Sigman, 1986; Dougherty & Haith, 1997; McCall & Carriger, 1993; Rose & Feldman, 1995, 1997). These results suggest that mental development may be more continuous than developmental psychologists previously thought. In addition, certain fundamental cognitive skills such as visual recognition memory and intermodal perception (discussed in the chapter titled "Basic Learning and Perception") seem to stay

FIGURE 10.5
Is Intelligence Stable
over Time?

The graph shows the correlation between IQ scores obtained in infancy and childhood
and IQ scores at age eighteen
years. Note that IQ scores
obtained before age four years
are poor predictors of subsequent IQ.

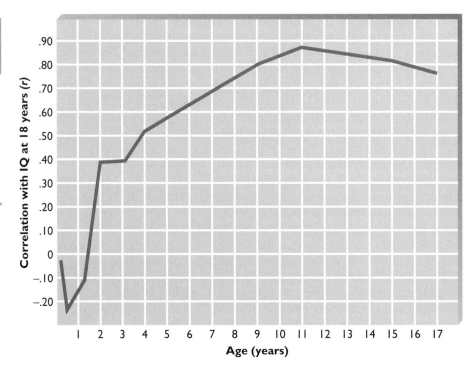

Source. Bayley Scales of Infant Development. Copyright © 1969 by the Psychological Corporation, a
Harcourt Assessment Company. Reproduced by permission. All rights reserved. "Bayley Scales of Infant
Development" is a registered trademark of The Psychological Corporation.

quite stable within individual children as they progress from infancy through childhood (Rose et al., 1997, 1998); it may be that these skills somehow play a specific role
in other higher-order mental processes that are usually associated with intelligence.

● **The Predictive Utility of IQ Tests**   What do IQ tests predict? IQ tests do a good
job of telling us which children will be successful in school and which will have difficulties. Most studies have found that the correlations between intelligence tests and
measures of educational achievement average about .50, with the correlations slightly
higher for elementary school children than for high school or college students (Brody
& Brody, 1976; Jensen, 1980). In addition, the correlations are strongest with academic
subjects that emphasize verbal skills, such as reading (Horn & Packard, 1985). One
reason IQ scores predict school achievement so successfully is that many of the skills
assessed in intelligence tests overlap with the skills essential to educational success.
Verbal fluency, the ability to solve arithmetic problems, and rote memory, some of the
abilities IQ tests measure, are part of most children's school routines. Thus IQ tests
predict best exactly what Binet originally designed them to foretell.

   Do IQ tests predict any developmental outcomes other than school success? IQ
scores are related to job status during adulthood, according to one research program.
In his longitudinal study of children with IQs of 140 or higher, Lewis Terman (Terman, 1925; Terman & Oden, 1959) found that many of these exceptionally bright individuals eventually became scientists, executives, and college faculty members. As
usual, however, we must be cautious about how we interpret correlational data. As
we saw earlier, IQ scores are strongly related to educational achievement. They are
also related to how many years an individual will actually spend in school (Neisser et
al., 1996). It may be that occupational success is the result of education and not a direct outcome of IQ (Ceci & Williams, 1997; Fulker & Eysenck, 1979; Jencks, 1972).

   Aside from these relationships, do IQ scores predict other measures of success in
life? Social scientists disagree. According to some, IQ scores predict economic status
in adulthood (Herrnstein & Murray, 1994); others claim that IQ scores do not necessarily forecast the amount of money an individual earns, physical or mental health,

job satisfaction, or general life satisfaction (Lewis, 1983; McClelland, 1973; Sternberg, 1995). The debate abounds with disagreements about the proper use of statistical techniques as well as whether various measures of IQ are valid (Fraser, 1995). Suffice it to say that this topic has strong roots in the nature-nurture controversy; generally, advocates of a nature position believe intelligence is a stable trait that affects later developmental outcomes, whereas those who favor a nurture position believe intelligence is malleable depending on the quality of a child's experiences.

RESEARCH APPLIED TO EDUCATION

Interpreting IQ Test Scores

T*he day seemed to drag on forever. Son Van Nguyen must have looked at the clock a hundred times before the 3:00 P.M. dismissal bell finally rang. He trudged slowly toward the school counselor's office to meet his family; they would be discussing his test results with the school psychologist. As he entered the office, he saw his parents already seated, silent and looking as apprehensive as he felt.*

After a brief greeting, the school psychologist launched into a description of the test Son had taken. Then she suddenly stopped.

"Do your parents understand English?" she asked.

"No," he replied softly.

"I should have realized that. Can you translate my comments for them?"

"I can try," responded Son as his confidence slowly resurfaced. "I often have to do that for my parents."

"The main thing you should tell them is that you did very well on many parts of the test." Son was visibly relieved. Maybe he had at least some intelligence, he thought.

The psychologist continued, "You just need to continue to work on your English and . . ."

"I borrowed some books from the library," interrupted Son as he pulled one from his backpack. "See? This one is all about Christopher Columbus." He stopped, looking up sheepishly as he realized he had not waited for the psychologist to finish.

"That's terrific!" she laughed. "Now can you please tell your parents what I said?"

B ecause of the controversy surrounding IQ tests—which (if any) tests are most valid, for example—and because scores on IQ tests can fluctuate markedly for any individual child, many psychologists advocate that educators and parents use caution when interpreting test scores. Here are several important aspects of testing to keep in mind:

A number of factors can affect a child's performance on an IQ test, including unfamiliarity with the adult administering the test and language and cultural barriers that may interfere with the child's performance. Therefore, IQ scores must be interpreted with caution.

1. *Recognize that a child may obtain a low score on a given test because of poor motivation, anxiety about taking a test, unfamiliarity with the English language, or vastly different cultural experiences.*   Psychologists who administer tests are trained to try to make the child feel comfortable, but it may be impossible to make him or her feel completely free of stress under the usual test-taking conditions: a separate, perhaps strange room, an unfamiliar adult, lots of questions with little feedback about the answers. Moreover, barriers created by language and cultural differences may be difficult to remove. These issues are addressed later in this chapter when we discuss cultural differences in IQ scores.

2. *Avoid labeling a child on the basis of an IQ score as an "underachiever" or a "slow learner," because this practice creates its own set of risks.*   For example, teachers and parents may lower expectations of that child, a phenomenon that can, in turn, further lower her achievement. This is an example of a "self-fulfilling prophecy."

3. *Be aware that IQ test scores usually do not have direct implications for specific remedial education practices or instructional techniques.*   The assignment of a child to a particular reading group or math skill level has less to do with the number the child received on an IQ test than with his successes or failures on various class assignments and observations of his behavior and problem-solving strategies in the classroom (Boehm, 1985; Bruer, 1994). In other words, optimizing performance in and out of the classroom, regardless of the scores on intelligence tests, should remain the primary goal of teachers and parents.

These caveats do not necessarily mean IQ tests are useless. They may give a clinician a good sense of the child's pattern of strengths and weaknesses, can assist in the diagnosis of learning problems, and give other clinical insights. However, care must be taken not to focus on the single number—the IQ score. Instead, school and clinical psychologists should use multiple sources of information about the child's level of functioning, including observations of classroom behaviors and personal history (Prifitera, Weiss, & Saklofske, 1998; Weinberg, 1989).

FOR YOUR REVIEW

- What assumptions do psychologists make about the distribution of IQ scores in the population?

- How is giftedness defined? What are the unique ways in which gifted individuals process information? What are the behavioral characteristics of gifted children?

- How is mental retardation defined? What are its causes? What are the unique ways in which these children process information?

- What are the major tests that have been used to assess intelligence in infants and children? What are the major features of each in terms of how they measure intelligence?

- What does research reveal about the stability of IQ? What kinds of outcomes do IQ scores predict?

- What cautions should be kept in mind when interpreting IQ scores?

Factors Related to Intelligence

KEY THEME
Nature/Nurture

In the chapter titled "Genetics and Heredity," we saw that genetics can influence intelligence. Chromosomal abnormalities and single-gene effects such as fragile X syndrome, Down syndrome, and PKU can have profound consequences for the child's intellectual growth. The higher correlations among IQ scores of identical twins reared apart compared with fraternal twins or nontwin siblings reared in the same environment and the strong correlations between IQs of adopted children and their biological parents also suggest a role for heredity. In fact, researchers have recently claimed to have located a specific gene associated with *g*, the general intelligence factor (Chorney et al., 1998). A particular allele on chromosome 6 was found to appear more frequently in very bright children than in children of average intellectual ability.

Yet even if we agree that genetic differences contribute, perhaps even substantially, to the child's intellectual competence, it would be a mistake to conclude that IQ scores are not influenced by environmental experiences (Angoff, 1988; Scarr, 1981). Consider two traits very strongly influenced by heredity: physical height and the presence of the trait for PKU. In each instance, the presence of the genotype bears a great resemblance to the phenotype. Yet it is also true that environmental factors can influence the eventual outcome for the child. Recall the discussion of secular trends in physical height in the chapter titled "Brain, Motor Skill, and Physical Development." Recall also from the chapter titled "Genetics and Heredity" that dietary modifications for infants born with PKU can result in nearly normal mental development. In each case, a highly canalized human characteristic is modified by the environment. Moreover, studies of early brain development demonstrate the critical role of experiences in how neurons form connections with one another. Individuals may differ in how readily neurons respond to experience, but the environment is still essential to understanding their eventual abilities (Garlick, 2002).

Consider also the phenomenon called the "Flynn effect." Across twenty countries in North America, Europe, and Asia, IQ scores have risen about 15 points every thirty years on culture-fair tests such as the Raven Progressive Matrices (Flynn, 1998, 1999). Perhaps better nutrition, increased access to schooling, or greater availability of technology (which may foster certain cognitive skills) are responsible (Neisser, 1998). By the same token, it would be difficult to argue for a genetic basis for these shifts in scores; large-scale changes in hereditary patterns occur across much longer time spans. Thus the ever-present role of the environment is an important factor to keep in mind as we discuss the roots of intelligence.

What factors are especially important in shaping the child's intellectual attainments? We begin by examining group differences in IQ scores, findings that have provided much of the backdrop for the nature-nurture debate. Next, we examine those elements of the child's home experience that may be crucial to mental growth as well as the role of the sociocultural environment in shaping specific mental skills. Finally, we consider the impact of early intervention programs on the intellectual attainment of children from culturally different backgrounds. In each case we will see that there are many conditions, even given the contributions of heredity, under which intelligence is not fixed but modified by the timing, extent, and range of environmental experiences.

Group Differences in IQ Scores

Children from different socioeconomic and ethnic backgrounds do not perform equally well on traditional IQ tests. One well-established finding is that African American children in the United States typically score 15 points lower than Caucasian children on tests such as the Stanford-Binet and the WISC (Jensen, 1980; Loehlin, Lindzey, & Spuhler, 1975). Another finding is that children from lower socioeconomic classes obtain lower IQ scores than those from middle and upper classes (Deutsch, Katz, & Jensen, 1968; Lesser, Fifer, & Clark, 1965). Of the many hypotheses put forward about the sources of these differences, some have rekindled the nature-nurture debate and others focus on the validity of IQ tests for children who are members of minority and lower socioeconomic groups.

● **Race, IQ, and Nature Versus Nurture**   In 1969, Arthur Jensen published a paper suggesting that racial differences in IQ scores could, in large part, be accounted for by heredity. According to Jensen, there is a high degree of *heritability* in IQ; that is,

KEY THEME
Nature/Nurture

about 80 percent of the variation in IQ scores in the population could be explained by genetic variation. He argued that because racial and ethnic subgroups within the population tend not to marry outside their groups, African American–Caucasian differences in IQ scores have a strong genetic component.

Jensen's propositions created a storm of controversy, one that has reemerged as a result of similar claims made more recently by Richard Herrnstein and Charles Murray (1994). One of the most immediate criticisms of Jensen's argument (which has also been applied to its modern-day counterpart) was that *within-group* estimates of heritability cannot be used to explain *between-group* differences in performance. Even if the heritability of IQ were .80 for both Caucasian and African American populations (actually the heritability estimates for IQ were derived solely from samples of Caucasian children and their families), other factors, such as differences in the environmental experiences of each group, could not be ruled out in explaining racial differences in IQ scores (Loehlin et al., 1975). For example, a 15-point difference in IQ could still arise if most Caucasian children grew up in enriched environments and most African American children experienced environments that did not promote optimal intellectual development.

A **cross-fostering study** by Sandra Scarr and Richard Weinberg (1976, 1978, 1983) that examined children who were raised in environments markedly different from those of their biological families demonstrated just how this effect might take place. In their transracial adoption study, Scarr and Weinberg selected 101 Caucasian middle-class families that had adopted African American children, most of whom were under one year of age at the time of adoption. Many of these families also had biological children of their own. The adoptive families were highly educated, were above average in occupational status and income, and had high IQ scores. The biological families of the adopted children had lower educational levels and lower-status occupations. Scarr and Weinberg found that the average IQ among the African American adopted children was 106, higher than the average score of both African American children and those in the general population. The researchers argued that because the adopted children were raised in environments that exposed them to Caucasian culture and the verbal and cognitive skills customarily assessed in IQ tests, they performed better than African American children with similar genetic backgrounds who did not have that experience. At the same time, however, the IQs of the adopted children were more strongly correlated with the educational levels of their biological parents ($r = 0.36$) than with the IQs of their adoptive parents ($r = 0.19$). Thus the role of heredity cannot be ruled out either.

Many researchers reject a genetic explanation of racial differences in IQ as too simplistic. We saw in the chapter titled "Genetics and Heredity" that heredity and environment interact in complex ways to produce varied developmental outcomes; neither by itself is sufficient to explain most human behaviors. In fact, because an individual's genotype influences the type of environment he or she will experience, heritability estimates may actually include environmental effects (Dickens & Flynn, 2001). Furthermore, in the United States race is a variable confounded by the other variables of social class, educational achievement, educational opportunities, and income. All of these factors can contribute to the types of learning experiences young children undergo. Parents with greater financial resources can provide the books, toys, and other materials that stimulate intellectual growth. Moreover, families with economic stability are likely to experience less stress than economically unstable families, a factor that can be related to intellectual performance, as we saw earlier in this chapter. Finally, a recent study shows that heritability estimates can vary depending on family background variables. For families in which parents were well educated, heritability of verbal IQ for children was estimated to be .74, whereas when parents were poorly educated, the heritability estimate was .26 (Rowe, Jacobson, & Van den Oord, 1999). Rather than settling the nature-nurture question, then, racial differences in IQ have served to highlight the complexity of interactions among variables associated with intelligence.

cross-fostering study   Research study in which children are reared in environments that differ from those of their biological parents.

● **Test Bias** A major hypothesis put forth to account for group differences in IQ scores is based on the notion of **test bias.** According to this view, the content of traditional tests is unfamiliar to children from some social or cultural backgrounds. In other words, traditional psychometric tests are not *culturally fair.* Recall the dilemma Son Van Nguyen faced at the beginning of this chapter and the erroneous conclusion he drew about his own intelligence based on his failure to define *inscription* and to answer the question "Who discovered America?" Unfortunately, his IQ test score may reflect the same conclusion. Individuals who have not encountered such specific information in their own cultural experiences will fail those items and score lower on many intelligence tests (Fagen & Holland, 2002).

What happens when tests that are more culturally fair are administered to children from varied sociocultural backgrounds? The research findings are mixed. In the chapter titled "Language," you were introduced to the Raven Progressive Matrices, a nonverbal test of reasoning ability that is assumed to contain minimal cultural bias. Caucasian children still score significantly higher on this test than African American children do (Jensen, 1980). Yet when another culturally fair test, the Kaufman Assessment Battery, was administered to children of different cultural backgrounds, the difference in test scores between Caucasian and African American children was smaller than when tests such as the WISC were given (Kaufman, Kamphaus, & Kaufman, 1985).

Finally, there are questions about whether minority children have the same experiences with, and attitudes toward, taking tests that majority children do. Some of the skills required to perform well on standardized tests include understanding directions, considering all response alternatives before selecting one, and attending to one item at a time (Oakland, 1982). Minority children may lack this basic "savvy" regarding how to take tests. Because most tests do not permit examiners to be flexible in administering them, they may underestimate minority children's skills (Miller-Jones, 1989). Moreover, minority children may score lower simply because they do not see the point of performing well or have not acquired the same drive to achieve in academic settings that is part of the majority culture (Gruen, Ottinger, & Zigler, 1970; Zigler & Butterfield, 1968). For some, IQ tests may even represent a part of the majority culture that is to be rejected outright (Ogbu, 1994). Still another factor to consider is the extent to which children are accustomed to having questions asked of them by adults. Greenfield (1997) points out that in Asian, African, and Latino cultures, children are expected not to speak to adults but to listen to them and respect their authority. By answering questions posed by an adult, the child may be violating cultural norms.

Not all researchers are convinced that test bias and motivational factors play a large part in explaining the lower IQ scores of certain groups of children (Jensen, 1980). Even for the skeptics, however, these ideas have highlighted the importance of structuring test situations so that *all* children are given the opportunity to display their best performance.

● **Stereotype Threat** How an individual thinks about his or her abilities in relation to negative stereotypes about gender or race can affect performance on different tasks, a concept called **stereotype threat.** This phenomenon has been demonstrated among adults: African American individuals initially primed to think that an upcoming test would assess their abilities scored lower on a challenging verbal test than did Caucasian individuals. However, there was no difference in performance when the groups were given instructions that did not emphasize ability testing (Steele & Aronson, 1995). Similar findings have been reported with upper and lower elementary and middle school Asian American girls given a standardized math test. Right before taking the test, each girl colored a picture that activated stereotypes about either "girls" or "Asians." A third group colored a neutral landscape scene. Figure 10.6 shows the performance of each of the groups on the math component of the Iowa Test of Basic Skills. For the youngest and oldest age groups, activating stereotypes about girls resulted in lower math test scores, whereas activating stereotypes about ethnicity resulted in higher scores (Ambady et al., 2001). (It is unclear why upper elementary

KEY THEME
Sociocultural Influence

test bias Idea that the content of traditional standardized tests does not adequately measure the competencies of children from diverse cultural backgrounds.

stereotype threat The psychological impact of negative social stereotypes in an individual.

FIGURE 10.6
Stereotype Threat and Test Performance

In a study of lower and upper elementary and middle school Asian American girls, Nalini Ambady and her colleagues found that activation of gender stereotypes resulted in lower math test scores but that activation of ethnic stereotypes resulted in higher scores at least for the youngest and oldest groups. These findings suggest that it is important to consider the phenomenon of stereotype threat in evaluating ethnic differences in intelligence test scores.

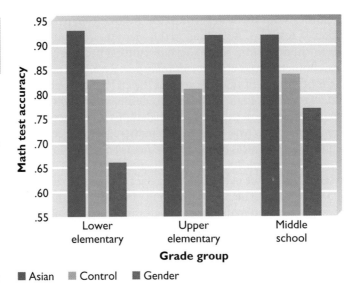

Source: Ambady et al., 2001.

KEY THEME
Nature/Nurture

students did not fit this pattern of performance.) Results such as these suggest that stereotype threat may be an important factor in interpreting racial and ethnic group differences in IQ scores.

The Role of Early Experiences

The generally lower performance of children from minority groups and lower socioeconomic classes on IQ tests has prompted many researchers to take a closer look at how interactions in the home, early experiences in preschool programs, and the values of the larger culture might affect intellectual development. Research has generally revealed that certain aspects of adult-child interactions are related to higher scores on IQ tests.

● **The HOME Inventory**   In 1970, an ambitious project got under way in Little Rock, Arkansas. Initiated by Bettye Caldwell and her associates (Caldwell & Bradley, 1978), the goal of the project was to identify characteristics of the young child's environment that might be related to later competence, including intellectual achievement. A sample of infants and their parents was recruited for a longitudinal study that would last eleven years.

The *Home Observation for Measurement of the Environment (HOME)* inventory was designed to measure a number of characteristics of the child's home surroundings, including the quality of caregiver-child interactions, the availability of objects and activities to stimulate the child, and the types of experiences family members provide to nurture the child's development (see Table 10.3 for the subscales and some sample items). Researchers collected data for the inventory through interviews and direct observations in the children's homes and gave children in the sample standard intelligence and school achievement tests.

The results identified several key features of the home environment as being related to subsequent IQ (Bradley, 1989). Significant correlations were found among measures of the home environment taken at age twelve months and children's IQ scores at ages three and four-and-a-half years. Particularly important were scales that measured parental emotional and verbal responsivity to the child, the availability of appropriate play materials, and parental involvement with the child (Bradley & Caldwell, 1976; Elardo, Bradley, & Caldwell, 1975). In addition, HOME scores at age two years were significantly related to language competencies at age three years (Elardo, Bradley, & Caldwell, 1977). The same three scales on the HOME inventory were especially related to the children's linguistic competence. A follow-up of these children

(1) Emotional and verbal responsivity of mother
Sample item: Mother caresses or kisses child at least once during visit.

(2) Avoidance of restriction and punishment
Sample item: Mother does not interfere with child's actions or restrict child's movements more than three times during visit.

(3) Organization of physical and temporal environment
Sample item: Child's play environment appears safe and free of hazards.

(4) Provision of appropriate play materials
Sample item: Mother provides toys or interesting activities for child during interview.

(5) Maternal involvement with child
Sample item: Mother tends to keep child within visual range and to look at the child often.

(6) Opportunities for variety in daily stimulation
Sample item: Child eats at least one meal per day with mother and father.

Source: Adapted from Elardo & Bradley, 1981.

TABLE 10.3

Subscales of the Home Observation for Measurement of the Environment (HOME)

The HOME Inventory assesses several features of the home environment. Subscales 1, 4, and 5 were found to be significantly correlated with the child's later IQ and language competence.

showed that parental involvement and availability of toys at age two years were significantly related to school achievement at age eleven years (Bradley, 1989).

This series of studies shows that important processes occur between children and their parents early in life that can have long-lasting implications for future intellectual achievement. For one thing, children who have responsive parents may develop a sense of control over their environments, and their resulting general socioemotional health may facilitate intellectual growth. In addition, the opportunity to play with toys may provide contexts for children to learn problem-solving skills from their parents, as well as the chance to develop knowledge from direct manipulation of the play materials. Language development is also enhanced because verbal interactions with parents during play and at other times teach children the properties of spoken speech (Bradley & Caldwell, 1984). One project demonstrated that when mothers provided an environment rich in learning experiences such as those described in the HOME studies, the difference in IQ scores between African American and Caucasian children dropped by 28 percent (Brooks-Gunn, Klebanov, & Duncan, 1996).

KEY THEME
Interaction Among Domains

EXAMINING RESEARCH METHODS

Using Correlations to Test Models of Causality

The HOME studies must be interpreted with caution because, as with any correlational research that uncovers relationships, we do not necessarily know the direction of influence. Parental responsiveness may have been responsible for children's IQ scores. But it is also possible that intelligent infants may have engendered more parental responsiveness and involvement simply because of their greater exploration of the environment or advanced verbal skills.

Some of these difficulties in interpretation are addressed with sophisticated statistical techniques, such as *structural equation modeling,* that allow researchers to evaluate hypotheses about the directions of influence in correlational relationships. Although the mathematical details of these approaches are beyond the scope of the present discussion, a study by Gottfried, Fleming, and Gottfried (1998) concerning the effects of the home environment on school-related motivation serves to illustrate the general tactics involved.

In their study, Gottfried and colleagues (1998) tested the prediction that a cognitively stimulating home environment would have a positive impact on children's academic *intrinsic motivation*—the tendency to be curious, interested, and persistent in school-related tasks. When children in the sample were eight years old, extensive information was collected on their home environments by using a portion of the HOME inventory, as well as two other measures, the Home Environment Survey (HES) and the Family Environment Survey (FES). These latter two measures assessed parental encouragement of learning, educational stimulation, and involvement with the child. Some sample items from these scales are, "Does your child have access to a real musical instrument?" and the true-or-false item, "Family members often go to the library." Children were tested on the Children's Academic Intrinsic Motivation Inventory at ages nine, ten, and thirteen for reading, social studies, science, math, and "school in general." This test assesses the extent to which children enjoy learning, seek out challenging tasks, show curiosity, and display an orientation toward mastering tasks. Of special interest, of course, was whether measures of the home environment predicted children's motivation scores. We will focus here on children's motivation scores for math.

In structural equation modeling, the researcher usually draws a diagram, called a *path diagram,* that illustrates the predicted pattern of cause-and-effect relationships among the variables. An important assumption in this technique is that the connections among variables are set out before the researcher has the opportunity to inspect the results. If you look at Figure 10.7 (and ignore the numbers for now), you can see that the path diagram indicates that the home environment is expected to predict math motivation; the arrows indicate the direction of suspected causality. Specifically, the researchers predicted the relationships designated in (a), (b), and (c). Notice also that the dimension of interest to the researchers, a "cognitively stimulating home environment," is denoted by a circle. The reason is that it is an underlying psychological construct that is not measured directly. It is approximated by a combination of the variables in the small squares, the specific measures of the home environment obtained by the researchers. The variable in the circle is seen as causing the scores on the different home environment measures to take on their specific values. How would the diagram look if, in contrast, motivation levels in children were hypothesized to be responsible for different levels of stimulation in the home?

Next, the "goodness-of-fit" of the model is tested statistically. In Figure 10.7, the results are indicated by the numbers along each arrow, which are called *path coefficients.* Similar to correlation coefficients, the numbers indicate how much of a change in the variable at the start of an arrow is associated with a change at the end of an arrow. As you can see by the starred (statistically significant) numbers, the results supported the idea that home environment predicted math motivation at age nine and that math motivation scores at successive ages were also related. (A secondary level of the statistical analysis also showed that the home environment predicted math motivation at age thirteen, depicted as (d) in the path diagram.) In addition, another statistical test indicated that the overall pattern of the data fit the predicted model.

FIGURE 10.7
An Example of Structural Equation Modeling

This diagram shows the causal relationship between the home environment and math motivation predicted by Gottfried, Fleming, and Gottfried (1998). The direction of the arrows shows that a cognitively stimulating home environment, as measured by the HOME inventory, the Home Environment Survey (HES), and the Family Environment Survey (FES), was thought to predict math motivation. The starred path coefficients show that the data are consistent with the predictions. Structural equation modeling allows researchers to come closer to understanding causal relations than simple correlational studies do.

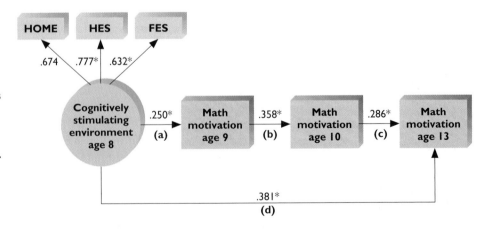

Source: Adapted from Gottfried, Fleming, & Gottfried, 1998.

An important caution about structural equation modeling is that because the analyses are essentially correlational, we can still not be absolutely sure that one variable or set of variables causes another to occur. What other cautions about correlational research might also apply to these results? What is the only research approach by which confidence about causality can be established? Could such an approach be used in the situation being examined by Gottfried and colleagues? Despite the limitations we are suggesting, however, structural equation modeling allows researchers to come closer to understanding causal relations than simple correlational studies do.

Gottfried, Fleming, and Gottfried's (1998) study did not directly explore the impact of home environment on IQ, but it does suggest a methodology that could be useful in untangling difficulties in interpreting research on this topic. How would you design such a study?

● **Early Intervention Programs**　During the 1960s, the idea of compensatory education became popular in the United States. Researchers wanted to see whether the poor performance of children from lower socioeconomic classes on IQ and achievement tests could improve if the children received the kinds of cognitive stimulation presumably available to middle-class children. If compensatory education programs worked, the idea that IQ is malleable or modifiable by experience would receive strong support, and a genetic explanation of class and race differences in IQ would be less tenable.

Today, interest in early education is further spurred by the belief that experiences during the first three or four years of life are crucial for optimal brain development. Because we now understand that neurotransmitter functioning, synaptic formation, and gene activation are influenced by environmental conditions, there is greater urgency to provide optimal learning environments for young children (Shore, 1997).

The first federally funded program for compensatory education was Project Head Start, begun in the 1960s as a preschool enrichment program for "underprivileged children." The program includes nutritional and medical assistance, as well as a structured educational program designed to provide cognitive stimulation. The first evaluations of Head Start were disappointing. In 1969, the Westinghouse Learning Corporation/Ohio University report compared the intellectual development of about four thousand children from similar backgrounds, half of whom had participated in the first Head Start programs around the country and half of whom did not participate. Essentially no differences were found in the intellectual performance of

KEY THEME
Nature/Nurture

One example of an early intervention program is **Project Head Start**, a federal program designed to provide nutritional and medical assistance, as well as school readiness skills, to children growing up in poverty. Children who attend Head Start show gains in some measures of educational achievement and at least short-term increases in IQ scores.

the two groups; both remained below the norms for their age groups. This evaluation, however, has been criticized on a number of grounds, including the fact that the evaluation was done prematurely, just barely after the program got off the ground.

● **SEE FOR YOURSELF**
psychology.college.hmco.com
Evaluating Head Start

Subsequent evaluations of Head Start have yielded more optimistic results. The Head Start Evaluation, Synthesis, and Utilization Project was an attempt to summarize all research on the impact of Head Start (McKey et al., 1985). This review concluded that Head Start produced significant effects on the intellectual performance of program participants, at least for the short term. Head Start children performed well in the first year or two after they started elementary school, showing average gains of 10 points in IQ score, but the effects of the program faded in subsequent years.

Another important early intervention project, the Carolina Abecedarian Project, begun in 1972, aimed to prevent the lower intellectual functioning of children at risk (Ramey & Campbell, 1981; Ramey, Lee, & Burchinal, 1989). A sample of 121 low-income, pregnant women with low educational achievement and low IQ scores (an average of 84) was selected. Once the infants were born, roughly half were assigned to the experimental group and half to the control group. Infants in the experimental group received medical care, nutritional supplements, and a structured program of day care that emphasized the development of cognitive, language, social, and motor skills. In addition, the researchers provided a toy-lending library and a home visiting program, as well as parent support groups. During the first year, few differences on Bayley scores were found between infants in the experimental and control groups. From age eighteen months onward, however, the IQs of the experimental group consistently exceeded those of the control group, even when the children reached young adulthood (see Figure 10.8) (Campbell & Ramey, 1994; Campbell et al., 2001). Yet some researchers remain pessimistic about the significance of these findings. For example, Herman Spitz (1986) pointed out that by age five years, the differences between the experimental and control groups diminished to an average of only 7 points. Also, scores for the experimental group never really increased (Spitz, 1999). Therefore, say the critics, the effects of this intensive intervention were not substantial.

An important issue concerns why the initial gains of Head Start and Abecedarian children "washed out" in successive years. Perhaps early intervention is not enough to overcome the pervasive and continuing effects of poverty and understimulating environments on children as they advance into the school years. Perhaps, too, IQ scores are not the best indicators of the impact of Head Start and other early intervention programs. One collaborative study of the effects of eleven early intervention programs showed that children who had participated were less likely than nonparticipants to be assigned to special education classes, less likely to be "held back" in grade, and more likely to cite their school achievements as a source of pride (Lazar &

FIGURE 10.8
Early Intervention and IQ

Children who participated in the Abecedarian Project from infancy have been followed longitudinally through early adulthood. As the graph shows, compared with a control group, participants in this program had higher IQ scores at each test time, suggesting a modest but long-term impact of intensive early intervention.

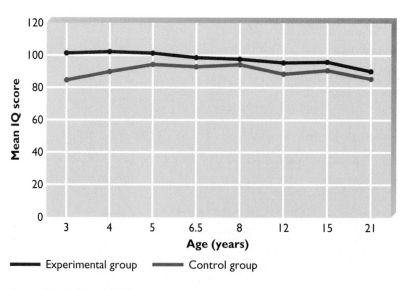

Source: Campbell et al., 2001.

Darlington, 1982). Edward Zigler, a key figure in the formulation of Project Head Start, and his colleagues have also found that Head Start children show notable gains in social competence (Zigler & Berman, 1983; Zigler & Trickett, 1978). Perhaps these multifaceted outcomes are just as important as gains in IQ scores.

Craig and Sharon Ramey (1998), pioneers in the Abecedarian Project, suggest that in order to be effective, early intervention programs need to target children early in development, include substantial contact with children and families who participate, and provide direct learning experiences for children. Programs should also provide a broad array of services, including health and social services, as well as transportation. Finally, in order to have long-lasting impact, continuous intervention and support should take place beyond the preschool years.

The Child's Sociocultural Environment

Children from different cultural backgrounds often display unique patterns of intellectual abilities. For example, the Inuit people of the Arctic region show exceptional visual-spatial skills compared with those of United States residents (Berry, 1966; Vernon, 1966). How does the larger culture within which the child lives influence his or her pattern of mental abilities?

The role of culture in intellectual development may be examined in terms of activities and behaviors essential for adaptation and survival. The Inuits depend on hunting and gathering in their native terrain, activities that require the ability to perceive small changes in large, expansive fields of vision; in this context, the prominence of their visual-spatial skills is understandable. Similarly, as we saw in the chapter titled "Cognition: Piaget and Vygotsky," Mexican children with extensive experience in making clay pottery were found to be more advanced on a Piagetian measure of intelligence, the conservation of quantity task, than children without experience in pottery making (Price-Williams, Gordon, & Ramirez, 1969). Intensive practice in specialized skills that are an integral part of one's cultural experience can heighten "intelligence" in those domains.

The degree to which culture emphasizes formal schooling can also influence patterns of intellectual activity. Cross-cultural studies have shown that children with formal education are more likely to use mnemonic strategies to learn lists of words and to classify objects according to a consistent rule (Sharp, Cole, & Lave, 1979; Wagner, 1978). Although memory and classification performance, the dependent measures in

KEY THEME
Sociocultural Influence

The child's sociocultural environment can influence specific patterns of intellectual skills. For example, among the Inuits, superior visual-spatial skills may be tied to that culture's emphasis on hunting in large, expansive terrains.

these studies, are not explicit indices of intelligence, they are cognitive skills that are frequently embedded in psychometric tests. Moreover, if intelligence is assumed to be reflected in IQ scores, children may learn specific skills in school that enable them to do well on intelligence tests (Ceci, 1991). Performing on a time-limited test, understanding and following directions, and being able to consider a number of response alternatives are all general test-taking skills that children are likely to absorb in school. Furthermore, the answers to specific questions found on intelligence tests, such as "Who discovered America?" or "What is the distance from New York to Los Angeles?" are usually learned in school.

Finally, cultures may differ in the ways intelligent behavior is conceptualized. For example, Latino immigrants place a high value on behaviors that are socially respectful and correct (Reese et al., 1995). Humility and personal self-knowledge are emphasized in certain Chinese traditions (Yang & Sternberg, 1997). Even in our own society, new theories describe notions such as "emotional intelligence," the ability to read and respond to the feelings of others, as well as to understand and regulate one's own emotions (Goleman, 1995; Mayer & Salovey, 1997). Children growing up in societies that promote concepts such as these may be encouraged to develop in ways that differ from those of cultures in which cognitive and academic skills are viewed as the exclusive components of intelligence.

FOR YOUR REVIEW

- What are the complexities involved in trying to assess the contributions of heredity to group differences in IQ?

- How might concepts like test bias and stereotype threat play a part in explaining group differences in IQ?

- Which specific aspects of the home environment are related to subsequent IQ scores in children?

- How do techniques like structural equation modeling help to address questions of causal relationships among variables?

- What has research revealed about the effects of early intervention programs for children? What factors are most important in promoting successful outcomes?

- How does the child's sociocultural environment influence intellectual abilities? What are some specific examples of this influence?

CHAPTER RECAP

SUMMARY OF DEVELOPMENTAL THEMES

■ **Nature/Nurture** *What roles do nature and nurture play in the development of intelligence?*

The nature-nurture debate becomes an especially thorny issue in the matter of intelligence. Few psychologists would dispute that heredity plays a role in the child's intellectual development. For example, early individual differences in the speed of infant habituation and recognition memory may signal differences in some aspects of later intellectual functioning. In addition, genetic effects such as Down syndrome and the high correlations between IQ scores of identical twins reared apart suggest a role for "nature." Yet research also shows that children's early experiences within the home, together with the intellectual skills touted by the larger culture, modulate how their genetic blueprints unfold.

■ **Sociocultural Influence** *How does the sociocultural context influence the development of intelligence?*

Culture broadly influences the kinds of skills that its members value and nurture and that are believed to constitute "intelligence." Is speed of executing tasks important? Are good visual-spatial or verbal skills essential for successful adaptation to the environment? A culture's demands and expectations frame the way intelligent behavior will be defined in the first place. From the narrower perspective of performance on standardized IQ tests, children who have experiences consistent with the knowledge tapped by test items will perform well, whereas those with more impoverished backgrounds will be at a disadvantage. Other sociocultural factors often associated with social class, such as parental emphasis on intellectual achievement or the amount of emotional stress within the family system, can also impinge on IQ test performance.

■ **Child's Active Role** *How does the child play an active role in the development of intelligence?*

Traditional psychometric theories have rarely assumed that the child plays an active role in affecting her intelligence. However, the information-processing perspective has focused on executive control skills, the child's ability to monitor his own cognitive processes, and other cognitive activities as significant contributors to intellectual development.

■ **Continuity/Discontinuity** *Is the development of intelligence continuous or discontinuous?*

Some would argue that intelligence does not really develop at all, that it is a stable, relatively unchanging, inborn human characteristic. Information-processing theorists, in contrast, see intelligence as largely the by-product of normal, continuous developmental processes wherein the child learns more complex relations among stimuli in the surrounding world and becomes capable of more sophisticated cognitive processing with age.

■ **Individual Differences** *How prominent are individual differences in the development of intelligence?*

From the psychometric perspective, the concept of intelligence is rooted in the assumption that individual differences exist in performance on certain mental tasks. Other theories, particularly Gardner's theory of multiple intelligences, stress the patterns of strength and weakness a given individual shows across a spectrum of domains. Studies of how the environment influences intelligence also suggest that an individual's score on an IQ test can be a function of the specific parenting practices she or he has experienced or other elements of the childhood environment.

■ **Interaction Among Domains** *How does the development of intelligence interact with development in other domains?*

Children who obtain high scores on intelligence tests are more likely to be successful in school and, as adults, to hold high-status jobs and be productive in those jobs. Thus, to some extent, IQ scores can predict certain aspects of success in life. According to more recent theoretical perspectives, the child's experiences in various domains can also influence intelligence. For example, in Gardner's theory of multiple intelligences, bodily-kinesthetic intelligence can be fostered through athletic experiences, and interpersonal intelligence can grow through extensive social experience.

▌ SUMMARY OF TOPICS

What Is Intelligence?

■ Definitions of intelligence vary in two major ways: (1) whether intelligence is seen as a global characteristic or as a set of separate abilities and (2) whether the emphasis is on the products or the processes of intelligent behavior.

Psychometric Approaches

■ The *psychometric model* of intelligence emphasizes individual differences in test scores.

■ Two historically important ideas were those of Spearman, who conceptualized a general intelligence factor called *g*, and Thurstone, who believed in seven primary mental abilities.

■ In Cattell and Horn's view, intelligence could be seen as having two components: *fluid intelligence*, which was free of cultural influence, and *crystallized intelligence*, which referred to culturally derived skills. Fluid intelligence shows an earlier developmental decline than crystallized intelligence.

Information-Processing Approaches

■ Information-processing models focus on the mental activities of individuals as they engage in problem solving. Speed of processing and working memory capacity are two information-processing activities thought to be involved in intelligence.

■ Sternberg's *triarchic theory* points to (1) the ability to adapt to the environment, (2) the ability to encode, combine, and compare stimuli, and (3) the ability to deal with novelty and to automatize as components of intelligence.

■ Gardner's theory of multiple intelligences states that individuals can differ in discrete skill areas such as language, music, mathematics, spatial perception, physical activities, personal awareness, social interaction, or nature.

Measuring Intelligence

■ IQ scores are normally distributed in the population. The mean IQ is 100 and the standard deviation is 15.

■ Individuals who fall beyond two standard deviations from the mean are considered to be exceptional. They may be categorized as either gifted or mentally retarded.

Standardized Tests of Intelligence

■ Intelligence is usually expressed in terms of the intelligence quotient, or IQ score.

■ IQ tests are designed by being administered to large groups of individuals to assess norms of performance and to establish the validity and reliability of the test.

■ Two tests of intelligence for infants are the Bayley Scales of Infant Development and the Fagan Test of Infant Intelligence. Both are generally used to identify children who are at risk for developmental delays.

■ School-age children are most frequently tested with the Stanford-Binet Intelligence Scales or the Wechsler Intelligence Scale for Children–III (WISC-III). These tests are based on the psychometric model and assess a range of verbal, visual-spatial, quantitative, and problem-solving skills. The Kaufman Assessment Battery (K-ABC) focuses more on children's mental processing skills.

Stability and Prediction

- For many children, IQ scores are stable over time, especially after age five years, although individual children can show dramatic fluctuations.

- Studies of infant attention and memory show that there are some developmental continuities in mental abilities.

- IQ scores generally predict academic success but are not necessarily related to other measures of life satisfaction.

Factors Related to Intelligence

- Intelligence is the result of the complex interplay between heredity and environment.

Group Differences in IQ Scores

- Social class and racial differences in IQ scores illustrate the difficulty of drawing simple conclusions about the sources of intelligence. One problem is that estimates of heritability do not necessarily explain between-group differences in scores.

- *Cross-fostering studies* of children who were raised in environments that differ from those of their biological parents indicate that IQ scores rise in enriched environments but that scores are still more strongly related to educational levels of biological parents than to IQ levels of adoptive parents.

- *Test bias*, the idea that the content of IQ tests may not be fair to children from different cultural backgrounds, can help to explain group differences in IQ scores. Other factors in the testing situation may also interfere with children's optimal performance.

- *Stereotype threat*, the negative psychological impact of being sensitized to a stereotype about gender or ethnicity, has been linked to diminished performance on standardized tests.

The Role of Early Experiences

- Studies using the HOME Inventory show that several factors in the child's home environment are related to higher IQ scores. Particularly important are parental responsiveness to the child, provision of appropriate play materials, and parental involvement with the child.

- Evaluations of the effectiveness of early intervention programs such as Head Start and the Abecedarian Project show intellectual gains by children who have participated. However, the increases shown by Head Start children often fade after a few years. Critics of the Abecedarian Project say that increases in IQ scores are modest at best. Some researchers argue that more intensive and continuous intervention is necessary to produce more dramatic outcomes.

The Child's Sociocultural Environment

- Children have been observed to display different patterns of intellectual skills depending on the environment in which they are raised, probably because of the intensive practice they receive in those domains.

- Formal schooling influences the development of cognitive skills such as memory and classification.

- Cultures differ in the ways they conceptualize intelligence. For example, some give greater priority to social respectfulness, whereas others emphasize the importance of personal knowledge.

CHAPTER 11

Emotion

Key Themes in Emotional Development

- **Nature/Nurture** What roles do nature and nurture play in emotional development?

- **Sociocultural Influence** How does the sociocultural context influence emotional development?

- **Child's Active Role** How does the child play an active role in the process of emotional development?

- **Continuity/Discontinuity** Is emotional development continuous or discontinuous?

- **Individual Differences** How prominent are individual differences in emotional development?

- **Interaction Among Domains** How does emotional development interact with development in other domains?

It's a quiet time on Sunday morning, just after a big breakfast, and Cindy admires her eight-month-old son Michael as he sits in his infant seat. He is looking at her so intently, raising his eyebrows a bit and scanning her face, gurgling contentedly. Suddenly the phone rings. Michael falls silent and opens his eyes wide. Cindy raises her eyebrows into two big arches and opens her mouth, making an exaggerated "Oohh" sound, suggesting surprise. Her baby eyes her with fascination, chortles, then smiles broadly. Cindy smiles back, chuckles, and says, "Must be Grandma calling to see how you are. Let me answer the phone, okay, honey?" She touches Michael affectionately under the chin as she gets up to reach for the phone. The baby lets out a shriek of delight and smiles again. Cindy can't help but laugh at the antics of her young son.

This scene, in all its simplicity, is a typical one in many families. Babies and caregivers revel in each other's company, and although the infant cannot yet speak, he participates fully in the interaction in nonverbal ways. The communication relies less on language than on both overt and subtle nuances in facial expressions and sounds that communicate emotional state. Some have characterized the back-and-forth nature of this exchange as a well-choreographed "waltz" wherein each partner looks to the other for cues about what to do next so the interaction proceeds smoothly and enjoyably. The episode also suggests some fundamental questions about the nature of human emotions and the forces that guide emotional development. Are our emotions innately determined, the result of a biological "prewiring"? Or are our displays and conceptions of emotions derived from learning the rules and conventions of our culture?

On the surface, the interaction between Cindy and her infant may suggest that nurture rather than nature is the determining factor, especially when the exchange is contrasted with interactions typical among the Gusii of Kenya. The Gusii culture places great emphasis on suppressing intense emotions, probably to maintain harmony in the small, tribal living units characteristic of that group. Consequently, mothers maintain a bland, neutral expression when interacting with their infants and try to inhibit strong shows of emotion from their children (Dixon et al., 1981). These differing cultural norms are reflected in the parenting styles of each culture and the behaviors children eventually display. At the same time, however, research with young infants suggests that emotions possess biological underpinnings as well.

In this chapter, we see how children's expression and understanding of emotions change with age. Many of these accomplishments are tied to advances in cognition that permit children to think about complex feeling states within themselves as well as in others. Part of the process of emotional growth also involves the child's ability to regulate his emotions—to cool down, for example, if he is feeling angry and frustrated. In addition, even though emotions are the personal expressions of the individual's moods or feeling states, they also function as a mode of communicating with others. Given the social dimension of emotions, we will investigate the role they play in the child's relationships with others, specifically in the special "attachments" that emerge between child and caregivers. What is the psychological significance of these early emotional bonds, and how do they influence the child's later development?

What Are Emotions?

Emotions are a complex set of behaviors produced in response to some external or internal event, or elicitor, that serve to motivate and direct thoughts and actions. Emotions include several components. First, they have a *physiological* component, involving changes in autonomic nervous system activities such as respiration and heart rate. Fear or anxiety, for example, may be accompanied by more rapid breathing, increased heart rate and blood pressure, and perspiration. Second, emotions include an *expressive* component, usually a facial display that signals the emotion. Smiles, grimaces, cries, and laughter overtly express a person's emotional state. Third, emotions have an *experiential* component, the subjective feeling or cognitive judgment of having an emotion (Izard, Kagan, & Zajonc, 1984; Sroufe, 1996). Just how a person interprets and evaluates an emotional state depends on his level of cognitive development and the past experiences he has had. For a child to be able to state, "I feel happy," he must recognize the internal cues and external contexts associated with "happiness," which are derived from experience. In addition, he must have a relatively mature concept of the self as a feeling, responding being, a sign of cognitive maturity.

The Functions of Emotions

What role do emotions play in the psychological development of the child? On one level, they serve to organize and regulate the child's own behavior. If a child is learning to ride a two-wheeled bicycle and succeeds in tottering down the sidewalk without keeling over, she undoubtedly will feel elated and probably more motivated to practice this new skill for a few more minutes or even hours. If, on the other hand, she falls repeatedly or even injures herself, she may feel angry and discouraged and quit riding for a few days. Thus the child's emotional states regulate what she will decide to do (Campos et al., 1983).

A child's emotional state can also influence cognitive processes. One example concerns the relationship between emotion and learning. Research indicates that children who show an interest in certain objects or topics—a strong feeling of attraction or pleasure—pay more attention to those stimuli and remember them better in a subsequent memory test compared with objects that do not interest them (Renninger, 1992).

Of special importance is the fact that emotions serve to initiate, maintain, or terminate interactions with others. The baby's cry or smile almost invariably prompts contact with the caregiver. A toddler's frustration and anger over an unshared toy may lead him to abandon a playmate temporarily. In fact, a social dialogue completely devoid of emotional content is unusual. "Moods," more enduring emotional states, may help us understand the child's personality attributes, such as the tendency to be shy, dependent, or aggressive. These traits, in turn, can influence the frequency and form of the child's social contacts. Thus understanding emotional development can increase our appreciation of a broad range of children's accomplishments in other domains.

KEY THEME
Interaction Among Domains

Measuring Emotions

Given the complex nature of emotions, measuring them becomes an important issue for researchers because all three dimensions—physiological, expressive, and cognitive—must be considered. One approach is to record changes in physiological

emotions Complex behaviors involving physiological, expressive, and experiential components produced in response to some external or internal event.

functions such as heart rate (acceleration or deceleration), heart rate variability (the individual's basic heart rate pattern), or electroencephalogram (EEG) patterns showing brain activity as affective stimuli are presented (Fox, 1991; Fox & Davidson, 1986). Newer technologies, such as *positron emission tomography* (PET) and *functional magnetic resonance imaging* (fMRI) (see the chapter titled "Brain, Motor Skill, and Physical Development"), are also being used to track the activities of the brain as emotions are being experienced (Cacioppo & Gardner, 1999). Another strategy is to conduct fine-grained analyses of the child's facial expressions or vocalizations. Tiny movements of the muscles in the brow, eye, and mouth regions produce the facial configurations associated with joy, sadness, anger, and other emotions (Izard & Dougherty, 1982). Similarly, the frequency, loudness, duration, and sound patterns of the child's vocalizations indicate emotion (Papoušek, Papoušek, & Koester, 1986). Often facial expressions, body movements, and vocalizations function as an ensemble of emotion indicators; for example, a facial expression of anger, raising arms upward, and crying combine to signal "pick me up" (Weinberg & Tronick, 1994). Finally, the child's interpretations of her own and others' emotions can be assessed through the use of self-report measures (e.g., "Tell me how often you felt cheerful in the last week") and tasks requiring the child to label, match, or produce emotional expressions ("Tell me how the person in this picture feels" or "Show me the person who feels sad").

Although each methodological approach has helped to illuminate aspects of the child's emotional life, researchers must be cautious when interpreting their data. When physiological changes such as decelerated heart rate occur as the infant watches a lively segment of "Sesame Street," is he experiencing interest or surprise? The emotion that corresponds to a specific reaction of the nervous system is not always clear. Likewise, an overt emotional expression such as crying might represent a number of possible internal emotional states, such as sadness, joy, or fear. Self-reports of the child's emotional states present their own difficulties. As we saw in the chapter titled "Studying Child Development," some children may answer researchers' questions based on the way they think they should reply rather than on how they really feel. Others may be reluctant to discuss their inner feelings at all. Despite these methodological difficulties, researchers have learned a good deal about emotional development in the last two decades.

EXAMINING RESEARCH METHODS

Using Structured Observations to Record Infants' Facial Expressions

Many studies of children's emotions rely on observations of children's facial expressions during positive or stressful events to obtain clues about their affective experiences. For example, in a recent study, Katherine Weinberg and her colleagues (Weinberg et al., 1999) observed six-month-old infants while they experienced two minutes of face-to-face interactions with their mothers and then a two-minute episode called the "still face." In the latter condition, mothers were instructed to look at the infant but not to make any facial expressions, talk, or touch their infant. The researchers were interested in whether boys and girls would react differently in these two situations. A detailed coding scheme called the AFFEX (formally called the System for Identifying Affect Expression by Holistic Judgment), developed by Carroll Izard and his associates (Izard & Dougherty, 1982), was one of the measures used to conduct the observations. A closer look at the AFFEX provides a good way of understanding some of the methodological issues associated with observational studies, including the concepts of reliability and validity mentioned in the chapter titled "Studying Child Development."

The AFFEX was developed to score ten facial expressions, including joy, interest, sadness, anger, and disgust. Each emotional expression is associated with discrete facial movements that are carefully described in the coding scheme. For example,

Figure 11.1 shows several components of the expression for anger, including brows lowered and drawn together, eyes narrowed or squinted, and the mouth squarish or angular. When all three components are present, the appearance of anger is said to be observed. Similarly, combinations of facial movements for other emotions are detailed in the coding scheme. Before they actually score data collected for a study, coders proceed through a rigorous training procedure that typically takes several hours. Observers are expected to agree with the master codes on a training tape at least 80 percent of the time; only then are they ready to begin scoring the data.

In the Weinberg et al. (1999) study, each second of videotape of the child's behaviors was coded by two observers. The percent of time the observers agreed in their judgments was between 82 and 95 percent for the emotions that were used in the study: joy, interest, sadness, and anger. Thus interrater *reliability*, the consistency of scores between two observers, was high.

Izard and Dougherty (1982) maintain that this scoring scheme also has good *construct validity*, that it measures what it is supposed to—in this case, particular emotions such as anger and joy. When the AFFEX was initially developed, groups of untrained adults were asked to make global judgments of the emotions expressed in twenty-five video segments of infants' faces. They agreed a substantial proportion of the time with a different group of raters who used the AFFEX to code these same tapes. Are there other methods that might be used to establish the validity of a coding scheme such as the AFFEX, perhaps even more convincingly? How can we come closer to knowing which emotions infants are experiencing internally as they are showing a particular facial expression?

 SEE FOR YOURSELF
psychology.college.hmco.com
Measuring Emotional Expressions

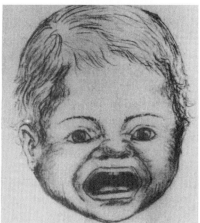

A

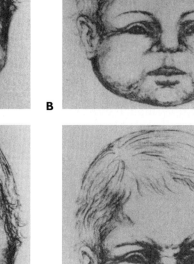

B

C

D

FIGURE 11.1
Identifying Facial Expressions of Anger in Infants

This series of drawings shows the elements of anger that are part of the AFFEX system for scoring facial expressions. Panel A shows the brows lowered and drawn together. Panel B shows the eyes narrowed. Panel C shows the angular or square-shaped mouth. When all of these elements appear together (as in Panel D), the emotion expressed is scored as anger.

Source: Izard & Dougherty, 1982.

As you will recall from the chapter titled "Studying Child Development," it is important for observers in studies such as these to be as objective as possible, that is, to avoid *observer bias*. Ideally they should be unaware of the conditions in which children are participating. Weinberg and colleagues (1999) faced a special challenge in this regard—how could they keep observers from knowing which infants were boys and which were girls? It was important to keep any stereotypes or expectations that observers had about the emotional expressions of males and females from biasing their judgments. Yet mothers often call their infants by name and dress them according to their sex. The researchers handled this problem by keeping the specific hypotheses and details of the study from both mothers and coders. They were told simply that the project involved "infant interactive and communicative behavior with mothers." Was this a satisfactory approach to this methodological problem? Is there an alternative way of handling this issue?

The results of the study indicated that for all infants the still face is a more stressful situation than normal face-to-face encounters, a finding that is explored further later in this chapter. In addition, boys expressed more anger than girls during both face-to-face and still-face situations. However, they also expressed more joy than girls, whereas girls expressed more interest. As this study shows, studying emotional expressions in infants requires painstaking attention to detail, a considerable investment of time in training reliable observers, and methodological challenges to establishing validity and objectivity.

Theoretical Perspectives on Emotional Development

Are human emotions biologically based, preprogrammed responses to specific environmental stimuli, or are they the products of the myriad learning experiences that accumulate over the course of infancy and childhood? Do emotions function in neat, discrete packages—anger being separate from sadness and fear? Or are different emotions simply points on a continuum of positive or negative arousal? These are some of the questions addressed by contemporary perspectives on emotion.

KEY THEME
Nature/Nurture

● **Biologically Based Explanations**   The main champions of a strong biological view of emotions are Paul Ekman and Carroll Izard. After studying people in various cultures, Ekman (1972, 1973) concluded that there are universal facial expressions for certain basic emotions that are interpreted in similar ways across cultures. Ekman showed photographs of six faces, each depicting a particular emotion—happiness, sadness, anger, fear, surprise, or disgust—to participants in the United States, Japan, Chile, Brazil, and Argentina. As they looked at each photograph, participants were asked to identify the emotion displayed. Ekman (1972) found a high degree of accuracy across cultures as to which emotions were represented. A recent meta-analysis of ninety-seven studies confirms what Ekman first reported—that individuals from a wide variety of cultures correctly recognize fundamental emotions, showing the highest degree of accuracy for happiness (Elfenbein & Ambady, 2002).

Similarly, Izard believes that because certain emotional expressions are displayed by very young infants, they are necessarily innate and have distinct adaptive value (Izard, 1978; Izard & Malatesta, 1987). When the newborn infant tastes a bitter substance such as quinine, for example, she will pull up her upper lip, wrinkle her nose, and squint her eyes, indicating she has detected the unpleasant stimulus. No learning is necessary to produce this reaction of disgust. The caregiver observing this signal might respond by removing a potentially harmful substance from the baby's mouth, thereby ensuring her well-being. The experience of emotion, Izard states, is the automatic product of the internal sensory feedback the individual receives from making the facial expression; wrinkling the face produces the feeling of disgust. Izard also maintains that once an emotion is activated, it in turn motivates the individual to

There are many cross-cultural similarities in the expression and interpretation of emotions. Most of us, for example, would recognize these Indian children's expressions as indicating happiness.

act. The experience of disgust, in other words, may lead the baby to spit out the distasteful substance. According to Izard and his colleagues, infants show a small set of discrete emotions, such as joy, anger, and fear, that function independently of one another. With development, these emotions become more interrelated and connected to cognition (Ackerman, Abe, & Izard, 1998). Furthermore, different patterns of expressing emotions eventually become organized as personality traits that can vary across individuals (Izard & Ackerman, 2000).

KEY THEME
Individual Differences

Both Ekman and Izard acknowledge that learning may play a role in emotional development, especially as children learn to control and regulate their emotions. They maintain, however, that the role of biological factors is paramount and that emotions originate in the genetic blueprints with which the child begins life.

● **A Cognitive-Socialization Explanation**   Michael Lewis and Linda Michalson (1983) have provided an alternative account of the emotional life of the child, one that emphasizes the cognitive activities involved in emotional experiences. According to these theorists, an environmental event does not directly produce an emotional expression. Instead, the child relies on cognitive processes to assess the event, how it compares with past events, and the social rules surrounding the event. Suppose, for example, the child encounters a barking dog. Whether he cries with fear or smiles at the noisy animal depends on his past experiences with dogs (has he ever been bitten?) and on what parents and others have instructed him to believe about animals ("Barking dogs will bite—stay away!" or "Some dogs get excited when they want to play—it's okay"). Cognitive processes thus act as *mediators,* or mental events that bridge the gap between environmental stimuli and the response the individual ultimately expresses. This conceptualization accounts for individual differences in emotional reactions when the same event produces different responses from two people.

KEY THEME
Interaction Among Domains

KEY THEME
Individual Differences
KEY THEME
Nature/Nurture

According to Lewis and Michalson, socialization plays an important role in shaping the time and the manner in which emotions are displayed. Children in our culture learn that it is appropriate to feel happy at birthday parties and sad when a friend's grandmother dies and that a smiling face and a sad face should be made under these respective circumstances. Socialization also guides the way emotions are managed. Young children in many cultures, for example, learn to inhibit expressions of fear and anger. Finally, socialization directs the way children label and interpret emotions. When the young child cries due to a physical injury and the parent says, "That hurts, doesn't it?" the interpretation provides pain as the reason for the tears. When crying is the response to the collapse of a tower of toy blocks, the parent may provide a different interpretation for the child, such as "That's frustrating." These kinds of communications serve as an important vehicle by which children learn how to interpret their own emotional states.

KEY THEME
Nature/Nurture

● **Emotion as Part of a Social Context**   For some theorists, such as Joseph Campos and Carol Saarni (Campos et al., 1994; Saarni, 1999; Saarni, Mumme, & Campos, 1998), emotions are deeply and inextricably intertwined with the social environment. Children's understanding of their own and others' emotions and how they regulate their emotional states arise from the crossroads of personal goals and social interactions with others. What the child wants and desires, as well as the reactions of those in the social environment, create the "mix" for experiences of emotions. Emotions serve to motivate the individual toward particular social actions. For example, the emotion of "pride" can be the outcome of glowing comments from the parents after a child produces a colorful drawing. For that same child, the experience of pride will likely motivate her to share a newly written poem with a visiting grandmother. Emotions also arise when the emotions of others are observed (e.g., a mother shows great fear at the sound of thunder) and when one remembers emotional experiences from the past.

Rather than describing discrete emotions such as joy or fear, contextual theorists emphasize the positive or negative tone of emotions and their intensity. Emotions are not conceptualized as *entities* but instead are viewed as *processes* embedded in social interactions (Barrett, 1998). In other words, it is of paramount importance to understand how they work or function. According to this perspective, considerable attention is necessarily given to the process of socialization and to the role of culture. How do families help children to regulate their emotions, to control, for example, angry outbursts or overt expressions of fear? How do different cultures conceptualize emotions and what emotional styles do they emphasize, being expressive or more restrained, for example? These are the types of research questions that are motivated by this important perspective on emotional development.

FOR YOUR REVIEW

- What are the three components of emotions? How are these related to the ways in which researchers measure emotions?

- What functions do emotions serve in the various aspects of the child's psychological life?

- What are the main ways in which biological, cognitive-socialization, and social-contextual theories of emotion differ from one another?

Expressing, Understanding, and Regulating Emotions

Researchers focus on emotional development from various angles. First, they examine whether children change in the way they express their own emotions. Do infants exhibit the full range of emotions that we see in adults, or does a developmental progression occur in the types of emotions children display? Second, do children change in their ability to understand emotions in themselves and others, to read facial expressions and interpret them, to know the circumstances that lead positive and negative emotions to arise, and to appreciate the consequences of different emotions? Finally, how do children change in the ways they regulate their emotions, and in particular in controlling their displays of negative emotions?

Early Emotional Development

Much of the groundwork for emotional development occurs during the first year or so of life. Parents and young infants frequently rely on nonverbal signals laden with emotional overtones to communicate with one another, as we saw with Cindy and Michael at the start of this chapter. Just what behaviors are infants capable of showing and "reading"?

● **Emotional Expression in Infancy** Even infants only a few days or weeks old are capable of producing the facial expressions associated with several emotions, including interest, distress, disgust, joy, sadness, anger, and surprise (Field et al., 1982; Izard, 1978; Izard et al., 1995). By seven months of age, the infant has added expressions of fear to his repertoire (Izard et al., 1980). The fact that these discrete facial expressions appear so early in infancy, before much learning can have taken place, provides strong support for the idea that emotional expressions are to some extent biologically determined. These emotions are often called **basic** (or *primary*) **emotions.**

KEY THEME
Nature/Nurture

Although even the earliest displays of basic emotions usually are recognized readily by adults, their form and the conditions that elicit them may change over the first few months. Two important emotional expressions in infancy, smiling and crying, demonstrate these changes. The smile is one of the most captivating and irresistible infant behaviors. In the newborn this behavior occurs primarily during the state of REM sleep, when dreaming is thought to occur, in bursts of several smiles in succession (Emde & Koenig, 1969). The mouth stretches sideways and up, producing a simple version of the smile. Although many hypotheses attempt to explain why very young infants produce this facial gesture (including the popular but mistaken notion that "gas" is responsible), the most consistent finding is that neonates smile when they experience a shift in physiological arousal state, such as when they fall asleep or become drowsy (Wolff, 1987). At approximately two weeks of age, the form of the smile changes. After the initial broadening of the lips, the corners of the lips retract even farther (with the mouth often opening), the cheek muscles contract, and the skin around the eyes wrinkles (Messinger, Fogel, & Dickson, 1999). Now the infant smiles during states of wakefulness, sometimes in response to familiar voices and sounds, sweet tastes, and pleasant food odors (Fogel, 1982; Steiner, 1979). By three months of age, smiles increase in frequency, and full-blown smiles—with open mouth and cheeks raised—become increasingly reserved for interactions in which the infant looks at a smiling mother (Messinger, Fogel, & Dickson, 2001). Because the "social smile" plays a substantial role in initiating and maintaining interactions between the infant and significant adults in her life, it is considered an important milestone in infant development. The shift from smiling as a reflexlike behavior to a controlled, voluntary response parallels the increasing maturation of the cerebral cortex, which is responsible for higher-order mental processes and deliberate, goal-directed behaviors.

KEY THEME
Child's Active Role

KEY THEME
Interaction Among Domains

Crying is another common way in which infants express emotion. Newborn babies cry for a variety of reasons, but primarily because they are hungry, cold, wet, in pain, or disturbed out of their sleep. The nature of the baby's distress is often reflected in the type of cry she emits. In an extensive study of eighteen infants observed in their homes, Peter Wolff (1969) identified three patterns of crying. The first is the *basic* (or *hungry*) *cry,* a rhythmical sequence consisting of a vocalization, a pause, an intake of air, and another pause. The second is the *angry cry,* in which extra air is forced through the vocal cords during the vocalization segment of the basic cry. Finally, in the *pain cry,* the infant produces a long vocalization followed by an even longer silence as he holds his breath and then gasps.

Like smiling, crying is a response that promotes contact between the infant and the caregiver. Mothers usually react to their young infants' cries promptly, especially an angry or a pain cry, and when they do, infants actually cry less in succeeding weeks and months (Bell & Ainsworth, 1972; Wolff, 1969). Usually the first order of

basic emotion Emotion such as joy, sadness, or surprise that appears early in infancy and seems to have a biological foundation. Also called *primary emotion.*

business is to make sure the infant's physical needs are met. Other effective techniques for soothing the crying infant include providing a pacifier, swaddling with a blanket, and tapping some part of his body, that is, providing some form of rhythmic or continuous stimulation (Brackbill, 1975). Picking up the baby and holding her on one's shoulder also is soothing, probably because this act provides the infant with a broad range of stimulation that distracts her from crying (Korner, 1972).

By the time the infant is about two months of age, the causes of crying are no longer purely physiological. An infant might cry when the caregiver puts him down in his crib or when a favorite toy is removed from his grasp. At about this time, a new type of cry emerges: the *fussy* or *irregular cry,* which varies in intensity, is less rhythmical, and seems to function as a demand for particular objects or actions. At eight months of age, the infant will pause in crying to see if the mother or other adults are receiving the message (Bruner, 1983). As the infant gains more voluntary control over his vocalizations, crying patterns become even more varied and controlled and are displayed in a wider range of situations to signal an assortment of messages. Individual differences in the crying patterns of some infants are useful in diagnosing developmental abnormalities. Malnourished infants, for example, display more variability in the pitch of their cries, whereas children who have suffered oxygen deprivation produce shorter, higher-pitched cries (Michelsson, Sirvio, & Wasz-Hockert, 1977; Zeskind, 1981).

● **Recognizing Others' Emotions**   Besides producing expressions themselves, infants are capable of discriminating and responding to emotional displays in others. Several remarkable studies conducted by Tiffany Field and her colleagues suggest that three-day-old infants are capable of imitating the facial expressions for happiness, surprise, and sadness when an adult models these expressions (Field et al., 1982, 1983). Infants widened their eyes and opened their mouths on "surprise" trials, drew back their lips on "happiness" trials, and tightened their mouths and furrowed their brows on "sadness" trials (see Figure 11.2). Although some researchers offer alternative explanations for these findings (see the chapter titled "Basic Learning and Perception"), many believe that infants have an early sensitivity to emotional expressions in others. In addition, researchers have shown that by three to four months of age, infants are able to distinguish among several expressions, particularly happiness as opposed to anger, surprise, and sadness (LaBarbera et al., 1976; Young-Browne, Rosenfeld, & Horowitz, 1977). They also tend to look less at sad faces and more at angry ones (Montague & Walker-Andrews, 2001).

Do infants derive meaning from the facial expressions they observe in others, or do they simply respond to changes in isolated facial features that contribute to these expressions (e.g., the upward curve of the mouth in the smile)? In the latter half of the first year, a phenomenon called **social referencing** suggests an infant's ability to interpret facial expressions. If infants are placed in an unfamiliar situation or encounter a strange object and are uncertain how to respond, they often will look to their caregivers for cues. The facial expression the caregiver displays typically will influence the infant's own emotional response and subsequent actions. For example, in one study, twelve-month-olds were placed on the shallow side of the visual cliff apparatus, which, as we saw in the chapter titled "Basic Learning and Perception," is used to assess the perception of depth. They were coaxed to move toward the place on the cliff where the surface appears to drop off. At this point, half of the participants' mothers posed a happy expression and the other half exhibited fear. Of the infants whose mothers smiled, 74 percent crossed the deep side of the cliff. In contrast, none of the infants whose mothers showed fear crossed the deep side. Moreover, these babies tended to produce fearful expressions on their own faces (Sorce et al., 1985). Thus infants not only "read" the expression they saw on their mothers' faces but also correctly interpreted its message.

Social referencing is a clear sign of the distinctly *interactive* nature of emotions. It is also a sign that infants begin to appreciate the referential nature of com-

---

KEY THEME
| **Individual Differences**

KEY THEME
| **Child's Active Role**

social referencing   Looking to another individual for emotional cues in interpreting a strange or ambiguous event.

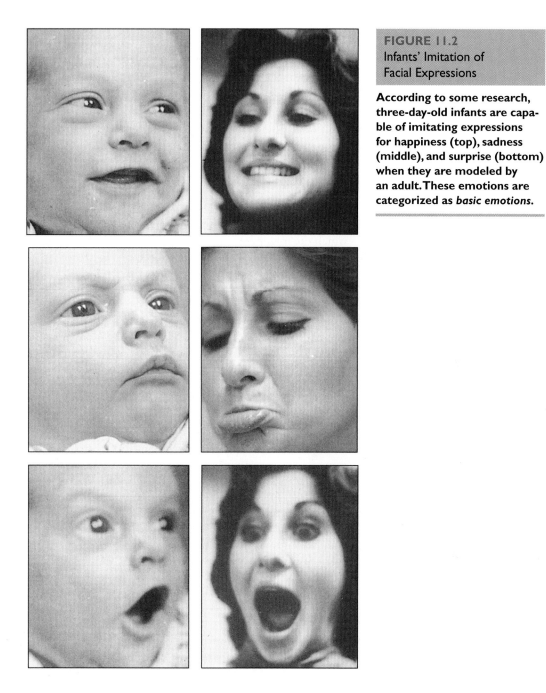

FIGURE 11.2
Infants' Imitation of
Facial Expressions

According to some research, three-day-old infants are capable of imitating expressions for happiness (top), sadness (middle), and surprise (bottom) when they are modeled by an adult. These emotions are categorized as *basic emotions*.

munication (see the chapter titled "Language"), as well as the intentions of others (see the chapter titled "Cognition: Piaget and Vygotsky"). When infants in one study heard an experimenter say "Iiuu" in a strong negative tone while looking at a toy, they were less likely to approach it than if she said "Nice!" However, if the experimenter made any of these comments while out of view, infants did not make use of the emotional tones in her messages (Moses et al., 2001). They seem to appreciate that by expressing emotions—but specifically in a social context—individuals intend to communicate something about objects, people, or events. In that sense, social referencing is linked to advances in cognition. It is probably also an early sign of the child's internalization of the views and values of parents, a process that will continue throughout the early years of childhood (Desrochers et al., 1994; Kochanska, 1994).

KEY THEME
Interaction Among Domains

● **Emotions as Regulators of Social Interactions**   Given infants' ability to express and identify emotions in the context of interactions with others, developmental psychologists now recognize that emotions serve an important function in regulating and modulating early social exchanges. This dynamic process begins at about two or three months of age, when the infant looks into the adult's eyes and produces a "social smile" or a cry, to which the adult responds. The adult vocalization or facial expression, in turn, often precipitates another emotional response from the infant. Such episodes of reciprocal, mutually engaging cycles of caregiver-child behaviors are called **interactive synchrony.** During the child's first year, interactive synchrony characterizes about 30 percent of face-to-face interactions between infant and caregiver (Tronick & Cohn, 1989).

At about three months, primary caregivers typically assume the major responsibility for guiding interactions, producing repetitions of exaggerated faces and vocalizations to which the infant pays rapt attention (Stern, 1974). Infants, without doubt, notice and react to their mothers' expressive displays. When mothers do not return a smile but show a still face or a neutral pose, infants respond with a quizzical or sober look, avert their gaze, and touch themselves or some nearby object (Toda & Fogel, 1993; Tronick et al., 1978). When mothers show a positive expression, infants follow suit. If mothers look depressed, infants react by averting their gaze and sometimes crying (Cohn & Tronick, 1983). By about six to nine months of age, infants more clearly take the initiative; their displays of positive affect now more often precede their mothers' (Cohn & Tronick, 1987). Thus, throughout early infancy, the child becomes an increasingly active partner in an emotionally toned, interactive "duet" with the caregiver.

But what about the other 70 percent of the time, when infant-caregiver interactions are *asynchronous,* or uncoordinated with each other? Edward Tronick and his colleagues believe these episodes, which constitute the majority of infant-caregiver relations, also play an important part in normal emotional development. A common occurrence after a sequence in which infant and caregiver are not coordinated is the infant's attempt to repair the "interactive error." When the mother looks sad, for example, the infant's subsequent gaze aversion or crying encourages the mother to modify her own behavior, and frequently she does (Cohn & Tronick, 1983). Thus episodes of asynchrony give infants opportunities to learn about the rules of interaction and, in cases in which they are able to repair an interaction, give them a sense of mastery or control over their environment (Tronick & Cohn, 1989).

Affective exchanges between infant and caregiver lay the groundwork for social behavior and emotional dispositions at later ages. Researchers have observed that depressed mothers tend to be less positive in face-to-face interactions with their infants (Campbell, Cohn, & Meyers, 1995). Perhaps as a consequence, infants of clinically depressed mothers express a good deal of negative affect in face-to-face interactions (Cohn et al., 1986). They tend to express more sadness and anger, and their negative affect extends to other adults who are not depressed (Field, 1995; Field et al., 1988; Pickens & Field, 1993). These infants also show brain wave patterns similar to those of depressed adults (Dawson, 1994; Field et al., 1995). Thus the dominance of negative emotions during early mother-child interactions culminates in a general mood or background emotional state that apparently pervades the child's own behaviors (Tronick, Ricks, & Cohn, 1982). The child may bring this general affective tone to new situations; for example, an anxious child is likely to interpret a new event as frightening, whereas a happy child may react with curiosity. Finally, the nature of the affective exchanges between mother and child influences the strength of the emotional bond, or *attachment,* between them. Infants who attempt to elicit responses from their mothers by smiling, vocalizing, or crying at six months of age are more likely to have healthy attachments at age one year than children who withdraw from such interactions (Tronick et al., 1982); depressed mothers tend to have children with poorer quality attachments (Teti et al., 1995). As is discussed later in this chapter, healthy attachments, in turn, are correlated with many other positive developmental outcomes in social and cognitive functioning. Hence the tone of these early interactions is a crucial facet of child development.

KEY THEME
Child's Active Role

interactive synchrony   Reciprocal, mutually engaging cycles of caregiver-child behaviors.

Later Emotional Development

By their second year, many children begin to show emotions that reflect a more complex understanding of the self and social relationships. Shame, guilt, and envy, for example, each require the child to understand the perspective of another person—that the person may be disappointed with the child, may be hurt, or may feel affection for a third party. Such emotions also require a consciousness about the self and one's relations to others, a facet of development described in the chapter titled "Self and Values" (Campos et al., 1983; Lewis, 1989). Accordingly, emotions such as envy and guilt are known as **self-conscious emotions.**

    The visible signs of self-conscious emotions can be multifaceted: a child displaying shame lowers her head and eyes, collapses her body, and often has an odd smile on her face (Lewis, Alessandri, & Sullivan, 1992). Asked to dance in front of people or told that he or she has failed a task, a preschooler might show embarrassment with a smiling face, a look away, and nervous body movements (Lewis & Ramsay, 2002). The expression of self-conscious emotions can change with age, too. At age two years, children show discernible signs of jealousy. The child may wedge himself between his mother and father as they are hugging or hit a sibling whom his parent just kissed (Cummings, Zahn-Waxler, & Radke-Yarrow, 1981). But as children get older, they are better able to manage their jealousy, especially in front of their parents (Miller, Volling, & McElwain, 2000). Basic emotions, such as fear, also undergo developmental changes, particularly in the types of stimuli that elicit them. Whereas early expressions of fear result from loud noises or strange people, later in childhood fear occurs as a response to more complex events, such as the possibility of failing in school or being rejected by peers (Morris & Kratchowill, 1983; Rutter & Garmezy, 1983). Thus, as the child's cognitive skills and social awareness grow, he expresses more complex emotions or more elaborate and controlled forms of the basic emotions.

● **Understanding Emotions**   With the advent of language, children can communicate feelings by verbalizing instead of just furrowing their brows and crying or making some other facial display. Children begin to use language to describe feeling

KEY THEME
Interaction Among Domains

KEY THEME
Interaction Among Domains

By age three or four, children's understanding of emotions includes knowledge about how to soothe others' negative emotions. Preschoolers might suggest hugging or sharing a toy with a distressed child, for example.

self-conscious emotion
Emotion such as guilt and envy that appears later in childhood and requires knowledge about the self as related to others.

states between eighteen and thirty-six months of age, shortly after they begin to talk. Inge Bretherton and Marjorie Beeghly (1982) asked mothers of twenty-eight-month-olds to keep a diary of their children's verbalizations that referred to psychological states. Besides being able to apply a wide range of terms to express both positive and negative feelings, these children were able to discuss the conditions that led to a specific emotion and the actions that followed as a consequence. Several children, for example, made statements similar to "Grandma mad. I wrote on wall," suggesting an understanding of the reasons for another's emotion. Another type of utterance made by several children—"I cry. Lady pick me up and hold me"—signifies an understanding that emotions may be related to subsequent actions.

From age three to four years and older, children use more varied and complex emotion words (Fabes, Eisenberg, et al., 2001). At this age, children also become more proficient in verbally describing the causes and consequences of emotions (Barden et al., 1980). They tend to agree that certain events, such as receiving a compliment, lead to happy emotions, whereas others, such as being shoved, lead to negative feelings. Furthermore, they are able to suggest ways to ameliorate another's negative emotions, such as hugging a crying sibling or sharing toys to placate an angered playmate (Fabes et al., 1988).

Between about ages eight and ten, many children understand the emotional behaviors prescribed by cultural rules (e.g., you are supposed to look happy when you receive a gift even if you don't like it) or behaviors necessary to obtain certain goals (you should smile even if you don't feel well if you want your mother to allow you to go to a friend's party). In such cases, the individual masks or "fakes" an emotional state. Paul Harris and his associates (Harris et al., 1986) examined this skill in using emotional **display rules,** the cultural guidelines governing when and how to express emotions, by asking six- and ten-year-olds to listen to stories in which the central character felt either a positive or a negative emotion but had to hide it. After hearing the story, children were to describe verbally the facial expression of the protagonist, along with how this person really felt. Even six-year-olds could state that the emotion displayed would not match the emotion felt, although ten-year-olds provided a fuller explanation. These results suggest that by the middle school years, children have developed a broad understanding of the social norms and expectations that surround the display of feelings.

KEY THEME
Interaction Among Domains

Knowledge about emotions can have significant ramifications for the child's social development. For example, five-year-old-children who are able to label correctly facial expressions of emotions are more likely to display positive social behaviors at age nine (Izard et al., 2001). Moreover, children who have substantial knowledge about the emotions that usually accompany given situations have higher scores on tests of moral development, are less likely to evidence behavior problems, and are better liked by their peers (Cook, Greenberg, & Kusche, 1994; Denham et al., 1990; Dunn, Brown, & Maguire, 1995). The reason may be that children who have greater knowledge about emotions are more likely to respond appropriately to the emotional expressions of their agemates.

Knowledge about emotions is probably gleaned, at least in part, from parents. Children who have greater knowledge about emotions—who can label emotional expressions on faces, describe the feelings of another person in an emotion-related situation, and talk about the causes of emotions—typically have mothers who discuss and explain emotions, often in the context of the child expressing a negative emotion himself. In other words, these mothers are good "coaches." On the other hand, when parents display more negative affect themselves or dismiss children's experiences of emotions (e.g., "You're overreacting!"), children's understanding of emotions is poorer and they are less socially competent (Denham et al., 1997; Dunn & Brown, 1994; Laible & Thompson, 2002). Parents who engage in such behaviors are probably missing opportunities to explain to their children the important elements of emotional responding. The extreme case is represented by children who are physically abused or neglected by their parents. These children have noticeable deficits in their

display rules   The cultural guidelines governing when, how, and to what degree to display emotions.

ability to identify the emotional expressions that correspond to particular situations, such as going to the zoo and getting a balloon or losing a pet dog to disease. Physically abused children, perhaps not surprisingly, have a bias toward selecting angry expressions (Pollak et al., 2000).

Emotional development in older children is closely affiliated with advances in cognition that allow them to think in more complex, abstract terms. By the time they enter school, children begin to understand that changes in thoughts may lead to changes in feelings—that thinking happier thoughts, for example, might make a sad mood go away (Weiner & Handel, 1985). In addition, they comprehend the possibility of experiencing two contrasting emotions at the same time, such as feeling happy at receiving a gift but disappointed that it cannot yet be opened (Brown & Dunn, 1996). As children approach adolescence, their concepts of emotions center increasingly on internal psychological states. That is, whereas younger children identify their own emotional states based on the situations they are in ("I'm happy when it's my birthday"), preadolescents and adolescents refer more frequently to their mental states ("I'm happy when I feel good inside") (Harris, Olthof, & Meerum Terwogt, 1981).

● **Regulating Emotions** In addition to becoming more adept at understanding various emotions, during the early and middle school years children generally become better able to regulate their own emotional states. Behaviors such as calming down after getting angry have important repercussions for the child's social relationships and perhaps even mental health (Cicchetti, Ackerman, & Izard, 1995). In fact, much of the development of emotion that we have described previously—expressing, recognizing, and understanding emotions, as well as socialization experiences regarding emotions—culminates in the ability to regulate one's affective state (Denham, 1998).

Emotion regulation actually has its earliest roots in infancy. In general, infants rely on caregivers to help them regulate their emotions with carrying, rocking, or soft vocalizations. Distraction also helps, at least in the short run (Harman, Rothbart, & Posner, 1997). Even young babies, however, make some attempts to regulate their own affective states, whether it be by sucking on a pacifier, by looking away if they become too aroused (as noted earlier in this chapter), or even by falling asleep (Kopp, 1989; Walden & Smith, 1997). Specific emotions may cause specific regulatory behaviors. For example, infants who experience fear when seeing an unpredictable mechanical toy withdraw from the stimulus or look at the mother. When frustrated and angered by the removal of an attractive toy, infants distract themselves or try to approach the toy (Buss & Goldsmith, 1998). Two-year-olds continue to use strategies such as distraction; when they are presented with a snack or a gift but must wait to obtain it, they typically shift their attention to other objects. Normally, this strategy alleviates their distress (Grolnick, Bridges, & Connell, 1996). But when young children focus on the source of their frustration, their anger tends to increase (Gilliom et al., 2002). By age three, many children show fewer tantrums and intense negative outbursts as they increasingly rely on language to communicate their intents and desires (Kopp, 1992). Physiological maturation probably contributes, too. Researchers suspect that early childhood is a time when the frontal portions of the brain, which control excitation and inhibition of emotion-linked behavior, are maturing (Fox, 1994; Schore, 1996).

One of the most important aspects of emotion regulation is what it predicts later in development. Infants who have difficulty regulating their emotions at six months of age, for example, are more likely to be noncompliant with their parents at age three (Stifter, Spinrad, & Braungart-Rieker, 1999). Similarly, preschoolers and elementary-age children who express a lot of anger, hostility, and other negative emotions show poorer social competence in school and are isolated from or rejected by peers (Eisenberg et al., 1997; Fabes et al., 2002; Hubbard, 2001). Perhaps of most concern, researchers have found that the inability to regulate negative emotions is part of the behavioral profile of children with conduct problems. In one study, preschool-age children, some of whom were identified as being at risk for behavior problems, were

KEY THEME
Interaction Among Domains

KEY THEME
Interaction Among Domains

KEY THEME
Individual Differences

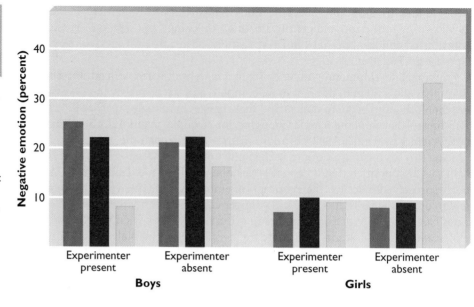

FIGURE 11.3
Emotion Regulation in Children at Risk for Conduct Problems

What happens when children who are at risk for behavior problems experience disappointment? In a study assessing this question, children who had been identified as being at high, medium, or low risk for conduct problems were given a prize that was disappointing to them. The graph shows that boys who were at risk showed a high percentage of negative emotions whether or not the experimenter was in the room with them. Low-risk boys were better able to regulate their negative feelings when someone was present in the room with them. Girls, in general, expressed fewer negative emotions regardless of whether or not they were with someone. The exception was low-risk girls, who expressed more negative emotions when alone.

Source: Cole, Zahn-Waxler, & Smith, 1994.

KEY THEME
Interaction Among Domains

KEY THEME
Nature/Nurture

invited to a laboratory to participate in several cognitive tasks. After each child finished the session, he or she was offered a prize that was undesirable and disappointing. The children's emotional expressions were observed in both the presence and absence of the experimenter. As Figure 11.3 indicates, boys who were at risk for conduct problems expressed more anger, speaking rudely and with obvious negative emotion, compared with low-risk boys. High-risk boys also maintained that anger for longer periods of time while in the presence of the experimenter. Low-risk boys showed anger, too, but only when they were alone. The pattern for girls differed: girls from almost all risk categories expressed fewer negative emotions. These results suggest that boys who are reported by parents and teachers to have fewer behavior problems are better able to manage their emotions when in a social setting. Boys with conduct problems, on the other hand, seem to have difficulty regulating their anger, a fact that could be a source of their generally disruptive behavior (Cole et al., 1994). The evidence linking emotion regulation and later social development continues to mount, not only for children in the United States but also for those in other cultures, such as Indonesia (Eisenberg, Pidada, & Liew, 2001).

The way children learn to manage their emotions depends, at least in part, on the kinds of experiences their parents provide (e.g., do parents provide opportunities for children to become aroused or to calm down?), as well as what children learn are the consequences of their own emotional displays (e.g., what happened when I had an angry tantrum versus when I "used my words"?). When parents become distressed at their children's display of negative emotions and punish them, children later tend to express more anger and hostility and have more behavior problems and poorer social functioning in school (Eisenberg, Fabes, et al., 1999; Fabes, Leonard, et al., 2001). On the other hand, when parents provide supportive coaching and guidance for children's expression of emotion—by helping children talk about how they feel and suggesting ways of dealing with their emotions—children are better able to soothe themselves and moderate their negative emotions (Gottman, Katz, & Hooven, 1997). The general emotional tone of interactions with parents may play a role, too. Nancy Eisenberg and her colleagues found that mothers who were more positive in their emotional expressivity, in contrast to mothers who generally expressed negative emotions, had children who were better able to regulate their own emotions. The children of more negative mothers also behaved more aggressively and were rated as less socially competent by parents and teachers (Eisenberg, Gershoff, et al., 2001). Finally,

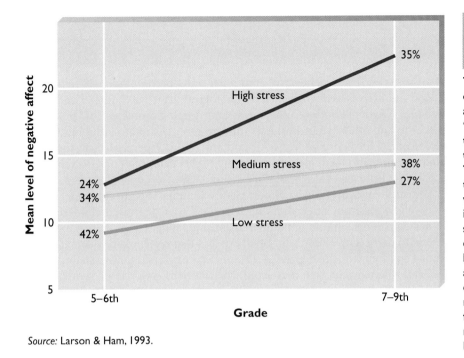

FIGURE 11.4
Frequency of Negative Affect Among Adolescents

To assess the types of emotions experienced by older children and adolescents, researchers "beeped" participants during their daily routines and asked them to report how they felt. The mean percentage of negative affect is shown along the vertical axis. The percentages indicated within the graph show the proportion of students in each grade reporting low, medium, or high stress associated with negative life events. Ninth-graders reported more negative affect than fifth-graders, and those who reported more stress in their lives were especially likely to experience negative emotions.

Source: Larson & Ham, 1993.

with development, children probably become more aware of their own emotional styles and seek out experiences that are compatible with their needs; some children may learn that sitting alone and playing is soothing, whereas others may seek the emotional release of a fast-paced basketball game (Thompson, 1994).

● **Emotions During Adolescence**   By many popular accounts, adolescence is a unique phase in emotional development. Many laypeople, as well as professionals, believe adolescence is a time of "storm and stress," of emotional turmoil and extreme moodiness. Does research substantiate this belief? Although the evidence is somewhat mixed, several studies suggest that adolescents do experience more negative emotions than children of other ages and, in fact, may be at risk for psychological problems such as depression (Larson & Lampman-Petraitis, 1989; Petersen & Hamburg, 1986; Rutter, 1991).

In one study, for example, fifth- through ninth-graders wore electronic pagers for one week as they went through their normal daily routines. At random times over the week, the researchers "beeped" the participants to indicate they should rate their mood just before the signal. In addition, the children and their parents filled out questionnaires assessing the number of positive and negative life events they experienced in the past six months. Figure 11.4 shows the results. Ninth-graders reported more negative affect than fifth-graders; moreover, for these young adolescents, negative emotions were associated with a greater number of negative life events, such as changing schools, breaking up with a boyfriend or girlfriend, or getting along poorly with parents (Larson & Ham, 1993). By grade ten, though, adolescents' emotional states become more stable and stop moving in a negative direction (Larson et al., 2002).

In addition, adolescents and their parents express increased negative emotions to each other from age twelve to about age fifteen, after which negativity declines. These parent-child interactions involve mutual reciprocal influences. Parents who receive a large amount of expressed negative affect from their adolescent children escalate in their own negative emotions over time, and, likewise, adolescents whose parents express negative emotions toward them increase in their negative affect (Kim et al., 2001). These results illustrate an important principle that we have introduced in this chapter and will discuss again in the chapter titled "The Family": that parents and their children are often involved in a mutually influencing spiral of interactions, sometimes affecting each other in important and enduring ways.

Adolescent Depression and Suicide

For some adolescents, negative emotional states become more extreme and manifest themselves as *depression*, a psychological disorder characterized by dejected mood for lengthy periods of time, eating and sleeping problems, low self-esteem, loss of energy, and other symptoms. According to recent estimates, roughly 35 percent of adolescents experience depressed mood and about 7 percent meet the criteria for clinical depression, with girls experiencing higher rates of depression than boys (Ge et al., 1994; Petersen et al., 1993; Wichstrøm, 1999).

The causes of depression in adolescents are complex and not completely understood by psychologists, but researchers have noticed that depressed children often have depressed parents. Studies of family relationships suggest that there is a genetic component to depression (Pike et al., 1996) but also that certain family climates are typical among children who are depressed. Parents who express less warmth and supportiveness and who participate in more conflicts with their children are more likely to have adolescents who are depressed (Ge, Best, et al., 1996; Greenberger & Chen, 1996; Messer & Gross, 1995). Children who witness or are victims of domestic violence are also at risk for depression (Downey et al., 1994; Sternberg et al., 1993). Perhaps these parents, whose poor parenting skills may be due to their own depression, weaken their children's ability to regulate their own emotions or influence their children to form negative ideas about social relationships (Cummings, 1995). The result is that the child, too, becomes depressed.

Why are adolescents especially vulnerable? Several explanations are possible. Cognitive growth may mean the adolescent thinks more about the self and the future. A switch from elementary to secondary school may mean adjustments in peer group relationships. Family relationships may be changing; parents may have reached a stage in their relationship at which they are considering divorce, for example (Petersen et al., 1993; Rutter, 1991). Changes in self-image may accompany the many biological changes in the body associated with puberty. For girls, depression is linked to issues of self-concept and interpersonal stress (Donnelly & Wilson, 1994; Rudolph & Hammen, 1999). Finally, some researchers believe that changes in hormone levels that occur during puberty may activate genes that put individuals at risk for psychological problems (Walker, 2002). Clearly, understanding and preventing depression in adolescents requires a consideration of several domains of development.

The most serious concern about adolescents who are depressed is their risk for committing suicide. Surveys suggest that 6 to 13 percent of adolescents have attempted suicide (Garland & Zigler, 1993). Between 1960 and 1990, the rate of adolescent suicide tripled (Bennett, 1994). Suicide is now the third leading cause of death among fifteen- to twenty-four-year-olds, and the fourth leading cause of death among children ages ten to fourteen (National Institute of Mental Health, 2002). Although the number of attempted suicides is greater in females than in males, completed suicides are more frequent among males than females. This difference is the consequence of the fact that males typically choose more lethal means of attempting suicide than females do. Homosexual male adolescents are at particular risk for suicide (Remafedi et al., 1998).

Some of the warning signs that a young person may be thinking about suicide include falling grades in school, drug or alcohol use, withdrawal from family or friends, or avoidance of social and sporting events. When these behaviors are combined with becoming especially quiet, changes in eating or sleeping patterns, giving away valued possessions, or talking or writing about suicide, the adolescent may be signaling a need for help. The Centers for Disease Control (1992) suggests that strategies to address the problem must include helping teachers and community leaders identify those most at risk, educating young people to become more knowledgeable about risk factors and intervention, developing screening, referral, and peer-support programs, support for crisis centers and hotlines, and reducing access to lethal means of suicide.

KEY THEME
Nature/Nurture

KEY THEME
Interaction Among Domains

SEE FOR YOURSELF
psychology.college.hmco.com
Preventing Suicide

FOR YOUR REVIEW

- What are the differences between basic and self-conscious emotions? Give some examples of basic emotions that researchers have observed in young infants. Give some examples of self-conscious emotions that emerge later in childhood.

- Why is the emergence of social referencing so significant in the course of emotional development?

- What are the dynamics of synchronous and asynchronous interactions between infant and caregiver? What is the significance of these types of interactions for later emotional development?

- What types of knowledge about emotions do children acquire in the years from preschool to adolescence?

- What strategies do children typically use to regulate their emotions?

- What is the significance of the child's ability to regulate his or her own emotions?

- How can parents and caregivers promote emotion knowledge and emotion regulation among children?

- What are the distinctive features of emotional development in adolescence?

- What factors are related to depression during adolescence?

Variations in Emotional Development

So far, our account of emotional development has emphasized commonalities across children in the expression and interpretation of emotions. Despite the generalities we have observed, however, there are noteworthy variations in emotional development among individuals and cultural groups.

Temperament

Emotions are not just transitory states of feeling and expression; often we discern a child's more enduring emotional mood and describe her personality as "cheerful" or "hostile," "easygoing" or "irritable." As we saw in the chapter titled "Genetics and Heredity," researchers have found that infants and children vary in *temperament*, a style of behavioral functioning that encompasses the intensity of expression of moods, distractibility, adaptability, and persistence. Individual differences among infants in these qualities often remain relatively stable over time and across different situations (Rothbart & Bates, 1998).

KEY THEME
Individual Differences

● **Patterns of Temperament**   Stella Chess and Alexander Thomas (1982, 1990, 1991) have offered one conceptualization of temperament, identifying three basic patterns that many children display:

■ The *easy* child generally has positive moods, regular body functions, a low to moderate energy level in responses, and a positive approach to new situations. This child establishes regular feeding and sleeping schedules right from early infancy and adapts quickly to new routines, people, and places.

■ The *difficult* child is often in a negative mood, has irregular body functions, shows high-intensity reactions, withdraws from new stimuli, and is slow to adapt to new situations. The difficult child sleeps and eats on an unpredictable schedule, cries a good deal (and loudly), and has trouble adjusting to new routines.

■ The *slow-to-warm-up* child is somewhat negative in mood, has a low level of activity and intensity of reaction, and withdraws from new stimuli. However, with repeated exposure to new experiences, she or he begins to show interest and involvement.

KEY THEME
Child's Active Role

Chess and Thomas (1991) note that children with different temperaments will evoke different patterns of reactions from their parents, teachers, and peers. "Easy" children usually elicit the most positive reactions from others, whereas children from the other two temperament categories typically draw more negative reactions. Later in life, children with "easy" temperaments may adjust more readily to important transitions, such as the start of school or making new friends. An important dimension of development, say Chess and Thomas, is the "goodness of fit" between the child's temperament and the demands placed on the child by the environment, specifically parents, teachers, peers, and others.

Other researchers have proposed alternative descriptions of temperament types. For example, Jerome Kagan and his colleagues (Kagan et al., 1984; Kagan, Reznick, & Snidman, 1988) noted that some infants tend to show wariness and fearfulness when they encounter unfamiliar people, objects, or events, and others react with interest, spontaneity, and sociability. Longitudinal studies show that both the first group, called *inhibited,* and the second, called *uninhibited,* tend to maintain their distinctive styles from infancy through adolescence.

Mary Rothbart and her colleagues (Rothbart, 1986; Rothbart, Derryberry, & Posner, 1994) have offered another increasingly popular description of temperament. Infants are thought to differ in terms of *reactivity,* or how easily the child becomes aroused in response to events in the environment. Some children react quickly and intensely, whereas others are slower to react and are generally calmer. A second dimension of temperament in this model is the ability to *regulate the self,* to adjust one's level of arousal and to soothe oneself. Some children are better able than others to shift their attention or to inhibit behaviors in order to bring themselves back to a calm state.

KEY THEME
Sociocultural Influence

One caution about categorizing infant styles concerns the cross-cultural dimensions of temperament. Although the preceding categories may capture individual differences in the emotional styles of Western infants, they may not apply to children from other cultures. For example, when Japanese mothers were asked to describe the behavioral styles of their infants, the "easy/difficult" dimension appeared in their responses, but so did unique qualities such as "self-assertiveness" (e.g., a tendency to like pleasant sounds, enjoy exercising the body, and feed quickly) (Shwalb, Shwalb, & Shoji, 1994). Cultural differences in parental expectations regarding children's temperament may, in turn, lead to differences in parenting styles that circle back to influence the child's style of responding to people and objects.

KEY THEME
Nature/Nurture

● **Biological Bases of Temperament** There are good reasons to believe that individual differences in temperament are rooted in biology. For example, children in Kagan's two temperament categories show different profiles of physiological responsiveness. Inhibited children show more pronounced cardiac reactions, a greater rise in blood pressure when changing from a sitting to a standing position, and more tension in skeletal muscles compared with uninhibited children. As adolescents, inhibited children exhibit a greater response of the brain stem to auditory stimulation (Woodward et al., 2001). Kagan and his colleagues postulate that differential responsiveness in the limbic system, the portion of the brain below the cortex that controls emotions, may lie at the root of temperament differences (Kagan, Snidman, & Arcus, 1993).

Infants who are prone to be irritable also show distinct patterns of brain wave functioning. In one study, infants were observed as they saw and heard novel stimuli; their level of motor activity and emotional responses were of particular interest. Then, when the infants were nine months of age, patterns of EEG activity were measured. Compared with other infants in the study, active, irritable children who were hard to soothe at four months of age showed greater brain wave activity in the right frontal lobe, the portion of the brain thought to be involved in the expression and processing of emotions (Tucker, 1981). These same infants, at twenty-four months of age, tended to be fearful and inhibited (Calkins, Fox, & Marshall, 1995).

Stephen Porges and his associates (Porges, Doussard-Roosevelt, & Maiti, 1994) have focused on *cardiac vagal tone* as a physiological component of temperament. This measure assesses the degree to which the heart is influenced by the vagus nerve, one of the principal nerves in the autonomic nervous system originating in the brain stem. Infants who show high baseline cardiac vagal tone tend to be reactive; they respond both positively and negatively in stressful situations compared with infants with low cardiac vagal tone (Gunnar et al., 1995; Huffman et al., 1998; Stifter, Fox, & Porges, 1989). In addition, infants who show declines in vagal tone while a series of novel stimuli are presented are more attentive and easier to soothe (Huffman et al., 1998). Perhaps these infants are better able to regulate their emotional states. It is interesting to note that these two patterns of physiological responding—reactivity and self-regulation—correspond to the two major dimensions of temperament proposed by Rothbart.

If individuals differ in the way their bodies tend to react emotionally, then it is logical to presume that genetics plays a role in temperament. As we noted in the chapter titled "Genetics and Heredity," studies comparing identical and fraternal twins and parents and children on dimensions of temperament suggest that they have a genetic component. Even so, most researchers of temperament agree that biology only sets in place certain predispositions. Any explanation of a child's personality development most certainly needs to include the complex interplay between initial behavior patterns and environmental experiences (Kagan, 1998; Rothbart & Bates, 1998).

● **Temperament and Later Development**   Does early temperament forecast any of the child's characteristics later in life? It appears so. For example, the extent to which an infant tends to show negative emotions at three months of age predicts poorer cognitive abilities for that child at age four years, even when factors such as the mother's responsiveness are ruled out as influences on the child (Lewis, 1993). In the domain of social relationships, preschool boys who tend to exhibit negative affect often have poorer social skills and lower status among their peers (Eisenberg et al., 1993). Similarly, infants who tend to express anger and frustration score higher on measures of aggression at age six to seven years than children who express less anger as infants (Rothbart, Ahadi, & Hershey, 1994). Likewise, a relationship exists between a child's negativism, short attention span, and swings in emotions at age three and hyperactivity, attention problems, and antisocial behavior in adolescence (Caspi et al., 1995). It seems that the relatively stable emotional style a particular child displays early in life may have a far-reaching impact on both cognitive and social functioning later on. According to some researchers, in fact, early temperament styles are likely to have a strong relationship to adult personality types (Rothbart, Ahadi, & Evans, 2000).

> **KEY THEME**
> **Interaction Among Domains**

Sex Differences in Emotions

According to the familiar stereotype, females are more emotionally expressive and more sensitive to the emotional states of others than are males. Do boys and girls actually differ in any facet of emotional development? It seems that for the most part the answer is yes—that girls are more emotionally expressive and more attuned to emotions than are boys.

During infancy and the preschool years, there do not appear to be strong, clear-cut sex differences. Some studies find that girls tend to show more positive emotions than boys (e.g., Matias & Cohn, 1993), but as we discussed at the start of this chapter, Weinberg and her colleagues (1999) found that boys were more expressive in general. By elementary school, though, girls show a greater range of emotions than boys. In one study, when seven- and twelve-year-olds played a game with a peer, girls were more likely than boys to show a positive or negative emotion when the peer made a comment such as "she looks friendly" or "she doesn't look nice" (Casey, 1993). Later in adolescence, girls smile more than boys both on their own initiative and in response to the smile of another (Hall & Halberstadt, 1986). Girls also begin to show more anxieties than boys during the school years—fears about tests, family issues, health, and other concerns (Orton, 1982; Scarr et al., 1981). Finally, some researchers report that girls are better than boys at decoding the emotional expressions of others (Brown & Dunn, 1996; Hall, 1978, 1984).

Girls may be more emotionally expressive than boys as a consequence of the kinds of experiences they have had with their caregivers. For example, mothers tend to be more facially expressive when they play with their preschool-aged daughters than with their sons.

KEY THEME
Nature/Nurture

Observations of parents' behaviors suggest that many of these sex differences may be taught or modeled directly. For example, mothers and fathers spend more time trying to get their infant daughters to smile than they do their infant sons (Moss, 1974). Mothers of preschoolers also mention feeling states more often and discuss a wider variety of emotions when they talk with their daughters than when conversing with their sons (Dunn, Bretherton, & Munn, 1987; Kuebli, Butler, & Fivush, 1995). Mothers are also more facially expressive when they play with their two-year-old girls than with boys, thus exposing girls to a greater range of emotions and displaying more social smiles to them (Malatesta et al., 1989). In general, parents encourage girls to maintain close emotional relationships and to show affection, whereas they instruct boys to control their emotions (Block, 1973). Thus, although biological explanations of sex differences cannot be ruled out completely, many of the emotional behaviors we see in males and females appear to be influenced by their learning histories.

Differences in how boys and girls regulate their emotions are of special interest to researchers trying to identify the precursors of adjustment difficulties in childhood. When girls experience challenges or problems, they tend to employ *internalizing* strategies for coping, such as worrying or becoming anxious or depressed. In contrast, when boys experience difficulties, they tend to engage in *externalizing* behaviors, such as aggression (Rossman, 1992; Zahn-Waxler, Cole, & Barrett, 1991). Understanding the sources of emotion regulation in boys and girls thus has implications for the treatment and prevention of psychological problems that are associated with each sex.

Cultural Differences in Emotions

KEY THEME
Sociocultural Influence

The tendency of children to express and detect emotions varies as a function of the culture in which they are raised. American children, for example, tend to smile more than Chinese infants (Camras et al., 1998). On the other end of the emotional spectrum, Chinese children are better able to identify fearful and sad situations than are American children, and they cry less (Borke, 1973; Camras et al., 1998). These differences may reflect the child's incorporation of particular cultural beliefs about emotions.

A recent study of two different cultural groups in rural Nepal further illustrates this concept. Pamela Cole and her colleagues (Cole, Bruschi, & Tamang, 2002) studied children in two small villages, each comprising a different ethnic group—one Brahman and the other Tamang. The Brahmins subscribe to a caste system in which strict rules dictate which social groups may interact. They are very oriented to status differences and the power of authority, and they have a great deal of pride in their own ethic group. The Tamang, on the other hand, place great value on community rather than on the individuals within the group. Resources are shared, and important decisions are made by consulting all group members, in accordance with their Buddhist values of selflessness. How do school-age children in these two very different cultures express emotions? All children were asked to react to scenarios likely to lead to an emotional reaction, such as having a friend snatch away a piece of candy or watching as a parent spills tea all over homework papers. Brahmin children, although they expected to feel anger in such situations, clearly stated that anger should not be expressed, primarily because authority needed to be respected and group orderliness preserved. Tamang children, in contrast, did not express anger; rather, they reported a feeling of *thiken*, or making the mind calm, in accordance with their Buddhist beliefs. American children, also participants in this study, endorsed anger as an appropriate response. This belief is consistent with the value we place on self-assertion and independence in our culture (Cole et al., 2002).

Cultural belief systems extend to the kinds of temperamental styles that are valued. A good example is the dimension of shyness and inhibition. In European American families, this personality profile is often seen as a liability; we expect our children to be outgoing, sociable, and eager to interact with the environment. In Chinese society, though, shyness is a valued trait. Parents and teachers believe that shy children are well behaved, and shy children have positive views of themselves (Chen, Rubin, & Li, 1997; Chen et al., 1999). These cultural beliefs are likely to be expressed in the socialization practices of parents and others.

Finally, cultures differ in the extent to which children are exposed to emotional events. Infants in northern Germany experience frequent separations from their mothers, whereas Japanese infants do not (Saarni et al., 1998). It should not be surprising, then, if children show varying patterns of emotional reactions to the same event—in this case, the mother's departure.

FOR YOUR REVIEW

- What are the different ways in which child temperament has been conceptualized?

- What is the evidence for a biological basis for temperament?

- How is temperament related to later development?

- How do boys and girls differ in the expression of emotions? What factors might be responsible for these differences?

- In what ways does the development of emotion vary across cultures?

Attachment: Emotional Relationships with Others

One of the most widely discussed and actively researched aspects of emotional and social development is **attachment,** the strong emotional bond that emerges between infant and caregivers. The concept of attachment occupies a prominent place in developmental psychology because of its link with successful cognitive, social, and emotional development throughout childhood.

How does attachment emerge between infant and caregiver? In what ways is this emotional bond expressed? What roles do the caregiver and infant play in its formation? What is the significance of attachment in the later development of the child? Do we observe the same patterns of attachment among children across cultures? In this portion of the chapter, we will examine the course of attachment in infancy and early childhood and explore the answers to these questions.

attachment Strong emotional bond that emerges between infant and caregiver.

The Origins of Attachment: Theoretical Perspectives

What forces govern the emergence of attachment? Historically, there have been two important perspectives on this question, learning theory and ethological theory.

KEY THEME
Nature/Nurture

● **Learning Theory**   Learning theorists believe that certain basic drives, such as hunger, are satisfied by **primary reinforcers,** rewards that gratify biological needs. In the case of the young infant, an important primary reinforcer is food. Other rewards, called **secondary reinforcers,** acquire their reinforcing qualities from their association with primary reinforcers. Because they are connected repeatedly with the reduction of the hunger drive, mothers acquire secondary reinforcing properties. Eventually the mother's presence in contexts outside feeding is rewarding to the infant.

Is the activity of feeding related to the emergence of infant-mother attachments, as learning theorists predict? Evidently not, according to a series of classic experiments conducted by Harry Harlow and his associates (Harlow & Zimmerman, 1959). These investigators separated infant monkeys from their mothers and provided them instead with extended contact with two surrogate mothers, one a figure made of wire mesh and the other a figure covered with terry cloth. The wire surrogate was equipped for feeding half of the monkeys; the terry-cloth surrogate fed the other half. The infant monkeys lived with both their surrogates for at least 165 days, during which time several observations were made of the monkeys' behaviors. One measure was the number of hours per day spent with each surrogate. As Figure 11.5 shows, infant monkeys preferred the cloth "mother" regardless of which surrogate was providing nourishment. In a subsequent test of attachment, when a frightening stimulus such as a mechanical spider was introduced into the monkeys' cage, the monkeys chose the cloth mother to run and cling to, even if they had been fed by the wire mother.

Harlow's findings challenged the view that attachments are based on the mother's acquisition of secondary-drive characteristics. The fact that the infant monkeys did not seek out the surrogate that fed them under either normal or stressful conditions led Harlow to conclude that "contact comfort," the security provided by a physically soothing object, played a greater role in attachment than the simple act of feeding.

KEY THEME
Nature/Nurture

● **The Ethological View**   Proponents of the ethological position state that attachments occur as the result of the infant's innate tendency to signal the caregiver and the caregiver's corresponding predisposition to react to these signals. As a result, infant and caregiver are brought together, a bond is forged between them, and the survival of the infant is ensured. In other words, attachment is an adaptive, biologically programmed response system that is activated early in the infant's development and follows many of the principles of *imprinting* described in the chapter titled "Themes and Theories."

The principal spokesperson for this perspective, John Bowlby (1958, 1969), initially was concerned with the detrimental effects of institutionalization on infants and young children. Scientists in the late 1940s had reported that children who spent extended periods of time in hospitals and orphanages during their early years often showed serious developmental problems, including profound withdrawal from social interactions, intellectual impairments, and, in some cases, physical delays (Skodak & Skeels, 1949; Spitz, 1946a). Bowlby proposed that the cause lay in the lack of a close emotional bond between child and primary caregiver.

Bowlby (1969) maintained that attachments develop in a fixed sequence:

■ In the first two months, infants emit *signaling behaviors*, such as crying and smiling, that bring the caregiver physically close to the infant. Infants emit these signals indiscriminately, but as caregivers respond, stable patterns of interaction emerge.

■ Between two and six months of age, smiles and cries become increasingly restricted to the presence of the caregiver, usually the mother.

■ From six to twelve months of age, clearer signs of the infant's strong attachment to the caregiver develop. At this point, most infants become visibly upset at the mother's departure, a phenomenon called **separation anxiety,** and also show signs of

primary reinforcer   Reward that gratifies biological needs or drives.

secondary reinforcer   Object or person that attains rewarding value because of its association with a primary reinforcer.

separation anxiety   Distress the infant shows when the caregiver leaves the immediate environment.

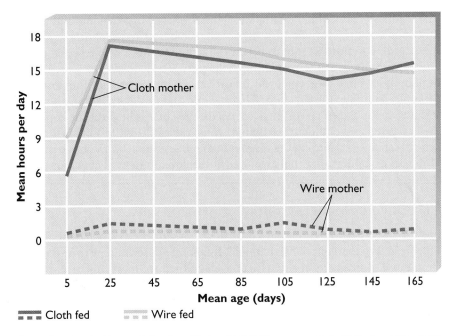

Source: Reprinted with permission from Harlow, H. F., & Zimmerman, R. R., "Affectional Responses in the Infant Monkey," *Science, 130,* 421–432. Copyright 1959 American Association for the Advancement of Science.

FIGURE 11.5
Forming Attachments:
The "Cloth Mother" and
"Wire Mother" Experiment

In Harlow's research, infant monkeys spent more time with a cloth surrogate mother than with a wire surrogate mother, regardless of which one fed them. This graph shows how much time infant monkeys spent with each surrogate as a function of feeding condition.

reunion behavior, happily greeting the mother on her return. Once they are able to move about, infants will ensure their nearness to their mothers by approaching and clinging to them. About the same time, they also display **stranger anxiety,** a wariness or fear at the approach of someone unfamiliar.

■ The final phase of attachment occurs at about three years of age, when the relationship between mother and child becomes more of a partnership and the child comes to appreciate the mother's feelings, motives, and goals.

Harlow's experiments showed that infant monkeys reared with surrogate mothers preferred the cloth mother even when the wire mother provided nourishment. Here, the infant monkey is actually nursing from the wire mother but still maintains contact with the cloth mother. These findings challenge the hypothesis that attachment arises from the caregiver's association with feeding the child.

reunion behavior The child's style of greeting the caregiver after a separation.

stranger anxiety Fear or distress an infant shows at the approach of an unfamiliar person.

The regularity with which infants show this sequence of behaviors and the adaptive function they serve, says Bowlby, suggests its biological and evolutionary basis.

According to Bowlby, infants become attached to those who respond consistently and appropriately to their signaling behaviors. Thus Bowlby saw the maladaptive development of institutionalized infants as a consequence of the absence of the dynamic, contingent interaction between child and caregiver. Although institutional settings met children's basic physical needs, they often did so at the convenience of the caregiver's schedule rather than in response to the child's behaviors. Bowlby's general scheme concerning the origins and course of attachment has framed literally hundreds of modern-day investigations of the development of attachment.

The Developmental Course of Attachment

For the most part, research has confirmed the sequence of behaviors outlined by Bowlby in the emergence of attachment. Infants can discriminate their mothers' faces from those of strangers at two days of age and their mothers' voices and odors a few days after that (DeCasper & Fifer, 1980; Field et al., 1984; MacFarlane, 1975). However, they emit their signals to anyone who is available. By about seven months of age, these indiscriminate behaviors give way to attachments to specific people, most notably the mother or primary caregiver. Stranger anxiety becomes full blown, and separation anxiety is usually manifested as well. In the months that follow, children show evidence of multiple attachments to fathers, substitute caregivers, and grandparents (Schaffer & Emerson, 1964).

At age two years most children continue to show strong attachments, but by age three years some of the manifestations of this bond begin to change. Separation distress diminishes for most children, probably due to advances in cognition. For example, children begin to appreciate the fact that even though the caregiver may depart for several hours, she always returns (Marvin, 1977). The impact of repeated experience with separation and reunion episodes may extend to a more general understanding that negative emotional experiences often yield to strong positive affect, that distress can be followed by stability (Schore, 1994). As children develop insights into the perspectives of others and as their communication skills improve, they can better understand the reasons for temporary separations and can express their emotions in ways other than crying or clinging. The Emotional Development chronology summarizes the sequence of changes in emotional development and attachment.

● **Measuring Attachment**   The **Strange Situation,** developed by Mary Ainsworth and her associates, is a standardized test frequently employed to measure the quality of the child's emotional ties to her mother (Ainsworth et al., 1978). Table 11.1 shows the eight episodes that compose this measure, which is administered in a laboratory setting.

On the basis of her extensive observations of the patterns of behaviors shown by infants, Ainsworth (Ainsworth et al., 1978) distinguished three patterns of attachment: *secure attachment* and two categories of *insecure attachment, avoidant* and *ambivalent attachment.* More recently, other researchers have identified still a third type of insecure attachment called *disorganized/disoriented attachment.* These attachment categories are described as follows:

Secure attachment   Children in this group show many clear signs of attachment by displaying stranger anxiety and separation protest and greeting the mother enthusiastically upon her return. They also use the mother as a **secure base** for exploration, exploring their new surroundings but looking or moving back to the mother as though to "check in" with her. They obviously feel comfortable in the presence of the mother and distressed and apprehensive in her absence.
Avoidant attachment   Infants in this category are less distressed when the mother leaves and less enthusiastic in greeting her when she returns. They tend to avoid or

---

KEY THEME
Interaction Among Domains

Strange Situation   Standardized test that assesses the quality of infant-caregiver attachment.

secure attachment   Attachment category defined by the infant's distress at separation from the caregiver and enthusiastic greeting upon his or her return. The infant also displays stranger anxiety and uses the caregiver as a secure base for exploration.

secure base   An attachment behavior in which the infant explores the environment but periodically checks back with the caregiver.

avoidant attachment   Insecure attachment in which the infant shows little separation anxiety and does not pay much attention to the caregiver's return.

TABLE 11.1	The Episodes of the Strange Situation		
Episode*	**Persons Present**	**Action**	**Attachment Behaviors Assessed**
1	Caregiver, baby, observer	Observer introduces mother and baby to experimental room and leaves.	
2	Caregiver, baby	Baby explores and plays while caregiver is passive.	Secure base
3	Stranger, caregiver, baby	Stranger enters room, converses with caregiver, and approaches baby.	Stranger anxiety
4	Stranger, baby	Caregiver leaves room unobtrusively.	Separation anxiety
5	Caregiver, baby	Caregiver returns and greets baby.	Reunion behavior
6	Baby	Caregiver leaves room, saying "bye-bye."	Separation anxiety
7	Stranger, baby	Stranger enters and orients to baby.	Stranger anxiety
8	Caregiver, baby	Caregiver returns and greets baby.	Reunion behavior

*Each episode except the first lasts for about three minutes.

Source: Adapted from Ainsworth et al., 1978.

ignore her, playing in isolation even when she is present in the room. All of these behaviors, according to Ainsworth, constitute a form of insecure attachment.

Ambivalent (or resistant) attachment   Tension characterizes the behaviors these children show toward their mothers. Although they display noticeable proximity-seeking behaviors when the mother is in the room, sometimes clinging excessively to her, they also show angry, rejecting behavior when she returns, even hitting or pushing her away. Some children in this category are extremely passive, showing limited exploratory play except for bouts of crying that are used as signals to be picked up and held. These children, too, are considered insecurely attached.

Disorganized/disoriented attachment   Children in this attachment category show fear of their caregivers, confused facial expressions, and an assortment of avoidant and ambivalent attachment behaviors in the Strange Situation (Main & Solomon, 1986). These behaviors are accompanied by physiological signs of stress (Hertsgaard et al., 1996).

In the United States, about 65 percent of infants are typically categorized as securely attached, about 20 percent as avoidantly attached, and about 10 percent as ambivalently attached (van IJzendoorn & Sagi, 1999). Other data suggest that perhaps as many as 15 percent of infants show signs of disorganized attachments (Lyons-Ruth & Jacobvitz, 1999).

A newer way to measure attachment is the *Q-sort*. In this method, mother and infant are observed for a specified period of time, after which the observer sorts

ambivalent (resistant) attachment   Insecure attachment in which the infant shows separation protest but also distress upon the caregiver's return.

disorganized/disoriented attachment   Infant-caregiver relations characterized by the infant's fear of the caregiver, confused facial expressions, and a combination of avoidant and ambivalent attachment behaviors.

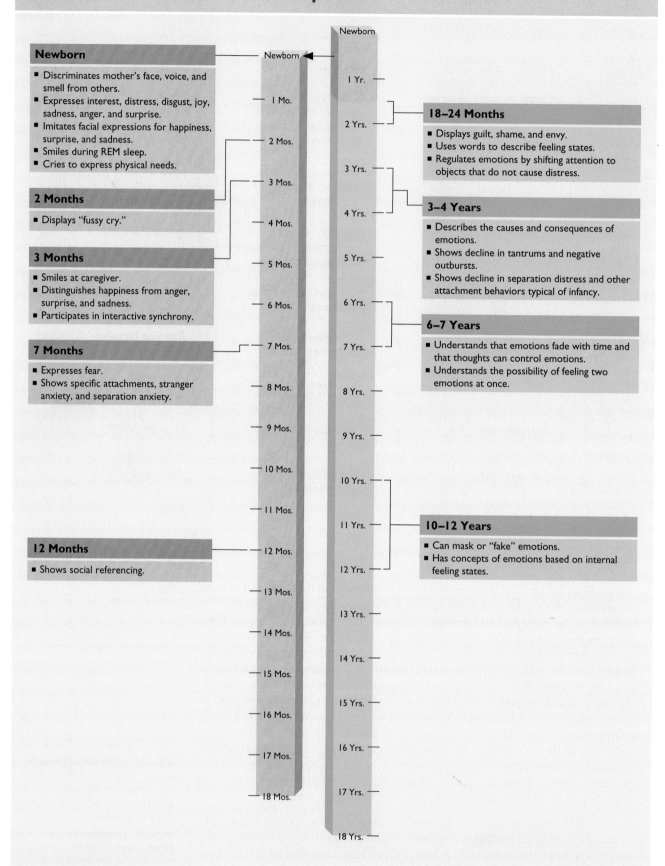

Newborn

- Discriminates mother's face, voice, and smell from others.
- Expresses interest, distress, disgust, joy, sadness, anger, and surprise.
- Imitates facial expressions for happiness, surprise, and sadness.
- Smiles during REM sleep.
- Cries to express physical needs.

2 Months

- Displays "fussy cry."

3 Months

- Smiles at caregiver.
- Distinguishes happiness from anger, surprise, and sadness.
- Participates in interactive synchrony.

7 Months

- Expresses fear.
- Shows specific attachments, stranger anxiety, and separation anxiety.

12 Months

- Shows social referencing.

18–24 Months

- Displays guilt, shame, and envy.
- Uses words to describe feeling states.
- Regulates emotions by shifting attention to objects that do not cause distress.

3–4 Years

- Describes the causes and consequences of emotions.
- Shows decline in tantrums and negative outbursts.
- Shows decline in separation distress and other attachment behaviors typical of infancy.

6–7 Years

- Understands that emotions fade with time and that thoughts can control emotions.
- Understands the possibility of feeling two emotions at once.

10–12 Years

- Can mask or "fake" emotions.
- Has concepts of emotions based on internal feeling states.

Newborn — Newborn — Newborn
1 Mo. — 1 Yr.
2 Mos. — 2 Yrs.
3 Mos. — 3 Yrs.
4 Mos. — 4 Yrs.
5 Mos. — 5 Yrs.
6 Mos. — 6 Yrs.
7 Mos. — 7 Yrs.
8 Mos. — 8 Yrs.
9 Mos. — 9 Yrs.
10 Mos. — 10 Yrs.
11 Mos. — 11 Yrs.
12 Mos. — 12 Yrs.
13 Mos. — 13 Yrs.
14 Mos. — 14 Yrs.
15 Mos. — 15 Yrs.
16 Mos. — 16 Yrs.
17 Mos. — 17 Yrs.
18 Mos. — 18 Yrs.

This chart describes the sequence of emotional development based on the findings of research. Children often show individual differences in the exact ages at which they display the various developmental achievements outlined here.

through a series of 90 cards containing descriptions of the mother-infant relationship. Several piles are created, from "least characteristic" to "most characteristic" of the child. The child's attachment score is based on the extent to which these ratings correlate with the characteristics of a securely attached child defined by a panel of experts on childhood attachment (Waters & Deane, 1985). The use of the Q-sort has permitted researchers to study attachment in a broader range of contexts and in a wider age range of children than has the Strange Situation (Thompson, 1998).

● **The Antedecents of Secure Attachment**   How do secure, high-quality attachments develop? Research by Mary Ainsworth and her colleagues (Ainsworth, Bell, & Stayton, 1971, 1972, 1974) suggests that the mother's style of interacting with her infant and her responsivity to the baby's signals are key factors.

KEY THEME
Nature/Nurture

Ainsworth and her associates visited the homes of twenty-six infants and their mothers for about four hours every three weeks during the entire first year of the infants' lives. When they were about one year old, the infants were brought to the laboratory to be tested in the Strange Situation and were classified according to the quality of attachment to their mothers. An attempt then was made to find relationships between the attachment classification and specific maternal behaviors observed earlier. The results of this study indicated that mothers of securely attached infants were *sensitive* to their children's signals, noticing their cues and interpreting them correctly. These mothers were *accepting* of their role as caregiver. They displayed *cooperation*; mothers of securely attached infants would wait until the child finished her activity or was in a good mood before imposing a request. They used gentle persuasion rather than assertive control. Mothers in this group were also *accessible,* providing quick responses to the child's signals, particularly crying. They were not distracted by their own thoughts and activities. In contrast, mothers of the insecurely attached group were often rigid, unresponsive, and demanding in their parenting style and did not feel positively about their role as caregiver.

A meta-analysis of sixty-six studies showed that maternal sensitivity is indeed strongly related to attachment (De Wolff & van IJzendoorn, 1997). However, the emotional tone of early mother-child interactions is also important to consider. Mothers of securely attached children have been found to be more affectionate, more positive, and less intrusive in their vocalizations than mothers of insecurely attached infants, toddlers, and young school-age children (Bates, Maslin, & Frankel, 1985; Isabella, 1993; Izard et al., 1991; Stevenson-Hinde & Shouldice, 1995). In a study of children who were about to enter school, those who were insecurely attached and who showed the most behavior problems two years later had mothers who displayed the highest levels of negativity and tension of all the participants (Moss et al., 1998).

Interactive synchrony also influences the emergence of attachments. One group of researchers observed the interactions of mothers and their infants at one, three, and nine months of age, recording each instance in which the infants' and mothers' behaviors co-occurred and produced a mutually satisfying outcome. For example, if the infant gazed at the mother, the mother verbalized, or if the infant fussed and cried, the mother soothed him. The infants' attachments were then assessed at one year of age. According to the results, securely attached infants had experienced a greater number of synchronous interactions in the prior months, a finding other researchers have replicated (Isabella, Belsky, & von Eye, 1989; Scholmerich et al., 1995). Therefore, in accounting for the emergence of secure attachment, it is important to consider maternal behavior *as it is related to the child's behavior.*

It is worth noting that siblings reared in the same family are at least moderately similar to each other in their attachment classifications and that identical twins are no more similar than fraternal twins in their attachment styles (O'Connor & Croft, 2001; van IJzendoorn et al., 2000). This pattern of results is consistent with the notion that the events that transpire within the family are a key ingredient in shaping attachments.

● **Attachments to Fathers**   Because mothers traditionally have fulfilled the role of primary caregiver, most of the emphasis in research has been on the emotional

Infants show clear signs of attachment to fathers, especially when fathers spend time in rewarding, mutually engaging interactions with them. Research shows that children who have healthy attachments to mothers *and* fathers show higher self-esteem and greater social competence than children who are securely attached to only one or neither parent.

KEY THEME
Child's Active Role

KEY THEME
Individual Differences

bond that develops between child and mother. With large numbers of women participating in the labor force, however, and challenges to the assumption that females have the exclusive role in child care, many caregiving responsibilities have been assumed by others either within or outside the family. Moreover, researchers in developmental psychology have begun to recognize the glaring absence of information on how another important family member, the father, interacts with his children. The result has been a growing literature on father-child interaction.

In general, fathers spend less time interacting with and caring for their children than mothers do. Nevertheless, many infants clearly do form attachments to their fathers. In the Strange Situation, infants show signs of separation anxiety when the father leaves the room and greet him on his return. They also use him as a secure base for exploration (Kotelchuk, 1976). In most cases, when infants are attached to their mothers, they are also attached to their fathers (Rosen & Burke, 1999). As is the case with mothers, when fathers spend time in face-to-face interactions with their infants, but particularly when they show sensitivity in their play, their infants show clear signs of attachment to them (Cox et al., 1992; Grossmann et al., 2002). Securely attached infants also tend to have fathers who are sociable, are agreeable, and express positive emotions (Belsky, 1996). Given the opportunity to be nurturant and responsive, fathers certainly can become partners in strong, secure attachments.

Children who have secure attachments to both mothers and fathers show higher self-esteem and greater social competence than children who have secure attachments to only one or to neither parent (Verschueren & Marcoen, 1999). Moreover, healthy relationships with fathers can buffer children who are at risk due to impaired interactions with their mothers. Recall how infants with depressed mothers often have poor quality interactions with them. One group of researchers found that infants with depressed mothers often had more positive interactions with their fathers (Hossain et al., 1994). In adolescence, a positive relationship with the father seems to protect children from the behavior problems associated with having a depressed mother (Tannenbaum & Forehand, 1994). In addition, attachments to fathers predict healthy friendship relationships for adolescents (Lieberman, Doyle, & Markiewicz, 1999). These studies suggest that fathers fulfill a role in the family that simply cannot be ignored.

● **Temperament and Attachment**   Caregivers are not solely responsible for the emergence of attachment. Because attachments form in the context of interactions between caregiver and infant, it seems reasonable to postulate that the infant's own style as a communication partner contributes significantly to the growth of an affectional bond.

Several researchers have reported a link between infant characteristics such as irritability and proneness to distress and subsequent attachment behaviors in the Strange Situation (Bates et al., 1985; Goldsmith & Alansky, 1987; Miyake, Chen, & Campos, 1985). For example, two-day-old infants' proneness to distress when a pacifier is removed from their mouths is related to insecure attachment at fourteen months of age (Calkins & Fox, 1992). Similarly, in a study of Dutch infants who were identified as very irritable newborns, 74 percent were classified as insecurely attached at eighteen months of age (van den Boom, 1994, 1995). Yet early irritability does not necessarily predispose children to become insecurely attached. In the same study of Dutch infants, a second group of irritable newborns and their mothers participated in an intervention program that resulted in only 28 percent being scored as insecurely attached later in infancy.

RESEARCH APPLIED TO PARENTING

Promoting Secure Attachment in Irritable Infants

The phone call turned out to be from Gwen, Cindy's close friend. The two of them had shared many life experiences since their childhood days, but Cindy still found it remarkable that they had had their babies within three months of each other. Cindy knew, though, that motherhood was a challenge for Gwen. Gwen's son, unlike Michael, was *hard to figure out and to keep happy. He didn't seem to like being held very much and was often cranky both before and after feeding. Gwen was a loving mother, but at times she was at her wits' end trying to think of ways to soothe her baby. When Cindy picked up the phone, she could tell from Gwen's voice that she was looking for advice on how to handle her difficult child.*

What can parents do if their infant is born with a "difficult" temperamental style, showing more negative than positive emotions, fussing and crying, and smiling infrequently? Research carried out in the Netherlands in which mother-child interaction was observed in the home monthly up until the infants were six months of age shows that mothers of irritable infants displayed distinct patterns of reactions. They exhibited less visual and physical contact with their babies, were less involved with them, and responded less when their babies smiled or showed other positive social behaviors (van den Boom & Hoeksma, 1994). Although many of the differences between mothers of irritable and nonirritable infants disappeared by the time their children were six months old, such negative parent-child interactions may predispose children to develop insecure attachments.

In a second study (van den Boom, 1994, 1995), mothers of irritable newborns were randomly assigned to either an intervention group or a control group when their infants were six months of age. During three in-home training sessions conducted every three weeks, mothers in the intervention group were taught to be more responsive to the cues their infants provided. The infants and mothers were observed again when the children were twelve, eighteen, twenty-four, and forty-two months of age. The benefits of the intervention were clear: children in the experimental group were far more likely to be securely attached than children in the control group, even into toddlerhood. These children were also more cooperative, displayed fewer behavior problems, and engaged in more activities and verbal interactions with their mothers than the control group children. Even though mothers had received training up to several years earlier, they continued to show responsive, sensitive parenting.

What exactly were mothers in the intervention group taught? Following are the essential ingredients of the training package:

1. *Attend to the infant's signals, especially by imitating the baby's behaviors and repeating one's own verbalizations.* If the infant coos, respond by making a similar sound. When speaking to the infant, say words slowly and repeat them. If the infant averts his gaze, remain silent, because gaze aversion often means the caregiver has not interpreted the child's signals correctly. These techniques aim to slow down the tempo of mother-infant interactions and to simplify them. The overall goal of these procedures is to help the mothers perceive and interpret infant signals accurately.

2. *Try to soothe the fussing or crying infant.* Because some infants seem to respond negatively to being cuddled or held in close physical contact, try to find a technique suitable for the particular child and her preferences, for example, feeding or vocalizing to her. Once an effective technique is identified, stick with it. Again, the idea is to avoid rapid changes in maternal behavior that might create further frustration and distress in the infant.

3. *Pay attention to the infant's positive signals instead of focusing on his negative behaviors.* Mothers of irritable infants are often so focused on their negative behaviors that they ignore the infant's positive signals. Create opportunities for positive interactions. Play with the infant using games and toys, paying attention to how he or she responds, especially if the response is a smile or a laugh.

In general, the goal of the program was to help mothers correctly read and respond to their own infants' signals, characteristics of mothering that Ainsworth's early studies identified as precursors of secure attachment. As the results described earlier indicate, infants who participated in this intervention showed many desirable outcomes even years after the intervention itself was terminated.

● **Attachment and Later Development**   The importance of attachment has been underscored by research findings showing that secure attachments are related to positive developmental outcomes in both social and cognitive spheres when children become older. Leah Matas and her associates assessed the quality of attachments of forty-eight infants when they were eighteen months of age (Matas, Arend, & Sroufe, 1978). Six months later, these same children were observed for the quality of their play and their problem-solving styles. Children who had earlier been categorized as securely attached were more enthusiastic and compliant with their mothers' suggestions in the problem-solving tasks and showed more positive affect and persistence than their insecurely attached counterparts. They also engaged in more symbolic play and displayed less crying and whining. Other researchers have noted that securely attached children show advantages in language acquisition and cognitive reasoning from toddlerhood well into the middle school years and adolescence. Perhaps the secure child's readiness to explore the environment provides the kind of intellectual stimulation that leads to better cognitive performance (Jacobsen, Edelstein, & Hofman, 1994; Meins, 1998). Perhaps, too, the style of maternal interaction that leads to secure attachment also promotes language and cognitive development.

Securely attached children have also been found to be more socially competent with their peers as preschoolers, showing more leadership, greater sympathy, less aggression, and less withdrawal from social interactions (DeMulder et al., 2000; Waters, Wippman, & Sroufe, 1979). They evidence stronger signs of "ego resiliency" at age five years, meaning they respond to problems in a flexible, persistent, and resourceful manner (Arend, Gove, & Sroufe, 1979). In contrast, insecurely attached infants, particularly those who show avoidant patterns, do not fare so well in the preschool years, according to other research. Children with this attachment classification are found to display many maladaptive and undesirable behaviors, such as high dependency, noncompliance, and poor social skills in peer interactions. They are described by teachers as hostile, impulsive, and withdrawn (Erickson, Sroufe, & Egeland, 1985; Laible & Thompson, 2000). Moreover, avoidant children tend to have negative representations of peers, interpret peers' behaviors as hostile, and become more fearful with age (Cassidy et al., 1996; Kochanska, 2001).

The effects of early attachments may carry over well into adolescence and the adult years. Adolescents who evidence secure attachments to their parents, in the sense of expressing affection for and trust in them, generally have high self-esteem, have a strong sense of personal identity, have fewer depressive symptoms, and display social competence (Cooper, Shaver, & Collins, 1998; Rice, 1990). They also engage in more constructive problem solving when discussing controversial topics, such as dating and household rules, with their parents (Kobak et al., 1993). Longitudinal data also suggest that children who showed the ambivalent attachment pattern as infants are more prone than secure infants to develop anxiety disorders and have poorer social competence in adolescence (Warren et al., 1997; Weinfield, Ogawa, & Sroufe, 1997).

● **Internal Working Models and Later Relationships**   One of the most provocative and interesting findings emerging in attachment research is that the quality of an individual's attachment during childhood may influence his interpersonal relationships as an adolescent or adult. In Bowlby's (1973) theory, as children experience ongoing interactions with parents, they develop mental frameworks of those relationships called **internal working models of relationships.** These internal working models can, in turn, influence representations of other close relationships that emerge later in life, such as those with friends and romantic partners. Secure attachments, according to the theory, help foster healthy close relationships later in life; insecure attachments, however, can forecast problems in subsequent close relationships. Consistent with this theory are the results of a meta-analysis of sixty-three studies of attachment that found that secure attachment was more strongly associated with friendship quality than with peer relations in general (Schneider, Atkinson, & Tardif, 2001). In a more direct exploration of how early representations of relationships are

internal working models of relationships   Mental frameworks of the quality of relationships with others, developed as a result of early ongoing interactions with caregivers.

related to later representations, Wyndol Furman and his colleagues (Furman et al., 2002) administered the Adult Attachment Interview to a group of high school seniors. This attachment measure requires participants to describe and evaluate their own childhood attachment relations; participants are then placed in the appropriate attachment category based on their responses. Working models of friendships and romantic partners were also assessed, using questions about support, caregiving, and cooperation in these relationships. The results showed a strong relationship between working models of relationships with parents and those with friends, but those with romantic relationships were less strong

Internal working models of relationships may even extend to how a parent conceptualizes his or her relationship and interacts with the child (Bowlby, 1973; Main, Kaplan, & Cassidy, 1985). Researchers have noted significant relationships between the attachment classifications given to parents through the Adult Attachment Interview and the attachment styles of their infants (Benoit & Parker, 1994; Steele, Steele, & Fonagy, 1996; Van IJzendoorn, 1995). Mothers who have positive concepts of their own attachments express more joy and pleasure in the relationship with their own child; they also display more emotional availability and use more positive and sensitive parenting behaviors (Aviezer et al., 1999; Pederson et al., 1998; Slade et al., 1999).

● **Cross-Cultural Variations in Patterns of Attachment**   Overall, children in most countries around the world show behaviors indicating secure attachment even if they have been reared in very different circumstances (Posada et al., 1995; Van IJzendoorn, 1995). Studies of children in Israel are good examples. Many Israeli infants are raised in the group setting of the kibbutz. While parents go to work, children are cared for by the *metapelet,* or caregiver, beginning sometime between six and twelve weeks of age and continuing after the first year. Children go to the group caregiving center (called the "children's house") in the morning and return home in the late afternoon, but most of their time is spent with the nonparental caregiver and peers. Do such arrangements interfere with the formation of attachments to mothers? One study showed that 80 percent of infants were securely attached to their mothers; interestingly, however, this finding held true only for infants who came home to sleep for the evening. Some infants sleep overnight at the "children's house," in keeping with more traditional practices of the kibbutz; among this group, only 48 percent were securely attached to their mothers (Sagi et al., 1994). Children raised on the kibbutz also showed notable attachments to their metapelet; 53 percent of infants were classified as securely attached to the caregiver (Sagi et al., 1985).

KEY THEME
Sociocultural Influence

Observations of infants in Germany show a different pattern of results. In one study, about 49 percent of infants were scored as avoidantly attached (Grossmann et al., 1985). As in the Ainsworth studies, these researchers noted a relationship between maternal sensitivity and infant attachment: securely attached infants had mothers who interacted with them in a warm, responsive manner. However, although mothers varied in the sensitivity of responding when infants were two months of age, they did not vary by the time the infants were ten months old; most mothers had *low* sensitivity ratings by this time. Grossmann and her colleagues interpreted their findings in the context of the different attitudes toward child rearing held by parents in Germany and the United States. The emphasis in German culture is on fostering independence in one's offspring, encouraging the development of an obedient child who does not make demands on the parents. Responding to the infant's every cry is considered inappropriate. Thus, German mothers' tendency to pick up their children less frequently and for shorter periods of time and to display less affection reflects the goals of socialization in that culture.

Finally, a recent study of Dogon mothers and infants in northwestern Africa found that, although infants assessed in the Strange Situation fell into the secure attachment category at the same rate as Western samples, no infants were classified as avoidant. Recall that in North America about 20 percent of infants are avoidant.

The researchers attribute the results to the fact that Dogon mothers feed their infants on demand, responding immediately to their infants' cries of hunger and distress. The high degree of responsiveness of mothers, say the researchers, makes avoidant behavior highly unlikely (True, Pisani, & Oumar, 2001).

Taken together, these studies suggest that the central ideas of attachment theory hold up under a wide variety of cultural circumstances. They show, in particular, that the mother's sensitivity and responsiveness is indeed related to the type of attachment style the infant displays. Yet some researchers caution that the Strange Situation may not take into account specific cultural practices as they relate to separation of the mother and infant. In Japan, for example, mothers and infants are rarely apart from one another, and infants respond with distress when the mother departs and then returns as part of the Strange Situation. Infants may be classified as insecure when they are really just responding to a breech of cultural practice (Takahashi, 1990). More broadly, say the critics, theorists need to consider the goals of socialization in a particular culture; not all cultures may value the emergence of independence and exploration as we do in our culture. Nor do all cultures define maternal sensitivity and responsiveness in the same way. Thus attachment should be studied within the context of a particular culture's belief systems and practices (Rothbaum et al., 2000).

● **Child Care and Attachment**   One of the most difficult decisions many parents face concerns alternative child care arrangements when they work. As Table 11.2 shows, almost 70 percent of mothers with preschool-age children work, and almost 60 percent of women with infants under one year of age are employed (U.S. Bureau of the Census, 2001). In fact, this latter group represents the fastest growing category of women in the labor force. A substantial number of children are therefore receiving nonparental care, many beginning very early in life. Does this form of early experience influence the formation of attachments?

One problem in answering this question is that many variables operate when the child receives nonparental care. Is it the mother's absence or the quality of substitute care that produces any observable effects on child behavior? These two factors are difficult to separate. Does it matter whether the child receives full-time or part-time care? Perhaps, but the tremendous variation in caregiving schedules has made this factor difficult to control in research studies. In addition, the kinds of alternative care children receive vary a great deal, ranging from a single caregiver coming to the home to out-of-home family daycare in which another parent provides care for several children to center-based care.

Studies conducted in the 1980s suggested that children in daycare behaved differently than home-reared children on some components of the Strange Situation. Although daycare children showed similar patterns of separation anxiety when the mother departed, a sizable minority showed avoidant responses when reunited with their mothers (Clarke-Stewart & Fein, 1983). This pattern was especially true for infants who received more than twenty hours per week of nonmaternal care, although even among this group over 50 percent of infants formed secure attachments (Belsky & Rovine, 1988). The most recent information, though, shows that early daycare experiences do not put children at risk for insecure attachments. In a major study involving more than one thousand infants attending ten centers, researchers found that children who attended daycare did not differ from home-reared children in their behaviors during reunions with their mothers and in overall attachment security. In addition, age at which daycare began, the amount of weekly time spent in daycare, the quality of care, and the type of care (e.g., home with a relative, home with a non-relative, center-based care) did not influence children's attachments in infancy or during the preschool years. There were some conditions under which insecure attachments were more likely, however: when maternal insensitivity co-occurred with extensive or poor quality child care. In these cases, children were particularly at risk for ambivalent attachments (NICHD Early Child Care Research Network, 1997; 2001).

Age of Child	Percentage of Women in the Labor Force		
	1975	*1985*	*2000*
Under 18	44.9	60.8	70.6
Under 6, total	36.7	53.4	62.8
Under 3	32.7	50.5	59.0
1 year or under	30.8	49.4	58.3
2 years	37.1	54.0	61.9
3–5 years	42.2	58.4	68.4
6–13 years	51.8	68.2	75.8
14–17 years	53.5	67.0	80.6

Source: Data from U.S. Bureau of the Census, 2001.

TABLE 11.2
Labor Force Participation Rates for Women with Children Under Age 18

This table shows the percentage of women with children under age eighteen who are employed outside the home (the table shows only the data for married women whose husbands are present in the home). The participation rates for this group of women have grown rapidly since 1975, especially for those with children age one year and under.

A recent study conducted in Australia reiterates that what is important is the attitude and behaviors of the mother. The researchers found that mothers who returned to work by the time an infant was five months of age and who were committed to combining their roles as mothers with their work roles were more likely to have secure infants. These mothers, as it turned out, were also less anxious about child care and were more sensitive in their parenting styles (Harrison & Ungerer, 2002). Taken together, the studies on child care and attachment indicate that what matters most is the context in which child care is taking place—the emotional climate that parents create in the home and the quality of the interactions infants have with their parents.

Disruptions in Attachment

In some contexts, the ideal pattern of caregiver-child interaction may be disrupted, for example, when mother and infant are physically separated during the early days of their partnership due to the infant's premature birth or when the child is placed for adoption and nonbiological parents assume the caregiving role. Other children are the victims of physical abuse or neglect. Is there any evidence that attachments suffer in such cases? A consideration of these issues will further illuminate the ways in which early caregiver-child relationships influence subsequent child development.

● **Prematurity**   The preterm infant looks and behaves differently from the infant with the benefit of a full thirty-eight weeks in utero. In all likelihood, the premature infant will be very small and fragile looking, less alert and responsive to stimulation, and more difficult to comfort. Cries, but not smiles, are very frequent (Goldberg, 1979). In addition, mothers and their premature infants usually are separated physically, sometimes for several weeks, while the babies receive the medical care necessary to ensure their well-being and even survival. If attachments were based largely on mutually rewarding infant-caregiver interactions, we might expect premature infants to develop insecure attachments with their mothers.

In the hospital nursery, mothers of premature infants indeed behave in a markedly different manner than mothers of full-term infants do. Mothers of premature babies touch, hold, and smile at their babies less often than do mothers of full-term infants (DiVitto & Goldberg, 1979). As their babies get older, however, mothers of premature infants actually become more active than mothers of full-term babies in stimulating them: They initiate and maintain more interactions, even to the point of being excessive. These behaviors may stem from the mother's desire to alter the premature's unresponsive pattern or to stimulate the child in an effort to spur slowed development. As Figure 11.6 shows, infants often react to these maternal behaviors by averting their gaze, as though to shut out the added stimulation (Field, 1977, 1982).

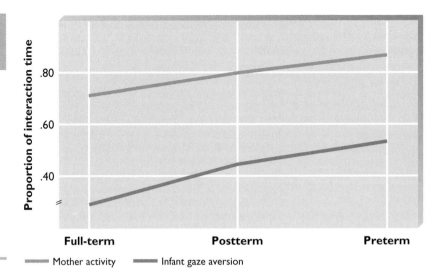

FIGURE 11.6
Maternal Interactions
with Premature Babies

After an initial period of inactivity following the births of their children, mothers of premature infants become more active in their exchanges with their infants than mothers of full- and postterm infants. At the same time, premature babies display more gaze aversion, as though they are seeking to terminate their mothers' overstimulation.

Source: Adapted from Field, 1982.

Given the differences in maternal styles with premature babies, is there a corresponding impact on the attachments of these infants? In a comparison of twenty full-term and twenty premature infants at eleven months of age, Ann Frodi and Ross Thompson (1985) observed no significant differences in the patterns of attachments. Most of the children in both groups were observed to be securely attached. By one year of age, many premature infants "rebound" from the negative effects of early birth, especially if they encounter a responsive, supportive environment. Mothers may also adapt their styles in later months to conform more closely with the rhythms and needs of the child. Thus the early developmental risk posed by prematurity does not automatically lead to persistent problems in mother-child relations or other developmental patterns. On the other hand, very-low-birthweight infants—those under 1,250 grams—have been found to be at risk for insecure attachments at nineteen months of age (Mangelsdorf et al., 1996). These infants in particular may present greater stresses and challenges for their caregivers.

● Adoption and Foster Care By the time they reach middle childhood and adolescence, adopted children show a noticeably higher incidence of psychological and academic problems compared with nonadopted children (Brodzinsky et al., 1984; Fergusson, Lynskey, & Horwood, 1995; Sharma, McGue, & Benson, 1998). They are at greater risk for substance abuse, health problems, emotional distress, and fighting (B. C. Miller et al., 2000). Because most adoptions involve the separation of the child from the biological parent during infancy, the disruption of the attachment process may be a factor.

KEY THEME
Continuity/Discontinuity

Investigations of this issue showed that separation of the infant from the biological parents at six to seven months of age can produce socioemotional difficulties even ten years later, particularly in the child's ability to form relationships with others (Yarrow et al., 1973). Separation at an earlier age, however, may have a lesser impact. When Leslie Singer and her colleagues assessed the attachments of adopted and nonadopted infants between thirteen and eighteen months of age, they found no difference in the classifications of attachments between these two groups (Singer et al., 1985). Most of the infants fell into the securely attached category. In this group, most of the adoptive placements had occurred at fairly early ages, the majority by three months of age. At this age children have not yet developed the early manifestations of attachment, such as stranger and separation anxiety. It is also important to keep in mind that maternal sensitivity is important for adopted children, just as it is for biological caregivers and their infants. In a recent Dutch study of 146 children adopted before six months of age, maternal sensitive responsiveness—more than such factors as the child's temperament or gender—predicted better cognitive and social functioning when these children were seven years old (Stams, Juffer, & van IJzendoorn, 2002).

Although the studies of adoption generally suggest that early placement is better for children than later placement, the findings on the importance of caregiver sensitivity have relevance for another group of children who experience disrupted relationships with their biological parents—foster children. Mary Dozier and her colleagues (Dozier et al., 2001) found that infants placed in foster homes at age eighteen months can still develop secure attachments provided that their caregivers both value relationships and had strong attachments to their own parents. This pattern occurred even if the infants had experienced neglect, physical abuse, and frequent turnover in caregivers. These data speak to the remarkable resilience of young children when they are provided with loving, nurturant homes.

● **Abuse**   Physically or psychologically abused children are at risk for an assortment of cognitive and socioemotional difficulties. Because the trauma that accompanies within-family violence can be enduring, especially with repeated episodes of abuse, it is not surprising that attachments between abused children and their parents take on an aberrant character.

Infants and toddlers who have been maltreated by their caregivers are likely to fall into the category of insecure attachment, called *disorganized/disoriented attachment*. Approximately 80 percent of maltreated infants fit this attachment profile (Carlson et al., 1989; Cicchetti, Toth, & Lynch, 1995). Like other attachment categories, the disorganized/disoriented pattern may predict later developmental outcomes. In one study, 71 percent of preschoolers who showed high levels of hostile behavior toward peers had been categorized as having disorganized attachments during infancy (Lyons-Ruth, Alpern, & Repacholi, 1993). In another, researchers found that when children with disorganized/disoriented attachments were six years old, they tended to be depressed, disorganized in behavior, and even self-destructive in response to questions about their parents or family life (Main et al.,1985). Disorganized children also tend to express more anger over time (Kochanska, 2001).

Why do these maladaptive attachments form? Abusive parents tend to react negatively to many of their children's social signals, even positive ones. When Ann Frodi and Michael Lamb (1980) observed the reactions of abusive and nonabusive mothers to videotapes of smiling and crying infants, abusive mothers were more aroused physiologically by both cries and smiles than were nonabusive mothers and were less willing to interact with an infant, even a smiling one. These findings suggest, at the very least, that the abused infant has an unwilling and psychologically distant interaction partner. In addition, mothers of disorganized/disoriented children tend to be intrusive and insensitive in their parenting styles independent of the temperamental characteristics of their children (Carlson, 1998).

Studies of premature and adopted children reveal that secure attachment relationships can develop in circumstances that are less than optimal during the early part of infancy. At the same time, however, when interactions between caregivers and infants deviate too widely from the ideal, especially in terms of the emotional tone of interactions, the consequences for the child can be serious and enduring.

● **Early Emotional Experiences and the Brain**   One of the most valuable outcomes of the studies that have been conducted on disrupted infant-caregiver attachments has been an accumulating appreciation for the role of early experiences in children's emotional lives. Recent physiological evidence suggests that changes in the functioning of the nervous system may accompany early social-emotional

WHAT DO YOU THINK?

Should a Child's Age Be Considered in Custody Cases?
psychology.college.hmco.com

KEY THEME

Interaction Among Domains

interactions and, furthermore, that the first two to three years of life may represent a critical period in laying down the "hard-wiring" of emotional responding.

One physiological system that has been examined is the action of the stress hormone *cortisol*. Researchers have observed that infants with a tendency to be fearful, inhibited, or angry sometimes show elevation of the amount of cortisol in their saliva, reflecting their experience of stress (Stansbury & Gunnar, 1994). In one study, though, inhibited infants with secure attachments did not show these typical elevations when confronted with fear-provoking stimuli, as indicated in Figure 11.7 (Nachmias et al., 1996). In contrast, inhibited infants who were insecurely attached did show a rise in levels of cortisol. Because these data are correlational, the usual precautions about interpreting the results apply. Nonetheless, there are some interesting potential implications of studies such as this one. Cortisol is released by the adrenal glands and can influence the hippocampus (which is involved in learning and memory), the frontal areas of the brain, and portions of the limbic system (connected with emotional responding). In animals, excessive exposure to cortisol results in the death of neurons and the atrophy of dendrites. Although the impact of too much exposure to cortisol on the human brain has not yet been studied directly, one implication is that early and prolonged exposure to stress can have negative consequences on the structure of important brain systems. Healthy attachments, however, might buffer those effects (Gunnar, 1998; Gunnar & White, 2001).

Another biochemical substance, the neurotransmitter norepinephrine, has also been implicated in early emotional development. Infant monkeys deprived of contact with their mothers show depressed levels of norepinephrine. Similarly, emotionally disturbed children who have suffered neglect show lower levels of norepinephrine than children not neglected (Rogeness & McClure, 1996). Researchers are beginning to explore the relationship of attachment with this biochemical system as well (Nelson & Panksepp, 1998).

We now know that many of the brain systems involved in emotional responding—the hippocampus, the amygdala, and the prefrontal cortex—are malleable and plastic in early infancy. Because of their malleability, they may be especially vulnerable to the differing types of emotional experiences, positive and negative,

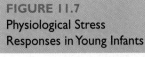

KEY THEME
Continuity/Discontinuity

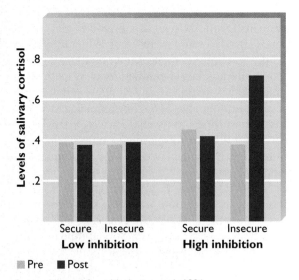

FIGURE 11.7
Physiological Stress Responses in Young Infants

In a study in which inhibited and uninhibited eighteen-month-olds were exposed to stressful situations (e.g., a noisy mechanical robot), inhibited children showed elevated levels of the stress hormone cortisol, but only if they were insecurely attached. The lightly shaded bars represent baseline levels of cortisol in the saliva prior to the fearful situation, and the darkly shaded bars represent levels of cortisol after the fearful event. These findings suggest that secure attachments might buffer the physiological stress responses of inhibited children.

Source: Adapted from Nachmias et al., 1996.

to which children are exposed (Post & Weiss, 1997). Given these findings, it is vital that researchers continue to explore the role that early emotional experiences play in development.

FOR YOUR REVIEW

- What theoretical perspectives have influenced our understanding of attachment?

- What changes in attachment behaviors are typically seen over the course of development? Which behaviors are special hallmarks of attachment?

- How is attachment accessed in young children? What categories are used to classify children?

- What factors have been shown to promote secure attachments?

- What are the consequences of attachment styles for later development?

- How are attachment behaviors similar or different across cultures? What is the significance of these findings?

- What is the impact of child care on attachment?

- What do the cases of prematurity, adoption, and abuse tell us about the concept of attachment?

- What is the relationship between early emotional experiences and the development of the brain?

CHAPTER RECAP

SUMMARY OF DEVELOPMENTAL THEMES

■ **Nature/Nurture** *What roles do nature and nurture play in emotional development?*

As has been stressed throughout this chapter, both nature and nurture contribute to the child's emotional development. Biology assumes a larger role in the child's early emotional capacities, for example, in the infant's ability to express and detect basic emotions such as joy and sadness. However, socialization and cognitive development become more prominent explanations for later emotional expression, particularly for self-conscious emotions such as guilt and envy. Ethologists and child temperament researchers also maintain that nature guides the formation of attachments between children and caregivers, but other researchers suggest that qualities of parenting style are equally important.

■ **Sociocultural Influence** *How does the sociocultural context influence emotional development?*

Different cultures place varying emphasis on emotionality itself and on the specific emotions considered appropriate to display. For example, Chinese infants smile and cry less than American infants. A culture's beliefs and values also can influence the child's responses in the Strange Situation. For example, Japanese children are more frequently classified as insecurely attached, but their behavior may simply reflect a response to changes in normative cultural practice.

■ **Child's Active Role** *How does the child play an active role in the process of emotional development?*

The child is hardly passive in the construction of his or her emotional repertoire. There are numerous examples of how the child plays an active role in emotional development, including the phenomenon of social referencing, the infant's role in producing interactive synchrony with the caregiver, and the role of the child's temperament in the formation of attachments.

■ **Continuity/Discontinuity** *Is emotional development continuous or discontinuous?*

Attachment patterns established during the first year of life endure for relatively long periods of time and forecast many desirable developmental outcomes. Thus many researchers believe that infancy is a sensitive period for the formation of attachments. Studies of adopted children in particular suggest that better socioemotional outcomes result when infants are placed with their adoptive parents prior to age six months.

■ **Individual Differences** *How prominent are individual differences in emotional development?*

Individual differences are especially evident in the enduring emotional moods infants and children display. For example, children may be "easy," "difficult," or "slow to warm up" in temperament or may display inhibited or uninhibited styles. These relatively stable individual differences may affect how parents and others react to the child and, in turn, influence other developmental outcomes such as attachment.

■ Interaction Among Domains   *How does emotional development interact with development in other domains?*

Emotions are closely intertwined with both cognition and social behavior. On the one hand, cognitive achievements, such as the ability to interpret social and personal experiences, lay the groundwork for advances in attachment and emotional expression. Similarly, children often learn about emotions through social experiences, such as interactions with their caregivers. On the other side of the equation, successful emotional development in the form of attachment is associated with positive social and cognitive achievements later in childhood. Children who are skilled at understanding, expressing, and regulating emotions also have better relations with their peers.

▮ Summary of Topics

What Are Emotions?

■ *Emotions* are a complex set of behaviors produced in response to some event; they motivate action.

■ Emotions have physiological, expressive, and experiential components.

The Functions of Emotions

■ Emotions can regulate overt actions, influence cognitive processing, and, most important, initiate, maintain, or terminate social interactions with others.

Measuring Emotions

■ Because of their varied dimensions, emotions can be measured in an assortment of ways. Physiological measures (such as heart rate, EEGs, and fMRI), analyses of observed facial expressions, and self-report measures have all been used to study emotions.

Theoretical Perspectives on Emotional Development

■ Ekman and Izard believe that emotions are biologically based. Cross-cultural similarities in the recognition of emotion expressions and the display by young infants of basic emotions (such as joy and disgust) are consistent with a biological point of view.

■ Cognitive-socialization theorists such as Lewis and Michalson emphasize the child's knowledge about the appropriate times and ways of expressing emotions. This knowledge is gleaned from socialization experiences.

■ Social-contextual theorists such as Campos and Saarni believe that emotions must be understood as processes embedded in social interactions. The positive or negative tone of emotions and their intensity, rather than categories of discrete emotions, are emphasized.

Expressing, Understanding, and Regulating Emotions

Early Emotional Development

■ *Basic emotions*, such as joy, sadness, and surprise, are observed in infants from birth.

■ The forms of emotional expressions, such as smiling and crying, change over the first year. Smiling shifts from a reflex-like behavior to a controlled, voluntary response important to social interactions with the caregiver. Crying changes from a way of expressing physical needs to include demands for objects and actions.

■ Young infants can discriminate and imitate basic facial expressions.

■ *Social referencing*, looking to another individual for emotional cues on how to act, indicates that the infant interprets emotional expressions as having meaning.

■ Infants' emotional expressions often co-occur in a synchronous manner with those of caregivers in a dynamic called *interactive synchrony*. Infants may learn important lessons about the rules of interaction and the ability to regulate interactions in the context of these, as well as of asynchronous interactions, as studies of depressed mothers and their infants show.

Later Emotional Development

■ Starting in the preschool years, children show *self-conscious emotions* such as shame, guilt, and jealousy.

■ Preschoolers begin to understand many of the situations that give rise to specific emotions and the consequences of displaying them. School-age children begin to appreciate cultural *display rules* that dictate when and how emotions should be displayed. They also understand that they can control emotions with their own thoughts and that sometimes two emotions can be experienced simultaneously.

■ Knowledge about emotions has important ramifications for children's social development and is learned, at least in part, from interactions with parents. Parents who discuss and explain emotions and who display less negative affect themselves have children with greater understanding of emotions.

■ An important developmental achievement is the ability to regulate one's emotions. Infants and young children distract themselves to alleviate distress, and older children use their growing language skills to regulate themselves. The ability to regulate emotions predicts behavioral conduct and the quality of social relationships later in childhood. Here, too, parents who provide supportive guidance and positively toned interactions have children who are better able to regulate their own emotions.

- Adolescents experience more negative emotions and have more negative emotional interactions with their parents than children of other ages. For some, adolescence is a time of increased risk for depression.

Variations in Emotional Development

Temperament

- *Temperament* is a style of behavioral functioning that may include intensity of reactions, distractibility, adaptability, and persistence. Different temperament categories include the easy, difficult, and slow-to-warm-up styles identified by Chess and Thomas, the inhibited versus uninhibited styles researched by Kagan and his colleagues, and the dimensions of reactivity and self-regulation focused on by Rothbart and her colleagues.

- Children with different temperament styles show differences in physiological responses such as heart rate, EEG patterns, and cardiac vagal tone. Thus there is reason to believe that biology plays some part in temperament.

- Early temperament styles predict social behaviors, peer relations, and cognitive functioning later in development.

Sex Differences in Emotions

- Among school-age children, girls are more emotionally expressive and more attuned to emotions than are boys. Research suggests that although a biological explanation cannot be ruled out, many of these sex differences may be modeled by or learned from parents.

Cultural Differences in Emotions

- Different cultures encourage the expression of some emotions over others, depending on the broader values and belief systems they hold. They may also value some temperament styles over others and vary in the degree to which they expose children to emotional situations.

Attachment: Emotional Relationships with Others

- *Attachment* is the strong emotional bond that emerges between infant and caregiver.

The Origins of Attachment: Theoretical Perspectives

- Learning theory has emphasized the mother's association with feeding (a *primary reinforcer*) and other activities the infant finds pleasurable. As a result of this association, she is said to acquire *secondary reinforcing* attributes. Harlow's classic experiments with surrogate monkeys showed that contact comfort played a more important role in attachment than feeding did.

- Ethological theorists view attachment as an innate, adaptive phenomenon that promotes proximity between infant and caregiver and thus ensures the infant's survival.

- Bowlby believed that attachment emerges in a series of four phases during which the infant becomes increasingly emotionally connected with the caregiver. Several behaviors mark the child's emerging attachment to the caregiver at about six months of age. These include *separation anxiety*, *reunion behavior*, and *stranger anxiety*.

The Developmental Course of Attachment

- Research has confirmed the general chronology of attachment behaviors first outlined by Bowlby.

- Attachment is measured by observing the infant's responses to the *Strange Situation*, a standardized laboratory task that assesses the infant's use of the mother as a *secure base* for exploration; stranger anxiety; separation anxiety; and reunion behavior. The different attachment categories include *secure attachment* and three categories of insecure attachment—*avoidant*, *ambivalent* (or *resistant*), and *disorganized/disoriented* attachment.

- Several variables predict the formation of secure attachments, including the sensitivity and responsiveness of the caregiver, the synchrony of child-caregiver interactions, and the temperament of the child. Fathers who are high on sensitivity and responsiveness are fully capable of being the objects of attachment.

- Security of attachment predicts a number of important developmental outcomes, including cognitive performance, social competence, and high self-esteem.

- The child's *internal working models of relationships*, derived from his or her attachment relationship, can forecast the nature of other close relationships later in life, such as close friendships and parenthood.

- Although the proportion of infants placed into the various attachment categories can vary cross-culturally, these studies still confirm that maternal sensitivity is an important factor in the emergence of secure attachment. However, it is important to consider the goals of socialization in a particular culture as attachment concepts are applied in different cultural contexts.

- The most recent data show that, in general, early experiences in child care do not lead to disruptions in attachment. Rather, it is important to consider the emotional climate of the home and the quality of interactions parents and infants have when both parents work.

Disruptions in Attachment

- Studies of premature infants, adoptees, foster children, and abused children indicate that attachments can form under less than optimal circumstances but that extreme deviations in caregiver-child interaction patterns can have serious negative consequences for the child.

- There is growing evidence to suggest that early emotional experiences are linked to changes in the underlying physiology of the central nervous system. Changes in the action of cortisol and neurotransmitters have been observed in young organisms that experience prolonged early stress.

CHAPTER 12
Self and Values

Key Themes in Self and Values

■ **Nature/Nurture** What roles do nature and nurture play in the development of the self and of values?

■ **Sociocultural Influence** How does the sociocultural context influence the development of the self and of values?

■ **Child's Active Role** How does the child play an active role in the development of the self and of values?

■ **Continuity/Discontinuity** Is the development of the self and of values continuous or discontinuous?

■ **Individual Differences** How prominent are individual differences in the development of the self and of values?

■ **Interaction Among Domains** How does the development of the self and of values interact with development in other domains?

Michael had just finished his math assignment when he heard the door slam. Then he heard the loud, angry voice. "Kids today!" his grandfather fumed to no one in particular. "A couple of 'em almost ran me down on the sidewalk. Didn't bother to apologize. One even yelled, 'Get out of my way!' as she chased after her friends. Kids don't respect anybody, not even themselves—wearing those weird clothes, dying their hair every color you can think of, poking holes in their ears, even their noses! I suppose if I had stopped 'em, they'd have taken a swing at me or even worse. . . ." His voice trailed off to a mutter.

Michael had heard such tirades before: how the world has changed, how young people today do not know right from wrong, how they are just plain troublemakers. Michael also worried about reports on the news: the first-grader who punched his teacher, the large number of sixth-graders who felt cheating was okay, the junior high students suspended for bringing knives and guns to school, and the shootings.

Did his grandfather have a valid point? Just what values do young people have today?

To instill in children a sense of satisfaction with who they are and to recognize the standards of conduct considered acceptable and ethical within their community are among the most important goals of society. We expect children and adults to take pride in their accomplishments, learn to judge right from wrong, and refrain from actions that harm family, friends, or neighbors. Broadly speaking, survival in a social community depends on helping, cooperation, and sharing, behaviors that benefit others. Children display an awareness of self and the consequences of their conduct, both good and bad, early on, but these understandings undergo noticeable changes with development.

Michael's grandfather believes his generation has witnessed a decline in a positive sense of self and in courtesy and concern for others. Although one might debate whether such a change has actually taken place, the concerns voiced by Michael's grandfather are not new. Philosophers, theologians, and scientists have argued for decades about whether human nature is good or evil and whether experience serves to channel children's inborn tendencies in either direction. In this sense, the nature-nurture debate remains embedded in contemporary discussions of the roots of self, moral behavior, and values. In this chapter, we look first at the nature of "self" and how it relates to self-esteem and identity. We consider too how self-regulation and self-control contribute to our development. We then examine several theories of moral development. Finally, we look at how and to what extent society promotes the development of prosocial values.

The Concept of Self

"I know how."

"Look! See what I did!"

"I'm smart."

"I'm stronger than you!"

"I'm really good at this!"

These declarations express in no uncertain terms what children believe they can do, what they think they are like, and how they feel about their abilities. The statements reveal the child's awareness of self. How does this understanding of **self**—as someone who is an independent, unique person, able to reflect on his or her own beliefs and characteristics—develop?

To answer this question, it will be useful to adopt a distinction first offered by William James (1892) more than a century ago. The distinction continues to be every bit as useful today (Harter, 1999). For James, there were two components of self: the "me," or *objective self*, and the "I," or *subjective self*. James's objective, or the "me" aspect of self, is often called *self-concept*. An individual's self-concept includes an understanding of his or her physical qualities, possessions and status, skills, and psychological characteristics, including personality, beliefs, and value systems.

The "I," or the subjective component, is made up of several key realizations about the self: (1) I can be an agent of change and can control events in my life (sense of autonomy); (2) my experiences are unique and accessible to no one else in exactly the same way (sense of individuality); (3) my past, present, and future are continuous (sense of stability); and (4) I can reflect on, that is, think about, my self (sense of reflection, or self-consciousness). All contribute to the sense of the subjective "I."

Self as Object

Self as object, the **self-concept,** consists of the unique set of traits and characteristics an individual holds to be true about himself or herself. The seeds of such awareness already may be sown in the infant's recognition of how his own body movements take place. For example, the attentional preferences of babies as young as three months suggest that they recognize when left and right position and movements of their legs, viewed on videotape, are inverted (Rochat & Morgan, 1995, 1998). Other research reveals that infants recognize their own voices, faces, and body movements as different from those of others, suggesting the origins of a rudimentary understanding of self as separate and distinct from other people and objects well before the end of the first year (Legerstee, Anderson, & Schaffer, 1998; Rochat & Striano, 2002; Tomasello, 1995). These capacities very likely serve as precursors to the representation of self as object. *Self-awareness*, however, is usually said to begin with the child's ability to declare or indicate in a fairly specific way, "That's me!" When do young children have this "idea of me"?

● **Self-recognition**   The household mirror has become a helpful research tool in answering the question of when self-recognition emerges. A toddler younger than fifteen to eighteen months shows little evidence of recognizing herself in a mirror. How do we know? If a spot of rouge, for example, is placed surreptitiously on her nose, it is not until she is older than this age that she will touch or rub her nose while looking in the mirror. Such behavior suggests that she has formed a concept of the details that ordinarily make up her appearance. In just a few more months she will also say, "That's me" when asked, "Who's that?" as she stares at a picture or a reflection of herself. Moreover, this self-recognition emerges about the same time in children from widely varying backgrounds (Cicchetti et al., 1997).

The implications of becoming aware of physical appearance can be enormous. For one thing, it may signal the appearance of self-conscious emotions, such as embarrassment, shame, and pride, that emerge in toddlers, as we saw in the discussion of

In touching her nose while looking in the mirror, this eighteen-month-old illustrates one way a toddler tells us something about the knowledge she has about herself. After having a small spot of rouge surreptitiously placed on the tip of her nose, she seems to be indicating by touching her nose that the reflection is of "me." Before about fifteen to eighteen months of age, children typically do not respond to their reflections in the mirror because they still have a very limited understanding of self.

self   Realization of being an independent, unique, stable, and self-reflective entity; the beliefs, knowledge, feelings, and characteristics the individual ascribes to himself or herself.

self-concept   Perceptions, conceptions, and values one holds about oneself.

emotional development in the chapter titled "Emotion" (Lewis et al., 1989). For another, self-recognition seems to develop hand in hand with a growing awareness of others as distinct individuals. For example, a toddler who displays self-recognition on the mirror task also is likely to attend to a partner of a similar age and to encourage that child to play with matching toys, an indication of increased interest in sharing and enjoyment of the other child's activities (Asendorpf & Baudonnière, 1993). Thus, at a very young age, children have begun to unwrap a major piece of the total package of their self-concept, the first of many steps in the development of their identities.

● **Self-definition**   A self-concept consists of much more than appearance. If asked to answer the question "Who are you?" a preschooler might say, "I'm a boy. I'm strong. I know the letters of the alphabet. I like pizza. I live with my mother and father. I go to nursery school." Thus, during the preschool years, knowledge of self extends beyond physical features to include activities the child likes and is good at, his possessions, and his relationships to others. In defining themselves, children at this age commonly establish a **categorical self,** that is, classify themselves in terms of membership in certain groups based on their sex, age, skills, what they own, where they live, and who their friends are.

Are very young children also aware of having psychological and social attributes? As we pointed out in the chapter titled "Cognition: Piaget and Vygotsky," preschoolers know quite a bit about their own mental activities. They possess knowledge of themselves that goes beyond appearance and actions. Thus responses such as "I have a friend" or "I'm a happy person" are among their self-descriptions. Preschoolers consistently select self-statements that reflect moods, feelings, achievements, and other psychological and social orientations. Self as object, as *me,* even for a young child, includes a sense of a psychological and social being (Damon & Hart, 1988; Harter, 1999).

Between five and seven years of age children increasingly coordinate the attributes they apply to themselves (Harter, 1999). When children reach about seven years of age, a new element enters their self-descriptions. Whereas younger children describe themselves in terms of typical categorical activities ("I run fast"), older children begin to make relational statements. For example, in response to the question "Who are you?" a fifth-grader might say, "I can run faster than anyone else in my class," "I'm not as pretty as my older sister," or "Other kids in my class are better than I am at math." Instead of itemizing their skills, actions, or social and psychological qualities, they compare their qualities with those of others (Ruble, 1983; Harter, 1999).

As children become older, they view self in terms of more abstract and increasingly differentiated qualities (Harter & Monsour, 1992); thus a global notion of self fails to capture the full complexity of this concept. Even preschool children have some understanding of domain-specific representations (DesRosiers et al., 1999; Marsh, Ellis, & Craven, 2002), but during the elementary school years children effectively distinguish self in terms of, for example, academic abilities, physical appearance, behavioral conduct, social skills, and athletic competence (Cole et al., 2001; Hymel et al., 1999).

Self tends to be evaluated very highly by preschoolers and somewhat less positively in the early elementary school years, as children acquire a better understanding of their limitations and strengths at that time. Their self-concepts show some positive increases in most domains in the later elementary school years but then tend to dip again as they enter the adolescent years. Moreover, gender differences exist in how favorable these different domains of self are perceived, as can be seen in Figure 12.1. In addition, the emphasis on portraying different domains of self increasingly focuses on the implications of those domains for social relationships. The change is evident in such responses from young adolescents as, "I play sports . . . because all the kids like athletes" and "I'm an honest person . . . people trust me because of it" (Damon & Hart, 1988).

During adolescence, self also begins to be viewed from multiple or even opposing perspectives. Susan Harter (1986) asked whether someone can have both positive and negative qualities. Can a person be both "smart" and "dumb" or "nice" and "nasty"? She found a substantial increase in the belief in this possibility between the

KEY THEME
Interaction Among Domains

categorical self Conceptual process, starting in the early preschool years, in which the child begins to classify himself or herself according to easily observable categories such as sex, age, or physical capacities.

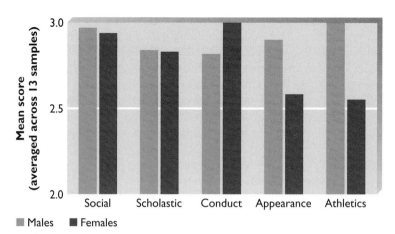

FIGURE 12.1
Evaluations of Self as
a Function of Gender

The different domains of self
are not always evaluated
equally. Females consistently
give less favorable ratings (on a
4-point scale) to their appearance and to their athletic ability
than do males. These data have
been averaged over thirteen
different studies carried out
by Susan Harter with children
from elementary school through
high school (Harter, 1999). In
addition, research cited by
Harter (1999) and carried out
by others in England, Ireland,
Australia, and many non-English
speaking countries, including
Switzerland, Italy, Holland,
China, Japan, and Korea, reveals
a similar pattern of findings.

Source: Harter, 1999, p. 131.

KEY THEME
Sociocultural Influence

seventh and ninth grades. The number of opposite perspectives, and concerns about
feeling confused or bothered by qualities of self that conflict when, for example, interacting with parents, with friends, in a romantic relationship, or as a member of the
classroom, become greatest during middle adolescence, as Figure 12.2 indicates
(Harter & Monsour, 1992).

The impetus for conflicting selves may arise from a desire to impress or gain increased acceptance or simply as part of experimentation during the teenage years.
Under these circumstances, "false" selves appear to be a normal and even healthy aspect of development. However, if, as may be the case for some adolescents, the incon-
sistencies arise from a belief that approval is contingent on "showing different faces"
at the expense of one's true self, these conflicts may lead to more serious consequences, such as feeling depressed and confused about self (Harter et al., 1996). Fortunately, concerns about conflicting selves typically lessen for most adolescents as
adolescents become older and establish a higher order coherent picture of self based
on principled ideas and comprehensive plans that include a more extended future
and greater understanding of their strengths and limitations.

Can cultural, religious, and social class differences, which are highly laden with
values in their own right, influence the development of self-concepts? William Damon and Daniel Hart (1988) believe such influence is likely. In some societies, for example, possessions or membership in the family or a social group may be far more
important in determining perceptions of self than individual qualities, abilities, and
achievements (Levine & White, 1986). To illustrate their point, Damon and Hart
(1988) studied children living in a fishing village in Puerto Rico. The residents were
relatively poor and had few educational and social services available to them. Children typically attended school for no more than three or four years, and obtaining a
job often depended on a network of family and social relationships. Compared with
middle-income youngsters from mainland regions of the United States, Puerto Rican children voiced far more apprehension about whether their *behavior* was good
or bad than whether they were competent or talented. A twelve-year-old might say it
is important to be nice and respect people because misbehavior would mean "everybody will hit me and hate me or not help me." Compared with their mainland counterparts, Puerto Rican children consistently expressed greater concern about whether
others approved of their actions than about their relative competence with respect to
some skill or capacity.

In still other cultures that place greater emphasis on contributions to the collective
community than on individual accomplishments—for example, the Samoan society
and in many Asian countries—evaluations of self in terms of particular competencies
may not be seen as desirable. As a consequence, greater modesty is demanded in describing one's personal qualities. Because children's views of themselves are heavily

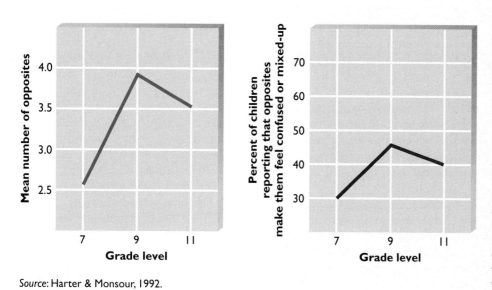

Source: Harter & Monsour, 1992.

FIGURE 12.2
Concerns About Opposing Attributes

From early to middle adolescence, students increasingly report conflicting descriptions of self that depend on whether their evaluations are framed within the perspective of classroom, friends, close relationships, or parents. Concerns about these conflicting views increase at the same time. However, both the number of opposite attributes assigned to self and concerns about their effects on defining self begin to decline in later adolescence, as young people establish a more integrated identity and recognize that contradictions may be normal and even of some value.

influenced by social structure and the expectations of the community, as well as styles of parenting and formal education, the picture of an emerging self in many societies may differ substantially from that typically observed in many Western nations.

● **Social Comparison**   During the early and middle school years, as we already indicated, children begin to reference others in describing themselves. Whether Jim feels he is nice or can run fast, or Ellen believes she is smart or throws a ball well, depends on how Jim or Ellen thinks he or she stacks up against agemates and friends. How important is this process, called **social comparison,** the tendency of people to use others as mirrors to evaluate their own abilities, interests, and values? The answer appears to be that it becomes increasingly important as children move through the elementary school years. For example, nine-year-olds who could not actually determine their success but were told they did better than, or not as well as, peers in a ball-throwing contest predicted future performance based on the feedback they received. If told they were successful, they expected to show continued superior ability; if told they were less successful, they expected to continue to perform more poorly than children who received no feedback. Five- and seven-year-olds, however, were unaffected by the information; they predicted they would do equally well, regardless of how they compared with others (Ruble et al., 1980).

Children, of course, observe things happening to others even in the preschool years. Two pieces of candy of unequal size shared between two four-year-olds can easily initiate conflict about who has the larger piece and is probably motivated by concerns about obtaining a fair share. And preschoolers are able to compare their performance to that of other children when asked to make judgments about a relatively simple task such as who drew a line farther within a winding path in a particular amount of time (Butler, 1998). At this age, however, observing others seems to be geared toward learning how to respond or to gain new skills for mastering a task (Butler, 1989; Ruble & Dweck, 1995).

In fact, young children frequently are unrealistic about their skills; they claim they will do far better than they actually can (Butler, 1990; Harter, 1999). Moreover, kindergartners rate themselves more positively than older children do and tend to ignore feedback to adjust their evaluations, particularly when information about failure is indicated (Ruble, Eisenberg, & Higgins, 1994). However, by attending to the attributes and qualities of others, children may gain a more realistic means of predicting how well they can do. For example, Diane Ruble (1987) found that children in kindergarten and first grade who more frequently made social comparisons involving achievement tended to have greater knowledge of their relative standing in the classroom.

KEY THEME
Child's Active Role

social comparison   Process in which individuals define themselves in relation to the skills, attributes, and qualities of others; an important contributor to self-concept during middle childhood.

This fifth-grade boy exhibits pride in the certificate of achievement he received as he describes his work on a project designed to save energy. Such positive feedback can play an important role in promoting continued academic effort. As he enters into and proceeds through the adolescent years, he will increasingly rely on his own standards for determining whether he has done a good job in the various activities he undertakes.

KEY THEME
Child's Active Role

KEY THEME
Nature/Nurture

effectance motivation Inborn desire theorized by Robert White to be the basis for the infant's and child's efforts to master and gain control of the environment.

Older school-age children engage in increasingly subtle, indirect social comparisons to determine how well they are doing, perhaps because more conspicuous forms of information gathering are perceived as inappropriate behaviors. For example, nine- or ten-year-olds are more likely than younger children to ask classmates, "What question are you on?" to assess their progress among peers (Pomerantz et al., 1995). On the other hand, the kind of educational environment in which children participate also influences this behavior. In Israel, for example, children in kibbutz schools, which place greater emphasis on cooperative activity than more traditional urban schools in that country, continue to be more likely to interpret glances among one another as efforts to increase mastery rather than as social comparisons (Butler & Ruzany, 1993).

As children approach the adolescent years and become more competent, they are less likely to look to others to evaluate how well they are doing; in some domains, such as academic achievement, they can use their own measures of performance on a task to judge success (Ruble & Flett, 1988). This may indicate an impending shift from social comparison to a more self-reliant and principled standard for evaluating self. This basis for a self-concept, rooted in internalized values and norms of mastery and competence, fits the criteria mature individuals use to evaluate their identities and often is observed in later adolescence and early adulthood. But throughout the early and middle adolescent years, concern with the views and expectations of others, especially peers, and in many cases parents and teachers, is far-reaching (Harter, 1999).

Self as Subject

Just as we can ask a child what she knows about her physical features or personal characteristics, so too can we ask whether she realizes that she influences and controls her surroundings, remains the same person over time, or is a unique individual. Such questions inquire about a child's understanding of her sense of agency or autonomy, individuality, and stability and her capacity to reflect on these abilities. What do children know about such matters?

● **The Sense of Agency**   The belief that a person can determine and influence his or her surroundings probably has its roots in infancy. Robert White (1959) suggested that babies are born with a desire to master their environment, an ambition he termed **effectance motivation.** The active infant repeatedly stacks blocks, bangs pots, smiles at caregivers, and plays peek-a-boo, activities that often lead to consequences that he anticipates. If he cries, he typically is picked up, rocked, and comforted. The one-year-old who says "Mama" or another new word often becomes the center of attention. From the feedback associated with these actions, infants may learn to expect outcomes and how to make them happen again. Eventually, they see themselves as being in control, capable of reaching desired goals, and having the means to do so as they interact with both their physical and social environments (Wachs & Combs, 1995). For example, when babies can make a mobile rotate rapidly by moving their heads on a pressure-sensitive pillow, they quickly learn to do so. But if their head movements on the pillow initially fail to have any consequences, they are far less likely to learn a contingency-related outcome when it is established (Watson, 1971; Watson & Ramey, 1972).

Many of the early accomplishments exhibited by infants are accompanied by positive emotional responses such as delight and laughter (Case, 1991; Harter, 1998). Toward the end of the first year and continuing into the second, children start to initiate efforts to share interesting sights and activities with caregivers and playmates, an important step in becoming aware of their ability to influence what others see and do. After about two years of age, many will protest the attempts of caregivers to help them in an activity such as dressing. Some researchers believe such protests further reveal an early desire to be an agent or to master an activity (Kagan, 1981; Lutkenhaus, Bullock, & Geppert, 1987). At about this same time, children also look to adults after completing a task as though to share their success or turn away and hunch their

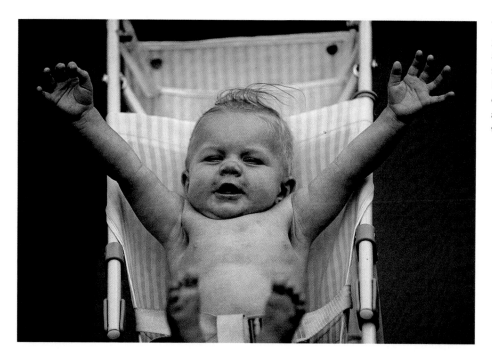

This infant may have already gained a rudimentary sense of agency. His outstretched arms seem to shout, "Pick me up!" His behavior illustrates one of the many ways even babies actively influence the things that happen to them.

shoulders after failure (Stipek, Recchia, & McClintic, 1992). The feedback mothers provide to two-year-olds following their efforts to solve a problem plays an important role in the way they subsequently respond to a challenging task. When mothers are more negative and critical, their children are increasingly likely to display shame in confronting a difficult problem as three-year-olds. When mothers are more supportive and provide a scaffold to assist in solving a problem, their children display greater persistence when confronted with an achievement-oriented task when they are older (Kelley, Brownell, & Campbell, 2000).

Children become increasingly sophisticated about how the world responds to their actions. For example, if asked, "How did you get to be the way you are?" a preschooler is likely to refer to uncontrollable factors ("I just grew . . . . My body just got bigger"), whereas a ten-year-old mentions her own efforts ("From getting good grades in school from studying"). By age thirteen, children also acknowledge the contributions of others to their sense of agency ("I learned from my parents, I even learned from friends, just listening to them and talking to them"). Older adolescents incorporate into their reasoning principled personal and moral qualities ("Well, I decided to be kind to people because I've seen lots of kids hurt other kids' feelings for no reason, and it's not right or fair") (Damon & Hart, 1988). Even in societies that have emphasized a more collective orientation, such as Russia, most children believe individual effort is an important aspect of achieving success and avoiding failure (Stetsenko et al., 1995). For example, elementary school children in Los Angeles, Tokyo, Berlin, Moscow, and Prague are in close agreement in their views that effort in particular, rather than other factors such as the teacher or luck or even ability, is the most important determinant of school performance (Little & Lopez, 1997).

Yet, within every community, individuals can differ substantially in their sense of self-determination and control. Some children are convinced that what happens to them depends on their actions, that their choices, decisions, and abilities govern whether outcomes are good or bad, successful or unsuccessful. When asked how to find a friend, such a child might say, "Go up to someone you like and ask them to play with you." When asked how to do well on a test, the child might answer, "Study for it and you'll get smarter!" Such children have a strong **mastery orientation,** a belief that success stems from trying hard; failures, these children presume, are conditions to be overcome by working more or by investing greater effort (Dweck & Elliott, 1983).

KEY THEME
Individual Differences

mastery orientation Belief that achievements are based on one's own efforts rather than on luck or other factors beyond one's control.

Positive feedback from a parent is an important element in a child's taking pride in her achievements. Even by helping out with routine chores, a child can gain a sense of mastery that generalizes to her efforts involving academic and other activities.

Other children, in contrast, believe luck, fate, or other people have an inordinate influence on what happens to them. When asked why he cannot catch a ball, such a child might say, "The others throw it too fast." When asked why he got a poor grade, he might say, "The teacher doesn't like me." His explanation for a good grade might be, "I was lucky." Such children often express little confidence in their ability and feel powerless to influence the future. They perceive themselves as being unable to achieve, perhaps because their efforts have not led to regular success. In place of a sense of mastery, they have a sense of **learned helplessness** (Dweck & Elliott, 1983).

These differing interpretations about success and failure are linked to another property of the belief system. To the extent that children think the characteristics they and others display are stable *entities*, that is, fixed or unchangeable qualities or traits such as being smart, friendly, or popular, the more vulnerable they are to a helpless orientation. As a consequence, when faced with a challenging situation, the focus tends to be on evaluating how well they perform or "measure up" rather than on what steps might be taken to improve their performance or activity. In contrast, when children hold beliefs that characteristics or traits of individuals are *incremental* or malleable and can therefore be changed, their focus in challenging situations is more likely to be directed toward learning procedures and strategies reflecting resilience and increased effort (Erdley et al., 1997; Heyman & Dweck, 1998). Why might this be so? If traits are seen as enduring characteristics, little can be done to change them; thus the child places greater emphasis on determining the degree to which he or she (and others) possesses them as indicated by *performance* on the problem or task. On the other hand, if traits are seen as temporary characteristics, then the child can focus on the processes required to improve on or modify them, that is, on better ways of *learning* the task or how to solve the problem (Dweck, 1999).

Differing beliefs about the degree to which traits are fixed or modifiable and the causes of success or failure have a powerful bearing on academic achievement, participation in athletics and other physical activities, efforts to establish social relationships, self-esteem, and career aspirations (Bandura et al., 2001; Chapman, Skinner, & Baltes, 1990; Heyman & Dweck, 1998). Children who display evidence of learned helplessness in school, for example, may be caught in a vicious cycle involving self-fulfilling anticipation of failure accompanied by excuses that they have little control over what happens to them (Bandura et al., 1996). They are especially likely to expect failure on tasks found difficult in the past and may avoid them when given further opportunity to work on them (Dweck, 1991; Erdley et al., 1997). Note that high abil-

learned helplessness   Belief that one has little control over situations, perhaps because of lack of ability or inconsistent outcomes.

ity is not the factor that determines a mastery orientation (Dweck, 1999). Deborah Phillips (1984) reported that nearly 20 percent of fifth-graders with high ability limit their goals and persistence in school activities. In the academic realm, this pattern occurs more frequently among girls than boys, perhaps because girls are more likely than boys to view their failures in terms of such uncontrollable factors as lack of ability (Crandall, 1969; Dweck, Goetz, & Strauss, 1980; Stipek & Hoffman, 1980).

A mastery-versus-helplessness orientation can be observed in kindergarteners and remains stable for up to five years (Ziegert et al., 2001). However, teachers can have an important influence on children's beliefs about their academic competence. When teachers provide a supportive, responsive learning environment, children come to believe that they have greater control over their understanding of academic materials and, as a consequence, become more actively engaged, as well as more successful in their efforts. Where learning environments are unsupportive, children are more likely to conclude that external factors are responsible for what happens, which, in turn, leads to less satisfaction and lower achievement in the classroom. Longitudinal data reveals that these differences in perceived control form a cyclic pattern of confidence and success that feed into and magnify individual differences in children's views of beliefs about their achievements and failures in the classroom (Skinner, Zimmer-Gembeck, & Connell, 1998).

RESEARCH APPLIED TO PARENTING

Preventing Learned Helplessness

The rule in Michael's house was that once homework was finished, the remaining time before bedtime was his to do with as he wished. He often played chess with his grandfather. This evening, however, his grandfather had become busy on another project. "Perhaps just as well," thought Michael as he reflected on the earlier exchange that had so angered his grandfather. Michael dialed his friend Jonathon. "Can you play some catch?" he queried when Jonathon answered the phone. "You must have finished your math already," Jonathon retorted. "I hate math, still have a lot more problems to do," he continued. But Michael quickly interjected, "You did really well on that last test." But before he could finish, Michael knew what Jonathon's reply would be: "I was lucky. The teacher asked the right questions. I wish I were good at math."

Children who gain little mastery over their environment or face conflicting and inconsistent reactions, such as those they might receive from abusive parents, are among the most likely to display learned helplessness. But even well-intentioned parents and teachers may unwittingly help to foster a sense of helplessness. For example, when parents generally believe they can promote their children's intellectual development, their children seem to benefit (Bandura et al., 1996). Moreover, the seeds of a sense of helplessness, Carol Dweck (1999) believes, are sown in preschoolers who tend to judge their performance on tasks as "good" or "bad." When the value of self becomes contingent on feeling worthy or unworthy, young children become especially vulnerable to learned helplessness.

A recent study conducted by Melissa Kamins and Carol Dweck (1999) provides some experimental evidence to indicate that certain types of feedback with respect to either criticism *or* praise can lead to a more helpless orientation when children are subsequently confronted with similar situations involving a setback. In this study five- and six-year-olds engaged in role-playing a series of four different stories that involved various tasks. In each of these tasks, children acted in the role of a doll, either making an error or completing the task successfully. At the end of each story the experimenter (who was engaged in role-playing as the teacher) provided one of three different types of feedback. When the task involved an error, the feedback from the "teacher" was directed either at the person (e.g., "I'm very disappointed in you"), at the outcome of the task ("That's not the right way to do it"), or at the process that

FIGURE 12.3
The Consequences of
Different Types of Feedback
for Learned Helplessness

When given praise or criticism
for their work on a task, children may hear comments that
are directed at them as a person ("good," "bad"), at the outcome ("right way to do it,"
"wrong way to do it"), or at
the process ("really tried
hard," "think of another way").
Hearing these different types
of feedback influences how children subsequently respond to a
setback on a similar task. Children who have heard person-
oriented feedback evaluate the
outcome of the new work less
positively (product rating),
view themselves has having
fewer positive abilities (self-
assessment), feel less happy
with themselves (affect), and
are less willing to continue
the activity (persistence) than
children who experience
process-oriented feedback and,
to a lesser extent, outcome-
oriented feedback. Moreover,
these kinds of responses are
produced even though errors
have not occurred in the previous tasks and children have
heard praise. The results suggest that the extent to which
children express a sense of
helplessness after experiencing
a setback is affected by the specific form of praise or criticism
they have heard in previous
similar situations.

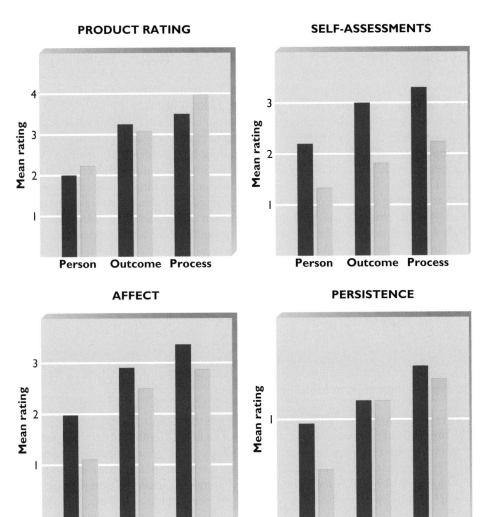

Source: Adapted from Kamins & Dweck, 1999.

contributed to the error in the task ("Maybe you can think of *another* way to do it").
(Special effort was made to ensure that the children understood they were role-
playing and that the scenarios were pretend situations.) When praise for success was
administered, the child heard something like, "I'm very proud of you," or "That's the
right way to do it," or "You must have tried really hard" for the person, outcome, and
process feedback conditions, respectively.

How would children respond after role-playing in a similar but new task when a
setback occurred? To answer this question the researchers asked children to evaluate
how well the new problem had been completed (product rating), how performance in
the task reflected abilities such as being good, bad, smart, not so smart, and so forth
(self-assessment), whether they felt happy or sad (affect), and their willingness to continue in the role-playing activity or to attempt to correct the error (persistence). The
results are shown in Figure 12.3. Higher scores indicate a more positive rating.

The results revealed a consistent pattern of reactions typical of helplessness when
the emphasis in the feedback had been on the person (and to a lesser extent, on the
outcome) than when the feedback focused on the process of completing the task effectively. Somewhat surprisingly, this relationship held up whether the children had
been exposed earlier to criticism or to praise in the role-playing activity, a finding reported by other researchers as well (Henderlong & Lepper, 2002). These findings and

the research of many others suggest that parents can take several steps to reduce the likelihood that children will acquire a sense of learned helplessness:

1. *Avoid frequent criticism and punishment, especially of younger children.* The younger child who is often criticized or punished for, say, being messy or failing to finish a task may be particularly susceptible to the belief that he is "bad." In arriving at this stable view of his personality, he may have little reason to try to do better or may shun similar challenges to avoid receiving further negative evaluations. Thus it is important that parents help the younger child to avoid feelings of shame or limited self-worth when evaluating behavior (Kelley et al., 2000).

2. *Motivate effort by identifying positive process approaches to problem solving.* As children become older and more knowledgeable, parents and teachers can promote a mastery orientation by emphasizing the various skills and procedures important to success, that is, what children can do to more effectively achieve a goal. Such feedback should help children to appreciate the malleability of traits and capacities.

3. *Attribute poor performance to factors other than ability.* When a child does perform poorly, a parent's or teacher's evaluation should focus on nonintellectual and temporary factors that may have reduced the child's performance rather than on her intrinsic ability, thereby inspiring effort when the next opportunity arises.

4. *View activities as opportunities to learn rather than as tests of ability.* Parents and teachers can encourage children to approach academic tasks as opportunities to learn rather than as situations in which their performance will be evaluated in terms of competence (or lack of competence) (Dweck, 1999; Erdley et al., 1997).

Younger children must be convinced that their failures and successes are not the outcome of being "bad" or "good." Older children should be assured that shortcomings in performance on, say, academic tasks stem less from lack of ability than from insufficient effort or some other factor that can be modified. Children who already have acquired an orientation to learned helplessness can benefit from *attribution retraining*, a procedure designed to change their beliefs about the cause of their failures. This procedure emphasizes tying lack of success more directly to poor or ineffective effort than to inability. Attribution retraining has become an effective method of replacing self-limiting styles and attitudes with positive approaches to success, a means of converting learned helplessness into a greater sense of mastery and agency (Dweck, 1986).

Schoolwork should be viewed as an opportunity for learning rather than as a situation in which performance is being evaluated. A child who takes pride in his work and believes that he can accomplish the tasks he is assigned often gains confidence and the motivation to be more successful.

● **The Sense of Individuality**   How does a child know that she cannot become someone else? In other words, what do children understand about individuality and uniqueness? In one study young people were asked, "What makes you different from everybody else in the world?" Preschoolers usually answered with their names ("'Cause there is only one person with my name"), their possessions, or specific features of their bodies. Eight- to ten-year-olds added comparative statements involving abilities, activities, and personality ("Well, I think I'm friendlier than most kids I know"). Young adolescents were more likely to list unique psychological and other traits ("Yeah, I worry too much and a lot of things that a lot of kids don't care about"). Older adolescents adopted even stronger views involving unique personal feelings and orientations ("Nobody else sees things or feels the same way about things as I do") (Damon & Hart, 1988).

The answer that emerges from this research is that the child gains his sense of individuality early and first links it to observable physical characteristics and features. As children grow, they begin to compare themselves with others, especially their private feelings and thoughts, and these qualities become the central criteria for their claim to uniqueness.

● **The Sense of Stability**   Is an individual essentially the same person today that she was a year ago or will be a year from now? As with the sense of individuality, a child's understanding of continuity begins quite early, but the explanation for this stability changes with development. Preschoolers have more difficulty than older children recognizing that changes in mood, weight, and even age or height are possible while still retaining one's identity (Bales & Sera, 1995). When asked, "If you change from year to year, how do you know it's still always you?" preschoolers cite their names ("My name, and then I would know if it was me if someone called me"), physical features, possessions, or other categorical qualities as proof. An eight- to ten-year-old is likely to refer to stable personal or internal qualities ("I know it's me because I still know the things I knew five years ago"). Young adolescents link the sense of continuity to others ("I'll still have my family. They always know I'm me and not someone else"). Older adolescents are likely to state their certainty more abstractly ("Well, nothing about me always stays the same, but I am always kind of like I was awhile ago") (Damon & Hart, 1988).

As in the case of individuality, children's sense of a stable self gradually expands from physical, highly observable attributes to include both inner psychological and broader contextual elements. Moreover, as children mature, they judge inner psychological qualities as increasingly important in decisions about their stability of self (Aboud & Skerry, 1983). Children and adolescents are also more likely to anticipate greater similarity between their present and future selves than between past and present selves (Hart, Fegley, & Brengelman, 1993). Still, anticipated changes in future selves are positive ones; children and adolescents expect to lose undesirable characteristics as they mature.

● **The Sense of Reflection**   When does the ability to reflect on or contemplate the self emerge? Perhaps not until early adolescence, when its advent, along with new ways of thinking abstractly, helps to explain the preoccupations of young teenagers with appearance and worth, that is, a growing self-consciousness about who they are (Elkind, 1981; Selman, 1980). Another consequence of the capacity to reflect on the self is a greater appreciation of how the mind contributes to experience. A fourteen-year-old may say, "I can fool myself into thinking I don't miss my lost puppy." Yet an older adolescent often realizes that completely controlling her feelings, even if she is unaware of them, may not be possible. Thus the sense of reflection forms the basis for eventually distinguishing between the influence of conscious and unconscious psychological processes on behavior (Damon & Hart, 1988).

KEY THEME
Interaction Among Domains

Self-esteem: Evaluating Self

A child's description of self often includes an evaluation component. **Self-esteem** or self-worth is specifically concerned with the positive feelings of merit and the extent

self-esteem   One's feelings of worth; extent to which one senses one's attributes and actions are good, desired, and valued.

to which the child believes his attributes and actions are good, desired, and valued (Davis-Kean & Sandler, 2001). This aspect of self appears to be related to social affiliations, success in school, and overall mental health (Dusek, 2000; Harter, 1999; Kling et al., 1999). For example, later life satisfaction and happiness have been linked to high self-esteem (Bachman, 1970; Crandall, 1973); depression, anxiety, and poor adjustment in school and social relationships have been associated with low self-esteem (Damon, 1983; Zimmerman et al., 1997).

● **Defining Self-esteem** How should we describe a child's self-esteem if the child takes pride in how smart she is, concludes that she is not very good at sports (but sports are unimportant anyway), and is unsure whether she is pretty enough to become a movie star? Work by Susan Harter and others (Harter, 1999; Eccles, Wigfield, et al., 1993; Marsh, Craven, & Debus, 1998) has revealed that children often give different evaluations of self when asked about academic competence, athletic skill, social acceptance, or physical appearance. Still, by about eight years of age, children can give answers to such global questions as "Do you like yourself?" and "Are you happy the way you are?" The responses to these broad inquiries, however, are not simple summations of all the different evaluations made with respect to specific attributes and abilities, and they can vary across situations and time (Harter, Waters, & Whitesell, 1998). What, then, are some of the factors that influence how a child arrives at a global sense of worth?

William James (1892) theorized that self-esteem depends on the success a person feels in areas in which she wants to succeed. Others emphasize that self-esteem originates in how a person thinks others see him; the *generalized other*—the combined perceived evaluations of parents, peers, and teachers influential in a person's life—helps to determine sense of worth (Cooley, 1902; Felson, 1993; Mead, 1934).

Both success in a highly regarded domain and the perceived evaluations of others do appear to affect self-esteem. Harter (1987) obtained ratings of how children viewed themselves in scholastic competence, athletic competence, social acceptance, physical appearance, and behavioral conduct and in terms of global success. Children were also asked how critical it was for them to do well in each of these domains. Harter reasoned that greater discrepancies between perceived competence and the importance of a domain, especially one highly valued, would be linked to lower self-esteem. Children also rated how others (parents, peers) viewed them, felt they were important, liked them, and so on.

KEY THEME
Individual Differences

For children in the third to eighth grades, the more an area rated as important outstripped a child's perception of her competence, the lower was the child's sense of her overall worth. In fact, children with low self-esteem seemed to have trouble disregarding the significance of domains in which they were not skilled (Harter, 1985). In contrast, children with high self-esteem minimized the value of those fields in which they were not especially competent and gained considerable satisfaction from areas in which they were relatively successful. But Harter found the perceived social support of others also correlated with the child's sense of self-worth. As Figure 12.4 shows, elementary school children with low discrepancy *and* high social support scores showed superior levels of self-worth. Children with high discrepancy and low social support displayed the lowest levels of self-esteem. Both factors contributed to overall sense of worth. Thus efforts to improve self-esteem in children may require both a supportive social milieu and the formation and acceptance of realistic personal goals.

KEY THEME
Child's Active Role

Are some domains more important than others for a child's overall sense of worth? The answer appears to be yes. Boys and girls of elementary and middle school age who are dissatisfied with and keenly concerned about their physical appearance tend to have lower self-esteem. Although discrepancies are also important in other domains, they correlate less highly with judgments of overall self-worth. Harter (1987, 1998) speculates that in American culture, the relationship stems from the enormous emphasis on physical appearance in movies, television, and teen magazines as the key to

KEY THEME
Interaction Among Domains

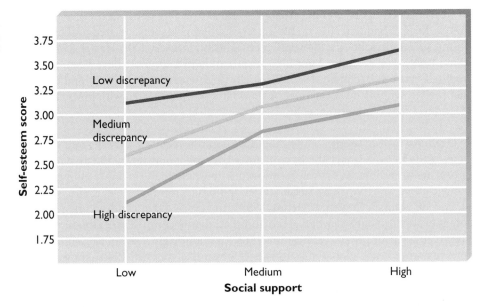

FIGURE 12.4
How Self-esteem Develops

Self-esteem reflects the combined influence of social support and the discrepancy between the child's perceived and desired competence in some ability or attribute. Harter divided elementary school children into three groups based on these two measures. Those with the highest self-esteem reported high social support and a low discrepancy between perceived and desired competence. Those with the lowest self-esteem reported low social support and a high discrepancy between perceived and desired competence. The findings suggest that parents, teachers, and others concerned with increasing self-esteem need to consider both the kind of social encouragement and positive regard they provide and children's own beliefs about what is important.

Source: Adapted from Harter, 1987.

KEY THEME
Interaction Among Domains

KEY THEME
Sociocultural Influence

success and acceptance. As children become older, discrepancy scores on social acceptance take on increasingly greater significance, whereas discrepancy scores on athletic competence show a decline in importance (Harter, 1987). Nevertheless, positive assessments of physical appearance continue to be an important predictor of higher self-esteem for boys and girls as they enter the adolescent years (DuBois et al., 2000; Lord, Eccles, & McCarthy, 1994).

● **Developmental Changes in Self-esteem**   In general, the self-esteem of children in early elementary school is high. Yet as they approach adolescence, self-esteem for a substantial portion, especially girls, declines (Block & Robins, 1993; Simmons & Blyth, 1987; Wigfield & Eccles, 1994). The change accompanies major transitions, such as the onset of puberty, entry into junior high school, and substantial realignments in friendship patterns. Often the decline accompanies a lowering of perceived competence in academic subjects such as math.

During the change to junior high, daily hassles tend to increase, whereas teacher support and extracurricular activities decline, all factors correlated with a decrease in self-esteem, especially among disadvantaged children regardless of ethnic or racial background (Seidman et al., 1994). However, when adolescents retain a warm, strong orientation toward others and perceive their parents as being attuned to and supportive of their efforts in decision making, they are more likely to maintain high self-esteem throughout these transitions (Lord et al., 1994). And as our earlier discussion of a sense of agency suggests, coping strategies that lead young people to attribute success to their competence and mastery are certainly another critical element in maintaining high self-esteem (Brooks, 1992).

Relatively little cross-cultural research on self-esteem has been reported, although several studies comparing children from the United States and Taiwan have revealed a consistent pattern: Taiwanese children report lower self-esteem than their counterparts in the United States (Chiu, 1992–1993; Stigler, Smith, & Mao, 1985; Turner & Mo, 1984). The reasons may stem from cultural practices in Taiwan that emphasize humility rather than pride in one's accomplishments or qualities and provide less opportunity to receive social or public displays of success in academic and other settings. Also, Taiwanese family-rearing patterns emphasize obedience rather than individual achievement, and although children in Taiwan often do excel academically, other ways of gaining high self-esteem may be less available to them.

CONTROVERSY: THINKING IT OVER

Is Praise Always a Good Thing?

In the discussion of ways to prevent learned helplessness, one finding by Kamins and Dweck (1999) may come as a surprise to many. Kamins and Dweck noted that praise directed toward children for success did not necessarily inoculate the children from reporting a greater sense of helplessness when faced with a setback in a new task. Are we to conclude that praise (such as "I am really proud of you," "You are really smart," "You are a star") is not a particularly good means of promoting effective behavior?

What Is the Controversy?

If there is one prescription that many parents and professionals in Western societies, and particularly in the United States, would offer for encouraging the development of a competent child, it very likely would be to praise generously for his or her accomplishments. As Carol Dweck (1999) points out, it is one of our most treasured assumptions. Enlightened parents attempt to (and often do) follow such a practice, and many teachers and others working with children are advised to unstintingly administer praise to promote learning. Yet in their recent examination of the effects of praise on children, Jennifer Henderlong and Mark Lepper (2002) have concluded that the research literature often paints a far different picture of its motivational consequences for children.

What Are the Opposing Arguments?

Learning theory has long recognized the importance of reinforcement for enhancing behavior. Telling a child that he or she is good or excellent or really smart after completing a task should be reinforcing and promote continuing efforts to engage in that behavior. Moreover, a common belief is that such praise helps to bring about and strengthen intrinsic motivation for accomplishing various goals. To top it off, praise is routinely viewed as an effective way of enhancing a child's self-esteem, another desirable goal, as our discussion of this concept has suggested.

Yet others have raised serious questions about the effectiveness of frequent praise. The concern is that praise, although a presumably positive source of feedback for a child, is nevertheless a *judgment*. As a consequence, it can lead a child to become increasingly concerned about performing well and to avoid risks (Henderlong & Lepper, 2002). In other words, the child may place greater value on receiving the praise at the expense of working autonomously or of learning from one's own mistakes. Morever, when given indiscriminately, such as for an easy task, praise may be interpreted by the child as indicating low ability. Thus frequent praise can have the paradoxical effect of lowering motivation and of promoting a kind of *contingent self-worth*, that is, of feeling worthy only when successful (Dweck, 1999).

What Answers Exist? What Questions Remain?

When is praise beneficial to a child? In their summary of the research literature, Henderlong and Lepper (2002) suggest a number of conditions under which some types of praise may have positive consequences for a child. These conditions include praise that is sincere and appropriate; that focuses on the type of effort, strategies, and self-corrections the child initiates in an activity rather than on his or her stable attributes (being good, smart, etc.); that encourages the child to be autonomous in his or her activity rather than serving as a way of controlling behavior; that emphasizes effectiveness in the task rather than social comparison; and that is informative in providing feedback about realistic expectations for the task.

Yet many questions remain about praise as a motivational tool. How could professionals and the public be so convinced of its unbridled value whereas still others have now come to question its general effects on children's development? Thus controversy continues over what kind of and how frequently praise should be administered. Moreover, virtually all of the research on the consequences of praise has been completed on children in the United States (Henderlong & Lepper, 2002). However, cultures differ dramatically in the extent to which children are praised. For example, could its effects on children be very different in a collectivist society in which the emphasis is on improving oneself for the good of the group rather than on self-enhancement? Methodological limitations in the research that has been carried out on this topic present further challenges to some of the conclusions about the effects of praise. Broad acceptance of the value of praise for self-esteem and of its motivational consequences for effort remains controversial and in need of further examination. What kinds of evidence must researchers obtain to decide whether this long-cherished assumption needs to be amended?

Identity

The burgeoning sense of self, along with the capacity to reflect on individual qualities, serves as the nucleus for the construction of an **identity,** a broad, coherent, internalized view of who a person is and what a person wants to be, believes, and values. A sense of identity solidifies and gives meaning to such fundamental questions about self as: Who am I? Why do I exist? What am I to become? The development of a healthy identity, as Erik Erikson pointed out (see the chapter titled "Themes and Theories"), is a lifelong process that builds on earlier gains in accepting and trusting others, in being encouraged to explore interests and desires, and in acquiring feelings of competence and skill. However, it undergoes further important changes during adolescence and early adulthood. By formulating a unified sense of self as an agent separate from others and as someone capable of reflecting on one's own agency, the adolescent creates a more fully integrated identity and sets the stage for developing a healthy personality to accompany the transition to mature adulthood (Blasi & Glodis, 1995). Nevertheless, the stagelike progression in the emergence of identity at this time has been challenged (e.g., Bosma & Kunnen, 2001). For example, alternative conceptualizations place greater emphasis on the view that one's identity is constantly being modified and adjusted as part of an individual's efforts to make sense out of the story of his or her life (Dien, 2000). Despite these differing perspectives, the adolescent period in identity development typically has generated the most interest from researchers.

● **The Adolescent Identity Crisis**   The period of adolescence has sometimes been viewed as filled with stress and uncertainty about self, riddled with sudden and frequent mood shifts, a time dubbed the **identity crisis.** Increased conflict with parents and the initiation of more risky and socially disruptive behavior are said to be a part of this developmental period as well (Arnett, 1999).

As they approach the teen years, children frequently engage in new ways of behaving and thinking that involve greater autonomy, independence, and expressions of intimacy with others. For example, teenagers increasingly view their actions and conduct as personal—their own business, so to speak (Smetana, 1988)—and believe that such things as family chores, eating habits, curfews, and personal appearance are up to them, not their parents. Needless to say, this view can introduce conflict within the family, especially for parents who wish to maintain control. Meta-analyses of the findings of numerous studies reveal that the frequency of conflict within the family is greatest early in adolescence and declines over the teenage years (Laursen, Coy, & Collins, 1998). For many adolescents, however, conflict is far less frequent than the idea of a crisis would suggest (Hill, 1987; Powers, Hauser, & Kilner, 1989).

KEY THEME
Continuity/Discontinuity

KEY THEME
Child's Active Role

identity (personal)   Broad, coherent, internalized view of who a person is and what a person wants to be, believes, and values that emerges during adolescence.

identity crisis   Period, usually during adolescence, characterized by considerable uncertainty about the self and the role the individual is to fulfill in society.

Parents are not always enthusiastic about some of the things their children do. During the adolescent years, decisions about dress and appearance are especially common sources of tension within families. However, these efforts to distinguish themselves are typically part of an ordinary developmental process accompanying the transition to mature adulthood and probably reflect the increasing independence young people desire, and may need, in their efforts to construct their own identity.

Mood disruptions are greater during the adolescent years than during other major periods of development (Arnett, 1999). Still, substantial differences among individuals are found here as well. Youth who experience negative life events—that is, who are less popular, are not doing well in school, and are experiencing stress within the family—are especially susceptible to mood shifts (Brooks-Gunn & Warren, 1989; Petersen et al., 1993). In addition, risk-taking behaviors that involve the potential for harm to self and others peak during the late adolescent years, although again substantial individual differences exist in these activities (Arnett, 1999).

One key to successfully negotiating this period appears to be a family, educational environment, and social milieu that support the needs and interests of adolescents (Eccles, Midgley, et al., 1993). For example, as children progress from elementary to junior high school, they find greater emphasis on control and discipline, less positive personal support from teachers, and more competitiveness and public evaluation of their work (Lord et al., 1994). Such changes may conflict with adolescents' need for fewer intellectual pressures and more opportunity to take charge in exploring and resolving uncertainties about their identity (Eccles, Midgley, et al., 1993). From bargaining over their choices of friends and activities to use of the telephone or the family car, adolescents also test new ways of communicating with and relating to parents and others in authority (Powers et al., 1989). Being able to establish a point of view seems to promote a strong sense of personal identity (Grotevant & Cooper, 1986; Hauser et al., 1987). Parents, teachers, and others play an important role in providing reassurance and support while permitting teenagers to weigh their ideas.

Cultural differences exist in the extent to which storm and stress during adolescence is reported as well (Arnett, 1999). Problems associated with the adolescent years seem to be most severe in Western and other cultures in which greater independence is encouraged and in which the transition from childhood to the adult world is relatively greater. Within the United States less conflict is reported between adolescents

KEY THEME
Individual Differences

KEY THEME
Sociocultural Influence

and adults in Mexican American families than in Caucasian American middle-class families (Suarez-Orozco & Suarez-Orozco, 1996). Nevertheless, as families assimilate Western culture over generations, the conflict seems to increase. For example, adolescents in those generations of Asian American families who have been in the United States longer are more likely to display greater evidence of characteristics suggestive of an identity crisis (Steinberg, 1996).

● **Ethnic Identity**   Among the factors affecting a young person's identity is ethnic and racial background. **Ethnic identity** refers to the sense of belonging to a specific cultural group as opposed to simply adopting its social practices, known more generally as *acculturation* (Phinney, 1990). Because the majority culture often views minority groups in a stereotypical and negative light, identifying with a minority ethnic or racial group was once thought to set the stage for personal conflict and confusion.

Early studies with preschool and younger children reported a bias for choosing dolls or pictures that depict the majority group, in this case Caucasian children, even by members of a minority group (Gray-Little & Hafdahl, 2000). But this measure may be methodologically biased, or other factors may be influencing children's choices; the preference has been observed even in the West Indies, where Caucasians are the minority. Other measures sometimes used to assess the value given to one's own racial group have not shown any disadvantage to children with a strong ethnic identity (Gray-Little & Hafdahl, 2000). In fact, two large-scale meta-analyses of self-esteem in majority and minority groups in the United States have revealed that self-esteem among African American children and adolescents, especially for girls, is higher than among Caucasians. It does, however, tend to be lower for Hispanic, Asian, and Native Americans than for Caucasians among both boys and girls (Gray-Little & Hafdahl, 2000; Twenge & Crocker, 2002).

Becoming comfortable with one's own ethnic identity can lead to greater acceptance of and a more positive attitude toward other ethnic groups (Phinney, Ferguson, & Tate, 1997; Valk, 2000). Valuing one's ethnicity seems to be fostered by responsive parents who are sensitive to ethnic issues (Phinney & Rosenthal, 1992). However, ethnic socialization for minority parents is carried out within, not at the expense of, broader child-rearing goals emphasized in most families: getting a good education, being a good human being, feeling satisfied about oneself, working hard, and so forth (Marshall, 1995).

FOR YOUR REVIEW

• What are the primary distinctions between self as object and self as subject? What are typical behaviors that illustrate these two characterizations of self?

• When do various aspects of self-concept appear, and what developmental transitions do they undergo? Distinguish between categorical self, social comparison, and the adolescent basis for self.

• How does effectance motivation begin and develop? What factors contribute to a mastery orientation and to learned helplessness? What steps can parents and teachers take to reduce learned helplessness?

• What contributes to high self-esteem and how do social and cultural differences influence it?

• What role does praise play in self-esteem and in promoting an achievement orientation?

• When is a child likely to develop a broad and coherent concept of self? What is an identity crisis? How important is ethnic identity for young people?

ethnic identity   The sense of belonging to a particular cultural group.

Self-regulation and Self-control

Impulsive and easily upset, infants and young children have difficulty behaving in a patient or deliberate manner. Eventually, however, parents and others demand that children acquire *effortful control*, the ability to suppress undesirable responses for less dominant ones that are considered socially or morally more acceptable. A three-year-old needs to stay away from an attractive fireplace, use the toilet, say thank you, and share and put away toys. Older children and teenagers assume ever greater responsibility for their actions and are expected to conform to socially accepted rules and standards. But becoming responsible and self-reliant can be a long and difficult transition. A mother may have great difficulty persuading her daughter, who is eager to show off her tricycle-riding prowess, that it is a playmate's turn. And countless parents have wrestled with how best to convince their children that completing their homework is an important way to prepare themselves for future success.

Self-regulation refers to the capacity to monitor and direct one's activities to achieve certain goals or meet the demands imposed by others. **Self-control,** a related concept, is the ability to comply with expectations of caregivers or other adults, especially in their absence. Both are important for instilling a sense of self and for achieving ethical and moral behavior.

Developmental Changes

For infants and young children, regulation of behavior might best be labeled *co-regulation* (Kopp, 1987) because children and their caregivers jointly manage behavior. In many families, efforts to limit activities begin when babies are about eight or nine months old. At this time, newly acquired motor skills increase risk of injury, heralding the need for restraining devices such as playpens and gates. Infants about one year of age may be warned to avoid dangerous or health-threatening objects and situations ("Don't touch the knife"; "Don't play with the cat litter"; "Hold on to my hand"). Efforts to preserve possessions ("Stay away from the VCR") and avoid harm to others ("Don't pinch") are also common concerns at about this time (Gralinski & Kopp, 1993).

As toddlers move beyond eighteen months of age, adults often supplement these *caregiving demands* with additional *demands for appropriate behavior,* such as keeping quiet and sitting up straight, and *demands for competent action,* such as helping to set the table or participating in social and family activities (Kuczynski & Kochanska, 1995). These efforts focus on encouraging acceptable social interactions, taking part in family routines and chores, and cultivating self-care and greater independence (e.g., walking rather than being carried) (Gralinski & Kopp, 1993). By the time children reach twenty-four to thirty months of age, parental demands may decline in frequency as children become familiar with and respond to requests more routinely (Kopp, 1987). Nevertheless, the frequency with which conflict occurs between parents and children in American families—for example, asking the child to delay a response, slow down an activity, stop an unacceptable behavior, pay attention, or help out with an uninteresting task—is typically still high, perhaps on the order of fifteen to twenty times per hour (Laible & Thompson, 2002). The commitment to comply with a "don't" uttered by caregivers appears to be acquired somewhat earlier and more rapidly by children in American families than consistency in responding to a "do." This difference may be due to parents' enforcement of the former more often than the latter or to their greater persistence in prohibiting negative behaviors, thus promoting more fear in children about initiating (or continuing to produce) these behaviors (Kochanska, 2002; Kochanska, Coy, & Murray, 2001). Girls also tend to be more compliant than boys (Kochanska, Murray, & Harlan, 2000).

Young children who are best able to engage in effortful control of behavior as toddlers are more effective in focusing and sustaining their attention to a task as early as

Toddlers are often asked to begin to regulate behaviors so that they are displayed in socially acceptable ways. One such activity that most toddlers are expected to master is control of body functions. Although it can be a stressful practice, this toddler has found a way to make "potty training" a more positive experience.

self-regulation Process by which children come to control their own behaviors in accordance with the standards of their caregivers and community, especially in the absence of other adults.

self-control Ability to comply with sociocultural prescriptions concerning ethical or moral behavior.

twelve months of age. In addition, caregivers who are supportive, responsive, accepting, sensitive, and emotionally available to their toddlers, who are able to justify to their children the need for children to act in certain ways, and who can point out the consequences of their youngsters' behaviors, offer a compromise or provide a benefit for alternative responses, and include positive or negative evaluations of their children's deeds are likely to have offspring who display more socially acceptable and compliant behaviors later in development (Kochanska et al., 2001; Laible & Thompson, 2002). Moreover, when mothers emphasize "do" over "don't" and behaving competently over inhibiting activities in their toddlers and preschoolers, fewer compliance and behavior problems arise at age five (Kuczynski & Kochanska, 1995).

KEY THEME
Child's Active Role

Children's self-initiated attempts to obey appear during the second year. A thirteen-month-old, for example, may look at, and perhaps even approach and touch, an electrical outlet while saying, "No, no!" Over the next few years, self-restraint improves rapidly. For example, in a **delay-of-gratification** task, in which the child is asked to wait some period of time before performing an activity or attaining some highly desired outcome (such as playing with an attractive toy or eating a piece of candy), eighteen-month-olds have great difficulty complying. Between two and three years of age, children become increasingly more effective in delaying their behavior (Vaughn, Kopp, & Krakow, 1984). Thus, although self-control begins with attempts by others to govern the young child's actions, their efforts are transferred and gradually relinquished as warnings and guidance become less direct and as the child takes on more responsibility for regulating his behavior. How does this shift come about?

The Influence of Language and Attention

KEY THEME
Interaction Among Domains

As we have just seen, both attentional factors and the communication pattern of the caregiver seem to be important components in facilitating compliance in children. Both also appear to be critical elements in the child's ability to regulate his or her own behavior without the assistance of an adult. As we learned in the chapter titled "Language," Lev Vygotsky (1962) and his students, particularly Alexander Luria (1961, 1969), theorized that language plays a pivotal role in behavioral regulation. A preschool child, for example, may engage in the expression of *private speech*, speech intended for no one else but that helps to direct attention to key dimensions and features of a task, to assist in establishing and organizing ways to carry out an activity, and to preserve important task-related information in memory (Meichenbaum, 1977). Yet children's observable private speech is not always correlated with effective problem solving. Perhaps this finding should be expected, as the production of private speech is more likely in especially challenging circumstances (Frauenglass & Diaz, 1985). Preschoolers at risk for behavior problems, however, tend to produce more spontaneous private speech than those who are not at risk. This finding raises the interesting possibility that the failure to progress from overt speech-for-self to internalized speech-for-self may contribute to greater risk for behavioral problems in some children (Winsler et al., 2000).

Attentional factors also seem important. For example, the child directed not to eat a marshmallow who says, "The marshmallow is yummy"—words that focus attention on the forbidden treat—or who talks about sad things such as falling and hurting himself—ideas that provide little diversion—shows less ability to inhibit his behavior than someone who sings a pleasant but distracting nursery rhyme such as "Three Blind Mice" (Mischel, Ebbesen, & Zeiss, 1972). A fidgety third-grader eager for recess might be better advised to direct her attention to reading a book of her choice rather than staring at the classroom clock. In fact, the more a child attends to a desired object, the more difficult it is to endure a continuing delay (Peake, Hebl, & Mischel, 2002).

For very young children, caregivers are more likely to initiate attempts to focus or distract the child. To illustrate this point, George Holden (1983) observed mothers and their two-and-a-half-year-olds as they completed grocery shopping, an activity

delay of gratification
Capacity to wait before performing a tempting activity or attaining some highly desired outcome; a measure of ability to regulate one's own behavior.

that can test the limits of most caregivers because grocery displays are enticing. In this setting, mothers were frequently forced to respond to their children's requests and used a variety of tactics to do so: reasoning, not responding, physically or verbally intervening, acknowledging children's desires, and attempting to distract children. Mothers who tried to anticipate conflicts, either by diverting children's attention in advance or by engaging them in an interesting conversation, were most effective in preventing conflict while grocery shopping. Sensitive and consistent mothers who learned to use strategies to direct, maintain, and redirect their children's attention appeared to be most successful in regulating their behavior (Holden & West, 1989; Kopp, 1987).

During the later preschool and early school years, children display their own attentional strategies to keep on track and support their goals. For example, in a delay-of-gratification task, preschoolers often place a tempting reward in front of themselves rather than a picture of it or some other, irrelevant item. In doing so, they increase their exposure to the forbidden object, look at it more, and have greater difficulty delaying their response to it. By age five, children are less likely to create such self-defeating arrangements. They prefer to wait with the tempting reward covered rather than uncovered (Mischel & Mischel, 1983). Some will even shield their eyes, play games with their hands and feet, or try to go to sleep to help manage the delay (Cournoyer & Trudel, 1991; Mischel, Shoda, & Rodriguez, 1989).

Older children show greater metacognitive understanding of helpful attentional and other tactics for regulating their activities (Holtz & Lehman, 1995; Mischel & Mischel, 1983). An eleven-year-old, for example, offered the following recommendation for distracting oneself: "You can take your mind off of it and think of Christmas or something like that. But the point is, think about something else." By this age, then, children have begun to reflect on ways they can most effectively control their behavior. The Development of Self and Self-regulation chronolgy summarizes major aspects of transitions in this ability, along with accomplishments in the development of self.

KEY THEME
Child's Active Role

Individual Differences

Even ten years later, those who at two years of age more successfully inhibited responses to attractive objects are better than other children at sustaining a goal and resisting distractions in order to complete a problem-solving task (Silverman & Ippolito, 1997). Adolescents who have greater self-regulatory capacities as preschoolers are described by their parents as more academically and socially competent and better able to handle frustration and temptation. They also are reported to be more attentive, deliberate, and intelligent and seem better able to tolerate stress and cope with social and personal problems, even when their intellectual performance is similar to peers less able to delay gratification (Mischel et al., 1989; Shoda, Mischel, & Peake, 1990).

Jeanne Block and Jack Block (1980) have identified yet another component of self-regulation, flexible and adaptive behavior in appropriate settings, that shows evidence of stable individual differences. Shouting, running, and responding impulsively, for example, may be unacceptable within the classroom but highly appropriate during recess. Some children display elasticity and are able to modify their behavior easily as the situation demands throughout childhood; others consistently show far less flexibility.

What accounts for these individual differences? Genetic factors may contribute, but researchers generally agree that socialization practices also play a significant role. Caregivers who encourage and use self-regulation provide opportunities for children to acquire skills, attitudes, and habits that promote persistence and effort and reduce frustration, yielding both social and academic benefits (Mischel et al., 1989). Parents also need to strike a proper balance between dispensing control and encouraging self-regulation. Overcontrolling adults tend to have grown up in families whose values emphasize considerable structure, order, and tradition (Block, 1971). Adults with

KEY THEME
Individual Differences

KEY THEME
Nature/Nurture

CHRONOLOGY: *Development of Self and Self-regulation*

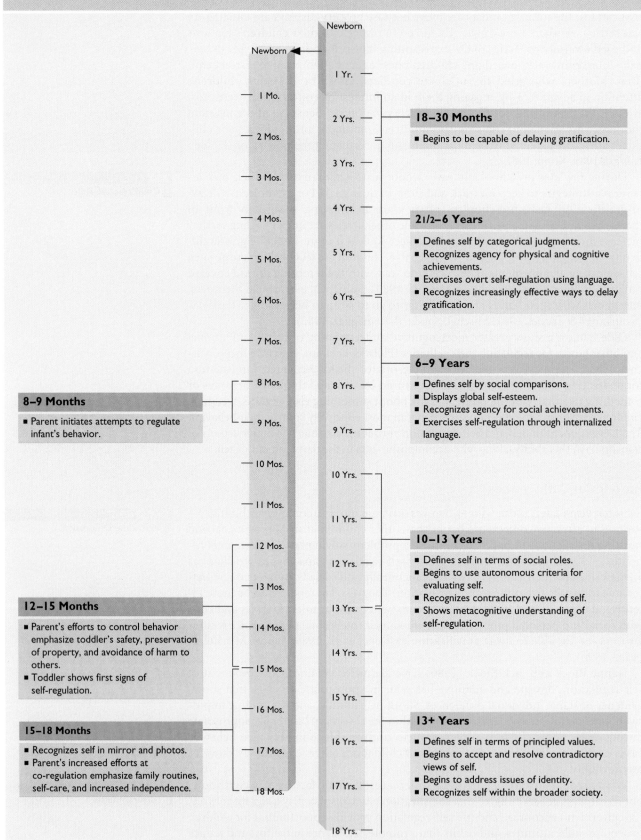

8–9 Months

- Parent initiates attempts to regulate infant's behavior.

12–15 Months

- Parent's efforts to control behavior emphasize toddler's safety, preservation of property, and avoidance of harm to others.
- Toddler shows first signs of self-regulation.

15–18 Months

- Recognizes self in mirror and photos.
- Parent's increased efforts at co-regulation emphasize family routines, self-care, and increased independence.

18–30 Months

- Begins to be capable of delaying gratification.

2 1/2–6 Years

- Defines self by categorical judgments.
- Recognizes agency for physical and cognitive achievements.
- Exercises overt self-regulation using language.
- Recognizes increasingly effective ways to delay gratification.

6–9 Years

- Defines self by social comparisons.
- Displays global self-esteem.
- Recognizes agency for social achievements.
- Exercises self-regulation through internalized language.

10–13 Years

- Defines self in terms of social roles.
- Begins to use autonomous criteria for evaluating self.
- Recognizes contradictory views of self.
- Shows metacognitive understanding of self-regulation.

13+ Years

- Defines self in terms of principled values.
- Begins to accept and resolve contradictory views of self.
- Begins to address issues of identity.
- Recognizes self within the broader society.

This chart describes the sequence in the development of understanding the self and self-regulation based on the findings of research. Children often show individual differences in the exact ages at which they display the various developmental achievements outlined here.

relatively little control, on the other hand, tend to have grown up in families that placed little emphasis on achievement and responsible behavior and in which each parent had different caregiving values.

FOR YOUR REVIEW

- What is the difference between self-regulation and self-control?

- How does compliant behavior change over development? What factors seem to promote it?

- What role do attentional and language processes play in delay of gratification?

- How stable are individual differences in self-regulation?

Moral Development

As children gain increasing knowledge of the self and greater skill in regulating their own behavior, they are expected to increasingly conform to the socially acceptable rules and regulations of their community. Theories of *moral development,* the process by which an individual comes to understand what society accepts as right and wrong, differ enormously in explaining how this change comes about.

Freud's Theory

Freud's theory focuses on *affective* dimensions of moral development. According to his perspective, the emotional relationships children have with their parents influence the degree to which they incorporate parental standards of conduct. Children *internalize* the standards of the parent as a by-product of the child's progression through the stages of psychosexual development. Freud believed a moral sense emerges near the end of the *phallic stage,* around age five or six years, when boys resolve the *Oedipal complex.* According to Freud, the boy experiences intense emotional conflict when his sexual attraction to his mother cannot be fulfilled and he comes to fear castration by his father (his competitor for his mother's affections).

The Oedipal conflict becomes resolved, Freud concluded, when the young boy suppresses his instinctual urges and allies himself with his powerful same-sex parent, his father. Through this process of *identification,* the child acquires his father's moral values and standards. The outcome is the formation of the **superego,** the component of the child's personality that functions both as a **conscience** (governing what not to do) and an **ego ideal** (governing appropriate and desirable behaviors). By acting in accordance with his parents' wishes, the child avoids feelings of guilt associated with violating these newly internalized values and standards.

Among the controversial aspects of Freud's theory is its prediction that girls will develop a weaker moral sense than boys (Turiel, 1998). In the counterpart to the Oedipal complex, dubbed the *Electra complex,* daughters experience a strong attachment to their fathers. However, because they cannot fear castration, the resolution of this conflict involves far less emotional intensity for girls than it does for boys. As a result, a girl's identification with her mother occurs with less force, and the superego or conscience, according to Freud, is not as strong.

Attempts to validate the various claims made by Freud have not met with great success. In fact, girls tend to display more guilt than boys (Kochanska et al., 2002). Moreover, positive emotional relationships and mutual responsiveness between mother and child are closely aligned with willingness to complete an assigned task and with a healthy conscience for *both* boys and girls (Kochanska, Aksan, & Koenig, 1995; Kochanska & Murray, 2000). The notion that moral development is inferior or incomplete in girls has been highly criticized for other reasons as well. For example, Carol Gilligan (1982) maintains that Freud's theory is a male's view of male

KEY THEME
Continuity/Discontinuity

superego In Freudian theory, a mental structure that monitors socially acceptable and unacceptable behavior.

conscience In Freudian theory, the part of the superego that defines unacceptable behaviors and actions, usually as also defined by the parents.

ego ideal In Freudian theory, the part of the superego that defines the positive standards for which an individual strives; acquired via parental rewarding of desired behaviors.

This young girl reflects on a transgression after being sent to her room. Research on moral development and the development of values has examined the roles of affect, reinforcement and punishment, and cognition in efforts to fully understand the socialization of culturally permissible behavior. All of these factors may play a part in the acquisition of behaviors that are considered socially acceptable and desirable in the community.

development that fails to explore the unique dimensions of the female experience as it pertains to morality.

Contemporary research also shows that children begin to develop a conscience well before the age at which Freud claimed the superego emerges. Early internalization of rules and an appreciation for right and wrong seem to arise in the child's second year of life, perhaps as the ability to recognize positive emotional reactions as well as anger or displeasure in the communications of caregivers and to regulate and inhibit behavior increases (Kochanska, 2002; Kochanska, Murray, & Coy, 1997; Kochanska, Tjebkes, & Forman, 1998). By age three years, some children willingly comply with the requests of their parents to complete certain activities (e.g., putting away toys) and avoid others (e.g., touching prohibited objects), even when the parents are no longer present (Kochanska, Aksan, & Koenig, 1995). Three-year-olds also notice flawed objects (e.g., a teddy bear with stuffing coming out or a broken cup), and, if led to believe the flaws are the consequence of their own behavior, they may voice apologies ("Sorry," "Didn't mean to"), offer reparations ("Put back in," "Clean up"), and exhibit distress ("Take this away," "I wanna go"), expressions of guilt and shame that are frequently manifestations of conscience (Kochanska, Casey, & Fukumoto, 1995). Thus the particulars of Freud's theory of moral development have failed to receive support. Nevertheless, his ideas about the internalization of society's standards, the central role of parents in the process, and the importance of the child's emotions for moral development have endured.

Social Learning Theory

Social learning theories emphasize the child's acquisition of *moral behaviors*, such as behaving acceptably and resisting temptation. According to social learning theory, the rewards and punishments dispensed by parents and others shape the child's conduct, as do the actions and verbalizations a child sees parents and others use. In this sense, moral values are learned just as any other behavior. Social learning theorists see morality as a process of incremental growth in appropriate actions and increasing conformity with the rules of society.

How convincingly does the social learning model explain moral development? Studies investigating the child's ability to resist temptation—for example, learning not to play with a forbidden toy—suggest that reinforcement history is indeed a factor in moral behavior. Children quickly learn not to touch an attractive toy if an

KEY THEME
Nature/Nurture

adult mildly reprimands them for initiating activities with it. In other words, they respond to the punishments the adult doles out.

Several factors influence children's tendency to transgress when left alone in the room with a forbidden toy after they have been punished. First, as social learning theory predicts, the timing of the punishment plays a role. Punishments are most effective if they closely follow the undesired behavior—for example, when the child first reaches for a forbidden toy rather than after he has picked it up. Second, providing a verbal explanation of why the toy is prohibited also has an effect. When children are told, for example, that the attractive toy might break if it is handled, they are much less likely to violate the adult's prohibition. According to social learning theorists, verbalizations facilitate the internalization of morally acceptable and unacceptable behaviors (Aronfreed, 1976).

Parents and others also serve as models. Children who observe a model commit a prohibited act, such as touching a forbidden toy, are more likely to perform the act themselves, whereas children observing a model who resists temptation will commit fewer transgressions (Rosenkoetter, 1973). However, models appear to be more powerful in *disinhibiting* than in inhibiting behavior that violates a rule or an expectation. Children are more likely to follow someone's deviant behaviors than his or her compliant ones (Hoffman, 1970).

Newer versions of social learning theory assign a larger role to cognitive processes in the emergence of moral values. In Albert Bandura's social cognitive theory (1986), children develop internalized standards of conduct, cognitive representations derived from observing others and processing their explanations for moral behavior. Children, especially to the extent to which they accept and accurately perceive communications, attempt to behave in ways consistent with those representations (Grusec & Goodnow, 1994). Nevertheless, describing changes in the child's ability to reason about moral questions has been left largely to other theorists, such as Jean Piaget and Lawrence Kohlberg.

> **KEY THEME**
> **Interaction Among Domains**

Cognitive-Developmental Theories

Cognitive-developmental explanations of moral development highlight the ways children *reason* about moral problems. Should a person ever steal, even if the transgression would help another person? Are there circumstances under which lying is acceptable? The child's capacity to think through the answers to such questions depends on his ability to consider the perspectives, needs, and feelings of others. In other words, moral development is intimately connected with advances in general thinking abilities. The two most prominent cognitive-developmental theorists concerned with moral development, Jean Piaget and Lawrence Kohlberg, have suggested stage theories in which children's reasoning about moral issues is qualitatively different depending on their level of development.

> **KEY THEME**
> **Interaction Among Domains**

> **KEY THEME**
> **Continuity/Discontinuity**

● **Piaget's Theory**   Piaget (1932/1965) derived many of his ideas about moral development from two contexts: as children played a formal game with a shared set of rules and as they encountered moral dilemmas created to assess thinking about ethical problems. For example, Piaget observed and interviewed children playing marbles, a popular children's game. Children were asked questions about this game: What are the rules? Can new rules be invented? Where do rules come from? Have they always been the same?

Preschoolers, Piaget stated, are not guided by rules. They engage in the activity for the pure pleasure it provides, and their play is largely solitary. Thus young children may hide marbles or throw them randomly, ignoring the formal rules of the game. By about age six, however, children come to regard rules as sacred and inviolable. Rules, handed down by adults, must be respected and have always existed in the same form; people played marbles in exactly the same way over the years. By about ten years of age, children understand rules to be the result of cooperation and mutual consent among all the participants in the game. Thus rules may be modified to suit the needs of the situation if all the players agree.

The second method Piaget used to study moral development consisted of noting responses of children to moral dilemmas, stories in which a central character committed a transgression. The intentions of that character and the consequences of his or her act varied, as the following stories illustrate:

> A. *A little boy who is called John is in his room. He is called to dinner. He goes into the dining room. But behind the door there was a chair, and on the chair there was a tray with fifteen cups on it. John couldn't have known that there was all this behind the door. He goes in, the door knocks against the tray, bang go the fifteen cups, and they all get broken!*

> B. *Once there was a little boy whose name was Henry. One day when his mother was out he tried to get some jam out of the cupboard. He climbed up onto a chair and stretched out his arm. But the jam was too high up and he couldn't reach it and have any. But while he was trying to get it he knocked over a cup. The cup fell down and broke.* (Piaget, 1932/1965, p. 122)

Which boy is naughtier? Younger children typically choose John, the child who broke more cups. According to Piaget, children younger than about ten are in the stage of moral development called **moral realism,** or *heteronomy*. They judge the rightness or wrongness of an act by the objective visible consequences—in this case, how many cups were broken. They do not consider the boys' intentions to behave well or improperly.

In the stage of moral realism, rules are viewed as unbreakable; if the rules are violated, the child sees punishment as the inevitable consequence. The belief in **immanent justice** is reflected in such statements as "That's God punishing me," made when the child accidentally falls off a bike after lying to her mother, for example. Although the fall is unrelated to the child's transgression, she believes the causal link exists. Children in this stage also believe that a punishment need not be related to the wrongful act if it is severe enough to teach a lesson. Thus stealing a friend's toy can be punished by any means, not necessarily by returning the toy or making reparations.

From a limited ability to reason about moral issues, children progress to **moral relativism,** or *autonomy*. Now the transgressor's motives are taken into account. Thus, Henry is named as the naughtier boy. In addition, the child no longer believes every violation will be punished. Punishments, however, should relate to the misdemeanor so that the individual appreciates the consequences of his act.

What precipitates the shift from moral realism to moral relativism? Piaget points to changes in the child's cognitive capabilities, especially decreasing egocentrism (see the chapter titled "Cognition: Piaget and Vygotsky"), as one important element. To understand another's intentions, for example, the child must be able to appreciate the point of view of that person as distinct from her own. Another important factor is the opportunity to interact with peers. Peer interactions force the child to consider the thoughts and feelings of others and eventually lead to an understanding of their intentions and motives. Parents can further promote the shift from realism to relativism, notes Piaget, by encouraging mutual respect and understanding, pointing out the consequences of the child's actions for others and articulating their needs and feelings as parents.

● **Evaluating Piaget**   How well does Piaget's theory stand up? Research confirms that reasoning about moral problems shifts as children grow older. With development children from diverse cultures, from different social classes, and of varying intellectual abilities more fully consider intentions in judging the actions of another person. Nevertheless, young children also can be sensitive to the intentions behind a given act (Zelazo, Helwig, & Lau, 1996). In addition, as early as the preschool years,

KEY THEME
Interaction Among Domains

moral realism   In Piaget's theory of moral development, the first stage of moral reasoning, in which moral judgments are made on the basis of the consequences of an act. Also called *heteronomy*.

immanent justice   Young child's belief that punishment will inevitably follow a transgression.

moral relativism   In Piaget's theory of moral development, the second stage of moral reasoning, in which moral judgments are made on the basis of the actor's intentions. Also called *autonomy*.

children recognize that actions that produce harmful psychological consequences (e.g., causing embarrassment, frightening another person) are as unacceptable as behaviors that produce physical harm (Helwig, Zelazo, & Wilson, 2001). As Piaget described, beliefs in immanent justice and arbitrary punishment decline with age (Hoffman, 1970; Lickona, 1976). Moreover, as children reach the stage of concrete operations, become less egocentric, and demonstrate improved ability to take the perspective of another, they are more likely to recommend punishment appropriate to the moral transgression (Lee, 1971). However, the manner in which *both* parents and peers reason with younger children influences the level of reasoning the children display concerning moral conflicts later in their development (Walker, Hennig, & Krettenauer, 2000). In other words, parents and not just peers (as Piaget claimed), have a significant impact on moral reasoning.

It is clear from Piaget's work that the child's conceptualization of what is moral becomes more elaborate and complex with age and that any attempt to understand moral development must include an explanation of the child's thought as well as behavior. Subsequent theorists, Lawrence Kohlberg in particular, have found Piaget's writings a useful springboard for their own theoretical formulations.

● **Kohlberg's Theory** Like Piaget, Kohlberg (1969, 1976) proposed a stage theory of moral development in which progress through each stage proceeds in a universal order and regression to earlier modes of thinking is rare. Kohlberg based his theory on children's responses to a set of dilemmas that put obedience to authority or the law in direct conflict with helping a person in need (e.g., "Should a man steal an overpriced drug that he cannot obtain legally in order to save his wife?").

Using an analysis of the reasoning of boys ranging in age from ten to sixteen, Kohlberg identified three general levels of moral orientation, each with two substages, to explain the varying responses of his participants (see Table 12.1). At the **preconventional level** the child's behavior is motivated by external pressures: avoidance of punishment, attainment of rewards, and preservation of self-interests. Norms of behavior are not yet derived from internalized principles, and the child's needs and desires are primary. At the **conventional level** conforming to the norms of the majority and maintaining the social order have become central to the child's reasoning. The child now considers the points of view of others, along with their intentions and motives. The child also feels a sense of responsibility to contribute to society and to uphold the laws and institutions that serve its members. Finally, at the **postconventional level** the individual has developed a fuller understanding of the basis for laws and rules. They are now seen as a social contract that all individuals must uphold because of shared responsibilities and duties. The individual recognizes the relative and sometimes arbitrary nature of rules, which may vary from group to group. Certain principles and values, in particular justice and human dignity, must be preserved at all costs. Kohlberg emphasized that changes in the child's perspective-taking ability are the basis for shifts in moral reasoning. According to Kohlberg, changes in perspective-taking ability are promoted by opportunities for children to discuss others' points of view, a position for which research provides some support (Walker et al., 2000).

● **Evaluating Kohlberg** Numerous investigations of Kohlberg's theory have confirmed stagelike transitions in moral reasoning. For example, Anne Colby and her colleagues (1983) followed Kohlberg's original sample of adolescent boys during a twenty-year period and noted that their responses to moral dilemmas fit within the developmental stages delineated by Kohlberg (see Figure 12.5). With few exceptions, participants progressed upward. Six- through fifteen-year-olds tested during a two-year period gained in moral reasoning and few children skipped stages or regressed to earlier forms of reasoning (Walker, 1989). Children also judge the sophistication of alternative responses to moral dilemmas in accordance with stage theory, as long as the alternatives are below their current level of reasoning about moral development (Boom, Brugman & van der Heijden, 2001).

KEY THEME
Continuity/Discontinuity

preconventional level In Kohlberg's theory, the first level of moral reasoning, in which morality is motivated by the avoidance of punishments and attainment of rewards.

conventional level In Kohlberg's theory, the second level of moral reasoning, in which the child conforms to the norms of the majority and wishes to preserve the social order.

postconventional level In Kohlberg's theory, the third level of moral reasoning, in which laws are seen as the result of a social contract and individual principles of conscience may emerge.

TABLE 12.1	Kohlberg's Six Substages of Moral Development	
Stage	**Motivation**	**Typical Moral Reasoning**
Preconventional Level		
1 **Punishment and obedience orientation**	The primary motive for action is the avoidance of punishment:	*Pro:* If you let your wife die, you will get in trouble. You'll be blamed for not spending the money to save her and there'll be an investigation of you and the druggist for your wife's death.
		Con: You shouldn't steal the drug because you'll be caught and sent to jail if you do. If you do get away, your conscience would bother you thinking how the police would catch up to you any minute. (Kohlberg, 1984, p. 52)
2 **Naive instrumental hedonism**	Actions are motivated by the desire for rewards:	*Pro:* If you do happen to get caught you could give the drug back and you wouldn't get much of a sentence. It wouldn't bother you much to serve a little jail term, if you have your wife when you get out.
		Con: He may not get much of a jail term if he steals the drug, but his wife will probably die before he gets out, so it wouldn't do him much good. If his wife dies, he shouldn't blame himself; it isn't his fault she has cancer. (Kohlberg, 1984, p. 52)
Conventional Level		
3 **Good-boy morality**	The child strives to avoid the disapproval of others (as distinct from avoidance of punishment):	*Pro:* No one will think you're bad if you steal the drug but your family will think you're an inhuman husband if you don't. If you let your wife die, you'll never be able to look anyone in the face again.
		Con: It isn't just the druggist who will think you're a criminal, everyone else will, too. After you steal it, you'll feel bad thinking how you've brought dishonor on your family and yourself; you won't be able to face anyone again. (Kohlberg, 1984, p. 52)
4 **Authority-maintaining morality**	An act is always wrong if it violates a rule or does harm to others:	*Pro:* You should steal it. If you did nothing you'd be letting your wife die, it's your responsibility if she dies. You have to take it with the idea of paying the druggist.
		Con: It is a natural thing. . . to want to save his wife but it's always wrong to steal. He still knows he's stealing and taking a valuable drug from the man who made it. (Kohlberg, 1984, p. 50)
Postconventional Level		
5 **Morality of contract and democracy**	The individual is concerned with self-respect and maintaining the respect of others. Laws must be obeyed, because they represent a social contract, but they may sometimes conflict with moral values:	*Pro:* The law wasn't set up for these circumstances. Taking the drug in this situation isn't really right, but it's justified to do it.
		Con: You can't completely blame someone for stealing, but extreme circumstances don't really justify taking the law in your own hands. You can't have everyone stealing when they get desperate. The end may be good, but the ends don't justify the means. (Kohlberg, 1984, p. 50)
6 **Morality of individual principles of conscience**	Individuals are concerned with upholding their personal principles and may sometimes feel it necessary to deviate from rules when the rules conflict with moral principles:	*Pro:* This is a situation that forces him to choose between stealing and letting his wife die. In a situation in which the choice must be made, it is morally right to steal. He has to act in terms of the principle of preserving and respecting life.
		Con: [The man] is faced with the decision of whether to consider other people who need the drug just as badly as his wife. [He] ought to act not according to his particular feelings toward his wife but considering the value of all the lives involved. (Kohlberg, 1984, p. 51)

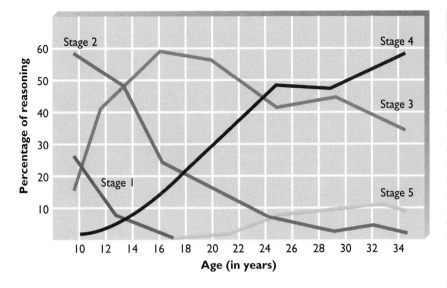

Source: Adapted from Colby et al., 1983.

FIGURE 12.5
The Development of Moral Reasoning

In a longitudinal follow-up study of Kohlberg's original sample, Anne Colby and her colleagues confirmed that participants showed consistent upward advances in moral reasoning with age. The graph shows the extent to which participants gave responses characteristic of each of Kohlberg's six stages from age ten through adulthood. With development, responses associated with the preconventional level (stages 1 and 2) declined, and responses associated with the conventional level (stages 3 and 4) increased. Few young adults moved to the postconventional level of moral reasoning.

KEY THEME
Sociocultural Influence

Cross-cultural studies in countries as diverse as India, Turkey, Japan, Nigeria, and Finland also have found that children show development of moral reasoning, from preconventional to conventional levels, without skipping stages and without regressing to previous stages. However, most individuals as adults still reason at the conventional level (see Figure 12.5). The highest level of moral maturity, what might be termed *moral excellence,* the kind, for example, displayed by Mahatma Gandhi, Martin Luther King, or Abraham Lincoln, probably requires more than postconventional reasoning about moral dilemmas. Such reasoning very likely must combine with high standards, a responsive conscience, a strong sense of personal agency and understanding of one's place in society, a sensitive and compassionate concern about others, and a willingness to act on one's convictions (Colby & Damon, 1992; Hart & Fegley, 1995; Walker & Pitts, 1998).

Moral development has been found to correlate positively with IQ and educational level, consistent with Kohlberg's emphasis on the cognitive basis of moral judgment. As with Piaget's theory, however, researchers have been unable to confirm some specific propositions in Kohlberg's outline of moral development. For example, do individuals within a stage respond consistently to different moral dilemmas, as Kohlberg maintains they should? In one study of seventy-five college students who responded to five moral dilemmas, not one person received the same stage score for all stories (Fishkin, Keniston, & MacKinnon, 1973). Thus, although individuals may exhibit a particular stage, they also display considerable variation in their reasoning about moral issues.

A major criticism of Kohlberg's theory is that it fails to capture the many modes of moral reasoning evident in individuals and different cultural groups. In responding to moral dilemmas, people growing up on the Israeli kibbutz often address the importance of the principle of happiness for everyone (Snarey, 1985). Asian cultures are more likely to emphasize the idea of the collective good and a harmonious social order than Western cultures. From this perspective, the desirable way to resolve disputes is to reconcile people who are in conflict rather than rely on laws to control their behavior. Thus families often preserve harmony by holding conferences to settle disputes. Kohlberg's moral dilemmas, which require a choice between rules and the needs of individuals to bring about justice, do not permit the expression of this cultural principle (Dien, 1982; Ma & Cheung, 1996). Evaluations of the appropriateness of telling the truth or lying also differ between Chinese and Canadian children, as might be predicted from the differing emphasis on modesty and humility reported for these two cultures (Lee et al., 1997). Likewise, Indian cultures emphasize the value of all life, not just human life; thus a most serious transgression, as expressed by

Kohlberg's theory of moral development has been criticized for failing to measure the values found in other cultures. Until researchers have a greater understanding of cultural values, such as those being conveyed by this mother in Somalia as she assists her children in studying the Koran, our understanding of the development of moral reasoning will remain incomplete.

orthodox Hindu children and adults, is eating beef, chicken, or fish (Shweder, Mahapatra, & Miller, 1987). Such a concept does not appear in Kohlberg's outline of moral development. Buddhist beliefs about limits to self and to the value of intervention in preventing suffering are also difficult to reconcile within Kohlberg's framework (Huebner & Garrod, 1991). Thus the movement of the individual toward the fullest understanding of the principle of justice, at least as conceptualized by Kohlberg, may be a singularly Western phenomenon.

The failure to consider alternative modes of moral reasoning has been an especially sensitive issue with respect to possible sex differences in moral development. In one early study, Kohlberg reported that most males function at the higher stage, whereas most females reason at the lower stage, within the conventional level of moral reasoning (Kohlberg & Kramer, 1969). The report provoked a strong reaction from some members of the psychological community and led Carol Gilligan to propose that moral development takes a different, not an inferior, course in females (Gilligan, 1982, 1988; Gilligan & Attanucci, 1988). Gilligan states that because females tend to be concerned with relationships, caregiving, and intimacy, they typically develop a **morality of care and responsibility** in contrast to the **morality of justice** described by Kohlberg. The morality of care and responsibility concerns self-sacrifice and relationships with others rather than the tension between rules and the needs and rights of the individual.

An eleven-year-old girl's response to the story about whether or not to steal a drug illustrates the ethic of care that Gilligan holds to be typical of females:

> *If he stole the drug, he might save his wife then, but if he did, he might have to go to jail, and then his wife might get sicker again, and he couldn't get more of the drug, and it might not be good. So, they should really just talk it out and find some other way to make the money.* (Gilligan, 1982, p. 28)

Although this girl's response might receive a low score in Kohlberg's system because of its seemingly wavering noncommittal nature, Gilligan believes it reflects a mature understanding of the crisis a relationship might undergo when a law is broken.

Are there sex differences in moral development? Of the large number of investigations based on Kohlberg's tasks, very few report substantial differences between males and females (Walker, 1984, 1991; Wark & Krebs, 1996). Both males and females tend to interpret moral decisions about impersonal situations (such as whether a man should steal a drug for his wife) in terms of justice and rights; decisions about dilemmas that they have personally confronted are more frequently made in terms of

morality of care and responsibility   Tendency to make moral judgments on the basis of concern for others.

morality of justice   Tendency to make moral judgments on the basis of reason and abstract principles of equity.

the ethic of care (Walker, 1996). Regardless of whether sex differences in moral development exist, Gilligan's work has shown that researchers need to expand their understanding of what constitutes moral values.

● **Morality as Domain-specific Knowledge**   As we have just seen, definitions of morality can vary enormously and are often embedded within the broad fabric of social knowledge and values represented in culture (Turiel & Wainryb, 1994; Turiel, 1998). But perhaps a distinction needs to be made between moral and societal beliefs. The *moral domain* consists of rules that regulate a person's own or another's rights or welfare; examples are the concepts of justice and responsibility toward others. The *societal domain* pertains to knowledge of **social conventions,** the rules that regulate social interactions such as how to dress appropriately for a given occasion and what degree of formality to use in speaking to someone, factors that can vary dramatically from one culture to another.

Elliot Turiel (1983) hypothesizes that the moral and societal domains develop along separate paths and that most theories of moral development have confused the two. Children begin distinguishing moral and social-conventional rules by age three (Smetana & Braeges, 1990). To illustrate, preschoolers will respond differently to transgressions of their playmates depending on whether the actions violate a social or a moral rule. When a child violates a moral rule, for example, by intentionally inflicting harm or taking another's possessions, other children typically react by physically intervening or making statements about the pain the victim experienced. On the other hand, when children observe another person violating a social convention, such as eating while standing instead of sitting, they either do not react or simply comment on the rules surrounding proper social behavior (Nucci & Turiel, 1978). In addition, when questioned about social-conventional transgressions, most children say such an act would be acceptable if no rule existed about it in school, whereas moral transgressions are wrong, are more serious, and should receive greater punishment, even if the school has no rule pertaining to them (Smetana, Schlagman, & Adams, 1993). Children and adolescents are also likely to be relatively intolerant about others holding moral beliefs with which they disagree but readily recognize that others need not share beliefs about social conventions (Wainryb et al., 2001). Moreover, disagreements with parents are far more likely to emerge with respect to social conventions than moral values as children move into and through adolescence in many different cultures (Smetana, 2002).

How do children come to appreciate the distinction between moral and social conventions? Perhaps through the greater emotional affect associated with moral transgressions than with social infractions. When a child observes a peer hitting someone or is a victim of retaliation himself, the abuse may arouse a high degree of emotion in him. For example, when first- and third-graders are asked to rate how they would feel if they were hit without provocation or if another child stole their toys, they are more likely to indicate a negative emotion than when they line up outside the wrong classroom. Furthermore, children frequently justify intervening in a moral transgression by referring to their own or the victim's emotional state (Arsenio & Ford, 1985). In addition, adults may react differently to transgressions associated with moral issues compared with social conventions; as a result, the child learns to discriminate between these two domains (Glassman & Zan, 1995).

● **Evaluating Cognitive-Developmental Theories**   Cognitive-developmental approaches fill a void left by Freudian and social learning theories by acknowledging that how the child thinks about moral situations and social conflict is every bit as important as how she feels or behaves. However, the approach also has shortcomings. A major concern is whether moral reasoning is related to moral behavior. Scores on reasoning tests do not always correlate with tendencies to avoid cheating, to help others, or to abide by rules (Richards et al., 1992). The closest relationships are found between moral reasoning and specific negative social behaviors, such as aggression and delinquency in adolescents (Blasi, 1980; Gregg, Gibbs, & Basinger, 1994).

KEY THEME
Interaction Among Domains

social conventions   Behavioral rules that regulate social interactions, such as dress codes and degrees of formality in speech.

Theory	Emphasis	Path of Development	Process of Moral Development
TABLE 12.2	The Major Theories of Moral Development		
Freudian	Affective dimensions	Stagelike	Resolution of Oedipal/Electra conflict followed by identification with same-sex parent
Social Learning	Moral behavior	Continuous	Reinforcement and modeling of standards of behavior followed by internalization of those standards
Cognitive-Developmental			
Piaget	Moral reasoning	Stagelike	Growth in cognitive and perspective-taking skills that lead to more abstract, other-oriented principles of morality
Kohlberg	Moral reasoning	Stagelike	
Turiel	Moral reasoning	Continuous	Growth in knowledge of moral rules as distinct from social conventions

Another limitation is that current formulations do not capture the full range of moral principles individuals use in making ethical judgments across different cultures and between the sexes (Gilligan, Lyons, & Hanmer, 1989; Turiel, 1998; Turiel & Wainryb, 1994).

Although they highlight different facets of moral progress, Freudian, social learning, and cognitive-developmental theories (summarized in Table 12.2) all portray the child as moving from a self-orientation to an other-orientation. They also share the view of a child motivated initially by external events, such as rewards and punishments, or the need to affiliate with his parents. With development, the standards of morality become internalized. Ultimately, however, a complete theory of moral development should describe the ways the affective, cognitive, and behavioral dimensions interact with one another. The importance of understanding these interactions is illustrated by the recent findings of a study conducted by Judith Smetana and her colleagues (Smetana et al., 1999). Maltreated and nonmaltreated preschoolers were equivalent in their judgments of the severity of various moral transgressions, such as hitting another child or not sharing a toy. However, maltreated children, compared with nonmaltreated children, reported different levels of affective reactions in such stories (e.g., that a perpetrator would feel less sadness when engaged in some transgression). Thus the findings suggest that the context in which children are socialized (e.g., maltreated versus nonmaltreated) can have different consequences for cognitive and affective measures used to provide insight into the topic of moral development. Perhaps research on more positive aspects of moral development can shed additional light on these complex interrelationships. It is to these more positive aspects that we turn next.

FOR YOUR REVIEW

- What kinds of responses are primarily emphasized in Freudian, social learning, and cognitive-developmental theories of moral development?

- How are the superego, the conscience, and the ego ideal formed in boys and girls according to Freud's theory?

- What findings provide support for the role of social learning in the acquisition of moral behavior?

- What are the basic elements of Piaget's theory of moral development? What elements of his theory are supported or refuted by research evidence?

- What are the primary stages of moral development according to Kohlberg? What kinds of data support his theory and what are some of the major criticisms of his perspective?

- What is the distinction between a morality of justice and a morality of care and responsibility? What evidence exists to suggest that the development of knowledge in the moral domain should be distinguished from the development of knowledge about social conventions?

Prosocial Behavior

A young child consoles a friend in distress, helps her pick up the pieces of a broken toy, or shares a snack. These **prosocial behaviors,** social actions performed to benefit others and perhaps the self, have come under increasing investigation in recent years as another way to understand the development of values and moral behavior in children. Among prosocial behaviors is **altruism,** behavior carried out to help others without expectation of rewards for oneself.

In contrast to research that focuses on justice and rights, prosocial and altruistic responses have a less obligatory, legalistic quality about them (Kahn, 1992). Acts of kindness or assistance are often discretionary but highly valued in many communities. Grade school children who tend to help others have better social skills (Eisenberg & Mussen, 1989), are more popular with peers (Gottman, Gonso, & Rasmussen, 1975; McGuire & Weisz, 1982), and are more self-confident, self-assured, and better adjusted than those who do not. Thus prosocial behaviors are associated with many desirable outcomes, particularly in children's social relationships. Therefore, it is important to understand what influences the emergence of these qualities.

The Development of Prosocial Behaviors and Altruism

Several contemporary theorists believe an essential element underlying prosocial or altruistic behavior is **empathy,** a vicarious, shared emotional response involving an understanding and appreciation of the feelings of others that includes sympathetic concern for the person in need of assistance (Eisenberg & Fabes, 1998). Perhaps humans are biologically predisposed to exhibit such a trait. Even infants show signs of sensitivity to the distress of others. Two- and three-day-olds may cry when other infants cry, but not in response to other, equally loud noises (Simner, 1971). In addition to crying, ten- to fourteen-month-olds may whimper or silently attend to expressions of distress from another person. Often they respond by soothing themselves, sucking their thumbs, or seeking a parent for comfort (Radke-Yarrow & Zahn-Waxler, 1984). Perhaps because the boundary between self and another individual is not yet clear at this age, consoling the self is a form of coping with another's distress, a self-focused emotional reaction more than a genuine prosocial behavior.

Between one and two years of age, empathy may promote new behaviors typically called *sympathy*: touching or patting the distressed person as though to provide solace, seeking assistance for the person, or even giving the person something to provide comfort, such as a cookie, blanket, or teddy bear. The person's emotional state may also be labeled with expressions such as "Cry," "Oh-oh!," or "Hurting" (Radke-Yarrow & Zahn-Waxler, 1984; Zahn-Waxler et al., 1992). Preschool children display more varied and complex responses, including comforting and helping the troubled child, asking questions of her, punishing the agent of the child's distress, protecting the child, and asking an adult for help.

Although many researchers report that helping and sharing increase with age, others note that older children may actually help or share less (Radke-Yarrow, Zahn-Waxler, & Chapman, 1983). Between ages six and sixteen, increasing concerns about

KEY THEME
Nature/Nurture

SEE FOR YOURSELF
psychology.college.hmco.com
Promoting the Development of Empathy

prosocial behavior Positive social action performed to benefit others.

altruism Behavior carried out to help another without expectation of reward.

empathy An understanding and sharing of the feelings of others.

Even preschoolers display care and concern about others. Here a boy brushes sand from the face of his younger sister in an effort to keep her from becoming upset. These kinds of actions suggest that prosocial behavior is an early aspect of human development. Moreover, its expression very likely is greatly influenced by the socialization practices of parents and other caregivers.

self-interests and the expectations of others and greater consideration of the consequences of their actions can enter into decisions about assisting a person in need or performing another prosocial activity (Krebs & Van Hesteren, 1994; Eisenberg et al., 1995). Nevertheless, a recent meta-analysis of research on children and adolescents revealed that prosocial behavior increases with age and generally continues to show positive, although smaller, increases throughout the teenage years (Fabes et al., 1999).

Are girls, often believed to be more nurturing, caring, and empathic than boys, also more altruistic? On the whole, children display few sex differences in the amount of helping and sharing they exhibit (Radke-Yarrow et al., 1983). For example, when in the presence of a crying baby, girls are no more likely to assist than boys (Zahn-Waxler, Friedman, & Cummings, 1983). But some sex differences are observed favoring girls and the differences tend to increase with age (Fabes et al., 1999). These differences are more evident when measures of prosocial behavior involve being kind or considerate rather than when the activity demands helping, comforting, or sharing. In addition, they are more likely to be found when self-reports rather than observational methods are used to measure prosocial activity (Eisenberg & Fabes, 1998).

● **The Relationship Between Empathy and Helping**   Behaving prosocially, such as attempting to alleviate distress in others, may be a way to relieve a child's own empathic distress (Hoffman, 1976, 1982). Thus, if a boy sees that a friend who has just fallen down on the playground is crying, he feels uncomfortable. He knows how painful a skinned knee feels and shares his friend's anguish. To feel better himself, the boy rushes to help his playmate to the school nurse's office.

How strong is the connection between empathy and prosocial behavior? When children are asked to report their feelings, a consistent link between empathy and assisting others has not always been shown. However, empathy assessed by using nonverbal measures, such as facial expressions (e.g., sadness) or behavioral gestures that connote empathy or lack of it (e.g., looking away from the distressed person), is related to helping and sharing. Moreover, as children grow older, the relationship grows distinctly stronger (Eisenberg, 1986; Eisenberg & Miller, 1987; Roberts & Strayer, 1996).

A younger child may show signs of empathic distress but not know what form, if any, the assistance should take (Hoffman, 1976). If a playmate is crying as the result of a fall, should she be helped to stand up or left alone? Should the child say something comforting or reassuring or simply keep silent? As children mature, they are better able to interpret the emotions they are feeling, may experience them more strongly, and learn about the range of prosocial behaviors they can express. The distinction between self and other also matures and with it the realization that the other person's distress can be relieved by taking some action. However, individual differences in helpfulness do exist (Hay et al., 1999). Children who show greater prosocial behaviors as preschoolers continue to do so as adolescents (Eisenberg, Guthries, et al., 1999). In addition, they are better able to take the perspective of another and therefore to feel sympathy for that individual. Unfortunately, if the emotional arousal is either too limited or becomes too great, children may either ignore another or focus on their own uncomfortable feelings at the expense of helping (Fabes et al., 1994; Miller et al., 1996; Young, Fox, & Zahn-Waxler, 1999).

KEY THEME
Individual Differences

ATYPICAL DEVELOPMENT

Conduct Disorders

Anywhere from nearly one half to two thirds of children and adolescents who are referred to mental health centers in the United States display some type of conduct disorder. Conduct disorders range from highly aggressive and violent behaviors directed toward people or animals to the destruction of property, deceitfulness, theft, and truancy. Many of these problem behaviors, particularly violent crimes, have shown a substantial increase during the past decade (Children's Defense Fund, 1996; Hennes, 1998). All of them share the common denominator of violating or seriously disregarding the social norms and rules of the family, school, or society.

The factors hypothesized to contribute to the development of conduct disorders in children and adolescents are as varied as the types of problem behaviors that are identified as antisocial. For example, genetic and temperamental predispositions, along with inconsistent and coercive parenting practices—especially when discipline is based on physical punishment (see the chapter titled "The Family") or includes abuse and maltreatment, frequent parental discord and conflict, or limited cognitive skills associated with perspective taking—may play some part in contributing to conduct disorders (Gabel, 1997; Horne, Glaser, & Calhoun, 1999). But is it possible that a child or adolescent who is aggressive and actually injures another person, who displays cruelty to pets, who intentionally and maliciously destroys another's property, or who often lies or engages in other threatening and harmful activities that violate the basic rights of others might be deficient in empathy? That is, are some children unable to emotionally share others' feelings and to understand the negative impact of their actions on others?

KEY THEME
Nature/Nurture

To examine this question, Douglas Cohen and Janet Strayer (1996) asked young people (ages fourteen to seventeen) who had been diagnosed as conduct disordered and were residing in a residential treatment center and a comparison group of normal young people from the same community to observe and respond to a videotaped set of vignettes depicting individuals in emotionally laden situations. They also completed a set of questionnaires about how certain types of situations made them feel (e.g., "Seeing [a child] who is crying makes me feel like crying" or "I am often very touched by the things that I see happen"). These various measures revealed that young people who display conduct disorders exhibit substantially less empathy than the comparison group; they are less good at identifying the emotions of others and showing responses concordant with and responsive to the emotional states of others.

Cohen and Strayer's research did not reveal why the differences in empathy between conduct-disordered and normal adolescents might exist. Perhaps family socialization practices that differ in the extent to which the youths' emotional needs are met or experienced are part of the answer. For example, concern for others is found more frequently in families in which warmth is high (see the chapter titled "The Family"), in which parents point out the consequences of harmful behavior, and in which altruistic activities are modeled (Robinson, Zahn-Waxler, & Emde, 1994). Perhaps, too, children who begin to engage in antisocial conduct become less sensitive to and less willing to interpret empathic cues in others, growing increasingly callous to such information. Children who show signs of behavioral problems as preschoolers display similar levels of concern for others as children who display normative behavior. But by six to seven years of age, they no longer exhibit as much concern for others (Hastings et al., 2000). These results raise the question of how important empathic training might be for effective treatment of children who display conduct disorders. Many therapeutic efforts, especially when begun later in development, have not always benefitted children with conduct disorders (Gabel, 1997; Horne et al., 1999); perhaps increased efforts to foster empathy constitute one approach that needs further consideration.

● **Prosocial Reasoning**   Just as moral reasoning associated with justice changes with development, so does reasoning associated with prosocial behavior. Nancy Eisenberg (1986) formulated prosocial dilemmas in which the interests of one person are in conflict with those of another individual or group. For example, a child on the way to a birthday party sees another child who has hurt her leg. Should she go find that child's parent in order to get her to a doctor? Or should she continue on to the birthday party so as not to miss the fun? In justifying their answers to such a dilemma, many preschool and some young school-age children in the United States use a *hedonistic orientation* in their reasoning, saying they would help to gain affection or material rewards such as candy or cake. A *needs-of-others orientation* prevails in the reasoning of early elementary school children, who typically express a concern for the physical or psychological needs of others ("He needs help"; "She's hurt"). An *approval and interpersonal orientation* is more prevalent in the middle childhood years as the child's responses increasingly take into consideration the reactions of others ("The child should help because the other person would like her"). During the later elementary years and into high school, a more *self-reflective, empathic orientation* emerges ("I'm trying to put myself in that person's shoes"). Older adolescents develop an *internalized orientation,* focusing on the importance of such emotions as happiness and pride to match internalized abstract principles of behavior concerned with fulfilling societal obligations, avoiding guilt, and maintaining self-respect.

TABLE 12.3
Levels of Prosocial Reasoning

Nancy Eisenberg has outlined the accompanying progression in prosocial reasoning. Children move from a concern with the self to a concern for others and show more internal, abstract bases for helping as they grow older.

Level	Age	Characteristics
Hedonistic orientation	Preschoolers and young elementary school children	Preoccupation with gain for the self as a result of being or not being altruistic
Needs-of-others orientation	Early and middle elementary school children	Concern for the physical and psychological needs of others although they may conflict with own
Approval and interpersonal orientation	Middle elementary and high school students	Reliance on stereotypes of good and bad and seeking approval from others for helping or not helping
Self-reflective, empathetic orientation	Late elementary and high school students	Concern for feelings of others and use of norms for prosocial behavior
Internalized orientation	High school students	Maintenance of self-respect for living up to internalized values and beliefs; belief in rights of all individuals and importance of fulfilling societal obligations

Source: Adapted from Eisenberg, 1986.

Table 12.3 outlines the stages of prosocial reasoning. As with other views of moral development, reasoning progresses from concern for external consequences to a more internalized, principled foundation. However, hedonistic responses do show some increase during the adolescent years, especially in boys (Eisenberg et al., 1995). As expected, level of orientation relates to behavior and how children are perceived by others. For example, children who reason hedonistically tend to donate toys, stickers, or other valued objects to other children less frequently and are evaluated less positively by peers than children of a similar age who reason at higher levels (Carlo et al., 1996; Eisenberg & Shell, 1986). The Moral and Prosocial Development chronology provides an additional summary of developmental changes for both moral and prosocial development.

KEY THEME
Sociocultural Influence

● **Cross-Cultural Investigations**   When asked to reason about prosocial dilemmas, children in other Western industrialized societies display similar patterns of development. German, Italian, and Polish children, for example, show the same progression from hedonistic to needs-of-others orientation that children in the United States do (Boehnke et al., 1989; Eisenberg et al., 1985). In other cultures, however, variations have been found. For example, elementary school children reared on the Israeli kibbutz reflect a more mature level of prosocial reasoning, voicing concern about the humaneness of the central character and the importance of internalized norms ("She has a duty to help others") (Eisenberg, Hertz-Lazarowitz, & Fuchs, 1990). A somewhat different picture emerges for children from the Maisin tribe, a coastal village society of Papua New Guinea. Here children maintain a needs-of-others orientation well into adolescence and even adulthood (Tietjen, 1986). These developmental patterns mirror the values emphasized by each culture. On the Israeli kibbutz, the goal of contributing to the good of the entire community is stressed, whereas among the Maisin, children are taught explicitly to be aware of and respond to the needs of specific others rather than to those of the larger social group.

Might children also show cross-cultural differences in their tendency to behave prosocially related to their prosocial reasoning? Nancy Graves and Theodore Graves (1983) studied the inhabitants of Aitutaki Island, one of the Cook Islands in the South Pacific. A tremendous economic shift, from a subsistence to an industrialized market economy, took place on parts of this island and produced corresponding changes in family structure and the roles of family members. Children living in the

Some children grow up in cultures in which they contribute to the needs of the entire community. Here children in India assist by carrying firewood to their local rural village. Children reared in group-oriented societies tend to engage in more prosocial behavior than children reared in settings that emphasize individualism.

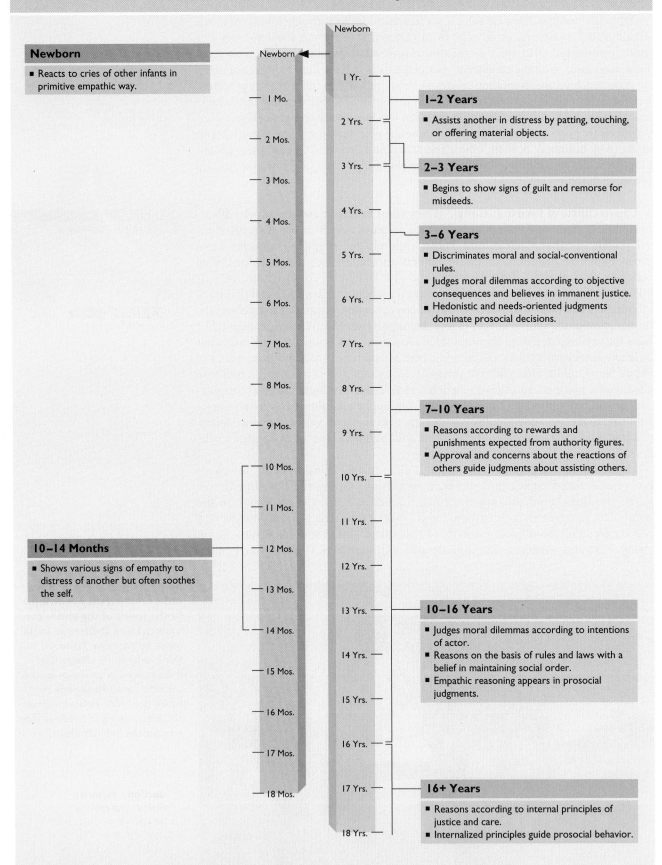

CHRONOLOGY: *Moral and Prosocial Development*

Newborn
- Reacts to cries of other infants in primitive empathic way.

Newborn

10–14 Months
- Shows various signs of empathy to distress of another but often soothes the self.

1–2 Years
- Assists another in distress by patting, touching, or offering material objects.

2–3 Years
- Begins to show signs of guilt and remorse for misdeeds.

3–6 Years
- Discriminates moral and social-conventional rules.
- Judges moral dilemmas according to objective consequences and believes in immanent justice.
- Hedonistic and needs-oriented judgments dominate prosocial decisions.

7–10 Years
- Reasons according to rewards and punishments expected from authority figures.
- Approval and concerns about the reactions of others guide judgments about assisting others.

10–16 Years
- Judges moral dilemmas according to intentions of actor.
- Reasons on the basis of rules and laws with a belief in maintaining social order.
- Empathic reasoning appears in prosocial judgments.

16+ Years
- Reasons according to internal principles of justice and care.
- Internalized principles guide prosocial behavior.

This chart describes the sequence in the development of moral and prosocial behavior based on the findings of research. Children often show individual differences in the exact ages at which they display the various developmental achievements outlined here.

unaffected rural villages grow up in extended families in which they make substantial contributions to family and community goals. They participate in most community affairs, are sent by elders to share food and goods with other village members, and bring the family contribution to church each week. In contrast, children growing up in urban, more modernized settings are reared in nuclear families and participate less in both family and community functions.

Graves and Graves (1983) observed that children five and six years of age in the urban communities were less likely to assist others in their homes and surrounding environs than were children in rural settings. The researchers conclude that prosocial behavior is more likely in societies in which the predominant ethic is one of interdependence and group orientation and in which the child participates in cooperative work experiences than it is in cultures that emphasize individualism and self-reliance. In general, children from traditional rural communities tend to be more cooperative than children from urban cultures (Eisenberg & Mussen, 1989). Also, children from more communal cultures (typical of Asian countries) tend to share more than children from cultures emphasizing individualism (typical of Western countries) (Rao & Stewart, 1999).

● **The Role of Socialization**   What role do child-rearing techniques play in the emergence of prosocial behavior? As social learning theory would predict, reinforcement can be influential. Both material rewards (e.g., money, candy, tokens) and social rewards ("You're a good boy!") increase the likelihood that children will share with or help others, although social rewards and acknowledgments seem to motivate greater care and concern for others (Grusec, 1991). Opportunities for observational learning are another potent factor. When a child sees someone make a donation to a needy person or group, he is likely to be charitable as well (Grusec & Skubiski, 1970).

What models do appears to be more important than what they say (Rushton, 1975); yet the nature of caregivers' verbal communications also has a bearing on prosocial behavior. When parents use **induction**—that is, explain why transgressions are wrong, provide a rationale for rules and regulations, present a reason for prosocial activity, and express disappointment at specific behaviors when exhibited inappropriately—their children are more likely to practice prosocial behaviors (Hastings et al., 2000; Hoffman, 1975; Krevans & Gibbs, 1996). For example, a parent might say, "Don't pull Sam's hair! That hurts him. You don't like to have your hair pulled, do you?" Such messages emphasize clear communication about standards for behavior, arouse empathic feelings, and stimulate perspective taking (Eisenberg & Mussen, 1989). In contrast, a far less effective means of fostering prosocial behavior involves **power assertion,** using forceful commands, physical punishment, or removal of material objects or privileges to influence behavior. For example, the parent might yell, "Stop that! You're not watching TV tonight!" as her son pulls his brother's hair.

Assigning responsibility to children, particularly for tasks that benefit others rather than oneself, also has an impact. For example, having adolescents contribute to household chores such as gardening, helping to prepare meals, keeping the family room clean, or other activities beneficial to the family as a whole is related to the production of more prosocial activities that benefit the family than is taking responsibility for tasks that only directly profit oneself, such as taking care of one's own room or cleaning up one's own space (Grusec, Goodnow, & Cohen, 1996). Moreover, prosocial actions are increased when children are "expected" to initiate and routinely complete these helping activities—that is, when children must self-regulate their actions in these realms rather than when they are requested to carry out the chores on particular occasions.

Another socialization technique that may be as effective as induction is to emphasize the child's prosocial characteristics. When a child is told, "I guess you're the kind of person who helps others whenever you can," her tendency to behave prosocially greatly increases (Mills & Grusec, 1989). Perhaps attributing to the child a sense of concern for others changes her self-concept and she strives to behave in a manner consistent with that image (Grusec, 1982). Parents do not make prosocial attributions

KEY THEME
Nature/Nurture

induction   Parental control technique that relies on the extensive use of reasoning and explanation, as well as the arousal of empathic feelings.

power assertion   Parental control technique that relies on the use of forceful commands, physical punishment, and removal of material objects or privileges.

about their children often, but it is precisely the rarity of these comments that may make them so powerful in the eyes of the child (Grusec, 1991).

● **Prosocial Behavior and Academic Achievement**   Recent research has revealed a surprisingly intriguing link between prosocial behavior and academic achievement. In one study carried out by Gian Caprara and colleagues (Caprara et al., 2000), eight- to nine-year-olds in a community near Rome, Italy, were revisited five years later as adolescents. In contrast to the more traditional focus, in which negative factors such as aggression in young children are studied as a condition predicting poor academic achievement, this study examined the consequences of prosocial behavior on success in the later school years. Teachers, peers, and the children themselves rated their willingness to help, share, be cooperative, and be kind. Even after controlling for level of early academic achievement as third-graders, the researchers found that higher levels of prosocial behavior displayed at this younger age subsequently predicted greater achievement in school as adolescents (Caprara et al., 2000). In another study carried out in Shanghai, China, a greater prosocial orientation among sixth-graders also was correlated with greater academic achievement two years later (Chen et al., 2000). These results suggest that educational environments might benefit from emphasizing prosocial behaviors as much as, if not more than, from the fairly widespread practice of focusing on reducing negative behaviors.

Additional Factors in Prosocial Behavior

**What Do You Think?**

What Role Should Schools Play in Promoting Values?
psychology.college.hmco.com

KEY THEME
Sociocultural Influence

Surprisingly, developmental researchers have seldom investigated the many potential influences that exposure to religious education and other social organizations such as scouting, boys' and girls' clubs, and other community programs may have on the development of prosocial responses and values. Yet many parents would claim that such activities also play a vital role in the development of socially acceptable behaviors. In one study of children given training in their Jewish or Christian faith, participants as young as ten years were found to distinguish between moral issues they considered to be unalterable (stealing, hitting, damaging another's property) and conventional religious practices that might change in certain circumstances or not apply to other individuals (dress customs, dietary laws, worship activities). Thus they can distinguish moral issues involving justice and human welfare associated with their religion from social conventions that arise from exposure to their particular faith (Nucci & Turiel, 1993). In other words, recognizing what is moral and what is socially determined very likely is influenced not only by parental teachings and school practices but also by the myriad other activities and examples to which children are exposed in their particular social contexts. Issues of fairness and rights, caring and cooperation, and duties and personal responsibility are among those that individuals in most cultures believe are too important to be left to just one component of the child's experiences.

FOR YOUR REVIEW

• What are the differences between prosocial behavior, altruism, and empathy?

• How does empathy develop and what is its relationship to prosocial behavior?

• To what extent are conduct disorders associated with lack of empathy?

• How do cross-cultural differences in child rearing influence displays of prosocial behavior?

• What roles do socialization practices such as the use of induction and power assertion techniques play in displays of prosocial behavior?

• What relationship exists between prosocial behavior and academic achievement?

• What other factors influence prosocial behavior?

CHAPTER RECAP

SUMMARY OF DEVELOPMENTAL THEMES

■ **Nature/Nurture**   *What roles do nature and nurture play in the development of the self and of values?*

Although early, biologically based tendencies for children to display a mastery orientation and empathy may exist, most researchers have described how the child's cognitions and social experiences shape self and values. For example, feedback from others certainly plays an enormous role in the child's characterization of self and prosocial behavior. Theorists such as Piaget and Kohlberg suggest that maturation contributes in part to changes in moral reasoning. But even they believe children's experiences with peers and other socializing agents play a large role in spurring moral reasoning.

■ **Sociocultural Influence**   *How does the sociocultural context influence the development of the self and of values?*

Children's evaluations of self are greatly determined by the extent to which they display autonomy, loyalty, cooperation, perseverance, and other qualities stressed by the culture. Self-esteem is affected by how well children live up to the society's expectations concerning beauty, athletic skill, academic ability, and other attributes the culture values. Moral reasoning and behavior further reflect the values of a culture. When responsibilities to the larger social group are emphasized, children tend to be more caring and display more prosocial reasoning than when the culture emphasizes the role of the individual. In addition, groups place different weights on law and justice versus other values, such as harmonious interactions with others. Children's responses to moral dilemmas often reflect their culture's unique beliefs.

■ **Child's Active Role**   *How does the child play an active role in the development of the self and of values?*

Caregivers take on initial responsibility for instituting standards for the behavior of young children. As children gain cognitive and social skills, they initiate efforts to control their own activities and are assumed to internalize the values of the larger society. Children also begin to recognize that they are competent individuals, capable of influencing and controlling their environment in realistic ways. Their judgments about the appropriateness of moral and prosocial actions are assumed to influence their behavior as well.

■ **Continuity/Discontinuity**   *Is the development of the self and of values continuous or discontinuous?*

Although the child's understanding of self undergoes many developmental changes, evidence that these changes are stagelike remains limited. Even the identity crisis, often considered a hallmark of adolescence, may not be experienced by all young people and reflects a culmination of many earlier, gradual changes. Several influential theories of moral development are stage theories, specifically those of Piaget and Kohlberg. The empirical evidence, however, suggests that reasoning about moral, prosocial, and other values may occur at several levels within the same individual. Although stage theories are popular, domain-specific approaches emphasizing continuous growth are prominent as well.

■ **Individual Differences**   *How prominent are individual differences in the development of the self and of values?*

Because the reactions of others play an important role in the development of self, children may differ enormously in how they view themselves and in how they interact with their world. Some may develop confidence and a sense of control; others may express considerable uncertainty and a sense of helplessness. As a result of their socialization experiences and opportunities to interact with peers, children also display considerable differences in their moral and prosocial values.

■ **Interaction Among Domains**   *How does the development of the self and of values interact with development in other domains?*

Cognitive skills, such as the ability to reason abstractly about the feelings and intentions of others, play a role in evaluations of self and moral judgments. Emotions such as empathy contribute to prosocial behaviors and altruism. Physical changes and capacities, as well as the social environment, can dramatically affect self-esteem and the emergence of identity. At the same time, development of the self and of values has an effect on other domains. For example, high self-esteem and prosocial activity are associated with healthy peer interactions. Development of the self and of values represents an important interaction among affect, cognition, and social experience.

SUMMARY OF TOPICS

The Concept of Self

■ Researchers concerned with the development of *self*—the beliefs, knowledge, and feelings an individual uses to describe his personal characteristics—make the distinction between self as *object* and self as *subject*.

Self as Object

■ Self as object consists of *self-concept*, the perceptions, ideas, and beliefs a person holds to be true of himself or herself.

■ Evidence exists that children begin to distinguish their own behaviors from those of others in the first year of life.

However, a sense of themselves as objects is first evident in their self-recognition at about fifteen to eighteen months of age.

- During the preschool years children typically define themselves in terms of a *categorical self*, that is, by referring to various categories that provide membership in one group or another. By the early school years, *social comparison* involving others becomes important. Effects on others and their relationships to broader sociocultural ideals become a central part of the adolescent's definitions of self.

Self as Subject

- Self as subject includes the child's sense of agency, individuality, stability, and reflection.

- Infants seem to be born with an intrinsic desire to gain control of their world. To the extent that an environment provides consistent feedback, children acquire an increasing sense of agency.

- Children with a *mastery orientation* believe they have considerable influence over what happens to them. Those who experience *learned helplessness* believe they have little influence over what happens to them. Mastery orientation and learned helpless are also determined in part by the extent to which children perceive their abilities as entity-based or as a result of their effort.

- Learned helplessness can be reduced by a focus on effort and by avoiding either praise or criticism of stable abilities.

Self-esteem: Evaluating Self

- *Self-esteem* consists of the positive or negative feelings a person has about himself. It stems from the evaluation of others, as well as the extent to which the child feels successful in those areas thought to be important.

- Self-esteem is very high in preschoolers but tends to decline in earlier elementary school, and for many, especially girls, it shows a further decline during the early adolescent years.

Identity

- *Identity* refers to the broad, coherent view that a person holds about oneself. Although Erik Erikson considered the acquisition of one's identity to be an important achievement during the adolescent years, others suggest it is an ongoing process that continues into adulthood.

- Although many adolescents may experience greater conflict with their parents as they explore new ways of behaving, most successfully negotiate the teenage years without undergoing an *identity crisis,* a period of great stress and uncertainty.

- Acquiring an *ethnic identity,* a sense of belonging to one's own ethnic and cultural minority group, seems to benefit children and their understanding of others.

Self-regulation and Self-control

- Initial efforts at *self-regulation* of behavior are instituted by adults and take the form of co-regulation involving caregiver and child. *Self-control* involves the child's regulation of behavior apart from the caregiver.

Developmental Changes

- Self-regulation efforts usually begin in the second half of the first year of life and continue throughout childhood. Self-initiated attempts to control behavior become more evident as children demonstrate increasing capacities for *delay of gratification* and other forms of compliance, planning, and orderly behavior.

The Influence of Language and Attention

- Verbal, attentional, and other cognitive mechanisms appear to be important in children's efforts to control their own behavior.

Individual Differences

- Differences in the ability of children to regulate their own behavior remain consistent throughout childhood.

Moral Development

- Moral development refers to the child's acquisition of the standards of conduct considered ethical within a culture.

Freud's Theory

- Freud's theory focuses on the affective relationship between child and parents. Through the process of identification and as a result of his or her emotional relationship with a parent, the child acquires a *superego,* a *conscience,* and an *ego ideal.* Guilt and other responses indicating internalization of parental and cultural standards begin to be evident in the second year and are displayed in a wide number of ways.

Social Learning Theory

- Social learning theory focuses on the display of moral behavior, such as children's ability to resist temptation. From this perspective, the reinforcements children receive from parents and other agents of socialization, as well as their observations of the behavior of others, are important for moral development.

Cognitive-Developmental Theories

- Cognitive-developmental theories emphasize the child's level of moral reasoning in conflict situations.

- Both Piaget and Kohlberg have outlined stages in the development of moral thought. In Piaget's theory, children progress from *moral realism* to *moral relativism* as their cognitive capabilities mature. In Kohlberg's view, most children advance through *preconventional, conventional,* and *postconventional* levels of moral reasoning. Both Piaget and Kohlberg maintain that the child's increasing perspective-taking skills are a major factor in these changes.

- Kohlberg's theory focuses on the development of a *morality of justice.* However, others suggest that consideration needs to be given to the development of a *morality of care and responsibility,* a form of morality that may be more evident among girls than boys.

- Newer domain-specific approaches to moral development distinguish between moral knowledge and social-conventional knowledge.

- The relationships among emotional, behavioral, and cognitive measures of moral development is not always strong. However, all theories portray the child as moving from a self-orientation to an other-orientation in consideration of what is moral and socially acceptable.

Prosocial Behavior

- *Prosocial behavior* may be performed for a number of reasons. However, *altruism* is a specific form of prosocial behavior in which the individual expects no rewards for himself or herself.

The Development of Prosocial Behaviors and Altruism

- Evidence for *empathy*, an understanding and sharing of the feelings of others, is displayed in early infancy. By the preschool years children engage in substantive effort to help others. Reasoning about prosocial behavior undergoes a developmental change from a focus on the concern with external consequences of acting in certain ways to a more internalized, principled basis for helping behavior.

- Children who are rewarded for prosocial behaviors and who observe parents and others acting prosocially tend to be more helpful than other children. Children whose parents use induction as a disciplinary technique and who grow up in cultures that emphasize group values are also more likely to demonstrate care and concern for others than children whose parents use *power assertion* as a disciplinary technique or who grow up in cultures emphasizing greater individualism.

- Children who display *conduct disorders* show lower levels of empathy than do normal children, especially once they enter the elementary school years.

- Prosocial behavior seems to be correlated with higher academic achievement.

Additional Factors in Prosocial Behavior

- Although little research exists, religious and other organized socialization programs also probably encourage children to engage in more prosocial behavior as they grow older.

CHAPTER 13

Gender

Key Themes in Gender Development

■ **Nature/Nurture**   What roles do nature and nurture play in gender development?

■ **Sociocultural Influence**   How does the sociocultural context influence gender development?

■ **Child's Active Role**   How does the child play an active role in the process of gender development?

■ **Continuity/Discontinuity**   Is gender development continuous or discontinuous?

■ **Individual Differences**   How prominent are individual differences in gender development?

■ **Interaction Among Domains**   How does gender development interact with development in other domains?

"*N*icky," one of the authors said to her then five-year-old son, "what do you think should be on the cover of this book? It's about children, you know."

"Well," he thought for a moment, "how about a picture of a child?"

"A boy or a girl?" asked the mother.

"How about one of each?" he suggested. The mother was pleased that her son chose a girl as well as a boy. She had tried hard to teach him to think about gender in nonstereotypical ways, and his willingness to include girls seemed to indicate that her efforts were successful.

"What should they be doing?" the mother continued.

"Well, how about having the boy play with a computer?" he quickly responded.

"And the girl?" she asked.

"I think she should have a tea party or something."

This five-year-old's response is consistent with many **gender stereotypes** that exist in our society, that is, our beliefs and expectations about the characteristics of females and males. Boys, according to these stereotypes, are active, aggressive, independent, and interested in science. Girls, on the other hand, are passive, nonaggressive, and socially oriented. At what ages and to what extent do children have knowledge of these stereotypes? Furthermore, are such common beliefs actually manifested in the everyday behaviors of children? Are any differences we might observe due to the biological makeup of males and females? What part does socialization play in this process? We will address these central questions in this chapter as we discuss **gender-role development,** the process by which children acquire the characteristics and behaviors prescribed for males and females in their culture.

Before the mid-1960s, most psychologists regarded the socialization of children into traditional masculine and feminine roles as both a natural and a desirable outcome of development. Behavioral sex differences were viewed as inevitable and were linked to comparable sex differences among nonhumans (Kohlberg, 1966; Mischel, 1966; Shaw & Darling, 1985). But changes in social values in the mid-1960s, especially those accompanying the women's movement, shifted the ways in which psychologists approached sex differences and gender-role socialization. Many of the questions that interest developmental psychologists today represent both a challenge to traditional assumptions about the nature and origins of gender roles and sex differences and a concerted effort to determine the developmental processes that underlie children's acquisition and enactment of gender roles.

gender stereotypes   Expectations or beliefs that individuals within a given culture hold about the behaviors characteristic of males and females.

gender-role development   Process by which individuals acquire the characteristics and behaviors prescribed by their culture for their sex. Also called *sex typing.*

Gender Stereotypes Versus Actual Sex Differences

Throughout the recorded history of Western civilization, females and males have been assumed to differ in temperament and interests, among other characteristics. Many of these beliefs persist unchanged in contemporary gender stereotypes.

The Stereotypes: What Are They?

Suppose a group of college students is asked to rate the "typical" boy or girl on a number of psychological attributes. Will they rate certain traits as more typical of males than of females, and vice versa? College students respond that characteristics such as independence, aggression, and self-confidence are associated with masculinity. In general, attributes such as these, which are associated with acting on the world, are classified as **instrumental.** In contrast, emotional expressiveness, kindness, and gentleness are linked with femininity. These perceived feminine characteristics are often classified as **expressive,** or associated with emotions and interactions with other people. Table 13.1 shows other traits often associated with masculinity and femininity (Martin, 1995).

TABLE 13.1
Stereotypic Characteristics Attributed to Males and Females

When college students were asked to rate a typical boy or girl on a number of personality traits, strong patterns emerged among traits that were seen as being associated with each sex. Male traits generally fall into a cluster called *instrumentality* and female traits into a cluster labeled *expressiveness.*

Item Type	Mean Typicality Ratings by Sex of Child Target[a]	
	Boys	Girls
Sex-typed Masculine[b]		
Self-reliant	5.05	3.69
Does dangerous things	4.96	2.57
Enjoys mechanical objects	5.57	2.68
Dominant	5.36	3.54
Enjoys rough play	6.09	3.07
Independent	4.95	3.59
Competitive	5.70	4.16
Noisy	5.78	3.93
Physically active	6.23	4.80
Aggressive	5.60	3.41
Conceited	4.38	3.46
Sex-typed Feminine[c]		
Gentle	3.21	5.36
Neat and clean	3.05	5.42
Sympathetic	3.42	5.33
Eager to soothe hurt feelings	3.35	5.33
Well-mannered	4.01	5.44
Cries and gets upset easily	3.20	4.95
Easily frightened	3.27	4.89
Soft-spoken	3.00	4.64
Helpful around the house	3.27	5.31
Gullible	3.74	4.33
Reliable	4.33	4.74
Truthful	4.31	4.91
Likeable	4.99	5.68
Nonsex-typed		
Adaptable	4.90	4.72

[a]Maximum scores = 7.0.
[b]Indicates that ratings for boys were significantly higher than for girls.
[c]Indicates that ratings for girls were significantly higher than for boys.

Source: Martin, 1995.

instrumental characteristics Characteristics associated with acting on the world; usually considered masculine.

expressive characteristics Characteristics associated with emotions or relationships with people; usually considered feminine.

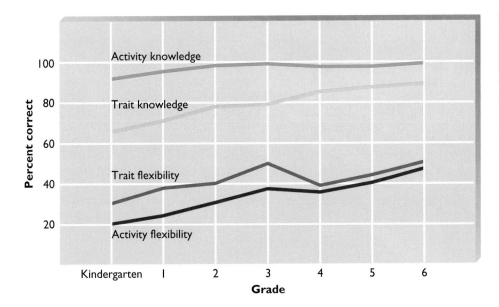

Source: Serbin, Powlishta, & Gulko, 1993.

FIGURE 13.1
Developmental Trends in Gender-Role Knowledge

When kindergartners through sixth-graders were asked to identify which of twenty stereotyped objects were masculine and which were feminine, all children gave at least 90 percent correct answers (see the line for "activity knowledge"). If they were asked to indicate whether objects could be used by both sexes, a developmental increase in flexibility was also observed (see the line for "activity flexibility"). In addition, knowledge of stereotyped traits and flexibility with regard to those traits both increased over the age span studied.

KEY THEME
Sociocultural Influence

These gender stereotypes are not limited to our own society. Researchers asked children and adults from thirty nations in North and South America, Europe, Africa, and Asia to indicate whether certain traits are more frequently associated with men or women in their culture. The results showed many cross-cultural similarities in the stereotypes adults attributed to males and females (Williams & Best, 1982).

Despite the many similarities in gender stereotypes across cultures, some differences occurred among nations in the specific characteristics attributed to males and females. For example, Italian adults stereotypically associated "endurance" with women, although most adults in other countries believed this is a masculine trait. Nigerian adults believed "affiliation" is neutral, whereas adults in other countries said it is a feminine characteristic. Thus we cannot say that specific characteristics are always attributed to males or to females. We can say, however, that the tendency to stereotype on the basis of sex is found in a variety of cultural settings.

Children's Knowledge of Gender Stereotypes

Children begin to acquire gender-role stereotypes and employ them as guides for their behavior at a surprisingly early age—from about two years onward. At eighteen months of age, infants prefer to look at toys stereotypically associated with their own sex (Serbin et al., 2001). By age two, children believe that girls are nonaggressive, talk a lot, play with dolls, and will grow up to be nurses or teachers. In contrast, they say that boys are aggressive, play with trucks and cars, and will grow up to be the boss (Kuhn, Nash, & Brucken, 1978). Preschoolers' knowledge about gender stereotypes includes personality traits, occupations, appearance qualities, and household activities that are associated with males and females (Bauer, Liebl, & Stennes, 1998; Poulin-Dubois et al., 2002). Their thinking about gender stereotypes even extends beyond these qualities to items that may serve as metaphors for masculinity and femininity; they believe, for example, that fir trees and bears are "for boys" and that maple trees and butterflies are "for girls" (Leinbach, Hort, & Fagot, 1997).

By age six or seven, children's knowledge of gender stereotypes is well established. Lisa Serbin and her colleagues (Serbin, Powlishta, & Gulko, 1993) asked five- through twelve-year-olds to state whether twenty stereotyped objects (e.g., *hammer, rifle, stove, broom*) belonged to male or female categories. As Figure 13.1 indicates, all children, regardless of age, showed extensive knowledge of the stereotypes. The figure also shows that children's knowledge of stereotyped personality traits (e.g., *gentle, emotional, adventurous, messy*) expands through the middle school years. As children

By two to three years of age, children show a fairly extensive understanding of gender stereotypes, the beliefs about the characteristics of males and females. Through the early and middle school years, this knowledge becomes even more fully elaborated.

grow older, however, their knowledge of stereotypes also becomes more flexible in that they are more likely to say that both males and females can possess certain traits (Katz & Ksansnak, 1994; Levy, Taylor, & Gelman, 1995; Serbin et al., 1993). Other researchers have found that flexibility concerning gender stereotypes is especially high right when young adolescents experience a life transition that may involve reevaluation of past beliefs: entering junior high school. Later in adolescence, when individuals are more likely to be thinking about their future roles and responsibilities, flexibility regarding gender stereotypes declines (Alfieri, Ruble, & Higgins, 1996). Some researchers have described this return to traditional beliefs about gender during adolescence as *gender intensification* (Galambos, Almeida, & Petersen, 1990).

What Sex Differences Actually Exist?

In light of such durable and pervasive stereotypes about "femaleness" and "maleness," it is logical to ask whether researchers have documented actual differences in the characteristics or behaviors of females and males. For many human traits, the data show that average differences *between* the sexes are smaller than the variability in performance *within* each sex. Nonetheless, in some domains the characteristics of females and males have been found to differ.

● **Physical Attributes**   Females and males physically differ in a number of ways, including the makeup of their chromosomes, their genitalia, and levels of certain hormones. Females are physically more mature at birth, whereas males show a special physical vulnerability during infancy. Compared with females, males are more likely to be miscarried, die in infancy, or develop hereditary diseases (Jacklin, 1989). Later in infancy and childhood, females walk, talk, and reach other developmental milestones earlier than males. Males, on the other hand, are more physically active and are more likely to engage in vigorous rough-and-tumble play (Eaton & Ennis, 1986; Pellegrini & Smith, 1998). By later childhood and adolescence, females reach puberty earlier and males develop greater height, weight, and muscle mass than females (Maccoby & Jacklin, 1974).

● **Cognition**   One aspect of cognition for which males and females have been thought to differ is in verbal abilities. The popular belief has been that girls are more

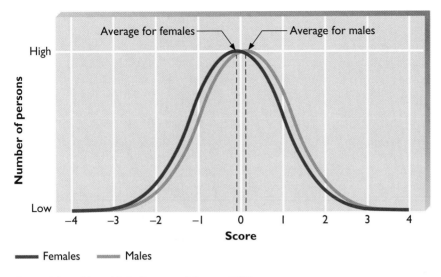

FIGURE 13.2
Sex Differences in
Mathematics Skills

Although sex differences in mathematics skills do exist, the differences are quite small. This graph illustrates the size of the average sex differences. The horizontal axis represents scores converted to a standardized form.

Source: Adapted from Hyde, Fennema, & Lamon, 1990.

skilled than boys at verbal tasks, a belief that was modestly substantiated by an early review of the relevant research (Maccoby & Jacklin, 1974). Meta-analyses of cognitive sex differences, however, indicate only small sex differences in verbal skills favoring females (Feingold, 1988; Hyde & Linn, 1988). Females have a slight advantage on tests that measure reading comprehension, spelling, word meaning, or grammar (Feingold, 1993; Halpern, 1997), but most researchers agree that the differences are not large enough to warrant much notice.

In another meta-analysis of more than a hundred studies of sex differences in mathematics skills, the investigators concluded that boys and girls showed no overall differences in performance (Hyde, Fennema, & Lamon, 1990). When the scores of participants of different ages and from specific groups were examined more closely, however, sex differences in certain aspects of mathematics performance did emerge. During elementary school, for example, girls showed a slight superiority over boys in the area of computation; in the high school and college years, on the other hand, males did moderately better than females on tests of mathematical problem solving. Among groups selected for exceptional performance (such as students in gifted and talented programs), males performed better than females in tests of mathematics. The scores of males on mathematics tests are more variable than the scores of females, at least for children in the United States (Feingold, 1992). When differences across all the studies are averaged, males show only a very slight advantage. Figure 13.2 illustrates the overall magnitude of this sex difference.

In fact, the only notable sex difference in cognitive skills currently supported by empirical evidence involves visual-spatial abilities. Visual-spatial skills include a number of processes, all of which require the ability to visualize and transform figures or objects in the mind. Figure 13.3 illustrates three tests of visual-spatial skills: spatial perception, mental rotation, and spatial visualization. As you can see, spatial perception tasks require participants to ignore distracting information to locate horizontal and vertical orientation. Mental rotation tasks demand that participants transform two- and three-dimensional figures "in their heads." Spatial visualization tasks require them to analyze relationships among different spatial representations.

In general, results indicate no sex differences on spatial visualization tasks. Males do, however, show superior performance on mental rotation and, to a lesser extent, spatial perception (the tasks depicted in the middle and top portions of Figure 13.3, respectively) (Linn & Peterson, 1985, 1986; Voyer, Voyer, & Bryden, 1995). As with mathematical skills, boys show greater variability in their visual-spatial scores than do girls in our society (Feingold, 1992). Sex differences in visual-spatial skills are evident in children by age four-and-a-half years (Levine et al., 1999), but the magnitude of sex differences in this domain increases with age (Voyer et al., 1995).

◉ SEE FOR YOURSELF
psychology.college.hmco.com
A Mental Rotation Test

FIGURE 13.3
Sex Differences in
Visual-Spatial Skills

Tests of visual-spatial skills typically assess spatial perception (top), mental rotation ability (middle), or spatial visualization (bottom). In the top panel, participants are asked to indicate which bottle has a horizontal water line. In the middle panel, participants must identify the two responses that depict rotated versions of the standard. In the bottom panel, participants are asked to identify the simple geometric figure on the top within the more complex figure underneath. Generally, males perform better than females on spatial perception and mental rotation tasks.

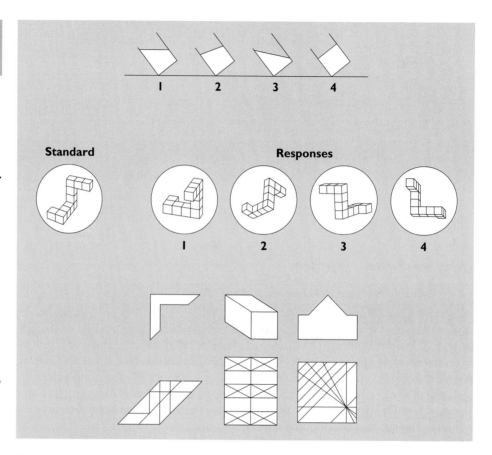

Source: Adapted from Linn & Petersen, 1985.

● **Social Behaviors**   Researchers who have examined the results of hundreds of studies of social behaviors and personality characteristics have concluded that few actual sex differences exist in the area of social behaviors (Feingold, 1994a; Maccoby & Jacklin, 1974). Although average scores of boys and girls consistently differ in some areas, the performance of children within each sex shows considerable variability.

One of the most consistent findings in the research on sex differences is that, beginning in the preschool years, males are more aggressive than females. They engage in more rough-and-tumble play, display more physical aggression, try to dominate peers, and subsequently display more antisocial behaviors than girls (Block, 1983; Huston, 1985; Loeber & Hay, 1997). Meta-analyses substantiate that sex differences in aggression are greatest among preschoolers and decrease through the college years (Eagly & Steffen, 1986; Hyde, 1984, 1986). Even though males generally are more aggressive than females, however, the magnitude of the sex difference varies as a function of where the aggression occurs and the type of aggression being measured. The largest sex differences are found in naturalistic settings, such as playgrounds, and when physical aggression is being measured. Conclusions about sex differences in aggression must be tempered by how this construct is defined, however. When aggression is described as an attempt to harm another person through manipulation, gossip, or excluding peers from a social group (called *indirect* or *relational aggression*), girls are found to be more aggressive than boys starting in the preschool years (Bjorkqvist, 1994; Crick, Casas, & Mosher, 1997; Crick & Grotpeter, 1995).

Other sex differences occur in the verbal and nonverbal behaviors that boys and girls use as they participate in social communication. Boys generally issue more directive statements (e.g., "Put that block over here!"), attempt to gain the floor, and engage in one-upmanship as they speak. Girls, on the other hand, tend to verbally reinforce their conversation partners and follow the ongoing themes of conversations (Carli & Bukatko, 2000). Girls are especially likely to display these affiliative behaviors

One of the most consistent sex differences is the tendency for boys to display more physical aggression than girls, especially during the preschool years. Girls, on the other hand, are more likely to show relational aggression than boys.

when they are interacting with other girls (Strough & Berg, 2000). Girls also display more social smiles and gazing than boys do, especially in late adolescence (Eisenberg & Lennon, 1983; Hall & Halberstadt, 1986).

● **Emotions** To some degree, girls show a heightened sensitivity to emotions compared with boys. For example, female children and adults from widely varying cultures are better than males at identifying the positive and negative emotions displayed on faces (Hall, 1984). Girls also tend to display more positive and negative emotions themselves (Casey, 1993), although boys tend to express one particular emotion—anger—more often than do girls (Hubbard, 2001). Females also show more anxieties and worrying about social and problem-solving situations than do males (Block, 1983; LaGreca & Lopez, 1998; Silverman, LaGreca, & Wasserstein, 1995). Such findings must be interpreted with caution, however, because females may simply be more likely than males to report their feelings and emotional states. The case of empathy provides a good example of this problem. Females report that they are more empathic and cry more than males do, but no sex differences emerge when physiological or unobtrusive measures are used to assess empathy (Eisenberg & Lennon, 1983).

In addition, some researchers have found sex differences in self-esteem. Surveys of middle-class girls indicate that when they reach adolescence, girls report a decline in their feelings about their self-worth (American Association of University Women, 1992). More recent research, however, indicates that the size of the difference in self-esteem between boys and girls is generally small (Kling et al., 1999) and that there is more variability in self-esteem within groups of boys and girls than there is between them (Eccles et al., 1999).

Perhaps of greatest concern is the fact that, beginning in adolescence, girls show a sharp rise in the rates of depression they experience compared with boys (see the chapter titled "Emotion"); by late adolescence, they are twice as likely as boys to be depressed. According to Susan Nolen-Hoeksma (2001), these findings can be understood as the result of several factors that girls experience to a greater degree than boys: greater exposure to stressful life events (e.g., sexual abuse), greater biological responses to stress, and coping styles that involve focusing inward on feelings of distress (Nolen-Hoeksma, 2001). Because adolescence is the time during which we usually begin to see this gender difference, researchers are trying to understand how the complex changes that occur at this developmental stage might be responsible.

Sex Differences in Perspective

Perhaps because of our tendency to think in terms of gender stereotypes, we might assume sex differences will be numerous. In fact, research on actual sex differences indicates that the behavior of people in general shows great variability and that males and females often are more alike than different. If the research indicates more similarities than differences between males and females, why do stereotypical beliefs persist? One explanation may be that we notice, and therefore retain our beliefs, when boys and girls display behaviors consistent with stereotypes. In contrast, when a girl or a boy behaves in a manner inconsistent with a stereotype, we ascribe this pattern to an individual difference. Thus, when Billy fights (a stereotypically masculine activity), we say that "boys will be boys." But when he cooks and helps around the house in stereotypically feminine tasks, we comment on how "helpful" (not how "feminine") he is compared with other boys his age. Perhaps, too, stereotypes result from the tendency of children (and adults) to form cognitive categories of social groups (Martin, 1991). On seeing one similarity among people in a group (e.g., in terms of physical characteristics), we may be tempted to conclude that they resemble one another in other ways, too.

FOR YOUR REVIEW

- What are the characteristics associated with masculine and feminine stereotypes? What do cross-cultural studies reveal about the nature of gender stereotypes?

- How do children's concepts of gender stereotypes change with age?

- What actual sex differences exist in the physical, cognitive, social, and emotional domains?

Theories of Gender-Role Development

What are the origins of sex differences in behavior? Even though contemporary research shows that actual sex differences in behavior are relatively few, boys and girls still show different profiles in some domains of behavior. Three major theoretical perspectives—biological, social learning, and cognitive theories—each make unique and important contributions to our understanding of these behaviors.

Biological Theories

KEY THEME
Nature/Nurture

Biologically based explanations for sex differences focus largely on the influence of chromosomes, hormones, and the structure of the brain on behavior. These factors often work in ways that illustrate the complex interactions of biological systems to produce sex-differentiated behaviors.

As we saw in the chapter titled "Genetics and Heredity," the presence of an X or a Y sex chromosome begins a complex process that leads to sexual differentiation. Between six and twelve weeks after conception, the XY chromosomal configuration leads to the development of testes and the secretion of a class of male hormones called **androgens,** a process that results in further sexual differentiation. The penis and scrotum develop in response to the metabolism of *testosterone,* an androgen that is actually present in both sexes but in greater amounts in males (Whalen, 1984). In the absence of an XY configuration and the associated greater amounts of androgens, the female structures develop (Breedlove, 1994; Hood et al., 1987). These differences in biological structures form the bases by which a child is labeled "boy" or "girl," the social categorization of biological sex.

● **Hormones and Behavior**   Prenatal exposure to hormones, particularly androgens, influences the developing fetus in ways that may have an impact on biology

androgen   Class of male or masculinizing hormones.

and, perhaps, postnatal behavior. Most important for our discussion, androgens influence the developing organization of the central nervous system and the brain (Gorski, 1980; MacLusky & Naftolin, 1981; Overman et al., 1997). Hormone-related sex differences in the central nervous system may, in turn, have important influences on behavior and abilities.

Take the example of aggression. Explanations of sex differences in aggression from a biological perspective have relied largely on experiments in which androgens were administered systematically to female animals during prenatal development. The animal studies show that these hormonally treated females subsequently display increased aggressive behaviors, such as threats and rough-and-tumble play, compared with normally developing females. These findings have been replicated in rats, monkeys, and a number of other species (Goy, 1970; Parsons, 1980).

Although this type of evidence implies a causal link between male hormones and aggression, some controversy concerning the relationship exists (Tieger, 1980). First, although hormones have been shown to precede and presumably influence certain behaviors, such as aggression, those behaviors may themselves have an impact on hormone levels. That is, levels of hormones, including testosterone, can also change *in response to* changes in the environment (Hood et al., 1987). Among nonhuman males, for example, increases in androgen levels frequently follow, rather than precede, an aggressive encounter (Hood et al., 1987). Thus the link between aggression and levels of androgens is not unidirectional, and it is difficult to make causal statements. Second, because human beings have a nervous system that differs in important ways from those of other species—particularly in the size of the cortex, which directs voluntary behavior—it is not clear that findings from animal studies can be generalized to humans (Fausto-Sterling, 1992). Nevertheless (and still keeping the aforementioned cautions in mind), the data from a recent study with humans show that the more testosterone women had in their bloodstream during pregnancy, the more likely their daughters were to show preferences for masculine activities when they were preschoolers. In contrast, social factors such as parental sex-role beliefs did not predict these girls' behaviors (Hines et al., 2002).

ATYPICAL DEVELOPMENT

Hormonal Disorders in Children

Among humans, there are several conditions in which genetic males or females may be exposed to a hormonal environment that is not typical for their sex. One such disorder is *congenital adrenal hyperplasia (CAH)*, a condition that occurs in about one in five thousand to one in fifteen thousand births (Miller & Levine, 1987). This genetic disorder causes a deficiency in the production of adrenal steroids, with the result that high levels of androgens begin to be produced during the prenatal period. If the child is a genetic female, for example, she will be born with masculinized genitalia. Usually her physical appearance is surgically corrected, hormone therapy is begun to regulate the levels of androgens circulating in her body, and the child is raised as a girl. Even following treatment, however, CAH girls have been found to show many behavioral patterns that are "typical" of boys. They prefer toys geared for boys, like rough-and-tumble play, and show enhanced visual-spatial skills (Collaer & Hines, 1995; Hampson, Rovet, & Altmann, 1998).

Among boys, a failure of androgen to bind with its receptors can result in *androgen insensitivity syndrome (AI)*. Because the boy is born with female-looking genitalia, he is usually raised as a girl; the disorder is typically discovered at puberty, when menstruation fails to begin (Breedlove, 1994). These children commonly show "female" play interests and visual-spatial skills that are poorer than those of normal females who served as controls (Collaer & Hines, 1995).

It is tempting to conclude from these unusual hormonal disorders that biological factors are responsible for sex differences in patterns of social behaviors and cognitive skills. CAH girls do, in fact, have masculine-typed behaviors and were exposed to unusually high levels of androgens even though they were later socialized as girls. AI boys have lower levels of androgens and, even though they are socialized as girls, their performance on some cognitive tasks is actually lower than that of the average female. Thus, it is difficult to argue simply for the effect of socialization on their behavior. On the other hand, studies of androgenized girls are difficult to interpret because parents were aware of their daughters' masculinized appearance at birth and may have tolerated or even encouraged more "boylike" behaviors. Moreover, their enhanced visual-spatial skills may be the result of their masculine play styles rather than hormone levels per se (Liben et al., 2002). Thus although these studies suggest a role for biology in the emergence of some sex-linked behaviors, it is still premature to rule out the effects of socialization.

● **Brain Lateralization**   A second way in which biology can influence sex differences in behavior is through the organization and functions of the brain. A prominent biological explanation for sex differences in visual-spatial skills involves the process known as *lateralization of the brain.* During the course of development, as we saw in the chapter titled "Physical Growth and Motor Skills," the two halves of the brain become increasingly specialized to handle different types of information, such as speech perception and speech production. According to one version of the lateralization hypothesis, girls' brains mature more quickly and lateralize earlier than boys'. Because verbal skills are thought to develop sooner than visual-spatial skills, and because rapid maturation of the brain is assumed to produce less eventual lateralization, the verbal skills of girls are presumed to be more evenly distributed across the hemispheres. Verbal processing in the right and left hemispheres, in turn, interferes with the visual-spatial processing that usually takes place predominantly in the right hemisphere. Because lateralization takes longer in boys, their cerebral hemispheres are thought to become more specialized than girls'. The net result is that their visual-spatial skills are stronger. Some research evidence confirms that children (regardless of sex) who mature early score better on verbal tasks than on spatial tasks, whereas the reverse pattern holds for late maturers (Waber, 1976).

Before we accept the lateralization hypothesis, however, we should note that there are also nonbiological explanations of sex differences in visual-spatial skills. One such explanation relies on the contrasting play experiences of boys and girls. According to this formulation, masculine play activities, such as using building blocks or video games, facilitate the development of visual-spatial skills in boys (Block, 1983; Greenfield, 1994). Evidence for this explanation was found in a study in which ten- to eleven-year-old boys and girls were given practice in playing either a visual-spatial or a verbal video game. The results showed that both boys and girls who played the visual-spatial game improved in their visual spatial skills, whereas those who played the word game did not improve (Subrahmanyam & Greenfield, 1994). Thus sex-typed play activities may account, at least in part, for sex differences in visual-spatial skills.

No one doubts that explanations of the development of gender roles must start on some level with biology. However, you have seen in the preceding discussion, as well as throughout this text, that biology and environment interact in complex and sometimes bidirectional ways. Elucidating the precise ways in which hormones and brain structures are responsible for or combine with experiences to produce the behavioral tendencies of boys and girls remains a major challenge for researchers.

Social Learning Theory

One of the primary mechanisms accounting for sex differences in behavior, social learning theorists maintain, is sex-differentiated treatment of boys and girls. According to this position, boys and girls are reinforced and punished differentially for specific behaviors, which leads them to behave in sex-typed ways. Girls, for example, may be rewarded for playing with dolls and punished for climbing trees, whereas boys may receive the opposite treatment. Thus, because children are motivated to seek reinforcement and avoid punishment, they will behave in a sex-typed fashion.

Children attend both to the consequences of their own behavior and to the consequences others face for their behavior. In fact, imitation, or modeling, may be an even more powerful means by which children learn gender roles. By observing the experiences of other people, children develop expectations for reinforcement and punishment of their own behavior. These expectations may influence their behavior as strongly as the actual experiences of reward or punishment do (Bandura, 1969, 1977a). Children have numerous opportunities to observe models behaving in gender-stereotypic ways in the home, in the outside world, and in the media. Recent studies show that gender stereotypes are frequently evident in television, video games, and children's literature (Dietz, 1998; Furnham & Mak, 1999; Turner-Bowker, 1996). They also show that, within families, women still do the bulk of household tasks such as cooking and cleaning (Coltrane, 2000). Each time a child sees that Dad fixes things around the house and Mom does the cleaning, or that most little boys play baseball and little girls play house, she is adding to her growing storehouse of sex-typed behaviors.

According to social learning theory, a powerful vehicle for the transmission of gender roles is imitation. Parents can be especially potent models for gender-typed behaviors. Thus the roles they take on in the household, as well as their attitudes and beliefs, can have an impact on the gender-role development of their children.

● **Imitation of Sex-Typed Behaviors**   Several factors influence whether children will imitate the sex-typed behaviors of others. Albert Bandura and other researchers have proposed that children's *attention* to models in the first place is influenced by both the sex of the model and the **sex typicality** of the model's behavior, that is, how characteristic it is of the model's own sex (Bandura, 1977a; Perry & Bussey, 1979). According to this hypothesis, boys would, in general, be more likely than girls to attend to the behavior of male models, although they would be less likely to attend to a male model who was exhibiting "feminine" behavior. The prediction that individuals will pay greater attention to same-sex models is based on the notion that observation of same-sex models should provide children with greater information about potential consequences for their own behavior. In addition, Bandura suggests, children *recognize* that certain behaviors are sex-typed, especially as they observe the frequency with which males and females, as a group, perform certain behaviors. Finally, Bandura (1977a) proposes that *motivational* factors, such as reward seeking and attempts to retain a sense of mastery, will influence behavior in a variety of realms. As children grow older, they rely less on others to regulate their behavior and more on *self-regulation,* based on personal standards of gender-appropriate behavior (Bandura, 1986).

Research has supported several of the predictions of social learning theory. Children are indeed more likely to imitate same-sex than other-sex models (Bussey & Bandura, 1984; Bussey & Perry, 1982). Thus same-sex parents, peers, and characters in the media can be powerful influences on the child. In addition, children are more likely to imitate models who behave in sex-typical ways than models who behave in sex-atypical ways (Perry & Bussey, 1979). Finally, self-regulation of sex-typed behavior does seem to increase with development, as a study by Kay Bussey and Albert Bandura (1992) shows. Two- to four-year-olds privately rated how they would feel if they played with a series of toys, some of which were masculine (e.g., a dump truck), some feminine (e.g., a baby doll), and some neutral (e.g., a xylophone). As Figure 13.4 shows, younger children expressed relatively neutral self-evaluations regarding playing with masculine and feminine toys. Older children, in contrast, indicated more positive self-evaluations when visualizing themselves playing with toys geared for their own sex.

Social learning theory makes an important contribution to our understanding of gender-role development in that it provides a way for us to understand how broader societal beliefs and values are transmitted to individual children. As Bussey and Bandura (1999) state, labeling boys as boys and girls as girls would have very little consequence if there were no social repercussions to acting in masculine and feminine ways.

sex typicality   Extent to which a behavior is usually associated with one sex as opposed to the other.

FIGURE 13.4
Self-Evaluations During
Same-Sex Activities

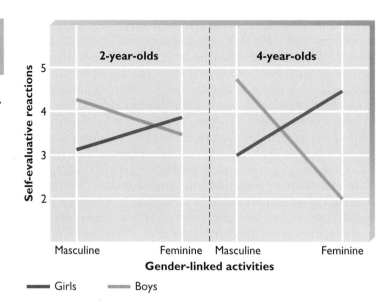

Two- and four-year-olds rated
how they would feel while playing with masculine, feminine,
or neutral toys. The higher the
score, the more favorable the
self-evaluation. As the graph
indicates, younger children,
especially girls, gave relatively
neutral self-evaluations for
playing with masculine and
feminine toys. In contrast,
older children said they would
feel better about themselves
when they played with same-
sex toys.

Source: Bussey & Bandura, 1992.

KEY THEME
Sociocultural Influence

● **Cross-Cultural Patterns of Sex Differences**   The contexts in which gender-
role development occurs are many and varied. Do gender roles differ according to
the beliefs and demands of a specific culture? Cross-cultural studies can shed some
light on biological versus social learning explanations for sex typing. If sex typing results solely from biological influences, we would expect to see great unanimity in
gender roles across periods of history and among different cultures. If, on the other
hand, gender roles reflect values that are peculiar to a given era or culture, we would
expect to see variability in the characteristics defined as masculine and feminine by
different cultures or at different points in time.

Perhaps the most comprehensive cross-cultural comparison of children and the
factors that influence their development was conducted by Beatrice Whiting and
Carolyn Pope Edwards. In their Six-Culture study, these researchers examined aggression, nurturance, help seeking, sociability, and other social behaviors in children
ages three to eleven living in Kenya, Okinawa, India, the Phillippines, Mexico, and the

Similar gender-typed behaviors
have been observed in several
different cultures, including
Mexico, this girl's home.
Women and girls are expected
to participate in household
tasks and the care of children.
Variations in gender roles
across cultures have also been
observed, however, suggesting
that biology alone cannot account for their occurrence.

United States (Whiting & Edwards, 1988; Whiting & Whiting, 1975). The results showed that differences between boys and girls were more exaggerated in some cultures than in others; in fact, they were least pronounced for the American children in the sample. Furthermore, sex differences between males and females diminished when both boys and girls were involved in household tasks, particularly the care of younger siblings. For example, Nyansango boys in East Africa scored higher than girls on their tendency to offer help and support to others; they were also as likely as girls to retreat from aggression. Interestingly, many boys in this culture tend to babies and perform other domestic chores, tasks that encourage nurturance and collaboration.

The finding that many resemblances were observed in the sex-typed behaviors of children from these diverse cultures is consistent with a biological explanation of gender-role development. At the same time, the variation that occurs in roles and characteristics across cultures points to the undeniable influence of socialization experiences (Best & Williams, 1993).

KEY THEME
Nature/Nurture

Cognitive-Developmental Theories

Cognitive-developmental theories focus on the ways children understand gender roles in general and themselves as males or females in particular. In cognitive-developmental theories, *gender* is emphasized as a conceptual category, a way of classifying people on the basis of their overt appearance or behaviors.

KEY THEME
Interaction Among Domains

● **Kohlberg's Cognitive-Developmental Theory** Lawrence Kohlberg (1966) proposed that gender roles emerge as a consequence of stagelike developments in cognition. The most basic of these cognitive milestones is acquisition of **gender identity,** the knowledge that self and others are female or male. This concept, which is acquired between ages two and three years, is crucial to later gender-role development because it provides a basic categorizing principle with which children begin to divide the world. After acquiring gender identity, around their fourth birthday children develop **gender stability,** a sense that gender does not change over time. Children who have acquired gender stability recognize that they were born one sex and will grow up to be a member of that same sex. Despite this knowledge, however, they may not yet be aware of the fact that genitalia determine biological sex. Rather, children assume external factors (such as clothing or hair length) are the determinants of sex. Thus a young boy may believe he was a baby boy and will grow up to be a "daddy" (gender stability), but only if his behavior and physical characteristics (such as hair length) remain masculine. By age six, most children acquire **gender constancy,** the awareness that changes in external characteristics, behaviors, or desires do not lead to a change in biological sex. Thus a boy may wear a dress and a girl may play with toy soldiers without altering their respective biological sexes. For Kohlberg, the acquisition of gender constancy marks the child's mature awareness of the concept of gender differentiation.

Because children value both their own sex and themselves, they are motivated to behave in a gender-typical fashion. From Kohlberg's perspective, cognitive development facilitates *self-socialization* among children. Kohlberg believed that children are internally motivated by their positive self- and same-sex evaluations to behave in a manner consonant with their conceptions of what is sex-appropriate. External motivators (such as reinforcements and punishments) are of minimal importance in the process of self-socialization.

Research has confirmed that children progress from attaining gender identity to gender stability and, finally, gender constancy from about two to nine years of age (Fagot, 1985; Slaby & Frey, 1975; Szkrybalo & Ruble, 1999). This trend appears among children from several cultures, including Argentina, Belize, Kenya, Nepal, and American Samoa (DeLisi & Gallagher, 1991; Munroe, Shimmin, & Munroe, 1984). At about eighteen months of age, children show some knowledge of gender categories by matching up the faces and voices of adult males and females (Poulin-Dubois, Serbin, & Derbyshire, 1998). Between ages two and three, most children are

gender identity Knowledge, usually gained by age three years, that one is male or female.

gender stability Knowledge, usually gained by age four years, that one's gender does not change over time.

gender constancy Knowledge, usually gained around age six or seven years, that one's gender does not change as a result of alterations in appearance, behaviors, or desires.

able to label themselves as male or female (Huston, 1985). Precisely when children develop this distinction can forecast subsequent patterns of behavior. Beverly Fagot and Mary Leinbach (1989) found that some children developed gender identity early (before age twenty-eight months) and others not until later. Boys and girls who were early identifiers engaged in significantly more gender-typical play, such as play with building toys for boys and doll play for girls, than did late identifiers. At two to three years of age, children who are able to apply gender labels correctly to others also have greater knowledge of gender stereotypes (Fagot, Leinbach, & O'Boyle, 1992).

How does gender identity develop? Perhaps parents and others provide this information directly by saying things to their young children such as "There's another little boy just like you" or "Be a good girl now, won't you?" Beverly Fagot's research also shows that children who are adept at using gender labels tend to have mothers who engage in sex-typed play with their children and espouse traditional beliefs about gender roles themselves (Fagot et al., 1992). Many researchers contend, however, that the messages about gender roles are so clear and pervasive in our society that, even aside from the role parents may play, children cannot help but notice them and categorize themselves as males or females.

● **Gender Schema Theory**   Another cognitive-developmental theory is *gender schema theory* (Bem, 1981; Martin & Halverson, 1981, 1987). Like Kohlberg's theory, gender schema theory stresses the importance of the acquisition of gender identity and children's intrinsic motivations to behave in a gender-typical manner. Unlike Kohlberg's theory, however, gender schema theory does not stress the attainment of gender constancy; rather, it focuses on the influence of children's active construction of gender knowledge on their behavior (Bem, 1981; Martin & Halverson, 1987; Signorella, 1987).

Carol Martin and Charles Halverson (1981) have proposed that children first acquire gender identity and then, in their attempts to create order in their social worlds, begin to construct two **gender schemas,** or cognitive organizing structures for information relevant to gender. The first one, the *same-sex/opposite-sex schema,* refers to the child's knowledge of one sex or the other. This is a fairly primitive cognitive structure composed largely of gender stereotypes, such as "boys fix cars" and "girls sew." Children also develop a second, more elaborate gender schema about behaviors relevant to their own sex. This *own-sex schema* provides a basis for guiding children's behavior. Thus, even though both boys and girls know that girls sew, girls are more likely to be motivated to learn to sew, whereas they may not want to learn how to fix a car. Researchers have confirmed that children explore and prefer neutral objects labeled as intended for their own sex more than they do for objects labeled for the other sex. Moreover, up to one week later, children remember more details about the "same-sex" objects than they do about the "other-sex" objects, even when they are offered a reward for remembering details (Bradbard et al., 1986; Martin, Eisenbud, & Rose, 1995).

According to Martin and Halverson (1981), children's gender schemas serve as a potent means of organizing information about their social worlds. Some children tend to be *gender schematic;* that is, they possess a strong gender schema, exhibit more consistent sex typing in their behavior, and process information along gender lines. In contrast, children who are *gender aschematic* possess a weaker gender schema, are less sex typed behaviorally, and focus their attention on aspects of information that are not related to gender. Gender-schematic children often distort information according to their beliefs about gender and are unlikely to remember events that are inconsistent with those beliefs. For example, gender-schematic children find it difficult to remember information about pictures of people engaged in sex-atypical activities, such as a boy playing with a doll, whereas they can easily remember information about people engaged in sex-typical activities, such as a girl playing with a tea set (Signorella, 1987; Welch-Ross & Schmidt, 1996). These effects are apparent as early as age twenty-five months, at least among boys (Bauer, 1993). Even more dramatic is the finding that children distort stereotype-inconsistent

gender schema   Cognitive organizing structure for information relevant to sex typing.

child's experiences in schools, in which teachers and the instructional materials they use can confirm (or disconfirm) early gender-role beliefs and behaviors.

The Influence of Parents

Traditionally, developmental psychologists have believed one of the most important sources of information about gender for children is the behavior of their parents and the environment parents create (Katz, 1987). Sometimes the messages are subtle. Parents commonly provide their children with sex-differentiated toys and room furnishings (Rheingold & Cook, 1975). They buy sports equipment, tools, and vehicles for their sons and dolls and doll furniture for their daughters. Boys' rooms typically are decorated in blue, girls' in yellow (Pomerleau et al., 1990). When parents supply boys and girls with different physical environments, they send messages that boys are indeed different from girls and set sex-related limits on the types of behavior that are acceptable and appropriate.

Another way in which parents influence their children's gender-role development is through their own general beliefs about masculine and feminine roles. Many parents believe children as young as two years differ along gender-stereotypic lines (McGuire, 1988). They report, for example, that their own sons like sports, enjoy using tools, and are energetic. On the other hand, parents of girls say their daughters like to be admired, enjoy playing with dolls, and like clothes. Parent's gender beliefs are related to their children's gender beliefs (Tenenbaum & Leaper, 2002). And those beliefs are frequently translated into sex-differentiated patterns in the types of chores boys and girls are assigned to do around the house: boys take out the garbage and mow the lawn; girls do more chores within the house, such as cleaning and cooking (Goodnow, 1988; Lackey, 1989). The tendency of children to participate in household tasks associated with their gender increases in early adolescence, especially if their own parents assume traditional roles in household tasks or parents openly encourage traditional chores (Antill et al., 1996; Crouter, Manke, & McHale, 1995).

● **Parental Behaviors**   Sometimes parents' messages about gender are more direct. Research shows that parents treat children differently on the basis of sex in early infancy, beginning at ages younger than those at which actual behavioral sex differences emerge (Fagot & Leinbach, 1987). Right in the first week following the birth of their child, parents of daughters describe their infants as more delicate and less strong and as having finer features than do parents of boys (Karraker, Vogel, & Lake, 1995). Adults play more roughly with a male infant, tossing him in the air and tickling him vigorously, than they do with a female infant (Huston, 1983). During infancy and childhood, girls are more likely than boys to be protected and sheltered by adults, whereas boys are given greater opportunities than girls to explore their environments (Block, 1983; Burns, Mitchell, & Obradovich, 1989). When their children are preschoolers, parents react more negatively when their daughters assert themselves than when their sons do. Fathers in particular tend to react positively when their daughters display compliant behavior and to reward their sons for assertiveness (Kerig, Cowan, & Cowan, 1993). In addition, parents give boys more positive evaluations and girls more negative evaluations when children are working on solving problems (Alessandri & Lewis, 1993). Both mothers and fathers use more emotion words when speaking with their preschool-age daughters than with their sons (Adams et al., 1995; Kuebli, Butler, & Fivush, 1995). Parents also respond positively to boys who play with blocks, manipulate objects, and engage in physical play. With girls they encourage play that involves dolls, domestic themes, and "pretending" (Fagot & Leinbach, 1987; Farver & Wimbarti, 1995; Lindsay, Mize, & Pettit, 1997). Fathers appear to be especially concerned about what they perceive as masculinity in their sons, at least during the preschool years (Jacklin, DiPietro, & Maccoby, 1984). Such concern is often expressed in parental interviews, as well as in the consistently negative manner in which fathers respond to sex-atypical behavior in their sons.

However, a meta-analysis of 172 studies of parents' differential socialization of girls and boys suggests that we must be cautious about how much weight we give to the role of direct parental reinforcement in accounting for the various facets of gender-role development. In general, the overall impact of parental behaviors was judged to be small in most areas of socialization, including achievement expectations, dependency, and aggression. The only socialization area that showed a significant effect was parental encouragement of sex-typed activities, such as doll play for girls and tool play for boys (Lytton & Romney, 1991).

There are several ways to interpret these somewhat surprising findings. First, it may be that children's participation in sex-typed play is a particularly important context for acquiring behaviors typical of masculinity and femininity. Recent studies show that children's activity interests and how they spend their leisure time are indeed gender-stereotyped—even more so than their beliefs about gender or their personality characteristics. Boys tend to prefer and engage in activities such as competitive sports and building, whereas girls prefer and participate in activities such as dancing, reading, and writing (McHale, Crouter, & Tucker, 1999, 2001). Even at age three, girls spend more of their weekend time in socializing, personal care activities, and educational activities, whereas boys engage in more video game playing (Huston et al., 1999). Some of these contexts are more conducive to fostering collaboration, whereas others tend to promote competition and assertiveness (Leaper, 2000). Second, children's gender-role socialization may be more heavily influenced by broader social forces than by parental behaviors (Harris, 1995; Martin & Ruble, 1997). For example, peer experiences and exposure to gender-typed media messages may be far more important in gender socialization than the behaviors encouraged by mothers and fathers.

● Gender Roles in Nontraditional Families

A series of profound changes in the traditional American family over the last several decades has had an impact on gender-role development. As we described in the chapter titled "Emotion," mothers increasingly are employed outside the home while their children are still young. These women may be providing their children with alternative models for feminine behavior.

In general, maternal employment facilitates the development of flexibility in children's conceptions of gender roles. Children with employed mothers are more likely to believe both males and females can exhibit a wide variety of behaviors and personality characteristics than are children whose mothers are not employed outside the home. The effects on daughters of employed mothers are particularly dramatic. Daughters of mothers who work outside the home show higher levels of achievement motivation and are more likely to have personality styles that blend male-typed and female-typed traits than are the daughters of nonworking mothers (Hoffman, 1979; Huston, 1983).

Psychologists are also interested in the effects of nontraditional mothers and fathers—those who take on approximately equal responsibility for child care—on children's gender-role development. Children whose mothers and fathers make a deliberate effort to share parenting are slower to adopt gender labels and show less knowledge of gender stereotypes during the children's preschool years (Fagot & Leinbach, 1995). Research shows that girls in particular profit from the involvement of fathers in child-oriented activities. Elementary school-age girls whose parents were less stereotyped in their marital and child-rearing roles also showed more independence and feelings of being in control over events in their lives (Hoffman & Kloska, 1995). In another research project that included traditional parents, as well as parents who shared equally in child-related responsibilities, adolescent girls from egalitarian families maintained high levels of school achievement, whereas girls from traditional families showed declines in science and mathematics achievement as they made the transition to seventh grade. Boys showed no differences in achievement associated with parenting styles (Updegraff, McHale, & Crouter, 1996).

When fathers assume a greater role in parenting, children show less knowledge of stereotypes and are slower to acquire gender labels.

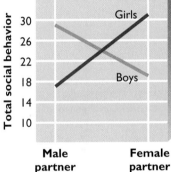

Source: Adapted from Jacklin & Maccoby, 1978.

FIGURE 13.5
Social Behavior as a Function of the Child's Play Partner

In a study by Jacklin and Maccoby, unacquainted two-year-olds were observed as they interacted with either a same-sex or an opposite-sex partner. The amount of social behavior (both positive overtures and negative acts such as aggression) was greater when children played with a peer of the same sex.

The Influence of Peers

An extremely powerful influence on children's gender-role development is the peer group. Peer groups not only provide children with opportunities for particular kinds of play but also offer a forum in which children can learn about social behavior and social interactions by watching models and obtaining feedback about their own behaviors. Although peers influence children in a variety of social dimensions, nowhere is their impact more marked than in the area of gender-role socialization (Carter, 1987).

● **Early Play Patterns**   The role of peers in gender-role development can be observed even among very young children. Carol Jacklin and Eleanor Maccoby (1978) observed same-sex and mixed-sex pairs of unacquainted two-year-olds to determine the influence of peers on toddlers' behavior. Children were dressed in a sex-neutral fashion (in yellow jumpsuits) and allowed to play in a room with their mothers present but nondirective. As Figure 13.5 shows, the toddlers' behavior varied as a function of the sex of their play partner even though the children were unaware of the true sex of the other child. In general, children displayed more social behaviors, both positive overtures and negative acts, when they played with a peer of the same sex. Girls were more likely to be passive when they played with a boy than when they played with a girl. In addition, girls in girl-girl pairs exhibited greater sharing of toys and were less likely to become upset and cry than when they were in mixed-sex pairs. Finally, boys were less likely to obey a verbal prohibition from a girl than from a boy. Already at this young age, the dynamics of peer interactions were markedly affected by the sex of the partners.

● **Peer Enforcement of Gender Roles**   Peers continue to exert a strong influence on children's adoption of sex-typical behaviors as they begin preschool. A number of studies have shown, for example, that children respond differentially to sex-typical and sex-atypical behavior in their peers. Children may reward behavior they like by complimenting a child or by engaging in mutual play, and they may punish a behavior they do not approve of by name calling. Preschoolers and kindergartners reliably punish boys who engage in sex-atypical behavior, such as playing with dolls, while rewarding them for engaging in sex-typical behavior, such as playing with trucks (Fagot, 1977; Lamb, Easterbrooks, & Holden, 1980; Lamb & Roopnarine, 1979). In contrast, girls are rewarded for engaging in sex-typical behavior, such as playing house, but apparently they experience no consequences when they engage in sex-atypical behavior (Fagot, 1977).

The pressures the peer group exerts apparently work. Children are responsive to the positive and negative feedback they receive from their peers. They are likely to continue to engage in a sex-typical behavior in response to reinforcement and to terminate behaviors their peers punish (Lamb et al., 1980). Furthermore, feedback from same-sex peers is especially important. Beverly Fagot (1978a) found that both girls and boys two years of age were more likely to continue a behavior if a same-sex peer responded positively and to discontinue a behavior if a same-sex peer reacted negatively. If the peer was of the other sex, however, the peer's feedback was largely ineffective.

● **Cross-Gender Behavior**   Some children (between 20 and 40 percent), more often girls than boys, fail to respond to their peers' disapproval of sex-atypical behavior (Sandberg et al., 1993). These children exhibit **cross-gender behavior;** that is, they adopt, in whole or in part, a variety of characteristics typical of the other sex (Fagot, 1977). Cross-gender boys, for example, exhibit a strong interest in feminine games and activities and play "dress-up" in girls' clothes. Cross-gender boys are likely to become social isolates over time because their male peers refuse to interact with them even when they play in a masculine fashion, and their female peers seem to merely tolerate their presence. Cross-gender girls, in contrast, appear to suffer very little for their sex-atypical behavior, at least in the preschool years.

The tendency of children to disapprove of cross-gender behavior is more pronounced in cultures that emphasize the importance of traditions and adhering to social norms (e.g., Taiwan) as opposed to freedom to break from traditions and individualism (e.g., Israel) (Lobel et al., 2001). This tendency also increases with age. When researchers interviewed kindergartners through sixth-graders to determine how these children would respond to hypothetical cases of cross-gender behavior in their peers, older children reported they would respond more negatively to cross-

KEY THEME
Sociocultural Influence

Both boys and girls may engage in cross-gender activities. However, it is usually easier for girls to cross gender boundaries than for boys; peers usually react more negatively in the latter case.

cross-gender behavior   Behavior usually seen in a member of the opposite sex. Term generally is reserved for behavior that is persistently sex atypical.

gender behavior than did younger children. Moreover, children stated they would respond more negatively to cross-gender behavior in their male peers than in their female peers. The degree of negativity children exhibited was particularly surprising. Children were virtually unanimous in their assertion that they would not want to play with a cross-gender child. Children's reports of how they would respond ranged from fairly innocuous comments (such as "I'd stay away") to statements indicating they would physically abuse cross-gender children (Carter & McCloskey, 1984).

Similar results were obtained when researchers asked preadolescents to describe the personal qualities of an actor who played a gender-inappropriate game with children of the opposite sex. If a boy actor played jumprope with a group of girls, he was viewed as significantly less popular than a female actor or a male actor playing a masculine game (Lobel et al., 1993). As we will see in the chapter titled "Peers," popularity with peers is, in turn, associated with other significant developmental outcomes. Children who are unpopular often have low self-esteem and poor academic achievement and may be prone to aggression. Thus cross-gender behavior can be stigmatizing and potentially far-reaching in its effects.

KEY THEME
Interaction Among Domains

CONTROVERSY: THINKING IT OVER

Is Gender Identity Disorder Really a Disorder?

According to the *Diagnostic and Statistical Manual of Mental Disorders* (DSM-IV) of the American Psychiatric Association (1994), cross-gender children may qualify for a diagnosis of *gender identity disorder* if they express a strong desire to be a member of the opposite sex or claim to be unhappy as a boy or a girl (American Psychiatric Association, 1994). Children may insist on wearing clothing or hairstyles of the opposite sex or may display significant problems at home or school, sometimes to the extent that parents seek out professional help (Zucker & Bradley, 2000).

What Is the Controversy?
The main point of contention is whether gender identity disorder is a genuine psychiatric problem residing within an individual or whether the problem lies in our broader society's intolerance for behaviors that violate gender boundaries. When these children experience distress, for example, is it because of some inner turmoil associated with personal adjustment issues or is it due to the highly negative reactions of peers and parents to cross-gender behaviors?

What Are the Opposing Arguments?
The criteria for mental disorder in the DSM-IV include an individual's experience of severe distress or increased risk of harm. Mental health professionals note that children with gender identity disorder are prone to depression and behavior problems similar to those of children with other clinical diagnoses (Zucker & Bradley, 2000). Therefore, some say that gender identity disorder is a legitimate psychiatric problem. Critics point out that gender identity disorder does not necessarily lead to adjustment problems later in adolescence and adulthood. Many of these children, for example, eventually identify themselves as homosexual, which is not a psychiatric condition in DSM-IV. Moreover, the distress children experience is not due to cross-gender behaviors—these children are perfectly happy when they perform such behaviors. It is the reactions of peers and others that cause them such great difficulty. The critics believe that gender identity disorder should be removed from DSM-IV (Bartlett, Vasey, & Bukowski, 2000).

What Answers Exist? What Questions Remain?
Research has shown that the degree to which children view themselves as compatible with their gender is indeed related to psychological adjustment. Preadolescents who express contentment with their own gender and see themselves as typical for their

sex have higher self-esteem, for example (Egan & Perry, 2001). Thus "fitting in" with one's gender is associated with indicators of mental health.

However, when children with gender identity disorder report distress, the cause is usually problems with peers or unhappiness at having to stop their cross-gender behaviors, not a disturbance of gender. Also important to consider is the fact that definitions of masculinity and femininity can vary across cultures and historical times. Nancy Bartlett and her colleagues point out that in other eras, for example, men who stayed at home with their children might have been seen as mentally ill for violating a gender norm (Bartlett et al., 2000).

Perhaps it would be helpful to conduct more longitudinal studies of cross-gender children to observe developmental changes in their adjustment, as well as the specific antecedents and consequences of their cross-gender behaviors. What other kinds of studies might be useful in sorting out the issues relevant to considering whether gender identity disorder is really a disorder?

● **Sex Segregation**   The influence of peers on sex typing in children's behavior is undoubtedly enhanced by the fact that boys and girls tend to interact in separate groups: starting at age three or four, boys play with boys and girls play with girls (Maccoby, 1988, 1990). This phenomenon is called **sex segregation.** In one observation of one hundred children on their preschool playgrounds, four-year-olds spent three times as much time with same-sex partners as with opposite-sex partners. By age six, they spent eleven times more time with peers of the same sex (Maccoby & Jacklin, 1987). In fact, only about 10 percent of young children's peer interactions are with members of the opposite sex (Martin & Fabes, 2001). This tendency to prefer same-sex peers persists at least until early adolescence (Maccoby, 1990). Interestingly enough, when young children are asked if a boy can join a group of girls playing with dolls (or if a girl can join a group of boys playing with trucks), almost 90 percent say "Yes" and justify their responses on moral grounds. It wouldn't be right or fair, they say, to exclude the member of the opposite sex (Killen et al., 2001). Yet when confronted with social interactions with an opposite-sex peer, elementary–school age children express more negative emotion toward and less liking of that child (Underwood, Schockner, & Hurley, 2001). Sex segregation is a potent phenomenon in the social lives of young children.

Eleanor Maccoby (1990, 2002) believes children's experiences in same-sex groups constitute an extremely powerful socialization environment. As boys play in their characteristic rough-and-tumble fashion or in team sports and games, they develop assertive, dominance-seeking styles of interaction. In contrast, girls' groups, which are oriented toward relationships and shared intimacy, promote cooperation and mutual support, as well as a tendency to preserve the cohesiveness of the group. A recent study of preschool and kindergarten children over a six-month period confirmed that as children spent more time in same-sex groups, their conformity with gender-stereotyped behaviors increased. Boys who spent more time with boys became more active and rough in their play. Similarly, girls who spent more time with girls played more calmly over time and engaged in more gender-stereotyped play, such as dressing up and interacting with dolls (Martin & Fabes, 2001).

Sex segregation begins to break down as children enter adolescence and begin to think about dating (Richards et al., 1998). The pressures of heterosexual interactions, however, may enhance rather than diminish the push toward conformity with gender-role norms (Eccles, 1987; Petersen, 1980). This pattern is particularly obvious among teenage girls, many of whom abandon "tomboyish" behaviors that were acceptable during an earlier period of development (Huston & Alvarez, 1990).

● **Adolescent Peer Influences**   Peer acceptance and rejection become increasingly important during adolescence. Although sex-typing pressures remain high, popularity among adolescents of both sexes relies more on positive personality characteristics, such as leadership abilities and politeness, than on merely the presence of

sex segregation Clustering of individuals into same-sex groups.

sex-typed behavior (Sigelman, Carr, & Begley, 1986). Thus the presence of cross-gender personality characteristics or behaviors may not lead to isolation from peers among older adolescents to the extent that it does for younger children (Huston & Alvarez, 1990; Katz & Ksansnak, 1994). Adolescents' greater tolerance for sex-atypical personality characteristics probably reflects their increasing cognitive abilities, specifically their ability to consider multiple dimensions as they make judgments about individuals, including abstract qualities such as trustworthiness or loyalty (Eccles, 1987).

KEY THEME
Interaction Among Domains

The Influence of Teachers and Schools

Teachers, like peers and parents, treat children differentially according to sex, reinforce and punish sex-typed behaviors, and model sex-typical behavior for their students. Moreover, schools may foster sex typing through the teaching materials and curriculum to which children are exposed. For example, one survey of children's readers found that although boys and girls were portrayed with almost equal frequency, girls were more often the characters in stories in need of rescue and boys were rarely shown doing housework or displaying emotions (Purcell & Stewart, 1990).

● **Teacher Attitudes and Behaviors**   Teachers, like other adults, may express stereotypical, gender-based views about the capacities of their students. They believe female students are feminine and male students are masculine, although more experienced teachers are less likely to hold stereotyped beliefs and more likely to treat students in an egalitarian fashion than are less experienced teachers (Fagot, 1978a; Huston, 1983). When teachers are asked to nominate their best students or those with the most potential, they are more likely to nominate boys than girls. They are especially likely to name boys as most skilled in mathematics. When asked to think of students who excel in language or social skill, teachers are more likely to name girls (BenTsvi-Mayer, Hertz-Lazarowitz, & Safir, 1989). These patterns in teacher responses occur despite the fact that actual sex differences in many of these domains are minimal.

In addition, teachers respond differently to students on the basis of sex as opposed to behavior. Boys, for example, receive more disapproval from teachers than girls do during preschool and elementary school, even when boys and girls engage in similar amounts of disruptive behavior (Huston, 1983; Serbin et al., 1973). Teachers' behavior may reflect a belief that boys are more likely than girls to cause trouble in the classroom unless rules are strictly enforced (Huston, 1983). On the other hand, teachers pay more attention to a girl when she sits quietly in the front of the classroom, whereas the amount of attention paid to a boy is high regardless of where he sits (Serbin et al., 1973). Within elementary school classrooms, teachers tend to call on boys more often than girls and give them more explicit feedback regarding their answers. When girls answer, they are more likely to receive a simple acceptance from the teacher ("okay"), whereas boys tend to receive more praise, constructive criticism, or encouragement to discover the correct answer (Sadker & Sadker, 1994). Thus boys receive more explicit academic instruction and tend to dominate classroom interactions.

Teachers can influence the degree to which children pay attention to stereotypes when they highlight gender as a relevant social grouping. In one study, teachers in one set of classrooms were told to behave in ways that emphasized gender groups. For example, they used separate bulletin boards to display girls' and boys' artwork and made frequent comments such as, "All the boys should be sitting down" or "Amber, you can come up for the girls." Teachers in this group made an average of 7.2 references to gender per twenty-minute time period. Compared with a control group in which teachers were instructed to refer to children as individuals rather than according to gender, children in the "gendered" classrooms showed significant increases in stereotyping over the course of four weeks (Bigler, 1995).

Research has shown that boys typically receive more attention from teachers than girls. Teachers can promote sex equity in the classroom by deliberately calling on girls to answer questions and by waiting a few moments to give girls a chance to participate.

RESEARCH APPLIED TO EDUCATION

Promoting Gender Equity in the Classroom

Now eight years old, Nicky is sitting in a circle with the other third-graders in his class, listening to Brittany read the story she wrote during Writing Workshop. The children seem captivated by her story; even the most restless among them sits quietly, eyes glued on the storyteller. When Brittany is done, Ms. Klein says, "Okay, does anyone have any questions or comments about Brittany's story? Go ahead, Brittany. You can call on someone." Hands fly up eagerly.

"Stephen," says Brittany.

"Why did you make the character live by a pond?" asks Stephen.

"Because he has a lot of animal friends that live there," she responds.

More hands churn in the air. "Nicky," she calls out next. "Wait a minute," says Ms. Klein. "Remember our rule. You have to call on a girl next."

"Reesha," Brittany calls out.

"I like how the words you picked make me think of beautiful pictures in my head," comments Reesha. "Thank you," responds Brittany, a little shyly.

Nicky's mother, observing all of this, thinks maybe her son feels slighted for being passed over. Later, when she asks him about this, he firmly proclaims, "All Ms. Klein is trying to do is to be fair to the boys and girls in the class. I didn't feel bad at all. I think it's the right thing to do."

Just as teacher behavior can perpetuate stereotypes, it can change sex-typing patterns among children in classroom settings. A collection of studies suggests some specific techniques teachers can use to reduce sex segregation, modify children's beliefs about gender, and promote the participation of girls in the classroom.

1. *Use reinforcement to facilitate cooperative cross-sex play.*   In one study involving preschoolers and kindergartners, teachers praised children who played in mixed-

sex groups by pointing out their cooperative play to the class and complimenting the children. Cross-sex play subsequently increased (Serbin, Connor, & Iler, 1979; Serbin, Tonick, & Sternglanz, 1977).

2. *Prepare lessons that explicitly allow children to question gender stereotypes about personal qualities, occupations, and activities.* Researchers in Dublin, Ireland, had student teachers present a series of lessons to children in the first through sixth grades. The lessons encouraged children to think of counterexamples to common stereotypes, for example, instances in which women show an interest in football or in which men have been observed to be warm and gentle. Discussions were supplemented by opportunities to meet people who worked in nontraditional roles, such as a male nurse and a female veterinary surgeon. In addition, children read poetry, read fairy tales, and had worksheets that brought up themes counter to traditional stereotypes. At the end of four months, children who had experienced the lessons had significantly lower stereotype scores than those in a control group (Gash & Morgan, 1993).

3. *Be conscious of the need to give girls a chance to participate.* One way to do this is to wait three to five seconds before calling on a student to answer a question. Girls, especially those who are shy or less confident, may need time to formulate their answers and decide they are willing to share them with the class. Also, do not just call on students who volunteer, because these are more likely to be boys. Teachers can even have an observer record the number of times they call on boys versus girls. Myra and David Sadker (1994) found that when teachers saw the results of such observations, and, further, when they received training on how to be more gender equitable, girls in their elementary and secondary school classrooms became more equal partners with boys in class participation.

- **Student Attitudes Toward Coursework** For several decades, research has indicated that students, teachers, and parents alike view some academic subjects as masculine and others as feminine (Huston, 1983). As we noted earlier, mathematics has generally been seen as a masculine activity and reading as feminine (Eccles, 1983; Eccles, Wigfield, et al., 1993; Huston, 1983; Yee & Eccles, 1988). Such sex typing has not been limited to American schoolchildren. In a study of first- through fifth-grade Chinese, Japanese, and American boys and girls, the investigators found that most children believed boys are better in mathematics and girls are better at reading (Lummis & Stevenson, 1990). Moreover, boys in these three societies predicted they would do better in mathematics in high school than girls predicted they would do, although no sex differences were found in children's predictions of their future reading skills.

Society's messages about girls' mathematical abilities may be changing, however. In a recent study including data from children in first through twelfth grades, researchers asked children to report how competent they felt in math. Although in the early grades boys clearly felt more capable in math than girls, the gender gap in beliefs declined with age such that by twelfth grade there was virtually no difference between boys and girls. The researchers suggest that one reason for this shift may be a general societal push for girls to participate in math courses and activities (Fredricks & Eccles, 2002).

- **Sex Differences in Academic Self-evaluations** Girls generally show greater self-criticism of their academic work than boys do. Karin Frey and Diane Ruble (1987) have studied instances of self- and peer criticism for academic work in classroom settings. Children between ages five and ten years were observed at work in academic tasks in their classrooms, and their spontaneous critical and complimentary comments about themselves and their peers were tallied. Several sex differences emerged in the nature of comments children made. Overall, both girls and boys made more self-compliments than self-criticisms, but boys made a greater number

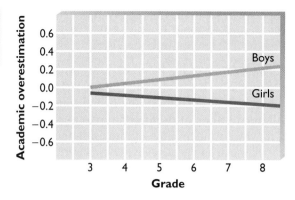

FIGURE 13.6
Gender Differences in
Academic Self-evaluations

In a study by Cole et al. (1999),
third- and sixth-graders were
asked to evaluate their scholastic competence each year for a
period of three years. Teachers
also evaluated children's academic abilities. The graph shows
that there are sex differences in
children's tendency to overestimate their academic abilities
starting at about fourth grade
and continuing through eighth
grade. (The y-axis shows a statistical estimate of the tendency
to overestimate such that a
higher positive number indicates greater overestimation.)

Source: Cole et al., 1999.

of self-congratulatory statements relative to self-criticisms than girls did. Boys complimented themselves and criticized their peers more than girls did, whereas girls
criticized themselves and complimented their peers more than boys did. Girls also
were more likely to attribute their failures to a lack of ability ("I'm so stupid") than
boys were. If girls tend to take greater responsibility for their own failures than boys
do, it is possible that there may be emotional consequences for them, for example,
greater anxiety and depression.

The link between emotions and academic self-evaluations was demonstrated in a
recent longitudinal study in which third- and sixth-graders were asked to evaluate
their scholastic competence each year for a period of three years. Teachers also evaluated children's academic abilities. Boys and girls were similar in their estimates of
their academic ability in grade three, but in successive years, their profiles diverged.
As Figure 13.6 illustrates, starting at about fourth grade and continuing through
eighth grade, boys tended to overestimate their academic abilities and girls tended
to underestimate theirs. In addition, symptoms of anxiety and depression were
negatively correlated with the tendency to overestimate one's abilities (Cole et al.,
1999). Thus gender differences in self-evaluations can have important connections
to children's emotional well-being.

The preceding findings should be a concern in light of the findings of a recent
cross-cultural study that found that in settings as diverse as Japan, Germany, and
Russia, girls who outperformed boys on academic measures did not see themselves
as more talented than boys (Stetsenko et al., 2000). Just why talented girls tend to un-
derplay their abilities and the repercussions of this tendency are key questions for developmental researchers.

WHAT **D**O
YOU **T**HINK?

**Are Single-Sex
Schools Better Than
Coed Schools?**
psychology.college.hmco.com

FOR YOUR REVIEW

- What are some indirect and direct ways in which parents influence children's gender-
  role development?

- What effects do nontraditional parents have on gender-role development?

- What do early play patterns reveal about the role of peers in gender-role development?

- What role do peers play in the enforcement of sex-typed behaviors?

- What are the consequences of cross-gender behaviors for boys and for girls?

- How does sex segregation contribute to the development of gender roles?

- In what ways do teachers sometimes contribute to sex-typed behaviors in children?

- In what specific ways can teachers promote gender equity in classrooms?

- What attitudes do boys and girls hold about academic subjects and academic
  self-evaluations?

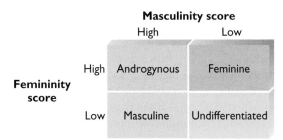

FIGURE 13.7
Classification of Sex Typing

In Sandra Bem's (1974, 1975) classification scheme, individuals who score high on traits associated with both masculinity and femininity are classified as "androgynous"; those scoring low on both dimensions are classified as "undifferentiated." "Feminine" and "masculine" individuals are those who score high on one sex-typing dimension and low on the other.

Alternative Conceptualizations of Gender

Changes in society's conceptions of the desirability of traditional sex typing have been reflected in changes in psychological theories. Conceptions of gender-role development have taken two relatively new directions. Rather than assuming that traditional masculine and feminine roles are the most desirable, some psychologists have suggested that blending both sets of traits may expand our ability to respond adaptively to the demands of our environments. Others maintain that male and female development differ, but in ways that can be valued and embraced.

Androgyny

Traditionally, psychologists treated masculinity and femininity as opposite ends of a bipolar dimension: by definition, the more masculine one was, the less feminine one could be. Sandra Bem (1974, 1975) challenged this view by proposing that masculinity and femininity are not mutually exclusive, as the bipolar formulation would suggest, but are separate, measurable dimensions of personality. Thus a person of either sex could be assertive in situations in which that behavior was necessary and nurturant when nurturance was required. From Bem's perspective, **androgyny,** the coexistence of both masculine and feminine characteristics, allows the individual to be maximally adaptive.

Psychological androgyny should not be confused with the ways the popular media present androgyny. From a psychological perspective, people whose physical appearance is ambiguous, neither distinctively male nor distinctively female, are not necessarily androgynous. In Bem's formulation, *androgynous* people are those who exhibit high levels of both masculine and feminine personality characteristics. People who are highly masculine and possess fewer feminine characteristics are designated as *masculine,* whereas those who are highly feminine and possess fewer masculine characteristics are designated as *feminine.* People who have few masculine and feminine characteristics are classified as *undifferentiated.* Figure 13.7 presents this classification scheme.

Psychological health and popularity with peers have been found to be associated with androgyny. For example, androgynous adolescents are better adjusted psychologically than are sex-typed or undifferentiated people (Ziegler, Dusek, & Carter, 1984). Similarly, androgynous adolescents are liked better by their peers and report feeling less lonely than other groups of adolescents (Avery, 1982; Massad, 1981). Androgynous adolescents also are more likely to have resolved identity crises than are nonandrogynous adolescents (Dusek, 1987). Finally, androgynous girls are more likely to attribute success to internal factors, such as their own efforts or hard work, than to external factors, such as chance or the influences of others (Huston, 1983).

How does an individual become androgynous? One possibility involves the child's growing ability to conceptualize the self and social roles in complex, abstract terms. Eccles (1987) has proposed that children cannot become androgynous before adolescence because they are still in the process of acquiring a gender role. During adolescence, however, children's abilities to conceptualize sex roles in a more

KEY THEME

Interaction Among Domains

androgyny Gender-role orientation in which a person possesses high levels of personality characteristics associated with both sexes.

abstract manner lead them to view gender-role stereotypes as descriptive statements about regularities in behavior rather than as prescriptions for acceptable behavior. Simultaneously, as adolescents strive to define their identities, they may consider factors other than gender as a means of characterizing themselves. Though androgynous role models are likely to foster gender-role transcendence, according to Eccles (1987), the convergence of cognitive developmental changes and the emergence of self-definition, rather than external factors such as models, allow children to transcend traditional roles and emerge as androgynous.

The Relational Approach

Instead of emphasizing the blending of male and female traits, some theorists maintain that the development of females is unique and different from the development of males. For example, in the chapter titled "Self and Values," we saw how Carol Gilligan (1982) defined a "morality of care and responsibility" for females, a distinctive orientation toward relationships that characterizes responses of females to moral dilemmas, in contrast to the "morality of justice" that typifies male responses. Similarly, Jean Baker Miller (1986) maintains that a central feature of female development, largely ignored by mainstream developmental psychology, is the tendency to seek out and maintain relationships with others. This tendency represents a marked departure from the widely held notion that child development is, in large part, the process of becoming independent, autonomous, and self-reliant. For females, development may mean more, not less, connection with others. Further, instead of characterizing these tendencies of females as "dependency," a term that has negative connotations, theorists of the relational school believe they are an important source of gratification and self-fulfillment (Miller, 1991; Surrey, 1991).

This framework opens up new interpretations for certain important developmental time periods. For example, adolescence has traditionally been seen as a phase in which children desire to separate from their parents, to realize their own potentials and strike out on their own. For females, however, breaking away from parents may not be the goal. Instead, the adolescent girl may wish to change the form of her relationships but still maintain them (Surrey, 1991). The dilemma of reconciling her inclinations toward relationship with her knowledge that the larger society expects her to "break away" may lead to intense conflicts for the adolescent female (Gilligan, Lyons, & Hanmer, 1990). Young girls who were at one time outspoken may become reluctant to verbalize their feelings; they may lose confidence in themselves, and their relationships with other females may suffer (Brown & Gilligan, 1992).

Researchers have begun to find other support for the idea that female development is distinct from male development in that it revolves around establishing and maintaining relationships with others. For example, in one study in which children were asked to talk about past events in their lives, eight-year-old girls mentioned more details about the social context and their relationships with other people than did boys (Buckner & Fivush, 1998). In another study, high self-esteem in female adolescents was positively correlated with a strong desire to help female friends, that is, to feel connected with them. In contrast, high self-esteem in male adolescents was related to assertiveness with male friends, that is, wanting to stand apart and get ahead of them (Thorne & Michaelieu, 1996). Finally, other research has shown that girls in the eighth and tenth grades were more likely than boys to agree with questionnaire items such as "When making a decision, I take other people's needs and feelings into account." That is, they endorsed items that contained an orientation toward relationships (Jones & Costin, 1995).

Parental socialization of girls may lead them to an orientation toward relationships. When mothers of preschoolers were observed conversing with their daughters, they spent more time than mothers of boys discussing their children's shared activities— that is, their relationships with others; mothers of boys tended to discuss compar-

KEY THEME

Nature/Nurture

According to the relational approach, girls' development is distinct from that of boys, revolving around the need to establish and maintain relationships with others. Rather than breaking away from parents during adolescence, for example, girls may desire to keep their connections with them.

isons of their children with peers more than mothers of girls did (Flannagan & Hardee, 1994). Some researchers argue that without additional empirical evidence, it is premature to conclude that males and females differ in their essential nature (Martin & Ruble, 1997). Nonetheless, the relational perspective has revealed important details about the nature of female development that had previously been overlooked.

FOR YOUR REVIEW

- What are the characteristics of individuals who are psychologically androgynous? What psychological benefits often accompany androgyny?

- How does the relational approach conceptualize gender-role development? What research findings are consistent with the relational point of view?

CHAPTER RECAP

SUMMARY OF DEVELOPMENTAL THEMES

■ Nature/Nurture   *What roles do nature and nurture play in gender development?*

According to some theorists, biological influences such as hormones and brain lateralization underlie sex differences in aggression and visual-spatial skill, and some experimental evidence is indeed consistent with such hypotheses. According to social learning theorists, the child's socialization experiences with parents and peers and in school contribute substantially to observed sex differences, as does the child's knowledge of gender-role stereotypes. Research shows that peers and teachers, and to some extent parents, treat boys and girls differently, providing support for the nurture position.

■ Sociocultural Influence   *How does the sociocultural context influence gender development?*

Most cultures hold stereotypical beliefs about gender roles, although the specific characteristics associated with each sex can vary. The particular behaviors exhibited by males and females can also vary according to culture. Such findings demonstrate that although the tendency to stereotype is widespread, the characteristics associated with each sex are not necessarily fixed. Changes within American society, such as the increased proportion of women employed outside the home, underscore the idea that children's gender-role development can be affected by shifting sociocultural trends.

■ **Child's Active Role**   *How does the child play an active role in the process of gender development?*

The child's active role in the construction of gender-based knowledge is emphasized in cognitive-developmental theories of gender development. For example, many children construct gender schemas based on their socialization experiences, schemas that in turn influence how they process gender-related information and how they themselves behave.

■ **Continuity/Discontinuity**   *Is gender development continuous or discontinuous?*

Theorists such as Lawrence Kohlberg describe gender development as a stagelike process. Kohlberg hypothesized that children progress through a sequence of attaining gender identity, gender stability, and gender constancy. In contrast, social learning theorists describe the cumulative and incremental effects of reinforcement and modeling on gender-role development. Research has confirmed that children pass through the general sequence of gender awareness outlined by Kohlberg, but has also provided support for social learning theory.

■ **Individual Differences**   *How prominent are individual differences in gender development?*

Some children acquire gender identity earlier than others; these children tend to behave in more sex-typed ways and have greater knowledge of gender stereotypes than children who acquire gender identity later in life. Later in childhood, some children tend to be gender schematic; that is, they tend to organize their world along sex-divided lines. These children may even distort information to make it consistent with their strong gender schemas. Finally, some children exhibit patterns of cross-gender behavior. These tendencies are usually met with negative feedback from peers, especially if the cross-gender child is a boy.

■ **Interaction Among Domains**   *How does gender development interact with development in other domains?*

Attainments in cognition are thought to be related to many aspects of gender-role development. Bandura describes cognitive processes, such as attention, that influence which models, male or female, children will imitate. Kohlberg suggests that general cognitive advances pave the way for gender knowledge, such as gender constancy. By the same token, the child's state of gender-role development can influence cognitive processing. Gender-schematic children, for example, may show memory distortions consistent with their gender-role beliefs.

SUMMARY OF TOPICS

Gender Stereotypes Versus Actual Sex Differences

- *Gender stereotypes* are the expectations or beliefs that individuals within a given culture hold about the behaviors characteristic of women and men. Children learn these stereotypes as part of the process of *gender-role development*.

The Stereotypes: What Are They?

- Stereotypes of masculinity center on *instrumentality*, qualities associated with acting on the world. Stereotypes of femininity center on *expressiveness*, qualities associated with emotions and relationships.

- Although there are many cross-cultural similarities in the content of gender stereotypes, there are also notable variations.

Children's Knowledge of Gender Stereotypes

- Children demonstrate knowledge of gender stereotypes as early as age two.

- With development, knowledge about stereotypes becomes more extensive but also more flexible.

What Sex Differences Actually Exist?

- Males and females differ in several physical qualities, including activity level, rate of maturity, and physical size.

- The most notable sex differences in cognition are in visual-spatial tasks. Males tend to perform better than females on tasks that require mental rotation and spatial perception.

- A consistent finding in the domain of social behaviors is that males are more aggressive than females, although definitions of aggression, context, and age all make a difference in how this quality is expressed.

- Girls show a heightened sensitivity to emotions and are more vulnerable than boys to depression.

Sex Differences in Perspective

- Actual sex differences are fewer than the stereotypes suggest, but the stereotypes persist because of basic ways in which humans process social information.

Theories of Gender-Role Development

Biological Theories

- Biological theories emphasize the role of hormones such as *androgens* and differences in the structures of male and female brains in explaining sex differences in behaviors such as aggression and visual-spatial skills.

- Although research evidence provides support for biological theories of sex differences, cautions are in order because of the complex and bidirectional ways in which biology and environment interact.

Social Learning Theory

- Social learning theory emphasizes the roles of reinforcement, imitation, and, eventually, self-regulation in producing sex-typed behaviors.

- An important factor influencing the likelihood of imitation is the *sex typicality* of the model's behavior.

- Variations in sex-typed behaviors across cultures suggest a role for socialization experiences.

Cognitive-Developmental Theories

- Kohlberg's theory hypothesizes that children's awareness of gender grows through successive notions of *gender identity*, *gender stability*, and *gender constancy*.

- Gender identity is usually formed by age three, an accomplishment that is linked to sex-typed preferences in play activities and knowledge of stereotypes.

- *Gender schema* theory states that children first form schemas of same-sex–opposite-sex and then form more elaborate schemas for their own sex.

- Some children rely more on gender schemas than others as they process social information, a tendency that often leads them to distort information about sex-atypical behaviors.

The Socialization of Gender Roles

The Influence of Parents

- From the birth of a child onward, many parents express stereotypical attitudes and beliefs about their male and female children. They also treat children differently based on their biological sex, especially in the kinds of activities and play they encourage in children.

- Children who have nontraditional parents show less knowledge of gender stereotypes, and girls show more independence and achievement.

The Influence of Peers

- Children show early preferences for same-sex peer groups, and peers are ardent enforcers of gender-role norms.

- Children who consistently display cross-gender behaviors are likely to be isolated from their peer groups.

- *Sex segregation* is a robust phenomenon through the early school years and provides differential socialization experiences for boys and girls.

The Influence of Teachers and Schools

- Teachers may contribute to gender-role socialization through their attitudes and behaviors. Teachers may have different expectations about the academic skills of boys and girls and often focus more attention on boys than on girls.

- Students' own beliefs about their academic skills may be sex typed, but at least in the domain of mathematics, girls' beliefs in their competence seem to be increasing.

- Girls often underestimate their academic abilities and attribute failures to lack of ability.

Alternative Conceptualizations of Gender

Androgyny

- Androgyny refers to a gender-role orientation in which the individual possesses many qualities associated with both masculinity and femininity.

- Androgyny has been found to be associated with psychological health.

The Relational Approach

- The relational approach attempts to define the elements of female development that are unique compared with those of male development.

CHAPTER 14
The Family

Key Themes in the Family

- **Sociocultural Influence**   How does the socio-cultural context influence family processes?

- **Child's Active Role**   How does the child play an active role in family processes?

- **Interaction Among Domains**   How do family processes interact with other domains of development?

Seven-year-old Joey looked at his loaded dinner plate and announced, "I'm not hungry. Can I just have dessert?" "No, you may not!" his embarrassed mother replied as she turned toward her house guest. "I can't think why he gets like this. He's stubborn as a mule." The guest wondered why no one mentioned that Joey, in full view of his mother, had eaten most of a gift box of cookies before dinner.

"I don't want this! It stinks! You stink!" Joey shouted. He pushed away his plate, got up from the table, and ran to the television, which he turned up to full volume.

"Turn that down this minute or go to your room!" his mother ordered. Joey ignored her. "He's been like this since his father and I split up," she told her guest in a lowered voice. "Everything's so different now. I feel like I have to be two parents instead of one. He used to be such a good boy." Spying Joey reaching for the cookie box, she warned, "Don't take that cookie!" Joey removed his hand from the box and gave his mother a mournful, pleading look. "All right, but just one!" she conceded. Joey took two and returned to the TV.

This episode represents only one brief experience in Joey's life, but the accumulation of experiences such as this within the context of the family can have a distinct effect on the developing child. Families are central to the process of **socialization,** the process by which children acquire the social knowledge, behaviors, and attitudes valued by the larger society. Parents, siblings, and others within the family unit are the people with whom the child usually spends the most time and forms the strongest emotional bonds, and they thus exert an undeniable influence in the child's life.

The study of the impact of the family is no simple matter. For one thing, the child's experiences within the family can be affected by other factors, such as divorce or parental employment status, that can change the nature of interpersonal dynamics within the family. Joey's family experiences both before and after his parents' separation, for example, can have potentially long-lasting effects on his development. Moreover, the direction of influence within families runs along several paths. Just as parents and siblings affect the child's behavior, the child affects the reactions of other family members. Because the family experience includes fluid, constantly changing effects and outcomes for its various members, studying the influence of the family presents a special research challenge to developmental psychologists.

In a sense, virtually every domain of development is deeply influenced by the family environment. Cognition, moral awareness, gender identity, and emotional growth are all nurtured largely within the family. In this chapter we focus on the roles specific family members play in the child's social development, with special attention to adaptive and maladaptive patterns of interaction. We will also see how the family itself is a structure in flux, shaped by cultural values and shifting demographic trends such as divorce and maternal employment. The effects of these changes in family structure on the individual child's development are a major concern for developmental psychologists.

socialization Process by which children acquire the social knowledge, skills, and attitudes valued by the larger society.

497

Understanding the Family

Historians, sociologists, and anthropologists who study the family as a social unit point to the changes in its structure and functions over the last two centuries. With the industrialization of nineteenth-century America, for example, the extended family, in which secondary relatives such as grandparents, aunts and uncles, or cousins lived in the same household as the primary family, gave way to the nuclear family, consisting solely of parents and their offspring living in a single household. Similarly, as we saw in the chapter titled "Themes and Theories," the modern notion that families are havens for nurturing the child's growth and development was not always prevalent. As we look back in history, we see that the family has been a changing social structure, and all signs indicate it will continue to take different shapes in the future to reflect larger social, economic, and historical trends.

The Demographics of the American Family

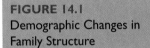

KEY THEME
Sociocultural Influence

No one family structure typifies contemporary American society. The 1950s model of a two-parent family with two children and a nonworking mother no longer applies. For example, as Figure 14.1 shows, only 69 percent of children younger than eighteen years lived with two parents in 2000, compared with 85 percent in 1970. Today 26 percent of American children live with only one parent (U.S. Bureau of the Census, 2001). High rates of divorce and single-parent births have contributed to this trend. Projections are that about 50 percent of current marriages will end in divorce (compared with about 15 percent in 1960), and about 32 percent of all births are to single women (Bumpass, 1990; U.S. Bureau of the Census, 2001, 2002). Moreover, about 5 percent of children live with their grandparents (U.S. Bureau of the Census, 2001), and a growing number live with gay or lesbian parents. Finally, more than 70 percent of married women with children younger than eighteen years work outside the home, compared with about 45 percent in 1975. All of these changes in family structure have distinct implications for the child's experiences within the family.

A Systems Approach

Many child development researchers have found it fruitful to focus on family dynamics, the interactions among all members of the group, rather than on the structure of the family per se as they study the impact of the family. An important influence on

FIGURE 14.1
Demographic Changes in Family Structure

The percentage of children living with two parents has declined since 1970, and the percentage living with a single parent (most frequently the mother) has increased dramatically. About one-fourth of American children live with a single parent. The higher rates of divorce and single-parent births have contributed to this trend.

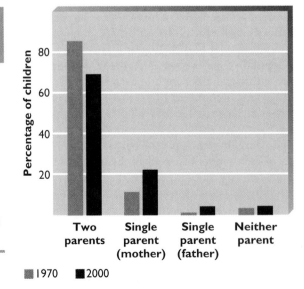

Source: Adapted from U.S. Bureau of the Census, 2001.

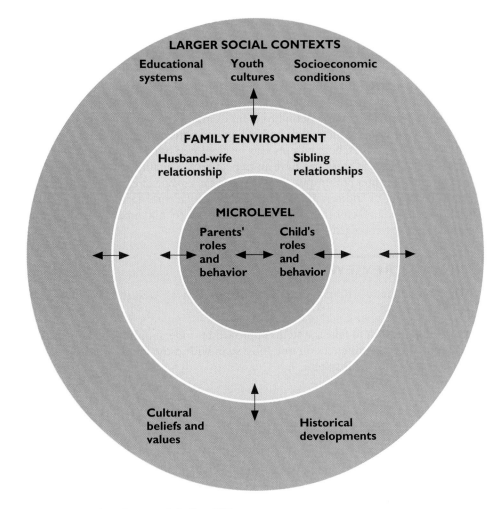

FIGURE 14.2
The Systems Model of
the Family

According to systems theorists, reciprocal influences among family members occur at three levels: the individual or microlevel, the family environment, and the larger social context. At the microlevel, parent and child influence each other directly. Within the family, relationships among particular individuals, such as husband and wife, can affect interactions with children. Finally, larger social factors, such as the presence of economic stress, can affect parent-child relations. The individual child's development is thus embedded in this network of multidirectional interactions.

Source: Adapted from Peterson & Rollins, 1987.

contemporary thinking about the family is **systems theory.** The premise is that all members influence one another simultaneously and the interactions flow in a circular, reciprocal manner. In systems theory (see Figure 14.2), the individual child's development is understood as being embedded in the complex network of multidirectional interactions among all family members (Bronfenbrenner, 1986; Cox & Paley, 1997).

Systems theory assumes that families undergo periods of stability and change. The family tends to adapt to maintain a state of *homeostasis,* or equilibrium. Thus, as children attain milestones such as going to school or entering adolescence, the family system must readjust to absorb the child's new routines or demands for independence. At other times families may experience crises, such as financial hardship, moving, or divorce. In these instances, changing external circumstances require the child and all other family members to adapt to the new situation. Systems theory, then, regards families as dynamic, self-regulating social groups (Minuchin, 1988).

Families usually contain several subsystems, such as the relations maintained between spouses, among siblings, and between parent and child. A single family member is usually a member of more than one subsystem at the same time. The child has a relationship with each parent, as well as with one or more siblings; mothers and fathers are spouses as well as parents. The quality of each of these separate relationships can have an impact on other relationships. Thus, for example, when parents have high-quality marital relationships, their relationships with their children are warmer, and their children show more favorable psychological adjustment (Davies & Scummings, 1998; Harold et al., 1997; Miller et al., 1993). Siblings have more positive interactions with one another, too (MacKinnon, 1988). Within the systems

systems theory Model for understanding the family that emphasizes the reciprocal interactions among various members.

model, family members have reciprocal influences on one another, and there are several layers of such interactions.

The family system itself is embedded in larger social networks, including the economic, political, legal, and educational forces that are part of the larger culture. Events in the workplace, school, and other extrafamilial settings can affect individual family members and hence the interactions that occur within the family unit. When one or both parents becomes unemployed, for example, the family experiences stress that often is expressed in increased conflict between parents and children (Flanagan, 1990). In other instances, both parents may be employed outside the home, and their experiences of stress at work can have an impact on the quality of interactions with their children (Crouter & Bumpus, 2001). The *social ecology* of child development—that is, the direct or indirect impact of broad sociocultural factors on the child's social, cognitive, and emotional growth—is critical to understand, according to developmental psychologists.

FOR YOUR REVIEW

- What major changes have occurred in the structure of American families in the past thirty years?

- What does it mean to take a systems approach to understanding the family? Give examples of how influences on one subsystem within the family can have consequences for another subsystem.

Parents and Socialization

In most cultures, the primary agents of the child's socialization are parents. As we will see in the next two chapters, teachers, peers, and broader social factors also play a significant role; but perhaps no other individuals in the child's life have the powerful influence on future behaviors, attitudes, and personality that parents do.

Parents affect children's socialization in three primary ways. First, they socialize their children through direct training, providing information or reinforcement for the behaviors they find acceptable or desirable. Parents may, for example, encourage their children to share with playmates or instruct them on how to become acquainted with an unfamiliar peer. Second, as they interact with their children, parents serve as important models for the children's attitudes, beliefs, and actions. For example, parents who are warm, engaging, and verbally stimulating tend to have children who are popular in school. Finally, parents manage other aspects of their children's lives that in turn can influence children's social development. Parents choose the neighborhood in which the family lives; they also may enroll children in sports programs, arrange birthday parties, and invite children's friends to spend the night, all of which influence children's peer networks (Parke et al., 1988; Parke & O'Neil, 1999).

Of course, parents' major concerns and activities shift as the child develops. Parents of infants focus on caregiving activities and helping the child to learn such skills as self-feeding, dressing, and toileting. By the time their child is two years old, parents begin more deliberate attempts at socialization. Parents of preschoolers help their children to regulate their emotions—to control angry outbursts, for example—and start to instill social skills, such as polite forms of speech and sharing during play with peers. Parents of elementary school children are likely to be concerned with their children's academic achievement. When their children approach adolescence, most parents encourage independent, rational, and value-based decision making as their youngsters prepare to enter their own adult lives.

Parental roles also shift with development. Throughout early childhood, parents closely monitor much of their children's activity. Once children enter school, parents play less of a supervisory role. They begin to expect their children to be cooperative members of the family by avoiding conflicts and sharing in household tasks. Parents and children begin to negotiate as they make decisions and solve family problems. Finally, during adolescence, parents observe children's participation in the larger social world, in school and community activities and close personal relationships with peers. While parents are encouraging independence in some domains, such as school achievement, they may also be exerting more control in other domains, such as their children's social activities (Maccoby, 1984; Maccoby & Martin, 1983; McNally, Eisenberg, & Harris, 1991).

As this quick sketch suggests, the child's own development often precipitates shifts in parental roles. As the child's language and cognitive skills mature, parents place greater expectations on her social communication behaviors. As she enters school, parents nurture greater independence. The physical changes associated with puberty often signal to parents that more mature child-adult interactions, such as deferring at times to the child's wishes rather than rigidly restricting his activities, are warranted (Steinberg, 1981). As systems theory suggests, the individual child's development within the family represents an ongoing give-and-take between child and parent, necessitating continual readjustment by all members to reinstate family equilibrium.

Styles of Parenting

Even the casual observer of parents interacting with their children in public places such as parks, shopping malls, and supermarkets will notice markedly different styles of parental behavior. Some parents are extremely controlling, using crisp, firm commands devoid of explanations to restrict their children's behavior. Others seem not to notice as their charges create chaos and pandemonium. Researchers have established that the pattern of interactions a parent adopts is an important variable in influencing the child's later development.

In a landmark series of observational studies, Diana Baumrind (1971, 1973) recorded the interpersonal and behavioral styles of nursery school children as they engaged in normal school activities. She also watched as they worked on a series of standardized problem-solving tasks, such as completing a set of puzzles. In addition, Baumrind gathered information on parenting styles by observing how mothers interacted with their children in both play and structured teaching settings, watching parents and their children in the home, and interviewing parents about their child-rearing practices. The children and parents were observed again when children were eight or nine years old. Based on these extensive observations, Baumrind identified several distinct patterns of parenting.

Some parents, Baumrind found, were extremely restrictive and controlling. They valued respect for authority and strict obedience to their commands and relied on coercive techniques, such as threats or physical punishment, rather than on reasoning or explanation, to regulate their children's actions. They were also less nurturant toward their children than other parents in the study. Baumrind identified this group as **authoritarian parents.** The second parenting style belonged to the group she called **permissive parents.** These parents set few limits and made few demands for mature behavior from their children. Children were permitted to make their own decisions about many routine activities such as TV viewing, bedtime, and mealtimes, for example. Permissive parents tended to be either moderately nurturant or cool and uninvolved. The third group of parents was high on both control and nurturance. These **authoritative parents** expected their children to behave in a mature fashion but tended to use rewards more than punishments to achieve their ends. They communicated their expectations clearly and provided explanations to help their children understand the reasons for their requests. They also listened to what their children had to say and encouraged a dialogue with them. Authoritative parents were distinctly supportive and warm in their interactions with their children. Figure 14.3 summarizes the characteristics of these three parental styles, as well as a fourth style, *uninvolved parents,* which has been described in later research and will be discussed shortly.

Research has shown that parents who expect mature behavior from their children, provide explanations for their requests, and are supportive and warm in their interactions have children who display instrumental competence. These parents display what is called an *authoritative style.*

authoritarian parent Parent who relies on coercive techniques to discipline the child and displays a low level of nurturance.

permissive parent Parent who sets few limits on the child's behavior.

authoritative parent Parent who sets limits on a child's behavior using reasoning and explanation and displays a high degree of nurturance.

FIGURE 14.3

FIGURE 14.3
Patterns of Parenting
as a Function of Control
and Nurturance

**Four parenting styles can
be identified in terms of the
extent to which parents set
limits on the child's behavior
(control) and the level of nurturance and responsiveness
they provide.**

NURTURANCE

	Responsive, child centered	Rejecting, parent centered
High on control, demanding	Authoritative	Authoritarian
Low on control, undemanding	Permissive	Uninvolved

CONTROL

Source: Adapted from Maccoby & Martin, 1983.

KEY THEME
Interaction Among Domains

Baumrind found a cluster of behavioral characteristics in children linked with
each parental style. The offspring of authoritative parents were friendly with peers,
cooperative with adults, independent, energetic, and achievement oriented. They also
displayed a high degree of self-control. This set of characteristics often is termed
instrumental competence. In marked contrast, children of authoritarian and permissive parents did not exhibit the social responsibility and independence associated
with instrumental competence. Children who had authoritarian parents appeared
unhappy; also, boys tended to be aggressive, whereas girls were likely to be dependent. Children of permissive parents, on the other hand, were low on self-control and
self-reliance.

The effects of parenting style extend to other dimensions of child development
and reach into the adolescent years. Authoritarian parenting, especially with its use
of coercive techniques for controlling behavior, is associated with less advanced
moral reasoning and less prosocial behavior (Boyes & Allen, 1993; Krevans & Gibbs,
1996), lower self-esteem (Loeb, Horst, & Horton, 1980), and poorer adjustment
to starting school (Barth, 1989). Extremely controlling parenting and the use of
coercive techniques are also associated with higher levels of aggression in children
(Maccoby & Martin, 1983), poor peer relations (Pettit et al., 1996; Putallaz, 1987), and
lower school achievement in adolescence (Dornbusch et al., 1987). In contrast, by the
time children reach adolescence, those with authoritative parents show more prosocial
behaviors, fewer problem behaviors such as substance abuse, greater academic
achievement, and higher self-confidence than adolescents whose parents use other
parenting styles (Baumrind, 1991; Lamborn et al., 1991; Radziszewska et al., 1996).

Researchers have also identified a fourth parenting style: the **uninvolved,** or
neglectful, **parent** (Maccoby & Martin, 1983). These parents seem to be uncommit-
ted to their parental role and emotionally detached from their children, often giving
greater priority to their own needs and preferences than to the child's. These parents
may be uninterested in events at the child's school, unfamiliar with his playmates,
and have only infrequent conversations with him (Pulkkinen, 1982). Uninvolved
parenting is related to children's lower self-esteem (Loeb et al., 1980), heightened
aggression (Hatfield, Ferguson, & Alpert, 1967), and lower control over impulsive
behavior (Block, 1971). As older adolescents, children with uninvolved parents show
more maladjustment, lack of creativity, and greater alcohol consumption than adolescents who experienced other parenting styles (Weiss & Schwarz, 1996). Some
researchers believe that uninvolved parenting may present the greatest risks of all to
healthy long-term development (Steinberg et al., 1994).

instrumental competence
Child's display of independence,
self-control, achievement orientation, and cooperation.

uninvolved parent Parent who
is emotionally detached from the
child and focuses on his or her
own needs as opposed to the
child's.

Why does authoritative parenting work so well? Several explanations are possible. First, when parents make demands for mature behavior from their children, they make explicit the responsibilities individuals have toward one another when they live in social groups. When parents set forth clear, consistent guidelines for behavior, they make the child's job of sorting out the social world much easier. Second, when parental demands are accompanied by reasonable explanations, the child is more likely to accept the limitations on her actions. Third, when parents take into account the child's responses and show affection, he is likely to acquire a sense of control over his actions and derive the sense that he has worth. Studies confirm that adolescents who have authoritative parents have a healthy sense of autonomy and personal responsibility, and feel a sense of control over their lives (Glasgow et al., 1997; Steinberg, Elmen, & Mounts, 1989). Thus the net outcome of authoritative parenting is a competent child who shows successful psychological adjustment.

Effective Parenting

Baumrind's research showed that the most desirable developmental outcomes are associated with parenting that has two key characteristics: responding to the child's needs and actions with warmth and nurturance and setting limits on the child's behavior. These themes echo the discussion of sensitive parenting and attachment presented in the chapter titled "Emotion."

No matter what the age of the child, whether he is a toddler exhibiting a fierce temper tantrum or an adolescent testing a curfew, research shows that parenting based on strong expressions of warmth, involvement with children's lives, and clear limit setting results in successful developmental outcomes. Even when families are faced with stresses and challenges, these techniques can mitigate potentially negative long-term outcomes for children.

● **Parental Warmth**   A series of recent studies has singled out parental warmth, the tendency of parents to express positive emotions and approval toward their children, as an important feature of effective parenting. Children whose parents express warmth and support tend to have higher self-esteem, greater empathy, and fewer behavioral problems (Cox & Harter, 2003; Zhou et al., 2002). Among adolescents, who may begin to experiment with risky behaviors, parental support and warmth are related to a decreased likelihood of teen pregnancy, less aggression, and less association with deviant peers (Scaramella et al., 1998; Young et al., 1995). On the other hand, parental negativity is related to less compliance on the part of the child, poor peer relationships, and delinquency (Deater-Deckard et al., 2001; Isley et al., 1999; Simons et al., 2001). Parental warmth may even serve as a protection of sorts for children who are highly aggressive as youngsters and who are at risk for later developmental problems. When these children experience warm and affectionate parenting, they are less likely to show the declines in empathy, school problems, and adulthood unemployment that many other children in this category display (Hastings et al., 2000; Kokko & Pulkkinen, 2000).

Parental warmth probably works in a number of ways. One outcome of parental warmth and supportiveness is the child's perception of his or her own competence. As we see in the chapter titled "Self and Values," parental support is an important contributor to the growth of children's self-esteem, which in turn has consequences for many other aspects of the child's social and cognitive development. Moreover, warm parents, in their expression of positive emotions, may encourage a process of "emotion matching" in their children. Positive parental emotions are associated with positive emotions in children (Kochanska, 1997). Similarly, Kee Kim and associates found that a high level of negative affect expressed by parents of adolescents predicted the rate at which adolescents increased their own expressions of negative affect (Kim et al., 2001).

A recent survey shows that many fathers and mothers report showing warmth and affection to their children every day (see Figure 14.4) (Child Trends, 2002b). Given the importance of parental warmth in child rearing, these statistics are encouraging to see.

◉ SEE FOR YOURSELF
psychology.college.hmco.com
Resources for Parents

KEY THEME
Interaction Among Domains

FIGURE 14.4
Expressing Parental Warmth

To what degree do mothers and fathers express warmth to their children? This graph shows the percentage of fathers and mothers who say they provide various visible signs of warmth to their children (under age 13) on a daily basis. Numerous studies confirm that parental warmth is a key feature of effective parenting.

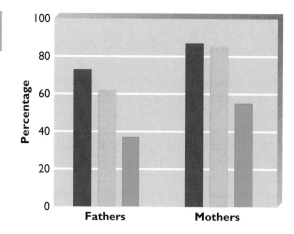

■ Hugged or showed physical affection to their children

▨ Told their child that they love him or her

▨ Told their child that they appreciated something he or she did

Source: Child Trends Databank, 2002b.

● **Parental Control**   Effective parenting also includes the ability of parents to control their children's behavior, setting limits when appropriate. However, researchers are finding that a distinction needs to be made between *behavioral control,* monitoring and regulating the child's actions, and *psychological control,* intrusive and domineering parenting that can interfere with the child's growing autonomy. Gregory Pettit and his colleagues found that adolescents whose parents were high on monitoring (that is, they were aware of their activities, friends, and how they spent their time) were less likely to become involved in delinquent behaviors. In contrast, parents who exerted a high degree of psychological control were more likely to display delinquent behaviors and also expressed higher levels of anxiety and depression (Pettit et al., 2001). Research is increasingly pointing to the importance of parents monitoring and supervising their children's behaviors (Herman et al., 1997); parents need to be involved! At the same time, parents must respect their children's need to develop a sense of identity and independent decision making. Oftentimes, overbearing and controlling parents are simply exerting their power in a style reminiscent of authoritarian parenting. It should not be surprising that the consequences of this approach to parental control are often negative (Barber & Harmon, 2002).

● **Punishment**   In recent decades, the most widely discussed parental control technique has been *punishment,* the administration of an aversive stimulus or withdrawal of rewards to decrease the frequency of undesirable behaviors (see the chapter titled "Basic Learning and Perception"). A form of power assertion, punishment can include spanking, sharp verbal rebukes, or the loss of such privileges as TV viewing time or playtime with friends.

Laboratory studies carried out in the tradition of learning theory show that certain ways of administering punishment are more effective than others. One important factor is making sure the punishment closely follows the child's transgression so that the child makes the connection between her behavior and the consequences. Another powerful factor is providing an explanation for why the behavior is not desirable (Parke, 1969). The effectiveness of punishment also depends on the consistency with which it is applied. As we saw in the case of Joey and the cookies at the beginning of the chapter, children become particularly disobedient and aggressive when parents prohibit a behavior on one occasion and permit it on another. Consistency among caregivers (**interagent consistency**) and consistency of one caregiver from one occasion to the next (**intra-agent consistency**) are both important in giving children clear, unambiguous messages about acceptable and unacceptable behaviors (Deur & Parke, 1970; Sawin & Parke, 1979).

interagent consistency
Consistency in application of disciplinary strategies among different caregivers.

intra-agent consistency
Consistency in a single caregiver's application of discipline from one situation to the next.

CONTROVERSY: THINKING IT OVER

Should Parents Spank Their Children?

Most often, when parents think of punishment, they think of spanking the child. In a survey of almost one thousand parents, Murray Straus and Julie Stewart found that 94 percent of parents of three- and four-year-olds reported striking their children in the previous year. Infants and adolescents were spanked less often (Straus & Stewart, 1999). However, even half of adolescents report being hit by their parents, with an average of six to eight times in a year (Straus & Donnelly, 1993). Thus, in the United States, many parents resort to physical punishment, at least on occasion, to control their child's behavior.

What Is the Controversy?

Many psychologists believe that physical tactics such as hitting and spanking should not be used at all. Some groups of lay individuals feel so strongly about the negative effects that they are working to make physical punishment of children illegal. Others maintain that moderate spanking in the context of a warm, supportive family life has no long-lasting negative effects.

What Are the Opposing Arguments?

Many researchers argue that by using physical punishment, parents are serving as models for aggression. Following the tenets of social learning theory, we should not be surprised if the chief lesson children learn from parents who spank is that physical aggression is a way to resolve conflicts (Parke & Slaby, 1983). Also, an overreliance on physical punishment may set the stage for child abuse (Parke & Collmer, 1975). Caught up in the escalating emotions of a confrontation with their children, parents who are already willing to spank, hit, or pinch do not have far to go before they cause more serious physical injury.

A contrasting position is that occasional spanking has no long-lasting negative effects. In fact, spanking, judiciously used, may be a necessary tactic when children are unrelentingly noncompliant. In this line of thinking, parents should consider spanking only when other nonphysical disciplinary tactics have failed. When parents are warm and supportive, however, an occasional spanking is not harmful; rather, it may be necessary to help children learn to be compliant and to regulate their own behavior (Baumrind, 1996).

What Answers Exist? What Questions Remain?

Some research suggests that the children of parents who use occasional spanking do not have different profiles from children whose parents never spank. In one study of twenty-one-month-olds, for example, children whose mothers used frequent physical punishment scored lower on their ability to regulate their behaviors. However, children whose mothers used occasional physical punishment did not differ from children whose mothers never spanked them—both fared better than the high-physical-punishment group (Power & Chapieski, 1986). Additional evidence suggests that the link between spanking and aggression in children, and spanking and child abuse, is not necessarily clear. For example, since 1995, when Sweden passed a law to ban physical punishment, aggression in teenagers has increased (and not decreased), as has the number of cases of child abuse (Baumrind, 1996).

Supporting the other side of the debate are the results of a recent meta-analysis of eighty-eight studies evaluating the impact of physical punishment on children. The findings indicated that physical punishment had a strong relationship to the child's immediate compliance. However, there was also a strong association between the use of physical punishment and child abuse. Lesser, but still significant, associations were found between increased use of physical punishment and heightened aggression, risk for mental health problems, and lower moral internalization in children (Gershoff, 2002).

The meta-analysis has been criticized for including studies in which physical punishment was more extreme than an occasional spanking (Baumrind, Larzelere, & Cowan, 2002). What kinds of studies might provide more compelling evidence about the appropriateness of spanking? Moreover, what are the potential effects on parents and children when experts take a position on an issue such as this one before the research fully settles the controversy?

RESEARCH APPLIED TO PARENTING

Managing Noncompliant Children

Afier her dinner guest left and Joey was put to bed (with yet another struggle), his mother sat exhausted on the couch and thought about the difficulties she was having in controlling her child's behavior. Her embarrassment in front of her guest was just a small problem compared to the negative cycle in which she and Joey always seemed to end up. She loved her child beyond words, but things were just too far out of control and she needed help. A friend had suggested that she see a clinical psychologist for advice. She went to her dresser drawer and pulled out the psychologist's card; she would call Dr. Nagle in the morning.

At the visit with Dr. Nagle two weeks later, Joey's mother described some examples of her son's noncompliant behavior. Dr. Nagle nodded knowingly and then spoke of the need for parents to maintain reasonable control over their child's behavior. "Just how can I do that?" asked Joey's mother. "I don't believe in spanking. What else can I do to get him to listen to me?" Dr. Nagle then proceeded to outline the elements of a parent behavior management program.

One of the most common problems parents face is the oppositional behavior their children show, often beginning at age two or three. A parent makes a request (e.g., "Time to go to bed"), and the child simply refuses to comply, adding a loud "No!" for emphasis. The child's response may reflect a healthy, growing desire for independence and self-assertion. But this pattern, if repeated for a length of time, can quickly lead to conflicts with parents and frustration on their part. For the child, persistent noncompliance has the potential to lead to major behavior problems, including aggression.

Rex Forehand and his colleagues (Forehand & McMahon, 1981; Wierson & Forehand, 1994) have described some basic behavior management techniques that can help parents control children's negative behaviors without resorting to spanking or physical punishment. They are based on having parents avoid two kinds of traps: a negative reinforcement trap and a positive reinforcement trap. In the first case, a parent issues a command, but the child whines, protests, and does not listen. If the parent gives in, the child has received a negative reinforcement, learning that whining will remove an aversive stimulus (the parent's commands). In the second case, the child's noncompliance receives a positive consequence—that is, extra attention— if parents spend a lot of time and effort talking with her about why she should obey. Therefore, parents should try to adhere to the following principles:

1. *Attend to the child's appropriate behavior each day.*   Children will learn that attention and rewards follow when they behave as parents expect them to. When attending to the child's desirable behavior, avoid using commands, questions, and criticisms, all of which are associated with the child's noncompliance.

2. *Ignore inappropriate behaviors that are minor, such as crankiness and whining.* The lack of attention should cause the behavior to decrease.

3. *Give clear, succinct commands and reward the child with verbal praise for following them.*   Do not engage in a long discussion with the child (which amounts to too much attention), but make sure the child understands what is expected.

One effective technique for managing a child's behavior is the use of "time-out," sending the child to a neutral area for a specific amount of time after she or he misbehaves. Time-out has been found to reduce or eliminate a variety of behavior problems among children.

4. *Use a technique called time-out if the child does not comply with a command.* Remove the child from all possible sources of reward, even subtle or accidental ones. Take him immediately to a quiet, neutral place and leave him alone there until a short period of time, usually two to five minutes, has elapsed. Time-out has been found to be effective in reducing or eliminating a variety of troublesome behaviors in children, including temper tantrums, fighting, and self-injurious behaviors (Varni, 1983). Time-out also gives both children and parents the opportunity to "cool down" after all parties have become aroused.

The techniques just described have been found to significantly reduce noncompliance in children who were referred to a clinic for their behavior problems. Not only did their behavior improve relative to their pretreatment baseline; it also compared favorably with that of a group of control children who had not been referred to the clinic (Forehand & Long, 1988). Although the focus of this intervention was on families experiencing serious difficulties with child behavior management, many parents can benefit from using the techniques just outlined.

Factors That Influence Parenting Strategies

As they engage in interactions with each other, parents and children interpret each other's behaviors; these judgments, in turn, influence the specific behaviors they display toward each other. In addition, parents hold beliefs about their own competence and effectiveness as parents; these beliefs are also related to the quality of parenting (Coleman & Karraker, 1998). Finally, children's behaviors, specifically the extent to which they escalate the intensity of interactions, can determine parental styles. In short, parenting strategies arise from a complex interplay of cognitions and reactions to the dynamics of the situation.

● **Parental Cognitions**   One way to understand parents' cognitions is in terms of their *attributions* about children's behaviors: Why are their children acting the way they do? Theodore Dix and Joan Grusec (1985; Dix, 1993) hypothesize that the kinds of attributions parents make about the causes of their children's behaviors will influence the parenting strategies they adopt. If, for example, a parent believes his three-year-old is throwing a tantrum at the dinner table because she wants her dessert

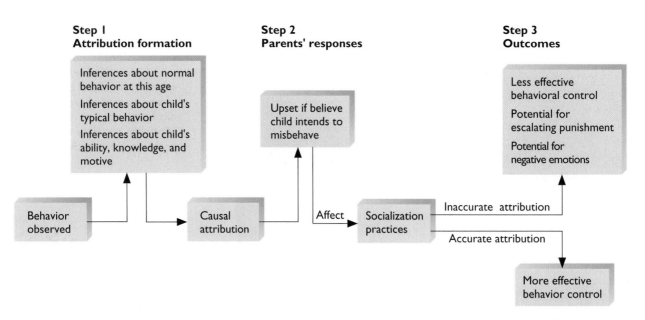

Step 1
Attribution formation

Step 2
Parents' responses

Step 3
Outcomes

Source: Adapted from Dix & Grusec, 1985.

FIGURE 14.5
The Attribution Model of Socialization

Dix and Grusec (1985) hypothesize that parents' judgments about the child's intentionality in misbehaving are critical in determining their response. Parents become more upset if they believe the child intended to transgress and select more forceful control strategies than they do if they believe the transgression was unintentional. If their attributions are correct, they will effectively control behavior. If they make an incorrect attribution, however, they will be less effective, may escalate the level of punishment, and may produce negative emotions in themselves and the child.

immediately, he will probably insist that she first eat all her vegetables. If, on the other hand, the parent suspects the child is ill, he will probably remove the child from the dinner table and nurture and console her.

Figure 14.5 presents a schematic diagram of Dix and Grusec's (1985) attribution model of socialization. The flow of events proceeds as follows. First, the parent observes the child's behavior and judges whether it is typical for the child or normative for her age group. The parent assesses whether the child has the skills, knowledge, and motive to behave intentionally in a certain way. Do most three-year-olds throw tantrums to get dessert? Is throwing a tantrum a typical behavior for that child? Parents make a causal attribution about the child's intentions. Next, parents' attributions affect their emotional and behavioral responses to the child. Parents become more upset and act more forcefully if they believe the child intends to misbehave—in this case, screaming for the explicit purpose of getting dessert. Finally, if parents have made the correct attribution, they will be effective in controlling the child. But if they are wrong, the child may continue to misbehave, and both parents and child may feel negative emotions rising.

Research confirms that parents make more attributions about children's intentions as the children get older. Furthermore, when parents believe that a child intends to misbehave, they feel more upset and think it is important to respond forcefully (Dix et al., 1986; Dix, Ruble, & Zambarano, 1989). Mothers who tend to attribute hostile intentions to children's actions are likely, in fact, to use harsh discipline practices; their children, in turn, tend to have problems with aggression in school (Nix et al., 1999).

Another dimension of parental cognitions is their beliefs about their own *efficacy:* Do parents see themselves as competent and able to control their children's behaviors? For example, some parents see themselves as powerless relative to their children. Oftentimes, in an attempt to regain their power and control, these parents engage in conflict and harsh discipline with their children (Bugental & Lewis, 1998; Bugental et al., 1997). However, their inconsistent style may send mixed messages to the child. For example, a harsh command might be followed by "just kidding" or some other form of appeasement (Bugental, Blue, & Cruzcosa, 1989). Children tend to become inattentive when they experience this type of ambiguous communication style from adults and may thus become unresponsive to their requests (Bugental et al., 1999). Parental beliefs about their own efficacy can be influenced by diverse factors, including financial stress (Brody, Flor, & Gibson, 1999), the degree to which the child's temperament challenges the parent (Teti & Gelfand, 1991), and the parent's "working models" of interpersonal relationships (Grusec, Hastings, & Mammone, 1994).

Finally, it is important to consider the different goals that parents have as they raise their children. These goals typically extend beyond simply controlling their children's behavior—parents want their children to be happy, have strong values, and have a trusting and loving relationship with them. Parents rely on different strategies depending on the goals they have in mind. When parents want to quickly resolve a disagreement with the child, for example, they most often use power assertion. When they wish to teach a child specific values, on the other hand, they tend to use explanation and open communication (Hastings & Grusec, 1998).

● **The Child's Characteristics and Behaviors**   In his **control theory,** Richard Bell (1968; Bell & Harper, 1977) suggests that children play a distinct role in the types of behaviors that parents display toward them. Parents and children have upper and lower limits of tolerance for the types of behavior each shows the other. When the behavior of one approaches the other's upper limit, the recipient tries to reduce the excessive behavior with increasing levels of intensity. Thus, for example, a parent whose son is having a temper tantrum might first try to talk to him, then remove him to his room, and finally resort to physical punishment. Likewise, if the child's behavior approaches the parent's lower limits—in the child's shyness or withdrawal at the doctor's office, for example—the parent may try to stimulate the child by coaching her to speak and then promising her a reward if she vocalizes.

Control theory implies that when children's behavior pushes parents to their upper limits, parents will respond with more forceful and firmer control techniques. Furthermore, some children may transgress to this extent more frequently than others. Support for this idea comes from research that shows that aggressive, difficult children elicit more negative reactions from adults than more compliant, non-aggressive children (Anderson, Lytton, & Romney, 1986). In addition, in a recent study of identical and fraternal twins and biologically related and unrelated siblings, genetic factors accounted for the relationship between parents' negativity and adolescent problem behaviors (Neiderhiser et al., 1999). The idea that the child's inborn temperament influences parental reactions is consistent with these data.

The research of Grazyna Kochanska and her colleagues is adding to the growing body of evidence that some children are easier to socialize than others. Some children, she finds, display *committed compliance*. Even as fourteen-month-old infants, these children seem eager to respond to their mothers, imitating them eagerly as they teach or complying quickly and enthusiastically with their requests. Other children may comply with parental requests only as particular situations demand, and still others seem to be generally unresponsive to their parents (Forman & Kochanska, 2001). These qualities of the child are, in turn, related to parenting styles. When children display committed compliance, for example, parents are less likely to use power-assertive techniques (Kochanska, 1997). Another study involving school-age children shows similar findings: Mothers who scolded, yelled, and used other ineffective discipline techniques reported that their children were very difficult to manage during their first five years of life. These children had frequent temper tantrums, were strong-willed, did not obey, and were very active (Stoolmiller, 2001).

Children's cognitions about their parents' demands probably also make a difference in how they react. Do children see their parents' requests as fair and appropriate? Are children motivated to comply? Do they feel internally motivated rather than pressured by others to respond? These are some of the factors that likely play a part in the tone and outcomes of parent-child interactions (Grusec & Goodnow, 1994). Researchers are just beginning to explore the role of children's cognitions in parent-child interactions.

KEY THEME
Child's Active Role

control theory Hypothesis about parent-child interactions suggesting that the intensity of one partner's behavior affects the intensity of the other's response.

Problems in Parenting

There is no doubt that being a parent presents special rewards but also distinct challenges. In some instances, such extreme maladaptive styles of interaction develop between parent and child that physical and psychological harm can occur to both. Understanding the dynamics of these families is essential to any attempt at intervention and also provides an even greater understanding of how all families, both healthy and dysfunctional, work as systems.

● **Coercive Cycles**   Sometimes, problems in parenting result from a pattern of escalating negative reciprocal interactions between parent and child called **coercive cycles.** Gerald Patterson and his colleagues (Patterson, 1982, 1986; Patterson, Reid, & Dishion, 1992) conducted extensive longitudinal studies of boys who exhibited pathological aggression and concluded that they acquired their behavior from routine family interactions in which both parents and children engaged in coercive behavior.

In Patterson's studies, preadolescent boys labeled as highly aggressive by schools, courts, or the families themselves were compared with nonaggressive boys from "normal" families over a period of several months. Detailed observations were made of family interactions in the home, including the sequences of behaviors displayed by parents, the target children, and their siblings. Patterson learned that the families of antisocial boys were characterized by high levels of aggressive interaction that rewarded coercive behaviors. When younger, the antisocial boys exhibited minor negative behaviors, such as whining, teasing, or yelling, in response to the aggression of another family member. About 70 percent of these behaviors were reinforced by the acquiescence of the child's interaction partner; in other words, the parent or sibling backed down, and the submission negatively reinforced the child's aggression. In addition, although parents were observed to nag, scold, or threaten their children, they seldom followed through on their threats. Such sequences between the target child and other family members occurred as often as hundreds of times each day in the aggressive families. Over time, the target boys' aggression escalated in frequency and progressed to physical assaults.

At this point, many parents attempted to control their sons' aggressive behaviors, but in doing so they too became highly aggressive. The chains of coercion increased in duration to form long bursts of negative interactions and often resulted in hitting between parent and child. After extended experience in these maladaptive familial exchanges, boys became out of control and acted violently in settings outside the home, such as the school. Aggression in school was related, in turn, to poor peer relations and academic failure, adding to the chain of negative events in the boys' lives.

Can such extreme patterns of aggression be controlled? Patterson and his colleagues have intervened in the maladaptive interactions of aggressive families by training parents in basic child management skills (Patterson et al., 1975). They focused on teaching parents to use discipline more effectively by dispensing more positive reinforcements for prosocial behaviors, using reasoning, disciplining consistently, and setting clear limits on even minor acts of aggression. Children significantly decreased their rates of deviant behavior after only a few weeks, and the results were maintained for as long as twelve months after the initial training period (Patterson & Fleischman, 1979). As an added benefit, parents' perceptions of their children became more positive (Patterson & Reid, 1973).

● **Child Abuse**   In 2000, more than 800,000 children in the United States were the victims of abuse or neglect (National Clearinghouse on Child Abuse and Neglect Information, 2002). Table 14.1 shows some of the characteristics of children who are the victims of maltreatment. Aside from the immediate physical and psychological consequences of abuse, children who are the victims of family violence are predisposed to a number of developmental problems. Maltreated infants and toddlers are more likely to be anxiously attached to their mothers than are children who are not

coercive cycles Pattern of escalating negative reciprocal interactions.

maltreated (Egeland & Sroufe, 1981a; Schneider-Rosen et al., 1985). These children are thus vulnerable to the social, emotional, and cognitive impairments associated with insecure attachment. Preschool and school-age children with a history of abuse score lower on tests of cognitive maturity and academic engagement and manifest low self-esteem and school learning problems (Eckenrode, Laird, & Doris, 1993; Hoffman-Plotkin & Twentyman, 1984; Shonk & Cicchetti, 2001). Emotionally, they may display withdrawal and passivity or, on the other hand, aggressive, oppositional patterns of behavior, patterns that are linked to their generally poor relationships with peers (Salzinger et al., 1993; Shonk & Cicchetti, 2001). They also frequently display symptoms of clinical depression (Sternberg et al., 1993). Finally, abused and neglected children are at risk for delinquency and violent criminal behavior in adulthood (Widom, 1989) and may be prone to become abusive parents themselves (Egeland, Jacobvitz, & Papatola, 1987).

The causes of abuse are neither simple nor easily ameliorated. Research on the interaction patterns in abusive families suggests that they differ in several respects from those in nonabusive families. Perhaps most significantly, parents in abusive families tend to rely on coercive or negative strategies to modify their children's behavior, even for routine or mild discipline problems. In one study, abusive and nonabusive mothers were observed as they engaged in a sequence of preparing a meal, playing, and cleaning up with their preschool-age children. Abusive mothers relied heavily on power-assertive techniques, such as threats, humiliation, or physical contact, to alter their children's behavior, whereas nonabusive mothers used predominantly positive strategies, including reasoning, bargaining, or modeling. Abusive mothers issued more than twice as many commands to their children as nonabusive mothers and also were inconsistent in reinforcing their children's compliance (Oldershaw, Walters, & Hall, 1986). As we saw earlier, inconsistent punishment usually leads to the persistence of undesirable behaviors in children.

Certain characteristics of children are also more commonly observed in abusive families. Parents often describe the abused child as irritable, difficult to put to sleep, and prone to excessive crying (Ounsted, Oppenheimer, & Lindsay, 1974). A group at special risk for abuse is premature infants, who tend to have high-pitched, aversive cries and a less attractive appearance (Parke & Collmer, 1975). Abusive parents become especially sensitized to some of the child's objectionable behaviors and show

KEY THEME
Interaction Among Domains

WHAT DO YOU THINK?

How Can Child Abuse Be Stopped?
psychology.college.hmco.com

KEY THEME
Child's Active Role

Number of Victims		826,162
Rate per 1,000		11.8
Gender	Male	48
	Female	52
Age of Victim	1 year and younger	14
	2–5 years old	24
	6–9 years old	25
	10–13 years old	20
	14–17 years old	15
	18 and older	1
Type of Maltreatment	Neglect	56
	Physical Abuse	21
	Sexual Abuse	11
	Psychological or Emotional Abuse	8
	Medical Neglect	2
	Other and Unknown	28

TABLE 14.1
Characteristics of Victims of Child Maltreatment

The table shows some of the characteristics of American children who experienced child abuse or neglect, as well as the specific type of maltreatment they experienced (expressed in terms of percentages), for the year 1999. The percentages for type of maltreatment reflect the fact that some children experience multiple forms of abuse and neglect.

Source: Child Trends Databank, 2002a.

heightened emotional reactivity to the child's cries or noncompliance (Frodi & Lamb, 1980; Wolfe et al., 1983). Older children in abusive families tend to be more aggressive and less compliant than children of similar ages from control families (Bousha & Twentyman, 1984; Egeland & Sroufe, 1981). Thus both parental and child factors may contribute to a pattern of physically and psychologically harmful interactions.

Finally, abusive families tend to be isolated from the outside world and have fewer sources of social support than nonabusive families. In one study, abusive parents reported they were less involved with the community than nonabusive parents were; they tended not to join sports teams, go to the library, or take classes (Trickett & Susman, 1988). In another study, some mothers who were at risk for becoming abusive because of their own family history had normal, positive relationships with their children. These mothers also had extensive emotional support from other adults, a therapist, or a mate. In contrast, high-risk mothers who subsequently became abusive experienced greater life stress and had fewer sources of psychological support (Egeland, Jacobvitz, & Sroufe, 1988).

How can the spiral of abuse be broken? Researchers suggest that interventions should teach basic parenting skills, provide parents with mechanisms to cope with their emotional tension, and offer social support such as child care or counseling services (Belsky, 1993; Wolfe, 1985). Especially promising are programs in which home visitors provide parent education and support (MacMillan et al., 1994). Moreover, observers have noted our society's general acceptance of violence as a means of solving problems. This tendency is evident in the widespread endorsement of physical punishment as a technique for disciplining children, as well as in the pervasive displays of violence in the media (Belsky, 1980, 1993; Hart & Brassard, 1987). Altering broader societal attitudes about violence may thus be an additional and necessary step in breaking the cycle of child abuse. Finally, a national study of more than six thousand households showed that violence toward children was more prevalent in families experiencing unemployment, substance abuse, and financial difficulties (Wolfner & Gelles, 1993). As daunting as the task may seem, a broad attack on more general social problems may help to ameliorate the problem of child abuse.

KEY THEME
Sociocultural Influence

ATYPICAL DEVELOPMENT

Posttraumatic Stress Disorder

Approximately one-fourth to one-half of children who are the victims of physical or sexual abuse experience the symptoms of posttraumatic stress disorder or PTSD (Dubner & Motta, 1999; Famularo et al., 1994; Wolfe, Sas, & Wekerle, 1994). This diagnosis was originally formulated in studies of adults' responses to extremely stressful events such as wars and natural disasters, but many of the symptoms have also been observed in children who have experienced psychological traumas. Chief among those symptoms is the reexperiencing of the traumatic event; children may show repetitive, intrusive thoughts or have vivid flashbacks of the episode. They may also show sleep disturbances and nightmares, have angry outbursts, suffer from stomachaches and headaches, display signs of depression, and have difficulties in school (Milgram, 1998; Yule, 1998).

Physiological changes in the central nervous system may accompany PTSD. Studies with animals and adult humans have shown that extreme stress is associated with decreases in the size of the hippocampus and declines in short-term memory performance (Bremner, 1999; Bremner & Narayan, 1998). More volatile functioning of the neurochemical system that responds to stress has also been observed in adults and adolescents who have experienced trauma (Golier & Yehuda, 1998; Southwick, Yehuda, & Charney, 1997). The possibility that stress can cause permanent changes to the structure of the brain and affect children's learning abilities is particularly disturbing.

KEY THEME
Interaction Among Domains

The most successful treatments of PTSD in children and adults have used a cognitive-behavioral approach (Foa & Meadows, 1997). Typically, the child is given relaxation training along with suggestions for how to control thoughts about the traumatic event. For example, in one study of four sexually abused children who were given this type of intervention, all four reported a decline in the symptoms of PTSD (Farrell, Hains, & Davies, 1998). Because of the seriousness of the problems associated with PTSD in children, many researchers are eager to devise more precise ways to diagnose and treat this disorder.

Cultural and Social Class Variations in Parenting

Do broader sociocultural beliefs and values play a role in parental socialization practices? If so, do children show specific patterns of behavior as a result of their different cultural experiences? Recent research suggests that the answer to both questions is yes.

KEY THEME
Sociocultural Influence

● **Cross-Cultural Differences** Beatrice Whiting and Carolyn Pope Edwards (1988) have provided an extended analysis of variations in parenting by comparing societies as diverse as rural Kenya, Liberia, and the Philippines with urban America. Despite vast differences in economic, social, and political conditions, many similar, overarching patterns are apparent in the ways parents socialize their children. With infants and toddlers, the universal emphasis is on nurturance, that is, providing routine care along with attention and support. By the time the child reaches age four or five years, most parents shift their focus to control, correcting or reprimanding misbehavior. Finally, when children reach school age, parents become concerned with training their children in the skills and social behavior their cultural group values.

At the same time, though, Whiting and Edwards (1988) observed notable differences. For example, mothers from rural villages in Kenya and Liberia emphasized training children to do chores responsibly and placed a high premium on obedience. From an early age, children were taught how to care for the family's fields and animals, and they assumed a major role in caring for younger siblings. Children were

Children's socialization experiences are influenced by cultural values and beliefs. For example, in rural Kenya, children care for the family's fields and animals and have responsibility for younger siblings. Children growing up in such communities were found to display a high degree of compliance to mothers' requests.

punished for performing tasks irresponsibly and were rarely praised. Consistent with this orientation to child rearing was the family's dependence on women and children for producing food. Because women in these cultures typically had an enormous workload, they delegated some tasks to children as soon as children were physically capable of managing them; because accidents and injury to infants and the family's resources must be prevented, deviant behaviors were not tolerated in children. Children growing up in these communities were highly compliant to mothers' commands and suggestions.

An even more controlling style characterized the Tarong community in the Philippines, in which subsistence farming was the mainstay but responsibilities for producing food were more evenly distributed among the group's members. When the mother did not rely so heavily on her children to work for the family's survival and when the goals of training were thus less clear, arbitrary commands and even punishing became more common. Children were scolded frequently for being in the way of adults or playing in inappropriate places. By middle childhood, Tarong children showed a marked decline in their tendency to seek attention from or be close to their parents.

These patterns provided a striking contrast to the "sociability" that characterized the middle-income American mothers in the sample. Interactions between mothers and children consisted of significant information exchange and warm, friendly dialogues. Mothers emphasized verbalization, educational tasks, and play, and they were liberal in their use of praise and encouragement. Because children in American society normally do not work to ensure the economic survival of the family unit, firm training and punishing were not part of these parents' styles. The emphasis on verbalization and educational activities was consistent with the high value Americans place on social interactions and schooling.

Other researchers examining parent-child relationships in Asian cultures have reaffirmed the idea that culture affects parenting styles. Japanese mothers use less physical punishment and more verbal reasoning to control their children than American mothers (Kobayashi-Winata & Power, 1989). Japanese culture emphasizes responsibilities and commitments to others, a socialization goal that is achieved more effectively through reasoning than through power-assertive techniques. Japanese children, in fact, comply with rules at home and in school more than their American counterparts do. Similarly, when Chinese parents are asked to describe their child-rearing practices, they report a greater emphasis on control and achievement in children than American parents (Chao, 1994; Lin & Fu, 1990). In Chinese society, character development and educational attainment are highly valued, and parental practices follow directly from these larger societal goals.

As Whiting and Edwards (1988) point out, parents around the world resemble one another in numerous ways because of the universal needs children have as they grow and develop. But it is also true that the specific ecology of each culture, its socialization goals, and the demands it places on the family unit can dramatically shape parenting practices and the course of the individual child's socialization.

● **Social Class and Ethnic Differences**   Reliable social class differences exist in parenting practices. Middle-class mothers use induction, or reasoning, as they discipline their children more frequently than do lower-class mothers, who tend to use power-assertive techniques. Middle-class mothers also praise their children liberally and generally verbalize more than lower-class mothers, who in turn more frequently utter such commands as "Do it because I say so!" and dispense less positive reinforcement (Hoffman, 1984).

Social class (typically defined by the father's occupation) by itself, however, is not a variable that provides neat or meaningful explanations, because it is usually associated with other variables, such as access to health care, nutrition, physical environment, and educational experiences. Moreover, even within low-income families, significant variations in parenting styles can occur; a single characteristic style may not exist. For example, among low-income families, older mothers and mothers who are more religious tend to rely less on power-assertive parenting styles than younger

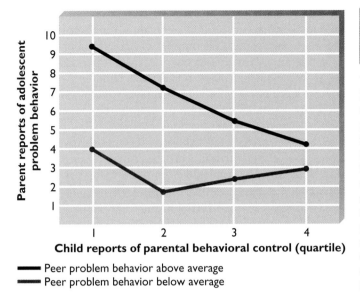

Child reports of parental behavioral control (quartile)

— Peer problem behavior above average
— Peer problem behavior below average

Source: Adapted from Mason et al., 1996.

FIGURE 14.6
Effective Parenting and
Peer Influences

The style of parenting that best predicts successful developmental outcomes may depend on other influences in the child's life. For example, researchers have found that for lower- and working-class adolescents, a more controlling style of parenting may lead to fewer problem behaviors if peers exert a negative influence. In this study, adolescents were divided into two groups: those who were above and below average in their exposure to negative peer influences. The amount of control parents exhibited was divided into four categories, from least to most control (where 1 was equal to least control). As the graph shows, for adolescents exposed to higher-than-average negative peer influences, greater parental control was associated with fewer behavior problems. Levels of parental control mattered less for adolescents exposed to lower-than-average negative peer influences.

mothers or those who are less religious (Kelley, Power, & Wimbush, 1992). Another factor to consider is how parenting practices might be related to the type of peer influence to which children are exposed. In one recent study, African American adolescents from lower- and working-class families were divided into two groups, those who were above and below average in their exposure to peer problem behaviors. As Figure 14.6 shows, for adolescents exposed to negative peer influences, fewer behavior problems occurred when parents exerted more control over their children. When exposure to negative peer influences was lower, the type of parental control made less of a difference (Mason et al., 1996). Although we have seen in much of this chapter that high parental control is associated with negative child outcomes, under some circumstances this type of parenting may actually be advantageous.

Vonnie McLoyd (McLoyd, 1990; McLoyd et al., 1994) has provided an extended analysis of the growing literature on families under economic stress that illuminates the effects of social class. Because African American children experience a disproportionate share of the problems of poverty (a rate of 41 percent for African American children at the time of her analysis compared with 13 percent for Caucasian children), McLoyd focused on the social and family dynamics that can affect this racial minority. In McLoyd's analysis, economic hardship has a serious negative impact on children's socioemotional development because of the psychological distress it causes parents. Parents under stress have a diminished ability to provide nurturant, consistent, involved care for their children. Children growing up with poverty are thus at risk for depression, poor peer relations, lower self-esteem, and conduct disorders. In one study of African American mothers, mothers' job loss was related to the tendency to report symptoms of depression. This fact was, in turn, related to their use of punishment and less parental nurturance (McLoyd et al., 1994). Similar findings have been reported for Caucasian middle-class families from the midwestern United States during a time of economic downturn. Rand Conger and his colleagues (Conger et al., 1992) found that parents who experienced economic hardship reported greater emotional distress; this factor, in turn, was related to less skillful parenting. The disruptions in parenting were associated with adjustment problems among the adolescent boys in the sample. These seventh-graders reported more feelings of hostility and depression than those whose families were not experiencing economic hardship. The effects of financial stress have been observed in many types of families. Both one- and two-parent families of African American and European American backgrounds show more negative parent-child relationships in the context of financial strain (Conger et al., 2002; Gutman & Eccles, 1999; Jackson et al., 2000).

The demands poverty makes on many African American families may be related to unique family structures that are adaptive for their situation and help them to cope. For example, a significant number of African American children grow up in an extended family. About 10 percent of African American children younger than eighteen years—three times as many as Caucasian children—grow up with a live-in grandparent (Beck & Beck, 1989). Extended family members often bring additional income, child care assistance, and emotional support and counseling to families under stress, especially when the parent is single (Wilson, 1986). Extensive networks of social support have, in turn, been associated with responsive and involved parenting styles among low-income African American mothers (Burchinal, Follmer, & Bryant, 1996). Among African American adolescents, those who perceived their families as having extensive social support from relatives also perceived their homes as being organized and their parents as being involved in their schooling; these beliefs were linked to fewer problem behaviors, greater self-reliance, and higher grades in school than for adolescents whose perceptions differed (Taylor, 1996). The higher levels of involvement of African American families in religion also have a positive impact on children. Children of religious parents show less aggression and depression than those whose parents are less involved in religion (Brody, Stoneman, & Flor, 1996). Thus, although economic stress can have a negative effect on family dynamics, it can also foster alternative family structures and socialization goals that help to meet the needs of children.

FOR YOUR REVIEW

- What are the characteristics of the four major styles of parenting? What child behaviors are associated with each parental style?

- What are some of the specific effects of parental warmth on the developing child?

- Which principles of learning theory help to explain effective punishment?

- What are some ways that parents can effectively manage the noncompliant behavior of their children?

- In what ways do parental cognitions play a role in parenting strategies?

- What are some ways in which the characteristics of the child can influence parenting strategies?

- How do coercive cycles of maladaptive parent-child interactions arise? What can be done to intervene in these maladaptive interactions?

- What are some of the factors associated with the incidence of child abuse?

- In what ways do parenting strategies vary across different cultural and socioeconomic groups?

Relationships with Mothers, Fathers, and Siblings

Because women traditionally have been seen as the primary caregivers for children, most studies of parenting practices in the psychological literature have focused on mothering. Two decades of research on fathers, however, as well as even more recent studies of sibling relationships, have provided a much broader understanding of how each distinct relationship within the family influences the individual child's development.

Mothering Versus Fathering: Are There Differences?

For the most part, mothers still bear most of the responsibility for child rearing in American society, whether or not they are employed outside the home. However, the

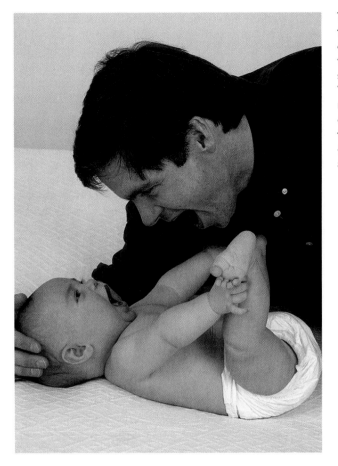

When given the opportunity, fathers respond to their children by touching, holding, and vocalizing to them in much the same way that mothers do. They do, however, engage in more physical play with their children than mothers. When fathers participate in child care, their children show favorable developmental outcomes.

number of fathers participating in child care is increasing. For example, the number of single fathers who have custody of their children rose to more than 3 million in 2000. In addition, fathers assume primary child care responsibilities in about 20 percent of the families in which both parents are employed (U.S. Bureau of the Census, 2001). Research resoundingly reveals that fathers are significant figures in their children's lives and are clearly competent in their parental role.

In this chapter, as well as in the chapter titled "Emotion," we have underscored maternal sensitivity and responsiveness as key factors in fostering optimal child development. Studies have shown that fathers are just as responsive as mothers to the signals of their infants, and, when given the opportunity, they interact with their babies in ways similar to mothers. One team of researchers measured the physiological responsiveness of mothers and fathers as they observed quiet, smiling, or crying babies on a video monitor (Frodi et al., 1978). Mothers and fathers showed similar changes in heart rate, blood pressure, and skin conductance when the babies smiled or cried. In another study of maternal and paternal behaviors toward infants in the newborn nursery, Ross Parke and Sandra O'Leary (1976) found that fathers were just as likely as mothers to hold, touch, and vocalize to their babies.

After the newborn period, fathers and mothers begin to manifest somewhat different styles of interacting with their infants. When they play face to face with their babies, fathers tend to provide physical and social stimulation in staccato bursts, whereas mothers tend to be more rhythmic and soothing (Yogman et al., 1977). Fathers engage in physical and unpredictable "idiosyncratic" play with their infants—throwing them up in the air, moving their limbs, and tickling them—whereas mothers spend more time in caregiving activities or calm games such as "pat-a-cake" (Lamb, 1997; Yogman, 1982). As a consequence, infants prefer fathers when they wish to play and seek out mothers when they desire care and comfort. This dichotomy in parental styles of interaction continues at least until middle childhood (Russell & Russell, 1987).

Despite their responsiveness and competence as parents, most fathers spend less time with their children than mothers do. In general, fathers spend about one-third the time mothers do in direct contact with their children, even when the mother works outside the home (Ishii-Kuntz & Coltrane, 1992; Lamb et al., 1987). This pattern has been found in diverse ethnic groups and cultures, including African American, Chinese, and Japanese families (Hossain & Roopnarine, 1994; Ishii-Kuntz, 1994; Sun & Roopnarine, 1996).

Why are fathers relatively uninvolved? Some may hold traditional beliefs about which family member should be responsible for child care. Another reason may be that fathers are not confident in their caregiving skills. Because males typically are not exposed to child care through such experiences as baby-sitting and home economics courses, they may feel insecure about feeding, bathing, or diapering a child (Lamb et al., 1987). On the other hand, some circumstances predict greater father involvement in child care: fewer hours at work, the fact that the mother works, and the father's memories of his own relationship with his father (Gottfried, Bathurst, & Gottfried, 1994; NICHD Early Child Care Research Network, 2000a; Radin, 1994). In some cases, the father may have learned to extend his caregiving role from observing the participation of his father; in other cases, he may be trying to have a better relationship with his own children than he had with his uninvolved father.

Demographers project that more and more children will be cared for by fathers for longer periods of time (Casper & O'Connell, 1998). It seems, then, that the concept of the father as an equal partner in parenthood is starting to emerge (Pleck & Pleck, 1997).

● **The Father's Influence on Child Development**   Do fathers have a different influence than mothers on the process of child development? During the 1960s and 1970s psychologists believed they do, based on studies of the effects of father absence, especially on boys. Boys growing up without fathers were more likely to have problems in academic achievement, gender-role development, and control of aggression (Biller, 1974; Lamb, 1981). An important theoretical construct driving much of the research was *identification:* the idea that boys assimilate the characteristics, attitudes, and behaviors of their fathers as they form an intense emotional bond with them. Presumably, boys without fathers did not have an identity figure or model for appropriate masculine, instrumentally competent behavior and thus suffered deficits in cognitive, social, and emotional domains.

Identification with the father may be less important than other variables, however. Michael Lamb (1987) points out that the effects of father absence may result not from the loss of a masculine identity figure for the son but from the loss of a source of emotional and financial support for the entire family. The tension and stress that result may produce maladaptive patterns of parenting, which in turn generate undesirable developmental outcomes for boys. Boys may be particularly vulnerable because they seem to be more generally susceptible than girls to the effects of deviant environments (Rutter, 1986).

A more contemporary view is that fathers make recognizable contributions to family life in general and child development in particular but that those contributions simply reflect aspects of good parenting. In other words, good fathering resembles good mothering, and the child will thrive by having two parents who fill those roles instead of just one. For example, one recent study showed that the mere presence of a father was not associated with benefits to children's development. Instead, it was only when fathers were nurturant and involved with their children that children showed higher cognitive and social functioning (Black, Dubowitz, & Starr, Jr., 1999). Several other studies also show that a father's warmth and involvement is associated with children's competence and academic achievement and with less rigid gender-role stereotypes (Radin, 1981, 1994; Wagner & Phillips, 1992). This influence holds true even when children live in single-parent families with their mothers but have contact with their biological fathers (Coley, 1998).

Siblings

Like parents, siblings serve as important sources of the child's social attitudes, beliefs, and behaviors. Although they may not wield as much power as parents, siblings certainly do attempt to control one another's behaviors (ask anyone who is not an only child!) and may be models for both desirable and undesirable actions. An emerging body of research on sibling relationships has provided yet another perspective on how families influence development.

● **The Only Child**   One way to assess the impact of siblings on development is to examine children who have none. Are there notable differences between only children and children with one or more sisters or brothers? Popular opinion depicts the only child as spoiled, demanding, self-centered, and dependent (Thompson, 1974). But research evidence suggests the contrary, that only children may enjoy the benefits of having their parents' exclusive attention. Toni Falbo and Denise Polit (1986) summarized the results of 115 studies of only children and concluded that overall, only children showed higher achievement and intelligence scores than children with siblings. In addition, only-borns ranked higher on measures of character—that is, tendencies toward leadership, personal control, and maturity—than children with siblings. No overall differences emerged between only children and children with siblings on assessments of sociability and personal adjustment.

> **KEY THEME**
> **Interaction Among Domains**

In explaining these findings, Falbo and Polit (1986) found support for the hypothesis that features of the parent-child relationship account for the advantages only children enjoy in certain domains. Only children were found to have more positive relationships with their parents than children having siblings. This effect probably occurs because parents of one child have more time to spend with their son or daughter and generally have high-quality interactions with their child (Falbo & Cooper, 1980). Parents and children in one study, for example, exchanged more information in mealtime conversations in one-child families than in families having two or three children (Lewis & Feiring, 1982). First-time parents are also more anxious about their child-rearing techniques and may thus be more vigilant and responsive to their child's behaviors (Falbo & Polit, 1986).

Falbo and Polit's (1986) meta-analysis showed that parent-child relations in one- and two-child families are actually more similar than different. Only when a third child is born does the quality of parent-child relations diminish significantly. Parents of more than two children probably become more relaxed about their child-rearing strategies and also have significantly more demands placed on their time. The result is less responsiveness and fewer deliberate attempts to instruct their children, aspects of parenting found to be related to cognitive achievements.

● **Family Size and Birth Order**   Children growing up in contemporary American society have fewer siblings than children in earlier eras. In 2000, the typical American family with children had one or two children (U.S. Bureau of the Census, 2001). Many children thus grow up with only one other sibling. Does the size of the family make any difference in child development?

> **KEY THEME**
> **Interaction Among Domains**

In general, children from smaller families have higher intelligence test scores, achieve higher levels of education, and display greater self-esteem (Blake, 1989; Wagner, Schubert, & Schubert, 1985). As we have just seen, one reason for these effects may be that parents in larger families have less time to spend with their children and may not provide the kind of cognitive stimulation children in smaller families receive. Another important factor is financial circumstances: Parents with a larger number of children often experience greater economic stress, which in turn may diminish the quality of their parenting (Rutter & Madge, 1976).

Regardless of family size, the child's birth order, whether first born or later born, can also be a factor in development. Like only children, first-borns tend to score higher on IQ tests and have higher achievement motivation than other children

(Glass, Neulinger, & Brim, 1974; Zajonc, Markus, & Markus, 1979). They also tend to be more obedient and socially responsible (Sutton-Smith & Rosenberg, 1970). All these effects probably stem from the greater attention parents give to their first children. Later-borns seem to have an advantage in the social sphere, however. Youngest siblings tend to have better peer relationships than first-borns and are more confident in social situations (Lahey et al., 1980; Miller & Maruyama, 1976).

● **The Impact of a Sibling's Arrival**   The birth of a sibling can have a dramatic effect on the life of a first-born child. Research on the consequences of a second child's arrival generally confirms that "sibling rivalry" is no myth. Judy Dunn and Carol Kendrick (1982) followed the progress of family relationships among forty first-born children who experienced the arrival of a sibling sometime between their first and fourth birthdays. Dunn and Kendrick observed normal home routines during the mother's last month of pregnancy and again when the baby sibling was one, eight, and fourteen months old. They also interviewed the mother at each stage about the older child's eating and sleeping habits, moods, and other routine behaviors.

For the majority of children, the arrival of a sister or brother led to marked changes in behavior; they became more demanding, clingy, unhappy, or withdrawn. Accompanying these changes in their behavior were significant decreases in maternal attention toward them; mothers engaged in less joint play, cuddling, and verbalization with their first-borns and in general initiated fewer interactions with them. At the same time, restrictive and punitive maternal behaviors increased. Over time, Dunn and Kendrick (1982) noted, two distinct patterns of sibling relationships emerged. Among some sibling pairs, almost all interactions eventually became friendly and positive; for others, a persistent pattern of hostility and aggression became the norm. The first pattern was more likely if mothers had previously prepared the older child for the newborn's arrival by referring to the infant as a person with needs and desires. Engaging the older child in caring for the infant also seemed to have positive consequences. In contrast, negative relationships between siblings resulted if the older child experienced a sharp drop in maternal contact. The discrepancy in pre- and postsibling maternal contact made the most difference: Children who had less contact with their mothers before the sibling's birth were less profoundly affected by her attention to the new infant.

This young boy's reaction to a new sibling is typical. Although many children become clingy, withdrawn, or demanding when a new sibling first arrives, these reactions can be diminished if parents prepare the older child for the infant's arrival and involve him in the infant's care. Adjustment is also more difficult if the older child perceives that he must compete for the parents' affection and attention.

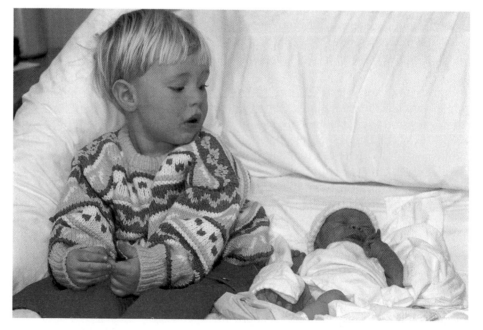

The timing of a sibling's arrival may also be important. Researchers have noted a drop in the security of a child's attachment to the mother following the birth of a second child. However, the decrease in attachment security was less noticeable if the older child was twenty-four months of age or younger (Teti et al., 1996). Younger children may not yet have the social cognitive capacities to see the new arrival as a threat or cause of change in family routines.

The arrival of a sibling demands a big adjustment for the older child, especially because another individual begins to compete for the parents' attention and affection. Siblings are aware of the differential treatment parents may knowingly or unwittingly bestow on them (Kowal & Kramer, 1997; McHale et al., 1995). The greater the perceived discrepancy is, the greater the sibling conflict will be (Dunn, 1988). But certainly not all aspects of sibling relationships are negative. Dunn and Kendrick (1982) noted that in certain circumstances, siblings fill a void in parent-child relationships. When the mother and her older child have difficulties in their interactions, siblings may provide the attention and affection missing from the maternal relationship, thus helping to keep the family system in equilibrium. When parents display a high degree of marital conflict or even undergo divorce, siblings show an increase in emotional closeness and positive, friendly behavior toward one another (Dunn, 1996).

● **Sibling Interactions Among Older Children**   How do older children interact as siblings? For one thing, children tend to fight more with their siblings than with their friends. When fifth- through eighth-graders were asked to describe conflicts with their siblings, they reported that they allowed quarrels with siblings to escalate, whereas they tried to resolve conflicts with friends. Most of the time, siblings fight about privacy and interpersonal boundaries (Raffaelli, 1989). Typically, parents do not intervene in sibling conflicts, and when they do not, those conflicts continue (Perozynski & Kramer, 1999). On the other hand, when parents discuss each child's needs (as opposed to using controlling tactics), subsequent conflicts between siblings are less likely (Kramer, Perozynski, & Chung, 1999). Siblings also express more positive behaviors with one another when their fathers, in particular, are nurturant and try to be fair to each child (Brody, Stoneman, & McCoy, 1992). Researchers have noted that the degree of conflict in sibling relationships is related to the amount of aggression a child shows in school, whereas the amount of warmth in sibling relationships is linked to emotional control and social competence in school (Garcia et al., 2000; Stormshak et al., 1996).

KEY THEME
Interaction Among Domains

Whether positive or negative in character, sibling relationships in early childhood tend to remain stable through middle childhood (Dunn, Slombowski, & Beardsall, 1994) and then typically change from middle childhood through adolescence. Duane Buhrmester and Wyndol Furman (1990) administered the Sibling Relationship Questionnaire to third-, sixth-, ninth-, and twelfth-graders to assess several dimensions of sibling interactions. Older siblings reported being more dominant and nurturant toward their younger siblings, and younger siblings confirmed that they received more often than dispensed dominance and nurturance. These differences between older and younger siblings apparently disappear over time, however. The older children in the sample reported having more egalitarian relationships with their siblings, as well as less intense feelings of both warmth and conflict. Initial differences in power and nurturance usually disappeared when the younger sibling was twelve years old, by which time she or he had become more competent and needed less guidance and emotional support.

Although the presence of siblings may mean the child has fewer opportunities to interact with parents, it also provides the context for developing other unique skills. Older siblings have opportunities to become nurturant and assertive, and younger siblings have more models for a range of behaviors than only children. Although many children grow up with siblings, we are just beginning to understand the role brothers and sisters play in child development.

- What are the major differences between mothers and fathers in parenting styles?

- In what ways do fathers make important contributions to child development?

- How do family size and birth order have an impact on child development?

- In what ways can parents facilitate a child's transition to having a new sibling?

- How do sibling interactions change as children get older?

Families in Transition

As we saw at the start of this chapter, the traditional nuclear family has been slowly disappearing from mainstream American society. Single-parent families, dual wage-earner families, and reconstituted families (in which adults who remarry bring their respective children into new families) are becoming more and more prevalent and offer new circumstances to which children must adapt. What are the effects of these emerging family structures on child development? Research shows that child development is influenced not so much by changes in family structure per se as by the ways in which structural changes affect interpersonal relations within the family.

Maternal Employment

In the past three decades, the percentage of married women with children in the labor force has increased dramatically. The working mother is now the norm. What is the effect of maternal employment on child development?

When psychologists compare children of employed mothers with children of women who remain at home, few differences emerge on measures of cognitive achievement and socioemotional development, at least among middle-class participants. If anything, daughters of employed mothers derive some benefit; they are likely to show greater independence, greater achievement, and higher self-esteem than daughters of nonworking mothers (Gottfried et al., 1994; Hoffman, 1989). Apparently these girls profit from having a successful, competent role model, at least as the larger society recognizes these qualities. (Women who remain at home "work" too, but traditionally have not been afforded recognition or status for that role.) When a mother returns to work seems not to be an important factor. In an analysis of data collected from several thousand participants in the National Longitudinal Survey of Youth, Elizabeth Harvey (1999) found that the timing of mother's entry or return to the work force was not associated with children's development. The number of hours mothers work can make a difference, however. Two recent studies of mostly Caucasian middle-class women found that the more hours mothers worked, the lower was the academic achievement of their preschool and early school-age children (Brooks-Gunn, Han, & Waldfogel, 2002; Goldberg, Greenberger, & Nagel, 1996). On the other hand, comprehensive longitudinal studies of children from infancy through age twelve have found that although academic achievement was negatively related to the number of hours the mothers worked when children were ages five and six, this relationship was modest and was not apparent as children grew older (Gottfried et al., 1994; Harvey, 1999).

For low-income families, maternal employment is related to some clear benefits for children. One longitudinal study examined 189 second-graders; most were born to adolescent mothers, and 41 percent lived in households with incomes below the poverty level. For this sample, maternal employment during the child's first three years was associated with greater household income, a higher-quality home environment as assessed by the HOME inventory (see the chapter titled "Intelligence"), and

KEY THEME

Interaction Among Domains

When mothers work, their children are less likely to hold stereotyped beliefs about gender, probably because they see both parents in multiple roles.

higher mathematics achievement in school for the child compared with the effects when mothers did not work (Vandell & Ramanan, 1992).

In general, the clearest effect of maternal employment involves the gender-role attitudes of both sons and daughters. As we saw in the chapter titled "Gender," when mothers work outside the home, their children are less likely than children of at-home mothers to hold stereotypical beliefs about males and females and more likely to see both sexes as competent (Hoffman, 1989). When both mother and father work, sons and daughters have the opportunity to see both parents in multiple roles—as powerful, competent wage earners and nurturant, warm caregivers—a factor that probably contributes to more egalitarian beliefs.

Overall, maternal employment is not a simple, "neat" variable in studying child development. Some mothers work out of sheer economic necessity, whereas others are more concerned with realizing personal or career goals, for example. As researchers point out, the impact of maternal employment is better understood through its effects on family dynamics, parental attitudes, and the alternative child care arrangements the family chooses (Beyer, 1995; Hoffman, 1989). It is to these factors that we now turn our attention.

● **Maternal Employment and Parent-Child Interaction**   Mothers who work full time outside the home spend less time caring for their children, whether infants or high school age, than mothers who stay at home (Hill & Stafford, 1980). In terms of direct, one-to-one mother-child interaction, however, no significant differences have been found between employed and nonemployed mothers (Richards & Duckett, 1994). Employed mothers often compensate for the time they miss with their children during the workweek by allocating more time for them during mornings and evenings (Ahnert, Rickert, & Lamb, 2000). Some studies show that fathers assume more responsibilities for child care when the mother works (Pederson et al., 1982; Pleck, 1983), although they sometimes find their new roles to be challenging, particularly in the early part of infancy (Grych & Clark, 1999; Vandell et al., 1997).

Overall, what matters more than whether or not the mother works is her attitude toward mothering and work and why she is working or staying home. In one study of mothers of infants, women who remained at home contrary to their preference had higher scores on tests of depression and stress than mothers who preferred to be at home and were not in the labor force and employed mothers who valued their positions in the work world (Hock & DeMeis, 1990). We saw earlier in this chapter that parental stress has been implicated as a factor in less consistent and less nurturant parenting. On the other hand, when maternal employment produces tension, parenting practices also may suffer. Researchers have found that mothers who worked more than forty hours per week, for example, were more anxious and unhappy and had less sensitive and less animated interactions with their infants than mothers who worked less than forty hours per week (Owen & Cox, 1988). In another recent study, parents who experienced higher levels of stress at work had more conflicts with their adolescent children (Crouter et al., 1999).

In general, family factors continue to predict child outcomes, even though when mothers work, their children may be enrolled in full-time child care. Variables such as child-rearing style, parental psychological well-being, and sensitivity are associated with children's cognitive and social development irrespective of the child's caregiving context (NICHD Early Child Care Research Group, 1998b).

● **The Effects of Daycare**   About one-fourth of children enter child care during the first five months after birth, according to one national survey. About half begin regular child care before they turn three (Singer et al., 1998). Child care arrangements take various forms, from in-home care provided by a relative or paid caregiver to group care in a formal, organized center. As Figure 14.7 shows, about 40 percent of children under age six are cared for by their parents. Of those who receive full-time nonparental care, the largest percentage attends organized child care centers. There has been a steady increase in the last thirty years in the proportion of children attending child care centers as opposed to family daycare or being cared for by a relative or a sitter (Hofferth, 1996).

One area in which some (but not all) researchers have noted an effect of daycare is in intellectual performance. Daycare children tend to outperform children reared at home by parents on standardized tests of IQ, as well as measures of problem-solving ability, creativity, language development, and arithmetic skills (Clarke-Stewart & Fein, 1983). Daycare programs that stress cognitive activities have a greater effect on IQ scores than those that simply provide caregiving (McCartney et al., 1985). Moreover, the effect of daycare on intellectual achievements shows up years later, when children are in elementary school. In one study that examined the academic achievements of sixth-graders, the amount of time children had spent in high-quality daycare centers during infancy was positively related to their mathematics grades and their tendency to be enrolled in programs for gifted children (Field, 1991). In two other studies, conducted in Sweden, children who had daycare experience performed better on measures of verbal and mathematics abilities and obtained better grades in school seven years later and beyond than children who had no experience with out-of-home care (Andersson, 1992; Broberg et al., 1997).

Daycare is also associated with effects in the realm of social development. Specifically, children with experience in daycare are more socially competent with peers. They show more frequent nonnegative interactions, more complex and reciprocal play, and more positive engagement with peers compared with children not in child care. Important to note is the finding that responsiveness of caregivers in daycare centers was associated with these positive peer interactions (NICHD Early Child Care Research Network, 2001). In addition to showing more positive behaviors, some studies suggest that daycare children may display more aggression with peers and noncompliance with adults (Bates et al., 1994; Baydar & Brooks-Gunn, 1991). However, a national study of more than one thousand children in daycare centers across the United States found that the amount of time spent in child care did not predict children's problem social behaviors at age three (NICHD Early Child Care

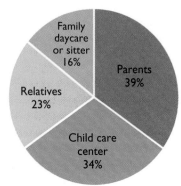

Source: National Center for Educational Statistics, 2001.

FIGURE 14.7
Child Care Arrangements for Children Age 6 and Under, 2000

This chart shows the percentage of American children who receive different forms of child care. Forty percent of infants, toddlers, and preschoolers are cared for by parents. Of the remainder, most attend a formal child care center.

Research shows that daycare has few negative effects on young children and may even facilitate cognitive and social development. High-quality centers generally have small group size, favorable staff-to-child ratios, and responsive, warm caregivers.

Research Network, 1998a). If there are negative effects, they may arise from more prolonged experiences in daycare or experiences in low-quality centers (Lamb, 1998).

It is important to remember that many studies of daycare have been conducted in high-quality centers, often associated with universities and populated by children from middle- to upper-class families. But not all parents have the opportunity or financial resources to send their children to such high-caliber programs. In a disturbing report on the quality of child care centers in the United States, only 14 percent of centers were judged to offer care that promotes children's development; most provided only custodial-level care, and 12 percent were found to jeopardize children's development (Children's Defense Fund, 1996). What are the effects of less-than-excellent programs on children? Research suggests that when children are enrolled in low-quality centers before age one, they have more difficulty with peers and are distractible and less task oriented in kindergarten than children who are enrolled at later ages and those who attend high-quality centers (Howes, 1990). Children in low-quality child care also tend to score lower on tests of cognitive and language skills than children in high-quality care (Burchinal et al., 2000; NICHD Early Child Care Research Network, 2000b; Peisner-Feinberg et al., 2001). Evidence is accumulating that quality of child care makes a difference. Thus it is essential that parents be aware of the elements of high-quality daycare.

● **Choosing a Daycare Center** Both the federal government and many states have set minimum requirements for daycare services that regulate the qualifications of teachers, staff-child ratios, the size and safety of the physical facility, and the provision of nourishing meals. Although the guidelines and laws provide for minimum standards, most parents are concerned with providing their children with the best possible care during the hours they are at work. Alison Clarke-Stewart (1993) has drawn on the expanding body of research findings on daycare to compile the following suggestions for parents:

■ Center-based care is more likely to include educational opportunities for children than home-based care, such as that provided by baby-sitters and family daycare. On the other hand, children are more likely to receive one-to-one supervision and authoritative discipline in home-based care.

■ Children are most likely to thrive intellectually and emotionally in programs that offer a balance between structured educational activities and an open, free environment.

◉ SEE FOR YOURSELF
psychology.college.hmco.com
Childcare Regulations

■ The caregiving environment should provide ample physical space (at least twenty-five square feet per child) and a variety of materials and activities to foster sensorimotor, social, and cognitive development.

■ Class size should be small (fewer than ten children) and should include children within a two-year age range. Small centers (fewer than thirty children) usually have better staff-child ratios than centers with more children.

■ The interaction style of the caregiver is a key aspect of quality care. The caregiver should be actively involved but not restrictive with the children. The caregiver should also be responsive and offer positive encouragement.

■ Caregivers who have training in child development and continuing opportunities for education are most likely to provide high-quality care.

■ The individual characteristics of the child should be taken into account. Some children will probably do well in a program that balances structure and openness; others may profit from either more structure or a more flexible and relaxed program.

Other important factors include a high staff-child ratio and low staff turnover. Research shows, for example, that when the staff-child ratio is at least one to three for infants, one to four for toddlers, and one to nine for preschoolers, the quality of caregiving and of children's activities within the center are both good. Likewise, when the overall class size is six or fewer for infants, twelve or fewer for toddlers, and eighteen or fewer for preschoolers, children have better quality experiences than those in larger groups (Howes, Phillips, & Whitebook, 1992).

In essence, the qualities of good daycare mirror the qualities of good parenting. In fact, the reason that factors such as good staff-child ratios and education of caregivers are important is because they are related to the quality of caregiving (NICHD Early Child Care Research Network, 2002). In choosing a daycare center, parents should seek a warm, responsive environment that provides the child, at least some of the time, with opportunities for structured play and prosocial learning.

The Effects of Divorce

As we pointed out at the start of this chapter, the statistics are dramatic: The divorce rate among couples in the United States has tripled since 1960, and estimates suggest that 40 percent of children will live through the divorce of their parents in the current decade (Cherlin, 1992; Furstenberg, 1994). Far from being an atypical event, divorce affects a significant proportion of American children. Unfortunately, the effects of divorce on children are rarely positive; the absence of one parent, the emotional and financial tension, and sometimes continuing conflicts between parents that accompany divorce frequently lead to a range of psychological problems for both boys and girls, at least in the period immediately following the breakup of the family. The ability of children to cope with the stresses of divorce, particularly in the long run, depends on a number of variables. Most important is the way parents manage the transition in family structure.

A major longitudinal study of the effects of divorce on parents and children conducted by E. Mavis Hetherington and her associates illuminated how parental separation affects children and how the nature of parent-child interactions changes (Hetherington, Cox, & Cox, 1982). The researchers compared two groups over a period of two years, a sample of forty-eight preschool-age, middle-class children whose parents divorced and another group of forty-eight middle-class children matched on several variables, such as age and sex, whose families were intact. In all the divorced families, mothers had custody of their children. During the course of the study, the researchers made several assessments of both parents and children, including parental interviews, observations of parent-child interactions in the laboratory and at home, observations and ratings of children's behavior in the home and at school, and personality tests.

The results of the study indicated that the worst period for most children was the first year after the divorce, when they exhibited many negative characteristics such as aggression, distractability, and noncompliance. The extent of their undesirable behaviors even surpassed those of children from intact families with a high level of conflict, and it was particularly noticeable in boys. Two years after the divorce, many of the effects on children had diminished, especially for girls. In a six-year follow-up, however, many boys continued to show patterns of aggression and noncompliance, academic difficulties, poor relations with peers, and extremely low self-esteem (Hetherington, 1989).

A look at family interaction styles after divorce helps to account for the poor initial adjustment of children. Hetherington and her colleagues noted that soon after they separated from their husbands, mothers tended to adopt a more authoritarian style of parenting (Hetherington et al., 1982). They gave out numerous commands and prohibitions and displayed little affection or responsiveness to their children. These mothers were undoubtedly having problems coping with their new status as single parents in both emotional and practical terms. At the same time, the fathers withdrew, participating little in the management of their children's behavior. Children, particularly boys, became less compliant, and mothers in turn responded with increased restrictiveness and punitiveness. Caught up in a spiral of frustration, helplessness, and feelings of incompetence, these mothers responded negatively to many of their children's behaviors, even those that were neutral or positive, and, despite their harsh threats, followed up on few of the directives they gave. The result was a coercive cycle of parent-child interaction such as that described earlier in this chapter and typified by this chapter's opening scene between Joey and his mother.

Other researchers have confirmed that many children show heightened aggression, lower academic achievement, disruptions in peer relationships, and depression after their parents' divorce than they had previously (Camara & Resnick, 1988; Stolberg & Anker, 1984; Wallerstein, Corbin, & Lewis, 1988). Sibling interactions also suffer. Carol MacKinnon (1989) observed elementary school-age children as they played games with their siblings in the laboratory. Siblings whose parents had been divorced for one year or longer showed more teasing, quarreling, physical attacks, and other negative behaviors toward one another than children from intact families. Children ages six to eight years seem to have the most difficulty adjusting to divorce; they are old enough to recognize the seriousness of the family's situation but do not yet have the coping skills to deal with feelings of sadness and guilt that often accompany the change in family structure (Wallerstein & Kelly, 1980). Older children often have a better understanding of divorce and the notion that conflicts between parents must somehow be resolved (Kurdek, 1989). However, even adolescents often suffer negative psychological consequences after their parents divorce. Adolescent boys in particular were found to be more likely to use alcohol or illicit drugs after their parents separated than boys in a control group whose parents remained married (Doherty & Needle, 1991).

For some individuals, the aftermath of divorce may last well into young adulthood. According to data collected as part of a major longitudinal study in Great Britain, young adults whose parents had previously divorced reported more depression, anxiety, and other emotional problems than adults from intact families (Chase-Lansdale, Cherlin, & Kiernan, 1995). In addition, in a twenty-year follow-up of her original sample, Hetherington (1999) found that young adults whose parents had divorced were less likely to finish high school, had smaller social networks, experienced more conflicts with siblings and friends, and had more conflicts in their own marriages. The results of another longitudinal study show that adults whose parents had divorced were more likely to experience a break-up of their own marriages (Amato, 1999).

● **Adjusting to Divorce**   The consequences of divorce are not always so grim for all children. Hetherington (1989) observed that after six years, some of the children in her original study recovered from the family crisis and showed a healthy adaptation to their new family lifestyle whether or not their mothers remarried. These

KEY THEME
Interaction Among Domains

children displayed few behavior problems, high self-esteem, successful academic performance, and positive relations with peers.

What factors were associated with this favorable pattern of adjustment? For one thing, mothers of children in this group had become less authoritarian and more authoritative in their parental style, encouraging independence but also providing a warm, supportive climate for their sons and daughters. If the mother was not available, many of these children had contact with some other caring adult, such as a relative, teacher, or neighbor. In addition, several children in this category had responsibility for the care of another individual: a younger sibling, an aging grandparent, or someone with a physical or emotional problem. These relationships may have offered children an opportunity to feel needed and provided an alternative source of emotional gratification and support. In contrast, mothers of children with long-lasting adjustment problems continued to manifest coercive styles of interaction. Mothers and sons were especially likely to fall into this pattern. Children are also more likely to show successful adjustment to divorce when conflict between divorced parents is low, when the child does not feel "caught" between the two parents, and when the child does not feel that he or she will be abandoned (Amato & Rezac, 1994; Buchanan, Maccoby, & Dornbusch, 1991; Wolchik et al., 2002). Maintaining a close relationship with grandparents can also help (Lussier et al., 2002).

Divorce represents a difficult transition for all members of the family. Some of the effects of divorce on children may actually be due to personal attributes in parents that are passed on genetically to children. Parents and children may share biological predispositions for low social and academic skills, and these may be the very characteristics that lead to marital problems for parents, as well as problematic postdivorce behaviors in children (O'Connor et al., 2000). However, research also suggests that a key variable to understanding the effects of divorce is the quality of relationships among all family members: the more conflict and negative emotion associated with the process and the more prolonged the maladaptive patterns of interaction, the worse the outcomes for the child. In addition, the child's overall adjustment needs to be considered in the broader context of factors such as socioeconomic status, neighborhood, and parental emotional state. These risk factors operate in a similar fashion whether the parents are divorced or not (Deater-Dekard & Dunn, 1999).

● **Custody Arrangements**   After divorce, most children reside with their mothers, in large part because of long-standing societal beliefs about the privileged nature of mother-child relationships. Yet when children live with their mothers after a divorce, they are more likely to experience economic hardship than if they live with their fathers. Studies have found that income for divorced women with children declines an average of 30 percent, whereas income for fathers declines much less or even increases (Burkhauser et al., 1991; Weitzman, 1985). Children living with their mothers also typically show a dramatic impairment in relationships with their fathers. For example, according to one national study, more than a third of the children in the sample did not see their fathers *at all* or saw them only a few times a year (Selzer, 1991).

Many states now have laws that favor joint custody of children following divorce. In most cases, this means both parents have equal responsibility for making decisions about the child's medical care and education; that is, they have *joint legal custody*. In other cases, children reside for substantial periods of time with each parent; this arrangement refers to *joint physical custody*. A recent meta-analysis of studies comparing the effects of joint custody versus sole custody shows that joint custody—whether it is legal or physical—generally has greater benefits for children. Children in joint custody display higher self-esteem and fewer behavioral and emotional problems than children in sole custody. An important factor related to these benefits is the ability of children to spend time with each parent; also, parents of children in joint custody tend to have fewer conflicts than parents in a sole-custody situation (Bauserman, 2002). Researchers have also reported that parental participation in a wide range of activities, even everyday ones such as shopping and watching TV together, predicted children's successful adjustment better than the frequency of special trips or activities (Clarke-Stewart & Hayward, 1996).

● **Relationships with Stepparents**   Approximately 75 to 80 percent of divorced individuals remarry, the majority within five years after their divorce (Cherlin, 1992). As a consequence, about 35 percent of children born in the early 1980s will live with a stepparent (Glick, 1989). For children who have just experienced the separation of their parents, the introduction of a new "parent" can represent yet another difficult transition even though parental remarriage holds the promise of greater financial security and emotional support for both parents and children (Zill, Morrison, & Coiro, 1993).

Like divorce, a parent's remarriage often leads to aggression, noncompliance, poor peer relations, and academic difficulties among children (Bray, 1988; Zill, 1988). In fact, children with stepparents often resemble children with single parents on measures of problem behavior, academic success, and psychological adjustment (Hetherington & Henderson, 1997). As Figure 14.8 shows, a survey of more than ten thousand children in grades six through twelve showed that children in stepfamilies look similar to children from single-parent families in the number of school-related problems experienced; both groups have more problems than children from two-parent families (Zill, 1994). The child usually has more difficulty adjusting when stepparents have larger numbers of their own children, when children from two previous marriages are assimilated into one family, and when the custodial parent and stepparent have a new biological child of their own (Hetherington, 1999; Hetherington, Henderson, & Reiss, 1999; Santrock & Sitterle, 1987; Zill, 1988). Adolescents have more problems adjusting to their new families than younger children, perhaps because their growing autonomy leads them to be more confrontational with parents (Brand, Clingempeel, & Bowen-Woodward, 1988; Hetherington & Jodl, 1994). Even if children had shown previous adjustment to the remarriage of their parents, problems can resurface in adolescence (Bray, 1999). In addition, girls in the middle school and adolescent years do not adjust as well as boys to parental remarriage; girls especially withdraw from their stepfathers (Brand et al., 1988; Vuchinich et al., 1991).

Drawing from data collected in a national survey of parent-adolescent relations, Frank Furstenberg (1987) found that stepparents had reservations about their ability to discipline and provide affection to stepchildren. At the same time, stepchildren corroborated that stepparents were less involved than their biological parents in care

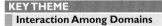

KEY THEME
Interaction Among Domains

Children often have a difficult time adjusting to the presence of stepparents, generally because stepparents do not take an active role in disciplining and showing affection to their "new" children. Problems are more likely to occur when children from each parent's prior marriage become part of the new "blended" family.

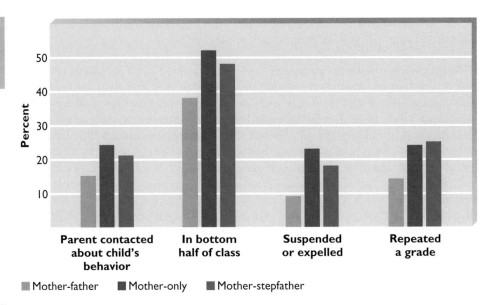

FIGURE 14.8
Family Type and Percentage of Children Experiencing Problems in School

According to a national study involving more than ten thousand children in grades six through twelve, children living in stepfamilies resemble those living in single-parent homes (with their mothers) in the patterns of difficulties they show in school. Both groups have more problems than children living in two-parent families, probably due to differences in parenting styles among the groups.

Source: Adapted from Zill, 1994.

and supervision. Other researchers examining stepparent-stepchild relationships over time confirm that stepparents typically do not fit the profile of authoritative parenting described earlier in this chapter (Hetherington & Jodl, 1994), and thus the benefits of that parenting style for children are not realized. If anything, stepparents often look like the disengaged parents described at the beginning of this chapter; they provide less support for and control over the behavior of their stepchildren compared with their biological children (Mekos, Hetherington, & Reiss, 1996). Moreover, when stepparents do exert control, adolescents tend to show greater aggression, noncompliance, and other problem behaviors (Kim, Hetherington, & Reiss, 1999).

Some difficulties in stepfamilies may stem from the uncertain social roles of stepparents. Stepparents believe that they should play an active role in parenting but are also reluctant to become too involved with their stepchildren (Fine, Coleman, & Ganong, 1999). The advice given by one sixteen-year-old stepson reveals just how delicate a balance stepparents must strike:

> *The stepparent first would be to give room to the children, but still on the same spectrum, keep control basically, keep disciplining but I wouldn't say that you should make them, kinda let them ease into it. You shouldn't jump into something right away which is completely new.* (Fine et al., 1999 p. 283)

Parental remarriage presents special challenges to all family members that researchers are just beginning to explore.

Single-Parent Families

At the start of this chapter, we pointed out that approximately one-third of American children are born to single mothers. A substantial number of these mothers, almost half, are of African American descent, and many live in conditions of poverty (U.S. Bureau of the Census, 2001). Children growing up in single-parent families are at greater risk for a broad array of developmental problems, including poor academic achievement, behavior problems, and high-risk behaviors such as substance abuse (Barber & Eccles, 1992; Demo & Acock, 1996; Turner, Irwin, & Millstein, 1991).

Information from several recent studies suggests some of the factors that are associated with more successful child outcomes in single-parent families. One of these is more involved parenting (Avenevoli, Sess, & Steinberg, 1999). In a study of almost two hundred inner-city African American and Latino families, most of whom earned less than $20,000 per year, adolescent boys from mother-only families showed fewer problem behaviors when mothers used effective discipline strategies (firm but warm), allowed for the child's growing autonomy, provided a structured family environment, and facilitated the growth of relationships with other male family members (Florsheim, Tolan, & Gorman-Smith, 1998). When parents are too punitive, however, children may not fare so well. In a study of 290 single-parent, poor families, most of whom were African American, children with fewer behavior problems and better school readiness had parents who were less likely to use harsh discipline (Zaslow et al., 1999). Another factor is the involvement of mothers in religion. Among single-parent, poor African American families in the rural south, maternal religiosity was related to use of "no-nonsense" parenting (firm but warm), higher quality of mother-child relationships, and more maternal involvement in school. These latter variables, in turn, were linked to the child's overall successful development in cognitive, social, and behavioral domains (Brody & Flor, 1998).

Studies of single-parent families, as well as families who are undergoing other types of transitions, emphasize that it is important to find ways to promote healthy, positive interactions between parents and children. Effective parents are involved and nurturant and provide firm, steady guidance to their children. When parents are stressed or distracted, or when they are unaware of the importance of parenting style, they are less likely to engage in successful interactions with their children. Assistance with child care, parent training programs, and counseling support for families experiencing stress are some of the societal programs that can be helpful.

FOR YOUR REVIEW

- What are some of the effects of maternal employment on child development? How are mother-child interactions affected?

- What has research shown about the effects of daycare on the cognitive and social development of children?

- What are some important factors to consider in selecting a daycare center?

- What are the effects of divorce on child development? What factors can help children adjust to the divorce of their parents?

- What are some typical characteristics of stepparent-child relationships?

- What factors are associated with successful outcomes in single-parent families?

CHAPTER RECAP

SUMMARY OF DEVELOPMENTAL THEMES

■ Sociocultural Influence *How does the sociocultural context influence family processes?*

Many goals parents have for their children's socialization are governed by attitudes the larger society holds, values and beliefs that change over time. Parents will emphasize cooperation, achievement, and sociability, for example, to the extent that the larger social group values these characteristics. Culture also influences who participates in child care and to what extent; in some cultures, for example, fathers and siblings take part in many routine child care tasks. Finally, economic and social trends, such as family size, single parenthood, maternal employment, alternative child care, divorce, and remarriage, can alter family structures. The changes in family dynamics these factors introduce can have far-reaching consequences for child development.

■ Child's Active Role *How does the child play an active role in family processes?*

As integral members of the family system, children can have significant effects on interactions with parents, siblings, and others. The dramatic physical and cognitive changes associated with development require parents and siblings to adapt to the rapidly altering capabilities and needs of the child. In general, parents and siblings react to the child's growing independence and competence by displaying less dominance and regulation. In addition, the child's behaviors may influence the parents' choice of discipline style; for example, aggressive, difficult children may elicit more authoritarian parenting and premature children may be at risk for abuse.

■ **Interaction Among Domains** *How do family processes interact with other domains of development?*

The child's experiences within the family, particularly the type of parenting style to which the child is exposed, can have broad consequences for development. For example, children who experience authoritarian parenting show less advanced moral reasoning, lower self-esteem, poorer relations with peers, poorer school adjustment, and higher levels of aggression than children who experience authoritative parenting. Similarly, interactions with siblings often provide children with opportunities to develop such social skills as nurturance and assertiveness. Finally, transitions in families can introduce both new opportunities and new stresses that can affect children's emotional, social, and cognitive development.

SUMMARY OF TOPICS

Understanding the Family

■ Families play a key role in the child's *socialization*, his or her acquisition of the social knowledge, skills, and attitudes valued by the larger society.

■ The demographics of the family have changed in the past thirty years such that more children live in single-parent families, with grandparents, with gay or lesbian parents, or in families in which both parents work outside the home.

■ Social scientists conceptualize the family in terms of *systems theory*, in which the reciprocal interactions among various members are recognized.

Parents and Socialization

■ Parenting has been categorized according to four general styles: *authoritarian*, *permissive*, *authoritative*, and *uninvolved*. The key dimensions in which these styles differ include the degree of parental warmth and the extent of parental control.

■ The child's instrumental competence is generally associated with authoritative parenting.

■ Parental warmth is related to a number of desirable outcomes among children, including higher self-esteem, greater empathy, and fewer behavioral problems such as aggression.

■ Desirable child outcomes, including fewer delinquent behaviors, are also associated with parental behavioral control, as distinguished from psychological control.

■ Parenting strategies can be influenced by the kinds of attributions parents make about children's behaviors, their beliefs in their own efficacy, and their socialization goals.

■ Characteristics of the child, such as his or her temperament style or degree of committed compliance, are often related to parenting strategies.

■ Problems in parenting, such as coercive cycles and child abuse, illustrate how power assertion can lead to escalating levels of violence within the family.

■ Cross-cultural and social class variations in parenting reflect the pressures exerted by larger social forces, such as the degree to which children must contribute to the family's subsistence or the amount of economic stress on parents.

Relationships with Mothers, Fathers, and Siblings

■ Even though fathers typically spend less time with their children than do mothers, they behave similarly when they are given the opportunity. One difference is that fathers engage in more physical interactions with their infants and young children than mothers.

■ Sensitive, responsive fathering is associated with many desirable outcomes in children in the cognitive and social domains.

■ The presence of siblings usually means that parents have less time to spend with later-born children, a factor that may help explain the generally higher achievement of only and first-born children.

■ Preschool-age children have both aggressive and prosocial exchanges, and older siblings are more dominant and nurturant than younger siblings. These differences among siblings diminish as they get older.

Families in Transition

■ Maternal employment is associated with higher levels of achievement, independence, and self-esteem in girls and less stereotyped gender-role attitudes in both boys and girls.

■ More important than the fact of maternal employment is the mother's interaction style and the quality of substitute care the child receives. Mothers who are satisfied with their life circumstances and who display adaptive parenting techniques tend to have well-adjusted children.

■ Studies of daycare generally show that children who attend high-quality daycare are more cognitively and socially competent than children who are reared solely at home by their parents. High-quality child care provides the same sensitive, responsive caregiving that good parenting provides.

■ Children whose parents divorce evidence socioemotional and academic difficulties, especially boys. Many effects disappear after the first year, particularly among girls.

■ Parental separation typically means increased stress on the family, a factor that can lead to ineffective parenting. Successful adjustment to divorce among children is associated with shifts from power-assertive to authoritative parenting, as well as low parental conflict after separation.

■ Children, especially adolescents, often have difficulty adjusting to the remarriage of their parents. These difficulties stem, in part, from the reluctance of stepparents to exhibit nurturance or control in their interactions with their stepchildren.

CHAPTER 15

Peers

Key Themes in Peer Relations

- **Sociocultural Influence**   How does the socio-cultural context influence peer relations?

- **Child's Active Role**   How does the child play an active role in peer relations?

- **Individual Differences**   How prominent are individual differences in peer relations?

- **Interaction Among Domains**   How do peer relations interact with other domains of development?

It was the start of the first day of school. Jan Nakamura, the third-grade teacher, surveyed her new charges as they played in the schoolyard before the bell rang. It was a familiar scene: the boys played a raucous game of kickball, cheering their teammates and urging victory. The girls gathered in small groups, talking with great animation about their summer experiences and their excitement about school. As always, certain children in both groups were the center of activity; they seemed to attract their agemates as a pot of honey draws bees. Other children seemed to fall into the background; few of their peers approached or spoke to them. Already Jan had a sense that third grade would be easier on some of these fresh new faces than others.

In many ways, Jan's intuitions were correct. She would find, as she learned to match names to faces in this year's class, that many of the playground stars made the transition to a new grade more easily than some of the less popular children. Research evidence suggests that the ability to have successful and rewarding interactions with peers during childhood can be the harbinger of successful later adjustment and that poor peer relations are often associated with a range of developmental problems. Boys and girls who have good peer relationships enjoy school more and are less likely to experience academic difficulties, drop out of school, or commit delinquent acts in later years than agemates who relate poorly with their peers (Bagwell, Newcomb, & Bukowski, 1998; Morison & Masten, 1991; Parker & Asher, 1987). Children who are accepted by their peers are also less likely to report feeling lonely, depressed, and socially anxious than children who are rejected (Boivin & Hymel, 1997; Cassidy & Asher, 1992; Crick & Ladd, 1993). Of course, the quality of peer relations is not the only factor that predicts later developmental outcomes. Nevertheless, experiences with peers play a substantial role in the lives of most children and thus have become an important focus of developmental research.

What do child development theorists say about the role of peers? Social learning theorists believe peers exert a powerful influence on the child's socialization by means of modeling and reinforcement. Piaget (1932/1965) and Vygotsky (1978) have discussed the ways in which peer contacts alter the child's cognitions, which can, in turn, direct social behavior. Piaget contends that peer interactions prompt, or even coerce, the child to consider the viewpoints of others, thus broadening her social perspective-taking ability and diminishing her egocentrism. The result is a greater capacity for social exchange. Vygotsky maintains that contact with peers, especially those who are more skilled in a given domain, stretches the child's intellectual and social capacities. As a result of experiences with peers, the child internalizes new modes of thinking and social interaction and then produces them independently.

The number of studies examining peer relations in childhood and adolescence has skyrocketed in the last two decades, due in part to a recognition of the prevalence of peer experiences in children's lives and the power of peers as socializing agents. Because we humans are "social" beings, it is not surprising that our childhood experiences in social groups play such a large part in making us what we are.

534

Developmental Changes in Peer Relations

Compared with any other human relationship, the special feature of peer relations is their egalitarian nature. In fact, strictly speaking, the term **peer** refers to a companion who is of approximately the same age and developmental level. Parent-child interactions are characterized by a distinct dominant-subordinate hierarchy that facilitates the child's socialization as parents use their authority to transmit information about social rules and behaviors. Peers, however, usually function as equals, and it is primarily among equals that children can forge such social skills as compromising, competing, and cooperating. Thus experiences with peers afford the child unique opportunities to construct social understanding and to develop social skills (Hartup, 1989; Youniss & Smollar, 1985).

Relationships with peers also contribute to the child's developing sense of self. Peers provide the child with direct feedback (verbal and sometimes nonverbal) about how well he is doing in the academic, social, and emotional realms, information that can significantly influence his self-esteem. Peers provide a natural comparison against which the child can gauge his own accomplishments (Furman & Robbins, 1985): "Am I really a good athlete?" "How am I doing as a student?" A child can answer questions such as these by comparing his own abilities with those of his peers.

The way in which children relate to their peers undergoes significant developmental changes. At first, peers are simply interesting (or, at times, annoying) companions in play, but eventually they assume a larger and more crucial part in the child's social and emotional life. Children's peer networks start out small. But as children enter daycare and school, and as their cognitive, language, and social skills develop, their peer networks expand, and their relationships with a subset of those peers grow in intensity.

KEY THEME

Interaction Among Domains

Early Peer Exchanges and Play

Infants show distinct reactions to peers even in the first few months of life. The sight of another baby often prompts a three-month-old to become generally aroused and active, a reaction that is very different from the ritualized greeting she usually reserves for her mother (Fogel, 1979) or the rapt and quiet attention she displays to her reflected image (Field, 1979). At six months, diffuse responses to peers give way to more specific signals, such as smiles, squeals, touching, and leaning in their direction (Hay, Nash, & Pedersen, 1983; Vandell, Wilson, & Buchanan, 1980). Older babies crawl toward one another and explore one another's facial features (Vandell & Mueller, 1980). Thus, from early on, infants recognize something special and interesting about strangers who resemble them in size and features. At the same time, most peer interactions during infancy are brief, lasting only a few seconds, and usually do not involve mutual exchanges of behaviors (Eckerman, Whatley, & Kutz, 1975; Vandell & Wilson, 1982).

In the second year, social exchanges with peers become longer and more coordinated. Two children will jointly manipulate toys and other objects, each child taking a turn playing and then offering the object to the playmate. Children also begin to play simple games together, such as hide-and-seek or tag, activities that require taking turns and switching roles (Howes, 1987a, 1987b). Later in toddlerhood, between ages two and three years, children engage in peer interactions more frequently. Instead of revolving around objects such as toys, these interactions contain many positive social and affiliative behaviors, such as giving attention, smiling, sharing, and cooperating (Bronson, 1981).

In her classic studies of children's play, Mildred Parten (1932) found that the peer relations of young children are characterized by three forms. In **solitary play,** children play alone with toys, apart from other children and without regard for what they are doing. One child might be stacking rings while another does a puzzle; neither notices or cares about the other's activities. In **parallel play,** children play independently

peer Companion of approximately the same age and developmental level.

solitary play Individual play, performed without regard for what others are doing.

parallel play Side-by-side, independent play that is not interactive.

KEY THEME
Sociocultural Influence

KEY THEME
Interaction Among Domains

while alongside or close to other children. Several children might be gathered at a sandbox, one digging with a shovel, another making "pies," and still another dragging a truck through the sand. Even though they are in close proximity, one child's activities do not influence the play of the others. In **cooperative play,** children interact. They share toys, follow one another, and make mutual suggestions about what to do next. Although Parten believed that a stagelike developmental progression takes place from solitary to parallel and then cooperative play, other research suggests that all three types of play occur among preschoolers (Barnes, 1971; Rubin, Maioni, & Hornung, 1976). The type of play exhibited by preschoolers may depend on the socialization goals of parents and teachers. For example, in Korean American preschools, teachers encourage individual academic achievement and task persistence rather than social interaction with other children. Korean American preschoolers engage in significantly less cooperative play and more parallel play than Anglo American preschoolers do (Farver, Kim, & Lee, 1995).

One of the most interesting forms of play seen in preschoolers is **social pretend play** (also called *sociodramatic play*), in which they invoke "make-believe" to change the functions of objects, create imaginary situations, and enact pretend roles, often with the cooperation of one or two peers (Rubin, Fein, & Vandenberg, 1983). Children use sticks and pots as band instruments, ride "magic carpets" together, and play "Mommy and Daddy." Growth in the child's cognitive, perspective-taking, and communication skills helps to explain these changes (Hartup, 1983; Howes, 1987a). To conceive of a stick as representing a flute, for example, the child must develop symbolic capabilities that allow him to let one object represent another. To play "Mommy," a young girl must relinquish her own perspective and appreciate another person's social role: what "mommies" do and how they speak to children. Finally, for complex and coordinated exchanges of pretend play to occur, such as when one child sets the table and prepares the food while the other cries like a baby, children must understand the rules of social dialogue and communication. When we watch three-year-olds engage in pretend play with one another, we are witnessing an intersection of their growing competence in several arenas: social, language, and cognitive skills (Howes, Unger, & Seidner, 1989).

The tendency for three- and four-year-olds to engage in social pretend play has been observed among children from diverse cultural backgrounds, including Chinese, Korean American, and Irish American groups, suggesting that this form of play may be a universal developmental acquisition. It is interesting to note that this is the age at which children from different cultures acquire a "theory of mind" (see the

Preschoolers often show social pretend play in which they invoke "make believe" to create imaginary situations, change the functions of objects, or enact pretend roles. Social pretend play has been observed in children from diverse cultures.

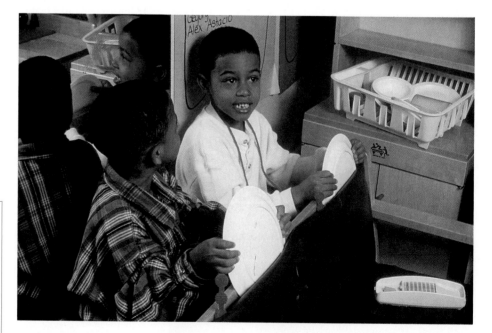

cooperative play   Interactive play in which children's actions are reciprocal.

social pretend play   Play that makes use of imaginary and symbolic objects and social roles, often enacted among several children. Also called *sociodramatic play.*

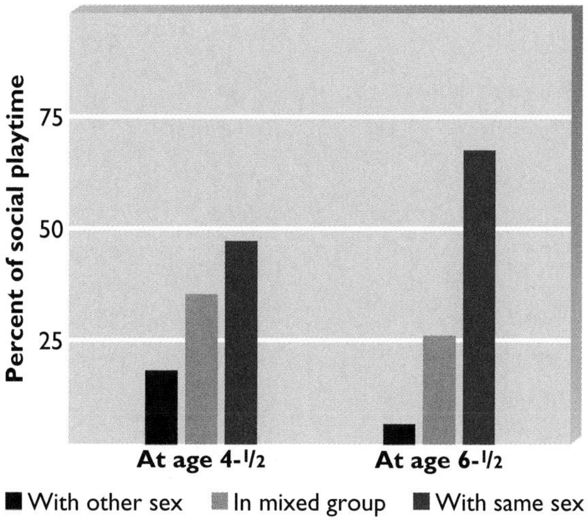

FIGURE 15.1
Changes in Time Spent with Same-Sex Friends During Early Childhood

The amount of time children spend with same-sex peers increases dramatically during early childhood, as this study of children's behavior during free play at school shows. At the same time, the proportion of time spent playing with opposite-sex peers decreases noticeably.

Source: Adapted from Maccoby & Jacklin, 1987.

chapter titled "Cognition: Piaget and Vygotsky") and that children who engage in pretend play are advanced in theory-of-mind tasks (Dunn & Hughes, 2001). At the same time, the child's background culture influences the specific content of pretend play. Korean American children, for example, typically enact family and everyday themes (e.g., eating, sleeping, going places) in their play, whereas American children display themes of danger (e.g., crashes, injuries) and fantasy characters (Farver & Shin, 1997). Irish American children spend substantial time pretending with toys purchased by their families, whereas Chinese children rely more on social routines than on props (Haight et al., 1999). Thus cultural values and resources are often vividly reflected in children's play.

KEY THEME
Sociocultural Influence

The School Years and Adolescence

Elementary school-age children begin to participate more in group activities than in the dyads (two-person groups) that characterize earlier peer relations. As noted in the chapter titled "Gender," they show a clear preference for same-sex peers and, to a lesser extent, for children who are racially similar. In fact, as Figure 15.1 shows, the tendency to play with other children of the same sex begins in the preschool years and grows stronger throughout the elementary school years (Maccoby & Jacklin, 1987). It's not that children dislike others of the opposite sex; they simply prefer to play with same-sex peers (Bukowski et al., 1993). They also prefer to associate with peers who have similar behavior styles; for example, aggressive children tend to "hang out" with other aggressive children (Cairns & Cairns, 1994). In general, quarrels and physical aggression with peers eventually wane, and prosocial behaviors such as sharing and helping others increase (Hartup, 1983).

A special form of play, called **rough-and-tumble play,** emerges around age two years and becomes more visible during the elementary school years, especially among boys. Children chase one another, pretend to fight, or sneak up and pounce on one another. Rough-and-tumble play differs from aggression in that children do not intend to hurt other players and in that it often occurs among children who like one another. Smiling and laughing typically accompany rough-and-tumble play, and children will frequently continue to play together after a bout, all signs that these interactions are friendly (Humphreys & Smith, 1987). Observations of children on school playgrounds during recess show that for some, episodes of rough-and-tumble play were routinely followed by organized games with rules. A playful chase, for example, often led to a game of tag. Thus rough-and-tumble play can provide a context for learning role exchange (e.g., "Now you chase *me*") and prosocial behaviors such as cooperation. On the other hand, especially among unpopular children, rough play

rough-and-tumble play
Active, physical play that carries no intent of imposing harm on another child.

Activity	United States	Europe	East Asia
Household labor	20–40 min	20–40 min	10–20 min
Paid labor	40–60 min	10–20 min	1–10 min
Schoolwork	3.0–4.5 hr	4.0–5.5 hr	5.5–7.5 hr
Total work time	**4–6 hr**	**4.5–6.5 hr**	**6–8 hr**
TV viewing	1.5–2.5 hr	1.5–2.5 hr	1.5–2.5 hr
Talking	2–3 hr	Insufficient data	45–60 min
Sports	30–60 min	20–80 min	1–20 min
Structured voluntary activities	10–20 min	1.0–20 min	0–10 min
Total free time	**6.5–8.0 hr**	**5.5–7.5 hr**	**4.0–5.5 hr**

TABLE 15.1

How Do Adolescents Spend Their Free Time?

Reed Larson has compiled the results of forty-five studies of how adolescents in various cultures spend their work and free time hours per day. A portion of the results is shown here. You should note that several of the activities in the "free time" include opportunities to interact with peers. What do the data suggest about cross-cultural differences in how adolescents spend their time?

Source: Larson, 2001.

KEY THEME
Interaction Among Domains

clique Peer group of five to ten children who frequently interact together.

crowd Large group of peers characterized by specific traits or reputation.

can end up in a real physical fight. The rough-and-tumble play of unpopular children escalated into aggression 28 percent of the time and was positively correlated with a measure of antisocial behavior (Pellegrini, 1988). In general, rough-and-tumble play seems to be a way for boys, especially, to establish their dominance and status (Pellegrini & Smith, 1998).

By the time they reach adolescence, children spend considerable free time with their peers, at least in the United States. In a review of forty-five studies of how adolescents in different countries spend their daily time (see Table 15.1), Reed Larson found that American youth have more unrestricted time than children in Europe or Asia and that much of this time is spent with friends (Larson, 2001). Although time spent with peers might provide important opportunities to develop social skills and supportive relationships, some research is beginning to indicate that the amount of unstructured time spent with peers without adult supervision is related to depression, conduct problems, and lower grades in school. On the other hand, free time spent with parents and other adults or participating in structured activities such as hobbies, sports, and extracurricular activities at school predicts better school success and fewer conduct problems (Mahoney, 2000; McHale, Crouter, & Tucker, 2001).

Peer relations during adolescence become more intense on one level and involve larger networks on another level. Adolescents form close, intimate friendships with a subset of their peers, often those who resemble themselves in certain traits, such as an orientation to academics (Iervolino et al., 2002). Many children also form **cliques,** groups of five to ten children, usually in the same class at school, who frequently interact together (Brown, 1989). Clique membership is frequently supplemented by identification with a **crowd,** a larger group of peers with a specific reputation, such as "jocks" or "brains." Members of crowds do not necessarily spend time together but share a label based on a stereotype. Interestingly, even though youngsters may see themselves as members of particular cliques, their membership in crowds is often identified or labeled by others (Brown, 1989). That is, a girl may not see herself as a "brain" but receive that label from peers who observe her academic achievements and studious behaviors. Membership in cliques and crowds in the middle and later school years reflects the child's growing need for group belonging at a time when he is orienting away from parents and other adults. At the same time, the values parents encourage can influence the crowds with which their adolescent children affiliate themselves. If a parent encourages achievement, for example, the child's academic success may place her in the group of "brains" (Brown et al., 1993). The norms of cliques and crowds can be powerful shapers of behavior; they often provide the adolescent with prescriptions on how to dress, act, and even what ambitions to have for the future. However, the degree to which the group has influence depends on how strongly the adolescent identifies with that group (Kiesner et al., 2002).

As adolescents approach young adulthood and feel more secure about their self-identities, they are less interested in cliques and crowds and become oriented once again toward relationships with individuals. In one study, third- through twelfth-graders were asked to list their closest friends in the entire school, as well as the people they spent time with (Shrum & Cheek, 1987). Analysis of the patterns of relationships among children showed a sharp decline toward later adolescence in the percentage of students who were members of cliques.

One other significant change in adolescence is that some peer relations begin to reflect interest in the opposite sex. The time spent with same-sex peers does not decline in adolescence, but time spent with an opposite-sex peer increases substantially during high school (Richards et al., 1998). As they grow older, and as they begin to spend increasing time with their romantic partners, adolescents spend less time with family members. Nonetheless, they still maintain close emotional ties with families, rating parents and romantic partners as their most influential relationships (Laursen & Williams, 1997).

The Development of Peer Relations chronology summarizes the major developmental changes in peer relations that we have discussed in this section.

FOR YOUR REVIEW

- What developmental outcomes usually accompany good peer relationships during childhood?

- What are the different forms of play exhibited by toddlers? What factors are related to the emergence of these different types of play?

- What are the characteristics of peer relationships during the elementary school years?

- What are the characteristics of peer relationships during adolescence?

Peer Group Dynamics

When we observe preschoolers or elementary school children, we see that they often associate in groups. Peer groups, however, become especially visible and significant during the middle school and early secondary school years (Crockett, Losoff, & Petersen, 1984). Adolescents frequently "hang out" in groups, desire to be members of the most popular groups, and look to the peer group for standards of appearance, conduct, and attitudes. Parents may find that their son or daughter *must* have a certain haircut or *must* buy a particular video game, only to discover that everyone else in the child's circle of friends has the same "look" or library of games. The social dynamics of large groups often differ from the dynamics of two-person groups, or dyads; the power exerted by the group in shaping how the child acts and thinks can be enormous.

Peer Group Formation

How do peer groups form in the first place? Undoubtedly, they coalesce on the basis of children's shared interests, backgrounds, or activities. Children associate with other members of their classroom, soccer team, or school band, for example. Other variables, such as socioeconomic status or ethnic and racial group membership, can also contribute. Youngsters often join with others of similar social class or ethnic/racial background (Clasen & Brown, 1985; Larkin, 1979). As we have seen in the chapter titled "Gender" and in this chapter, gender is another powerful variable;

WHAT DO YOU THINK?

Are Children's Lives Too Structured?
psychology.college.hmco.com

CHRONOLOGY: *Development of Peer Relations*

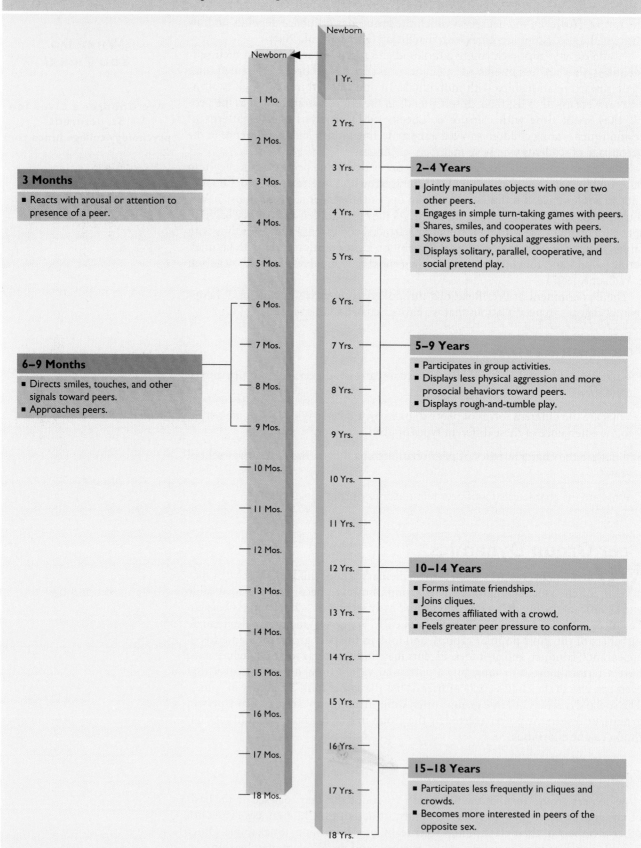

Newborn

Newborn

— 1 Mo.

— 2 Mos.

3 Months
- Reacts with arousal or attention to presence of a peer.

— 3 Mos.

— 4 Mos.

— 5 Mos.

— 6 Mos.

— 7 Mos.

6–9 Months
- Directs smiles, touches, and other signals toward peers.
- Approaches peers.

— 8 Mos.

— 9 Mos.

— 10 Mos.

— 11 Mos.

— 12 Mos.

— 13 Mos.

— 14 Mos.

— 15 Mos.

— 16 Mos.

— 17 Mos.

— 18 Mos.

Newborn

1 Yr.

2 Yrs.

3 Yrs.

2–4 Years
- Jointly manipulates objects with one or two other peers.
- Engages in simple turn-taking games with peers.
- Shares, smiles, and cooperates with peers.
- Shows bouts of physical aggression with peers.
- Displays solitary, parallel, cooperative, and social pretend play.

4 Yrs.

5 Yrs.

6 Yrs.

7 Yrs.

5–9 Years
- Participates in group activities.
- Displays less physical aggression and more prosocial behaviors toward peers.
- Displays rough-and-tumble play.

8 Yrs.

9 Yrs.

10 Yrs.

11 Yrs.

12 Yrs.

10–14 Years
- Forms intimate friendships.
- Joins cliques.
- Becomes affiliated with a crowd.
- Feels greater peer pressure to conform.

13 Yrs.

14 Yrs.

15 Yrs.

16 Yrs.

15–18 Years
- Participates less frequently in cliques and crowds.
- Becomes more interested in peers of the opposite sex.

17 Yrs.

18 Yrs.

This chart describes the sequence of peer relations based on the findings of research. Children often show individual differences in the exact ages at which they display the various developmental achievements outlined here.

During adolescence, peer groups form on the basis of shared interests or common activities. Mixed-sex interactions are more likely to occur than in the earlier years of childhood.

groups, for the most part, tend to be of the same sex throughout childhood and early adolescence.

A particularly enlightening description of how peer groups form and operate can be found in a classic experiment called the Robber's Cave Study, named after the state park in Oklahoma where it took place. Muzafer Sherif and his colleagues invited twenty-two fifth-grade boys who did not know one another to participate in a summer camp program (Sherif et al., 1961). The boys were divided into two groups housed in separate parts of the state park. Initially, each group participated in its own program of typical camp activities—hiking, crafts, structured games—and was unaware of the existence of the other group. In this initial period of the experiment, each group began to develop a unique identity, and individual members performed distinct roles in relation to this group identity. One group became "tough"; the boys swore, acted rough, and ridiculed those who were "sissies." Members of the other group were polite and considerate. As group solidarity grew, members decided to name themselves, the former calling themselves the Rattlers and the latter the Eagles.

The experimenters found that when they deliberately structured certain situations to encourage cooperation, group identities could be further strengthened. One day, for example, each group returned to the campsite only to find that the staff had not prepared dinner; only the uncooked ingredients were available. The boys quickly took over, dividing up the tasks so that some cooked, others prepared drinks, and so forth. Some boys assumed a leadership role, directing the suppertime activities, and others followed their directives. It was quite apparent that the boys had a strong sense of identity with the group and that the group had a clear structure. In other words, for both the Rattlers and the Eagles, there was strong intragroup cooperation and identity.

Another change in circumstances made the group identities even more pronounced. The camp counselors arranged for the Rattlers and Eagles to meet and organized a series of competitions for them, including games such as baseball and tug-of-war. The effects of losing in these competitions were dramatic. The losing group became very disharmonious and conflict ridden. Members accused one another of causing the loss, and some boys who had previously enjoyed status and prestige were demoted in standing if they had contributed to the group's humiliation.

After these initial conflicts, however, group identity became stronger than ever. The effects of competition on behavior *between* the groups were even more pronounced. The Rattlers and Eagles verbally antagonized each other and retaliated for a loss in the day's competition by raiding each other's campsites and stealing possessions such as comic books and clothing. Each episode forged intragroup identity but also increased intergroup hostility.

In the last phase of this social experiment, the counselors attempted to lessen the bad feelings between the Rattlers and the Eagles by having them share meals or watch movies together. Instead of promoting harmony between the groups, however, this tactic produced continuing hostilities, punctuated with fights and verbal assaults. In contrast, when the experimenters created situations in which the two groups had to work together to achieve some common goal, antagonisms between them began to crumble. One hot day, for example, when the counselors "discovered" that the water pipeline for the campsites was broken, boys from both Rattlers and Eagles began to search together for the broken pipes. On another occasion, the food delivery truck broke down; again, the boys all worked together to restart the engine. The acrimonious behavior between the two groups diminished, and boys from the two groups actually began to form friendships with one another.

Few studies of the formation and function of peer groups match the scope of the Robber's Cave Study. However, a more recent series of studies sheds further light on the factors that promote peer group identity. Rebecca Bigler and her colleagues (Bigler, Jones, & Lobliner, 1997) divided children in each of several summer school classrooms into a "blue" group and a "yellow" group. For some children, their assignment to a group was based on a biological characteristic, whether their hair color was light or dark. For others, assignment to a group was random. Teachers in both groups were instructed to emphasize group membership with verbal comments and by other overt actions such as seating children and having them line up for recess according to their groups. Children in all the groups also wore T-shirts denoting the color of the group they were in. The researchers also included a control group in which children wore either yellow or blue T-shirts but did not experience emphasis on the groups from their teachers. At the end of four weeks, children were asked a series of questions evaluating their attitudes toward their own group (the in-group) and the other group (the out-group). Children in the experimental conditions showed a strong tendency to ascribe positive traits to *all* members of the in-group and *none* of the members of the out-group. The control group, in contrast, did not show this pattern. Thus, when adults actively use obvious perceptual categories to describe children's groups, children exhibit strong favoritism toward their own group and bias against the out-group. In-group favoritism does not operate in all circumstances, however. In a subsequent study, Bigler and her colleagues manipulated the status of the "yellow" and "blue" groups by featuring photographs of past winners of athletic and academic competitions on posters placed around the classrooms. They purposely showed more "winners" from the yellow group. Under these conditions, children in the low-status group, the "blue" group, did not show a bias toward their own group, whereas children in the high-status group did (Bigler, Brown, & Markell, 2001). These studies, together with the Robbers Cave study, reveal important information about the factors that influence peer group dynamics. They provide clues, in particular, about the strategies that either promote or break down animosities among children's groups, findings that have implications for interventions aimed at reducing gender or racial and ethnic biases.

Dominance Hierarchies

The scene: a standard laboratory playroom on a university campus. Six elementary school boys, strangers to one another, are brought together to play for forty-five minutes, five days in a row. Beginning the first day, researchers discover, the boys establish dominance hierarchies, distinct levels of social power in the relationships among group members. Some boys initiate more activity, verbally persuade the other group members to act a certain way, or use aggression to get their way. Others play a more submissive role, giving in to the actions of the dominant boys. Based on the frequencies with which they display these behaviors, each boy can be rated as most or least dominant or somewhere in between (Pettit et al., 1990).

KEY THEME
Individual Differences

As laboratory studies and field experiments such as the Robber's Cave Study show, the dominance relations among members of the peer group form quickly and remain stable over a period of months or even longer (Strayer & Strayer, 1976). Especially among younger children, dominance is established through physical power and aggression; the most powerful children are those who physically coerce or threaten the other members of the group into compliance. The basis of dominance changes, however, as group members get to know one another. When preschoolers are observed over the period of a school year, for example, their aggression is highly correlated with dominance in the beginning of the year but is unrelated to dominance by the end of the year (LaFreniere & Charlesworth, 1983). As children approach adolescence, the basis for dominance shifts from physical power to characteristics such as intelligence, creativity, and interpersonal skill (Pettit et al., 1990; Savin-Williams, 1980).

What function do dominance hierarchies serve in the social behavior of children? First, groups can more easily meet their objectives when certain individuals within the group assume a leadership role. Ethologists have long observed that many species of animals, especially primates, have clear lines of power that probably enhance the obtaining of food, protection against natural enemies, and control of reproduction. Among children, dominance hierarchies can serve to get games going on the playground or accomplish school projects that require group efforts. Second, dominance hierarchies make social relationships more predictable for members of the group. Each individual has a specific role, whether as leader or follower, and the behaviors associated with those roles are often clearly defined (Savin-Williams, 1979). Finally, dominance hierarchies are thought to control aggression among members of the group. Usually, once the most dominant members of the group have emerged, few other members resort to aggression. In one naturalistic observation of preschool children's free play, only 20 percent of the interactions among children were classified as counterattacks to aggression (Strayer & Strayer, 1976).

Peer Pressure and Conformity

One of the most widely accepted beliefs about peer groups is that they control the behavior of children, sometimes more than parents and other adults would like. And in fact, peer pressure *is* a very real phenomenon. When seventh- through twelfth-graders were asked to rate how much pressure they felt from agemates in several domains, they did report pressure, and the greatest pressure was to simply be involved with peers: spend time with them, go to parties, and otherwise associate with them (Brown, Clasen, & Eicher, 1986; Clasen & Brown, 1985). They also felt pressure to excel and to complete their education. Contrary to popular opinion, however, they reported the least peer pressure to engage in misconduct, such as smoking, drinking, or having sexual relations. Older adolescents, however, felt more pressure to engage in misconduct than younger adolescents.

How willing are children to conform to these peer pressures? Again, when researchers ask them, children give different answers depending on their age (Berndt, 1979; Brown, Clasen, & Eicher, 1986; Gavin & Furman, 1989). Relative to other ages, vulnerability to peer pressure peaks in early adolescence, usually between the sixth and ninth grades (see Figure 15.2). Note in Figure 15.2, though, that in terms of actual conformity scores, most children would not succumb to peer pressure; their average ratings are in the middle of the rating scale and correspond to a neutral response (Berndt, 1999). By late adolescence the influence of peers on conformity declines even further.

For some children, though, the peer group plays an important part in influencing behaviors and choices. By virtue of their style of parenting, parents may be responsible for adolescents' tendencies to seek out the peer group. When parents of adolescents are unresponsive to their children and maintain their power and restrictiveness, their children tend to be more noticeably oriented to their peer group (Bogenschneider et al., 1998; Fuligni & Eccles, 1993). Adolescents who develop an extreme orientation to their peer group, to the extent that they will ignore parents and schoolwork in order to remain popular, are more likely to become involved with

KEY THEME

Child's Active Role

◉ SEE FOR YOURSELF

psychology.college.hmco.com

Risky Behaviors in Adolescents

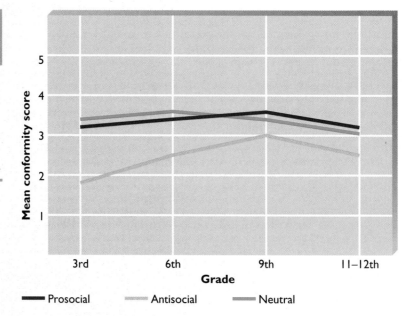

FIGURE 15.2

Developmental Changes in Conformity to Peer Pressure

Conformity to peer pressure, whether it involves prosocial, antisocial, or neutral behavior, peaks in early adolescence, then declines. The higher numbers in this graph represent greater willingness to conform.

Source: Adapted from Berndt, 1979.

alcohol and drug use, to skip classes, and to demonstrate other problem behaviors (Fuligni et al., 2001).

Researchers now believe that studying "peer pressure" as a general phenomenon is not as revealing as examining the roles that *specific* peers play in the child's development. For example, some friends may be more influential than others, and their influence may be greater in some domains than in others, such as aggression as opposed to school achievement. In addition, a child's vulnerability to peer influences probably depends to some degree on his level of emotional and cognitive development (Berndt, 1999; Hartup, 1999). Thus a full understanding of peer influences will have to take these complexities into account.

KEY THEME
Interaction Among Domains

FOR YOUR REVIEW

- What do research findings reveal about the factors that promote the formation of peer group identities?

- What do research findings reveal about the factors that can lessen hostilities between groups of peers?

- How do dominance hierarchies form in children's peer groups? What functions do they serve?

- When does conformity to peer pressure reach its peak? What factors are related to a stronger orientation to the peer group?

Peers as Agents of Socialization

Like parents, teachers, and the media, peers are the child's source of information about the "do's and don'ts" of the social world. Because children have such extensive social relations with their peers, there are few more potent sources of feedback on acceptable and unacceptable behaviors. Peers socialize their agemates in two main ways: as models and as reinforcers. In their behaviors, peers also reflect the values of the larger society.

Peers as Models

According to social learning theory, the greater the similarity between a model and an observer, the more likely it is that the observer will imitate the model's behavior (Bandura, 1969). Peers therefore are prime candidates for prompting imitation in children. Although peer imitation declines by middle childhood, it occurs quite frequently in the early years. In one study, the number of imitative acts occurring in the free play of preschoolers averaged 14.82 per hour (Abramovitch & Grusec, 1978).

There is ample evidence that a host of social behaviors can be transmitted through peer modeling. Display of aggression is a prime example. When children observe a peer acting aggressively with toys, they spontaneously perform similar aggressive acts (Hicks, 1965). On the opposite end of the spectrum, models can promote sharing and other altruistic acts in child observers (Elliott & Vasta, 1970; Hartup & Coates, 1967). Peer models can also influence gender-role behaviors. Most children are reluctant to play with toys meant for the opposite sex. Yet if a peer model displays cross-sex play, children's tendency to follow suit increases (Kobasigawa, 1968; Wolf, 1973).

A powerful variable influencing imitation is the model's competence as perceived by the child observer, especially when new skills or behaviors are involved. Children prefer older, friendly models who are similar to themselves in background and interests (Brody & Stoneman, 1981; Hartup & Coates, 1967; Rosekrans, 1967). Especially in the realm of social behaviors, children may imitate competent peer models over adult models because they see the behaviors selected by peers as more appropriate for themselves.

Peers as Reinforcers

Peers not only model certain behaviors but also actively reinforce their friends' behaviors. Peers communicate clear signals about the social behaviors they prefer and those they won't tolerate, messages that may either maintain or inhibit the child's behaviors. Consider the case of sex-typed behaviors. Researchers observed the reactions of peers as preschool-age children engaged in sex-appropriate or inappropriate play in their nursery schools (Lamb & Roopnarine, 1979). They found that boys who engaged in male-typed activities such as playing ball or chase received more praise and approval (mostly from other boys) than girls did when they attempted these same behaviors. Similarly, peers more frequently reinforced girls than boys who played with dolls or kitchen items or assumed female character roles. Peers controlled behavior through punishment, too, although it was reserved largely for cross-sex activities.

In the same way, peer reactions can regulate the frequency of other social behaviors, such as aggression. In their observations of aggression among preschoolers, Gerald Patterson and his colleagues noted that about three-fourths of the aggressive behaviors that took place were reinforced by victims' compliance or submission (Patterson, Littman, & Bricker, 1967). The consequence was that aggressors maintained their combative styles of interaction. If a peer responded with counteraggression, however, the perpetrator was less likely to repeat the action with that child, choosing either another victim or another behavior. Thus peers powerfully affect one another by means of their positive and negative reactions.

Peer Popularity and Social Competence

Parents, teachers, and others who have the opportunity to observe children over time usually notice the two extreme ends of the sociability spectrum: Some children seem to be at the center of many activities, from school projects to playground games, whereas others are ridiculed or ignored. Frequently the patterns of peer acceptance that become established in the early school years persist for years afterward, along with the psychological rewards or disappointments that accompany them. Psychologists have uncovered several factors related to peer acceptance and popularity and have applied this knowledge to helping children at the unpopular extreme of the spectrum.

EXAMINING RESEARCH METHODS

Using Questionnaires to Assess Peer Status

Given the relationship between peer acceptance and later development described at the start of this chapter, the task of identifying children with problems in this domain is all the more important. One way that psychologists have assessed the quality of peer relations is to administer questionnaires to children, asking about the social standing of their agemates.

Peer assessments frequently consist of a **sociometric nomination** measure in which children are asked to name a specified number of peers (usually between three and five) who fit a certain criterion. For example, children might be asked to "name three classmates you especially like (or dislike)" or "list three peers you would like to walk home from school with." The number of positive or negative nominations the child receives from other children serves as a measure of his popularity. Alternatively, children are sometimes asked to rate each peer in the class or group on a **sociometric rating scale,** a series of items such as "How much do you like to be with this person at school?" The target child's average rating by the other children is the index of peer acceptance.

Peer nomination measures, in turn, are used to classify children's *peer status.* *Popular* children receive many more positive ("like") than negative ("dislike") nominations. *Rejected* children, in contrast, receive few positive but many negative nominations. *Neglected* children receive low numbers of nominations in either category; although they lack friends, they are not actively disliked (Asher & Dodge, 1986). *Controversial* children receive high numbers of both positive and negative nominations. They have a high degree of "social impact" because they are active and visible, but they are generally not preferred as social partners (Coie, Dodge, & Coppotelli, 1982). Finally, *average* children do not receive extreme scores on peer nomination measures. Figure 15.3 summarizes these categories of peer status.

The use of sociometric questionnaires, although important to research on peer relations, raises some interesting questions. First, do researchers and children agree on the connotations of popularity? In one study, fourth- and fifth-graders were shown photographs of three children; one was described as popular, one was described as unpopular, and one was presented as neutral. Children were asked to imagine several different social encounters with each of the children (e.g., meeting in the lunch room) and to rate how positive and negative these interactions would be. Children were also asked to rate how much they liked each target child. The results showed that although unpopular targets were liked less than the other two targets, popular children were not liked any more than neutral targets (LaFontana & Cillessen, 1998). Other researchers have found that popular peers, as defined by children, are viewed as more aggressive, dominant, and "stuck up" than popular children as defined by sociometric measures (LaFontana & Cillessen, 2002; Parkhurst & Hopmeyer, 1998). Thus researchers' and children's notions of popularity may not have exactly the same meaning. What are some of the circumstances in which each type of information might be useful?

Second, most sociometric measures assess an individual child's one-on-one relationships with a few children. However, as the Robbers Cave study so vividly demonstrated, much of children's experience with peers is in the context of larger groups. Because understanding children's leadership, dominance, and status requires an examination of their functioning in a broader social network, researchers are now calling for new approaches that capture the complexities of children's peer networks (Cairns, Xie, & Leung, 1998). One such approach involves creating *composite social maps* of children's peer group relations. In order to create one, several children are asked to report with whom various *other* children associate; these reports are tallied up and diagrammed (see Figure 15.4 for an example) (Kinder-

KEY THEME
Individual Differences

sociometric nomination
Peer assessment measure in which children are asked to name a specific number of peers who fit a certain criterion, such as "peers you would like to walk home with."

sociometric rating scale   Peer assessment measure in which children rate peers on a number of social dimensions.

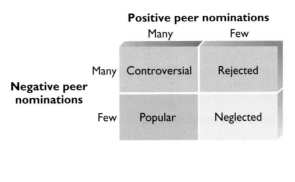

Positive peer nominations

	Many	Few
Many	Controversial	Rejected
Few	Popular	Neglected

Negative peer nominations

FIGURE 15.3
Classifications of Peer Status

The number of positive and negative peer nominations received determines whether a child's peer status is classified as controversial, rejected, neglected, or popular. Average children receive less extreme scores on peer nomination measures.

mann, 1998). What types of questions might researchers begin to study once they have identified these broader peer networks?

The issues raised here suggest a very important point regarding the use of questionnaires in research—the nature of the questions themselves matters a great deal. Perhaps that fact seems obvious, but researchers need to be aware of how subtle changes in wording may have important ramifications for the information they collect. Thus asking a child to name a peer she would like to walk home with may be tapping a different underlying construct than asking who is popular and what a popular person is like. Similarly, asking children whom they prefer to "hang out" with might yield different kinds of information than asking peers to report on who "hangs out" with whom.

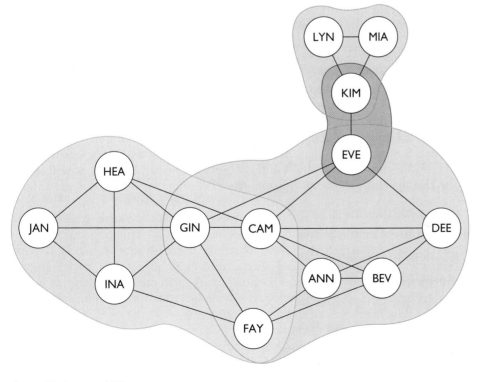

FIGURE 15.4
A Composite Social Map

Illustrated here is a composite social map for girls in a fourth-grade classroom. Children are asked to report on the social affiliations of others in their classroom, and their responses are tallied and diagrammed. The map shows four peer groups of various sizes in this particular classroom, some of them with overlapping members.

Source: Kindermann, 1998.

Characteristics of Popular and Unpopular Children

KEY THEME
Individual Differences

What exactly is it about unpopular children that makes them so unappealing to their agemates and places them so consistently in an undesirable status? This is a particularly important question for those attempting to intervene in these children's "at-risk" circumstances. Peer popularity, as defined by sociometric measures, is related to a number of variables, some of which lie within the child's control and some of which, unfortunately, do not.

- **Physical Attractiveness** When asked to rate photographs of unfamiliar children, both preschool- and elementary school-age children believe children with attractive faces are more friendly, intelligent, and socially competent than unattractive children (Dion & Berscheid, 1974; Langlois & Stephan, 1981). Correlations between children's ratings of peers' attractiveness and sociometric measures of peer acceptance typically range between +0.35 and +0.50, indicating a moderately strong relationship between these two variables (Cavior & Dokecki, 1973; Lerner & Lerner, 1977). Body type makes a difference too. For example, boys with broad shoulders and large muscles are the most popular, and short, chubby boys are the least popular (Staffieri, 1967). The reasons for these stereotypic beliefs are unknown, but they can lead to self-fulfilling behaviors in children who have been labeled (Hartup, 1983). For example, a child who receives peer attention because of attractiveness may have numerous opportunities to develop the social skills that lead to even greater peer acceptance. Finally, as we saw in "Brain, Motor Skill, and Physical Development," boys who mature early and girls who mature later during adolescence are more likely to be accepted by peers.

KEY THEME
Interaction Among Domains

- **Motor Skills** Another factor related to peer acceptance is the child's proficiency in motor activities. Both boys and girls who are coordinated, strong, and skilled in activities such as throwing a ball are rated as more popular by peers and as more socially competent by their teachers and parents (Hops & Finch, 1985). It may be that the value our society places on athletic prowess is reflected in children's preferences in playmates. Alternatively, motor skill may facilitate the manipulation of objects and game playing that constitute the majority of children's shared activities. Those who are talented in this arena will naturally have more peer contacts and eventually be better liked.

KEY THEME
Sociocultural Influence

KEY THEME
Child's Active Role

- **Social Skills** One of the most important factors in peer acceptance is the constellation of social behaviors displayed by popular and unpopular children. Researchers who have observed the overt activities of accepted and unaccepted peers have learned that each presents a distinct behavioral profile. In general, popular children engage in prosocial, cooperative, and normative behaviors and show a high degree of social skill. In contrast, about 50 percent of rejected children are aggressive (Bierman, Smoot, & Aumiller, 1993) and about 20 percent are highly socially withdrawn (Volling et al., 1993). Both of these types of rejected children, as well as neglected children, display socially inappropriate behaviors for which they receive little social reinforcement (Parkhurst & Asher, 1992; Pettit et al., 1996).

For example, when Gary Ladd (1983) observed third- and fourth-grade students during recess, he noted several differences in the behavioral styles of popular and rejected children. Popular children spent more time in cooperative play, social conversation, and other positive social interactions with peers than their rejected counterparts. Rejected children, on the other hand, spent more time engaging in antagonistic behaviors such as arguing and playing in a rough-and-tumble fashion, or playing or standing alone at a distance from peers.

According to the results of another study that examined the peer-directed behaviors of first- and third-grade boys, neglected and controversial children display still other clusters of behaviors (Coie & Dodge, 1988). Neglected boys were the least aggressive of any group observed. They tended to engage in isolated activities and had low visibility with peers. Controversial boys were intellectually, athletically, or so-

Children who lack social skills may be rejected or neglected by their peers. In contrast, popular children display prosocial behaviors and a wide range of social knowledge.

cially talented and very active, but they were sometimes prone to anger and rule violations. The mixture of their positive and negative social behaviors thus elicited a similarly mixed reaction from their classmates. Thus children may be unpopular with their peers for a number of reasons, ranging from social withdrawal to outright aggression.

The social competence of popular children becomes markedly apparent when they are asked to enter a group of unfamiliar children who are already at play. Kenneth Dodge and his colleagues observed as individual kindergartners entered a room where two other children they did not know were already playing with blocks (Dodge et al., 1983). Popular, rejected, and neglected children used different tactics to gain entry into the group, with popular children generally the most successful. Rejected children tended to disrupt the group's ongoing activity by pushing the blocks off the table or making intrusive statements, usually about themselves (e.g., "I have a baby brother"). In return, their peer hosts responded negatively to them. Neglected children were not disruptive but employed another ineffective strategy. Instead of making some verbal or nonverbal attempt to join the group, these children passively watched as their peers played—and they were ignored. Popular children seemed to know exactly what to do. Rather than calling attention to themselves or disrupting the group's activities, they made statements about their peers or what they were doing, such as "That looks like a fun game you are playing." These diplomatic verbalizations paved the way for their smooth integration into the group.

Popular children are particularly effective at maintaining cohesive social interactions with their peers. When Betty Black and Nancy Hazen (1990) observed the social entry behaviors of preschool-age children, they found that disliked children made significantly more irrelevant comments when they spoke with peers. The following segment illustrates how such a conversation might go:

> *Mary:* We're being witches here, and I am the mean witch.
> *Sandy:* My mom is taking me to get shoes today. (p. 387)

In contrast, children who were liked tended to maintain organized, thematically coherent conversations with their peers.

● **Emotion Regulation** Research is increasingly pointing to a link between children's ability to regulate their own emotions and the reactions they receive from peers. For example, in one recent study, peers reported that children they had categorized as

KEY THEME
Interaction Among Domains

rejected were irritable and inattentive in their behaviors. Peers saw them as complaining and getting upset when things went wrong and as being easily distracted (Pope & Bierman, 1999). In fact, rejected children do tend to express more anger, both in their facial expressions and their verbalizations, in contexts such as losing a game (Hubbard, 2001). Or they may show inappropriate happiness as they behave aggressively with their peers (Arsenio, Cooperman, & Lover, 2000). Observations of preschool- and kindergarten-age children also show that there is a relationship between the ability to inhibit undesirable behaviors and social competence with peers. Children who are able to control their behaviors (e.g., who are attentive and follow directions) tend to express fewer negative emotions and generally have more positive interactions with their classmates (Fabes et al., 1999). This pattern of findings has been observed in varying cultures, such as Indonesia, for example (Eisenberg, Picada, & Liew, 2001).

Observations of popular children show that they display a range of socioemotional skills that their more unpopular agemates often lack. But does their skill actually cause their popularity, or do children develop reputations that precipitate subsequent successful or maladaptive patterns of social interaction? A child who is initially rejected because of his appearance, for example, may develop an aggressive style in retaliation. Gary Ladd and his associates examined this question more closely by observing preschool children in the playground during three six-week intervals at the beginning, middle, and end of the academic year (Ladd, Price, & Hart, 1988). Episodes of cooperative play, arguments, and other positive and negative forms of interaction were recorded. In addition, children's sociometric status was assessed at each of these three points in time. The results showed that children who engaged in more cooperative play at the beginning of the school year made gains in peer acceptance by the end of the school year, whereas children who frequently argued showed a decline in acceptance by the middle of the school year. These results are consistent with the idea that children's behaviors precede their social status.

Perhaps of most concern is the finding that once children are rejected by peers, they are on a trajectory that oftentimes leads to lower school achievement and emotional problems. In another study, Ladd observed children both in the fall and spring of their kindergarten year, noting their peer status, peer interactions, classroom participation, and emotional adjustment over the school year. The data fit the model depicted in Figure 15.5. Rejected children were subjected to more negative treatment from peers (e.g., exclusion from peer activities, victimization) and participated less in classroom activities, which in turn predicted lower achievement and emotional

FIGURE 15.5
The Impact of Peer Rejection

Peer rejection is associated with negative consequences among children, including emotional and academic problems. To study more closely the dynamics of this process, Eric Buhs and Gary Ladd (2001) monitored kindergarten children's peer status, peer interactions, classroom participation, and eventual adjustment over the school year. They found that the results of the study generally supported a model like that depicted here.

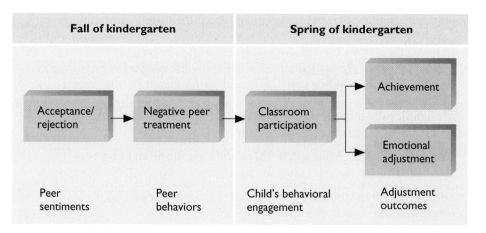

Source: Buhs & Ladd, 2001.

difficulties (Buhs & Ladd, 2001). Given the developmental pathway that many rejected children follow, finding ways to help them negotiate their social world, especially as they begin school, seems all the more important.

Social Withdrawal

Some children are "loners." They have few or no friends, and they end up playing or doing their schoolwork on their own, even if surrounded by other children. Along with aggression, social withdrawal is considered by many child development experts to be one of the two most important indicators of a behavior problem (Rubin & Asendorpf, 1993). Withdrawn children are prone to express anxiety, loneliness, negative conceptions of themselves, and depression (Boivin & Hymel, 1997; Rubin, Hymel, & Mills, 1989). Moreover, lack of social contact is a feature of several clinical categories of psychopathology (Rubin & Asendorpf, 1993).

Children may have limited interactions with their peers for a number of reasons. Some children may simply prefer to play by themselves, curling up with a book or becoming involved with an interesting toy. This pattern is usually noted in the preschool and early school years and is not necessarily an indication that the child is at risk for abnormal development. If this pattern persists, however, peers may react negatively and outrightly reject the child (Rubin, 1993). A second pattern is that of the shy child, who is nervous about being in new environments or with strangers but generally desires social interactions. This characteristic may stem from a biologically based temperament that results in the child's wariness and inhibition (Kagan, Snidman, & Arcus, 1993). Early negative experiences due to a shy temperament can escalate into more severe social withdrawal as the childhood years progress. A third category is children who desire social interactions but, because of their inept social skills, are avoided by their peers. These children may react with aggression, which further contributes to their isolation (Rubin & Asendorpf, 1993).

Researchers are just beginning to understand some of the factors, aside from biological temperament, that may contribute to social withdrawal in children. For example, Rosemary Mills and Kenneth Rubin (1993) found that mothers of four-year-olds who were withdrawn were highly controlling and directive when attempting to teach their children how to interact with peers. They also expressed more anger, disappointment, and guilt about their children's behaviors than mothers of aggressive and "average" children. The reactions of peers may make a difference too. First-grade children do not seem to think about social withdrawal as a liability when asked to rate the likability of children described in vignettes. By age ten, though, social withdrawal was viewed as an abnormal behavior (Younger, Gentile, & Burgess, 1993). Interestingly, even in China, where adults value shyness as a personality trait, children shift from positive to negative evaluations of shy children at around age twelve (Chen, Rubin, & Li, 1995). These studies, along with the different patterns of social withdrawal described here, suggest the complex nature of this style of social functioning.

Despite these complexities, it is important that researchers continue to examine the nature of social withdrawal in childhood because of its potential lingering impact even well into adulthood. Kenneth Rubin gives one example in a letter he received from a fifty-one-year-old individual who had read about his research:

I recall one instance in my third year of grade school and my teacher approached me after recess with the enquiry "have you no one to play with—I have noticed you standing by yourself at recess for several days now." I recalled replying and LYING— "yes I've friends." The teacher was observant and I give her credit for this, however, I wish, oh how I wish, something had been done about my isolation at the tender age of 7 or 8. It has been a long, lonely road. (Rubin & Asendorpf, 1993, p. 4)

The Origins of Social Competence

What factors are responsible for the skilled social behaviors of some children and the seeming social ineptness of others? Researchers draw their answers from a number of perspectives, from the early attachment relationships children form with their caregivers to capabilities in processing the subtle cues that form such an integral part of social interactions.

• **Attachment Relationships** As we saw in the chapter titled "Emotion," infants who are securely attached to their caregivers are predisposed to have positive peer relations in toddlerhood (Waters, Wippman, & Sroufe, 1979). A plausible hypothesis is that in their relationships with caregivers, children have the opportunity to learn and practice a variety of social skills, such as turn taking, compromise, and effective communication. Once honed and refined, these abilities can later be employed with peers and other individuals in the child's life. Attachment also teaches children about emotional ties: how to recognize affection and how to show it. This knowledge about the central ingredients of relationships and the "internal working models" they construct regarding relationships may assist children as they expand their social worlds (Hay, 1985; Sroufe, 1983). Longitudinal studies confirm that children and adolescents who have more positive relationships with peers tended to have secure attachments with their parents during infancy and toddlerhood (Booth et al., 1995; Sroufe, Egeland, & Carlson, 1999; Youngblade & Belsky, 1992). Other researchers have noted that seven-to twelve-year-olds who reported positive relationships with their mothers also had positive cognitions about relationships with peers. For example, those who characterized their mothers as being indifferent made similar judgments about interactions with peers (Rudolph, Hammen, & Burge, 1995). On the other hand, adolescents who have a close, involved relationship with their parents also feel close and secure with their friends (Lieberman, Doyle, & Markiewicz, 1999).

KEY THEME
Interaction Among Domains

• **Parental Influences** Parents play an influential role in the relationships their children form with peers. Broadly speaking, parents who exhibit an authoritative style (see the chapter titled "The Family")—that is, are responsive, are nurturant, and provide verbal explanations—tend to have children who are popular and who display prosocial behaviors with peers. In contrast, children of authoritarian, power-assertive parents are more likely to be classified as rejected (Dekovic & Janssens, 1992; Hart et al., 1992; Pettit et al., 1996).

Parents serve as important models of social competence for their children; they may also provide explicit instruction on appropriate ways to behave in social situations. In one study, mothers of popular and unpopular preschoolers were observed as they introduced their children to a pair of peers busily playing with blocks. Mothers of unpopular children tended to disrupt the ongoing play and use their authority to incorporate their own child into the group. In many ways, their behaviors resembled those of the unpopular children we discussed earlier. In contrast, mothers of popular children encouraged them to become involved in play without intervening in the activity of the host peers. Moreover, in a subsequent interview, these mothers displayed greater knowledge of how to encourage their children to make friends, resolve conflicts, and display other positive social behaviors (Finnie & Russell, 1988). Others have noted that compared with parents of less popular children, parents of popular and socially competent children are generally less disagreeable and demanding and express less negative affect when they play with their children (Isley et al., 1999; Putallaz, 1987). In addition, both mothers and fathers of unpopular children have been found to shift conversations to irrelevant topics, speak while someone else is talking, and ignore their children's requests. Perhaps not surprisingly, their children showed similar ineffective communication styles (Black & Logan, 1995).

Finally, parents can influence children's social competence on another level: by managing their children's social activities. Parents vary in the extent to which they

Parents influence peer-group relations by structuring the kinds of opportunities children have to socialize with age-mates. They also serve as models of social competence and may provide instruction on how to behave in social situations.

create opportunities for their children to interact with peers, experiences that provide the context for the emergence of social skills. Some parents seek out play groups for their preschoolers, enroll them in nursery school, or periodically get together with friends who have children. When parents deliberately arrange peer contacts for their preschoolers, their children have a greater variety of playmates and a larger number of consistent play partners, display more prosocial behaviors at preschool, and have higher sociometric status (at least among boys) than when parents do not make such efforts (Ladd & Golter, 1988; Ladd & Hart, 1992). Opportunities to interact with peers provide the child with a natural arena to discover those behaviors that generate positive responses from peers and those that do not.

● **Daycare**   When children have more experiences with peers because they are enrolled in daycare (as many children do in today's society), they show greater social competence than children reared solely at home by their parents. Carollee Howes (1987a) conducted an extensive longitudinal study of the peer relationships of one-to six-year-olds who were enrolled in child care programs. Among her findings was the discovery that popular or average-status children had entered child care at earlier ages (about ten to nineteen months on average) than rejected children (about thirty to thirty-three months). Early experience was not the sole important factor, however. Howes found that the stability of the peer group was significant as well. Toddlers who had spent a year or more *with the same peers* were more socially competent in that they showed more cooperative forms of play. These children were also rated by teachers as having fewer difficulties than children who had moved to a different group. Evidently, experiences with peers indeed provide an excellent context for mastering social skills, especially if there is sustained contact with familiar agemates.

● **Social-Cognitive Development**   The studies of peer group entry strategies described earlier vividly illustrate that the social competence of children includes an array of intertwined cognitive and behavioral skills. An information-processing model of social competence formulated by Nicki Crick and Kenneth Dodge (see Figure 15.6) suggests more precisely how cognitions and behaviors are related and where problems in social functioning might occur (Crick & Dodge, 1994).

According to the model, the first step in processing social information is to focus on the correct cues. For example, suppose a boy initiates a conversation with a peer. It is more important for the child to encode the peer's facial expression ("Is that a

KEY THEME
Interaction Among Domains

FIGURE 15.6
Social Competence:
An Information-
Processing Model

Crick and Dodge (1994) have proposed a six-step model of social competence based on the child's growing social information-processing skills. The process begins when the child is able to correctly encode and then interpret a social cue. Next, the child generates a set of social goals and possible responses to achieve them. Finally, the child evaluates those responses and enacts the behavior he or she internally selected. Children low in social competence may have difficulties at any step in this model.

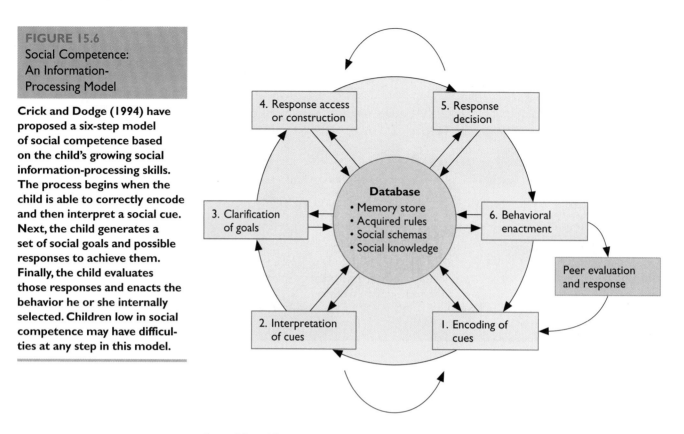

Source: Adapted from Crick & Dodge, 1994.

KEY THEME
Child's Active Role

KEY THEME
Interaction Among Domains

smile or a sneer?") than the color of her clothing. Second, the child must meaningfully interpret the social cues based on his past experiences. Most children would interpret a scowl on a peer's face as a sign of hostility and a smile as a mark of friendliness. In the third step of processing, the child selects a goal for the situation, such as retaliating against an aggressor or making a friend. Fourth, the child generates one or more potential behavioral responses. If he perceives the peer as hostile, he may contemplate avoiding her or matching her hostility. If he reads her signals as friendly, he may consider smiling back or beginning to talk. Fifth, the child evaluates the potential consequences of each possible behavior. Hostility and aggression could lead to physical harm whereas avoidance might not, and hence avoidance might be preferable. Finally, the child enacts the chosen response verbally or physically, monitors the outcome of his behavior, and, if necessary, modifies it, engaging in the six-step cycle over again. This model thus includes a number of steps at which things can go wrong to disrupt a smooth, mutually rewarding social interaction.

Studies of peer relations suggest that popular children are more skillful than unpopular (and, in particular, rejected) children at several steps in the model. First, they are better able to encode and decipher social information correctly. In one study, elementary school children were asked to label the emotions depicted in sets of pictures. For example, one was a series of faces depicting anger, happiness, sadness, disgust, surprise, and fear. Rejected children were less able than popular children to correctly identify the emotions represented in these stimuli (Monfries & Kafer, 1987).

Second, some rejected children tend to make incorrect attributions about the behaviors of peers. In one experiment, researchers asked children to view videotaped episodes of an actor destroying a second actor's toy with either hostile, prosocial, accidental, or ambiguous intent. Both rejected and neglected children tended to attribute hostile intentions to the actor's actions, even when the acts were accidental or prosocial. Popular children were more often correct in their judgments (Dodge, Murphy, & Buchsbaum, 1984). Numerous studies have confirmed that aggressive children in particular tend to make more hostile attributions about the intentions of others than nonaggressive children (Orobio de Castro et al., 2002). The tendency to hold negative beliefs about peers is linked to two factors: prior negative experiences with parents and past low social acceptance from peers (MacKinnon-Lewis, Rabiner, & Starnes, 1999). As a result of these mistaken attributions, aggressive children often retaliate with further negative behavior. Children who exhibit this style of overattributing hostile intent are called *reactive-aggressive* (Crick & Dodge, 1996).

Third, some rejected children tend to suggest inappropriate strategies to resolve social problems and have difficulty devising alternative paths to attain their social goals (Rubin & Krasnor, 1986). Researchers typically assess social problem-solving skills by presenting children with hypothetical social dilemmas and examining their proposed solutions. Researchers in one study asked kindergartners to react to a series of dilemmas in which, for example, one child takes away another's toy. Unpopular children were much more likely than popular children to recommend an aggressive solution, such as "Punch him" or "She could beat her up." A preference for aggressive solutions to problems is typical of children who are *proactive aggressive* (Crick & Dodge, 1996). In addition, when Kenneth Rubin and Linda Krasnor observed children's strategies for handling social problems in naturalistic settings, they noted that rejected children were rigid in their attempts (Rubin & Krasnor, 1986). If, for example, a rejected child failed to convince another child to give him an object, he simply repeated the same unsuccessful behavior. Popular children often tried a different approach to attaining their goal, indicating a broader and more flexible repertoire of social problem-solving skills.

Popular children thus possess social knowledge that leads to successful interactions with their peers and also behave in ways that manifest this expertise. They know what strategies are needed to make friends (e.g., ask others their names, invite them to do things) and can describe prosocial behaviors that tend to foster peer relationships (e.g., be generous, keep promises) (Wentzel & Erdley, 1993). They also recognize that the achievement of their social goals may require time and work and adjust their behaviors according to the sometimes subtle demands of the situation (Asher, 1983). Rejected children, on the other hand, have a more limited awareness of how to solve social problems, believing particularly in the effectiveness of aggression. Unfortunately, their antagonistic actions frequently lead to a spiral of continuing rejection. As they become disassociated from more socially skilled, popular peers, they have fewer opportunities to learn the basics of successful social interaction from them. Moreover, the child who receives consistently negative feedback from peers would probably be hard pressed to be positive, cooperative, and friendly. In this context, it is perhaps not surprising that aggression tends to remain a fairly stable trait, at least in the early school years (Ladd & Burgess, 1999). Neglected children have their own special problems. Rubin and Krasnor (1986) believe children in this special category do not display social cognitive deficits but insecurities and anxieties about the consequences of their social actions. What they need is more self-confidence in their abilities to interact with and be accepted by their peers.

RESEARCH APPLIED TO EDUCATION

Helping the Victims of Aggression

Jan's attention was drawn to the loud shouts of a circle of boys at the back of the playground. As she approached, she saw two boys in the middle of the circle, one waving clenched fists and yelling at the other. Quickly she stepped in and broke up the fight, fortunately before anyone got hurt. She recognized the older of the two boys; he was a fourth-grader who had a reputation for being a "bully." The other child was a small, frightened-looking second-grader who was on the verge of tears. Jan knew she would have some talking to do to both of them and probably to their parents as well.

One way to help children who are the victims of bullies is to encourage their physical development so that they do not send cues suggesting "weakness" to potential aggressors. Building the victim's confidence by encouraging special abilities and talents can also be beneficial.

Researchers have documented many of the characteristics of children who are rejected, particularly those who are aggressive with their peers. But what about children who are the victims of aggression? About 9 percent of children are chronic targets of peer aggression, a pattern that can begin as early as kindergarten age. Being a victim is associated with poorer school adjustment, anxiety, low self-esteem, loneliness, and depression (Boulton & Underwood, 1992; Egan & Perry, 1998; Kochenderfer & Ladd, 1996; Olweus, 1993a). Given these characteristics of victims, is there anything parents (and perhaps teachers) can do to stop this negative cycle?

Dan Olweus has studied the problem of bullies and victims among children in grades one through nine in Norway and Sweden. He has found that victims are often anxious, sensitive, and quiet children who react to bullying by crying and giving in. Often they are physically weaker than most children their age and generally have few friends. Olweus believes this pattern of passive characteristics signals to other children that they are unlikely to retaliate against aggression (Olweus, 1993a). Other researchers, including those who have studied children from varying cultures such as China, have confirmed that chronic victims tend to be unassertive and submissive when they are with their peers (Schwartz, Chang, Farver, 2001; Schwartz, Dodge, & Coie, 1993). A major intervention program to deal with the problems of bullying was launched in Norway over a three-year period. The program involved about twenty-five hundred students from forty-two elementary and junior high schools, as well as their parents and teachers. Advice to the parents of chronic victims included the following:

1. *Help the child to develop self-confidence by encouraging special talents or abilities he displays.*   Children who gain confidence are more likely to be assertive and refuse to tolerate the behaviors of bullies.

2. *Encourage the child to undertake some form of physical training or participate in sports.*   By doing so he will feel less anxiety about his body and send out "signals" of strength rather than weakness to potential aggressors.

3. *Help the child get to know a friendly student in the class who has similar interests or is also looking for a friend.*   A relationship with another peer can help with feelings of loneliness and depression.

4. *Encourage the child's attempts to become involved with people or activities outside the family.*   This suggestion is especially helpful if the family tends to attempt to protect the child every time he is attacked.

This advice was combined with several other programmatic changes involving the school, including teachers' institution of class rules against bullying, better supervision of lunch and recess, talks with the parents of bullies, and promotion of more positive classroom experiences and cooperative learning (Olweus, 1993b). The results showed a 50 percent reduction in the number of children being bullied (and in those acting as bullies as well). In addition, the incidence of other antisocial behavior such as thefts and vandalism was reduced, and the social climate of the classroom became more positive. A key to the program's success was the involvement of *all* children in the program (not just bullies and victims), greater supervision of children during the school day, and good communication between teachers and parents (Olweus, 1994, 1997).

A small proportion of victims of bullying are aggressive themselves (Olweus, 1978; Schwartz et al., 1993). Many of these children come from homes in which they are treated harshly by parents, in some cases even abused (Schwartz et al., 1997). For this subgroup of victims, intervention strategies may have to take a different course than for children who fit the more prevalent pattern of being chronically passive and submissive.

👁 **SEE FOR YOURSELF**
psychology.college.hmco.com
Preventing Bullying

FIGURE 15.7
Training Social Skills

Training Social Skills

Can children be taught the elements of socially skilled behavior and thereby gain greater acceptance from their peers? Answering this question is important in light of findings that the longer children experience rejection from peers, the more likely they are to have academic, social, and psychological problems (DeRosier, Kupersmidt, & Patterson, 1994). Several forms of intervention, usually employed in schools and clinical settings, have produced improvements in children's interpersonal strategies.

● **Modeling** One effective training technique is *modeling,* that is, exposing children to live or recorded models displaying desirable behaviors. For example, one research team presented a group of socially withdrawn preschoolers with short videotapes depicting young children engaging in social behaviors accompanied by a narration of their thoughts (Jakibchuk & Smeriglio, 1976). The soundtrack included the following self-directed statements as the model approached a group of peers: "Those children over there are playing together. . . . I would like to play with them. But I'm afraid. I don't know what to do or say. . . . This is hard. But I'll try. . . . I'm close to them. I did it. Good for me. . . ." Compared with their baseline behaviors, withdrawn children who watched these videotapes for four days increased the number of their social interactions and in turn were the objects of more positive social behaviors from others. Figure 15.7 shows dramatic results when children who received this treatment were compared with children who received no intervention at

In an experiment that evaluated the effects of several treatment strategies with socially withdrawn preschoolers, researchers found that children who observed a model approach a group of peers while verbalizing his thoughts later increased their number of social interactions compared with the pretreatment (or baseline) period. These children also experienced more positive social behaviors from others. The graphs show both measures for this treatment group compared with a group that saw a neutral film and with a no-treatment control group. These last two groups were included to ensure that any gains in social behavior were not the result of simple contact with the experimenters or exposure to a film per se.

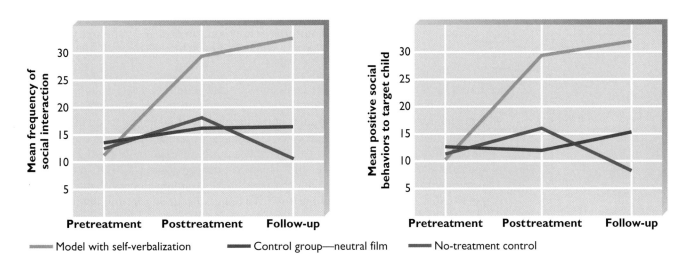

Source: Adapted from Jakibchuk & Smeriglio, 1976.

all or who saw a film on another subject. From the perspective of social learning theory, by identifying with the model, observing how the model acted, and noting the positive consequences of the model's behavior, children were able to expand their repertoire of social behaviors and increase their likelihood of performing those behaviors.

● **Reinforcement**   A second type of intervention uses social or material *reinforcement* to shape socially skilled behaviors and increase their frequency, a technique of operant conditioning (see the chapter titled "Basic Learning and Perception"). Suppose a withdrawn child merely looks at a group of peers playing on the opposite side of the room. The teacher or parent immediately reacts with a "Good!" or a pat on the head. Next, the young child might take a few steps in the direction of the group. Again, the adult promptly delivers a reinforcer. The teacher or parent rewards each successive approximation to the target behavior—in this case, joining the group—until the child has actually entered the group. In general, direct reinforcement of social behaviors is a very effective technique, especially for increasing their frequency (Schneider & Byrne, 1985).

Sometimes the operant approach is combined with other techniques, such as modeling. In one investigation, withdrawn nursery school children received social reinforcement whenever they interacted with their peers. Those who also saw a model demonstrating social interactions showed the greatest gains in the amount of time spent with peers (O'Connor, 1972).

● **Coaching**   The most popular training technique has been *coaching*, or direct instruction in displaying an assortment of social behaviors. In this approach, a verbal presentation of the "right" and "wrong" ways to act is frequently accompanied by discussion about why certain techniques work and by opportunities for children to *role-play*, or act out the desirable behaviors. The goal is to expand children's knowledge of socially desirable behaviors and develop social problem-solving skills. For example, in one social skills training program, elementary school children learn how to join a conversation:

> *Teacher:* Chances are that if you don't know how to start talking with another person or join in when others are talking, you won't be a part of many conversations. . . . For example, pretend that some of your classmates are talking about a TV show that you happened to see last night and you want to get in on the conversation. . . . What you might do is walk over to the group and, when there is a slight pause in the talking, say something like, "Are you talking about 'Star Trek'? I saw that and really liked it a lot too." At this point you have joined the conversation.
>
> Next, you want to make sure that you participate in what's going on. You should listen and add comments to what is being said. . . . Can you give me different examples of how you can now add to or take part in a conversation or what else you would say? (Michelson et al., 1983, pp. 116–117)

Karen Bierman (1986) has added still another component to a social skills training program based on coaching: conducting the intervention as a cooperative activity among both popular and unpopular peers. Each target child in her group of preadolescents met with two socially accepted classmates for ten half-hour sessions to produce a film together but also to receive coaching on expressing feelings, asking questions, and displaying leadership. This two-pronged approach led to greater improvements in conversational skills than social skills training alone, possibly because peers could observe firsthand the positive changes occurring in initially unskilled children and could reinforce them immediately.

Children as young as four years can profit from training programs that explicitly teach social skills. George Spivack and Myrna Shure (1974) provided preschoolers and kindergartners with several months of instruction on how to solve social problems. Situations such as the following were presented: "This girl wants that boy to get his wagon out of the way so she can ride by." Children were asked to generate solutions to the problems and then asked to evaluate the solutions' merits. Children were also taught other skills, such as how to evaluate the emotional expressions of others and how to cope with their own feelings of frustration. At the end of the program, the participants showed significant gains in their ability to solve social problems. Moreover, aggressive children showed fewer disruptive and more prosocial behaviors and withdrawn children became more socially active, even one year after the formal instruction ended. One factor to notice is the emphasis this program had on emotion knowledge and emotion management. Recent research suggests that emotion knowledge is indeed a key predictor of social skills and peer acceptance (Mostow et al., 2002).

KEY THEME
Interaction Among Domains

FOR YOUR REVIEW

- What methods do researchers use to assess children's peer status?

- What are some of the characteristics displayed by popular children? What are some of the specific elements of their socioemotional behaviors?

- What are some of the influences on the development of children's social competence?

- How do popular and rejected children differ in the ways they process social information?

- What are some techniques for promoting children's social skills?

Children's Friendships

Certain peer relations are special. They are marked by shared thoughts and experiences, trust, intimacy, and joy in the other's company. Children's relationships with friends differ from those with other peers. Friends express more emotion and loyalty toward each other, see each other more frequently, and both cooperate and disagree more than mere acquaintances do (Bigelow, Tesson, & Lewko, 1992; Hartup & Sancilio, 1986; Newcomb & Bagwell, 1995). Even though childhood friendships may not endure, their impact on social and emotional development can rival that of the family and may provide a needed buffer when children feel psychological strains. Friendships are also an important source of cognitive and social support (Hartup, 1996).

Children's Patterns and Conceptions of Friendship

About 80 percent of three- to four-year-olds spend a substantial amount of time with at least one peer who is a "strong associate" or friend. Most preschoolers observed in their nursery school classrooms spend at least 30 percent of their time with one other peer, usually someone of the same sex (Hinde et al., 1985). For the three-year-old, however, the concept of *friend* does not encompass the full range of psychological complexities that it does for the older child. At this age, the term is virtually synonymous with *playmate.*

Preschoolers' activities with friends usually consist of games, object sharing, and pretend sequences (e.g., "You be the baby and I'll be the Mommy"). Conversations between friends often contain a good deal of social comparison, a search for differences as well as similarities. Preschool children are fascinated not so much by the specific *things* they have in common as by the fact that they *have* things in common. Hence the following typical conversation recorded by Jeffrey Parker and John Gottman (1989):

Child A: We both have chalk in our hands.
Child B: Right!

Preschoolers try to avoid disagreements and negative affect in their interactions with friends more so than older children do (Gottman & Parkhurst, 1980). Preschoolers especially value friends who give them positive feedback, prefer to play with them over other children, and engage in low levels of conflict with them (Ladd, Kochenderfer, & Coleman, 1996).

In the middle school years (roughly ages eight through twelve), children are very concerned with being accepted by their peers and avoiding the insecurity peer rejection brings; both factors motivate friendship formation. Most friends are of the same age and sex, although relationships with younger and older children occasionally occur as well. Cross-sex friendships are rare, however, constituting only about 5 percent of the mutual friendships reported in one study of more than seven hundred third- and fourth-graders (Kovacs, Parker, & Hoffman, 1996). Researchers in another study even found their fifth-grade participants to be openly resistant to the idea that they might have a friend of the opposite sex (Buhrmester & Furman, 1987). By the time children approach preadolescence, the time they spend with same-sex friends surpasses the time they spend with either parent.

Friendship partners may change, though, over the childhood years. As part of a comprehensive longitudinal study of the social development of children beginning in fourth grade, Robert and Beverly Cairns (1994) asked children to name their best friends each year through eleventh grade. Figure 15.8 shows that the friend named in fourth grade was unlikely to be named again in successive years. Friendships can even shift within a time span of a few weeks. When Robert Cairns and his colleagues observed the nature of fourth- and seventh-graders' friendships, they found that children who mutually nominated each other as friends the first time they were interviewed usually did not name each other as close friends three weeks later (Cairns et al., 1995). However, the tendency for children to have new mutual friends at different points in time may depend on the characteristics of the child. In another project, children who switched friends more frequently over the four weeks of a summer camp session tended to be perceived by other children as playful, humorous, and "gossipy," but also as aggressive, unreliable, and untrustworthy; that is,

KEY THEME
▌ **Individual Differences**

FIGURE 15.8
Changes in Best Friends

In a longitudinal study of best friends, Cairns and Cairns (1994) found that children named as best friends in fourth grade were seldom renamed as best friends in successive years. Friendships may therefore be less stable than generally thought. On the other hand, other research suggests that the stability of friendships over time may depend on the specific personality characteristics of individual children.

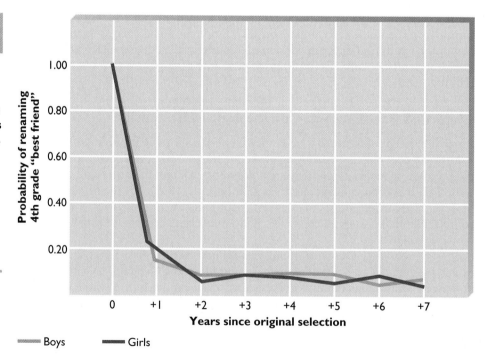

Source: Cairns & Cairns, 1994.

they had qualities that probably both attracted and disappointed friends (Parker & Seal, 1996).

In middle childhood, friendship interactions typically include conflicts as well as cooperation (Hartup et al., 1993), and gossip becomes a predominant format for communication, as the following episode between two girls illustrates:

> E: Oh, see, um, you know that tub she gave us for the spider?
> M: Yeah.
> E: She acts like she owns the whole thing.
> M: The whole spider.
> E: I know.   (Parker & Gottman, 1989, p. 114)

Parker and Gottman (1989) believe gossip allows children to sample the attitudes and beliefs of their agemates without taking the risk of revealing their own views. Because gossip involves the sharing of "privileged" information, it also solidifies the child's membership in the friendship circle.

During this age period, the internal psychological aspects of friendship grow in importance. When sixth-graders are asked, "How do you know that someone is your best friend?," they respond with statements such as "I can talk to her about my problems" or "He'll keep a secret if you tell him." In other words, intimacy and trust as well as loyalty, generosity, and helpfulness become integrated into the child's understanding of friendship (Berndt, 1981). Girls in particular speak of the value they place on intimacy in friendship relations. Girls cite the importance of sharing confidences and private feelings with friends far more frequently than boys do and find that their same-sex friendships provide more support than boys find in their friendships (Buhrmester & Furman, 1987; Furman & Buhrmester, 1992; Jones & Dembo, 1989). This tendency, however, may stem in part from their stereotyped knowledge that female relationships are *supposed* to be close (Bukowski & Kramer, 1986).

Sex differences in concepts of friendship are accompanied by heightened differences in the structure of boys' and girls' friendship networks during the middle school years. Boys' friendships are usually *extensive;* their circle of friends is larger, and play is frequently enacted in groups. For boys, friendship is oriented around shared activities, especially sports (Erwin, 1985). In contrast, girls' friendships tend to be *intensive.* Girls have smaller networks of friends, but they engage in more intensive affective communication and self-disclosure. Girls usually play with only one other girl and may even be reluctant to include a third girl in the relationship. Girls also become more distressed over the breakup of a friendship (Eder & Hallinan, 1978; Maccoby & Jacklin, 1987; Waldrop & Halverson, 1975). It may be that these sex differences in friendship patterns are derived from the games children play. Boys are encouraged to play group games and team sports, such as baseball, which involve a number of children and do not promote intimacy and close interaction. Girls' games, such as "house" and "dolls," involve smaller groups and provide an ideal environment for the exchange of thoughts and emotions. Another possibility is that sex differences in friendships are due to larger socialization forces that foster sensitivity to others and affective sharing in girls and autonomy and emotional reserve in boys (Winstead, 1986).

By adolescence, the importance of close friendship is firmly solidified. Adolescents from diverse cultures such as China and Iceland claim strong loyalty to their close friends (Keller et al., 1998). In our culture, adolescents say they value the ability to share thoughts and feelings with friends and expect mutual understanding and self-disclosure in friendships (Bigelow & LaGaipa, 1975; Furman & Bierman, 1984). They share problems, solutions to those problems, and private feelings with friends. These qualities fit the needs of individuals who are struggling to define who they are and who they will become. A sample exchange between two adolescent friends drawn from Parker and Gottman's (1989) research illustrates these themes:

Boys and girls differ in the patterns of their friendships and the types of activities they engage in with friends. Boys tend to have larger networks of friends, and they tend to participate in shared activities with them. Girls' networks, on the other hand, are smaller and center on affective communication and self-disclosure.

A: I don't know. Gosh,
I have no idea what I want to do. And it really doesn't bother me that much that I don't have my future planned. [laughs]

B: [laughs]

A: [laughs] Like it bothers my Dad a lot, but it doesn't bother me.

B: Just tell your dad what I always tell my Dad: "Dad, I *am*."

A: [laughs] Exactly!

B: "And whatever happens tomorrow, I *still* will be!"

Adolescents continue to prefer same-sex friends, although the frequency of boy-girl interactions increases. At this age, similarities in attitudes about academics, dating, drinking, smoking, and drug use influence whether children become friends (Dishion, Andrews, & Crosby, 1995; Epstein, 1983; Tolson & Urberg, 1993). Adolescent friendships become more selective with age; teenagers have fewer mutual friends than younger children do, but mutual friends comprise a greater proportion of their total network of friends. The tendency for girls to have smaller friendship networks than boys, observed earlier in childhood, disappears (Urberg et al., 1995). Adolescents also say that the time they spend with their friends is the most enjoyable part of their day (Csikszentmihalyi & Larson, 1984). Friendship is thus a key element in the social and emotional life of the older child.

How Children Become Friends

How do two previously unacquainted children form a friendship? What behaviors must occur to produce an affiliative bond between these two peers? A time-intensive investigation by John Gottman (1983) provides a fascinating glimpse into the process of friendship formation among children who initially met as strangers. Gottman's method involved tape-recording the conversations of eighteen unfamiliar dyads ages three to nine years as they played in their homes for three sessions. Even in this short time, friendships among some of the pairs began to emerge. In all cases, each member of the pair was within one year of the age of the other. Some were same-sex pairs, others opposite-sex. The behaviors of the child whose home it was (the host child) and the visiting child (the guest) were coded separately; the sequences of behaviors these children displayed—that is, how one child's behavior influenced the other's—were also analyzed.

Children who "hit it off" in the first play session showed several distinct patterns of interaction. First, they were successful in exchanging information, as in the following conversation one pair had:

A: Hey, you know what?

B: No, what?

A: Sometime you can come to my house.

Children who became friends made efforts to establish a common ground by finding activities they could share or by identifying similarities and differences between them.

In addition, any conflicts that occurred as they played were successfully resolved, either by one member of the dyad explaining the reason for the disagreement or by one child complying with the other child's demands, as long as they were not excessive or unreasonable. Alternatively, as activities escalated from simply coloring side by side ("I'm coloring mine green") to one child issuing a command ("Use blue. That'd be nice"), children who became friends tempered potential conflict by de-escalating the intensity of play (in this case, going back to side-by-side coloring) or using another element of play that was "safe"—namely, information exchange (e.g., "I don't have a blue crayon. Do you?"). In contrast, children who did not become friends often persisted in escalating their play until the situation was no longer amicable. Children who became friends thus modulated their interactions to preserve a positive atmosphere. Over time, other social processes also came into play; clear communication and self-disclosure (the revelation of one's feelings) were among these.

Generally speaking, children become friends with agemates who resemble themselves on a number of dimensions. Young children and their friends often share similar play styles and language skills (Dunn & Cutting, 1999; Rubin et al., 1994). Among older children, friends are similar in temperament, popularity, and the tendency to behave prosocially or aggressively (Haselager et al., 1998). By becoming friends with like-minded agemates, children select contexts in which some of their own initial tendencies—their aggression or prosocial behavior, for example—may become even more accentuated. In fact, friends become more similar to one another as their relationship continues (Newcomb, Bukowski, & Bagwell, 1999).

KEY THEME
Child's Active Role

The Functions of Friendship

By virtue of their special qualities, friendships contribute to the child's development in ways that differ from other, more transient peer interactions. Friendships involve a distinct sense of mutual reciprocity between peers and a significant affective investment from each child (Hartup & Stevens, 1999). Thus they provide a fertile ground for the child's social and emotional development.

Because friendships include the sharing of affection and emotional support, especially among older children, they may play a vital role in protecting children from anxiety and stress, particularly when there are problems in the family. For example, boys seem to adjust better to the practical and psychological consequences of divorce when they have friends (Wallerstein & Kelly, 1980). Likewise, when children come from harsh, punitive home environments, they are at risk for becoming the victims of peer aggression and for behaving aggressively and defiantly; however, this risk is diminished for children who have friends (Criss et al., 2002; Schwartz et al., 2000). Children who have close and intimate friendships have higher levels of self-esteem, experience less anxiety and depression, and are more sociable in general than those with few close friends (Buhrmester, 1990; Mannarino, 1978). Because many studies of friendship are correlational, the direction of influence is not always clear. That is, less anxious children may be more capable of forming intimate friendships, or the reverse may be true: Friendships may make them less anxious. Nonetheless, it is reasonable to hypothesize that friends provide an important source of social support for and feedback about one's competence and self-worth. In fact, as Figure 15.9 shows, having even just one "best friend" can mean less loneliness for the child (Parker & Asher, 1993; Renshaw & Brown, 1993).

Interactions with friends also provide a context for the development of certain social skills, such as cooperation, competition, and conflict resolution. In one study, researchers observed teams of four- and five-year-olds playing a game in which cooperation led to both partners winning, whereas competition led to losses for both (Matsumoto et al., 1986). Teachers independently rated the degree of friendship for each pair of children. The results showed that the greater the degree of friendship,

KEY THEME
Interaction Among Domains

FIGURE 15.9
Friendship as a Buffer Against Loneliness

Having even one "best friend" can significantly lower children's reports of loneliness. In this study, third- through sixth-graders filled out a questionnaire assessing their feelings of loneliness and social dissatisfaction partway through the school year. A high score indicated greater feelings of loneliness. Children who had a reciprocal relationship with at least one friend had significantly lower loneliness scores than children who had no such relationship.

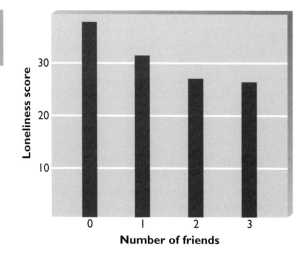

Source: Renshaw & Brown, 1993.

the more the children cooperated to win the game. Because of their investment in friendships, when children have conflicts with friends they frequently seek to negotiate and resolve those conflicts rather than letting the argument escalate or terminating the friendship (Fonzi et al., 1997; Laursen, Hartup, & Koplas, 1996). In observing four-year-olds in nursery school over a period of several weeks, Willard Hartup and his colleagues noted instances of spontaneous conflict in which one child attempted to influence another but met with resistance (Hartup et al., 1988). They found that when conflicts occurred between friends, children were more likely to either negotiate and bargain or physically turn away from the situation. When conflicts occurred between nonfriends, children were more likely to stand firm and insist on their original goal.

Finally, the relationship styles cultivated in friendships may extend to relations with others later in life. Harry Stack Sullivan (1953) believed the capacity for intimacy nurtured by same-sex friendships in childhood provides the foundation for intimacy in more mature adult relationships. The failure to acquire this capacity in the formative years of childhood may impair a person's later functioning as a romantic partner, spouse, or parent. Recent studies confirm that there is a correlation between relational styles used with friends and romantic partners (Furman, 1999). For example, adolescents who perceive their friendships as supportive also tend to see their romantic relationships as supportive (Connolly, Furman, & Konarski, 2000).

Although friends can have exceedingly positive benefits for development, research has revealed that friendships may not always be emotionally supportive. Among rejected children, for example, interactions with their friends tend to be more negative than among other children (Rubin, Bukowski, & Parker, 1998). Friends can also be a factor in deviant behavior, especially among children who are predisposed to have conduct problems themselves. Thomas Dishion and his colleagues (Dishion, Patterson, & Griesler, 1994) observed that ten-year-old aggressive boys who had been rejected by most of their peers often became friends with other aggressive boys. Over time, they conversed more about deviant behavior such as substance abuse and delinquency, a form of talk that deviant peers typically reward each other for (Dishion et al., 1996). By age fourteen, association with antisocial friends was found to contribute statistically to the tendency to engage in deviant behaviors. These findings suggest that breaking the cycle of antisocial behavior may require more than intervening in an individual child's pattern of behaviors; monitoring his or her friendship networks may be just as important. Adolescence is an especially vulnerable time for the negative influences of antisocial friends (Berndt, Hawkins, & Jiao, 1999). In addition, association with deviant friends is especially likely when parents fail to be nurturant and involved and to monitor their adolescents' behaviors (Ary et al., 1999; Scaramella et al., 2002).

Our knowledge of the impact of friendships on child development is relatively incomplete compared to other influences. However, this area of research is likely to grow considering the accumulating evidence that "the company they keep" has important repercussions for the pathways of development (Hartup, 1996).

FOR YOUR REVIEW

- What are the qualities of children's friendships during the preschool, middle childhood, and adolescent years?

- What factors influence the formation of children's friendships?

- How do friendships contribute to the child's social and emotional development?

CHAPTER RECAP

SUMMARY OF DEVELOPMENTAL THEMES

■ Sociocultural Influence *How does the sociocultural context influence peer relations?*

As more children in our society enter daycare, they also have more extensive experiences with peers than previous generations. In general, children who spend more time with peers show advances in social development and often tend to prefer cooperation to competition. Culture can also influence childrens' play styles and the standards that shape peer acceptance. For example, our society highly values athletic capabilities and social skill, and consequently children who are proficient in these domains typically enjoy more peer popularity.

■ Child's Active Role *How does the child play an active role in peer relations?*

On one level, many of the physical qualities the child possesses influence the reactions of peers. Physical attractiveness, body build, motor skill, and rate of maturation all engender different responses from other children. On another level, the child's social and emotional skills clearly affect how peers react. Children who can accurately read the emotions of others, gauge the consequences of their own behaviors on others, and employ the strategies that facilitate effective social interactions are more popular with their peers. Similarly, children who are aggressive and display physical power often rise to the top of peer group dominance hierarchies but may become unpopular with peers, as evidenced when those peers are asked to name children they like or prefer to associate with.

■ Individual Differences *How prominent are individual differences in peer relations?*

Children vary in the extent to which they are accepted by their peers. Some children are popular, whereas others are rejected, neglected, or controversial. A child's popularity may be linked to aspects of physical appearance, motor skills, and social skills. Children may also show individual differences in their tendency to keep the same friends over time.

■ Interaction Among Domains *How do peer relations interact with other domains of development?*

First, healthy relations with peers are associated with a number of successful developmental outcomes in other arenas. Popular children do well in school, have high levels of self-esteem, and suffer fewer emotional difficulties, such as depression, than unpopular children. Second, the ability to interact successfully with peers is related to attainments in several other developmental domains. Children who are reared in a positive emotional environment and are skillful in deciphering emotional cues tend to be more socially competent with peers. The formation of early emotional attachments and growth in social knowledge may also play a role. The child's emerging cognitive capabilities, especially perspective-taking skills, allow the child to think about the reactions and expectations of others and to anticipate the consequences of his or her own behaviors. Successful peer interaction is thus both a product of and a contributor to the child's emotional, cognitive, and social achievements.

SUMMARY OF TOPICS

- Good peer relationships during childhood are related to academic success, fewer problem behaviors, and healthy socioemotional adjustment.

Developmental Changes in Peer Relations

- Infants show a direct interest in peers through visual attention, smiles, and touches.

- By age two, children show coordinated social interactions with peers.

- Preschoolers typically engage in three forms of play: *solitary play*, *parallel play*, and *cooperative play*. They also engage in *social pretend play*, a form of play that is linked to advances in cognition, language, and social understanding.

- Peer groups assume greater importance for children during the school years, when they associate in same-sex groups and groups based on other similarities.

- *Rough-and-tumble play* is often observed, especially among boys, and may function as a way to establish dominance.

- Adolescents form larger groups called *cliques* and *crowds*, but they also form more intense relationships with friends. Toward the end of adolescence, romantic relationships start to become important.

Peer Group Dynamics

- Children typically show strong identity with the peer groups they join, especially when groups compete against one another. Intergroup hostilities can be reduced by having groups work together on some common goal.

- Peer groups show in-group favoritism when their group is highly defined and when their group has high status.

- Peer groups quickly form dominance hierarchies, organized structures in which some children become leaders and some become followers. Dominance hierarchies seem to serve adaptive social functions, such as controlling aggression.

- Susceptibility to peer pressure heightens during early adolescence but declines as young adulthood approaches. For some children, extreme orientation to the peer group is associated with deviant behaviors.

Peers as Agents of Socialization

- Peers can serve as important models for social behaviors, such as aggression and sex-typed behaviors.

- Peers actively reinforce children's behaviors through their positive and negative reactions.

Peer Popularity and Social Competence

- Peer acceptance is typically measured through assessment devices such as *sociometric nominations*, *sociometric rating scales*, or composite social maps.

- The child's peer status is related to his or her physical attractiveness, motor skills, social skills, and emotion regulation. Popular children engage in prosocial behaviors, know how to enter peer groups, and effectively maintain cohesive social interactions.

- Social competence has its roots in the child's earliest attachment relationships but is also influenced by parental styles of social interaction, as well as by opportunities to interact with peers, as is afforded in daycare.

- Socially competent children are skilled at perceiving social cues and have good social problem-solving ability.

- Modeling, reinforcement, and coaching are some of the techniques used to enhance social skills in children who display problem behaviors such as aggression and social withdrawal.

Children's Friendships

- Preschoolers view friends as peers to play with, but with development, children come to value friends for their psychological qualities. Children approaching adolescence, for example, see friends as providers of intimacy and trust.

- Children form friendships by keeping social interactions positive in tone, exchanging information, and at later ages, through self-disclosure.

- Friendships provide a context for developing skills such as cooperation and conflict resolution and may help the child learn the benefits of intimacy in relationships. Friendships can also provide a context for the development of problem behaviors.

CHAPTER 16

Beyond Family and Peers

Key Themes in Media, Computers, Schools, and Neighborhoods

- **Sociocultural Influence** How does the sociocultural context influence the child's experiences with media, computers, schools, and the neighborhood?

- **Child's Active Role** How does the child play an active role in experiences with media, computers, schools, and the neighborhood?

- **Interaction Among Domains** How do the child's experiences with media, computers, schools, and the neighborhood interact with development in other domains?

Jeremy slammed the door behind him, flicked the lock, and headed to the refrigerator. It was his regular routine after school. Come home, get a snack, and turn on the television to watch cartoons. He wasn't allowed to go out to play; too dangerous, his mother claimed. If he had already seen the cartoons, he might play a video game for awhile. But because he couldn't have anyone over until his mother returned from work, that wasn't much fun, either. He dreamed of living in a house with a big yard, maybe even a swimming pool in the back and a park nearby. But that wasn't the neighborhood he was living in.

Children grow up in many different contexts. In contrast to Jeremy, some go to soccer practice or music lessons after school or stay at the school until a parent picks them up an hour or two later. Some spend their time chatting on the computer with their friends. Some, like Jeremy, watch a lot of television.

Historically, of course, parents and peers have played a major role in socializing children and helping them build their cognitive skills, and they continue to serve this function in contemporary society. Nevertheless, formal education in the schools and, in more recent decades, computers and the information highway, along with television, videocassette and digital recorders, and computer activities have begun to play a significant part in these processes as well.

A host of questions have sprung up concerning television, computers, and other recent technological marvels and their effects on children. What are children learning from these increasingly ubiquitous sources of information? Do they get "hooked" on television and computer games? What aspects of cognitive or social development might these cultural innovations be affecting? In addition, schools have both pedagogical and social effects on development. Questions about academic and social success and their relationship to the programs that schools offer, as well as the role of teachers in these processes, continue to be of concern to parents and educators. Finally, neighborhoods offer a means of further exploring potential influences of the broader context in which children live.

Television

American children watch a great deal of television. Babies as young as six months of age attend to television and on average are exposed to more than one hour per day (Hollenbeck & Slaby, 1979). As Figure 16.1 shows, the time children spend attending to television increases dramatically during the preschool years, especially after age two-and-a-half, peaks between ages ten to twelve, and declines during adolescence, when radio listening increases (D. R. Anderson et al., 1986; Brown et al., 1990; Calvert et al., 1982). Children, at least in the United States, spend

SEE FOR YOURSELF
psychology.college.hmco.com
Children and Media

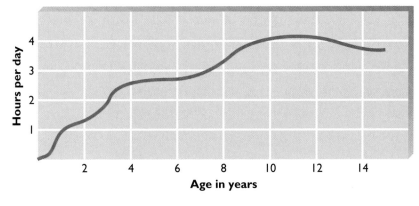

Source: Adapted from Liebert & Sprafkin, 1988.

FIGURE 16.1
Hours of TV Watching as a Function of Children's Age

The amount of time children spend watching television increases throughout early childhood, peaks at about age ten or twelve years, and then declines in adolescence.

more time watching television than at any other activity except sleep (Roberts et al., 1999). In fact, by high school graduation, three years will, on average, have been given to watching television (Strasburger, 1993). Moreover, with the advent of cable television, videocassette recorders (VCR), and digital games, children have more opportunities than ever to spend time in front of a television screen.

Television viewing among children shows large individual differences. Some three- to five-year-olds watch very little television; others watch as much as seventy-five hours per week. Individual patterns of TV viewing remain stable over the years. Thus the television-viewing habits children acquire in early childhood can be relatively long lasting (Huston & Wright, 1998).

As they grow older, children also show changes in the types of programs they prefer to watch. Preschoolers are more likely to view educational programs designed for children, such as *Sesame Street* or *Mister Rogers' Neighborhood,* and cartoons. Interest in child-centered educational programs is relatively greater among younger preschoolers than older children (Wright et al., 2001). By ages five to seven, children begin to watch comedies and entertainment shows aimed at general audiences, shows that make increasing demands on their ability to comprehend plots and themes (Huston et al., 1990). Boys tend to watch more television than girls (Huston & Wright, 1998) and African American children more than European American children (Comstock, 1991). Children from lower socioeconomic levels are more frequent viewers than children from higher-income backgrounds (Greenberg, 1986).

Children's Comprehension of Television Programs

Contrary to popular belief, television viewing is usually not a passive process in which a mesmerized child sits gazing at the screen. The fact that preferences for shows change with age is just one example of the ways children actively control their TV viewing. Daniel Anderson and his colleagues have conducted numerous studies demonstrating that children's selection of television programs is influenced by their ability to comprehend content (Anderson & Burns, 1991). Certain formal, or structural, features of television serve to draw the viewer in, particularly such sound effects as laughter, music, and children's and women's voices. Other features, such as visual cuts, motion, and special sound effects, hold the child's attention (Alwitt et al., 1980; Schmitt, Anderson, & Collins, 1999). But the formal features of television programs are not the sole determinants of what children watch.

When preschoolers watch segments of *Sesame Street* in which the comprehensibility of the program has been altered, that is, presented in a foreign language or played backward, attention declines even though the formal features remain constant (Anderson et al., 1981). In other words, children actively direct their attention to

KEY THEME
Child's Active Role

Young children in most families spend many hours watching television. As a consequence, television can have a powerful influence on their development. According to some estimates, as much as one-third of a child's waking life will have been spent watching television, and a good portion of the programming young children see will be cartoons.

KEY THEME
Interaction Among Domains

those portions of the show that they most readily understand; they are not influenced by sound effects or visual cuts alone. Many television shows have complex plots and use subtle cues that require inferences about characters' motives, intentions, and feelings. In addition, most programs contain changes of scene that require viewers to integrate information across several scenes. Research indicates that clear developmental differences exist in children's ability to understand information from television shows, differences that accompany changes in cognitive processing.

Preschoolers can understand short story segments and remember the most central elements of each story (Lorch, Bellack, & Augsbach, 1987). When the plots and themes of television shows thicken, however, young children have difficulties. More specifically, when they watch programs designed for general audiences, younger children are less likely than older children to remember the *explicit* content, that is, the discrete scenes that are essential to understanding the plot. Even when they do remember explicit information, younger children frequently fail to grasp the *implicit* content communicated by relationships among scenes (Collins et al., 1978). For example, young children may fail to understand a character's motive for aggression if the message is communicated in two scenes separated by several other sequences (Collins, 1983).

Children's general knowledge and previous experiences can affect their comprehension of the programs they watch. Suppose, for example, that children are asked to retell the content of a show about a murder and the suspect's eventual capture. Children frequently mention *script-based* knowledge (see the chapter titled "Cognition: Information Processing"), drawing from their general storehouse of information on the events that surround the relationships between police and criminals. Older children are more likely than younger children, however, to describe content specific to the program they watched, such as the fact that some police officers in the show did not wear uniforms (Collins, 1983). As children's general knowledge about the world grows, their comprehension of more detailed, specific information in television programs expands as well.

Other research has shown that children's growing verbal competency underlies their ability to understand TV programs. When five-year-olds were given standardized IQ tests and tested on their memory of the central and incidental events in a thirty-five-minute television program, their scores on the verbal subscales of the tests correlated significantly with their ability to comprehend the show's central events (Jacobvitz, Wood, & Albin, 1989).

One other important developmental change is in children's ability to recognize that most television programming is fictional. Children under four years of age often have difficulty distinguishing the boundaries between events that occur on television and those that take place in the real world (Flavell et al., 1990; Jaglom & Gardner, 1981). For example, preschoolers may think that *Sesame Street* is a place where others live, that individuals portrayed on television can see and hear their viewers, and that the things seen on TV exist inside it (Nikken & Peeters, 1988). Nevertheless, not until they are older than two years of age do children seem to realize that information presented on television can help them solve a problem such as finding a toy in a room after having just seen someone on television hiding it in that room (Schmitt & Anderson, 2002; Troseth & DeLoache, 1998).

Many five- and six-year-olds do not fully understand that television characters are actually actors playing roles; not until age eight and older do the majority of children grasp this concept. However, even kindergartners realize that cartoons are fantasy. They are also quite accurate about deciding whether their favorite programs occur as part of real life or just on television. In fact, they tend to be biased in assuming that most television programming does not occur in real life (Wright et al., 1994). Thus the developmental course seems to progress from failing to make a distinction between events on television and events in the real world to a belief that few events depicted on television occur in the real world to, finally, a more complete understanding of which events occurring on television are fictional and which are not (Wright et al., 1994).

Television's Influence on Cognitive and Language Development

KEY THEME
Interaction Among Domains

Today many preschoolers in the United States and most Western countries have ready access to programs specifically designed to teach cognitive skills to preschool children. But they also learn a lot more, according to research on educational television. Evaluations of the effects of such shows as *Sesame Street* demonstrate that television can teach children a range of problem-solving, mathematical, reading, and language skills (Huston & Wright, 1998).

● **Cognition** *Sesame Street* was specifically designed to provide entertaining ways to teach children, especially those who might be underprepared for school, the letters of the alphabet, counting, vocabulary, and similar school-readiness skills. The programs also deliberately include both male and female characters from many racial and ethnic backgrounds. Preschoolers, many from disadvantaged backgrounds, who watched the show most frequently were found to show the greatest gains on several skills, including writing their names and knowing letters, numbers, and forms (see Figure 16.2). Frequent viewers also obtained higher scores on a standardized vocabulary test, adapted better to school, and had more positive attitudes toward school and people of other races than nonwatchers (Bogatz & Ball, 1972; Rice et al., 1990). Thus the show had effects not only on children's cognitive skills but also on their prosocial attitudes.

Not only does educational programming have immediate effects on children's cognitive abilities, but evidence is also accumulating to indicate that these effects can

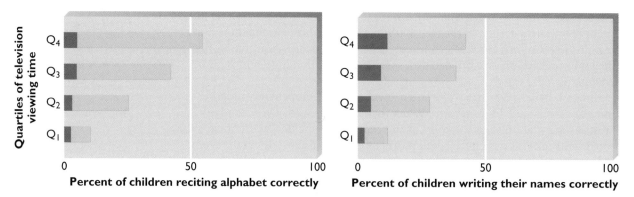

Before watching *Sesame Street*   After watching *Sesame Street*

Source: Adapted from Liebert & Sprafkin, 1988.

FIGURE 16.2
Television and Enhancement of Language Skills

Preschoolers who watched *Sesame Street* showed gains in a number of prereading skills, including the ability to recite the alphabet and write their names. The graph indicates that children who watched the show the most displayed the greatest gains in performance. (Children in quartile 1 rarely watched the show; those in quartile 2 watched two to three times per week; those in quartile 3 watched four to five times per week; and those in quartile 4 watched more than five times per week.)

be long lasting. For example, children in low-income families who spent relatively greater amounts of time watching *Sesame Street* and other television shows geared to educational goals at two and three years of age did well on measures of reading, math, language abilities, and other indicators of school readiness three years later (Wright et al., 2001). This effect may, in part, stem from their increased interest in continuing to watch informative television as they become older. Moreover, a recent longitudinal study carried out on high schoolers in working- and middle-class families for whom television viewing habits had been recorded as preschoolers suggests a positive impact of having watched informative educational programming more than a decade earlier. Compared with those who watched more violent or entertainment-oriented shows as preschoolers, those who watched more educational programming had higher grades in English, math, and science, read more books, and were more achievement oriented as teenagers (D. R. Anderson et al., 2001). This relationship was somewhat greater for males than females, although a similar pattern was found for both sexes. Because the data on long-term effects of television viewing are correlational in nature, it is not possible to completely rule out other factors that could account for the positive relationships that were observed in the longitudinal study. For example, either individual differences or parental encouragement of educational and achievement goals throughout childhood may help to explain these findings. Nevertheless, the results considerably blunt many of the strong objections that have been raised about television's negative influence on development, especially if children are observing programming designed to be educationally informative.

It is not uncommon to read criticisms in the popular press arguing that television viewing contributes to an inability to maintain a long attention span, difficulty in concentrating, lower task perseverance, and a reduced capacity to think (Mielke, 1994). How sound are these criticisms? Although many gaps continue to exist in our knowledge about this matter, meta-analyses and major reviews of the research further suggest that television viewing, at least when done in moderation, is not such an undesirable activity (Anderson & Collins, 1988; Neuman, 1991). However, those who watch television a great deal of time do poorly on academic achievement tests. Thus there may be a curvilinear relationship between television viewing and academic achievement; a moderate level of television viewing, especially if it consists primarily of educational programming, may be beneficial. A great deal of TV viewing, especially when it involves a lot of programming that contains violence, may be harmful.

● **Language**   Language skills may also be influenced by television. Mabel Rice and her colleagues (1990) suggest that television promotes children's language development. Many programs targeted for children include simplified speech, repetitions, recasts, and elaboration on the meanings of words. As we saw in the chapter titled "Language," these devices can enhance the child's acquisition of vocabulary and syntax (Rice, 1983). Parents also sometimes use television as a "video picture book" in which events portrayed on the show stimulate verbal exchanges and language learning. For example, when mothers watch television with their preschoolers, they frequently identify objects, repeat new words, ask questions, or relate the content of the show to the child's own experiences (Lemish & Rice, 1986).

Is there direct evidence that television can function as a vehicle for vocabulary acquisition? Investigators exposed three- and five-year-olds to twenty new words in a fifteen-minute animated television story and found that both age groups showed gains in comprehension after only two viewings. Three-year-olds learned an average of one to two new words, and five-year-olds learned four to five words (Rice & Woodsmall, 1988). These findings are all the more impressive considering the brevity of the children's exposure to new vocabulary items and the limited efforts of the experimenters to highlight or exaggerate the new words.

Television's Influence on Social Development

Whipping a towel over his shoulders, a seven-year-old jumps off the couch after watching the movie *Superman* on television. A brother and sister brandish toy swords, the brother mimicking the action of a favorite cartoon character. These common scenes in American households illustrate the power of television to influence children's behavior by providing models for direct imitation. Sometimes the messages are more subtle: a male announcer's authoritative voice decrees that this toy is the one all your friends want or that a sugary cereal is fortified with vitamins. When mostly men's voices appear in television commercials, the indirect message is that males more than females have the knowledge and authority to make such definitive statements. Whether by directly providing models for children to imitate or by indirectly offering messages about social categories, television can promote behaviors as diverse as aggression and sex typing. Psychologists and social policymakers have been particularly concerned about how television affects the child's social behavior and understanding, for better or worse.

These photos, taken from Bandura's classic experiments, illustrate with stark clarity the power of imitation in influencing children's aggression. In the top row, an adult model displays various aggressive actions against a "Bobo doll." The middle and bottom rows depict the sequence of imitative aggression shown by a male and female participant in the experiment. Their behaviors closely mimic the specific actions they had previously seen the adult perform.

FIGURE 16.3
The Effect of Watching
Modeled Aggression

After children saw a live, filmed, or live dressed-up "cartoon" model behave aggressively in the laboratory (bottom three bars), they were much more likely to imitate the model's aggression than were children who had seen no model at all or viewed a model behaving nonaggressively.

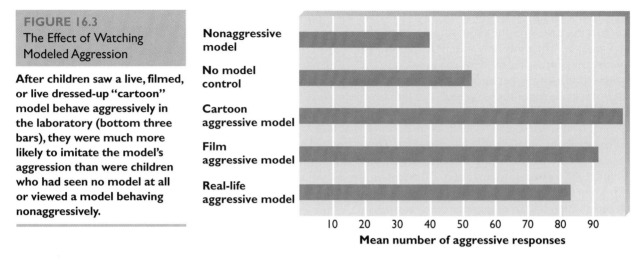

Source: Adapted from Bandura & Walters, 1963.

● **Aggression**   Any child who turns on the television in the United States has an extraordinarily good chance of encountering a portrayal of violence. Approximately 60 percent of the programming shown between 6:00 A.M. and 11:00 P.M. contains violent scenes (and sometimes many of them). Moreover, that rate is even higher in children's programming, especially cartoons (Center for Communication and Social Policy, 1998). As a consequence, children will see an average of 10,000 acts of violence every year (Federman, 1996, 1997, 1998). Does this heavy dose of televised violence viewing produce aggression in children? Hundreds of research studies have examined this issue, and the consensus is clearly yes; meta-analyses of the large number of studies investigating the relationship arrive at the same conclusion: A small but consistent causal relationship exists between viewing aggression on TV and aggressive behavior in children (Comstock & Scharrer, 1999; Huston, Watkins, & Kunkel, 1989; Wood, Wong, & Chachere, 1991).

In keeping with the principles of social learning theory, a regular diet of viewing aggressive models may suggest to the child that physical attacks are acceptable in a person's repertoire of behaviors. Two processes could be operating. First, children can learn new acts of aggression from the models they observe. Second, aggressive behaviors already in the child's repertoire may be disinhibited (Bandura, 1969). Albert Bandura and his colleagues (Bandura, Ross, & Ross, 1963a, 1963b) designed a number of laboratory studies to explore the effects of viewing aggression. For example, nursery school children in one experiment were randomly assigned to one of five experimental conditions. The first group watched from behind a one-way mirror as a model in the next room performed a series of unusual acts of physical and verbal aggression on a plastic, inflated Bobo doll. For example, the model hit the doll with a hammer, kicked it, and said, "Hit the Bobo doll!" and "Kick the Bobo doll!" A second group of children watched a model perform the same actions, but the presentation was on film. A third group watched an adult disguised as a cartoon figure behave like the models in the previous two conditions. A fourth group observed an adult model behaving in a nonaggressive manner, sitting quietly and ignoring the Bobo doll and the toys associated with aggressive behavior. The last group of children saw no model at all.

Figure 16.3 shows the mean number of aggressive responses displayed by children in each condition. Children who had seen an aggressive model performed a large number of imitative aggressive acts, copying even the subtle details of the model's behaviors. In addition, they frequently added their own forms of physical and verbal aggression. Moreover, the performance of children in the film-model group was no different from that of children who saw the real-life model. Models on film were just as powerful as "live" models in eliciting aggression.

Field experiments and large-scale correlational studies add to the evidence connecting violence on television with aggression. Lynette Friedrich and Aletha Stein (1973) found that preschool children who viewed violent cartoons declined on several measures of self-control, including the ability to tolerate delays, obedience to school rules, and task perseverance. At the same time, children who saw prosocial programs displayed higher tolerance for delays, more rule obedience, and greater task perseverance than control children. One study of almost one thousand children showed that aggression and televised violence are actually linked in a reciprocal way (Huesmann, Lagerspetz, & Eron, 1984). The investigators asked each child's peers to rate how aggressive the child was, and they also noted how much television violence each child watched. The number of violent TV shows children watched at the start of the study predicted how aggressive they were three years later. In turn, aggression also influenced TV viewing. Children who were aggressive at the start of the study watched more violent shows three years later than they did initially. The findings are consistent with a bidirectional model of influence: children become more aggressive after a diet of violent television, and their aggression seems to stimulate even more viewing of violent shows. The tendency to view high amounts of violence as preschoolers correlates not only with more aggression in adolescence but also with poorer academic success (D. R. Anderson et al., 2001).

> **KEY THEME**
> **Interaction Among Domains**

Can parents do anything to mitigate the potentially harmful consequences of certain television shows on their children's behavior? One obvious tactic is to limit the amount of time children are permitted to watch violent programs. Another is to suggest prosocial methods of conflict resolution when violence is displayed (Dorr, 1986). In a school-based intervention program, 170 children who frequently watched violent programs were divided into an experimental and a control group. During a period of six to eight weeks, children in the experimental group participated in regular training sessions in which they were taught, after watching high-action, "superhero" shows, that (1) the behaviors of aggressive TV characters are not representative of the way most people act, (2) aggressive scenes on TV are not real but are staged by means of special effects and camera techniques, and (3) the average person uses more positive strategies to resolve interpersonal problems than those shown on violent TV programs. During the same time period, control participants saw nonviolent shows and engaged in neutral discussions. By the end of the study, children in the experimental group were significantly less aggressive than the control children, demonstrating that the real-life behaviors of children can be modified by effecting changes in their attitudes about television (Huesmann et al., 1983).

● **Prosocial Behavior**　Just as television can encourage negative social behaviors, it can foster prosocial development. Friedrich and Stein (1973) found that children who watched *Mister Rogers' Neighborhood* for a four-week period showed increases in prosocial interpersonal behaviors. Other researchers have also found that programs that contain messages about cooperation, altruism, and sharing promote these behaviors in children (Sprafkin, Liebert, & Poulos, 1975). A meta-analysis of 190 studies of prosocial television indicates that such programs can have powerful effects. In fact, the statistical findings indicated that the effects of prosocial programming are even greater than the effects of antisocial programming on children's behavior (Hearold, 1986).

● **Gender Stereotypes**　Television does occasionally portray males and females in nontraditional roles: Fathers cook and care for their children, and women are employed outside the home. These programs, however, are not standard fare on commercial television. Working women, when they are shown, are likely to be employed in gender-typical roles (e.g., as secretaries and nurses); if they occupy positions of authority, they are often cast as villains (Huston & Alvarez, 1990). Consistent with stereotypes of female behavior, girls and women on television act nurturantly, passively, or emotionally. In contrast, males are more frequently the central characters of television shows, and they act forcefully, have more power and authority than women, and display reason rather than emotion (Lovdal, 1989; Signorielli, 1989). Portrayal of these gender stereotypes may be declining, but they continue to exist in much of television programming. Moreover, the greatest stereotyping tends to be found in programs aimed at children (Comstock, 1991; Signorielli, 1993).

Children's attention to these stereotypes very likely depends on other developmental changes children undergo. For example, five-year-old boys who demonstrate gender constancy (see the chapter titled "Gender") are more likely to watch male characters on television and prefer programs that contain a greater proportion of males than five-year-old boys who do not display gender constancy (Luecke-Aleksa et al., 1995). In addition, gender-constant boys are more likely to watch shows created for adult entertainment, particularly sports and action shows, than their counterparts who still do not exhibit gender constancy. This difference in viewing preferences does not seem to be linked to earlier maturity in other cognitive abilities.

In contrast, gender constancy in five-year-old girls has relatively little effect on their television preferences or viewing habits. Perhaps this sex difference reflects the greater attractiveness of male roles on much of television and, therefore, accounts for such programs' increased interest value for boys who have gained gender constancy. Alternatively, perhaps this sex difference reflects a lessened need on the part of girls to exploit television as a basis for gender-role differentiation.

● **Ethnic Considerations**   The characters on American television are predominantly white. African Americans are occasionally shown, but Hispanic, Asian, and Native American individuals are rarely seen (Greenberg & Brand, 1994). Unfortunately, this portrait applies even more strongly to commercial *entertainment* programs for children, although in both commercial and public *educational* programming for children about one-fourth to more than one-third of the characters are minorities, and minorities are becoming represented in increasing numbers on American television (Calvert, 1999). Relatively little research has been carried out to determine how important the representation of ethnic minorities may be to young children. However, African American young people tend to prefer to watch and identify with African American characters (Greenberg & Brand, 1994). The extent to which they do so has been found to be positively related to self-esteem (McDermott & Greenberg, 1984) and, in some cases, although not consistently, to positive attitudes about their own race (Graves, 1993).

● **Consumer Behavior**   Because of their tremendous spending power, either directly or through their parents, children are the targets of a significant number of television commercials. Of concern to many child advocates is the proliferation of television shows linked to specific toys (e.g., cartoon shows that portray the same characters as toys) and product endorsements for expensive items, such as athletic shoes, by popular sports figures and other celebrities, all of which put pressure on children to spend money.

Children do respond to the messages of commercials. For one thing, they frequently request the cereals and other foods they see advertised (Taras et al., 1989). By age three, children distinguish commercials from other programming, but they do not always recognize commercials as messages specifically intended to influence their behavior; four- and five-year-olds, for example, believe "commercials are to help and entertain you" (Ward, Reale, & Levinson, 1972). Young children are especially likely to confuse programs with commercials if toys or cartoon characters appear in both (Wilson & Weiss, 1992). It is usually not until children are eight years of age or older that they understand that commercials are intended to influence viewers' buying habits (Ward et al., 1972). Because young children are not able to critically evaluate the information presented to them in commercials, they may pressure their parents to purchase expensive toys and clothes, heavily sugared foods, and other products (Kunkel & Roberts, 1991).

In more recent years, controversy has swirled around the introduction of Channel One in public schools. This program consists of ten minutes of news and two minutes of commercials for products of interest to young people. If a school agrees to air these broadcasts to students, free televisions are provided. It has become a popular idea in American school systems; approximately 12,000 schools and an estimated 40 percent of children in grades six through twelve were viewing the program in 1995 (Wartella, 1995). In general, students seem to learn about current events from such programming, and it is liked by teachers and principals (Johnston, Brzezinski, & Anderman, 1994). But the commercials also are reported to be effective as well; students more positively evaluate and express greater interest in buying the products that are advertised (Brand & Greenberg, 1994). Other companies are providing school computer labs with free equipment in which the advertising is available on a small part of the screen continuously. In addition, based on information provided when the student logs on, these companies are collecting information about the age and gender of children working with the computer, as well as the kinds of Web sites they visit. Although schools are being provided with state-of-the-art computer facilities, critics worry about the potential invasion of privacy and the consequences of what could be interpreted as school-sanctioned commercialism from these kinds of arrangements.

RESEARCH APPLIED TO PARENTING

Encouraging Critical Skills in Television Viewing

Jeremy finished his homework just before his mother came home. Fortunately, there still was enough daylight for his best friend, Aaron, to come over for a visit. As soon as he arrived, the conversation turned to the afternoon's television fare. "Hey, did you see that movie on Channel 5? That car chase was awesome." "Yeah," Aaron replied. "But I really liked the way he jumped off the bridge before it blew up. He was lucky there weren't any alligators in the river!" "Huh? That was the least of his worries. There must have been twenty crooks trying to shoot him to get the money. I sure didn't think he was going to get away," Jeremy replied.

As we have seen, television holds enormous promise to enhance children's intellectual and social functioning. However, there is also clear evidence of potential dangers, especially when television viewing takes up much of a child's time or is directed at programs that are age inappropriate. Apart from the option not to have a television set available in the home (an alternative that relatively few parents defend), what steps might parents take to promote positive benefits from this medium? Any recommendations will, of course, depend on the maturity of the child, as well as the values caregivers wish to promote. However, developmental psychologists and others concerned about the influence of television on children generally agree with the following guidelines:

1. *Be aware of how much time is being spent watching television and what is being watched.* Parents may not always realize how much of the day their children spend in front of the television set, what they are watching, or how the program is affecting them. Continuous supervision may not be possible when parents are busy with other household duties or away at work. However, knowing what children are watching, and for how long, is the first step in understanding what they might be learning from television.

2. *Decide what is acceptable to watch.* Even very young children may be attracted to programming that is frightening or inappropriate, not because they necessarily enjoy it but because the rapid pace of events or some other convention of the programming is attracting their attention. Parents have the responsibility to determine which programs are permissible and ensure that children limit their television viewing to those programs. Recognize, however, that as children become older and more

The effects of television viewing on children's development
probably depend on the types
of programs watched, as well
as how much time is spent
in front of the television set.
When parents view television
programs along with their children, opportunities become
available for parents to promote a variety of critical skills
in their children's thinking.

independent, parental monitoring will be more difficult (Cantor & Wilson, 1988). Older
children must learn to take increasing responsibility for their own television viewing.

   3. *Establish acceptable times for watching television.*   Family members need to
know when they can watch television. For example, can the television be on during
the dinner hour? Is watching television permitted if homework, chores, or other obligations are not yet finished? How late in the evening is television viewing allowed?

   4. *Watch television with children whenever possible.*   When jointly watching programs with their children, parents have the opportunity to discuss such things as what
is real and what is fantasy, how conflict might be resolved other than through violence,
the stereotypes being portrayed, the goals of advertising, and many other issues presented through this medium that are valued or not approved within the household. In
addition, by commenting on the material, parents can stimulate vocabulary development and provide different perspectives that may promote cognitive and social skills.
Unfortunately, coviewing involving active discussion of television content appears to
be infrequent in most families (Huston & Wright, 1998).

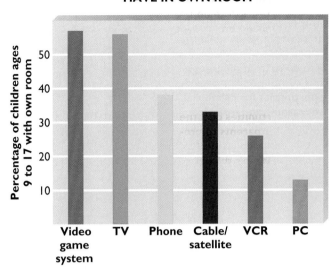

Source: Adapted from Nickelodeon/Yankelovich Youth Monitor™, 1999.

FOR YOUR REVIEW

- How much time do children of different ages spend viewing television? What kinds of programs are they attending to, and how are they watching them?

- What do children comprehend about television programming?

- How are cognitive and language development influenced by viewing television?

- What influences does television viewing have on social development?

- How might caregivers influence television viewing for their children?

Computers

Perhaps there is no more visible symbol of the technological age than the computer. Just as most adults in many countries are now likely to encounter computers in their daily experiences, so are children. For example, within the United States approximately 80 percent of children between the ages of six and eight years work with a computer in school. Furthermore, as can be seen in Figure 16.4, the availability of computers in the homes of school-age children in the United States has increased dramatically within the last few years (Nickelodeon/Yankelovich, 1999). The number of young people who have computers in their own rooms, compared with many other types of modern electronic equipment, remains relatively low (see Figure 16.4). Nevertheless, more than one-fourth of all children under age eighteen in the United States currently operate a home computer for educational and entertainment purposes, as well as for communicating with others. These percentages may not be too different for children in some other countries (Light, 1997). Nearly three-fourths of nine- to seventeen-year-olds who have computers in their homes use them for playing games (Nickelodeon/Yankelovich, 1999), and children spend the largest proportion of time on the computer in this activity (Roberts et al., 1999).

What is the effect of computers on children's development? Does experience with computers influence the ways children tackle problem solving and other cognitive tasks? Are young "keyboard junkies" who spend long hours glued to the video screen

FIGURE 16.4
Availability of Personal Computers and Other Technologies

The availability of personal computers to school-age children in the United States has increased dramatically over the past few years. Now more than half of American children between six and seventeen years of age have computers at home (see graph on left). Of the 80% of nine- to seventeen-year-olds who have their own rooms, many have computers in them, although they are still more likely to have other electronic equipment, such as a television, video game system, or telephone in their rooms (see graph on right).

The introduction of computers into the classroom may have some surprising benefits. For example, when children use computers in school, they often do so in small groups. Thus computers can provide opportunities for collaborative learning and may also promote socialization skills.

missing other critical experiences, particularly the social interactions crucial to their socioemotional development? The pervasive presence of computers in today's world makes these questions well worth exploring. The emerging answer is clear: there is no such thing as an "effect of computers" per se on child development. What matters, rather, is the way children use them (Behrman, 2000).

Academic Mastery and Cognition

The first relatively widespread use of computers in education began in the 1960s, when **computer-assisted instruction (CAI)** was touted as a valuable, efficient educational tool. CAI programs serve primarily to supplement classroom instruction, providing highly structured tutorial information along with drill-and-practice exercises in content areas such as mathematics and reading. Several principles are presumed to make CAI programs effective teaching tools. First, the child can work through a lesson at her own pace, reviewing topics if necessary. CAI thus provides an individually paced learning experience in which the content can be tailored to the specific needs of the student. Second, the child receives immediate feedback about the correctness of his responses to questions and exercises and may even receive periodic summaries of performance. Finally, CAI programs often employ sound effects and graphics designed to promote the child's attention to and interest in the material being presented.

How effective are CAI approaches to instruction? Meta-analyses of hundreds of studies have shown that on average, students with CAI experience improve in achievement test scores and that this effect is moderately strong (Lepper & Gurtner, 1989). CAI is especially effective with elementary school and special-needs children, who seem to profit most from individualized approaches to learning (Kulik, Kulik, & Bangert-Drowns, 1985; Niemiec & Walberg, 1987).

Newer educational software places less emphasis on rote memorization and more on providing children with opportunities to use higher-order thinking skills as they master academic subjects. To date, the effects of these efforts have been mixed (Roschelle et al., 2000). For example, math education programs designed to encour-

computer-assisted instruction (CAI) Use of computers to provide tutorial information and drill-and-practice routines.

age children to think more fully seem to have positive effects, whereas those that are oriented toward making repetitive math learning more fun seem to have no, and perhaps even detrimental, effects on learning (Wenglinsky, 1998). In general, however, the areas in which computer learning seems to have the greatest benefits are in science and mathematics (Roschelle et al., 2000). Being able to visualize and observe simulations of scientific concepts appears to encourage children to engage in levels of thinking generally more advanced than had been thought possible (Gordin & Pea, 1995; White & Fredriksen, 1998). Another factor associated with computers that may have powerful benefits is the opportunity to work on real-world problems that are available through the Internet. More specifically, with increased access to recently collected data from scientific research, children and adolescents can engage in the very same types of activities of experimentation, design, and reflection that scientists and researchers carry out in their efforts to make contributions to understanding the environment, society, and the physical and biological world.

Other major advantages of the computer, especially with Internet access, stem from the opportunity to learn about issues and topics that simply would not be available to most children any other way. For example, with very little investment, children can explore and even design art and music, choreograph dramatic scenes, acquire information about other cultures (both existing and extinct), and communicate with other peoples. They can also find others who share similar academic interests and activities. As a consequence of these opportunities, children become more willing to take on more difficult academic problems (Roschelle et al., 2000).

Among the cognitive skills that may be enhanced are spatial representation, iconic skills, and increased ability to attend to multiple events, as is often required in action game playing associated with the computer and video games (Subrahmanyam et al., 2001). The limited research carried out on the impact of computers on these abilities suggests positive effects (e.g., Greenfield, 1998; Greenfield & Cocking, 1996).

> **KEY THEME**
> Interaction Among Domains

Social Development

Contrary to popular opinion, the interactions a child has with the computer do not necessarily displace other activities of a more social nature, nor is computer use itself necessarily a solitary activity (Crook, 1992). In one survey of more than five hundred children, those with computers at home resembled nonowners in the frequency with which they visited friends, participated in club meetings, and engaged in sports (Lieberman, 1985). Furthermore, children who work on computer projects in school tend to collaborate and share ideas more in these settings than they do in other school activities (Hawkins et al., 1982). In one observation of four-year-olds who had a computer in their child care center, 63 percent of the time they spent at the computer was in joint participation with a peer and 70 percent of the interactions consisted of active sharing of the computer (Muller & Perlmutter, 1985). Thus, rather than inhibiting social interactions, computer activities may actually promote them, especially when teachers encourage group problem solving as opposed to individual projects (Bergin, Ford, & Hess, 1993).

> **KEY THEME**
> Interaction Among Domains

Older children and adolescents do spend much of their time at the computer alone. Adolescents who put in relatively large amounts of time on the computer—for example, more than two hours a day—report fewer and poorer social interactions with parents and friends (Sanders et al., 2000). Nevertheless, a substantial portion of children's involvement with the computer, especially after it is no longer a novelty in the home, is devoted to communicating and maintaining social relationships with others via e-mail, instant messaging, playing games with others, or in chat rooms (Subrahmanyam et al., 2000; Subrahmanyam et al., 2001). Of course, one major concern is what kinds of social interactions may be occurring during some of these on-line activities, especially with individuals with whom the young person is not acquainted.

Sex Differences

Ask children ranging from kindergarten age to twelfth grade to rate the word *computer* on a scale labeled M (for "male") at one end and F (for "female") at the other. Ask them also to rate how much they like the item. Researchers who have followed these and other procedures have found that children place computers toward the "male" side of the rating scale. In general, boys like computers more than girls do (Culley, 1993), and children sometimes perceive school computers as "belonging more" to boys (Cassell & Jenkins, 1998). Yet these gender differences are apparent primarily at the elementary and high school levels and are not present at younger ages; preschoolers and kindergartners are much less likely to display these stereotypes, at least with respect to interest in the computer (Bergin et al., 1993; Collis & Ollila, 1990; Krendl & Broihier, 1992). Moreover, the gender gap appears to be narrowing; girls now indicate that they use their home computers as much as boys do (Subrahmanyam et al., 2000). And boys and girls use the Internet about equally often, although the sites they access may differ (Clark, 2001). New computer games designed for girls have helped to reduce the disparity (Subrahmanyam & Greenfield, 1998), as has the increasing availability of web sites responsive to girls' interests (Subrahmanyam et al., 2000).

CONTROVERSY: THINKING IT OVER

What Regulations Should Exist for Children's Access to the Internet?

With the emergence of new technologies often come new challenges and dilemmas for parents and society. Because computers and the Internet have become such a prevalent part of the environment for many children, this new resource has generated its own set of controversies.

What Is the Controversy?

As we have just seen, many positive advantages can exist for children using the Internet. These benefits may come from being able to move from one site to another in exploring or addressing a question and in obtaining in-depth information about a topic. But readily accessible sites may provide access to some material not considered appropriate for children, including ways to engage in violent activity, information from groups that promote hatred and bigotry, and sexually explicit imagery. Children also may be constantly bombarded with advertising and other images that can promote certain points of view that children have difficulty understanding and that parents may find objectionable.

What Are the Opposing Arguments?

The issues related to this matter bear closely on questions of free speech and rights to information. Few would argue in support of the unfettered availability to children of some types of material. Parents can take steps in limiting their children's exposure to unacceptable information in the home. However, applying the same restrictions to the schools and, particularly, to children's access to the Internet in public libraries or other public places may be far more difficult. Should filters and blocking devices be installed on computers in these publicly accessible locations as well? Would such restrictions be inappropriate in public facilities given that they interfere with the rights of adults? Still others are concerned that efforts to regulate public sites, and even efforts by parents in the home, may promote a false sense of security among caregivers that overlooks the myriad ways in which inappropriate material can become available to their children via the computer.

Other debates arise over how to determine when it becomes reasonable for children and adolescents to have access to various kinds of information—for example, in cases in which a young person (and his or her parents) may feel uncomfortable or unwilling to discuss sexuality with their children. The timetable for such access may differ considerably depending on a child's age, the parents' beliefs about such matters, and community standards (National Research Council and Institute of Medicine, 2001). Additionally, young people must ultimately learn to engage in responsible use of the Internet, an educational goal that could receive little attention when parents and others rely on filters or blocking devices to monitor web site activity.

What Answers Exist? What Questions Remain?

Parents may need to become more fully aware of how their children are using the computer. For example, whereas only 30 percent of parents think their adolescent children have ever corresponded with a stranger via e-mail, more than 50 percent of teenagers report having done so. Moreover, whereas only 17 percent of parents believe that their teenage children have provided personal information over the computer, 45 percent of young people report having done so (Penn, Schoen, & Berland Associates, 2000). In addition, little research exists on what children are actually viewing on the Internet. Perhaps it would also be valuable to establish web sites to offer balanced and healthy information on topics about which young people might otherwise search for and find more controversial material. There is also a growing need for psychologists and educators to develop programs to teach children and adolescents about appropriate on-line computer usage. Indeed, in order to address the question about what regulations are needed for children's access to the Internet, perhaps it is important to first ask to what extent *mentoring* or *monitoring* is needed to effectively deal with the problem (National Research Council and Institute of Medicine, 2001).

FOR YOUR REVIEW

- How has computer use changed over the past several decades?

- What benefits do computers provide in the mastery of academic material? What has been their impact on social development?

- How do boys and girls differ in their use of and attitudes toward computers?

- What controversies exist concerning children's access to computers?

School

The main aim of education is to provide children with the skills necessary to function as independent, responsible, and contributing members of society. Schools reinforce cultural practices for how to get things done (Matusov, Bell, & Rogoff, 2002). Academic accomplishment and the development of cognitive skills are the chief points of emphasis. For example, school experience cultivates rote memory, classification, and logical reasoning (Morrison, Smith, & Dow-Ehrensberger, 1995; Rogoff, 1981). One especially important goal of schooling is the development of literacy, the ability to read and write using the symbol system of the culture's language. Literacy is virtually a prerequisite for survival in most societies; more and more jobs in the professional and technical sectors require not only reading and writing skills but also the ability to communicate, reason, and apply mathematical and scientific concepts (Jackson & Hornbeck, 1989). Yet as we discussed in the chapter titled "Cognition: Piaget and Vygotsky," societies vary in the extent to which they stress the experience of formal schooling; rural and agrarian subcultures in some countries, for example, do not have compulsory schooling.

FIGURE 16.5
High School Completion
Rates in the United States

Although the percentage
of young adults who have
completed high school has
remained relatively stable in
the United States since 1980,
the greatest gains in completion rates have been made
in young adults of Hispanic
origin. However, this group
still remains below African
Americans, who, in turn, fall
below Caucasians in percentage completing high school.

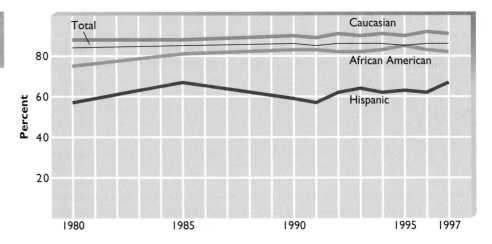

Note: Because of changes in the survey questionnaire and data collection methodology beginning in 1994,
percentages for earlier years may not be strictly comparable. Percentages are not shown separately for
non-Hispanic Asians/Pacific Islanders and American Indians/Alaska Natives, but they are included in the total.
Sources: Kaufman, Klein, & Frase, 1999; U.S. Bureau of the Census (various years).

In some measure, most children in the United States and many other countries
attain the basic goals educators and parents have set for academic achievement in
school. For example, in the United States between 1980 and 1997 approximately 85
percent of young adults had completed high school. However, these completion
rates are not the same for young adults of different ethnic backgrounds, as can be
seen in Figure 16.5.

How well are children learning in schools? Major national surveys often conclude
that academic achievement among American students is not high and compares un-
favorably with that of students from other industrialized countries. For example, by
age seventeen, less than half of American students are able to read and understand
complicated information (Gonzales et al., 2000), although no comparison with
other countries exists for this kind of information. However, the United States ranks
below many countries in student performance on tests in science and mathematics,
as indicated by the results of the Third International Mathematics and Science
Study (TIMSS). This research project has included evaluations of academic performance by fourth-graders and twelfth-graders, as well as for eighth-graders
whose relative level of performance is shown in Figure 16.6. Because children in
many East Asian and European nations perform better than those in the United
States, the findings are among those that have created enormous concern about the
adequacy of our educational system. Major improvements in the United States educational system may be needed, but a closer look at the methodologies used in studies involving international comparisons is also worthwhile for explaining some of
the findings.

EXAMINING RESEARCH METHODS

Interpreting Cross-Cultural Test Results

To many in the United States who take great pride in this country's scientific
accomplishments, and where considerable sums of money are expended on education (Vogel, 1996), the results of cross-cultural comparisons involving TIMSS and
other projects are both alarming and perplexing. Have American schools shirked
their commitment to academic excellence? Has the educational system failed? What
steps must be carried out to improve competence in these, and perhaps other, subject areas? Or are there other possible explanations for why nations rank high or low
on such tests?

MATHEMATICS		SCIENCE	
Nation	**Average**	**Nation**	**Average**
Singapore	604	Chinese Taipei	569
Korea, Republic of	587	Singapore	568
Chinese Taipei	585	Hungary	552
Hong Kong SAR	582	Japan	550
Japan	579	Korea, Republic of	549
Belgium-Flemish	558	Netherlands	545
Netherlands	540	Australia	540
Slovak Republic	534	Czech Republic	539
Hungary	532	England	538
Canada	531	Finland	535
Slovenia	530	Slovak Republic	535
Russian Federation	526	Belgium-Flemish	535
Australia	525	Slovenia	533
Finland[a]	520	Canada	533
Czech Republic	520	Hong Kong SAR	530
Malaysia	519	Russian Federation	529
Bulgaria	511	Bulgaria	518
Latvia-LSS[b]	505	**United States**	**515**
United States	**502**	New Zealand	510
England	496	Latvia-LSS[b]	503
New Zealand	491		
Lithuania[c]	482	Italy	493
Italy	479	Malaysia	492
Cyprus	476	Lithuania[c]	488
Romania	472	Thailand	482
Moldova	469	Romania	472
Thailand	467	(Israel)	468
(Israel)	466	Cyprus	460
Tunisia	448	Moldova	459
Macedonia, Republic of	447	Macedonia, Republic of	458
Turkey	429	Jordan	450
Jordan	428	Iran, Islamic Republic of	448
Iran, Islamic Republic of	422	Indonesia	435
Indonesia	403	Turkey	433
Chile	392	Tunisia	430
Philippines	345	Chile	420
Morocco	337	Philippines	345
South Africa	275	Morocco	323
		South Africa	243
International average of 38 nations	487	International average of 38 nations	488

FIGURE 16.6
Average Mathematics and Science Achievement Scores, 1999.

This table presents the average scores of eighth-graders for the thirty-eight nations included in the Third International Mathematics and Science Study. Although these findings typically receive considerable interest from politicians, educators, and others, the methodological problems that often accompany comparisons of performance by young people from different nations may be substantial, and the policy implications for education are not always clear.

■ Average is significantly higher than the U.S. average

■ Average does not differ significantly from the U.S. average

Average is significantly lower than the U.S. average

Note: Eighth grade in most nations. Parentheses indicate nations not meeting international sampling and/or other guidelines. The international average is the average of the national averages of the thirty-eight nations.

[a] The shading of Finland may appear incorrect; however, statistically, its placement is correct.
[b] Designated LSS because only Latvian-speaking schools were tested, which represents 61 percent of the population.
[c] Lithuania tested the same cohort of students as other nations, but later in 1999, at the beginning of the next school year.

Source: Gonzales et al., 2000.

Cross-cultural research is exceedingly difficult. No matter what issue is under investigation, translating a questionnaire or research task so that it asks an equivalent question in different languages or is understood with the same meaning by participants whose customs differ is not always a certainty. Good research projects go to great lengths to overcome these problems. However, other obstacles to sound research involving large-scale international research projects such as TIMSS may be far more difficult to manage.

One question is how to obtain equivalent populations of students for participation. For example, in comparing the performance of twelfth-graders, in which students in the United States did not do well, drop-out rates need to be considered. Because individuals leaving school before completion of the twelfth grade might be expected to score generally lower on the tests than students who complete their high school education, nations who have a higher proportion of their students remaining in school in this grade could be penalized. The difficulty of equating the proportion of the eligible population taking part in a study, however, is not unique to cross-cultural research. For example, in the United States, the lowest average SAT scores tend to be reported in those states that have the highest proportion of students taking the exam (Rotberg, 1998).

Another issue relating to the population tested is the age of the participants and the number of years, as well as types, of schooling they have received. In the case of the TIMSS project, some participants, depending on the age at which they entered the educational system, had received from ten to fourteen years of formal schooling before completing the twelfth-grade exam; moreover, the countries that scored highest tended to have older students (Rotberg, 1998). And although great effort was made to include participants from all kinds of schools, countries differed in their inclusion of students from vocational schools, apprenticeship programs, and private schools. Because of these differences, the proportion of children representing different socioeconomic backgrounds may not be equivalent across the various countries. Nor would it be easy to equate for such factors, because nations vary tremendously in the types of schooling available to their children, as well as in their standards of living. Information may not be available to take steps to statistically control for these types of differences, making comparisons even more difficult to interpret.

A final concern with respect to the TIMSS project is that no information was provided concerning curricula instituted in the educational programs of various nations. Children in the United States, for example, scored relatively well on science when tested at the third and fourth grades (Vogel, 1997). But that may be because science education begins in this country's schools much earlier than it does in many other countries. In contrast, by eighth grade, for example, children in schools in other countries are tackling algebra and geometry, whereas in the United States they are often still covering arithmetic.

Thus issues relating to student preparation, as well as methodological problems associated with selectivity, representation, and other characteristics of the student sample, only compound the problem of making meaningful sense of the data. Are international tests really the best way to compare children's competencies with respect to math, science, or any other subject matter? At present, they are one of the few ways of doing so. But could a nation's scientific and technological education efforts be evaluated more effectively using other measures of success (Gibbs & Fox, 1999)? Perhaps a good place to begin is by identifying those factors within the curriculum that contribute to high performance in children regardless of where they are being educated (Rotberg, 1998).

KEY THEME
Interaction Among Domains

Families and Peers as Agents Mediating School Achievement

Several factors aside from aspects of the school curriculum itself are associated with academic success. Not surprisingly, parents are of paramount importance. Consider,

FIGURE 16.7 A Model of Parental Influences on Children's Academic Achievement

One model of children's academic achievement suggests that parental involvement and support of children's autonomy predict children's "inner resources." These resources include children's feelings of control, competence, and autonomy. These characteristics, in turn, predict academic achievement. Research has found support for the major elements of this model.

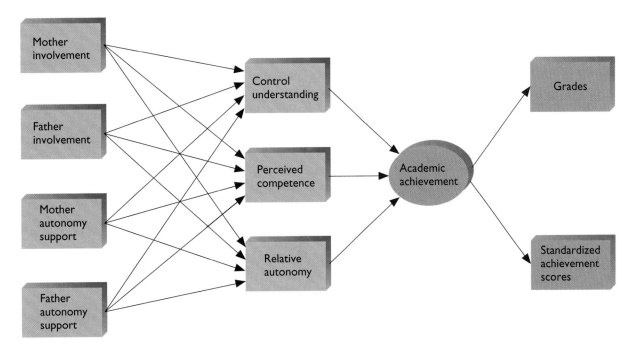

Source: Grolnick, Ryan, & Deci, 1991.

for example, a model proposed by Wendy Grolnick and her colleagues (Grolnick, Ryan, & Deci, 1991) and illustrated in Figure 16.7. According to these researchers, parental support for their children's autonomy (e.g., encouraging independent decision making) and involvement with their children (such as spending time talking with them about the children's problems) are related to the strength of children's "inner resources." That is, children develop feelings of competence, autonomy, and control, which in turn influence academic performance. To test these ideas, the researchers measured both parental and child qualities that were components of the model, as well as children's academic success. Using sophisticated statistical techniques, they were able to show the relationships they had predicted. Other researchers have confirmed that authoritative parenting (characterized by warmth and extensive verbal explanation) and the social support parents provide predict, at least indirectly, exactly how well children will do in school during middle childhood and adolescence (DeBaryshe, Patterson, & Capaldi, 1993; Dubow et al., 1991; Steinberg et al., 1992). Frequent transitions in parenting (e.g., divorce and remarriage followed by another divorce) and a more discordant family climate are also related to less positive outcomes in school (Kurdek, Fine, & Sinclair, 1995).

Peers make a difference, too. As early as fourth grade, children tend to sort themselves into groups that have different levels of school motivation, and children who are members of a particular group at the start of the school year become even more aligned with the group's motivation level by the end of this period (Kindermann, 1993). For example, when a student at the beginning of the school year has friends who consider themselves disruptive in school, that student will begin to demonstrate more disruptive behavior as the school year progresses (Berndt & Keefe, 1995).

Peers may also enhance or offset the effects of different parenting styles on children's academic achievement. Laurence Steinberg and his associates found that among Asian American adolescents, for example, peer support for academic excellence lessened the negative effects of authoritarian parenting on academic achievement. For Caucasian adolescents, peer support for achievement complemented parents' tendency to be authoritative (Steinberg, Dornbusch, & Brown, 1992). A supportive family context may be an important factor in encouraging children to gain the interpersonal and cognitive skills that will lead to interactions with peers who promote academic success in the first place (Kurdek et al., 1995; Steinberg, 1996).

The availability of a mentor can also be an important contributor to success in the schools for adolescents. For example, research on Big Brother and Big Sister programs has revealed a positive influence on grades, attendance, and perceived competence with respect to academic subjects (Grossman & Tierney, 1998). Perhaps a bit surprising, however, is that many of these benefits seemed to be mediated by adolescents establishing better parental relationships rather than as a direct consequence of the mentor's activities with the student (Rhodes, Grossman, & Resch, 2000).

Still another factor that can affect academic performance of older children is whether they hold jobs before or after school. In general, adolescents who work more than fifteen to twenty hours per week attain poorer grades and show less commitment to school than adolescents who work fewer hours or not at all (Steinberg et al., 1982; Steinberg, Fegley, & Dornbusch, 1993).

School and Classroom Size

Schools can vary substantially in their organization and structure. Although the one-room classroom is rarely found today, schools can be large or small depending on the community, and they are likely to increase in size in the upper grades. Some children may also attend crowded classrooms, thus limiting the amount of time teachers can spend with each child. What are some of the effects of these factors on children's achievement?

KEY THEME
Child's Active Role

● **School Size** Although some controversy surrounds the importance of school size, any significant effects researchers have found usually favor students from smaller schools (Moore & Lackney, 1993; Rutter, 1983b). In a major study of thirteen high schools ranging in size from thirteen to more than two thousand students, researchers noted that students from smaller schools were less alienated, participated more in school activities, felt more competent, and found themselves more challenged (Barker & Gump, 1964). Students in smaller schools may need to fill more roles, particularly leadership roles such as editing the school newspaper or being captain of the band, for which positive feedback from parents, teachers, and peers is received. They are also likely to identify strongly with the school and develop a greater sense of personal control and responsibility. Furthermore, participating in school-based extracurricular programs seems to reduce the likelihood that young people will drop out of school, especially among those who are less academically competitive (Mahoney & Cairns, 1997).

● **Class Size** Class size is another important aspect of school structure. Many countries around the world, as well as numerous states within the United States, have invested huge amounts of money to reduce class size (Ehrenberg et al., 2001b). For example, the number of students per teacher in elementary school classrooms in the United States has fallen from 25.1 to 18.3 over the past three decades; a similar decrease, from 19.7 to 14.0, has occurred in secondary schools (Ehrenberg et al., 2001b). Although research has not always revealed a consistent benefit from such efforts, the general consensus is that children in small classes, especially in the earlier grades, show academic advances over children in large classes (Ehrenberg et al., 2001a). Perhaps the most influential of these studies was carried out in Tennessee and involved seventy-six schools. Kindergarten children and teachers were randomly assigned to classes of dif-

Many factors can influence children's success in school. Encouraging boys and girls to be engaged in classroom activities is one important factor. Perhaps because teachers can retain their attention more effectively, students in classrooms with fewer numbers of children seem to do better academically than students in classrooms with higher numbers of classmates.

ferent sizes (thirteen to seventeen versus twenty-two to twenty-five pupils per class). By the end of first grade, children in the small classes showed marked improvement in performance on standardized tests of reading and mathematics compared with children from regular-size classes. The benefits of small classes were especially pronounced for minority children (Finn & Achilles, 1990).

The long-term consequences of smaller class size have also been investigated. Children in small classes in kindergarten through third grade in the Tennessee study continued to do better than their classmates assigned to larger classes, even after entering regular-size classrooms beginning in fourth grade (Mosteller, 1995). The benefits of the smaller-class experience were exhibited by children in later grades as well. Moreover, when small class sizes were introduced to the poorest districts in the state, children in these districts moved from displaying reading and mathematics scores that were well below average to scores above average for the state.

Why do smaller classes work? For one thing, teachers probably have greater enthusiasm and higher morale when they are not burdened with large numbers of students. Teachers also have more time to spend with individual children, and students are more likely to be attentive and engaged in classroom activities and show fewer behavioral problems in small classes (Finn & Achilles, 1990; Mosteller, 1995). But it is likely that benefits of reduced class size emerge only when teachers are trained to take advantage of the opportunities of working with smaller numbers of students (Bennett, 1998; Ehrenberg et al., 2001a, 2001b).

School Transitions

In addition to the size of the school and the classroom, the school transitions children are expected to make at specific ages may influence development. Most children begin kindergarten at age five or six, and the way in which they adjust to this first experience of school frequently determines how much they will like later grades. A second important transition occurs in adolescence, when entering junior or senior high school makes new academic and social demands on them.

● **Starting School** Few occasions in a child's life are as momentous as the first day of school. Parents typically find this a time of mixed emotions, of eager anticipation about the child's future accomplishments coupled with anxieties about whether school will provide positive and rewarding experiences for their child. Children have many major adjustments to handle, including accommodating to a teacher and a new physical environment, making new friends, and mastering new academic challenges. Success in making the initial transition to school can set the tone for later academic and socioemotional development.

Not surprisingly, children who bring to school certain entry-level skills, such as a battery of positive social behaviors (e.g., cooperativeness in their preschool play or friendliness in their interactions with peers), and who exhibit cognitive and linguistic maturity (e.g., ability to engage in or be ready for school-related activities as a result of preschool and family experiences) do better in kindergarten (Entwisle, 1995; Ladd, Birch, & Buhs, 1999; Ladd & Price, 1987). Gary Ladd and his colleagues (Ladd et al., 1999), testing several hundred kindergartners throughout the school year, found that positive behavioral orientations exhibited by children in the first weeks of kindergarten fostered the formation of friendships and peer acceptance, whereas antisocial behaviors resulted in children being less liked by peers over the year and having greater conflict with teachers. Cognitive and linguistic maturity directly facilitated classroom participation and higher achievement. In addition, classroom participation, which ultimately plays an important part in contributing to achievement in kindergarten, was influenced by the relationships children established with their peers and their teachers. The negative qualities displayed by some children (lack of friends, peer rejection, poor teacher-child relationship) seemed to be increasingly detrimental for adjustment to this new environment (Ladd et al., 1999). These findings confirm that many factors working within the school, as well as the qualities children bring to the school environment, affect their early academic success.

The presence of familiar peers in the kindergarten classroom also facilitates peer acceptance (Ladd & Price, 1987) and is related to more positive attitudes toward school and fewer anxieties at the start of the school year. In general, factors promoting continuity between the preschool and kindergarten experiences seem beneficial to the child's adjustment, suggesting that parents should consider ways to foster their children's friendships with peers who will be future classmates. These results underscore the fact that the transition to school can be a particularly crucial time and that successes in one domain, peer relations, are related to successes in another, competence in school.

Another major controversy that surrounds this first school transition is the age of the child upon school entry. Some researchers claim the younger members of the classroom do not perform as well academically as the older members and continue to have difficulty in the later school years (Breznitz & Teltsch, 1989; May, Kundert, & Brent, 1995). Others, however, have pointed out methodological and other problems in this research and have failed to find evidence that younger and older children in the classroom differ in any meaningful way (Alexander & Entwisle, 1988; Shepard & Smith, 1986). Frederick Morrison and his colleagues have carried out further work on this issue with Canadian schoolchildren (Morrison, Griffith, & Alberts, 1997). They found that younger children do tend to score below older children on reading and mathematics achievement tests at the end of the school year. However, the same is true even at the beginning of the school year. In fact, when measures of progress in reading and mathematics were used as the criteria, younger first-graders gained just as much as older first-graders did. Furthermore, the first-graders, whether younger or older, gained more than children who remained in kindergarten but could have been enrolled in first grade. Although additional research needs to be carried out, these findings suggest that entrance age by itself may not be an important factor in academic progress and that children should not be delayed in entering school on that basis alone.

● **A Second Transition: Junior High**   Another important transition occurs later in many children's schooling careers, when they move from elementary school to a middle or junior high school. In the United States, this transition is usually the visible signal of childhood's end and the beginning of adolescence. Once again children must adapt to a new physical environment, new teachers, and, often, new peers; and

Entry into junior high or middle school is a source of new opportunities for learning, as well as new challenges and difficulties. In making the change, students such as these in the school cafeteria often find themselves in a much larger school and as a result may need to build new friendships.

now, rather than staying with the same classmates in the same room for most of the school day, they move from class to class, each usually with its own set of students. Frequently the difference in student body size is dramatic. In one study, the mean school size from grade six to grade seven increased from 466 to 1,307, and the mean number of children in each grade went from 59 to 403 (Simmons et al., 1987). It is no wonder that many researchers report a decline in school satisfaction and academic motivation in pre- and early adolescence, as well as a drop in grades and participation in extracurricular activities (Eccles, Midgley, et al., 1993; Hirsch & Rapkin, 1987; Schulenberg, Asp, & Petersen, 1984; Simmons & Blyth, 1987).

Some researchers have also observed a decline in self-esteem at this time, particularly among preadolescent girls, and an increase in physical complaints (Hirsch & Rapkin, 1987; Simmons et al., 1979). Early-maturing sixth-grade girls display better images of themselves when they attend schools with kindergarten through eighth-grade classes, presumably because they feel less pressured to adopt dating and other activities that become prevalent among seventh- and eighth-graders. On the other hand, those girls entering puberty at more typical ages and at about the same time at which they enter a new school program or undergo other significant transitions tend to have lower self-images and more difficulties in school, possibly because multiple changes in life are difficult to handle (Simmons et al., 1987). Boys and girls who feel they have little control over their academic progress and are less personally invested in succeeding in school also benefit by not having to undergo a school transition between fifth and sixth grades (Rudolph et al., 2001).

For some adolescents, the difficulties encountered during school transitions continue to be reflected in lower self-esteem, high levels of depression, and greater drug and alcohol use through the later school years (Rudolph et al., 2001). These difficulties may even set in motion a pattern of academic decline that leads them to drop out of school (Eccles et al., 1997; Eccles & Midgley, 1989). Perhaps school transitions do not fit the specific developmental needs of many preadolescents. At a time during which youngsters seek stronger peer associations and a supportive climate for resolving identity issues, they confront an educational environment that is more impersonal than elementary school and fragments peer relationships. Compared with elementary school, junior high school classrooms also tend to emphasize greater teacher control and discipline, offer fewer personal and positive teacher-student interactions, use a

KEY THEME
Interaction Among Domains

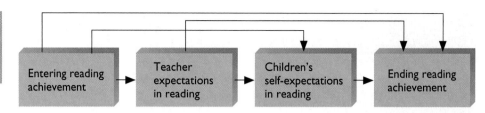

Source: Kuklinski & Weinstein, 2001, p. 1557.

FIGURE 16.8
Teacher Expectancy Effects
on Children's Reading
Achievement

**Teacher expectancies may
not only have a direct effect
on reading achievement but
can also influence behavior
by modifying children's own
expectations for themselves, as
this model suggests. Margaret
Kuklinsky and Rhona Weinstein
(2001) obtained support for this
model, especially in classrooms
in which teacher expectancies
could be recognized easily by
children. The impact of the
children's own self-perceptions
pertain-ing to reading, as influenced by teacher expectations,
was especially evident when
children were in fifth grade but
far less evident in earlier
grades.**

**WHAT DO
YOU THINK?**

**Is Classroom Tracking
Beneficial?**
psychology.college.hmco.com

higher standard of evaluating student competence while focusing on more public eval-uation of the quality of work, and can often be less cognitively challenging as class-rooms become more teacher directed and provide fewer opportunities for student-initiated learning (Eccles, Midgley, et al., 1993; Eccles & Roeser, 1999).

What happens when alternatives to the traditional junior high school and high school structures are instituted? When teachers offer greater academic and personal counseling, contact parents when students are absent, and encourage communication with parents and when students are assigned to classes with many of the same class-mates, students show higher levels of academic success, less psychological dysfunction, and a substantially lower school dropout rate than students who experience more tra-ditional school changes (Felner & Adan, 1988; Felner, Ginter, & Primavera, 1982).

Teachers: Key Agents of Influence

No single factor in the school experience plays a more critical role in student achieve-ment and self-esteem than teachers. The expectations teachers have of students, their classroom management strategies, and the climate they create in the classroom are all major elements in student success or failure.

● **The Role of Expectations**   A highly publicized study by Robert Rosenthal and Lenore Jacobson (1968) documented how teachers' expectations of students' per-formance can affect students' actual attainments. The researchers told teachers that certain elementary school children could be expected to show sudden gains in intel-lectual skills during the course of the school year based on their scores on an IQ test administered at the beginning of the term. In reality, the students they designated as "rapid bloomers" were chosen randomly. An IQ test administered at the end of the school year revealed that the targeted children indeed showed significantly greater improvement than other students in the class, an outcome called the *Pygmalion ef-fect*. The investigators explained the findings by suggesting that teachers somehow treated the targeted children differently based on their beliefs about the children's in-tellectual potential, thereby creating a self-fulfilling prophecy.

Differing expectations, especially when they are clearly evident to students, have consequences for achievement, as well. Margaret Kuklinski and Rhona Weinstein (2001) looked at children in grades one through five to determine whether teacher expectations affected performance on reading achievement. As Figure 16.8 suggests, the researchers anticipated that teacher expectations about reading ability would in-fluence not only achievement in reading at the end of the school year but also the children's own self-perceptions of their reading ability. These self-perceptions would, in turn, also influence their reading achievement. The results of the study generally supported these hypotheses, especially in classrooms in which teacher expectations were more readily apparent to children, although children's self-perceptions tended not to become a factor until they reached the fifth grade.

Other studies have confirmed that high achievers *are* treated differently in the classroom by many teachers; they are given more opportunities to participate, given more time to answer questions, receive more praise for being correct, and receive less criticism than lower achievers (Minuchin & Shapiro, 1983). In other words, the class-

One of the most important factors in a child's school experience is teacher encouragement. This boy is receiving the kind of assistance with writing that will promote learning. Effective teachers are involved in all phases of instruction, provide clear feedback, and create a positive emotional climate in the classroom.

room climate is most supportive for those who have already demonstrated success, whereas those who most need the teacher's attention and encouragement may actually get it least.

● **Classroom Management Strategies**   Students achieve most in school when their teachers maximize the time spent in actual learning. This statement may seem obvious, but not all school time is spent in direct instruction. Effective teachers plan their lessons well, monitor the entire classroom continuously, minimize the time spent in disciplining children who misbehave, and keep transitions between activities brief and smooth (Brophy, 1986). They make sure there is little "dead time" in the classroom when students are unoccupied, and they keep the focus on instruction.

Another key ingredient in a teacher's success is active involvement in the learning process. This means teachers remain personally involved in every phase of instruction, from the initial presentation of a new lesson to supervising the individual work of students. *Involvement* also refers to the teacher's enjoyment and knowledge of students. Even when students are working in groups, teachers who guide the discussion or progress of the group will foster higher levels of mastery and greater feelings of competence than those who leave students completely on their own (Brophy, 1986; Skinner & Belmont, 1993). Effective teachers also provide students with clear feedback on the quality of their performance and on what is expected of them (Rutter, 1983).

Creating peer-centered learning experiences can be an effective means of involving students in the educational enterprise of the school. In studies of **cooperative learning,** students work in groups rather than individually to solve academic problems. These groups, for example, may consist of four or five students, some boys and some girls, with a range of abilities and from diverse backgrounds. The teacher is usually instrumental in introducing a topic or set of materials, but then the team members work and study together on the problems, quizzing one another until they decide collectively that they understand the unit. Cooperative learning has been found to increase affiliations among students from diverse backgrounds (e.g., cross-racial friendships), improve self-esteem, and produce more favorable attitudes toward academic achievement (Slavin, 1990).

As an illustration of the effectiveness of cooperative learning, Hanna Shachar and Shlomo Sharan (1994) compared the communication and achievement skills of 197 eighth-graders assigned to cooperative learning classrooms in history and geography with those of 154 students in classrooms taught by traditional teacher-led methods.

cooperative learning   Peer-centered learning experience in which students work together in small groups to solve academic problems.

An important form of learning is *cooperative learning,* in which small groups of students work together. The four students participating in this project can learn a great deal from each other. Students engaged in cooperative learning, compared with those who receive more traditional methods of instruction, often display significantly higher performance in subject matters on which they work as a group.

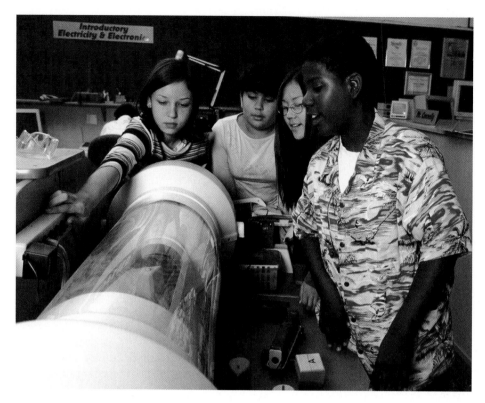

The study, carried out in Israel, included Jewish students from Western and Middle Eastern backgrounds. The classes were taught for six months. The cooperative learning groups were reconstituted several times throughout the year to give students the opportunity to work with a number of different peers. At the end of the year, a video-taped discussion of a topic in history and geography involving six-person groups revealed that those who participated in cooperative learning expressed themselves more frequently, were more likely to take a personal position and expand on the ideas brought up by another student, and were less likely to interrupt their peers than students who participated in traditional classrooms. The gains in communication skills were especially great for Middle Eastern students; those with this background who came from the traditional classroom were far less likely to express themselves than their peers from Western backgrounds. Gains in scores on achievement tests in history were also much higher among students who participated in the cooperative groups than among students in the traditional classroom.

One form of peer-centered education is called **collaborative learning.** Here students work jointly on the same problems, often without competing with other groups but with the goal of arriving at solutions jointly, solutions that would be unlikely to arise from students working by themselves (Littleton & Häkkinen, 1999). For example, in one study fourth-graders worked in pairs on mathematics and spatial reasoning problems, some that required rote learning and copying and some that required formal reasoning (Phelps & Damon, 1989). After six sessions of collaboration, children showed significant gains in performance on math and spatial problems compared with a control group of children who did not participate in collaborative efforts. This effect occurred for tasks that required formal reasoning but not for those that required rote learning or copying. Another interesting outcome was that the superiority of boys over girls on spatial problems at the start of the study significantly diminished. In fact, other research indicates that cooperative and collaborative learning may be especially beneficial in certain areas for students, such as, for example, girls learning math or science. These gains could come about because girls now have a chance to take on leadership roles or because cooperative or collaborative learning more closely fits their preferred style of learning and helps to maintain interest in these subjects (Eccles & Roeser, 1999; Peterson, Johnson, & Johnson, 1991).

collaborative learning   Peer-centered learning in which students work together on academic problems with the goal of arriving at solutions that are more effective than solutions that could have been derived from individual effort alone.

● **The Classroom Climate**   One possible factor associated with cooperative and collaborative learning efforts may be the perception that the teacher and the school are promoting *autonomy* or increased student initiative within the classroom, a perception that appears to be beneficial to student progress (Boggiano et al., 1992; Valeski & Stipek, 2001). Children who view their teachers as giving them greater responsibility within the classroom have higher self-esteem scores than those who perceive teachers as controlling and directive (Ryan & Grolnick, 1986). Moreover, teachers who display the kinds of qualities associated with good parenting—that is, who have high expectations for their students and who show caring, supportive, and nurturant qualities in contrast to an emphasis on negative feedback in their educational approach—are more effective in promoting student adjustment to the classroom and high academic performance in early adolescence (Linney & Seidman, 1989; Rutter, 1983; Rutter et al., 1979; Wentzel, 2002).

Children as early as first grade are able to recognize the strength of their interpersonal relationship with a teacher. When they perceive that teachers care about them, children have more favorable attitudes toward school (Valeski & Stipek, 2001). Moreover, teacher-child relationships that begin early in the schooling process have long-term outcomes. Bridget Hamre and Robert Pianta (2001) asked kindergarten teachers in a small community to assess their personal relationships with each of their students. Nearly 200 of these students were followed through eighth grade. Those reported to have had a negative relationship with the teacher as kindergartners, for example, conflict and overdependency, continued to have difficulties with school over the next eight years. However, if children who displayed behavior problems in kindergarten were able to develop positive relationships with their kindergarten teachers, it helped to counter behavioral difficulties in the later school years, a finding that has considerable implications for the importance of a young student's relationship with his or her teacher and academic success.

Cultural Differences in School Achievement

The school experience is not the same for children of different racial and ethnic backgrounds. Children who attend school bring with them attitudes about school that are first nurtured within their families, as well as cultural beliefs that may be in synchrony or in conflict with the predominant belief system of the school (Gibson & Ogbu, 1991). For example, are schools a vehicle for economic and personal advancement? Cultural and ethnic groups may vary in their responses to this question. Is verbal, rational expression (which schools emphasize) the optimal means of human communication as opposed to emotional or spiritual sharing? Again, cultures differ in the extent to which they value these skills. One of the major challenges facing educators is how to ensure the academic success of children who come from a range of cultural-ethnic backgrounds.

● **School Achievement Among Minority Children**   A persistent finding in past research on school achievement in the United States is that children from some minority groups—for example, African American children—score significantly lower than Caucasian children on many measures of academic performance. In the 1960s, the prevailing explanation for the school difficulties of minority children centered on the *cultural deficit hypothesis,* the notion that some deficiency in the backgrounds of minority children hindered their preparation for the academic demands of school. However, Herbert Ginsberg (1972) pointed out that rather than being culturally deficient, minority children are culturally *different;* that is, the behaviors minority children display help them to adapt to their specific life circumstances. For example, rather than having poor language skills, African American children display rich images and poetic forms when speaking to one another in Black English. According to the **cultural compatibility hypothesis,** school instruction produces greater improvements in learning if it is consistent with the practices of the child's own culture (Tharp, 1989).

An example of an educational intervention specifically designed to be compatible with the child's cultural background is the Kamehameha Early Education Program

KEY THEME
Sociocultural Influence

cultural compatibility hypothesis   Theory that school instruction is most effective if it is consistent with the practices of the child's background culture.

(KEEP) in Hawaii (Tharp et al., 1984). Like many minority children in other parts of the United States, youngsters of native Hawaiian ancestry have been the lowest achieving in the state. The KEEP program was instituted as an early education program in language arts for kindergartners through third-graders. Several unique features of the program were tied to the practices and beliefs of traditional Hawaiian culture. Because collaboration and cooperation are highly valued in that society, classrooms were organized into small groups of four to five children working on independent projects under the close supervision of a teacher. Teachers made a deliberate attempt to establish warm, nurturant relationships with their charges through the frequent use of praise and the avoidance of authoritarian methods of control. The program also capitalized on the tendency of native Hawaiian children to engage their peers in rich and animated verbal interactions. Each day teachers conducted small-group discussions of some academic topic and did not discourage children's interruptions, overlapping speech, and rapidly paced discussions. In addition, reading was taught with the aim of developing comprehension as opposed to mechanics, and children were encouraged to relate personal experiences that were triggered by reading a given text.

What were the results of this broad-based intervention? Participants in KEEP scored at approximately the national norms on several tests of reading achievement, whereas control participants from similar low-income backgrounds continued to place below national averages (Tharp et al., 1984). The KEEP program is an excellent example of how modifying classroom practices to incorporate cultural patterns of language, communication, and social organization can enhance the school performance of children.

● **African American Culture and Education**   In a study of children in the first two years of school, Karl Alexander and Doris Entwisle (1988) found that African American and Caucasian first-graders did not differ significantly on a standardized test of verbal and quantitative achievement when they were assessed at the beginning of the school year. But by the end of the year and during the second year, the scores of African American and Caucasian students began to diverge noticeably. In keeping with the cultural compatibility hypothesis, some have argued that for many African American students, a conflict exists between their background culture and the social and cognitive structure of traditional schools. For example, the spiritualism, expressiveness, and rich oral tradition characteristic of the African American heritage frequently clash with the materialism, emotional control, and emphasis on printed materials characteristic of European Americans and their schools (Boykin, 1986; Heath, 1989; Slaughter-Defoe et al., 1990). Some African American children may also perceive that academic success does not necessarily lead to occupational or economic success, and therefore do not take academic performance seriously (Ogbu, 1974). Furthermore, many African American children believe they will do well in school even though past performance indicates they are likely to do otherwise. These children may need not only to overcome the hurdles imposed by racism and economic hardship but also to more fully understand what behaviors will be necessary to achieve their expectations, that is, to become motivated to master the academic materials and skills necessary to achieve their goals (Alexander, Entwisle, & Bedinger, 1994; Steinberg, 1996).

In focusing on cultural differences, however, researchers need to recognize that they may be unwittingly contributing to stereotypes. After all, many children in all cultural and ethnic groups in the United States are doing well in school. In fact, children of immigrant families in the United States, who are often poor and members of minority groups, generally do better in mathematics and English courses in high school than children of native families (Fuligni, 1997). What factors are contributing to their success? Tom Luster and Harriette McAdoo (1994, 1996) have provided some answers for African American children, and the answers should not be too surprising. African American children who are high achieving, just as other children who are high achieving, experience relatively supportive home environments in which mothers display self-esteem and are members of smaller families whose incomes are above the poverty line. Luster and McAdoo (1996) followed African American chil-

KEY THEME
Interaction Among Domains

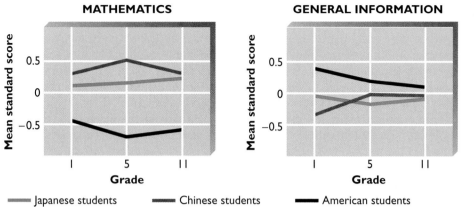

Source: Reprinted with permission from H. W. Stevenson, C. Chen, and S. Y. Lee, "Mathematics Achievement of Chinese, Japanese, and American Children: Ten Years Later," *Science, 259,* 53–58. Copyright 1993 American Association for the Advancement of Science. Visit us at http://www.sciencemag.org

FIGURE 16.9
Mathematics Achievement and General Information Scores as a Function of Sociocultural Context

Chinese and Japanese students score higher than American students on tests of mathematics achievement beginning in first grade, and their superiority in this area continues throughout high school. However, on tests of general information, children from all three cultures perform at similar levels, especially in the higher grades. The better performance on mathematics tests by East Asian children may reflect both school- and family-related cultural influences.

dren from preschool age until young adulthood. All the children lived in families with low socioeconomic status during the preschool period. Consistent with our earlier discussion emphasizing the importance of parents in promoting school success, the cognitive competence and academic motivation these children brought to the public school setting, as well as their degree of social adjustment, predicted performance on achievement tests during the elementary school years. Children of mothers who were more involved with their children's schooling also tended to do better in the lower grades, although this relationship did not hold up during adolescence. However, parents' expectations for success in the classroom were correlated with achievement throughout the school years. These findings further confirm the important role families play in the education of African American children, just as in the education of all children (Fuligni, 1997; Steinberg, 1996).

● **Achievement Among Asian Children**   Beginning in the mid-1980s, Harold Stevenson and his associates have conducted comparative research on the academic abilities of Taiwanese Chinese, Japanese, and American students. This research has been guided by an effort to understand why Asian students seem to do particularly well in the areas of mathematics and science. First- and fifth-grade students from middle- to upper-class backgrounds in all three countries were tested on a battery of specially designed cognitive tasks that assessed, among other things, spatial relations, perceptual speed, auditory and verbal memory, and vocabulary, along with reading and mathematics achievement (Stevenson, Lee, & Stigler, 1986).

Most noteworthy about the findings was that American children scored far lower in mathematics than the other two groups (see Figure 16.9). The distinctive patterns of achievement could not be explained by superior cognitive skills in any one group. The researchers found no predictive relationships between scores on the various cognitive assessments and scores on achievement tests. In fact, the children's cognitive profiles were quite similar across cultural groups by the time they reached fifth grade (Stevenson et al., 1985). When again tested in eleventh grade, American children continued to lag well behind the Chinese and Japanese in mathematics achievement, although, as Figure 16.9 shows, on age-appropriate tests of general information (e.g., "What are two things a plant needs in order to grow?" or "Why has it been possible to make smaller computers in recent years?"), the Asian children were not superior to the American children (Stevenson, Chen, & Lee, 1993).

In a subsequent study, Chuansheng Chen and Harold Stevenson included comparisons between Caucasian American and Asian American high school students on mathematics achievement (Chen & Stevenson, 1995). Asian Americans scored higher than Caucasian Americans but somewhat lower than Taiwan Chinese or Japanese students on mathematics tests. What accounts for this pattern of findings? Stevenson's research group reported significant differences in children's school routines and parents' attitudes and beliefs among the Taiwan Chinese, Japanese, and American groups, as well as differences between Asian American and Caucasian American families. For example, during the year Taiwan Chinese and Japanese children attend school about fifty more days than American children do. Furthermore, Asian high school students spend close to fifty hours a week in school and students in the United States about thirty-six hours a week (Fuligni & Stevenson, 1995).

The percentage of classroom time actually spent in academic activities also differs. For fifth-grade students, the figures were 64.5 percent of the time for American children, 91.5 percent for Taiwan Chinese children, and 87.4 for Japanese children. Furthermore, American children studied language arts more than twice as long as they did mathematics, whereas the Asian children spent equal amounts of time on each subject. Thus the American children received far less instruction in mathematics than their Taiwanese and Japanese counterparts did (Stevenson, Lee, & Stigler, 1986). In addition, the Asian teachers were far more likely to use their time in mathematics classes directly teaching the entire class, whereas American children spent more than half their time in mathematics classes working alone (Stigler, Lee, & Stevenson, 1987).

Stevenson's research group also examined attitudes and behaviors related to homework. American children devoted substantially less time to doing homework—an average of 46 minutes per day among fifth-graders, according to mothers' estimates—compared with 114 and 57 minutes for Taiwanese and Japanese children, respectively. American mothers were not dissatisfied with the small amount of homework their children received, nor were Taiwan Chinese and Japanese mothers dissatisfied with the large amounts their children were assigned (Stevenson, Lee, & Stigler, 1986). In addition, compared with American students, high school students, their peers, and their parents in the two Asian cultures seemed to expect higher standards and voiced greater concern about education, with Asian Americans surpassing their Caucasian American counterparts on these measures (Chen & Stevenson, 1995). American high school students were also far more likely to work, date, and engage in other leisure time activities than East Asian students. Finally, East Asian students were also more likely than American students to believe their own effort was the best route to accomplishments; Asian Americans outscored Caucasian Americans on this measure as well (Chen & Stevenson, 1995). Indeed, effort is a central component of the socialization process in many Asian cultures, that is, the procedures by which one achieves a goal are considered extremely important (Bempechat & Drago-Severson, 1999).

These data confirm that a number of factors other than pure cognitive ability determine the child's level of achievement in school. As we have seen throughout this section, the events that transpire in the classroom, parental attitudes, and larger cultural influences are all related to patterns of academic success or failure. If we are concerned about the educational attainments of students and their overall psychological development, research on the influence of schools reveals that there are many ways to more fully engage children of all ability levels and diverse sociocultural backgrounds (Steinberg, 1996).

ATYPICAL DEVELOPMENT

Educating Youths with Serious Emotional Disturbances

The goal of public education in the United States is to help all children achieve to the highest level they can. As a consequence, schools are responsible for educating every child regardless of his or her background or ability. Children enter the public schools with various strengths and sometimes with disabilities. In fact, approximately 11 percent of students in the United States have one or more disabilities (Wagner, 1995). How well do such students do? There is no simple story to tell about the success of children with disabilities in the schools, because enormous variability occurs among this population of children. Some children—for example, those with sensory impairments—are just as likely to further their educations beyond high school as youngsters in the general population but may not do as well in the labor market. Others, such as those with learning disabilities, often obtain jobs quickly after high school, although they are less likely to pursue further education.

One group of youth, those with serious emotional disturbances who display problems over a long period of time—such as unexplained difficulty in learning, inability to establish satisfying interpersonal relationships with peers or adults, pervasive depression or fears, or other inappropriate behaviors or emotions in normal circumstances—seem to have an especially difficult time both in school and afterward. These children typically become disengaged from school, as evidenced by frequent absenteeism and failure to make friends among schoolmates. The consequence is often poor school performance and dropping out. Only a relatively small proportion continue their educations (Wagner, 1995).

Are there ways the schools can improve on these outcomes? One concern is that these students be provided the kind of support they need to achieve their goals. For example, the few special services they are likely to receive are academic (tutoring, slower-paced instructions, and so forth) rather than assistance with emotional or behavioral problems. Moreover, the vast majority of youth with serious emotional disturbances are expected to compete just as other students do despite their additional needs and different career goals. Under these sink-or-swim conditions, perhaps it is little wonder that youngsters with serious emotional disorders often find school frustrating and difficult; even those who do graduate still have difficulty obtaining jobs.

What interventions might help these children? As repeatedly observed in our discussion of the impact of school on children, the involvement of parents in promoting learning, holding high expectations for their children's efforts, and becoming involved in the school seems to contribute to success for youngsters with serious emotional disorders (Henderson, 1994). However, schools may need to offer these students more, and perhaps earlier, vocational and technical courses that maintain their interest in education and provide the job skills needed for success (Wagner, Blackorby, & Hebbeler, 1993). When student interest is maintained, participation in regular courses in the later school years is likely to be more positive. Finally, fostering integration with other students, through sports, hobbies, or other social activities, along with greater collaboration with mental health and social service agencies to address the specific needs of individual children, can also yield positive outcomes for youngsters with serious emotional disturbances (Wagner, 1995).

School Violence

In recent years violence in the schools has become a growing concern. Violent behavior may range from attacks on children or teachers that result in physical and psychological damage, to even death. Youth violence resulting in deaths in the schools in the United States increased substantially in the late 1980s in disadvantaged urban schools among African American and Hispanic youths. However, in the latter half of the 1990s, violence was reported increasingly frequently in suburban and rural communities and at the hands of middle-class Caucasian American youths (National Research Council and Institute of Medicine, 2002b). Shootings in schools have resulted in deaths not only in the United States but also in Western Europe and other nations. Fortunately, such incidents remain quite rare. Nevertheless, they have received enormous attention in the media and have contributed to considerable public alarm (M. Anderson et al., 2001).

The violence associated with inner-city schools often appears to be an extension of the violence found in urban neighborhoods (National Research Council and Institute of Medicine, 2002b). Problems involving poverty, racial segregation, and illegal drug activity very likely spill over from the neighborhood and into the school in urban communities and typically involve specific grievances held by the perpetrators against particular individuals. However, in suburban and rural schools the violence seems more like the kind of "rampage" shootings by adults that occur in workplaces

SEE FOR YOURSELF
psychology.college.hmco.com
School Violence

or in other public locations (National Research Council and Institute of Medicine, 2002b). Although the youths who commit violence in suburban and rural communities also hold grievances, their dissatisfactions tend to be more abstract and less concerned with specific issues or threats. Case studies of a number of these rampage-type events reported by researchers reveal few similarities among the students committing these acts of violence other than that the perpetrators are virtually always male. But among other factors shared by some of the perpetrators are a recent drop in grades, the tendency to be associated with or engage in delinquent behavior, serious mental health problems (not typically recognized by either parents or the school), and easy access to guns. The stereotyped picture of a child who is a member of a dysfunctional family, who is a loner, and whom adults believe to be at high risk for committing violence is not usually supported in the cases that have been studied. Although the youths who committed lethal violence were often members of some student groups and informal cliques—that is, they were not completely outside the configuration of social participation with other peers—they were more likely to be only marginally associated with the group. At least some adults had hints that these boys might commit violent acts; however, the gap between the young persons who displayed such clues and their parents or others who might have been able to obtain help was never bridged. Some of the youths' friends had an even greater sense of the potential danger of violence. However, they, too, failed to communicate this information to appropriate authorities who might have been able to intervene.

Perhaps many steps can be taken to reduce or eliminate such rampages in the future and to make schools safer. For example, more extensive mental health services should be provided in the schools for children in need of them. Additionally, greater efforts may be required to limit young people's access to weapons such as guns, because their use has been the primary means by which violent acts resulting in death have occurred. However, the most important step in reducing violent lethal behavior may be to establish a climate, not just in the schools but in other locations within the community as well, in which adults and young people can communicate with each other and work together to provide a supportive network committed to the safety and well-being of all youth (National Research Council and Institute of Medicine, 2002b).

FOR YOUR REVIEW

- What are some of the difficulties in making cross-cultural comparisons of academic performance?

- What factors—apart from classroom experience itself—predict academic success?

- How do school and class size influence performance in the classroom?

- Why are school transitions difficult and what practices can be implemented to make them easier for children?

- What is the role of teacher expectations for success in the classroom?

- What are some classroom management strategies that appear to promote achievement? Why do peer cooperation and collaboration seem to be effective?

- How does the classroom climate and a teacher's style of interaction with children affect their development?

- How does the cultural compatibility hypothesis help to explain school achievement among children from an ethnic minority group? What factors seem to facilitate learning among minority children? Why do Asian children outperform American children in mathematics?

- What responsibility does public education have toward children who are emotionally disturbed? How successful are such children in the classroom?

- What explanations exist for violent behavior in schools?

Neighborhoods

In many cultures and societies, rearing children is considered a communal effort. Even in the United States, with its emphasis on the family as the bedrock for the transmission of cultural values and beliefs, neighbors and other community members often provide resources to families in their efforts to create a supportive rearing environment (National Research Council and Institute of Medicine, 2002a). Of course, at one time, neighbors might often have included distant family members. But today, increased family mobility, less visibility in the community because of long absences for work, more heterogenous interests among the residents, and the deterioration of some areas as a result of crime, drugs, and poverty have made questions about the neighborhood's role in development—that is, the broader ecological context in which children live—even more important.

KEY THEME
Sociocultural Influence

Do Neighborhoods Matter?

A recent review by Tama Leventhal and Jeanne Brooks-Gunn (2000) of the literature on their effects on developmental outcomes indicates that neighborhoods do matter. They matter, for example, with respect to school readiness and achievement; children who grow up in neighborhoods in which the residents have higher socioeconomic status do better in school and are more likely to graduate from high school and to attend college. Neighborhoods matter, too, with respect to behavioral and emotional problems; both are more likely to be present among children residing in neighborhoods with lower socioeconomic status. And youths living in neighborhoods with higher socioeconomic status tend to delay engaging in sexual activity and are less likely to bear children as teenagers.

These findings are probably not too surprising. However, a more important question is how neighborhoods might influence these kinds of outcomes (Jencks & Mayer, 1990). Leventhal and Brooks-Gunn (2000) propose three different pathways by which neighborhoods can have an impact. One pathway is via the availability of institutional resources such as libraries, educational programs, and museums designed to promote achievement. Such resources also extend to the availability of quality child care and the presence of good schools and medical services and, in the case of adolescents, employment opportunities that encompass visible opportunities for "getting ahead" through the acquisition of job-relevant skills. The benefits of high-quality child care and good schools are well documented, although evidence that other institutional resources make a difference needs more thorough research.

A second pathway by which neighborhoods may have an effect on development is through the parenting styles caregivers engage in and the interpersonal support networks that are available to parents. Indeed, parenting is affected by a mother's perception of the neighborhood, such as how safe it is. As an illustration, mothers who have a negative view of their neighborhoods are more likely to show greater supervision of their children's activities than mothers who view their neighbors as a source of help (O'Neil, Parke, & McDowell, 2001). Nevertheless, more restrictive parental practices in poorer, high-crime neighborhoods may be beneficial to children, as the findings of a recent study carried out by Rosario Ceballo and Vonnie McLoyd (2002) indicate. Perhaps such parental practices reduce opportunities for children to be influenced by peers who may encourage them to engage in less desirable activities (Jarrett, 1997). Even so, an important beneficial component to children of concerned and involved parents in poor neighborhoods continues to be nurturance rather than harsh and inconsistent socialization practices (Brody et al., 2001). When parents have greater social support from family and friends within the community, the negative effects that often accompany increased parental stress in poor neighborhoods may also be reduced.

Yet a third pathway for influences on development occurs through the individual and community-level offerings provided within neighborhoods to supervise young people and to reduce the risks that they may experience. This pathway is sometimes referred to in terms of the norms or collective efforts of neighbors (Leventhal &

Brooks-Gunn, 2000). The social cohesion—that is, the willingness of residents to intervene or establish alternatives such as athletic activities, after-school programs, and social clubs designed to promote the values and goals of the community—may differ substantially from one neighborhood to another. Yet when residents are willing to take the initiative in monitoring or overseeing the doings of children and youths, neighborhoods tend to experience less violence and fewer deviant behaviors among the young (Brody et al., 2001; Elliott et al., 1996; Sampson, Raudenbush, & Earls, 1997).

These various neighborhood effects on development are not large (Caspi et al., 2000; Leventhal & Brooks-Gunn, 2000). For example, research involving identical twins growing up in a range of communities suggests that neighborhood differences account for about 5 percent of the variability associated with their mental health. Although this impact may seem small, when the interventions designed to improve institutional resources, interpersonal support, and the norms and collective efforts of a community are extended to a large number of children within a neighborhood, the costs are small and the benefits quite high. Thus social policies designed to enhance the institutional resources within the community, parental perceptions of support and other features that uphold desirable parenting practices, and the individual and collective efforts of the community members to monitor and assist in the supervision of children and adults may be important avenues for promoting child and youth development.

War and Children

👁 SEE FOR YOURSELF
psychology.college.hmco.com
War and Children

Perhaps no other tragedy aside from natural calamities such as earthquakes, floods, or famine is more disruptive to neighborhoods than war. But wars often have an impact on large numbers of communities and are the result of human motivation; they are therefore subject to a form of intervention that is not available for many other kinds of disasters. The consequences of war for young people can be devastating. As a result of conflicts between 1990 and 2000, perhaps as many as 2 million children around the world have lost their lives, 6 million have been injured or disabled, 12 million have been left homeless, and 1 million have been orphaned (UNICEF, 2002).

Of children who experience and survive war in their neighborhoods, a high percentage, typically on the order of 40 to 50 percent, display posttraumatic stress disorder (PTSD), a disorder that was described with respect to physical and sexual abuse in the chapter titled "The Family." In the case of war, multiple factors may contribute to the appearance of PTSD. Children may witness violent acts such as killing, rape, and torture (or even experience some of these) or see the physical manifestations of war, including dead bodies or destroyed buildings. They may also be subjected to homelessness, starvation, relocation to refugee camps, and separation from family and friends. All of these factors can contribute to the occurrence of PTSD (Allwood, Bell-Dolan, & Husain, 2002), and the extent of stress reported by children is influenced by the degree to which they report experiencing the more traumatizing aspects of war (Smith et al., 2001).

In general, the symptoms of PTSD are most evident within the first year of exposure to war events; after one year, they decline. However, some stressors, such as relocation and separation from family, may be ongoing for years, and, as a consequence, children may remain vulnerable to PTSD for long periods of times (Thabet & Vostanis, 2000). Nevertheless, some children show exceptional resilience in the face of such tragedy. At the present time, researchers know little about the factors that might promote this resilience; however, the availability of some kind of social support is often theorized to be one important element (Cairns & Dawes, 1996). That support usually comes from a mother. Her reactions to the war experience do have an impact on the child's level of distress (Smith et al., 2001).

Effective ways to treat children experiencing the stresses of war remain uncertain (Yule, 2000). Perhaps a first step is to establish a secure environment for children, often an extremely difficult task given the possibilities of continued conflict, the uncertainties associated with living under refugee conditions, and the suspicions that can pervade attitudes toward others who may not be well known by the children. Psychosocial intervention efforts designed to assist the mothers of children exposed to war so that they, in turn, can be more helpful to their children show promise of positive benefits (Dybdahl, 2001).

Vast amounts of support may be needed for children who have experienced this kind of disruption in their lives. Well-designed research to evaluate the procedures that can help the most should be a priority until such time as neighborhoods are safe, no matter where children reside.

FOR YOUR REVIEW

- What aspects of development are known to be influenced by the neighborhood?

- How might the neighborhood have its influence on developmental outcomes?

- What are the most serious outcomes for children experiencing war, and what procedures may be most effective in dealing with these consequences?

CHAPTER RECAP

SUMMARY OF DEVELOPMENTAL THEMES

■ **Sociocultural Influence** *How does the sociocultural context influence the child's experiences with media, computers, schools, and the neighborhood?*

The society in which the child grows up determines what kind of exposure she will have to television, computers, schools, and neighborhood resources. Not all cultures emphasize formal schooling, and not all children have access to television or computers. In terms of school, the child's cultural background may either harmonize or conflict with the predominant values of the educational system. In the latter case, the child may experience academic failure as well as lower self-esteem. The KEEP model suggests that the child's academic performance climbs when educational practices are compatible with his culture. In addition, exposure to war varies considerably depending on the society in which a child grows up.

■ **Child's Active Role** *How does the child play an active role in experiences with media, computers, schools, and the neighborhood?*

In their television viewing, children actively direct their attention to programs they understand. In their school experiences, children show greater academic achievement and higher self-esteem when school structures facilitate their greater participation in the educational process. In addition, educational techniques such as peer collaboration, classroom autonomy, and computer activities in group contexts all seem to foster development by promoting the child's active involvement.

■ **Interaction Among Domains** *How do the child's experiences with media, computers, schools, and the neighborhood interact with development in other domains?*

As children's cognitive skills grow, so does their ability to comprehend information portrayed on television. At the same time, television programs can enhance cognitive growth in such areas as prereading skills. Moreover, television can influence social behavior through the strong messages it portrays about violence, prosocial acts, and gender-role stereotypes. Experiences with computers also can facilitate cognitive and social development. Children's developmental accomplishments affect their school experience, and vice versa. Children who have good peer relations are more likely to adjust well to school in the first place. Once in school, children typically have experiences that can promote their intellectual advancement, peer relations, and self-concept. For example, open classrooms can enhance peer interaction skills, and the academic feedback students receive can influence self-esteem. Peer learning techniques especially foster developmental accomplishments in many domains.

SUMMARY OF TOPICS

Television

- Among the most frequent activities in which children engage is watching television. Children tend to watch increasing amounts of television as they become older, until they reach adolescence.

Children's Comprehension of Television Programs

- Although the formal features of television often guide their attention, children actively attend to the portions of programs they comprehend. As children's cognitive and verbal skills expand, so does their ability to comprehend both the explicit and implicit elements of programs.

Television's Influence on Cognitive and Language Development

- Television can promote certain prereading skills, such as knowledge of the alphabet and numbers. Children who watch relatively greater amounts of educational television as preschoolers continue to demonstrate greater academic achievement during the high school years.
- Television can also promote language development and increase children's vocabularies.

Television's Influence on Social Development

- Children who observe aggressive events on television learn such behaviors and can demonstrate them in similar situations. Viewing high levels of violence on television is associated with greater aggression in children and youth.
- Prosocial behaviors can be learned via television and may be even more influential on children's behavior than violent content.
- Gender stereotypes are commonly exhibited in television programming. Children's attention to these stereotypes appears to be dependent on an understanding of their own gender.
- Children's understanding of commercials may not be clear. When children view commercials on television, they tend to request the products.
- Parents can take a number of steps to encourage positive benefits from television. These include being aware of their children's viewing habits, selecting acceptable programs for viewing at appropriate times, and commenting on the programming to assist children in their understanding of it.

Computers

- Most children now have access to computers either in the home, at school, or in both locations.

Academic Mastery and Cognition

- Computer-assisted instruction may result in gains in achievement in various subjects. The largest gains in achievement occur when children are required to think more fully about a

topic. Gains are most frequently reported in the areas of mathematics and science.
- Among the cognitive skills that appear to benefit from children's use of computers and other electronic technologies are spatial representation, iconic skills, and the ability to attend to multiple events.

Social Development

- Children and adolescents spend a substantial portion of their time on computers engaging in social interactions, as, for example, in using e-mail and other communication opportunities.
- Controversy exists over how to regulate access to the Internet, as some material available on it may not be suitable for children. A major unresolved issue is the extent to which children should be either educated about or monitored in the use of the Internet.

Sex Differences

- Although boys may still use computers more than girls for game playing, the difference has declined over the years for other uses, including word processing and accessing the Internet.

School

- Assisting children in acquiring the academic skills needed in society is the main goal of schools.
- Criticisms have been leveled at the schools because cross-cultural comparisons of performance by children suggest that students in the United States lag in the acquisition of some academic skills. Interpreting cross-cultural research is difficult because of the many methodological problems associated with collecting information in other countries.

Families and Peers as Agents Mediating School Achievement

- The resources children bring to the school as a result of family and peer experiences can have a large impact on their academic success.

School and Classroom Size

- Schools vary greatly in their organization and structure.
- Children who attend smaller schools seem to show benefits not always found among children who attend larger schools.
- The number of pupils in classrooms in the United States has declined over the past several decades. Smaller classes, especially during the early grades, appear to have positive consequences for children.

School Transitions

- Children who initially demonstrate good skills with respect to social behaviors and cognitive and linguistic skills on entering school tend to be more successful in school. Entering school along with familiar peers has some advantages for young children. Those children in the classroom who are younger show similar gains during the school year as those who are older.

■ The transition from elementary to junior high school can be difficult for many children, especially if they experience other developmental transitions at the same time. The kinds of interactions that occur in the more advanced grades may be difficult for some children if they feel they have little control over their academic progress or are not personally invested in succeeding in the classroom.

Teachers: Key Agents of Influence

■ Teacher expectations about student performance can have important consequences on IQ and academic achievement.

■ Children actively involved in the learning process do better in school. Studies of *cooperative learning* and *collaborative learning* reveal more favorable academic outcomes for students. These results provide some support for the theories of Piaget and Vygotsky concerning the importance of peers for learning and the value of a scaffold for facilitating learning.

Cultural Differences in School Achievement

■ Research demonstrates that children's academic performance rises when educational tactics incorporate elements of their culture, that is, are *culturally compatible* with their background.

■ Children in Asian societies display higher levels of achievement than American children in the areas of mathematics and science. These differences may arise from the amount of time spent in learning about these subjects, demands for homework, the concerns of parents for successful school performance, and the central role that effort plays in the socialization process in many Asian cultures.

■ The schools are not well equipped to provide appropriate educational experiences for children with serious emotional problems.

School Violence

■ The past two decades have seen an increase in lethal school violence within the public schools.

■ In urban communities, school violence tends to reflect an extension of violence found in the neighborhood. In suburban and rural communities, the violence is more likely the result of a youth engaging in a "rampage." Few commonalities are shared by the perpetrators, and although both adults and peers may show some signals that anticipate these actions, the signs are often not sufficiently visible to lead others to intervene.

Neighborhoods

■ In many cultures and societies, the socialization efforts of parents are often supplemented by neighbors and other community members.

Do Neighborhoods Matter?

■ The neighborhoods in which children grow up do have an effect on academic success, mental health, and sexual behavior.

■ The mechanisms by which a neighborhood influences development include the availability of institutional resources within the community, the parenting style practiced in response to the safety and support network perceived to exist in the neighborhood, and the individual and collective efforts of community residents to supervise and monitor the development of youth.

War and Children

■ Large numbers of children are killed and injured and experience homelessness, loss of family members, and relocation to refugee settlements as a result of war.

Accommodation   In Piagetian theory, a component of adaptation; process of modification in thinking (schemes) that takes place when old ways of understanding something no longer fit.

Adaptation   In Piagetian theory, the inborn tendency to adjust or become more attuned to conditions imposed by the environment; takes place through assimilation and accommodation.

Age-history confound   In longitudinal studies, the co-occurrence of historical factors with changes in age; affects the ability to interpret results.

Allele   Alternate form of a specific gene; provides a genetic basis for many individual differences.

Altruism   Behavior carried out to help another without expectation of reward.

Ambivalent (resistant) attachment   Insecure attachment in which the infant shows separation protest but also distress upon the caregiver's return.

Amniocentesis   Method of sampling the fluid surrounding the developing fetus by insertion of a needle. Used to diagnose fetal genetic and developmental disorders.

Amniotic sac   Fluid-filled, transparent protective membrane surrounding the fetus.

Analogical transfer   Ability to employ the solution to one problem in other, similar problems.

Androgen   Class of male or masculinizing hormones.

Androgyny   Gender-role orientation in which a person possesses high levels of personality characteristics associated with both sexes.

Animism   Attribution of lifelike qualities to inanimate objects.

Artificialism   Belief that naturally occurring events are caused by people.

Assimilation   In Piagetian theory, a component of adaptation; process of interpreting an experience in terms of current ways (schemes) of understanding things.

Attachment   Strong emotional bond that emerges between infant and caregiver.

Attention   State of alertness or arousal that allows the individual to focus on a selected aspect of the environment.

Authoritarian parent   Parent who relies on coercive techniques to discipline the child and displays a low level of nurturance.

Authoritative parent   Parent who sets limits on a child's behavior using reasoning and explanation and displays a high degree of nurturance.

Autobiographical memory   Memory for specific events in one's own life.

Autosomes   Twenty-two pairs of homologous chromosomes. The two members of each pair are similar in size, shape, and genetic function. The two sex chromosomes are excluded from this class.

Avoidant attachment   Insecure attachment in which the infant shows little separation anxiety and does not pay much attention to the caregiver's return.

Babbling   Consonant-vowel utterances that characterize the infant's first attempts to vocalize.

Basic emotion   Emotion such as joy, sadness, or surprise that appears early in infancy and seems to have a biological foundation. Also called *primary emotion*.

Behavior analysis   Learning theory perspective that explains the development of behavior according to the principles of classical and operant conditioning.

Behavior genetics   Study of how characteristics and behaviors of individuals, such as intelligence and personality, are influenced by the interaction between genotype and experience.

Broca's area   Portion of the cerebral cortex that controls expressive language.

Canalization   Concept that the development of some attributes is governed primarily by the genotype and only extreme environmental conditions will alter the phenotypic pattern for these attributes.

Canonical babbling   Repetition of simple consonant-vowel combinations in well-formed syllables.

Cardinality   Principle that the last number in a set of counted numbers refers to the number of items in that set.

Case study   In-depth description of psychological characteristics and behaviors of an individual, often in the form of a narrative.

Catch-up growth   Increase in growth rate after some factor, such as illness or poor nutrition, has disrupted the expected, normal growth rate.

Categorical perception   Inability to distinguish among sounds that vary on some basic physical dimension except when those sounds lie at opposite sides of a critical juncture point on that dimension.

Categorical self   Conceptual process, starting in the early preschool years, in which the child begins to classify himself or herself according to easily observable categories such as sex, age, or physical capacities.

Centration   In Piagetian theory, tendency of the child to focus on only one aspect of a problem.

Cephalocaudal development   Pattern in which organs, systems, and motor movements near the head tend to develop earlier than those near the feet.

Chorionic villus sampling   Method of sampling fetal chorionic cells. Used to diagnose embryonic genetic and developmental disorders.

Chromosomes   Threadlike structures of DNA, located in the nucleus of cells, that form a collection of genes. A human body cell normally contains forty-six chromosomes.

Chronosystem   In Bronfenbrenner's ecological systems theory, the constantly changing temporal component of the environment that can influence development.

Clinical method   Flexible, open-ended interview method in which questions are modified in reaction to the child's responses.

Clique   Peer group of five to ten children who frequently interact together.

Codominance   Condition in which individual, unblended characteristics of two alleles are reflected in the phenotype.

Coercive cycles   Pattern of escalating negative reciprocal interactions.

Cognition   Processes involved in thinking and mental activity, such as attention, memory, and problem solving.

Cognitive-developmental theory   Theoretical orientation, most frequently associated with Piaget, emphasizing the active construction of psychological structures to interpret experience.

Cohort effects   Characteristics shared by individuals growing up in a given sociohistorical context that can influence developmental outcomes.

Collaborative learning   Peer-centered learning in which students work together on academic problems with the goal of arriving at solutions that are more effective than solutions that could have been derived from individual effort alone.

Computer-assisted instruction (CAI)   Use of computers to provide tutorial information and drill-and-practice routines.

Concept   Definition of a set of information on the basis of some general or abstract principle.

Concordance rate   Percentage of pairs of twins in which both members have a specific trait identified in one twin.

Concrete operational stage   In Piagetian theory, the third stage of development, from approximately seven to eleven years of age, in which thought is logical when stimuli are physically present.

Conditioned response (CR)   Learned response that is exhibited to a previously neutral stimulus (CS) as a result of pairing the CS with an unconditioned stimulus (UCS).

Conditioned stimulus (CS)   Neutral stimulus that begins to elicit a response similar to the unconditioned stimulus (UCS) with which it has been paired.

Conscience   In Freudian theory, the part of the superego that defines unacceptable behaviors and actions, usually as also defined by the parents.

Conservation tasks   Problems that require the child to make judgments about the equivalence of two displays; used to assess stage of cognitive development.

Control theory   Hypothesis about parent-child interactions suggesting that the intensity of one partner's behavior affects the intensity of the other's response.

Conventional level   In Kohlberg's theory, the second level of moral reasoning, in which the child conforms to the norms of the majority and wishes to preserve the social order.

Cooing   Vowel-like utterances that characterize the infant's first attempts to vocalize.

Cooperative learning   Peer-centered learning experience in which students work together in small groups to solve academic problems.

Cooperative play   Interactive play in which children's actions are reciprocal.

Core knowledge hypothesis   The idea that infants possess innate knowledge of certain properties of objects.

Correlation coefficient (r)   Statistical measure, ranging from +1.00 to -1.00, that summarizes the strength and direction of the relationship between two variables; does not provide information about causation.

Correlational study   Study that assesses whether changes in one variable are accompanied by systematic changes in another variable.

Cross-cultural study   Study that compares individuals in different cultural contexts.

Cross-fostering study   Research study in which children are reared in environments that differ from those of their biological parents.

Cross-gender behavior   Behavior usually seen in a member of the opposite sex. Term generally is reserved for behavior that is persistently sex atypical.

Crossing over   Process during the first stage of meiosis when genetic material is exchanged between autosomes.

Cross-sectional study   A study in which individuals of different ages are examined at the same point in time.

Crowd   Large group of peers characterized by specific traits or reputation.

Crystallized intelligence   Mental skills derived from cultural experience.

Cultural compatibility hypothesis   Theory that school instruction is most effective if it is consistent with the practices of the child's background culture.

Debriefing   Providing research participants with a statement of the true goals of a study after initially deceiving them or omitting information about its purposes.

Deferred imitation   Ability to imitate a model's behavior hours, days, and even weeks after observation.

Delay of gratification   Capacity to wait before performing a tempting activity or attaining some highly desired outcome; a measure of ability to regulate one's own behavior.

Deoxyribonucleic acid (DNA)   Long, spiral staircaselike sequence of molecules created by nucleotides identified with the blueprint for genetic inheritance.

Dependent variable   Behavior that is measured; suspected effect of an experimental manipulation.

Development   Physical and psychological changes in the individual over a lifetime.

Developmental psychology   Systematic and scientific study of changes in human behaviors and mental activities over time.

Deviation IQ   IQ score computed by comparing the child's performance with that of a standardization sample.

Dishabituation   See *Recovery from habituation.*

Disorganized/disoriented attachment   Infant-caregiver relations characterized by the infant's fear of the caregiver, confused facial expressions, and a combination of avoidant and ambivalent attachment behaviors.

Display rules   The cultural guidelines concerning when, how, and to what degree to display emotions.

Dominant allele   Allele whose characteristics are reflected in the phenotype even when part of a heterozygous genotype. Its genetic characteristics tend to mask the characteristics of other alleles.

Dynamic systems theory   A theoretical orientation that explains development as the emerging organization arising from the interaction of many different processes.

Ecological systems theory   Bronfenbrenner's theory that development is influenced by experiences arising from broader social and cultural systems as well as a child's immediate surroundings.

Ectopic pregnancy   Implantation of the fertilized ovum in a location outside of the uterus.

Effectance motivation   Inborn desire theorized by Robert White to be the basis for the infant's and child's efforts to master and gain control of the environment.

Egocentrism   Preoperational child's inability to separate his or her own perspective from those of others.

Ego ideal   In Freudian theory, the part of the superego that defines the positive standards for which an individual strives; acquired via parental rewarding of desired behaviors.

Elaboration   Memory strategy in which individuals link items to be remembered in the form of an image or a sentence.

Elicited imitation A way of assessing memory in which children must reconstruct a unique sequence of actions that they have seen in the past; usually used with preverbal children.

Embryonic period Period of prenatal development during which major biological organs and systems form. Begins about the tenth to fourteenth day after conception and ends about the eighth week after conception.

Emotions Complex behaviors involving physiological, expressive, and experiential components produced in response to some external or internal event.

Empathy An understanding and sharing of the feelings of others.

Empiricism Theory that environmental experiences shape the individual; more specifically, that all knowledge is derived from sensory experiences.

Episodic memory Memory for events that took place at a specific time and place.

Equilibration In Piagetian theory, an innate self-regulatory process that, through accommodation and assimilation, results in more organized and powerful schemes for adapting to the environment.

Ethnic identity The sense of belonging to a particular cultural group.

Ethnography Set of methods, including observations and interviews, used by researchers to describe the behaviors and underlying meaning systems within a given culture.

Ethology Theoretical orientation and discipline concerned with the evolutionary origins of behavior and its adaptive and survival value in animals, including humans.

Executive function Portion of the information-processing system that coordinates various component processes in order to achieve some goal.

Exosystem In Bronfenbrenner's ecological systems theory, environmental settings that indirectly affect the child by influencing the various microsystems forming the child's immediate environment.

Expansion Repetition of a child's utterance along with more complex forms.

Experimental design Research method in which one or more independent variables are manipulated to determine the effect on other, dependent variables.

Expressive aphasia Loss of the ability to speak fluently.

Expressive characteristics Characteristics associated with emotions or relationships with people; usually considered feminine.

Expressive style Type of early language production in which the child uses many social words.

Externality effect Tendency for infants younger than two months to focus on the external features of a complex stimulus and explore the internal features less systematically.

Failure to thrive Label applied to any child whose growth in height or weight is below the third percentile for children of the same age.

Fast-mapping Deriving meanings of words from the contexts in which they are spoken.

Fetal alcohol syndrome (FAS) Cluster of fetal abnormalities stemming from mother's consumption of alcohol; includes growth retardation, defects in facial features, and intellectual retardation.

Fetal blood sampling Method of withdrawing blood from the umbilical cord of the fetus. Used to diagnose genetic disorders, especially those that affect the blood.

Fetal monitoring device Medical device used to monitor fetal heartbeat during delivery.

Fetal period Period of prenatal development, from about the eighth week after conception to birth, marked by rapid growth and preparation of body systems for functioning in the postnatal environment.

Field experiment Experiment conducted in a "natural," real-world setting such as the child's home or school.

Fluid intelligence Biologically based mental abilities that are relatively uninfluenced by cultural experiences.

Focus on states Preoperational child's tendency to treat two or more connected events as unrelated.

Formal operational stage In Piagetian theory, the last stage of development, from approximately eleven to fifteen years of age, in which thought is abstract and hypothetical.

Fragile X syndrome Disorder associated with a pinched region of the X chromosome; a leading genetic cause of mental retardation in males.

Fraternal twins Siblings who share the same womb at the same time but originate from two different eggs fertilized by two different sperm cells. Also called *dizygotic twins*.

Gametes Sperm cells in males, egg cells in females, normally containing only twenty-three chromosomes.

Gender constancy Knowledge, usually gained around age six or seven years, that one's gender does not change as a result of alterations in appearance, behaviors, or desires.

Gender identity Knowledge, usually gained by age three years, that one is male or female.

Gender schema Cognitive organizing structure for information relevant to sex typing.

Gender stability Knowledge, usually gained by age four years, that one's gender does not change over time.

Gender stereotypes Expectations or beliefs that individuals within a given culture hold about the behaviors characteristic of males and females.

Gender-role development Process by which individuals acquire the characteristics and behaviors prescribed by their culture for their sex. Also called *sex typing*.

Gene Large segment of nucleotides within a chromosome that codes for the production of proteins and enzymes. These proteins and enzymes underlie traits and characteristics inherited from one generation to the next.

Genetic counseling Medical and counseling specialty concerned with determining and communicating the likelihood that prospective parents will give birth to a baby with a genetic disorder.

Genetic screening Systematic search using a variety of tests to detect individuals at developmental risk due to genetic anomalies.

Genomic imprinting Instances of genetic transmission in which the expression of a gene is determined by whether the particular allelic form has been inherited from the mother or the father.

Genotype Total genetic endowment inherited by an individual.

Germinal period Period lasting about ten to fourteen days following conception before the fertilized egg becomes implanted in the uterine wall. Also called *period of the zygote*.

Gestational age Age of fetus derived from onset of mother's last menstrual period.

Glial cells Brain cells that provide the material from which myelin is created, nourish neurons, and provide a scaffolding for neuron migration.

Grammar Rules pertaining to the structure of language.

Habituation Gradual decline in intensity, frequency, or duration of a response over repeated or lengthy occurrences of the same stimulus.

Heritability Proportion of variability in the phenotype that is estimated to be accounted for by genetic influences within a known environmental range.

Heterozygous   Genotype in which two alleles of a gene are different. The effects on a trait will depend on how the two alleles interact.

Homozygous   Genotype in which two alleles of a gene are identical, thus having the same effects on a trait.

Hormones   Chemicals produced by various glands that are secreted directly into the bloodstream and can therefore circulate to influence cells in other locations of the body.

Human genome   Entire inventory of nucleotide base pairs that compose the genes and chromosomes of humans.

Hypothetical reasoning   Ability to systematically generate and evaluate potential solutions to a problem.

Identical twins   Two individuals who originate from a single zygote (one egg fertilized by one sperm), which early in cell division separates to form two separate cell masses. Also called *monozygotic twins*.

Identity (personal)   Broad, coherent, internalized view of who a person is and what a person wants to be, believes, and values that emerges during adolescence.

Identity   In Eriksonian psychosocial theory, the acceptance of both self and society, a concept that must be achieved at every stage but is especially important during adolescence.

Identity crisis   Period, usually during adolescence, characterized by considerable uncertainty about the self and the role the individual is to fulfill in society.

Imaginary audience   Individual's belief that others are examining and evaluating him or her.

Immanent justice   Young child's belief that punishment will inevitably follow a transgression.

Implicit leaning   Abstract knowledge not available to conscious reflection acquired incidentally from processing structured information.

Imprinting   Form of learning, difficult to reverse, during a sensitive period in development in which an organism tends to stay near a particular stimulus.

Independent variable   Variable manipulated by the experimenter; the suspected cause.

Individual differences   Unique characteristics that distinguish a person from other members of a larger group.

Induction   Parental control technique that relies on the extensive use of reasoning and explanation as well as the arousal of empathic feelings.

Infantile amnesia   Failure to remember events from the first two to three years of one's life.

Information processing   Theoretical approach that views humans as having a limited ability to process information, much like computers.

Informed consent   Participant's formal acknowledgment that he or she understands the purposes, procedures, and risks of a study and agrees to participate in it.

Inner speech   Interiorized form of private speech.

Instrumental characteristics   Characteristics associated with acting on the world; usually considered masculine.

Instrumental competence   Child's display of independence, self-control, achievement orientation, and cooperation.

Intelligence quotient (IQ)   Numerical score received on an intelligence test.

Interactive synchrony   Reciprocal, mutually engaging cycles of caregiver-child behaviors.

Interagent consistency   Consistency in application of disciplinary strategies among different caregivers.

Intermodal perception   Coordination of sensory information to perceive or make inferences about the characteristics of an object.

Internal working models of relationships   Mental frameworks of the quality of relationships with others, developed as a result of early ongoing interactions with caregivers.

Intersubjectivity   Mutual attention and shared communication that take place between the child and caregiver or learner and expert.

Intra-agent consistency   Consistency in a single caregiver's application of discipline from one situation to the next.

Joint attention   Episodes in which the child shares the same "psychological space" with another individual.

Karyotype   Pictorial representation of an individual's chromosomes.

Kinetic cue   Perceptual information provided by movement of eyes, head, or body. Important source of information for depth perception.

Lagging-down growth   Decrease in growth rate after some factor, such as a congenital or hormonal disorder, has accelerated the expected, normal growth rate.

Landmark   Distinctive location or cue that the child uses to negotiate or represent a spatial environment.

Lateralization   Process by which one hemisphere of the brain comes to dominate the other, for example, processing of language in the left hemisphere or of spatial information in the right hemisphere.

Learned helplessness   Belief that one has little control over situations, perhaps because of lack of ability or inconsistent outcomes.

Learning   Relatively permanent change in behavior as a result of such experiences as exploration, observation, and practice.

Limited-resource model   Information-processing model that emphasizes the allocation of finite energy within the cognitive system.

Long-term memory   Memory that holds information for extended periods of time.

Longitudinal study   Research in which the same participants are repeatedly tested over a period of time, usually years.

Macrosystem   In Bronfenbrenner's ecological systems theory, major historical events and the broad values, practices, and customs promoted by a culture.

Mastery orientation   Belief that achievements are based on one's own efforts rather than on luck or other factors beyond one's control.

Maternal blood screening   Tests performed on a woman's blood to determine if the fetus she is carrying has an increased risk for some types of chromosomal and metabolic disorders.

Means-ends behavior   Deliberate behavior employed to attain a goal.

Meiosis   Process of cell division that forms the gametes; normally results in twenty-three chromosomes in each human egg and sperm cell rather than the full complement of forty-six chromosomes.

Memory span   Number of stimulus items that can be recalled after a brief interval of time.

Memory strategy   Mental activity, such as rehearsal, that enhances memory performance.

Menarche   First occurrence of menstruation.

Mesosystem   In Bronfenbrenner's ecological systems theory, the environment provided by the interrelationships among the various settings of the microsystem.

Meta-analysis   Statistical examination of a body of research studies to assess the effect of the common central variable.

Metacognition   Awareness and knowledge of cognitive processes.

Metalinguistic awareness   Ability to reflect on language as a communication tool and on the self as a user of language.

Metamemory   Understanding of memory as a cognitive process.

Metaphor   Figurative language in which a term is transferred from the object it customarily designates to describe a comparable object or event.

Microgenetic approach   A research approach in which detailed trial-to-trial observations are made of individual children's performance.

Microsystem   In Bronfenbrenner's ecological systems theory, the immediate environment provided in such settings as the home, school, workplace, and neighborhood.

Mitosis   Process of cell division that takes place in most cells of the human body and results in a full complement of identical material in the forty-six chromosomes in each cell.

Moral realism   In Piaget's theory of moral development, the first stage of moral reasoning, in which moral judgments are made on the basis of the consequences of an act. Also called *heteronomy*.

Moral relativism   In Piaget's theory of moral development, the second stage of moral reasoning, in which moral judgments are made on the basis of the actor's intentions. Also called *autonomy*.

Morality of care and responsibility   Tendency to make moral judgments on the basis of concern for others.

Morality of justice   Tendency to make moral judgments on the basis of reason and abstract principles of equity.

Morphology   Rules of how to combine the smallest meaningful units of language to form words.

Motherese/parentese   Simple, repetitive, high-pitched speech of caregivers to young children; includes many questions.

Multistore model   Information-processing model that describes a sequence of mental structures through which information flows.

Mutation   Sudden change in molecular structure of a gene; may occur spontaneously or be caused by an environmental event such as radiation.

Mutual exclusivity bias   Tendency for children to assume that unfamiliar words label new objects.

Myelin   Sheath of fatty cells that insulates and speeds neural impulses by about tenfold.

Natural domains   Concepts or categories that children acquire especially rapidly and effortlessly.

Naturalistic observation   Study in which observations of naturally occurring behavior are made in real-life settings.

Nature-nurture debate   Ongoing theoretical controversy over whether development is the result of the child's genetic endowment or the kinds of experiences the child has had.

Negative correlation   Relationship in which changes in one variable are accompanied by systematic changes in another variable in the opposite direction.

Negative punishment   Removal or loss of a desired stimulus or reward that weakens or decreases the frequency of a preceding response.

Negative reinforcement   Removal of an aversive stimulus that strengthens a preceding response.

Neuron   Nerve cell within the central nervous system that is electrochemically designed to transmit messages between cells.

Niche picking   Tendency to actively select an environment compatible with a genotype.

Nominals   Words that label objects, people, or events; the first type of words most children produce.

Norms   Measures of average values and variations in some aspect of development, such as physical size and motor skill development, in relation to age.

Nucleotide   Repeating basic building block of DNA consisting of nitrogen-based molecules of adenine, thymine, cytosine, and guanine.

Object concept   Realization that objects exist even when they are not within view. Also called *object permanence*.

Observational learning   Learning that takes place by simply observing another person's behavior.

Observer bias   Tendency of researchers to interpret ongoing events as being consistent with their research hypotheses.

One-to-one correspondence   Understanding that two sets are equivalent in number if each element in one set can be mapped onto a unique element in the second set with none left over.

Operation   In Piagetian theory, a mental action such as reversibility.

Operational definition   Specification of variables in terms of measurable properties.

Ordinality   Principle that a number refers to an item's order within a set.

Organization   In Piagetian theory, the inborn tendency for structures and processes to become more systematic and coherent. Also memory strategy in which individuals reorder items to be remembered on the basis of category or some other higher-order relationship.

Overextension   Tendency to apply a label to a broader category than the term actually signifies.

Overregularization   Inappropriate application of syntactic rules to words and grammatical forms that show exceptions.

Parallel play   Side-by-side, independent play that is not interactive.

Participant reactivity   Tendency of individuals who know they are under observation to alter natural behavior.

Peer   Companion of approximately the same age and developmental level.

Perception   Process of organizing and interpreting sensory information.

Perceptual differentiation   Process postulated by Eleanor and James Gibson in which experience contributes to the ability to make increasingly finer perceptual discriminations and to distinguish stimulation arising from each sensory modality.

Perinatal period   Period beginning about the seventh month of pregnancy and continuing until about four weeks after birth.

Permissive parent   Parent who sets few limits on the child's behavior.

Personal fable   Belief that one is unique and perhaps even invulnerable.

Perspective taking   Ability to take the role of another person and understand what that person is thinking, is feeling, or knows.

Phenotype   Observable and measurable characteristics and traits of an individual; a product of the interaction of the genotype with the environment.

Phenylketonuria (PKU)   Recessive genetic disorder in which phenylalanine, an amino acid, fails to be metabolized. Unless dietary changes are made to reduce intake of phenylalanine, severe mental retardation occurs.

Phoneme   Smallest unit of sound that changes the meanings of words.

Phonology   Fundamental sound units and combinations of units in a given language.

Placenta   Support organ formed by cells from both blastocyst and uterine lining; serves as exchange site for oxygen, nutrients, and waste products.

Plasticity   Capacity of immature systems, including regions of the brain and the individual neurons within those regions, to take on different functions as a result of experience.

Polygenic   Phenotypic characteristic influenced by two or more genes.

Positive correlation   Relationship in which changes in one variable are accompanied by systematic changes in another variable in the same direction.

Positive punishment   An aversive stimulus that serves to weaken or decrease the frequency of a preceding response.

Positive reinforcement   Occurrence of a stimulus that strengthens a preceding response. Also known as a *reward*.

Postconventional level   In Kohlberg's theory, the third level of moral reasoning, in which laws are seen as the result of a social contract and individual principles of conscience may emerge.

Postnatal development   Period in development following birth.

Power assertion   Parental control technique that relies on the use of forceful commands, physical punishment, and removal of material objects or privileges.

Pragmatics   Rules for using language effectively within a social context.

Preconventional level   In Kohlberg's theory, the first level of moral reasoning, in which morality is motivated by the avoidance of punishments and attainment of rewards.

Prenatal development   Period in development from conception to the onset of labor.

Preoperational stage   In Piagetian theory, the second stage of development, from approximately two of seven years of age, in which thought becomes symbolic in form.

Prepared childbirth   Type of childbirth that involves practicing procedures during pregnancy and childbirth that are designed to minimize pain and reduce the need for medication during delivery. Also called *natural childbirth*.

Primacy effect   Tendency for individuals to display good recall for early items in a list.

Primary reinforcer   Reward that gratifies biological needs or drives.

Private speech   Children's vocalized speech to themselves that directs behavior.

Processing speed   The rapidity with which cognitive activities are carried out.

Production deficiency   Failure of children under age seven years to spontaneously generate memory strategies.

Productive language   Meaningful language spoken or otherwise produced by an individual.

Prosocial behavior   Positive social action performed to benefit others.

Prosody   Patterns of intonation, stress, and rhythm that communicate meaning in speech.

Protodeclarative communication   Use of a gesture to call attention to an object or event.

Protoimperative communication   Use of a gesture to issue a command or request.

Proximodistal development   Pattern in which organs and systems of the body near the middle tend to develop earlier than those near the periphery.

Psychometric model   Theoretical perspective that quantifies individual differences in test scores to establish a rank order of abilities.

Psychosocial theory of development   Erikson's theory that personality develops through eight stages of adaptive functioning to meet the demands framed by society.

Puberty   Developmental period during which a sequence of physical changes takes place that transforms the person from an immature individual to one capable of reproduction.

Quasi-experiment   Study in which the assignment of individuals to experimental groups is determined by their natural experiences.

Questionnaire   Set of standardized questions administered to individuals in written form.

Random assignment   Use of principles of chance to assign participants to treatment and control groups; avoids systematic bias.

Range of reaction   Range of phenotypic differences possible as a result of different environments interacting with a specific genotype.

Realism   Inability to distinguish between mental and physical entities.

Recall memory   Ability to reproduce stimuli that one has previously encountered.

Recast   Repetition of a child's utterance with grammatical corrections.

Recency effect   Tendency for individuals to show good recall for the last few items in a list.

Receptive aphasia   Loss of the ability to comprehend speech.

Receptive language   Ability to comprehend spoken speech.

Recessive allele   Allele whose characteristics do not tend to be expressed when part of a heterozygous genotype. Its genetic characteristics tend to be masked by other alleles.

Recognition memory   Ability to identify whether a stimulus has been previously encountered.

Recovery from habituation   Reinstatement of the intensity, frequency, or duration of a response to a stimulus that has changed. Also called *dishabituation*.

Referential communication   Communication in situations that require the speaker to describe an object to a listener or to evaluate the effectiveness of a message.

Referential style   Type of early language production in which the child uses mostly nominals.

Reflex   Involuntary movement in response to touch, light, sound, or other form of stimulation; controlled by subcortical neural mechanisms.

Rehearsal   Memory strategy that involves repetition of items to be remembered.

Reliability   Degree to which a measure will yield the same results if administered repeatedly.

Representational insight   The child's ability to understand that a symbol or model can stand for a real-life event.

Reunion behavior   The child's style of greeting the caregiver after a separation.

Reversibility   In Piagetian theory, the ability to mentally reverse or negate an action or a transformation.

Rhythmical stereotypies   Repeated sequences of movements, such as leg kicking, hand waving, or head banging, that have no apparent goal.

Rough-and-tumble play   Active, physical play that carries no intent of imposing harm on another child.

Saccade   Rapid eye movement to inspect an object or view a stimulus in the periphery of the visual field.

Scaffolding   Temporary aid provided by one person to encourage, support, and assist a lesser-skilled person in carrying out a task or completing a problem. The model provides knowledge and skills that are learned and gradually transferred to the learner.

Scheme   In Piagetian theory, the mental structure underlying a coordinated and systematic pattern of behaviors or thinking applied across similar objects or situations.

Scientific method   Use of objective, measurable, and repeatable techniques to gather information.

Script   Organized scheme or framework for commonly experienced events.

Secondary reinforcer   Object or person that attains rewarding value because of its association with a primary reinforcer.

Secular trend   Consistent pattern of change over generations.

Secure attachment   Attachment category defined by the infant's distress at separation from the caregiver and enthusiastic greeting upon his or her return. The infant also displays stranger anxiety and uses the caregiver as a secure base for exploration.

Secure base   An attachment behavior in which the infant explores the environment but periodically checks back with the caregiver.

Self   Realization of being an independent, unique, stable, and self-reflective entity; the beliefs, knowledge, feelings, and characteristics the individual ascribes to himself or herself.

Self-concept   Perceptions, conceptions, and values one holds about oneself.

Self-conscious emotion   Emotion such as guilt and envy that appears later in childhood and requires more knowledge about the self as related to others.

Self-control   Ability to comply with sociocultural prescriptions concerning ethical or moral behavior.

Self-esteem   One's feelings of worth; extent to which one senses one's attributes and actions are good, desired, and valued.

Self-regulation   Process by which children come to control their own behaviors in accordance with the standards of their caregivers and community, especially in the absence of other adults.

Semantic bootstrapping hypothesis   Idea that children derive information about syntax from the meanings of words.

Semantic memory   Memory for general concepts or facts.

Semantics   Meanings of words or combinations of words.

Sensation   Basic information in the external world that is processed by the sensory receptors.

Sensitive period   Brief period during which specific kinds of experiences have significant positive or negative consequences for development and behavior. Also called *critical period*.

Sensorimotor stage   In Piagetian theory, the first stage of cognitive development, from birth to approximately two years of age, in which thought is based primarily on action.

Sensory register   Memory store that holds information for very brief periods of time in a form that closely resembles the initial input.

Separation anxiety   Distress the infant shows when the caregiver leaves the immediate environment.

Sequential study   Study that examines groups of children of different ages over a period of time; usually shorter than a longitudinal study.

Sex segregation   Clustering of individuals into same-sex groups.

Sex typicality   Extent to which a behavior is usually associated with one sex as opposed to the other.

Sickle cell disease   Genetic blood disorder common in regions of Africa and other areas where malaria is found and among descendants of these regions. Abnormal blood cells carry insufficient oxygen.

Sickle cell trait   Symptoms shown by those possessing a heterozygous genotype for sickle cell anemia.

Single-case design   Study that follows only one or a few participants over a period of time, with an emphasis on systematic collection of data.

Skeletal maturity   Extent to which cartilage has ossified to form bone; provides the most accurate estimate of how much additional growth will take place in the individual.

Smooth visual pursuit   Consistent, unbroken tracking by the eyes that serves to maintain focus on a moving visual target.

Social comparison   Process in which individuals define themselves in relation to the skills, attributes, and qualities of others; an important contributor to self-concept during middle childhood.

Social conventions   Behavioral rules that regulate social interactions, such as dress codes and degrees of formality in speech.

Social learning theory   Theoretical approach emphasizing the importance of learning through observation and imitation of behaviors modeled by others.

Social policy   The programs and plans established by local, regional, or national public and private organizations and agencies designed to achieve a particular social purpose or goal.

Social pretend play   Play that makes use of imaginary and symbolic objects and social roles, often enacted among several children. Also called *sociodramatic play*.

Social referencing   Looking to another individual for emotional cues in interpreting a strange or ambiguous event.

Socialization   Process by which children acquire the social knowledge, skills, and attitudes valued by the larger society.

Sociohistorical theory   Vygotsky's developmental theory emphasizing the importance of cultural tools, symbols, and ways of thinking that the child acquires from more knowledgeable members of the community.

Sociometric nomination   Peer assessment measure in which children are asked to name a specified number of peers who fit a certain criterion, such as "peers you would like to walk home with."

Sociometric rating scale   Peer assessment measure in which children rate peers on a number of social dimensions.

Solitary play   Individual play, performed without regard for what others are doing.

Sound localization   Ability to determine a sound's point of origin.

Spermarche   The first ejaculation of sperm by males entering puberty.

Stage   Developmental period during which the organization of thought and behavior is qualitatively different from that of an earlier or later period.

Stereopsis   Ability to perceive a single image of an object even though perceptual input is binocular and differs slightly for each eye; significant source of cues for depth perception.

Stereotype threat   The psychological impact of negative social stereotypes in an individual.

Strange Situation   Standardized test that assesses the quality of infant-caregiver attachment.

Stranger anxiety   Fear or distress an infant shows at the approach of an unfamiliar person.

Structured interview   Standardized set of questions administered orally to participants.

Structured observation   Study in which behaviors are recorded as they occur within a situation constructed by the experimenter, usually in the laboratory.

Sudden infant death syndrome (SIDS)   Sudden, unexplained death of an infant or a toddler as a result of cessation of breathing during sleep.

Superego   In Freudian theory, a mental structure that monitors socially acceptable and unacceptable behavior.

Syntax   Grammatical rules that dictate how words can be combined.

Systems theory   Model for understanding the family that emphasizes the reciprocal interactions among various members.

Telegraphic speech   Early two-word speech that contains few modifiers, prepositions, or other connective words.

Temperament   Stable, early-appearing constellation of individual personality attributes believed to have a hereditary basis; includes sociability, emotionality, and activity level.

Teratogen   Any environmental agent that can cause deviations in prenatal development. Consequences may range from behavioral problems to death.

Test bias   Idea that the content of traditional standardized tests does not adequately measure the competencies of children from diverse cultural backgrounds.

Theory   Set of ideas or propositions that helps to organize or explain observable phenomena.

Theory of mind   Awareness of the concept of mental states, both one's own and those of others.

Triarchic theory   Theory developed by Robert Sternberg that intelligence consists of three major components: (1) the ability to adapt to the environment, (2) the ability to employ fundamental information-processing skills, and (3) the ability to deal with novelty and automatize processing.

Trisomy   Condition in which an extra chromosome is present.

Turn taking   Alternating vocalization by parent and child.

Turnabout   Element of conversation that requests a response from the child.

Ultrasonography   Method of using sound wave reflections to obtain a representation of the developing fetus. Used to estimate gestational age and detect fetal physical abnormalities.

Umbilical cord   Conduit of blood vessels through which oxygen, nutrients, and waste products are transported between placenta and embryo.

Unconditioned response (UCR)   Response that is automatically elicited by the unconditioned stimulus (UCS).

Unconditioned stimulus (UCS)   Stimulus that, without prior training, elicits a reflexlike response (unconditioned response).

Underextension   Application of a label to a narrower class of objects than the term signifies.

Uninvolved parent   Parent who is emotionally detached from the child and focuses on his or her own needs as opposed to the child's.

Utilization deficiency   Phenomenon by which a memory strategy, when first applied, may fail to improve memory in a noticeable way.

Validity   Degree to which an assessment procedure actually measures the variable under consideration.

Variable   Factor having no fixed or constant value in a given situation.

Vergence   Ability of the eyes to rotate in opposite directions to fixate on objects at different distances; improves rapidly during first few months after birth.

Viability   Ability of the baby to survive outside the mother's womb.

Visual accommodation   Visuomotor process by which small involuntary muscles change the shape of the lens of the eye so that images of objects seen at different distances are brought into focus on the retina.

Visual acuity   Ability to make fine discriminations among elements in a visual array by detecting contours, transitions in light patterns that signal borders and edges.

Visual cliff   Experimental apparatus used to test depth perception in which the surface on one side of a glass-covered table is made to appear far below the surface on the other side.

Vocabulary spurt   Period of rapid word acquisition that typically occurs early in language development.

Wernicke's area   Portion of the cerebral cortex that controls language comprehension.

Williams syndrome   Dominant genetic disorder involving the deletion of a set of genes that results in affected individuals typically having a strong social orientation, good musical ability, and some unusual capabilities; accompanied by mental retardation and severe deficits in numerical and spatial ability.

Working memory   Short-term memory store in which mental operations such as rehearsal and categorization take place.

X chromosome   Larger of the two sex chromosomes associated with genetic determination of sex. Normally females have two X chromosomes and males only one.

Y chromosome   Smaller of the two sex chromosomes associated with genetic determination of sex. Normally males have one Y chromosome and females none.

Zone of proximal development   Range of various kinds of support and assistance provided by an expert (usually an adult) who helps children to carry out activities they currently cannot complete but will later be able to accomplish independently.

Zygote   Fertilized egg cell.

Abbassi, V. (1998). Growth and normal puberty. *Pediatrics, 102,* 507–511.

Abel, E. L. (1981). Behavioral teratology of alcohol. *Psychological Bulletin,* 90, 564–581.

Abel, E. L. (1989). *Behavioral teratogenesis and behavioral mutagenesis: A primer in abnormal development.* New York: Plenum Press.

Aboud, F. E., & Skerry, S. (1983). Self and ethnic concepts in relation to ethnic constancy. *Canadian Journal of Behavioral Science, 15,* 14–26.

Abramovitch, R., & Grusec, J. E. (1978). Peer imitation in a natural setting. *Child Development, 49,* 60–65.

Achenbach, T. M., Howell, C. T., Aoki, M. F., & Rauh, V. A. (1993). Nine-year outcome of the Vermont Intervention Program for Low Birth Weight Infants. *Pediatrics, 91,* 45–55.

Ackerman, B. P., Abe, J. A., & Izard, C. E. (1998). Differential emotions theory and emotional development. In M. F. Mascolo & S. Griffin (Eds.), *What develops in emotional development?* (pp. 85–106). New York: Plenum.

Acredolo, L. P., & Goodwyn, S. W. (1988). Symbolic gesturing in normal infants. *Child Development, 59,* 450–466.

Acredolo, L. P., & Goodwyn, S. W. (1990a). Sign language among hearing infants: The spontaneous development of symbolic gestures. In V. Volterra & C. J. Erting (Eds.), *From gesture to language in hearing and deaf children.* New York: Springer-Verlag.

Acredolo, L. P., & Goodwyn, S. W. (1990b). Sign language in babies: The significance of symbolic gesturing for understanding language development. In R. Vasta (Ed.), *Annals of child development* (Vol. 7, pp. 1–42). Greenwich, CT: JAI Press.

Acredolo, L. P., Pick, H. L., Jr., & Olsen, M. G. (1975). Environmental differentiation and familiarity as determinants of children's memory for spatial location. *Developmental Psychology, 11,* 495–501.

Adair, R., Zuckerman, B., Bauchner, H., Philipp, B., & Levenson, S. (1992). Reducing night waking in infancy: A primary care intervention. *Pediatrics, 89,* 585–588.

Adams, R. J., & Courage, M. L. (1998). Human newborn color vision: Measurement with chromatic stimuli varying in excitation purity. *Journal of Experimental Child Psychology, 68,* 22–34.

Adams, S., Kuebli, J., Boyle, P. A., & Fivush, R. (1995). Gender differences in parent-child conversations about past emotions: A longitudinal investigation. *Sex Roles, 33,* 309–323.

Adi-Japha, E., & Freeman, N. H. (2001). Development of differentiation between writing and drawing systems. *Developmental Psychology, 37,* 101–114.

Adler, S. A., Gerhardstein, P., & Rovee-Collier, C. (1998). Levels-of-processing effects in infant memory? *Child Development, 69,* 280–294.

Adler, S. P. (1992). Cytomegalovirus and pregnancy. *Current Opinions in Obstetrics and Gynecology, 4,* 670–675.

Adoh, T. O., & Woodhouse, J. M. (1994). The Cardiff Acuity Test used for measuring visual acuity development in toddlers. *Vision Research, 34,* 555–560.

Adolph, K. E. (1997). Learning in the development of infant locomotion. *Monographs of the Society for Research in Child Development, 62*(3, Serial No. 251).

Adolph, K. E. (2000). Specificity of learning: Why infants fall over a veritable cliff. *Psychological Science, 11,* 290–295.

Adolph, K. E., Vereijken, B., & Denny, M. A. (1998). Learning to crawl. *Child Development, 69,* 1299–1312.

Agustines, L. A., Lin, Y. G., Rumney, P. J., Lu, M. C., Bonebrake, R., Asrat, T., & Nageotte, M. (2000). Outcomes of extremely low-birth-weight infants between 500 and 750 g. *American Journal of Obstetrics and Gynecology, 182,* 1114–1116.

Ahmed, A., & Ruffman, T. (1998). Why do infants make A not B errors in a search task, yet show memory for location of hidden objects in a non-search task? *Developmental Psychology, 34,* 441–453.

Ahnert, L., Rickert, H., & Lamb, M. E. (2000). Shared caregiving: Comparisons between home and child-care settings. *Developmental Psychology, 36,* 339–351.

Ainsworth, M. D. S., Bell, S. M., & Stayton, D. J. (1971). Individual differences in Strange Situation behavior of one-year-olds. In H. R. Schaffer (Ed.), *The origins of human social relations.* London: Academic Press.

Ainsworth, M. D. S., Bell, S. M., & Stayton, D. J. (1972). Individual differences in the development of some attachment behaviors. *Merrill-Palmer Quarterly, 18,* 123–143.

Ainsworth, M. D. S., Bell, S. M., & Stayton, D. J. (1974). Infant-mother attachment and social development: "Socialization" as a product of reciprocal responsiveness to signals. In M. R. Richards (Ed.), *The integration of the child into a social world.* London: Cambridge University Press.

Ainsworth, M. D. S., Blehar, M. C., Waters, E., & Wall, S. (1978). *Patterns of attachment: A psychological study of the strange situation.* Hillsdale, NJ: Erlbaum.

Akhtar, N., Carpenter, M., & Tomasello, M. (1996). The role of discourse novelty in early word learning. *Child Development, 67,* 635–645.

Akhtar, N., Jipson, J., & Callanan, M. A. (2001). Learning words through overhearing. *Child Development, 72,* 416–430.

Alaimo, K., Olson, C. M., & Frongillo, E. A., Jr. (2001). Food insufficiency and American school-aged children's cognitive, academic, and psychosocial development. *Pediatrics, 108,* 44–53.

Alan Guttmacher Institute. (1993). *Facts in Brief, March* (pp. 1–2). Chicago: Alan Guttmacher Innstitute.

Alessandri, S. M., & Lewis, M. (1993). Parental evaluation and its relation to shame and pride in young children. *Sex Roles, 29,* 335–343.

Alexander, J. M., Carr, M., & Schwanenflugel, P. J. (1995). Development of metacognition in gifted children: Directions for future research. *Developmental Review, 15,* 1–37.

Alexander, K. L., & Entwisle, D. R. (1988). Achievement in the first 2 years of school: Patterns and processes. *Monographs of the Society for Research in Child Development, 53*(2, Serial No. 218).

Alexander, K. L., Entwisle, D. R., & Bedinger, S. D. (1994). When expectations work: Race and socioeconomic differences in school performance. *Social Psychology Quarterly, 57,* 283–299.

Alfieri, T., Ruble, D. N., & Higgins, E. T. (1996). Gender stereotypes during adolescence: Developmental changes and the transition to junior high school. *Developmental Psychology, 32,* 1129–1137.

Allaire, A. D. (2001). Complementary and alternative medicine in the labor and delivery suite. *Clinical Obstetrics and Gynecology, 44,* 681–691.

Allen, J. P., Philliber, S., Herrling, S., & Kuperminc, G. P. (1997). Preventing teen pregnancy and academic failure: Experimental evaluation of a developmentally based approach. *Child Development, 64,* 729–742.

Allwood, M. A., Bell-Dolan, D., & Husain, S. A. (2002). Children's trauma and adjustment reactions to violent and nonviolent war experiences. *Journal of the American Academy of Child and Adolescent Psychiatry, 41,* 450–457.

Als, H., Lawhon, G., Duffy, F. H., McAnulty, G. B., Gibes-Grossman, R., Blickman, J. G. (1994). Individualized developmental care for the very low-birth-weight preterm infants: Medical and neurofunctional effects. *Journal of the American Medical Association, 272,* 853–858.

Alsaker, F. D. (1992). Pubertal timing, overweight, and psychological adjustment. *Journal of Early Adolescence, 12,* 396–419.

Alwitt, L. F., Anderson, D. R., Lorch, E. P., & Levin, S. R. (1980). Preschool children's visual attention to attributes of television. *Human Communication Research, 7,* 52–67.

Amato, P. R. (1999). Children of divorced parents as young adults. In E. M. Hetherington (Ed.), *Coping with divorce, single parenting, and remarriage* (pp. 147–163). Mahwah, NJ: Erlbaum.

Amato, P. R., & Rezac, S. J. (1994). Contact with nonresident parents, interparental conflict, and children's behavior. *Journal of Family Issues, 15,* 191–207.

Ambady, N., Shih, M., Kim, A., & Pittinsky, T. L. (2001). Stereotype susceptibility in children: Effects of identity activation on quantitative performance. *Psychological Science, 12,* 385–390.

American Academy of Pediatrics Committee on Drugs. (2001). The transfer of drugs and other chemicals into human milk. *Pediatrics, 108,* 776–789.

American Academy of Pediatrics Committee on Environmental Health. (1997). Environmental tobacco smoke: A hazard to children. *Pediatrics, 99,* 639–642.

American Academy of Pediatrics. Committee on Substance Abuse and Committee on Children with Disabilities. (1993). Fetal alcohol syndrome and fetal alcohol effects. *Pediatrics, 91,* 1004–1006.

American Academy of Pediatrics Task Force on Infant Sleep Position and Sudden Infant Death Syndrome. (2000). Changing concept of sudden infant death syndrome: Implications for infant sleeping environment and sleep position. *Pediatrics, 105,* 650–656.

American Association on Mental Retardation. (2002). *Definition of mental retardation.* Retrieved December 12, 2002, from http://www.aamr.org/Policies/faq_mental_retardation.shtml

American Association of University Women. (1992). *How schools shortchange girls.* Washington, DC: AAUW Educational Foundation.

American College of Obstetricians and Gynecologists. (1994). Substance abuse in pregnancy. *ACOG Technical Bulletin No. 195.*

American College of Obstetricians and Gynecologists Committee on Ethics. (2002). Sex selection. *Ethics in Obstetrics and Gynecology* (pp. 85–88). Washington, DC: The American College of Obstetricians and Gynecologists.

American Psychiatric Association. (1994). *Diagnostic and statistical manual of mental disorders* (4th ed.). Washington, DC.

American Psychiatric Association. (2002). *Fact sheet: Attention deficit/hyperactivity disorder.* Retrieved December 9, 2002, from http://www.psych.org/publicinfo/adhdfactsheet42401.pdf

Anand, K. J. S., and the International Evidence-Based Group for Neonatal Pain. (2001). Consensus statement for the prevention and management of pain in the newborn. *Archives of Pediatric and Adolescent Medicine, 155,* 173–180.

Andersen, R. E., Crespo, C. J., Bartlett, S. J., Cheskin, L. J., & Pratt, M. (1998). Relationship of physical activity and television watching with body weight and level of fatness among children: Results from the Third National Health and Nutrition Examination Survey. *Journal of the American Medical Association, 279,* 938–942.

Anderson, A. H., Clark, A., & Mullen, J. (1994). Interactive communication between children: Learning how to make language work in dialogue. *Journal of Child Language, 21,* 439–463.

Anderson, D. R., & Burns, J. (1991). Paying attention to television. In J. Bryant & D. Zillmann (Eds.), *Responding to the screen: Reception and reaction processes* (pp. 3–25). Hillsdale, NJ: Erlbaum.

Anderson, D. R., & Collins, P. A. (1988). *The impact of children's education: Television's influence on cognitive development* (Working Paper No. 2). Washington, DC: Office of Educational Research and Improvement.

Anderson, D. R., Huston, A. C., Schmitt, K. L., Lineberger, D. L., & Wright, J. C. (2001). Early childhood television viewing and adolescent behavior: The recontact study. *Monographs of the Society for Research in Child Development, 66*(Serial No. 264).

Anderson, D. R., Lorch, E. P., Field, D. E., Collins, P. A., & Nathan, J. G. (1986). Television viewing at home: Age trends in visual attention and time with TV. *Child Development, 57,* 1024–1033.

Anderson, D. R., Lorch, E. P., Field, D. E., & Sanders, J. (1981). The effects of TV program comprehensibility on preschool children's television viewing behavior. *Child Development, 52,* 151–157.

Anderson, K. E., Lytton, H., & Romney, D. M. (1986). Mothers' interactions with normal and conduct-disordered boys: Who affects whom? *Developmental Psychology, 22,* 604–609.

Anderson, M., Kaufman, J., Simon, T. R., Barrios, L., Paulozzi, L., Ryan, G., et al. (2001). School-associated violent deaths in the United States, 1994–1999. *Journal of the American Medical Association, 286,* 2695–2702.

Andersson, B. (1992). Effects of day-care on cognitive and socioemotional competence of thirteen-year-old Swedish schoolchildren. *Child Development, 63,* 20–36.

Anglin, J. M. (1993). Vocabulary development: A morphological analysis. *Monographs of the Society for Research in Child Development, 59* (5, Serial No. 242).

Angoff, W. H. (1988). The nature-nurture debate: Aptitudes and group differences. *American Psychologist, 43,* 713–720.

Anisfeld, M. (1996). Only tongue protrusion modeling is matched by neonates. *Developmental Review, 16,* 149–161.

Annett, M. (1973). Laterality of childhood hemiplegia and the growth of speech and intelligence. *Cortex, 9,* 4–33.

Antell, S. E., & Keating, D. P. (1983). Perception of numerical invariance in neonates. *Child Development, 54,* 695–701.

Antill, J. K., Goodnow, J. J., Russell, G., & Cotton, S. (1996). The influence of parents and family context on children's involvement in household tasks. *Sex Roles, 34,* 215–236.

Antonov, A. N. (1947). Children born during the siege of Leningrad in 1942. *Journal of Pediatrics, 30,* 250–259.

Apgar, V. (1953). A proposal for a new method of evaluation of the newborn infant. *Anesthesia and Analgesia: Current Researches, 32,* 260–267.

Arend, R., Gove, F. L., & Sroufe, L. A. (1979). Continuity of individual adaptation from infancy to kindergarten: A predictive study of ego-resiliency and curiosity in preschoolers. *Child Development, 50,* 950–959.

Ariès, P. (1962). *Centuries of childhood: A social history of family life* (R. Baldick, Trans.). New York: Vintage.

Arnett, J. J. (1999). Adolescent storm and stress, reconsidered. *American Psychologist, 54,* 317–326.

Arnold, D. S., & Whitehurst, G. J. (1994). Accelerating language development through picture book reading: A summary of dialogic reading and its effects. In D. K. Dickinson (Ed.), *Bridges to literacy: Children, families, and schools* (pp. 103–128). Cambridge, MA: Blackwell.

Aronfreed, J. (1976). Moral development from the standpoint of a general psychological theory. In T. Lickona (Ed.), *Moral development and moral behavior.* New York: Holt, Rinehart & Winston.

Arsenio, W. F., Cooperman, S., & Lover, A. (2000). Affective predictors of preschoolers' aggression and peer acceptance: Direct and indirect effects. *Developmental Psychology, 36,* 438–448.

Arsenio, W. F., & Ford, M. E. (1985). The role of affective information in social-cognitive development: Children's differentiation of moral and conventional events. *Merrill-Palmer Quarterly, 31,* 1–17.

Artigal, J. M. (1991). *The Catalan immersion program: A European point of view.* Norwood, NJ: Ablex.

Ary, D. V., Duncan, T. E., Biglan, A., Metzler, C. W., Noell, J. W., & Smolkowski, K. (1999). Development of adolescent problem behavior. *Journal of Abnormal Child Psychology, 27,* 141–150.

Asendorpf, J. B., & Baudonnière, P-M. (1993). Self-awareness and other-awareness: Mirror self-recognition and synchronic imitation among unfamiliar peers. *Developmental Psychology, 29,* 88–95.

Asher, S. R. (1983). Social competence and peer status: Recent advances and future directions. *Child Development, 54,* 1427–1434.

Asher, S. R., & Dodge, K. A. (1986). The identification of socially rejected children. *Developmental Psychology, 22,* 444–449.

Ashima-Takane, Y., Goodz, E., & Derevensky, J. L. (1996). Birth order effects on early language development: Do secondborn children learn from overheard speech? *Child Development, 67,* 621–634.

Ashley-Koch, A., Yang, Q., & Olney, R. S. (2000). Sickle hemoglobin (HbS) allele and sickle cell disease: A HuGE review. *American Journal of Epidemiology, 151,* 839–845.

Ashmead, D. H., Clifton, R. K., & Perris, E. E. (1987). Precision of auditory localization in human infants. *Developmental Psychology, 23,* 641–647.

Ashmead, D. H., Hill, E. W., & Talor, C. R. (1989). Obstacle perception by congenitally blind children. *Perception & Psychophysics, 46,* 425–433.

Aslin, R. N. (1987a). Motor aspects of visual development in infancy. In P. Salapatek & L. Cohen (Eds.), *Handbook of infant perception: From sensation to perception* (Vol. 1, pp. 43–113). Orlando, FL: Academic Press.

Aslin, R. N. (1987b). Visual and auditory development in infancy. In J. D. Osofsky (Ed.), *Handbook of infant development* (2nd ed., pp. 5–97). New York: Wiley.

Aslin, R. N. (1993). Perception of visual direction in human infants. In C. Granrud (Ed.), *Visual perception and cognition in infancy* (pp. 91–119). Hillsdale, NJ: Erlbaum.

Aslin, R. N. (2000). Why take the cog out of infant cognition? *Infancy, 1,* 463–470.

Aslin, R. N., Jusczyk, P. W., & Pisoni, D. B. (1998). Speech and auditory processing during infancy: Constraints on and precursors to language. In W. Damon (Series Ed.) & R. Siegler & D. Kuhn (Vol. Eds.), *Handbook of child psychology: Vol. 2. Cognition, perception, and language* (5th ed., pp. 147–198). New York: Wiley.

Aslin, R. N., Pisoni, D. B., & Jusczyk, P. W. (1983). Auditory development and speech perception in infancy. In M. M. Haith & J. J. Campos (Eds.), *Handbook of child psychology: Vol. II. Infancy and developmental psychobiology* (pp. 573–687). New York: Wiley.

Aslin, R. N., & Smith, L. B. (1988). Perceptual development. *Annual Review of Psychology, 39,* 435–473.

Astington, J. W., Harris, P. L., & Olson, D. R. (1988). *Developing theories of mind.* New York: Cambridge University Press.

Atkinson, R. C., & Shiffrin, R. M. (1968). Human memory: A proposed system and its control processes. In K. W. Spence & J. T. Spence (Eds.), *The psychology of learning and motivation: Advances in research and theory* (Vol. 2, pp. 90–95). New York: Academic Press.

Au, T. K.-F., Knightly, L. M., Jun, S.-A., & Oh, J. S. (2002). Overhearing a language during childhood. *Psychological Science, 13,* 238–243.

Avenevoli, S., Sess, F. M., & Steinberg, L. (1999). Family structure, parenting practices, and adolescent adjustment: An ecological examination. In E. M. Hetherington (Ed.), *Coping with divorce, single parenting, and remarriage* (pp. 65–90). Mahwah, NJ: Erlbaum.

Avery, A. W. (1982). Escaping loneliness in adolescence: The case for androgyny. *Journal of Youth and Adolescence, 11,* 451–459.

Aviezer, O., Sagi, A., Joels, T., & Ziv, Y. (1999). Emotional availability and attachment representations in kibbutz infants and their mothers. *Developmental Psychology, 35,* 811–821.

Avis, J., & Harris, P. L. (1991). Belief-desire reasoning among Baka children: Evidence for a universal conception of mind. *Child Development, 62,* 460–467.

Aylward, G. P., Pfeiffer, S. I., Wright, A., & Verhulst, S. J. (1989). Outcome studies of low birth weight infants published in the last decade: A meta-analysis. *Journal of Pediatrics, 115,* 515–520.

Bachevalier, J., Brickson, M., & Hagger, C. (1993). Limbic-dependent recognition memory in monkeys develops early in infancy. *Neuro Report, 4,* 77–80.

Bachevalier, J., Hagger, C., & Mishkin, M. (1991). Functional maturation of the occipitotemporal pathway in infant rhesus monkeys. In N. A. Lassen, D. H. Ingvar, M. E. Raichle, & L. Friberg (Eds.), *Brain work and mental activity* (pp. 231–240). Copenhagen: Munksgaard.

Bachman, J. G. (1970). *The impact of family background and intelligence on tenth grade boys: Vol. 2. Youth in transition.* Ann Arbor: Survey Research Center, Institute for Social Research.

Backscheider, A. G., Shatz, M., & Gelman, S. A. (1993). Preschoolers' ability to distinguish living kinds as a function of regrowth. *Child Development, 64,* 1242–1257.

Bader, A. P., & Phillips, R. D. (1999). Father's proficiency at recognizing their newborns by tactile cues. *Infant Behavior and Development, 22,* 405–409.

Bagwell, C. L., Newcomb, A. F., & Bukowski, W. M. (1998). Preadolescent friendship and peer rejection as predictors of adult adjustment. *Child Development, 69,* 140–153.

Bahrick, L. E. (1983). Infants' perception of substance and temporal synchrony in multimodal events. *Infant Behavior and Development, 6,* 429–451.

Bahrick, L. E. (2002). Generalization of learning in three-and-a-half-month-old infants on the basis of amodal relations. *Child Development, 73,* 667–681.

Bahrick, L. E., & Lickliter, R. (2000). Intersensory redundancy guides attentional selectivity and perceptual learning in infancy. *Developmental Psychology, 36,* 190–201.

Bahrick, L. E., Netto, D., & Hernandez-Reif, M. (1998). Intermodal perception of adult and child faces and voices by infants. *Child Development, 69,* 1263–1275.

Baillargeon, R. (1987a). Object permanence in 31/2- and 41/2-month-old infants. *Developmental Psychology, 23,* 655–664.

Baillargeon, R. (1987b). Young children's reasoning about the physical and spatial characteristics of a hidden object. *Cognitive Development, 2,* 179–200.

Baillargeon, R. (1995). Physical reasoning in infancy. In M. S. Gazzaniga (Ed.), *The cognitive neurosciences* (pp. 181–204). Cambridge, MA: MIT Press.

Baillargeon, R. (2001). Infants' physical knowledge: Of acquired expectations and core principles. In E. Dupoux (Ed.), *Language, brain, and cognitive development: Essays in honor of Jacques Mehler* (pp. 341–361). Cambridge, MA: MIT Press.

Baillargeon, R., & DeVos, J. (1991). Object permanence in young infants: Further evidence. *Child Development, 62,* 1227–1246.

Baille, M.-F., Arnaud, C., Cans, C., Grandjean, H., du Mazaubrun, C., & Rumeau-Rouquette, C. (1996). Prevalence, aetiology, and care of severe and profound hearing loss. *Archives of Disease in Childhood, 75,* 129–132.

Baker-Sennett, J., Matusov, E., & Rogoff, B. (1993). Planning as a developmental process. In H. W. Reese (Ed.), *Advances in child development and behavior* (Vol. 24, pp. 254–281). San Diego, CA: Academic Press.

Baker-Ward, L., Ornstein, P. A., & Holden, D. J. (1984). The expression of memorization in early childhood. *Journal of Experimental Child Psychology, 37,* 555–575.

Balaban, M. T., Anderson, L. M., & Wisniewski, A. B. (1998). Lateral asymmetries in infant melody perception. *Developmental Psychology, 34,* 39–48.

Baldwin, J. M. (1930). [Autobiography]. In C. Murchison (Ed.), *A history of psychology in autobiography* (Vol. 1). Worcester, MA: Clark University Press.

Bale, J. F., Jr., Zimmerman, B., Dawson, J. D., Souza, I. E., Petheram, S. J., & Murph, J. R. (1999). Cytomegalovirus transmission in child care homes. *Archives of Pediatrics and Adolescent Medicine, 153,* 75–79.

Bales, D. W., & Sera, M. D. (1995). Preschoolers' understanding of stable and changeable characteristics. *Cognitive Development, 10,* 69–107.

Balint, J. P. (1998). Physical findings in nutritional deficiencies. *Pediatric Clinics of North America, 45,* 245–260.

Ball, W., & Tronick, E. (1971). Infant responses to impending collision: Optical and real. *Science, 171,* 818–820.

Ballard, B. D., Gipson, M. T., Guttenberg, W., & Ramsey, K. (1980). Palatability of food as a factor influencing obese and normal-weight children's eating habits. *Behavior Research and Therapy, 18,* 598–600.

Bandura, A. (1969). *Principles of behavior modification.* New York: Holt, Rinehart & Winston.

Bandura, A. (1977a). Self-efficacy: Toward a unifying theory of behavioral change. *Psychological Review, 84,* 191–215.

Bandura, A. (1977b). *Social learning theory.* Englewood Cliffs, NJ: Prentice-Hall.

Bandura, A. (1986). *Social foundations of thought and action: A social cognitive theory.* Englewood Cliffs, NJ: Prentice-Hall.

Bandura, A. (1989). Social cognitive theory. In R. Vasta (Ed.), *Annals of child development: Vol. 6. Six theories of child development: Revised formulations and current issues* (pp. 1–60). Greenwich, CT: JAI Press.

Bandura, A., Barbaranelli, C., Caprara, G. V., & Pastorelli, C. (1996). Multifaceted impact of self-efficacy beliefs on academic functioning. *Child Development, 67,* 1206–1222.

Bandura, A., Barbaranelli, C., Caprara, G. V., & Pastorelli, C. (2001). Self-efficacy beliefs as shapers of children's aspirations and career trajectories. *Child Development, 72,* 187–206.

Bandura, A., Ross, D., & Ross, S. A. (1963a). Imitation of film-mediated aggressive models. *Journal of Abnormal and Social Psychology, 66,* 3–11.

Bandura, A., Ross, D., & Ross, S. A. (1963b). Vicarious reinforcement and imitative learning. *Journal of Abnormal and Social Psychology, 67,* 601–607.

Bandura, A., & Walters, R. H. (1959). *Adolescent aggression.* New York: Ronald Press.

Bandura, A., & Walters, R. H. (1963). *Social learning and personality development.* New York: Holt, Rinehart & Winston.

Banks, M. S., Aslin, R. N., & Letson, R. D. (1975). Sensitive period for the development of human binocular vision. *Science, 190,* 675–677.

Barber, B. K., & Harmon, E. L. (2002). Violating the self: Parental psychological control of children and adolescents. In B. K. Barber (Ed.), *Parental psychological control of children and adolescents* (pp. 15–52). Washington, DC: American Psychological Association.

Barber, B. L., & Eccles, J. S. (1992). Long-term influence of divorce and single-parenting on adolescent family- and work-related values, behaviors, and aspirations. *Psychological Bulletin, 111,* 108–126.

Barden, R. C., Zelko, F., Duncan, S. W., & Masters, J. C. (1980). Children's consensual knowledge about the experiential components of emotion. *Journal of Personality and Social Psychology, 39,* 968–976.

Barela, J. A., Jeka, J. J., & Clark, J. E. (1999). The use of somatosensory information during the acquisition of independent upright stance. *Infant Behavior and Development, 22,* 87–102.

Barinaga, M. (1994). Looking to development's future. *Science, 266,* 561–564.

Barkeling, B., Ekman, S., & Rössner, S. (1992). Eating behaviour in obese and normal weight 11-year-old children. *International Journal of Obesity, 16,* 355–360.

Barker, R., & Gump, P. (1964). *Big school, small school: High school size and student behavior.* Stanford, CA: Standard University Press.

Barkley, R. A. (1997). *ADHD and the nature of self-control.* New York: Guilford Press.

Barnes, K. (1971). Preschool play norms: A replication. *Developmental Psychology, 5,* 99–103.

Barnhart, H. X., Caldwell, M. B., Thomas, P., Mascola, L., Ortiz, I., Hus, H. W., et al. (1996). Natural history of human immunodeficiency virus disease in perinatally infected children: An analysis from the Pediatric Spectrum of Disease Project. *Pediatrics, 97,* 710–716.

Baron-Cohen, S. (1995). *Mindblindness: An essay on autism and theory of mind.* Cambridge, MA: MIT Press.

Baron-Cohen, S., Tager-Flusberg, H., & Cohen, D. J. (1993). *Understanding other minds: Perspectives from autism.* New York: Oxford University Press.

Barr, R., Dowden, A., & Hayne, H. (1996). Developmental changes in deferred imitation by 6- to 24-month-old infants. *Infant Behavior and Development, 19,* 159–170.

Barrett, K. C. (1998). A functionalist perspective to the development of emotions. In M. F. Mascolo & S. Griffin (Eds.), *What develops in emotional development?* (pp. 109–133). New York: Plenum.

Barrett, M. D. (1985). Issues in the study of children's single-word speech. In M. D. Barrett (Ed.), *Children's single-word speech.* Chichester, UK: Wiley.

Barrett, M. D. (1986). Early semantic representations and early word usage. In S. A. Kuczaj & M. D. Barrett (Eds.), *The development of word meaning.* New York: Springer-Verlag.

Barrett, M. D. (1989). Early language development. In A. Slater & G. Bremner (Eds.), *Infant development* (pp. 211–241). London: Erlbaum.

Barth, J. M. (1989, April). *Parent-child relationships and children's transition to school.* Paper presented at the biennial meeting of the Society for Research in Child Development, Kansas City, MO.

Bartlett, N. H., Vasey, P. L., & Bukowski, W. M. (2000). Is gender identity disorder in children a mental disorder? *Sex Roles, 43,* 753–785.

Baruch, C., & Drake, C. (1997). Tempo discrimination in infants. *Infant Behavior and Development, 20,* 573–577.

Basser, L. S. (1962). Hemiplegia of early onset and the faculty of speech with special reference to the effects of hemispherectomy. *Brain, 85,* 427–460.

Bates, E. (1979). *The emergence of symbols: Cognition and communication in infancy.* New York: Academic Press.

Bates, E., Bretherton, I., & Snyder, L. (1988). *From first words to grammar.* Cambridge, UK: Cambridge University Press.

Bates, E., Camaioni, L., & Volterra, V. (1975). The acquisition of performatives prior to speech. *Merrill-Palmer Quarterly, 21,* 205–224.

Bates, E., Marchman, V., Thal, D., Fenson, L., Dale, P., Reznick, J. S., et al. (1994). Developmental and stylistic variation in the composition of early vocabulary. *Journal of Child Language, 21,* 85–123.

Bates, J., Marvinney, D., Kelly, T., Dodge, K., Bennett, T., & Pettit, G. (1994). Child-care history and kindergarten adjustment. *Developmental Psychology, 30,* 690–700.

Bates, J. E., Maslin, C. A., & Frankel, K. A. (1985). Attachment security, mother-child interaction, and temperament as predictors of behavior-problem ratings at age three years. In I. Bretherton & E. Waters (Eds.), *Growing points of attachment theory and research. Monographs of the Society for Research in Child Development, 50*(1–2, Serial No. 209).

Bauer, P. J. (1993). Memory for gender-consistent and gender-inconsistent event sequences by twenty-five-month-old children. *Child Development, 64,* 285–297.

Bauer, P. J. (2002). Long-term recall memory: Behavioral and neuro-developmental changes in the first 2 years of life. *Current Directions in Psychological Science, 11,* 137–141.

Bauer, P. J., Liebl, M., & Stennes, L. (1998). PRETTY is to DRESS as BRAVE is to SUITCOAT: Gender-based property-to-property inferences by 4-1/2-year-old children. *Merrill-Palmer Quarterly, 44,* 355–377.

Bauer, P. J., & Mandler, J. M. (1992). Putting the horse before the cart: The use of temporal order in recall of events by one-year-old children. *Developmental Psychology, 28,* 441–452.

Bauer, P. J., Schwade, J. A., Wewerka, S. S., & Delaney, K. (1999). Planning ahead: Goal-directed problem solving by 2-year-olds. *Developmental Psychology, 35,* 1321–1337.

Bauer, P. J., Wenner, J. A., Dropik, P. L., & Wewerka, S. S. (2000). Parameters of remembering and forgetting in the transition from infancy to early childhood. *Monographs of the Society for Research in Child Development, 65*(4, Serial No. 263).

Baum, C. G., & Foreham, R. (1984). Social factors associated with adolescent obesity. *Journal of Pediatric Psychology, 9,* 293–302.

Baumrind, D. (1971). Current patterns of parental authority. *Developmental Psychology Monographs, 4*(1, Pt. 2).

Baumrind, D. (1972). From each according to her ability. *School Review, 80,* 161–197.

Baumrind, D. (1991). The influence of parenting style on adolescent competence and substance abuse. *Journal of Early Adolescence, 11,* 56–94.

Baumrind, D. (1993). The average expectable environment is not good enough: A response to Scarr. *Child Development, 64,* 1299–1317.

Baumrind, D. (1996). Parenting: The discipline controversy revisited. *Family Relations, 45,* 405–414.

Baumrind, D., Larzelere, R. E., & Cowan, P. A. (2002). Ordinary physical punishment: Is it harmful? Comment on Gershoff (2002). *Psychological Bulletin, 128,* 580–589.

Bauserman, R. (2002). Child adjustment in joint-custody versus sole-custody arrangements: A meta-analytic review. *Journal of Family Psychology, 16,* 91–102.

Baydar, N., & Brooks-Gunn, J. (1991). Effects of maternal employment and child care arrangements on preschoolers' cognitive and behavioral outcomes: Evidence from the children of the National Longitudinal Survey of Youth. *Developmental Psychology, 27,* 932–945.

Bayley, N. (1949). Consistency and variability in the growth of intelligence from birth to eighteen years. *Journal of Genetic Psychology, 75,* 165–196.

Bayley, N. (1993). *Bayley Scales of Infant Development* (2nd ed.). San Antonio: The Psychological Corporation.

Beauchamp, G. K., & Cowart, B. J. (1990). Preference for high salt concentrations among children. *Developmental Psychology, 26,* 539–545.

Beauchamp, G. K., & Moran, M. (1982). Dietary experience and sweet taste preferences in human infants. *Appetite, 3,* 139–152.

Beauchamp, T. L., Faden, R. R., Wallace, R. J., Jr., & Walters, L. (1982). *Ethical issues in social science research.* Baltimore, MD: Johns Hopkins University Press.

Beaudet, A. L., Scriver, C. R., Sly, W. S., & Valle, D. (1995). Genetics, biochemistry, and molecular basis of variant human phenotypes. In C. R. Scriver, A. L. Beaudet, W. S. Sly, & D. Valle (Eds.), *The metabolic and molecular bases of inherited disease,* Vol. I (7th ed., pp. 53–118). New York: McGraw-Hill.

Beck, R. W., & Beck, S. H. (1989). The incidence of extended households among middle-aged black and white women. *Journal of Family Issues, 10,* 147–168.

Becker, A. B., Manfreda, J., Ferguson, A. C., Dimich-Ward, H., Watson, W. T. A., Chan-Yeung, M. (1999). Breast-feeding and environmental tobacco smoke exposure. *Archives of Pediatric and Adolescent Medicine, 153,* 689–691.

Becker, J. (1989). Preschoolers' use of number words to denote one-to-one correspondence. *Child Development, 60,* 1147–1157.

Beckett, K. (1995). Fetal rights and "crack moms": Pregnant women in the war on drugs. *Contemporary Drug Problems, 22,* 587–612.

Behl-Chadha, G. (1996). Basic-level and superordinate-like categorical representations in early infancy. *Cognition, 60,* 105–141.

Behrman, R. E. (Ed.). (2000). Children and computer technology [Special issue]. *The Future of Children, 10*(2).

Beilin, H. (1989). Piagetian theory. In R. Vasta (Ed.), *Annals of child development: Vol. 6. Six theories of child development: Revised formulations and current issues* (pp. 85–131). Greenwich, CT: JAI Press.

Beilin, H., & Fireman, G. (1999). The foundation of Piaget's theories: Mental and physical action. *Advances in child development and behavior* (Vol. 27, pp. 221–246). San Diego: Academic Press.

Bell, M. A., & Fox, N. A. (1992). The relations between frontal brain electrical activity and cognitive development during infancy. *Child Development, 63,* 1142–1163.

Bell, R. Q. (1968). A reinterpretation of the direction of effects in studies of socialization. *Psychological Review, 75,* 81–95.

Bell, R. Q., & Harper, L. V. (1977). *Child effects on adults.* Hillsdale, NJ: Erlbaum.

Bell, S. M., & Ainsworth, M. D. S. (1972). Infant crying and maternal responsiveness. *Child Development, 43,* 1171–1190.

Belsky, J. (1980). Child maltreatment: An ecological integration. *American Psychologist, 35,* 320–335.

Belsky, J. (1981). Early human experience: A family perspective. *Developmental Psychology, 17,* 3–23.

Belsky, J. (1993). Etiology of child maltreatment: A developmental-ecological analysis. *Psychological Bulletin, 114,* 413–434.

Belsky, J. (1996). Parent, infant, and social-contextual antecedents of father-son attachment security. *Developmental Psychology, 32,* 905–913.

Belsky, J., & Rovine, M. J. (1988). Nonmaternal care in the first year of life and the security of infant-parent attachment. *Child Development, 59,* 157–167.

Bem, S. L. (1974). The measurement of psychological androgyny. *Journal of Consulting and Clinical Psychology, 42,* 155–162.

Bem, S. L. (1975). Sex role adaptability: One consequence of psychological androgyny. *Journal of Personality and Social Psychology, 31,* 634–643.

Bem, S. L. (1981). Gender schema theory: A cognitive account of sex-typing. *Psychological Review, 88,* 354–364.

Bem, S. L. (1983). Gender schema theory and its implications for child development: Raising gender aschematic children in a gender schematic society. *Signs, 8,* 598–616.

Bempechat, J., & Drago-Severson, E. (1999). Cross-national differences in academic achievement: Beyond etic conceptions of children's understanding. *Review of Educational Research, 69,* 287–314.

Bender, B. G., Harmon, R. J., Linden, M. G., & Robinson, A. (1995). Psychosocial adaptation of 39 adolescents with sex chromosome abnormalities. *Pediatrics, 96,* 302–308.

Bender, B. G., Linden, M. G., & Robinson, A. (1987). Environment and developmental risk in children with sex chromosome abnormalities. *Journal of the Academy of Child and Adolescent Psychiatry, 26,* 499–503.

Bendersky, M., & Lewis, M. (1999). Prenatal cocaine exposure and neonatal condition. *Infant Behavior and Development, 22,* 353–366.

Bennett, N. (1998). Annotation: Class size and the quality of educational outcomes. *Journal of Child Psychology and Psychiatry, 39,* 797–804.

Bennett, W. J. (1994). *The index of leading cultural indicators: Facts and figures on the state of American society.* New York: Simon & Schuster.

Bennetto, L., Pennington, B. F., & Rogers, S. J. (1996). Intact and impaired memory functions in autism. *Child Development, 67,* 1816–1835.

Benoit, D., & Parker, K. (1994). Stability and transmission of attachment across three generations. *Child Development, 65,* 1444–1456.

Benson, J. B. (1997). The development of planning: It's about time. In S. L. Friedman & E. K. Scholnick (Eds.), *The developmental psychology of planning: Why, how, and when do we plan?* (pp. 43–75). Mahwah, NJ: Erlbaum.

BenTsvi-Mayer, S., Hertz-Lazarowitz, R., & Safir, M. P. (1989). Teachers' selections of boys and girls as prominent pupils. *Sex Roles, 21,* 231–245.

Bercu, B. B. (1996). Growing conundrum: Growth hormone treatment of the non-growth hormone deficient child. *Journal of the American Medical Association, 276,* 567–568.

Bergin, D. A., Ford, M. E., & Hess, R. D. (1993). Patterns of motivation and social behavior associated with microcomputer use of young children. *Journal of Educational Psychology, 85,* 437–445.

Behrman, R. E. (Ed.). (2000). Children and computer technology [Special issue]. *The Future of Children, 10*(2).

Berk, L. E. (1986). Relationship of elementary school children's private speech to behavioral accompaniment to task, attention, and task performance. *Developmental Psychology, 22,* 671–680.

Berk, L. E. (1992). Children's private speech: An overview of theory and the status of research. In R. M. Diaz & L. E. Berk (Eds.), *Private speech: From social interaction to self-regulations* (pp. 17–53). Hillsdale, NJ: Erlbaum.

Berko, J. (1958). The child's learning of English morphology. *Word, 14,* 150–177.

Berndt, T. J. (1979). Developmental changes in conformity to peers and parents. *Developmental Psychology, 15,* 608–616.

Berndt, T. J. (1981). Relations between social cognition, nonsocial cognition, and social behavior: The case of friendship. In J. H. Flavell & L. D. Ross (Eds.), *Social cognitive development: Frontiers and possible futures.* Cambridge, UK: Cambridge University Press.

Berndt, T. J. (1999). Friends' influence on school adjustment. In W. A. Collins & B. Laursen (Eds.), *Minnesota Symposia on Child Psychology: Vol. 30. Relationships as developmental contexts* (pp. 85–107). Mahwah, NJ: Erlbaum.

Berndt, T. J., Hawkins, J. A., & Jiao, Z. (1999). Influences of friends and friendships on adjustment to junior high school. *Merrill-Palmer Quarterly, 45,* 13–41.

Berndt, T. J., & Keefe, K. (1995). Friends' influence on adolescents' adjustment to school. *Child Development, 66,* 1312–1329.

Berry, J. W. (1966). Temne and Eskimo perceptual skills. *International Journal of Psychology, 1,* 207–229.

Bertenthal, B. I. (1993). Infants' perception of biomechanical motions: Intrinsic image and knowledge-based constraints. In C. Granrud (Ed.), *Visual perception and cognition in infancy* (pp. 175–214). Hillsdale, NJ: Erlbaum.

Berthier, N. E. (1996). Learning to reach: A mathematical model. *Developmental Psychology, 32,* 811–823.

Berthier, N. E., DeBlois, S., Poirier, C. R., Novak, M. A., & Clifton, R. K. (2000). Where's the ball? Two- and three-year-olds reason about unseen events. *Developmental Psychology, 36,* 394–401.

Berthier, N. E., & Robin, D. J. (1998). Midreach correction in 7-month-olds. *Journal of Motor Behavior, 30,* 290–300.

Berthoud-Papandropoulou, I. (1978). An experimental study of children's ideas about language. In A. Sinclair, R. J. Jarvella, & W. J. M. Levelt (Eds.), *The child's conception of language* (pp. 55–64). Heidelberg: Springer-Verlag.

Best, C. T., Hoffman, H., & Glanville, B. B. (1982). Development of infant ear asymmetries for speech and music. *Perception and Psychophysics, 31,* 75–85.

Best, C. T., McRoberts, G. W., LaFleur, R., & Silver-Isenstadt, J. (1995). Divergent developmental patterns for infants' perception of two nonnative consonant contrasts. *Infant Behavior and Development, 18,* 339–350.

Best, D. L., & Williams, J. E. (1993). A cross-cultural viewpoint. In A. E. Beall & R. J. Sternberg (Eds.), *The psychology of gender* (pp. 215–248). New York: Guilford Press.

Betts, P. (2000) Which children should receive growth hormone treatment: Long term side effects possible with high doses. *Archives of Disease in Childhood, 83,* 177–178.

Beyer, S. (1995). Maternal employment and children's academic achievement: Parenting styles as mediating variable. *Developmental Review, 15,* 212–253.

Bialystok, E. (1986). Factors in the growth of linguistic awareness. *Child Development, 57,* 498–510.

Bialystok, E. (1999). Cognitive complexity and attentional control in the bilingual mind. *Child Development, 70,* 636–644.

Bialystok, E. (2001). *Bilingualism in development: Language, literacy, and cognition.* Cambridge, UK: Cambridge University Press.

Biederman, J., Faraone, S. V., Keenan, K., Knee, D., & Tsuang, M. T. (1990). Family-genetic and psychosocial risk factors in DSM-III attention deficit disorder. *Journal of the American Academy of Child and Adolescent Psychiatry, 29,* 526–533.

Bierman, K. L. (1986). Process of change during social skills training with preadolescents and its relation to treatment outcome. *Child Development, 57,* 230–240.

Bierman, K. L., Smoot, D. L., & Aumiller, K. (1993). Characteristics of aggressive-rejected, aggressive (nonrejected), and rejected (nonaggressive) boys. *Child Development, 64,* 139–151.

Bigelow, B. J., & LaGaipa, J. J. (1975). Children's written descriptions of friendship: A multidimensional analysis. *Developmental Psychology, 11,* 857–858.

Bigelow, B. J., Tesson, G., & Lewko, J. H. (1992). The social rules that children use: Close friends, other friends, and "other kids" compared to parents, teachers, and siblings. *International Journal of Behavioral Development, 15,* 315–335.

Bigler, R. S. (1995). The role of classification skill in moderating environmental effects on children's gender stereotyping: A study of the functional use of gender in the classroom. *Child Development, 66,* 1072–1087.

Bigler, R. S., Brown, C. S., & Markell, M. (2001). When groups are not created equal: Effects of group status on the formation of intergroup attitudes in children. *Child Development, 72,* 1151–1162.

Bigler, R. S., Jones, L. C., & Lobliner, D. B. (1997). Social categorization and the formation of intergroup attitudes in children. *Child Development, 68,* 530–543.

Bijou, S. W. (1989). Behavior analysis. In R. Vasta (Ed.), *Annals of child development: Vol 6. Six theories of child development: Revised formulations and current issues* (pp. 61–83). Greenwich, CT: JAI Press.

Biller, H. B. (1974). *Paternal deprivation: Family, school, sexuality and society.* Lexington, MA: Heath.

Billing, L., Eriksson, M., Jonsson, B., Steneroth, G., & Zetterström, R. (1994). The influence of environmental factors on behavioral problems in 8-year-old children exposed to amphetamine during fetal life. *Child Abuse & Neglect, 18,* 3–9.

Binet, A., & Simon, T. (1905). Méthodes nouvelles pour le diagnostic du niveau intellectuel des anormaux. *L'Anée Psychologique, 11,* 191–244.

Birch, L. L., & Davison, K. K. (2001). Family environmental factors influencing the developing behavioral controls of food intake and childhood overweight. *Pediatric Clinics of North America, 48,* 893–907.

Birdsong, D., & Molis, M. (2001). On evidence for maturational constraints in second-language acquisition. *Journal of Memory and Language, 44,* 235–249.

Biro, F. M., McMahon, R. P., Striegel-Moore, R., Crawford, P. B., Obarzanek, E., Morrison, J. A., et al. (2001). Impact of timing of pubertal maturation on growth in black and white female adolescents: The National Heart, Lung, and Blood Institute Growth and Health Study. *Journal of Pediatrics, 138,* 636–643.

Bithoney, W. G., Van Sciver, M. M., Foster, S., Corson, S., & Tentindo, C. (1995). Parental stress and growth outcome in growth-deficient children. *Pediatrics, 96,* 707–711.

Bivens, J. A., & Berk, L. E. (1990). A longitudinal study of the development of elementary school children's private speech. *Merrill-Palmer Quarterly, 36,* 443–463.

Bjorklund, D. F., & Harnishfeger, K. K. (1990). The resources construct in cognitive development: Diverse sources of evidence and a theory of inefficient inhibition. *Developmental Review, 10,* 48–71.

Bjorklund, D. F., Ornstein, P. A., & Haig, J. R. (1977). Development of organization and recall: Training in the use of organizational techniques. *Developmental Psychology, 13,* 175–183.

Bjorklund, D. F., & Rosenblum, K. E. (2002). Context effects in children's selection and use of simple arithmetic strategies. *Journal of Cognition and Development, 3,* 225–242.

Bjorkqvist, K. (1994). Sex differences in physical, verbal, and indirect aggression: A review of recent research. *Sex Roles, 30,* 177–188.

Black, B., & Hazen, N. L. (1990). Social status and patterns of communication in acquainted and unacquainted preschool children. *Developmental Psychology, 26,* 379–387.

Black, B., & Logan, A. (1995). Links between communication patterns in mother-child, father-child, and child-peer interactions and children's social status. *Child Development, 66,* 255–271.

Black, M. M., Dubowitz, H., & Starr, R. H., Jr. (1999). African American fathers in low income, urban families: Development, behavior, and home environment of their three-year-old children. *Child Development, 70,* 967–978.

Black, M. M., & Rollins, H. A., Jr. (1982). The effects of instructional variables on young children's organization and recall. *Journal of Experimental Child Psychology, 33,* 1–19.

Blake, J. (1989). Number of siblings and educational attainment. *Science, 245,* 32–36.

Blampied, N. M., & France, K. G. (1993). A behavioral model of infant sleep disturbance. *Journal of Applied Behavior Analysis, 26,* 477–492.

Blasco, P. A. (1994). Primitive reflexes: Their contribution to the early detection of cerebral palsy. *Clinical Pediatrics, 33,* 388–397.

Blasi, A. (1980). Bridging moral cognition and moral action: A critical review of the literature. *Psychological Bulletin, 88,* 1–45.

Blasi, A., & Glodis, K. (1995). The development of identity: A critical analysis from the perspective of the self as subject. *Developmental Review, 15,* 404–433.

Blass, E. M., Ganchrow, J. R., & Steiner, J. E. (1984). Classical conditioning in newborn humans 2–48 hours of age. *Infant Behavior and Development, 7,* 223–235.

Blinkov, S. M., & Glezer, I. I. (1968). *The human brain in figures and tables: A quantitative handbook.* New York: Basic Books.

Block, J. H. (1971). *Lives through time.* Berkeley, CA: Bancroft Books.

Block, J. H. (1973). Conceptions of sex role: Some cross-cultural and longitudinal perspectives. *American Psychologist, 28,* 512–526.

Block, J. H. (1983). Differential premises arising from differential socialization of the sexes: Some conjectures. *Child Development, 54,* 1335–1354.

Block, J. H., & Block, J. (1980). The role of ego-control and ego-resiliency in the organization of behavior. In W. A. Collins (Ed.), *The Minnesota symposia on child psychology: Vol. 13. Development of cognition, affect, and social relations.* Hillsdale, NJ: Erlbaum.

Block, J. H., & Robins, R. W. (1993). A longitudinal study of consistency and change in self-esteem from early adolescence to early adulthood. *Child Development, 64,* 909–923.

Bloom, B. S. (1982). The role of gifts and markers in the development of talent. *Exceptional Children, 48,* 510–522.

Bloom, L. (1973). *One word at a time.* The Hague: Mouton.

Bloom, L. (1991). *Language development from two to three.* Cambridge, UK: Cambridge University Press.

Bloom, L. (1998). Language acquisition in its developmental context. In W. Damon (Series Ed.) & D. Kuhn & R. S. Siegler (Vol. Eds.), *Handbook of child psychology: Vol. 2: Cognition, perception, and language.* (5th ed., pp. 309–370). New York: Wiley.

Bloom, L., Lightbown, P., & Hood, L. (1975). Structure and variation in child language and the acquisition of grammatical morphemes. *Monographs of the Society for Research in Child Development, 40* (2, Serial No. 160).

Bloom, L., & Tinker, E. (2001). The intentionality model of language acquisition. *Monographs of the Society for Research in Child Development, 66*(4 Serial No. 267).

Bloom, P. (1990). Syntactic distinctions in child language. *Journal of Child Language, 17,* 343–355.

Bloom, P. (2000). *How children learn the meanings of words.* Cambridge, MA: MIT Press.

Bock, J. K., & Hornsby, M. E. (1981). The development of directives: How children ask and tell. *Journal of Child Language, 8,* 151–163.

Boddy, J., Skuse, D., & Andrews, B. (2000). The developmental sequelae of nonorganic failure to thrive. *Journal of Child Psychology and Psychiatry, 41,* 1003–1014.

Boehm, A. (1985). Educational applications of intelligence testing. In B. B. Wolman (Ed.), *Handbook of intelligence* (pp. 933–964). New York: Wiley.

Boehnke, K., Silbereisen, R. K., Eisenberg, N., Reykowski, J., & Palmonari, A. (1989). Developmental pattern of prosocial motivation: A cross-national study. *Journal of Cross-Cultural Psychology, 20,* 219–243.

Bogartz, R. S., & Shinskey, J. L. (1998). On perception of a partially occluded object in 6-month-olds. *Cognitive Development, 13,* 141–163.

Bogartz, R. S., Shinskey, J. L., & Schilling, T., H. (2000). Object permanence in five-and-a-half-month-olds? *Infancy, 1,* 403–428.

Bogartz, R. S., Shinskey, J. L., & Speaker, C. J. (1997). Interpreting infant looking: The event set × event set design. *Developmental Psychology, 33,* 408–422.

Bogatz, G., & Ball, S. (1972). *The second year of Sesame Street: A continuing evaluation.* Princeton, NJ: Educational Testing Service.

Bogenschneider, K., Wu, M., Raffaeilli, M., & Tsay, J. C. (1998). Parent influences on adolescent peer orientation and substance abuse: The interface of parenting practices and values. *Child Development, 69,* 1672–1688.

Boggiano, A. K., Shields, A., Barrett, M., Kellam, T., Thompson, E., Simons, J., & Katz, P. (1992). Helplessness deficits in students: The role of motivation orientation. *Motivation and Emotion, 16,* 271–296.

Boivin, M., & Hymel, S. (1997). Peer experiences and social self-perceptions: A sequential model. *Developmental Psychology, 33,* 135–145.

Bongaerts, T. (1999). Ultimate attainment in foreign language pronunciation: The case of very advanced foreign language learners. In D. Birdsong (Ed.), *Second language acquisition and the critical period hypothesis* (pp. 133–159). Mahwah, NJ: Erlbaum.

Bookstein, F. L., Sampson, P. D., Streissguth, A. P., & Barr, H. M. (1996). Exploiting redundant measure of dose and developmental outcome: New methods from the behavioral teratology of alcohol. *Developmental Psychology, 32,* 404–415.

Boom, J., Brugman, D., & van der Heijden, P. G. M. (2001). Hierarchical structure of moral stages assessed by a sorting task. *Child Development, 72*, 535–548.

Booth, C. L., Rose-Krasnor, L., McKinnon, J., & Rubin, K. H. (1995). Predicting social adjustment in middle childhood: The role of preschool attachment security and maternal style. *Social Development, 3*, 189–204.

Borke, H. (1973). The development of empathy in Chinese and American children between three and six years of age: A cross-culture study. *Developmental Psychology, 9*, 102–108.

Borke, H. (1975). Piaget's mountains revisited: Changes in the egocentric landscape. *Developmental Psychology, 11*, 240–243.

Bornstein, M. H., Haynes, O. M., Pascual, L., Painter, K. M., & Galperín, C. (1999). Play in two societies: Pervasiveness of process, specificity of structure. *Child Development, 70*, 317–331.

Bornstein, M. H., & Sigman, M. D. (1986). Continuity in mental development from infancy. *Child Development, 57*, 251–274.

Bornstein, M. H., Tal, J., Rahn, C., Galperín, G. Z., Pêcheux, M., Lamour, M., et al. (1992). Functional analysis of the contents of maternal speech to infants of 5 and 13 months in four cultures: Argentina, France, Japan, and the United States. *Developmental Psychology, 28*, 593–603.

Borstelmann, L. J. (1983). Children before psychology: Ideas about children from antiquity to the late 1800s. In W. Kessen (Ed.), *Handbook of child psychology: Vol. I. History, theory, and methods* (4th ed., pp. 1–40). New York: Wiley.

Bosma, H. A., & Kunnen, E. S. (2001). Determinants and mechanisms in ego identity development: A review and synthesis. *Developmental Review, 21*, 39–66.

Bouchard, T. J., Jr. (1984). Twins reared together and apart: What they tell us about human diversity. In S. W. Fox (Ed.), *Individuality and determinism: Chemical and biological bases.* New York: Plenum Press.

Bouchard, T. J., Jr. (1997). IQ similarity in twins reared apart: Findings and responses to critics. In R. J. Sternberg & E. Grigorenko (Eds.), *Intelligence, heredity and environment* (pp. 126–160). New York: Cambridge University Press.

Bouchard, T. J., Jr., Lykken, D. T., McGue, M., Segal, N. L., & Tellegen, A. (1990). Sources of human psychological differences: The Minnesota Study of Twins Reared Apart. *Science, 250*, 223–228.

Boulton, M. J., & Underwood, K. (1992). Bully/victim problems among middle school children. *British Journal of Educational Psychology, 62*, 73–87.

Bousha, D. M., & Twentyman, C. Y. (1984). Mother-child interactional style and abuse, neglect, and control groups: Naturalistic observations in the home. *Journal of Abnormal Psychology, 93*, 106–114.

Bowerman, M. (1978). The acquisition of word meaning: An investigation of some current conflicts. In N. Waterson & C. Snow (Eds.), *The development of communication.* New York: Wiley.

Bowlby, J. (1958). The nature of the child's tie to his mother. *International Journal of Psychoanalysis, 39*, 350–373.

Bowlby, J. (1969). *Attachment and loss: Vol. 1. Attachment.* New York: Basic Books.

Bowlby, J. (1973). *Attachment and loss. Vol. 2. Separation: Anxiety and anger.* New York: Basic Books.

Boyes, M. C., & Allen, S. G. (1993). Styles of parent-child interaction and moral reasoning in adolescence. *Merrill-Palmer Quarterly, 39*, 551–570.

Boykin, A. W. (1986). The triple quandary and the schooling of Afro-American children. In U. Neisser (Ed.), *The school achievement of minority children: New perspectives.* Hillsdale, NJ: Erlbaum.

Boysson-Bardies, B. de, Halle, P., Sagart, L., & Durand, C. (1989). A crosslinguistic investigation of vowel formants in babbling. *Journal of Child Language, 16*, 1–17.

Brackbill, Y. (1975). Continuous stimulation and arousal level in infancy: Effects of stimulus intensity and stress. *Child Development, 46*, 364–369.

Brackbill, Y., McManus, K., & Woodward, L. (1985). *Medication in maternity: Infant exposure and maternal information.* Ann Arbor: University of Michigan Press.

Bradbard, M. R., Martin, C. L., Endsley, R. C., & Halverson, C. F. (1986). Influence of sex stereotypes on children's exploration and memory: A competence versus performance distinction. *Developmental Psychology, 22*, 481–486.

Bradley, R. H. (1989). The use of the HOME inventory in longitudinal studies of child development. In M. H. Bornstein & N. A. Krasnegor (Eds.), *Stability and continuity in mental development: Behavioral and biological perspectives* (pp. 191–215). Hillsdale, NJ: Erlbaum.

Bradley, R. H., & Caldwell, B. M. (1976). The relation of infants' home environments to mental test performance at fifty-four months: A follow-up study. *Child Development, 47*, 1172–1174.

Bradley, R. H., & Caldwell, B. M. (1984). The relation of infants' home environments to achievement test performance in first grade: A follow-up study. *Child Development, 55*, 803–809.

Braine, M. D. S. (1976). Children's first word combinations. *Monographs of the Society for Research in Child Development, 41*(1, Serial No. 164).

Brainerd, C. J. (1978a). *Piaget's theory of intelligence.* Englewood Cliffs, NJ: Prentice-Hall.

Brainerd, C. J. (1978b). The stage question in cognitive-developmental theory. *Brain and Behavioral Science, 2*, 173–213.

Brainerd, C. J. (1996). Piaget: A centennial celebration. *Psychological Science, 7*, 191–195.

Brainerd, C. J., & Gordon, L. L. (1994). Development of verbatim and gist memory for numbers. *Developmental Psychology, 30*, 163–177.

Brainerd, C. J., & Mojardin, A. H. (1998). Children's and adults' spontaneous false memories: Long-term persistence and mere-testing effects. *Child Development, 69*, 1361–1377.

Brand, E., Clingempeel, W. E., & Bowen-Woodward, K. (1988). Family relationships and children's psychological adjustment in stepmother and stepfather families: Findings and conclusions from the Philadelphia Stepfamily Research Project. In E. M. Hetherington & J. D. Arasteh (Eds.), *Impact of divorce, single-parenting, and stepparenting on children* (pp. 299–324). Hillsdale, NJ: Erlbaum.

Brand, J. E., & Greenberg, B. S. (1994). Commercials in the classroom: The impact of Channel One advertising. *Journal of Advertising Research, 34*, 18–27.

Bray, J. H. (1988). Children's development during early remarriage. In E. M. Hetherington & J. D. Arasteh (Eds.), *Impact of divorce, single parenting, and stepparenting on children* (pp. 279–298). Hillsdale, NJ: Erlbaum.

Bray, J. H. (1999). From marriage to remarriage and beyond: Findings from the Developmental Issues in Stepfamilies Research Project. In E. M. Hetherington (Ed.), *Coping with divorce, single parenting, and remarriage* (pp. 253–271). Mahwah, NJ: Erlbaum.

Brazelton, T. B. (1973). *Neonatal Behavioral Assessment Scale.* Philadelphia: J. B. Lippincott.

Brazelton, T. B., Nugent, J. K., & Lester, B. M. (1987). Neonatal Behavioral Assessment Scale. In J. D. Osofsky (Ed.), *Handbook of infant development* (2nd ed., pp. 780–817). New York: Wiley.

Breedlove, S. M. (1994). Sexual differentiation of the human nervous system. *Annual Review of Psychology, 45*, 389–418.

Bregman, J. (1998). Developmental outcome in very low birthweight infants: Current status and future trends. *Pediatric Clinics of North America, 45*, 673–690.

Bremner, A., & Bryant, P. (2001). The effect of spatial cues on infants' responses in the AB task, with and without a hidden object. *Developmental Science, 4*, 408–415.

Bremner, J. D. (1999). Does stress damage the brain? *Biological Psychiatry, 45*, 797–805.

Bremner, J. D., & Narayan, M. (1998). The effects of stress on memory and the hippocampus throughout the life cycle: Implications for childhood development and aging. *Development and Psychopathology, 10*, 871–885.

Bremner, J. G. (1978). Egocentric versus allocentric spatial coding in nine-month-old infants: Factors influencing the choice of code. *Developmental Psychology, 14*, 346–355.

Bremner, J. G. (1998). From perception to action: The early development of knowledge. In F. Simion & G. Butterworth (Eds.), *The development of sensory, motor and cognitive capacities in early infancy* (pp. 239–255). East Sussex, England: Psychology Press.

Bremner, J. G., & Bryant, P. E. (1977). Place versus response as the basis for spatial errors made by young infants. *Journal of Experimental Child Psychology, 23*, 162–171.

Brenner, R. A., Simons-Morton, B. G., Bhaskar, B., Mehta, N., Melnick, V., Revenis, M., et al. (1998). Prevalence and predictors of the prone sleep position among inner-city infants. *Journal of the American Medical Association, 280*, 341–346.

Bretherton, I., & Beeghly, M. (1982). Talking about internal states: The acquisition of an explicit theory of mind. *Developmental Psychology, 18*, 906–921.

Breznitz, Z., & Teltsch, T. (1989). The effect of school entrance age on academic achievement and social-emotional adjustment of children: Follow-up study of fourth graders. *Psychology in the Schools, 26*, 62–68.

Brisk, M. (1998). *Bilingual education: From compensatory to quality schooling.* Mahwah, NJ: Erlbaum.

Broberg, A. G., Wessels, H., Lamb, M. E., & Hwang, C. P. (1997). Effects of day care on the development of cognitive abilities in 8-year-olds: A longitudinal study. *Developmental Psychology, 33,* 62–69.

Brody, E. B., & Brody, N. (1976). *Intelligence: Nature, determinants, and consequences.* New York: Academic Press.

Brody, G. H., & Flor, D. L. (1998). Maternal resources, parenting practices, and child competence in rural, single-parent African American families. *Child Development, 69,* 803–816.

Brody, G. H., Flor, D. L., & Gibson, N. M. (1999). Linking maternal efficacy beliefs, developmental goals, parenting practices, and child competence in rural single-parent African American families. *Child Development, 70,* 1197–1208.

Brody, G. H., Ge, X., Conger, R., Gibbons, F. X., Murry, V. M., Gerrard, M., & Simons, R. L. (2001). The influence of neighborhood disadvantage, collective socialization, and parenting on African American children's affiliation with deviant peers. *Child Development, 72,* 1231–1246.

Brody, G. H., & Stoneman, Z. (1981). Selective imitation of same-age, older, and younger peer models. *Child Development, 52,* 717–720.

Brody, G. H., & Stoneman, Z. (1994). Sibling relationships and their association with parental differential treatment. In E. M. Hetherington, D. Reiss, & R. Plomin (Eds.), *Separate social worlds of siblings* (pp. 129–142). Hillsdale, NJ: Erlbaum.

Brody, G. H., Stoneman, Z., & Flor, D. (1996). Parental religiosity, family processes, and youth competence in rural, two-parent African American families. *Developmental Psychology, 32,* 696–706.

Brody, G. H., Stoneman, Z., & McCoy, J. K. (1992). Associations of maternal and paternal direct and differential behavior with sibling relationships: Contemporaneous and longitudinal analyses. *Child Development, 63,* 82–92.

Brody, N. (1992). *Intelligence* (2nd ed.). San Diego: Academic Press.

Brodzinsky, D. M., Schecter, D. E., Braff, A. M., & Singer, L. M. (1984). Psychological and academic adjustment in adopted children. *Journal of Consulting and Clinical Psychology, 52,* 582–590.

Bronfenbrenner, U. (1977). Toward an experimental ecology of human development. *American Psychologist, 32,* 513–531.

Bronfenbrenner, U. (1986). Ecology of the family as a context for human development: Research perspectives. *Developmental Psychology, 22,* 723–742.

Bronfenbrenner, U. (1989). Ecological systems theory. In R. Vasta (Ed.), *Annals of child development: Vol 6. Six theories of child development: Revised formulations and current issues* (pp. 187–251). Greenwich, CT: JAI Press.

Bronfenbrenner, U. (1995). Developmental ecology through space and time: A future perspective. In P. Moen, G. H. Elder, & K. Luescher (Eds.), *Examining lives in context: Perspectives on the ecology of human development* (pp. 619–647). Washington, DC: American Psychological Association.

Bronfenbrenner, U., & Ceci, S. J. (1994). Nature-nurture reconceptualized in developmental perspective: A bioecological model. *Psychological Review, 101,* 568–586.

Bronson, G. W. (1994). Infants' transitions toward adult-like scanning. *Child Development, 65,* 1243–1261.

Bronson, W. (1981). Toddlers' behavior with age-mates: Issues of interaction, cognition, and affect. In L. Lipsitt (Ed.), *Monographs on infancy* (Vol. 1). Norwood, NJ: Ablex.

Brook, C. G. D. (2000). Which children should receive growth hormone treatment: Reserve it for the GH deficient. *Archives of Disease in Childhood, 83,* 176.

Brooks, P. J., & Tomasello, M. (1999). Young children learn to produce passives with nonce verbs. *Developmental Psychology, 35,* 29–44.

Brooks, R. B. (1992). Self-esteem during the school years: Its normal development and hazardous decline. *Pediatric Clinics of North America, 39,* 537–550.

Brooks-Gunn, J. (1989). Pubertal processes and the early adolescent transition. In W. Damon (Ed.), *Child development today and tomorrow* (pp. 155–176). San Francisco: Jossey-Bass.

Brooks-Gunn, J., & Chase-Lansdale, P. L. (1995). Adolescent parenthood. In M. H. Bornstein (Ed.), *Handbook of parenting: Vol. 3. Status and social conditions of parenting* (pp. 113–149). Mahwah, NJ: Erlbaum.

Brooks-Gunn, J., Han, W. J., & Waldfogel, J. (2002). Maternal employment and child cognitive outcomes in the first three years of life: The NICHD study of early child care. *Child Development, 73,* 1052–1072.

Brooks-Gunn, J., Klebanov, P. K., & Duncan, G. J. (1996). Ethnic differences in children's intelligence test scores: Role of economic deprivation, home environment, and maternal characteristics. *Child Development, 67,* 396–408.

Brooks-Gunn, J., Klebanov, P. K., Liaw, F., & Spiker, D. (1993). Enhancing the development of low-birthweight, premature infants: Changes in cognition and behavior over the first three years. *Child Development, 64,* 736–754.

Brooks-Gunn, J., & Ruble, D. (1980). Menarche: The interaction of physiology, cultural, and social factors. In A. J. Dan, E. A. Graham, & C. P. Beecher (Eds.), *The menstrual cycle: A synthesis of interdisciplinary research* (pp. 141–159). New York: Springer-Verlag.

Brooks-Gunn, J., & Warren, M. P. (1989). Biological and social contributions to negative affect in young adolescent girls. *Child Development, 60,* 40–55.

Brophy, J. (1986). Teacher influences on student achievement. *American Psychologist, 41,* 1069–1077.

Brown, A. L. (1990). Domain-specific principles affect learning and transfer in children. *Cognitive Science, 14,* 107–133.

Brown, A. L., Campione, J. C., Ferrara, R. A., Reeve, R. A., & Palincsar, A. S. (1991). Interactive learning and individual understanding: The case of reading and mathematics. In L. T. Landsmann (Ed.), *Culture, schooling, and psychological development* (pp. 136–170). Norwood, NJ: Ablex.

Brown, A. L., Kane, M. J., & Echols, C. H. (1986). Young children's mental models determine analogical transfer across problems with a common goal structure. *Cognitive Development, 1,* 103–121.

Brown, A. L., & Scott, M. S. (1971). Recognition memory for pictures in preschool children. *Journal of Experimental Child Psychology, 11,* 401–412.

Brown, B. B. (1989). The role of peer groups in adolescents' adjustment to secondary school. In T. J. Berndt & G. W. Ladd (Eds.), *Peer relationships in child development* (pp. 188–215). New York: Wiley.

Brown, B. B., Clasen, D. R., & Eicher, S. A. (1986). Perceptions of peer pressure, peer conformity dispositions, and self-reported behavior among adolescents. *Developmental Psychology, 22,* 521–530.

Brown, B. B., Mounts, N., Lamborn, S. D., & Steinberg, L. (1993). Parenting practices and peer group affiliation in adolescence. *Child Development, 64,* 467–482.

Brown, J. D., Childers, K. W., Bauman, K. E., & Koch, G. G. (1990). The influences of new media and family structure on young adolescents' television and radio use. *Communication Research, 17,* 65–82.

Brown, J. L., & Pollitt, E. (1996, February). Malnutrition, poverty and intellectual development. *Scientific American, 274,* 38–43.

Brown, J. R., & Dunn, J. (1996). Continuities in emotion understanding from three to six years. *Child Development, 67,* 789–802.

Brown, L. K., Lourie, K. J., & Pao, M. (2000). Children and adolescents living with HIV and AIDS: A review. *Journal of Child Psychology and Psychiatry, 41,* 81–96.

Brown, L. M., & Gilligan, C. (1992). *Meeting at the crossroads: Women's psychology and girls' development.* Cambridge, MA: Harvard University Press.

Brown, M. L. (2001). The effects of environmental tobacco smoke on children: Information and implications for PNPs. *Journal of Pediatric Health Care, 15,* 280–286.

Brown, P. J., & Konner, M. (1987). An anthropological perspective on obesity. *Annals of the New York Academy of Sciences, 499,* 29–46.

Brown, R. (1973). *A first language: The early stages.* Cambridge, MA: Harvard University Press.

Bruck, K. (1962). Temperature regulation in the newborn infant. *Biological Neonatorum, 3,* 65–119.

Bruck, M. (1993). Word recognition and component phonological processing skills of adults with childhood diagnosis of dyslexia. *Developmental Review, 13,* 258–268.

Bruck, M., & Ceci, S. J. (1999). The suggestibility of children's memory. *Annual Review of Psychology, 50,* 419–439.

Bruer, J. T. (1994). Classroom problems, school culture, and cognitive research. In K. McGilly (Ed.), *Classroom lessons: Integrating cognitive theory and classroom practice* (pp. 273–290). Cambridge, MA: MIT Press.

Bruer, J. T. (1999). *The myth of the first three years.* New York: Free Press.

Bruer, J. T. (2001). A critical and sensitive period primer. In D. B. Bailey, J. T. Bruer, F. J. Symons, & J. W. Lichtman (Eds.), *Critical thinking about critical periods* (pp. 3–26). Baltimore, MD: Brookes.

Bruner, J. S. (1981). Intention in the structure of action and interaction. In L. P. Lipsitt (Ed.), *Advances in infancy research* (Vol. 1, pp. 41–56). Norwood, NJ: Ablex.

Bruner, J. S. (1983). *Child's talk: Learning to use language.* New York: W. W. Norton.

Bryant-Waugh, R., & Lask, B. (1995). Annotation: Eating disorders in children. *Journal of Child Psychology and Psychiatry, 36,* 191–202.

Buchanan, C. M., Maccoby, E. E., & Dornbusch, S. M. (1991). Caught between parents: Adolescents' experience in divorced homes. *Child Development, 62,* 1008–1029.

Buckner, J. P., & Fivush, R. (1998). Gender and self in children's autobiographical narratives. *Applied Cognitive Psychology, 12,* 407–429.

Bugental, D. B., Blue, J. B., & Cruzcosa, M. (1989). Perceived control over caregiving outcomes: Implications for child abuse. *Developmental Psychology, 25,* 532–539.

Bugental, D. B., & Lewis, J. (1998). Interpersonal power repair in response to threats to control from dependent others. In M. Kofta, G. Weary, & G. Sedek (Eds.), *Personal control in action: Cognitive and motivational mechanisms* (pp. 341–362). New York: Plenum.

Bugental, D. B., Lyon, J. E., Krantz, J., & Cortez, V. (1997). Who's the boss? Accessibility of dominance ideation among individuals with low perceptions of interpersonal power. *Journal of Personality and Social Psychology, 72,* 1297–1309.

Bugental, D. B., Lyon, J. E., Lin, E. K., McGrath, E. P., & Bimbela, A. (1999). Children "tune out" in response to the ambiguous communication styles of powerless adults. *Child Development, 70,* 214–230.

Buhrmester, D. (1990). Intimacy of friendship, interpersonal competence, and adjustment during preadolescence and adolescence. *Child Development, 61,* 1101–1111.

Buhrmester, D., & Furman, W. (1987). The development of companionship and intimacy. *Child Development, 58,* 1101–1113.

Buhrmester, D., & Furman, W. (1990). Perceptions of sibling relationships during middle childhood and adolescence. *Child Development, 61,* 1387–1398.

Buhs, E. S., & Ladd, G. W. (2001). Peer rejection as an antecedent of young children's school adjustment: An examination of mediating processes. *Developmental Psychology, 37,* 550–560.

Buitendijk, S., & Bracken, M. B. (1991). Medication in early pregnancy: Prevalence of use and relationship to maternal characteristics. *American Journal of Obstetrics and Gynecology, 165,* 33–40.

Bukowski, W. M., Gauze, C., Hoza, B., & Newcomb, A. F. (1993). Differences and consistency between same-sex and other-sex peer relationships during early adolescence. *Developmental Psychology, 29,* 255–263.

Bukowski, W. M., & Kramer, T. L. (1986). Judgments of the features of friendship among early adolescent boys and girls. *Journal of Early Adolescence, 6,* 331–338.

Bumpass, L. L. (1990). What's happening to the American family? Interactions between demographic and institutional change. *Demography, 27,* 483–498.

Burchinal, M. R., Follmer, A., & Bryant, D. M. (1996). The relations of maternal social support and family structure with maternal responsiveness and child outcomes among African American families. *Developmental Psychology, 32,* 1073–1083.

Burchinal, M. R., Roberts, J. E., Riggins, R., Jr., Zeisel, S. A., Neebe, E., & Bryant, D. (2000). Relating quality of center-based child care to early cognitive and language development longitudinally. *Child Development, 71,* 338–357.

Burgess, T. (2001). Determinants of transmission of HIV from mother to child. *Clinical Obstetrics and Gynecology, 44,* 198–209.

Burkhauser, R. V., Duncan, G. J., Hauser, R., & Bernsten, R. (1991). Wife or frau, women do worse: A comparison of men and women in the United States and Germany after marital dissolution. *Demography, 28,* 353–360.

Burns, A. L., Mitchell, G., & Obradovich, S. (1989). Of sex role and strollers: Female and male attention to toddlers at the zoo. *Sex Roles, 20,* 309–315.

Bushnell, E. W. (1981). The ontogeny of intermodal relations: Vision and touch in infancy. In R. D. Walk & H. L. Pick, Jr. (Eds.), *Intersensory perception and sensory integration* (pp. 5–36). New York: Plenum Press.

Bushnell, I. W. R., Sai, F., & Mullin, J. T. (1989). Neonatal recognition of the mother's face. *British Journal of Developmental Psychology, 7,* 3–15.

Buss, K. A., & Goldsmith, H. H. (1998). Fear and anger regulation in infancy: Effects on the temporal dynamics of affective expression. *Child Development, 69,* 359–374.

Bussey, K., & Bandura, A. (1984). Influence of gender constancy and social power on sex-linked modeling. *Journal of Personality and Social Psychology, 47,* 1292–1302.

Bussey, K., & Bandura, A. (1992). Self-regulatory mechanisms governing gender development. *Child Development, 63,* 1236–1250.

Bussey, K., & Perry, D. G. (1982). Same-sex imitation: The avoidance of cross-sex models or the acceptance of same-sex models? *Sex Roles, 8,* 773–784.

Bussey, K., & Bandura, A. (1999). Social cognitive theory of gender development and differentiation. *Psychological Bulletin, 106,* 676–713.

Butler, J., Abrams, B., Parker, J., Roberts, J. M., & Laros, R. K., Jr. (1993). Supportive nurse-midwife care is associated with a reduced incidence of cesarean section. *American Journal of Obstetrics and Gynecology, 168,* 1407–1413.

Butler, R. (1989). Mastery versus ability appraisal: A developmental study of children's observations of peers' work. *Child Development, 60,* 1350–1361.

Butler, R. (1990). The effects of mastery and competitive conditions on self-assessment at different ages. *Child Development, 61,* 201–210.

Butler, R. (1998). Age trends in the use of social and temporal comparison for self-evaluation: Examination of a novel developmental hypothesis. *Child Development, 69,* 1054–1073.

Butler, R., & Ruzany, N. (1993). Age and socialization effects on the development of social comparison motives and normative ability assessment in kibbutz and urban children. *Child Development, 64,* 532–543.

Butler, S. C., Berthier, N. E., & Clifton, R. K. (2002). Two-year-olds' search strategies and visual tracking in a hidden displacement task. *Developmental Psychology, 38,* 581–590.

Butler, S. C., Caron, A. J., & Brooks, R. (2000). Infant understanding of the referential nature of looking. *Journal of Cognition and Development, 1,* 359–377.

Butz, A. M., Pulsifer, M., Marano, N., Belcher, H., Lears, M. K., & Royall, R. (2001). Effectiveness of a home intervention for perceived child behavioral problems and parenting stress in children with in utero drug exposure. *Archives of Pediatric and Adolescent Medicine, 155,* 1029–1037.

Caccia, N., Johnson, J. M., Robinson, G. E., & Barna, T. (1991). Impact of prenatal testing on maternal-fetal bonding: Chorionic villus sampling versus amniocentesis. *American Journal of Obstetrics and Gynecology, 165,* 1122–1125.

Cacioppo, J. T., & Gardner, W. L. (1999). Emotion. *Annual Review of Psychology, 50,* 191–214.

Cairns, E., & Dawes, A. (1996). Children: Ethnic and political violence: A commentary. *Child Development, 67,* 129–139.

Cairns, R. B. (1992). The making of developmental science: The contributions and intellectual heritage of James Mark Baldwin. *Developmental Psychology, 28,* 17–24.

Cairns, R. B. (1998). The making of developmental psychology. In W. Damon (Series Ed.) & R. Lerner (Vol. Ed.), *Handbook of child psychology: Vol. 1. Theoretical models of human development* (5th ed., pp. 25–105). New York: Wiley.

Cairns, R. B., & Cairns, B. D. (1994). *Lifelines and risks: Pathways of youth in our time.* Cambridge, UK: Cambridge University Press.

Cairns, R. B., Leung, M., Buchanan, L., & Cairns, B. D. (1995). Friendships and social networks in childhood and adolescence: Fluidity, reliability, and interrelations. *Child Development, 66,* 1330–1345.

Cairns, R. B., & Ornstein, P. A. (1979). Developmental psychology. In E. Hearst (Ed.), *The first century of experimental psychology.* Hillsdale, NJ: Erlbaum.

Cairns, R., Xie, H., & Leung, M. (1998). The popularity of friendship and the neglect of social networks: Toward a new balance. In W. K. Bukowski & A. H. Cillessen (Eds.), *New directions for child development: No. 80. Sociometry then and now: Building on six decades of measuring children's experiences in the peer group* (pp. 25–53). San Francisco: Jossey-Bass.

Caldwell, B. M., & Bradley, R. H. (1978). *Home Observation for Measurement of the Environment.* Little Rock: University of Arkansas.

Calkins, S. D., & Fox, N. A. (1992). The relations among infant temperament, security of attachment, and behavioral inhibition at twenty-four months. *Child Development, 63,* 1456–1472.

Calkins, S. D., Fox, N. A., & Marshall, T. R. (1995). Behavioral and physiological antecedents of inhibition in infancy. *Child Development, 67,* 523–540.

Calvert, S. (1999). *Children's journeys through the information age.* New York: McGraw-Hill.

Calvert, S. L., Huston, A. C., Watkins, B. A., & Wright, J. C. (1982). The relationship between selective attention to televised forms and children's comprehension of content. *Child Development, 53,* 601–610.

Camara, K. A., & Resnick, G. (1988). Interparental conflict and cooperation: Factors moderating children's post-divorce adjustment. In E. M. Hetherington & J. Arasteh (Eds.), *Impact of divorce, single-parenting, and stepparenting on children* (pp. 169–195). Hillsdale, NJ: Erlbaum.

Campbell, F. A., Pungello, E., Miller-Johnson, S., Burchinal, M., & Ramey, C. T. (2001). The development of cognitive and academic abilities: Growth curves from an early childhood educational experiment. *Developmental Psychology, 37,* 231–242.

Campbell, F. A., & Ramey, C. T. (1994). Effects of early intervention on intellectual and academic achievement: A follow-up study of children from low-income families. *Child Development, 65,* 684–698.

Campbell, S. B., Cohn, J. F., & Meyers, T. (1995). Depression in first-time mothers: Mother-infant interaction and depression chronicity. *Developmental Psychology, 31,* 349–357.

Campione, J. C., Brown, A. L., & Ferrara, R. A. (1982). Mental retardation and intelligence. In R. J. Sternberg (Ed.), *Handbook of human intelligence.* Cambridge, UK: Cambridge University Press.

Campos, J. J., Barrett, K. C., Lamb, M. E., Goldsmith, H. H., & Stenberg, C. (1983). Socioemotional development. In M. M. Haith & J. J. Campos (Eds.), *Handbook of child psychology: Vol. II. Infancy and developmental psychobiology* (pp. 783–915). New York: Wiley.

Campos, J. J., Langer, A., & Krowitz, A. (1970). Cardiac responses on the visual cliff in prelocomotor human infants. *Science, 170,* 196–197.

Campos, J., Mumme, D., Kermoian, R. , & Campos, R. G. (1994). A functionalist perspective on the nature of emotion. In N. Fox (Ed.), The development of emotion regulation: Behavioral and biological considerations. *Monographs of the Society for Research in Child Development, 59*(2–3, Serial No. 240).

Camras, L. A., Oster, H., Campos, J., Campos, R., Ujie, T., Miyake, K., et al. (1998). Production of emotional facial expressions in European, American, Japanese, and Chinese infants. *Developmental Psychology, 34,* 616–628.

Canfield, R. L., & Smith, E. G. (1996). Number-based expectations and sequential enumeration by 5-month-olds. *Developmental Psychology, 32,* 269–279.

Cantalupo, C., & Hopkins, W. D. (2001). Asymmetric Broca's area in great apes: A region of the ape brain is uncannily similar to one linked with speech in humans. *Nature, 414,* 505.

Cantor, J., & Wilson, B. J. (1988). Helping children cope with frightening media presentations. *Current Psychology: Research and Reviews, 7,* 58–75.

Caprara, G. V., Barbaranelli, C., Pastorelli, C., Bandura, A., & Zimbardo, P. G. (2000). Prosocial foundations of children's academic achievement. *Psychological Science, 11,* 302–306.

Capron, A. M. (1998). Punishing mothers. *Hastings Center Report, 28,* 31–33.

Carey, S. (1978). The child as word learner. In M. Halle, J. Bresnan, & G. A. Miller (Eds.), *Linguistic theory and psychological reality.* Cambridge, MA: MIT Press.

Carey, S. (1985). *Conceptual changes in childhood.* Cambridge, MA: MIT Press.

Carey, S. (2001). On the very possibility of discontinuities in conceptual development. In E. Dupoux (Ed.), *Language, brain, and cognitive development: Essays in honor of Jacques Mehler* (pp. 303–324). Cambridge, MA: MIT Press.

Carli, L. L., & Bukatko, D. (2000). Gender, communication, and social influence: A developmental perspective. In T. Eckes & H. M. Trautner (Eds.), *The developmental social psychology of gender* (pp. 295–331). Mahwah, NJ: Erlbaum.

Carlo, G., Koller, S. H., Eisenberg, N., Da Silva, M. S., & Frohlich, C. B. (1996). A cross-national study on the relations among prosocial moral reasoning, gender role orientations, and prosocial behaviors. *Developmental Psychology, 32,* 231–240.

Carlson, E. A. (1998). A prospective longitudinal study of attachment disorganization/disorientation. *Child Development, 69,* 1107–1128.

Carlson, S. M., Moses, L. J., & Hix, H. R. (1998). The role of inhibitory processes in young children's difficulties with deception and false belief. *Child Development, 69,* 672–691.

Carlson, V., Cicchetti, D., Barnett, D., & Braunwald, K. (1989). Contributions of the study of maltreated infants to the development of the disorganized ("D") type of attachment relationship. In D. Cicchetti & V. Carlson (Eds.), *Child maltreatment: Theory and research on the causes and consequences of child abuse and neglect* (pp. 495–528).Cambridge, UK: Cambridge University Press.

Carmichael, C. A., & Hayes, B. K. (2001). Prior knowledge and exemplar encoding in children's concept acquisition. *Child Development, 72,* 1071–1090.

Carpenter, M., Akhtar, N., & Tomasello, M. (1998). Fourteen- through 18-month-old infants differentially imitate intentional and accidental actions. *Infant Behavior and Development, 21,* 315–330.

Carpenter, M., Nagell, K., & Tomasello, M. (1998). Social cognition, joint attention, and communicative competence from 9 to 15 months of age. *Monographs of the Society for Research in Child Development, 63* (4, Serial No. 176).

Carroll, J. B. (1993). *Human cognitive abilities: A survey of factor-analytic studies.* New York: Cambridge University Press.

Carter, D. B. (1987). The roles of peers in sex role socialization. In D. B. Carter (Ed.), *Current conceptions of sex roles and sex-typing: Theory and research* (pp. 101–121). New York: Praeger.

Carter, D. B., & Levy, G. D. (1988). Cognitive aspects of early sex-role development: The influence of gender schemas on preschoolers' memories and preferences for sex-typed toys and activities. *Child Development, 59,* 782–792.

Carter, D. B., & McCloskey, L. A. (1984). Peers and the maintenance of sex-typed behavior: The development of children's understanding of cross-gender behavior in their peers. *Social Cognition, 2,* 294–314.

Casasola, M., & Cohen, L. B. (2000). Infants' association of linguistic labels with causal actions. *Developmental Psychology, 36,* 155–168.

Case, R. (1985). *Intellectual development: A systematic reinterpretation.* New York: Academic Press.

Case, R. (1991). Stages in the development of the young child's first sense of self. *Developmental Review, 11,* 210–230.

Case, R. (1992). *The mind's staircase: Exploring the conceptual underpinnings of children's thought and knowledge.* Hillsdale, NJ: Erlbaum.

Case, R., Kurland, D. M., & Goldberg, J. (1982). Operational efficiency and the growth of short term memory span. *Journal of Experimental Child Psychology, 33,* 386–404.

Casey, B. J., Thomas, K. M., & McCandless, B. (2001). Applications of magnetic resonance imaging to the study of development. In C. A. Nelson & M. Luciana (Eds.), *Handbook of developmental cognitive neuroscience* (pp. 137–148). Cambridge, MA: MIT Press.

Casey, R. J. (1993). Children's emotional experience: Relations among expression, self-report, and understanding. *Developmental Psychology, 29,* 119–129.

Casper, L. M., & O'Connell, M. (1998). Work, income, the economy, and married fathers as child care providers. *Demography, 35,* 243–250.

Caspi, A., Henry, B., McGee, R. O., Moffitt, T. E., & Silva, P. A. (1995). Temperamental origins of child and adolescent behavior problems: From age three to age fifteen. *Child Development, 66,* 55–68.

Caspi, A., Taylor, A., Moffitt, T. E., & Plomin, R. (2000). Neighborhood deprivation affects children's mental health: Environmental risks identified in a genetic design. *Psychological Science, 11,* 338–342.

Cassel, W. S., Roebers, C. E. M., & Bjorklund, D. F. (1996). Developmental patterns of eyewitness responses to repeated and increasingly suggestive questions. *Journal of Experimental Child Psychology, 61,* 116–133.

Cassell, J., & Jenkins, H. (1998). Chess for girls? Feminism and computer games. In J. Cassell & H. Jenkins (Eds.), *From Barbie to Mortal Kombat: Gender and computer games* (pp. 2–45). Cambridge, MA: MIT Press.

Cassidy, J., & Asher, S. R. (1992). Loneliness and peer relations in young children. *Child Development, 63,* 350–365.

Cassidy, J., Kirsh, S. J., Scolton, K. L., & Parke, R. D. (1996). Attachment and representations of peer relationships. *Developmental Psychology, 32,* 892–904.

Castles, A., Datta, H., Gayan, J., & Olson, R. K. (1999). Varieties of developmental reading disorder: Genetic and environmental influences. *Journal of Experimental Child Psychology, 72,* 73–94.

Cattell, J. M. (1890). Mental tests and measurements. *Mind, 15,* 373–381.

Cattell, R. B. (1971). *Abilities: Their structure, growth, and action.* Boston: Houghton Mifflin.

Cavior, N., & Dokecki, P. R. (1973). Physical attractiveness, perceived attitude similarity, and academic achievement as contributors to interpersonal attraction among adolescents. *Developmental Psychology, 9,* 44–54.

Ceballo, R., & McLoyd, V. C. (2002). Social support and parenting in poor, dangerous neighborhoods. *Child Development, 73,* 1310–1321.

Ceci, S. J. (1991). How much does schooling influence general intelligence and its cognitive components? A reassessment of the evidence. *Developmental Psychology, 27,* 703–722.

Ceci, S. J., & Bruck, M. (1993). Suggestibility of the child witness: A historical review and synthesis. *Psychological Bulletin, 113,* 403–439.

Ceci, S. J., Ross, D. F., & Toglia, M. P. (1987). Suggestibility of children's memory: Psychological implications. *Journal of Experimental Psychology: General, 116,* 38–49.

Ceci, S. J., & Williams, W. M. (1997). Schooling, intelligence, and income. *American Psychologist, 52,* 1051–1058.

Celera Genomics Sequencing Team. (2001). The sequence of the human genome. *Science, 291,* 1304–1351.

Center for Communication and Social Policy. (1998). *National Television Violence Study* (Vol. 3). Newbury Park, CA: Sage

Centers for Disease Control. (1991). Premarital sexual experience among adolescent women-United States, 1970–1988. *Morbidity and Mortality Weekly Report, 39,* 929–932.

Centers for Disease Control. (1992). Youth suicide prevention programs: A resource guide. Atlanta: U.S. Department of Health and Human Services, Public Health Service.

Centers for Disease Control. (1993). Rates of Cesarean delivery—United States 1991. *Morbidity and Mortality Weekly Report, 42,* 285–289.

Centers for Disease Control and Prevention. (2000). State-specific pregnancy rates among adolescents-United States, 1992–1995. *Morbidity and Mortality Weekly Report, 49,* 605–611.

Centers for Disease Control and Prevention, National Center for Health Statistics. (2000). *Individual growth charts.* Retrieved January 13, 2003, from http://www.cdc.gov/growthcharts/

Centers for Disease Control and Prevention, National Health and Nutrition Examination Survey, National Center for Health Statistics. (2002). *Overweight among U.S. children and adolescents.* Retrieved January 13, 2003, from http://www.cdc.gov/nchs/nhanes.htm

Chan, K., Ohlsson, A., Synnes, A., Lee, D. S. C., Chien, L.-Y., Lee, S. K., and the Canadian Neonatal Network. (2000). Survival, morbidity, and resource use of infants of 25 weeks' gestational age or less. *American Journal of Obstetrics and Gynecology, 185,* 220–226.

Chao, R. K. (1994). Beyond parental control and authoritarian parenting style: Understanding Chinese parenting through the cultural notion of training. *Child Development, 65,* 1111–1119.

Chapman, M., Skinner, E. A., & Baltes, P. B. (1990). Interpreting correlations between children's perceived control and cognitive performance: Control, agency, or means-ends beliefs? *Developmental Psychology, 26,* 246–253.

Charpak, N., Ruiz, J. G., de Calume, Z. F., & Charpak, Y. (1997). Kangaroo mother versus "traditional" care for newborn infants < 2000 grams: A randomized, controlled trial. *Pediatrics, 100,* 682–688.

Chase-Lansdale, P. L., Cherlin, A. J., & Kiernan, K. E. (1995). The long-term effects of parental divorce on the mental health of young adults: A developmental perspective. *Child Development, 66,* 1614–1634.

Chasnoff, I. J. (1986). Perinatal addiction: Consequences of intrauterine exposure to opiate and nonopiate drugs. In I. J. Chasnoff (Ed.), *Drug use in pregnancy: Mother and child.* Lancaster, UK: MTP Press.

Chasnoff, I. J. (1992). Cocaine, pregnancy, and the growing child. *Current Problems in Pediatrics, 22,* 302–321.

Chavajay, P., & Rogoff, B. (1999). Cultural variation in management of attention by children and their caregivers. *Developmental Psychology, 35,* 1079–1090.

Chavkin, W. (2001). Cocaine and pregnancy: Time to look at the evidence. *Journal of the American Medical Association, 285,* 1626–1627.

Chen, C., & Stevenson, H. W. (1995). Motivation and mathematics achievement: A comparative study of Asian-American, Caucasian-American, and East Asian high school students. *Child Development, 66,* 1215–1234.

Chen, J. Q., & Gardner, H. (1997). Alternative assessment from a multiple intelligences theoretical perspective. In D. P. Flanagan, J. L. Genshaft, & P. L. Harrison (Eds.), *Contemporary intellectual assessment* (pp. 105–121). New York: Guilford.

Chen, X., Li, D., Li, Z., Li, B., & Liu, M. (2000). Sociable and prosocial dimensions of social competence in Chinese children: Common and unique contributions to social, academic, and psychological adjustment. *Developmental Psychology, 36,* 302–314.

Chen, X., Rubin, K. H., & Li, D. (1997). Maternal acceptance and social and school adjustment: A four-year longitudinal study. *Merrill-Palmer Quarterly, 43,* 663–681.

Chen, X., Rubin, K. H., & Li, Z. (1995). Social functioning and adjustment in Chinese children: A longitudinal study. *Developmental Psychology, 31,* 531–539.

Chen, X., Rubin, K. H., Li, B., & Li, D. (1999). Adolescent outcomes of social functioning in Chinese children. *International Journal of Behavioral Development, 23,* 199–223.

Chen, Z., & Daehler, M. W. (1989). Positive and negative transfer in analogical problem-solving by 6-year-olds. *Cognitive Development, 4,* 327–344.

Chen, Z., & Klahr, D. (1999). All other things being equal: Acquisition and transfer of the control of variables strategy. *Child Development, 70,* 1098–1120.

Chen, Z., Sanchez, R. P., & Campbell, T. (1997). From beyond to within their grasp: The rudiments of analogical problem solving in 10- and 13-month-olds. *Developmental Psychology, 33,* 790–801.

Cherlin, A. J. (1992). *Marriage, divorce, remarriage* (Rev. ed.). Cambridge, MA: Harvard University Press.

Chess, S., & Thomas, A. (1982). Infant bonding: Mystique and reality. *American Journal of Orthopsychiatry, 52,* 213–222.

Chess, S., & Thomas, A. (1990). Continuities and discontinuities in temperament. In L. N. Robins & M. Rutter (Eds.). *Straight and devious pathways from childhood to adolescence* (pp. 205–220). Cambridge, UK: Cambridge University Press.

Chess, S., & Thomas, A. (1991). Temperament and the concept of goodness of fit. In J. Strelau & A. Angleitner (Eds.), *Explorations in temperament: International perspectives on theory and measurement* (pp. 15–28). New York: Plenum.

Chi, M. T. H. (1978). Knowledge structure and memory development. In R. Siegler (Ed.), *Children's thinking: What develops?* (pp. 73–96). Hillsdale, NJ: Erlbaum.

Chiappe, P., & Siegel, L. S. (1999). Phonological awareness and reading acquisition in English- and Punjabi-speaking Canadian children. *Journal of Educational Psychology, 91,* 20–28.

Chibucos, T., & Kail, P. R. (1981). Longitudinal examination of father-infant interaction and infant-father interaction. *Merrill-Palmer Quarterly, 27,* 81–96.

Child Trends Databank. (2002a). *Child maltreatment.* Retrieved December 23, 2002, from http://www.childtrendsdatabank.org/family/thefamily/40ChildMaltreatment.htm

Child Trends Databank. (2002b). *Parental warmth and affection.* Retrieved December 23, 2002, from http://www.childtrendsdatabank.org/family/thefamily/52ParentalWarmthAffection.htm

Childers, J. B., & Tomasello, M. (2001). The role of pronouns in young children's acquisition of the English transitive construction. *Developmental Psychology, 37,* 739–748.

Chilosi, A. M., Cipriani, P., Bertuccelli, B., Pfanner, L., & Cioni, G. (2001). Early cognitive and communication development in children with focal brain lesions. *Journal of Child Neurology, 16,* 309–316.

Children's Defense Fund. (1996). *The state of America's children: Yearbook.* Washington, DC: Author.

Children's Defense Fund. (2001). *The state of America's children: Yearbook.* Washington, DC: Author.

Chiu, L. H. (1992–93). Self-esteem in American and Chinese (Taiwanese) children. *Current Psychology: Research & Reviews, 11,* 309–313.

Choi, S. (1998). Verbs in early lexical and syntactic development in Korean. *Linguistics, 36,* 755–780.

Choi, S., & Gopnik, A. (1995). Early acquisition of verbs in Korean: A cross-linguistic study. *Journal of Child Language, 22,* 497–529.

Chomsky, N. (1980). *Rules and representations.* New York: Columbia University Press.

Chomsky, N. (1986). *Knowledge of language: Its nature, origin, and use.* New York: Praeger.

Chorney, M. J., Chorney, K., Seese, N., Owen, M. J., Daniels, J., McGuffin, P., et al. (1998). A quantitative trait locus associated with cognitive ability in children. *Psychological Science, 9,* 159–166.

Chugani, H. T. (1994). Development of regional brain glucose metabolism in relation to behavior and plasticity. In G. Dawson & K. Fischer (Eds.), *Human behavior and the developing brain* (pp. 153–175). New York: Guilford.

Cicchetti, D., Ackerman, B., & Izard, C. (1995). Emotions and emotion regulation in developmental psychopathology. *Development and Psychopathology, 7,* 1–10.

Cicchetti, D., Rogosch, F. A., Toth, S. L., & Spagnola, M. (1997). Affect, cognition, and the emergence of self-knowledge in the toddler offspring of depressed mothers. *Journal of Experimental Child Psychology, 67,* 338–362.

Cicchetti, D., Toth, S. L., & Lynch, M. (1995). Bowlby's dream comes full circle: The application of attachment theory to risk and psychopathology. *Advances in Clinical Child Psychology, 17,* 1–75.

Clark, E. V. (1973). What's in a word? On the child's acquisition of semantics in his first language. In T. E. Moore (Ed.), *Cognitive development and the acquisition of language* (pp. 27–63). New York: Academic Press.

Clark, W. (2001, Autumn). Kids and teens on the net. *Canadian Social Trends,* No. 62 (Catalogue Number 11-008-XPE). Retrieved November 27, 2002, from http://www.statcan.ca/english/IPS/Data/11-008-XPE20010025821.htm

Clarke-Stewart, K. A. (1993). *Daycare* (rev. ed.). Cambridge, MA: Harvard University Press.

Clarke-Stewart, K. A., & Fein, G. G. (1983). Early childhood programs. In M. M. Haith & J. J. Campos (Eds.), *Handbook of child psychology: Vol. II. Infancy and developmental psychobiology* (4th ed., pp. 917–999). New York: Wiley.

Clarke-Stewart, K. A., & Hayward, C. (1996). Advantages of father custody and contact for the psychological well-being of school-age children. *Journal of Applied Developmental Psychology, 17,* 239–270.

Clarkson, M. G. (1996). Infants' intensity discrimination: Spectral profiles. *Infant Behavior and Development, 19,* 181–190.

Clarren, S. K., Alvord, E. C., Suni, S. M., & Streissguth, A. P. (1978). Brain malformations related to prenatal exposure to ethanol. *Journal of Pediatrics, 92,* 64–67.

Clasen, D. R., & Brown, B. B. (1985). The multidimensionality of peer pressure in adolescence. *Journal of Youth and Adolescence, 14,* 451–468.

Clearfield, M. W., & Mix, K. S. (1999). Number versus contour length in infants' discrimination of small visual sets. *Psychological Science, 10,* 408–411.

Clearfield, M. W., & Mix, K. S. (2001). Amount versus number: Infants' use of area and contour length to discriminate small sets. *Journal of Cognition and Development, 2,* 243–260.

Clifton, R., Muir, D. W., Ashmead, D. H., & Clarkson, M. G. (1993). Is visually guided reaching in early infancy a myth? *Child Development, 64,* 1099–1110.

Clifton, R., Perris, E., & Bullinger, A. (1991). Infants' perception of auditory space. *Developmental Psychology, 27,* 187–197.

Cohen, D., & Strayer, J. (1996). Empathy in conduct-disordered and comparison youth. *Developmental Psychology, 32,* 988–998.

Cohen, L. B., & Oakes, L. M. (1993). How infants perceive a simple causal event. *Developmental Psychology, 29,* 421–433.

Cohen, R. L. (1966). Experimental and clinical chemateratogenesis. *Advances in Pharmacology, 4,* 263–349.

Cohn, J. F., Matias, R., Tronick, E. Z., Connell, D., & Lyons-Ruth, D. (1986). Face-to-face interactions of depressed mothers and their infants. In E. Z. Tronick & T. M. Field (Eds.), *New directions for child development: No. 34. Maternal depression and infant disturbance.* San Francisco: Jossey-Bass.

Cohn, J. F., & Tronick, E. Z. (1983). Three-month-old infants' reaction to simulated maternal depression. *Child Development, 54,* 185–193.

Cohn, J. F., & Tronick, E. Z. (1987). Mother-infant face-to-face interaction: The sequence of dyadic states at 3, 6, and 9 months. *Developmental Psychology, 23,* 68–77.

Coie, J. D., & Dodge, K. A. (1988). Multiple sources of data on social behavior and social status in the school: A cross-age comparison. *Child Development, 59,* 815–829.

Coie, J. D., Dodge, K. A., & Coppotelli, H. (1982). Dimensions and types of social status: A cross-age perspective. *Developmental Psychology, 18,* 557–570.

Colby, A., & Damon, W. (1992). *Some do care: Contemporary lives of moral commitment.* New York: Free Press.

Colby, A., Kohlberg, L., Gibbs, J., & Lieberman, M. (1983). A longitudinal study of moral judgment. *Monographs of the Society for Research in Child Development, 48*(1–2, Serial No. 200).

Cole, D. A., Martin, J. M., Peeke, L. A., Seroczynski, A. D., & Fier, J. (1999). Children's over- and underestimation of academic competence: A longitudinal study of gender differences, depression, and anxiety. *Child Development, 70,* 459–473.

Cole, D. A., Maxwell, S. E., Martin, J. M., Peeke, L. G., Seroczynski, A. D., Tram, J. M., et al. (2001). The development of multiple domains of child and adolescent self-concept: A cohort sequential longitudinal design. *Child Development, 72,* 1723–1746.

Cole, P. M., Bruschi, C. J., & Tamang, B. L. (2002). Cultural differences in children's emotional reactions to difficult situations. *Child Development, 73,* 983–996.

Cole, P. M., Zahn-Waxler, C., & Smith, K. D. (1994). Expressive control during a disappointment: Variations related to preschoolers' behavior problems. *Developmental Psychology, 30,* 835–846.

Coleman, P. K., & Karraker, K. H. (1998). Self-efficacy and parenting quality: Findings and future applications. *Developmental Review, 18,* 47–85.

Coley, R. L. (1998). Children's socialization experiences and functioning in single-mother households: The importance of fathers and other men. *Child Development, 69,* 219–230.

Coley, R. L., & Chase-Lansdale, P. L. (1998). Adolescent pregnancy and parenthood: Recent evidence and future directions. *American Psychologist, 53,* 152–166.

Collaer, M. L., & Hines, M. (1995). Human behavioral sex differences: A role for gonadal hormones during early development? *Psychological Bulletin, 118,* 55–107.

Collins, J. A. (1995). A couple with infertility. *Journal of the American Medical Association, 274,* 1159–1164.

Collins, W. A. (1983). Social antecedents, cognitive processing, and comprehension of social portrayals on television. In E. T. Higgins, D. N. Ruble, & W. W. Hartup (Eds.), *Social cognition and social development* (pp. 110–133). Cambridge, UK: Cambridge University Press.

Collins, W. A., Maccoby, E. E., Steinberg, L., Hetherington, E. M., & Bornstein, M. H. (2000). Contemporary research on parenting: The case for nature and nurture. *American Psychologist, 55,* 218–232.

Collins, W. A., Wellman, H., Keniston, A. H., & Westby, S. D. (1978). Age-related aspects of comprehension and inference from a televised dramatic narrative. *Child Development, 49,* 389–399.

Collis, B., & Ollila, L. (1990). The effects of computer use on grade 1 children's gender stereotypes about reading, writing, and computer use. *Journal of Research and Development in Education, 24,* 14–20.

Coltrane, S. (2000). Research on household labor: Modeling and measuring the social embeddedness of routine family work. *Journal of Marriage and the Family, 62,* 1208–1233.

Comeau, L., Cormier, P., Grandmaison, È., & Lacroix, D. (1999). A longitudinal study of phonological processing skills in children learning to read in a second language. *Journal of Educational Psychology, 91,* 29–43.

Committee on Genetics. (1994). American Academy of Pediatrics: Prenatal genetic diagnosis for pediatricians. *Pediatrics, 93,* 1010–1014.

Committee on Genetics. (1996). Newborn screening fact sheet. *Pediatrics, 98,* 473–501.

Comstock, G. (1991). *Television and the American child.* Orlando, FL: Academic Press.

Comstock, G. & Scharrer, E. (1999). *Television: What's on, who's watching, and what it means.* San Diego: Academic Press.

Conger, R. D., Conger, K. J., Elder, G. H., Jr., Lorenz, F. O., Simons, R. L., & Whitbeck, L. B. (1992). A family process model of economic hardship and adjustment of early adolescent boys. *Child Development, 63,* 526–541.

Conger, R. D., Wallace, L. E., Sun, Y., Simons, R. L., McLoyd, V. C., & Brody, G. H. (2002). Economic pressure in African American families: A replication and extension of the family stress model. *Developmental Psychology, 38,* 179–193.

Connolly, J., Furman, W., & Konarski, R. (2000). The role of peers in the emergence of heterosexual romantic relationships in adolescence. *Child Development, 71,* 1395–1408.

Connors, F., & Olson, R. K. (1990). Reading comprehension in dyslexic and normal readers: A component-skills analysis. In D. A. Balota, G. B. Flores d'Arcais, & K. Rayner (Eds.), *Comprehension processes in reading.* Hillsdale, NJ: Erlbaum.

Conway, A. R. A., Cowan, N., Bunting, M. F., Therriault, D. J., & Minkoff, S. R. B. (2002). A latent variable analysis of working memory capacity, short-term memory capacity, processing speed, and general fluid intelligence. *Intelligence, 30,* 163–184.

Cook, E. T., Greenberg, M. T., & Kusche, C. (1994). The relations between emotional understanding, intellectual functioning, and disruptive behavior problems in elementary-school-aged children. *Journal of Abnormal Child Psychology, 22,* 205–219.

Cooley, C. H. (1902). *Human nature and the social order.* New York: Scribner's.

Cooper, M. L., Shaver, P. R., & Collins, N. L. (1998). Attachment styles, emotion regulation, and adjustment in adolescence. *Journal of Personality and Social Psychology, 74,* 1380–1397.

Copper, R. L., Goldenberg, R. L., Cliver, S. P., DuBard, M. B., Hoffman, H. J., & Davis, R. O. (1993). Anthropometric assessment of body size differences of full-term male and female infants. *Obstetrics and Gynecology, 81,* 161–164.

Corina, D. P., McBurney, S. L., Dodrill, C., Hinshaw, K., Brinkley, J., & Ojemann, G. (1999). Functional roles of Broca's area and supramarginal gyrus: Evidence from cortical stimulation mapping of a deaf signer. *NeuroImage, 10,* 570–581.

Costanzo, P. R., & Woody, E. Z. (1979). Externality as a function of obesity in children: Pervasive style or eating-specific attribute? *Journal of Personality and Social Psychology, 37,* 2286–2296.

Costanzo, P. R., & Woody, E. Z. (1985). Domain-specific parenting styles and their impact on the child's development of particular deviance: The example of obesity proneness. *Journal of Social and Clinical Psychology,* 425–445.

Cournoyer, M., & Trudel, M. (1991). Behavioral correlates of self-control at 33 months. *Infant Behavior and Development, 14,* 497–503.

Coustan, D. R., & Felig, P. (1988). Diabetes mellitus. In G. N. Burrow & T. F. Ferris (Eds.), *Medical complications during pregnancy* (3rd ed.). Philadelphia: W.B. Saunders.

Cowan, N. (1999). The differential maturation of two processing rates related to digit span. *Journal of Experimental Child Psychology, 72,* 193–209.

Cowan, N., Wood, N. L., Wood, P. K., Keller, T. A., Nugent, L. D., & Keller, C. V. (1998). Two separate verbal processing rates contribute to short-term memory span. *Journal of Experimental Psychology: General, 127,* 141–160.

Cox, M., & Harter, K. S. M. (2003). Parent-child relationships. In M. H. Bornstein, L. Davidson, C. Keyes, & K. Moore (Eds.), *Well-being: Positive development across the lifespan.* Mahwah, NJ: Erlbaum.

Cox, M. J., Owen, T. J., Henderson, V. K., & Margand, N. A. (1992). Prediction of infant-father and infant-mother interaction. *Developmental Psychology, 28,* 474–483.

Cox, M. J., & Paley, B. (1997). Families as systems. *Annual Review of Psychology, 48,* 243–267.

Coyle, T. R., & Bjorklund, D. F. (1997). Age differences in, and consequences of, multiple- and variable-strategy use on a multitrial sort-recall task. *Developmental Psychology, 33,* 372–380.

Crain-Thoreson, C., & Dale, P. S. (1992). Do early talkers become early readers? Linguistic precocity, preschool language, and emergent literacy. *Developmental Psychology, 28,* 421–429.

Crandall, R. (1973). The measurement of self-esteem and related concepts. In J. P. Robinson & P. R. Shaver (Eds.), *Measures of social psychological attitudes* (rev. ed.). Ann Arbor: Institute for Social Research.

Crandall, V. C. (1969). Sex differences in expectancy of intellectual and academic reinforcement. In C. P. Smith (Ed.), *Achievement-related motives in children* (pp. 11–45). New York: Russell Sage.

Cratty, B. J. (1986). *Perceptual and motor development in infants and children* (3rd ed.). Englewood Cliffs, NJ: Prentice-Hall.

Crawford, P. B., Story, M., Wang, M. C., Ritchie, L. D., & Sabry, Z. I. (2001). Ethnic issues in the epidemiology of childhood obesity. *Pediatric Clinics of North America, 48,* 855–875.

Crick, N. R., Casas, J. F., & Mosher, M. (1997). Relational and overt aggression in preschool. *Developmental Psychology, 33,* 579–588.

Crick, N. R., & Dodge, K. A. (1994). A review and reformulation of social information-processing mechanisms in children's social adjustment. *Psychological Bulletin, 115,* 74–101.

Crick, N. R., & Dodge, K. A. (1996). Social information-processing mechanisms in reactive and proactive aggression. *Child Development, 67,* 993–1002.

Crick, N. R., & Grotpeter, J. K. (1995). Relational aggression, gender, and social-psychological adjustment. *Child Development, 66,* 710–722.

Crick, N. R., & Ladd, G. W. (1993). Children's perceptions of their peer experiences: Attributions, loneliness, social anxiety, and social avoidance. *Developmental Psychology, 29,* 244–254.

Criss, M. M., Pettit, G. S., Bates, J. E., Dodge, K. A., & Lapp, A. L. (2002). Family adversity, positive peer relationships, and children's externalizing behavior: A longitudinal perspective on risk and resilience. *Child Development, 73,* 1220–1237.

Crockett, L., Losoff, M., & Petersen, A. C. (1984). Perceptions of the peer group and friendship in early adolescence. *Journal of Early Adolescence, 4,* 155–181.

Crook, C. (1992). Cultural artifacts in social development: The case of computers. In H. McGurk (Ed.), *Childhood social development: Contemporary perspectives* (pp. 207–231). Hove, UK: Erlbaum.

Cross, J. C., Werb, Z., & Fisher, S. J. (1994). Implantation and the placenta: Key pieces of the development puzzle. *Science, 266,* 1508–1518.

Crouter, A. C., & Bumpus, M. F. (2001). Linking parents' work stress to children's and adolescents' psychological adjustment. *Current Directions in Psychological Science, 10,* 156–159.

Crouter, A. C., Bumpus, M. F., Maguire, M. C., & McHale, S. M. (1999). Linking parents' work pressure and adolescent's well-being: Insights into dynamics in dual-earner families. *Developmental Psychology, 35,* 1453–1461.

Crouter, A. C., Manke, B. A., & McHale, S. M. (1995). The family context of gender intensification in early adolescence. *Child Development, 66,* 317–329.

Crouter, A. C., McHale, S. M., & Tucker, C. J. (1999). Does stress exacerbate parental differential treatment of siblings? A pattern-analytic approach. *Journal of Family Psychology, 13,* 286–299.

Crowley, K., & Siegler, R. S. (1998). Explanation and generalization in young children's strategy learning. *Child Development, 70,* 304–316.

Csibra, G. (2001). Illusory contour figures are perceived as occluding surfaces by 8-month-old infants. *Developmental Science, 4,* F7–F11.

Csikszentmihalyi, M., & Larson, R. (1984). *Being adolescent.* New York: Basic Books.

Culley, L. (1993). Gender equity and computing in secondary schools. In J. Benyon & H. McKay (Eds.), *Computers into classrooms* (pp. 73–95). London: Falmer Press.

Cummings, E. M. (1995). Security, emotionality, and parental depression: A commentary. *Developmental Psychology, 31,* 425–427.

Cummings, E. M., Zahn-Waxler, C., & Radke-Yarrow, M. (1981). Young children's responses to expressions of anger and affection by others in the family. *Child Development, 52,* 1274–1282.

Cunningham, J. D. (1993). Experiences of Australian mothers who gave birth either at home, at a birth centre, or in hospital labour wards. *Social Science and Medicine, 36,* 475–483.

Curtiss, S. (1977). *Genie: A psycholinguistic study of a modern-day "wild child."* New York: Academic Press.

Cuttler, L., Silvers, J. B., Singh, J., Marrero, U., Finkelstein, B., Tannin, G., & Neuhauser, D. (1996, August 21). Short stature and growth hormone therapy: A national study of physician recommendation patterns. *Journal of the American Medical Association, 276,* 531–537.

Cycowicz, Y. M., Friedman, D., Snodgrass, J. G., & Duff, M. (2001). Recognition and source memory for pictures in children and adults. *Neuropsychologia, 39,* 255–267.

Daehler, M. W., & Bukatko, D. (1977). Recognition memory for pictures in very young children: Evidence from attentional preferences using a continuous presentation procedure. *Child Development, 48,* 693–696.

Dahl, R. E., Scher, M. S., Williamson, D. E., Robles, N., & Day, N. (1995). A longitudinal study of prenatal marijuana use: Effects on sleep and arousal at age 3 years. *Archives of Pediatric and Adolescent Medicine, 149,* 145–150.

Dalterio, S., & Bartke, A. (1979). Perinatal exposure to cannabinoids alters male reproductive function in mice. *Science, 205,* 1420–1422.

Damon, W. (1983). *Social and personality development: Infancy through adolescence.* New York: W. W. Norton.

Damon, W., & Hart, D. (1988). *Self-understanding in childhood and adolescence.* New York: Cambridge University Press.

Daniels, K. (1989). Waterbirth: The newest form of safe, gentle and joyous birth. *Journal of Nurse-Midwifery, 34,* 198–205.

Daniels, K., & Taylor, K. (1993). Formulating selection policies for assisted reproduction. *Social Science & Medicine, 37,* 1473–1480.

Dapretto, M., & Bjork, E. L. (2000). The development of word retrieval abilities in the second year and its relation to early vocabulary growth. *Child Development, 71,* 635–648.

Dark, V. J., & Benbow, C. P. (1993). Cognitive differences among the gifted: A review and new data. In D. K. Detterman (Ed.), *Current topics in human intelligence. Vol. 3. Individual differences and cognition* (pp. 85–120). Norwood, NJ: Ablex.

Darwin, C. (1877). A biographical sketch of an infant. *Mind, 2,* 285–294.

Dasen, P. R. (1972). Cross-cultural Piagetian research: A summary. *Journal of Cross-Cultural Psychology, 3,* 23–39.

Davies, P. T., & Scummings, E. M. (1998). Exploring children's emotional security as a mediator of the link between marital relations and child adjustment. *Child Development, 69,* 124–139.

Davis, B. L., MacNeilage, P. F., Matyear, C. L., & Powell, J. K. (2000). Prosodic correlates of stress in babbling: An acoustical study. *Child Development, 71,* 1258–1270.

Davis, S. C., & Roberts, I. A. G. (1996). Bone marrow transplant for sickle cell disease: An update. *Archives of Disease in Childhood, 75,* 448–450.

Davis-Kean, P. E., & Sandler, H. M. (2001). A meta-analysis of measures of self-esteem for young children: A framework for future measures. *Child Development, 72,* 887–906.

Davison, K. K., & Birch, L. L. (1999). Weight status, parent reaction, and self-concept in five-year-old girls. *Pediatrics, 107,* 46–53.

Dawson, G. (1994). Development of emotion expression and emotion regulation in infancy. In G. Dawson & K. W. Fischer (Eds.), *Human behavior and the developing brain* (pp. 346–379). New York: Guilford.

Dawson, G., Munson, J., Estes, A., Osterling, J., McPartland, J., Toth, K., et al. (2002). Neurocognitive function and joint attention ability in young children with autism spectrum disorder versus developmental delay. *Child Development, 73,* 345–358.

Day, N. L., & Richardson, G. A. (1994). Comparative teratogenicity of alcohol and other drugs. *Alcohol Health and Research World, 18,* 42–48.

Deák, G. O., & Bauer, P. J. (1996). The dynamics of preschoolers' categorization choices. *Child Development, 67,* 740–767.

Deater-Deckard, K., & Dunn, J. (1999). Multiple risks and adjustment in young children growing up in different family settings: A British community study of stepparent, single mother, and nondivorced families. In E. M. Hetherington (Ed.), *Coping with divorce, single parenting, and remarriage* (pp. 65–90). Mahwah, NJ: Erlbaum.

Deater-Deckard, K., Pike, A., Petrill, S. A., Cutting, A. L., Hughes, C., & O'Connor, T. G. (2001). Nonshared environmental processes in social-emotional development: An observational study of identical twin differences in the preschool period. *Developmental Science, 4,* F1–F6.

DeBaryshe, B. D. (1993). Joint picture-book reading correlates of early oral language skill. *Journal of Child Language, 20,* 455–461.

DeBaryshe, B. D., Patterson, G. R., & Capaldi, D. M. (1993). A performance model for academic achievement in early adolescent boys. *Developmental Psychology, 29,* 795–804.

DeCasper, A. J., & Fifer, W. P. (1980). Of human bonding: Newborns prefer their mothers' voices. *Science, 208,* 1174–1176.

DeCasper, A. J., Lecanuet, J.-P., Busnel, M.-C., Granier-Deferre, C., & Maugeais, R. (1994). Fetal reactions to recurrent maternal speech. *Infant Behavior and Development, 17,* 159–164.

DeCasper, A. J., & Spence, M. J. (1986). Prenatal maternal speech influences newborns' perception of speech sounds. *Infant Behavior and Development, 9,* 133–150.

Declercq, E. R. (1993). Where babies are born and who attends their births: Findings from the revised 1989 United States Standard Certificate of Live Birth. *Obstetrics and Gynecology, 81,* 997–1004.

de Fockert, J. W., Rees, G., Frith, C. D., & Lavie, N. (2001). The role of working memory in visual selective attention. *Science, 291,* 1803–1806.

DeFries, J. C., Gervais, M. C., & Thomas, E. A. (1978). Response to 30 generations of selection for open-field activity in laboratory mice. *Behavior Genetics, 8,* 3–13.

de Haan, M., & Nelson, C. A. (1997). Brain activity differentiates face and object processing in 6-month-olds. *Developmental Psychology, 35,* 1113–1121.

Dekovic, M., & Janssens, J. (1992). Parents' child-rearing style and child's sociometric status. *Developmental Psychology, 28,* 925–932.

DeLisi, R., & Gallagher, A. M. (1991). Understanding of gender stability and constancy in Argentinian children. *Merrill-Palmer Quarterly, 37,* 483–502.

DeLoache, J. (1987). Rapid change in the symbolic functioning of young children. *Science, 238,* 1556–1557.

DeLoache, J. S. (2000). Dual representation and young children's use of scale models. *Child Development, 71,* 329–338.

DeLoache, J. S., & Smith, C. M. (1999). Early symbolic representation. In I. E. Sigel (Ed.), *Development of mental representation: Theories and applications* (pp. 61–86). Mahwah, NJ: Erlbaum.

Demany, L., McKenzie, B., & Vurpillot, E. (1977). Rhythm perception in early infancy. *Nature, 266,* 718–719.

Demmler, G. J. (1991). Summary of a workshop on surveillance for congenital cytomegalovirus disease. *Review of Infectious Diseases, 13,* 315–329.

Demo, D. H., & Acock, A. C. (1996). Family structure, family process, and adolescent well-being. *Journal of Research on Adolescence, 6,* 457–488.

Dempster, F. N. (1981). Memory span: Sources of individual and developmental differences. *Psychological Bulletin, 89,* 63–100.

DeMulder, E. K., Denham, S., Schmidt, M., & Mitchell, J. (2000). Q-sort assessment of attachment security during the preschool years: Links from home to school. *Developmental Psychology, 36,* 274–282.

Denham, S. A. (1998). *Emotional development in young children.* New York: Guilford.

Denham, S. A., McKinley, M., Couchoud, E. A., & Holt, R. (1990). Emotional and behavioral predictors of preschool ratings. *Child Development, 61,* 1145–1152.

Denham, S. A., Mitchell-Copeland, J., Strandberg, K., Auerbach, S., & Blair, K. (1997). Parental contributions to preschoolers' emotional competence: Direct and indirect effects. *Motivation and Emotion, 21,* 65–86.

Dennis, W. (1960). Causes of retardation among institutional children: Iran. *Journal of Genetic Psychology, 96,* 47–59.

Dennis, W., & Dennis, M. G. (1940). The effect of cradling practices upon the onset of walking in Hopi children. *Journal of Genetic Psychology, 56,* 77–86.

Dennison, B., Rockwell, H. L., & Baker, S. L. (1997). Excess fruit juice consumption by preschool-aged children is associated with short stature and obesity. *Pediatrics, 99,* 15–22.

DeRosier, M. E., Kupersmidt, J. B., & Patterson, C. J. (1994). Children's academic and behavioral adjustment as a function of the chronicity and proximity of peer rejection. *Child Development, 65,* 1799–1813.

DesRosiers, F., Vrsalovic, W. T., Knauf, D. E., Vargas, M., & Busch-Rossnagel, N. A. (1999). Assessing the multiple dimensions of the self-concept of young children: A focus on Latinos. *Merrill-Palmer Quarterly, 45,* 543–566.

Desrochers, S., Ricard, M., Decarie, T. G., & Allard, L. (1994). Developmental synchrony between social referencing and Piagetian sensorimotor causality. *Infant Behavior and Development, 17,* 303–309.

Deur, J. L., & Parke, R. D. (1970). Effects of inconsistent punishment on aggression in children. *Developmental Psychology, 2,* 403–411.

Deutsch, M., Katz, I., & Jensen, A. R. (1968). *Social class, race, and psychological development.* New York: Holt, Rinehart & Winston.

De Wolff, M. S., & van IJzendoorn, M. H. (1997). Sensitivity and attachment: A meta-analysis on parental antecedents of attachment. *Child Development, 68,* 571–591.

Devoe, L. D., Murray, C., Youssif, A., & Arnaud, M. (1993). Maternal caffeine consumption and fetal behavior in normal third-trimester pregnancy. *American Journal of Obstetrics and Gynecology, 168,* 1105–1112.

de Villiers, P. A., & de Villiers, J. G. (1979). Form and function in the development of sentence negation. *Papers and Reports in Child Language, 17,* 57–64.

Dhont, M., De Sutter, P., Ruyssinck, G., Martens, G., & Bekaert, A. (1999). Perinatal outcome of pregnancies after assisted reproduction: A case-control study. *American Journal of Obstetrics and Gynecology, 181,* 688–695.

Diamond, A. (1985). The development of the ability to use recall to guide action as indicated by infants' performance on A–B. *Child Development, 56,* 868–883.

Diamond, A. (1991). Neuropsychological insights into the meaning of object concept development. In S. Carey & R. Gelman (Eds.), *The epigenesis of mind: Essays on biology and cognition* (pp. 67–110). Hillsdale, NJ: Erlbaum.

Diamond, A., & Goldman-Rakic, P. S. (1989). Comparison of human infants and rhesus monkeys on Piaget's A–B task: Evidence for dependence on dorsolateral prefrontal cortex. *Experimental Brain Research, 74,* 24–40.

Diamond, A., Prevor, M. B., Callender, G., & Druin, D. P. (1997). Prefrontal cortex cognitive deficits in children treated early and continuously for PKU. *Monographs of the Society for Research in Child Development, 62*(4, Serial No. 252).

Diaz, R. M., & Klingler, C. (1991). Towards an explanatory model of the interaction between bilingualism and cognitive development. In E. Bialystok (Ed.), *Language processing in bilingual children* (pp. 167–192). Cambridge, UK: Cambridge University Press.

Diaz, R. M., Neal, C. J., & Vachio, A. (1991). Maternal teaching in the zone of the proximal development: A comparison of low- and high-risk dyads. *Merrill-Palmer Quarterly, 37,* 83–108.

Dick, D. M., Rose, R. J., Viken, R. J., & Kaprio, J. (2000). Pubertal timing and substance use: Associations between and within families across late adolescence. *Developmental Psychology, 36,* 180–189.

Dickens, W. T., & Flynn, J. R. (2001). Heritability estimates versus large environmental effects: The IQ paradox resolved. *Psychological Review, 108,* 346–369.

Dick-Read, G. (1959). *Childbirth without fear.* New York: Harper & Row.

Dien, D. S. (1982). A Chinese perspective on Kohlberg's theory of moral development. *Developmental Review, 2,* 331–341.

Dien, D. S.-F. (2000). The evolving nature of self-identity across four levels of history. *Human Development, 43,* 1–18.

Dietz, T. L. (1998). An examination of violence and gender role portrayals in video games: Implications for gender socialization and aggressive behavior. *Sex Roles, 38,* 425–442.

DiMatteo, M. R., Lepper, H. S., Damush, T. M., Morton, S. C., Carney, M. F., Pearson, M., & Kahn, K. L. (1996). Cesarean childbirth and psychosocial outcomes: A meta-analysis. *Health Psychology, 15,* 303–314.

Dion, K. K., & Berscheid, E. (1974). Physical attractiveness and peer perception among children. *Sociometry, 37,* 1–12.

Dishion, T. J., Andrews, D. W., & Crosby, L. (1995). Anti-social boys and their friends in early adolescence: Relationship characteristics, quality, and interactional process. *Child Development, 66,* 139–151.

Dishion, T. J., Patterson, G. R., & Griesler, P. C. (1994). Peer adaptations in the development of antisocial behavior: A confluence model. In L. R. Huesmann (Ed.), *Aggressive behavior: Current perspectives* (pp. 61–95). New York: Plenum.

Dishion, T. J., Spracklen, K. M., Andrews, D. W., & Patterson, G. R. (1996). Deviancy training in male adolescent friendships. *Behavior Therapy, 27,* 373–390.

DiVitto, B., & Goldberg, S. (1979). The effect of newborn medical status on early parent-infant interactions. In T. M. Field, A. M. Sostek, S. Goldberg, & H. H. Shuman (Eds.), *Infants born at risk.* New York: S. P. Medical & Scientific Books.

Dix, T. (1993). Attributing dispositions to children: An interactional analysis of attribution in socialization. *Personality and Social Psychology Bulletin, 19,* 633–643.

Dix, T. H., & Grusec, J. E. (1985). Parent attribution processes in the socialization of children. In I. E. Sigel (Ed.), *Parental belief systems: The psychological consequences for children.* Hillsdale, NJ: Erlbaum.

Dix, T. H., Ruble, D. N., Grusec, J. E., & Nixon, S. (1986). Social cognition in parents: Inferential and affective reactions to children of three age levels. *Child Development, 57,* 879–894.

Dix, T. H., Ruble, D. N., & Zambarano, R. J. (1989). Mothers' implicit theories of discipline: Child effects, parent effects, and the attribution process. *Child Development, 60,* 1373–1391.

Dixon, S., Tronick, E., Keeler, C., & Brazelton, T. B. (1981). Mother-infant interaction among the Gusii of Kenya. In T. M. Field, A. M. Sosteck, P. Vietze, & P. H. Leiderman (Eds.), *Culture and early interactions* (pp. 149–168). Hillsdale, NJ: Erlbaum.

Dixon, W. E., Jr., & Shore, C. (1997). Temperamental predictors of linguistic style during multiword acquisition. *Infant Behavior and Development, 20,* 99–103.

Dixon, W. E., Jr., & Smith, P. H. (2000). Links between early temperament and language acquisition. *Merrill-Palmer Quarterly, 46,* 417–440.

Dodge, K. A., Murphy, R. R., & Buchsbaum, K. (1984). The assessment of intention-cue detection skills in children: Implications for developmental psychopathology. *Child Development, 55,* 163–173.

Dodge, K. A., Pettit, G. S., & Bates, J. E. (1994). Socialization mediators of the relation between socioeconomic status and child conduct problems. *Child Development, 65,* 649–665.

Dodge, K. A., Schlundt, D. C., Schocken, I., & Delugach, J. D. (1983). Social competence and children's sociometric status: The role of peer group entry strategies. *Merrill-Palmer Quarterly, 29,* 309–336.

Doherty, W. J., & Needle, R. H. (1991). Psychological adjustment and substance use among adolescents before and after parental divorce. *Child Development, 62,* 328–337.

Donnelly, M., & Wilson, R. (1994). The dimensions of depression in early adolescence. *Personality and Individual Differences, 17,* 425–430.

Dooley, S. L. (1999). Routine ultrasound in pregnancy. *Clinical Obstetrics and Gynecology,* 737–748.

Dornbusch, S. M., Ritter, P. L., Leiderman, P. H., Roberts, D. F., & Fraleigh, M. J. (1987). The relation of parenting style to adolescent school performance. *Child Development, 58,* 1244–1257.

Dorr, A. (1986). *Television and children: A special medium for a special audience.* Beverly Hills: Sage.

Dougherty, T. M., & Haith, M. M. (1997). Infant expectations and reaction time as predictors of childhood speed of processing and IQ. *Developmental Psychology, 33,* 146–155.

Downey, G., Feldman, S., Khuri, J., & Friedman, S. (1994). Maltreatment and childhood depression. In W. M. Reynolds & H. F. Johnston (Eds.), *Handbook of depression in children and adolescents: Issues in clinical child psychology* (pp. 481–508). New York: Plenum.

Dozier, M., Stovall, K. C., Albus, K. E., & Bates, B. (2001). Attachment for infants in foster care: The role of caregiver state of mind. *Child Development, 72,* 1467–1477.

Dreher, M. C., Nugent, J. K., & Hudgins, R. (1994). Prenatal marijuana exposure and neonatal outcomes in Jamaica: An ethnographic study. *Pediatrics, 93,* 254–260.

Drewett, R., Wolke, D., Asefa, M., Kaba, M., & Tessema, F. (2001). Malnutrition and mental development: Is there a sensitive period? A nested case-control study. *Journal of Child Psychology and Psychiatry, 42,* 181–187.

Drewett, R. F., Corbett, S. S., & Wright, C. M. (1999). Cognitive and educational attainments at school age of children who failed to thrive in infancy: A population-based study. *Journal of Child Psychology and Psychiatry, 40,* 551–561.

Dromi, E. (1999). Early lexical development. In M. Barrett (Ed.), *The development of language* (pp. 99–131). East Sussex, UK: Psychology Press.

Drotar, D. (1991). The family context of nonorganic failure to thrive. *American Journal of Orthopsychiatry, 61,* 23–34.

Drug and Therapeutics Committee of the Lawson Wilkins Pediatric Endocrine Society. (1995). Guidelines for the use of growth hormone in children with short stature. *Journal of Pediatrics, 127,* 857–867.

DuBois, D. L., Tevendale, H. D., Burk-Braxton, C., Swenson, L. P., & Hardesty, J. L. (2000). Self-system influences during early adolescence: Investigation of an integrative model. *Journal of Early Adolescence, 20,* 12–43.

Dubner, A. E., & Motta, R. W. (1999). Sexually and physically abused foster care children and posttraumatic stress disorder. *Journal of Consulting and Clinical Psychology, 67,* 367–373.

Dubow, E. F., Tisak, J., Causey, D., Hryshko, A., & Reid, G. (1991). A two-year longitudinal study of stressful life events, social support, and social problem-solving skills: Contributions to children's behavioral and academic adjustment. *Child Development, 62,* 583–599.

Dunham, P., & Dunham, F. (1995). Developmental antecedents of taxonomic and thematic strategies at 3 years of age. *Developmental Psychology, 31,* 483–493.

Dunn, J. (1988). Connections between relationships: Implications of research on mothers and siblings. In R. A. Hinde & J. Stevenson-Hinde (Eds.), *Relationships within families: Mutual influences.* Oxford: Clarendon Press.

Dunn, J. (1996). Brothers and sisters in middle childhood and early adolescence: Continuity and change in individual differences. In G. H. Brody (Ed.), *Sibling relationships: Their causes and consequences* (pp. 31–46). Norwood, NJ: Ablex.

Dunn, J., Bretherton, I., & Munn, P. (1987). Conversations about feeling states between mothers and their young children. *Developmental Psychology, 23,* 132–139.

Dunn, J., & Brown, J. R. (1994). Affect expression in the family, children's understanding of emotions, and their interactions with others. *Merrill Palmer Quarterly, 40,* 120–137.

Dunn, J., Brown, J. R., & Maguire, M. (1995). The development of children's moral sensibility: Individual differences and emotion understanding. *Developmental Psychology, 31,* 649–659.

Dunn, J., & Cutting, A. L. (1999). Understanding others, and individual differences in friendship interactions in young children. *Social Development, 8,* 201–219.

Dunn, J., & Hughes, C. (2001). "I got some swords and you're dead!": Violent fantasy, antisocial behavior, and moral sensibility in young children. *Child Development, 72,* 491–505.

Dunn, J., & Kendrick, C. (1982). *Siblings: Love, envy, and understanding.* Cambridge, MA: Harvard University Press.

Dunn, J., & McGuire, S. (1994). Young children's nonshared experiences: A summary of studies in Cambridge and Colorado. In E. M. Hetherington, D. Reiss, & R. Plomin (Eds.), *Separate social worlds of siblings: The impact of nonshared environment on development* (pp. 111–128). Hillsdale, NJ: Erlbaum.

Dunn, J., Slombowski, C., & Beardsall, L. (1994). Sibling relationships from the preschool period through middle childhood and early adolescence. *Developmental Psychology, 30,* 315–324.

Dusek, J. B. (1987). Sex roles and adjustment. In D. B. Carter (Ed.), *Current conceptions of sex roles and sex typing: Theory and research* (pp. 211–222). New York: Praeger.

Dusek, J. B. (2000). Commentary on the special issue: The maturing of self-esteem research with early adolescents. *Journal of Early Adolescence, 20,* 231–240.

Durik, A. M., Hyde, J. S., & Clark, R. (2000). Sequelae of Cesarean and vaginal deliveries: Psychosocial outcomes for mothers and infants. *Developmental Psychology, 36,* 251–260.

Durston, S., Hulshoff, H. E., Casey, B. J., Giedd, J. N., Buitelaar, J. K., & van Engeland, H. (2001). Anatomical MRI of the developing human brain: What have we learned? *Journal of the American Academy of Adolescent Psychiatry, 40* 1012–1020.

Dweck, C. S. (1986). Motivational processes affecting learning. *American Psychologist, 41,* 1040–1048.

Dweck, C. S. (1991). Self-theories and goals: Their role in motivation, personality, and development. In R. Diestbier (Ed.), *Nebraska Symposium on Motivation, 1990* (Vol. 36, pp. 199–235). Lincoln: University of Nebraska Press.

Dweck, C. S. (1999). *Self-theories: Their role in motivation, personality, and development.* Philadelphia, PA: Psychology Press.

Dweck, C. S., & Elliott, E. S. (1983). Achievement motivation. In E. M. Hetherington (Ed.), *Handbook of child psychology: Vol. IV. Socialization, personality, and social development* (4th ed., pp. 643–691). New York: Wiley.

Dweck, C. S., Goetz, T. E., & Strauss, N. L. (1980). Sex differences in learned helplessness: IV. An experimental and naturalistic study of failure generalization and its mediators. *Journal of Personality and Social Psychology, 38,* 441–452.

Dybdahl, R. (2001). Children and mothers in war: An outcome study of a psychosocial intervention program. *Child Development, 72,* 1214–1230.

Dye, N. S. (1986). The medicalization of birth. In P. S. Eakins (Ed.), *The American way of birth.* Philadelphia: Temple University Press.

Eagly, A. H., & Steffen, V. J. (1986). Gender and aggressive behavior: A meta-analytic review of the social psychological literature. *Psychological Bulletin, 100,* 309–330.

East, P. L., & Jacobson, L. J. (2001). The younger siblings of teenage mothers: A follow-up of their pregnancy risk. *Developmental Psychology, 37,* 254–264.

Eaton, W., & Ennis, L. (1986). Sex differences in human motor activity level. *Psychological Bulletin, 100,* 19–28.

Ebrahim, S. H., Luman, E. T., Floyd, R. L.,Murphy, C. C., Bennett, D. M., & Boyle, C. A. (1998). Alcohol consumption by pregnant women in the United States during 1988–1995. *Obstetrics and Gynecology, 92,* 187–192.

Eccles, J. (1983). Expectancies, values, and academic behaviors. In J. T. Spence (Ed.), *Achievement and achievement motives: Psychological and sociological approaches.* San Francisco: W.H. Freeman.

Eccles, J. S. (1987). Adolescence: Gateway to androgyny? In D. B. Carter (Ed.), *Current conceptions of sex roles and sex typing: Theory and research* (pp. 225–241). New York: Praeger.

Eccles, J., Barber, B., Jozefowicz, D., Malenchuk, O., & Vida, M. (1999). Self-evaluations of competence, task values, and self-esteem. In N. G. Johnson, M. C. Roberts, & J. Worell (Eds.), *Beyond appearance: A new look at adolescent girls* (pp. 53–83). Washington, DC: American Psychological Association.

Eccles, J. S., Lord, S. E., Roeser, R. W., Barber, B. L., & Jozefowicz, D. M. H. (1997). The association of school transitions in early adolescence with developmental trajectories through high school. In J. Schulenberg, J. Maggs, & K. Hurrelmann (Eds.), *Health risks and developmental transitions during adolescence* (pp. 283–320). New York: Cambridge University Press.

Eccles, J. S., & Midgley, C. (1989). Stage/environment fit: Developmentally appropriate classrooms for early adolescents. In R. E. Ames & C. Ames (Eds.), *Research on motivation in education* (Vol. 3, pp. 139–186). San Diego, CA: Academic Press.

Eccles, J. S., Midgley, C., Wigfield, A., Buchanan, C. M., Reuman, D., Flanagan, C., & Mac Iver, D. (1993). Development during adolescence: The impact of stage-environment fit on young adolescents' experiences in schools and families. *American Psychologist, 48,* 90–101.

Eccles, J. S., & Roeser, R. W. (1999). School and community influences on human development. In M. H. Bornstein & M. E. Lamb (Eds.), *Developmental psychology: An advanced textbook* (4th ed., pp. 503–554). Mahwah, NJ: Erlbaum.

Eccles, J., Wigfield, A., Harold, R. D., & Blumenfeld, P. (1993). Age and gender differences in children's self- and task perceptions during elementary school. *Child Development, 64,* 830–847.

Eckenrode, J., Laird, M., & Doris, J. (1993). School performance and disciplinary problems among abused and neglected children. *Developmental Psychology, 29,* 53–62.

Eckerman, C. O., Whatley, J. L., & Kutz, S. L. (1975). Growth of social play with peers during the second year of life. *Developmental Psychology, 11,* 42–49.

Eder, D., & Hallinan, M. T. (1978). Sex differences in children's friendships. *American Sociological Review, 43,* 237–250.

Egan, S. K., & Perry, D. G. (1998). Does low self-regard invite victimization? *Developmental Psychology, 34,* 299–309.

Egan, S. K., & Perry, D. G. (2001). Gender identity: A multidimensional analysis with implications for psychosocial adjustment. *Developmental Psychology, 37,* 451–463.

Egeland, B., Jacobvitz, D., & Papatola, K. (1987). Intergenerational continuity of abuse. In R. J. Gelles & J. B. Lancaster (Eds.), *Child abuse and neglect: Biosocial dimensions.* Hawthorne, NY: Aldine de Gruyter.

Egeland, B., Jacobvitz, D., & Sroufe, L. A. (1988). Breaking the cycle of abuse. *Child Development, 59,* 1080–1088.

Egeland, B., & Sroufe, L. A. (1981). Attachment and early maltreatment. *Child Development, 52,* 44–52.

Ehrenberg, R. G., Brewer, D. J., Gamoran, A., & Willms, J. D. (2001a). Class size and student achievement. *Psychological Science in the Public Interest, 2,* 1–30.

Ehrenberg, R. G., Brewer, D. J., Gamoran, A., & Willms, J. D. (2001b, November). Does class size matter? *Scientific American, 285,* 79–85.

Ehri, L. C. (1998). Grapheme-phoneme knowledge is essential for learning to read words in English. In J. L. Metsala & L. C. Ehri (Eds.), *Word recognition in beginning literacy* (pp. 3–40). Mahwah, NJ: Erlbaum.

Eilers, R. E., & Berlin, C. (1995). Advances in early detection of hearing loss in infants. *Current Problems in Pediatrics, 25,* 60–66.

Eimas, P. D., Siqueland, E. R., Jusczyk, P., & Vigorito, J. (1971). Speech perception in infants. *Science, 171,* 303–306.

Eisenberg, N. (1986). *Altruistic emotion, cognition, and behavior.* Hillsdale, NJ: Erlbaum.

Eisenberg, N., Boehnke, K., Schuhler, P., & Silbereisen, R. K. (1985). The development of prosocial behavior and cognition in German children. *Journal of Cross-Cultural Psychology, 16,* 69–82.

Eisenberg, N., Carol, G., Murphy, B., & Van Court, P. (1995). Prosocial development in late adolescence: A longitudinal study. *Child Development, 66,* 1179–1197.

Eisenberg, N., & Fabes, R. A. (1998). Prosocial development. In W. Damon (Series Ed.) & N. Eisenberg (Vol. Ed.), *Handbook of child psychology: Vol. 3. Social, emotional, and personality development* (5th ed., pp. 701–778). New York: Wiley.

Eisenberg, N., Fabes, R. A., Bernzweig, J., Karbon, M., Poulin, R., & Hanish, L. (1993). The relations of emotionality and regulation to preschoolers' social skills and sociometric status. *Child Development, 64,* 1418–1438.

Eisenberg, N., Fabes, R. A., Shepard, S. A., Guthrie, I. K., Murphy, B. C., & Reiser, M. (1999). Parental reactions to children's negative emotions: Longitudinal reactions to the quality of children's social functioning. *Child Development, 70,* 513–534.

Eisenberg, N., Fabes, R. A., Shepard, S. A., Murphy, B. C., Guthrie, I. K., Jones, S., et al. (1997). Contemporaneous and longitudinal prediction of children's social functioning from regulation and emotionality. *Child Development, 68,* 642–664.

Eisenberg, N., Gershoff, E. T., Fabes, R. A., Shepard, S. A., Cumberland, A. J., Losoya, S. H., et al. (2001). Mother's emotional expressivity and children's behavior problems and social competence: Mediation through children's regulation. *Developmental Psychology, 37,* 475–490.

Eisenberg, N., Guthrie, I. K., Murphy, B. C., Shepard, S. A., Cumberland, A., & Carlo, G. (1999). Consistency and development of prosocial dispositions: A longitudinal study. *Child Development, 70,* 1360–1372.

Eisenberg, N., Hertz-Lazarowitz, R., & Fuchs, I. (1990). Prosocial moral judgment in Israeli kibbutz and city children: A longitudinal study. *Merrill-Palmer Quarterly, 36,* 273–285.

Eisenberg, N., & Lennon, R. (1983). Sex differences in empathy and related capacities. *Psychological Bulletin, 94,* 100–131.

Eisenberg, N., & Miller, P. A. (1987). The relation of empathy to prosocial and related behaviors. *Psychological Bulletin, 101,* 91–119.

Eisenberg, N., & Mussen, P. H. (1989). *The roots of prosocial behavior in children.* Cambridge, UK: Cambridge University Press.

Eisenberg, N., Pidada, S., & Liew, J. (2001). The relations of regulation and negative emotionality to Indonesian children's social functioning. *Child Development, 72,* 1747–1763.

Eisenberg, N., & Shell, R. (1986). Prosocial moral judgment and behavior in children: The mediating role of cost. *Personality and Social Psychology Bulletin, 12,* 426–433.

Eizenman, D. R., & Bertenthal, B. I. (1998). Infants' perception of object unity in translating and rotating displays. *Developmental Psychology, 34,* 426–434.

Ekman, P. (1972). Universals and cultural differences in facial expressions of emotion. In J. K. Cole (Ed.), *Nebraska symposium on motivation, 1971.* Lincoln: University of Nebraska Press.

Ekman, P. (1973). Cross-cultural studies of facial expression. In P. Ekman (Ed.), *Darwin and facial expression.* New York: Academic Press.

Elardo, R., & Bradley, R. H. (1981). The Home Observation for Measurement of the Environment (HOME) scale: A review of research. *Developmental Review, 1,* 113–145.

Elardo, R., Bradley, R. H., & Caldwell, B. M. (1975). The relation of infants' home environments to mental test performance from six to thirty-six months: A longitudinal analysis. *Child Development, 46,* 71–76.

Elardo, R., Bradley, R., & Caldwell, B. M. (1977). A longitudinal study of the relation of infants' home environments to language development at age three. *Child Development, 48,* 595–603.

Eley, T. C. (1997). General genes: A new theme in developmental psychopathology. *Current Directions in Psychological Science, 6,* 90–95.

Elfenbein, H. A., & Ambady, N. (2002). On the universality and cultural specificity of emotion recognition: A meta-analysis. *Psychological Bulletin, 128,* 203–235.

Elias, S., & Simpson, J. L. (1997). Prenatal diagnosis. In D. L. Rimoin, J. M. Connor, & R. E. Pyeritz (Eds.), *Emery and Rimoin's principles and practices of medical genetics* (3rd ed., Vol. 1, pp. 563–580). New York: Churchill Livingstone.

Eliez, S., & Reiss, A. L. (2000). Genetics of childhood disorders: 77 Fragile X syndrome. *Journal of the American Academy of Child and Adolescent Psychiatry, 39,* 264–266.

Elkind, D. (1976). *Child development and education.* New York: Oxford.

Elkind, D. (1981). *Children and adolescents: Interpretive essays on Jean Piaget* (3rd ed.). New York: Oxford University Press.

Elkind, D., Koegler, R. R., & Go, E. (1964). Studies in perceptual development: 2. Part-whole perception. *Child Development, 35,* 81–90.

Ellemberg, D., Lewis, T. L., Liu, C. H., & Maurer, D. (1999). Development of spatial and temporal vision during childhood. *Vision Research, 39,* 2325–2333.

Elliott, D. S., Wilson, W. J., Huizinga, D., Sampson, R. J., Elliott, A., & Rankin, B. (1996). The effects of neighborhood disadvantage on adolescent development. *Journal of Crime and Delinquency, 33,* 389–426.

Elliott, R., & Vasta, R. (1970). The modeling of sharing: Effects associated with vicarious reinforcement, symbolization, age, and generalization. *Journal of Experimental Child Psychology, 10,* 8–15.

Ellis, B. J., & Garber, J. (2000). Psychosocial antecedents of variation in girls' pubertal timing: Maternal depression, stepfather presence, and marital and family stress. *Child Development, 71,* 273–287.

Emde, R. N., & Hewitt, J. K. (Eds.). (2001). *Infancy to Early Childhood: Genetic and environmental influences on developmental change.* New York: Oxford University Press.

Emde, R. N., & Koenig, K. L. (1969). Neonatal smiling, frowning and rapid eye movement states. *Journal of the American Academy of Child Psychiatry, 8,* 57–67.

Emde, R. N., Plomin, R., Robinson, J., Corley, R., DeFries, J., Walker, D. W., et al. (1992). Temperament, emotion, and cognition at fourteen months:

The MacArthur longitudinal twin study. *Child Development, 63,* 1427–1455.

Emmons, L. (1996). The relationship of dieting to weight in adolescents. *Adolescence, 31,* 167–178.

Emory, E. K., Schlackman, L. J., & Fiano, K. (1996). Drug-hormone interactions on neurobehavioral responses in human neonates. *Infant Behavior and Development, 19,* 213–220.

Eng, T. R., & Butler, W. T. (Eds.). (1997). *The hidden epidemic: Confronting sexually transmitted disease.* Washington, DC: Institute of Medicine, National Academy Press.

Engle, R. W. (2002). Working memory capacity as executive attention. *Current Directions in Psychological Science, 11,* 19–23.

Engle, R. W., Kane, M. J., & Tuholski, S. W. (1999). Individual differences in working memory capacity and what they tell us about controlled attention, general fluid intelligence, and functions of the prefrontal cortex. In A. Miyake & P. Shah (Eds.), *Models of working memory: Mechanisms of active maintenance and executive control* (pp. 102–134). New York: Cambridge University Press.

Enright, M. K., Rovee-Collier, C. K., Fagen, J. W., & Caniglia, K. (1983). The effects of distributed training on retention of operant conditioning in human infants. *Journal of Experimental Child Psychology, 36,* 512–524.

Entwisle, D. (1995). The role of schools in sustaining early childhood program benefits. *The Future of Children: Long-term Outcomes of Early Childhood Programs, 5,* 133–143.

Epstein, C. J. (1989). Down syndrome (Trisomy 21). In C. R. Scriver, A. L. Beaudet, W. S. Sly, & D. Valle (Eds.), *The metabolic basis of inherited disease* (6th ed., Vol. I, pp. 291–326). New York: McGraw-Hill.

Epstein, C. J. (1995). Down syndrome (Trisomy 21). In C. R. Scriver, A. L. Beaudet, W. S. Sly, & D. Valle (Eds.), *The metabolic and molecular bases of inherited disease* (7th ed., Vol. I, pp. 749–794). New York: McGraw-Hill.

Epstein, J. L. (1983). Examining theories of adolescent friendship. In J. L. Epstein & N. L. Karweit (Eds.), *Friends in school.* San Diego: Academic Press.

Erbe, R. W., & Levy, H. L. (1997). Neonatal screening. In D. L. Rimoin, J. M. Connor, & R. E. Pyeritz (Eds.), *Emery and Rimoin's principles and practices of medical genetics* (3rd ed., Vol. 1, pp. 581–593). New York: Churchill Livingstone.

Erdley, C. A., Cain, K. M., Loomis, C. C., Dumas-Hines, F., & Dweck, C. S. (1997). Relations among children's social goals, implicit personality theories, and responses to social failure. *Developmental Psychology, 33,* 263–272.

Erhardt, D., & Hinshaw, S. P. (1994). Initial sociometric impressions of attention-deficit hyperactivity disorder and comparison boys: Predictions from social behaviors and from nonbehavioral variables. *Journal of Consulting and Clinical Psychology, 62,* 833–842.

Erickson, M. F., Sroufe, L. A., & Egeland, B. (1985). The relationship between quality of attachment and behavior problems in preschool in a high-risk sample. In I. Bretherton & E. Waters (Eds.), *Growing points of attachment theory and research. Monographs of the Society for Research in Child Development, 50*(1–2, Serial No. 209).

Erikson, E. H. (1950). *Childhood and society.* New York: W. W. Norton.

Ernst, M., Moolchan, E. T., & Robinson, M. L. (2001). Behavioral and neural consequences of prenatal exposure to nicotine. *Journal of the Academy of Adolescent Psychiatry, 40,* 630–641.

Eron, L. D., Huesmann, L. R., & Zelli, A. (1991). The role of parental variables in the learning of aggression. In D. J. Pepler & K. H. Rubin (Eds.), *The development and treatment of childhood aggression* (pp. 169–188). Hillsdale, NJ: Erlbaum.

Erwin, P. (1985). Similarity of attitudes and constructs in children's friendships. *Journal of Experimental Child Psychology, 40,* 470–485.

Eskenazi, B., Stapleton, A. L., Kharrazi, M., & Chee, W. Y. (1999). Associations between maternal decaffeinated and caffeinated coffee consumption and fetal growth and gestational duration. *Epidemiology, 10,* 242–249.

Eskritt, M., & Lee, K. (2002). "Remember where you last saw that card": Children's production of external symbols as a memory aid. *Developmental Psychology, 38,* 254–266.

Espy, K. A., & Kaufmann, P. M. (2002). Individual differences in the development of executive function in children: Lessons from the delayed response and A-not-B tasks. In D. L. Molfese & V. J. Molfese (Eds.), *Developmental variations in learning: Applications to social, executive function, language, and reading skills* (pp. 113–137). Mahwah, NJ: Erlbaum.

European Collaborative Study. (2001). Fluctuations in symptoms in human immunodeficiency virus-infected children: The first 10 years of life. *Pediatrics, 108,* 116–122.

Eveleth, P. B., & Tanner, J. M. (1990). *Worldwide variation in human growth* (2nd ed.). Cambridge, UK: Cambridge University Press.

Everman, D. B., & Cassidy, S. B. (2000). Genetics of childhood disorders: 12 Genomic imprinting: Breaking the rules. *Journal of the American Academy of Child and Adolescent Psychiatry, 39,* 386–389.

Ezzell, C. (2000, July). Beyond the human genome. *Scientific American, 283,* 64–69.

Eyler, F. D., Behnke, M., Conlon, M., Woods, N. W., & Wobie, K. (1998). Birth outcomes from a prospective matched study of prenatal crack cocaine use: II. Interactive and dose effects on neurobehavioral assessment. *Pediatrics, 101,* 237–241.

Fabes, R. A., Eisenberg, N., Hanish, L. D., & Spinrad, T. L. (2001). Preschoolers' spontaneous emotion vocabulary: Relations to likability. *Early Education and Development, 12,* 11–27.

Fabes, R. A., Eisenberg, N., Jones, S., Smith, M., Guthries, I, Poulin, R., et al. (1999). Regulation, emotionality, and preschoolers' socially competent peer interactions. *Child Development, 70,* 432–442.

Fabes, R. A., Eisenberg, N., Karbon, M., Troyer, D., & Switzer, G. (1994). The relations of children's emotion regulation to their vicarious emotional responses and comforting behaviors. *Child Development, 65,* 1678–1693.

Fabes, R. A., Eisenberg, N., McCormick, S. E., & Wilson, M. S. (1988). Preschoolers' attributions of the situational determinants of others' naturally occurring emotions. *Developmental Psychology, 24,* 376–385.

Fabes, R. A., Hanish, L. D., Martin, C. L., & Eisenberg, N. (2002). Young children's negative emotionality and social isolation: A latent growth curve analysis. *Merrill Palmer Quarterly, 48,* 284–307.

Fabes, R. A., Leonard, S. A., Kupanoff, K., & Martin, C. L. (2001). Parental coping with children's negative emotions: Relations with children's emotional and social responding. *Child Development, 72,* 907–920.

Fackelmann, K. (1998). It's a girl! Is sex selection the first step to designer children? *Science News, 154,* 350–351.

Fagan, J. F., & Holland, C. R. (2002). Equal opportunity and racial differences in IQ. *Intelligence, 30,* 361–387.

Fagan, J. F., & Montie, J. E. (1988). The behavioral assessment of cognitive well-being in the infant. In J. Kavanagh (Ed.), *Understanding mental retardation: Research accomplishments and new frontiers.* Baltimore: Paul H. Brookes.

Fagan, J. F., & Singer, L. T. (1983). Infant recognition memory as a measure of intelligence. In L. P. Lipsitt (Ed.), *Advances in infancy research* (Vol. 2). Norwood, NJ: Ablex.

Fagan, J. F., III. (1974). Infant recognition memory: The effects of length of familiarization and type of discrimination task. *Child Development, 45,* 351–356.

Fagot, B. I. (1977). Consequences of moderate cross-gender behavior in preschool children. *Child Development, 48,* 902–907.

Fagot, B. I. (1978). The influence of sex of child on parental reactions to toddler children. *Child Development, 49,* 459–465.

Fagot, B. I. (1985). Changes in thinking about early sex role development. *Developmental Review, 5,* 83–98.

Fagot, B. I., & Leinbach, M. D. (1987). Socialization of sex roles within the family. In D. B. Carter (Ed.), *Current conceptions of sex roles and sex typing: Theory and research* (pp. 89–100). New York: Praeger.

Fagot, B. I., & Leinbach, M. D. (1989). The young child's gender schema: Environmental input, internal organization. *Child Development, 60,* 663–672.

Fagot, B. I., & Leinbach, M. D. (1995). Gender knowledge in egalitarian and traditional families. *Sex Roles, 32,* 513–526.

Fagot, B. I., Leinbach, M. D., & O'Boyle, C. (1992). Gender labeling, gender stereotyping, and parenting behaviors. *Developmental Psychology, 28,* 225–230.

Falbo, T., & Cooper, C. R. (1980). Young children's time and intellectual ability. *Journal of Genetic Psychology, 173,* 299–300.

Falbo, T., & Polit, D. F. (1986). Quantitative review of the only child literature: Research evidence and theory development. *Psychological Bulletin, 100,* 176–189.

Famularo, R., Fenton, T., Kinscherff, R., Ayoub, C., & Barnum, R. (1994). Maternal and child posttraumatic disorder in cases of child maltreatment. *Child Abuse and Neglect, 18,* 27–36.

Fancher, R. E. (1998). Alfred Binet, general psychologist. In G. A. Kimble & M. Wertheimer (Eds.), *Portraits of pioneers in psychology* (Vol. 3, pp. 67–83). Washington, DC: American Psychological Association.

Fangman, J. J., Mark, P. M., Pratt, L., Conway, K. K., Healey, M. L., Oswald, J. W., & Uden, D. L. (1994). Prematurity prevention programs: An analysis of successes and failures. *American Journal of Obstetrics and Gynecology, 170,* 744–750.

Fantz, R. L. (1961, May). The origin of form perception. *Scientific American, 204,* 66–72.

Farooqi, I. S., & O'Rahilly, S. (2000). Recent advances in the genetics of severe childhood obesity. *Archives of Disease in Childhood, 83,* 31–34.

Farr, K. A. (1995). Fetal abuse and the criminalization of the behavior during pregnancy. *Crime and Delinquency, 41,* 235–245.

Farrar, M. J. (1992). Negative evidence and grammatical morpheme acquisition. *Developmental Psychology, 28,* 90–98.

Farrell, S. P., Hains, A. A., & Davies, W. H. (1998). Cognitive behavioral interventions for sexually abused children exhibiting PTSD symptomology. *Behavior Therapy, 29,* 241–255.

Farrington, D. P. (1991). Childhood aggression and adult violence: Early precursors and later-life outcomes. In D. J. Pepler & K. H. Rubin (Eds.), *The development and treatment of childhood aggression* (pp. 5–29). Hillsdale, NJ: Erlbaum.

Farver, J. M., Kim, Y. K., & Lee, Y. (1995). Cultural differences in Korean- and Anglo-American preschoolers' social interaction and play behaviors. *Child Development, 66,* 1088–1099.

Farver, J. M., & Shin, Y. L. (1997). Social pretend play in Korean- and Anglo-American preschoolers. *Child Development, 68,* 544–556.

Farver, J. M., & Wimbarti, S. (1995). Paternal participation in toddlers' pretend play. *Social Development, 4,* 17–31.

Fausto-Sterling, A. (1992). *Myths of gender: Biological theories about women and men* (2nd ed.). New York: Basic Books.

Federal Interagency Forum on Child and Family Statistics. (1999). *Backgrounder: Healthy eating index shows most children and adolescents have a diet that is poor or needs improvement.* Retrieved January 13, 2003, from http://childstats.gov/ac1999/heirel.asp

Federman, J. (1996). *National Television Violence Study I.* Thousand Oaks, CA: Sage.

Federman, J. (1997). *National Television Violence Study II.* Thousand Oaks, CA: Sage.

Federman, J. (1998). *National Television Violence Study III.* Thousand Oaks, CA: Sage.

Feigenson, L., Carey, S., & Hauser, M. (2002). The representations underlying infants' choice of more: Object files versus analog magnitudes. *Psychological Science, 13,* 150–156.

Feinberg, M. E., & Hetherington, E. M. (2000). Sibling differentiation in adolescence: Implications for behavioral genetic theory. *Child Development, 71,* 1512–1524.

Feingold, A. (1988). Cognitive gender differences are disappearing. *American Psychologist, 43,* 95–103.

Feingold, A. (1992). Sex differences in variability in intellectual abilities: A new look at an old controversy. *Review of Educational Research, 62,* 61–84.

Feingold, A. (1993). Cognitive gender differences: A developmental perspective. *Sex Roles, 29,* 91–112.

Feingold, A. (1994). Gender differences in personality: A meta-analysis. *Psychological Bulletin, 116,* 429–456.

Feldman, D. (1979). The mysterious case of extreme giftedness. In H. Passow (Ed.), *The gifted and talented.* Chicago: University of Chicago Press.

Feldman, H. A. (1982). Epidemiology of toxoplasma infections. *Epidemiological Review, 4,* 204–213.

Feldman, H., Goldin-Meadow, S., & Gleitman, L. (1978). Beyond Herodotus: The creation of language by linguistically deprived children. In A. Locke (Ed.), *Action, gesture, and symbol: The emergence of language* (pp. 351–418). New York: Academic Press.

Feldman, P. J., Dunkel-Schetter, C., Sandman, C. A., & Wadhwa, P. D. (2000). Maternal social support predicts birth weight and fetal growth in human pregnancy. *Psychosomatic Medicine, 62,* 715–725.

Feldman, R., Weller, A., Sirota, L., & Eidelman, A. I. (2002). Skin-to-skin contact (kangaroo care) promotes self-regulation in premature infants: Sleep-wake cyclicity, arousal modulation, and sustained exploration. *Developmental Psychology, 38,* 194–207.

Feldman, W., Feldman, E., & Goodman, J. T. (1988). Culture versus biology: Children's attitudes toward fatness and thinness. *Pediatrics, 81,* 190–194.

Felner, R. D., & Adan, A. M. (1988). The School Transitional Environment Project: An ecological intervention and evaluation. In R. H. Price, E. L. Cowan, R. P. Lorion, I. Serrano-Garcia, & J. Ramos-McKay (Eds.), *14 ounces of prevention: A casebook for practitioners.* Washington, DC: American Psychological Association.

Felner, R. D., Ginter, M., & Primavera, J. (1982). Primary prevention during school transitions: Social support and environmental structure. *American Journal of Community Psychology, 10,* 277–290.

Felson, R. B. (1993). The (somewhat) social self: How others affect self-appraisals. In J. Suls (Ed.), *Psychological perspectives on the self* (Vol. 4, pp. 1–26). Hillsdale, NJ: Erlbaum.

Fenson, L., Dale, P. S., Reznick, J. S., Bates, E., Thal, D. J., & Pethick, S. J. (1994). Variability in early communicative development. *Monographs of the Society for Research in Child Development, 59* (5, Serial No. 242).

Ferber, R. (1985). *Solve your child's sleep problems.* New York: Simon and Schuster.

Fergusson, D. M., Lynskey, M., & Horwood, L. J. (1995). The adolescent outcomes of adoption: A 16-year longitudinal study. *Journal of Child Psychology and Psychiatry and Allied Disciplines, 36,* 597–615.

Fergusson, D. M., Woodward, L. J., & Horwood, L. J. (1998). Maternal smoking during pregnancy and psychiatric adjustment in late adolescence. *Archives of General Psychiatry, 55,* 721–727.

Fernald, A. (1985). Four-month-olds prefer to listen to motherese. *Infant Behavior and Development, 8,* 181–195.

Fernald, A. (1991). Prosody in speech to children: Prelinguistic and linguistic functions. In R. Vasta (Ed.), *Annals of child development: Vol. 8.* London: Jessica Kingsley.

Fernald, A., & Mazzie, C. (1991). Prosody and focus in speech to infants and adults. *Developmental Psychology, 27,* 209–221.

Fernald, A., & Morikawa, H. (1993). Common themes and cultural variations in Japanese and American mothers' speech to infants. *Child Development, 64,* 637–656.

Fernald, A., Swingley, D., & Pinto, J. P. (2001). When half a word is enough: Infants can recognize spoken words using partial phonetic information. *Child Development, 72,* 1003–1015.

Ferrier, S., Dunham, P., & Dunham, F. (2000). The confused robot: Two-year-olds' responses to breakdowns in conversation. *Social Development, 9,* 337–347.

Feuerstein, R., Rand, Y., & Rynders, J. (1988). *Don't accept me as I am: Helping "retarded" people to excel.* New York: Plenum.

Field, J., Muir, D., Pilon, R., Sinclair, M., & Dodwell, P. (1980). Infants' orientation to lateral sounds from birth to three months. *Child Development, 51,* 295–298.

Field, T. (1979). Differential behavior and cardiac responses of 3-month-olds to a mirror and a peer. *Infant Behavior and Development, 2,* 179–184.

Field, T. (1991). Quality infant day-care and grade school behavior and performance. *Child Development, 6,* 863–870.

Field, T. (1995). Infants of depressed mothers. *Infant Behavior and Development, 18,* 1–13.

Field, T., Fox, N. A., Pickens, J., & Nawrocki, T. (1995). Relative right frontal EEG activation in 3- to 6-month-old infants of "depressed" mothers. *Developmental Psychology, 31,* 358–363.

Field, T., Healy, B., Goldstein, S., Perry, S., Bendell, D., Schanberg, S., et al. (1988). Infants of depressed mothers show "depressed" behavior even with nondepressed adults. *Child Development, 59,* 1569–1579.

Field, T., Scafidi, F., Pickens, J., Prodromidis, M., Pelaez-Nogueras, M., Torquati, J., et al. (1998). Polydrug-using adolescent mothers and their infants receiving early intervention. *Adolescence, 33,* 117–143.

Field, T. M. (1977). Effects of early separation, interactive deficits, and experimental manipulations on infant-mother face-to-face interactions. *Child Development, 48,* 763–771.

Field, T. M. (1982). Affective displays of high-risk infants during early interactions. In T. Field & A. Fogel (Eds.), *Emotion and early interaction* (pp. 110–125). Hillsdale, NJ: Erlbaum.

Field, T. M., Cohen, D., Garcia, R., & Greenberg, R. (1984). Mother-stranger face discrimination by the newborn. *Infant Behavior and Development, 7,* 19–25.

Field, T. M., Woodson, R., Cohen, D., Greenberg, R., Garcia, R., & Collins, K. (1983). Discrimination and imitation of facial expressions by term and preterm neonates. *Infant Behavior and Development, 6,* 485–489.

Field, T. M., Woodson, R., Greenberg, R., & Cohen, D. (1982). Discrimination and imitation of facial expressions by neonates. *Science, 218,* 179–181.

Fillmore, L. W., & Meyer, L. (1992). The curriculum and linguistic minorities. In P. Jackson (Ed.), *Handbook of research on curriculum* (pp. 626–658). New York: Macmillan.

Finch, E. (1978). *Clinical assessment of short stature.* Unpublished medical school thesis, Yale University.

Fine, M. (1988). Sexuality, schooling, and adolescent females: The missing discourse of desire. *Harvard Educational Review, 58,* 29–53.

Fine, M. A., Coleman, M., & Ganong, L. H. (1999). A social constructionist multi-method approach to understanding the stepparent role. In E. M. Hetherington (Ed.), *Coping with divorce, single parenting, and remarriage* (pp. 273–294). Mahwah, NJ: Erlbaum.

Finn, J. D., & Achilles, C. M. (1990). Answers and questions about class size: A statewide experiment. *American Educational Research Journal, 27,* 557–577.

Finnie, V., & Russell, A. (1988). Preschool children's social status and their mothers' behavior and knowledge in the supervisory role. *Developmental Psychology, 24,* 789–801.

Fioravanti, F., Inchingolo, P., Pensiero, S., & Spanio, M. (1995). Saccadic eye movement conjugation in children. *Vision Research, 35,* 3217–3228.

Fischbein, S. (1981). Heredity-environment influences on growth and development during adolescence. In L. Gedda, P. Parisi, & W. E. Nance (Eds.), *Twin research 3: Pt. B. Program in clinical and biological research* (pp. 43–50). New York: Liss.

Fischer, K. W. (1980). A theory of cognitive development: The control and construction of hierarchies of skills. *Psychological Review, 87,* 477–531.

Fischer, K. W., & Bidell, T. (1991). Constraining nativist inferences about cognitive capacities. In S. Carey & R. Gelman (Eds.), *The epigenesis of mind: Essays on biology and cognition* (pp. 199–235). Hillsdale, NJ: Erlbaum.

Fischer, K. W., & Bidell, T. R. (1998). Dynamic development of psychological structures in action and thought. In W. Damon (Series Ed.) & R. Lerner (Vol. Ed.), *Handbook of child psychology: Vol.1. Theoretical models of human development* (5th ed., pp. 467–561). New York: Wiley.

Fischer, K. W., & Farrar, M. J. (1988). Generalizations about generalization: How a theory of skill development explains both generality and specificity. In A. Demetriou (Ed.), *The neo-Piagetian theories of cognitive development: Toward an integration.* North-Holland: Elsevier.

Fischer, K. W., & Pipp, S. L. (1984). Processes of cognitive development: Optimal level and skill acquisition. In R. J. Sternberg (Ed.), *Mechanisms of cognitive development* (pp. 45–80). New York: W.H. Freeman.

Fisher, C. (2002). Structural limits on verb mapping: The role of abstract structure in 2.5-year-olds' interpretations of novel verbs. *Developmental Science, 5,* 55–64.

Fisher, C. B. (1994). Reporting and referring research participants: Ethical challenges for investigators studying children and youth. *Ethics & Behavior, 4,* 87–95.

Fisher, C. B., Higgins D'Alessandro, A., Rau, J. M. B., Kuther, T. L., & Belanger, S. (1996). Referring and reporting research participants at risk: Views from urban adolescents. *Child Development, 67,* 2086–2100.

Fishkin, J., Keniston, K., & MacKinnon, C. (1973). Moral reasoning and political ideology. *Journal of Personality and Social Psychology, 27,* 109–119.

Fivush, R. (1984). Learning about school: The development of kindergartners' school scripts. *Child Development, 55,* 1697–1709.

Fivush, R. (1997). Event memory in early childhood. In N. Cowan (Ed.), *The development of memory in childhood* (pp. 139–161). East Sussex, UK: Psychology Press.

Fivush, R., Haden, C., & Adam, S. (1995). Structure and coherence of preschoolers' personal narratives over time: Implications for childhood amnesia. *Journal of Experimental Child Psychology, 60,* 32–56.

Fivush, R., Kuebli, J., & Clubb, P. A. (1992). The structure of events and event representations: A developmental analysis. *Child Development, 63,* 188–201.

Fivush, R., & Schwarzmueller, A. (1998). Children remember childhood: Implications for childhood amnesia. *Applied Cognitive Psychology, 12,* 455–473.

Flanagan, C. A. (1990). Change in family work status: Effects on parent-adolescent decision making. *Child Development, 61,* 163–177.

Flannagan, D., & Hardee, S. D. (1994). Talk about preschoolers' interpersonal relationships: Patterns related to culture, SES, and gender of child. *Merrill-Palmer Quarterly, 40,* 523–537.

Flavell, J. H. (1963). *The developmental psychology of Jean Piaget.* New York: Van Nostrand Reinhold.

Flavell, J. H. (1970). Developmental studies of mediated memory. In H. W. Reese & L. P. Lipsitt (Eds.), *Advances in child development and behavior* (Vol. 5, pp. 182–211). New York: Academic Press.

Flavell, J. H. (1978). The development of knowledge about visual perception. In C. B. Keasey (Ed.), *Nebraska symposium on motivation* (Vol. 25, pp. 43–76). Lincoln: University of Nebraska Press.

Flavell, J. H. (1992). Cognitive development: Past, present, and future. *Developmental Psychology, 28,* 998–1005.

Flavell, J. H. (1993). Young children's understanding of thinking and consciousness. *Current Directions in Psychological Science, 2,* 40–43.

Flavell, J. H. (1996). Piaget's legacy. *Psychological Science, 7,* 200–203.

Flavell, J. H., Beach, D. H., & Chinsky, J. M. (1966). Spontaneous verbal rehearsal in a memory task as a function of age. *Child Development, 37,* 283–299.

Flavell, J. H., Flavell, E. R., Green, F. L., & Korfmacher, J. E. (1990). Do young children think of television images as pictures or real objects? *Journal of Broadcasting & Electronic Media, 34,* 399–419.

Flavell, J. H., & Green, F. L. (1999). Development of intuitions about the controllability of different mental states. *Cognitive Development, 14,* 133–146.

Flavell, J. H., Green, F. L., & Flavell, E. R. (1995). The development of children's knowledge about attentional focus. *Developmental Psychology, 31,* 706–712.

Flavell, J. H., & Wellman, H. M. (1977). Metamemory. In R. V. Kail & J. W. Hagen (Eds.), *Perspectives on the development of memory and cognition* (pp. 3–33). Hillsdale, NJ: Erlbaum.

Flavell, J. H., Zhang, X-D, Zou, H., Dong, Q., & Qi, S. (1983). A comparison of the appearance-reality distinction in the People's Republic of China and the United States. *Cognitive Psychology, 15,* 459–466.

Fletcher-Flinn, C. M., & Thompson, G. B. (2000). Learning to read with underdeveloped phonemic awareness but lexicalized phonological recoding: A case study of a 3-year-old. *Cognition, 74,* 177–208.

Flick, L., Vemulapalli, C., Stulac, B. B., & Kemp, J. S. (2001). The influence of grandmothers and other senior caregivers on sleep position used by African American infants. *Archives of Pediatrics and Adolescent Medicine, 155,* 1231–1237.

Flieller, A. (1999). Comparison of the development of formal thought in adolescent cohorts aged 10 to 15 years (1967–1996 and 1972–1993). *Developmental Psychology, 35,* 1048–1058.

Florsheim, P., Tolan, P., & Gorman-Smith, D. (1998). Family relationship, parenting practices, the availability of male family members, and the behavior of inner-city boys in single-mother and two-parent families. *Child Development, 69,* 1437–1447.

Flynn, J. R. (1998). IQ gains over time: Toward finding the causes. In U. Neisser (Ed.), *The rising curve: Long-term gains in IQ and related measures* (pp. 25–66). Washington, DC: American Psychological Association.

Flynn, J. R. (1999). Searching for justice: The discovery of IQ gains over time. *American Psychologist, 54,* 5–20.

Foa, E. B., & Meadows, E. A. (1997). Psychosocial treatments for posttraumatic stress disorder: A critical review. *Annual Review of Psychology, 48,* 449–480.

Fodor, J. A. (1983). *The modularity of mind.* Cambridge, MA: MIT Press.

Fodor, J. A . (1992). A theory of the child's theory of mind. *Cognition, 44,* 283–296.

Fogel, A. (1979). Peer- vs. mother-directed behavior in 1- to 3-month-old infants. *Infant Behavior and Development, 2,* 215–226.

Fogel, A. (1982). Early adult-infant face-to-face interaction: Expectable sequences of behavior. *Journal of Pediatric Psychology, 7,* 1–22.

Fomon, S. J. (1993). *Nutrition of normal infants.* St. Louis, MO: Mosby-Yearbook.

Fonzi, A., Schneider, B. H., Tani, F., & Tomada, G. (1997). Predicting children's friendship status from their dyadic interaction in structured situations of potential conflict. *Child Development, 68,* 496–506.

Forehand, R., & Long, N. (1988). Outpatient treatment of the acting out child: Procedures, long term follow-up data, and clinical problems. *Advances in Behavior Research and Therapy, 10,* 129–177.

Forehand, R., & McMahon, R. (1981). *Helping the noncompliant child.* New York: Guilford.

Forman, D. R., & Kochanska, G. (2001). Viewing imitation as child responsiveness: A link between teaching and discipline domains of socialization. *Developmental Psychology, 37,* 198–206.

Foulon, W., Villena, I., Stray-Pedersen, B., Decoster, A., Lappalainen, M., Pinon, J.-M., et al. (1999). Treatment of toxoplasmosis during pregnancy: A multicenter study of impact on fetal transmission and children's sequelae at age 1 year. *American Journal of Obstetrics and Gynecology, 180,* 410–415.

Fox, N. A. (1991). If it's not left, it's right: Electroencephalograph asymmetry and the development of emotion. *American Psychologist, 46,* 863–872.

Fox, N. A. (1994). Dynamic cerebral processes underlying emotion regulation. In N. A. Fox (Ed.), *The development of emotion regulation: Biological and behavioral considerations. Monographs of the Society for Research in Child Development, 59* (Nos. 2–3, Serial No. 240).

Fox, N. A., & Davidson, R. J. (1986). Psychophysiological measures of emotion: New directions in developmental research. In C. E. Izard & P. B. Read (Eds.), *Measuring emotions in infants and children* (Vol. 2). Cambridge, UK: Cambridge University Press.

Fox, R., Aslin, R. N., Shea, S. L., & Dumais, S. T. (1980). Stereopsis in human infants. *Science, 207,* 323–324.

Fraiberg, S. (1977). *Insights from the blind.* New York: Basic Books.

Franco, P., Groswasser, J., Hassid, S., Lanquart, J. P., Scaillet, S., & Kahn, A. (1999). Prenatal exposure to cigarette smoking is associated with a decrease in arousal in infants. *Journal of Pediatrics, 135,* 34–38.

Frank, D. A., Augustyn, M., Knight, W. G., Pell, T., & Zuckerman, B. (2001). Growth, development, and behavior in early childhood following prenatal cocaine exposure: A systematic review. *Journal of the American Medical Association, 285,* 1613–1625.

Frankenburg, W. K., Dodds, J., Archer, P., Shapiro, H., & Bresnick, B. (1992). The Denver II: A major revision and restandardization of the Denver Developmental Screening Test. *Pediatrics, 89,* 91–97.

Franklin, C., Grant, D., Corcoran, J., O'Dell-Miller, P., & Bultman, L. (1997). Effectiveness of prevention programs for adolescent pregnancy: A meta-analysis. *Journal of Marriage and the Family, 59,* 551–567.

Fraser, S. (1995). *The bell curve wars: Race, intelligence, and the future of America.* New York: Basic Books.

Frauenglass, M. H., & Diaz, R. M. (1985). Self-regulatory functions of children's private speech: A critical analysis of recent challenges to Vygotsky's theory. *Developmental Psychology, 21,* 357–364.

Frazier, J. A., & Morrison, F. J. (1998). The influence of extended-year schooling on growth of achievement and perceived competence in early elementary school. *Child Development, 69,* 495–517.

Fredriks, A. M., Van Buren, S., Burgmeijer, R. J. F., Meulmeester, J. F., Beuker, R J., Brugman, E., et al. (2000). Continuing positive secular growth change in the Netherlands 1955–1997. *Pediatric Research, 47,* 316–323.

Fredricks, J. A., & Eccles, J. S. (2002). Children's competence and value beliefs from childhood through adolescence: Growth trajectories in two male-sex-typed domains. *Developmental Psychology, 38,* 519–533.

Freedland, R. L., & Bertenthal, B. I. (1994). Developmental changes in interlimb coordination: Transition to hands-and-knees crawling. *Psychological Science, 5,* 26–32.

Freedman, D. (1979). Ethnic differences in babies. *Human Nature, 2,* 26–43.

Freire, A., & Lee, K. (2001). Face recognition in 4- to 7-year-olds: Processing of configural, featural, and paraphernalia information. *Journal of Experimental Child Psychology, 80,* 347–371.

Frey, K. S., & Ruble, D. N. (1987). What children say about classroom performance: Sex and grade differences in perceived competence. *Child Development, 58,* 1066–1078.

Fried, P. A., Watkinson, B., & Gray, R. (1998). Differential effects on cognitive functioning in 9- to 12-year-olds prenatally exposed to cigarettes and marijuana. *Neurotoxicology and Teratology, 20,* 293–306.

Friedman, J. M., & Polifka, J. E. (1996). *The effects of drugs on the fetus and nursing infant: A handbook for health care professionals.* Baltimore: Johns Hopkins University Press.

Friedmann, T. (1997, June). Overcoming the obstacles of gene therapy. *Scientific American, 276,* 96–102.

Friedrich, L. K., & Stein, A. H. (1973). Aggressive and prosocial television programs and the natural behavior of preschool children. *Monographs of the Society for Research in Child Development, 38*(4, Serial No. 151).

Frishmuth, G. J. (1998). Ectopic pregnancy. In L. A. Wallis et al. (Eds.), *Textbook of women's health* (pp. 709–713). Philadelphia: Lippincott-Raven.

Frith, U. (1993). Autism. *Scientific American, 268,* 108–114.

Frith, U., & Happé, F. (1999). Theory of mind and self-consciousness: What is it like to be autistic? *Mind & Language, 14,* 1–22.

Frodi, A. M., & Lamb, M. E. (1980). Child abusers' responses to infant smiles and cries. *Child Development, 51,* 238–241.

Frodi, A. M., Lamb, M. E., Leavitt, L. A., & Donovan, W. L. (1978). Fathers' and mothers' responses to infant smiles and cries. *Infant Behavior and Development, 1,* 187–198.

Frodi, A. M., & Thompson, R. (1985). Infants' affective responses in the strange situation: Effects of prematurity and of quality of attachment. *Child Development, 56,* 1280–1290.

Fuligni, A. J. (1997). The academic achievement of adolescents from immigrant families: The roles of family background, attitudes, and behavior. *Child Development, 68,* 351–363.

Fuligni, A. J., & Eccles, J. S. (1993). Perceived parent-child relationships and early adolescents' orientation toward peers. *Developmental Psychology, 29,* 622–632.

Fuligni, A. J., Eccles, J. S., Barber, B. L., & Clements, P. (2001). Early adolescent peer orientation and adjustment during high school. *Developmental Psychology, 37,* 28–36.

Fuligni, A. J., & Stevenson, H. W. (1995). Time use and mathematics achievement among American, Chinese, and Japanese high school students. *Child Development, 66,* 830–842.

Fulker, O. W., & Eysenck, H. J. (1979). Nature, nurture and socio-economic status. In H. J. Eysenck (Ed.), *The structure and measurement of intelligence.* Berlin: Springer-Verlag.

Furman, W. (1999). Friends and lovers: The role of peer relationships in adolescent romantic relationships. In W. A. Collins & B. Laursen (Eds.), *Minnesota symposia on child psychology: Vol. 30. Relationships as developmental contexts* (pp. 133–154). Mahwah, NJ: Erlbaum.

Furman, W., & Bierman, K. L. (1984). Children's conceptions of friendship: A multimethod study of developmental changes. *Developmental Psychology, 20,* 925–931.

Furman, W., & Buhrmester, D. (1992). Age and sex differences in perceptions of networks of personal relationships. *Child Development, 63,* 103–115.

Furman, W., & Robbins, P. (1985). What's the point? Issues in the selection of treatment objectives. In B. H. Schneider, K. H. Rubin, & J. E. Ledingham (Eds.), *Children's peer relations: Issues in assessment and intervention.* New York: Springer-Verlag.

Furman, W., Somin, V. A., Shaffer, L., & Bouchey, H. A. (2002). Adolescents' working models and styles for relationships with parents, friends, and romantic partners. *Child Development, 73,* 241–255.

Furnham, A., & Mak, T. (1999). Sex-role stereotyping in television commercials: A review and comparison of fourteen studies done on five continents over 25 years. *Sex Roles, 41,* 413–437.

Furstenberg, F. F. (1994). History and current status of divorce in the United States. *The Future of Children, 4,* 29–43.

Furstenberg, F. F., Jr. (1987). The new extended family: The experience of parents and children after remarriage. In K. Paley & M. Ihinger-Tallman (Eds.), *Remarriage and stepparenting* (pp. 42–61). New York: Guilford Press.

Furstenberg, F. F., Jr., Brooks-Gunn, J., & Chase-Lansdale, P. L. (1989). Teenaged pregnancy and childbearing. *American Psychologist, 44,* 313–320.

Fuson, K. C., & Kwon, Y. (1992). Korean children's understanding of multidigit addition and subtraction. *Child Development, 63,* 491–506.

Gabbe, S. G., & Turner, L. P. (1997). Reproductive hazards of the American lifestyle: Work during pregnancy. *American Journal of Obstetrics and Gynecology, 176,* 826–832.

Gabel, S. (1997). Conduct disorder in grade-school children. In J. D. Noshpitz (Series Ed.) & P. F. Kernberg & J. R. Bemporad (Vol. Eds.), *Handbook of child and adolescent psychiatry* (Vol. 2, pp. 309–401). New York: Wiley.

Gaddis, A., & Brooks-Gunn, J. (1985). The male experience of pubertal change. *Journal of Youth and Adolescence, 14,* 61–69.

Gagnon, M., & Ladouceur, R. (1992). Behavioral treatment of child stutterers: Replication and extension. *Behavior Therapy, 23,* 113–129.

Galambos, N. L., Almeida, D. M., & Petersen, A. C. (1990). Masculinity, femininity, and sex role attitudes in early adolescence. *Child Development, 61,* 1905–1914.

Gallahue, D. L. (1989). *Understanding motor development: Infants, children, adolescents.* Indianapolis, IN: Benchmark Press.

Galler, J. R., Ramsey, F. C., Morley, D. S., Archer, E., & Salt, P. (1990). The long-term effects of early kwashiorkor compared with marasmus. IV. Performance on the National High School Entrance Exam. *Pediatric Research, 28,* 235–239.

Gallistel, C. R., Brown, A. L., Carey, S., Gelman, R., & Keil, F. C. (1991). Lessons from animal learning for the study of cognitive development. In S. Carey & R. Gelman (Eds.), *The epigenesis of mind: Essays on biology and cognition* (pp. 3–36). Hillsdale, NJ: Erlbaum.

Galton, F. (1883). *Inquiries into human faculty and its development.* London: Macmillan.

Gannon, P. J., Holloway, R. L., Broadfield, D. C., & Braun, A. R. (1998). Asymmetry of chimpanzee planum temporale: Humanlike pattern of Wernicke's brain language area homolog. *Science, 279,* 220–222.

Garabino, J. (1982). Sociocultural risk: Dangers to competence. In C. Kopp & J. Krakow (Eds.), *Child development in a social context.* Reading, MA: Addison-Wesley.

Garber, A. P., Schreck, R., & Carlson, D. E. (1997). Fetal loss. In D. L. Rimoin, J. M. Connor, & R. E. Pyeritz (Eds.), *Emery and Rimoin's principles and practices of medical genetics* (3rd ed., Vol. 1, pp. 677–686). New York: Churchill Livingstone.

Garcia, M. M., Shaw, D. S., Winslow, E. B., & Yaggi, K. E. (2000). Destructive sibling conflict and the development of conduct problems in young boys. *Developmental Psychology, 36,* 44–53.

Gardner, B. T., & Gardner, R. A. (1971). Two-way communication with an infant chimpanzee. In A. M. Schrier & F. Stollnitz (Eds.), *Behavior of nonhuman primates.* New York: Academic Press.

Gardner, D., Harris, P. L., Ohmoto, M., & Hamasaki, T. (1988). Japanese children's understanding of the distinction between real and apparent emotion. *International Journal of Behavioral Development, 11,* 203–218.

Gardner, H. (1983). *Frames of mind: The theory of multiple intelligences.* New York: Basic Books.

Gardner, H. (1986). The waning of intelligence tests. In R. J. Sternberg & D. K. Detterman (Eds.), *What is intelligence?* (pp. 73–76). Norwood, NJ: Ablex.

Gardner, H. (1998). Are there additional intelligences? The case for naturalistic, spiritual, and existential intelligences. In J. Kane (Ed.), *Education, information, and transformation: Essays on learning and thinking* (pp. 111–131). Upper Saddle River, NJ: Prentice Hall.

Gardner, W., & Rogoff, B. (1990). Children's deliberateness of planning according to task circumstances. *Developmental Psychology, 26,* 480–487.

Garland, A. F., & Zigler, E. (1993). Adolescent suicide prevention: Current research and social policy implications. *American Psychologist, 48,* 169–182.

Garlick, D. (2002). Understanding the nature of the general factor of intelligence: The role of individual differences in neural plasticity as an explanatory mechanism. *Psychological Review, 109,* 116–136.

Gash, H., & Morgan, M. (1993). School-based modifications of children's gender-related beliefs. *Journal of Applied Developmental Psychology, 14,* 277–287.

Gathercole, S. F., Hitch, G. J., Service, E., & Martin, A. J. (1997). Phonological short-term memory and new word learning in children. *Developmental Psychology, 33,* 966–979.

Gavin, L. A., & Furman, W. (1989). Age differences in adolescent's perceptions of their peer groups. *Developmental Psychology, 25,* 827–834.

Ge, X., Best, K. M., Conger, R. D., & Simons, R. L. (1996). Parenting behaviors and the occurrence and co-occurrence of adolescent depressive symptoms and conduct problems. *Developmental Psychology, 32,* 717–731.

Ge, X., Conger, R. D., & Elder, G. H., Jr. (1996). Coming of age too early: Pubertal influences on girls' vulnerability to psychological distress. *Child Development, 67,* 3386–3400.

Ge, X., Lorenz, F. O., Conger, R. D., Elder, G. H., Jr., & Simons, R. L. (1994). Trajectories of stressful life events and depressive symptoms during adolescence. *Developmental Psychology, 30,* 467–483.

Geary, D. C., Bow-Thomas, C. C., Fan, L., & Siegler, R. S. (1993). Even before formal instruction, Chinese children outperform American children in mental addition. *Cognitive Development, 8,* 517–529.

Geldart, S., Maurer, D., & Carney, K. (1999). Effects of the height of the internal features of faces on adult's aesthetic ratings and 5-month-old's looking times. *Perception, 28,* 839–850.

Gelman, R. (1969). Conservation acquisition: A problem of learning to attend to relevant attributes. *Journal of Experimental Child Psychology, 7,* 167–187.

Gelman, R., & Baillargeon, R. (1983). A review of some Piagetian concepts. In J. H. Flavell & E. M. Markman (Eds.), *Handbook of child psychology. Vol. III. Cognitive development* (4th ed., pp. 167–230). New York: Wiley.

Gelman, R., & Cordes, S. (2001). Counting in animals and humans. In E. Dupoux (Ed.), *Language, brain, and cognitive development: Essays in honoe of Jacques Mehler* (pp. 279–301). Cambridge, MA: MIT Press.

Gelman, R., & Gallistel, C. R. (1978). *The child's understanding of number.* Cambridge, MA: Harvard University Press.

Gelman, R., & Meck, E. (1983). Preschoolers' counting: Principles before skill. *Cognition, 13,* 343–359.

Gelman, R., Spelke, E. S., & Meck, E. (1983). What preschoolers know about animate and inanimate objects. In D. Rogers & J. A. Sloboda (Eds.), *The acquisition of symbolic skills.* New York: Plenum.

Gelman, R., & Williams, E. M. (1998). Enabling constraints for cognitive development: Domain specificity and epigenesis. In W. Damon (Series Ed.) & D. Kuhn & R. S. Siegler (Vol. Eds.), *Handbook of child psychology: Vol. 2. Cognition, perception, and language* (5th ed., pp. 575–630). New York: Wiley.

Gelman, S. A., Coley, J. D., Rosengren, K. S., Hartman, E., & Pappas, A. (1998). Beyond labeling: The role of maternal input in the acquisition of richly structured categories. *Monographs of the Society for Research in Child Development, 63*(1, Serial No. 253).

Gelman, S. A., & Kremer, K. E. (1991). Understanding natural cause: Children's explanations of how objects and their properties originate. *Child Development, 62,* 396–414.

Gershkoff-Stowe, L. (2001). The course of children's naming errors in early word learning. *Journal of Cognition and Development, 2,* 131–155.

Gershkoff-Stowe, L., & Smith, L. B. (1997). A curvilinear trend in naming errors as a function of early vocabulary growth. *Cognitive Psychology, 34,* 37–71.

Gershoff, E. T. (2002). Corporal punishment by parents and associated child behaviors and experiences: A meta-analytic and theoretical review. *Psychological Bulletin, 128,* 539–579.

Geschwind, M., & Galaburda, A. M. (1987). *Cerebral lateralization.* Cambridge, MA: MIT Press.

Gesell, A., & Thompson, H. (1934). *Infant behavior: Its genesis and growth.* New York: McGraw-Hill.

Gesell, A., & Thompson, H. (1938). *The psychology of early growth.* New York: Macmillan.

Gewirtz, J. L., & Peláez-Nogueras, M. (1992). B. F. Skinner's legacy to human infant behavior and development. *American Psychologist, 47,* 1411–1422.

Ghim, H-R. (1990). Evidence for perceptual organization in infants: Perception of subjective contours by young infants. *Infant Behavior and Development, 13,* 221–248.

Gibbs, W. W., & Fox, D. (1999, October). The false crisis in science education. *Scientific American, 281,* 87–88, 92.

Gibson, E. J. (1969). *Principles of perceptual learning and development.* New York: Appleton.

Gibson, E. J. (1982). The concept of affordances in development: The renascence of functionalism. In W. A. Collins (Ed.), *The Minnesota symposia on child psychology: Vol. 15. The concept of development.* Hillsdale, NJ: Erlbaum.

Gibson, E. J. (1988). Exploratory behavior in the development of perceiving, acting, and the acquiring of knowledge. *Annual Review of Psychology, 39,* 1–41.

Gibson, E. J., Gibson, J. J., Pick, A. D., & Osser, H. (1962). A developmental study of the discrimination of letter-like forms. *Journal of Comparative and Physiological Psychology, 55,* 897–906.

Gibson, E. J., & Spelke, E. S. (1983). The development of perception. In J. H. Flavell & E. M. Markman (Eds.), *Handbook of child psychology: Vol. III. Cognitive development* (4th ed., pp. 1–76). New York: Wiley.

Gibson, E. J., & Walker, A. (1984). Development of knowledge of visual-tactual affordances of substance. *Child Development, 55,* 453–460.

Gibson, J. J. (1966). *The senses considered as perceptual systems.* Boston: Houghton Mifflin.

Gibson, J. J. (1979). *The ecological approach to visual perception.* Boston: Houghton Mifflin.

Gibson, M., & Ogbu, J. (Eds.). (1991). *Minority status and schooling: A comparative study of immigrant and involuntary minorities.* New York: Garland.

Giedd, J. N., Blumenthal, J., Molloy, E., & Castellanos, F. X. (2001). Brain imaging of attention deficit/hyperactivity disorder. *Annals of the New York Academy of Sciences, 931,* 33–49.

Gilbert, W. M., Nesbitt, T. S., & Danielsen, B. (1999). Childbearing beyond age 40: Pregnancy outcome in 24,032 cases. *Obstetrics and Gynecology, 93,* 9–14.

Giles, J. W., Gopnik, A., & Heyman, G. D. (2002). Source monitoring reduces the suggestibility of preschool children. *Psychological Science, 13,* 288–291.

Gilligan, C. (1982). *In a different voice: Psychological theory and women's development.* Cambridge, MA: Harvard University Press.

Gilligan, C. (1988). Remapping the moral domain: New images of self in relationship. In C. Gilligan, J. V. Ward, J. M. Taylor, & B. Bardige (Eds.), *Mapping the moral domain* (pp. 3–19). Cambridge, MA: Harvard University Press.

Gilligan, C., & Attanucci, J. (1988). Two moral orientations: Gender differences and similarities. *Merrill-Palmer Quarterly, 34,* 223–237.

Gilligan, C., Lyons, N. P., & Hanmer, T. J. (Eds.). (1990). *Making connections: The relational worlds of adolescent girls at Emma Willard School.* Cambridge, MA: Harvard University Press.

Gilliom, M., Shaw, D. S., Beck, J. E., Schonberg, M. A., & Lukon, J. L. (2002). Anger regulation in disadvantaged preschool boys: Strategies, antecedents, and the development of self-control. *Developmental Psychology, 38,* 222–235.

Ginsberg, H. P. (1972). *The myth of the deprived child: Poor children's intellect and education.* Englewood Cliffs, NJ: Prentice-Hall.

Ginsburg, H. P. & Opper, S. (1988). *Piaget's theory of intellectual development* (3rd ed.). Englewood Cliffs, NJ: Prentice-Hall.

Ginsburg, H. P., Pappas, S., & Seo, K. H. (2001). Everyday mathematical knowledge: Asking young children what is developmentally appropriate. In S. L. Golbeck (Ed.), *The Rutgers invitational symposium on education series: Psychological perspectives on early childhood education: Reframing dilemmas in research and practice* (pp. 181–219). Mahwah, NJ: Erlbaum.

Glasgow, K. L., Dornbusch., S. N., Troyer, L., Steinberg, L., & Ritter, P. (1997). Parenting styles, adolescents' attributions, and educational outcomes in nine heterogeneous high schools. *Child Development, 68,* 507–529.

Glass, D. C., Neulinger, J., & Brim, O. G. (1974). Birth order, verbal intelligence, and educational aspiration. *Child Development, 45,* 807–811.

Glassman, M., & Zan, B. (1995). Moral activity and domain theory: An alternative interpretation of research on young children. *Developmental Review, 15,* 434–457.

Gleason, J. B., & Perlmann, R. Y. (1985). Acquiring social variation in speech. In H. Giles & R. N. St. Clair (Eds.), *Recent advances in language, communication, and social psychology* (pp. 86–111). London: Erlbaum.

Gleason, J. B., & Weintraub, S. (1978). Input language and the acquisition of communicative competence. In K. Nelson (Ed.), *Children's language* (Vol. 1, pp. 171–222). New York: Gardner Press.

Gleitman, L. R., Gleitman, H., & Shipley, E. F. (1972). The emergence of the child as grammarian. *Cognition, 1,* 137–164.

Gleitman, L. R., Newport, E. L., & Gleitman, H. (1984). The current status of the motherese hypothesis. *Journal of Child Language, 11,* 43–79.

Glick, P. C. (1989). Remarried families, stepfamilies, and stepchildren: A brief demographic analysis. *Family Relations, 38,* 24–27.

Glynn, L. M., Wadhwa, P. O., Dunkel-Schetter, C., Chicz-DeMet, A., & Sandman, C. A. (2001). When stress happens matters: Effects of earthquake timing on stress responsivity in pregnancy. *American Journal of Obstetrics & Gynecology, 184,* 637–642.

Gogate, L. J., Bahrick, L. E., & Watson, J. D. (2000). A study of multimodal motherese: The role of temporal synchrony between verbal labels and gestures. *Child Development, 71,* 878–894.

Goldberg, M. C., Maurer, D., & Lewis, T. L. (2001). Developmental changes in attention: The effects of endogenous cueing and of distractors. *Developmental Science, 4,* 209–219.

Goldberg, S. (1979). Premature birth: Consequences for the parent-infant relationship. *American Scientist, 67,* 582–590.

Goldberg, W. A., Greenberger, E., & Nagel, S. K. (1996). Employment and achievement: Mothers' work involvement in relation to children's achievement behaviors and mothers' parenting behaviors. *Child Development, 67,* 1512–1527.

Golden, F. (1998, September 21). Boy? Girl? Up to you. *Time,* pp. 82–83.

Goldenberg, R. L., Clivar, S. P., Cutter, G. R., Hoffman, H. J., Cassady, G., Davis, R. O., & Nelson, K. G. (1991). Black-white differences in newborn anthropometric measurements. *Obstetrics and Gynecology, 78,* 782–788.

Goldfield, B. A., & Reznick, J. S. (1990). Early lexical acquisition: Rate, content, and the vocabulary spurt. *Journal of Child Language, 17,* 171–183.

Goldsmith, H. H., & Alansky, J. A. (1987). Maternal and infant temperamental predictors of attachment: A meta-analytic review. *Journal of Consulting and Clinical Psychology, 55,* 805–816.

Goldsmith, H. H., Buss, K. A., & Lemery, K. S. (1997). Toddler and childhood temperament: Expanded content, stronger genetic evidence, new evidence for the importance of environment. *Developmental Psychology, 33,* 891–905.

Goleman, D. (1995). *Emotional intelligence.* New York: Basic Books.

Golier, J., & Yehuda, R. (1998). Neuroendocrine activity and memory-related impairments in posttraumatic stress disorder. *Development and Psychopathology, 10,* 857–869.

Golinkoff, R. M., Harding, C. G., Carlson, V., & Sexton, M. E. (1984). The infant's perception of causal events: The distinction between animate and inanimate objects. In L. L. Lipsitt & C. Rovee-Collier (Eds.), *Advances in infancy research. Vol. 3.* Norwood, NJ: Ablex.

Golinkoff, R. M., Mervis, C. B., & Hirsh-Pasek, K. (1994). Early object labels: The case for a developmental lexical principles framework. *Journal of Child Language, 21,* 125–155.

Golombok, S., Cook, R., Bish, A., & Murray, C. (1995). Families created by the new reproductive technologies: Quality of parenting and social and emotional development of the children. *Child Development, 66,* 285–298.

Golombok, S., MacCallum, F., & Goodman, E. (2001). The "test-tube" generation: Parent-child relationships and the psychological well-being of in vitro fertilization in children at adolescence. *Child Development, 72,* 599–608.

Golombok, S., MacCallum, F., Goodman, E., & Rutter, M. (2002). Families with children conceived by donor insemination: A follow-up at stage twelve. *Child Development, 73,* 952–968.

Gonzales, P., Calsyn, C., Jocelyn, L., Mak., Kastberg, D., Arafeh, T., et al. (2000). *Pursuing excellence: Comparisons of international eigth-grade mathematics and science achievement from a U.S. perspective, 1995 and 1999* (N CES 2001 028). Retrieved December 9, 2002, from http://nces.ed.gov/pubs2001/2001028.pdf

Goodnow, J. (1988). Children's household work: Its nature and functions. *Psychological Bulletin, 103,* 5–26.

Goodwin, S. W., & Acredolo, L. P. (1993). Symbolic gesture versus word: Is there a modality advantage for onset of symbol use? *Child Development, 64,* 688–701.

Gopnik, A. (1996). The post-Piaget era. *Psychological Science, 7,* 221–225.

Gopnik, A., & Meltzoff, A. N. (1986). Relations between semantic and cognitive development in the one-word stage: The specificity hypothesis. *Child Development, 57,* 1040–1053.

Gopnik, A., & Meltzoff, A. N. (1987). The development of categorization in the second year and its relation to other cognitive and linguistic attainments. *Child Development, 58,* 1523–1531.

Gopnik, A., & Meltzoff, A. N. (1992). Categorization and naming: Basic-level sorting in eighteen-month-olds and its relation to language. *Child Development, 63,* 1091–1103.

Gopnik, A., & Rosati, A. (2001). Duck or rabbit? Reversing ambiguous figures and understanding ambiguous representations. *Developmental Science, 4,* 175–183.

Gordin, D., & Pea, R. D. (1995). Prospects for scientific visualization as an educational technology. *The Journal of Learning Science, 4,* 249–279.

Gordon, I., & Slater, A. (1998). Nativism and empiricism: The history of two ideas. In A. Slater (Ed.), *Perceptual development: Visual, auditory, and speech perception in infancy* (pp. 73–103). East Sussex, UK: Psychology Press.

Gorski, P. A. (1991). Developmental intervention during neonatal hospitalization: Critiquing the state of the science. *Pediatric Clinics of North America, 38,* 1469–1479.

Gorski, R. A. (1980). Sexual differentiation of the brain. In D. T. Krieger & J. C. Hughes (Eds.), *Neuroendocrinology.* New York: Rockefeller University Press.

Gortmaker, S. L., Must, A., Sobol, A. M., Peterson, K., Colditz, G. A., & Dietz, W. H. (1996). Television viewing as a cause of increasing obesity among children in the United States, 1986–1990. *Archives of Pediatrics and Adolescent Medicine, 150,* 356–362.

Goswami, U. (1996). Analogical reasoning and cognitive development. In H. W. Reese (Ed.), *Advances in child development and behavior* (Vol. 26, pp. 91–138). San Diego: Academic Press.

Gottlieb, G. (2000). Environmental and behavioral influences on gene activity. *Current Directions in Psychological Science, 9,* 93–97.

Gottesman, I. I., & Shields, J. (1982). *Schizophrenia: The epigenetic puzzle.* Cambridge, UK: Cambridge University Press.

Gottfried, A. E., Bathurst, K., & Gottfried, A. W. (1994). Role of maternal and dual-earner employment status in children's development. In A. E. Gottfried, & A. W. Gottfried (Eds.), *Redefining families: Implications for children's development.* New York: Plenum.

Gottfried, A. E., Fleming, J. S., & Gottfried, A. W. (1998). Role of cognitively stimulating home environment in children's academic intrinsic motivation: A longitudinal study. *Child Development, 69,* 1448–1460.

Gottfried, G. M. (1997). Using metaphors as modifiers: Children's production of metaphoric compounds. *Journal of Child Language, 24,* 567–601.

Gottlieb, G. (1991). Experimental canalization of behavioral development: Theory. *Developmental Psychology, 27,* 4–13.

Gottlieb, G. (1995). Some conceptual deficiencies in "developmental" behavior genetics. *Human Development, 38,* 131–141.

Gottlieb, G., Wahlsten, D., & Lickliter, R. (1998). The significance of biology for human development: A developmental psychobiological systems view. In W. Damon (Series Ed.) & R. Lerner (Vol. Ed.), *Handbook of child psychology: Vol. 1. Theoretical models of human development* (5th ed., pp. 233–273). New York: Wiley.

Gottman, J. M. (1983). How children become friends. *Monographs of the Society for Research in Child Development, 48*(2, Serial No. 201).

Gottman, J. M., Gonso, J., & Rasmussen, B. (1975). Social interaction, social competence, and friendship in children. *Child Development, 46,* 709–718.

Gottman, J. M., Katz, L. F., & Hooven, C. (1997). *Metaemotion: How families communicate emotionally.* Mahwah, NJ: Erlbaum.

Gottman, J. M., & Parkhurst, J. T. (1980). A developmental theory of friendship and acquaintanceship processes. In W. A. Collins (Ed.), *The Minnesota symposia on child development: Vol. 13. Development of cognition, affect, and social relations.* Hillsdale, NJ: Erlbaum.

Goubet, N., & Clifton, R. K. (1998). Object and event representation in 6½-month-old infants. *Developmental Psychology, 34,* 63–76.

Goy, R. (1970). Early hormonal influences on the development of sexual and sex-related behavior. In F. Schmitt, G. Quarton, T. Melnechuck, & G. Adelman (Eds.), *The neurosciences: Second study program.* New York: Rockefeller University Press.

Graham, S. A., & Poulin-Dubois, D. (1999). Infants' reliance on shape to generalize novel labels to animate and inanimate objects. *Journal of Child Language, 26,* 295–320.

Gralinski, J. H., & Kopp, C. B. (1993). Everyday rules for behavior: Mothers' requests to young children. *Developmental Psychology, 29,* 573–584.

Grandjean, H., Larroque, D., Levi, S., and the Eurofetus Study Group. (1999). The performance of routine ultrasonographic screening of pregnancies in the Eurofetus Study. *American Journal of Obstetrics and Gynecology, 181,* 446–454.

Grantham-McGregor, S., Powell, C., Walker, S., Change, S., & Fletcher, P. (1994). The long-term follow-up of severely malnourished children who participated in an intervention program. *Child Development, 65,* 428–439.

Graves, N. B., & Graves, T. D. (1983). The cultural context of prosocial development: An ecological model. In D. L. Bridgeman (Ed.), *The nature of prosocial development: Interdisciplinary theories and strategies.* New York: Academic Press.

Graves, S. B. (1993). Television, the portrayal of African Americans, and the development of children's attitudes. In G. L. Berry & J. K. Asamen (Eds.), *Children and television: Images in a changing sociocultural world* (pp. 179–190). Newbury Park, CA: Sage.

Gray-Little, B., & Hafdahl, A. R. (2000). Factors influencing racial comparisons of self-esteem: A quantitative review. *Psychological Bulletin, 126,* 26–54.

Greenberg, B. S. (1986). Minorities and the mass media. In J. Bryant & D. Zillman (Eds.), *Perspectives on mass media effects.* Hillsdale, NJ: Erlbaum.

Greenberg, B. S., & Brand, J. E. (1994). Minorities and the mass media: 1970s to 1990s. In J. Bryant & D. Zillmann (Eds.), *Media effects: Advances in theory and research* (pp. 273–314). Hillsdale, NJ: Erlbaum.

Greenberger, E., & Chen, C. (1996). Perceived family relationships and depressed mood in early and late adolescence: A comparison of European and Asian Americans. *Developmental Psychology, 32,* 707–716.

Greenfield, P. M. (1984). A theory of the teacher in the learning activities of everyday life. In B. Rogoff & J. Lave (Eds.), *Everyday cognition: Its development in social context.* Cambridge, MA: Harvard University Press.

Greenfield, P. M. (1994). Video games as cultural artifacts. *Journal of Applied Developmental Psychology, 15,* 3–12.

Greenfield, P. M. (1997). You can't take it with you: Why ability assessments don't cross cultures. *American Psychologist, 52,* 1115–1124.

Greenfield, P. M. (1998). The cultural evolution of IQ. In U. Neisser (Ed.), *The rising curve: Long-term gains in IQ and related measures* (pp. 85–94). Washington, DC: American Psychological Association.

Greenfield, P. M., & Cocking, R. R. (Eds.). (1996). *Interacting with video.* Norwood, NJ: Ablex.

Greenhoot, A. F., Ornstein, P. A., Gordon, B. N., & Baker-Ward, L. (1999). Acting out the details of a pediatric check-up: The impact of interview condition and behavioral style on children's memory reports. *Child Development, 70,* 363–380.

Greenhouse, L. (2000, October 5). Justices consider limits of the legal response to risky behavior by pregnant women. *New York Times,* p. A6.

Greenough, W. T., Black, J. E., & Wallace, C. S. (1987). Experience and brain development. *Child Development, 58,* 539–559.

Gregg, V., Gibbs, J. C., & Basinger, K. S. (1994). Patterns of developmental delay in moral judgment by male and female delinquents. *Merrill-Palmer Quarterly, 40,* 538–553.

Greif, E. B., & Gleason, J. B. (1980). Hi, thanks, and goodbye: More routine information. *Language in Society, 9,* 159–166.

Greif, E. B., & Ulman, K. J. (1982). The psychological impact of menarche on early adolescent females: A review of the literature. *Child Development, 53,* 1413–1430.

Gressens, P. (2000). Mechanisms and disturbances of neuronal migration. *Pediatric Research, 48,* 725–730.

Grimes, D. A. (1995). The morbidity and mortality of pregnancy: Still risky business. *American Journal of Obstetrics and Gynecology, 170,* 1489–1494.

Grimshaw, G. M., Adelstein, A., Bryden, M. P., & MacKinnon, G. E. (1998). First-language acquisition in adolescence: Evidence for a critical period for language development. *Brain and Language, 63,* 237–255.

Grolnick, W. S., Bridges, L. J., & Connell, J. P. (1996). Emotion regulation in two-year-olds: Strategies and emotional expression in four contexts. *Child Development, 67,* 928–941.

Grolnick, W. S., Ryan, R. M., & Deci, E. L. (1991). Inner resources for school achievement: Motivational mediators of children's perceptions of their parents. *Journal of Educational Psychology, 83,* 508–517.

Groome, L. J., Swiber, M. J., Atterbury, J. L., Bentz, L. S., & Holland, S. B. (1997). Similarities and differences in behavioral state organization during sleep periods in the perinatal infant before and after birth. *Child Development, 68,* 1–11.

Grossman, J. B., & Tierney, J. P. (1998). Does mentoring work? An impact study of the Big Brothers/Big Sisters. *Evaluation Review, 22,* 403–426.

Grossmann, K., Grossmann, K. E., Spangler, G., Suess, G., & Unzner, L. (1985). Maternal sensitivity and newborns' orientation responses as related to quality of attachment in northern Germany. In I. Bretherton & E. Waters (Eds.), *Growing points of attachment theory and research. Monographs of the Society for Research in Child Development, 50* (1–2, Serial No. 209).

Grossmann, K., Grossmann, K. E., Fremmer-Bombik, E., Kindler, H., Scheurer-Englisch, H., & Zimmermann, P. (2002). The uniqueness of the child-father attachment relationship: Fathers' sensitive and challenging play as a pivotal variable in a 16-year longitudinal study. *Social Development, 11,* 307–331.

Grotevant, H. D., & Cooper, C. R. (1986). Individuation in family relationships. *Human Development, 29,* 82–100.

Gruen, G., Ottinger, D., & Zigler, E. (1970). Level of aspiration and the probability learning of middle- and lower-class children. *Developmental Psychology, 3,* 133–142.

Grunseit, A., Kippax, S., Aggleton, P., & Baldo, M.,& Slutkin, G. (1997). Sexuality education and young people's sexual behavior: A review of studies. *Journal of Adolescent Research, 12,* 421–453.

Grusec, J. E. (1982). The socialization of altruism. In N. Eisenberg (Ed.), *The development of prosocial behavior.* New York: Academic Press.

Grusec, J. E. (1991). Socializing concern for others in the home. *Developmental Psychology, 27,* 338–342.

Grusec, J. E. (1992). Social learning theory and developmental psychology: The legacies of Robert Sears and Albert Bandura. *Developmental Psychology, 28,* 776–786.

Grusec, J. E., & Goodnow, J. J. (1994). Impact of parental discipline methods on the child's internalization of values: A reconceptualization of current points of view. *Developmental Psychology, 30,* 4–19.

Grusec, J. E., Goodnow, J. J., & Cohen, L. (1996). Household work and the development of concern for others. *Developmental Psychology, 32,* 999–1007.

Grusec, J. E., Hastings, P., & Mammone, N. (1994). Parenting cognitions and relationship schemas. In J. G. Smetana (Ed.), *Beliefs about parenting: Origins and developmental implications* (pp. 5–19). San Francisco: Jossey-Bass.

Grusec, J. E., & Skubiski, L. (1970). Model nurturance, demand characteristics of the modeling experiment, and altruism. *Journal of Personality and Social Psychology, 14,* 352–359.

Grych, J. H., & Clark, R. (1999). Maternal employment and development of the father-infant relationship in the first year. *Developmental Psychology, 35,* 893–903.

Guerra, B., Lazzarotto, T., Quarta, S., Lanari, M., Bovicelli, L., Nicolosi, A., & Landini, M. P. (2000). Prenatal diagnosis of symptomatic congenital cytomegalovirus infection. *American Journal of Obstetrics and Gynecology, 183,* 476–482.

Guinan, M. E. (1995). Artificial insemination by donor: Safety and secrecy. *Journal of the American Medical Association, 273,* 890–891.

Gunnar, M. R. (1998). Quality of early care and buffering of neuroendocrine stress reactions: Potential effects on the developing brain. *Preventive Medicine, 27,* 208–211.

Gunnar, M. R., Porter, F., Wolf, C., Rigatuso, J., & Larson, M. (1995). Neonatal stress reactivity: Predictions to later emotional development. *Child Development, 66,* 1–13.

Gunnar, M. R., & White, B. P. (2001). Salivary cortisol measures in infant and child assessment. In L. T. Singer & P. S. Zeskind (Eds.), *Biobehavioral assessment of the infant* (pp. 167–189). New York: Guilford Press.

Gunston, G. D., Burkimsher, D., Malan, H, & Sive, A. A. (1992). Reversible cerebral shrinkage in kwashiorkor: An MRI study. *Archives of Disease in Childhood, 67,* 1030–1032.

Guntheroth, W. G., & Spiers, P. S. (2001). Thermal stress in sudden infant death: Is there an ambiguity with the rebreathing hypothesis? *Pediatrics, 107,* 693–698.

Gutman, L. M. , & Eccles, J. S. (1999). Financial strain, parenting behaviors, and adolescents' achievement: Testing model equivalence between African American and European American single- and two-parent families. *Child Development, 70,* 1464–1476.

Guttentag, R. E. (1987). Memory and aging: Implications for theories of memory development during childhood. *Developmental Review, 5,* 56–82.

Hafner-Eaton, C., & Pearce, L. K. (1994). Birth choices, the law, and medicine: Balancing individual freedoms and protection of the public's health. *Journal of Health Politics, Policy and Law, 19,* 813–835.

Hagay, Z. J., Biran, G., Ornoy, A., & Reece, E. A. (1996). Congenital cytomegalovirus infection: A long-standing problem still seeking a solution. *American Journal of Obstetrics and Gynecology, 174,* 241–245.

Hahn, C.-S., & DiPietro, J. A. (2001). In vitro fertilization and the family: Quality of parenting, family functioning, and child psychosocial adjustment. *Developmental Psychology, 37,* 37–48.

Haight, W. L., Wang, X., Fung, H., Williams, K., & Mintz, J. (1999). Universal, developmental, and variable aspects of young children's play: A cross-cultural comparison of pretending at home. *Child Development, 70,* 1477–1488.

Hainline, L. (1998). The development of basic visual abilities. In A. Slater (Ed.), *Perceptual development: Visual, auditory, and speech perception in infancy* (pp. 5–50). East Sussex, UK: Psychology Press.

Hainline, L., & Riddell, P. M. (1995). Binocular alignment and vergence in early infancy. *Vision Research, 35,* 3229–3236.

Haith, M. M. (1990). Progress in the understanding of sensory and perceptual processes in early infancy. *Merrill-Palmer Quarterly, 36,* 1–26.

Haith, M. M. (1997). The development of future thinking as essential for the emergence of skill in planning. In S. L. Friedman & E. K. Scholnick (Eds.), *The developmental psychology of planning: Why, how, and when do we plan?* (pp. 25–42). Mahwah, NJ: Erlbaum.

Haith, M. M. (1998). Who put the cog in cognition? Is rich interpretation too costly? *Infant Behavior and Development, 21,* 167–179.

Hakuta, K. (1999). The debate on bilingual education. *Journal of Developmental & Behavioral Pediatrics, 20,* 36–37.

Hakuta, K., & Diaz, R. M. (1985). The relationship between degree of bilingualism and cognitive ability: A critical discussion and some new longitudinal data. In K. E. Nelson (Ed.), *Children's language* (Vol. 5, pp. 319–344). Hillsdale, NJ: Erlbaum.

Hakuta, K., & Mostafapour, E. F. (1996). Perspectives from the history and politics of bilingualism amd bilingual education in the United States. In I. Parasnis (Ed.), *Cultural and language diversity and the deaf experience* (pp. 38–50). Cambridge, UK: Cambridge University Press.

Hall, G. S. (1891). The contents of children's minds on entering school. *Pedagogical Seminary, 1*, 139–173.

Hall, J. A. (1978). Gender effects in decoding nonverbal cues. *Psychological Bulletin, 85*, 845–857.

Hall, J. A. (1984). *Nonverbal sex differences: Communication accuracy and expressive style.* Baltimore: Johns Hopkins University Press.

Hall, J. A., & Halberstadt, A. G. (1986). Smiling and gazing. In J. S. Hyde & M. C. Linn (Eds.), *The psychology of gender: Advances through meta-analysis* (pp. 136–158). Baltimore: Johns Hopkins University Press.

Halpern, C. T., Udry, J. R., Campbell, B., & Suchindran, C. (1999). Effects of body fat on weight concerns, dating, and sexual activity: A longitudinal analysis of black and white adolescent girls. *Developmental Psychology, 35*, 721–736.

Halpern, D. F. (1986). *Sex differences in cognitive abilities.* Hillsdale, NJ: Erlbaum.

Halpern, D. F. (1997). Sex differences in intelligence: Implications for education. *American Psychologist, 52*, 1091–1102.

Halpern, L. F., MacLean, W. E., Jr., & Baumeister, A. A. (1995). Infant sleep-wake characteristics: Relation to neurological status and the prediction of developmental outcome. *Developmental Review, 15*, 255–291.

Hampson, E., Rovet, J. F., & Altmann, D. (1998). Spatial reasoning in children with congential adrenal hyperplasia due to 21-hydroxylase deficiency. *Developmental Neuropsychology, 14*, 299–320.

Hamre, B. K., & Pianta, R. C. (2001). Early teacher-child relationships and the trajectory of children's outcomes through eighth grade. *Child Development, 72*, 625–638.

Han, J. J., Leichtman, M. D., & Wang, Q. (1998). Autobiographical memory in Korean, Chinese, and American children. *Developmental Psychology, 34*, 701–713.

Hansen, J. D. L. (1990). Malnutrition review. *Pediatric Reviews and Communication, 4*, 201–212.

Hanson, J.W. (1986). Teratogen update: Fetal hydantoin effects. *Teratology, 33*, 349–353.

Hanson, J. W. (1997). Human teratology. In D. L. Rimoin, J. M. Connor, & R. E. Pyeritz (Eds.), *Emory and Rimoin's principles and practices of medical genetics* (3rd Ed., Vol. 1, pp. 697–724). New York: Churchill Livingstone.

Harbison, R. D., & Mantilla-Plata, B. (1972). Prenatal toxicity, maternal distribution and placental transfer of tetrahydrocannabinol. *Journal of Pharmacology and Experimental Therapeutics, 180*, 446–453.

Hareven, T. (1985). Historical changes in the family and the life course: Implications for child development. In A. B. Smuts & J. W. Hagen (Eds.), *History and research in child development. Monographs of the Society for Research in Child Development, 50*(4–5, Serial No. 211).

Harley, K., & Reese, E. (1999). Origins of autobiographical memory. *Developmental Psychology, 35*, 1338–1348.

Harlow, H. F., & Zimmerman, R. R. (1959). Affectional responses in the infant monkey. *Science, 130*, 421–432.

Harman, C., Rothbart, M. K., & Posner, M. I. (1997). Distress and attention interactions in early infancy. *Motivation and Emotion, 21*, 27–43.

Harnishfeger, K. K., & Pope, S. (1996). Intending to forget: The development of cognitive inhibition in directed forgetting. *Journal of Experimental Child Psychology, 62*, 292–315.

Harold, G. T., Fincham, F. D., Osborne, L. N., & Conger, R. D. (1997). Mom and Dad are at it again: Adolescent perceptions of marital conflict and adolescent psychological distress. *Developmental Psychology, 33*, 333–350.

Harpin, V., Chellappah, G., & Rutter, N. (1983). Responses of the newborn infant to overheating. *Biology of the Neonate, 44*, 65–75.

Harriman, A. E., & Lukosius, P. A. (1982). On why Wayne Dennis found Hopi children retarded in age at onset of walking. *Perceptual and Motor Skills, 55*, 79–86.

Harris, J. R. (1995). Where is the child's environment? A group socialization theory of development. *Psychological Review, 102*, 458–489.

Harris, J. R. (1998). *The nurture assumption: Why children turn out the way they do.* New York: Free Press.

Harris, J. R. (2000). Socialization, personality development, and the child's environments: Comment on Vandell (2000). *Developmental Psychology, 36*, 711–723.

Harris, P. L., Brown, E., Marriott, C., Whittall, S., & Harmer, S. (1991). Monsters, ghosts and witches: Testing the limits of the fantasy-reality distinction. *British Journal of Developmental Psychology, 9*, 105–123.

Harris, P. L., Donnelly, K., Guz, G. R., & Pitt-Watson, R. (1986). Children's understanding of the distinction between real and apparent emotion. *Child Development, 57*, 895–909.

Harris, P. L., & Kavanaugh, R. D. (1993). Young children's understanding of pretense. *Monographs of the Society for Research in Child Development, 58* (1, Serial No. 231).

Harris, P. L., Olthof, T., & Meerum Terwogt, M. (1981). Children's knowledge of emotion. *Journal of Child Psychology and Psychiatry, 22*, 247–261.

Harris, R. T. (1991, March). Anorexia nervosa and bulimia nervosa in female adolescents. *Nutrition Today* pp. 30–34.

Harrison, L. J., & Ungerer, J. A. (2002). Maternal employment and infant-mother attachment security at 12 months postpartum. *Developmental Psychology, 38*, 758–773.

Harrison, M. R. (1996). Fetal surgery. *American Journal of Obstetrics and Gynecology, 174*, 1255–1264.

Hart, C. H., De Wolf, D. M., Wozniak, P., & Burts, D. C. (1992). Maternal and paternal disciplinary styles: Relations with preschoolers' playground behavioral orientations and peer status. *Child Development, 63*, 879–892.

Hart, D., & Fegley, S. (1995). Prosocial behavior and caring in adolescence: Relations to self-understanding and social judgment. *Child Development, 66*, 1346–1359.

Hart, D., Fegley, S., & Brengelman, D. (1993). Perceptions of past, present and future selves among children and adolescents. *British Journal of Developmental Psychology, 11*, 265–282.

Hart, E. L., Lahey, B. B., Loeber, R., Applegate, B., & Frick, P. J. (1995). Developmental change in attention-deficit hyperactivity disorder in boys: A four-year longitudinal study. *Journal of Abnormal Child Psychology, 23*, 729–749.

Hart, S. N., & Brassard, M. R. (1987). A major threat to children's mental health. *American Psychologist, 42*, 160–165.

Harter, S. (1986a). Cognitive-developmental processes in the integration of concepts about emotions and the self. *Social Cognition, 4*, 119–151.

Harter, S. (1986b). Processes underlying the construct, maintenance and enhancement of the self-concept in children. In J. Suls & A. Greenwald (Eds.), *Psychological perspectives on the self* (Vol. 3, pp. 136–182). Hillsdale, NJ: Erlbaum.

Harter, S. (1987). The determinants and mediational role of global self-worth in children. In N. Eisenberg (Ed.), *Contemporary topics in developmental psychology* (pp. 219–242). New York: Wiley.

Harter, S. (1998). The development of self-representations. In W. Damon (Series Ed.) & N. Eisenberg (Vol. Ed.), *Handbook of child psychology: Vol. 3. Social, emotional, and personality development* (5th ed., pp. 553–617). New York: Wiley.

Harter, S. (1999). *The construction of the self: A developmental perspective.* New York: Guilford Press.

Harter, S., Marold, D. B., Whitesell, N. R., & Cobbs, G. (1996). A model of the effects of perceived parent and peer support on adolescent false self behavior. *Child Development, 67*, 360–374.

Harter, S., & Monsour, A. (1992). Developmental analysis of conflict caused by opposing attributes in the adolescent self-portrait. *Developmental Psychology, 28*, 251–260.

Harter, S., Waters, P., & Whitesell, N. R. (1998). Relational self-worth: Differences in perceived worth as a person across interpersonal contexts among adolescents. *Child Development, 69*, 756–766.

Hartshorn, K., Rovee-Collier, C., Gerhardstein, P., Bhatt, R. S., Klein, P. J., Aaron, F., et al. (1998). Developmental changes in the specificity of memory over the first year of life. *Developmental Psychobiology, 33*, 61–78.

Hartup, W. W. (1983). Peer relations. In E. M. Hetherington (Ed.), *Handbook of child psychology: Vol. IV. Socialization, personality, and social development* (4th ed., pp. 103–196). New York: Wiley.

Hartup, W. W. (1989). Social relationships and their developmental significance. *American Psychologist, 44*, 120–126.

Hartup, W. W. (1996). The company they keep: Friendships and their developmental significance. *Child Development, 67*, 1–13.

Hartup, W. W. (1999). Constraints on peer socialization: Let me count the ways. *Merrill-Palmer Quarterly, 45*, 172–183.

Hartup, W. W., & Coates, B. (1967). Imitation of a peer as a function of reinforcement from the peer group and rewardingness of the model. *Child Development, 38*, 1003–1016.

Hartup, W. W., French, D. C., Laursen, B., Johnston, M. K., & Ogawa, J. R. (1993). Conflict and friendship relations in middle childhood: Behavior in a closed field situation. *Child Development, 64,* 445–454.

Hartup, W. W., Laursen, B., Stewart, M. I., & Eastenson, A. (1988). Conflict and the friendship relations of young children. *Child Development, 59,* 1590–1600.

Hartup, W. W., & Sancilio, M. F. (1986). Children's friendships. In E. Shopler & G. B. Mesibov (Eds.), *Social behavior in autism.* New York: Plenum Press.

Hartup, W. W., & Stevens, N. (1999). Friendships and adaptation across the life span. *Current Directions in Psychological Science, 3,* 76–79.

Harvey, E. (1999). Short-term and long-term effects of early parental employment on children of the National Longitudinal Survey of Youth. *Developmental Psychology, 35,* 445–459.

Haselager, G. J. T., Hartup, W. W., van Lieshout, C. F. M., & Riksen-Walraven, J. M. A. (1998). Similarities between friends and nonfriends in middle childhood. *Child Development, 69,* 1198–1208.

Hastings, P. D., & Grusec, J. E. (1998). Parenting goals as organizers of responses to parent-child disagreement. *Developmental Psychology, 34,* 465–479.

Hastings, P. D., Zahn-Waxler, C., Robinson, J., Usher, B., & Bridges, D. (2000). The development of concern for others in children with behavior problems. *Developmental Psychology, 36,* 531–546.

Hatfield, J. S., Ferguson, L. R., & Alpert, R. (1967). Mother-child interaction and the socialization process. *Child Development, 38,* 365–414.

Haubenstricker, J., & Seefeldt, V. (1986). Acquisition of motor skills during childhood. In V. Seefeldt (Ed.), *Physical activity and well-being.* Reston, VA: American Alliance for Health, Education, Recreation, and Dance.

Hauck, F. R., & Hunt, C. E. (2000). Sudden infant death syndrome in 2000. *Current Problems in Pediatrics, 30,* 241–261.

Hauser, S. T., Powers, S. I., Noam, G. G., & Bowlds, M. K. (1987). Family interiors of adolescent ego development trajectories. *Family Perspectives, 21,* 263–282.

Hawkins, J., Sheingold, K., Gearhart, M., & Berger, C. (1982). Microcomputers in classrooms: Impact on the social life of elementary classrooms. *Journal of Applied Developmental Psychology, 3,* 361–373.

Hawn, P. R., & Harris, L. J. (1983). Hand differences in grasp duration and reaching in two- and five-month old infants. In G. Young, S. Segalowitz, C. M. Carter, & S. E. Trehub (Eds.), *Manual specialization and the developing brain.* New York: Academic Press.

Hay, D. F. (1985). Learning from relationships in infancy: Parallel attainments with parents and peers. *Developmental Review, 5,* 122–161.

Hay, D. F., Castle, J., Davies, L., Demetriou, H., & Stimson, C. A. (1999). Prosocial action in very early childhood. *Journal of Child Psychology and Psychiatry, 40,* 905–916.

Hay, D. F., Nash, A., & Pedersen, J. (1983). Interaction between 6-month-old peers. *Child Development, 54,* 557–562.

Hayne, H., & Rovee-Collier, C. (1995). The organization of reactivated memory. *Child Development, 66,* 893–906.

Hearold, S. (1986). A synthesis of 1043 effects of television on social behavior. In G. A. Comstock (Ed.), *Public communications and behavior* (Vol. 1, pp. 65–133). New York: Academic Press.

Heath, S. B. (1989). Oral and literate traditions among black Americans living in poverty. *American Psychologist, 44,* 367–373.

Hebb, D. O. (1980). *Essay on mind.* Hillsdale, NJ: Erlbaum.

Held, R., Birch, E., & Gwiazda, J. (1980). Stereoacuity in human infants. *Proceedings of the National Academy of Sciences of the U.S.A., 77,* 5572–5574.

Helwig, C. C., Zelazo, P. D., & Wilson, M. (2001). Children's judgments of psychological harm in normal and noncanonical situations. *Child Development, 72,* 66–81.

Henderlong, J., & Lepper, M. R. (2002). The effects of praise on children's intrinsic motivation: A review and synthesis. *Psychological Bulletin, 128,* 774–795.

Henderson, A. A. (1994). *A new generation of evidence: The family is critical to student achievement.* Washington, DC: National Committee for Citizens in Education.

Henifin, M. S. (1993). New reproductive technologies: Equity and access to reproductive health care. *Journal of Social Issues, 49,* 61–74.

Hennes, H. (1998). A review of violence statistics among children and adolescents in the United States. *Pediatric Clinics of North America, 45,* 269–280.

Henry J. Kaiser Family Foundation. (2000). Sex education in America: A series of national surveys of students, parents, teachers, and principals. Retrieved October 24, 2002, from http://www.kff.org/content/2000/3048/SexED.pdf

Hepper, P. G., & Shahidullah, B. S. (1994). Development of fetal hearing. *Archives of Disease in Childhood, 71,* F81–F87.

Herman, M. R., Dornbusch, S. M., Herron, M. C., & Herting, J. R. (1997). The influence of family regulation, connection, and psychological autonomy on six measures of adolescent functioning. *Journal of Adolescent Research, 12,* 34–67.

Herpetz-Dahlmann, B., Müller, B., Herpetz, S., Heussen, N., Hebebrand, J., & Remschmidt, H. (2001). Prospective 10-year follow-up in adolescent anorexia nervosa: Course, outcome, psychiatric comorbidity, and psychosocial adaptation. *Journal of Child Psychology and Psychiatry, 42,* 603–612.

Herrnstein, R. J., & Murray, C. (1994). *The bell curve: Intelligence and class structure in American life.* New York: Free Press.

Hertsgaard, L., Gunnar, M., Erickson, M. F., & Nachmias, M. (1996). Adrenocortical responses to the Strange Situation in infants with disorganized/disoriented attachment relationships. *Child Development, 66,* 1100–1106.

Hetherington, E. M. (1989). Coping with family transitions: Winners, losers, and survivors. *Child Development, 60,* 1–14.

Hetherington, E. M. (1999). Social capital and the development of youth from nondivorced, divorced, and remarried families. In W. A. Collins & B. Laursen (Eds.), *Minnesota symposia on child psychology: Vol. 30. Relationships as developmental contexts* (pp. 177–209). Mahwah, NJ: Erlbaum.

Hetherington, E. M., Cox, M., & Cox, R. (1982). Effects of divorce on parents and children. In M. Lamb (Ed.), *Nontraditional families* (pp. 233–288). Hillsdale, NJ: Erlbaum.

Hetherington, E. M., & Henderson, S. H. (1997). The effects of divorce on fathers and their children. In M. E. Lamb (Ed.), *The role of the father in child development* (pp. 191–211). New York: Wiley.

Hetherington, E. M., & Henderson, S. H., & Reiss, D. (1999). Adolescent siblings in stepfamilies: Family functioning and adolescent adjustment. *Monographs of the Society for Research in Child Development, 64*(4, Serial No. 259).

Hetherington, E. M., & Jodl, K. M. (1994). Stepfamilies as settings for child development. In A. Booth & J. Dunn (Eds.), *Stepfamilies: Who benefits? Who does not?* (pp. 55–79). Hillsdale, NJ: Erlbaum.

Heyman, G. D., & Dweck, C. S. (1998). Children's thinking about traits? Implications for judgments of the self and others. *Child Development, 69,* 391–403.

Hicks, D. J. (1965). Imitation and retention of film-mediated aggressive peer and adult models. *Journal of Personality and Social Psychology, 2,* 97–100.

Hilgard, J. R. (1932). Learning and maturation in preschool children. *Journal of Genetic Psychology, 41,* 36–56.

Hill, C. R., & Stafford, F. P. (1980). Parental care of children: Time diary estimates of quantity, predictability, and variety. *Journal of Human Resources, 15,* 219–289.

Hill, J. P. (1987). Research on adolescents and their families: Past and prospect. In C. E. Irwin (Ed.), *Adolescent social behavior and health* (pp. 13–31). San Francisco: Jossey-Bass.

Hinde, R. A. (1989). Ethological and relationships approaches. In R. Vasta (Ed.), *Annals of child development: Six theories of child development: Revised formulations and current issues* (Vol. 6, pp. 251–285). Greenwich, CT: JAI Press.

Hinde, R. A., Titmus, G., Easton, D., & Tamplin, A. (1985). Incidence of "friendship" and behavior to strong associates versus non-associates in preschoolers. *Child Development, 56,* 234–245.

Hines, M., Golombok, S., Rust, J., Johnston, K. J., Golding, J., & ALSPAC Study Team. (2002). Testosterone during pregnancy and gender role behavior of preschool children: A longitudinal population study. *Developmental Psychology, 73,* 1678–1687.

Hiscock, H., & Wake, M. (2002). Randomised controlled trial of behavioural infant sleep intervention to improve infant sleep and maternal mood. *British Medical Journal, 324,* 1062–1065.

Hirsch, B. J., & Rapkin, B. D. (1987). The transition to junior high school: A longitudinal study of self-esteem, psychological symptomatology, school life, and social support. *Child Development, 58,* 1235–1243.

Hirschfeld, L. A., & Gelman, S. A. (1994). Toward a topography of mind: An introduction to domain specificity. In L. A. Hirschfeld & S. A. Gelman (Eds.), *Mapping the mind: Domain specificity in cognition and culture* (pp. 3–35). Oxford, UK: Oxford University Press.

Hirsch-Pasek, K., Gleitman, L. R., & Gleitman, H. (1978). What does the brain say to the mind? A study of the detection and report of ambiguity by young children. In A. Sinclair, R. J. Jarvella, & W. J. M. Levelt (Eds.), *The child's conception of language* (pp. 97–132). Berlin: Springer-Verlag.

Ho, C. S., & Bryant, P. (1997). Phonological skills are important in learning to read Chinese. *Developmental Psychology, 33,* 946–951.

Hock, E., & DeMeis, D. K. (1990). Depression in mothers of infants: The role of maternal employment. *Developmental Psychology, 26,* 285–291.

Hoff, E., & Naigles, L. (2002). How children use input to acquire a lexicon. *Child Development, 73,* 418–433.

Hoff, T. L. (1992). Psychology in Canada one hundred years ago: James Mark Baldwin at the University of Toronto. *Canadian Psychology, 33,* 683–694.

Hofferth, S. (1996). Child care in the United States today. *The Future of Children, 6*(2), 41–61.

Hoff-Ginsberg, E. (1986). Function and structure in maternal speech: Their relation to the child's development of syntax. *Developmental Psychology, 22,* 155–163.

Hoff-Ginsberg, E. (1991). Mother-child conversation in different social classes and communicative settings. *Child Development, 62,* 782–796.

Hoffman, L. W. (1979). Maternal employment: 1979. *American Psychologist, 34,* 859–865.

Hoffman, L. W. (1984). Maternal employment and the young child. In M. Perlmutter (Ed.), *The Minnesota symposia on child psychology: Vol. 17. Parent-child interaction and parent-child relations in child development.* Hillsdale, NJ: Erlbaum.

Hoffman, L. W. (1989). Effects of maternal employment in the two-parent family. *American Psychologist, 44,* 283–292.

Hoffman, L. W., & Kloska, D. D. (1995). Parents' gender-based attitudes toward marital roles and child rearing: Development and validation of new measures. *Sex Roles, 32,* 273–295.

Hoffman, M. L. (1970). Moral development. In P. H. Mussen (Ed.), *Carmichael's manual of child psychology* (Vol. 2, pp. 261–359). New York: Wiley.

Hoffman, M. L. (1975). Altruistic behavior and the parent-child relationship. *Journal of Personality and Social Psychology, 31,* 937–943.

Hoffman, M. L. (1976). Empathy, role-taking, guilt, and the development of altruistic motives. In T. Lickona (Ed.), *Moral development and behavior: Theory, research, and social issues* (pp. 124–143). New York: Holt, Rinehart & Winston.

Hoffman, M. L. (1982). Development of prosocial motivation: Empathy and guilt. In N. Eisenberg (Ed.), *The development of prosocial behavior* (pp. 281–313). New York: Academic Press.

Hoffman-Plotkin, D., & Twentyman, C. (1984). A multimodal assessment of behavioral and cognitive deficits in abused and neglected preschoolers. *Child Development, 52,* 13–30.

Høien, T., Lundberg, I., Stanovich, K. E., & Bjaalid, I. K. (1995). Components of phonological awareness. *Reading and Writing: An Interdisciplinary Journal, 7,* 171–188.

Holden, G. W. (1983). Avoiding conflict: Mothers as tacticians in the supermarket. *Child Development, 54,* 233–240.

Holden, G. W., & West, M. J. (1989). Proximate regulation by mothers: A demonstration of how differing styles affect young children's behavior. *Child Development, 60,* 64–69.

Hollenbeck, A. R., & Slaby, R. G. (1979). Infant visual and vocal responses to television. *Child Development, 50,* 41–45.

Hollich, G., Hirsh-Pasek, K., & Golinkoff, R. M. (2000). Breaking the language barrier: An emergentist coalition model of word learning. *Monographs of the Society for Research in Child Development, 65*(3, Serial No. 262).

Holtz, B. A., & Lehman, E. B. (1995). Development of children's knowledge and use of strategies for self-control in a resistance-to-distraction task. *Merrill-Palmer Quarterly, 41,* 361–380.

Honzik, M. P., Macfarlane, J. W., & Allen, L. (1948). The stability of mental test performance between two and eighteen years. *Journal of Experimental Education, 17,* 309–329.

Hood, K. E., Draper, P., Crockett, L. J., & Petersen, A. C. (1987). The ontogeny and phylogeny of sex differences in development: A biopsychosocial synthesis. In D. B. Carter (Ed.), *Current conceptions of sex roles and sex typing: Theory and research* (pp. 49–77). New York: Praeger.

Hopkins, B., & Westra, T. (1990). Motor development, maternal expectations, and the role of handling. *Infant Behavior and Development, 13,* 117–122.

Hops, H., & Finch, M. (1985). Social competence and skill: A reassessment. In B. H. Schneider, K. H. Rubin, & J. E. Ledingham (Eds.), *Children's peer relations: Issues in assessment and intervention* (pp. 23–39). New York: Springer-Verlag.

Horn, J. L. (1968). Organization of abilities and the development of intelligence. *Psychological Review, 75,* 242–259.

Horn, J. L. (1994). Theory of fluid and crystallized intelligence. In R. J. Sternberg (Ed.), *Encyclopedia of human intelligence* (Vol. 1, pp. 443–451). New York: Macmillan.

Horn, J. L., & Cattell, R. B. (1967). Refinement and test of the theory of fluid and crystallized ability intelligences. *Journal of Educational Psychology, 57,* 253–270.

Horn, J. L., & Noll, J. (1997). Human cognitive capabilities: Gf-Gc theory. In D. P. Flanagan, J. L. Genshaft, & P. L. Harrison (Eds.), *Contemporary intellectual assessment* (pp. 53–91). New York: Guilford.

Horn, J. M., & Packard, T. (1985). Early identification of learning problems: A meta-analysis. *Journal of Educational Psychology, 77,* 349–360.

Horne, A. M., Glaser, B. A., & Calhoun, G. B. (1999). Conduct disorders. In R. T. Ammerman, M. Hersen, & C. G. Last (Eds.), *Handbook of prescriptive treatments for children and adolescents* (2nd ed., pp. 84–101). Boston: Allyn & Bacon.

Horowitz, F. D. (2000). Child development and the PITS: Simple questions, complex answers, and developmental theory. *Child Development, 71,* 1–10.

Hosmer, L. (2001). Home birth. *Clinical Obstetrics and Gynecology, 44,* 671–680.

Hossain, Z., Field, T., Gonzalez, J., Malphurs, J., Del Valle, C., & Pickens, J. (1994). Infants of "depressed" mothers interact better with their nondepressed fathers. *Infant Mental Health Journal, 15,* 348–357.

Hossain, Z., & Roopnarine, J. L. (1994). African-American fathers' involvement with infants: Relationship to their functioning style, support, education, and income. *Infant Behavior and Development, 17,* 175–184.

Hotz, V. J., McElroy, S. W., & Sanders, S. G. (1997). The costs and consequences of teenage childbearing for mothers. In R. A. Maynard (Ed.), *Kids having kids* (pp. 55–94). Washington, DC: Urban Institute.

Howe, M. L. & Courage, M. L. (1993). On resolving the enigma of infantile amnesia. *Psychological Bulletin, 113,* 305–326.

Howe, M. L., & Courage, M. L. (1997). The emergence and early development of autobiographical memory. *Psychological Review, 104,* 499–523.

Howes, C. (1987a). Peer interaction of young children. *Monographs of the Society for Research in Child Development, 53* (1, Serial No. 217).

Howes, C. (1987b). Social competence with peers in young children. *Developmental Review, 7,* 252–272.

Howes, C. (1990). Can age of entry and the quality of childcare predict adjustment in kindergarten? *Developmental Psychology, 26,* 292–303.

Howes, C., Phillips, D. A., & Whitebook, M. (1992). Thresholds of quality: Implications for the social development of children in center-based child care. *Child Development, 63,* 449–460.

Howes, C., Unger, O., & Seidner, L. B. (1989). Social pretend play in toddlers: Parallels with social play and with solitary pretend. *Child Development, 60,* 77–84.

Hoyert, D. L., Freedman, M. A., Strobino, D. M., & Guyer, B. (2001). Annual summary of vital statistics: 2000. *Pediatrics, 108,* 1241–1255.

Hsieh, F.-J., Shyu, M.-K., Sheu, B.-C., Lin, S.-P., Chen, C.-P., & Huang, F.-Y. (1995). Limb defects after chorionic villus sampling. *Obstetrics and Gynecology, 85,* 84–88.

Hsu, H.-C., & Fogel, A. (2001). Infant vocal development in a dynamic mother-infant communication system. *Infancy, 2,* 87–109.

Hubbard, J. A. (2001). Emotion expression processes in children's peer interaction: The role of peer rejection, aggression, and gender. *Child Development, 72,* 1426–1438.

Hubel, D. H., & Wiesel, T. N. (1979, September). Brain mechanisms of vision. *Scientific American, 241,* pp. 150–162.

Hudson, J. A., Shapiro, L. R., & Sosa, B. B. (1995). Planning in the real world: Preschool children's scripts and plans for familiar events. *Child Development, 66,* 984–998.

Huebner, A., & Garrod, A. (1991). Moral reasoning in a karmic world. *Human Development, 34,* 341–352.

Huesmann, L. R., Eron, L. D., Klein, R., Brice, P., & Fischer, P. (1983). Mitigating the imitation of aggressive behaviors by changing children's attitudes about media violence. *Journal of Personality and Social Psychology, 44,* 899–910.

Huesmann, L. R., Lagerspetz, K., & Eron, L. D. (1984). Intervening variables and the TV violence-aggression relation: Evidence from two countries. *Developmental Psychology, 20,* 746–775.

Huffman, L. C., Bryan, Y. E., del Carmen, R., Pedersen, F. A., Doussrad-Roosevelt, J. A., & Porges, S. W. (1998). Infant temperament and cardiac vagal tone: Assessments at twelve weeks of age. *Child Development, 69,* 624–635.

Hughes, C., & Russell, J. (1993). Autistic children's difficulty with mental disengagement from an object: Its implications for theories of autism. *Developmental Psychology, 29,* 498–510.

Humphreys, A. P., & Smith, P. K. (1987). Rough and tumble, friendship, and dominance in schoolchildren: Evidence for continuity and change with age. *Child Development, 58,* 201–212.

Huntley-Fenner, G., & Cannon, E. (2000). Preschoolers' magnitude comparisons are mediated by a preverbal counting mechanism. *Psychological Science, 11,* 147–152.

Hur, Y.-M., & Bouchard, T. J., Jr. (1995). Genetic influences on perceptions of childhood family environment: A reared apart twin study. *Child Development, 1995,* 330–345.

Hurley, J. C., & Underwood, M. K. (2002). Children's understanding of their research rights before and after debriefing: Informed assent, confidentiality, and stopping participation. *Child Development, 73,* 132–143.

Husain, M., & Kennard, C. (1997). Distractor-dependent frontal neglect. *Neuropsychologia, 35,* 829–841.

Huston, A. C. (1983). Sex typing. In E. M. Hetherington (Ed.), *Handbook of child psychology: Vol. IV. Socialization, personality, and social development* (4th ed., pp. 387–467). New York: Wiley.

Huston, A. C. (1985). The development of sex typing: Themes from recent research. *Developmental Review, 5,* 1–17.

Huston, A. C., & Alvarez, M. M. (1990). The socialization context of gender role development in early adolescence. In R. Montemayor, G. R. Adams, & T. P. Gullota (Eds.), *From childhood to adolescence: A transitional period?* (pp. 156–179). Newbury Park, CA: Sage.

Huston, A. C., Watkins, B. A., & Kunkel, D. (1989). Public policy and children's television. *American Psychologist, 44,* 424–433.

Huston, A. C., & Wright, J. C. (1998). Mass media and children's development. In W. Damon (Series Ed.) & R. Lerner (Vol. Ed.), *Handbook of child psychology: Vol. 4. Child psychology in practice* (5th ed., pp. 999–1058). New York: Wiley.

Huston, A. C., Wright, J. C., Marquis, J., & Green, S. B. (1999). How young children spend their time: Television and other activities. *Developmental Psychology, 35,* 912–925.

Huston, A. C., Wright, J. C., Rice, M. L., Kerkman, D., & St. Peters, M. (1990). Development of television viewing patterns in early childhood: A longitudinal investigation. *Developmental Psychology, 26,* 409–420.

Huttenlocher, J., Haight, W., Bryk, A., Seltzer, M., & Lyons, T. (1991). Early vocabulary growth: Relation to language input and gender. *Developmental Psychology, 27,* 236–248.

Huttenlocher, J., Newcombe, N., & Sandberg, E. H. (1994). The coding of spatial location in young children. *Cognitive Psychology, 27,* 115–148.

Huttenlocher, P. R. (1994). Synaptogenesis in human cerebral cortex. In G. Dawson & K. W. Fischer (Eds.), *Human behavior and the developing brain* (pp. 137–152). New York: Guilford.

Hyde, J. S. (1984). How large are gender differences in aggression? A developmental meta-analysis. *Developmental Psychology, 20,* 722–736.

Hyde, J. S. (1986). Gender differences in aggression. In J. S. Hyde & M. C. Linn (Eds.), *The psychology of gender: Advances through meta-analysis* (pp. 51–66). Baltimore: Johns Hopkins University Press.

Hyde, J. S., Fennema, E., & Lamon, S. J. (1990). Gender differences in mathematics performance: A meta-analysis. *Psychological Bulletin, 107,* 139–155.

Hyde, J. S., & Linn, M. C. (1988). Gender differences in verbal ability: A meta-analysis. *Psychological Bulletin, 104,* 53–69.

Hymel, S., & Franke, S. (1985). Children's peer relations: Assessing self-perceptions. In B. H. Schneider, K. H. Rubin, & J. E. Ledingham (Eds.), *Children's peer relations: Issues in assessment and intervention* (pp. 75–91). New York: Springer-Verlag.

Hymel, S., LeMare, L., Ditner, E., & Woody, E. Z. (1999). Assessing self-concept in children: Variations across self-concept domains. *Merrill-Palmer Quarterly, 45,* 602–623.

Iervolino, A. C., Pike, A., Manke, B., Reiss, D., Hetherington, E. M., & Plomin, R. (2002). Genetic and environmental influences in adolescent peer socialization: Evidence from two genetically sensitive designs. *Child Development, 73,* 162–174.

Ingram, D. (1999). Phonological acquisition. In M. Barrett (Ed.), *The development of language* (pp. 73–97). Hove, UK: Psychology Press.

Inhelder, B., & Piaget, J. (1958). *The growth of logical thinking from childhood to adolescence.* New York: Basic Books.

International Human Genome Mapping Consortium. (2001). A physical map of the human genome. *Nature, 409,* 934–941.

Isabella, R. A. (1993). Origins of attachment: Maternal interactive behavior across the first year. *Child Development, 64,* 605–621.

Isabella, R. A., Belsky, J., & von Eye, A. (1989). Origins of infant-mother attachment: An examination of interactional synchrony during the infant's first year. *Developmental Psychology, 25,* 12–21.

Isensee, W. (1986, September 3). *The Chronicle of Higher Education,* 33.

Ishii-Kuntz, M. (1994). Paternal involvement and perception toward fathers' roles: A comparison between Japan and the United States. *Journal of Family Issues, 15,* 30–48.

Ishii-Kuntz, M., & Coltrane, S. (1992). Predicting the sharing of household labor: Are parenting and housework distinct? *Sociological Perspectives, 35,* 629–647.

Isley, S. L., O'Neil, R., Clatfelter, D., & Parke, R. D. (1999). Parent and child expressed affect and children's social competence: Modeling direct and indirect pathways *Developmental Psychology, 35,* 547–560.

Iverson, J. M., & Goldin-Meadow, S. (2001). The resilience of gesture in talk: Gesture in blind speakers and listeners. *Developmental Science, 4,* 416–422.

Izard, C., & Ackerman, B. P. (2000). Motivational, organizational, and regulatory functions of discrete emotions. In M. Lewis & J. M. Haviland-Jones (Eds.), *Handbook of emotions* (2nd ed., pp. 253–280). New York: Guilford Press.

Izard, C., Fine, S., Schultz, D., Mostow, A., Ackerman, B., & Youngstrom, E. (2001). Emotion knowledge as a predictor of social behavior and academic competence in children at risk. *Psychological Science, 12,* 18–23.

Izard, C. E. (1978). On the ontogenesis of emotions and emotion-cognition relationships in infancy. In M. Lewis & L. A. Rosenblum (Eds.), *The development of affect* (pp. 389–413). New York: Plenum Press.

Izard, C. E., & Dougherty, L. M. (1982). Two complementary systems for measuring facial expressions in infants and children. In C. E. Izard (Ed.), *Measuring emotions in infants and children* (Vol. 1, pp. 97–126). Cambridge, UK: Cambridge University Press.

Izard, C. E., Fantauzzo, C. A., Castle, J. M., Haynes, O. M., Rayias, M. F., & Putnam, P. H. (1995). The ontogeny and significance of infants' facial expressions in the first 9 months of life. *Developmental Psychology, 31,* 997–1013.

Izard, C. E., Haynes, O. M., Chisolm, G., & Baak, K. (1991). Emotional determinants of infant-mother attachment. *Child Development, 62,* 906–917.

Izard, C. E., Huebner, R. R., Risser, D., McGinnes, G., & Dougherty, L. (1980). The young infant's ability to produce discrete emotion expressions. *Developmental Psychology, 16,* 132–140.

Izard, C. E., Kagan, J., & Zajonc, R. B. (1984). Introduction. In C. E. Izard, J. Kagan, & R. B. Zajonc (Eds.), *Emotions, cognition, and behavior* (pp. 1–14). Cambridge, UK: Cambridge University Press.

Izard, C. E., & Malatesta, C. Z. (1987). Perspectives on emotional development: I. Differential emotions theory of early emotional development. In J. D. Osofsky (Ed.), *Handbook of infant development* (2nd ed., pp. 494–554). New York: Wiley.

Jaccard, J., Dittus, P. J., & Gordon, V. V. (1998). Parent-adolescent congruency in reports of adolescent sexual behavior and in communications about sexual behavior. *Child Development, 69,* 247–261.

Jacklin, C. N. (1989). Female and male: Issues of gender. *American Psychologist, 44,* 127–133.

Jacklin, C. N., DiPietro, J. A., & Maccoby, E. E. (1984). Sex-typing behavior and sex-typing pressure in child/parent interaction. *Archives of Sexual Behavior, 13,* 413–425.

Jacklin, C. N., & Maccoby, E. E. (1978). Social behavior at thirty-three months in same-sex and mixed-sex dyads. *Child Development, 49,* 557–569.

Jackson, A. P., Brooks Gunn, J., Huang, C. C., & Glassman, M. (2000). Single mothers in low-wage jobs: Financial strain, parenting, and preschoolers' outcomes. *Child Development, 71,* 1409–1423.

Jackson, A. W., & Hornbeck, D. W. (1989). Educating young adolescents: Why we must restructure middle grade schools. *American Psychologist, 44,* 831–836.

Jackson, J. F. (1993). Human behavioral genetics, Scarr's theory, and her views on interventions: A critical review and commentary on their implications for African American children. *Child Development, 64,* 1318–1332.

Jacobs, P. A., & Hassold, T. J. (1995). The origin of numerical chromosome abnormalities. *Advances in Genetics, 33,* 101–133.

Jacobsen, T., Edelstein, W., & Hofman, V. (1994). A longitudinal study of the relation between representations of attachment in childhood and cognitive functioning in childhood and adolescence. *Developmental Psychology, 30,* 112–124.

Jacobson, J. L., & Jacobson, S. W. (1996). Methodological considerations in behavioral toxicology in infants and children. *Developmental Psychology, 32,* 390–403.

Jacobvitz, R. S., Wood, M., & Albin, K. (1989, April). *Cognitive skills and young children's comprehension of television.* Paper presented at the biennial meeting of the Society for Research in Child Development, Kansas City, MO.

Jaglom, L. M., & Gardner, H. (1981). The preschool television viewer as anthropologist. In H. Kelly & H. Gardner (Eds.), *New directions in child development: Viewing children through television* (pp. 9–30). San Francisco: Jossey-Bass.

Jahns, L., Siega-Riz, A. M., & Popkin, B. M. (2001). The increasing prevalence of snacking among U.S. children from 1977 to 1996. *Journal of Pediatrics, 138,* 493–498.

Jakibchuk, Z., & Smeriglio, V. L. (1976). The influence of symbolic modeling on the social behavior of preschool children with low levels of social responsiveness. *Child Development, 47,* 838–841.

James, S. (1978). Effect of listener age and situation on the politeness of children's directives. *Journal of Psycholinguistic Research, 7,* 307–317.

James, W. (1890). *The principles of psychology.* New York: Henry Holt.

James, W. (1892). *Psychology: The briefer course.* New York: Henry Holt.

Janicki, M. P., & Dalton, A. J. (2000). Prevalence of dementia and impact on intellectual disability services. *Mental Retardation, 38,* 276–288.

Jarrett, R. L. (1997). Bringing families back in: Neighborhoods' effects on child development. In J. Brooks-Gunn, G. J. Duncan, & J. L. Aber (Eds.), *Neighborhood poverty: Vol. 2. Policy implications in studying neighborhoods* (pp. 48–64). New York: Russell Sage Foundation.

Jegalian, K., & Lahn, B. T. (2001, February). Why the Y is so weird. *Scientific American, 284,* pp. 56–61.

Jencks, C. (1972). *Inequality: A reassessment of the effect of family and schooling in America.* New York: Basic Books.

Jencks, C., & Mayer, S. (1990). The social consequences of growing up in a poor neighborhood. In L. E. Lynn & M. F. H. McGeary (Eds.), *Inner-city poverty in the United States* (pp. 111–186). Washington, DC: National Academy Press.

Jensen, A. R. (1969). How much can we boost IQ and scholastic achievement? *Harvard Educational Review, 39,* 1–123.

Jensen, A. R. (1980). *Bias in mental testing.* New York: Free Press.

Jensen, A. R. (1982). The chronometry of intelligence. In R. J. Sternberg (Ed.), *Advances in the psychology of human intelligence* (Vol. 1, pp. 255–310). Hillsdale, NJ: Erlbaum.

Jensen, A. R., & Munroe, E. (1979). Reaction time, movement time, and intelligence. *Intelligence, 3,* 121–126.

Johnson, J., & Newport, E. (1989). Critical period effects in second language learning: The influence of maturational state on the acquisition of English as a second language. *Cognitive Psychology, 21,* 60–99.

Johnson, K. E., & Mervis, C. M. (1997). First steps in the emergence of verbal humor: A case study. *Infant Behavior and Development, 20,* 187–196.

Johnson, M. (1991). Infant and toddler sleep: A telephone survey of parents in one community. *Journal of Developmental and Behavioral Pediatrics, 12,* 108–114.

Johnson, M. H. (1992). Imprinting and the development of face recognition: From chick to man. *Current Directions in Psychological Science, 1,* 52–55.

Johnson, M. H. (2000). Functional brain development in infants: Elements of an interactive specialization framework. *Child Development, 71,* 75–81.

Johnson, M. H., Dziurawiec, S., Ellis, H. D., & Morton, J. (1991). Newborns' preferential tracking of face-like stimuli and its subsequent decline. *Cognition, 40,* 1–21.

Johnson, M. H., Farroni, T., Brockbank, M., & Simion, F. (2000). Preferential orienting to faces in 4-month-olds: Analysis of temporal-nasal visual field differences. *Developmental Science, 3,* 41–45.

Johnson, S. P., Bremner, J. G., Slater, A. M., & Mason, U. C. (2000). The role of good form in young infant's perception of partly occluded objects. *Journal of Experimental Child Psychology, 76,* 1–25.

Johnson, S. P., & Mason, U. (2002). Perception of kinetic illusory contours by two-month-old infants. *Child Development, 73,* 22–34.

Johnston, J., Brzezinski, E. J., & Anderman, E. M. (1994). *Taking the measure of Channel One: A three year perspective.* Ann Arbor, MI: University of Michigan, Institute for Social Research.

Joint Committee on Infant Hearing. (2000). Year 2000 Position Statement: Principles and Guidelines for Early Hearing Detection and Intervention Program. *Pediatrics, 106,* 798–817.

Jones, D. C., & Costin, S. E. (1995). Friendship quality during adolescence: The contributions of relationship orientations, instrumentality, and expressivity. *Merrill-Palmer Quarterly, 41,* 517–535.

Jones, G. P., & Dembo, M. H. (1989). Age and sex role differences in intimate friendships during childhood and adolescence. *Merrill-Palmer Quarterly, 35,* 445–462.

Jones, H. E., & Bayley, N. (1941). The Berkeley Growth Study. *Child Development, 12,* 167–173.

Jones, K. L., & Smith, D. W. (1973). Recognition of the fetal alcohol syndrome in early infancy. *Lancet, 2,* 999–1001.

Jones, M. C. (1965). Psychological correlates of somatic development. *Child Development, 36,* 899–911.

Jones, S. S. (1996). Imitation or exploration? Young infants' matching of adults' oral gestures. *Child Development, 67,* 1952–1969.

Joseph, R. (2000). Fetal brain behavior and cognitive development. *Developmental Review, 20,* 81–98.

Joyce, B. A., Keck, J. F., & Gerkensmeyer, J. (2001). Evaluation of pain management interventions for neonatal circumcision pain. *Journal of Pediatric Health Care, 15,* 105–114.

Jusczyk, P. W., & Aslin, R. N. (1995). Infants' detection of sound patterns of words in fluent speech. *Cognitive Psychology, 29,* 1–23.

Jusczyk, P. W., Cutler, A., & Redanz, L. (1993). Infants' sensitivity to predominant stress patterns in English. *Child Development, 64,* 675–687.

Jusczyk, P. W., Friederici, A. D., Wessels, J. M. I., Svenkerud, V. Y., & Jusczyk, A. M (1993). Infants' sensitivity to the sound patterns of native language words. *Journal of Memory and Language, 32,* 402–420.

Jusczyk, P. W., Hirsh-Pasek, K., Kemler Nelson, D. G., Kennedy, L. J., Woodward, A. & Piwoz, J. (1992). Perception of acoustic correlates of major phrasal units by young infants. *Cognitive Psychology, 24,* 252–293.

Jusczyk, P. W., & Hohne, E. A. (1997). Infants' memory for spoken words. *Science, 277,* 1984–1986.

Kagan, J. (1981). *The second year: The emergence of self-awareness.* Cambridge, MA: Harvard University Press.

Kagan, J. (1984). *The nature of the child.* New York: Basic Books.

Kagan, J. (1994). *Galen's prophecy: Temperament in human nature.* New York: Basic Books.

Kagan, J. (1998). Biology and the child. In W. Damon (Series Ed.) & N. Eisenberg (Vol. Ed.), *Handbook of child psychology: Vol. 3. Social, emotional, and personality development* (5th ed., pp. 177–235). New York: Wiley.

Kagan, J., Arcus, D., Snidman, N., Feng, W. Y., Hendler, J., & Greene, S. (1994). Reactivity in infants: A cross-national comparison. *Developmental Psychology, 30,* 342–345.

Kagan, J., Reznick, J. S., & Snidman, N. (1988). Biological basis of childhood shyness. *Science, 240,* 167–171.

Kagan, J., Snidman, N., & Arcus, D. M. (1992). Initial reactions to unfamiliarity. *Current Directions in Psychological Science, 1,* 171–174.

Kagan, J., Snidman, N., & Arcus, D. (1993). On the temperamental categories of inhibited and uninhibited children. In K. H. Rubin & J. B. Asendorpf (Eds.), *Social withdrawal, inhibition, and shyness in children* (pp. 19–28). Hillsdale, NJ: Erlbaum.

Kahn, P. H., Jr. (1992). Children's obligatory and discretionary moral judgments. *Child Development, 63,* 416–430.

Kahneman, D. (1973). *Attention and effort.* Englewood Cliffs, NJ: Prentice-Hall.

Kail, R. (1986). Sources of age differences in speed of processing. *Child Development, 57,* 969–987.

Kail, R. (1990). *The development of memory in children* (3rd ed.). New York: W.H. Freeman.

Kail, R. (1991a). Development of processing speed in childhood and adolescence. In H. W. Reese (Ed.), *Advances in child development and behavior* (Vol. 23, pp. 151–185). San Diego, CA: Academic Press.

Kail, R. (1991b). Processing time declines exponentially during childhood and adolescence. *Developmental Psychology, 27,* 259–266.

Kaitz, M., Lapidot, P., Bronner, R., & Eidelman, A. I. (1992). Parturient women can recognize their infants by touch. *Developmental Psychology, 28,* 35–39.

Kaitz, M., Shiri, S., Danziger, S., Hershko, Z., & Eidelman, A. I. (1994). Fathers can also recognize their newborns by touch. *Infant Behavior and Development, 17,* 205–207.

Kajii, T., Kida, M., & Takahashi, K. (1973). The effect of thalidomide intake during 113 human pregnancies. *Teratology, 8,* 163–166.

Kamins, M. L., & Dweck, C. S. (1999). Person versus process praise and criticism: Implications for contingent self-worth and coping. *Developmental Psychology, 35,* 835–847.

Kanner, L. (1943). Autistic disturbances of affective contact. *Nervous Children, 2,* 217–250.

Kaplan, H., & Dove, H. (1987). Infant development among the Ache of Eastern Paraguay. *Developmental Psychology, 23,* 190–196.

Kaplowitz, P. B., Slora, E. J., Wasserman, R. C., Pedlow, S. E., & Herman-Giddens, M. E. (2001). Earlier onset of puberty in girls: Relation to increased body mass index and race. *Pediatrics, 108,* 347–353.

Karmiloff-Smith, A. (1995). Annotation: The extraordinary cognitive journey from foetus through infancy. *Journal of Child Psychology and Psychiatry, 36,* 1293–1313.

Karraker, K. H., Vogel, D. A., & Lake, M. A. (1995). Parents' gender-stereotyped perceptions of newborns: The eye of the beholder revisited. *Sex Roles, 33,* 687–701.

Katz, P. A. (1987). Variations in family constellation: Effects on gender schemata. In L. S. Liben & M. L. Signorella (Eds.), *New directions for child development: No. 38. Children's gender schemata* (pp. 39–56). San Francisco: Jossey-Bass.

Katz, P. A., & Ksansnak, K. R. (1994). Developmental aspects of gender role flexibility and traditionality in middle childhood and adolescence. *Developmental Psychology, 30,* 272–282.

Katzman, D. K., Golden, N. H., Neumark-Sztainer, D., Yager, J., & Strober, M. (2000). From prevention to prognosis: Clinical research update on adolescent eating disorders. *Pediatric Research, 47,* 709–712.

Kaufman, A. S. (2001). WAIS-III IQs, Horn's theory, and generational changes from young adulthood to old age. *Intelligence, 29,* 131–167.

Kaufman, A. S., Kamphaus, R. W., & Kaufman, N. L. (1985). New directions in intelligence testing: The Kaufman Assessment Battery for Children (K-ABC). In B. B. Wolman (Ed.), *Handbook of intelligence* (pp. 663–698). New York: Wiley.

Kaufman, A. S., & Kaufman, N. L. (1983). *K-ABC administration and scoring manual.* Circle Pines, MN: American Guidance Service.

Kaufman, P., Klein, S., & Frase, M. (1999). *Dropout rates in the United States, 1997.* Washington, DC: U.S. Department of Education, National Center for Education Statistics.

Kaye, K., & Marcus, J. (1981). Infant imitation: The sensorimotor agenda. *Developmental Psychology, 17,* 258–265.

Kayne, M. A., Greulich, M. B., & Albers, L. L. (2001). Doulas: An alternative yet complementary addition to care during childbirth. *Clinical Obstetrics and Gynecology, 44,* 692–703.

Keel, P. K., Fulkerson, J. A., & Leon, G. R. (1997). Disordered eating precursors in pre- and early adolescent girls and boys. *Journal of Youth and Adolescence, 26,* 203–216.

Keeney, T. J., Cannizzo, S. R., & Flavell, J. H. (1967). Spontaneous and induced rehearsal in a recall task. *Child Development, 38,* 953–966.

Keil, F. C. (1989). *Concepts, kinds, and cognitive development.* Cambridge, MA: MIT Press.

Keller, M., Edelstein, W., Schmid, C., Fang, F., & Fang, G. (1998). Reasoning about responsibilities and obligations in close relationships: A comparison across two cultures. *Developmental Psychology, 34,* 731–741.

Kelley, S. A., Brownell, C. A., & Campbell, S. B. (2000). Mastery motivation and self-evaluative affect in toddlers: Longitudinal relations with maternal behavior. *Child Development, 71,* 1061–1071.

Kelley, M. L., Power, T. G., & Wimbush, D. D. (1992). Determinants of disciplinary practices in low-income black mothers. *Child Development, 63,* 573–582.

Kellman, P. J. (1996). The origins of object perception. In R. Gelman & T. Au (Eds.), *Perceptual and cognitive development* (pp. 3–48). New York: Academic Press.

Kellman, P. J., & Arterberry, M. E. (1998). *The cradle of knowledge: Development of perception in infancy.* Cambridge, MA: MIT Press.

Kellman, P. J., & Banks, M. S. (1998). Infant visual perception. In W. Damon (Series Ed.) & R. Siegler & D. Kuhn (Vol. Eds.), *Handbook of child psychology: Vol. 2. Cognition, perception, and language* (5th ed., pp. 103–146). New York: Wiley.

Kellman, P. J., & Spelke, E. S. (1983). Perception of partly occluded objects in infancy. *Cognitive Psychology, 15,* 483–524.

Kelly, M. H. (1992). Using sound to solve syntactic problems: The role of phonology in grammatical category assignments. *Psychological Review, 99,* 349–364.

Kemler Nelson, D. G., Hirsh-Pasek, K., Jusczyk, P. W., & Cassidy, K. W. (1989). How the prosodic cues in motherese might assist language learning. *Journal of Child Language, 16,* 55–68.

Kemp, J. S., Livne, M., White, D. K., & Arfken, C. L. (1998). Softness and potential to cause rebreathing: Differences in bedding used by infants at high and low risk for sudden infant death syndrome. *Journal of Pediatrics, 132,* 234–239.

Kendler, K. S., Prescott, C. A., Neale, M. C., & Pedersen, N. L. (1997). Temperance Board registration for alcohol abuse in a national sample of Swedish male twins, born 1902–1949. *Archives of General Psychiatry, 54,* 178–184.

Kennedy, C. R. (2000). Neonatal screening for hearing impairment. *Archives of Disease in Childhood, 83,* 377–383.

Keogh, J., & Sugden, D. (1985). *Movement skill development.* New York: Macmillan.

Kerig, P. K., Cowan, P. A., & Cowan, C. P. (1993). Marital quality and gender differences in parent-child interaction. *Developmental Psychology, 29,* 931–939.

Kersten, A. W. (1998). A division of labor between nouns and verbs in the representation of motion. *Journal of Experimental Psychology: General, 127,* 34–54.

Kersten, A. W., & Smith, L. B. (2002). Attention to novel objects during verb learning. *Child Development, 73,* 93–109.

Kiesner, J., Cadinu, M., Poulin, F., & Bucci, M. (2002). Group identification in early adolescence: Its relation with peer adjustment and its moderator effect on peer influence. *Child Development, 73,* 196–208.

Kilbride, H., Castor, C., Hoffman, E., & Fuger, K. L. (2000). Thirty-six-month outcome of prenatal cocaine exposure for term or near-term infants: Impact of early case management. *Journal of Developmental and Behavioral Pediatrics, 21,* 19–26.

Killen, M., Pisacane, K., Lee Kim, J., & Ardila Rey, A. (2001). Fairness or stereotypes? Young children's priorities when evaluating group exclusion and inclusion. *Developmental Psychology, 37,* 587–596.

Kim, J. E., Hetherington, E. M., & Reiss, D. (1999). Associations among family relationships., antisocial peers, and adolescents' externalizing behaviors: Gender and family type differences. *Child Development, 70,* 1209–1230.

Kim, K. H. S., Relkin, N. R., Lee, K., & Hirsch, J. (1997). Distinct cortical areas associated with native and second languages. *Nature, 388,* 171–174.

Kim, K. J., Conger, R. D., Lorenz, F. O., & Elder, G. H., Jr. (2001). Parent-adolescent reciprocity in negative affect and its relation to early adult social development. *Developmental Psychology, 37,* 775–790.

Kindermann, T. (1998). Children's development within peer groups: Using composite social maps to identify peer networks and to study their influences. In W. K. Bukowski & A. H. Cillessen (Eds.), *New Directions for Child Development: No. 80. Sociometry then and now: Building on six decades of measuring children's experiences in the peer group* (pp. 55–82). San Francisco: Jossey-Bass.

Kindermann, T. A. (1993). Natural peer groups as contexts for individual development: The case of children's motivation in school. *Developmental Psychology, 29,* 970–977.

Kinsbourne, M., & Hiscock, M. (1983). The normal and deviant development of functional lateralization of the brain. In M. M. Haith & J. C. Campos (Eds.), *Infancy and developmental psychobiology: Vol. II. Handbook of child psychology* (pp. 157–280). New York: Wiley.

Kinsman, S. B., Romer, D., Furstenberg, F. F., & Schwartz, D. F. (1998). Early sexual initiation: The role of peer norms. *Pediatrics, 102,* 1185–1192.

Kirby, D. (1997). *No easy answers: Research findings on programs to reduce teen pregnancy.* Washington, DC: National Campaign to Prevent Teen Pregnancy.

Kirkpatrick, S. W., & Sanders, D. M. (1978). Body image stereotypes: A developmental comparison. *Journal of Genetic Psychology, 132,* 87–95.

Kisilevsky, B. S., Hains, S. M. J., & Low, J. A. (1999). Differential maturation of fetal responses to vibroacoustic stimulation in a high risk population. *Developmental Science, 2,* 234–245.

Kisilevsky, B. S., & Low, J. A. (1998). Human fetal behavior: 100 years of study. *Developmental Review, 18,* 1–29.

Kisilevsky, B. S., & Muir, D. W. (1991). Human fetal and subsequent newborn responses to sound and vibration. *Infant Behavior and Development, 14,* 1–26.

Klaczynski, P. A. (2000). Motivated scientific reasoning biases, epistemological beliefs, and theory polarization: A two-process approach to adolescent cognition. *Child Development, 71,* 1347–1366.

Klaczynski, P. A. (2001). Analytic and heuristic processing influences on adolescent reasoning and decision-making. *Child Development, 72,* 844–861.

Klahr, D. (1978). Goal formation, planning, and learning by preschool problem solvers or: "My socks are in the dryer." In R. S. Siegler (Ed.), *Children's thinking: What develops?* (pp. 181–212). Hillsdale, NJ: Erlbaum.

Klahr, D. (1989). Information-processing approaches. In R. Vasta (Ed.), *Annals of child development: Vol 6. Six theories of child development: Revised formulations and current issues* (pp. 133–185). Greenwich, CT: JAI Press.

Klahr, D., Chen, Z., & Toth, E. E. (2001). Cognitive development and science education: Ships that pass in the night or beacons of mutual illumination? In S. M. Carver & D. Klahr (Eds.), *Cognition and instruction: Twenty-five years of progress* (pp. 75–119). Mahwah, NJ: Erlbaum.

Klahr, D., & Dunbar, K. (1988). Dual space search during scientific reasoning. *Cognitive Science, 12,* 1–55.

Klahr, D., Fay, A. L., & Dunbar, K. (1993). Heuristics for scientific experimentation: A developmental study. *Cognitive Psychology, 25,* 111–146.

Klahr, D., & MacWhinney, B. (1998). Information processing. In W. Damon (Series Ed.) & D. Kuhn & R. S. Siegler (Vol. Eds.), *Handbook of child psychology: Vol. 2. Cognition, perception, and language* (5th ed., pp. 631–678). New York: Wiley.

Klahr, D., & Robinson, M. (1981). Formal assessment of problem solving and planning processes in preschool children. *Cognitive Psychology, 13,* 113–148.

Klaus, M., & Kennell, J. (1982). *Parent-infant bonding.* St. Louis: C. V. Mosby.

Klebanov, P. K., Brooks-Gunn, J., & McCormick, M. C. (1994). Classroom behavior of very low birth weight elementary school children. *Pediatrics, 94,* 700–708.

Klebanov, P. K., Brooks-Gunn, J., & McCormick, M. C. (2001). Maternal coping strategies and emotional distress: Results of an early intervention program for low birth weight young children. *Developmental Psychology, 37,* 654–667.

Klein, P. D. (1997). Multiplying the problems of intelligence by eight: A critique of Gardner's theory. *Canadian Journal of Education, 22,* 377–394.

Klesges, R. C., Haddock, C. K., Stein, R. J., Klesges, L. M., Eck, L. H., & Hanson, C. L. (1992). Relationship between psychosocial functioning and body fat in preschool children: A longitudinal investigation. *Journal of Consulting and Clinical Psychology, 60,* 793–796.

Klima, E. S., & Bellugi, U. (1966). Syntactic regularities in the speech of children. In J. Lyons & R. J. Wales (Eds.), *Psycholinguistic papers: The proceedings of the 1966 Edinburgh conference.* Edinburgh: Edinburgh University Press.

Kling, K. C., Hyde, J. S., Showers, C. J., & Buswell, B. N. (1999). Gender differences in self-esteem: A meta-analysis. *Psychological Bulletin, 125,* 470–500.

Knowles, R. V. (1985). *Genetics, society and decisions.* Columbus, OH: Merrill.

Kobak, R. R., Cole, H. E., Ferenz-Gillies, R., & Fleming, W. S. (1993). Attachment and emotion regulation during mother-teen problem-solving: A control theory analysis. *Child Development, 64,* 231–245.

Kobasigawa, A. (1968). Inhibitory and disinhibitory effects of models on sex-inappropriate behavior in children. *Psychologia, 11,* 86–96.

Kobayashi-Winata, H., & Power, T. G. (1989). Child rearing and compliance: Japanese and American families in Houston. *Journal of Cross-Cultural Psychology, 20,* 333–356.

Kochanska, G. (1994). Beyond cognition: Expanding the search for the early roots of internalization and conscience. *Developmental Psychology, 30,* 20–22.

Kochanska, G. (1997). Mutually responsive orientation between mothers and their young children: Implications for early socialization. *Child Development, 68,* 94–112.

Kochanska, G. (2001). Emotional development in children with different attachment histories: The first three years. *Child Development, 72,* 474–490.

Kochanska, G. (2002). Committed compliance, moral self, and internalization: A mediational model. *Developmental Psychology, 38,* 339–351.

Kochanska, G., Aksan, N., & Koenig, A. L. (1995). A longitudinal study of the roots of preschoolers' conscience: Committed compliance and emerging internalizations. *Child Development, 66,* 1752–1769.

Kochanska, G., Casey, R. J., & Fukumoto, A. (1995). Toddlers' sensitivity to standard violation. *Child Development, 66,* 643–656.

Kochanska, G., Coy, K. C., & Murray, K. T. (2001). The development of self-regulation in the first four years of life. *Child Development, 72,* 1091–1111.

Kochanska, G., Gross, J. N., Lin, M.-H., & Nichols, K. E. (2002). Guilt in young children: Development, determinants, and relations with a broader system of standards. *Child Development, 73,* 461–482.

Kochanska, G., & Murray, K. T. (2000). Mother-child responsive orientation and conscience development: From toddler to early school age. *Child Development, 71,* 417–431.

Kochanska, G., Murray, K., & Coy, K. C. (1997). Inhibitory control as a contributor to conscience in childhood: From toddler to early school age. *Child Development, 68,* 263–277.

Kochanska, G., Murray, K. T., & Harlan, E. T. (2000). Effortful control in early childhood: Continuity and change, antecedents, and implications for social development. *Developmental Psychology, 36,* 220–232.

Kochanska, G., Tjebkes, T. L., & Forman, D. R. (1998). Children's emerging regulation of conduct: Restraint, compliance, and internalization from infancy to the second year. *Child Development, 69,* 1378–1389.

Kochenderfer, B. J., & Ladd, G. W. (1996). Peer victimization: Cause or consequence of school maladjustment? *Child Development, 67,* 1305–1317.

Koff, E., & Rierdan, J. (1995). Preparing girls for menstruation: Recommendations from adolescent girls. *Adolescence, 30,* 795–811.

Kohlberg, L. (1966). A cognitive-developmental analysis of children's sex-role concepts and attitudes. In E. E. Maccoby (Ed.), *The development of sex differences* (pp. 82–173). Stanford, CA: Stanford University Press.

Kohlberg, L. (1969). Stage and sequence: The cognitive-developmental approach to socialization. In D. A. Goslin (Ed.), *The handbook of socialization theory and research* (pp. 347–380). Chicago: Rand McNally.

Kohlberg, L. (1976). Moral stages and moralization: The cognitive developmental approach. In T. Lickona (Ed.), *Moral development and moral behavior: Theory, research, and social issu*es (pp. 31–53). New York: Holt, Rinehart & Winston.

Kohlberg, L. (1984). *Essays on moral development: Vol. 2. The psychology of moral development.* San Francisco: Harper & Row.

Kohlberg, L., & Kramer, R. (1969). Continuities and discontinuities in childhood moral development. *Human Development, 12,* 93–120.

Kokko, K., & Pulkkinen, L. (2000). Aggression in childhood and long-term unemployment in adulthood: A cycle of maladaptation and some protective factors. *Developmental Psychology, 36,* 463–472.

Kolata, G. (2001, September 28). Fertility ethics authority approves sex selection. *New York Times,* p. A16.

Kopp, C. (1989). Regulation of distress and negative emotions: A developmental view. *Developmental Psychology, 25,* 343–354.

Kopp, C. B. (1987). The growth of self-regulation: Caregivers and children. In N. Eisenberg (Ed.), *Contemporary topics in developmental psychology* (pp. 34–55). New York: Wiley.

Kopp, C. B. (1992). Emotional distress and control in young children. In N. Eisenberg & R. A. Fabes (Eds.), *Emotion and its regulation in early development [New Directions in Child Development,* No. 55, pp. 41–56). San Francisco: Jossey-Bass.

Kopp, C. B., & McCall, R. B. (1980). Stability and instability in mental performance among normal, at-risk, and handicapped infants and children. In P. B. Baltes & O. G. Grim, Jr. (Eds.), *Life-span development and behavior* (Vol. 4). New York: Academic Press.

Korner, A. F. (1972). State as a variable, as obstacle, and mediator of stimulation in infant research. *Merrill-Palmer Quarterly, 18,* 77–94.

Korner, A. F. (1987). Preventive intervention with high-risk newborns: Theoretical, conceptual, and methodological perspectives. In J. D. Osofsky (Ed.), *Handbook of infant development* (2nd ed.). New York: Wiley.

Kosslyn, S. M., Gazzaniga, M. S., Galaburda, A. M., & Rabin, C. (1999). Hemispheric specialization. In M. J. Zigmond, F. E. Bloom, S. C. Landis, J. L. Roberts, & L. R. Squire (Eds.), *Fundamental neuroscience* (pp. 1521–1542). New York: Academic Press.

Kotelchuk, M. (1976). The infant's relationship to the father: Experimental evidence. In M. E. Lamb (Ed.), *The role of the father in child development* (pp. 329–344). New York: Wiley.

Kovacs, D. M., Parker, J. G., & Hoffman, L. W. (1996). Behavioral, affective, and social correlates of involvement in cross-sex friendship in elementary school. *Child Development, 67,* 2269–2286.

Kowal, A., & Kramer, L. (1997). Children's understanding of potential differential treatment. *Child Development, 68,* 113–126.

Kraemer, H. C., Korner, A., Anders, T., Jacklin, C. N., & Dimiceli, S. (1985). Obstetric drugs and infant behavior: A re-evaluation. *Journal of Pediatric Psychology, 10,* 345–353.

Krafchuk, E. E., Tronick, E. Z., & Clifton, R. K. (1983). Behavioral and cardiac responses to sound in preterm infants varying in risk status: A hypothesis of their paradoxical reactivity. In T. Field & A. Sostek (Eds.), *Infants born at risk: Physiological, perceptual, and cognitive processes* (pp. 99–128). New York: Grune & Stratton.

Kramer, L., Perozynski, L. A., & Chung, T. (1999). Parental responses to sibling conflict: The effects of development and parent gender. *Child Development, 70,* 1401–1414.

Kranzler, J. H., Rosenbloom, A. L., Proctor, B., Diamond, F. B., Jr., & Watson, M. (2000). Is short stature a handicap? A comparison of the psychosocial functioning of referred and nonreferred children with normal short stature and children with normal stature. *Journal of Pediatrics, 136,* 96–102.

Krascum, R. M., & Andrews, S. (1998). The effects of theories on children's acquisition of family-resemblance structures. *Child Development, 69,* 333–346.

Krauss, R. H., & Glucksberg, S. (1969). The development of communication. *Child Development, 40,* 255–266.

Krebs, D. L., & Van Hesteren, F. (1994). The development of altruism: Toward an integrative model. *Developmental Review, 14,* 103–158.

Krechevsky, M. (1994). *Project Spectrum preschool assessment handbook.* Cambridge, MA: Harvard Project Zero.

Krendl, K. A., & Broihier, M. (1992). Student responses to computers: A longitudinal study. *Journal of Educational Computing Research, 8,* 215–227.

Kreutzer, M. A., Leonard, S. C., & Flavell, J. H. (1975). An interview study of children's knowledge about memory. *Monographs of the Society for Research in Child Development, 40*(1, Serial No. 159).

Krevans, J., & Gibbs, J. C. (1996). Parents' use of inductive discipline: Relations to children's empathy and prosocial behavior. *Child Development, 67,* 3263–3277.

Kroll, J. (1977). The concept of childhood in the Middle Ages. *Journal of the History of the Behavioral Sciences, 13,* 384–393.

Krowchuck, D. P., Kreiter, S. R., Woods, C. R., Sinal, S. H., & DuRant, R. H. (1998). Problem dieting behavior among young adolescents. *Archives of Pediatric and Adolescent Medicine, 152,* 884–888.

Krumhansl, C. L., & Jusczyk, P. W. (1990). Infants' perception of phrase structure in music. *Psychological Science, 1,* 70–73.

Kuczaj, S. A., Borys, R. H., & Jones, M. (1989). On the interaction of language and thought: Some thoughts and developmental data. In A. Gellatly, D. Rogers, & J. A. Sloboda (Eds.), *Cognition and social worlds* (pp. 163–189). Oxford: Clarendon Press.

Kuczynski, L., & Kochanska, G. (1995). Function and content of maternal demands: Developmental significance of early demands for competent action. *Child Development, 66,* 616–628.

Kuczynski, L., Zahn-Waxler, C., & Radke-Yarrow, M. (1987). Development and content of imitation in the second and third year of life: A socialization perspective. *Developmental Psychology, 23,* 276–282.

Kuebli, J., Butler, S., & Fivush, R. (1995). Mother-child talk about past emotions: Relations of maternal language and child gender over time. *Cognition and Emotion, 9,* 265–283.

Kuhl, P. K. (1987). Perception of speech and sound in early infancy. In P. Salapatek & L. Cohen (Eds.), *Handbook of infant perception: From perception to cognition* (Vol. 2, pp. 275–382). Orlando, FL: Academic Press.

Kuhl, P. K., & Miller, J. D. (1978). Speech perception by the chinchilla: Identification functions for synthetic VOT stimuli. *Journal of the Acoustical Society of America, 63,* 905–917.

Kuhl, P. K., & Padden, D. M. (1983). Enhanced discriminability at the phonetic boundary for the place feature in macaques. *Journal of the Acoustical Society of America, 73,* 1003–1010.

Kuhl, P. K., Williams, K. A., Lacerda, F., Stevens, K. N., & Lindblom, B. (1992). Linguistic experience alters phonetic perception in infants by 6 months of age. *Science, 255,* 606–608.

Kuhn, D. (2000a). Metacognitive development. *Current Directions in Psychological Science, 9,* 178–181.

Kuhn, D. (2000b). Theory of mind, metacognition, and reasoning: A lifespan perspective. In P. Mitchell & K. J. Riggs (Eds.), *Children's reasoning and the mind* (pp. 301–326). Hove, UK: Psychology Press.

Kuhn, D., Garcia-Mila, M., Zohar, A., & Andersen, C. (1995). Strategies of knowledge acquisition. *Monographs of the Society for Research in Child Development, 60* (No. 4, Serial No. 245).

Kuhn, D., Nash, S. C., & Brucken, L. (1978). Sex role concepts of two- and three-year-olds. *Child Development, 49,* 445–451.

Kuhn, D., & Pearsall, S. (2000). Developmental origins of scientific thinking. *Journal of Cognition and Development, 1,* 113–129.

Kuhn, D., Schauble, L., & Garcia-Mila, M. (1992). Cross-domain development of scientific reasoning. *Cognition and Instruction, 9,* 285–327.

Kuklinski, M. R., & Weinstein, R. S. (2001). Classroom and developmental differences in a path model of teacher expectancy effects. *Child Development, 72,* 1554–1578.

Kulik, J. A., Kulik, C. C., & Bangert-Drowns, R. L. (1985). Effectiveness of computer-based education in elementary schools. *Computers in Human Behavior, 1,* 59–74.

Kunkel, D., & Roberts, D. (1991). Young minds and marketplace values: Issues in children's television advertising. *Journal of Social Issues, 47,* 57–72.

Kunzig, R. (1998, August). Climbing through the brain. *Discover, 19,* 61–69.

Kuppermann, M., Gates, E., & Washington, A. E. (1996). Racial ethnic differences in prenatal diagnostic test use and outcomes: Preferences, socioeconomics, or patient knowledge? *Obstetrics and Gynecology, 87,* 675–682.

Kurdek, L. A. (1989). Siblings' reactions to parental divorce. *Journal of Divorce, 12,* 203–219.

Kurdek, L. A., Fine, M. A., & Sinclair, R. J. (1995). School adjustment in sixth graders: Parenting transitions, family climate, and peer norm effects. *Child Development, 66,* 430–445.

LaBarbera, J. D., Izard, C. E., Vietze, P., & Parisi, S. A. (1976). Four- and six-month-old infants' visual responses to joy, anger, and neutral expressions. *Child Development, 47,* 535–538.

Lackey, P. N. (1989). Adults' attitudes about assignments of household chores to male and female children. *Sex Roles, 20,* 271–281.

Ladd, G. W. (1983). Social networks of popular, average, and rejected children in school settings. *Merrill-Palmer Quarterly, 29,* 283–307.

Ladd, G. W., Birch, S. H., & Buhs, E. S. (1999). Children's social and scholastic lives in kindergarten: Related spheres of influence? *Child Development, 70,* 1373–1400.

Ladd, G. W., & Burgess, K. B. (1999). Charting the relationship trajectories of aggressive, withdrawn, and aggressive/withdrawn children during early grade school. *Child Development, 70,* 910–929.

Ladd, G. W., & Golter, B. S. (1988). Parents' management of preschooler's peer relations: Is it related to children's social competencies? *Developmental Psychology, 24,* 109–117.

Ladd, G. W., & Hart, C. H. (1992). Creating informal play opportunities: Are parents' and preschoolers' initiations related to children's competence with peers? *Developmental Psychology, 28,* 1179–1187.

Ladd, G. W., Kochenderfer, B. J., & Coleman, C. C. (1996). Friendship quality as a predictor of young children's early school adjustment. *Child Development, 67,* 1103–1118.

Ladd, G. W., & Price, J. M. (1987). Predicting children's social and school adjustment following the transition from preschool to kindergarten. *Child Development, 58,* 1168–1189.

Ladd, G. W., Price, J. M., & Hart, C. H. (1988). Predicting preschoolers' peer status from their playground behaviors. *Child Development, 59,* 986–992.

LaFontana, K. M., & Cillessen, A. H. N. (1998). The nature of children's stereotypes of popularity. *Social Development, 7,* 301–320.

LaFontana, K. M., & Cillessen, A. H. N. (2002). Children's perceptions of popular and unpopular peers: A multimethod assessment. *Developmental Psychology, 38,* 635–647.

LaFreniere, P., & Charlesworth, W. R. (1983). Dominance, attention, and affiliation in a preschool group: A nine-month longitudinal study. *Ethology and Sociobiology, 4,* 55–67.

LaGreca, A. M., & Lopez, N. (1998). Social anxiety among adolescents: Linkages with peer relations and friendships. *Journal of Abnormal Child Psychology, 26,* 83–94.

Lahey, B. B., Hammer, D., Crumrine, P. L., & Forehand, R. L. (1980). Birth order sex interactions in child behavior problems. *Developmental Psychology, 16,* 608–615.

Laible, D. J., & Thompson, R. A. (2000). Mother-child discourse, attachment security, shared positive affect, and early conscience development. *Child Development, 71,* 1424–1440.

Laible, D. J., & Thompson, R. A. (2002). Mother-child conflict in the toddler years: Lessons in emotion, morality, and relationships. *Child Development, 73,* 1187–1203.

Lalonde, C. E., & Werker, J. F. (1995). Cognitive influences on cross-language speech perception in infancy. *Infant Behavior and Development, 18,* 459–475.

Lamaze, F. (1970). *Painless childbirth: Psychoprophylactic method.* Chicago: Henry Regnery.

Lamb, M. E. (1981). *The role of the father in child development* (rev. ed.). New York: Wiley.

Lamb, M. E. (1987). Introduction: The emergent American father. In M. E. Lamb (Ed.), *The father's role: Cross-cultural perspectives* (pp. 111–142). Hillsdale, NJ: Erlbaum.

Lamb, M. E. (1997). The development of father–infant relationships. In M. E. Lamb (Ed.), *The role of the father in child development* (3rd ed., pp. 104–120). New York: Wiley.

Lamb, M. E. (1998). Nonparental child care: Context, quality, correlates, and consequences. In W. Damon (Series Ed.) & I. E. Sigel & K. A. Renninger (Vol. Eds.), *Handbook of child psychology: Vol. 4. Child psychology in practice* (5th ed., pp. 73–133). New York: Wiley.

Lamb, M. E., Easterbrooks, M. A., & Holden, G. (1980). Reinforcement and punishment among preschoolers: Characteristics and correlates. *Child Development, 51,* 1230–1236.

Lamb, M. E., Pleck, J. H., Charnov, E. L., & Levine, J. A. (1987). A biosocial perspective on paternal behavior and involvement. In J. B. Lancaster, J. Altmann, A. S. Rossi, & L. R. Sherrod (Eds.), *Parenting across the life span: Biosocial dimensions* (pp. 111–142). New York: Aldine de Gruyter.

Lamb, M. E., & Roopnarine, J. L. (1979). Peer influences on sex-role development in preschoolers. *Child Development, 50,* 1219–1222.

Lamborn, S. D., Mounts, N. S., Steinberg, L., & Dornbusch, S. M. (1991). Patterns of competence and adjustment among adolescents from authoritative, authoritarian, indulgent, and neglectful families. *Child Development, 62,* 1049–1065.

Lampl, M., Veldhuis, J. D., & Johnson, M. L. (1992). Saltation and stasis: A model of human growth. *Science, 258,* 801–803.

Landau, S., Lorch, E. P., & Milich, R. (1992). Visual attention to and comprehension of television in attention-deficit hyperactivity disordered and normal boys. *Child Development, 63,* 928–937.

Landesman-Dwyer, S., Keller, L. S., & Streissguth, A. P. (1978). Naturalistic observations of newborns: Effects of maternal alcohol intake. *Alcoholism, 2,* 171–177.

Langlois, J. H., & Stephan, C. (1981). Beauty and the beast: The role of physical attractiveness in the development of peer relations and social behavior. In S. S. Brehm, S. H. Kassin, & F. X. Gibbons (Eds.), *Developmental social psychology* (pp. 152–168). New York: Oxford University Press.

Larkin, R. W. (1979). *Suburban youth in cultural crisis.* New York: Oxford University Press.

Larson, R. W. (2001). How U.S. children and adolescents spend time: What it does (and doesn't) tell us about development. *Current Directions in Psychological Science, 10,* 160–164.

Larson, R. W., & Ham, M. (1993). Stress and "storm and stress" in early adolescence: The relationship of negative events with dysphoric affect. *Developmental Psychology, 29,* 130–140.

Larson, R. W., & Lampman-Petraitis, C. (1989). Daily emotional stress as reported by children and adolescents. *Child Development, 60,* 1250–1260.

Larson, R. W., Moneta, G., Richards, M. H., & Wilson, S. (2002). Continuity, stability, and change in daily emotional experience across adolescence. *Developmental Psychology, 73,* 1151–1165.

Laskari, A., Smith, A. K., & Graham, J. M., Jr. (1999). Williams-Beuren syndrome: An update and review for the primary physician. *Clinical Pediatrics, 38,* 189–208.

Latz, S., Wolf, A. W., & Lozoff, B. (1999). Cosleeping in context: Sleep practices and problems in young children in Japan and the United States. *Archives of Pediatrics and Adolescent Medicine, 153,* 339–346.

Laursen, B., Coy, K. C., & Collins, W. A. (1998). Reconsidering changes in parent-child conflict across adolescence: A meta-analysis. *Child Development, 69,* 817–832.

Laursen, B., Hartup, W. W., & Koplas, A. L. (1996). Towards understanding peer conflict. *Merrill-Palmer Quarterly, 42,* 76–102.

Laursen, B., & Williams, V. A. (1997). Perceptions of interdependence and closeness in family and peer relationships among adolescents with and without romantic partners. In S. Shulman & W. Andrew Collins (Eds.), *New Directions for Child Development: No. 78. Romantic relationships in adolescence: Developmental perspectives* (pp. 3–20). San Francisco: Jossey-Bass.

Lawson, M. (1980). Development of body build stereotypes, peer ratings, and self-esteem in Australian children. *Journal of Psychology, 104,* 111–118.

Lazar, I., & Darlington, R. (1982). Lasting effects of early education: A report from the Consortium for Longitudinal Studies. *Monographs of the Society for Research in Child Development, 47*(2–3, Serial No. 195).

Leaper, C. (2000). Gender, affiliation, assertion, and the interactive context of parent-child play. *Developmental Psychology, 36,* 381–393.

LeBoyer, F. (1975). *Birth without violoence.* New York: Knopf.

Lecanuet, J.-P. (1998). Foetal responses to auditory and speech stimuli. In A. Slater (Ed.), *Perceptual development: Visual, auditory, and speech perception in infancy* (pp. 317–355). East Sussex, UK: Psychology Press.

Lederberg, A. R., Prezbindowski, A. K., & Spencer, P. E. (2000). Word-learning skills of deaf preschoolers: The development of novel mapping and rapid word-learning strategies. *Child Development, 71,* 1571–1585.

Lee, B. C. P., Kuppusamy, K. G. R., El-Ghazzawy, O., Gordon, R. E., Lin, W., & Haacke, M. (1999). Hemispheric language dominance in children demonstrated by functional magnetic resonance imaging. *Journal of Child Neurology, 14,* 78–82.

Lee, K., Cameron, C. A., Xu, F., Fu, G., & Board, J. (1997). Chinese and Canadian children's evaluations of lying and truth telling: Similarities and differences in the context of pro- and antisocial behavior. *Child Development, 68,* 924–934.

Lee, L. C. (1971). The concommitant development of cognitive and moral modes of thought: A test of selected deductions from Piaget's theory. *Genetic Psychology Monographs, 83,* 93–146.

Lee, R. V. (1988). Sexually transmitted infections. In G. N. Burrow & T. F. Ferris (Eds.), *Medical complications during pregnancy* (pp. 389–424). Philadelphia: W.B. Saunders.

Leekam, S. R., Lopez, B., & Moore, C. (2000). Attention and joint attention in preschool children with autism. *Developmental Psychology, 36,* 261–273.

Legerstee, M., Anderson, D., & Schaffer, A. (1998). Five- and eight-month-old infants recognize their faces and voices as familiar and social stimuli. *Child Development, 69,* 37–50.

Leiblum, S. R. (1997). Introduction. In S. R. Leiblum (Ed.), *Infertility: Psychological issues and counseling strategies* (pp. 3–19). New York: Wiley.

Leinbach, M. D., Hort, B. E., & Fagot, B. I. (1997). Bears are for boys: Metaphorical associations in young children's gender stereotypes. *Cognitive Development, 12,* 107–130.

Lemish, D., & Rice, M. (1986). Television as a talking picture book: A prop for language acquisition. *Journal of Child Language, 13,* 251–274.

Lenneberg, E. (1967). *Biological foundations of language.* New York: Wiley.

Leonard, L. B. (1998). *Children with specific language impairment.* Cambridge, MA: MIT Press.

Leonard, L. B., Newhoff, M., & Meselam, L. (1980). Individual differences in early child phonology. *Applied Psycholinguistics, 1,* 7–30.

Lepper, M. R., & Gurtner, J. (1989). Children and computers: Approaching the twenty-first century. *American Psychologist, 44,* 170–178.

Lerner, R. M., & Lerner, J. V. (1977). Effects of age, sex, and physical attractiveness on child-peer relations, academic performance, and elementary school adjustment. *Developmental Psychology, 13,* 585–590.

Leslie, A. M. (1982). The perception of causality in infants. *Perception, 11,* 15–30.

Leslie, A. M. (1984). Spatiotemporal continuity and the perception of causality in infants. *Perception, 13,* 287–305.

Leslie, A. M. (1994). ToMM, ToBy, and Agency: Core architecture and domain specificity. In L. A. Hirschfield & S. A. Gelman (Eds.), *Mapping the mind: Domain specificity in cognition and culture* (pp. 119–148). Cambridge, UK: Cambridge University Press.

Leslie, A. M., & Keeble, S. (1987). Do six-month-olds perceive causality? *Cognition, 25,* 265–288.

Lesser, G. S., Fifer, F., & Clark, D. H. (1965). Mental abilities of children of different social-class and cultural groups. *Monographs of the Society for Research in Child Development, 30*(4, Serial No. 102).

Lester, B. M., & Brazelton, T. B. (1982). Cross-cultural assessment of neonatal behavior. In D. Wagner & H. W. Stevenson (Eds.), *Cultural perspectives on child development* (pp. 20–53). San Francisco: W.H. Freeman.

Lester, B. M., & Dreher, M. (1989). Effects of marijuana use during pregnancy on newborn cry. *Child Development, 60,* 765–771.

LeVay, S., & Hamer, D. H. (1994, May). Evidence for a biological influence in male homosexuality. *Scientific American, 270,* 43–57.

Leventhal, T., & Brooks-Gunn, J. (2000). The neighborhoods they live in: The effects of neighborhood residence on child and adolescent outcomes. *Psychological Bulletin, 126,* 309–337.

Levine, R., Dixon, S., LeVine, S., Richman, A., Leiderman, P. M., Keefer, C. H., & Brazelton, T. B. (1994). *Child care and culture: Lessons from Africa.* New York: Cambridge University Press.

Levine, R., & White, M. (1986). *Human conditions: The cultural basis for educational development.* New York: Routledge & Kegan Paul.

Levine, S. C., Huttenlocher, J., Taylor, A., & Langrock, A. (1999). Early sex differences in spatial skill. *Developmental Psychology, 35,* 940–949.

Levine, S. C., Jordan, N. C., & Huttenlocher, J. (1992). Development of calculation abilities in young children. *Journal of Experimental Child Psychology, 53,* 72–103.

Levitin, D. J., & Bellugi, U. (1998). Musical abilities in individuals with Williams' syndrome. *Music Perception, 15(4),* 357–389.

Levitt, M. J., Guacci-Franco, N., & Levitt, J. L. (1993). Convoys of social support in childhood and early adolescence: Structure and function. *Developmental Psychology, 29,* 811–818.

Levy, G. D., Taylor, M. G., & Gelman, S. A. (1995). Traditional and evaluative aspects of flexibility in gender roles, social conventions, moral rules, and physical laws. *Child Development, 66,* 515–531.

Levy, Y. (1999). Early metalinguistic competence: Speech monitoring and repair behavior. *Developmental Psychology, 35,* 822–834.

Lew, A. R., Bremner, J. G., & Lefkovitch, L. P. (2000). The development of relational landmark use in six- to twelve-month old infants in a spatial orientation task. *Child Development, 71,* 1179–1190.

Lew, A. R., & Butterworth, G. (1997). The development of hand-mouth coordination in 2- to 5-month-old infants: Similarities with reaching and grasping. *Infant Behavior and Development, 20,* 59–69.

Lewis, M. (1983). On the nature of intelligence. In M. Lewis (Ed.), *Origins of intelligence.* New York: Plenum Press.

Lewis, M. (1989, April). *Self and self-conscious emotions.* Paper presented at the biennial meeting of the Society for Research in Child Development, Kansas City, MO.

Lewis, M. (1993). Early socioemotional predictors of cognitive competency at 4 years. *Developmental Psychology, 29,* 1036–1045.

Lewis, M. D. (2000). The promise of dynamic systems approaches for an integrated account of human development. *Child Development, 71,* 36–45.

Lewis, M., Alessandri, S., & Sullivan, M. (1992). Differences in shame and pride as a function of children's gender and task difficulty. *Child Development, 63,* 630–638.

Lewis, M., & Feiring, C. (1982). Some American families at dinner. In L. M. Laosa & I. E. Sigel (Eds.), *Families as learning environments for children* (pp. 115–145). New York: Plenum Press.

Lewis, M., & Michalson, L. (1983). *Children's emotions and moods: Developmental theory and measurement.* New York: Plenum Press.

Lewis, M., & Ramsay, D. (2002). Cortisol response to embarrassment and shame. *Child Development, 73,* 1034–1045.

Lewis, T. L., Maurer, D., & Kay, D. (1978). Newborns' central vision: Whole or hole? *Journal of Experimental Child Psychology, 26,* 193–203.

Lewkowicz, D. J. (2000). The development of intersensory temporal perception: An epigenetic systems/limitations view. *Psychological Bulletin, 126,* 281–308.

Liben, L. S., & Downs, R. M. (1993). Understanding person-space-map relations: Cartographic and developmental perspectives. *Developmental Psychology, 29,* 739–752.

Liben, L. S., Susman, E. J., Finkelstein, J. W., Chinchilli, V. M., Kunselman, S., Schwab, J., et al. (2002). The effects of sex steroids on spatial perform-

ance: A review and an experimental clinical investigation. *Developmental Psychology, 38,* 236–253.

Lickliter, R., & Bahrick, L. E. (2000). The development of infant intersensory perception: Advantages of a comparative convergent-operations approach. *Psychological Bulletin, 126,* 260–280.

Lickona, T. (1976). Research on Piaget's theory of moral development. In T. Lickona (Ed.), *Moral development and behavior: Theory, research, and social issues* (pp. 219–240). New York: Holt, Rinehart & Winston.

Lieberman, D. (1985). Research on children and microcomputers: A review of utilization and effect studies. In M. Chen & W. Paisley (Eds.), *Children and microcomputers: Research on the newest medium.* Beverly Hills: Sage.

Lieberman, M., Doyle, A., & Markiewicz, D. (1999). Developmental patterns in security of attachment to mother and father in late childhood and early adolescence: Associations with peer relations. *Child Development, 70,* 202–213.

Liebert, R. M., & Sprafkin, J. (1988). *The early window: Effects of television on children and youth* (3rd ed.). New York: Pergamon Press.

Liggon, C., Weston, J., Ambady, N., Colloton, M., Rosenthal, R., & Reite, M. (1992). Content-free voice analysis of mothers talking about their failure-to-thrive children. *Infant Behavior and Development, 15,* 507–511.

Light, P. (1997). Annotation: Computers for learning: Psychological perspectives. *Journal of Child Psychology and Psychiatry, 38,* 497–504.

Lightfoot, D. (1982). *The language lottery: Toward a biology of grammars.* Cambridge, MA: MIT Press.

Lillard, A. S. (1997). Other folks' theories of mind and behavior. *Psychological Science, 8,* 268–274.

Lillard, A. S. (1998). Ethnopsychologies: Cultural variation in theories of mind. *Psychological Bulletin, 123,* 3–32.

Lillard, A. S., & Flavell, J. H. (1992). Young children's understanding of different mental states. *Developmental Psychology, 28,* 626–634.

Limb, C. J., & Holmes, L. B. (1994). Anencephaly: Changes in prenatal detection and birth status, 1972 through 1990. *American Journal of Obstetrics and Gynecology, 170,* 1333–1338.

Lin, C. C., & Fu, V. R. (1990). A comparison of child-rearing practices among Chinese, immigrant Chinese, and Caucasian-American parents. *Child Development, 61,* 429–433.

Lindegren, M. L., Steinberg, S., & Byers, R. H. (2000). Epidemiology of HIV/AIDS in children. *Pediatric Clinics of North America, 47,* 1–20.

Lindsay, E. W., Mize, J., & Pettit, G. S. (1997). Differential play patterns of mothers and fathers of sons and daughters: Implications for children's gender role development. *Sex Roles, 37,* 643–661.

Linn, M. C., & Petersen, A. C. (1985). Emergence and characterization of sex differences in spatial ability: A meta-analysis. *Child Development, 56,* 1479–1498.

Linn, M. C., & Petersen, A. C. (1986). A meta-analysis of differences in spatial ability: Implications for mathematics and science achievement. In J. S. Hyde & M. C. Linn (Eds.), *The psychology of gender: Advances through meta-analysis* (pp. 67–101). Baltimore: Johns Hopkins University Press.

Linney, J. A., & Seidman, E. N. (1989). The future of schooling. *American Psychologist, 44,* 336–340.

Little, T. D., & Lopez, D. F. (1997). Regularities in the development of children's causality beliefs about school performance across six sociocultural contexts. *Developmental Psychology, 33,* 165–175.

Littleton, K., & Häkkinen, P. (1999). Learning together: Understanding the processes of computer-based collaborative learning. In P. Dillenbourg (Ed.), *Collaborative learning: Cognitive and computational approaches* (pp. 20–30). New York: Pergamon.

Littschwager, J. C., & Markman, E. M. (1994). Sixteen- and 24-month-olds' use of mutual exclusivity as a default assumption in second-label learning. *Developmental Psychology, 30,* 955–958.

Lobel, T. E., Bempechat, J., Gewirtz, J. C., Shoken-Tpaz, T., & Bashe, E. (1993). The role of gender-related information and self-endorsement of traits in preadolescents' inferences and judgments. *Child Development, 64,* 1285–1294.

Lobel, T. E., Gruber, R., Govrin, N., & Mashraki Pedhatzur, S. (2001). Children's gender-related inferences and judgments: A cross-cultural study. *Developmental Psychology, 37,* 839–846.

Locke, J. (1961). *An essay concerning human understanding.* London: J. M. Deut and Sons. (Original work published in 1690)

Locke, J. (1964). Some thoughts concerning education. In P. Gay (Ed.), *John Locke on education*. New York: Teacher's College. (Original work published in 1693).

Lockman, J. J., & Thelen, E. (1993). Developmental biodynamics: Brain, body, behavior connections. *Child Development, 64*, 953–959.

Loeb, R. C., Horst, L., & Horton, P. J. (1980). Family interaction patterns associated with self-esteem in preadolescent girls and boys. *Merrill-Palmer Quarterly, 26*, 203–217.

Loeber, R., & Hay, D. F. (1997). Key issues in the development of aggression and violence from childhood to early adulthood. *Annual Review of Psychology, 48*, 371–410.

Loehlin, J. C., Lindzey, G., & Spuhler, J. N. (1975). *Racial differences in intelligence.* San Francisco: W.H. Freeman.

Loewenstein, J., & Gentner, D. (2001). Spatial mapping in preschoolers: Close comparisons facilitate far mappings. *Journal of Cognition and Development, 2*, 189–219.

Lombroso, P. J. (2000). Genetics of childhood disorders: 16. Angleman syndrome: A failure to process. *Journal of the American Academy of Child and Adolescent Psychiatry, 39*, 931–933.

Lorch, E. P., Bellack, D. R., & Augsbach, L. H. (1987). Young children's memory for televised stories: Effects of importance. *Child Development, 58*, 453–463.

Lord, S. E., Eccles, J. S., & McCarthy, K. A. (1994). Surviving the junior high school transition: Family processes and self-perceptions as protective and risk factors. *Journal of Early Adolescence, 14*, 162–199.

Lorenz, J. M., Wooliever, D. E., Jetton, J. R., & Paneth, N. (1997). A quantitative review of mortality and developmental disability in extremely premature newborns. *Archives of Pediatric and Adolescent Medicine, 152*, 425–435.

Lorenz, K. Z. (1966). *On aggression* (M. K. Wilson, Trans.). New York: Harcourt, Brace, & World. (Original work published 1963)

Lovdal, L. T. (1989). Sex role messages in television commercials: An update. *Sex Roles, 21*, 715–724.

Lu, G. C., Rouse, D. J., DuBard, M., Cliver, S., Kimberlin, D., & Hauth, J. C. (2001). The effect of the increasing prevalence of maternal obesity on prenatal morbidity. *American Journal of Obstetrics and Gynecology, 185*, 845–849.

Lubinski, D., Webb, R. M., Morelock, M. J., & Benbow, C. P. (2001). Top 1 in 10,000: A 10-year follow-up of the profoundly gifted. *Journal of Applied Psychology, 86*, 718–729.

Ludington-Hoe, S. M., & Swinth, J. Y. (1996). Developmental aspects of kangaroo care. *Journal of Obstetric and Gynecological Neonatal Nursing, 25*, 691–703.

Luecke-Aleksa, D. R., Anderson, D. R., Collins, P. A., & Schmitt, K. L. (1995). Gender constancy and television viewing. *Developmental Psychology, 31*, 773–780.

Luke, B., Avni, M., Min, L., & Misiumas, R. (1999). Work and pregnancy: The role of fatigue and the "second shift" on antenatal morbidity. *American Journal of Obstetrics and Gynecology, 181*, 1172–1179.

Lummis, M., & Stevenson, H. W. (1990). Gender differences in beliefs and achievement: A cross-cultural study. *Developmental Psychology, 26*, 254–263.

Luria, A. R. (1961). *The role of speech in the regulation of normal and abnormal behavior.* New York: Liveright.

Luria, A. R. (1969). Speech and formation of mental processes. In M. Cole & I. Maltzman (Eds.), *A handbook of contemporary Soviet psychology.* New York: Basic Books.

Lussier, G., Deater-Deckard, K., Dunn, J., & Davies, L. (2002). Support across two generations: Children's closeness to grandparents following parental divorce and remarriage. *Journal of Family Psychology, 16*, 363–376.

Luster, T., & McAdoo, H. P. (1994). Factors related to the achievement and adjustment of young African American children. *Child Development, 65*, 1080–1994.

Luster, T., & McAdoo, H. P. (1996). Family and child influences on educational attainment: A secondary analysis of the High/Scope Perry Preschool data. *Developmental Psychology, 32*, 26–39.

Luthar, S. S., Cicchetti, D., & Becker, B. (2000). The construct of resilience: A critical evaluation and guidelines for future work. *Child Development, 71*, 543–562.

Lutkenhaus, P., Bullock, M., & Geppert, U. (1987). Toddlers' actions: Knowledge, control, and the self. In F. Halisch & J. Kuhl (Eds.), *Motivation, intention, and volition* (pp. 145–161). Berlin: Springer.

Lykken, D. T. , McGue, M. Tellegen, A., & Bouchard, T. J., Jr. (1992). Emergenesis: Genetic traits that may not run in families. *American Psychologist, 47*, 1565–1577.

Lyon, T. D., & Flavell, J. H. (1993). Young children's understanding of forgetting over time. *Child Development, 64*, 789–800.

Lyons-Ruth, K., Alpern, L., & Repacholi, B. (1993). Disorganized infant attachment classification and maternal psychosocial problems as predictors of hostile-aggressive behavior in preschool children. *Child Development, 64*, 572–585.

Lyons-Ruth, K., & Jacobvitz, D. (1999). Attachment disorganization: Unresolved loss, relational violence, and lapses in behavioral and attentional strategies. In J. Cassidy & P. R. Shaver (Eds.), *Handbook of attachment: Theory, research, and clinical applications* (pp. 520–554). New York: Guilford Press.

Lytton, H., & Romney, D. M. (1991). Parents' differential socialization of boys and girls: A meta-analysis. *Psychological Bulletin, 109*, 267–296.

Ma, H. K., & Cheung, C.-K. (1996). A cross-cultural study of moral stage structure in Hong Kong Chinese, English, and Americans. *Journal of Cross-Cultural Psychology, 27*, 700–713.

Maccoby, E. E. (1984). Socialization and developmental change. *Child Development, 55*, 317–328.

Maccoby, E. E. (1988). Gender as a social category. *Developmental Psychology, 24*, 755–765.

Maccoby, E. E. (1990). Gender and relationships: A developmental account. *American Psychologist, 45*, 513–520.

Maccoby, E. E. (2002). Gender and group process: A developmental perspective. *Current Directions in Psychological Science, 11*, 54–58.

Maccoby, E. E., & Jacklin, C. N. (1974). *The psychology of sex differences.* Stanford, CA: Stanford University Press.

Maccoby, E. E., & Jacklin, C. N. (1987). Gender segregation in childhood. In H. W. Reese (Ed.), *Advances in child development and behavior* (Vol. 20, pp. 239–287). Orlando, FL: Academic Press.

Maccoby, E. E., & Martin, J. A. (1983). Socialization in the context of the family: Parent-child interaction. In E. M. Hetherington (Ed.), *Handbook of child psychology: Vol. IV. Socialization, personality, and social development* (4th ed., pp. 1–101). New York: Wiley.

Mackey, M. M. (2001). Use of water in labor and birth. *Clinical Obstetrics, 44*, 733–749.

MacFarlane, J. A. (1975). Olfaction in the development of social preferences in the human neonate. In M. A. Hofer (Ed.), *Parent-infant interaction.* Amsterdam: Elsevier.

MacKinnon, C. E. (1988). Influences on sibling relations in families with married and divorced parents. *Journal of Social Issues, 9*, 469–477.

MacKinnon, C. E. (1989). Sibling interactions in married and divorced families: Influence of ordinal position, socioeconomic status, and play context. *Journal of Divorce, 12*, 221–251.

MacKinnon-Lewis, C., Rabiner, D., & Starnes, R. (1999). Predicting boys' social acceptance and aggression: The role of mother-child interactions and boys' beliefs about peers. *Developmental Psychology, 35*, 632–639.

MacKinnon-Lewis, C., Volling, B. L., Lamb, M. E., Dechman, K., Rabiner, D., & Curtner, M. E. (1994). A cross-contextual analysis of boys' social competence: From family to school. *Developmental Psychology, 30*, 325–333.

MacLusky, N. J., & Naftolin, F. (1981). Sexual differentiation of the nervous system. *Science, 211*, 1294–1303.

MacMillan, H. L., MacMillan, J. H., Offord, D. R., Griffith, L., & MacMillan, A. (1994). Primary prevention of child abuse and neglect: A critical review. Part I. *Journal of Child Psychology, Psychiatry, and Allied Disciplines, 35*, 835–856.

MacWhinney, B. (1998). Models of the emergence of language. *Annual Review of Psychology, 49*, 199–227.

Madi, B. C., Sandall, J., Bennett, R., & MacLeod, C. (1999). Effects of female relative support in labor: A randomized controlled trial. *Birth, 26*, 4–8.

Maffeis, C., Schutz, Y., Zaffanello, M., Piccoli, R., & Pinelli, L. (1994). Elevated energy expenditure and reduced energy intake in obese prepubertal children: Paradox of poor dietary reliability in obesity? *Journal of Pediatrics, 124*, 348–354.

Maggioni, A., & Lifshitz, F. (1995). Nutritional management of failure to thrive. *Pediatric Nutrition, 42,* 791–810.

Magnusson, D., Stattin, H., & Allen, V. (1986). Differential maturation among girls and its relations to social adjustment: A longitudinal perspective. In P. B. Baltes, D. L. Featherman, & R. M. Lerner (Eds.), *Life-span development and behavior* (Vol. 7, pp. 136–172). Hillsdale, NJ: Erlbaum.

Mahoney, J. L. (2000). School extracurricular activity participation as a moderator in the development of antisocial behavior patterns. *Child Development, 71,* 502–516.

Mahoney, J. L., & Cairns, R. B. (1997). Do extracurricular activities protect against early school dropout? *Developmental Psychology, 33,* 241–253.

Main, M., Kaplan, N., & Cassidy, J. (1985). Security in infancy, childhood, and adulthood: A move to the level of representation. In I. Bretherton & E. Waters (Eds.), *Growing points of attachment theory and research. Monographs of the Society for Research in Child Development, 50*(1–2, Serial No. 209).

Main, M., & Solomon, J. (1986). Discovery of a disorganized/disoriented attachment pattern. In T. B. Brazelton & M. W. Yogman (Eds.), *Affective development in infancy* (pp. 95–124). Norwood, NJ: Ablex.

Malatesta, C. Z., Culver, C., Tesman, J. R., & Shepard, B. (1989). The development of emotion expression during the first two years of life. *Monographs of the Society for Research in Child Development, 54*(1–2, Serial No. 219).

Malina, R. M. (1980). Biosocial correlates of motor development during infancy and early childhood. In L. S. Greene & F. E. Johnstone (Eds.), *Social and biological predictors of nutritional status, physical growth, and neurological development* (pp. 143–171). New York: Academic Press.

Malina, R. M., & Bouchard, C. (1991). *Growth, maturation, and physical activity.* Champaign, IL: Human Kinetics.

Mandler, J. M. (1988). How to build a baby: On the development of an accessible representational system. *Cognitive Development, 3,* 113–136.

Mandler, J. M. (1997). Development of categorization: Perceptual and conceptual categories. In G. Bremner, A. Slater, & G. Butterworth (Eds.), *Infant development: Recent advances* (pp. 163–189). East Sussex, UK: Psychology Press.

Mandler, J. M. (1998). Representation. In W. Damon (Series Ed.) & D. Kuhn & R. S. Siegler (Vol. Eds.), *Handbook of child psychology: Vol. 2. Cognition, perception, and language* (5th ed., pp. 255–308). New York: Wiley.

Mandler, J. M., Fivush, R., & Reznick, J. S. (1987). The development of contextual categories. *Cognitive Development, 2,* 339–354.

Mandler, J. M., & McDonough, L. (1993). Concept formation in infancy. *Cognitive Development, 8,* 291–318.

Mandler, J. M., & McDonough, L. (1995). Long-term recall of event sequences in infancy. *Journal of Experimental Child Psychology, 59,* 457–474.

Mandler, J. M., & McDonough, L. (1998). Studies in inductive inference in infancy. *Cognitive Psychology, 37,* 60–96.

Mandler, J. M., & McDonough, L. (2000). Advancing downward to the basic level. *Journal of Cognition and Development, 1,* 379–403.

Mangelsdorf, S. C., Plunkett, J. W., Dedrick, C. F., Berlin, M., Meisels, S. J., McHale, J. L., & Dichtellmiller, M. (1996). Attachment security in very low birth weight infants. *Developmental Psychology, 32,* 914–920.

Mannarino, A. P. (1978). Friendship patterns and self-concept development in preadolescent males. *Journal of Genetic Psychology, 133,* 105–110.

Maratsos, M. P. (1983). Some current issues in the study of the acquisition of grammar. In J. H. Flavell & E. M. Markman (Eds.), *Handbook of child psychology: Vol. III. Cognitive development* (4th ed., pp. 707–786). New York: Wiley.

Maratsos, M. P. (1989). Innateness and plasticity in language acquisition. In M. L. Rice & R. L. Schiefelbusch (Eds.), *The teachability of language* (pp. 105–125). Baltimore: Paul H. Brookes.

Marcus, G. F. (1996). Why do children say "breaked"? *Current Directions in Psychological Science, 5,* 81–85.

Marcus, G. F., Pinker, S., Ullman, M., Hollander, M., Rosen, T. J., & Xu, F. (1992). Overregularization in language acquisition. *Monographs of the Society for Research in Child Development, 57*(4 Serial No. 228).

Marcus, G. F., Vijayan, S., Bandi Rao, S., & Vishton, P. M. (1998). Rule learning by seven-month-old infants. *Science, 283,* 77–80.

Marean, G. C., Werner, L. A., & Kuhl, P. K. (1992). Vowel categorization by very young infants. *Developmental Psychology, 28,* 395–405.

Mareschal, D., & Johnson, S. P. (2002). Learning to perceive object unity: A connectionist account. *Developmental Science, 5,* 151–172.

Markman, E. M. (1987). How children constrain the possible meanings of words. In U. Neisser (Ed.), *Concepts and conceptual development: Ecological and intellectual factors in categorization* (pp. 255–287). Cambridge, UK: Cambridge University Press.

Markman, E. M. (1990). Constraints children place on word meanings. *Cognitive Science, 14,* 57–77.

Markman, E. M., & Hutchinson, J. E. (1984). Children's sensitivity to constraints on word meaning: Taxonomic versus thematic relations. *Cognitive Psychology, 16,* 1–27.

Markman, E. M., & Wachtel G. F. (1988). Children's use of mutual exclusivity to constrain the meanings of words. *Cognitive Psychology, 20,* 121–157.

Marlier, L., Schaal, B., & Soussignan, R. (1998). Neonatal responsiveness to the odor of amniotic and lacteal fluids: A test of perinatal chemosensory continuity. *Child Development, 69,* 611–623.

Marr, D. B., & Sternberg, R. J. (1987). The role of mental speed in intelligence: A triarchic perspective. In P. A. Vernon (Ed.), *Speed of information-processing and intelligence* (pp. 271–294). Norwood, NJ: Ablex.

Marsh, H. W., Craven, R., & Debus, R. (1998). Structure, stability, and development of young children's self-concepts: A multicohort-multioccasion study. *Child Development, 69,* 1030–1053.

Marsh, H. W., Ellis, L. A., & Craven, R. G. (2002). How do preschool children feel about themselves? Unraveling measurement and multidimensional self-concept structure. *Developmental Psychology, 38,* 376–393.

Marshall, D. H., Drummey, A. B., Fox, N. A., & Newcombe, N. S. (2002). An event-related potential study of item recognition memory in children and adults. *Journal of Cognition and Development, 3,* 201–224.

Marshall, S. (1995). Ethnic socialization of African American children: Implications for parenting, identity development, and academic achievement. *Journal of Youth and Adolescence, 24,* 377–396.

Martin, C. L. (1991). The role of cognition in understanding gender effects. In H. W. Reese (Ed.), *Advances in child development and behavior* (Vol. 23, pp. 113–149). San Diego, CA: Academic Press.

Martin, C. L. (1995). Stereotypes about children with traditional and nontraditional gender roles. *Sex Roles, 33,* 727–751.

Martin, C. L., Eisenbud, L., & Rose, H. (1995). Children's gender-based reasoning about toys. *Child Development, 66,* 1453–1471.

Martin, C. L., & Fabes, R. A. (2001). The stability and consequences of young children's same-sex peer interactions. *Developmental Psychology, 37,* 431–446.

Martin, C. L., & Halverson, C. F. (1981). A schematic processing model of sex typing and stereotyping in children. *Child Development, 52,* 1119–1134.

Martin, C. L., & Halverson, C. F. (1987). The roles of cognition in sex role acquisition. In D. B. Carter (Ed.), *Current conceptions of sex roles and sex typing: Theory and research* (pp. 123–137). New York: Praeger.

Martin, C. L., & Ruble, D. N. (1997). A developmental perspective of self-construals and sex differences: Comment on Cross and Madson (1997). *Psychological Bulletin, 122,* 45–50.

Martin, J., Martin, D. C., Lund, C. A., & Streissguth, A. P. (1977). Maternal alcohol ingestion and cigarette smoking and their effects on newborn conditioning. *Alcoholism: Clinical and Experimental Research, 1,* 243–247.

Marvin, R. S. (1977). An ethological-cognitive model for the attenuation of mother-child attachment behavior. In T. M. Alloway, L. Krames, & P. Pliner (Eds.), *Advances in the study of communication and affect: Vol. 3. The development of social attachments* (pp. 25–60). New York: Plenum Press.

Masataka, N. (1996). Perception of motherese in a signed language by 6-month-old infants. *Developmental Psychology, 32,* 874–879.

Mason, C. A., Cauce, A. M., Gonzales, N., & Hiraga, Y. (1996). Neither too sweet nor too sour: Problem peers, maternal control, and problem behavior in African American adolescents. *Child Development, 67,* 2115–2130.

Massad, C. M. (1981). Sex role identity and adjustment during adolescence. *Child Development, 52,* 1290–1298.

Massaro, D. W., & Cowan, N. (1993). Information processing models: Microscopes of mind. In L. W. Porter & M. R. Rosenzweig (Eds.), *Annual Review of Psychology, 34,* 383–425.

Masten, A. S., & Coatsworth, J. D. (1998). The development of competence in favorable and unfavorable environments: Lessons from research on successful children. *American Psychologist, 53,* 205–220.

Matusov, E., Bell, N., & Rogoff, B. (2002). Schooling as cultural process: Working together and guidance by children from schools differing in collaborative practices. In R. V. Kail & H. W. Reese (Eds.), *Advances in child development* (Vol. 29, pp. 129–160). San Diego: Academic Press.

Masur, E. F. (1982). Mothers' responses to infants' object-related gestures: Influences on lexical development. *Journal of Child Language, 9,* 23–30.

Matas, L., Arend, R. A., & Sroufe, L. A. (1978). Continuity of adaptation in the second year: The relationship between quality of attachment and later competence. *Child Development, 49,* 547–556.

Matias, R., & Cohn, J. F. (1993). Are max-specified infant facial expressions during face-to-face interaction consistent with differential emotions theory? *Developmental Psychology, 29,* 524–531.

Matsumoto, D., Haan, N., Yabrove, G., Theodorou, P., & Carney, C. C. (1986). Preschoolers' moral actions and emotions in prisoner's dilemma. *Developmental Psychology, 22,* 663–670.

Mattson, S. N., Riley, E. P., Gramling, L., Delis, D. C., & Jones, K. L. (1997). Heavy prenatal alcohol exposure with or without physical features of fetal alcohol syndrome leads to IQ deficits. *Journal of Pediatrics, 131,* 718–721.

Mattys, S. L., & Jusczyk, P. W. (2001). Do infants segment words or recurring contiguous patterns? *Journal of Experimental Psychology: Human Perception and Performance, 27,* 644–655.

Maurer, D. (1983). The scanning of compound figures by young infants. *Journal of Experimental Child Psychology, 35,* 437–448.

Maurer, D., Lewis, T. L., Brent, H. P., & Levin, A. V. (1999). Rapid improvement in the acuity of infants after visual input. *Science, 286,* 108–110.

May, D. C., Kundert, D. K., & Brent, D. (1995). Does delayed school entry reduce later grade retentions and use of special education services? *Remedial and Special Education, 16,* 288–294.

Mayberry, R. I., & Nicoladis, E. (2000). Gesture reflects language development: Evidence from bilingual children. *Current Directions in Psychological Science, 9,* 192–196.

Mayer, J. D., & Salovey, P. (1997). What is emotional intelligence? In P. Salovey & D. J. Sluyter (Eds.), *Emotional development and emotional intelligence: Educational implications* (p. 3–34). New York: Basic Books.

McAnarney, E. R. (1987). Young maternal age and adverse neonatal outcome. *American Journal of Diseases of Children, 141,* 1053–1059.

McAnarney, E. R., & Stevens-Simon, C. (1990). Maternal psychological stress/depression and low birth weight. *American Journal of Diseases of Children, 144,* 789–792.

McArdle, J. J., Ferrer Caja, E., Hamagami, F., & Woodcock, R. W. (2002). Comparative longitudinal structural analyses of the growth and decline of multiple intellectual abilities over the life span. *Developmental Psychology, 38,* 115–142.

McBride, W. G. (1961). Thalidomide and congenital abnormalities. *Lancet, 2,* 1358.

McCall, R. B. (1979). *Infants.* Cambridge, MA: Harvard University Press.

McCall, R. B., Appelbaum, M. I., & Hogarty, P. S. (1973). Developmental changes in mental performance. *Monographs of the Society for Research in Child Development, 38*(3, Serial No. 150).

McCall, R. B., & Carriger, M. S. (1993). A meta-analysis of infant habituation and recognition memory performance as predictors of later IQ. *Child Development, 64,* 57–79.

McCall, R. B., Hogarty, P. S., & Hurlburt, N. (1972). Transitions in sensorimotor development and the prediction of childhood IQ. *American Psychologist, 27,* 728–748.

McCall, R. B., Parke, R. D., & Kavanaugh, R. D. (1977). Imitation of live and televised models in children one to three years of age. *Monographs of the Society for Research in Child Development, 42*(3, Serial No. 171).

McCartney, K., Harris, M. J., & Bernieri, F. (1990). Growing up and growing apart: A developmental meta-analysis of twin studies. *Psychological Bulletin, 107,* 226–237.

McCartney, K., Scarr, S., Phillips, D., & Grajek, S. (1985). Day care as intervention: Comparisons of varying quality programs. *Journal of Applied Developmental Psychology, 6,* 247–260.

McCartney, K., & Nelson, K. (1981). Children's use of scripts in story recall. *Discourse Processes, 4,* 59–70.

McCarty, M. E., Clifton, R. K., Ashmead, D. H., Lee, P., & Goubet, N. (2001) How infants use vision for grasping objects. *Child Development, 72,* 973–987.

McClelland, D. C. (1973). Testing for competence rather than for "intelligence." *American Psychologist, 28,* 1–14.

McClintock, M. K., & Herdt, G. (1996). Rethinking puberty: The development of sexual attraction. *Current Directions in Psychological Science, 5,* 178–183.

McCord, J. (1977). A comparative study of two generations of native Americans. In R. F. Meier (Ed.), *Theory in criminology* (pp. 83–92). Beverly Hills, CA: Sage.

McCormick, M. C. (1997). The outcomes of very low birth weight infants: Are we asking the right questions? *Pediatrics, 99,* 869–875.

McCormick, M. C., McCarton, C., Tonascia, J., & Brooks-Gunn, J. (1993). Early educational intervention for very low birth weight infants: Results from the Infant Health and Development Program. *Journal of Pediatrics, 123,* 527–533.

McDermott, S., & Greenberg, B. (1984). Parents, peers and television as determinants of Black children's esteem. In R. Bostrom (Ed.), *Communication yearbook* (Vol. 8, pp. 164–177). Beverly Hills, CA: Sage.

McDonald, M. A., Sigman, M., Espinosa, M. P., & Neumann, C. G. (1994). Impact of temporary food shortage on children and their mothers. *Child Development, 65,* 404–415.

McGhee, P. E. (1979). *Humor: Its origin and development.* San Francisco: W.H. Freeman.

McGinniss, M. J., & Kaback, M. M. (1997). Carrier screening. In D. L. Rimoin, J. M. Connor, & R. E. Pyeritz (Eds.), *Emery and Rimoin's principles and practices of medical genetics* (3rd ed., Vol. 1, pp. 535–543). New York: Churchill Livingstone.

McGraw, M. B. (1935). *Growth: A study of Johnny and Jimmy.* New York: Appleton-Century-Crofts.

McGraw, M. B. (1939). Swimming behavior of the human infant. *Journal of Pediatrics, 15,* 485–490.

McGregor, J. A., & French, J. I. (1991). *Chlamydia trachomatis* infection during pregnancy. *American Journal of Obstetrics and Gynecology, 165,* 1782–1789.

McGue, M. (1999). The behavioral genetics of alcoholism. *Current Directions in Psychological Science, 8,* 109–115.

McGuire, J. (1988). Gender stereotypes of parents with two-year-olds and beliefs about gender differences in behavior. *Sex Roles, 19,* 233–240.

McGuire, K. D., & Weisz, J. R. (1982). Social cognition and behavior correlates of preadolescent chumship. *Child Development, 53,* 1478–1484.

McGuire, P. K., Robertson, D. A. T., David, A. S., Kitson, N., Frackowiak, R. S. J., & Frith, C. D. (1997). Neural correlates of thinking in sign language. *NeuroReport, 8,* 695–697.

McGurk, H., & MacDonald, J. (1976). Hearing lips and seeing voices. *Nature* (London), *264,* 746–748.

McHale, S. M., Crouter, A. C., & Tucker, C. J. (1999). Family context and gender role socialization in middle childhood: Comparing boys to girls and sisters to brothers. *Child Development, 70,* 990–1004.

McHale, S. M., Crouter, A. C., & Tucker, C. J. (2001). Free-time activities in middle childhood: Links with adjustment in early adolescence. *Child Development, 72,* 1764–1778.

McHale, S. M., Crouter, A. C., McGuire, S. A., & Updegraff, K. A. (1995). Congruence between mothers' and fathers' differential treatment of siblings: Links with family relations and children's well-being. *Child Development, 66,* 116–128.

McHale, S. M., Updegraff, K. A., Jackson-Newsom, J., Tucker, C. J., & Crouter, A. C. (2000). When does parents' differential treatment have negative implications for siblings? *Social Development, 9,* 149–172.

McIlhaney, J. S., Jr. (2000). Sexually transmitted infection and teenage sexuality. *American Journal of Obstetrics and Gynecology, 183,* 334–339.

McKey, R. H., Condelli, L., Granson, H., Barrett, B., McConkey, C., & Plantz, M. (1985). *The impact of Head Start on children, families and communities* (Final report of the Head Start Evaluation, Synthesis and Utilization Project). Washington, DC: U.S. Government Printing Office.

McKusick, V. A., & Amberger, J. S. (1997). Morbid anatomy of the human genome. In D. L. Rimoin, J. M. Connor, & R. E. Pyeritz (Eds.), *Emery and Rimoin's principles and practices of medical genetics* (3rd ed., Vol. 1, pp. 137–234). New York: Churchill Livingstone.

McLoyd, V. C. (1990). The impact of economic hardship on black families and children: Psychological distress, parenting, and socioemotional development. *Child Development, 61,* 311–346.

McLoyd, V. C. (1998). Changing demographics in the American population: Implications for research on minority children and adolescents. In V. C. McLoyd & L. Steinberg (Eds.), *Studying minority adolescents* (pp. 3–28). Mahwah, NJ: Erlbaum.

McLoyd, V. C., Epstein Jayaratne, T., Ceballo, R., & Borquez, J. (1994). Unemployment and work interruption among African American single mothers: Effects on parenting and adolescent socioemotional functioning. *Child Development, 65,* 562–589.

McManus, I. C., & Bryden, M. P. (1991). Geschwind's theory of cerebral lateralization: Developing a formal, causal model. *Psychological Bulletin, 110,* 237–253.

McNally, S., Eisenberg, N., & Harris, J. D. (1991). Consistency and change in maternal child-rearing practices and values: A longitudinal study. *Child Development, 62,* 190–198.

Mead, G. H. (1934). *Mind, self, and society.* Chicago: University of Chicago Press.

Medin, D. L. (1989). Concepts and conceptual structure. *American Psychologist, 44,* 1469–1481.

Meichenbaum, D. (1977). *Cognitive-behavior modification: An integrative approach.* New York: Plenum Press.

Meins, E. (1998). The effects of security of attachment and maternal attribution of meaning on children's linguistic acquisitional style. *Infant Behavior and Development, 21,* 237–252.

Mekos, D., Hetherington, E. M., & Reiss, D. (1996). Sibling differences in problem behavior and parental treatment in nondivorced and remarried families. *Child Development, 67,* 2148–2165.

Meltzoff, A., & Borton, R. (1979). Intermodal matching by human neonates. *Nature* (London), *282,* 403–404.

Meltzoff, A. N. (1995). What infant memory tells us about infantile amnesia: Long-term recall and deferred imitation. *Journal of Experimental Child Psychology, 59,* 497–515.

Meltzoff, A. N., & Kuhl, P. K. (1994). Faces and speech: Intermodal processing of biologically relevant signals in infants and adults. In D. J. Lewkowicz & R. Lickliter (Eds.), *The development of intersensory perception: Comparative perspectives* (pp. 335–370). Hillsdale, NJ: Erlbaum.

Meltzoff, A. N., & Moore, M. K. (1999). Persons and representation: Why infant imitation is important for theories of human development. In J. Nadel & G. Butterworth (Eds.), *Imitation in infancy* (pp. 9–35). Cambridge, UK: Cambridge University Press.

Mennella, J. A., & Beauchamp, G. K. (1996). The human infant's response to vanilla flavors in mother's milk and formula. *Infant Behavior and Development, 19,* 13–19.

Merimee, T. J., Zapf, J., & Froesch, E. R. (1981). Dwarfism in the Pygmy: An isolated deficiency of insulin-like Growth Factor I. *New England Journal of Medicine, 305,* 965–968.

Mervis, C. (1984). Early lexical development: The contributions of mother and child. In C. Sophian (Ed.), *Origins of cognitive skills* (pp. 330–370). Hillsdale, NJ: Erlbaum.

Mervis, C. B. (2001, August). *Cognition and personality in Williams syndrome.* Paper presented at the workshop on Separability of Cognitive Functions: What Can Be Learned from Williams Syndrome? University of Massachusetts, Amherst.

Mervis, C., & Crisafi, M. (1982). Order of acquisition of subordinate-, basic-, and superordinate-level categories. *Child Development, 53,* 267–273.

Messer, D. J. (1981). The identification of names in maternal speech to infants. *Journal of Psycholinguistic Research, 10,* 69–77.

Messer, S. C., & Gross, A. M. (1995) Childhood depression and family interaction: A naturalistic observation study. *Journal of Clinical Child Psychology, 24,* 77–88.

Messinger, D. S., & Fogel, A. (1998). Give and take: The development of conventional infant gestures. *Merrill-Palmer Quarterly, 44,* 566–590.

Messinger, D. S., Fogel, A., & Dickson, K. L. (1999). What's in a smile? *Developmental Psychology, 35,* 701–708.

Messinger, D. S., Fogel, A., & Dickson, K. L. (2001). All smiles are positive, but some smiles are more positive than others. *Developmental Psychology, 37,* 642–653.

Meyer, M., & Fienberg, S. (1992). *Assessing evaluation studies: The case of bilingual education strategies.* Washington, DC: National Academy Press.

Meyer, M. B., & Tonascia, J. A. (1977). Maternal smoking, pregnancy complications, and perinatal mortality. *American Journal of Obstetrics and Gynecology, 128,* 494–502.

Michel, G. F. (1988). A neuropsychological perspective on infant sensorimotor development. In C. Rovee-Collier & L. P. Lipsitt (Eds.), *Advances in infancy research* (Vol. 5, pp. 1–37). Norwood, NJ: Ablex.

Michelson, L., Sugai, D. P., Wood, R. P., & Kazdin, A. E. (1983). *Social skills assessment and training with children.* New York: Plenum Press.

Michelsson, K., Sirvio, P., & Wasz-Hockert, O. (1977). Pain cry in fullterm asphyxiated newborn infants correlated with late findings. *Acta Paediatrica Scandinavica, 66,* 611–616.

Michotte, A. (1963). *The perception of causality.* New York: Basic Books.

Mielke, K. W. (1994). On the relationship between television viewing and academic achievement. *Journal of Broadcasting & Electronic Media, 38,* 361–366.

Milgram, N. A. (1998). Children under stress. In T. H. Ollendick & M. Hersen (Eds.), *Handbook of child psychopathology* (3rd ed., pp. 505–533). New York: Plenum.

Milich, R. (1984). Cross-sectional and longitudinal observations of activity level and sustained attention in a normative sample. *Journal of Abnormal Child Psychology, 12,* 261–275.

Miller, A. L., Volling, B. L., & McElwain, N. L. (2000). Sibling jealousy in a triadic context with mothers and fathers. *Social Development, 9,* 433–457.

Miller, B. C., Benson, B., & Galbraith, K. A. (2001). Family relationships and adolescent pregnancy risk: A research synthesis. *Developmental Review, 21,* 1–38.

Miller, B. C., Fan, X., Christensen, M., Grotevant, H. D., & van Dulmen, M. (2000). Comparison of adopted and nonadopted adolescents in a large, nationally representative sample. *Developmental Psychology, 71,* 1458–1473.

Miller, J. B. (1986). *Toward a new psychology of women.* Boston: Beacon Press.

Miller, J. B. (1991). The development of women's sense of self. In J. V. Jordan, A. G. Kaplan, J. B. Miller, I. P. Stiver, & J. L. Surrey (Eds.), *Women's growth in connection* (pp. 11–26). New York: Guilford.

Miller, J. G. (1999). Cultural psychology: Implications for basic psychological theory. *Psychological Science, 10,* 85–91.

Miller, J. M., Jr., & Boudreaux, M. C. (1999). A study of antenatal cocaine use-chaos in action. *American Journal of Obstetrics and Gynecology, 180,* 1427–1431.

Miller, L. T., & Vernon, P. A. (1996). Intelligence, reaction time, and working memory in 4- to 6-year-old children. *Intelligence, 22,* 155–190.

Miller, N. B., Cowan, P. A., Cowan, C. P., Hetherington, E. M., & Clingempeel, W. G. (1993). Externalizing in preschoolers and early adolescents: A cross-study replication of a family model. *Developmental Psychology, 29,* 3–18.

Miller, N., & Maruyama, G. (1976). Ordinal position and peer popularity. *Journal of Personality and Social Psychology, 33,* 123–131.

Miller, P. A., Eisenberg, N., Fabes, R. A., & Shell, R. (1996). Relations of moral reasoning and vicarious emotion to young children's prosocial behavior toward peers and adults. *Developmental Psychology, 32,* 210–219.

Miller, P. H., & Harris, Y. R. (1988). Preschoolers' strategies of attention on a same-different task. *Developmental Psychology, 24,* 628–633.

Miller, P. H., Woody-Ramsey, J., & Aloise, P. A. (1991). The role of strategy effortfulness in strategy effectiveness. *Developmental Psychology, 27,* 738–745.

Miller, W. L., & Levine, L. S. (1987). Molecular and clinical advances in congenital adrenal hyperplasia. *Journal of Pediatrics, 111,* 1–17.

Miller-Jones, D. (1989). Culture and testing. *American Psychologist, 44,* 360–366.

Mills, D. L., Coffey-Corina, S. A., & Neville, H. J. (1993). Language acquisition and cerebral specialization in 20-month-old infants. *Journal of Cognitive Neuroscience, 5,* 317–334.

Mills, D. L., Coffey-Corina, S. A., & Neville, H. J. (1994). Variability in cerebral organization during primary language acquisition. In G. Dawson & K. W. Fischer (Eds.), *Human behavior and the developing brain* (pp. 427–455). New York: Guilford.

Mills, D. L., Coffey-Corina, S., & Neville, H. J. (1997). Language comprehension and cerebral specialization from 13 to 20 months. *Developmental Neuropsychology, 13,* 397–445.

Mills, R. S. L., & Grusec, J. E. (1989). Cognitive, affective, and behavioral consequences of praising altruism. *Merrill-Palmer Quarterly, 35,* 299–326.

Mills, R. S. L., & Rubin, K. H. (1993). Socialization factors in the development of social withdrawal. In K. H. Rubin & J. B. Asendorpf (Eds.), *Social withdrawal, inhibition, and shyness in childhood* (pp. 117–148). Hillsdale, NJ: Erlbaum.

Minuchin, P. P. (1988). Relationships within the family: A systems perspective on development. In R. A. Hinde & J. Stevenson-Hinde (Eds.), *Relationships within families: Mutual influences.* Oxford: Clarendon Press.

Minuchin, P. P., & Shapiro, E. K. (1983). The school as a context for social development. In E. M. Hetherington (Ed.), *Handbook of child psychology: Vol. IV. Socialization, personality, and social development* (pp. 197–274). New York: Wiley.

Mischel, H. N., & Mischel, W. (1983). The development of children's knowledge of self-control strategies. *Child Development, 54,* 603–619.

Mischel, W. (1966). A social learning view of sex differences in behavior. In E. E. Maccoby (Ed.), *The development of sex differences* (pp. 56–81). Stanford, CA: Stanford University Press.

Mischel, W., Ebbesen, E. B., & Zeiss, A. R. (1972). Cognitive and attentional mechanisms in delay of gratification. *Journal of Personality and Social Psychology, 21,* 204–218.

Mischel, W., Shoda, Y., & Rodriguez, M. L. (1989). Delay of gratification in children. *Science, 244,* 933–938.

Mitchell, E. A., & Milerad, J. (1999). *Smoking and sudden infant death syndrome.* Paper series prepared for International Consultation on Environmental Tobacco Smoke and Child Health. Geneva, Switzerland. Retrieved October 21, 2002, from http://www5.who.int/tobacco/repository/tld67/mitchell.pdf

Mitchell, E. A., Thach, B. T., Thompson, J. M. D., Williams, S. (1999). Changing infants' sleep position increases risk of sudden infant death syndrome. *Archives of Pediatrics and Adolescent Medicine, 153,* 1136–1141.

Mitchell, E. A., Tuohy, P. G., Brunt, J. M., Thompson, J. M. D., Clements, M. S., Stewart, A. W., et al. (1997). Risk factors for sudden infant death syndrome following the prevention campaign in New Zealand: A prospective study. *Pediatrics, 100,* 835–840.

Mittendorf, R., Williams, M. A., Berkey, C. S., & Cotter, P. F. (1990). The length of uncomplicated human gestation. *Obstetrics and Gynecology, 75,* 929–932.

Mittendorf, R., Williams, M. A., Berkley, C. S., Lieberman, E., & Monson, R. R. (1993). Predictors of human gestational length. *American Journal of Obstetrics and Gynecology, 168,* 480–484.

Mix, K. S., Levine, S. C., & Huttenlocher, J. (1999). Early fraction calculation ability. *Developmental Psychology, 35,* 164–174.

Mix, K. S., Huttenlocher, J., & Levine, S. C. (2002). *Quantitative development in infancy and early childhood*: London, Oxford University Press.

Miyake, K., Chen, S., & Campos, J. J. (1985). Infant temperament, mother's mode of interaction, and attachment in Japan: An interim report. In I. Bretherton & E. Waters (Eds.), *Growing points of attachment theory and research. Monographs of the Society for Research in Child Development, 50*(1–2, Serial No. 209).

Miyake, A., Friedman, N. P., Rettinger, D. A., Shah, P., & Hegarty, M. (2001). How are visuospatial working memory, executive functioning, and spatial abilities related? A latent variable analysis. *Journal of Experimental Psychology: General, 130,* 621–640.

Moely, B. E., Olson, F. A., Halwes, T. G., & Flavell, J. H. (1969). Production deficiency in young children's clustered recall. *Developmental Psychology, 1,* 26–34.

Moffat, R., & Hackel, A. (1985). Thermal aspects of neonatal care. In A. Gottfried & J. Gaiter (Eds.), *Infant stress under intensive care* (pp. 171–197). Baltimore: University Park Press.

Moldavsky, M., Lev, D., & Lerman-Sagie, T. (2001). Behavioral phenotypes of genetic syndromes: A reference guide to physicians. *Journal of the American Academy of Adolescent Psychiatry, 40,* 749–761.

Mondloch, C. J., Lewis, T. L., Budreau, D. R., Maurer, D., Dannemiller, J. L., Stephens, B. R., & Kleiner-Gathercoal, K. A. (1999). Face perception during early infancy. *Psychological Science, 10,* 419–422.

Monfries, M. M., & Kafer, N. F. (1987). Neglected and rejected children: A social-skills model. *Journal of Psychology, 121,* 401–407.

Montague, D. P. F., & Walker-Andrews, A. S. (2001). Peekaboo: A new look at infants' perception of emotion expressions. *Developmental Psychology, 37,* 826–838.

Moon, C., Cooper, R. P., & Fifer, W. P. (1993). Two-day-olds prefer their native language. *Infant Behavior and Development, 16,* 494–500.

Moon, R. Y., & Biliter, W. M. (2001). Infant sleep position policies in licensed child care centers after Back to Sleep campaign. *Pediatrics, 106,* 576–580.

Moon, R. Y., Patel, K. M., & McDermott Shaefer, S. J. (2000). Sudden infant death syndrome in child care settings. *Pediatrics, 106,* 295–300.

Moore, G. T., & Lackney, J. A. (1993). School design: Crisis, educational performance, and design patterns. *Children's Environments, 10,* 99–112.

Moore, K. L., & Persaud, T. V. N. (1998). *Before we are born: Essentials of embryology and birth defects* (5th ed.). Philadelphia: W.B. Saunders.

Morison, P., & Masten, A. S. (1991). Peer reputation in middle childhood as a predictor of adaptation in adolescence: A seven-year follow-up. *Child Development, 62,* 991–1007.

Morrelli, G., Rogoff, B., Oppenheim, D., & Goldsmith, D. (1992). Cultural variation in infants' sleeping arrangements: Questions of independence. *Developmental Psychology, 28,* 604–613.

Morris, R., & Kratchowill, T. (1983). *Treating children's fears and phobias.* New York: Pergamon Press.

Morrison, F. J., Griffith, E. M., & Alberts, D. M. (1997). Nature-nurture in the classroom: Entrance age, school readiness, and learning in children. *Developmental Psychology, 33,* 254–262.

Morrison, F. J., Smith, L., & Dow-Ehrensberger, M. (1995). Education and cognitive development: A natural experiment. *Developmental Psychology, 31,* 789–799.

Morrongiello, B. A. (1984). Auditory temporal pattern perception in 6- and 12-month-old infants. *Developmental Psychology, 20,* 441–448.

Morrongiello, B. A., Fenwick, K. D., & Chance, G. (1990). Sound localization acuity in very young infants: An observer-based testing procedure. *Developmental Psychology, 26,* 75–84.

Morrongiello, B. A., Fenwick, K. D., & Chance, G. (1998). Crossmodal learning in newborn infants: Inferences about properties of auditory-visual events. *Infant Behavior and Development, 21,* 543–554.

Moses, L. J., Baldwin, D. A., Rosicky, J. G., & Tidball, G. (2001). Evidence for referential understanding in the emotions domain at twelve and eighteen months. *Child Development, 72,* 718–735.

Mosko, S., Richard, C., & McKenna, J. (1997). Infant arousals during mother-infant bed sharing: Implications for infant sleep and sudden infant death syndrome research. *Pediatrics, 100,* 841–849.

Moss, E., Rousseau, D., Parent, S., St.-Laurent, D., & Saintonge, J. (1998). Correlates of attachment at school age: Maternal reported stress, mother-child interaction, and behavior problems. *Child Development, 69,* 1390–1405.

Moss, H. A. (1974). Early sex differences and mother-infant interaction. In R. C. Friedman, R. M. Richart, & R. L. Vande Wiele (Eds.), *Sex differences in behavior* (pp. 149–163). New York: Wiley.

Mosteller, F. (1995, Summer/Fall). The Tennessee study of class size in the early school grades. *The Future of Children, 5*(2), pp. 113–127.

Mostow, A. J., Izard, C. E., Fine, S., & Trentacosta, C. J. (2002). Modeling emotional, cognitive, and behavioral predictors of peer acceptance. *Child Development, 73,* 1775–1787.

MTA Cooperative Group. (1999). A 14-month randomized clinical trial of treatment strategies for attention-deficit/hyperactivity disorder: Multimodal treatment study of children with ADHD. *Archives of General Psychiatry, 56,* 1073–1086.

Mueller, R. F., & Cook, J. (1997). Mendelian inheritance. In D. L. Rimoin, J. M. Connor, & R. E. Pyeritz (Eds.), *Emery and Rimoin's principles and practices of medical genetics* (3rd ed., Vol. 1, pp. 87–102). New York: Churchill Livingstone.

Mullen, M. K. (1994). Earliest recollections of childhood: A demographic analysis. *Cognition, 52,* 55–79.

Mullen, M. K., & Yi, S. (1995). The cultural context of talk about the past: Implications for the development of autobiographical memory. *Cognitive Development, 10,* 407–419.

Muller, A. A., & Perlmutter, M. (1985). Preschool children's problem-solving interactions at computers and jigsaw puzzles. *Journal of Applied Developmental Psychology, 6,* 173–186.

Munakata, Y. (2001). Task dependency in infant behavior: Toward an understanding of the processes underlying cognitive development. In F. Lacerda & C. von Hofsten & M. Heimann (Eds.), *Emerging cognitive abilities in early infancy* (pp. 29–52). Mahwah, NJ: Erlbaum.

Munakata, Y., Bauer, D., Stackhouse, T., Landgraf, L., & Huddleston, J. (2002). Rich interpretation vs. deflationary accounts in cognitive development: The case of means-ends skills in 7–month-olds. *Cognition, 83,* B43–B53.

Munakata, Y., McClelland, J. L., Johnson, M. H., & Siegler, R. (1997). Rethinking infant knowledge: Toward an adaptive process account of successes and failures in object permanence tasks. *Psychological Review, 104,* 686–713.

Munroe, R. H., Shimmin, H. S., & Munroe, R. L. (1984). Gender understanding and sex role preference in four cultures. *Developmental Psychology, 20,* 673–682.

Mussen, P. H., & Jones, M. C. (1957). Self-conceptions, motivations, and interpersonal attitudes of late and early maturing boys. *Child Development, 28,* 243–256.

Mussen, P. H., & Jones, M. C. (1958). The behavior inferred motivations of late and early maturing boys. *Child Development, 29,* 61–67.

Myers, J., Jusczyk, P. W., Kemler Nelson, D. G., Charles-Luce, J., Woodward, A. L., & Hirsh-Pasek, K. (1996). Infants' sensitivity to word boundaries in fluent speech. *Journal of Child Language, 23,* 1–30.

Nachmias, M., Gunnar, M., Mangelsdorf, S., Parritz, R., & Buss, K. (1996). Behavioral inhibition and stress reactivity: Moderating role of attachment security. *Child Development, 67,* 508–522.

Nahmias, A. J., Keyserling, H. L., & Kernick, G. M. (1983). Herpes simplex. In J. S. Remington & J. O. Klein (Eds.), *Infectious diseases of the fetus and newborn infant.* Philadelphia: W.B. Saunders.

Naigles, L. (1990). Children use syntax to learn verb meanings. *Journal of Child Language, 17,* 357–374.

Naito, M., & Miura, H. (2001). Japanese children's numerical competencies: Age- and schooling-related influences on the development of number concepts and addition skills. *Developmental Psychology, 37,* 217–230.

Najarian, S. P. (1999). Infant cranial molding deformation and sleep position: Implications for primary care. *Journal of Pediatric Health Care, 13,* 173–177.

Nakamura, K. (2001). The acquisition of polite language by Japanese children. In K. E. Nelson, A. Aksu-Koc, & C. E. Johnson (Eds.), *Children's language: Developing narrative and discourse competence* (Vol. 10, pp. 93–112). Mahwah, NJ: Erlbaum.

Namy, L. L., & Waxman, S. R. (1998). Words and gestures: Infants' interpretations of different forms of symbolic reference. *Child Development, 69,* 295–308.

Náñez, J. E., Sr., & Yonas, A. (1994). Effects of luminance and texture motion on infant defensive reactions to optical collision. *Infant Behavior and Development, 17,* 165–174.

Nathanielsz, P. W. (1996). The timing of birth. *American Scientist, 84,* 562–569.

National Center for Education Statistics. (2001). *Child care.* Retrieved on December 20, 2002, from http://childstats.gov/ac2002/indicators.asp?IID=43&id=1

National Clearinghouse for English Language Acquisition. (2002). Retrieved November 8, 2002 from http://ncela.gwu.edu/states/stateposter.pdf

National Clearinghouse on Child Abuse and Neglect Information. (2002a). *Child maltreatment 1997: Reports from the states to the Child Abuse and Neglect Data System.* Washington, DC: Department of Health and Human Services.

National Clearinghouse on Child Abuse and Neglect Information. (2002b). *National Child Abuse and Neglect Data System (NCANDS) summary of key findings from calendar year 2000.* Retrieved December 20, 2002, from http://www.calib.com/nccanch/pubs/factsheets/canstats.cfm

National Institute on Drug Abuse. (1995). *Drug use among racial/ethnic minorities.* Bethesda, MD: Author.

National Institute of Mental Health. (1996). *Attention deficit hyperactivity disorder* (NIH Publication No. 96-3572). Washington, DC: U.S. Government Printing Office.

National Institute of Mental Health. (2002). *Suicide facts.* Retrieved December 12, 2002, from http://www.nimh.nih.gov/research/suifact.htm

National Research Council, Committee on Mapping and Sequencing the Human Genome. (1988). *Mapping and sequencing the human genome.* Washington, DC: National Academy Press.

National Research Council and Institute of Medicine. (2001). *Nontechnical strategies to reduce children's exposure to inappropriate material on the Internet: Summary of a workshop* (Joah G. Iannotta, Ed.). Washington, DC: National Academies Press.

National Research Council and Institute of Medicine. (2002a). *Community programs to promote youth development* (J. Eccles & J. A. Gootman, Eds.). Washington, DC: National Academies Press.

National Research Council and Institute of Medicine. (2002b). *Deadly lessons: Understanding lethal school violence* (M. H. Moore, C. V. Petrie, A. A. Braga, & B. L. McLaughlin, Eds.). Washington, DC: National Academies Press.

Nazzi, T., Bertoncini, J., & Mehler, J. (1998). Language discrimination by newborns: Towards an understanding of the role of rhythm. *Journal of Experimental Psychology: Human Perception and Performance, 24,* 756–766.

Nazzi, T., & Gopnik, A. (2001). Linguistic and cognitive abilities in infancy: When does language become a tool for categorization? *Cognition, 80,* B11–B20.

Nazzi, T., Kemler Nelson, D. G., Jusczyk, P. W., & Juczyk, A. M. (2000). Six-month-olds' detection of clauses embedded in contiguous speech: Effects of prosodic well-formedness. *Infancy, 1,* 123–147.

Needham, A. (2001). Object recognition and object segregation in 4.5-month-old infants. *Journal of Experimental Child Psychology, 78,* 3–24.

Needham, A., & Baillargeon, R. (1998). Effects of prior experience in 4.5-month-old infant's object segregation. *Infant Behavior and Development, 21,* 121–149.

Needham, A., & Modi, A. (2000). Infant's use of prior experiences with objects in object segregation: Implications for object recognition in infancy. In H. W. Reese (Ed.), *Advances in child development and behavior* (Vol. 27, pp. 100–135). San Diego: Academic Press.

Needleman, H. L., & Bellinger, D. (Eds.) (1994). *Prenatal exposure to toxicants: Developmental consequences.* Baltimore: Johns Hopkins University Press.

Neiderhiser, J. M., Reiss, D., Hetherington, E. M., & Plomin, R. (1999). Relationships between parenting and adolescent adjustment over time: Genetic and environmental contributions. *Developmental Psychology, 35,* 680–692.

Neimark, E. D. (1979). Current status of formal operations research. *Human Development, 22,* 60–67.

Neisser, U. (Ed.). (1998). *The rising curve: Long-term gains in IQ and related measures.* Washington, DC: American Psychological Association.

Neisser, U., Boodoo, G., Bouchard, T. J., Jr., Boykin, A. W., Brody, N., Ceci, S. J., et al. (1996). Intelligence: Knowns and unknowns. *American Psychologist, 51,* 77–101.

Nelson, C. A. (1995). The ontogeny of human memory: A cognitive neuroscience perspective. *Developmental Psychology, 31,* 723–738.

Nelson, C. A. (1999). Change and continuity in neurobehavioral development: Lessons from the study of neurobiology and neural plasticity. *Infant Behavior and Development, 22,* 415–429.

Nelson, C. A. (1999). Neural plasticity and human development. *Current Directions in Psychological Science, 8,* 42–45.

Nelson, C. A. (2000). Neural plasticity and human development: The role of early experience in sculpting memory systems. *Developmental Science, 3,* 115–136.

Nelson, C. A., & Monk, C. S. (2001). The use of event-related potentials in the study of cognitive development. From C. A. Nelson & M. Luciano (Eds.), *Handbook of developmental cognitive neuroscience* (pp. 125–136). Cambridge, MA: MIT Press.

Nelson, C. A., Monk, C. S., Lin, J., Carver, L. J., Thomas, K. M., & Truwit, C. L. (2000). Functional neuroanatomy of spatial working memory in children. *Developmental Psychology, 36,* 109–116.

Nelson, E. E., & Panksepp, J. (1998). Brain substrates of infant-mother attachment: Contributions of opioids, oxytocin, and norepinephrine. *Neuroscience and Biobehavioral Reviews, 22,* 437–452.

Nelson, K. (1973). Structure and strategy in learning to talk. *Monographs of the Society for Research in Child Development, 38*(1–2, Serial No. 149).

Nelson, K. (1993a). Events, narratives, memory: What develops? In C. A. Nelson (Ed.), *Memory and affect in development. The Minnesota symposia on child psychology* (Vol. 26, pp. 1–24). Hillsdale, NJ: Erlbaum.

Nelson, K. (1993b). The psychological and social origins of autobiographical memory. *Psychological Science, 4,* 7–14.

Nelson, K., & Gruendel, J. (1981). Generalized event representations: Basic building blocks of cognitive development. In M. E. Lamb & A. L. Brown (Eds.), *Advances in developmental psychology* (Vol. 1, pp. 131–158). Hillsdale, NJ: Erlbaum.

Nemeth, M. (1997, August 19). Looking for moral anchors. *Maclean's, 109,* 17–18.

Neu, M. (1999). Parents' perception of skin-to-skin care with their preterm infants requiring assisted ventilation. *Journal of Obstetric, Gynecologic, and Neonatal Nursing, 28,* 157–164.

Neuman, S. B. (1991). *Literacy in the television age.* Norwood, NJ: Ablex.

Neville, H., Mehler, J., Newport, E., Werker, J. F., & McClelland, J. (2001). Language. *Developmental Science, 4,* 293–312.

Newborg, J., Stock, J. R., & Wnek, L. (1984). *Battelle Developmental Inventory.* Allen, TX: LINC Associates.

Newcomb , A. F., & Bagwell, C. L. (1995). Children's friendship relations: A meta-analytic review. *Psychological Bulletin, 117,* 306–347.

Newcomb, A. F., Bukowski, W. M., & Bagwell, C. L. (1999). Knowing the sounds: Friendship as a developmental context. In W. A. Collins & B. Laursen (Eds.), *Minnesota symposia on child psychology: Vol. 30. Relationships as developmental contexts* (pp. 63–84). Mahwah, NJ: Erlbaum.

Newcombe, N., & Huttenlocher, J. (1992). Children's early ability to solve perspective-taking problems. *Developmental Psychology, 28*, 635–643.

Newcombe, N. S., & Huttenlocher, J. (2000). *Making space: The development of spatial representation and reasoning.* Cambridge, MA: MIT Press.

Newcombe, N. S., Huttenlocher, J., & Learmonth, A. (2000). Infants' coding of location in continuous space. *Infant Behavior and Development, 22*, 483–510.

Newcomer, S., & Baldwin, W. (1992). Demographics of adolescent sexual behavior, contraception, pregnancy, and STDs. *Journal of School Health, 62*, 265–270.

Newport, E. L. (1977). Motherese: The speech of mothers to young children. In N. J. Castellan, D. B. Pisoni, & G. Potts (Eds.), *Cognitive theory* (Vol. 2). Hillsdale, NJ: Erlbaum.

Newport, E. L. (1990). Maturational constraints on language learning. *Cognitive Science, 14*, 11–28.

Newton, N. (1955). *Maternal emotions.* New York: P. B. Hoeber.

NICHD Early Child Care Research Network. (1997). The effects of infant child care on infant-mother attachment security: Results of the NICHD study of early child care. *Child Development, 68*, 860–879.

NICHD Early Child Care Research Network. (1998a). Early child care and self-control, compliance, and problem behavior at twenty-four and thirty-six months. *Child Development, 69*, 1145–1170.

NICHD Early Child Care Research Network. (1998b). Relations between family predictors and child outcomes: Are they weaker for children in child care? *Developmental Psychology, 34*, 1119–1128.

NICHD Early Child Care Research Network. (2000a). Factors associated with fathers' caregiving activities and sensitivity to young children. *Journal of Family Psychology, 14*, 200–219.

NICHD Early Child Care Research Network. (2000b). The relations of child care to cognitive and language development. *Child Development, 71*, 960–980.

NICHD Early Child Care Research Network. (2001a). Child care and children's peer interaction at 24 and 36 months: The NICHD study of early child care. *Developmental Psychology, 72*, 1478–1500.

NICHD Early Child Care Research Network. (2001b). Child-care and family predictors of preschool attachment and stability from infancy. *Developmental Psychobiology, 37*, 847–862.

NICHD Early Child Care Research Network. (2002). Child-care structure → Process → Outcome: Direct and indirect effects of child-care quality on young children's development. *Psychological Science, 13*, 199–206.

Nickelodeon/Yankelovich Youth Monitor(tm). (1999). *1999 Management Summary: Planet Youth.* Norwalk, CT: Yankelovich Partners.

Niemiec, R., & Walberg, H. J. (1987). Comparative effects of computer-assisted instruction: A synthesis of reviews. *Journal of Educational Computing Research, 3*, 19–37.

Nikken, P., & Peeters, A. L. (1988). Children's perceptions of television reality. *Journal of Broadcasting and Electronic Media, 32*, 417–423.

Nilsson, L. (1990). *A child is born.* New York: Dell.

Ninio, A., & Bruner, J. S. (1978). The achievement and antecedents of labelling. *Journal of Child Language, 5*, 1–15.

Nix, R. L., Pinderhughes, E. E., Dodge, K. A., Bates, J. E., Pettit, G. S., & McFadyen-Ketchum, S. A. (1999). The relation between mothers' hostile attribution tendencies and children's externalizing problems: The mediating role of mother's harsh discipline practices. *Child Development, 70*, 896–909.

Nobre, A. C., & Plunkett, K. (1997). The neural system of language: Structure and development. *Current Opinion in Neurobiology, 7*, 262–268.

Nolen-Hoeksma, S. (2001). Gender differences in depression. *Current Directions in Psychological Science, 10*, 173–176.

Noll, R. B., Vannatta, K., Koontz, K., Kalinyak, K., Bukowski, W. M., & Davies, W. H. (1996). Peer relationships and emotional well-being of youngsters with sickle cell disease. *Child Development, 67*, 423–436.

Norbeck, J. S., & Tilden, V. P. (1983). Life stress, social support, and emotional disequilibrium in complications of pregnancy: A prospective, multivariate study. *Journal of Health and Social Behavior, 24*, 30–46.

Northrup, H., & Volcik, K. A. (2000). Spina bifida and neural tube defects. *Current Problems in Pediatrics, 30*, 317–332.

Novak, G. (1996). *Developmental psychology: Dynamic systems and behavioral analyses.* Reno, NV: Context Press.

Nucci, L. P., & Turiel, E. (1978). Social interactions and the development of social concepts in preschool children. *Child Development, 49*, 400–407.

Nucci, L. P., & Turiel, E. (1993). God's word, religious rules, and their relation to Christian and Jewish children's concepts of morality. *Child Development, 64*, 1475–1491.

Nugent, J. K., Lester, B. M., Greene, S. M., Wieczorek-Doering, D., & O'Mahony, P. (1996). The effects of maternal alcohol consumption and cigarette smoking during pregnancy on acoustic cry analysis. *Child Development, 67*, 1806–1815.

Oakes, L. M. (1994). Development of infants' use of continuity cues in their perception of causality. *Developmental Psychology, 30*, 869–879.

Oakes, L. M., & Cohen, L. B. (1990). Infant perception of a causal event. *Cognitive Development, 5*, 193–207.

Oakes, L. M., Coppage, D. J., & Dingel, A. (1997). By land or by sea: The role of perceptual similarity in infants' categorization of animals. *Developmental Psychology, 33*, 396–407.

Oakland, T. D. (1982). Nonbiased assessment in counseling: Issues and guidelines. *Measurement and Evaluation in Guidance, 15*, 107–116.

Oakley, D., Murray, M. E., Murtland, T., Hayashi, R., Andersen, H. F., Mayes, F., & Rooks, J. (1996). Comparisons of outcomes of maternity care by obstetricians and certified nurse-midwives. *Obstetrics and Gynecology, 88*, 923–929.

Ochs, E. (1988). *Culture and language development: Language acquisition and language socialization in a Samoan village.* New York: Cambridge University Press.

Ochs, E. (1990). Indexicality and socialization. In J. W. Stigler, R. A. Shweder, & G. Herdt (Eds.), *Cultural psychology* (pp. 287–308). Cambridge, UK: Cambridge University Press.

O'Connor, R. D. (1972). Relative efficacy of modeling, shaping, and the procedures for modification of social withdrawal. *Journal of Abnormal Psychology, 79*, 327–334.

O'Connor, T. G., Caspi, A., DeFries, J. C., & Plomin, R. (2000). Are associations between parental divorce and children's adjustment genetically mediated? An adoption study. *Developmental Psychology, 36*, 429–437.

O'Connor, T. G., & Croft, C. M. (2001). A twin study of attachment in preschool children. *Child Development, 72*, 1501–1511.

O'Connor, T. G., Deater-Deckard, K., Fulker, D., Rutter, M., & Plomin, R. (1998). Genotype-environment correlations in late childhood and early adolescence: Antisocial behavioral problems and coercive parenting. *Developmental Psychology, 34*, 970–981.

Ogbu, J. U. (1974). *The next generation: An ethnography of education in an urban neighborhood.* New York: Academic Press.

Ogbu, J. U. (1994). From cultural differences to differences in cultural frame of reference. In P. M. Greenfield & R. R. Cocking (Eds.), *Cross-cultural roots of minority child development* (pp. 365–391). Hillsdale, NJ: Erlbaum.

Oldershaw, L., Walters, G. C., & Hall, D. K. (1986). Control strategies and noncompliance in abusive mother-child dyads: An observational study. *Child Development, 57*, 722–732.

Olson, R. K. (1994). Language deficits in "specific" reading disability. In M. A. Gernsbacher (Ed.), *Handbook of psycholinguistics* (pp. 895–916). New York: Academic Press.

Olson, S. L., Bayles, K., & Bates, J. E. (1986). Mother-child interaction and children's speech progress: A longitudinal study of the first two years. *Merrill-Palmer Quarterly, 32*, 1–20.

Olweus, D. (1978). *Aggression in schools: Bullies and their whipping boys.* Washington, DC: Hemisphere.

Olweus, D. (1993a). Bullies on the playground: The role of victimization. In C. H. Hart (Ed.), *Children on playgrounds* (pp. 85–128). Albany: State University of New York Press.

Olweus, D. (1993b). *Bullying at school: What we know and what we can do.* Oxford, UK: Blackwell.

Olweus, D. (1994). Bullying at school: Long-term outcomes for the victims and an effective school-based intervention program. In L. R. Huesmann (Ed.), *Aggressive behavior: Current perspectives* (pp. 97–130). New York: Plenum.

Olweus, D. (1997). Tackling peer victimization with a school-based intervention program. In D. P. Frye & K. Bjorkqvist (Eds.), *Cultural variation in conflict resolution: Alternatives to violence* (pp. 215–231). Mahwah, NJ: Erlbaum.

O'Neil, R., Parke, R. D., & McDowell, D. J. (2001). Objective and subjective features of children's neighborhoods: Relations to parental regulatory strategies and children's social competence. *Applied Developmental Psychology, 22,* 135–155.

Orlebeke, J. F., Knol, D. L., & Verhulst, F. C. (1999). Child behavior problems increased by maternal smoking during pregnancy. *Archives of Environmental Health, 54,* 15–19.

Ornoy, A., Michailevskay, V., Lukashov, I., Barttamburger, R., & Harel, S. (1996). The developmental outcome of children born to heroin-dependent mothers, raised at home or adopted. *Child Abuse & Neglect, 20,* 385–396.

Ornstein, P. A., Baker-Ward, L., & Naus, M. J. (1988). The development of mnemonic skill. In F. E. Weinert & M. Perlmutter (Eds.), *Memory development: Universal changes and individual differences* (pp. 31–50). Hillsdale, NJ: Erlbaum.

Ornstein, P. A., & Naus, M. J. (1978). Rehearsal processes in children's memory. In P. A. Ornstein (Ed.), *Memory development in children* (pp. 69–99). Hillsdale, NJ: Erlbaum.

Ornstein, P. A., Naus, M. J., & Liberty, C. (1975). Rehearsal and organizational processes in children's memory. *Child Development, 46,* 818–830.

Orobio de Castro, B., Veerman, J. W., Koops, W., Bosch, J. D., & Monshouwer, H. J. (2002). Hostile attribution of intent and aggressive behavior: A meta-analysis. *Child Development, 73,* 916–934.

Orton, G. L. (1982). A comparative study of children's worries. *Journal of Psychology, 110,* 153–162.

O'Shea, T. M., Klinepeter, K. L., Goldstein, D. J., Jackson, B. W., & Dillard, R. G. (1997). Survival and developmental disability in infants with birth weights of 501 to 800 grams, born between 1979 and 1994. *Pediatrics, 100,* 982–986.

Osterling, J., & Dawson, G. (1994). Early recognition of children with autism: A study of first birthday home videotapes. *Journal of Autism and Developmental Disorders, 24,* 247–257.

Ounsted, C., Oppenheimer, R., & Lindsay, J. (1974). Aspects of bonding failure: The psychopathology and psychotherapeutic treatment of families of battered children. *Developmental Medicine and Child Neurology, 16,* 447–452.

Overman, W. H., Bachevalier, J., Schuhmann, E., & McDonough-Ryan, P. (1997). Sexually dimorphic brain-behavior development. In N. Krasnegor, G. R. Lyon, & P. S. Goldman-Rakic (Eds.), *Development of the prefrontal cortex: Evolution, neurobiology, and behavior* (pp. 337–357). Baltimore: Paul H. Brookes.

Overton, W. (1998). Developmental psychology: Philosophy, concepts, and methodology. In W. Damon (Series Ed.) & R. Lerner (Vol. Ed.), *Handbook of child psychology: Vol. 1. Theoretical models of human development* (5th ed., pp. 107–188). New York: Wiley.

Owen, M. T., & Cox, M. J. (1988). Maternal employment and the transition to parenthood. In A. E. Gottfried & A. W. Gottfried (Eds.), *Maternal employment and children's development: Longitudinal research* (pp. 85–119). New York: Plenum Press.

Palacios, J. (1996). Proverbs as images of children and childrearing. In C. P. Hwang, M. E. Lamb, & I. E. Sigel (Eds.), *Images of childhood* (pp. 75–98). Mahwah, NJ: Erlbaum.

Palincsar, A. S., & Brown, A. L. (1984). Reciprocal teaching of comprehension-fostering and comprehension-monitoring activities. *Cognition and Instruction, 1,* 117–175.

Palincsar, A. S., & Brown, A. L. (1986). Interactive teaching to promote independent learning from text. *The Reading Teacher, 39,* 771–777.

Palisin, H. (1986). Preschool temperament and performance on achievement tests. *Developmental Psychology, 22,* 766–770.

Palmer, S. E., & Kimchi, R. (1986). The information processing approach to cognition. In T. J. Knapp & L. C. Robertson (Eds.), *Approaches to cognition: Contrasts and controversies* (pp. 37–77). Hillsdale, NJ: Erlbaum.

Pääbo, S. (2001). The human genome and our view of ourselves. *Science, 291,* 1219–1220.

Paltrow, L. M., Cohen, D. W., & Carey, C. A. (2000). *Year 2000 overview: Governmental responses to pregnant women who use alcohol and other drugs.* Philadelphia, PA: Women's Law Project, National Advocates for Pregnant Women.

Papoušek, H., Papoušek, M., & Koester, L. S. (1986). Sharing emotionality and sharing knowledge: A microanalytic approach to parent-infant communication. In C. E. Izard & P. B. Read (Eds.), *Measuring emotions in infants and children* (Vol. 2). Cambridge, UK: Cambridge University Press.

Papoušek, M. (1992). Early ontogeny of vocal communication in parent-infant interactions. In H. Papoušek, U. Jürgens, & M. Papoušek (Eds.), *Non-verbal vocal communication: Comparative and developmental approaches* (pp. 230–261). Cambridge, UK: Cambridge University Press.

Parke, R. D. (1969). Effectiveness of punishment as an interaction of intensity, timing, agent nurturance, and cognitive structuring. *Child Development, 40,* 213–235.

Parke, R. D., & Collmer, C. W. (1975). Child abuse: An interdisciplinary analysis. In E. M. Hetherington (Ed.), *Review of child development research* (Vol. 5, pp. 509–590). Chicago: University of Chicago Press.

Parke, R. D., MacDonald, K. B., Beitel, A., & Bhavnagri, N. (1988). The role of the family in the development of peer relationships. In R. D. Peters & R. J. McMahon (Eds.), *Social learning and systems approaches to marriage and the family* (pp. 17–44). New York: Brunner/Mazel.

Parke, R. D., & O'Leary, S. (1976). Father-mother-infant interaction in the newborn period: Some findings, some observations, and some unresolved issues. In K. F. Riegel & J. Meacham (Eds.), *The developing individual in a changing world: Vol. 2. Social and environmental issues* (pp. 653–663). The Hague: Mouton.

Parke, R. D., & O'Neil, R. (1999). Social relationships across contexts: Family-peer linkages. In W. A. Collins & B. Laursen (Eds.), *Minnesota Symposia on Child Psychology: Vol. 30. Relationships as developmental contexts* (pp. 211–239). Mahwah, NJ: Erlbaum.

Parke, R. D., & Slaby, R. G. (1983). The development of aggression. In E. M. Hetherington (Ed.), *Handbook of child psychology: Vol. IV. Socialization, personality, and social development* (4th ed., pp. 547–641). New York: Wiley.

Parker, J. G., & Asher, S. R. (1987). Peer relations and later personal adjustment: Are low-accepted children at risk? *Psychological Bulletin, 102,* 357–389.

Parker, J. G., & Asher, S. R. (1993). Friendship and friendship quality in middle childhood: Links with peer group acceptance and feelings of loneliness and social dissatisfaction. *Developmental Psychology, 29,* 611–621.

Parker, J. G., & Gottman, J. M. (1989). Social and emotional development in a relational context: Friendship interaction from early childhood to adolescence. In T. M. Berndt & G. W. Ladd (Eds.), *Peer relations in childhood* (pp. 95–131). New York: Wiley.

Parker, J. G., & Seal, J. (1996). Forming, losing, renewing, and replacing friendships: Applying temporal parameters to the assessment of children's friendship experiences. *Child Development, 67,* 2248–2268.

Parkhurst, J. T., & Asher, S. R. (1992). Peer rejection in middle school: subgroup differences in behavior, loneliness, and interpersonal concerns. *Developmental Psychology, 28,* 231–241.

Parkhurst, J. T., & Hopmeyer, A. (1998). Sociometric popularity and peer-perceived popularity: Two distinct dimensions of peer status. *Journal of Early Adolescence, 18,* 125–144.

Parsons, J. E. (1980). Psychosexual neutrality: Is anatomy destiny? In J. E. Parsons (Ed.), *The psychobiology of sex differences and sex roles* (pp. 3–29). New York: Hemisphere.

Parten, M. B. (1932). Social participation among pre-school children. *Journal of Abnormal and Social Psychology, 32,* 243–269.

Pascalis, O., de Schonen, S., Morton, J., Deruelle, C., & Fabre-Grenet, M. (1995). Mother's face recognition by neonates: A replication and an extension. *Infant Behavior and Development, 18,* 79–85.

Pass, R. F. (1987). Congenital and perinatal infections due to viruses and toxoplasma. In N. Kretchmer, E. J. Quilligan, & J. D. Johnson (Eds.), *Prenatal and perinatal biology and medicine: Vol. 2. Disorder, diagnosis, and therapy* (pp. 213–302). New York: Harwood Academic Publishers.

Patterson, G. R. (1982). *A social learning approach: Vol. 3. Coercive family process.* Eugene, OR: Castalia.

Patterson, G. R. (1986). Performance models for antisocial boys. *American Psychologist, 41,* 432–444.

Patterson, G. R., & Fleischman, M. J. (1979). Maintenance of treatment effects: Some considerations concerning family systems and follow-up data. *Behavior Therapy, 10,* 168–185.

Patterson, G. R., Littman, R. A., & Bricker, W. (1967). Assertive behavior in children: A step toward a theory of aggression. *Monographs of the Society for Research in Child Development, 32*(5, Serial No. 113).

Patterson, G. R., & Reid, J. B. (1973). Intervention for families of aggressive boys: A replication study. *Behavior Research and Therapy, 11,* 383–394.

Patterson, G. R., Reid, J. B., & Dishion, T. J. (1992). *A social learning approach: IV. Antisocial boys.* Eugene, OR: Castalia.

Patterson, G. R., Reid, J. B., Jones, R. R., & Conger, R. E. (1975). *A social learning approach: Vol. 1. Families with aggressive children.* Eugene, OR: Castalia.

Paxton, S. J., Wertheim, E. H., Gibbons, K., Szmukler, G. I., Hillier, L., & Petrovich, J. L. (1991). Body image satisfaction, dieting beliefs, and weight loss behaviors in adolescent girls and boys. *Journal of Youth and Adolescence, 20,* 362–379.

Peak, K., & Del Papa, F. S. (1993). Criminal justice enters the womb: Enforcing the "right" to be born drug-free. *Journal of Criminal Justice, 21,* 245–263.

Peake, P. K., Hebl, M., & Mischel, W. (2002). Strategic attention deployment for delay of gratification in working and waiting situations. *Developmental Psychology, 38,* 313–326.

Peckham, C. S., & Logan, S. (1993). Screening for toxoplasmosis during pregnancy. *Archives of Disease in Childhood, 68,* 3–5.

Pederson, D. R., Gleason, K. E., Moran, G., & Bento, S. (1998). Maternal attachment representations, maternal sensitivity, and the infant-mother attachment relationship. *Developmental Psychology, 34,* 925–933.

Pederson, F. A., Cain, R., Zaslow, M., & Anderson, B. (1982). Variation in infant experience associated with alternative family organization. In L. Laosa & I. Sigel (Eds.), *Families as learning environments for children* (pp. 203–222). New York: Plenum Press.

Peisner-Feinberg, E. S., Burchinal, M., Clifford, R., Culkin, M., Howes, C., Kagan, S., & Yazejian, N. (2001). The relation of preschool child-care quality to children's cognitive and social developmental trajectories through second grade. *Child Development, 72,* 1534–1553.

Pellegrini, A. D. (1988). Elementary-school children's rough-and-tumble play and social competence. *Developmental Psychology, 24,* 802–806.

Pellegrini, A. D., & Smith, P. K. (1998). Physical activity play: The nature and function of a neglected aspect of play. *Child Development, 69,* 577–598.

Peltonen, L., & McKusick, V. A. (2001). Dissecting human disease in the postgenomic era. *Science, 291,* 1224–1229.

Penn, Schoen, & Berland Associates. (2000, September). *Web savvy and safety: How kids and parents differ in what they know, whom they trust.* Retrieved November 27, 2002, from http://www.microsoft.com/PressPass/press/2000/Nov00/SafetyWebsitesPR.asp

Pennington, B. F. (1998). Dimensions of executive functions in normal and abnormal development. In N. A. Krasnegor, G. R. Lyon, & P. S. Goldman-Rakic (Eds.), *Development of the prefrontal cortex: Evolution, neurobiology, and behavior* (pp. 265–281). Baltimore, MD: Brookes.

Pennisi, E. (2001). The human genome: News. *Science, 291,* 1177–1180.

Perner, J., & Ruffman, T. (1995). Episodic memory and autonoetic consciousness: Developmental evidence and a theory of childhood amnesia. *Journal of Experimental Child Psychology, 59,* 516–548.

Perozynski, L., & Kramer, L. (1999). Parental beliefs about managing sibling conflict. *Developmental Psychology, 35,* 489–499.

Perry, D. G., & Bussey, K. (1979). The social learning theory of sex differences: Imitation is alive and well. *Journal of Personality and Social Psychology, 37,* 1699–1712.

Pérusse, L., & Chagnon, Y. C. (1997). Summary of human linkage and association studies. *Behavior Genetics, 27,* 359–372.

Petersen, A. C. (1980). Biopsychosocial processes in the development of sex-related differences. In J. Parsons (Ed.), *The psychobiology of sex differences and sex roles* (pp. 31–55). New York: Hemisphere.

Petersen, A. C. (1988). Adolescent development. *Annual Review of Psychology, 39,* 583–607.

Petersen, A. C., Compas, B. E., Brooks-Gunn, J., Stemmler, M., Ey, S., & Grant, K. E. (1993). Depression in adolescence. *American Psychologist, 48,* 155–168.

Petersen, A. C., & Hamburg, B. (1986). Adolescence: A developmental approach to problems and psychopathology. *Behavior Therapy, 13,* 480–499.

Peterson, C., & Whalen, N. (2001). Five years later: Children's memory for medical emergencies. *Applied Cognitive Psychology, 15,* S7–S24.

Peterson, C. A., & Siegal, M. (1999). Representing inner worlds: Theory of mind in autistic, deaf, and normal hearing children. *Psychological Science, 10,* 126–129.

Peterson, G. W., & Rollins, B. C. (1987). Parent-child socialization. In M. B. Sussman & S. K. Steinmetz (Eds.), *Handbook of marriage and the family* (pp. 471–507). New York: Plenum Press.

Peterson, R. P., Johnson, D. W., & Johnson, R. T. (1991). Effects of cooperative learning on perceived status of male and female pupils. *Journal of Social Psychology, 131,* 717–735.

Petitto, L. A., Holowka, S., Sergio, L. E., & Ostry, D. (2001). Language rhythms in baby hand movements. *Nature, 413,* 35–36.

Petitto, L. A., & Marentette, P. F. (1991). Babbling in the manual code: Evidence for the ontogeny of language. *Science, 251,* 1493–1496.

Pettit, G. S., Clawson, M. A., Dodge, K. A. & Bates, J. E. (1996). Stability and change in peer-rejected status: The role of child behavior, parenting, and family ecology. *Merrill-Palmer Quarterly, 42,* 267–294.

Pettit, G. S., Dodge, K. A., Bakshi, A., & Coie, J. D. (1990). The emergence of social dominance in young boys' play groups: Developmental differences and behavioral correlates. *Developmental Psychology, 26,* 1017–1025.

Pettit, G. S., Laird, R. D., Dodge, K. A., Bates, J. E., & Criss, M. M. (2001). Antecedents and behavior-problem outcomes of parental monitoring and psychological control in early adolescence. *Child Development, 72,* 583–598.

Phelps, E., & Damon, W. (1989). Problem solving with equals: Peer collaboration as a context for learning mathematics and spatial concepts. *Journal of Educational Psychology, 81,* 639–646.

Phenylketonuria. (2000, October 16–18). Phenylketonuria (PKU): Screening and management. *NIH Consensus Statement, 17,* 1–33.

Phillips, D. (1984). The illusion of incompetence among academically competent children. *Child Development, 55,* 2000–2016.

Phinney, J. S. (1990). Ethnic identity in adolescents and adults: Review of research. *Psychological Bulletin, 108,* 499–514.

Phinney, J. S., Ferguson, D. L., & Tate, J. D. (1997). Intergroup attitudes among ethnic minority adolescents: A causal model. *Child Development, 68,* 955–969.

Phinney, J. S., & Rosenthal, D. A. (1992). Ethnic identity in adolescence: Process, context and outcome. In G. R. Adams, T. P. Gullotta, & R. Montemayor (Eds.), *Adolescent identity formation* (pp. 145–172). Newbury Park, CA: Sage.

Piaget, J. (1929). *The child's conception of the world.* London: Routledge & Kegan Paul.

Piaget, J. (1930). *The child's conception of physical causality.* London: Routledge & Kegan Paul.

Piaget, J. (1952a). *The child's conception of number.* New York: W. W. Norton.

Piaget, J. (1952b). *The origins of intelligence in children.* New York: W. W. Norton.

Piaget, J. (1954). *The construction of reality in the child.* New York: Basic Books.

Piaget, J. (1962). *Play, dreams, and imitation in childhood.* New York: W. W. Norton.

Piaget, J. (1965). *The moral judgment of the child.* New York: Free Press. (Original work published 1932)

Piaget, J. (1971). *Biology and knowledge: An essay on the relationship between organic regulations and cognitive processes.* Chicago: University of Chicago Press.

Piaget, J. (1974). *Understanding causality.* New York: W.W. Norton.

Pianta, R. C., & Egeland, B. (1994). Predictors of instability in children's mental test performance at 24, 48, and 96 months. *Intelligence, 18,* 145–163.

Pick, A. D. (1965). Improvement of visual and tactual discrimination. *Journal of Experimental Psychology, 69,* 331–339.

Pick, H. L., Jr. (1987). Information and the effects of early perceptual experience. In N. Eisenberg (Ed.), *Contemporary topics in developmental psychology* (pp. 59–76). New York: Wiley.

Pick, H. L., Jr. (1992). Eleanor J. Gibson: Learning to perceive and perceiving to learn. *Developmental Psychology, 28,* 787–794.

Pickens, J. (1994). Perception of auditory-visual distance relations by 5-month-old infants. *Developmental Psychology, 30,* 537–544.

Pickens, J., & Field, T. (1993). Facial expressivity in infants of depressed mothers. *Developmental Psychology, 29,* 986–988.

Piecuch, R. E., Leonard, C. H., & Cooper, B. A. (1998). Infants with birth weight 1,000–1,499 grams born in three time periods: Has outcome changed over time? *Clinical Pediatrics, 37,* 537–546.

Pierce, J. W., & Wardle, J. (1997). Cause and effect beliefs and self-esteem of overweight children. *Journal of Child Psychology and Psychiatry, 38,* 645–650.

Pike, A., McGuire, S., Hetherington, E. M., Reiss, D., & Plomin, R. (1996). Family environment and adolescent depressive symptoms and antisocial behavior: A multivariate genetic analysis. *Developmental Psychology, 32,* 590–603.

Pillemer, D. B. (1998). *Momentous events, vivid memories.* Cambridge, MA; Harvard University Press.

Pillemer, D. B., & White, S. H. (1989). Childhood events recalled by children and adults. In H. W. Reese (Ed.), *Advances in child development and behavior* (Vol. 21, pp. 297–340). San Diego: Academic Press.

Pillow, B. H. (1988). Young children's understanding of attentional limits. *Child Development, 59,* 38–46.

Pineau, A., & Streri, A. (1990). Intermodal transfer of spatial arrangement of the component parts of an object in infants aged 4–5 months. *Perception, 19,* 795–804.

Pinker, S. (1984). *Language learnability and language development.* Cambridge, MA: Harvard University Press.

Pinker, S. (1987). The bootstrapping problem in language acquisition. In B. MacWhinney (Ed.), *Mechanisms of language acquisition.* Hillsdale, NJ: Erlbaum.

Pinneau, S. R. (1961). *Changes in intelligence quotient: Infancy to maturity.* Boston: Houghton Mifflin.

Pinyerd, B. J. (1992). Assessment of infant growth. *Journal of Pediatric Health Care, 6,* 302–308.

Pipe, M., Gee, S., Wilson, J. C., & Egerton, J. M. (1999). Children's recall 1 or 2 years after an event. *Developmental Psychology, 35,* 781–789.

Pisarska, M. D., & Carson, S. A. (1999). Incidence and risk factors for ectopic pregnancy. *Clinical Obstetrics and Gynecology, 42,* 2–8.

Platt, L. D., Koch, R., Hanley, W. B., Levy, H. L., Matalon, R., Rouse, B., et al. (2000). The International Study of Pregnancy Outcome in Women with Maternal Phenylketonuria: Report of a 12-year study. *American Journal of Obstetrics and Gynecology, 182,* 326–333.

Pleck, E. H., & Pleck, J. H. (1997). Fatherhood ideals in the United States: Historical dimensions. In M. E. Lamb (Ed.), *The role of the father in child development* (3rd ed., pp. 33–48). New York: Wiley.

Pleck, J. H. (1983). Husbands' paid work and family roles: Current research issues. In H. Z. Lopata & J. H. Pleck (Eds.), *Research in the interweave of social roles: Families and jobs* (pp. 91–105). Greenwich, CT: JAI Press.

Plomin, R. (1996). Nature and nurture. In M. R. Merriens & G. G. Branigan (Eds.), *The developmental psychologists* (pp. 3–20). New York: McGraw-Hill.

Plomin, R., Corley, R., DeFries, J. C., & Fulker, D. W. (1990). Individual differences in television viewing in early childhood: Nature as well as nurture. *Psychological Science, 1,* 371–377.

Plomin, R., DeFries, J. C., & Fulker, D. (1988). The Colorado Adoption Project. In R. Plomin, J. C. DeFries, & D. Fulker (Eds.), *Nature and nurture during infancy and early childhood* (pp. 37–76). Cambridge, UK: Cambridge University Press.

Plomin, R., DeFries, J. C., & McClearn, G. E. (1990). *Behavioral genetics: A primer* (2nd ed.). New York: W.H. Freeman.

Plomin, R., DeFries, J. C., McClearn, G. E., & McGuffin, P. (2001). *Behavioral genetics* (4th ed.). New York: Worth.

Plomin, R., Owen, M. J., & McGuffin, P. (1994). The genetic basis of complex human behaviors. *Science, 264,* 1733–1739.

Plomin, R., Reiss, D., Hetherington, E. M., & Howe, G. W. (1994). Nature and nurture: Genetic contributions to measures of the family environment. *Developmental Psychology, 30,* 32–43.

Plomin, R., & Rutter, M. (1998). Child development, molecular genetics, and what to do with genes once they are found. *Child Development, 69,* 1223–1242.

Plunkett, K. (1995). Connectionist approaches to language acquisition. In P. Fletcher & B. MacWhinney (Eds.), *The handbook of child language* (pp. 36–72). Oxford, UK: Blackwell.

Plunkett, K., & Marchman, V. A. (1996). Learning from a connectionist model of the acquisition of the English past tense. *Cognition, 61,* 299–308.

Polka, L. M., & Werker, J. F. (1994). Developmental changes in perception of nonnative vowel contrasts. *Journal of Experimental Psychology: Human Perception and Performance, 20,* 421–435.

Pollak, S. D., Cicchetti, D., Hornung, K., & Reed, A. (2000). Recognizing emotion in faces: Developmental effects of child abuse and neglect. *Developmental Psychology, 36,* 679–688.

Pollard, I. (2000). Substance abuse and parenthood: Biological mechanisms–bioethical challenges. *Women & Health, 30,* 1–24.

Pollitt, E. (1994). Poverty and child development: Relevance of research in developing countries to the United States. *Child Development, 65,* 283–295.

Pollitt, E. (1996). Timing and vulnerability in research on malnutrition and cognition. *Nutrition Reviews, 54,* S49-S55.

Pollitt, E., Gorman, K. S., Engle, P. L., Martorell, R., & Rivera, J. (1993). Early supplementary feeding and cognition. *Monographs of the Society for Research in Child Development, 58*(7, Serial No. 235).

Pollock, L. A. (1983). *Forgotten children: Parent-child relations from 1500–1900.* Cambridge, UK: Cambridge University Press.

Pomerantz, E. M., Ruble, D. N., Frey, K. S., & Greulich, F. (1995). Meeting goals and confronting conflict: Children's changing perceptions of social comparison. *Child Development, 66,* 723–738.

Pomerleau, A., Bolduc, D., Malcuit, G., & Cossette, L. (1990). Pink or blue: Environmental gender stereotypes in the first two years of life. *Sex Roles, 22,* 359–367.

Poole, D. A., & Lindsay, D. S. (2002). Reducing child witnesses' false reports of misinformation from parents. *Journal of Experimental Child Psychology, 81,* 117–140.

Poole, D. A., & White, L. T. (1991). Effects of question repetition on the eyewitness testimony of children and adults. *Developmental Psychology, 27,* 975–986.

Poole, D. A., & White, L. T. (1993). Two years later: Effects of question repetition and retention interval on the eyewitness testimony of children and adults. *Developmental Psychology, 29,* 844–853.

Pope, A. W., & Bierman, K. L. (1999). Predicting adolescent peer problems and antisocial activities: The relative roles of aggression and dysregulation. *Developmental Psychology, 35,* 335–346.

Pope, S., & Kipp, K. K. (1998). The development of efficient forgetting: Evidence from directed-forgetting tasks. *Developmental Review, 18,* 86–123.

Porges, S. W., Doussard-Roosevelt, J. A., & Maiti, A. K. (1994). Vagal tone and the physiological regulation of emotion. In N. A. Fox (Ed.), *The development of emotion regulation: Biological and behavioral considerations. Monographs of the Society for Research in Child Development, 59*(2–3, Serial No. 240).

Porter, F. L., Grunau, R. E., & Anand, K. J. S. (1999). Long-term effects of pain in infants. *Journal of Developmental and Behavioral Pediatrics, 20,* 253–261.

Porter, R. H., Balogh, R. D., & Makin, J. W. (1988). Olfactory influences on mother-infant interaction. In C. Rovee-Collier & L. P. Lipsitt (Eds.), *Advances in infancy research* (Vol. 5, pp. 39–68). Norwood, NJ: Ablex.

Posada, G., Gao, Y., Wu, F., Posada, R., Tascon, M., Schoelmerich, A., et al. (1995). The secure-base phenomenon across cultures: Children's behaviors, mothers' preferences, and experts' concepts. In E. Waters, B. E. Vaughn, G. Posada, & K. Kondo-Ikemura (Eds.), *Caregiving, cultural, and cognitive perspectives on secure-base behavior and working models: New growing points of attachment theory and research. Monographs of the Society for Research in Child Development, 60* (Nos. 2–3, Serial No. 244).

Post, R. M., & Weiss, S. R. B. (1997). Emergent properties of neural systems: How focal molecular neurobiological alterations can affect behavior. *Development and Psychopathology, 9,* 907–929.

Poulin-Dubois, D., Lepage, A., & Ferland, D. (1996). Infants' concept of animacy. *Cognitive Development, 11,* 19–36.

Poulin-Dubois, D., Serbin, L. A., & Derbyshire, A. (1998). Toddlers' intermodal and verbal knowledge about gender. *Merrill-Palmer Quarterly, 44,* 338–354.

Poulin-Dubois, D., Serbin, L. A., Eichstedt, J. A., Sen, M. G., & Beissel, C. F. (2002). Men don't put on make-up: Toddlers' knowledge of the gender stereotyping of household activities. *Social Development, 11,* 166–181.

Power, T. G., & Chapieski, M. L. (1986). Childrearing and impulse control in toddlers: A naturalistic investigation. *Developmental Psychology, 22,* 271–275.

Powers, S. I., Hauser, S. T., & Kilner, L. A. (1989). Adolescent mental health. *American Psychologist, 44,* 200–208.

Prader, A. (1978). Catch-up growth. *Postgraduate Medical Journal, 54,* 133–146.

Prather, P. A., & Bacon, J. (1986). Developmental differences in part/whole identification. *Child Development, 57,* 549–558.

Pratt, M. W., Green, D., MacVicar, J., & Bountrogianni, M. (1992). The mathematical parent: Parental scaffolding, parenting style, and learning outcomes in long-division mathematics homework. *Journal of Applied Developmental Psychology, 13,* 17–34.

Premack, D. (1971). Language in chimpanzee? *Science, 172,* 808–822.

Pressley, M., & Levin, J. R. (1977). Task parameters affecting the efficacy of a visual imagery learning strategy in younger and older children. *Journal of Experimental Child Psychology, 24,* 53–59.

Preyer, W. (1888–1889). *The mind of the child* (H. W. Brown, Trans.). New York: Appleton. (Original work published in 1882)

Price-Williams, D., Gordon, W., & Ramirez, M. (1969). Skill and conservation: A study of pottery-making children. *Developmental Psychology, 1,* 769.

Pride, P. G., Drugan, A., Johnson, M. P., Isada, N. B., & Evans, M. I. (1993). Prenatal diagnosis: Choices women make about pursuing testing and acting on abnormal results. *Clinical Obstetrics and Gynecology, 36,* 496–509.

Prifitera, A., Weiss, L. G., & Saklofske, D. H. (1998). The WISC-III in context. In A. Prifitera & D. H. Saklofske (Eds.), *WISC-III clinical use and interpretation: Scientist-practitioner perspectives* (pp. 1–38). San Diego, CA: Academic Press.

Proffitt, D. R., & Bertenthal, B. I. (1990). Converging operations revisited: Assessing what infants perceive using discrimination measures. *Perception & Psychophysics, 47,* 1–11.

Pulkkinen, L. (1982). Self-control and continuity from childhood to adolescence. In P. B. Baltes & O. G. Brim (Eds.), *Life-span development and behavior* (Vol. 4, pp. 63–105). New York: Academic Press.

Purcell, P., & Stewart, L. (1990). Dick and Jane in 1989. *Sex Roles, 22,* 177–185.

Putallaz, M. (1987). Maternal behavior and children's sociometric status. *Child Development, 58,* 324–340.

Quinn, P. C., Eimas, P. D., & Rosenkranz, S. L. (1993). Evidence for representations of perceptually similar natural categories by 3-month-old and 4-month-old infants. *Perception, 22,* 463–475.

Radin, N. (1981). The role of the father in cognitive, academic, and intellectual development. In M. E. Lamb (Ed.), *The role of the father in child development.* New York: Wiley.

Radin, N. (1982). Primary caregiving and role-sharing fathers. In M. E. Lamb (Ed.), *Nontraditional families: Parenting and child development* (pp. 379–427). Hillsdale, NJ: Erlbaum.

Radke-Yarrow, M., & Zahn-Waxler, C. (1984). Roots, motives, and patterns of children's prosocial behavior. In E. Staub, D. Bar-Tel, J. Karylowski, & J. Reykowski (Eds.), *Development and maintenance of prosocial behavior* (pp. 81–99). New York: Plenum Press.

Radke-Yarrow, M., Zahn-Waxler, C., & Chapman, M. (1983). Children's prosocial dispositions and behavior. In E. M. Hetherington (Ed.), *Handbook of child psychology: Vol. IV. Socialization, personality, and social development* (4th ed., pp. 469–545). New York: Wiley.

Radziszewska, B., Richardson, J. L., Dent, C. W., & Flay, B. R. (1996). Parenting style and adolescent depressive symptoms, smoking, and academic achievement: Ethnic, gender, and SES differences. *Journal of Behavioral Medicine, 19,* 289–305.

Radziszewska, B., & Rogoff, B. (1988). Influence of adult and peer collaborators on children's planning skills. *Developmental Psychology, 24,* 840–848.

Radziszewska, B., & Rogoff, B. (1991). Children's guided participation in planning imaginary errands with skilled adult or peer partners. *Developmental Psychology, 27,* 381–389.

Raffaelli, M. (1989, April). *Conflict with siblings and friends in late childhood and early adolescence.* Paper presented at the biennial meeting of the Society for Research in Child Development, Kansas City, MO.

Rakic, P. (1981). Developmental events leading to laminar and areal organization of the neocortex. In F. O. Schmitt, F. G. Worden, G. Adelman, & S. G. Dennis (Eds.), *The organization of the cerebral cortex: Proceedings of a neurosciences research program colloquium.* Cambridge, MA: MIT Press.

Rallison, M. L. (1986). *Growth disorders in infants, children, and adolescents.* New York: Wiley.

Ram, A., & Ross, H. S. (2001). Problem-solving, contention, and struggle: How siblings resolve a conflict of interests. *Child Development, 72,* 1710–1722.

Ramenghi, L. A., Griffith, G. C., Wood, C. M., & Levene, M. I. (1996). Effect of non-sucrose sweet tasting solution on neonatal heel prick responses. *Archives of Disease in Childhood, 74,* F129–F131.

Ramey, C. T., Bryant, D. M., & Suarez, T. M. (1987). Early intervention: Why, for whom, how, at what cost? In N. Gunzenhauser (Ed.), *Infant stimulation: For whom, what kind, when, and how much?* (Johnson & Johnson Baby Products Company Pediatric Round Table Series No. 13, pp. 170–180). Skilman, NJ: Johnson & Johnson.

Ramey, C. T., Bryant, D. M., Wasik, B. H., Sparling, J. J., Fendt, K. H., & LaVange, L. M. (1992). Infant Health and Development Program for low birth weight, premature infants: Program elements, family participation, and child intelligence. *Pediatrics, 89,* 454–465.

Ramey, C. T., & Campbell, F. A. (1981). Educational intervention for children at risk for mild retardation: A longitudinal analysis. In P. Mittler (Ed.), *Frontiers of knowledge in mental retardation: Vol. 1. Social, educational, and behavioral aspects* (pp. 47–57). Baltimore: University Park Press.

Ramey, C. T., Lee, M. W., & Burchinal, M. R. (1989). Developmental plasticity and predictability: Consequences of ecological change. In M. H. Bornstein & N. A. Krasnegor (Eds.), *Stability and continuity in mental development: Behavioral and biological perspectives* (pp. 217–233). Hillsdale, NJ: Erlbaum.

Ramey, C. T., & Ramey, S. L. (1998). Early intervention and early experience. *American Psychologist, 53,* 109–120.

Rao, N., & Stewart, S. M. (1999). Cultural influences on sharer and recipient behavior: Sharing in Chinese and Indian preschool children. *Journal of Cross-Cultural Psychology, 30,* 219–241.

Rapport, M. D. (1995). Attention-deficit hyperactivity disorder. In M. Hersen & R. T. Ammerman (Eds.), *Advanced abnormal psychology* (pp. 353–373). Hillsdale, NJ: Erlbaum.

Ratner, H. H. (1984). Memory demands and the development of young children's memory. *Child Development, 55,* 2173–2191.

Raven, J. C. (1962). *Coloured progressive matrices.* London: H. K. Lewis and Co.

Reece, E. A., Hobbins, J. C., Mahoney, M. J., & Petrie, R. H. (1995). *Handbook of medicine of the fetus & mother.* Philadelphia: J. B. Lippincott.

Reese, E., & Fivush, R. (1993). Parental styles for talking about the past. *Developmental Psychology, 29,* 596–606.

Reese, E., Haden, C. A., & Fivush, R. (1993). Mother-child conversations about the past: Relationships of style and memory over time. *Cognitive Development, 8,* 403–430.

Reese, L., Balzano, S., Gallimore, R., & Goldenberg, C. (1995). The concept of *educación*: Latino family values and American schooling. *International Journal of Educational Research, 23,* 57–81.

Reilly, J. J., & Dorosty, A. R. (1999). Epidemic of obesity in UK children. *Lancet, 354,* 1874–1875.

Reisman, J. E. (1987). Touch, motion, and proprioception. In P. Salapatek & L. Cohen (Eds.), *Handbook of infant perception: From sensation to perception* (Vol. 1, pp. 265–303). Orlando, FL: Academic Press.

Reiss, D., Neiderhiser, J. M., Hetherington, E. M., & Plomin, R. (2000). *The relationship code: Deciphering genetic and social patterns in adolescent development.* Cambridge, MA: Harvard University Press.

Reissland, N. (1988). Neonatal imitation in the first hour of life: Observations in rural Nepal. *Developmental Psychology, 24,* 464–469.

Remafedi, G., French, S., Story, M., Resnick, M. D., & Blum, R. (1998). The relationship between suicide risk and sexual orientation: Results of a population-based study. *American Journal of Public Health, 88,* 57–60.

Renninger, K. A. (1992). Individual interest and development: Implications for theory and practice. In K. A. Renninger, S. Hidi, & A. Krapp (Eds.), *The role of interest in learning and development* (pp. 361–395). Hillsdale, NJ: Erlbaum.

Renshaw, P. D. & Brown, P. J. (1993). Loneliness in middle childhood: Concurrent and longitudinal predictors. *Child Development, 64,* 1271–1284.

Repacholi, B. M., & Gopnik, A. (1997). Early reasoning about desires: Evidence from 14- and 18-month-olds. *Developmental Psychology, 33,* 12–21.

Resnick, L. B. (1986). The development of mathematical intuition. In M. Perlmutter (Ed.), *Perspectives on intellectual development: The Minnesota symposia on child psychology* (Vol. 19). Hillsdale, NJ: Erlbaum.

Resnick, L. B. (1995). Inventing arithmetic: Making children's intuitions work at school. In C. A. Nelson (Ed.), *Basic and applied perspectives on learning, cognition, and development. Minnesota Symposia on Child Psychology* (Vol. 28, pp. 75–101). Mahwah, NJ: Erlbaum.

Resnick, L. B., & Singer, J. A. (1993). Protoquantitative origins of ratio reasoning. In T. P. Carpenter, E. Fennema, & T. A. Romberg (Eds.), *Rational numbers: An integration of research* (pp. 107–130). Hillsdale, NJ: Erlbaum.

Reyna, V. F., & Brainerd, C. J. (1995). Fuzzy-trace theory: An interim synthesis. *Learning and Individual Differences, 7,* 1–75.

Reznick, J. S., & Goldfield, B. A. (1992). Rapid change in lexical development in comprehension and production. *Developmental Psychology, 28,* 406–413.

Rheingold, H. L., & Cook, K. V. (1975). The contents of boys' and girls' rooms as an index of parents' behavior. *Child Development, 46,* 459–463.

Rhodes, J. E., Grossman, J. B., & Resch, N. L. (2000). Agents of change: Pathways through which mentoring relationihips influence adolescents' academic adjustment. *Child Development, 71,* 1662–1671.

Rice, K. G. (1990). Attachment in adolescence: A narrative and meta-analytic review. *Journal of Youth and Adolescence, 19,* 511–538.

Rice, M. L. (1983). The role of television in language acquisition. *Developmental Review, 3,* 211–224.

Rice, M. L., Huston, A. C., Truglio, R., & Wright, J. (1990). Words from "Sesame Street": Learning vocabulary while viewing. *Developmental Psychology, 26,* 421–428.

Rice, M. L., & Woodsmall, L. (1988). Lessons from television: Children's word learning when viewing. *Child Development, 59,* 420–429.

Richards, H. G., Bear, G. G., Stewart, A. L., & Norman, A. D. (1992). Moral reasoning and classroom conduct: Evidence for a curvilinear relationship. *Merrill-Palmer Quarterly, 38,* 176–190.

Richards, H. G., Frentzen, B., Gerhardt, K. J., McCann, M. E., & Abrams, R. M. (1992). Sound levels in the human uterus. *Obstetrics and Gynecology, 80,* 186–190.

Richards, J. E. (2000). Localizing the development of covert attention in infants with scalp event-related potentials. *Developmental Psychology, 36,* 91–108.

Richards, J. E., & Holley, F. B. (1999). Infant attention and the development of smooth pursuit tracking. *Developmental Psychology, 35,* 856–867.

Richards, M. H., Crowe, P. A., Larson, R., & Swarr, A. (1998). Developmental patterns and gender differences in the experience of peer companionship during adolescence. *Child Development, 69,* 154–163.

Richards, M. H., & Duckett, E. (1994). The relationship of maternal employment to early adolescent daily experience with and without parents. *Child Development, 65,* 225–236.

Rimoin, D. L., Connor, J. M., & Pyeritz, R. E. (1997). Nature and frequency of genetic disease. In D. L. Rimoin, J. M. Connor, & R. E. Pyeritz (Eds.), *Emery and Rimoin's principles and practices of medical genetics* (3rd ed., Vol. 1, pp. 31–34). New York: Churchill Livingstone.

Ris, M. D., Williams, S. E., Hunt, M. M., Berry, H. K., & Leslie, N. (1994). Early-treated phenylketonuria: Adult neuropsychologic outcome. *Journal of Pediatrics, 124,* 388–392.

Robbins, W. J., Brody, S., Hogan, A. G., Jackson, C. M., & Green, C. W. (Eds.). (1928). *Growth.* New Haven: Yale University Press.

Roberts, D. F., Foehr, U. G., Rideout, V. J., & Brodie, M. (1999). *Kids and media at the new millennium: A comprehensive national analysis of children's media use.* Menlo Park, CA: The Henry J. Kaiser Family Foundation.

Roberts, J. E., Burchinal, M., & Durham, M. (1999). Parents' reports of vocabulary and grammatical development of African American preschoolers: Child and environment associations. *Child Development, 70,* 92–106.

Roberts, L. (1991). Does the egg beckon sperm when the time is right? *Science, 252,* 214.

Roberts, W., & Strayer, J. (1996). Empathy, emotional expressiveness, and prosocial behavior. *Child Development, 67,* 449–470.

Robertson, M. A. (1984). Changing motor patterns during childhood. In J. R. Thomas (Ed.), *Motor development during childhood and adolescence.* Minneapolis, MN: Burgess.

Robin, D. J., Berthier, N. E., & Clifton, R. K. (1996). Infants' predictive reaching for moving objects in the dark. *Developmental Psychology, 32,* 824–835.

Robinson, A., & Clinkenbeard, P. R. (1998). Giftedness: An exceptionality examined. *Annual Review of Psychology, 49,* 117–139.

Robinson, A., & de la Chappelle, A. (1997). Sex chromosome abnormalities. In D. L. Rimoin, J. M. Connor, & R. E. Pyeritz (Eds.), *Emery and Rimoin's principles and practices of medical genetics* (3rd ed., Vol. 1, pp. 973–997). New York: Churchill Livingstone.

Robinson, J. L., Kagan, J., Reznick, J. S., & Corley, R. (1992). The heritability of inhibited and uninhibited behavior: A twin study. *Developmental Psychology, 28,* 1030–1037.

Robinson, J. L., Zahn-Waxler, C., & Emde, R. N. (1994). Patterns of development in early empathic behavior: Environmental and child constitutional influences. *Social Development, 3,* 125–145.

Robinson, T. N. (2001). Television viewing and childhood obesity. *Pediatric Clinics of North America, 48,* 1017–1026.

Robinson, T. N., Chang, J. Y., Haydel, K. F., & Killen, J. D. (2001). Overweight concerns and body dissatisfaction among third-grade children: The impacts of ethnicity and socioeconomic status. *Journal of Pediatrics, 138,* 181–187.

Rochat, P. (1993). Hand-mouth coordination in the newborn: Morphology, determinants, and early development of a basic act. In G. J. P. Savelsbergh (Ed.), *The development of coordination in infancy* (pp. 265–288). Amsterdam, The Netherlands: Elsevier.

Rochat, P., & Goubet, N. (1995). Development of sitting and reaching in 5- to 6-month-old infants. *Infant Behavior and Development, 18,* 53–68.

Rochat, P., & Morgan, R. (1995). Spatial determinants in perception of self-produced leg movements by 3- to 5-month-old infants. *Developmental Psychology, 31,* 626–636.

Rochat, P., & Morgan, R. (1998). Two functional orientations of self-exploration in infancy. *British Journal of Developmental Psychology, 16,* 139–154.

Rochat, P., & Striano, T. (1999). Social-cognitive development in the first year. In P. Rochat (Ed.), *Early social cognition: Understanding in the first months of life* (pp. 3–34). Mahwah, NJ: Erlbaum.

Rochat, P., & Striano, T. (2002). Who's in the mirror? Self-other discrimination in specular images by four- and nine-month-old infants. *Child Development, 73,* 35–46.

Roesler, T. A., Barry, P. C., & Bock, S. A. (1994). Factitious food allergy and failure to thrive. *Archives of Pediatrics and Adolescent Medicine, 148,* 1150–1155.

Roffwarg, H. P., Muzio, J. N., & Dement, W. C. (1966). Ontogenetic development of the human sleep-dream cycle. *Science, 152,* 604–619.

Rogeness, G. A., & McClure, E. B. (1996). Development and neurotransmitter-environmental interactions. *Development and Psychopathology, 8,* 183–199.

Rogoff, B. (1981). Schooling and the development of cognitive skills. In H. C. Triandis & A. Heron (Eds.), *Handbook of cross-cultural psychology: Developmental psychology* (Vol. 4). Boston: Allyn & Bacon.

Rogoff, B. (1998). Cognition as a collaborative process. In W. Damon (Series Ed.) & D. Kuhn & R. S. Siegler (Vol. Eds.), *Handbook of child psychology: Vol. 2. Cognition, perception, and language* (5th ed., pp. 679–744). New York: Wiley.

Rogoff, B., Mistry, J., Göncü, A., & Mosier, C. (1993). Guided participation in cultural activity by toddlers and caregivers. *Monographs of the Society for Research in Child Development, 58*(8, Serial No. 236).

Roid, G. (2003). *Stanford-Binet Intelligence Scales.* Boston: Houghton Mifflin.

Rönnqvist, L., & von Hofsten, C. (1994). Neonatal finger and arm movements as determined by a social and an object context. *Early Development & Parenting, 3,* 81–94.

Rosch, E., Mervis, C. B., Gray, W. D., Johnson, D. M., & Boyes-Braem, P. (1976). Basic objects in natural categories. *Cognitive Psychology, 8,* 382–439.

Roschelle, J. M., Pea, R. D., Hoadley, C. M., Gordin, D. N., & Means, B. M. (2000, Fall/Winter). Changing how and what children learn in school with computer-based technologies. *Future of Children, 10*(2), 76–101.

Rose, S. A., & Feldman, J. F. (1995). Prediction of IQ and specific cognitive abilities at 11 years from infancy measures. *Developmental Psychology, 31,* 685–696.

Rose, S. A., & Feldman, J. F. (1997). Memory and speed: Their role in the relation of infant information processing to later IQ. *Child Development, 68,* 630–641.

Rose, S. A., Feldman, J. F., Futterweit, L. R., & Jankowski, J. J. (1997). Continuity in visual recognition memory: Infancy to 11 years. *Intelligence, 24,* 381–392.

Rose, S. A., Feldman, J. F., Futterweit, L. R., & Jankowski, J. J. (1998). Continuity in tactual-visual cross-modal transfer: Infancy to 11 years. *Developmental Psychology, 34,* 435–440.

Rose, S. A., Feldman, J. F., & Jankowski, J. J. (2001a). Attention and recognition memory in the 1st year of life: A longitudinal study of preterm and full-term infants. *Developmental Psychology, 37,* 135–151.

Rose, S. A., Feldman, J. F., & Jankowski, J. J. (2001b). Visual short-term memory in the first year of life: Capacity and recency effects. *Developmental Psychology, 37,* 539–549.

Rose, S. A., Gottfried, A. W., & Bridger, W. H. (1981). Cross-modal transfer in 6-month-old infants. *Developmental Psychology, 17,* 661–669.

Rosekrans, M. A. (1967). Imitation in children as a function of perceived similarity to a social model and vicarious reinforcement. *Journal of Personality and Social Psychology, 7,* 307–315.

Rosen, K. S., & Burke, P. B. (1999). Multiple attachment relationships within families: Mothers and fathers with two young children. *Developmental Psychology, 35,* 436–444.

Rosenberg, K. R., & Trevathen, W. R. (2001, November). The evolution of human birth. *Scientific American, 285,* 72–77.

Rosenblith, J. F., & Sims-Knight, J. E. (1985). *In the beginning: Development in the first two years of life.* Monterey, CA: Brooks/Cole.

Rosenblum, L. D., Schmuckler, M. A., & Johnson, J. A. (1997). The McGurk effect in infants. *Perception & Psychophysics, 59,* 347–357.

Rosengren, K. S., Gelman, S. A., Kalish, C. W., & McCormick, M. (1991). As time goes by: Children's early understanding of growth in animals. *Child Development, 62,* 1302–1320.

Rosenkoetter, L. I. (1973). Resistance to temptation: Inhibitory and disinhibitory effects of models. *Developmental Psychology, 8,* 80–84.

Rosenshine, B., & Meister, C. (1994). Reciprocal teaching: A review of research. *Review of Educational Research, 64,* 479–530.

Rosenthal, R., & Jacobson, L. (1968). *Pygmalion in the classroom: Teacher expectation and pupils' intellectual development.* New York: Holt, Rinehart & Winston.

Ross, G. S. (1980). Categorization in infancy. *Developmental Psychology, 16,* 391–396.

Rossman, B. R. (1992). School-age children's perceptions of coping with distress: Strategies for emotion regulation and the moderation of adjustment. *Journal of Child Psychology and Psychiatry, 33,* 1373–1397.

Rotberg, I. C. (1998). Interpretation of international test scores. *Science, 280,* 1030–1031.

Rothbart, M. K. (1986). Longitudinal home observations of infant temperament. *Developmental Psychology, 22,* 356–365.

Rothbart, M. K., Ahadi, S. A., & Evans, D. E. (2000). Temperament and personality: Origins and outcomes. *Journal of Personality and Social Psychology, 78,* 122–135.

Rothbart, M. K., Ahadi, S. A., & Hershey, K. L. (1994). Temperament and social behavior in childhood. *Merrill-Palmer Quarterly, 40,* 21–39.

Rothbart, M. K., & Bates, J. E. (1998). Temperament. In W. Damon (Series Ed.) & N. Eisenberg (Vol. Ed.), *Handbook of child psychology: Vol. 3. Social, emotional, and personality development* (5th ed., pp. 105–176). New York: Wiley.

Rothbart, M. K., Derryberry, D., & Posner, M. I. (1994). A psychobiological approach to the development of temperament. In J. E. Bates & T. D. Wachs (Eds.), *Temperament: Individual differences at the interface of biology and behavior* (pp. 83–116). Washington, DC: American Psychological Association.

Rothbaum, F., Weisz, J., Pott, M., Miyake, K., & Morelli, G. (2000). Attachment and culture: Security in the United States and Japan. *American Psychologist, 55,* 1093–1104.

Rothberg, A. D., & Lits, B. (1991). Psychosocial support for maternal stress during pregnancy: Effect on birth weight. *American Journal of Obstetrics and Gynecology, 165,* 403–407.

Rouse, B., Matalon, R., Koch, R., Azen, C., Levy, H., Hanley, W., et al. (2000). Maternal phenylketonuria syndrome: Congenital heart defects, microcephaly, and developmental outcomes. *Journal of Pediatrics, 136,* 57–61.

Rousseau, J. J. (1895). *Émile or treatise on education* (W. H. Payne, Trans.). New York: Appleton. (Original work published 1762)

Rovee-Collier, C. (1999). The development of infant memory. *Current Directions in Psychological Science, 8,* 80–85.

Rovee-Collier, C. K. (1987). Learning and memory in infancy. In J. D. Osofsky (Ed.), *Handbook of infant development* (2nd ed., pp. 98–148). New York: Wiley.

Rovee-Collier, C. K. (1995). Time windows in cognitive development. *Developmental Psychology, 31,* 147–169.

Rovee-Collier, C. K., Evancio, S., & Earley, L. A. (1995). The time window hypothesis: Spacing effects. *Infant Behavior and Development, 18,* 69–78.

Rovee-Collier, C. K., Greco-Vigorito, C., & Hayne, H. (1993). The time window hypothesis: Implications for categorization and memory modification. *Infant Behavior and Development, 16,* 149–176.

Rovee-Collier, C. K., & Hayne, H. (1987). Reactivation of infant memory: Implications for cognitive development. In H. W. Reese (Ed.), *Advances in child development and behavior* (Vol. 20, pp. 185–238). San Diego, CA: Academic Press.

Rovee-Collier, C., Schechter, A., Shyi, G. C. W., & Shields, P. (1992). Perceptual identification of contextual attributes and infant memory retrieval. *Developmental Psychology, 28,* 307–318.

Rovee-Collier, C. K., & Shyi, G. (1992). A functional and cognitive analysis of infant long-term retention. In M. L. Howe, C. J. Brainerd, & V. F. Reyna (Eds.), *Development of long-term retention* (pp. 3–55). New York: Springer-Verlag.

Rowe, D. C., Jacobson, K. C., & Van den Oord, E. J. C. G. (1999). Genetic and environmental influences on vocabulary IQ: Parental education level as moderator. *Child Development, 70,* 1151–1162.

Rozin, P. (1990). Development in the food domain. *Developmental Psychology, 26,* 555–562.

Rubin, K. H. (1993). The Waterloo Longitudinal Project: Correlates and consequences of social withdrawal from childhood to adolescence. In K. H. Rubin & J. B. Asendorpf (Eds.), *Social withdrawal, inhibition, and shyness in childhood* (pp. 291–314). Hillsdale, NJ: Erlbaum.

Rubin, K. H., & Asendorpf, J. B. (1993). Social withdrawal, inhibition, and shyness in childhood: Conceptual and definitional issues. In K. H. Rubin & J. B. Asendorpf (Eds.), *Social withdrawal, inhibition, and shyness in childhood* (pp. 3–17). Hillsdale, NJ: Erlbaum.

Rubin, K. H., Bukowski, W., & Parker, J. G. (1998). Peer interactions, relationships, and groups. In W. Damon (Series Ed.) & N. Eisenberg (Vol. Ed.), *Handbook of child psychology. Vol. 3. Social, emotional, and personality development* (5th ed., pp. 619–700). New York: Wiley.

Rubin, K. H., Fein, G. G., & Vandenberg, B. (1983). Play. In E. M. Hetherington (Ed.), *Handbook of child psychology: Vol. IV. Socialization, personality, and social development* (4th ed., pp. 693–744). New York: Wiley.

Rubin, K. H., Hymel, S., & Mills, R. S. L. (1989). Sociability and social withdrawal in childhood: Stability and outcomes. *Journal of Personality, 57,* 238–255.

Rubin, K. H., & Krasnor, L. R. (1986). Social-cognitive and social behavioral perspectives on problem-solving. In M. Perlmutter (Ed.), *The Minnesota symposia on child psychology: Vol. 18. Cognitive perspectives on children's social and behavioral development.* Hillsdale, NJ: Erlbaum.

Rubin, K. H., Lynch, D., Coplan, R., Rose-Krasnor, L., & Booth, C. L. (1994). "Birds of a feather...": Behavioral concordances and preferential personal attraction in children. *Child Development, 65,* 1778–1785.

Rubin, K. H., Maioni, T. L., & Hornung, M. (1976). Free play behaviors in middle- and lower-class preschoolers: Parten and Piaget revisited. *Child Development, 47,* 414–419.

Ruble, D. N. (1983). The development of social-comparison processes and their role in achievement-related self-socialization. In E. T. Higgins, D. Ruble, & W. W. Hartup (Eds.), *Social cognition and social development: A sociocultural perspective* (pp. 134–157). Cambridge, UK: Cambridge University Press.

Ruble, D. N. (1987). The acquisition of self-knowledge: A self-socialization perspective. In N. Eisenberg (Ed.), *Contemporary topics in developmental psychology* (pp. 243–270). New York: Wiley.

Ruble, D. N., Boggiano, A. K., Feldman, N. S., & Loebl, J. H. (1980). Developmental analysis of the role of social comparison in self-evaluation. *Developmental Psychology, 16,* 105–115.

Ruble, D. N., & Brooks-Gunn, J. (1982). The experience of menarche. *Child Development, 53,* 1557–1566.

Ruble, D. N., & Dweck, C. (1995). Self-conceptions, person conception, and their development. In N. Eisenberg (Ed.), *Review of personality and social psychology: Development and social psychology: The interface* (Vol. 15, pp. 109–139). Thousand Oaks, CA: Sage.

Ruble, D. N., Eisenberg, R., & Higgins, E. T. (1994). Developmental changes in achievement evaluation: Motivational implications of self-other differences. *Child Development, 65,* 1095–1110.

Ruble, D. N., & Flett, G. L. (1988). Conflicting goals in self-evaluative information seeking: Developmental and ability level analyses. *Child Development, 59,* 97–106.

Rudolph, K. D., & Hammen, C. (1999). Age and gender as determinants of stress exposure, generation, and reactions in youngsters: A transactional perspective. *Child Development, 70,* 660–677.

Rudolph, K. D., Hammen, C., & Burge, D. (1995). Cognitive representations of self, family, and peers in school-age children: Links with social competence and sociometric status. *Child Development, 66,* 1385–1402.

Rudolph, K. D., Lambert, S. F., Clark, A. G., & Kurlakowsky, K. D. (2001). Negotiating the transition to middle school: The role of self-regulatory processes. *Child Development, 72,* 929–946.

Ruff, H. A., Capozzoli, M., & Weissberg, R. (1998). Age, individuality, and context as factors in sustained visual attention during the preschool years. *Developmental Psychology, 34,* 454–464.

Ruff, H. A., & Kohler, C. J. (1978). Tactual visual transfer in 6-month-old infants. *Infant Behavior and Development, 1,* 259–264.

Ruff, H. A., & Lawson, K. R. (1990). Development of sustained, focused attention in young children during free play. *Developmental Psychology, 26,* 85–93.

Ruff, H. A., & Rothbart, M. K. (1996). *Attention and early development: Themes and variations.* New York: Oxford University Press.

Ruffman, T., Slade, L., & Crowe, E. (2002). The relation between children's and mothers' mental state language and theory-of-mind understanding. *Child Development, 73,* 734–751.

Rumbaugh, D. M., Gill, T. V., & von Glasersfeld, E. C. (1973). Reading and sentence completion by a chimpanzee (*Pan*). *Science, 182,* 731–733.

Runyan, D. K., Hunter, W. M., Socolar, R. R. S., Amaya-Jackson, L., English, D., Landsverk, J., et al. (1998). Children who prosper in unfavorable environments: The relationship to social capital. *Pediatrics, 101,* 12–18.

Rushton, J. P. (1975). Generosity in children: Immediate and long-term effects of modeling, preaching, and moral judgment. *Journal of Personality and Social Psychology, 31,* 459–466.

Russell, G., & Russell, A. (1987). Mother-child and father-child relationships in middle childhood. *Child Development, 58,* 1573–1585.

Rutter, M. (1983). School effects on pupil progress: Research findings and policy implications. *Child Development, 54,* 1–29.

Rutter, M. (1986). Meyerian psychobiology, personality development, and the role of life experiences. *American Journal of Psychiatry, 143,* 1077–1087.

Rutter, M. (1990). Psychosocial resilience and protective mechanisms. In J. Rolf, A. S. Masten, D. Cicchetti, K. H. Neuchterlein, & S. Weintraub (Eds.), *Risk and protective factors in the development of psychopathology* (pp. 79–101). New York: Cambridge University Press.

Rutter, M. (1991). Age changes in depressive disorders: Some developmental considerations. In J. Garber & K. A. Dodge (Eds.), *The development of emotion regulation and dysregulation* (pp. 273–300). Cambridge, UK: Cambridge University Press.

Rutter, M. (2002). Nature, nurture, and development: From evangelism through science toward policy and practice. *Child Development, 73,* 1–21.

Rutter, M., & Garmezy, N. (1983). Developmental psychopathology. In E. M. Hetherington (Ed.), *Handbook of child psychology: Vol. IV. Socialization, personality, and social development* (4th ed., pp. 775–911). New York: Wiley.

Rutter, M., & Madge, N. (1976). *Cycles of disadvantage.* London: Heinemann.

Rutter, M., Maughan, B., Mortimore, P., Ouston, J., & Smith, A. (1979). *Fifteen thousand hours: Secondary schools and their effects on children.* Cambridge, MA: Harvard University Press.

Rutter, M., & Silberg, J. (2002). Gene-environment interplay in relation to emotional and behavioral disturbance. *Annual Review of Psychology, 53,* 463–490.

Rutter, M., Silberg, J., O'Connor, T., & Simonoff, E. (1999a). Genetics and child psychiatry: I. Advances in quantitative and molecular genetics. *Journal of Child Psychology and Psychiatry, 40,* 3–18.

Rutter, M., Silberg, J., O'Connor, T., & Simonoff, E. (1999b). Genetics and child psychiatry: II. Empirical research findings. *Journal of Child Psychology and Psychiatry, 40,* 19–55.

Ryan, R. M., & Grolnick, W. S. (1986). Origins and pawns in the classroom: Self-report and projective assessments of individual differences in children's perceptions. *Journal of Personality and Social Psychology, 50,* 550–558.

Saarni, C. (1998). Issues of cultural meaningfulness in emotional development. *Developmental Psychology, 34,* 647–652.

Saarni, C. (1999). *The development of emotional competence.* New York: Guilford.

Saarni, C., Mumme, D. L., & Campos, J. J. (1998). Emotional development: Action, communication, and understanding. In W. Damon (Series Ed.) & N. Eisenberg (Vol. Ed.), *Handbook of child psychology: Vol. 3. Social, emotional, and personality development* (5th ed., pp. 237–309). New York: Wiley.

Sachs, S. (2001, August 15). Clinic's pitch to Indian emigres: It's a boy. *New York Times,* pp. A1, B6.

Sadker, M. & Sadker, D. (1994). *Failing at fairness: How America's schools cheat girls.* New York: Charles Scribner's Sons.

Sagi, A., Lamb, M. E., Lewkowicz, K. S., Shoham, R., Dvir, R., & Estes, D. (1985). Security of infant-mother, -father, and -metapelet attachments among kibbutz-reared Israeli children. In I. Bretherton & E. Waters (Eds.), *Growing points of attachment theory and research. Monographs of the Society for Research in Child Development, 50*(1–2, Serial No. 209).

Sagi, A., Van IJzendoorn, M. H., Aviezer, O., Donnell, F., & Mayseless, O. (1994). Sleeping out of home in a kibbutz communal arrangement: It makes a difference for mother-child attachment. *Child Development, 65,* 991–1004.

Saigal, S., Hoult, L. A., Streiner, D. L., Stoskopf, B. L., & Rosenbaum, P. L. (2000). School difficulties at adolescence in a regional cohort of children who were extremely low birth weight. *Pediatrics, 105,* 325–331.

Saffran, J. R. (2001). Words in a sea of sounds: The output of infant statistical learning. *Cognition, 81,* 149–169.

Saffran, J. R., Aslin, R. N., & Newport, E. (1996). Statistical learning by 8-month-olds. *Science, 274,* 1926–1928.

Saffran, J. R., & Griepentrog, G. J. (2001). Absolute pitch in infant auditory learning: Evidence for developmental reorganization. *Developmental Psychology, 37,* 74–85.

Saffran, J. R., Loman, M. M., & Robertson, R. R. W. (2000). Infant memory for musical experiences. *Cognition, 77,* B15–B23.

Sakala, C. (1993). Midwifery care and out-of-hospital birth settings: How do they reduce unnecessary cesarean section births? *Social Science and Medicine, 37,* 1233–1250.

Salapatek, P. (1975). Pattern perception in early infancy. In L. B. Cohen & P. Salapatek (Eds.), *Infant perception: From sensation to cognition* (Vol. 1, pp. 143–248). New York: Academic Press.

Saltzman, R. L., & Jordan, M. C. (1988). Viral infections. In G. N. Burrow & T. F. Ferris (Eds.), *Medical complications during pregnancy.* Philadelphia: W.B. Saunders.

Salzinger, S., Feldman, R. S., Hammer, M., & Rosario, M. (1993). The effects of physical abuse on children's social relationships. *Child Development, 64,* 169–187.

Samarapungavan, A. (1992). Children's judgments in theory choice tasks: Scientific rationality in childhood. *Cognition, 45,* 1–32.

Sameroff, A. J. (1972). Learning and adaptation in infancy: A comparison of models. In H. W. Reese (Ed.), *Advances in child development and behavior* (Vol. 7, pp. 170–214). New York: Academic Press.

Sameroff, A. J. (1994). Developmental systems and family functioning. In R. D. Parke & S. G. Kellam (Eds.), *Exploring family relationships with other social contexts* (pp. 199–214). Hillsdale, NJ: Erlbaum.

Sameroff, A. J., & Chandler, P. J. (1975). Reproductive risk and the continuum of caretaking casualty. In F. D. Horowitz (Ed.), *Review of child development research* (Vol. 4, pp. 187–244). Chicago: University of Chicago Press.

Sameroff, A. J., Seifer, R., Baldwin, A., & Baldwin, C. (1993). Stability of intelligence from preschool to adolescence: The influence of social and family risk factors. *Child Development, 64,* 80–97.

Sampson, P. D., Streissguth, A. P., Bookstein, F. L., Little, R. E., Clarren, S. K., Dehaene, P., et al. (1997). The incidence of fetal alcohol syndrome and the prevalence of alcohol-related neurodevelopmental disorder. *Teratology, 56,* 317–326.

Sampson, R. J., Raudenbush, S. W., & Earls, F. (1997). Neighborhoods and violent crime: A multilevel study of collective efficacy. *Science, 277,* 918–924.

Samuels, M., & Bennett, H. Z. (1983). *Well body, well earth: The Sierra Club environmental health sourcebook.* San Francisco: Sierra Club Books.

Samuels, M., & Samuels, N. (1986). *The well pregnancy book.* New York: Summit Books.

Samuelson, L. K., & Smith, L. B. (1998). Memory and attention make smart word learning: An alternative account of Akhtar, Carpenter, and Tomasello. *Child Development, 69,* 94–104.

Samuelson, L. K., & Smith, L. B. (2000). Children's attention to rigid and deformable shape in naming and non-naming tasks. *Child Development, 71,* 1555–1570.

Sandberg, D. E., Brook, A. E., & Campos, S. P. (1994). Short stature: A psychosocial burden requiring growth hormone therapy? *Pediatrics, 94,* 832–840.

Sandberg, D. E., Meyer-Bahlburg, H. F., Ehrhardt, A. A., & Yager, T. J. (1993). The prevalence of gender-atypical behavior in elementary school. *Journal of the American Academy of Child and Adolescent Psychiatry, 32,* 306–314.

Sandberg, E. H., & Huttenlocher, J. (2001). Advanced spatial skills and advance planning: Components of 6-year-olds' navigational map use. *Journal of Cognition and Development, 2,* 51–70.

Sanders, C. E., Field, T. M., Diego, M., & Kaplan, M. (2000). The relationship of Internet use to depression and social isolation among adolescents. *Adolescence, 35,* 237–242.

Santrock, J. W., & Sitterle, K. A. (1987). Parent-child relationships in stepmother families. In K. Pasley & M. Ihinger-Tallman (Eds.), *Remarriage and stepparenting: Current research and theory* (pp. 273–299). New York: Guilford Press.

Saudino, K. J. (1997). Moving beyond the heritability question: New directions in behavioral genetic studies of personality. *Current Directions in Psychological Science, 6,* 86–90.

Savage-Rumbaugh, E. S., Murphy, J., Sevcik, R. A., Brakke, K. E., Williams, S. L., & Rumbaugh, D. M. (1993). Language comprehension in ape and child. *Monographs of the Society for Research in Child Development, 58*(3–4, Serial No. 233).

Savin-Williams, R. C. (1979). Dominance hierarchies in groups of early adolescents. *Child Development, 50,* 923–935.

Savin-Williams, R. C. (1980). Dominance hierarchies in groups of middle to late adolescent males. *Journal of Youth and Adolescence, 9,* 75–85.

Sawin, D. B., & Parke, R. D. (1979). The effects of interagent inconsistent discipline on children's aggressive behavior. *Journal of Experimental Child Psychology, 28,* 525–538.

Saxe, G. B., Guberman, S. R., & Gearhart, M. (1987). Social processes in early number development. *Monographs of the Society for Research in Child Development, 52* (2, Serial No. 216).

Saxton, M. (1997). The contrast theory of negative input. *Journal of Child Language, 24,* 139–161.

Scaramella, L. V., Conger, R. D., Simons, R. L., & Whitbeck, L. B. (1998). Predicting risk for pregnancy by late adolescence: A social contextual perspective. *Developmental Psychology, 34,* 1233–1245.

Scaramella, L. V., Conger, R. D., Spoth, R., & Simons, R. L. (2002). Evaluation of a social contextual model of delinquency: A cross-study replication. *Child Development, 73,* 175–195.

Scarborough, H. S., & Dobrich, W. (1993). On the efficacy of reading to preschoolers. *Developmental Review, 14,* 245–302.

Scarr, S. (1981). Genetics and the development of intelligence. In S. Scarr (Ed.), *Race, social class, and individual differences in IQ.* Hillsdale, NJ: Erlbaum.

Scarr, S. (1992). Developmental theories for the 1990s: Development and individual differences. *Child Development, 63,* 1–19.

Scarr, S. (1993). Biological and cultural diversity: The legacy of Darwin for development. *Child Development, 64,* 1333–1353.

Scarr, S., & McCartney, K. (1983). How people make their own environments: A theory of genotype environment effects. *Child Development, 54,* 424–435.

Scarr, S., Webber, P. L., Weinberg, R. A., & Wittig, M. A. (1981). Personality resemblance among adolescents and their parents in biologically related and adoptive families. *Journal of Personality and Social Psychology, 40,* 885–898.

Scarr, S., & Weinberg, R. A. (1976). IQ test performance of black children adopted by white families. *American Psychologist, 31,* 726–739.

Scarr, S., & Weinberg, R. A. (1977). Intellectual similarities within families of both adopted and biological children. *Intelligence, 1,* 170–191.

Scarr, S., & Weinberg, R. A. (1978). The influence of "family background" on intellectual attainment. *American Sociological Review, 43,* 674–692.

Scarr, S., & Weinberg, R. A. (1983). The Minnesota adoption studies: Genetic differences and malleability. *Child Development, 54,* 260–267.

Schachar, R., Mota, V., Logan, G. D., Tannock, R., & Klim, P. (2000). Confirmation of an inhibitory control deficit in attention-deficit/hyparactivity disorder. *Journal of Abnormal Child Psychology, 28,* 227–235.

Schachter, F. F. (1982). Sibling deidentification and split-parent identification: A family tetrad. In M. E. Lamb & B. Sutton-Smith (Eds.), *Sibling relationships: Their nature and significance across the life-span* (pp. 123–151). Hillsdale, NJ: Erlbaum.

Schaffer, H. R., & Emerson, P. E. (1964). The development of social attachments in infancy. *Monographs of the Society for Research in Child Development, 29*(3, Serial No. 94).

Schauble, L. (1996). The development of scientific reasoning in knowledge-rich contexts. *Developmental Psychology, 32,* 102–119.

Scheper-Hughes, N. (1992). *Death without weeping: The violence of everyday life in Brazil.* Berkeley: University of California Press.

Schieffelin, B. B., & Ochs, E. (1983). A cultural perspective on the transition from prelinguistic to linguistic communication. In R. M. Golinkoff (Ed.), *The transition from prelinguistic to linguistic communication* (pp. 115–131). Hillsdale, NJ: Erlbaum.

Schlegel, A., & Barry, H. III. (1991). *Adolescence: An anthropological inquiry.* New York: Free Press.

Schlinger, H.D., Jr. (1992). Theory in behavior analysis: An application to child development. *American Psychologist, 47,* 1396–1410.

Schmitt, K. A., & Anderson, D. R. (2002). Television and reality: Toddlers' use of visual information from video to guide behavior. *Media Psychology, 4,* 51–76.

Schmitt, K. L., Anderson, D. R., & Collins, P. A. (1999). Form and content: Looking at visual features of television. *Developmental Psychology, 35,* 1156–1167.

Schmuckler, M. A., & Fairhall, J. L. (2001). Visual-proprioceptive intermodal perception using point light displays. *Child Development, 72,* 949–962.

Schneider, B. H., Atkinson, L., & Tardif, C. (2001). Child-parent attachment and children's peer relations: A quantitative review. *Developmental Psychology, 37,* 86–100.

Schneider, B. H., & Byrne, B. M. (1985). Children's social skills training: A meta-analysis. In B. H. Schneider, K. H. Rubin, & J. E. Ledingham (Eds.), *Children's peer relations: Issues in assessment and intervention* (pp. 179–192). New York: Springer-Verlag.

Schneider, W. (2000). Research on memory development: Historical trends and current themes. *International Journal of Behavioral Development, 24,* 407–420.

Schneider-Rosen, K., Braunwald, K., Carlson, V., & Cicchetti, D. (1985). Current perspectives on attachment theory: Illustrations from the study of maltreated infants. In I. Bretherton & E. Waters (Eds.), *Growing points of attachment theory and research. Monographs of the Society for Research in Child Development, 50*(1–2, Serial No. 209).

Scholmerich, A., Fracasso, M. P., Lamb, M. E., & Broberg, A. (1995). Interactional harmony at 7- and 10-months-of-age predicts security of attachment as measured by Q-sort ratings. *Social Development, 4,* 62–74.

Schore, A. N. (1994). *Affect regulation and the origin of the self: The neurobiology of emotional development.* Hillsdale, NJ: Erlbaum.

Schore, A. N. (1996). The experience-dependent maturation of a regulatory system in the orbital prefrontal cortex and the origin of developmental psychopathology. *Development and Psychopathology, 8,* 59–87.

Schulenberg, J., Asp, C. E., & Petersen, A. (1984). School from the young adolescent's perspective: A descriptive report. *Journal of Early Adolescence, 4,* 107–130.

Schwartz, D., Chang, L., & Farver, J. M. (2001). Correlates of victimization in Chinese children's peer groups. *Developmental Psychology, 37,* 520–532.

Schwartz, D., Dodge, K. A., & Coie, J. D. (1993). The emergence of chronic peer victimization in boys' play groups. *Child Development, 64,* 1755–1772.

Schwartz, D., Dodge, K. A., Pettit, G. S., & Bates, J. E. (1997). The early socialization of aggressive victims of bullying. *Child Development, 68,* 665–675.

Schwartz, D., Dodge, K. A., Pettit, G. S., Bates, J. E., & Conduct Problems Prevention Research Group. (2000). Friendship as a moderating factor in the pathway between early harsh home environment and later victimization in the peer group. *Developmental Psychology, 36,* 646–662.

Scott, K. D., Berkowitz, G., & Klaus, M. (1999). A comparison of intermittent and continuous support during labor: A meta-analysis. *American Journal of Obstetrics and Gynecology, 180,* 1054–1059.

Scoville, R. (1983). Development of the intention to communicate: The eye of the beholder. In L. Feagans, C. Garvey, & R. Golinkoff (Eds.), *The origins and growth of communication* (pp. 109–122). Norwood, NJ: Ablex.

Scriver, C. R., Beaudet, A. L., Sly, W. S., & Valle, D. (1995). *The metabolic and molecular bases of inherited disease,* Vol I. New York: McGraw-Hill.

Secker-Walker, R. H., Vacek, P. M., Flynn, B. S., & Mead, P. B. (1997). Smoking in pregnancy, exhaled carbon monoxide, and birth weight. *Obstetrics and Gynecology, 89,* 648–653.

Segall, M. H., Campbell, D. T., & Herskovits, M. J. (1966). *The influence of culture on perception.* New York: Bobbs-Merrill.

Seidman, E., Allen, L., Aber, J. L., Mitchell, C., & Feinman, J. (1994). The impact of school transitions in early adolescence on the self-system and perceived social context of poor urban youth. *Child Development, 65,* 507–522.

Seitz, V., & Apfel, N. H. (1994). Effects of a school for pregnant students on the incidence of low-birthweight deliveries. *Child Development, 65,* 666–676.

Selman, R. L. (1980). *The growth of interpersonal understanding: Developmental and clinical analysis.* New York: Academic Press.

Selzer, J. A. (1991). Relationships between fathers and children who live apart: The father's role after separation. *Journal of Marriage and the Family, 53,* 79–101.

Sen, M. G., Yonas, A., & Knill, D. C. (2001). Development of infants' sensitivity to surface contour information for spatial layout. *Perception, 30,* 167–176.

Senghas, A., & Coppola, M. (2001). Children creating language: How Nicaraguan Sign Language acquired a spatial grammar. *Psychological Science, 12,* 323–328.

Serbin, L. A., Connor, J. M., & Iler, I. (1979). Sex-stereotyped and non-stereotyped introductions of new toys in the preschool classroom: An observational study of teacher behavior and its effects. *Psychology of Women Quarterly, 4,* 261–265.

Serbin, L. A., O'Leary, K. D., Kent, R. N., & Tonick, I. J. (1973). A comparison of teacher response to the preacademic and problem behavior of boys and girls. *Child Development, 44,* 796–804.

Serbin, L. A., Poulin-Dubois, D., Colburne, K. A., Sen, M. G., & Eichstedt, J. A. (2001). Gender stereotyping in infancy: Visual preferences for and knowledge of gender-stereotyped toys in the second year. *International Journal of Behavioral Development, 25*, 7–15.

Serbin, L. A., Powlishta, K. K., & Gulko, J. (1993). The development of sex typing in middle childhood. *Monographs of the Society for Research in Child Development, 58* (No. 2, Serial No. 232).

Serbin, L. A., Tonick, I. J., & Sternglanz, S. H. (1977). Shaping cooperative cross-sex play. *Child Development, 48*, 924–929.

Shachar, H., & Sharan, S. (1994). Talking, relating, and achieving: Effects of cooperative learning and whole-class instruction. *Cognition and Instruction, 12*, 313–353.

Shah, N. R., & Bracken, M. B. (2000). A systematic review and meta-analysis of prospective studies on the association between maternal cigarette smoking and preterm delivery. *American Journal of Obstetrics and Gynecology, 182*, 465–472.

Shahar, S. (1990). *Childhood in the Middle Ages.* London: Routledge.

Shantz, C. (1983). Social cognition. In J. H. Flavell & E. M. Markman (Eds.), *Handbook of child psychology: Vol. III. Cognitive development* (4th ed., pp. 495–555). New York: Wiley.

Sharma, A. R., McGue, M. K., & Benson, P. L. (1998). The psychological adjustment of United States adopted adolescents and their nonadopted siblings. *Child Development, 69*, 791–802.

Sharp, D., Cole, M., & Lave, C. (1979). Education and cognitive development: The evidence from experimental research. *Monographs of the Society for Research in Child Development, 44*(1–2, Serial No. 178).

Shatz, C. J. (1992, September). The developing brain. *Scientific American,* pp. 60–67.

Shatz, M., & Gelman, R. (1973). The development of communication skills: Modification in the speech of young children as a function of listener. *Monographs of the Society for Research in Child Development, 38*(5, Serial No. 152).

Shaw, E., & Darling, J. (1985). *Strategies of being female.* Brighton, UK: Harvester Press.

Shepard, L. A., & Smith, M. L. (1986). Synthesis of research on school readiness and kindergarten retention. *Educational Leadership, 44*, 78–86.

Sherif, M., Harvey, O. J., White, B. J., Hood, W. R., & Sherif, C. W. (1961). *Inter-group conflict and cooperation: The Robber's Cave experiment.* Norman: University of Oklahoma Press.

Shinskey, J. L., & Munakata, Y. (2001). Detecting transparent barriers: Clear evidence against the means-end deficit account of search failures. *Infancy, 2*, 395–404.

Shoda, Y., Mischel, W., & Peake, P. K. (1990). Predicting adolescent cognitive and self-regulatory competencies from preschool delay of gratification: Identifying diagnostic conditions. *Developmental Psychology, 26*, 978–986.

Shonk, S. M., & Cicchetti, D. (2001). Maltreatment, competency deficits, and risk for academic and behavioral maladjustment. *Developmental Psychology, 37*, 3–17.

Shore, R. (1997). *Rethinking the brain: New insights into early development.* New York: Families and Work Institute.

Shostak, M. (1981). *Nisa: The life and words of a !Kung woman.* Cambridge, MA: Harvard University Press.

Shrum, W., & Cheek, N. H. (1987). Social structure during the school years: Onset of the degrouping process. *American Sociological Review, 52*, 218–223.

Schumuckler, M. A., & Fairhall, J. L. (2001). Visual-proprioceptive intermodal perception using point light displays. *Child Development, 72*, 949-962.

Sen, M. G., Yonas, A., & Knill, D. C. (2001). Development of infant's sensitivity to surface contour information for spatial layout. *Perception, 30*, 167–176.

Shwalb, B. J., Shwalb, D. W., & Shoji, J. (1994). Structure and dimensions of maternal perceptions of Japanese infant temperament. *Developmental Psychology, 30*, 131–141.

Shwe, H. I., & Markman, E. M. (1997). Young children's appreciation of the mental impact of their communicative signals. *Developmental Psychology, 33*, 630–636.

Shweder, R., Goodnow, J., Hatano, G., LeVine, R., Markus, H., & Miller, P. (1998). The cultural psychology of development: One mind, many mentalities. In W. Damon (Series Ed.) & N. Eisenberg (Vol. Ed.), *Handbook of child psychology: Vol. 3. Social, emotional, and personality development* (5th ed., pp. 237–309). New York: Wiley.

Shweder, R. A., Mahapatra, M., & Miller, J. G. (1987). Culture and moral development. In J. Kagan & S. Lamb (Eds.), *The emergence of morality in young children* (pp. 1–83). Chicago: University of Chicago Press.

Siegal, M. (1988). Children's knowledge of contagion and contamination as causes of illness. *Child Development, 59*, 1353–1359.

Siegel, L. S. (1993). Phonological processing deficits as the basis of a reading disability. *Developmental Review, 13*, 246–257.

Siegel, L. S. (1998). Phonological processing deficits and reading disabilities. In J. L. Metsala & L. C. Ehri (Eds.), *Word recognition in beginning literacy* (pp. 191–160). Mahwah, NJ: Erlbaum.

Siegler, R. S. (1989). Mechanisms of cognitive development. In M. R. Rosenzweig & L. W. Porter (Eds.), *Annual Review of Psychology, 40*, 353–379.

Siegler, R. S. (1994). Cognitive variability: A key to understanding cognitive development. *Current Directions in Psychological Science, 3*, 1–5.

Siegler, R. S. (1996). *Emerging minds: The process of change in children's thinking.* New York: Oxford University Press.

Siegler, R. S. (1997). Concepts and methods for studying cognitive change. In E. Amsel & K. A. Renninger (Eds.), *Change and development: Issues of theory, method, and application* (pp. 77–97). Mahwah, NJ: Erlbaum.

Siegler, R. S. (1998). *Children's thinking* (3rd ed.). Upper Saddle River, NJ: Prentice-Hall.

Siegler, R. S., & Crowley, K. (1991). The microgenetic method: A direct means for studying cognitive development. *American Psychologist, 46*, 606–620.

Siegler, R. S., & Ellis, S. (1996). Piaget on childhood. *Psychological Science, 7*, 211–215.

Siegler, R. S., & Jenkins, E. (1989). *How children discover new strategies.* Hillsdale, NJ: Erlbaum.

Siegler, R. S., & Richards, D. D. (1982). The development of intelligence. In R. J. Sternberg (Ed.), *Handbook of human intelligence* (pp. 897–971). Cambridge, UK: Cambridge University Press.

Siegler, R. S., & Robinson, M. (1982). The development of numerical understandings. In H. W. Reese & L. P. Lipsitt (Eds.), *Advances in child development and behavior* (Vol. 16, pp. 242–312). New York: Academic Press.

Siegler, R. S., & Shrager, J. (1984). Strategy choices in addition and subtraction: How do children know what to do? In C. Sophian (Ed.), *Origins of cognitive skills* (pp. 229–293). Hillsdale, NJ: Erlbaum.

Siegler, R. S., & Stern, E. (1998). Conscious and unconscious strategy discoveries: A microgenetic analysis. *Journal of Experimental Psychology: General, 127*, 377–397.

Sigelman, C. K., Carr, M. B., & Begley, N. L. (1986). Developmental changes in the influence of sex-role stereotypes on person perception. *Child Study Journal, 16*, 191–205.

Signorella, M. L. (1987). Gender schemata: Individual differences and context effects. In L. S. Liben & M. L. Signorella (Eds.), *New directions for child development: No. 38. Children's gender schemata.* San Francisco: Jossey-Bass.

Signorielli, N. (1989). Television and conceptions about sex roles: Maintaining conventionality and the status quo. *Sex Roles, 21*, 341–360.

Signorielli, N. (1993). Television, the portrayal of women, and children's attitudes. In G. Berry & J. K. Asamen (Eds.), *Children and television: Images in a changing sociocultural world* (pp. 229–242). Newbury Park, CA: Sage.

Silberstein, L., Gardner, H., Phelps, E., & Winner, E. (1982). Autumn leaves and old photographs: The development of metaphor preferences. *Journal of Experimental Child Psychology, 34*, 135–150.

Silver, L. M. (1998, September 21). A quandary that isn't: Picking a baby's sex won't lead to disaster. *Time,* p. 83.

Silverman, I. W., & Ippolito, M. F. (1997). Goal-directedness and its relation to inhibitory control among toddlers. *Infant Behavior and Development, 20*, 271–273.

Silverman, W. K., LaGreca, A. M., & Wasserstein, S. (1995). What do children worry about? Worries and their relation to anxiety. *Child Development, 66*, 671–686.

Simcock, G., & Hayne, H. (2002). Breaking the barrier? Children fail to translate their preverbal memories into language. *Psychological Science, 13*, 225–231.

Simmons, R. G., & Blyth, D. A. (1987). *Moving into adolescence: The impact of pubertal change and school context.* Hawthorne, NY: Aldine de Gruyter.

Simmons, R. G., Blyth, D. A., & McKinney, K. L. (1983). The social and psychological effects of puberty on white females. In J. Brooks-Gunn & A. C. Petersen (Eds.), *Girls at puberty* (pp. 229–272). New York: Plenum Press.

Simmons, R. G., Blyth, D. A., Van Cleave, E. F., & Bush, D. M. (1979). Entry into early adolescence: The impact of school structure, puberty, and early dating on self-esteem. *American Sociological Review, 44,* 948–967.

Simmons, R. G., Burgeson, R., Carlton-Ford, S., & Blyth, D. A. (1987). The impact of cumulative change in early adolescence. *Child Development, 58,* 1220–1234.

Simner, M. L. (1971). Newborn's response to the cry of another infant. *Developmental Psychology, 5,* 136–150.

Simon, T. J., Hespos, S. J., & Rochat, P. (1995). Do infants understand simple arithmetic? A replication of Wynn (1992). *Cognitive Development, 10,* 253–269.

Simons, R., Chao, W., Conger, R., & Elder, G. H. (2001). Quality of parenting as a mediator of the effect of childhood defiance on adolescent friendship choices and delinquency. *Journal of Marriage and Family, 63,* 63–79.

Sinclair, D. (1985). *Human growth after birth* (4th ed.). New York: Oxford University Press.

Singer, J. D., Fuller, B., Keiley, M. K., & Wolf, A. (1998). Early child-care selection: Variation by geographic location, maternal characteristics, and family structure. *Developmental Psychology, 34,* 1129–1144.

Singer, L. M., Brodzinsky, D. M., Ramsay, D., Steir, M., & Waters, E. (1985). Mother-infant attachment in adoptive families. *Child Development, 56,* 1543–1551.

Singer, L. T., Arendt, R., Fagan, J., Minnes, S., Salvator, A., Bolek, T., & Becker, M. (1999). Neonatal visual information processing in cocaine-exposed and non-exposed infants. *Infant Behavior and Development, 22,* 1–15.

Singer, L. T., Arendt, R., Minnes, S., Salvator, A., Siegel, A. C., & Lewis, B. A. (2001). Developing language skills of cocaine-exposed infants. *Pediatrics, 107,* 1057–1064.

Singer, L. T., Salvator, A., Guo, S., Collin, M., Lilien, L., & Baley, J. (1999). Maternal psychological distress and parenting after the birth of a very low-birth-weight infant. *Journal of the American Medical Association, 281,* 799–805.

Singh, L. Morgan, J. L., & Best, C. T. (2002). Infants listening preferences. Baby talk or happy talk? *Infancy, 3,* 365–394.

Sininger, Y. S., Doyle, K. J., & Moore, J. K. (1999). The case for early identification of hearing loss in children: Auditory system development, experimental auditory deprivation, and development of speech and hearing. *Pediatric Clinics of North America, 46,* 1–14.

Siqueland, E. R., & Lipsitt, L. P. (1966). Conditioned head turning in human newborns. *Journal of Experimental Child Psychology, 4,* 356–376.

Sireteanu, R. (1999). Switching on the infant brain. *Science, 286,* 59–61.

Skinner, B. F. (1953). *Science and human behavior.* New York: Macmillan.

Skinner, B. F. (1957). *Verbal behavior.* New York: Appleton-Century-Crofts.

Skinner, B. F. (1971). *Beyond freedom and dignity.* New York: Knopf.

Skinner, B. F. (1974). *About behaviorism.* New York: Knopf.

Skinner, E. A., & Belmont, M. J. (1993). Motivation in the classroom: Reciprocal effects of teacher behavior and student engagement across the school year. *Journal of Educational Psychology, 85,* 571–581.

Skinner, E. A., Zimmer-Gembeck, M. J., & Connell, J. P. (1998). Individual differences and the development of perceived control. *Monographs of the Society for Research in Child Development, 63*(2–3, Serial No. 254).

Skodak, M., & Skeels, H. M. (1949). A final follow-up study of one hundred adopted children. *Pedagogical Seminary and Journal of Genetic Psychology, 75,* 85–125.

Slaby, R. G., & Frey, K. S. (1975). Development of gender constancy and selective attention to same-sex models. *Child Development, 46,* 849–856.

Slade, A., Belsky, J., Aber, J. L., & Phelps, J. L. (1999). Mothers' representations of their relationships with their toddlers: Links to adult attachment and observed mothering. *Developmental Psychology, 35,* 611–619.

Slater, A., Johnson, S. P., Brown, E., & Badenoch, M. (1996). Newborn infants' perception of partly occluded objects. *Infant Behavior and Development, 19,* 145–148.

Slater, A., Quinn, P. C., Brown, E., & Hayes, R. (1999). Intermodal perception at birth: Intersensory redundancy guides newborn infant's learning of arbitrary auditory-visual pairings. *Developmental Science, 2,* 333–338.

Slater, A., Rose, D., & Morison, V. (1984). New-born infants' perception of similarities and differences between two- and three-dimensional stimuli. *British Journal of Developmental Psychology, 3,* 211–220.

Slater, A., Von der Schulenburg, C., Brown, E., Badenoch, M., Butterworth, G., Parsons, S., & Samuels, C. (1998). Newborn infants prefer attractive faces. *Infant Behavior and Development, 21,* 345–354.

Slaughter-Defoe, D. T., Nakagawa, K., Takanishi, R., & Johnson, D. J. (1990). Toward cultural/ecological perspectives on schooling and achievement in African- and Asian-American children. *Child Development, 61,* 363–383.

Slavin, R. E. (1990). *Cooperative learning: Theory, research, and practice.* Englewood Cliffs, NJ: Prentice Hall.

Slomkowski, C., & Dunn, J. (1996). Young children's understanding of other people's beliefs and feelings and their connected communication with friends. *Developmental Psychology, 32,* 442–447.

Smetana, J. G. (1988). Concepts of self and social conventions: Adolescents' and parents' reasoning about hypothetical and actual family conflicts. In M. R. Gunnar & W. A. Collins (Eds.), *The Minnesota symposia on child psychology: Vol. 21. Development during the transition to adolescence.* Hillsdale, NJ: Erlbaum.

Smetana, J. (2002). Culture, autonomy, and personal jurisdiction in adolescent-parent relationships. In R. V. Kail & H. W. Reese (Eds.), *Advances in child development and behavior* (Vol. 29, pp. 52–89). San Diego: Academic Press.

Smetana, J. G., & Braeges, J. L. (1990). The development of toddlers' moral and conventional judgments. *Merrill-Palmer Quarterly, 36,* 329–346.

Smetana, J. G., Schlagman, N., & Adams, P. W. (1993). Preschool judgments about hypothetical and actual transgressions. *Child Development, 64,* 202–214.

Smetana, J. G., Toth, S. L., Cicchetti, D., Bruce, J., Kane, P., & Daddis, C. (1999). Maltreated and nonmaltreated preschoolers' conceptions of hypothetical and actual moral transgressions. *Developmental Psychology, 35,* 269–281.

Smilkstein, G., Helsper-Lucas, A., Ashworth, C., Montano, D., & Pagel, M. (1984). Prediction of pregnancy complications: An application of the biopsychosocial model. *Social Sciences & Medicine, 18,* 315–321.

Smith, L., Fagan, J. F., & Ulvund, S. E. (2002). The relation of recognition memory in infancy and parental socioeconomic status to later intellectual competence. *Intelligence, 30,* 247–259.

Smith, L. B. (1989). From global similarities to kinds of similarities: The construction of dimensions in development. In S. Vosniadou & A. Ortony (Eds.), *Similarity and analogical reasoning* (pp. 146–178). New York: Cambridge University Press.

Smith, L. B. (1995). Self-organizing processes in learning to learn words: Development is not induction. In C. A. Nelson (Ed.), *Basic and applied perspectives on learning, cognition, and development. The Minnesota symposia in child psychology* (Vol. 28). Mahwah, NJ: Erlbaum.

Smith, L. B. (1999). Children's noun learning: How general learning processes make specialized learning mechanisms. In B. MacWhinney (Ed.), *The emergence of language* (pp. 277–303). Mahwah, NJ: Erlbaum.

Smith, L. B. (1999). Do infants possess innate knowledge structures? The con side. *Developmental Science, 2,* 133–144.

Smith, L. B., Thelen, E., Titzer, R., & McLin, D. (1999). Knowing in the context of acting: The task dynamics of the A-not-B error. *Psychological Review, 106,* 235–260.

Smith, P., Perrin, S., Yule, W., & Rabe-Hesketh, S. (2001). War exposure and maternal reactions in the psychological adjustment of children from Bosnia-Hercegovina. *Journal of Child Psychology and Psychiatry, 42,* 395–404.

Smith, R. (1999, March). The timing of birth. *Scientific American, 280,* 68–75.

Smith, T. E. (1988). Parental control techniques: Relative frequencies and relationships with situational factors. *Journal of Family Issues, 9,* 155–176.

Snarey, J. R. (1985). Cross-cultural universality of social-moral development: A critical review of Kohlbergian research. *Psychological Bulletin, 97,* 202–232.

Snow, C. E. (1977). The development of conversation between babies and mothers. *Journal of Child Language, 4,* 1–22.

Snow, C. E. (1984). Parent-child interaction and the development of communicative ability. In R. L. Schiefelbusch & J. Pickar (Eds.), *The acquisition of communicative competence* (pp. 69–107). Baltimore: University Park Press.

Snow, C. E. (1987). Relevance of the notion of a critical period to language acquisition. In M. H. Bornstein (Ed.), *Sensitive periods in development.* Hillsdale, NJ: Erlbaum.

Snow, C. E. (1993). Families as social contexts for literacy development. In C. Daiute (Ed.), *The development of literacy through social interaction. New Directions for Child Development. No. 61* (pp. 11–24). San Francisco: Jossey-Bass.

Sobal, J., & Stunkard, A. J. (1989). Socioeconomic status and obesity: A review of the literature. *Psychological Bulletin, 105,* 260–275.

Society for Research in Child Development. (1996). Ethical standards for research with children. In *Directory of members.* Ann Arbor, MI: Author.

Society for Research in Child Development. (2002). *About the society.* Retrieved September 23, 2002, from http://www.srcd.org/index.html

Sodian, B., Zaitchik, D., & Carey, S. (1991). Young children's differentiation of hypothetical beliefs from evidence. *Child Development, 62,* 753–766.

Sontag, L. W., Baker, C. T., & Nelson, V. L. (1958). Mental growth and personality development: A longitudinal study. *Monographs of the Society for Research in Child Development, 23*(2, Serial No. 68).

Sophian, C., Garyantes, D., & Chang, C. (1997). When three is less than two: Early developments in children's understanding of fractional quantities. *Developmental Psychology, 33,* 731–744.

Sorce, J. F., Emde, R. N., Campos, J., & Klinnert, M. D. (1985). Maternal emotional signaling: Its effect on the visual cliff behavior of 1-year-olds. *Developmental Psychology, 21,* 195–200.

Southwick, S. M., Yehuda, R., & Charney, D. S. (1997). Neurobiological alterations in PTSD: Review of the clinical literature. In C. S. Fullerton & R. J. Ursano (Eds.), *Posttraumatic stress disorder: Acute and long-term responses to trauma and disaster* (pp. 241–266). Washington, DC: American Psychiatric Press.

Spear, L. P. (2000). Neurobehavioral changes in adolescence. *Current Directions in Psychological Science, 9,* 111–114.

Spearman, C. (1904). "General intelligence," objectively determined and measured. *American Journal of Psychology, 15,* 72–101.

Spearman, C. (1923). *The nature of "intelligence" and the principles of cognition.* London: Macmillan.

Spearman, C. (1927). *The abilities of man.* London: Macmillan.

Spears, W., & Hohle, R. (1967). Sensory and perceptual processes in infants. In Y. Brackbill (Ed.), *Infancy and early childhood* (pp. 51–121). New York: Free Press.

Spelke, E., Breinlinger, K., Macomber, J., & Jacobson, K. (1992). Origins of knowledge. *Psychological Review, 99,* 605–632.

Spelke, E., & Hespos, S. (2001). Continuity, competence, and the object concept. In E. Dupoux (Ed.), *Language, brain, and cognitive development: Essays in honor of Jacques Mehler* (pp. 325–340). Cambridge, MA: MIT Press.

Spelke, E. S. (1976). Infants' intermodal perception of events. *Cognitive Psychology, 8,* 553–560.

Spelke, E. S. (1985). Perception of unity, persistence and identity: Thoughts on infants' conceptions of objects. In J. Mehler & R. Fox (Eds.), *Neonate cognition: Beyond the blooming, buzzing confusion* (pp. 89–113). Hillsdale, NJ: Erlbaum.

Spelke, E. S., & Newport, E. L. (1998). Nativism, empiricism, and the development of knowledge. In W. Damon (Series Ed.) & R. Lerner (Vol. Ed.), *Handbook of child psychology: Vol. 1. Theoretical models of human development* (5th ed., pp. 275–340). New York: Wiley.

Spelke, E. S., & Owsley, C. J. (1979). Intermodal exploration and knowledge in infancy. *Infant Behavior and Development, 2,* 13–27.

Spence, M. J., & Freeman, M. S. (1996). Newborn infants prefer the maternal low-pass filtered voice, but not the maternal whispered voice. *Infant Behavior and Development, 19,* 199–212.

Spencer, J. P., Smith, L. B., & Thelen, E. (2001). Tests of a dynamic systems account of the A-not-B error: The influence of prior experience on the spatial memory abilities of two-year-olds. *Child Development, 72,* 1327–1346.

Spencer, J. P., Vereijken, B., Diedrich, F. J., & Thelen, E. (2000). Posture and the emergence of manual skills. *Developmental Science, 3,* 216–233.

Spitz, H. H. (1986). *The raising of intelligence.* Hillsdale, NJ: Erlbaum.

Spitz, H. H. (1999). Attempts to raise intelligence. In M. Anderson (Ed.), *The development of intelligence* (pp. 275–293). Hove, UK: Psychology Press.

Spitz, R. (1946a). Anaclitic depression. *Psychoanalytic Study of the Child, 2,* 313–342.

Spitz, R. (1946b). Hospitalism: A follow-up report. *Psychoanalytic Study of the Child, 2,* 113–117.

Spivack, G., & Shure, M. B. (1974). *Social adjustment of young children.* San Francisco: Jossey-Bass.

Sprafkin, J. N., Liebert, R. M., & Poulos, R. W. (1975). Effects of a prosocial televised example on children's helping. *Journal of Experimental Child Psychology, 20,* 119–126.

Sprauve, M. E. (1996) Substance abuse and HIV in pregnancy. *Clinical Obstetrics and Gynecology, 39,* 316–332.

Spreen, O., Tupper, D., Risser, A., Tuokko, H., & Edgell, D. (1984). *Human developmental neuropsychology.* New York: Oxford University Press.

Sroufe, L. A. (1983). Infant-caregiver attachment and patterns of adaptation in preschool: The roots of maladaptation and competence. In M. Perlmutter (Ed.), *The Minnesota symposia on child psychology: Vol. 16. Development and policy concerning children with special needs.* Hillsdale, NJ: Erlbaum.

Sroufe, L. A. (1996). *Emotional development: The organization of life in the early years.* New York: Cambridge University Press.

Sroufe, L. A., Egeland, B., & Carlson, E. A. (1999). One social world: The integrated development of parent-child and peer relationships. In W. A. Collins & B. Laursen (Eds.), *Minnesota symposia on child psychology: Vol. 30. Relationships as developmental contexts* (pp. 241–261). Mahwah, NJ: Erlbaum.

Staffieri, J. R. (1967). A study of social stereotypes of body image in children. *Journal of Personality and Social Psychology, 7,* 101–104.

Stagno, S., & Cloud, G. A. (1994). Working parents: The impact of day care and breast-feeding on cytomegalovirus infections in offspring. *Proceedings of the National Academy of Science, USA, 91,* 2384–2389.

Stams, G. J. M., Juffer, F., & van IJzendoorn, M. H. (2002). Maternal sensitivity, infant attachment, and temperament in early childhood predict adjustment in middle childhood: The case of adopted children and their biologically unrelated parents. *Developmental Psychology, 38,* 806–821.

Stanovich, K. E. (1993). A model for studies of reading disability. *Developmental Review, 13,* 225–245.

Stansbury, K., & Gunnar, M. R. (1994). Adrenocortical activity and emotion regulation. In N. A. Fox (Ed.), The development of emotion regulation: Biological and behavioral considerations. *Monographs of the Society for Research in Child Development, 59*(2–3, Serial No. 240).

Stanwood, G. D., & Levitt, P. (2001). The effects of cocaine on the developing nervous system. In C. A. Nelson & M. Luciana (Eds.), *Handbook of developmental cognitive neuroscience* (pp. 519–536). Cambridge, MA: MIT Press.

Stark, R. E. (1986). Prespeech segmental feature detection. In P. Fletcher & M. Garman (Eds.), *Language acquisition: Studies in first language development* (pp. 15–32). Cambridge, UK: Cambridge University Press.

Statistics Canada. (1999). Retrieved January 13, 2003, from http:\\www.statcan.ca

Steele, C. D., Wapner, R. J., Smith, J. B., Haynes, M. K., & Jackson, L. G. (1996). Prenatal diagnosis using fetal cells isolated from maternal peripheral blood: A review. *Clinical Obstetrics and Gynecology, 39,* 801–813.

Steele, C. M., & Aronson, J. (1995). Stereotype threat and the intellectual test performance of African Americans. *Journal of Personality and Social Psychology, 69,* 797–811.

Steele, H., Steele, M., & Fonagy, P. (1996). Associations among attachment classifications of mothers, fathers, and their infants. *Child Development, 67,* 541–555.

Stein, J. H., & Reiser, L. W. (1994). A study of white middle-class adolescent boys' responses to "semenarche" (the first ejaculation). *Journal of Youth and Adolescence, 23,* 373–384.

Stein, L. K. (1999). Factors influencing the efficacy of universal newborn hearing screening. *Pediatric Clinics of North America, 46,* 95–105.

Steinberg, L. (1981). Transformations in family relations at puberty. *Developmental Psychology, 17,* 833–840.

Steinberg, L. (1996). *Beyond the classroom: Why school reform has failed and what parents need to do.* New York: Simon & Schuster.

Steinberg, L., Dornbusch, S. M., & Brown, B. B. (1992). Ethnic differences in adolescent achievement: An ecological perspective. *American Psychologist, 47,* 723–729.

Steinberg, L., Elmen, J. D., & Mounts, N. S. (1989). Authoritative parenting, psychosocial maturity, and academic success among adolescents. *Child Development, 60,* 1424–1436.

Steinberg, L., Fegley, S., & Dornbusch, S. M. (1993). Negative impact of part-time work on adolescent adjustment: Evidence from a longitudinal study. *Developmental Psychology, 29,* 171–180.

Steinberg, L., Greenberger, E., Garduque, L., & McAuliffe, S. (1982). High school students in the labor force: Some costs and benefits to schooling and learning. *Educational Evaluation and Policy Analysis, 4,* 363–372.

Steinberg, L., Lamborn, S. D., Darling, N., Mounts, N. S., & Dornbusch, S. (1994). Over-time changes in adjustment and competence among adolescents from authoritative, authoritarian, indulgent, and neglectful families. *Child Development, 65,* 754–770.

Steinberg, L., Lamborn, S. D., Dornbusch, S. M., & Darling, N. (1992). Impact of parenting practices on adolescent achievement: Authoritative parenting, school involvement, and encouragement to succeed. *Child Development, 63,* 1266–1281.

Steiner, J. E. (1979). Human facial expressions in response to taste and smell stimulation. In H. W. Reese & L. P. Lipsitt (Eds.), *Advances in child development and behavior* (Vol. 13, pp. 257–295). New York: Academic Press.

Stern, D. N. (1974). The goal and structure of mother-infant play. *Journal of the American Academy of Child Psychiatry, 13,* 402–421.

Sternberg, K. J., Lamb, M. E., Greenbaum, C., Cichetti, D., Dawud, S., Cortes, R. M., et al. (1993). Effects of domestic violence on children's behavior problems and depression. *Developmental Psychology, 29,* 44–52.

Sternberg, R. J. (1981). A componential theory of intellectual giftedness. *Gifted Child Quarterly, 25,* 86–93.

Sternberg, R. J. (1982). *Intelligence applied.* New York: Harcourt.

Sternberg, R. J. (1985). *Beyond IQ: A triarchic theory of human intelligence.* Cambridge, UK: Cambridge University Press.

Sternberg, R. J. (1986). Triarchic theory of intellectual giftedness. In R. J. Sternberg & J. E. Davidson (Eds.), *Conceptions of giftedness* (pp. 223–243). Cambridge, UK: Cambridge University Press.

Sternberg, R. J. (1995). Testing common sense. *American Psychologist, 50,* 912–927.

Sternberg, R. J. (1998). Applying the triarchic theory of human intelligence in the classroom. In R. J. Sternberg & W. M. Williams (Eds.), *Intelligence, instruction, and assessment: Theory into practice* (pp. 1–15). Mahwah, NJ: Erlbaum.

Sternberg, R. J. (2001). Successful intelligence: Understanding what Spearman had rather than what he studied. In J. M. Collis & S. Messick (Eds.), *Intelligence and personality: Bridging the gap in theory and measurement* (pp. 347–373). Mahwah, NJ: Erlbaum.

Sternberg, R. J., Conway, B. E., Ketron, J. L., & Bernstein, M. (1981). People's conceptions of intelligence. *Journal of Personality and Social Psychology, 41,* 37–55.

Sternberg, R. J., & Frensch, P. A. (1993). Mechanisms of transfer. In D. K. Detterman & R. J. Sternberg (Eds.), *Transfer on trial: Intelligence, cognition, and instruction* (pp. 25–38). Norwood, NJ: Ablex.

Sternberg, R. J., & Kaufman, J. C. (1998). Human abilities. *Annual Review of Psychology, 49,* 479–502.

Sternberger, J. (1992). A performance constraint on compensatory lengthening in child phonology. *Language and Speech, 35,* 207–218.

Stetsenko, A., Little, T. D., Gordeeva, T., Grasshof, M., & Oettingen, G. (2000). Gender effects in children's beliefs about school performance: A cross-cultural study. *Child Development, 71,* 517–527.

Stetsenko, A., Little, T. D., Oettingen, G., & Baltes, P. B. (1995). Agency, control, and means-ends beliefs about school performance in Moscow children: How similar are they to beliefs of western children? *Developmental Psychology, 31,* 285–299.

Stevenson, D. K., et al. (1998). Very low birth weight outcomes of the National Institute of Child Health and Human Development Neonatal Research Network, January 1993 through December 1994. *American Journal of Obstetrics and Gynecology, 179,* 1632–1639.

Stevenson, H. W., Chen, C., & Lee, S. (1993). Mathematics achievement of Chinese, Japanese, and American children: Ten years later. *Science, 259,* 53–58.

Stevenson, H. W., Lee, S., & Stigler, J. W. (1986). Mathematics achievement of Chinese, Japanese, and American children. *Science, 231,* 693–699.

Stevenson, H. W., Stigler, J. W., Lee, S., Lucker, G. W., Kitamura, S., & Hsu, C. (1985). Cognitive performance and academic achievement of Japanese, Chinese, and American children. *Child Development, 56,* 718–734.

Stevenson, R. E., Allen, W. P., Pai, S., Best, R., Seaver, L. H., Dean, J., & Thompson, S. (2000). Decline in prevalence of neural tube defects in a high-risk region of the United States. *Pediatrics, 106,* 677–683.

Stevenson-Hinde, J., & Shouldice, A. (1995). Maternal interactions and self-reports related to attachment classifications at 4.5 years. *Child Development, 66,* 583–596.

Stewart Woods, N., Davis Eyler, F., Conlon, M., Behnke, M., & Wobie, K. (1998). Pygmalion in the cradle: Observer bias against cocaine-exposed infants. *Developmental and Behavioral Pediatrics, 19,* 283–285.

Stice, E., Presnell, K., & Bearman, S. K. (2001). Relation of early menarche to depression, eating disorders, substance abuse, and comorbid psychopathology among adolescent girls. *Developmental Psychology, 37,* 608–619.

Stifter, C. A., Fox, N. A., & Porges, S. W. (1989). Facial expressivity and vagal tone in five- and ten-month-old infants. *Infant Behavior and Development, 12,* 127–137.

Stifter, C. A., Spinrad, T. L., & Braungart-Rieker, J. M. (1999). Toward a developmental model of child compliance: The role of emotion regulation in infancy. *Child Development, 70,* 21–32.

Stigler, J. W., Lee, S., & Stevenson, H. W. (1987). Mathematics classrooms in Japan, Taiwan, and the United States. *Child Development, 58,* 1272–1285.

Stigler, J. W., Smith, S., & Mao, L.-W. (1985). The self-perception of competence by Chinese children. *Child Development, 56,* 1259–1270.

Stiles, J., Delis, D. C., & Tada, W. L. (1991). Global-local processing in preschool children. *Child Development, 62,* 1258–1275.

Stipek, D., & Hoffman, J. M. (1980). Children's achievement related expectancies as a function of academic performance histories and sex. *Journal of Educational Psychology, 72,* 861–865.

Stipek, D., Recchia, S., & McClintic, S. (1992). Self-evaluation in young children. *Monographs of the Society for Research in Child Development, 57*(1, Serial No. 226).

Stoel-Gammon, C., & Otomo, K. (1986). Babbling development of hearing-impaired and normally hearing subjects. *Journal of Speech and Hearing Disorders, 51,* 33–41.

Stolberg, A. L., & Anker, J. M. (1984). Cognitive and behavioral changes in children resulting from parental divorce and consequent environmental changes. *Journal of Divorce, 8,* 184–197.

Stoolmiller, M. (2001). Synergistic interaction of child manageability problems and parent-discipline tactics in predicting future growth in externalizing behavior for boys. *Developmental Psychology, 37,* 814–825.

Stormshak, E. A., Bellanti, C. J., Bierman, K. L., & the Conduct Problems Prevention Group. (1996). The quality of sibling relationships and the development of social competence and behavioral control in aggressive children. *Developmental Psychology, 32,* 79–89.

Strasburger, V. C. (1993). Children, adolescents, and the media: Five crucial issues. *Adolescent Medicine: State of the Art Review, 4,* 479–493.

Stratton, K. R., Howe, C. J., & Battaglia, F. C. (Eds.). (1996). *Fetal alcohol syndrome: Diagnosis, epidemiology, prevention and treatment.* Washington, DC: National Academy Press.

Straus, M. A., & Donnelly, D. A. (1993). Corporal punishment of adolescents by American parents. *Youth and Society, 24,* 419–442.

Straus, M. A., & Stewart, J. H. (1999). Corporal punishment by American parents: National data on prevalence, chronicity, severity, and duration, in relation to child and family characteristics. *Clinical Child and Family Psychology Review, 2,* 55–70.

Strauss, R. (1999). Childhood obesity. *Current Problems in Pediatrics, 29,* 5–29.

Strayer, F. F., & Strayer, J. (1976). An ethological analysis of social agonism and dominance relations among preschool children. *Child Development, 47,* 980–989.

Streiner, D. L., Saigal, S., Burrows, E., Stoskopf, B., & Rosenbaum, P. (2001). Attitudes of parents and health care professionals toward active treatment of extremely premature infants. *Pediatrics, 108,* 152–157.

Streissguth, A. P., Barr, H. M., Bookstein, F. L., Sampson, P. D., & Olson, H. C. (1999). The long-term neurocognitive consequences of prenatal alcohol exposure: A 14-year study. *Psychological Science, 10,* 186–190.

Streissguth, A. P., Bookstein, F. L., Sampson, P. D., & Barr, H. M. (1995). Attention: Prenatal alcohol and continuities of vigilence and attentional problems from 4 through 14 years. *Development and Psychopathology, 7,* 419–446.

Streissguth, A. P., Sampson, P. D., Barr, H. M., Bookstein, F. L., & Olson, H. C. (1994). The effects of prenatal exposure to alcohol and tobacco: Contributions from the Seattle Longitudinal Prospective Study and implications for public policy. In H. L. Needleman & D. Bellinger (Eds.), *Prenatal exposure to toxicants: Developmental consequences* (pp. 148–183). Baltimore: Johns Hopkins University Press.

Streissguth, A. P., Treder, R., Barr, H. M., Shepard, T., Bleyer, A., & Martin, D. (1984). Prenatal aspirin and offspring IQ in a large group. *Teratology, 29,* 59A–60A.

Stricker, J. M., Miltenberger, R. G., Garlinghouse, M. A., Deaver, C. M., & Anderson, C. A. (2001). Evaluation of an awareness enhancement device for the treatment of thumb sucking in children. *Journal of Applied Behavior Analysis, 34,* 77–80.

Strough, J., & Berg, C. A. (2000). Goals as a mediator of gender differences in high-affiliation dyadic conversations. *Developmental Psychology, 36,* 117–125.

Strutt, G. F., Anderson, D. R., & Well, A. D. (1975). A developmental study of the effects of irrelevant information on speeded classification. *Journal of Experimental Child Psychology, 20*, 127–135.

Styne, D. M. (2001). Childhood and adolescent obesity. *Pediatric Clinics of North America, 48*, 832–862.

Suarez-Orozco, C., & Suarez-Orozco, M. (1996). *Transformations: Migration, family life and achievement motivation among Latino adolescents.* Palo Alto, CA: Stanford University Press.

Subrahmanyam, K., & Greenfield, P. M. (1994). Effect of video game practice on spatial skills in girls and boys. *Journal of Applied Developmental Psychology, 15*, 13–32.

Subrahmanyam, K., & Greenfield, P. M. (1998). Computer games for girls: What makes them play? In J. Cassell & H. Jenkins (Eds.), *From Barbie to Mortal Kombat: Gender and computer games* (pp. 46–71). Cambridge, MA: MIT Press.

Subrahmanyam, K., Greenfield, P., Kraut, R., & Gross, E. (2001). The impact of computer use on children's and adolescents' development. *Journal of Applied Developmental Psychology, 22*, 7–30.

Subrahmanyam, K., Kraut, R. E., Greenfield, P. M., & Gross, E. F. (2000, Fall/Winter). The impact of computer use on children's activities and development. *Future of Children, 10*(2), 123–144.

Sugarman, S. (1982). Developmental change in early representational intelligence: Evidence from spatial classification strategies and related verbal expressions. *Cognitive Psychology, 14*, 410–449.

Sugarman, S. (1983). *Children's early thought: Developments in classification.* New York: Cambridge University Press.

Sullivan, H. S. (1953). *The interpersonal theory of psychiatry.* New York: W. W. Norton.

Sullivan, S. A., & Birch, L. L. (1990). Pass the sugar, pass the salt: Experience dictates preference. *Developmental Psychology, 26*, 546–551.

Sun, L. C., & Roopnarine, J. L. (1996). Mother-infant, father-infant interaction and involvement in childcare and household labor among Taiwanese families. *Infant Behavior and Development, 19*, 121–129.

Super, C. M. (1976). Environmental effects on motor development: The case of "African infant precocity." *Developmental Medicine and Child Neurology, 18*, 561–567.

Super, C. M., & Harkness, S. (1982). The infant's niche in rural Kenya and metropolitan America. In L. Adler (Ed.), *Cross-cultural research at issue* (pp. 247–255). New York: Academic Press.

Super, C. M., & Harkness, S. (1997). The cultural structuring of child development. In J. W. Berry (Ed.), *Handbook of cross-cultural psychology: Vol. 2. Basic processes and human development* (2nd ed., pp. 1–39). Boston: Allyn & Bacon.

Surrey, J. L. (1991). The "self-in-relation": A theory of women's development. In J. V. Jordan, A. G. Kaplan, J. B. Miller, I. P. Stiver, & J. L. Surrey (Eds.), *Women's growth in connection* (pp. 162–180). New York: Guilford.

Sutton-Smith, B., & Rosenberg, B. G. (1970). *The sibling.* New York: Holt, Rinehart & Winston.

Swain, I. U., Zelazo, P. R., & Clifton, R. K. (1993). Newborn infants' memory for speech sounds retained over 24 hours. *Developmental Psychology, 29*, 312–323.

Swanson, H. L., Mink, J., & Bocian, K. M. (1999). Cognitive processing deficits in poor readers with symptoms of reading disabilities and ADHD: More alike than different? *Journal of Educational Psychology, 91*, 321–333.

Szkrybalo, J., & Ruble, D. N. (1999). "God made me a girl": Sex-category constancy judgments and explanation revisited. *Developmental Psychology, 35*, 392–402.

Taddio, A., Goldbach, M., Ipp, M., Stevens, B., & Koren, G. (1995). Effect of neonatal circumcision on pain responses during vaccination in boys. *Lancet, 345*, 291–292.

Tager-Flusberg, H. (1985). Putting words together: Morphology and syntax in the preschool years. In J. B. Gleason (Ed.), *The development of language.* Columbus, OH: Charles E. Merrill.

Takahashi, K. (1990). Are the key assumptions of the Strange Situation procedure universal? A view from Japanese research. *Human Development, 33*, 23–30.

Takei, W. (2001). How do deaf infants attain first signs? *Developmental Science, 4*, 71–78.

Tallal, P., Miller, S. L., Bedi, G., Byma, G., Wang, X., Nagarajan, S. S., et al. (1996). Language comprehension in language-learning impaired children improved with acoustically modified speech. *Science, 271*, 81–84.

Tallal, P., Miller, S. L., Jenkins, W. M., & Merzenich, M. M. (1997). The role of temporal processing in developmental language-based learning disorders: Research and clinical implications. In B. Blachman (Ed.), *Foundations of reading acquisition and dyslexia: Implications for early intervention* (pp. 49–66). Mahwah, NJ: Erlbaum.

Tam, C. W. Y., & Stokes, S. F. (2001). Form and function of negation in early developmental Cantonese. *Journal of Child Language, 28*, 373–391.

Tamis-LeMonda, C. S., Bornstein, M. H., & Baumwell, L. (2001). Maternal responsiveness and children's achievement of language milestones. *Child Development, 72*, 748–767.

Tanapat, P., Hastings, N. B., & Gould, E. (2001). Adult neurogenesis in the hippocampal formation. In C. A. Nelson & M. Luciana (Eds.), *Handbook of developmental cognitive neuroscience* (pp. 93–105). Cambridge, MA: MIT Press.

Tannenbaum, L., & Forehand, R. (1994). Maternal depressive mood: The role of the father in preventing adolescent behavior problems. *Behavior Research and Therapy, 32*, 321–326.

Tanner, J. M. (1978). *Fetus into man: Physical growth from conception to maturity.* Cambridge, MA: Harvard University Press.

Tanner, J. M. (1990). *Foetus into man: Physical growth from conception to maturity* (rev. ed.). Cambridge, MA: Harvard University Press.

Tannock, R., & Martinussen, R. (2001). Reconceptualizing ADHD. *Educational Leadership, 59*, 20–25.

Taras, H. L., Sallis, J. F., Patterson, T. L., Nader, P. R., & Nelson, J. A. (1989). Television's influence on children's diet and physical activity. *Journal of Developmental and Behavioral Pediatrics, 10*, 176–180.

Tardieu, M., Mayaux, M.-J., Seibel, N., Funck-Brentano, I., Straub, E., Teglas, J. P., & Blanche, S. (1995). Cognitive assessment of school-age children infected with maternally transmitted human immunodeficiency virus type 1. *Journal of Pediatrics, 126*, 375–379.

Tardif, T. (1996). Nouns are not always learned before verbs: Evidence from Mandarin speakers' early vocabularies. *Developmental Psychology, 32*, 492–504.

Tardif, T., Gelman, S. A., & Xu, F. (1999). Putting the "noun bias" in context: A comparison of English and Mandarin. *Child Development, 70*, 620–635.

Tardif, T., & Wellman, H. M. (2000). Acquisition of mental state language in Mandarin- and Cantonese-speaking children. *Developmental Psychology, 36*, 25–43.

Taubes, G. (1998). As obesity rates rise, experts struggle to explain why. *Science, 1998*, 1367–1368.

Taylor, H. G., Klein, N., & Hack, M. (2000). School-age consequences of birth-weight less than 750g: A review and update. *Developmental Neuropsychology, 17*, 289–321.

Taylor, H. G., Klein, N., Minich, N. M., & Hack, M. (2001). Long-term family outcomes for children with very low birth weights. *Archives of Pediatrics & Adolescent Medicine, 155*, 155–161.

Taylor, R. D. (1996). Adolescents' perceptions of kinship support and family management practices: Association with adolescent adjustment in African American families. *Developmental Psychology, 32*, 687–695.

Teller, D. Y. (1998). Spatial and temporal aspects of infant color vision. *Vision Research, 38*, 3275–3282.

Tenenbaum, H. R., & Leaper, C. (2002). Are parents' gender schemas related to their children's gender-related cognitions? A meta-analysis. *Developmental Psychology, 38*, 615–630.

Terman, L. M. (1916). *The measurement of intelligence.* Boston: Houghton Mifflin.

Terman, L. M. (1925). *Genetic studies of genius: Vol. 1. Mental and physical traits of a thousand gifted children.* Stanford, CA: Stanford University Press.

Terman, L. M. (1954). The discovery and encouragement of exceptional talent. *American Psychologist, 9*, 221–238.

Terman, L. M., & Oden, M. H. (1959). *Genetic studies of genius: Vol. 4. The gifted group at midlife.* Stanford, CA: Stanford University Press.

Terrace, H. S., Pettito, L. A., Sanders, R. J., & Bever, T. G. (1979). Can an ape create a sentence? *Science, 206*, 891–900.

Teti, D. M., & Gelfand, D. M. (1991). Behavioral competence among mothers of infants in the first year: The mediational role of maternal self-efficacy. *Child Development, 62*, 918–929.

Teti, D. M., Gelfand, D. M., Messinger, D. S., & Isabella, R. (1995). Maternal depression and the quality of early attachment: An examination of infants, preschoolers, and their mothers. *Developmental Psychology, 31*, 364–376.

Thabet, A. A., & Vostanis, P. (2000). Posttraumatic stress disorder reactions in children of war: A longitudinal study. *Child Abuse & Neglect, 24*, 291–298.

Tharp, R. G. (1989). Psychocultural variables and constants: Effects on teaching and learning in schools. *American Psychologist, 44*, 349–359.

Tharp, R. G., Jordan, C., Speidel, G. E., Au, K. H., Klein, T. W., Calkins, R. P., et al. (1984). Product and process in applied developmental research: Education and the children of a minority. In M. E. Lamb, A. L. Brown, & B. Rogoff (Eds.), *Advances in developmental psychology* (Vol. 3, pp. 91–141). Hillsdale, NJ: Erlbaum.

Thelen, E. (1996). The improvising infant: Learning about learning to move. In M. R. Merrens & G. G. Brannigan (Eds.), *The developmental psychologists: Research adventures across the life span* (pp. 21–36). New York: McGraw-Hill.

Thelen, E., Skala, K. D., & Kelso, J. A. S. (1987). The dynamic nature of early coordination: Evidence from bilateral leg movements in young infants. *Developmental Psychology, 23*, 179–186.

Thelen, E., & Smith, L. B. (1994). *A dynamic systems approach to the development of cognition and action.* Cambridge, MA: MIT Press.

Thelen, E., and Smith, L. B. (1998). Dynamic systems theories. In W. Damon (Series Ed.) & R. Lerner (Vol. Ed.), *Handbook of child psychology: Vol. 1. Theoretical models of human development* (5th ed., pp. 563–634). New York: Wiley.

Thelen, E., & Ulrich, B. D. (1991). Hidden skills: A dynamic systems analysis of treadmill stepping during the first year. *Monographs of the Society for Research in Child Development, 56*(1, Serial No. 223).

Thierry, K. L., & Spence, M. J. (2002). Source-monitoring training facilitates preschoolers' eyewitness memory performance. *Developmental Psychology, 38*, 428–437.

Thoman, A. (1993). Obligation and option in the premature nursery. *Developmental Review, 13*, 1–30.

Thomas, D. G., & Lykins, M. S. (1995). Event-related potential measures of 24-hour retention in 5-month-old infants. *Developmental Psychology, 31*, 946–957.

Thompson, C. (1982). Cortical activity in behavioural development. In J. W. T. Dickerson & H. McGurk (Eds.), *Brain and behavioural development* (pp. 131–167). London: Surrey University Press.

Thompson, R. A. (1990). Vulnerability in research: A developmental perspective on risk research. *Child Development, 61*, 1–16.

Thompson, R. A. (1994). Emotion regulation: A theme in search of definition. In N. A. Fox (Ed.), *The development of emotion regulation. Monographs of the Society for Research in Child Development, 59* (Nos. 2–3, Serial No. 240).

Thompson, R. A. (1996). Attachment and emotional development: From clinic to research to policy. In M. R. Merrens & G. G. Brannigan (Eds.), *The developmental psychologists: Research adventures across the life span* (pp. 69–87). New York: McGraw-Hill.

Thompson, R. A. (1998). Early sociopersonality development. In W. Damon (Series Ed.) & N. Eisenberg (Vol. Ed.), *Handbook of child psychology: Vol. 3. Social, emotional, and personality development* (5th ed., pp. 25–104). New York: Wiley.

Thompson, R. A., & Nelson, C. A. (2001). Developmental science and the media: Early brain development. *American Psychologist, 56*, 5–15.

Thompson, V. D. (1974). Family size: Implicit policies and assumed psychological outcomes. *Journal of Social Issues, 30*, 93–124.

Thorn, F., Gwaizda, J., Cruz, A. V., Bauer, J. A., & Held, R. (1994). The development of eye alignment, convergence and sensory binocularity in young infants. *Investigative Ophthalmology and Visual Science, 35*, 544–553.

Thorndike, R. L. (1994). g. *Intelligence, 19*, 145–155.

Thorne, A., & Michaelieu, Q. (1996). Situating adolescent gender and self-esteem with personal memories. *Child Development, 67*, 1374–1390.

Thornton, S. (1999). Creating the conditions for cognitive change: The interaction between task structures and specific strategies. *Child Development, 70*, 588–603.

Thurstone, L. L. (1938). *Primary mental abilities.* Chicago: University of Chicago Press.

Thurstone, L. L. (1947). *Multiple factor analysis.* Chicago: University of Chicago Press.

Tieger, T. (1980). On the biological basis of sex differences in aggression. *Child Development, 51*, 943–963.

Tietjen, A. M. (1986). Prosocial moral reasoning among children and adults in a Papua New Guinea society. *Developmental Psychology, 22*, 861–868.

Tincoff, R., & Jusczyk, P. W. (1999). Some beginnings of word comprehension in 6-month-olds. *Psychological Science, 10*, 172–175.

Toda, S., & Fogel, A. (1993). Infant response to the still-face situation at 3 and 6 months. *Developmental Psychology, 29*, 532–538.

Toda, S., Fogel, A., & Kawai, M. (1990). Maternal speech to three-month-old infants in the United States and Japan. *Journal of Child Language, 17*, 279–294.

Tolmie, J. L. (1997). Down syndrome and other autosomal trisomies. In D. L. Rimoin, J. M. Connor, & R. E. Pyeritz (Eds.), *Emery and Rimoin's principles and practices of medical genetics* (3rd ed., Vol. 1, pp. 925–945). New York: Churchill Livingstone.

Tolson, J. M., & Urberg, K. A. (1993). Similarity between adolescent best friends. *Journal of Adolescent Research, 8*, 274–288.

Tomasello, M. (1995). Understanding the self as social agent. In P. Rochat (Ed.), *The self in infancy: Theory and research* (pp. 449–460). Amsterdam: North Holland-Elsevier.

Tomasello, M. (1998). Uniquely primate, uniquely human. *Developmental Science, 1*, 1–16.

Tomasello, M. (2000). Do young children have adult syntactic competence? *Cognition, 74*, 209–253.

Tomasello, M., Akhtar, N., Dodson, K., & Rekau, L. (1997). Differential productivity in young children's use of nouns and verbs. *Journal of Child Language, 24*, 373–387.

Tomasello, M., & Brooks, P. (1998). Young children's earliest transitive and intransitive contructions. *Cognitive Linguistics, 8*, 375–395.

Tomasello, M., & Brooks, P. J. (1999). Early syntactic development: A construction grammar approach. In M. Barrett (Ed.), *The development of language* (pp. 161–190). Hove, UK: Psychology Press.

Tomasello, M., Conti-Ramsden, G., & Ewert, B. (1990). Young children's conversations with their mothers and fathers: Differences in breakdown and repair. *Journal of Child Language, 17*, 115–130.

Tomasello, M., & Farrar, M. J. (1986). Joint attention and early language. *Child Development, 57*, 1454–1463.

Tomasello, M., Strosberg, R., & Akhtar, N. (1996). Eighteen-month-old children learn words in non-ostensive contexts. *Journal of Child Language, 23*, 157–176.

Tongsong, T., Wanapirak, C., Sirivatanapa, P., Piyamongkol, W., Sirichotiyakul, S. & Yampochai, A. (1998). Amniocentesis-related fetal loss: A cohort study. *Obstetrics and Gynecology, 92*, 64–67.

Tough, S. C., Greene, C. A., Svenson, L. W., & Belik, J. (2000). Effects of in vitro fertilization on low birth weight, preterm delivery, and multiple birth. *Journal of Pediatrics, 136*, 618–622.

Touwen, B. C. L. (1974). The neurological development of the infant. In J. A. Davis & J. Dobbing (Eds.), *Scientific foundations of paediatrics* (pp. 615–625). Philadelphia: W.B. Saunders.

Trainor, L. J. (1996). Infant preferences for infant-directed versus non-infant-directed play songs and lullabies. *Infant Behavior and Development, 19*, 83–92.

Trainor, L. J., & Heinmiller, B. M. (1998). The development of evaluative responses to music: Infants prefer to listen to consonance over dissonance. *Infant Behavior and Development, 21*, 77–88.

Trehub, S. E., Bull, D., & Thorpe, L. A. (1984). Infants' perception of melodies: The role of melodic contour. *Child Development, 55*, 821–830.

Trehub, S. E., Thorpe, L. A., & Morrongiello, B. A. (1985). Infants' perception of melodies: Changes in a single tone. *Infant Behavior and Development, 8*, 213–223.

Trehub, S. E., Unyk, A. M., & Trainor, L. J. (1993). Maternal singing in cross-cultural perspective. *Infant Behavior and Development, 16*, 285–295.

Treiber, F., & Wilcox, S. (1980). Perception of a "subjective" contour by infants. *Child Development, 51*, 915–917.

Trevathen, W. R. (1987). *Human birth: An evolutionary perspective.* New York: Aldine de Gruyter.

Trickett, P. K., & Susman, E. J. (1988). Parental perceptions of child-rearing practices in physically abusive and nonabusive families. *Developmental Psychology, 24*, 270–276.

Tronick, E. Z. (1987). The Neonatal Behavioral Assessment Scale as a biomarker of the effects of environmental agents on the newborn. *Environmental Health Perspectives, 74,* 185–189.

Tronick, E. Z., Als, H., Adamson, L., Wise, S., & Brazelton, T. E. (1978). The infant's response to entrapment between contradictory messages in face-to-face interaction. *Journal of the American Academy of Child Psychiatry, 17,* 1–13.

Tronick, E. Z., & Cohn, J. F. (1989). Infant-mother face-to-face interaction: Age and gender differences in coordination and the occurrence of miscoordination. *Child Development, 60,* 85–92.

Tronick, E. Z., Ricks, M., & Cohn, J. F. (1982). Maternal and infant affective exchange: Patterns of adaptation. In T. Field & A. Fogel (Eds.), *Emotion and early interaction* (pp. 83–100). Hillsdale, NJ: Erlbaum.

Troseth, G. L., & DeLoache, J. S. (1998). The medium can obscure the message: Young children's understanding of video. *Child Development, 69,* 950–965.

Tröster, H., & Brambring, M. (1993). Early motor development in blind infants. *Journal of Applied Developmental Psychology, 14,* 83–106.

True, M. M., Pisani, L., & Oumar, F. (2001). Infant-mother attachment among the Dogon of Mali. *Child Development, 72,* 1451–1466.

Tschopp, C., Viviani, P., Reicherts, M., Bullinger, A., Rudaz, N., Mermoud, C., & Safran, A. B. (1999). Does visual sensitivity improve between 5 and 8 years? A study of automated visual field examination. *Vision Research, 39,* 1107–1119.

Tucker, D. M. (1981). Lateral brain function, emotion, and conceptualization. *Psychological Bulletin, 89,* 19–46.

Tucker, G. R., & d'Anglejan, A. (1972). An approach to bilingual education: The St. Lambert experiment. In M. Swain (Ed.), *Bilingual schooling: Some experiences in Canada and the United States* (pp. 15–21). Ontario: Ontario Institute for Studies in Education.

Turiel, E. (1998). The development of morality. In W. Damon (Series Ed.) & N. Eisenberg (Vol. Ed.), *Handbook of child psychology: Vol. 3. Social, emotional, and personality development* (5th ed., pp. 863–932). New York: Wiley.

Turiel, E., & Wainryb, C. (1994). Social reasoning and the varieties of social experiences in cultural contexts. In H. Reese (Ed.), *Advances in child development and behavior* (Vol. 25, pp. 289–326).

Turkheimer, E., Goldsmith, H. H., & Gottesman, I. I. (1995). Commentary. *Human Development, 38,* 142–153.

Turner, G., Webb, S., Wake, S., & Robinson, H. (1996). Prevalence of fragile X syndrome. *American Journal of Medical Genetics, 64,* 196–197.

Turner, R. A., Irwin, C. E., & Millstein, S. G. (1991). Family structure, family processes, and experimenting with substances during adolescence. *Journal of Research on Adolescence, 1,* 93–106.

Turner, S. M., & Mo, L. (1984). Chinese adolescents' self-concept as measured by the Offer Self-Image Questionnaire. *Journal of Youth and Adolescence, 13,* 131–142.

Turner-Bowker, D. M. (1996). Gender stereotyped descriptors in children's picture books: Does "Curious Jane" exist in the literature? *Sex Roles, 35,* 461–488.

Twenge, J. M., & Crocker, J. (2002). Race and self-esteem: Meta-analyses comparing Whites, Blacks, Hispanics, Asians, and American Indians and comment on Gray-Little and Hafdahl (2000). *Psychological Bulletin, 128,* 371–408.

Ullian, E. M., Sapperstein, S. K., Christopherson, K. S., & Barres, B. A. (2001). Control of synapse number by glia. *Science, 291,* 657–661.

Underwood, L. E. (1991, March/April). Normal adolescent growth and development. *Nutrition Today,* pp. 11–16.

Underwood, M. K., Schockner, A. E., & Hurley, J. C. (2001). Children's responses to same- and other-gender peers: An experimental investigation with 8-, 10-, and 12-year-olds. *Developmental Psychology, 37,* 362–372.

UNICEF. (2002). *The State of the World's Children 2002.* Retrieved November 27, 2002, from http://www.unicef.org/sowc02/

United Nations. (2001, October). *Population and vital statistics report* (Series A, Vol. 53, No. 4). New York: Author.

U.S. Bureau of the Census. (1998). *Statistical abstract of the United States* (118th ed.). Washington, DC: U.S. Government Printing Office.

U.S. Bureau of the Census. (1999). *Statistical abstract of the United States* (119th ed.). Washington, DC: U.S. Government Printing Office.

U.S. Bureau of the Census. (various years). *October current population survey.* Washington, DC: U.S. Government Printing Office.

U.S. Bureau of the Census. (2001). *Statistical abstract of the United States* (121st ed.). Washington, DC: U.S. Government Printing Office.

U.S. Department of Education. (1993). *National excellence: A case for developing America's talent.* Washington, DC: Office of Educational Research and Improvement.

U.S. Department of Education. (1996). *1996 trends in academic programs.* Washington, DC: U.S. Government Printing Office.

Updegraff, K. A., McHale, S. M., & Crouter, A. C. (1996). Gender roles in marriage: What do they mean for girls' and boys' school achievement? *Journal of Youth and Adolescence, 25,* 73–88.

Urberg, K. A., Degirmencioglu, S. M., Tolson, J. M., & Halliday-Scher, K. (1995). The structure of adolescent peer networks. *Developmental Psychology, 31,* 540–547.

Uttal, D. H., Gregg, V. H., Tan, L. S., Chamberlin, M. H., & Sines, A. (2001). Connecting the dots: Children's use of a systematic figure to facilitate mapping and search. *Developmental Psychology, 37,* 338–350.

Uttal, D. H., & Wellman, H. M. (1989). Young children's representation of spatial information acquired from maps. *Developmental Psychology, 25,* 128–138.

Uzgiris, I. (1968). Situational generality of conservation. In I. E. Sigel & F. H. Hooper (Eds.), *Logical thinking in children* (pp. 40–52). New York: Holt, Rinehart & Winston.

Valdez-Menchaca, M. C., & Whitehurst, G. J. (1992). Accelerating language development through picture book reading: A systematic extension to Mexican day care. *Developmental Psychology, 28,* 1106–1114.

Valeski, T. N., & Stipek, D. J. (2001). Young children's feelings about school. *Child Development, 72,* 1198–1213.

Valian, V. (1986). Syntactic categories in the speech of young children. *Developmental Psychology, 22,* 562–579.

Valk, A. (2000). Ethnic identity, ethnic attitudes, self-esteem, and esteem toward others among Estonian and Russian adolescents. *Journal of Adolescent Research, 15,* 637–651.

Valsiner, J. (1998). The development of the concept of development: Historical and epistemological perspectives. In W. Damon (Series Ed.) & R. Lerner (Vol. Ed.), *Handbook of child psychology: Vol.1. Theoretical models of human development* (5th ed., pp. 189–232). New York: Wiley.

Van Balen, F. (1998). Development of IVF children. *Developmental Review, 18,* 30–46.

Van de Carr, R., & Lehrer, M. (1996). *While you're expecting: Creating your own prenatal classroom.* Atlanta, GA: Humanics Trade.

Vandell, D. L. (2000). Parents, peers, and other socializing influences. *Developmental Psychology, 36,* 699–710.

Vandell, D. L., Hyde, J. S., Plant, E. A., & Essex, M. J. (1997). Fathers and "others" as child care providers during the first year: Predictors of parents' emotional well-being and marital relationships. *Merrill-Palmer Quarterly, 43,* 361–385.

Vandell, D. L., & Mueller, E. C. (1980). Peer play and friendships during the first two years. In H. C. Foot, A. J. Chapman, & J. R. Smith (Eds.), *Friendship and social relations in children.* New York: Wiley.

Vandell, D. L., & Ramanan, J. (1992). Effects of early and recent maternal employment on children from low-income families. *Child Development, 63,* 938–949.

Vandell, D. L., & Wilson, K. S. (1982). Social interaction in the first year of life: Infants' social skills with peers versus mother. In K. H. Rubin & H. S. Ross (Eds.), *Peer relationships and social skills in childhood.* New York: Springer-Verlag.

Vandell, D. L., Wilson, K. S., & Buchanan, N. R. (1980). Peer interaction in the first year of life: An examination of its structure, content, and sensitivity to toys. *Child Development, 51,* 481–488.

Vandenberg, S. G., & Vogler, G. P. (1985). Genetic determinants of intelligence. In B. B. Wolman (Ed.), *Handbook of intelligence.* New York: Wiley.

van den Boom, D. C. (1994). The influence of temperament and mothering on attachment and exploration: An experimental manipulation of sensitive responsiveness among lower-class mothers with irritable infants. *Child Development, 65,* 1457–1477.

van den Boom, D. C. (1995). Do first-year intervention effects endure? Follow-up during toddlerhood of a sample of Dutch irritable infants. *Child Development, 66,* 1798–1816.

van den Boom, D. C., & Hoeksma, J. B. (1994). The effects of infant irritability on mother-infant interaction: A growth-curve analysis. *Developmental Psychology, 30,* 581–590.

Van IJzendoorn, M. H. (1995). Adult attachment representations, parental responsiveness and infant attachment: A meta-analysis on the predictive validity of the Adult Attachment Interview. *Psychological Bulletin, 117,* 387–403.

van IJzendoorn, M. H., Moran, G., Belsky, J., Pederson, D., Bakermans Kranenburg, M. J., & Kneppers, K. (2000). The similarity of siblings' attachments to their mother. *Child Development, 71,* 1086-1098.

van IJzendoorn, M. H., & Sagi, A. (1999). Cross-cultural patterns of attachment. In J. Cassidy & P. R. Shaver (Eds.), *Handbook of attachment: Theory, research, and clinical applications* (pp. 713–734). New York: Guilford Press.

Van Rooy, C., Stough, C., Pipingas, A., Hocking, C., & Silberstein, R. B. (2001). Spatial working memory and intelligence: Biological correlates. *Intelligence, 29,* 275–292.

Varni, J. W. (1983). *Clinical behavioral pediatrics: An interdisciplinary biobehavioral approach.* New York: Pergamon Press.

Vaughn, B. E., Kopp, C. B., & Krakow, J. B. (1984). The emergence and consolidation of self-control from eighteen to thirty months of age: Normative trends and individual differences. *Child Development, 55,* 990–1004.

Vaughn, B. E., Taraldson, B., Crichton, L., & Egeland, B. (1980). Relationships between neonatal behavioral organization and infant behavior during the first year of life. *Infant Behavior and Development, 3,* 78–89.

Vernon, P. A. (1983). Speed of information processing and general intelligence. *Intelligence, 7,* 53–70.

Vernon, P. E. (1966). Educational and intellectual development among Canadian Indians and Eskimos. *Educational Review, 18,* 79–91.

Verschueren, K., & Marcoen, A. (1999). Representation of self and socio-emotional competence in kindergartners: Differential and combined effects of attachment to mothers and fathers. *Child Development, 70,* 183–201.

Vihman, M. M. (1998). Early phonological disorders. In J. E. Bernthal & N. W. Bankson (Eds.), *Articulation and phonological development* (4th ed., pp. 63–110). Boston: Allyn & Bacon.

Vinter, A., & Perruchet, P. (2000). Implicit learning in children is not related to age: Evidence from drawing behavior. *Child Development, 71,* 1223–1240.

Vogel, G. (1996). Asia and Europe top in world, but reasons hard to find. *Science, 274,* 1296.

Vogel, G. (1997). U.S. kids score well in primary grades. *Science, 276,* 1642.

Vohr, B. R., Wright, L. L., Dusick, A. M., Mele, L., Verter, J., Steichen, J. J., et al. (2000). Neurodevelopmental and functional outcomes of extremely low birth weight infants in the National Institute of Child Health and Human Development Neonatal Research Network, 1993–1994. *Pediatrics, 105,* 1216–1226.

Volling, B. L., MacKinnon-Lewis, C., Rabiner, D., & Baradaran, L. P. (1993). Children's social competence and sociometric status: Further exploration of aggression, social withdrawal, and peer rejection. *Development and Psychopathology, 5,* 459–483.

von Hofsten, C., & Rönnqvist, L. (1993). The structuring of neonatal arm movement. *Child Development, 64,* 1046–1057.

von Hofsten, C., & Rosander, K. (1997). Development of smooth pursuit tracking in young infants. *Vision Research, 37,* 1799–1810.

Vorhees, C. V. (1986). Principles of behavioral teratology. In E. P. Riley & C. V. Vorhees (Eds.), *Handbook of behavioral teratology.* New York: Plenum Press.

Voyer, D., Voyer, S., & Bryden, M. P. (1995). Magnitude of sex differences in spatial abilities: A meta-analysis and consideration of critical variables. *Psychological Bulletin, 117,* 250–270.

Vuchinich, S., Hetherington, E. M., Vuchinich, R. A., & Clingempeel, W. G. (1991). Parent-child interaction and gender differences in early adolescents' adaptation to stepfamilies. *Developmental Psychology, 27,* 618–626.

Vurpillot, E. (1968). The development of scanning strategies and their relation to visual differentiation. *Journal of Experimental Child Psychology, 6,* 632–650.

Vurpillot, E., & Ball, W. A. (1979). The concept of identity and children's selective attention. In G. A. Hale & M. Lewis (Eds.), *Attention and cognitive development* (pp. 23–42). New York: Plenum Press.

Vuyk, R. (1981). *Overview and critique of Piaget's genetic epistemology 1965–1980* (Vols. 1 & 2). New York: Academic Press.

Vygotsky, L. S. (1962). *Thought and language* (E. Hanfmann & G. Vakar, Trans.). Cambridge, MA: MIT Press.

Vygotsky, L. S. (1978). *Mind in society: The development of higher psychological processes.* Cambridge, MA: Harvard University Press.

Waber, D. P. (1976). Sex differences in cognition: A function of maturation rate? *Science, 192,* 572–574.

Wachs, T. D., & Combs, T. T. (1995). The domains of infant mastery motivation. In R. H. McTurk & G. A. Morgan (Eds.), *Mastery motivation: Origins, conceptualizations, and applications* (pp. 147–164). Norwood, NJ: Ablex.

Waddington, C. H. (1971). Concepts of development. In E. Tobach, L. R. Aronson, & E. Shaw (Eds.), *The biopsychology of development* (pp. 17–23). San Diego, CA: Academic Press.

Wadhwa, P. D., Sandman, C. A., Porto, M., Dunkel-Schetter, C., & Garite, T. J. (1993). The association between prenatal stress and infant birth weight and gestational age at birth: A prospective investigation. *American Journal of Obstetrics and Gynecology, 169,* 858–865.

Wagner, B. M., & Phillips, D. A. (1992). Beyond beliefs: Parent and child behaviors and children's perceived academic competence. *Child Development, 63,* 1380–1391.

Wagner, D. A. (1978). Memories of Morocco: The influence of age, schooling, and environment on memory. *Cognitive Psychology, 10,* 1–28.

Wagner, L. (2001). Aspectual influences on early tense comprehension. *Journal of Child Language, 28,* 661–681.

Wagner, M. E., Schubert, H. J. P., & Schubert, D. S. P. (1985). Family size effects: A review. *Journal of Genetic Psychology, 146,* 65–78.

Wagner, M. M. (1995, Summer/Fall). Outcomes for youths with serious emotional disturbance in secondary school and early adulthood. *The Future of Children, 5*(2), pp. 90–112.

Wagner, M. M., Blackorby, J., & Hebbeler, K. (1993). *Beyond the report card: The multiple dimensions of secondary school performance of students with disabilities: A report from the National Longitudinal Transition Study of Special Education Students.* Menlo Park, CA: SRI International.

Wainryb, C., Shaw, L. A., Laupa, M., & Smith, K. R. (2001). Children's, adolescents', and young adults' thinking about different types of disagreements. *Developmental Psychology, 37,* 373–386.

Walden, T. A., & Smith, M. C. (1997). Emotion regulation. *Motivation and Emotion, 21,* 7–25.

Waldenström, U. (1999). Experience of labor and birth in 1111 women. *Journal of Psychosomatic Research, 47,* 471–482.

Waldrop, M. F., & Halverson, C. F. (1975). Intensive and extensive peer behavior: Longitudinal and cross-sectional analyses. *Child Development, 46,* 19–26.

Walk, R. D. (1968). Monocular compared to binocular depth perception in human infants. *Science, 162,* 473–475.

Walker, E. F. (2002). Adolescent neurodevelopment and psychopathology. *Current Directions in Psychological Science, 11,* 24–28.

Walker, L., Hennig, K. H., & Krettenauer, T. (2000). Parent and peer contexts for children's moral reasoning development. *Child Development, 71,* 1033–1048.

Walker, L. J. (1984). Sex differences in the development of moral reasoning: A critical review. *Child Development, 55,* 677–691.

Walker, L. J. (1989). A longitudinal study of moral reasoning. *Child Development, 60,* 157–166.

Walker, L. J. (1991). Sex differences in moral reasoning. In W. M. Kurtines & J. L. Gewirtz (Eds.), *Handbook of moral behavior and development: Vol. 2. Research* (pp. 333–364). Hillsdale, NJ: Erlbaum.

Walker, L. J. (1996). Is one sex morally superior? In M. R. Merrens & G. G. Brannigan (Eds.), *The developmental psychologists: Research adventures across the life span* (pp. 173–186). New York: McGraw-Hill.

Walker, L. J., & Pitts, R. C. (1998). Naturalistic conceptions of moral maturity. *Developmental Psychology, 34,* 403–419.

Walker-Andrews, A. S., Bahrick, L. E., Raglioni, S. S., & Diaz, I. (1991). Infant's bimodal perception of gender. *Ecological Psychology, 3,* 55–75.

Walker-Andrews, A. S., & Lennon, E. M. (1985). Auditory-visual perception of changing distance by human infants. *Child Development, 56,* 544–548.

Wallerstein, J. S., Corbin, S. B., & Lewis, J. M. (1988). Children of divorce: A ten-year study. In E. M. Hetherington & J. Arasteh (Eds.), *Impact of divorce, single-parenting, and stepparenting on children* (pp. 198–214). Hillsdale, NJ: Erlbaum.

Wallerstein, J. S., & Kelly, J. B. (1980). *Surviving the breakup: How children and parents cope with divorce.* New York: Basic Books.

Walsh, B. T., & Devlin, M. J. (1998). Eating disorders: Progress and problems. *Science, 280,* 1387–1390.

Ward, S., Reale, G., & Levinson, D. (1972). Children's perceptions, explanations, and judgments of television advertising. In E. A. Rubenstein, G. A. Comstock, & J. P. Murray (Eds.), *Television and social behavior: Vol. 4. Television in day-to-day life: Patterns of use* (pp. 468–490). Washington, DC: U.S. Government Printing Office.

Wark, G. R., & Krebs, D. L. (1996). Gender and dilemma differences in real-life moral judgment. *Developmental Psychology, 32,* 220–230.

Warkany, J., & Schraffenberger, E. (1947). Congenital malformations induced in rats by roentgen rays. *American Journal of Roentgenology and Radium Therapy, 57,* 455–463.

Warren, S. L., Huston, L., Egeland, B., & Sroufe, L. A. (1997). Child and adolescent anxiety disorders and early attachment. *Journal of the American Academy of Child and Adolescent Psychiatry, 36,* 637–644.

Wartella, E. (1995). The commercialization of youth: Channel One in context. *Phi Delta Kappan,* 448–451.

Wass, T. S., Persutte, W. H., & Hobbins, J. C. (2001). The impact of prenatal alcohol exposure on frontal cortex development in utero. *American Journal of Obstetrics and Gynecology, 185,* 737–742.

Waterhouse, L., Fein, D., & Modahl, C. (1996). Neurofunctional mechanisms in autism. *Psychological Review, 103,* 457–489.

Waters, E., & Deane, K. E. (1985). Defining and assessing individual differences in attachment relationships: Q-methodology and the organization of behavior in infancy and early childhood. In I. Bretherton & E. Waters (Eds.), *Growing points of attachment theory and research. Monographs of the Society for Research in Child Development, 50* (1–2, Serial No. 209).

Waters, E., Wippman, J., & Sroufe, L. A. (1979). Attachment, positive affect, and competence in the peer group: Two studies in construct validation. *Child Development, 50,* 821–829.

Watson, A. C., Nixon, C. L., Wilson, A., & Capage, L. (1999). Social interaction skills and theory of mind in young children. *Developmental Psychology, 35,* 386–391.

Watson, J. B. (1930). *Behaviorism.* New York: W. W. Norton.

Watson, J. S. (1971). Cognitive-perceptual development in infancy: Settings for the seventies. *Merrill-Palmer Quarterly, 17,* 139–152.

Watson, J. S., & Ramey, C. T. (1972). Reactions to response-contingent stimulation in early infancy. *Merrill-Palmer Quarterly, 18,* 219–227.

Waxman, S. R., & Booth, A. E. (2000). Principles that are invoked in the acquisition of words, but not facts. *Cognition, 77,* B33–B43.

Weber-Fox, C. M., & Neville, H. J. (1996). Maturational contraints on functional specializations for language processing: ERP and behavioral evidence in bilingual speakers. *Journal of Cognitive Neuroscience, 8,* 231–256.

Wechsler, D. (1991). *Wechsler intelligence scale for children-Third edition: Manual.* New York: The Psychological Corporation.

Weinberg, M. K., & Tronick, E. Z. (1994). Beyond the face: An empirical study of infant affective configurations of facial, vocal, gestural, and regulatory behaviors. *Child Development, 65,* 1503–1515.

Weinberg, R. (1989). Intelligence and IQ: Landmark issues and great debates. *American Psychologist, 44,* 98–104.

Weinberg, W. K., Tronick, E. Z., Cohn, J. F., & Olson, K. L. (1999). Gender differences in emotional expressivity and self-regulation during early infancy. *Developmental Psychology, 35,* 175–188.

Weinberger, S. E., & Weiss, S. T. (1988). Pulmonary diseases. In G. N. Burrow & T. F. Ferris (Eds.), *Medical complications of pregnancy* (3rd ed., pp. 448–484). Philadelphia: W.B. Saunders.

Weiner, B., & Handel, S. J. (1985). A cognition-emotion-action sequence: Anticipated emotional consequences of causal attributions and reported communication strategy. *Developmental Psychology, 21,* 102–107.

Weinfield, N. S., Ogawa, J. R., & Sroufe, L. A. (1997). Early attachment as a pathway to adolescent peer competence. *Journal of Research on Adolescence, 7,* 241–265.

Weisner, T. S. (1996). Why ethnography should be the most important method in the study of human development. In A. C. R. Jessor & R. A. Shweder (Eds.), *Ethnography and human development* (pp. 305–324). Chicago: University of Chicago Press.

Weiss, L. H., & Schwarz, J. C. (1996). The relationship between parenting types and older adolescents' personality, academic achievement, adjustment, and substance abuse. *Child Development, 67,* 2101–2114.

Weitzman, L. J. (1985). *The divorce revolution: The unexpected social and economic consequences for women and children in America.* New York: Free Press.

Weitzman, M., Gortmaker, S., & Sobol, A. (1992). Maternal smoking and behavior problems of children. *Pediatrics, 90,* 342–349.

Weizman, Z. O., & Snow, C. E. (2001). Lexical input as related to children's vocabulary acquisition: Effects of sophisticated exposure and support for meaning. *Developmental Psychology, 37,* 265–279.

Welch-Ross, M. K. (1995). An integrative model of the development of autobiographical memory. *Developmental Review, 15,* 338–365.

Welch-Ross, M. K., & Schmidt, C. R. (1996). Gender-schema development and children's constructive story memory: Evidence for a developmental model. *Child Development, 67,* 820–835.

Wellman, H. M. (1977). The early development of intentional memory. *Human Development, 20,* 86–101.

Wellman, H. M. (1990). *The child's theory of mind.* Cambridge, MA: MIT Press.

Wellman, H. M., Cross, D., & Watson, J. (2001). Meta-analysis of theory-of-mind development: The truth about false belief. *Child Development, 72,* 655–684.

Wellman, H. M., & Estes, D. (1986). Early understanding of mental entities: A reexamination of childhood realism. *Child Development, 57,* 910–923.

Wellman, H. M., & Hickling, A. K. (1994). The mind's "I": Children's conception of the mind as an active agent. *Child Development, 65,* 1564–1580.

Wellman, H. M., & Lempers, J. D. (1977). The naturalistic communicative abilities of two-year-olds. *Child Development, 48,* 1052–1057.

Welsh, M. C. (2002). Developmental and clinical variations in executive functions. In D. L. Molfese & V. J. Molfese (Eds.), *Developmental variations in learning: Applications to social, executive function, language, and reading skills* (pp. 139–185). Mahwah, NJ: Erlbaum.

Wenglinsky, H. (1998). *Does it compute? The relationship between educational technology and student achievement in mathematics.* Princeton, NJ: Educational Testing Service.

Wentzel, K. R. (2002). Are effective teachers like good parents? Teaching styles and student adjustment in early adolescence. *Child Development, 73,* 287–301.

Wentzel, K. R., & Erdley, C. A. (1993). Strategies for making friends: Relations to social behavior and peer acceptance in early adolescence. *Developmental Psychology, 29,* 819–826.

Werker, J. F. (1989). Becoming a native listener. *American Scientist, 77,* 54–59.

Werker, J. F., & Desjardins, R. N. (1995). Listening to speech in the 1st year of life: Experiential influences on phoneme perception. *Current Directions in Psychological Science, 4,* 76–81.

Werker, J. F., & Lalonde, C. E. (1988). Cross-language speech perception: Initial capabilities and developmental change. *Developmental Psychology, 24,* 672–683.

Werker, J. F., & Tees, R. C. (1984). Cross-language speech perception: Evidence for perceptual reorganization during the first year of life. *Infant Behavior and Development, 7,* 49–63.

Werner, E. E. (1972). Infants around the world: Cross-cultural studies of psychomotor development from birth to two years. *Journal of Cross-Cultural Psychology, 3,* 111–134.

Werner, E. E. (1995). Resilience in development. *Current Directions in Psychological Science, 4,* 81–85.

Wertsch, J. V. (1985). *Vygotsky and the social formation of mind.* Cambridge, MA: Harvard University Press.

Wertsch, J. V., & Tulviste, P. (1992). L. S. Vygotsky and contemporary developmental psychology. *Developmental Psychology, 28,* 548–557.

Wertz, D. C., & Fletcher, J. C. (1993). Feminist criticism of prenatal diagnosis: A response. *Clinical Obstetrics and Gynecology, 36,* 541–567.

Wertz, D. C., & Fletcher, J. C. (1998). Ethical and social issues in prenatal sex selection: A survey of geneticists in 37 nations. *Social Science & Medicine, 46,* 255–273.

West, T. A., & Bauer, P. J. (1999). Assumptions of infantile amnesia: Are there differences between early and later memories? *Memory, 7,* 257–278.

Wexler, K. (1982). A principle theory for language acquisition. In E. Wanner & L. Gleitman (Eds.), *Language acquisition: The state of the art* (pp. 288–315). Cambridge: Cambridge University Press.

Whalen, C. K., Jamner, L. D., Henker, B., Delfino, R. J., & Lozano, J. M. (2002). The ADHD Spectrum and everyday life: Experience sampling of adolescent moods, activities, smoking, and drinking. *Child Development, 73,* 209–227.

Whalen, J., Gallistel, C. R., & Gelman, R. (1999). Nonverbal counting in humans: The psychophysics of number representation. *Psychological Science, 10,* 130–137.

Whalen, R. E. (1984). Multiple actions of steroids and their antagonists. *Archives of Sexual Behavior, 13,* 497–502.

Whitaker, R. C., Wright, J. A., Pepe, M. S., Seidel, K. D., & Dietz, W. H. (1997). Predicting obesity in young adulthood from childhood and parental obesity. *New England Journal of Medicine, 337,* 869–873.

White, B. Y., & Fredriksen, J. R. (1998). Inquiry, modeling, and metacognition: Making science accessible to all students. *Cognition and Instruction, 16*(63), 90–91.

White, R. W. (1959). Motivation reconsidered: The concept of competence. *Psychological Review, 66,* 297–333.

Whitehurst, G. J., Arnold, D. S., Epstein, J. N., Angell, A. L., Smith, M., & Fischel, J. E. (1994). A picture book reading intervention in day care and home for children from low-income families. *Developmental Psychology, 30,* 679–689.

Whitehurst, G. J., & Fischel, J. E. (2000). Reading and language impairments in conditions of poverty. In D. V. M. Bishop & L. B. Leonard (Eds.), *Speech and language impairments in children: Causes, characteristics, intervention and outcome* (pp. 53–71). Hove, UK: Psychology Press.

Whiting, B. B., & Edwards, C. P. (1988). *Children of different worlds.* Cambridge, MA: Harvard University Press.

Whiting, B. B., & Whiting, J. W. M. (1975). *Children of six cultures: A psychocultural analysis.* Cambridge, MA: Harvard University Press.

Wichstrøm, L. (1999). The emergence of gender difference in depressed mood during adolescence: The role of intensified gender socialization. *Developmental Psychology, 35,* 232–245.

Widom, C. S. (1989). The cycle of violence. *Science, 244,* 160–166.

Wierson, M., & Forehand, R. (1994). Parent behavioral training for child noncompliance: Rationale, concepts, and effectiveness. *Current Directions in Psychological Science, 4,* 146–150.

Wigfield, A., & Eccles, J. S. (1994). Children's competence beliefs, achievement values, and general self-esteem: Changes across elementary and middle school. *Journal of Early Adolescence, 14,* 107–138.

Winner, E. (2000). The origins and ends of giftedness. *American Psychologist, 55,* 159–169.

Winsler, A., Carlton, M. P., & Barry, M. J. (2000). Age-related changes in preschool children's systematic use of private speech in a natural setting. *Journal of Child Language, 27,* 665–687.

Willats, P. (1990). Development of problem-solving strategies in infancy. In D. F. Bjorklund (Ed.), *Children's strategies: Contemporary views of cognitive development* (pp. 23–66). Hillsdale, NJ: Erlbaum.

Williams, J. E., & Best, D. L. (1982). *Measuring sex stereotypes: A thirty nation study.* Beverly Hills, CA: Sage.

Williams, J. M., & Currie, C. (2000). Self-esteem and physical development in early adolescence: Pubertal timing and body image. *Journal of Early Adolescence, 20,* 120–149.

Willig, A. C., & Ramirez, J. D. (1993). The evaluation of bilingual education. In M. B. Arias & U. Casanova (Eds.), *Bilingual education: Politics, practice, research.* Chicago: National Society for the Study of Education.

Willinger, M., Ko, C.-W., Hoffman, H. J., Kessler, R. C., & Corwin, M. J. (2000). Factors associated with caregivers' choice of infant sleep position, 1994–1998: The National Infant Sleep Position Study. *Journal of the American Medical Association, 283,* 2135–2142.

Wilson, B. J., & Weiss, A. J. (1992). Developmental differences in children's reactions to a toy advertisement linked to a toy-based cartoon. *Journal of Broadcasting and Electronic Media, 36,* 371–394.

Wilson, J. G. (1977). Current status of teratology: General principles and mechanisms derived from animal studies. In J. G. Wilson & F. C. Fraser (Eds.), *Handbook of teratology: Vol. 1. General principles and etiology* (pp. 47–74). New York: Plenum Press.

Wilson, M. N. (1986). The black extended family: An analytical consideration. *Developmental Psychology, 22,* 246–258.

Wimmer, H., & Perner, J. (1983). Beliefs about beliefs: Representation and constraining function of wrong beliefs in young children's understanding of deception. *Cognition, 13,* 103–128.

Winner, E. (1979). New names for old things: The emergence of metaphoric language. *Journal of Child Language, 6,* 469–491.

Winner, E. (1986, August). Where pelicans kiss seals. *Psychology Today,* pp. 25–35.

Winner, E. (1996). *Gifted children: Myths and realities.* New York: Basic Books.

Winner, E. (1997). Exceptionally high intelligence and schooling. *American Psychologist, 52,* 1070–1081.

Winsler, A., Diaz, R. M., Atencio, D. J., McCarthy, E. M., & Chabay, L. A. (2000). Verbal self-regulation over time in preschool children at risk for attention and behavior problems. *Journal of Child Psychology and Psychiatry, 41,* 875–886.

Winstead, B. A. (1986). Sex differences in same-sex friendships. In V. J. Derlaga & B. A. Winstead (Eds.), *Friendship and social interaction* (pp. 81–99). New York: Springer-Verlag.

Wolchik, S. A., West, S. G., Westover, S., Sandler, I. N., Martin, A., Lustig, J., et al. (2002). The children of divorce parenting intervention: Outcome evaluation of an empirically based program. In T. A. Revenson & A. R. D'Augelli (Eds.), *A quarter century of community psychology: Readings from the American Journal of Community Psychology* (pp. 409–444). New York: Kluwer Academic/Plenum Publishers.

Wolf, T. M. (1973). Effects of live modeled sex-inappropriate play behavior in a naturalistic setting. *Developmental Psychology, 9,* 120–123.

Wolfe, D. A. (1985). Child-abusive parents: An empirical review and analysis. *Psychological Bulletin, 97,* 462–482.

Wolfe, D. A., Fairbank, J., Kelly, J. A., & Bradlyn, A. S. (1983). Child abusive parents' physiological responses to stressful and non-stressful behavior in children. *Behavioral Assessment, 5,* 363–371.

Wolfe, D. A., Sas, L., & Wekerle, C. (1994). Factors associated with the development of post-traumatic stress disorder among child victims of sexual abuse. *Child Abuse and Neglect, 18,* 37–50.

Wolff, P. H. (1969). The natural history of crying and other vocalizations in early infancy. In B. Foss (Ed.), *Determinants of infant behavior* (Vol. 4). London: Methuen.

Wolff, P. H. (1987). *The development of behavioral states and the expression of emotions in early infancy.* Chicago: University of Chicago Press.

Wolfner, G. D., & Gelles, R. J. (1993). A profile of violence toward children: A national study. *Child Abuse and Neglect, 17,* 197–212.

Wood, D. J., Bruner, J. S., & Ross, G. (1976). The role of tutoring in problem solving. *Journal of Child Psychology and Psychiatry, 17,* 89–100.

Wood, W., Wong, F. Y., & Chachere, J. G. (1991). Effects of media violence on viewers' aggression in unconstrained social interaction. *Psychological Bulletin, 109,* 371–383.

Woodward, A. L. (2000). Constraining the problem space in early word learning. In R. M. Golinkoff, K. Hirsh-Pasek, L. Bloom, L. B. Smith, A. L. Woodward, N. Akhtar, M. Tomasello, & G. Hollich (Eds.), *Becoming a word learner: A debate on lexical acquisition* (pp. 81–114). New York: Oxford University Press.

Woodward, S. A., McManis, M. H., Kagan, J., Deldin, P., Snidman, N., Lewis, M., & Kahn, V. (2001). Infant temperament and the brainstem auditory evoked response in later childhood. *Developmental Psychology, 37,* 533–538.

Woolfe, T., Want, S. C., & Siegal, M. (2002). Signposts to development: Theory of mind in deaf children. *Child Development, 73,* 768–778.

Worobey, J. (1985). A review of Brazelton-based interventions to enhance parent-infant interaction. *Journal of Reproductive and Infant Psychology, 3,* 64–73.

Wright, J. C., Huston, A. C., Murphy, K. C., St. Peters, M., Piñon, M., Scantlin, R., & Kotler, J. (2001). The relations of early television viewing to school readiness and vocabulary of children from low-income families: The Early Window Project. *Child Development, 72,* 1347–1366.

Wright, J. C., Huston, A. C., Reitz, A. L., & Piemyat, S. (1994). Young children's perceptions of television reality: Determinants and developmental differences. *Developmental Psychology, 30,* 229–239.

Wright, J. C., Murphy, K. C., St Peters, M., Piñon, M., Scantlin, R., & Kotler, J. (2001). The relations of early television viewing to school readiness and vocabulary of children from low-income families: The Early Window Project. *Child Development, 72,* 1347–1366.

Wright, K. (1998, May). Human in the age of mechanical reproduction. *Discover, 19,* pp. 79–84.

Wynn, K. (1992a). Addition and subtraction by human infants. *Nature, 358,* 749–750.

Wynn, K. (1992b). Children's acquisition of the number words and the counting system. *Cognitive Psychology, 24,* 220–251.

Wynn, K. (1998). Psychological foundations of number: Numerical competence in human infants. *Trends in Cognitive Science, 2,* 296–303.

Xu, F., & Spelke, E. S. (2000). Large number discrimination in 6-month-olds. *Cognition, 74,* B1–B11.

Yakovlev, P. I., & Lecours, A. R. (1967). The myelogenetic cycles of regional maturation of the brain. In A. Minkowski (Ed.), *Regional development of the brain in early life.* Oxford: Blackwell.

Yale, M. E., Messinger, D. S., Cobo-Lewis, A. B., Oller, D. K., & Eilers, R. E. (1999). An event-based analysis of the coordination of early child vocalizations and facial actions. *Developmental Psychology, 35,* 505–513.

Yang, S., & Sternberg, R. J. (1997). Conceptions of intelligence in ancient Chinese philosophy. *Journal of Theoretical and Philosophical Psychology, 17,* 101–119.

Yarrow, L. J., Goodwin, M. S., Manheimer, H., & Milowe, I. D. (1973). Infancy experiences and cognitive and personality development at 10 years. In L. J. Stone, H. T. Smith, & L. B. Murphy (Eds.), *The competent infant: Research and commentary* (pp. 1274–1281). New York: Basic Books.

Yazigi, R. A., Odem, R. R., & Polakoski, K. L. (1991). Demonstration of specific binding of cocaine to human spermatozoa. *Journal of the American Medical Association, 266,* 1956–1959.

Yee, D. K., & Eccles, J. S. (1988). Parent perceptions and attributions for children's math achievement. *Sex Roles, 19,* 317–333.

Yendovitskaya, T. V. (1971). Development of attention. In A. V. Zaporozhets & D. B. Elkonin (Eds.), *The psychology of preschool children* (pp. 65–88). Cambridge, MA: MIT Press.

Yogman, M. W. (1982). Observations on the father-infant relationship. In S. H. Cath, A. R. Gurwitt, & J. M. Ross (Eds.), *Father and child: Developmental and clinical perspectives.* Boston: Little, Brown.

Yogman, M. W., Dixon, S., Tronick, E., Als, H., Adamson, L., Lester, B. M., & Brazelton, T. B. (1977, April). *The goals and structure of face-to-face interaction between infants and their fathers.* Paper presented at the biennial meeting of the Society for Research in Child Development, New Orleans.

Yonas, A., & Owsley, C. (1987). Development of visual space perception. In P. Salapatek & L. Cohen (Eds.), *Handbook of infant perception: From perception to cognition* (Vol. 2, pp. 79–122). Orlando, FL: Academic Press.

Yoon, P. W., Olney, R. S., Khoury, M. J., Sappenfield, W. M., Chavez, G. F., & Taylor, D. (1997). Contribution of birth defects and genetic diseases to pediatric hospitalizations. *Archives of Pediatrics & Adolescent Medicine, 151,* 1096–1103.

Young, M. H., Miller, B. C., Norton, M. C., & Hill, E. J. (1995). The effect of parental supportive behaviors on life satisfaction of adolescent offspring. *Journal of Marriage and Family, 57,* 813–822.

Young, S. K., Fox, N. A., & Zahn-Waxler, C. (1999). The relations between temperament and empathy in 2-year-olds. *Developmental Psychology, 35,* 1189–1197.

Youngblade, L. M., & Belsky, J. (1992). Parent-child antecedents of 5-year-olds' close friendships: A longitudinal analysis. *Developmental Psychology, 28,* 700–713.

Young-Browne, G., Rosenfeld, H. M., & Horowitz, F. D. (1977). Infant discrimination of facial expression. *Child Development, 48,* 555–562.

Younger, A., Gentile, C., & Burgess, K. (1993). Children's perceptions of social withdrawal: Changes across age. In K. H. Rubin & J. B. Asend-orpf (Eds.), *Social withdrawal, inhibition, and shyness in childhood* (pp. 215–235). Hillsdale, NJ: Erlbaum.

Youniss, J., & Smollar, J. (1985). *Adolescent relations with mothers, fathers, and friends.* Chicago: University of Chicago Press.

Yule, W. (1998). Posttraumatic stress disorder in children and its treatment. In T. W. Miller (Ed.), *Children of trauma: Stressful life events and their effects on children and adolescents* (pp. 219–243). Madison, CT: International Universities Press.

Yule, W. (2000). Emmanuel Miller lectures from pogroms to "ethnic cleansing": Meeting the needs of war affected children. *Journal of Child Psychology and Psychiatry, 41,* 695–702.

Zagon, I. S., & McLaughlin, P. J. (1984). An overview of the neurobehavioral sequelae of perinatal opioid exposure. In J. Yanai (Ed.), *Neurobehavioral teratology* (pp. 197–234). New York: Elsevier.

Zahn-Waxler, C., Cole, P. M., & Barrett, K. C. (1991). Guilt and empathy: Sex differences and implications for the development of depression. In J. Garber & K. Dodge (Eds.), *The development of emotion regulation and dysregulation* (pp. 243–272). New York: Cambridge University Press.

Zahn-Waxler, C., Friedman, S. L., & Cummings, E. M. (1983). Children's emotions and behaviors in response to infants' cries. *Child Development, 54,* 1522–1528.

Zahn-Waxler, C., Radke-Yarrow, M., Wagner, E., & Chapman, M. (1992). Development of concern for others. *Developmental Psychology, 28,* 126–136.

Zajonc, R. B., Markus, H., & Markus, G. B. (1979). The birth order puzzle. *Journal of Personality and Social Psychology, 37,* 1325–1341.

Zaslow, M. J., Dion, M. R., Morrison, D. R., Weinfield, N., Ogawa, J., & Tabors, P. (1999). Protective factors in the development of preschool-age children of young mothers receiving welfare. In E. M. Hetherington (Ed.), *Coping with divorce, single parenting, and remarriage* (pp. 193–223). Mahwah, NJ: Erlbaum.

Zebrowitz, L. A., Kendall-Tackett, K., & Fafel, J. (1991). The influence of children's facial maturity on parental expectations and punishments. *Journal of Experimental Child Psychology, 52,* 221–238.

Zelazo, N. A., Zelazo, P. R., Cohen, K. M., & Zelazo, P. D. (1993). Specificity of practice effects on elementary neuromotor patterns. *Developmental Psychology, 29,* 686–691.

Zelazo, P., & Frye, D. (1998). Cognitive complexity and control: 2. The development of executive function in childhood. *Current Directions in Psychological Science, 7,* 121–125.

Zelazo, P. D., Helwig, C. C. & Lau, A. (1996). Intention, act, and outcome in behavioral prediction and moral judgment. *Child Development, 67,* 2478–2492.

Zelazo, P. R. (1983). The development of walking: New findings and old assumptions. *Journal of Motor Behavior, 15,* 99–137.

Zelazo, P. R. (1998). McGraw and the development of unaided walking. *Developmental Review, 18,* 449–471.

Zeskind, P. S. (1981). Behavioral dimensions and cry sounds of infants of differential fetal growth. *Infant Behavior and Development, 4,* 297–306.

Zhou, Q., Eisenberg, N., Losoya, S. H., Fabes, R. A., Reiser, M., Guthrie, I. K., et al. (2002). The relations of parental warmth and positive expressiveness to children's empathy-related responding and social functioning: A longitudinal study. *Developmental Psychology, 73,* 893–915.

Ziegert, D. I., Kistner, J. A., Castro, R., & Robertson, B. (2001). Longitudinal study of young children's responses to challenging achievement situations. *Child Development, 72,* 609–624.

Ziegler, C. B., Dusek, J. B., & Carter, D. B. (1984). Self-concept and sex-role orientation: An investigation of multidimensional aspects of personality development on adolescence. *Journal of Early Adolescence, 4,* 25–39.

Zigler, E. (1967). Familial mental retardation: A continuing dilemma. *Science, 155,* 292–298.

Zigler, E., & Berman, W. (1983). Discerning the future of early childhood intervention. *American Psychologist, 38,* 894–906.

Zigler, E., & Butterfield, E. C. (1968). Motivational aspects of changes in IQ test performance of culturally deprived nursery school children. *Child Development, 39,* 1–14.

Zigler, E., & Hodapp, R. M. (1986). *Understanding mental retardation.* Cambridge, UK: Cambridge University Press.

Zigler, E., & Trickett, P. K. (1978). IQ, social competence, and evaluation of early childhood intervention programs. *American Psychologist, 33,* 789–798.

Zill, N. (1988). Behavior, achievement, and health problems among children in stepfamilies: Findings from a national survey of child health. In E. M. Hetherington & J. D. Arasteh (Eds.), *Impact of divorce, single-parenting, and stepparenting on children.* Hillsdale, NJ: Erlbaum.

Zill, N. (1994). Understanding why children in stepfamilies have more learning and behavior problems than children in nuclear families. In A. Booth & J. Dunn (Eds.), *Stepfamilies: Who benefits? Who does not?* (pp. 97–106) Hillsdale, NJ: Erlbaum.

Zill, N., Morrison, D. R., & Coiro, M. J. (1993). Long-term effects of parental divorce on parent-child relationships, adjustment, and achievement in young adulthood. *Journal of Family Psychology, 7,* 1–13.

Zimet, G. D., Owens, R., Dahms, W., Cutler, M., Litvene, M., & Cuttler, L. (1997). Psychosocial outcome of children evaluated for short stature. *Archives of Pediatric and Adolescent Medicine, 151,* 1017–1023.

Zimmerman, M. A., Copeland, L. A., Shope, J. T., & Dielman, T. E. (1997). A longitudinal study of self-esteem: Implications for adolescent development. *Journal of Youth and Adolescence, 26,* 117–142.

Zucker, K. J., & Bradley, S. J. (2000). Gender identity disorder. In C. H. Zeanah, Jr. (Ed.), *Handbook of infant mental health* (2nd ed., pp. 412–424). New York: Guilford Press.

Zuckerman, B., & Bresnahan, K. (1991). Developmental and behavioral consequences of prenatal drug and alcohol exposure. *Pediatric Clinics of North America, 38,* 1387–1406.

Text Credits

Chapter 1: *Figure 1.1* From EMERGING MINDS: THE PROCESS OF CHANGE IN CHILDREN'S THINKING by Robert S. Siegler. Copyright © 1996 by Oxford University Press, Inc. Used by permission of Oxford University Press, Inc. *Figure 1.4* From Garabino, J., "Sociocultural Risk: Dangers to Competence," in C. Kopp and J. Krakow (Eds.), *Child Development in a Social Context*. Copyright © 1982. Used by permission of Addison-Wesley.

Chapter 2: *Figure 2.1* Adapted from Ram, A., & Ross, H.S. (2001). Problem-solving, contention, and struggle: How siblings resolve a conflict of interests. CHILD DEVELOPMENT, 72, 1710–1722. Table 3, p. 1715. Reprinted by permission. *Figure 2.5* From Gagnon, M., & Ladouceur, R. (1992). "Behavioral treatment of child stutterers: Replication and extension," *Behavior Therapy, 23,* pp. 113–129. Copyright © 1992 by the Association for Advancement of Behavior Therapy. Reprinted by permission of the publisher. *Figure 2.7* Cole, D.A., Maxwell, S.E., Martin, J.M., Peeke, L.G., Seroczynski, A.D., Tram, J.M., Hoffman, K.B., Ruiz, M.D., Jacquez, F., & Maschman, T. (2001). The development of multiple domains of child and adolescent self-concept: A cohort sequential longitudinal design. *Child Development, 72,* 1723–1746. Figure 3, p. 1735. Reprinted by permission.

Chapter 3: *Figure 3.1* Adapted from Isensee, W. (September 3, 1986). *The Chronicle of Higher Education.* Used with permission. *Figure 3.11* From Turkheimer, Goldsmith, & Gottesman, "Commentary," *Human Development, 38,* pp. 142–153. Copyright © 1995. Reprinted by permission of S. Karger AG, Basel, Switzerland. *Table 3.5* "IQ and Degrees of Relatedness: Similarities of Genetically Related and Unrelated Individuals Who Live Together and Apart." *Intelligence, genes, and success: Scientists respond to the Bell Curve,* pp. 45–70. Copyright © 1997. Used by permission of Springer-Verlag, and the author.

Chapter 4: *Figure 4.3* Moore: *The Developing Human: Critically Oriented Embryology,* p. 182. Copyright © 1998. Used by permission of W.B. Saunders, and the author. *Figure 4.4* Reprinted from PEDIATRIC CLINICS OF NORTH AMERICA, V47: 1–20, Lindgren et al: "Epidemiology of HIV/AIDS in Children." Copyright © 2000, with permission from Elsevier Science. *Figure 4.7* From Brooks-Gunn, Kiebanov, Liaw, & Spiker, "Enhancing the Development of Low-Birthweight, Premature Infants: Changes in Cognition and Behavior Over the First Three Years," *Child Development, 64,* 736–754. Used by permission of Society for Research in Child Development. *Table 4.5* "Nutritional Need Differences Between Nonpregnant and Pregnant Women Ages 24 and Over" From Reece, E.A., Hobbins, J.C., Mahoney, M.J., and Petrie, R.H. (1995) HANDBOOK OF MEDICINE OF THE FETUS AND THE MOTHER. Copyright © 1995. Used by permission of Lippincott Williams and Wilkins (http://lwww.com). *Table 4.7* "The Apgar Scoring System" From V.

Apgar, "A Proposal for a New Method of Evaluation of the Newborn Infant," *Anesthesia and Analgesia: Current Researches, 32,* 260–267. Copyright © 1953. Used by permission of Lippincott Williams & Wilkins. Visit our website at www.anesthesia-analgesia.org.

Chapter 5: *Figure 5.3* Illustration by John W. Karapelou © 1998. Reprinted with permission of artist. www.karapelou.com *Figure 5.4* Reprinted from NEUROPSYCHOLOGIA, 28, Huttenlocher, P. R., "Morphometric Study of Human Cerebral Cortex Development," pp. 517–527, Copyright 1990, with permission from Elsevier Science Ltd, The Boulevard, Langford Lane, Kidlington OX5 1GB, UK. *Figure 5.8* From Brown and Pollitt, "Malnutrition, Poverty and Intellectual Development," *Scientific American, 274* (Feb. 1996), pp. 38–43. Used by permission of Dimitry Schildlovsky. *Figure 5.10* From R. Strauss, "Childhood Obesity," *Current Problems in Pediatrics, 29,* January 1999, p. 11. Copyright © 1999. Used by permission of MOSBY, Inc. *Figure 5.11* From Marshall, W.A., & Tanner, J.M., "Puberty," in Falkner & J. M. Tanner (eds.), *Human Growth,* vol. 2, 2/e, p. 196. Copyright © 1986. Used by permission of Plenum Publishing Corporation. *Figure 5.12* From X Ge, R.D. Conger, & G.H. Elder, Jr., "Coming of age too early: Pubertal influences on girls' vulnerability to psychological distress," *Child Development, 67,* p. 3394. Copyright © 1996. Used by permission of Society for Research in Child Development.

Chapter 6: *Figure 6.3* Figure adapted from "Pattern Perception in Early Infancy" by P. Salapatek in INFANT PERCEPTION: From Sensation to Cognition, Vol. 1 by L. B. Cohen and P. Salapatek (Eds.), copyright © 1975 by Academic Press, reproduced by permission of the publisher. *Figure 6.4* Johnson, S.P., & Mason, U. (2002). Perception of kinetic illusory contours by two-month-old infants. *Child Development, 73,* p. 24. Reprinted with permission of the Society for Research in Child Development. *Figure 6.6* From Treiber et al., "Perception of a 'Subjective' Contour by Infants," *Child Development, 51,* 915–917. Used by permission of Society for Research in Child Development. *Figure 6.7* Adapted from Spelke, E. S., "Perception of Unity, Persistence and Identity: Thoughts on Infants' Conceptions of Objects." In J. Mehler and R. Fox (Eds.), NEONATE COGNITION: BEYOND THE BLOOMING, BUZZING CONFUSION. Copyright © 1985. Reprinted by permission of E. S. Spelke. *Figure 6.8* Adolph, K.E. (2000). Specificity of learning: Why infants fall over a veritable cliff. PSYCHOLOGICAL SCIENCE, 11, 290–295, 2000. Reprinted by permission of Blackwell Publishing Ltd., UK. *Figure 6.11* Pick, A. D. (1965). Improvement of visual and tactical discrimination. *Journal of Experimental Psychology, 69,* 331–339. Copyright © 1969 by the American Psychological Association. Adapted by permission. *Figure 6.12* Gopnik, A., & Rosati, A. (2001). Duck or Rabbit? Reversing ambiguous figures and understanding ambiguous representations. DEVELOPMENTAL SCIENCE, 4, 175–183. Reprinted by permission of Blackwell Publishing Ltd., UK.

Chapter 7: *Figure 7.1* Fernald, A. (1985). Four-month-olds prefer to listen to motherese. *Infant Behavior and Development, 8,* 181–195. Reprinted with permission of Ablex Publishing Corporation. *Figure 7.2* From Bates, Thal, Fenson, Dale, Reznick, Reilley, & Hartung, "Developmental and Stylistic Variation in the Composition of Early Vocabulary," *Journal of Child Language, 21,* pp. 85–123. Copyright © 1994. Reprinted with the permission of Cambridge University Press. *Figure 7.3* Adapted from Goldfield, B. A. & Reznick, J. S., "Early Lexical Acquisition: Rate, Content, & the Vocabulary Spurt," *Journal of Child Language, 17,* 171–183. Copyright © 1990. Reprinted with the permission of Cambridge University Press. *Figure 7.4* Adapted from Kraus et al., "The Development of Communication," *Child Development, 40,* 255–266. Used by permission of Society for Research in Child Development. *Figure 7.7* Reprinted from *Current Opinion in Neurobiology,* Vol. 7, Nobre & Plunkett, "The neural system of language: Structure and development," pp. 262–268, Copyright 1997, with permission from Elsevier Science. *Figure 7.8* Figure A1 from Raven's Standard Progressive Matrices. Used by permission of J.C. Raven Ltd. *Figure 7.9* Winsler, A., Carleton, M.P., & Barry, M.J. (2000). Age-related changes in preschool children's systematic use of private speech in a natural setting. JOURNAL OF CHILD LANGUAGE, 27, 665–687. Reprinted with the permission of Cambridge University Press.

Chapter 8: *Figure 8.2,* "Do Infants Have an Object Concept?" adapted from Baillargeon, R. (1987). "Object Permanence in 3½ – 4½ month-old infants." DEVELOPMENTAL PSYCHOLOGY, 23, 655–664. Copyright © 1987 by the American Psychological Association. Adapted with permission. *Figure 8.3* Spelke, E., Breinlinger, K., Macomber, J., & Jacobson, K. (1992). Origins of knowledge. PSYCHOLOGICAL REVIEW, 99, 605–632. Copyright © 1999 by the American Psychological Association. Adapted with permission. *Figure 8.5* Reprinted from *Cognition,* Vol. 25, A.M. Leslie and S. Keeble, "Do six-month-olds perceive causality?," Copyright 1987, with permission from Elsevier Science. *Figure 8.8* Adapted from K. Wynn, "Addition and subtraction by human infants." *Nature, 358,* pp. 749–750. Reprinted by permission from Nature, copyright 1992 Macmillan Magazines Ltd.; Visit our website at www.nature.com. *Figure 8.9* Feigenson, L., Carey, S., & Hauser, M. (2002). The representations underlying infants' choice or more: Object files versus analog magnitudes. PSYCHOLOGICAL SCIENCE, 13, 150–156. Reprinted by permission of Blackwell Science. *Figure 8.10* From THE ORIGINS OF INTELLECT: PIAGET'S THEORY, 2/e, by John L. Phillips. © 1975 by W.H. Freeman and Company. Used with permission.

Chapter 9: *Figure 9.2* Figure "Comparing Houses," from E. Vurpillot, from "The Development of Scanning Strategies and Their Relation to Visual Differentiation," by E. Vurpillot in *Journal of Experimental Child Psychology,* Volume 6, 632–650, copyright © 1968 by Academic Press, reproduced by permission of the publisher. *Figure 9.3* Adapted from J.F. Fagan, "Infant Recognition Memory: The Effects of Length...," *Child Development, 45,* pp. 351–356. Copyright © 1974. Used by permission of Society for Research in Child Development. *Figure 9.5* Reprinted from *Infant Behavior & Development,* Vol. 18, Rovee-Collier et al., "The time-window hypothesis," pp. 69–78, Copyright 1995, with permission from Elsevier Science. *Figure 9.6* "Developmental Changes in Memory Span," from "Memory Span: Sources of Individual and Developmental Differences," by F.N. Dempster, *Psychological Bulletin, 89,* 1981, pp. 63–100. Copyright © 1981 by the American Psychological Association. Reprinted with permission. *Figure 9.7* Adapted from Ornstein, Naus, & Liberty, "Rehearsal and Organization Processes in Children's Memory," *Child Development, 46,* pp. 818–830. Copyright © 1975. Used by permission of Society for Research in Child Development. *Figure 9.8* Eskritt, M., & Lee, K. (2002). "Remember where

you last saw that card": Children's production of external symbols as a memory aid. DEVELOPMENTAL PSYCHOLOGY, 38, 254–266. Copyright © 2002 by the American Psychological Association. Reprinted with permission. *Figure 9.12* R.S. Siegler & E. Stern, "Conscious and unconscious strategy discoveries: A microgenetic analysis," *Journal of Experimental Psychology: General, 127,* 1998, pp. 377–397. Copyright © 1998 by the American Psychological Association. Reprinted with permission. *Figure 9.13* Adapted from Z. Chen, R.P. Sanchez, and T. Campbell, "From beyond to within their grasp: The rudiments of analogical problem solving in 10- and 13-month-olds," *Developmental Psychology, 33,* 1997, pp. 790–801. Copyright © 1997 by the American Psychological Association. Reprinted with permission.

Chapter 10: *Figure 10.4* Simulated items similar to those from the *Wechsler Intelligence Scale for Children–Revised.* Copyright © 1974 by The Psychological Corporation. *Figure 10.6* Ambady, N., Shih, M., Kim, A., & Pittinsky, T.L. (2001). Stereotype susceptibility in children: Effects of identity activation on quantitative performance. *Psychological Science, 12,* 385–390. Copyright © 2001 by Blackwell Science Publishers. Reprinted with permission. *Figure 10.7* Adapted from A.E. Gottfried, J.S. Fleming, & A.W. Gottfried, "Role of cognitively stimulating home environment in children's academic intrinsic motivation: A longitudinal study," *Child Development, 69,* pp. 1448–1460. Copyright © 1998. Used by permission of Society for Research in Child Development. *Table 10.1* Siegler, R.S., and Richards, D.D. (1982). The development of intelligence. In R.J. Sternberg (Ed.), HANDBOOK OF HUMAN INTELLIGENCE. Cambridge: Cambridge University Press. Reprinted with the permission of Cambridge University Press. *Table 10.3* Table from "The Home Observation of the Environment (HOME) Scale: A Review of Research," by R. Elardo, & R.H. Bradley *in Developmental Review,* Volume 1, 113–145, copyright © 1981 by Academic Press, reproduced by permission of the publisher.

Chapter 11: *Figure 11.3* Cole, Zahn-Waxler, & Smith, "Expressive Control During a Disappointment: Variations Related to Preschoolers' Behavior Problems," *Developmental Psychology, 30,* 1994, pp. 835–846. Copyright © 1994 by the American Psychological Association. Reprinted with permission. *Figure 11.4* R. Larson & M. Ham, "Stress and 'Storm and Stress' in Early Adolescence: The Relationship of Negative Effects with Dysphoric Affect," *Developmental Psychology, 29,* 1993, p. 136. Copyright © 1993 by the American Psychological Association. Reprinted with permission. *Figure 11.6* Adapted from T.M. Field, "Affective Displays of High-Risk Infants During Early Interactions," in T. Field and A. Fogel (eds.), *Emotion and Early Interaction,* p. 109. Copyright © 1982 by Lawrence Erlbaum Associates, Inc. Reprinted by permission of Lawrence Erlbaum Associates, Inc. *Figure 11.7* Adapted from M. Nachmias, M. Gunnar, S. Mangelsdorf, R. Parritz, and K. Buss, "Behavioral inhibition and stress reactivity: Moderating role of attachment security," *Child Development, 67,* pp. 508–522. Copyright © 1996. Used by permission of Society for Research in Child Development.

Chapter 12: *Figure 12.1* Harter, Susan (1999). THE CONSTRUCTION OF THE SELF: A DEVELOPMENTAL PERSPECTIVE, p. 131. Reprinted by permission of Guilford Publications, Inc. *Figure 12.2* Harter, S., & Monsour, A., "Developmental Analysis of Conflict Caused by Opposing Attributes in the Adolescent Self-Portrait," DEVELOPMENTAL PSYCHOLOGY, 28, pp. 251–260. Copyright © 1992 by the American Psychological Association. Reprinted with permission. *Figure 12.3* M.L. Kamins & C.S. Dweck, "Person versus process praise and criticism: Implications for contingent self-worth and coping," *Developmental Psychology, 35,* pp. 835–847. Copyright © 1999 by the American Psychological Association. Reprinted with permission. *Figure 12.4* Adapted from Harter, S., "The Determinants and Mediational Role of Global Self-Worth in Children," in N. Eisenberg (Ed.), *Contemporary Topics In Developmental Psychology*, p. 227. Copyright © 1987. This material is used by permission of John Wiley & Sons, Inc. *Figure 12.5* Colby, A., Kohlberg, L., Gibbs, J., and Lieberman, M. (1983). A longitudinal study of moral judgment. *Monographs of the Society for Research in Child Development*, *48* (No. 1–2, Serial No. 200). The Society for Research in Child Development.

Chapter 13: *Figure 13.1* Serbin, L.A., Powlishta, K.K., & Gulko, J. "The development of sex typing in middle childhood" from *Monographs of the Society for Research in Child Development*. Used with permission. *Figure 13.2* Adapted from Hyde, J.S., Fennema, E., and Lamon, S. J., "Gender Differences in Mathematics Performance: A Meta-Analysis." PSYCHOLOGICAL BULLETIN, 107, 139–155. Copyright © 1990 by the American Psychological Association. Adapted with permission. *Figure 13.3* Linn, M.C., and Peterson, A.C. (1988). Emergence and characterization of sex difference in spatial ability: A meta-analysis. *Child Development*, *56*, 1479–1498. © The Society of Research for Child Development, Inc. *Figure 13.4* Adapted from "Self-regulatory mechanisms governing gender development" by K. Bussy and A. Bandura from *Child Development*, Vol. 63, p. 1243. Copyright © 1992 The Society for Research in Child Development, Inc. Used with permission. *Figure 13.5* "Social Behavior as a Function of the Child's Play Partner" adapted from Jacklin, C.N. et al., "Social Behavior at 33 Months," *Child Development*, *49*, 557–559. © The Society of Research for Child Development, Inc. Used by permission. *Figure 13.6* From D.A. Cole, J.M. Martin, L. Peeke, A.D. Seroczynski, and J. Fier, "Children's over- and underestimation of academic competence: A longitudinal study of gender differences, depression, and anxiety," *Child Development*, *70*, pp. 459–473. Copyright © 1999. Reprinted with permission of the Society for Research in Child Development. *Table 13.1* C.L. Martin, "Stereotypes about Children with Traditional and Nontraditional Gender Roles," *Sex Roles*, *33*, pp. 727–751. Copyright © 1995 by Plenum Publishing Corporation. Reprinted by permission of Plenum Publishing Corporation.

Chapter 14 *Figure 14.2* Peterson, G.W., and Rollins, B.C. (1987). Parent-child socialization. In M.B. Sussman and S.K. Steinmetz (Eds.), *Handbook of Marriage and the Family*. Reprinted by permission of Plenum Publishing Corporation. *Figure 14.3* Adapted from Maccoby, E. E., & Martin, J. A., "Socialization in the Context of the Family: Parent-Child Interaction," in E. M. Hetherington (Ed.), HANDBOOK OF CHILD PSYCHOLOGY, Vol. 4. Socialization, Personality, and Social Development. Copyright © 1983. This material is used by permission of John Wiley & Sons, Inc. *Figure 14.5* Adapted from Dix, T. H., & Grusec, J. E., "Parent Attribution in the Socialization of Children," in I. E. Sigel (Ed.), *Parental Belief Systems: The Psychological Consequences For Children*. Copyright © 1985 by Lawrence Erlbaum Associates, Inc. Reprinted by permission of Lawrence Erlbaum Associates, Inc. *Figure 14.6* Mason, C. A., Cauce, A.M., Gonzales, N., & Hiraga, Y. (1996). Neither Too Sweet Nor Too Sour: Problem Peers, Maternal Control, and Problem Behavior in African American Adolescents. *Child Development*, *67*, 2115–2130. © Society for Research in Child Development, Inc. Reprinted by permission. *Figure 14.8* Nicholas Zill, Ph.D., "Understanding Why Children in Stepfamilies Have More Learning and Behavior Problems Than Children in Nuclear Families," in A. Booth & J. Dunn (Eds.), *Stepfamilies: Who Benefits? Who Does Not?* Copyright © 1994 by Lawrence Erlbaum Associates, Inc. Reprinted by permission of Lawrence Erlbaum Associates, Inc.

Chapter 15: *Figure 15.1* Figure from "Gender Segregation in Childhood," by Maccoby, H.H., and Jacklin, C.N. in H.W. Reese (Ed.), ADVANCES IN CHILD DEVELOPMENT AND BEHAVIOR, Vol.

20, copyright © 1987 by Academic Press, reproduced by permission of the publisher. *Figure 15.2* Adapted from Berndt, "Developmental Changes in Conformity to Peers and Parents," *Developmental Psychology*, *15*, pp. 608–616. Copyright © 1979 by the American Psychological Association. Adapted with permission. *Figure 15.6* N.R. Crick & K.A. Dodge, "A review and reformulation of social information-processing mechanisms in children's social adjustment," *Psychological Bulletin*, *115*, pp. 74–101. Copyright © 1994 by the American Psychological Association. Reprinted with permission. *Figure 15.7* Adapted from Jakibchuk, Z. et al., "The Influence of Symbolic Modeling on the Social Behavior..." *Child Development*, *47*, 838–841. *Figure 15.8* Cairns, R.B., & Cairns, B.D., *Lifelines and Risks: Pathways of Youth in Our Time*. Copyright © 1994. Reprinted with the permission of Cambridge University Press. *Figure 15.9* From Renshaw, P.D., & Brown, P.J., "Loneliness in Middle Childhood: Concurrent and Longitudinal Predictors," *Child Development*, *64*, 1271–1284. Copyright © 1993. Reprinted with permission of the Society for Research in Child Development.

Chapter 16 *Figure 16.1* From R.M. Liebert and J. Sprafkin, *The Early Window: Effects of Television on Children and Youth*, 3/e. Copyright © 1988 by Allyn & Bacon. Reprinted by permission. Use of this material without written permission from the publisher is prohibited. Please visit us at www.abacon.com. *Figure 16.2* The first year of *Sesame Street*: An evaluation; a report to the Children's Television Workshop, by Samual Ball and Gerry Ann Bogatz. Princeton, NJ: Educational Testing Service, © 1970. *Figure 16.7* Grolnick, W.S., Ryan, R.M., & Deci, E.L. (1991). "Inner Resources for School Achievement: Motivational Mediators of Children's Perceptions of Their Parents," JOURNAL OF EDUCATIONAL PSYCHOLOGY, 83, p. 515. Copyright © 1991 by the American Psychological Association. Reprinted with permission. *Figure 16.8* Kuklinski, M.R. and Weinstein, R.S. (2001). Classroom and Developmental Differences in a Path Model of Teacher Expectancy Effects. CHILD DEVELOPMENT, 72, 1554–1578. Reprinted with permission.

Photo Credits

Chapter 1: **p. 1** © Ariel Skelley/Corbis. **p. 4** © Tom & Dee Ann McCarthy/Corbis. **p. 6** © Don Smetzer/Stone/Getty Images. **p. 9** © Will Hart/PhotoEdit. **p. 11** © Sean Sprague/The Image Works. **p. 12** Erich Lessing/Art Resource. **p. 14** Archives of the History of American Psychology. **p. 16** Photo courtesy of Mitzi M. Wertheim. **p. 20** Mark Wise/Stock Boston. **p. 21** © Bill Anderson/Photo Researchers. **p. 27** Erik Homburger/Stock Montage. **p. 28** © Earl & Nazima Kowall/Corbis. **p. 31** © Elizabeth Harris. **p. 33** Thomas McAvoy/Life Magazine © Time Warner Inc.

Chapter 2: **p. 38** © Eastcott/The Image Works. **p. 41** © Laura Dwight. **p. 48** Legerstee, M., Anderson, D., & Shaffer, A. (1998). Five- and eight-month-old infants recognize their faces as familiar and social stimuli. *Child Development*, *69*, 37–50. **p. 53** © Elizabeth Crews. **p. 57** © Michael Paras.

Chapter 3: **p. 63** © Spencer Grant/Photo Researchers. **p. 68** © CNRI/Science Photo Library/Photo Researchers. **p. 75** Courtesy of Williams Syndrome Association. **p. 78** © Rosenan/Custom Medical Stock Photo. **p. 80** © Billie Carstens/Denver Children's Hospital. **p. 81** © Laura Dwight. **p. 87** © B. E. Barnes/PhotoEdit. **p. 91** © Rachel Epstein/The Image Works. **p. 95** © David Grossman/The Image Works. **p. 99** © Robert Brenner/PhotoEdit.

Chapter 4: **p. 104** © Laurence Monneret/Stone/Getty Images. **p. 107** © David Philips/SS/Photo Researchers. **pp. 110–111** © Lennart Nilsson/Albert Bonniers Forlag AB, A CHILD IS BORN. **p. 114** © Hank Morgan/Photo Researchers. **p. 119** © George Steinmetz. **p. 130** ©

David Young-Wolff/PhotoEdit. **p. 133** © Peter Essick/Aurora. **p. 134** © Gale Zucker/Stock Boston. **p. 135** © Jules Perrier/Corbis. **p. 139** © Sean Cayton/The Image Works. **p. 142** © Elizabeth Crews.

Chapter 5: p. 147 © Rudi Von Briel/PhotoEdit. **p. 149** Courtesy of Dr. Joy Hirsch, Head, The Functional MRI Laboratory, Memorial Sloan-Kettering Cancer Center, New York. **p. 152** © Oliver Meckes/Ottawa/Photo Researchers. **p. 156** William McCauley/Corbis. **p. 159** Myrleen Ferguson Cate/PhotoEdit. **p. 162** © Laura Dwight. **p. 164** © Lionel Delevingne/Stock Boston. **p. 167** © Suzanne Arms/The Image Works. **p. 171** © Debbi Morello/Black Star. **p. 178** © David Young-Wolff/PhotoEdit.

Chapter 6: p. 189 © Robert Ullmann. **p. 194** © Ron Chapple/Taxi/Getty Images. **p. 195** © Nadja Reissland. **p. 202** © John Lamb/The Image Bank/Getty Images. **p. 203** © PhotoDisc 2004. **p. 217** Steiner, J.E. (1979). Human facial expressions in response to taste and smell stimulation. In H.W. Reese & L.P. Lipsitt (Eds.), *Advances in child development and behavior* (Vol. 13). New York: Academic Press. **p. 219** © Laura Dwight. **p. 224** © Betty Press.

Chapter 7: p. 228 © Dorothy Little Greco/The Image Works. **p. 236** © Laura Dwight. **p. 240** © Bruce Dale/National Geographic Society Image Collection. **p. 242** © Philip & Karen Smith/Stone/Getty Images. **p. 246** Sheila Sheridan. **p. 254** Reprinted by permission from Nature: Kim, K.H.S., Relkin, N.R., Lee, K., & Hirsch, J. (1997). Distinct cortical areas associated with native and second languages. *Nature, 388,* 171–174. Copyright 1997 Macmillan Magazines Ltd. **p. 258** © Laura Dwight. **p. 261** © Robert Brenner/PhotoEdit. **p. 265** © Norbert Schafer/Corbis.

Chapter 8: p. 270 © Elizabeth Crews. **p. 274** © Laura Dwight/PhotoEdit. **p. 278** © Laura Dwight. **p. 287** © Adele Diamond. **p. 292** Mandler, J.M. (1997). Development of categorization: Perceptual and conceptual categories. In G. Bremner, A. Slater, & G. Butterworth (eds.), *Infant development: Recent advances.* East Sussex, UK: Psychology Press. Reprinted by permission of Psychology Press Limited, Hove, UK. **p. 293** © Myrleen Ferguson Cate/PhotoEdit. **p. 303** Archives of the History of American Psychology. **p. 304** © Eastcott/Momatiuk/The Image Works.

Chapter 9: p. 310 © LWA-Dan Tardiff/Corbis. **p. 319** Courtesy of Carolyn Rovee-Collier. **p. 326** © Esbin-Anderson/The Image Works. **p. 327** © Laura Dwight. **p. 331** Dr. Peter Willatts. **p. 332** © Michael Newman/PhotoEdit. **p. 338** © Syracuse Newspapers/Michelle Gabel/The Image Works. **p. 340** © Elizabeth Crews.

Chapter 10: p. 346 © Ellen Senisi/The Image Works. **p. 350** © Betty Press. **p. 353** © Felicia Martinez/PhotoEdit. **p. 354** © Elizabeth Crews. **p. 365** © Michael Newman/PhotoEdit. **p. 373** © Michael Newman/PhotoEdit. **p. 375** © John Eastcott/YVA Momatiuk/Stock Boston.

Chapter 11: p. 379 © Elizabeth Crews. **p. 385** © DPA/The Image Works. **p. 389** Reprinted with permission from Field, T.M., Woodson, R., Greenberg, R., & Cohen, D. (1982). Discrimination and imitation of facial expressions by neonates. *Science, 218,* 179–181. Copyright 1982 American Association for the Advancement of Science. **p. 391** © Tony Freeman/PhotoEdit. **p. 400** © Michael Newman/Photo Edit. **p. 403** Harlow Primate Laboratory, University of Wisconsin. **p. 408** © Laura Dwight/PhotoEdit.

Chapter 12: p. 420 © Tomas Spangler/The Image Works. **p. 422** © Laura Dwight/PhotoEdit. **p. 426** © Rachel Epstein/The Image Works. **p. 427** © George Shelley/Corbis. **p. 428** © Ron Dahlquist/Superstock. **p. 431** © Andy Sacks/Stone/Getty Images. **p. 437** © M. Fredericks/The Image Works. **p. 439** © Laura Dwight. **p. 444** © Laura Dwight/Corbis. **p. 450** © R. Lord/The Image Works. **p. 454** © Elizabeth Crews. **p. 457** © Sean Sprague/The Image Works.

Chapter 13: p. 464 © Elyse Lewin/The Image Bank/Getty Images. **p. 468** © Hazel Hankin/Stock Boston. **p. 471** © Richard Hutchings/PhotoEdit. **p. 475** Michael Newman/PhotoEdit. **p. 476** Bob Daemmrich. **p. 483** © Michael Newman/PhotoEdit. **p. 484** © Bob Daemmrich/The Image Works. **p. 488** © Mary Kate Denny/PhotoEdit. **p. 493** © Michael Newman/PhotoEdit.

Chapter 14: p. 496 © Ariel Skelley/Corbis. **p. 501** © Annie Griffiths Belt/Material World Woman's Project. **p. 507** © Goodman/Monkmeyer. **p. 513** © VictorEngleberg. **p. 517** © Laura Dwight. **p. 520** © Philip & Karen Smith. **p. 523** © Cindy Charles/PhotoEdit. **p. 525** © Paul Conklin. **p. 529** © M. Bridwell/PhotoEdit.

Chapter 15: p. 533 © Bob Daemmrich. **p. 536** © Laura Dwight. **p. 541** © Michael Newman/PhotoEdit. **p. 549** © Bob Daemmrich/Stock Boston. **p. 553** © Michael Newman/PhotoEdit. **p. 556** © Tony Freeman/PhotoEdit. **p. 562 (left)** © Laura Dwight. **p. 562 (right)** © Myrleen Ferguson Cate/PhotoEdit.

Chapter 16: p. 567 © David Silverman/Getty Images. **p. 570** © McLaughlin/The Image Works. **p. 573** © Albert Bandura. **p. 578** © Juan Silva/The Image Bank/Getty Images. **p. 580** © Mark Richards/PhotoEdit. **p. 589** © Peter Hvizdak/The Image Works. **p. 591** © David R. Frazier. **p. 593** © Elizabeth Crews/The Image Works. **p. 594** © Michael Newman/PhotoEdit.

Resource Center
Stockton
Riverside College